Textbook on Land Law

Textbook on
Land Law

Nineteenth edition

Aruna Nair
Associate Professor of Law, University of Oxford

OXFORD
UNIVERSITY PRESS

OXFORD
UNIVERSITY PRESS

Great Clarendon Street, Oxford, OX2 6DP,
United Kingdom

Oxford University Press is a department of the University of Oxford.
It furthers the University's objective of excellence in research, scholarship,
and education by publishing worldwide. Oxford is a registered trade mark of
Oxford University Press in the UK and in certain other countries.

© Aruna Nair and Judith-Anne MacKenzie 2023

The moral rights of the authors have been asserted.

Sixteenth edition 2016
Seventeenth edition 2018
Eighteenth edition 2020

All rights reserved. No part of this publication may be reproduced, stored in
a retrieval system, or transmitted, in any form or by any means, without the
prior permission in writing of Oxford University Press, or as expressly permitted
by law, by licence or under terms agreed with the appropriate reprographics
rights organization. Enquiries concerning reproduction outside the scope of the
above should be sent to the Rights Department, Oxford University Press, at the
address above.

You must not circulate this work in any other form
and you must impose this same condition on any acquirer.

Public sector information reproduced under Open Government Licence v3.0
(http://www.nationalarchives.gov.uk/doc/open-government-licence/open-government-licence.htm)

Published in the United States of America by Oxford University Press
198 Madison Avenue, New York, NY 10016, United States of America

British Library Cataloguing in Publication Data

Data available

Library of Congress Control Number: 2023937476

ISBN 978–0–19–285883–2

Printed in the UK by
Bell & Bain Ltd., Glasgow

Links to third party websites are provided by Oxford in good faith and
for information only. Oxford disclaims any responsibility for the materials
contained in any third party website referenced in this work.

CONTENTS

Preface	vii
Table of cases	ix
Table of statutes	xxii
Table of statutory instruments	xxix
Who's who	xxxi

PART I Introduction — 1

1. Estates in land — 3
2. Interests in land — 14

PART II The freehold estate — 33

3. Buying a house — 35
4. The contract — 41
5. Unregistered land — 69
6. Registered land — 87
7. Acquisition of an estate by adverse possession — 141

PART III Legal estates — 171

8. The freehold estate — 173
9. The leasehold estate — 182
10. Obligations of landlord and tenant — 238
11. Enforcement of leasehold covenants — 258
12. Remedies for breach of leasehold covenants — 281

PART IV Trusts — 301

13. Express and implied trusts — 303
14. Trusts of land — 315
15. Settled Land Act settlements — 348
16. The rule against perpetuities — 350
17. Co-ownership — 355
18. Trusts of the family home — 382
19. Proprietary estoppel — 410

PART V	Licences and rights to the family home	431
20	Licences and their enforcement	433
21	Special rights in relation to the family home	451

PART VI	Rights in land	463
22	Mortgages and charges	465
23	Priorities in relation to mortgages and charges	498
24	Easements and profits à prendre	515
25	Freehold covenants	576

PART VII	In conclusion	613
26	What is land?	615

Bibliography		628
Glossary		629
Index		639

PREFACE

This book originated in the 1980s, when Judith-Anne MacKenzie became concerned that many very able postgraduate students found Land Law horribly difficult to cope with and sometimes confusing. She adopted a new approach to the subject, which concentrated on its modern and practical aspects rather than heavily emphasising its historical aspects. This style of teaching eventually took the form of a book, *A Practical Approach to Land Law*, which first appeared in 1986 and which later developed into the current text. The running case study, 'Trant Way', has provided an entertaining and accessible introduction to the fundamentals of land law for generations of law students and has influenced the teaching of land law for the better for many years.

This is the first edition of the textbook since Judith-Anne MacKenzie's retirement in 2021, updated to take account of changes to the land law of England and Wales that have occurred since the previous edition. Having first joined her as a co-author on the book in 2018, I have done my best to ensure that the updates to the textbook maintain its accessible style and modern feel and remain relevant to Trant Way and all its characters. Updates discussed in this edition include *Penninstone Holdings Ltd v Rock Ferry Waterfront Trust* [2021] EWCA Civ 1029, a case involving the escheat of a registered freehold title; *Nasrullah v Rashid* [2018] EWCA Civ 685 on the effect of adverse possession of registered land by a fraudulent registered proprietor; *Global 100 Ltd v Laleva* [2021] EWCA Civ 1835, on the role of intention in defining whether a contract to occupy land creates a lease or a licence; the Leasehold Reform (Ground Rent) Act 2022, which removes landlord's ability to charge significant sums as ground rent under new long leases in England and Wales; *Procter v Procter* [2021] EWCA Civ 167 on the question whether two joint tenants can grant a lease to themselves and another joint tenant; *Ali v Khatib* [2022] EWCA Civ 481 on the circumstances in which 'occupation rent' is payable by a co-owner in occupation to a co-owner who is not in occupation; *Hudson v Hathaway* [2022] EWCA Civ 1648 on the effect of changing intentions on a trust of the family home and the need for detrimental reliance where a common intention constructive trust is being recognised; and the important new Supreme Court decision on the remedy in proprietary estoppel cases, *Guest v Guest* [2022] UKSC 27.

Finally, I must express my gratitude to the staff of the Land Registry for the copy of the register of title for 1 Trant Way, which appears as Form 6.1 and for permission to reproduce the transfer form as Form 6.2.

The law is stated as at 6 March 2022.

Some information about the author

Dr Aruna Nair is a Fellow and Tutor in Law at Hertford College, Oxford, where she teaches the law of trusts and land law. She is also an Associate Professor in the Faculty of Law at the University of Oxford, where she lectures on aspects of the law on land registration and trustee duties. She was previously a lecturer at King's College London and, before that, a research assistant with the Property, Family and Trusts team at the Law Commission for England and Wales.

TABLE OF CASES

United Kingdom

88 Berkeley Road NW9, Re [1971] Ch 648 . . . 372

A-G v Blake [2001] AC 268 . . . 602
Abbahall Ltd v Smee [2003] 1 All ER 465 . . . 627
Abbey National Building Society v Cann [1989] 2 FLR 265 . . . 125
Abbey National Building Society v Cann [1991] 1 AC 56 . . . 115, 117, 119, 122, 126, 216
Abbeyfield (Harpenden) Society Ltd v Woods [1968] 1 WLR 374 . . . 197
Abbott v Abbott [2007] UKPC 53 . . . 392, 407
Adealon International Proprietary Ltd v Merton LBC [2007] 1 WLR 1604 . . . 535, 536, 540
Adekunle v Ritchie [2007] BPIR 1177 . . . 370, 404
AG Securities v Vaughan [1990] 1 AC 417 . . . 194, 195, 199
Akici v LR Butlin Ltd [2006] 1 WLR 201 . . . 292
Aldin v Latimer Clark, Muirhead & Co [1894] 2 Ch 437 . . . 245, 246
Alexander v Alexander [2011] EWHC 2721 (Ch) . . . 325
Ali v Dinc [2020] EWHC 3055 . . . 56, 97
Ali v Khatib [2022] EWCA Civ 149 . . . 334
Alker v Collingwood Housing Association [2007] 1 WLR 2230 . . . 249
Allcard v Skinner (1887) 36 ChD 145 . . . 512
Allen v Greenwood [1980] Ch 119 . . . 522, 573
Amsprop Trading Ltd v Harris Distribution Ltd [1997] 1 WLR 1025 . . . 279, 580
Antoine v Barclays Bank [2019] EWCA Civ 2846 . . . 134
Antoniades v Villiers [1990] 1 AC 417 . . . 193, 194, 195
Appah v Parncliffe Investments Ltd [1964] 1 WLR 1064 . . . 191, 193
Argyle Building Society v Hammond (1985) 49 P & CR 148 . . . 136, 137
Arkwright v Gell (1839) 5 M & W 203 . . . 548
Armstrong and Holmes Ltd v Holmes [1993] 1 WLR 1482 . . . 48, 72
Ashburn Anstalt v Arnold [1989] 1 Ch 1 . . . 205, 444, 445, 448, 449, 511
Ashe v National Westminster Bank plc [2008] 1 WLR 710 . . . 496, 497
Asher v Whitlock (1865) LR 1 QB 1 . . . 141, 153
Ashworth Frazer Ltd v Gloucester CC [2001] 1 WLR 2180 . . . 252, 253
Aslan v Murphy (Nos 1 and 2) [1990] 1 WLR 766 . . . 193, 196
Aspden v Elvy [2012] EWHC 1387 (Ch), [2012] 2 FLR 435 . . . 407, 455
Attwood v Bovis Homes Ltd [2001] Ch 379 . . . 520, 522
Austerberry v Corporation of Oldham (1885) 29 ChD 750 . . . 584, 586
Avonridge Property Co Ltd v Mashru see London Diocesan Fund v Phithwa

Bagum v Hafiz and Hai [2016] Ch 241 . . . 340–1
Bailey v Barnes [1894] 1 Ch 25 . . . 483
Bailey v Stephens (1862) 12 CB NS 91 . . . 520
Bailey Ltd (C. H.) v Memorial Enterprises see C. H. Bailey Ltd v Memorial Enterprises Ltd
Baker v Craggs [2018] EWCA Civ 1126 . . . 127, 132
Baker v Craggs [2017] Ch 295 . . . 128
Bakewell Management Ltd v Brandwood [2004] 2 AC 519 . . . 548
Ballard's Conveyance, Re [1937] Ch 473 . . . 590
Bank of Baroda v Dhillon [1998] 1 FLR 524 . . . 484, 511
Bank of Ireland Home Mortgages Ltd v Bell [2001] 2 FLR 809 . . . 336, 339–40, 456, 511
Bannister v Bannister [1948] 2 All ER 133 . . . 308
Barclays Bank v Guy (No. 1) [2008] EWCA Civ 452 . . . 137
Barclays Bank Ltd v Bird [1954] Ch 274 . . . 488
Barclays Bank plc v Alcorn [2002] All ER (D) 146 . . . 486
Barclays Bank plc v Zaroovabli [1997] Ch 321 . . . 127
Barnes v Phillips [2015] EWCA Civ 1056 . . . 406
Baron Bernstein of Leigh v Skyviews & General Ltd [1978] QB 479 . . . 623, 624
Barrett v Halifax Building Society (1995) 28 HLR 634 . . . 483
Barrett v Morgan (1999) 1 WLR 1109 . . . 223
Barrett v Morgan [2000] 2 AC 264 . . . 223
Basham, Re [1986] 1 WLR 1498 . . . 412, 415, 420, 421
Batchelor v Marlow [2003] 1 WLR 764 . . . 527, 528, 571
Bates v Donaldson [1896] 2 QB 241 . . . 253
Bath Rugby Ltd v Greenwood [2021] EWCA Civ 1927 . . . 594
Batsford Estates (1983) Company Ltd v Taylor [2006] 2 P&CR 5 . . . 149
Baxter v Four Oaks Properties Ltd [1965] Ch 816 . . . 596
Baxter v Mannion [2011] 1 WLR 1594 . . . 98, 134, 138, 157

Beard, Re [1908] 1 Ch 383 . . . 175
Beardman v Wilson (1868) LR 4 CP 57 . . . 217
Beesly v Hallwood Estates Ltd [1960] 1 WLR 549 . . . 249
Bellcourt Estates Ltd v Adesina [2005] 18 EG 150 . . . 220
Benn v Hardinge (1992) 66 P&CR 246 . . . 565, 571
Berkley v Poulett (1976) 242 EG 39 . . . 619
Berrisford v Mexfield Housing Co-operative Ltd [2011] UKSC 52 . . . 192, 201–3, 220, 233
Beswick v Beswick [1966] Ch 538 . . . 581
Bettison v Langton [2002] 1 AC 27 . . . 530, 531
BHP Petroleum Ltd v Chesterfield Ltd [2002] Ch 194 . . . 273, 275
Biggs v Hoddinott [1898] 2 Ch 307 . . . 477
Bignold, ex parte (1834) 4 Deac & Ch 259 . . . 488
Billson v Residential Apartments Ltd [1992] 1 AC 494 . . . 294, 295
Binions v Evans [1972] Ch 359 . . . 308, 309, 349, 443, 445, 449
Bird v Syme-Thomson [1979] 1 WLR 440 . . . 120
Birmingham Citizens Permanent Building Society v Caunt [1962] Ch 883 . . . 480, 486
Blathwayt v Baron Cawley [1976] AC 397 . . . 178
Bocardo SA v Star Energy UK Onshore Ltd [2010] 1 AC 380 . . . 623, 624, 625
Bolling v Hobday (1882) 31 WR 9 . . . 154
Bond v Nottingham Corpn [1940] Ch 429 . . . 562
Borman v Griffith [1930] 1 Ch 493 . . . 213, 538, 543, 546
Borwick, Re [1933] Ch 657 . . . 178
Boyer v Warbey [1953] 1 QB 234 . . . 241, 269
Bradburn v Lindsay [1983] 2 All ER 408 . . . 564
Bradley v Carritt [1903] AC 253 . . . 477
Breams Property Investment Co Ltd v Stroulger [1948] 2 KB 1 . . . 203, 219, 267
Brent LBC v Cronin (1997) 30 HLR 43 . . . 191
Bridges v Mees [1957] Ch 475 . . . 143
Bridle v Ruby [1989] QB 169 . . . 547, 552
Brikom Investments Ltd v Carr [1979] QB 467 . . . 419
Bristol and West v Bartlett [2003] 1 WLR 284 . . . 485
British General Insurance Co Ltd v Attorney-General (1945) 12 LJNCCR 113 . . . 485
British Railways Board v Glass [1965] Ch 538 . . . 520
Broomfield v Williams [1987] 1 Ch 602 . . . 544
Brown v Wilson (1949), unreported . . . 222
Browne v Flower [1911] 1 Ch 219 . . . 243
Brunner v Greenslade [1971] Ch 993 . . . 597
Bruton v London & Quadrant Housing Trust [1998] QB 834 . . . 230, 232

Bruton v London & Quadrant Housing Association [2001] 1 AC 406 . . . 187, 196, 215, 230–2, 233, 234, 435
Buchanan-Wollaston's Conveyance, Re [1939] Ch 738 . . . 314
Buckinghamshire County Council v Moran [1990] Ch 623 . . . 146, 148, 150
Buckland v Butterfield (1820) 2 Brod & Bing 54 . . . 618
Bull v Bull [1955] 1 QB 234 . . . 313, 330, 363, 378, 381
Bull v Hutchens (1863) 32 Beav 615 . . . 75
Bullock v Dommitt (1796) 2 Chit 608 . . . 257
Burgess v Rawnsley [1975] Ch 429 . . . 371, 374, 375
Burns v Burns [1984] 1 Ch 317 . . . 390, 392, 405, 406, 407, 454
Burrows v Lang [1901] 2 Ch 502 . . . 529
Bury v Pope (1588) Cro Eliz 118 . . . 551

C. H. Bailey Ltd v Memorial Enterprises Ltd [1974] 1 WLR 728 . . . 229
Calisher v Forbes (1871) LR 7 Ch App 109 . . . 500
Camelot Guardians v Khoo [2018] EWHC 2296 . . . 193, 194, 198
Cameron Ltd v Rolls-Royce plc [2008] L&TR 22 . . . 198
Campbell v Chief Land Registrar [2022] EWHC 200 . . . 52
Campbell v Griffin [2001] EWCA Civ 990, [2001] W & TLR 981 . . . 4419
Campbell v Holyland (1877) 7 ChD 166 . . . 482
Cannan v Grimley (1850) 9 CB 634 . . . 220
Capehorn v Harris [2015] EWCA Civ 955, [2016] 2 FLR 1026 . . . 407, 455
Cardiothoracic Institute v Shrewdcrest Ltd [1986] 1 WLR 368 . . . 213
Cargill v Gotts [1981] 1 WLR 441 . . . 548
Carl-Zeiss Stiftung v Herbert Smith & Co (No. 2) [1969] 2 Ch 276 . . . 307
Carter v Cole [2006] EWCA Civ 398 . . . 521
Carter v Wake (1877) 4 ChD 605 . . . 482
Caunce v Caunce [1969] 1 WLR 286 . . . 82, 345
CDC 2020 plc v George Ferreira (2005) 35 EG 112 . . . 565
Celsteel Ltd v Alton House Holdings Ltd [1985] 1 WLR 204 . . . 111, 532, 562
Central London Property Trust Ltd v High Trees House Ltd [1947] KB 130 . . . 411
Chadwick v Collinson [2014] EWHC 3055 . . . 376
Chaffe v Kingsley [2000] 79 P&CR 404 . . . 525, 540
Chandler v Kerley [1978] 1 WLR 693 . . . 437
Chartered Trust plc v Davies (1997) 76 P&CR 396 . . . 228, 229, 246

Chaudhary v Yavuz [2011] EWCA Civ 1314 . . . 120, 445, 553
Chelsea Yacht and Boat Club Ltd v Pope [2000] 1 WLR 1941 . . . 620
Cheltenham & Gloucester plc v Krausz [1997] 1 All ER 21 . . . 483, 486
Cheltenham and Gloucester Building Society v Norgan [1996] 1 WLR 343 . . . 486
Chester v Buckingham Travel Ltd [1981] 1 WLR 96 . . . 242
China & South Sea Bank Ltd v Tan Soon Gin [1990] 1 AC 536 . . . 493
Chowood Ltd v Lyall [1930] 2 Ch 156 . . . 135
Chowood's Registered Land, Re [1933] Ch 574 . . . 135
Church of England Building Society v Piskor [1954] Ch 553 . . . 215, 216
Churston Golf Club Ltd v Haddock [2019] EWCA Civ 544 . . . 524, 602
Cinderella Rockerfellas Ltd v Rudd [2003] 1 WLR 2423 . . . 620
Citibank International plc v Kessler (1999) EGCS 40 . . . 478
Citro, Re [1991] Ch 142 . . . 337, 338
City and Metropolitan Properties Ltd v Greycroft Ltd [1987] 1 WLR 1085 . . . 270
City of London Brewery Co Ltd v Tenant (1873) LR 9 Ch App 212 . . . 522
City of London Building Society v Flegg [1988] AC 54 . . . 81, 115, 116, 343, 345, 511
City of London Corporation v Fell [1994] 1 AC 458 . . . 262, 265
City Permanent Building Society v Miller [1952] Ch 840 . . . 111
Cityland and Property (Holdings) Ltd v Dabrah [1968] Ch 166 . . . 470, 477
Clapman v Edwards [1938] 2 All ER 507 . . . 449
Clarke v Meadus [2010] EWHC 3117 (Ch) . . . 362
Clore v Theatrical Properties Ltd [1936] 3 All ER 483 . . . 442
Coatsworth v Johnson (1886) 55 LJ QB 220 . . . 210
Cobbe v Yeoman's Row Management Ltd [2006] 1 WLR 2964, [2008] 1 WLR 1752 . . . 59, 60, 62, 411, 414, 415, 416, 418, 421
Colin Dawson Windows Ltd v King's Lynn, West Norfolk BC [2005] 2 P&CR 19 . . . 149
Colls v Home & Colonial Stores Ltd [1904] AC 179 . . . 522, 573
Commission for the New Towns v Cooper (Great Britain) Ltd [1995] Ch 259 . . . 44, 45, 48, 54
Commonwealth of Australia v Verwayen (1990) 170 CLR 394 . . . 422
Co-operative Insurance Society Ltd v Argyll Stores (Holdings) Ltd [1996] Ch 286 . . . 282

Co-operative Insurance Society Ltd v Argyll Stores (Holdings) Ltd [1998] AC 1 . . . 282, 283, 284
Copeland v Greenhalf [1952] 1 Ch 488 . . . 526
Corbett v Halifax Building Society [2003] 1 WLR 964 . . . 20, 495
Cordell v Second Clanfield Properties Ltd [1969] 2 Ch 9 . . . 535
Cornish v Brook Green Laundry Ltd [1959] 1 QB 394 . . . 210
Cory v Davies [1923] 2 Ch 95 . . . 537
Cottage Holiday Associates Ltd v Customs and Excise Commissioners [1983] 1 QB 735 . . . 184
Coventry v Lawrence [2014] UKSC 13 . . . 573
Cowcher v Cowcher [1972] 1 WLR 425 . . . 304
Cowell v Rosehill Racecourse Co Ltd (1937) 56 CLR 605 . . . 439
Cowper v Laidler [1903] 2 Ch 337 . . . 562
Crabb v Arun DC [1976] 1 Ch 179 . . . 410, 412, 420
Crago v Julian [1992] 1 WLR 372 . . . 217
Crancour Ltd v Da Silvaesa [1986] 1 EGLR 80 . . . 190, 193
Crest Nicholson Residential (South) Ltd v McAllister [2004] 1 WLR 2409 . . . 592, 594
Cricklewood Property and Investment Trust Ltd v Leighton's Investment Trust Ltd [1945] AC 221 . . . 626
Crow v Wood [1971] 1 QB 77 . . . 523, 524, 602
Cuckmere Brick Co v Mutual Finance Ltd [1971] Ch 949 . . . 494
Curley v Parks [2005] 1 P&CR DG 15 . . . 385

D'Eyncourt v Gregory (1866) LR 3 Eq 382 . . . 619
Dalton v Angus (1881) 6 App Cas 740 . . . 523, 547, 552
Dalton v Pickard [1926] 2 KB 545 . . . 220
Dance v Triplow [1992] 1 EGLR 190 . . . 556
Daniel v North (1809) 11 East 372 . . . 550
Dano Ltd v Earl Cadogan [2003] 2 P&CR 10 . . . 579
Dano Ltd v Earl Cadogan, The Times, 2 June 2003 (CA) . . . 579
Darby v Read (1675) Rep t Finch 226 . . . 474
Darling v Clue (1864) 4 F & F 329 . . . 551
Das v Linden Mews Ltd [2003] 2 P&CR 4 . . . 521
Davey v Durrant (1857) 1 De G&J 535 . . . 493
Davies v Davies [2016] EWCA Civ 463 . . . 424
Davies v Du Paver [1953] 1 QB 184 . . . 554, 556
Davis v Jackson [2017] EWHC 698 . . . 332, 333, 334
Davis v Lisle [1936] 2 KB 434 . . . 438
Davis v Whitby [1974] Ch 186 . . . 551
Dayani v Bromley LBC [1999] 3 EGLR 144 . . . 256

Dean and Chapter of the Cathedral and Metropolitan Church of Christ Canterbury v Whitbread (1995) 72 P&CR 9 . . . 185
Dearle v Hall (1823) 3 Russ 1 . . . 500, 501, 506
Design Progression Ltd v Thurloe Properties Ltd [2005] 1 WLR 1 . . . 254, 255
Dewar v Dewar [1975] 1 WLR 1532 . . . 307
Dewar v Goodman [1909] AC 72 . . . 268
Dhillon v Barclays Bank [2020] EWCA Civ 619 . . . 139
DHN Food Distributors v Tower Hamlets LBC [1976] 1 WLR 852 . . . 444
Dickinson v Grand Junction Canal Co Ltd (1852) 7 Exch 282 . . . 522
Diligent Finance Ltd v Alleyne (1972) 23 P&CR 346 . . . 73
Dillwyn v Llewellyn (1862) 4 De G F & J 517 . . . 308, 416, 420, 445
Dobbin v Redpath [2007] 4 All ER 465 . . . 604
Doe d Clarke v Smaridge (1845) 7 QB 957 . . . 214
Doe d Gray v Stanion (1836) 1 M & W 700 . . . 185
Doe d Hanley v Wood (1819) 2 B & Ald 724 . . . 437
Doe d Henniker v Watt (1828) 8 B & C 308 . . . 241
Doe d Lockwood v Clarke (1807) 8 East 185 . . . 2219
Doe d Shore v Porter (1789) 3 TR 13 . . . 219
Dolphin's Conveyance, Re [1970] Ch 654 . . . 595, 596
Downsview Nominees Ltd v First City Corporation Ltd (No. 1) [1993] AC 295 . . . 492
Dowse v Bradford MBC [2020] UKUT 202 . . . 161
Drake v Whipp (1995) 28 HLR 531 . . . 385, 393, 459
Draper's Conveyance, Re [1969] 1 Ch 486 . . . 371
Dudley Muslim Association v Dudley Metropolitan Borough Council [2015] EWCA Civ 1123 . . . 63
Duke v Wynne [1990] 1 WLR 766 . . . 193
Dunbar v Plant [1998] FLR 157 . . . 375–6
Duncliffe v Caerfelin Properties Ltd [1989] 2 EGLR 38 . . . 269
Dunraven Securities v Holloway (1982) 264 EG 709 . . . 292
Duppa v Mayo (1669) Saund 282 . . . 293
Duval v 11–13 Randolph Crescent Ltd [2020] UKSC 18 . . . 245
Dyce v Hay (1865) 1 Macq 305 . . . 525, 570
Dyce v Lady James Hay (1852) 1 Macq 305 . . . 517
Dyer v Dyer (1788) 2 Cox 92 . . . 307

Earl of Leicester v Wells-next-the-Sea Urban District Council [1973] Ch 110 . . . 590
Eaton v Swansea Waterworks Co (1851) 17 QB 267 . . . 548
Ecclesiastical Commissioners for England v Kino (1880) 14 ChD 213 . . . 565
Ecclesiastical Commissioners for England's Conveyance, Re [1936] Ch 430 . . . 580
Edgar, Re [1939] 1 All ER 635 . . . 178
Edginton v Clark [1964] 1 QB 367 . . . 152
Edwards v Kumaraswamy [2016] UKSC 40 . . . 248
Egerton v Harding [1975] QB 62 . . . 523
Elitestone Ltd v Morris [1997] 1 WLR 687 . . . 619
Ellenborough Park, Re [1956] Ch 131 . . . 517–21, 519, 521, 524, 525, 526, 528, 559
Elliott v Johnson (1866) LR 2 QB 120 . . . 268
Elliston v Reacher [1908] 2 Ch 374 . . . 596
Elwood v Goodman [2014] Ch 442 . . . 599
EMI Group Ltd v O & H Q1 Ltd [2016] EWHC 529 (Ch) . . . 272
Emile Elias & Co Ltd v Pine Groves Ltd [1993] 1 WLR 305 . . . 596
England Environmental (Northern) Ltd v Arthur Jones & Sons (Contractors) Ltd [2017] EWHC 1903 (Ch) . . . 552–3
Errington v Errington [1952] 1 KB 290 . . . 197, 442, 443, 444
Esso Petroleum Co Ltd v Fumegrange Ltd [1994] 2 EGLR 90 . . . 190
Etridge v Royal Bank of Scotland see Royal Bank of Scotland v Etridge
Eves v Eves [1975] 1 WLR 1338 . . . 388, 389
Expert Clothing Service & Sales Ltd v Hillgate House Ltd [1986] 1 Ch 340 . . . 288, 290, 291, 292, 293

Facchini v Bryson [1952] 1 TLR 1386 . . . 197
Fairclough v Swan Brewery Co Ltd [1912] AC 565 . . . 477
Faiz v Burnley BC [2021] EWCA Civ 55 . . . 288
Family Housing Association v Jones [1990] 1 WLR 779 . . . 196, 199
Farnol Eades Irvine & Co Ltd, Re [1915] 1 Ch 22 . . . 482
Farrar v Farrars Ltd (1888) 40 ChD 395 . . . 495
Fearn v Board of Trustees of the Tate Gallery [2023] UKSC 4 . . . 529
Federated Homes Ltd v Mill Lodge Properties Ltd [1980] 1 WLR 594 . . . 591, 592, 593, 594, 597
Ferrishurst Ltd v Wallcite Ltd [1999] Ch 355 . . . 116
First National Bank v Thompson [1996] Ch 231 . . . 215
First National Bank plc v Syed [1991] 2 All ER 250 . . . 486

First National Securities v Hegarty [1984] 1 All ER 139 . . . 374
Firstpost Homes Ltd v Johnson [1995] 1 WLR 1567 . . . 45
Fitzgerald v Firbank [1897] 2 Ch 96 . . . 436
Fitzkriston LLP v Panayi [2008] EWCA Civ 283 . . . 207
Flexman v Corbett [1930] 1 Ch 672 . . . 242
Footwear Corp Ltd v Amplight Properties Ltd [1998] 3 All ER 52 . . . 254
Foster, Re [1938] 3 All ER 357 . . . 580
Foster v Robinson [1951] 1 KB 149 . . . 197, 220
Four-Maids Ltd v Dudley Marshall (Properties) Ltd [1957] Ch 317 . . . 480
Fowler v Barron [2008] 2 FLR 831 . . . 405–6, 407
Freeguard v Royal Bank of Scotland plc [2002] EWHC 2509 . . . 494
French v Barcham [2009] 1 WLR 1124 . . . 332, 333, 334
Fuller v Happy Shopper Markets Ltd [2001] 2 EGLR 32 . . . 286
Fuller's Contract, Re [1933] Ch 652 . . . 363
Furness v Bond (1888) 4 TLR 457 . . . 199

Gafford v Graham (1998) 77 P&CR 73 . . . 603
Gardner v Rowe (1828) 5 Russ. 258 . . . 304
Garfitt v Allen (1887) 37 ChD 48 . . . 488
Gayford v Moffat (1868) LR 4 Ch App 133 . . . 549
Geary v Rankine [2012] EWCA Civ 555, [2012] 2 FCR 461 . . . 407, 455
George Legge & Son Ltd v Wenlock Corporation [1938] AC 204 . . . 548
Gibbs v Lakeside Developments Ltd [2018] EWCA Civ 2874 . . . 295
Gibson v Revenue & Customs Prosecution Office [2008] EWCA Civ 645 . . . 384
Gillett v Holt [2001] Ch 210 . . . 413, 419, 420, 429
Gissing v Gissing [1971] AC 886 . . . 384, 386–9, 390, 391, 392, 393, 399, 402, 427
Glass v Kencakes Ltd [1966] 1 QB 611 . . . 292
Global 100 Ltd v Laleva [2021] EWCA Civ 1835 . . . 194, 198
Godden v Merthyr Tydfil Housing Association [1997] NPC 1 . . . 50
Goldberg v Edwards [1950] Ch 247 . . . 523, 541
Goodman v Gallant [1986] Fam 106 . . . 358, 362, 366, 397
Goodman v J. Eban Ltd [1954] 1 QB 550 . . . 45
Gore v Carpenter (1990) 60 P&CR 456 (ChD) . . . 375
Gouldsworth v Knights (1843) 11 M & W 337 . . . 215
Gow v Grant [2012] UKSC 29 . . . 460
GoWest Ltd v Spigarola [2003] QB 1140 . . . 254

Grand Junction Co Ltd v Bates [1954] 2 QB 160 . . . 469, 470
Grant v Edmondson [1931] 1 Ch 1 . . . 268
Grant v Edwards [1986] Ch 638 . . . 388, 427
Gray v Taylor [1998] 1 WLR 1093 . . . 190, 197
Greasely v Cooke [1980] 1 WLR 1306 . . . 419, 420, 421, 445
Great Northern Railway Co v Arnold (1916) 33 TLR 114 . . . 219
Green v Ashco Horticultural Ltd [1966] 1 WLR 889 . . . 529
Greenwich Healthcare National Health Service Trust v London and Quadrant Housing Trust [1998] 1 WLR 1749 . . . 562
Gregg v Richards [1926] Ch 521 . . . 545
Grigsby v Melville [1972] 1 WLR 355 . . . 526
Grindal v Hooper [1999] EGCS 150 . . . 373
Grossman v Hooper [2001] 2 EGLR 82 . . . 50, 51
Grundt v Great Boulder Pty Gold Mines Ltd (1937) 59 CLR 641 . . . 420
Guest v Guest [2022] UKSC 27 . . . 411, 414–16, 423–4

Habermann v Koehler (1996) 73 P&CR 515 . . . 445, 447
Habermann v Koehler (No. 2) [2000] TLR 825 . . . 425, 447, 448
Hadjiloucas v Crean [1988] 1 WLR 1006 . . . 193
Halifax plc and Bank of Scotland v Curry Popeck [2008] EWHC 1692 (Ch) . . . 109, 425
Hall v Ewin (1887) 37 ChD 74 . . . 588
Hall v Hall [1982] 3 FLR 379 . . . 389, 390
Halsall v Brizell [1957] Ch 169 . . . 446–7, 598–600
Hamilton v Geraghty (1901)1 SRNSW Eq 81 . . . 449
Hammersmith LBC v Monk [1992] 1 AC 478 . . . 184, 224, 225, 229
Hammond v Farrow [1904] 2 KB 332 . . . 207
Hammond v Mitchell [1991] 1 WLR 1127 . . . 459
Handel v St Stephen's Close [1994] 1 EGLR 70 . . . 526
Hanning v Top Deck Travel Group Ltd [1993] 68 P&CR 14 . . . 548
Hannon v 169 Queen's Gate Ltd, The Times, 23 November 1999 . . . 598
Hansford v Jago [1921] 1 Ch 322 . . . 539
Hardwick v Johnson [1978] 1 WLR 683 . . . 437
Hardy v Haselden [2011] EWCA Civ 1387 . . . 202
Harmer v Jumbil (Nigeria) Tin Areas Ltd [1921] 1 Ch 200 . . . 246
Harrison v Malet (1886) 3 TLR 58 . . . 247
Harrow LBC v Qazi [2004] 1 AC 983 . . . 225
Harvey v Pratt [1965] 1 WLR 1025 . . . 199
Haskell v Marlow [1928] 2 KB 45 . . . 256

Hastings & Thanet Building Society v Goddard [1970] 1 WLR 1544 . . . 490
Haywood v Brunswick Permanent Benefit Building Society (1881) 8 QBD 403 . . . 586
Haywood v Mallalieu (1883) 25 ChD 357 . . . 523
Heathe v Heathe (1740) 2 Atk 121 . . . 361
Hemingway Securities Ltd v Dunraven Ltd [1995] 1 EGLR 61 . . . 277–8
Herbert v Doyle [2010] EWCA Civ 1095 . . . 62
Heslop v Burns [1974] 1 WLR 1241 . . . 197
Hill v Barclay (1810) 16 Ves Jun 402 . . . 283, 284
Hill v Booth [1930] 1 KB 381 . . . 206
Hill v Tupper (1863) 2 Hurl & C 121 . . . 436, 519
Hillingdon Estates Co v Stonefield Estates Ltd [1952] Ch 627 . . . 65
HKRUK II (CHC) Ltd v Heaney [2010] EWHC 2245 (Ch) . . . 563
Hodgson v Marks [1971] Ch 892 . . . 114, 120
Hodson and Howes's Contract, Re (1887) 35 ChD 668 . . . 489
Hoffmann v Fineberg [1949] Ch 245 . . . 290, 292
Holbeck Hall Hotel v Scarborough BC [2000] QB 836 . . . 523, 564
Holland v Hodgson (1872) LR 7 CP 328 . . . 619
Hollins v Verney (1884) 13 QBD 304 . . . 551
Holmes, Re (1885) 29 ChD 786 . . . 500
Hood v Oglander (1865) 34 Beav 513 . . . 179
Hooper v Sherman [1994] NPC 153 . . . 44
Hope v Walter [1900] 1 Ch 257 . . . 66
Hopgood v Brown [1955] 1 WLR 213 . . . 446
Horrocks v Forray [1976] 1 WLR 230 . . . 437
Horsey Estate Ltd v Steiger [1899] 2 QB 79 . . . 268, 293
Horsham Properties Group Ltd v Clark [2009] 1 WLR 1255 . . . 480, 484, 485, 486
Houga v Allen [2014] 1 WLR 2889 . . . 165
Houlder Bros v Gibbs [1925] 1 Ch 575 . . . 252
Hounslow LBC v Twickenham Garden Developments Ltd [1971] Ch 233 . . . 437, 439
Housden v The Conservators of Wimbledon and Putney Commons [2008] 1 WLR 1172 . . . 554
Howe v Gossop [2021] EWHC 637 . . . 60
Hudson v Hathway [2022] EWCA Civ 1648 . . . 19, 45, 366, 369, 380, 407
Hughes v Cook (1994), The Independent, 21 March 1994 . . . 146
Hughes v Williams (1806) 12 Ves Jr 493 . . . 492
Hulme v Brigham [1943] KB 152 . . . 619
Hunt v Luck [1902] 1 Ch 428 . . . 82, 83, 125, 511
Hunter v Babbage [1994] EGCS 8 . . . 374
Hunter v Canary Wharf Ltd [1997] AC 655 . . . 191
Hurst v Picture Theatres Ltd [1915] 1 KB 1 . . . 434, 439, 442
Hussein v Mehlman [1992] 2 EGLR 87 . . . 227, 228, 281
Hussey v Palmer [1972] 1 WLR 1286 . . . 384, 389
Hyman v Van den Bergh [1908] 1 Ch 167 . . . 556, 557
Hypo-Mortgage Services Ltd v Robinson (1997), The Times, 2 January 1997 . . . 120

IAM Group PLC v Chowdrey [2012] EWCA Civ 505, [2012] 2 P&CR 13 . . . 162–3
IDC Group Ltd v Clark [1992] EGLR 187 . . . 436
Industrial Properties (Barton Hill) Ltd v Associated Electrical Industries Ltd [1977] 1 QB 580 . . . 215, 216
Ingram v IRC [1997] 4 All ER 395 . . . 229, 230
Ingram v IRC [2001] 1 AC 293 . . . 229, 230
Inns, Re [1947] Ch 576 . . . 312, 326
International Drilling Fluids Ltd v Louisville Investments (Uxbridge) Ltd [1986] Ch 513 . . . 253
International Tea Stores v Hobbs [1903] 2 Ch 165 . . . 541
Inwards v Baker [1965] 2 QB 29 . . . 416, 420, 421, 445, 446
Iron Trades Employers Insurance Association Ltd v Union Land & House Investors Ltd [1937] Ch 313 . . . 478
Ives (E. R.) Investment Ltd v High [1967] 2 QB 379 . . . 81, 446, 447, 449, 599
Ivimey v Stocker (1866) LR 1 Ch App 396 . . . 549

Jamaica Life Assurance Society v Hillsborough Ltd [1989] 1 WLR 1101 . . . 591
James v Evans [2003] 3 EGLR 1 . . . 63
James v Stevenson [1893] AC 162 . . . 565
James Jones & Sons Ltd v Earl of Tankerville [1909] 2 Ch 440 . . . 437
Jared v Clements [1903] 1 Ch 428 . . . 21
Javad v Mohammed Aqil [1991] 1 WLR 1007 . . . 213
Jelson Ltd v Derby County Council [1999] 3 EGLR 91 . . . 46, 48
Jennings v Rice [2003] 1 P&CR 8 . . . 422, 423, 424
Jeune v Queen's Cross Properties Ltd [1974] Ch 97 . . . 283, 284
Jones v Challenger [1961] 1 QB 176 . . . 314
Jones v Jones (1876) 1 QBD 279 . . . 178
Jones v Kernott [2011] UKSC 53, [2011] 3 WLR 1121 . . . 363, 364, 366, 368–9, 385, 395, 396, 397, 398, 400–3, 406, 407, 455
Jones v Lavington [1903] 1 KB 253 . . . 245
Jones v Morgan [2002] 1 EGLR 125 . . . 476
Jones v Price [1965] 2 QB 618 . . . 523, 524
Jones v Pritchard [1908] 1 Ch 630 . . . 523, 562

Jordeson v Sutton, Smithcoates & Drypool Gas Co Ltd [1898] 2 Ch 614 . . . 523
Joscelyne v Nissen [1970] 2 QB 86 . . . 52, 67
Joyce v Epsom and Ewell Borough Council [2012] EWCA Civ 1398 . . . 417, 426

Kay v Lambeth Borough Council [2005] QB 352 . . . 233
Kay v Lambeth Borough Council [2006] 2 AC 465 . . . 233
Keay v Morris Homes (West Midlands) Ltd [2012] 1 WLR 2855 . . . 43, 51, 56
Kelly v Monck (1795) 3 Ridg Parl Rep 205 . . . 178
Kensington Mortgage Co Ltd v Mallon [2019] EWHC 2512 . . . 97
Kent v Kavanagh [2007] Ch 1 . . . 537, 539
Keppell v Bailey (1834) 2 My &K 517 . . . 585
Kernott v Jones [2010] 1 WLR 2401 . . . 368, 401
Keshwala v Bhalsod [2021] EWCA Civ 492 . . . 295
Keymer v Summers (1769) Bull NP 74 . . . 551
Kilcarne Holdings Ltd v Targetfollow (Birmingham) Ltd [2005] 2 P & CR 8 . . . 56, 397
Kilgour v Gaddes [1904] 1 KB 457 . . . 549, 555
Killick v Second Covent Garden Property Co Ltd [1973] 1 WLR 658 . . . 252, 253
Kinane v Mackie-Conteh [2005] EWCA Civ 45, [2005] WTLR 345 . . . 61, 428, 473, 489
Kinch v Bullard [1999] 1 WLR 423 . . . 372
King, Re [1963] Ch 459 . . . 270
King v David Allen & Sons (Billposting) Ltd [1916] 2 AC 54 . . . 442
King's Trusts, Re (1892) 29 LR Ir 401 . . . 176
Kingsnorth Finance Co Ltd v Tizard [1986] 1 WLR 783 . . . 82, 83, 307, 384, 456
Knight v Fernley [2021] EWHC 1343 . . . 128, 132
Knightsbridge Estates Trust Ltd v Byrne [1939] Ch 441 . . . 476
Kreglinger v New Patagonia Meat & Cold Storage Co Ltd [1914] AC 25 . . . 474, 477
Kuznetsov v London Borough of Camden [2019] EWHC 805 . . . 44

Lace v Chantler [1944] KB 368 . . . 184, 200, 202, 203, 220
Ladies' Hosiery and Underwear Ltd v Parker [1930] 1 Ch 304 . . . 214
Lagan Navigation Co v Lambeg Bleaching, Dyeing & Finishing Co Ltd [1927] AC 226 . . . 562
Lake v Gibson (1729) 1 Eq Rep 290 . . . 363
Lalani v Crump Holdings Ltd [2007] EWHC 47 (Ch), [2007] 08 EG 136 (CS) . . . 428
Lane v Cox [1897] 1 QB 415 . . . 242

Lashbrook v Cock (1816) 2 Mer 70 . . . 361
Laskar v Laskar [2008] 1 WLR 2695 . . . 370, 385, 404–5
Lavender v Betts [1942] 2 All ER 72 . . . 243
Lawrence v Fen Tigers Ltd [2014] 2 WLR 433 . . . 563
Leach v Jay (1878) 9 ChD 42 . . . 153
Lee Parker v Izzet [1971] 1 WLR 1688 . . . 283
Leigh v Jack (1879) 5 Ex D 264 . . . 149, 150
Leigh v Taylor [1902] AC 157 . . . 619
Les Laboratoires Servier v Apotex Inc [2014] 3 WLR 1257 . . . 165
Lewen v Dodd (1595) Cro Eliz 443 . . . 361
Lewis v Frank Love Ltd [1961] 1 WLR 261 . . . 476
Liden v Burton [2016] Fam Law 687 . . . 412
Link Lending Ltd v Bustard [2010] EWCA Civ 424 . . . 114, 118, 123
Liverpool City Council v Irwin [1977] AC 239 . . . 238, 529, 536
Liverpool Corporation v Coghill & Sons Ltd [1918] 1 Ch 307 . . . 548
Lloyd v Banks (1868) LR 3 Ch App 488 . . . 21
Lloyd v Dugdale [2002] 2 P&CR 13 . . . 425, 445
Lloyds Bank plc v Byrne & Byrne [1993] 1 FLR 369 . . . 337, 338
Lloyds Bank plc v Carrick [1996] 4 All ER 630 . . . 42, 78, 447
Lloyds Bank plc v Rosset [1989] Ch 350 . . . 117, 125, 126, 392
Lloyds Bank plc v Rosset [1991] 1 AC 107 . . . 117, 126, 388, 391–2, 407
Lock v Pearce [1893] 2 Ch 271 . . . 289
Lodge v Wakefield City Council [1995] 38 EG 136 . . . 146
London & Blenheim Ltd v Ladbrooke Parks Ltd [1992] 1 WLR 1278 . . . 526, 527
London County Council v Allen [1914] 3 KB 642 . . . 587
London Diocesan Fund v Phithwa [2005] 1 WLR 3956 . . . 274, 295
Long v Gowlett [1923] 2 Ch 177 . . . 543, 544
Long v Tower Hamlets LBC [1998] Ch 197 . . . 207
Low v Fry (1935) 51 TLR 322 . . . 54
Lurcott v Wakeley [1911] 1 KB 905 . . . 257
Luxe Holding Ltd v Midland Resources Holding Ltd [2010] EWHC 1399 . . . 64
Lynn Shellfish Ltd v Loose [2017] AC 599 . . . 531, 552
Lysaght v Edwards (1876) 2 ChD 499 . . . 64
Lyttelton Times Company Ltd v Warners Ltd [1907] AC 476 . . . 246

McAdams Homes Ltd v Robinson [2004] EWCA Civ 214 . . . 520
McCann v UK [2008] 47 EHRR 913 . . . 225

McCausland v Duncan Lawrie Ltd [1997] 1 WLR 38 . . . 43
McDonald v McDonald [2017] AC 273 . . . 30
McDonagh v Bank of Scotland plc [2019] 4 WLR 12 . . . 495
Macepark (Whittlebury) Ltd v Sargeant [2003] 1 WLR 2284 . . . 521
Macleay, Re (1875) LR 20 Eq 186 . . . 179
MacLeod v Gold Harp Properties Ltd [2014] EWCA 1084 . . . 134, 137
McNerny v Lambeth Borough Council [1989] 19 EG 77 . . . 249
Malaysian Credit Ltd v Jack Chia-MPH Ltd [1986] 1 AC 549 . . . 364
Malory Enterprises Ltd v Cheshire Homes (UK) Ltd [2002] Ch 216 . . . 117, 118, 135, 136
Manchester Airport plc v Dutton [2000] 1 QB 133 . . . 191
Manchester City Council v Pinnock [2010] USKC 45 . . . 30
Manfield & Sons Ltd v Botchin [1970] 2 QB 612 . . . 185, 203, 214
Mann v Lovejoy (1826) Ry & M 355 . . . 214
Marjorie Burnett Ltd v Barclay [1981] 1 EGLR 41 . . . 250
Markham v Paget [1908] 1 Ch 697 . . . 243
Marlborough Knightsbridge Management Ltd v Fivaz [2021] EWCA Civ 989 . . . 619
Marquess of Zetland v Driver [1939] Ch 1 . . . 590, 593
Marr v Collie [2017] UKPC 17 . . . 368, 370
Mars Capital Finance Ltd v Hussain [2021] EWHC 2416 . . . 52
Marten v Flight Refuelling Ltd [1962] Ch 115 . . . 590, 591
Martin v Smith (1874) LR 9 Ex 50 . . . 213
Massey v Boulden [2003] 1 WLR 1792 . . . 521
Matchmove Ltd v Dowding [2016] EWCA Civ 1233 . . . 62
Matharu v Matharu (1994) 68 P&CR 93 . . . 441
Matthews v Goodday (1861) 31 LJ Ch 282 . . . 473
Matthey v Curling [1922] 2 AC 180 . . . 226
Maughan, Re (1885) 14 QBD 956 . . . 211
Mayo, Re [1943] Ch 302 . . . 313, 324
Medforth v Blake [2000] Ch 86 . . . 495
Mellor v Spateman (1669) 1 Saund 339 . . . 530
Mellor v Watkins (1874) LR 9 QB 400 . . . 222
Meretz Investments NV v ACP Ltd [2007] Ch 197 . . . 493
Midland Bank v Cooke [1995] 4 All ER 562 . . . 394–5, 395, 396, 454, 459
Midland Bank Trust Co Ltd v Green [1981] AC 513 . . . 20, 77, 78, 510
Midland Railway Co's Agreement, Re [1971] 1 Ch 725 . . . 200
Midtown Ltd v City of London Real Property Co Ltd (2005) 4 EG 166 (CS) . . . 522
Mikeover Ltd v Brady [1989] 3 All ER 618 . . . 194
Milebush Properties Ltd v Tameside Metropolitan Borough Council [2010] EWHC 1022 . . . 46
Miller v Emcer Products Ltd [1956] Ch 304 . . . 241, 523
Millgate Developments Ltd v Alexander Devine Children's Cancer Trust [2020] UKSC 45 . . . 605
Millman v Ellis (1996) 71 P&CR 158 . . . 538
Mills v Silver [1991] Ch 271 . . . 552
Milmo v Carreras [1946] KB 306 . . . 217
Milverton Group Ltd v Warner World Ltd [1995] 2 EGLR 28 . . . 265
Mint v Good [1951] 1 KB 517 . . . 255
Mitchell v Mosley [1914] 1 Ch 438 . . . 623
Moncrieff v Jamieson [2007] 1 WLR 2620 . . . 121, 527–8
Moody v Steggles (1879) 12 ChD 261 . . . 520
Moore, Re (1888) 39 ChD 116 . . . 176
Morley v Bird (1798) 3 Ves Jr 628 . . . 364
Morrells of Oxford Ltd v Oxford United Football Club Ltd [2001] Ch 459 . . . 587, 588, 590
Mortgage Corporation v Shaire [2001] Ch 743 . . . 337–9, 340, 456
Mortgage Express v Lambert [2017] Ch 93 . . . 97, 512
Mortimer v Bailey [2005] 2 P&CR 9 . . . 603
Moule v Garrett (1872) LR 7 Ex 101 . . . 263
Mounsey v Ismay (1865) 3 Hurl & C 486 . . . 528
Multiservice Bookbinding Ltd v Marden [1979] Ch 84 . . . 477
Murphy v Gooch [2007] EWCA Civ 603 . . . 332
Mutual Life Assurance Society v Langley (1886) 32 ChD 460 . . . 500

N3 Living Ltd v Burgess Property Investments Ltd [2020] EWHC 1711 . . . 344
Nash v Eads (1880) 25 Sol J 95 . . . 493
Nasrullah v Rashid [2018] EWCA Civ 685 . . . 136, 144, 151
National and Provincial Building Society v Lloyd [1996] 1 All ER 630 . . . 486
National Carriers Ltd v Panalpina (Northern) Ltd [1981] AC 675 . . . 226, 228, 229
National Provincial Bank Ltd v Hastings Car Mart Ltd [1964] Ch 665 . . . 444
National Provincial Bank v Ainsworth [1965] AC 1175 . . . 444, 456, 457
National Westminster Bank plc v Skelton [1993] 1 WLR 72 . . . 480
NCR Ltd v Riverland Portfolio No. 1 Ltd [2005] 22 EG 134 . . . 253
Neaverson v Peterborough Rural District Council [1902] 1 Ch 557 . . . 552
Neocleous v Rees [2019] EWCH 2462 (Ch) . . . 45

Table of cases

Newman v Jones, unreported, quoted in Handel v St Stephen's Close [1994] 1 EGLR 70 . . . 526, 528
Newton Abbot Cooperative Society Ltd v Williamson & Treadgold Ltd [1952] Ch 286 (Devonia case) . . . 590
Nickerson v Barraclough [1981] Ch 426 . . . 535, 536, 560
Nielson-Jones v Fedden [1975] Ch 222 . . . 373
Nisbet & Potts' Contract, Re [1906] 1 Ch 386 . . . 154
No.1 West India Quay (Residential) Ltd v East Tower Apartments Ltd [2018] EWCA Civ 250 . . . 254
North Eastern Properties Ltd v Coleman [2010] 1 WLR 2715 . . . 51
Northchurch Estates Ltd v Daniels [1947] Ch 117 . . . 249, 250
Norwich and Peterborough Building Society v Steed [1993] Ch 116 . . . 136, 137
NRAM Ltd v Evans [2017] EWCA Civ 1013 . . . 134, 137
Nweze v Nwoko [2004] EWCA Civ 379 . . . 46, 48

Oak Co-operative Building Society v Blackburn [1968] Ch 730 . . . 73
Ocean Estates Ltd v Pinder [1969] 2 AC 19 . . . 148
Odey v Barber [2008] 2 WLR 618 . . . 549
Odogwu v Vastguide Ltd [2009] EWHC 3565 . . . 135
Ofulue v Bossert [2009] Ch 1 . . . 169
Ofulue v Bossert [2009] 1 AC 990 . . . 152
Old Grovebury Manor Farm v W Seymour Plant Sales [1979] 3 All ER 504 . . . 251
Olympia & York Canary Wharf Ltd v Oil Property Investments Ltd [1994] 2 EGLR 48 . . . 253
O'Neill v Holland [2022] EWCA Civ 1583 . . . 407
Orchard Trading Estate Management Ltd v Johnson Security Ltd [2002] 18 EG 155 . . . 601
Owen v Gadd [1956] 2 QB 99 . . . 243
Oxley v Hiscock [2005] Fam 211 . . . 368, 392, 394, 395, 401, 402

P & A Swift Investments v Combined English Stores Group plc [1989] AC 632 . . . 267, 582
P & S Platt Ltd v Crouch [2004] 1 P&CR 18 . . . 544
Paddington Building Society v Mendelsohn (1985) 50 P&CR 244 . . . 115, 116
Paine v Meller (1801) 6 Ves Jr 349 . . . 65
Palk v Mortgage Services Funding plc [1993] Ch 330 . . . 480, 482, 483, 493–4
Pallant v Morgan [1953] Ch 43 . . . 58
Palmer v Fletcher (1663) 1 Lev 122 . . . 245
Pankhania v Chandegra [2012] EWCA Civ 1438 . . . 362
Paradine v Jane (1647) Al 26 . . . 226
Parc (Battersea) Ltd v Hutchinson [1999] 2 EGLR 33 . . . 217
Parker v Boggon [1947] KB 346 . . . 253
Parker v Jones [1910] 2 KB 32 . . . 251
Parker v Taswell (1858) 2 De G & J 559 . . . 210
Parker v Webb (1693) 3 Salk 5 (91 ER 656) . . . 265
Parshall v Hackney [2013] EWCA Civ 240 . . . 150, 151
Pascoe v Turner [1979] 1 WLR 431 . . . 410, 420, 440, 455
Pawlett v Attorney-General (1667) Hardres 465 . . . 475
Payne v Inwood (1996) 74 P&CR 42 . . . 543, 544
Payne v Webb (1874) LR 19 Eq 26 . . . 361
Peace v Morris (1869) LR 5 Ch App 227 . . . 490
Peacock v Custins [2002] 1 WLR 1815 . . . 520
Peat v Chapman (1750) 1 Ves Sen 542 . . . 361
Peckham v Ellison [2000] 79 P&CR 276 . . . 540
Peck's Contract, Re [1893] 2 Ch 315 . . . 543
Pennell v Payne [1995] QB 192 . . . 222, 245
Penniall v Harborne (1848) 11 QB 368 . . . 257
Pennistone Holdings Ltd v Rock Ferry Waterfront Trust [2021] EWCA Civ 1029 . . . 9, 10
Perera v Vandiyar [1953] 1 WLR 672 . . . 243
Perry v Fitzhowe (1846) 8 QB 757 . . . 562
Pettit v Pettit [1970] AC 777 . . . 387, 390, 402
Phené v Popplewell (1862) 12 CB NS 334 . . . 220
Phillips v Mobil Oil Co Ltd [1989] 1 WLR 888 . . . 72, 271
Phipps v Pears [1965] 1 QB 76 . . . 529, 542, 564
Pile v Pile [2022] EWHC 2036 . . . 358
Pimms Ltd v Tallow Chandlers Co [1964] 2 QB 547 . . . 253
Pinewood Estate, Re [1958] Ch 280 . . . 595
Pinnington v Galland (1853) 9 Exch 1 . . . 540
Pitt v PHH Asset Management Ltd [1994] 1 WLR 327 . . . 48
Plimmer v Wellington Corporation (1884) 9 App Cas 699 . . . 440, 441
Port v Griffith [1938] 1 All ER 295 . . . 246
Poste Hotels Ltd v Cousins [2020] EWHC 582 . . . 528
Poster v Slough Estates Ltd [1968] 1 WLR 1515 . . . 81
Powell v McFarlane (1979) 38 P&CR 452 . . . 145, 147
Proctor v Proctor [2021] EWCA Civ 167 . . . 185, 195
Procter v Procter [2022] EWHC 1202 . . . 358
Prudential Assurance Co Ltd v London Residuary Body [1992] 2 AC 386 . . . 200, 201, 202, 203, 205, 220, 229, 511

Prudential Assurance Co Ltd v Waterloo Real Estate Inc [1999] 2 EGLR 85 . . . 146
Pugh v Savage [1970] 2 QB 373 . . . 520, 550, 554
Pugh v Savage [1974] 1 WLR 1427 . . . 547
Purchase v Lichfield Brewery Co [1915] 1 KB 184 . . . 269
PW & Co v Milton Gate Investments Ltd [2004] Ch 142 . . . 223, 230
Pye (J. A.) (Oxford) Ltd v Graham [2000] Ch 676 . . . 147, 166
Pye (J. A.) (Oxford) Ltd v Graham [2001] Ch 804 . . . 147
Pye (J. A.) (Oxford) Ltd v Graham [2003] 1 AC 419 . . . 147, 150, 151, 166, 169
Pye (J. A.) (Oxford) Ltd v United Kingdom [2005] 3 EGLR 1 . . . 167
Pye (J. A.) (Oxford) Ltd v United Kingdom [2007] ECHR 700 . . . 166–7, 169

Quigley v Masterson [2011] EWHC 2529 (Ch) . . . 372

R v Inhabitants of Hermitage (1692) Carth 239 . . . 565
R v Inhabitants of Horndon-on-the-Hill (1816) 4 M & S 562 . . . 438
R v Lam [2022] EWCA Crim 448 . . . 384, 407
R v Tower Hamlets LBC, ex parte Von Goetz [1999] QB 1019 . . . 211
R v Westminster City Council, ex parte Leicester Square Coventry Street Association (1989) 87 LGR 675 . . . 585
R (Beresford) v Sunderland City Council [2004] 1 AC 889 . . . 548, 549
R (Best) v Chief Land Registrar [2015] EWCA Civ 17, [2016] QB 23 . . . 164, 165
R (HCP (Hendon) Ltd) v Chief Land Registrar [2020] EWHC 1278 . . . 102
R (Smith) v Land Registry [2009] EWHC 328 (Admin) . . . 165
R G Kensington Co Ltd v Hutchinson IDH Ltd [2003] 2 P&CR 195 . . . 46, 48
Race v Ward (1855) 4 El & Bl 702 . . . 522
Rainbow Estates Ltd v Tokenhold Ltd [1999] Ch 64 . . . 284
Raja v Austin Gray (a firm) [2002] EWCA Civ 1965 . . . 493, 496
Raja v Lloyds TSB Bank plc (2001) Lloyds Rep Bank 113 . . . 487
Ramsden v Dyson [1866] LR 1 HL 129 . . . 411, 416, 428
Rawlings v Rawlings [1964] P 398 . . . 314
Rawlin's Case (1587) Jenk 254 . . . 216
Rawlinson v Ames [1925] Ch 96 . . . 55, 209
Record v Bell [1991] 1 WLR 853 . . . 49, 50
Red House Farms (Thornden) Ltd v Catchpole [1977] 2 EGLR 125 . . . 145

Rees v Skerrett [2001] 1 WLR 1541 . . . 529, 564
Reeve v Lisle [1902] AC 461 . . . 476
Regan v Paul Properties Ltd [2007] Ch 135 . . . 563
Regency Villas Title Ltd v Diamond Resorts (Europe) Ltd [2019] AC 553 . . . 525, 528, 529
Regent Oil Co Ltd v J. A. Gregory (Hatch End) Ltd [1966] Ch 402 . . . 588
Regis Property Co Ltd v Redman [1956] 2 QB 612 . . . 529
Reid v Bickerstaff [1909] 2 Ch 305 . . . 598
Remon v City of London Real Property Co Ltd [1921] 1 KB 49 . . . 214
Renals v Cowlishaw (1878) 9 ChD 125 . . . 590, 592
Rhone v Stephens [1994] 2 AC 310 . . . 585, 587, 588, 599, 602
Richards v Rose (1853) 9 Exch 218 . . . 540
Richmond v Savill [1926] 2 KB 530 . . . 220
Rickett v Green [1910] 1 KB 253 . . . 269
Roake v Chadha [1984] 1 WLR 40 . . . 592
Robert Leonard Developments Ltd v Wright [1994] NPC 49 . . . 67
Robinson v Kilvert (1889) 41 ChD 88 . . . 246
Robson v Hallet [1967] 2 QB 939 . . . 438
Rochefoucauld v Boustead [1897] 1 Ch 196 . . . 308
Rochester Poster Services v Dartford BC (1991) 63 P&CR 88 . . . 191
Roe v Siddons (1888) 22 QBD . . . 519
Rogers v Hosegood [1900] 2 Ch 388 . . . 590
Rollerteam Ltd v Riley [2017] Ch 109 . . . 52
Romulus Trading Co Ltd v Comet Properties Ltd [1996] 2 EGLR 70 . . . 246
Ropaigealach v Barclays Bank plc [1999] 1 QB 263 . . . 480, 484, 486
Royal Bank of Scotland v Etridge [2002] 2 AC 773 . . . 513
Rudge v Richens (1873) LR 8 CP 358 . . . 485
Rugby School (Governors) v Tannahill [1934] 1 KB 695 . . . 291
Rugby School (Governors) v Tannahill [1935] 1 KB 87 . . . 292
Russel v Russel (1783) 1 Bro CC 269 . . . 472
Rye v Rye [1962] AC 496 . . . 542

Sainsbury's Supermarkets Ltd v Olympia Homes Ltd [2006] 1 P&CR 17 . . . 76, 101, 105
Salt v Marquess of Northampton [1892] AC 1 . . . 474
Salvin's Indenture, Re [1938] 2 All ER 498 . . . 609
Samuel v Jarrah Timber & Wood Paving Co Ltd [1904] AC 323 . . . 476
Sanderson v Berwick-upon-Tweed Corporation (1884) 13 QBD 547 . . . 244
Saner v Bilton (1876) 7 ChD 815 . . . 256

Santley v Wilde [1899] 2 Ch 474 . . . 466
Sarson v Roberts [1895] 2 QB 395 . . . 247
Saunders v Vautier (1841) 4 Beav 115 . . . 305, 322
Savva v Hussein (1997) 73 P&CR 150 . . . 291, 292, 297
Sayers v Collyer [1885] 28 ChD 103 . . . 603
Scala House & District Property Co Ltd v Forbes [1974] QB 575 . . . 291, 292, 293, 295
Scott v Bradley [1971] 1 Ch 850 . . . 54
Scott v Southern Pacific Mortgages [2014] UKSC 52 . . . 64, 65, 216
Scottish Equitable plc v Thompson [2003] HLR 48 . . . 485
Seaman v Vawdrey (1810) 16 Ves Jr 390 . . . 565
Sefton v Tophams Ltd [1967] 1 AC 50 . . . 588
Segal Securities Ltd v Thoseby [1963] 1 QB 887 . . . 288, 289
Shanly v Ward (1913) 29 TLR 714 . . . 253
Sharpe, In re [1980] 1 WLR 219 . . . 443, 446
Shelfer v City of London Electric Lighting Co Ltd [1895] 1 Ch 287 . . . 562, 563
Shiloh Spinners Ltd v Harding [1973] AC 691 . . . 81
Shropshire County Council v Edwards (1982) 46 P&CR 270 . . . 591
Sidney Bolsom Investment Trust Ltd v E Karmios & Co (London) Ltd [1956] 1 QB 529 . . . 417
Silven Properties v Royal Bank of Scotland plc [2004] 1 WLR 997 . . . 492, 493, 494, 494, 495
Simmons v Dobson [1991] 1 WLR 720 . . . 549
Simper v Foley (1862) 2 John & H 555 . . . 565
Sims v Dacorum Borough Council [2014] UKSC 63. . . 225
Skipton Building Society v Clayton (1993) 66 P&CR 223 . . . 205
Sledmore v Dalby (1996) 72 P&CR 196 . . . 421, 423
Small v Oliver & Saunders (Developments) Ltd [2006] 3 EGLR 141 . . . 590, 594, 596, 602
Smallwood v Sheppards [1895] 2 QB 627 . . . 184
Smith and Snipes Hall Farm Ltd v River Douglas Catchment Board [1949] 2 KB 500 . . . 279, 581, 583
Smith v Brudenell-Bruce [2002] 2 P&CR 4 . . . 558
Smith v Marrable (1843) 11 M & W 5 . . . 247
Southern Pacific Mortgages Ltd v Scott [2015] AC 385 . . . 115
Southward Housing Co-operative v Walker [2016] Ch 443 . . . 202, 203
Southwark LBC v Tanner [2001] 1 AC 1 . . . 243, 244
Sovmots Investments Ltd v Secretary of State for the Environment [1979] AC 144 . . . 543
Spectrum Investment Co v Holmes [1981] 1 WLR 221 . . . 154

Spencer's Case (1583) 5 Co Rep 16a . . . 267, 268, 269, 270, 277, 278, 583, 588, 600
Spiro v Glencrown Properties Ltd [1994] Ch 537 . . . 47
Spring House (Freehold) Ltd v Mount Cook Land Ltd [2001] EWCA Civ 1833 . . . 241–2
St Helen's Smelting Co Ltd v Tipping (1862) 11 ER 1483 . . . 522
Stack v Dowden [2007] 2 AC 432 . . . 332, 333, 358, 362, 363, 364, 365–7, 368, 370, 376, 385, 386, 392, 395, 396, 397, 398, 400, 401, 403, 404, 405, 406–7, , 442–8, 454, 455, 461
Stafford v Lee (1992) 65 P&CR 172 . . . 537
Staffordshire and Worcestershire Canal Navigation v Birmingham Canal Navigation [1866] LR 1 HL 254 . . . 554
Standard Chartered Bank Ltd v Walker [1982] 1 WLR 1410 . . . 493, 494
Starling v Lloyds TSB Bank plc [2000] Lloyd's Rep 8 . . . 478
State Bank of India v Sood [1997] Ch 276 . . . 343, 345, 511
Steadman v Steadman [1976] AC 536 . . . 55
Stockholm Finance Ltd v Garden Holdings Inc [1995] LTL (26 October 1995) . . . 118–19
Stokes v Anderson [1991] 1 FLR 391 . . . 427
Strand Securities v Caswell [1965] Ch 958 . . . 119, 212
Street v Mountford [1985] AC 809 . . . 191, 192, 194, 196, 197, 198, 199, 205, 230, 231
Stromdale & Ball Ltd v Burden [1952] Ch 223 . . . 26
Surrendra Overseas Ltd v Government of Sri Lanka [1997] 1 WLR 565 . . . 497
Surrey County Council v Bredero Homes Ltd [1993] 1 WLR 1361 . . . 602
Sutton v Mishcon de Reya, The Times, 28 January 2004 . . . 453
Sweet v Summer [2004] 4 All ER 288 . . . 536
Swift 1st v Chief Land Registrar [2015] EWCA Civ 330 . . . 136
Swift 1st Ltd v Colin [2012] Ch 206 . . . 489
Sykes v Harry [2001] QB 1014 . . . 249
System Floors Ltd v Ruralpride Ltd [1995] 1 EGLR 48 . . . 268

Tamares (Vincent Square) Ltd v Fairpoint Properties (Vincent Square) Ltd [2007] 1 WLR 2148 . . . 563
Tanner v Tanner [1975] 1 WLR 1346 . . . 437, 449, 456
Target Home Loans Ltd v Clothier [1994] 1 All ER 439 . . . 483
Taylor v Caldwell (1863) 3 B & S 826 . . . 227
Taylors Fashions Ltd v Liverpool Victoria Trustees Co Ltd [1982] 1 QB 133 . . . 414, 415, 418–19

Tebb v Hodge (1869) LR 5 CP 73 . . . 472
Tehidy Minerals Ltd v Norman [1971] 2 QB 528 . . . 552, 556, 558
Terunnanse v Terunnanse [1968] AC 1086 . . . 442
Texaco Antilles Ltd v Kernochan [1973] AC 609 . . . 597, 604
Thamesmead Town Ltd v Allotey (1998) 37 EG 161 . . . 599, 600
Thatcher v Douglas (1995) 146 NLJ 282 . . . 447
Thomas v Clydesdale Bank PLC [2010] EWHC 2755 (QB) . . . 117, 124
Thomas v Hayward (1869) LR 4 Ex 311 . . . 268
Thomas v Ken Thomas Ltd [2007] 1 EGLR 31 . . . 289
Thomas v Sorrell (1673) Vaugh 330 . . . 433
Thompson v Foy [2010] 1 P & CR 16 . . . 114, 116, 118, 119, 122
Thorner v Major [2009] 1 WLR 776 . . . 59, 60, 411, 413–14, 417–18, 428–9
Thorpe v Brumfitt (1873) LR 8 Ch App 650 . . . 518
Thursby v Plant (1690) 1 Saund 230 . . . 262
Tichbourne v Weir (1892) 67 LT 735 . . . 153
Tickner v Buzzacott [1965] Ch 426 . . . 214
Tiltwood, Sussex, Re [1978] Ch 269 . . . 604
Timmins v Rowlinson (1765) 3 Burr 1603 . . . 219
Timson v Ramsbottom (1836) 2 Keen 35 . . . 500
Tito v Waddell (No. 2) [1977] Ch 106 . . . 599
Toomes v Conset (1745) 3 Atk 261 . . . 475
Tootal Clothing Ltd v Guinea Properties Management Ltd [1992] 2 EGLR 80 . . . 49, 51, 56
Topplan Estates Ltd v Townley [2005] 1 EGLR 90 . . . 147
Total Oil Great Britain Ltd v Thompson Garages (Biggin Hill) Ltd [1972] 1 QB 318 . . . 228
TSB Bank plc v Marshall [1998] 3 EGLR 100 . . . 338
Tse Kwong Lam v Wong Chit Sen [1983] 1 WLR 1349 . . . 493
Tulk v Moxhay (1848) 2 Ph 774 . . . 277, 278, 280, 296, 585–9, 597, 609

Union Lighterage Co v London Graving Dock [1902] 2 Ch 557 . . . 548
Union of London & Smith's Bank Ltd's Conveyance, Re [1933] Ch 611 . . . 595
United Bank of Kuwait plc v Sahib [1997] Ch 107 . . . 473, 489
University of Westminster, Re [1998] 3 All ER 1014 . . . 604

Van Haarlem v Kasner (1992) 64 P&CR 214 . . . 292, 295
Vernon v Bethall (1762) 2 Eden 110 . . . 475
Verrall v Great Yarmouth BC [1981] 1 QB 202 . . . 440

Wakeham v Wood [1981] 43 P&CR 40 . . . 603
Wall v Collins [2007] Ch 390, [2007] EWCA Civ 444 . . . 518, 519, 541, 542, 566, 567, 571
Wallis's Caytown Bay Holiday Camp Ltd v Shell-Mex and BP Ltd [1975] QB 94 . . . 150
Walsh v Lonsdale (1882) 21 ChD 9 . . . 27, 64 210–11, 236, 472
Ward v Day (1864) 5 B & S 359 . . . 288
Ward v Duncombe [1893] AC 369 . . . 500
Ward v Kirkland [1967] Ch 194 . . . 538
Warmington v Miller [1973] QB 877 . . . 210
Warner v Jacob (1882) 20 ChD 220 . . . 493
Warren v Keen [1954] 1 QB 15 . . . 255, 256
Wasdale, Re [1899] 1 Ch 163 . . . 500
Waterlow v Bacon (1866) LR 2 Eq 514 . . . 565
Waterman v Boyle [2009] EWCA Civ 115 . . . 528
Watts v Stewart [2016] EWCA Civ 1247 . . . 197, 199
Wayling v Jones (1993) 69 P&CR 170 . . . 419
Webb v Bird (1861) 10 CB (NS) 268 . . . 523
Webb v Pollmount [1966] Ch 584 . . . 114
Webb v Russell (1789) 3 TR 393 . . . 583
Webb's Lease, Re [1951] Ch 808 . . . 540
Wedd v Porter [1916] 2 KB 91 . . . 256
Weg Motors Ltd v Hales [1962] Ch 49 . . . 241
West Bromwich Building Society v Wilkinson [2005] 1 WLR 2303 . . . 485
Westminster City Council v Clarke [1992] 2 AC 288 . . . 196
Weston v Lawrence Weaver Ltd [1961] 1 QB 402 . . . 562
Wheaton v Maple [1893] 3 Ch 48 . . . 549
Wheeldon v Burrows (1879) 12 ChD 31 . . . 535, 537–40, 541, 544, 545, 546, 560
Wheeler v J. J. Saunders Ltd [1996] Ch 19 . . . 539
White v Amirtharaja [2021] EWHC 330 affirmed on appeal [2022] EWCA Civ 11 . . . 146
White v City of London Brewery Co (1889) 42 ChD 237 . . . 492
White v Williams [1922] 1 KB 727 . . . 546
White Rose Cottage, Re [1965] Ch 940 . . . 489
Whitgift Homes v Stocks [2001] 48 EG 130 (CS) . . . 597
Wilkes v Spooner [1911] 2 KB 473 . . . 83
William Aldred's Case (1610) 9 Co Rep 57b . . . 525
William Old International Ltd v Arya [2009] EWHC 599 (Ch) . . . 246
Williams v Earle (1868) LR 3 QB 739 . . . 268
Williams v Hensman (1861) 1 John & H 546 . . . 373, 374, 375
Williams v Kiley (trading as CK Supermarkets Ltd) [2003] 1 EGLR 47 . . . 598
Williams v Morgan [1906] 1 Ch 804 . . . 482
Williams v Sandy Lane (Chester) Ltd [2007] 1 EGLR 10 . . . 547, 550, 566

Williams & Glyn's Bank Ltd v Boland [1981] AC 487 . . . 82, 114, 115, 116, 120, 124, 125, 313, 330, 343, 345, 384, 511

Willmott v Barber (1880) 15 Ch D 96 . . . 414

Wimbledon and Putney Commons Conservators v Dixon (1875) 1 Ch D 362 . . . 520

Windeler v Whitehall [1990] 1 FLR 505 . . . 384

Winter Garden Theatre (London) Ltd v Millennium Productions Ltd [1948] AC 173 . . . 439

Winterburn v Bennett [2017] 1 WLR 646 . . . 555

Wong v Beaumont Property Trust Ltd [1965] 1 QB 173 . . . 523, 536

Wood v Leadbitter (1845) 13 M & W 838 . . . 439

Wood v Manley (1839) 11 Ad & El 34 . . . 437

Wood v Waddington [2015] EWCA Civ 538 . . . 544, 545

Woodall v Clifton [1905] 2 Ch 257 . . . 267, 271

Woolnough, Re [2002] WTLR 595 . . . 374, 375

Woolwich Building Society v Dickman (1996) 72 P&CR 470 . . . 513

Worthington v Morgan (1849) 16 Sim 547 . . . 82

Wright v Macadam [1949] 2 KB 744 . . . 524, 526, 541, 542, 545, 560, 569

Wright v Robert Leonard (Developments) Ltd [1994] NPC 49 . . . 50

Wright v Williams (1836) 1 M & W 77 . . . 554

Wrotham Park Estate Co v Parkside Homes Ltd [1974] 1 WLR 798 . . . 602

Yaxley v Gotts [2000] Ch 162 . . . 57, 59, 60, 62, 427, 428

Zarb v Parry [2011] EWCA Civ 1306, [2012] 1 WLR 1240 . . . 149, 152, 161–2, 163

TABLE OF STATUTES

Administration of Estates Act 1925 . . . 2, 9, 174
  s 33(1) . . . 305
  s 46A . . . 376
Administration of Justice Act 1970
  s 36 . . . 483, 484, 486
  s 36(2) . . . 486
Administration of Justice Act 1973
  s 8 . . . 486
  s 8(3) . . . 486

Capital Transfer Tax Act 1984 . . . 72
Civil Partnership Act 2004 . . . 73, 77, 453, 457, 458
  s 65 . . . 454
  s 72 . . . 383
  s 81 . . . 185
  s 82 . . . 457
  Sch 5, Pt 2
    para 21 . . . 383
  Sch 8
    para 1 . . . 185
  Sch 9
    Pt 1 . . . 457
Coal Industry Act 1994
  s 7(3) . . . 623
Common Law Procedure Act 1852 . . . 293, 294
  s 210 . . . 293
  s 210A . . . 293
Commonhold and Leasehold Reform Act 2002 . . . 628
  Pt 1 . . . 179-180
  s 31(7) . . . 532
  ss 168–169 . . . 294
Commons Act 2006 . . . 112, 113, 533, 534
  s 9 . . . 531
Commons Registration Act 1965 . . . 112, 530, 531, 533
Companies Act 2006
  s 102 . . . 9, 10
Consumer Credit Act 1974
  s 94 . . . 476
  s 173 . . . 476
Contract (Rights of Third Parties) Act 1999 . . . 279-280, 581
  s 7(1) . . . 581
Conveyancing Act 1881 . . . 592
  s 6(2) . . . 543, 544
  s 10 . . . 269
Coronavirus Act 2020 . . . 190
County Courts Act 1984 . . . 294
  s 138(9A) . . . 295
Courts and Legal Services Act 1990
  ss 104–107 . . . 478

Criminal Law Act 1977
  s 5 . . . 486
  s 6 . . . 152, 214, 294, 480, 486

Defective Premises Act 1972
  s 4 . . . 248, 249
Domestic Violence and Matrimonial Proceedings Act 1976 . . . 458

Enterprise Act 2002
  s 261 . . . 484
Equality Act 2010 . . . 178
Estates of Decreased Person (Forfeiture Rule and Law of Succession) Act 2011
  s 1 . . . 376

Family Law Act 1996 . . . 73, 453, 457, 458, 459
  s 30 . . . 457
  s 30(3) . . . 490
  s 31 . . . 457
  s 31(10) . . . 116
  s 31(10)(b) . . . 457
  s 33 . . . 457
  s 36 . . . 450, 458
  s 42 . . . 458
  s 62(1)(a) . . . 458
  s 62(3) . . . 458
Family Law (Scotland) Act 2006 . . . 460
Financial Services Act 1986 . . . 47
Financial Services Act 2012 . . . 478
Financial Services and Markets Act 2000 . . . 478, 487
Forfeiture Act 1982
  s 2(1) . . . 375
  s 2(2) . . . 375

Homes (Fitness for Human Habitation) Act 2018 . . . 246, 247
  s 1 . . . 247
Housing Act 1974
  s 125 . . . 284
Housing Act 1985
  Pt VI . . . 285
  s 610 . . . 605
Housing Act 1988 . . . 218, 440
  Pt I . . . 219
  s 27 . . . 285
Housing Act 2004 . . . 247
Human Rights Act (HRA) 1998 . . . 29, 30, 143, 156, 166, 169, 179, 286, 294
  s 1 . . . 29

s 3 . . . 30
s 4 . . . 30
s 6 . . . 30
Sch 1 (European Convention on Human Rights) . . . 29

Infrastructure Act 2015 . . . 626
ss 34–36 . . . 39
ss 43–48 . . . 624
s 43(1) . . . 624
s 43(2) . . . 624
s 43(3) . . . 624
s 44(1) . . . 625
s 44(2) . . . 625
s 44(3) . . . 625
s 44(4) . . . 625
s 45 . . . 625
s 46 . . . 625
s 47(1) . . . 625
s 50 . . . 626
Sch 5 . . . 39
Inheritance Tax Act 1984 . . . 126
Insolvency Act 1986 . . . 221, 337, 456
s 313 . . . 484
s 335A . . . 336, 337
s 335A(3) . . . 337
Interpretation Act 1978 . . . 618
s 5 . . . 45
Sch 1 . . . 618

Judicature Acts 1873–5 . . . 269

Land Charges Act (LCA) 1925 . . . 2, 71
s 3(6)(b) . . . 276
Land Charges Act (LCA) 1972 . . . 34, 36, 71, 72, 75, 76, 78, 79, 84, 609
Class A . . . 71, 76
Class B . . . 71, 76
Class C . . . 71
Class C(i) . . . 71, 73, 74, 76, 213, 505, 506, 507, 510
Class C(ii) 72, 74, 76
Class C(iii) . . . 72, 73, 76, 213, 505, 506
Class C(iv) . . . 72, 73, 76–7, 78, 213, 276
Class D . . . 72, 213
Class D(i) . . . 72, 73, 76–7
Class D(ii) . . . 73, 76–7
Class D(iii) . . . 73, 74, 76, 78
Class E . . . 73
Class F . . . 73, 76, 213
Class G . . . 610
s 1 . . . 71, 79
s 2 . . . 534
s 2(4) . . . 71, 212
s 2(4)(iv) . . . 77
s 2(5) . . . 589
s 2(8) . . . 71

s 4(2) . . . 76
s 4(5) . . . 76, 77, 213
s 4(6) . . . 76, 77, 212, 213, 589
s 4(8) . . . 76, 213
s 9 . . . 75
s 10(4) . . . 79
s 11(5) . . . 79
s 11(6) . . . 79
s 17(1) . . . 76, 77
Land Registration Act (LRA) 1925 . . . 2, 36, 89, 99, 111, 113, 132, 136, 137, 143
s 3(viii) . . . 617
s 20(1) . . . 599
s 25(2) . . . 470
s 28 . . . 501
s 40 . . . 67
s 50(1) . . . 589
s 69 . . . 135
s 70 . . . 345
s 70(1) . . . 113
s 70(1)(a) . . . 111, 532
s 70(1)(f) . . . 105, 135, 156
s 70(1)(g) . . . 78, 114, 116, 117, 119, 120, 122, 123, 126, 216, 345, 391, 425, 447
s 70(1)(k) . . . 111
s 75 . . . 144
s 75(1) . . . 143, 155, 156, 166
s 75(2) . . . 155
s 82(3) . . . 135
s 85 . . . 471
s 87 . . . 471
s 102(2) . . . 501
Land Registration Act (LRA) 1986 . . . 119
s 5 . . . 501
Land Registration Act (LRA) 2002 . . . 26, 34, 37, 77, 87, 88, 89, 92, 94, 95, 97, 98, 99, 111, 112, 113, 124, 126, 132, 134, 135, 141, 142, 144, 152, 153, 155, 156, 157, 158, 160, 163, 164, 166, 168, 206, 208, 276, 344, 348, 479, 501, 508, 509, 532, 545, 606, 608, 611
s 2(a) . . . 99
s 3 . . . 98
s 3(1) . . . 99
s 3(3) . . . 98
s 3(4) . . . 98
s 4 . . . 99, 100, 208, 470, 471, 511
s 4(1)(c) . . . 208
s 4(1)(g) . . . 471, 490
s 4(8) . . . 471
s 6 . . . 86
s 6(2) . . . 471
s 6(4) . . . 100
s 6(6) . . . 100
s 7 . . . 86
s 7(1) . . . 100
s 7(2)(b) . . . 208
s 7(4) . . . 176

s 9 . . . 101
s 9(2) . . . 102
s 9(3) . . . 102
s 9(4) . . . 103
s 9(5) . . . 103
s 10 . . . 101
s 10(2) . . . 102
s 10(3) . . . 102
s 11 . . . 104, 105, 532
s 11(2)–(3) . . . 104
s 11(4)–(5) . . . 104
s 11(4)(c) . . . 105, 126, 155
s 11(6) . . . 105
s 11(7) . . . 106
s 12 . . . 532
s 12(3)–(5) . . . 105
s 12(6) . . . 102106
ss 15–22 . . . 97
s 23(1)(a) . . . 470
s 25 . . . 470
s 26 . . . 97, 344
s 26(1) . . . 97
s 26(2)(a) . . . 97
s 26(3) . . . 344
s 27 . . . 106, 110, 308, 470, 502
s 27(1) . . . 107, 208, 502, 533, 559, 560
s 27(2) . . . 106, 112, 208
s 27(2)(d) . . . 533
s 27(2)(f) . . . 123, 471, 479, 502
s 27(4) . . . 601
s 27(7) . . . 112, 542, 545
s 28 . . . 108, 109, 110, 126, 502, 503, 504
s 29 . . . 108, 109, 110, 126, 128, 212, 213, 342, 344, 502, 504, 506, 533
ss 29–30 501
s 29(1) . . . 109, 110, 123
s 29(2) . . . 110, 503
s 29(3) . . . 112, 503, 533
s 29(4) . . . 110, 502
s 30 . . . 108, 109, 502, 504, 533
s 31 . . . 126
s 32 . . . 589
s 32(1) . . . 95, 502
s 32(3) . . . 95
s 33 . . . 96, 110
s 37 . . . 103
s 40 . . . 601
s 41(1) . . . 96, 97
s 41(2) . . . 97
s 42(2) . . . 96
s 44(1) . . . 96
s 46(2) . . . 96
s 49 . . . 509
s 49(3) . . . 509
s 49(4) . . . 509
s 49(5) . . . 509
s 49(6) . . . 509

s 51 . . . 471
s 58 . . . 94, 95, 135, 136, 137, 571
s 58(1) . . . 95
s 58(2) . . . 95
s 62 . . . 102
s 62(1) . . . 103
s 62(2) . . . 103
s 65 . . . 132
s 71 . . . 103
s 71(a) . . . 104
s 86 . . . 126
s 92(2)(a)(iii) . . . 108
s 92(2)(b) . . . 108
ss 96–98 . . . 138, 157
s 96 . . . 157
s 98 . . . 160, 162
s 98(1) . . . 160
s 98(3) . . . 160
s 98(5) . . . 160
ss 107–113 . . . 98
s 116 . . . 109, 425, 448, 504, 512
s 117 . . . 113
s 131 . . . 133
s 132 . . . 89
s 134 . . . 263
Sch 1 . . . 91, 104, 105, 106
   para 2 . . . 155
   para 3 . . . 208, 532
Sch 2 . . . 107, 112
   para 3 . . . 208
   para 6 . . . 601
   para 7 . . . 601
   para 8 . . . 502
Sch 3 . . . 91, 92, 110, 111, 112, 125, 212, 503, 504, 506
   para 1 . . . 111, 116, 212
   para 2 . . . 78, 111, 113, 114, 115, 116, 118, 119, 122, 123, 125, 126, 155, 163, 212, 345, 425, 503, 511
   para 2(a) . . . 116
   para 2(b) . . . 123
   para 2(c) . . . 123, 124
   para 2(d) . . . 116
   para 3 . . . 111–3, 114, 116, 121, 126, 533
   paras 3(1)–(2) . . . 112
   paras 4–9 . . . 111, 113
   paras 10–14 . . . 111, 113
Sch 4 . . . 132, 133, 135, 136, 137, 138
   para 2 . . . 132
   para 3 . . . 135
   para 3(2) . . . 133
   para 3(3) . . . 133
   para 4 . . . 134
   para 5 . . . 132, 134, 138, 496
   para 6 . . . 135, 138
   para 6(2) . . . 133, 138
   para 6(3) . . . 133

Sch 6 . . . 134, 138, 152, 157, 158, 159, 163, 164, 165
   para 1 . . . 158
   para 4 . . . 160
   para 4(c) . . . 163
   para 5 . . . 158, 159, 164
   para 5(2) . . . 159
   para 5(3) . . . 159
   para 5(4) . . . 160, 161
   para 5(4)(c) . . . 161, 162
   para 6 . . . 158, 160
   para 7 . . . 158
   paras 8(2)–(4) . . . 157
   para 8(2) . . . 152
   para 11(1) . . . 157
   para 11(2) . . . 152
   para 12 . . . 157
Sch 8 . . . 132, 133, 138, 139
   para 1(a) . . . 133
   para 1(b) . . . 133
   para 5 . . . 133
Sch 9 . . . 98
Sch 11
   para 33(4) . . . 457
Sch 12
   para 18(1) . . . 155
   para 20 . . . 263
Land Transfer Act 1862 . . . 88
Land Transfer Act 1897 . . . 88
Landlord and Tenant Act 1927 . . . 252, 254
   s 19 . . . 255
   s 19(1) . . . 254
   s 19(1)(a) . . . 252
Landlord and Tenant Act 1954 . . . 190, 219
Landlord and Tenant Act 1985 . . . 247
   s 8 . . . 247
   ss 9A–9C . . . 247
   s 9A(1) . . . 247
   s 9A(2) . . . 247
   s 10 . . . 247
   ss 11–14 . . . 248
   s 11 . . . 227, 230, 231, 248
   s 12(1) . . . 248
   s 12(2) . . . 248
   s 13 . . . 248
   s 14 . . . 247
   s 17 . . . 284
Landlord and Tenant Act 1988 . . . 254
   s 1(3) . . . 254
   s 1(6) . . . 254
   s 4 . . . 254, 255
Landlord and Tenant (Covenants) Act 1995 . . . 204, 212, 258, 259, 260, 261, 262, 263–4, 268, 271, 272, 273, 275, 276, 278, 280, 299, 588, 600
   s 1 . . . 261
   s 1(2) . . . 263

s 1(3) . . . 212, 259
s 2 . . . 277
s 2(1)(a) . . . 276
s 3 . . . 275
s 3(5) . . . 278, 280
s 3(6)(a) . . . 275
s 4 . . . 275
s 5 . . . 271
s 5(2)(b) . . . 275
s 6 . . . 273
s 6(2)(b) . . . 275
s 7 . . . 273
s 8 . . . 273
s 11 . . . 273
s 11(1) . . . 272
s 11(2)(b) . . . 272
s 11(3)(b) . . . 273
s 16 . . . 272
ss 17–20 . . . 263, 270, 272
ss 17–21 . . . 264
s 17 . . . 264
s 18(2) . . . 264
s 18(3) . . . 264
s 19 . . . 264
s 20(6) . . . 72
s 22 . . . 254
s 23(1) . . . 276
s 23(3) . . . 276
s 24(2) . . . 272
s 24(4) . . . 272, 275
s 25 . . . 272, 273, 274, 275
s 25(1)(a) . . . 271
s 28(1) . . . 274, 275, 276
s 30(4) . . . 279
s 30(4)(a) . . . 272
s 30(4)(b) . . . 276
Law of Property Act (LPA) 1922
   s 145 . . . 250
   Sch 15 . . . 250
Law of Property Act (LPA) 1925 . . . 2, 74, 174, 183, 184, 187, 199, 259, 260, 309, 312, 315, 316, 342, 344, 346, 350, 371, 468, 470, 483, 542, 617, 618, 620
   s 1 . . . 18, 183, 184
   s 1(1) . . . 9, 18, 22, 23, 171, 174, 175, 177, 183, 186, 622
   s 1(1)(b) . . . 11
   s 1(2) . . . 18, 19, 21, 22, 23, 175, 531, 601
   s 1(2)(a) . . . 21, 107, 566
   s 1(2)(b) . . . 19, 21, 22, 107
   s 1(2)(c) . . . 21, 22
   s 1(2)(d) . . . 21, 23
   s 1(2)(e) . . . 21, 23, 107
   s 1(3) . . . 9, 10, 19, 23, 174, 175, 531, 559
   s 1(6) . . . 317, 360
   s 2(1) . . . 80, 128
   s 2(1)(ii) . . . 343

s 2(3) . . . 128
s 7(1) . . . 175
s 13 . . . 472
s 25(1) . . . 324
s 26(3) . . . 326
s 27 . . . 343, 344, 345
s 27(2) . . . 345
s 29 . . . 345
s 30 . . . 314, 338, 378, 381, 511
s 34(1) . . . 357, 371
s 34(2) . . . 305, 312, 358, 386, 396
s 36(1) . . . 305, 312, 358, 386, 396
s 36(2) . . . 371, 373, 374, 375
s 36(3) . . . 375
s 36(4) . . . 375
s 40 . . . 41, 53–6, 78, 209, 308, 374, 444, 561
s 40(2) . . . 56, 472
s 49(1) . . . 67
ss 52–54 . . . 52, 53
s 52 . . . 26, 53, 241
s 52(1) . . . 19, 84, 106, 206, 208, 217, 221, 232, 308, 531, 560
s 52(2)(c) . . . 220
s 53 . . . 19
s 53(1)(b) . . . 47, 304, 305, 306, 308, 361, 388
s 53(1)(c) . . . 369, 380, 473
s 53(2) . . . 47, 304, 305, 389
s 54(2) . . . 47, 207, 214, 217, 220, 235, 241, 269, 541, 542
s 56 . . . 279, 579–80, 581, 582, 584, 596, 597
s 56(1) . . . 579
s 62 . . . 112, 212, 213, 524, 533, 534, 535, 540–6, 567–8, 575, 607, 609
s 62(1) . . . 540
s 62(4) . . . 543
s 76(6) . . . 592
s 77 . . . 263
s 77(5) . . . 592
s 78 . . . 279, 582, 583, 584, 591, 592, 593, 594, 597
s 78(1) . . . 583
s 79 . . . 262, 263, 272, 296, 588, 592, 593
s 80(3) . . . 592
s 84 . . . 572, 604, 605, 611
s 84(1B) . . . 604
s 84(2) . . . 603
ss 85–87 . . . 22, 467, 470
s 85 . . . 468–9
s 85(1) . . . 479
s 85(2) . . . 469
s 86 . . . 468, 469
s 86(1) . . . 479
s 86(2) . . . 469
s 87 . . . 468, 469–471
s 87(1) . . . 479
s 88 . . . 489
s 88(1) . . . 484, 489

s 88(2) . . . 482
s 89(1) . . . 484, 489
s 89(2) . . . 482
s 91(2) . . . 482, 483, 489
s 93 . . . 481
s 94 . . . 509
s 94(2) . . . 509
s 96(1) . . . 479
s 98 . . . 479
s 99 . . . 478
s 99(1) . . . 480
s 100 . . . 479
s 101 . . . 484, 487, 489
s 101(1)(i) . . . 483, 488
s 101(1)(ii) . . . 480
s 101(1)(iii) . . . 487, 489
s 103 . . . 483
s 104 . . . 489
s 104(1) . . . 484
s 105 . . . 485
s 108 . . . 480
s 109 . . . 487
s 136 . . . 449, 584
s 137 . . . 473, 500
s 137(3) . . . 501
s 137(4) . . . 501
s 141 . . . 267, 269, 270, 276, 277, 278
s 142 . . . 267, 269, 270, 276, 277, 278
s 146 . . . 289, 290, 291, 292, 293, 294, 297, 298, 469
s 146(2) . . . 295
s 146(4) . . . 295, 297, 469
s 149(3) . . . 186, 187, 205
s 149(6) . . . 185, 201, 202, 205, 219, 220, 235
s 150 . . . 222
s 153 . . . 221, 236, 601
s 163(2) . . . 352
s 185 . . . 221
s 196(3) . . . 372
s 196(4) . . . 372
s 198 . . . 75
s 198(1) . . . 75
s 199(1)(ii) . . . 21
s 205 . . . 12, 195, 542, 617
s 205(1)(ii) . . . 542
s 205(1)(ix) . . . 617, 618, 620, 623
s 205(1)(xix) . . . 10
s 205(1)(xxi) . . . 77
s 205(1)(xxvii) . . . 11, 174, 184
Sch 5, form no 1 . . . 470
Law of Property Act (LPA) 1969 . . . 604
s 23 . . . 70
s 25 . . . 74
s 28(4) . . . 603
Law of Property Act (LPA) 2002 . . . 19
Law of Property (Amendment) Act 1926 . . . 175
Sch . . . 175

Law of Property (Joint Tenants) Act
1964 . . . 354, 380
s 3 . . . 380
Law of Property (Miscellaneous Provisions) Act
1989 . . . 26, 40, 41, 42, 43, 44, 47, 54, 56, 59,
60, 62, 473
s 1 . . . 26, 40, 208, 210
s 2 . . . 41, 42, 43, 44, 45, 46, 47, 48, 49, 50, 51,
52, 53, 54, 56, 57, 59, 61, 62, 63, 67, 209,
308, 374, 427, 472, 473, 489, 531, 561
s 2(1)–(3) . . . 42
s 2(1) . . . 43, 49, 50, 58
s 2(2) . . . 43
s 2(3) . . . 43, 45, 46
s 2(4) . . . 52
s 2(5) . . . 42, 43, 46, 47, 57, 58, 61, 63, 427
s 2(5)(a) . . . 47
s 3 . . . 66
Leasehold Property (Repairs) Act 1938 . . . 283, 284
Leasehold Reform (Ground Rent)
Act 2022 . . . 188, 206, 251
s 9 . . . 251
Legal Aid, Sentencing and Punishment of
Offenders Act (LASPOA) 2012
s 144 . . . 164, 165
s 144(1) . . . 164
s 144(7) . . . 164
Limitation Act 1980 . . . 103, 104, 106, 142, 143,
146, 151, 157, 176, 496, 497
s 15 . . . 142, 151, 153, 155, 157, 497
s 15(2) . . . 151
s 17 . . . 143, 154, 166, 497
s 18 . . . 154
s 20 . . . 497
s 28 . . . 151
s 29 . . . 497
s 30 . . . 497
s 32 . . . 151
s 38(2) . . . 151
Sch 1
para 1 . . . 148, 151
para 3 . . . 497
para 5 . . . 148
para 8 . . . 151
para 8(4) . . . 150
Local Government and Housing Act
1989 . . . 211
Local Land Charges Act 1975 . . . 39
s 10 . . . 39
Localism Act 2011
s 208 . . . 563

Matrimonial Causes Act 1973
Pt II . . . 383
s 25(2) . . . 383
Matrimonial Homes Act 1967 . . . 73

Matrimonial Proceedings and Property Act
1970 . . . 383
s 37 . . . 454, 455
Mental Capacity Act 2005
s 67 . . . 151
Sch 6
para 25 . . . 151
Mental Health Act 1983 . . . 118, 151, 553
Mortgage Repossessions (Protection of Tenants,
etc) Act 2010 . . . 487

National Trust Act 1937
s 8 . . . 588

Official Secrets Acts . . . 292

Perpetuities and Accumulations Act
1964 . . . 350, 352
Perpetuities and Accumulations Act (PAA)
2009 . . . 350, 353–4
s 1 . . . 353
s 5 . . . 353
s 5(2) . . . 353
s 12 . . . 353
s 13 . . . 354
s 14 . . . 354
s 15 . . . 353
s 16 . . . 254
s 18 . . . 354
Petroleum Act 1998
s 4B(4)–(6) . . . 626
Petroleum (Production) Act 1934
s 1 . . . 623
s 2 . . . 623
Prescription Act 1832 . . . 546, 547, 550, 551,
552, 553–8, 560, 561, 567, 570
s 1 . . . 553, 554, 558
s 2 . . . 553, 554, 558
s 3 . . . 557, 558
s 4 . . . 556, 558
s 7 . . . 553, 555
s 8 . . . 553, 555
Protection from Eviction Act 1977 . . . 285
s 1(3) . . . 243, 285
s 1(3A) . . . 243, 285
s 2 . . . 294
s 3 . . . 214, 440
s 3A . . . 219
s 3(2A) . . . 440
s 3(2B) . . . 440
s 5 . . . 440
s 5(1) . . . 219
s 5(1A) . . . 440
Public Trustee Act 1906
s 4(3) . . . 639

Real Property Act 1845
  s 5 . . . 581
Recorded Delivery Service Act 1962
  s 1 . . . 372
  Sch 1, para 1 . . . 372
Rent Act 1977 . . . 218
Rent Acts . . . 191, 196, 434, 541
Rentcharges Act 1977 . . . 22, 601
  s 1 . . . 22
  s 2 . . . 601
Renting Homes (Wales) Act 2016 . . . 247
Rights of Light Act 1959 . . . 557, 573

Senior Courts Act 1981 . . . 602
  s 37 . . . 489
  s 50 . . . 562
Settled Land Act (SLA) 1882 . . . 310, 315, 348
Settled Land Act (SLA) 1925 . . . 2, 72, 113, 309, 311, 312, 315, 322, 348, 349, 483, 500, 617
  s 107 . . . 348
  s 117(1)(ix) . . . 617
Statute of Frauds 1677 . . . 49, 55, 308
  s 7 . . . 308
Statute of Westminster the First 1275 . . . 551
Supreme Court Act 1981
  s 49(1) . . . 211
Supreme Court of Judicature Act 1873 . . . 18, 211, 459
  s 25(11) . . . 210
Supreme Court of Judicature Act 1875 . . . 18, 211, 459

Tenures Abolition Act 1660 . . . 6
Town and Country Planning Act 1990
  s 72 . . . 602
  s 106 . . . 46
  s 237 . . . 563
Tribunals, Courts and Enforcement Act 2007 . . . 293
  Pt 3 . . . 286
  Sch 12 . . . 286
Trustee Act (TA) 1925 . . . 2, 320
  s 34(2) . . . 321, 360
  s 36 . . . 321, 322
  s 39 . . . 321, 343, 374
  s 40 . . . 321
  s 41 . . . 321
  s 44 . . . 321
  s 68(6) . . . 617
  s 68(18) . . . 321
Trustee Act 2000 . . . 323, 328, 329
  s 1 . . . 329
  s 8 . . . 323
  s 8(1) . . . 323
Trusts of Land and Appointment of Trustees Act (TOLATA) 1996 . . . 2, 10, 174, 179, 309, 312, 314, 315, 316, 317, 318, 319, 320, 322, 323, 324, 330, 332, 333, 334, 335, 337, 338, 340, 341, 342, 343, 344, 345, 346, 348, 359, 378, 379, 380, 456, 484, 622, 640
  Pt 1 . . . 319
  Pt II . . . 322
  s 1(1) . . . 316, 319, 320
  s 1(1)(a) . . . 316, 320
  s 1(2)(a) . . . 217, 316
  s 1(2)(b) . . . 316
  s 2(1) . . . 316
  s 2(6) . . . 316, 317
  s 3 . . . 317, 373, 617
  s 3(1) . . . 317
  s 3(2) . . . 317
  s 4(1) . . . 317, 324, 325
  s 5 . . . 314
  s 6 . . . 325, 343
  s 6(1) . . . 322, 323, 326, 328, 329
  s 6(2) . . . 323, 327
  s 6(3) . . . 323, 346
  s 6(4) . . . 323
  s 6(5) . . . 328, 341
  s 6(6) . . . 328, 341, 343
  s 7 . . . 323, 325
  s 7(1) . . . 379
  s 7(3) . . . 323, 379
  s 8 . . . 323, 326, 342
  s 8(1) . . . 325, 328
  s 8(2) . . . 325, 341
  s 9 . . . 328, 329
  s 9(1) . . . 323, 325, 328
  s 9(2) . . . 342
  s 9(7) . . . 328, 329
  s 9(8) . . . 329
  s 9A . . . 329, 341
  s 9A(1) . . . 329
  s 9A(2) . . . 329
  s 9A(6) . . . 329
  s 10(1) . . . 342
  s 10(3) . . . 326
  s 11 . . . 327
  s 11(1) . . . 327, 335, 341
  s 11(2)(a) . . . 327
  s 11(2)(b) . . . 317
  s 12 . . . 330, 331, 332, 333, 347, 379, 511
  s 12(1) . . . 330, 331, 333
  s 12(1)(b) . . . 331
  s 12(2) . . . 331, 333
  s 13 . . . 331, 332, 333, 379
  s 13(3) . . . 331
  s 13(5) . . . 331
  s 13(6) . . . 331, 332, 333
  s 14 . . . 324, 326, 331, 332, 335, 336, 337, 338, 339, 340, 341, 378, 379, 380, 395, 456, 483, 484, 511
  s 14(1) . . . 335
  s 14(2) . . . 335

s 14(2)(a) . . . 336
s 15 . . . 332, 333, 336, 337, 338, 339, 340, 341, 347, 484
s 15(1) . . . 336, 338
s 15(1)(a) . . . 339, 341
s 15(1)(b) . . . 339, 381
s 15(1)(c) . . . 339, 341
s 15(1)(d) . . . 341
s 15(2) . . . 336
s 15(3) . . . 336, 338, 381
s 16 . . . 344
s 16(1) . . . 342
s 16(2) . . . 342, 343
s 16(3) . . . 342
s 16(4) . . . 346
s 16(5) . . . 346
s 16(7) . . . 343
ss 19–21 . . . 321, 322
s 19 . . . 321, 322, 324
s 19(1)(a) . . . 322
s 19(1)(b) . . . 322
s 19(2) . . . 322
s 25(1) . . . 316
s 25(2) . . . 617
Sch 1 . . . 316, 317
  para 1(1) . . . 317
  para 1(2) . . . 317
  para 3 . . . 318
  para 5(1) . . . 318
  para 5(2) . . . 318
Sch 2
  para 4(3) . . . 371
Sch 3
  para 3 . . . 316
  para 4 . . . 316
  para 4(1) . . . 343
  para 23 . . . 336
Sch 4 . . . 617

Wales Act 2017
  s 25 . . . 626

European Union Legislation
Treaty of Rome
  Art 48 . . . 478

International Instruments
European Convention for the Protection of Human Rights and Freedoms (ECHR) . . . 29, 165, 178, 286
  Art 6 . . . 30, 98, 166, 167, 286
  Art 8 . . . 30, 179, 286, 287
  Art 9 . . . 179
  Art 14 . . . 30, 179
  First Protocol, Art 1 . . . 29, 30, 113, 166, 167, 169, 286, 287, 484
  Sixth Protocol . . . 29

TABLE OF STATUTORY INSTRUMENTS

Land Charges Rules 1974
  r 22 . . . 75
Land Registration Rules 1925 . . . 111
  r 40 . . . 589
Land Registration Rules (LRR) 2003 (SI 2003/1417), as amended . . . 89
  r 2 . . . 89
  r 21 . . . 100
  r 28 . . . 103, 104
  r 35 . . . 589
  r 57 . . . 103
  r 103 . . . 470
  r 114 . . . 496
  r 115 . . . 496

Onshore Hydraulic Fracturing (Protected Areas) Regulations 2016 . . . 626

Taking Control of Goods Regulations 2012 . . . 286

Unfair Terms in Consumer Contracts Regulations . . . 476

WHO'S WHO

Property	Characters	Estates, interests etc.	Topics considered	Chaps
TRANT HOUSE	Vernon Venables	Freehold owner and prospective vendor	Introduction to basic concepts in land law, including the multiplicity of estates and interests in land	1, 2
	Vernon's wife, Vanessa Venables			
	Vernon's mother			
	Penelope Price	Possible purchaser		
	Ted Topling	Tenant of flat in stables		
	Unnamed owner of neighbouring cottage			
	Another neighbour who owns a pony			
	Vernon's bank or building society			
TRANT WAY				
1.	Victor Venn	Freehold owner and vendor	Registered title—sale and purchase of freehold house	3
	Mr and Mrs Armstrong	Purchasers	Investigation of title; transfer and registration	6
			Co-ownership	17
	Wanda Waynflete	Previous owner	Mistakes on the register; alteration and indemnity	6
	Double Gloucester Building Society	Mortgagees, after purchase by the Armstrongs	Mortgages and charges	22
2.	Victoria Ventnor	Freehold owner and vendor	Unregistered title—sale and purchase of freehold house	3

(Continued...)

WHO'S WHO

Property	Characters	Estates, interests etc.	Topics considered	Chaps
	Barbara Bell	Purchaser	The contract	4
			Investigations of title; conveyance	5
			First registration	6
	Bob Bell: Barbara's father	Occupier of top floor 'granny flat'	Licences; enforcement of licences; protection from molestation	20; 21
3.	Oscar Oregano	Adverse possessor or 'squatter'	Adverse possession	7
	Nicholas Oregano: Oscar's nephew			
4.	David Derby	Freehold owner	Types of freehold estate	8
	David's niece Erica and nephews: Frank and Hal			
	David's friend: George			
5.	Fingall Forest	Freehold owner and landlord of Gerald Gruyère and James Harding	Leasehold estate; obligations of landlord and tenant; running of covenants on assignment of lease and reversion	9, 10, 11
	Gerald Gruyère	Weekly tenant of basement flat		
	James Harding	Tenant of maisonette under 99-yr. lease granted in 2012 (a 'new' lease for purposes of L&T (Covs) Act, 1995)		
	Wensleydale Bank plc	Mortgagee of James Harding's 99-yr. lease	Mortgages	22
	Gerald Gruyère keeps dustbin in landlord's garden	Easement of storage	Easements	24

6.	Irene Ivy	Former freehold owner and landlord of John Jarlsberg	Obligations of landlord and tenant; running of covenants on assignment of lease and reversion	10, 11
	John Jarlsberg	Former tenant under 40-yr. lease, granted in 1979 (an 'old' lease for purposes of L&T (Covs) Act, 1995)		
	Liam Lyle	Current freehold owner		
	Keith Kale	Current tenant		
7.	Martin Mount	Freehold owner and landlord of Nigel Norman	Enforcement of leasehold covenants in head leases and subleases; remedies for breach	11, 12
	Nigel Norman	Tenant under 99-yr. lease, and landlord of Olav Orion and Paula Primrose		
7A	Olav Orion	Monthly periodic tenant of 7A		11, 12
7B	Paula Primrose	Monthly periodic tenant of 7B		
8.	Alice, Brian, Colin, David, Eric and Fanny	Co-owners	Co-ownership, severance of joint tenancy; disputes between co-owners; TOLATA 1996, s. 14	14, 17
9.	Mary Brown, her wife, Janet Brown and their two daughters	Freehold owner	Trusts of land under TOLATA 1996	14
10.	Sidney Search and Frederick Find	Partners in firm of chartered surveyors, tenants under 99-yr. lease	Co-ownership	17
11.	Mark Mould	Freehold owner	Resulting and constructive trusts	18
	his wife, Sally Mould		Home rights	21
12.	Mildred Mumps	Freehold owner and mortgagor	Cohabitants' property rights at end of relationship; home rights; protection from molestation	20, 21
	Henry Newton: Mildred's unmarried partner			
	Red Leicester Building Society	Mortgagee		22, 23
	Royal Windsor Bank	Prospective second mortgagee		22, 23

(Continued...)

WHO'S WHO

Property	Characters	Estates, interests etc.	Topics considered	Chaps
12A	Laura Lymeswold	Occupier of the basement flat	*Nature of a licence; 'lease or licence?'; enforcement of licences*	20, 23
14.	Nigel Neep	Freehold owner Grazes his goat on Fieldy Farm Uses a footpath across Fieldy Farm	*Easements and profits*	24
	Nigel's bank	Possible mortgagee	*Grant of informal mortgages*	22
15.	Un-named past freehold owner (in 1947)		*Easements; their grant and transmission*	24
	Charles Chive	Current freehold owner Benefits from a drain running under 16 Trant Way		
16.	Un-named past freehold owner (in 1947)		*Easements; their grant and transmission*	24
	Marjorie Marjoram (until 1980)	Former freehold owner		
	Dan Dill	Current freehold owner Provides drainage to No 15 Enjoys a view over Fieldy Farm Provides the only point of acess to 16A		
16A	Marjorie Marjoram	Freehold owner until 1980, when she divided the then 16 and sold the part which became 16A to Basil Borage	*Easements; their grant and transmission*	24
	Basil Borage	Purchased freehold in 1980		

Fieldy Farm (behind 14–16 Trant Way)	Farmer George	Freehold owner of a large farm, which neighbours some of the properties towards the end of Trant Way Maintains fence separating farm from 14 Trant Way	*Easements and profits* 24
17.	Olive Orange (died 1995)	Freehold owner in 1988 and covenantee	*Freehold covenants: grant and running of covenants* 25
	Paul Peach	Current freehold owner	
18.	Olive Orange	Freehold owner in 1988	*Freehold covenants: grant and running of covenants* 25
	Robert Raspberry	Purchaser of freehold in 1988 and covenantor	
	Silvia Strawberry	Current freehold owner	
19.	Daniel Date	Freehold owner in 1988	*Freehold covenants: grant of covenants* 25
20. Also called 'The Old Rectory'	Big Builders Ltd	Freehold owner in 1999 Divided property and constructed the new Rectory Crescent on the land forming part of the old 20 Trant Way	*Freehold covenants: building schemes* 25

RECTORY CRESCENT
(formerly 20 Trant Way)

1	Alfred Alpha	Freehold owners	*Freehold covenants: building schemes* 25
2	Bertie Beta		
3	Gail Gamma		
4	Dolly Delta		
5	Ewan Epsilon		
6	Oscar Omega		

PART I
Introduction

Trant Way

In this part, we will introduce you to Trant Way, a road in the fictitious town of Mousehole in the county of Stilton, which is used throughout the book to illustrate the application of land law rules in practical situations. We hope that these examples are helpful; but, in case you lose track of the stories, we include a table of the properties and the characters you will meet in the following chapters immediately before this Introduction. You do not have to read it: it is just a reference section to refer to if you forget 'Who's Who' in Trant Way.

Most of the properties in Trant Way are occupied as houses or flats, but the basic land law covered in this book is just as relevant to non-residential property.

The structure of this book

In the first two chapters, we follow prospective purchasers who are viewing properties in Trant Way and discover:

- what is meant by 'owning land' (in Chapter 1); and
- how one person may have rights over land owned by another (in Chapter 2).

In these two chapters we are, as it were, getting the chess pieces up on the board, and telling you what they are called and how they move. Some of the material in these two chapters may seem rather theoretical but, if you can get a basic understanding of the concepts described, it will make the rest of your study of land law much easier.

Looking ahead, you may like to know that in Part II we will work through the process of acquiring **title** to a piece of land, and then spend the rest of the book looking at some of the rights over land in more detail. We leave discussion of the question 'What is land?' to the end of the book. It is one of the more technical areas of the subject, and we think you will find it easier to follow at a later stage, although there is a brief introductory section about this topic in Chapter 1.

1925 property legislation

Finally, this is a convenient place in which to mention the property legislation which was passed in 1925 and which came into force on 1 January 1926. This legislation consolidated earlier amendments to land law, put into statutory form some common law rules, and introduced further reforms. This turning-point in land law was contained in the following statutes:

Settled Land Act 1925

Trustee Act 1925

Law of Property Act 1925

Land Registration Act 1925

Administration of Estates Act 1925

Land Charges Act 1925

These statutes have been amended by later enactments and in some cases are superseded by later statutes. For convenience we have used the following abbreviations throughout the book, giving the year in each case, in order to avoid confusion where there are two or more statutes with similar names:

SLA—Settled Land Act

LPA—Law of Property Act

LRA—Land Registration Act

More recently, the Trusts of Land and Appointment of Trustees Act 1996 introduced major changes to the important area of trusts of land. You will find that Act referred to in this book as TOLATA 1996.

Note on Bibliography

You will find a Bibliography immediately after Chapter 26, but may like to note now the abbreviations we use for four main textbooks, which are as follows:

Cheshire and Burn, *Cheshire and Burn's Modern Law of Real Property*, 18th edn., Oxford University Press, 2011 : Cheshire and Burn.

Dixon, *Modern Land Law*, 12th edn., Routledge, 2021 : Dixon.

Gray and Gray, *Elements of Land Law*, 5th edn., Oxford University Press, 2008 : Gray and Gray.

Megarry and Wade, *The Law of Real Property*, 9th edn., Sweet & Maxwell, 2019 : Megarry and Wade.

Smith, *Property Law*, 10th edn., Pearson, 2020 : Smith.

1

Estates in land

1.1	Introducing Trant Way and Trant House **3**	1.6	Reducing the number of legal estates **8**
1.2	Viewing Trant House **3**	1.7	The two modern legal estates **9**
1.3	What am I buying? **5**	1.8	What is land? **11**
1.4	Tenure **6**	1.9	Who else may have rights over Trant House? **12**
1.5	Estates in land **6**		

1.1 Introducing Trant Way and Trant House

Since Trant Way exists only in our imagination, we must explain that we visualise it as a road on the outskirts of an old country town. The town has grown considerably over the past 50 years (although so far it has avoided a ring road), and many of the outlying houses have been built on land which was once farmland. Thus the houses in Trant Way which are nearest to the centre of the town stand in a typically suburban environment, whereas the houses at the further end of the road are in more rural surroundings.

One of these more rural properties, Trant House (see Figure 1.1), has just come onto the market, and the house agent's particulars include the following details:

> ... a freehold property, offering spacious accommodation ... set in delightful grounds of approx. 2 acres, with open views to rear ... property includes converted stables containing two self-contained flats, suitable for permanent occupation or for use as holiday lets ...

Penelope Price is looking for a house in the area in which she can run a bed-and-breakfast business. She likes the sound of Trant House and arranges to view it.

1.2 Viewing Trant House

When Penelope arrives at the property she finds that a long drive leads from the gate to the house. Half-way up it, a smaller drive branches off and runs through a boundary wall towards a small cottage, called Trant Cottage. Penelope decides that she must find out more about this.

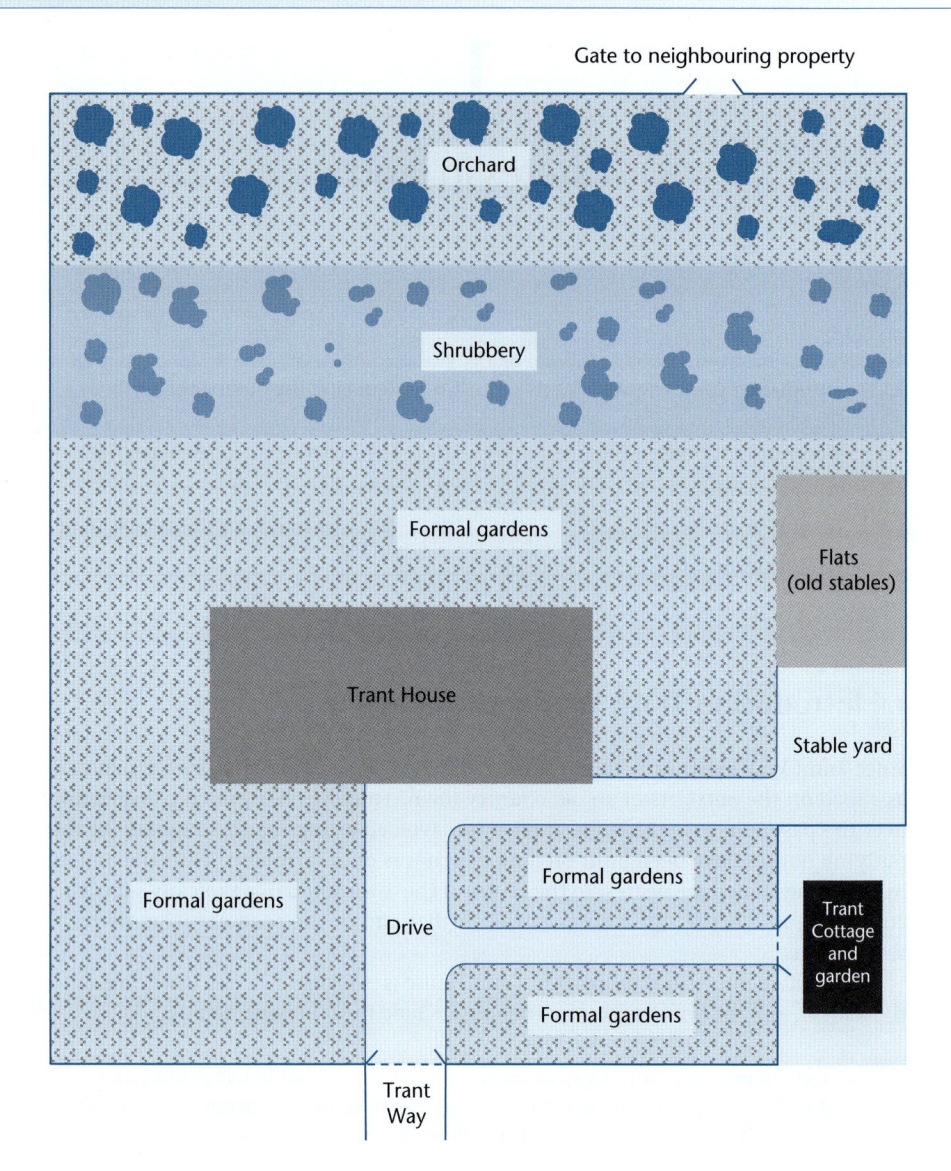

Figure 1.1 Trant House

She is shown around Trant House by Vernon Venables, who explains that he has lived here with his wife and family for many years, having bought the house in 1979. Their children are now grown up, with families of their own, and he and his wife no longer need such a large house. After going all over the house, which seems comfortable and well maintained, Penelope is taken out to look at the additional accommodation in the converted stables. It is obvious that both flats are currently occupied, and Vernon explains that one of them is let to a mature student, Ted Topling, who is following a three-year course in Applied Astronomy at Mousehole University. Vernon tells Penelope that the other flat was specially converted into a 'granny annexe' for his mother, who came to live with the family when his father died a few years ago. He mentions that converting the stables was a very expensive job. Fortunately for him, his mother contributed towards the cost of fitting out her flat, but he had to get quite a large loan to finance the rest of the work and intends to pay this off when he sells Trant House. He adds that his mother will be moving with them when they find a new house.

The grounds around the house prove to be most attractive. The grounds to the front of the house have been landscaped as a formal garden. Beyond this there are flower beds and a shrubbery, and then a large area of rough grassland, which the house agent's details describe as 'the orchard'. Penelope is rather surprised to see a pony grazing here, and Vernon tells her that it belongs to one of his neighbours, 'who has always grazed his ponies here'.

Vernon asks Penelope if she has any questions, and she takes the opportunity to ask about the drive at the front, which appears to be shared with the neighbouring property. She is told that Trant Cottage used to belong to Trant House, and was then reached by the main drive. When the cottage was sold off many years ago (before Vernon bought the property), the new owner was allowed to continue to use the Trant House drive, and occupants of the cottage have done so ever since. Talking about this reminds Vernon that, when the previous owner of Trant House sold the cottage, there was some agreement between him and the buyer that neither of them would carry on any sort of business or trade on their respective properties. He is rather vague about the details, but is sure that 'the lawyers will know'.

Penelope asks if she can have another look around the inside of the house, and having done so, goes away to think it all over. For her, as for most purchasers, thinking it over will involve all sorts of questions about how she will use the property, what sort of alterations she might make and, most important of all, how she will finance her purchase. One question that she probably will not ask herself is: what am I buying? The answer seems obvious: I am buying a house and some land. For a lawyer, however, the answer is rather different and in the next section we will explain what someone who is 'buying a house' is really buying.

1.3 What am I buying?

Under the system of landholding which operates in England and Wales, all land in England and Wales is 'held of' the Crown. This is an idea which dates from the Norman Conquest in 1066, when William the Conqueror claimed all the land by right of conquest. After the Conquest, the king gave rights over land to his most powerful supporters in exchange for the promise of certain 'services' (such as fighting for the king in his wars or sending men to do so). In turn, each of these supporters ('lords') granted their own followers similar rights, in exchange for their loyalty and services.

The result was that no one in England, other than the Crown, can simply acquire ownership of land, in the same way that you can acquire ownership of a pen or a book. You can only ever acquire a right over land for a particular period of time ('*an estate* in land'), and on terms that once obliged you to perform services for the benefit of another person ('**tenure**'). Each person was said to hold the land 'of' their feudal lord, to whom they owed services and who could terminate their right if they failed to render due performance of the services. Their lord in turn would owe services to their own lord, further up the chain, culminating at last in the large landowners who held their land directly of the Crown. Only the Crown could hold land free from any feudal relationship and for an unlimited period of time ('allodial land'). Although most of the links in this chain have now vanished, and the vast majority of land in England and Wales is now held directly of the Crown (see 1.4), this formal structure persists even today. As a result, an individual cannot simply own the land on which he or she lives or runs a business. What the individual does in fact own is a collection of rights and duties in relation to the land, one of the most important rights being to take and retain possession of the land and to make use of it for a period of time (the 'estate in land').

1.4 Tenure

During the medieval period, different kinds of 'tenure' developed, according to the nature of the services to be performed by the tenant. (Note that here 'tenant' means a person with tenure of an estate and not, as the word is now used, someone who has a lease. The word comes from the Latin *'tenere'*, meaning 'to hold'). Some of these came to be described as *'freehold tenures'*, because they could be held only by free men (i.e., not by the unfree serfs or villeins, who were obliged to remain in the area in which they had been born and to work for the local lord).

The substance of this system has now almost entirely disappeared in the modern law. In 1290, the Statute of Quia Emptores ('Whoever buys . . .') made it impossible to create new tenures. Over time, the duty to perform services under the remaining tenures was gradually replaced by ('commuted to') obligations to pay fixed sums of money; these in turn became increasingly valueless as a result of inflation. Finally, most surviving tenures were abolished by the Tenures Abolition Act 1660.

The result is that the vast majority of 'freehold' land in England and Wales is held directly of the Crown on the tenure of 'free and common socage'. '**Socage**' once referred to a duty to provide agricultural services—the word derives from the term 'sokeman', which referred to a type of free tenant—but these services were first commuted to money and then disappeared. Thus, almost anyone who buys freehold land in England and Wales will technically be entering a tenurial relationship with the Crown, holding their land of the Crown on the tenure of free and common socage. However, since this relationship imposes no duties on the tenant, its practical consequences are minimal. Its most important practical consequence is that, if the tenant's 'estate in land' comes to an end, there is a possibility that the land will '**escheat**' to the Crown (see 1.7.1.1).

1.5 Estates in land

The term 'estate', derived from the word *'status'*, is used to describe the period of time during which a particular person can hold the land—that is, how long they can possess it, excluding all others. It remains practically important for a person buying land to know what 'estate' in the land they are buying, since this will determine how long they can keep the land.

Throughout the book, we will be talking about **freehold and leasehold estates**, and we need to look briefly at how these developed.

1.5.1 The old rules relating to freehold estates

An estate in land which could be held by a free person on free tenure came to be known as a freehold estate, and over the years three main types of freehold estate developed.

1.5.1.1 The life estate

At the outset, it was usual to grant the right to possess and use land only for the life of the tenant, who accordingly could be said to have a *'life estate'*. The king or lesser noble who granted the estate depended on the loyalty of his tenants and would make grants only to those personally known to him.

1.5.1.2 The fee simple

As time went by, grants to a tenant 'and his heirs' became more common, with the result that the right to possession would last longer than the lifetime of the original tenant since it could pass to his children or other descendants. In a further development, it became possible for the tenant to **transfer** the estate (i.e., on a sale or by gift) and the right to possession of the land would continue as long as there was an heir to inherit from the *current* owner. The heirs need not be the descendants of the original tenant but could be the descendants of a person to whom that original tenant had transferred their rights, for example by gift or sale (a 'transferee'). The heading to this section describes this estate as a '**fee simple**' and we need to examine the meaning of this term.

The word *fee* denoted an interest in land that could be inherited and the word *simple* meant that the estate could be inherited by the 'general heirs', rather than some more limited class of relatives (see 1.5.1.3). On the death of the current owner, the estate would pass to his heir (in earlier times a landowner was usually male, since married women were unable to hold property in their own right until the nineteenth century). The heir was identified according to complicated rules. If the deceased had children, the heir would be his eldest son. If the eldest son had died before his father but had himself left a son, that grandson would be his grandfather's heir. If there were no sons to inherit, any daughters inherited the estate jointly. If the deceased had no descendants, his heir would be one of his blood relations, found among his brothers or sisters (or their descendants), or more remotely among his uncles, aunts or cousins. At a later stage, one of the deceased's ancestors, such as his father or grandfather, might be entitled to inherit. It was therefore possible for a fee simple estate to pass to a fairly distant relation. In 1540, it also became possible for a freehold to be disposed of by will, so that a freeholder could name someone who was not a blood relation as his heir. If the deceased owner had no relations at all and had also failed to make a will (dying '**intestate**', without a will or 'testament'), the estate would then come to an end. When this happened, the estate would 'escheat' to the heirs of the lord who had originally granted the estate or, if they could not be identified, to the Crown (see 1.7.1.1).

1.5.1.3 The fee tail

As just explained, the fee simple estate was inheritable by general heirs, the heir being drawn from a wide range of relatives of the deceased. In the case of a **fee tail**, however, the estate was still inheritable (denoted by the word 'fee'), but the heir had to come from a more limited class. A fee tail would be created by a grant to a tenant and the 'heirs of the body', meaning the lineal descendants of the *original* tenant. Sometimes this class was limited even further, to the 'heirs of the body male' (or, very rarely, 'female'). In such a case, the estate could not pass to an heir of the wrong gender, nor could it pass to the ascendants or siblings of the original tenant. Unlike a fee simple, the estate could not pass to the descendants of someone to whom the original tenant in fee tail had sold or transferred his estate. It would pass only to his direct descendants of the correct gender. The fact that the estate was limited or 'cut down' in this way led to it being described as a fee 'tail' (from the French word *'tailler'*—to cut down).

If no heir of the right sort existed, the estate would come to an end and the property *reverted* to the fee simple owner who had originally created this more limited estate (or, if he had already died, would pass to his general heir). The person who had the right to recover the property should the **entail** come to an end was said to have a '**reversion**'.

1.5.2 The leasehold estate

Once the owner of a freehold estate was free to deal with his estate as he chose, the practice developed of permitting another person to take possession of the land for a fixed time, usually in exchange for rent. In modern terms, we would say that the freehold owner 'let' the land or 'granted a lease' of it. This was in essence a commercial development, and although the relationship between landlord and tenant resembles that of tenure (i.e., the tenant 'holds' of the landlord), in this case the tenant usually paid for his use of the land with money, rather than by the performance of services.

Originally, letting the land in this way was regarded as creating only a contractual relationship between the parties. Over time, however, the tenant's position improved and the courts treated him as having a right to possession of the land which he could enforce against the landlord and also against any other person who dispossessed him. Recognition of this right meant that a tenant holding under a lease could also be said to have an estate in the land, a right to possession for a period of time.

1.6 Reducing the number of legal estates

In the past, all of the freehold and leasehold estates described so far were recognised and protected in the common law courts and so were described as 'legal' estates, as opposed to the 'equitable interests', which were only protected by the Chancellor as a matter of equity (see 2.4). Today, however, only two of those estates retain their legal status, and the other former legal estates now take effect only in equity.

This change was introduced by the 1925 property legislation (see the Introduction to Part I), as one of the measures designed to further its aim of simplifying the process of buying and selling land. Before that legislation came into force, dealings with land were complicated by the existence of limited freehold legal estates. This was because it was possible for a fee simple owner to create a number of smaller legal estates out of the fee simple, so as to give successive interests in the property to current and later generations of his family. The fee simple owner might have, for example:

- given a life estate to an elderly relative;
- created a fee tail in favour of his eldest son, which would entitle the son and his direct descendants to possession of the land when the previous life estate ended; and
- disposed of the reversion on the fee tail which would arise if the direct line died out (see 1.5.1.3).

This process was known as 'making a **settlement**', and we will tell you more about it in Chapter 13. At the moment all you need to know is that this practice of dividing up the legal fee simple could cause difficulties on a later sale of the estate, even if the settlement had come to an end. Any prospective purchaser would want to be satisfied that the seller owned the estate being offered for sale, and the fact that the fee simple could be fragmented into smaller estates made the process of investigating the seller's title more complicated, since the purchaser would need evidence that any smaller estates granted in the past had come to an end.

The solution to this problem adopted in 1925 was to provide that, from 1 January 1926, the smaller freehold estates should take effect only in equity, leaving one freehold estate (the fee simple) and the leasehold estate to continue as the two remaining legal estates. As a result, there are today only two estates in land which are recognised at law.

1.7 The two modern legal estates

The two legal estates which exist today are set out in LPA 1925, s. 1(1):

> The only estates and interests in land which are capable of subsisting or of being conveyed or created at law are –
> (a) an estate in fee simple absolute in possession;
> (b) a term of years absolute.

Section 1(3) of the Act provides:

> All other estates, interests, and charges in or over land take effect as equitable interests.

1.7.1 Estate in fee simple absolute in possession ('freehold estate')

This is now the only freehold estate which can exist at law, and it is normal practice to refer to it as 'the freehold estate' rather than using its full name. You may remember that the particulars of sale for Trant House describe it as 'a freehold property', and this tells us that Vernon owns a **fee simple absolute in possession**. Although for practical purposes one may speak of 'a freehold estate', it is important to understand the precise meaning of the full words, which you will certainly encounter throughout the 1925 legislation. Each part of those words has a technical meaning, which we will consider briefly.

1.7.1.1 Fee simple

We have already explained that originally this term indicated that the estate was inheritable by 'the general heirs' of the current tenant (see 1.5.1.2). Rather confusingly, the 1925 legislation retains this term, although the Administration of Estates Act 1925 abolished the old concept of the heir and introduced new statutory rules of inheritance, with the result that one cannot really define a fee simple today by describing it as an estate 'inherited by the general heirs' (See 8.2). What remains true is that the fee simple is an estate which can last indefinitely, as long as there are persons entitled to take the property under the provisions of the will of the previous owner, or under the statutory rules that apply when someone dies 'intestate' (without a will). Very occasionally no person entitled to the estate can be discovered after the rules have been applied. In such cases the estate will at this point come to an end and the land will revert to the Crown, in a process known as 'escheat'.

This can happen, as in the recent case of *Pennistone Holdings Ltd v Rock Ferry Waterfront Trust* [2021] EWCA Civ 1029, when a foreign company that holds a freehold estate in England and Wales is dissolved. When an English company that holds freehold land is dissolved, s. 102 of the Companies Act 2006 provides that the freehold estate is not terminated but simply passes to the Crown as 'bona vacantia' (unowned property). This means that the freehold estate continues to exist in the hands of the Crown and can be passed on to a third party by the Crown. However, the Companies Act 2006 does not govern a company that is registered in another jurisdiction. Where such a company holds freehold land in England and Wales, its dissolution will lead to the termination of the freehold estate, leaving the Crown as its absolute owner. As Lewison LJ held in *Pennistone Holdings Ltd v Rock Ferry Waterfront Trust*, this means that any transfer of the land by the Crown involves the creation of a new fee simple estate, rather than the transfer of the fee simple previously held by the dissolved company, with possible consequences for third parties (see 6.3.4).

1.7.1.2 'Absolute'

The explanation of the word **'absolute'** gives rise to further complications. The word indicates that the fee simple should not be subject to any restriction which would prevent it lasting as long as there are persons entitled to inherit. So, if you try to give Fred a fee simple estate 'until he qualifies as a solicitor', the gift cannot be of a legal fee simple estate. The estate will not necessarily last forever (as long as there is someone to inherit) because it will end earlier should Fred ever become a solicitor. This sort of arrangement is called a **'determinable fee'** and, together with its relative the **'conditional fee'**, it now takes effect as an equitable interest. (For further details of determinable and conditional fees, see Chapter 8.)

1.7.1.3 'In possession'

The final words in the legal term for a freehold estate are **'in possession'**. This means that the estate must give the owner rights immediately, rather than being one which is to give the owner the use of the land at some time in the future. Thus, if you give Paul a fee simple estate to start in five years' time, you have not given him a legal estate and he will have only an equitable interest. Future interests in land are dealt with in more detail in Chapters 13 to 16.

It should be noted that the estate owner does not have to have a right to *physical* possession of the land itself in order to have a legal estate. For example, the property may be let to another person, in which case the tenant under the lease will be entitled to physical possession of the land, while the landlord only has the right to receive the rent payable under the lease and will only become entitled to physical possession when the lease comes to an end. In this case the landlord still has a legal estate because LPA 1925, s. 205(1)(xix), provides that:

> 'Possession' includes receipt of rents and profits or the right to receive the same, if any.

1.7.1.4 Former legal estates which become equitable interests under LPA 1925, s. 1(3)

It will be obvious that there are many kinds of arrangement which one may wish to make concerning a piece of land, but which now cannot amount to a legal estate in fee simple. Examples of arrangements which fall into this category include: an interest for life; an interest to start at some time in the future, a future interest; or a determinable or conditional fee simple, a right that will terminate or arise when some condition is met. Arrangements of this sort can still be made, but they create equitable interests which have to operate by means of a 'trust'. In such a case, the legal fee simple is held by trustees on trust for those entitled to the equitable interests (see 2.6 and Part IV).

For some 60 years after the 1925 property legislation, an **entailed interest** (the former fee tail estate; see 1.5.1.3) was one of the equitable interests which operated behind a trust. However, major changes in this area of law were introduced by the TOLATA 1996, and it is no longer possible to create an entailed interest, even in equity (see 14.1.2.3).

1.7.2 Term of years absolute ('leasehold estate')

The '**term of years absolute**' is the full, correct name for what is more commonly called a lease. It has remained as a legal estate but it is inferior to the fee simple estate because it is of necessarily limited duration. The essential requirement is that a lease must be for a fixed 'term of years', though this can include periods of less than a year (LPA 1925, s. 205(1)(xxvii)) and can include arrangements such as weekly or monthly tenancies. The word 'absolute' does not seem to add anything to the meaning because a lease does not cease to be a legal estate merely because it will terminate on the occurrence of some event (e.g., if the rent is unpaid). Section 1(1)(b) of LPA 1925 does not require that the term of a legal lease should start at the date of grant (i.e., unlike the freehold estate, it does not have to be 'in possession', see 1.7.1.3). Thus, subject to certain rules (see 9.2 and 9.3), it is possible to grant a lease now, to take effect at some time in the future.

It should be noted that the owner of a term of years does not hold the land of the Crown. The leaseholder derives his or her title from that of the landlord, who will be either the owner of a fee simple estate or of a longer leasehold estate. The lease is of considerable importance in land law and it is considered in detail in Chapters 9–12.

1.7.3 Legal estates in Trant House

Both of the two modern legal estates can be found in the Trant House property. We have already noted that the description of the property as 'freehold' tells us that Vernon holds the fee simple absolute in possession in the property. In addition, one of the flats in the converted stables has been 'let' to the student, Ted. Provided that this letting satisfies the legal requirements for a lease and has been made in the correct form (which is covered in Chapter 9), a legal term of years absolute will have been created, which Ted will hold as a tenant from Vernon as his landlord.

1.8 What is land?

When Penelope was looking over Trant House, she was particularly impressed by the very lovely gardens. She has always dreamt of having gardens like these and thinks that they will also be a great attraction to possible guests for her business. She noticed that a major feature of the gardens is the presence of a number of statues, which appear to be antiques and to have been part of the gardens for some considerable time. She also noticed that the gardens contain a stunning display of scented roses and Vernon explained that rose growing had been his main hobby for some time and that he had won prizes for his champion roses, some of which he had cultivated himself. She is also very interested in tapestries that seem to have been used as wall coverings in some of the rooms of the house, in place of wallpaper. Penelope is now worried that Vernon may want to move or sell the statues and tapestries (which seem very valuable) and that he is certainly likely to want to remove some or all of the roses.

Penelope is starting to ask herself questions about what she is actually buying. The estate agent's particulars just mention the house, gardens, and orchard: they say nothing about statues, tapestries, or plants. She wonders whether, if nothing is said in the conveyancing documents about these items, she will get them if she buys the property. In essence, she is starting to wonder what actually constitutes land.

Unfortunately, the answer to Penelope's concern is one of the most complex and technical aspects of land law. Indeed, it is quite difficult to understand this issue fully until you have learnt a great deal about the estates and interests in land. Accordingly, we think it best to consider this issue in detail at the end of the book (see Chapter 26). However, you will need a working concept of 'land' from the start of your studies, so some basic ideas are covered here. Also, in some courses this issue is tackled at an early stage. If that is true for you, we suggest that you read Chapters 1 and 2 and then Chapter 26.

The traditional answer to what constitutes land is that land is the physical land down to the centre of the earth and up to the 'heavens' (skies). 'Land' also includes everything physically attached to the land. Thus Trant House and its foundations are also land. Since the roses are necessarily embedded in the land, they are also land. As far as the tapestries are concerned, the issue of whether they are part of the land may depend on the degree to which they are fixed to the walls and the purpose of that fixing. Is it just to display the tapestries conveniently or is it to incorporate them more fully into the design of the house? The statues may well just be placed on top of the land, rather than fixed to it. In that case they may not constitute land. However, if they can be regarded as forming part of the integral design of the garden, they may be taken to have become part of the land. The cases on this important topic are covered in Chapter 26 and you should look there if you need more detailed answers.

The whole issue of defining land is, however, made even more complex by the fact that not only physical things fixed to land are regarded by the law as being land. In addition, legal estates and most interests in land are also 'land'.

As we have seen already, in fact only the Crown can be said to hold land itself; others can only hold an estate or interest in land. Thus, part of the answer to the question, 'What is land?' is that estates and interests can be regarded as land.

It is, of course, always possible for a document to provide its own definition of land for the purpose of that document. Thus the document transferring Trant House to Penelope could specifically exclude the roses. If it does not, they will transfer without being mentioned because they are certainly affixed to the land. If Vernon removed them, he could be sued successfully by Penelope. This can be important because vendors often forget to tell their conveyancer that they want to take such items with them. In most cases it is not worth bringing a court action but, where what is removed is significant, it may be, particularly if the items removed can be restored to the property.

For most of your work on land law, the most important definition of land will be that provided by s. 205 of the LPA 1925 because that definition applies to the 1925 legislation as a whole (see 26.1.1 for this provision). If you look at it, you will see that it mixes together physical things which are land (such as buildings) with the estates and interests that can also be land. Do not worry; all of this is explained in much more detail in Chapter 26.

1.9 Who else may have rights over Trant House?

In this chapter we have told you about the two legal estates in land and explained that the house agent's description of Trant House as 'a freehold property' means that, if this description is accurate, the vendor, Vernon, holds the 'fee simple absolute in possession' in the property.

In addition to Vernon, a number of other people may have rights over the property. Some of these rights are covered in the next chapter, but we suggest that before you go any further you may like to look back at the account of Penelope's visit to the property (1.2), and see if you can identify some of the other people who might claim to have rights over it.

FURTHER READING

Cheshire and Burn, *Cheshire and Burn's Modern Law of Real Property*, 18th edn., Oxford University Press, 2011, Chapter 2.

Megarry and Wade, *The Law of Real Property*, 9th edn., Sweet and Maxwell, 2019, Chapters 2–4.

Both of these accounts are very detailed and may contain more historical information than is needed to understand the modern law.

You can visit the online resources to test your knowledge of this chapter with self-test questions at **www.oup.com/he/nair19e/**.

2

Interests in land

2.1	Introduction 14	2.6	Examples of equitable interests 23
2.2	Rights which others may have over Trant House 14	2.7	A multiplicity of rights 28
2.3	Interests in land 17	2.8	Modern approach to protection of rights 29
2.4	Distinction between law and equity 18	2.9	Human rights 29
2.5	Examples of legal interests 21	2.10	Classification of property 30

2.1 Introduction

If you did as was suggested at the end of Chapter 1, and looked back at the description of Penelope's visit to Trant House, you have probably identified a number of people, other than Vernon, who might have rights over the property.

They include:

- the owner of the neighbouring Trant Cottage;
- the neighbour who has always grazed his ponies in the orchard;
- Vernon's wife;
- Vernon's mother;
- Ted, the student who rents one of the flats; and
- the person or institution from whom Vernon borrowed the money to pay for the stable conversion.

It is possible that any or all of these people could have rights over Trant House, and that such rights could be enforced not only against Vernon, the fee simple owner, but also against anyone who acquires the property from him.

2.2 Rights which others may have over Trant House

In this section, we will look at the people identified and consider the rights which each might have. On what we know at present, we will not be able to decide whether anyone does in fact have rights over Trant House, but the information gathered by Penelope provides an opportunity to introduce you to some of the rights which can exist over land and which are considered in detail later on in this book.

If Penelope does decide to buy Trant House, she (or her legal adviser) will have to find out much more about these possible rights, because if they do exist and can be enforced against her, they could have a considerable effect on her use and enjoyment of the land.

2.2.1 The owner of the neighbouring Trant Cottage

Penelope has learnt two things about the owner of the cottage: he appears to have a right to use part of the Trant House drive and he may have a right to prevent the property being used for trade or business purposes.

2.2.1.1 Right to use the drive

This could mean that the owner of Trant Cottage has a right of way over part of the grounds of Trant House. Such a right may be an easement. Easements are rights attached to one piece of land, entitling its occupants to do something on another's property, or preventing the owner of that property from interfering with the passage of some benefit to the first piece of land. Thus one may have a right to walk or drive over one's neighbour's land (a right of way), or perhaps the right to prevent the neighbour building so as to block the passage of light to one's windows (a right to light). In each case there is a piece of land which is benefited by the easement and a piece of land which is burdened with it. There are many types of easement, such as rights to storage or drainage, the right to water, and a great number of others. A list of common examples is given in Chapter 24, in which there is more detail about the characteristics of easements and how they are created. However, it may be helpful to mention here that the land benefited by an easement is known as the **dominant tenement**, and the land over which an easement is exercised as the **servient tenement**.

2.2.1.2 Right to prevent the use of Trant House for business or trade

Such a right, if it exists, would have arisen from an undertaking by the former owner of Trant House, made in the document ('the **conveyance**' or 'the **transfer**') by which the legal estate in the cottage was transferred to its new owner. Such an undertaking is known as a '*restrictive covenant*' and, subject to certain rules, it can be enforced not only against the estate owner who made it, but also against later owners of the estate in the land. We will cover these **covenants** later in this chapter (see 2.6.5) and will then look at them in greater detail in Chapter 25. It is obvious that if such a restriction did exist and could be enforced against Penelope, she would not be able to carry out her plan of running a bed-and-breakfast business at Trant House, and so would probably decide not to buy the property unless she could negotiate a release from the covenant from the person who is entitled to enforce it.

2.2.2 The neighbour who has always grazed ponies in the orchard

It is possible that this neighbour has a right very similar to an easement, known as a **'profit à prendre'** (from the French word 'prendre', which means 'to take'). This is a right to take something from land which belongs to another estate owner: for example, to cut wood or to dig gravel. The right to take grass or other plants from land by grazing is a well-established profit, and, if the practice of grazing ponies in the Trant House orchard satisfies the relevant rules for the recognition and creation of profits à prendre (considered in Chapter 24), Penelope, or any other future owner of the property, might find that this use of the land could not be prevented.

2.2.3 Vernon's wife

Penelope did not meet Vanessa Venables, but learned of her existence from Vernon. Without knowing more about the couple's circumstances, there is no way of knowing what, if any, rights Vanessa may in fact have over Trant House, but there are several possibilities.

2.2.3.1 Rights of a co-owner

When the property was bought, the legal estate may have been conveyed to both Vernon and Vanessa, so that they hold it as joint legal owners. **Co-ownership** of property, especially of the family home, has become increasingly common during the last 60 years and co-ownership is explained in Chapter 17.

2.2.3.2 Rights of a beneficiary under a trust

Even if Vanessa is not a co-owner of the legal estate, she may have rights to the property arising under a trust. This could have been created formally, or have arisen informally, either by agreement between the couple or as a result of contributions made by Vanessa to buying or improving Trant House.

Trusts play a very important part in land law. They are explained briefly later in this chapter (2.6.2), and then trusts relating to land are covered in detail in Part IV.

2.2.3.3 Rights of a spouse or civil partner

If Vanessa does not own the legal estate jointly with her husband, she will nonetheless have statutory rights of occupation, known as 'home rights', which arise in cases of marriage and civil partnership. The rights prevent the partner who owns the property from excluding the other partner as long as the marriage or civil partnership lasts, and in some cases can be enforced against anyone who buys the property (see 21.3.3).

2.2.4 Vernon's mother

For a number of years now, Vernon's mother has been allowed to occupy one of the flats in the old stables as her home. In legal terms, she appears to be a 'licensee', that is, someone who is on another's property with his permission or '**licence**', and is therefore not a trespasser. Family arrangements of this sort, although usually made with the best of intentions, can cause problems because the parties to them often give little or no thought to the legal implications of what they are doing. If relationships break down, the licensee may claim to have a right to remain in the property and/or to be entitled to a share in its value. We will look at cases in which this has occurred in Chapters 18 and 19, but for the moment you should simply be aware that it could happen. Vernon says that his mother will be moving out with him and his wife, but if she changed her mind his mother might claim that she has a right to continue to live in the flat:

- because the arrangements with her son gave her a **lease** of the flat, so that she is a tenant, not a licensee; or
- because her son promised her that she could live there for the rest of her life and, relying on this, she spent money on fitting out the flat, 'estopping' him from denying her right to remain in occupation; or

- because her financial contributions evidence an intention that she become a beneficiary under a trust, entitling her to remain in occupation or to have a right to a share in the value of Trant House.

Any of these claims could give rise to rights which might be enforceable against a **purchaser** of the property and, if Penelope decides to buy the house, the presence of the vendor's elderly mother living in self-contained accommodation at Trant House might very well ring alarm bells with Penelope's legal adviser.

2.2.5 Ted, the student who occupies the other flat

In the previous chapter, we noted that Ted holds a leasehold estate in part of the old stable block at Trant House. This means that, as far as Penelope is concerned, he is another person who has rights which might be enforceable against her. In Chapter 9, we will see that a lease can be granted for a fixed term (for example, for 10 years) or it may be a **periodic tenancy**, which will run on from one period to another, such as from week to week or from month to month, until one party ends it by giving notice to the other. Without knowing more about the arrangements between Vernon and Ted, we cannot say whether Ted would be able to stay on in the flat when the whole property is sold, but it is certainly very likely that his lease might bind Penelope if she buys Trant House.

2.2.6 The lender who provided the money for the stable conversion

We know that Vernon borrowed a considerable amount of money for the conversion of the stables and that he has not yet repaid the loan. It is almost certain that the lender (most probably a bank or building society) would have required Vernon to provide security for the loan by granting a mortgage (sometimes also called a 'charge') over Trant House. Under a mortgage, the lender acquires rights over the property and is entitled to sell it if the borrower fails to repay the loan. We know that Vernon is planning to repay his debt out of the money which he will get when he sells Trant House. If he did this, the mortgage would be 'discharged' and would not affect Penelope. However, if Vernon did not repay the money, Penelope might very possibly take the property subject to the mortgage and would be at risk of having to pay off Vernon's mortgage or risk losing the property to the lender. In practice, it is very unlikely that Penelope's legal adviser would allow her to hand over the purchase money before the adviser had ensured that the mortgage would be discharged—but unlikely things do sometimes happen, both in real life and in exam questions!

2.3 Interests in land

In the previous section, we noted a number of rights which benefit someone other than the estate owner, and which can be enforced against the estate owner and possibly against anyone who acquires the estate from the owner. In the terminology adopted by the 1925 property legislation, such rights are known as *'interests in land'*, but they are often referred to as **encumbrances** (because they burden or 'encumber' the land), and they can also be described as *'third-party rights'*. All three terms are used interchangeably in this book, and we want to emphasise here that they are just three different ways of describing the same sort of rights.

Whatever terminology is used, the important thing to notice about these rights is that they are divided into two main categories:

- rights recognised by law, which are legal interests in land;
- rights recognised only by equity, which are equitable interests in land.

In the rest of this chapter, we explain the meaning of this distinction and set out the most important legal and equitable interests.

2.4 Distinction between law and equity

Historically, English law was administered in two different sets of courts. There were courts of 'common law' and courts of 'equity'. Courts of equity were ruled by the Lord Chancellor and other judges in Chancery, and gave remedies to litigants in circumstances in which the common law courts were not able to provide a remedy. While the courts of equity have been important to the development of many areas of English law, adding to the common law in a number of ways, they were particularly important in land law. This was because they recognised many types of interest in land that the common law courts did not recognise—'equitable interests'—and gave remedies to the holders of these rights that were unavailable to them in the common law courts.

As a result of the Supreme Court of Judicature Acts 1873 and 1875, the courts of common law and the courts of equity have been fused for well over a century. This means that it is no longer necessary to go to a separate court to enforce an equitable interest. However, the distinction between legal and equitable interests remains important in the modern law for a number of reasons.

2.4.1 Differences in content

As we saw in Chapter 1, s. 1 of the LPA 1925 lists all the legal estates and legal interests that can still exist in English law. Section 1(1) provides that only a fee simple absolute in possession or a term of years absolute can take effect as a legal estate. Meanwhile, s. 1(2) provides:

> The only interests or charges in or over land which are capable of subsisting or of being conveyed or created at law are—
>
> (a) An easement, right, or privilege in or over land for an interest equivalent to an estate in fee simple absolute in possession or a term of years absolute;
> (b) A **rentcharge** in possession issuing out of or charged on land being either perpetual or for a term of years absolute;
> (c) A charge by way of legal mortgage;
> (d) [Land tax, tithe rentcharge] and any other similar charge on land which is not created by an **instrument**;
> (e) Rights of entry exercisable over or in respect of a legal term of years absolute, or annexed, for any purpose, to a legal rentcharge.

Thus today, an interest in land takes effect as a *legal* interest only if it is of a type listed in s. 1(2) and has been granted for a period equivalent to one of the two legal estates. The requirement that a right must have been granted for a period equivalent to one of the two legal estates means that such rights must be either capable of lasting forever (i.e., for a period equivalent to a fee simple absolute in possession or, as s. 1(2)(b) puts it, 'perpetual') or for a fixed period (i.e., equivalent to a term of years absolute or lease).

Any interest which does not satisfy the requirements of s. 1(2) takes effect as an *equitable* interest (s. 1(3)). Thus, for example, if a right of way is given to a neighbour 'until the new road is constructed', this cannot be a legal easement because it is for an uncertain period. Accordingly, it exists only in equity. There are also many equitable interests that have no equivalents at common law and which s. 1(2) of the LPA 1925 does not affect at all. Among the most important of these are rights under trusts, restrictive covenants, and estate contracts (see 2.6).

2.4.2 Differences in formality rules

Usually, in order to consensually create ('grant') or transfer ('convey') a legal estate or interest in land it is necessary to use a 'deed'. LPA 1925, s. 52(1) provides:

> All conveyances of land or any interest therein are void for the purpose of conveying or creating a legal estate unless made by deed.

A deed is a document which has been executed in accordance with certain formalities in order to ensure that its validity can be proved (see 2.6.4). With limited exceptions, legal estates and interests in land can only be created by the use of such a formal document, which will usually have been drafted by a lawyer. Under the LRA 2002, there may also be requirements to register the transaction, applying to HM Land Registry to alter the official register of title of the affected land to reflect the creation of the new legal interest or the change in the identity of the owner of the existing legal estate or interest (see Chapter 6).

By contrast, although there is a requirement of signed writing for the creation and transfer of equitable interests in LPA 1925, s. 53, this is a much less demanding formality requirement. Unlike a deed, the requirement of signed writing can be satisfied by an informally expressed note or even an email, as for example in *Hudson v Hathway* [2022] EWCA Civ 1648 (see 17.5.5). There are also many ways in which equitable interests can arise without any formality at all. Among the most important of these are the doctrine of proprietary estoppel, discussed in Chapter 19, and the rules recognising the existence of so-called 'resulting' and 'constructive' trusts, discussed in Chapter 13.

2.4.3 Different effect on third parties

A major difference between legal and equitable interests is found in the rules governing the enforceability of those rights against a third party. Legal interests were said to be **rights in rem**; that is, rights in the land itself ('in the thing', from the Latin word *res*, meaning 'thing') and hence generally could be enforced against any person who interfered with the interest-holder's use of the land, including any later buyer of the land. This was expressed by saying that legal rights were 'good against the world'. Meanwhile, equitable interests began life as **rights in personam**; that is, rights which were enforceable against certain categories of person, because it was considered to be fair or equitable that they should take subject to them.

In considering the evolution of equitable interests, you may find it helpful to note Maitland's brief but memorable explanation (see Maitland, *Equity* (1936) at pp. 112–15). The Court of Chancery is pictured as working through the list of people who might acquire rights from a trustee holding a legal estate: which of them, in fairness, should be bound by the equitable rights of the beneficiary under the trust? Over the years, the court has decided that it would be fair to enforce such rights against:

- those who inherit rights from the trustee;
- those who take rights from the trustee as a gift ('donees' or '**volunteers**'); and
- those who buy rights from the trustee, either knowing about the beneficiary's rights or deliberately closing their eyes to them.

The rule which ultimately came to apply to equitable interests was that they bound everyone who took rights from the holder of the legal estate affected by the equitable interest, *except* a bona fide purchaser for value of that legal estate without notice of the equitable interest (sometimes known as 'equity's darling'). As a result of major changes introduced by the 1925 legislation, this doctrine is of less importance today, but it can still be of some significance (see 5.5.2 and 6.6.3) and so we need to tell you a little more about it here.

2.4.3.1 The purchaser must be bona fide

This means that the purchaser must act in good faith. This part of the rule seems to be duplicated by the requirement that the purchaser should not have notice of the right, and it is difficult to see what is added by this phrase. However, Lord Wilberforce in *Midland Bank Trust Co. Ltd v Green* [1981] AC 513 at p. 528 considered that:

> it would be a mistake to suppose that the requirement of good faith extended only to the matter of notice . . . good faith is a . . . separate test which may have to be passed even though absence of notice is proved.

We cannot point to any cases in which a purchaser without notice has failed the good faith test. In *Corbett v Halifax Building Society* [2003] 1 WLR 964 (considered further at 22.10.3) deception of the vendor seems to have had no relevance. However, Megarry and Wade, para. 5-007, fn 16, suggests that good faith might be relevant if a purchaser induced a vendor to sell at an undervalue due to fraud or coercion.

2.4.3.2 The purchaser must give value

It is necessary for the person who acquires the estate to give value if he or she is to rely on the notice rule. Thus a donee (or 'volunteer') takes a gift of land subject to any equitable interests that there may be. 'Value' includes money, money's worth, and some other forms of consideration, such as marriage.

A person who acquires an estate for value is described as a 'purchaser for value'. This may seem unnecessarily long-winded, since in ordinary speech 'purchaser' means 'buyer' and so includes the notion of taking for value. However, for the lawyer, 'purchaser' has the technical meaning of 'one who takes by act of the parties rather than by operation of law'. This means that he has had the property transferred to him in the appropriate way by the previous owner, rather than having it vested in him automatically by operation of some rule of law, such as that which vests a bankrupt's property in his trustee in bankruptcy or the deceased's property in his **personal representatives**. In this sense then, even a donee is a purchaser and so in a context like this it is necessary to state specifically that the person acquiring the estate is a purchaser *for value*.

2.4.3.3 The purchaser must acquire a legal estate

The purchaser must buy a legal estate, rather than an equitable interest in the land. Thus, if the purchaser is to be safe, he or she must have acquired the legal estate before discovering that the equitable interest exists.

2.4.3.4 The purchaser must not have notice of the equitable interest

There are three types of **notice**: actual notice; constructive notice; and imputed notice.

- *Actual notice*. This is quite straightforward and applies where the purchaser has actual knowledge of the existence of the equitable interest. It is not necessary for the purchaser to obtain this information from any particular source and he or she may even discover the truth from a complete outsider (*Lloyd v Banks* (1868) LR 3 Ch App 488).
- *Constructive notice*. When the notice rule was first created by the courts of equity, clever purchasers soon realised that they could obtain an advantage if they declined to make any investigations which might lead to the discovery of equitable interests. Equity was quick to extend the rule to prevent purchasers deliberately 'turning a blind eye' in this way, as such behaviour was evidence of a lack of good faith on the part of the purchaser. The means used was to say that the purchasers would be deemed to know of interests which they would have discovered if they had asked the usual questions about the property and so were bound by such interests. This constructive notice rule is preserved in modern law, for unregistered land, by LPA 1925, s. 199(1)(ii).
- *Imputed notice*. A purchaser is also deemed to have notice of an equitable interest if his or her agent has either actual or constructive notice of it. This rule is essential, since most purchasers do not conduct their own conveyancing. Thus, if a conveyancer obtains actual notice of an equitable interest, the purchaser, as the conveyancer's client, is also regarded as having notice of it (*Jared v Clements* [1903] 1 Ch 428).

2.5 Examples of legal interests

As we have seen, a complete list of legal interests in land is found in s. 1(2) of LPA 1925. These include:

- easements and profits à prendre (LPA 1925, s. 1(2)(a));
- rentcharges (LPA 1925, s. 1(2)(b));
- legal mortgages (LPA 1925, s. 1(2)(c));
- other land charges that are not created by instrument (LPA 1925, s. 1(2)(d)); and
- rights of entry (LPA 1925, s. 1(2)(e)).

We have already told you a little about easements and profits à prendre (see 2.2.1.1 and 2.2.2) and will not say any more about them at this point, but we do need to look at the other legal interests listed in s. 1(2).

2.5.1 Rentcharges (s. 1(2)(b))

Section 1 of the Rentcharges Act 1977 defines a rentcharge as 'any annual or other periodic sum charged on or issuing out of land, except (a) rent reserved by a lease or tenancy, or (b) any sum payable by way of interest'. The first thing to note about this is that the term does *not* refer to rent which is payable under a lease or to interest on a debt which is payable under a mortgage (see 2.5.2). Instead, it describes other arrangements whereby land is charged with the payment to someone of an annual or periodic sum. If the money is not paid, the person with the benefit of the rentcharge (the 'rent owner') is entitled to enter upon the land in order to enforce payment.

At one time, and in certain parts of the country, it was rare for an estate in fee simple to be sold for a single payment of money; instead, the vendor took a lump sum plus a rentcharge securing an annual payment. However, the Rentcharges Act 1977 prevented the creation of any new rentcharges of this type, provided that any existing ones are to end 60 years after the Act came into force, and gave the estate owner of the charged land the right to redeem the rentcharge earlier on the payment of compensation.

The 1977 Act did not, however, abolish rentcharges altogether and they may still be created for certain purposes. Thus it is still possible to leave a property to a person, subject to a rentcharge obliging him to make a periodical payment to your widow or widower, or to some other member of your family, in order to provide for the maintenance of that person. This sort of rentcharge gives rise to a trust of the land and is considered at 14.1.2.3.

It is also still possible to create 'estate rentcharges', which are used to ensure that the estate owner of the charged land makes a payment towards the upkeep of facilities on other land. An example of this type is the rentcharge obliging the estate owner to pay an annual sum towards the maintenance of a road on a neighbour's property. These rentcharges are a means of providing for the enforcement of positive covenants in freehold land and they are considered further in Chapter 25.

For a rentcharge to be a legal interest in land it must last for the same period as one of the two legal estates; that is, either in perpetuity or for a fixed period.

2.5.2 Charge by way of legal mortgage (s. 1(2)(c))

A mortgage is used to charge an estate in land with the repayment of a debt (or the performance of some other obligation). For example, the borrower, who grants the mortgage over his estate and is called the **mortgagor**, provides security for a loan by granting a mortgage to the lender, who is known as the **mortgagee**. The grant of a mortgage gives the mortgagee an estate or interest in the property, and if the borrower fails to repay the loan, the mortgagee may take the mortgagor's property and sell it to satisfy the debt.

Granting a **charge by way of legal mortgage** is one of the three ways in which a legal mortgage may be created after 1925 (LPA 1925, ss. 85–7). The other two methods of mortgaging property are not mentioned in LPA 1925, s. 1(2), because they operate by giving the mortgagee a legal estate in the property (in fact, a very long lease), and are therefore legal by virtue of s. 1(1). The charge by way of legal mortgage does not create an estate in the land but takes effect as a legal interest under s. 1(2). The mortgagee acquires the same rights over the mortgaged property whichever method of creation is used.

There is much more about mortgages in Chapters 22 and 23.

2.5.3 ... and any other similar charge on land which is not created by an instrument (s. 1(2)(d))

The rather peculiar wording of this section is due to the repeal of the first four words, which originally referred to 'land tax' and 'tithe rentcharge'. The charges in this category are all created by statute and are rarely encountered.

2.5.4 Rights of entry (s. 1(2)(e))

This heading includes rights of entry included in leases or attached to rentcharges. It is usual to include in a lease a clause which allows the landlord to recover, or 're-enter', the property (i.e., to forfeit the lease), should the tenant be in breach of any of his obligations under the lease. This right is a legal right in itself under s. 1(2)(e) and is regarded as an interest in land. A similar right is usually included in a rentcharge, so that the rent owner may enter and recover the land should the owner of the charged estate fail to pay the sums due.

Table 2.1 provides a simplified summary of rights in relation to land recognised by law.

Table 2.1 Summary of rights to land recognised at law

Allodial land	The Crown		By right of conquest
Legal estates s. 1(1) LPA 1925	(a) Fee simple absolute in possession		Freehold
			Free and common socage
	(b) Term of years absolute		Leasehold
			May be for a period of less than a year
Legal interests in land s. 1(2) LPA 1925	(a) Easement or profit		Must be for a term equivalent to one of the two legal estates
	(b) Rentcharge in possession		Must be for a term equivalent to one of the two legal estates
	(c) Charge by way of legal mortgage		The modern method of creating a mortgage
	(d) Statutory charges		
	(e) Rights of entry		Must arise in relation to a lease or a legal rentcharge

2.6 Examples of equitable interests

2.6.1 Introduction

As has been explained, equitable interests in land were developed by the Chancellor and his court in circumstances in which the common law courts were not able to provide a remedy. The range of equitable interests was also enlarged considerably in 1926 by the addition of a number of rights which until then had been legal, but ceased to be so as a result of the statutory reforms (LPA 1925, s. 1(2) and (3)). This change was covered in the previous sections, noting, for example, that the grant of an easement or profit à prendre for an uncertain period no longer creates a legal interest and takes effect only in equity. Nothing more needs to be said about this newer type of equitable interest, and in what follows we will concentrate on the 'traditional' equitable interests, which continue to be of great importance today.

2.6.2 The interest of a beneficiary under a trust of the legal estate

Trusts are extremely important in land law and are considered further in Part IV. However, it is not possible to proceed very far with a study of this subject without having a basic idea of what a trust is, and so a brief explanation will be included here.

A trust arises when property is held by a person or persons 'on trust' for another person or persons. Thus, Teresa may hold an estate in land on trust for Bob. Teresa is called a 'trustee', while Bob is called a 'beneficiary'. While the trustee is the holder of the legal estate in land, it is her job to use these rights for the benefit of the beneficiary. It is the beneficiary who is entitled to receive benefits from the use of the estate (called 'the *beneficial interest*'), while the trustee must not use the estate for her own benefit.

Historically, common law did not recognise this trust structure and would not help the beneficiary if the trustee used the estate for his own benefit. Equity did, however, protect the beneficiary, who accordingly came to have an enforceable right to the property. Thus even today the rights of the beneficiary are enforceable only in equity and not at law.

Where there is a trust of the legal estate in land, it is sometimes said that there are therefore effectively two 'owners' of the land:

- the trustee who holds the legal estate, who is called 'the legal owner'; and
- the beneficiary who holds the beneficial interest, who is called 'the beneficial owner'.

As Maitland has explained, this does not mean that the trustee and the beneficiary have identical rights to the land, with the trustee's rights being recognised in a common law court and the beneficiary's rights being recognised in Chancery: if that had been the case, with different courts in the same jurisdiction reaching different conclusions about who owned a particular piece of land, it would have led to 'civil war and utter anarchy' (*Equity* (1936), p. 17). Instead, the terms 'legal owner' and 'beneficial owner', applied to a trustee and a beneficiary like Teresa and Bob, describe rights that have different content. Teresa, the trustee, is the legal owner in the sense that she has the legal right to exclude strangers from the land and powers to deal with the estate, selling or leasing or mortgaging it as required. Meanwhile, Bob is the beneficial owner in the sense that he can require the trustee to use these rights and powers only for his benefit, and can hold Teresa to account if she uses her rights and powers improperly (for her own benefit, negligently, or inconsistently with the terms of the trust).

In addition to trusts which are created expressly by the owner of property, there are situations which the courts will interpret as giving rise to a trust, sometimes to give effect to the presumed intention of the owner, but on other occasions very much against his or her will. It is this sort of trust that might have arisen at Trant House, if Vernon's mother had contributed to the cost of acquiring or converting the property. Trusts which are recognised by the courts in this way, without express creation, are said to be 'implied', 'resulting', or 'constructive' trusts. We will look at them in more detail in Chapters 13 and 18.

2.6.3 Interests under estate contracts and options

2.6.3.1 Estate contracts

Equitable interests also arise from the special way in which equity treats contracts to create or transfer legal estates or interests (**estate contracts**). If, for example, a contract is made between Vernon and Penelope for the sale and purchase of the freehold estate in Trant House, different remedies for breach of that contract are available at law and in equity.

The legal remedy is that of *damages* for breach of contract. If Vernon refuses to perform his contract and convey the freehold to Penelope, for example, a court could order him to pay Penelope a sum of money reflecting the amount of the loss she has suffered because of his failure to perform the contract. Equity, however, goes further and may give an order for *specific performance* of the contract. Specific performance is an order which will make the parties to a contract perform their promises—in our example, a court could order Vernon to convey the estate or order Penelope to pay the promised purchase price. Specific performance is a remedy which lies in the discretion of the court, which the court will normally award only where damages are considered to be inadequate to compensate for the loss caused by the breach of contract. However, specific performance of a contract to convey a legal estate or interest in land is routinely awarded, because it is thought that land is so unique that damages will rarely be an adequate substitute for a failure to receive the very estate or interest in land that has been promised.

The application of an equitable maxim that, 'Equity regards as done that which ought to be done', produces the result that a contract to convey property which can be specifically enforced is regarded as creating an equitable interest in that property. The operation of this rule can best be explained by reference to our example of the sale by Vernon to Penelope. 'That which ought to be done' is Vernon's conveyance of the estate to Penelope. From the time that the contract is made, therefore, equity acts as though that conveyance had already been completed. As a result, Penelope is treated as having an equitable interest in the land from the date that the contract is made, while Vernon retains the legal estate until the **deed** transferring the legal estate is made (see further at 4.6).

2.6.3.2 Options

Under a contract for an option, an estate owner gives the other party the right to acquire an estate in the property at some time in the future. For example, Vera, the fee simple owner of a bungalow, may agree that, if Peter wishes to buy the property, he may do so at any time within the next 10 years. Peter thus acquires an option in respect of the bungalow. He is under no obligation to buy it, but has the right to do so if he wishes. By contrast, Vera is bound by the agreement and is under a contractual duty to sell to Peter if asked to do so. The agreement between them creates a sort of half-way situation, in which the prospective vendor is bound but the prospective purchaser remains free.

If Vera later refuses to sell the bungalow to Peter within the 10-year period, equity will compel her to do so by means of the remedy of specific performance. This is another situation in which equity 'regards as done that which ought to be done', and as a result Peter is regarded as having an equitable interest in the property from the time when he acquired the option.

This special way in which equity treats contracts to create or convey estates or interests in land leads us on to the third type of equitable interest: interests which are created where formality requirements for creating legal rights are not observed.

2.6.4 Interests which are not created formally

2.6.4.1 Formal requirements at law

As has been explained, in order to create or transfer a legal estate or interest in land it is usually necessary to use a 'deed' as required by s. 52 of the LPA 1925. Additional requirements for the creation or transfer of certain legal estates or interests are imposed by LRA 2002, but we will postpone consideration of these until Chapter 6, and will concentrate here on the nature of a deed.

A deed is a document which has been executed in accordance with certain formalities in order to ensure that its validity can be proved. The nature of the formalities required depends on the date at which the deed was executed.

(a) *Deeds executed before 31 July 1990* Deeds made before this date are subject to the traditional rules which required a deed to be *signed, sealed, and delivered*. At one time it was a person's seal that was essential in order to prove the authenticity of a document, but for many years the habit of using sealing wax and a real seal had been abandoned and the seal was represented by a red sticker on the document, or even by a printed circle containing the letters 'LS' (from the Latin phrase *'locus sigilli'*—'the place of the seal'). It should be noted that, in relation to these older documents, no witness was necessary but most deeds were in fact witnessed.

(b) *Deeds made on or after 31 July 1990* Since 31 July 1990, the Law of Property (Miscellaneous Provisions) Act 1989, s. 1, has required that to be a deed a document must:

- make it clear on the face of the document that it is intended to be a deed; and
- be signed by the person executing the deed in the presence of a witness who attests the signature (this means that the witness sees the deed being signed and then signs the deed as a witness); and
- be delivered by the person executing or by someone else on his or her behalf.
- So the document must be *signed, witnessed, and delivered*.

Delivery

In the case of both the old and the new rules it is technically necessary for the deed to be delivered formally. This used to be done by the person concerned placing a hand on the seal on the document and saying, 'I deliver this as my act and deed'. Today formal delivery is usually dispensed with, a practice which was approved in *Stromdale & Ball Ltd v Burden* [1952] Ch 223.

How do you know if a document is a deed?

The changes introduced by the Law of Property (Miscellaneous Provisions) Act 1989 have simplified the creation of deeds for the parties involved, but seem to have made the concept of a deed more difficult to understand! The difference between a deed and a document which is merely 'in writing' is less obvious now, but the distinction between the two is essential because, as we have seen, most legal estates and interests cannot be created or transferred unless a deed is used. Since 31 July 1990, the distinguishing characteristics of a deed are that the signature of the party executing it is witnessed and the document is stated to be a deed (for example, by some phrase such as 'This Deed of Conveyance is made the first day of September 1999', or by the document recording that it is signed 'as a deed'—see Forms 5.1 and 6.2). A written document which does not satisfy these requirements is not a deed, and in general will not create or transfer a legal estate or interest.

2.6.4.2 Help from equity when formal requirements not observed

At law an attempt to create an estate or interest without a deed will be totally ineffective. It may be, however, that the attempted grant can be treated as a contract to create the estate or interest. Contracts relating to land are now themselves subject to strict formalities (see Chapter 4), but in the earlier law less formality was required and frequently the courts were able to deduce the existence of a contract from the circumstances surrounding the ineffective grant.

Where such a contract could be identified, specific performance of that contract might be available in equity to compel the creation of a legal estate or interest in the proper form, by requiring one party to make a grant by deed. Moreover, the maxim that equity regards as done that which ought to be done might enable equity to treat the person entitled to the grant as already having the interest in equity (see 2.6.3).

We may illustrate this principle with the following example.

- If Len purports to grant a lease of a flat to Tom for 10 years but without using a deed, Tom does not obtain a legal lease.
- If Tom could satisfy the court that a valid contract for a lease exists, he could seek an order for specific performance to compel Len to grant the lease by deed.
- If specific performance could be granted, equity would 'regard as done that which ought to be done', i.e., it would act as though Len had complied with an order for specific performance and had granted the lease in the correct form.
- As a result, equity would regard Tom as having an equitable lease in the property for 10 years.

An example of such an equitable lease may be found in *Walsh v Lonsdale* (1882) 21 ChD 9 (considered further at 9.3.2.3).

A similar process operates to give rise to other rights, such as equitable easements and equitable mortgages, where the correct formalities for granting these interests have not been observed, but the court is able to identify a contract to grant such an interest.

2.6.5 Interests arising under restrictive covenants

A further example of equity's willingness to provide a remedy when the law would not do so relates to restrictive covenants. Covenants are promises made in a deed. A restrictive covenant is a promise by the promisor, or 'covenantor', not to do certain things on his land. If, for example, Pip is buying a house he might covenant with the vendor not to carry on a business on the premises. The common law will enforce this promise against Pip, the original covenantor, as a matter of contract. If Pip later sells the property to Quentin, however, the common law will not enforce the covenant against Quentin, because he was not a party to the original contract. This is the ordinary contractual rule which requires 'privity of contract'.

However, in certain circumstances, which are explained in Chapter 25, equity will enforce the covenant against Quentin. The person who is seeking to enforce the covenant will therefore have a right which is enforceable in equity against the owner for the time being of the property, and so has an equitable interest in that land. Thus if the owner of the cottage next to Trant House does indeed have such an interest (2.2.1.2), it is likely that he or she could prevent Penelope from using the property as bed-and-breakfast accommodation.

2.6.6 Other rights to equitable relief

Having told you about some equitable interests, we must mention briefly some more rights which have on occasion been described by the courts as 'mere' equities. A person is sometimes said to have an 'equity' when that person has a right to some form of equitable remedy, such as a right to have a transaction set aside for fraud or undue influence, or to have a document rectified for mistake. In some cases, most notably those involving estoppel, the courts regard themselves as having a wide discretion to choose the form of relief most appropriate to the circumstances. In the past, these rights to relief appeared to operate only between the parties personally concerned, but increasingly now they are regarded as enforceable against successors in title (that is, against the current owner of land formerly owned by the person subject to the equity).

2.6.7 Proprietary estoppel

Before leaving this introductory account of equitable developments, it is necessary to refer briefly to '**proprietary estoppel**', which in recent years has come to play an important part in many areas of land law. In general, rules of estoppel operate to prevent a party denying matters which he or she has previously asserted or represented. The doctrine is used by both law and equity, and we shall see some examples of legal estoppel when we come to consider leases (**tenancy by estoppel**—9.3.4; and surrender by operation of law—9.5.2.3(2)). At law, the representation must relate to existing fact, but equity, in its traditional role of restraining unconscionable behaviour, applies the concept more widely.

In a particular form of equitable estoppel, called 'proprietary estoppel', equity may prevent an estate owner denying representations made by him which have led the representee to believe that he has, or will have, some rights in the representor's land and to act to his detriment in reliance on that belief. In some cases the equity (right to relief) which arises from such an estoppel is enforceable not only against the representor, but also against anyone who acquires the land from him. Thus it is just possible that if Vernon's mother wants to remain in her flat after Trant House is sold (see 2.2.4), she might claim that her son represented to her that she could live there for the rest of her life. This, coupled with her expenditure on the property (arguably a 'detriment') might give her a right to some relief in equity which could bind Penelope or any other purchaser of Trant House.

Proprietary estoppel is considered in more detail in Chapters 19 and 20. However, you will come across other references to estoppel in the course of reading this book, and in particular should note a new application of the principle as a replacement for the old doctrine of part performance of a contract (see 4.4 and 4.5).

2.7 A multiplicity of rights

It will be obvious from what has been said so far that one piece of land may be subject to a large number of interests all at the same time. Indeed the doctrine of estates may be responsible for encouraging the development of such multiple interests, because it encourages one to think in terms of owning rights in land rather than of owning the land itself. As we shall see, in England and Wales land law is not really concerned with absolute rights but rather with balancing the relative claims to land which may be made by a number of people. Thus one piece of land could be subject to all the following rights at the same time:

- a fee simple owned by Amy;
- a 99-year lease granted by Amy to Bob;
- a weekly tenancy granted by Bob to Carol;
- a legal mortgage of the freehold granted by Amy to a building society;
- an equitable mortgage of the 99-year lease granted by Bob to his bank;
- a right of way over the property granted in perpetuity to David, the owner of the house next door (a legal easement);
- an estate rentcharge granted by Amy to Eric, a neighbouring owner, to ensure that Amy contributes to the cost of maintaining a shared drive;
- a restrictive covenant enforceable by another neighbour, Fred, which prevents the land from being used for business purposes.

2.8 Modern approach to protection of rights

Over time the traditional methods of protection of estates and interests in land have become increasingly unsatisfactory, particularly because the traditional approach to checking for ownership of estates and for any interests in the land depended upon inspection of the documents relating to the property, which might readily be damaged, lost, destroyed, or tampered with. Therefore, the concept of having registers to cover such matters developed. Over time, this started with the possibility of registering some interests in land (leading to the Land Charges Register, see Chapter 5) and moved on to the concept of registering the estates in land and including in those registrations the majority of interests relating to the registered estate (the Land Registry, see Chapter 6). As far as the owner of a right to land was concerned, the new systems might mean that he or she needed to have the right put on a register and, in the absence of registration, the right would not be binding on a purchaser. You will see the extent to which registration has become important in Chapters 5 and 6.

2.9 Human rights

In addition to the purely land law protections that may be available to the owner of an estate or interest in land, you will need to bear in mind that in some cases human rights arguments might be relevant. The study of human rights may largely be the subject of your other studies, either as part of constitutional and administrative law or as a subject in its own right. However, it is important to be able to identify cases in which an argument under the Human Rights Act 1998 (HRA 1998), which incorporates the European Convention of Human Rights into English law, may be appropriate in the land law context. We deal with the case law as and when it becomes relevant throughout this text but it is worth starting out with some basic points in mind, as you start to acquire your knowledge of land law.

HRA 1998, s. 1 describes the rights it protects as 'Convention rights' and these are defined in s. 1 by reference to the Articles of the Convention and of the First and Sixth Protocols to it (you will find the text of the Convention in Sch. 1 of the Act). Of the

16 Articles included in this definition, the four which are most likely to be of significance in a land law context are:

Art. 6—right to a fair trial;

Art. 8—right to respect for private and family life, including right to respect for the home;

Art. 14—prohibition of discrimination; and

Art. 1 of the First Protocol—peaceful enjoyment of possession.

In looking at these rights you should note that although the first part of each Article appears to give an absolute right, in each case (except that of the prohibition of discrimination) the opening statement is qualified by further provisions which set out the circumstances in which the right may be limited or excluded by individual states.

One important point to note is that, although there are disputes about its exact effect, the courts have generally taken the view that these human rights do not have 'horizontal effect', so that it is not open to a person to argue that a non-state entity (like a landlord or a mortgagee that is not a public authority) has a duty to respect their human rights. The Supreme Court took a very robust approach to the issue of horizontal effect in *McDonald v McDonald* [2017] AC 273. In *McDonald*, parents had borrowed money, secured by the grant of a mortgage, in order to buy a property as a home for their daughter, who had a severe mental illness. They granted their daughter a series of short tenancies of the premises. When they failed to make payments on the loan secured by the mortgage, the mortgagee appointed a receiver that took over the power to manage the rights of the parents as landlord (see 22.8.1.7 for this remedy of a mortgagee). On the expiry of the daughter's latest short lease, the receiver sought a possession order. Despite the fact that a forced move could have very serious implications for this tenant's right to respect for her home under Article 8 of the European Convention, the Supreme Court was not prepared to conclude that Convention rights operated as between individuals, as opposed to between a state entity and an individual. They therefore considered that the Convention and HRA 1998 did not require the court to consider the 'proportionality' of an order for possession. This has meant that human rights arguments have most commonly been relevant in cases in which a person is renting property from a local council, which is a public authority, and owes a duty to act compatibly with the Convention under s. 6 of the HRA 1998 (as, for example, in Manchester City Council v Pinnock [2010] USKC 45). Such arguments can also be relevant where some rule of land law is found in a statute, which the court may be asked to interpret compatibly with Convention rights (s. 3 of the HRA 1998) or declare to be incompatible with the Convention (s. 4 of the HRA 1998).

2.10 Classification of property

Although we are leaving questions about the statutory definition of land, and other technical matters, until the last chapter, we must make a brief mention here of the lawyers' classification of property and a few of the technical terms connected with it.

2.10.1 Real and personal property

Property is divided into two main categories: 'real' property and 'personal' property (or 'realty' and 'personalty'). **Real property** consists of all the estates and interests in land which we will be considering in this book, with the exception of leases which, for historical reasons, are regarded as a form of personal property. The reason for this is explained in Chapter 26, but you should note that 'real property' got its name from the fact that in early law it was protected by a 'real action' (i.e., an action to recover the *'res'* or 'thing').

2.10.2 Personal property

Personal property is divided into three categories: **choses in possession**, **choses in action**, and **chattels real**.

2.10.2.1 Choses in possession

Tangible objects other than land which can be physically possessed (such as cars, books, and clothes) are called 'choses in possession'. *'Chose'* is another word which, like *'res'*, means 'thing' but this time lawyers use French rather than Latin.

2.10.2.2 Choses in action

Intangible rights, other than those relating to land, of which one cannot take physical possession and which depend for their existence on enforcement by the courts are called 'choses in action'. In this category are placed debts, copyrights, and patents, among other rights.

2.10.2.3 Chattels real

Leases, which are estates in land, but were classified as personal property, are known technically as 'chattels real', because although they are chattels (another name for personal property) they became much like real property, as is explained in Chapter 26.

FURTHER READING

On origins and nature of equity

Hanbury and Martin, *Modern Equity*, 21st edn., Sweet & Maxwell, 2018, Chapter 1 (History and Principles—in particular paras. 1-001–1-008 and 1-024–1-042).

Maitland, *Equity*, Cambridge University Press, 1936, Lectures 1 and 11 (The Origins of Equity).

Megarry and Wade, *The Law of Real Property*, 9th edn., Sweet & Maxwell, 2019, paras. 4-003–4-029.

On the doctrine of notice

Cheshire and Burn, *Cheshire and Burn's Modern Law of Real Property*, 18th edn., Oxford University Press, 2011, pp. 83–91.

Hanbury and Martin, *Modern Equity*, 21st edn., Sweet & Maxwell, 2018, paras. 1-042–1-046.

You can visit the online resources to test your knowledge of this chapter with self-test questions at **www.oup.com/he/nair19e/**.

PART II
The freehold estate

Introduction

This part is largely about the acquisition of a fee simple estate in land. A lot of this material is also relevant to acquiring an existing long lease from the current leaseholder, but details of how such leases are originally created will be dealt with in Chapter 9, in which the term of years absolute is discussed in detail.

Although estates and interests in land may be acquired by way of gift, either in the lifetime of the donor or by will on death, this part concentrates on acquisitions for value and, in the main, covers the process by which a purchaser buys an estate in land from a vendor. Although land law and conveyancing are normally taught separately, they are in fact inextricably linked: the law relating to conveyancing is unintelligible without an understanding of the underlying structure of land law, and land law seems pointless unless one has an appreciation of how the theory of the law is applied in practice. This book concentrates on the rules of land law rather than those of conveyancing but sets the land law rules in their conveyancing context as this makes it easier to appreciate their purpose. To this end we will consider in Chapters 3–6 the steps necessary to purchase two properties, one registered and the other unregistered, Nos. 1 and 2 Trant Way. Chapter 7 then considers how a freehold estate can be acquired without the consent of a previous owner, by 'adverse possession' (sometimes known as 'squatter's title').

3

Buying a house

3.1 The properties and the parties **35**
3.2 Two systems of title **36**
3.3 Outline of the conveyancing process **38**

3.1 The properties and the parties

Two freehold properties are currently for sale in Trant Way, Mousehole, Stilton.

3.1.1 1 Trant Way

This property is a large Victorian house with a garden. The current owner of the fee simple is Victor Venn. Mr Venn bought the property in 1992 but is now obliged to move to another part of the country. Mr and Mrs Armstrong (Arnold and Arriety) are interested in buying the property for £450,000.

3.1.2 2 Trant Way

Number 2 is another large house but it has been divided up so that the top floor provides a separate 'granny flat', with its own internal front door but sharing the street door with the rest of the house and using the internal stairs for access. The current fee simple owner is Victoria Ventnor who bought the property in 1988. Barbara Bell is interested in buying the house for £475,000. Barbara has an elderly father, Bob Bell, and she hopes that he will agree to come and live in the top-floor flat so that she can 'keep an eye on him'.

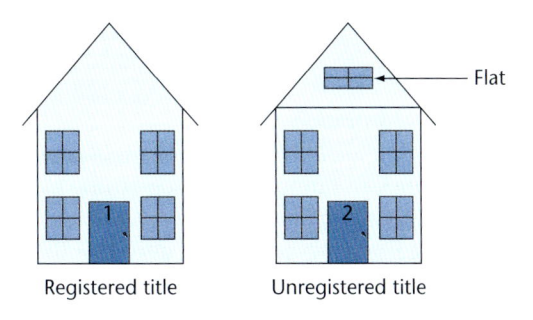

Figure 3.1 1 and 2 Trant Way

3.2 Two systems of title

3.2.1 What the buyer wants to know

As you saw in Chapters 1 and 2, prospective purchasers of any property (or normally their legal advisers) have two main concerns.

First, they must be sure that the vendor of the property is really entitled to sell it. Thus a buyer must insist on proof that the vendor's title to the land is good and that he or she can pass to the purchaser the estate which has been offered for sale. Otherwise, a stranger with a better title to land than the vendor may come along and evict the purchaser after the sale.

Secondly, the purchaser will want to know whether any third parties have rights to the land which might interfere with the purchaser's intended use. These third-party rights might, for example, include covenants restricting use, rights of way, tree preservation orders, or mortgages obliging the owner of the estate to make payments to a creditor.

Concern about these matters will lead the purchaser, or the purchaser's representatives, to make extensive enquiries before the purchase of the estate is finally concluded.

3.2.2 Registered and unregistered systems

Unfortunately for the student of English land law, there are two totally separate systems of proving title to land and investigating third-party rights in it. The newer (and now more common) system is the registered land system; the older system is the unregistered system of conveyancing. The enquiries to be made by a purchaser differ depending on whether the title to the estate is registered or unregistered. For the student this means learning two importantly different sets of laws: one mainly governed by statute, the Land Registration Act 2002, which repealed and replaced the earlier Land Registration Act 1925 (see Chapter 6); the other governed by the old rules of common law and equity, as amended by statute, chiefly now the Law of Property Act 1925 and the Land Charges Act 1972 (see Chapter 5).

3.2.3 Which system applies?

The first thing you must ascertain when dealing with any piece of land is which system of conveyancing is to be applied to it. In other words, you must find out whether the relevant estate in the land is registered or not. It may surprise you to find that the old unregistered system of title is still in operation almost a century after the introduction of compulsory registration by the LRA 1925. This is a result of the policy of phased introduction, which is explained later, but undoubtedly the whole process has taken far longer than was expected in 1925, and recent statutory changes are designed to extend registration of title more quickly.

3.2.3.1 Areas of compulsory registration

Although there had been some limited voluntary registration of title before 1926, it was LRA 1925 which provided that, in future, registration of title to land was to become compulsory when the land was sold or otherwise dealt with, in areas designated as *areas of compulsory registration*. As it was not possible to introduce the registration system to the whole country immediately (largely due to cost), the practice was adopted of making only certain places areas of compulsory registration and gradually increasing those areas as time went on. Originally it was thought that the whole country would soon be covered, but economic depression, followed by World War II, and then further recession, held up the extension of the system. However, the last areas, including our imaginary town of Mousehole, became compulsory registration areas on 1 December 1990. Accordingly, now all land in England and Wales stands in an area of compulsory registration and any person dealing with a property simply needs to ask the Land Registry whether the title has in fact been registered or will need to be registered for the first time by the new owner.

3.2.3.2 Has the title to the estate been registered?

One has to ask this question because estates do not have to be registered as soon as the area in which the land stands became an area of compulsory registration. To require this would involve estate owners in unexpected costs, for land registry fees are payable on all registrations. Instead, estates have to be registered at the time of the first dealing for value with certain estates in the land (usually the sale of the freehold or a grant of a long lease) after the area became a compulsory area. Thus, in Mousehole, all estates which have been dealt with since 1990 should have been registered at the Land Registry. Accordingly, the title to 1 Trant Way will be registered (last dealing in 1992), while the title to 2 Trant Way will not be registered (last dealing in 1988).

Triggering registration
From 1997 onwards, the occasions which give rise to compulsory registration have been considerably extended, so that the duty to apply for first registration now arises not only on dealings for value, but on dispositions by way of gift and on those made by personal representatives (who pass property to those entitled to it on the death of the previous owner), and by trustees (on transfers to beneficiaries or on the appointment of new trustees). In addition, a legal estate becomes registrable if the owner creates over it a first legal charge (a mortgage), even though the owner is not transferring the estate itself (see 6.3.2).

The requirements for first registration are set out in Chapter 6, but you should note that the extension of events triggering a requirement of registration has led to a very real increase in the number of titles coming onto the register. The current intention is that all land in England and Wales should become subject to the land registration system by 2030 (see Ruoff and Roper, looseleaf edn., para. 1.013).

Voluntary registration
While most registered land has been entered on the register in compliance with the requirements for compulsory registration, there are also cases in which registration is appropriate on a voluntary basis. For example, a developer planning to build a large housing estate on land which is currently unregistered may choose to register the title to the whole estate voluntarily, before embarking on the sales of individual plots that would trigger compulsory registration. The developer can then agree an estate plan for all the new properties with the Land Registry before selling the individual plots. This makes conveyancing of each plot of land easier and is convenient for the developer, the purchasers, and the registry. Voluntary registration is also sometimes used to solve a problem which has arisen in relation to the property—for example, if the title deeds have been destroyed in a fire or lost. In these cases, voluntary registration can avoid many difficulties when the estate owner comes to sell, because the registry entry will replace the missing deeds and provide a buyer of land with more certainty over time (for the notion of registering and then 'upgrading' an uncertain title, see 6.3.3.2).

As we shall see in Chapter 6, it is now considered desirable to extend registration of title as rapidly and thoroughly as possible. The Land Registry encourages landowners to seek voluntary registration by offering reduced fees for the process and by drawing attention to the advantages of registered title which, under LRA 2002, include improved protection against squatters (see Chapter 7).

How to find out if title has been registered
At present, the result of the gradual introduction of registration is that the title to some estates in some land will be registered, while the title to others will not. If you are not sure whether a registration has been made you can find out by making an 'index map search', which will tell you whether an estate in that land has been registered (but which will not reveal any other information, such as the name of the estate owner). Further details may be obtained by making a full search of the register, which, since 3 December 1990, can be done without the consent of the estate owner.

3.2.3.3 Unregistered land
Any land which is not shown as being registered on the Land Registry index map is necessarily unregistered land. As such it is covered by the older system of conveyancing rules which are substantially different, particularly as regards the protection of third-party rights. According to Land Registry's latest business strategy, published on its website in 2022 around 88 per cent of the land mass of England and Wales has been registered. Nevertheless, it remains necessary to have an understanding of how the older system works, because it is still far from being redundant.

3.3 Outline of the conveyancing process

3.3.1 A two-stage process
Conveyancing is usually conducted in two stages. First, there may be an informal, oral agreement between vendor and purchaser; this will normally have no legal effect because contracts to convey land are subject to strict formality requirements (see 4.2). Next, the parties will enter into a contract, in which the purchaser agrees to buy, and the vendor agrees to sell, the property. The contract will place the vendor under a legally binding *obligation* to convey the legal estate, but it cannot actually transfer that estate since there are even stricter formality requirements for dealing with legal estates in land. After a period of time, the contract will be performed or 'completed' by the transfer or conveyance of the legal estate by the vendor to the purchaser, complying with these strict formalities.

The interval between contract and completion used to be quite long, and was the stage at which the main investigation of the vendor's title took place. Nowadays, however, a full investigation of title usually precedes the exchange of contracts, and as a result the period between contract and completion is often shortened. The consequence of this change, however, has been to lengthen the period between the informal agreement to buy the property and the formal making of the contract. Until the contract is concluded neither party is legally bound to continue with the transaction and either of them can withdraw from the negotiations without liability. It is this freedom from obligation which, in times of rising house prices, can lead to the practice of 'gazumping', in which the vendor accepts a higher offer from another purchaser. Although the vendor is legally free to do this, the original purchaser may well feel aggrieved, especially if he or she has already incurred the expense of surveyors' and solicitors' fees. On the other hand, it may be the purchaser who withdraws, for a variety of reasons which could include receiving an unfavourable surveyor's report, finding a cheaper property, or simply changing his or her mind. (A threat of withdrawal by the purchaser, with the object of obtaining a reduction in price, is sometimes described as 'gazundering'.) In 2019, it was indicated that the government was giving consideration to the promotion of 'reservation agreements' as a standard part of the conveyancing process; these are agreements where each side pays a deposit which may be lost if either party pulls out before the exchange of contracts. However, at the time of writing and given the effect of the pandemic in 2020 and 2021, no decision has been made yet.

For the purposes of this book, it is convenient to deal with questions relating to the contract before going on to matters of title, but you should remember that this is not necessarily the order in which these topics will present themselves in real life.

3.3.2 Steps before a contract is concluded

Before they enter into contracts to buy 1 and 2 Trant Way, Mr and Mrs Armstrong and Miss Bell will want confirmation of certain information about the properties: they will want to know how much the council tax is, whether the price includes any fittings, such as carpets, whether there have been any disputes in respect of the land (e.g., boundary disputes) and, no doubt, a good deal else. Where the buyers are borrowing part of the purchase price from a bank or a building society that is willing to lend in exchange for a mortgage of the purchased land, the prospective mortgagee will also want more information about the property in order to be confident that it is good security for the loan. In addition, the buyers' solicitors may wish to query portions of the draft contract which each will have received from the vendor's solicitor.

At this stage, it is also usual to make a search about the property in the local land charges register.

3.3.2.1 Local land charges

These registers are maintained under the Local Land Charges Act 1975. They contain details of a variety of 'charges' (burdens) on the land. Thus you might discover from searching the local land charges register that the property is in a smoke control zone, or that a tree in the garden is the subject of a tree preservation order, or that the local authority has a claim against the land because the council tax has not been paid. You might also discover planning restrictions or that the building is listed as being of outstanding architectural or historical importance. As all these matters might have a considerable effect upon the use to which the land can be put, it is essential that a purchaser should know about them.

Oddly, a purchaser of an estate will be bound by any charge which exists, even if it has not been registered. However, a search is still worthwhile because, if a purchaser obtains an official search certificate, compensation can be claimed under the Local Land Charges Act 1975, s. 10 if later a charge is discovered which was not revealed by the search. This right to compensation arises whether the search was clean because the charge had not been registered or because a mistake was made when issuing the certificate. The compensation is paid by the registry, even if the loss is due to the mistake of some third party who has failed to register a charge (the registry may seek to recover from the third party any sums so paid).

The responsibility for maintaining the registers of local land charges was originally a matter for the local authority in whose area the property stood. However, in 2015 the responsibility for local land charges was passed to the Land Registry. This was done by ss. 34–6 of, and Schedule 5 to, the Infrastructure Act 2015, which came into force in April 2015, and which introduced a phased process by which control of the local land charges registries would pass to Land Registry. Note that the local land charges registers remain separate registers but their operation is now, for convenience, managed by the Land Registry.

3.3.3 The contract

Once a purchaser is satisfied with the answers to whatever enquiries are made at this stage, has made any necessary arrangements to finance the transaction, and has had any surveyor's report on the property that has been sought, the point will have been reached at which the parties are ready to conclude a legally binding contract. Once this has been done, each party is legally obliged to give effect to the transaction, unless the other party is in breach of the terms of the contract. The detailed requirements for the creation of contracts relating to land are covered in Chapter 4.

3.3.4 Investigating title

At some stage in the process of selling a property the vendor should be required to prove ownership of the title being sold. The means by which this is done varies depending upon whether the title to the land is registered or unregistered. Basically, if the title is registered the purchaser will investigate the register, while if the title is unregistered the purchaser will need to see the title deeds to the property. The methods used to protect third-party rights also differ between the two systems and the searches to be made by the purchaser will accordingly be different.

Thus there are two very different processes ahead of Barbara Bell and the Armstrongs, who respectively are buying 2 Trant Way (unregistered title), and 1 Trant Way (registered title) (see 3.2.3.2) and we will follow their progress and consider the two systems in more detail in Chapters 5 and 6.

3.3.5 Completing the transaction

Once both parties have made all the necessary arrangements, the time will have arrived for the purchaser to pay the purchase price and the vendor to transfer the legal estate in the land to the purchaser. The vendor will also be obliged to give possession of the property to the purchaser. This transfer is usually called 'completion'. Obviously it requires a further document, and you will recall from Chapter 2 (see 2.4.2) that the document used to dispose of a legal estate must be a 'deed', a document which is signed, witnessed, and delivered (Law of Property (Miscellaneous Provisions) Act 1989, s. 1). If the land is *unregistered*, the deed is called a 'conveyance' and it has the immediate effect of conveying the legal estate to the purchasers without the need for further formalities (although there may be a requirement to apply for first registration of the title if the purchasers are to *keep* the legal estate they have received by deed: see 6.3.2.3). If the title to the land is *registered*, the deed used is called a 'transfer' and the legal title will not pass to the purchasers until Land Registry has responded to the transfer by changing the title register. As explained in Chapter 6, there has been some discussion about the possibility of replacing the two-step process of a paper transfer by the vendor and subsequent registration by Land Registration with a single electronic transfer that simultaneously effects registration (see 6.2.1).

You can visit the online resources to test your knowledge of this chapter with self-test questions at **www.oup.com/he/nair19e/**.

4

The contract

4.1	Introduction **41**	4.5	Estoppel and s. 2 **57**
4.2	Contracts made on or after 27 September 1989 **42**	4.6	Effect of the contract: passing of the equitable interest **64**
4.3	Contracts made before 27 September 1989 **53**	4.7	Remedies for breach of contract **66**
4.4	Part performance after the 1989 Act **56**	4.8	Application to 2 Trant Way **67**

4.1 Introduction

To some extent, a contract for the sale of an estate or an interest in land is just like any other contract. It must comply with the basic requirements for a contract, which you may have studied in a contract law course—that is, there must have been an offer and an acceptance, there must be 'consideration' (something of value given in exchange), and the parties must have intended to create a legal relationship. However, contracts to sell land are special, partly due to the considerable value of land and partly because such contracts do not merely create personal obligations but also give rise to equitable interests that can affect third parties (see 2.6.3). As a result, it is not surprising that for many centuries there have been additional rules relating to these contracts which require certain formalities to be observed.

The nature of these formalities will depend upon the date at which the contract was made:

- contracts made on or after 27 September 1989 are governed by the Law of Property (Miscellaneous Provisions) Act 1989, s. 2;
- contracts made before 27 September 1989 are governed by the old rules contained in the LPA 1925, s. 40, which was repealed by the 1989 Act.

You might think that most contracts made under the old law would by now either have been performed or have come before the courts, but in fact cases could continue to arise for some years yet. One of the reasons for this is that, as we explained in Chapter 2, a contract to grant a legal estate may give rise to an equitable interest in the property that is, in principle, capable of being enforced against a later buyer of the land. Parties who rely on informal arrangements of this type, made before 27 September 1989, may continue to enjoy rights under them for many years before any dispute arises; since the rights under the contract can be enforced against third parties, they will continue to matter even if the original contracting parties have died or ceased to have any rights in relation to the land.

In *Lloyds Bank plc v Carrick* [1996] 4 All ER 630, for example, the defendant relied upon a contract with her brother-in-law, entered into in the early 1980s, against a mortgagee that was seeking possession of the property in the 1990s. In such a case, it will be necessary to show that the alleged contract satisfied the requirements of the law in force at the date of its creation, and accordingly it seems likely that, for some time to come, one will have to be familiar with the old rules as well as with the new ones.

We will start by looking at the new rules, and will then consider the old ones more briefly.

4.2 Contracts made on or after 27 September 1989

4.2.1 Law of Property (Miscellaneous Provisions) Act 1989, s. 2

Any contract relating to land which is made on or after 27 September 1989 must:

- be made in writing;
- contain all the terms agreed between the parties; and
- be signed by each of the parties.

These requirements are imposed by s. 2 of the Law of Property (Miscellaneous Provisions) Act 1989 (which is referred to hereafter as 'the 1989 Act').

Section 2(1)–(3) provides:

> (1) A contract for the sale or other disposition of an interest in land can only be made in writing and only by incorporating all the terms which the parties have expressly agreed in one document or, where contracts are exchanged, in each.
>
> (2) The terms may be incorporated in a document either by being set out in it or by reference to some other document.
>
> (3) The document incorporating the terms or, where contracts are exchanged, one of the documents incorporating them (but not necessarily the same one) must be signed by or on behalf of each party to the contract.

These provisions are now considered in detail.

4.2.2 Requirements of s. 2

4.2.2.1 Contracts for the sale or other disposition of an interest in land

The effect of this phrase is that s. 2 applies to a wide range of transactions. Obviously, the words would cover the sale of a fee simple and of an existing long lease, but they also include a contract for the original grant of some leases, and contracts to grant a wide range of other interests in land, such as mortgages and easements. Section 2(5) creates a number of specific exceptions, including contracts to grant very short leases and contracts concluded at public auction. These are considered at 4.2.3. There have also been a number of instances when disputes arose as to which agreements are covered by s. 2 and which are not. These cases are considered at 4.2.4, after all of the basic elements of s. 2 have been considered.

4.2.2.2 The contract must be made in writing

There is no alternative to this requirement. The only way in which a contract relating to land can be made on or after 27 September 1989 is in writing: an oral agreement between the parties will not create a contract to dispose of an interest in land, unless one of the exceptions in s. 2(5) applies (see 4.2.3).

You will see later on that equitable concepts such as estoppel or the constructive trust may assist a party who relies on an agreement which does not satisfy the Act's requirements (see 4.5) but, even so, this does not give the agreement the force of a valid contract at law as opposed to in equity.

4.2.2.3 Any variation of the contract must comply with s. 2

It was established in *McCausland v Duncan Lawrie Ltd* [1997] 1 WLR 38 at p. 49H that the requirements of s. 2 apply to any subsequent variation of the contract. The Court of Appeal explained in *Keay v Morris Homes (West Midlands) Ltd* [2012] 1 WLR 2855 para. 31 that this is because:

> when the parties to a contract agree to vary it, they are in fact entering into a new contract, and an agreement to vary an existing contract for the sale or other disposition of an interest in land will only do so validly if made in a written and signed document that itself contains or incorporates all the terms of the original agreement and so itself complies with s. 2.

4.2.2.4 The written contract must incorporate all the terms which the parties have expressly agreed

This requirement is set out in s. 2(1), and s. 2(2) then goes on to provide that the terms agreed by the parties may be incorporated in the contract either by setting them out in it, or by referring to some other document which contains them. Failure to do this will invalidate the contract.

Since the 1989 Act has been in operation, a number of cases have come before the courts in which it has been alleged that a term which forms part of the agreement has not been incorporated in the written contract and that the contract is accordingly void. The attempt by one party to escape from an agreement often appears to be somewhat unmeritorious, and occasionally the court has succeeded in holding them to their bargains. In some cases the court has done this by treating the missing terms as a separate contract, the omission of which does not invalidate the contract relating to an interest in land. By contrast, there have been other decisions in which the court has refused to adopt this approach, and has treated the whole contract as void because certain terms have been omitted. These cases are considered at 4.2.5.

4.2.2.5 The written contract may take the form of one document, which both parties sign, or of identical documents, each signed by one party and then exchanged

This requirement is derived from s. 2(1) and (3). The provision for the exchange of contracts perpetuates the method which conveyancers have developed over the years for concluding contracts for the sale of estates in land. The normal procedure is for two identical copies of the contract to be prepared. One copy is signed by the vendor and the other by the purchaser and, when the time comes to create a binding contract, the parties exchange their copies. As a result of the exchange, each party holds a copy of the contract signed by the other.

Contracts by correspondence

The terms of s. 2(1) and (3) may seem to produce the result that it is no longer possible to create what are known as 'contracts by correspondence'. Under the old rules, and in contract law generally, an enforceable contract can come into existence as a result of a written offer and a written acceptance contained in letters passing between the parties, or through correspondence between them confirming the terms of a previously made oral agreement. The courts have considered the effect under the 1989 Act of such 'contracts by correspondence' in a number of cases, including two important decisions by the Court of Appeal.

In *Hooper v Sherman* [1994] NPC 153 an unmarried couple agreed that the man would transfer his interest in the family home to the woman in return for being released from his mortgage obligations. This arrangement was confirmed by letters between the parties' solicitors, but some delay was caused by the mortgagees and eventually the man refused to complete. The Court of Appeal held that, while neither letter by itself constituted a contract, a bilateral contract came into existence through the exchange of the letters. Morritt LJ, in a dissenting judgment, took the view that the letters were no more than confirmation of the oral agreement, and were not enough for the purposes of s. 2 of the 1989 Act.

In *Commission for the New Towns v Cooper (Great Britain) Ltd* [1995] Ch 259 the documents in question again took the form of letters passing between the plaintiff and the defendant, purporting to record and confirm an oral agreement reached at a meeting between the parties. The facts of the case are complicated because the defendant had deliberately planned to mislead the plaintiff and had engineered the discussions at the meeting in such a way that the plaintiff was not aware of the true effect of the proposals to which it agreed. The Court of Appeal found for the plaintiff on a number of grounds, one of them being that the correspondence between the parties did not constitute an exchange of contracts for the purpose of s. 2. In the view of the court, written offers and acceptances can no longer, in themselves, give rise to a written contract: they are merely the process by which the agreement is reached. For s. 2 to be satisfied, the terms of any agreement have to be finally reduced to a document that has either been signed by both parties or exchanged in the traditional way (identical copies signed by vendor and purchaser and then exchanged).

It was only at a late stage of the proceedings in *Commission for the New Towns v Cooper (Great Britain) Ltd* that the Court of Appeal was reminded of its decision in *Hooper v Sherman*. The court was, however, able to find reasons for not following this earlier decision, on the basis that the letters in *Hooper v Sherman* had been exchanged *after* all the terms of the agreement had been settled by the parties and simply recorded the terms of that agreement, rather than the letters themselves constituting the offer and the acceptance. Both Stuart-Smith LJ and Evans LJ indicated that, if the cases could not be distinguished, they were willing to treat *Hooper v Sherman* as decided 'per incuriam', so that it need not be followed.

This issue was recently considered by the High Court in *Kuznetsov v London Borough of Camden* [2019] EWHC 805. In that case, the local council had sent a signed letter to the owner of a leasehold flat, advising him to obtain a valuation of his flat from a surveyor and offering to buy the property at a price reflecting that valuation. The leaseholder alleged that he had added a sentence to the bottom of this letter, accepting the offer and adding his own signature, before returning it to the council; he argued that this constituted an exchange of contracts for the purposes of s. 2 and sued the council on the contract. The council asked the court to strike out his claim on the basis that he had no arguable case, on the authority of *Commission for the New Towns v Cooper (Great Britain) Ltd*. They argued that the decision of the Court of Appeal meant that no 'contract by correspondence' could ever satisfy s. 2, because the terms of the contract had to be fully agreed by the parties before they were reduced to writing. The High Court rejected this argument, holding that it was at least arguable that *Commission for the New Towns v Cooper (Great Britain) Ltd* was authority only for a narrower rule that the correspondence had to result in a single document containing all the terms and signed by both parties. On this basis, since the claimant's signed acceptance of the offer from the council appeared on the same letter initially signed by the council, it was possible that s. 2 might have been satisfied.

4.2.2.6 The written contract must be signed by both parties

This requirement of s. 2(3) can be satisfied either by both parties signing the same document, or by each party signing a copy and then exchanging them.

The requirement of 'signature' was considered in *Firstpost Homes Ltd v Johnson* [1995] 1 WLR 1567. Here the purchaser prepared a letter to himself from the vendor, in which she agreed to sell him land which was identified 'on the enclosed plan'. The purchaser signed the plan but not the letter, and sent both plan and letter to the vendor, who signed both of them. After the vendor's death, the purchaser sought to enforce the contract against the vendor's personal representatives, but the Court of Appeal held that the requirements of s. 2(3) as to the signature were not satisfied, and accordingly there was no valid contract. The court regarded the letter and the plan as two documents, not one ('Something enclosed with the letter is not . . . the same document as the letter'—per Peter Gibson LJ at p. 1573); it was the letter which set out the terms of the agreement, incorporating the details of the plan by referring to it; and, accordingly, it was the letter which should have been signed by both parties. The purchaser sought to meet this point by arguing that he was identified as the addressee on the letter and that earlier authorities showed that the typing or printing of the name of a party as addressee, in a document prepared by that party, was a sufficient signature. The Court of Appeal, however, rejected this argument, saying that it was an artificial use of language to describe the typing or printing of a name in this way as a signature, and quoting with approval the words of Denning LJ in *Goodman v J. Eban Ltd* [1954] 1 QB 550:

> In modern English usage, when a document is required to be 'signed' by someone, that means that he must write his name with his own hand upon it.

In consequence, the court held that the relevant document, the letter, was not signed in accordance with s. 2(3), and accordingly there was no written contract within the provisions of s. 2. However, s. 5 of the Interpretation Act 1978 gives a very wide meaning to 'writing' and thus the situation is not as straightforward as first appears because electronic documents can amount to writing. It seems, therefore, that a signature can be more than something written on paper with a pen or pencil. This became relevant in *Neocleous v Rees* [2019] EWHC 2462 (Ch), where it was held that an automatically generated footer on an electronic document could render the document 'signed' for the purposes of s. 2(3), as long as the inclusion of the footer was for the purpose of authenticating the document as sent by the person sending the email. The judge distinguished *Firstpost Homes Ltd v Johnson* on the basis that, there, the party's name and address had appeared on the letter simply to evidence that he was its addressee, rather than being deliberately inserted by him for the purpose of authenticating the letter as his own. In *Hudson v Hathway* [2022] EWCA Civ 1468, the Court of Appeal affirmed the correctness of *Neocleous v Rees* on this point, holding that 'deliberately subscribing one's name to an email' amounts to a signature for the purposes of s. 2 and other formality rules requiring signed writing.

Although it may seem self-evident from the wording of s. 2(3), it must be emphasised that it is the parties to the *contract* who are required to sign it. The reason for emphasising this is that, sometimes, the parties to a contract for the disposition of land need not be the parties to the eventual conveyance: it is possible that A might contract with B to sell the land to C, the eventual purchaser. This is quite common, for example, where a developer gets planning permission to build on a site on the condition that they allocate some part of the land for purposes favoured by the planning authority (such arrangements are known as 'section 106 agreements', after s. 106 of the Town and Country Planning Act 1990). The developer might then contract with the council that they will sell part of the land to a named third party who will carry out the purpose (e.g., where the purpose is to use the land for affordable housing, a housing association). In such cases, assuming such contracts fall within the purview of s. 2 in the first place (see 4.2.4.2 below), it has been asked whether the signature of the eventual purchaser is also needed for the contract to be valid.

This issue has been considered in two High Court decisions, *Jelson Ltd v Derby County Council* [1999] 3 EGLR 91, and *RG Kensington Co Ltd v Hutchinson IDH Ltd* [2003] 2 P&CR 195, which reached different conclusions. In *Jelson*, it was held that the signature of the eventual purchaser was also needed for the contract to satisfy s. 2. However, this view was rejected by Neuberger J in *Kensington*, who held that the interpretation adopted in *Jelson* could not be supported. He pointed out that s. 2(3) referred specifically to the signature of 'each party to the contract' and added that the interpretation relied on by the developer:

> would involve an impermissible re-writing and extension . . . of s. 2(3) [and] would also involve giving s. 2 a greater degree of interference with Common Law rights and freedom to contract than it naturally bears.

The decision in *Jelson* was also considered by the Court of Appeal in *Nweze v Nwoko* [2004] EWCA Civ 379. While the Court of Appeal was ultimately able to distinguish *Jelson* on the basis that the agreement in *Nweze v Nwoko* concerned a contract that the land would eventually be sold without specifying the identity of the intended purchaser (see 4.2.4.2), they did describe the decision as 'open to criticism' on the signature point ([2004] EWCA Civ 379 at paras. 21 and 35). More recently, in *Milebush Properties Ltd v Tameside Metropolitan Borough Council* [2010] EWHC 1022, the High Court refused to follow *Jelson*, arguing that its interpretation of s. 2 would 'substantially frustrate' s. 106 of the Town and Country Planning Act 1990, which enables councils to ensure that grants of planning permission can be made conditional on the landowner's agreement to grant rights to third parties. Although High Court decisions have equal weight, therefore, and the Court of Appeal in *Nweze v Nwoko* did not decide the point, it seems that the decision in *Kensington* is more likely to be followed than the decision in *Jelson*.

4.2.3 Contracts which do not have to satisfy s. 2

Section 2(5) specifies certain types of contract which do not have to comply with the main provisions of s. 2, and which accordingly may be made without a written contract.

4.2.3.1 Contracts to grant short leases

While most leases have to be granted by deed, certain leases for not more than three years may be granted more informally: in writing or even by word of mouth (LPA 1925,

s. 54(2); see 9.3.1.1). In these circumstances, it would seem inappropriate to require a written contract to grant a lease when the actual grant does not need to be in writing, and accordingly s. 2(5)(a) excludes contracts for such leases from the general requirements of s. 2.

4.2.3.2 Contracts made in the course of a public auction

These contracts have always had their own rules, and the usual rule is that the contract is concluded on the fall of the auctioneer's gavel.

4.2.3.3 Contracts regulated under the Financial Services Act 1986

This exclusion covers certain contracts for investments which happen to include an interest of some kind in land. An example might be a unit trust or a debenture (a debenture is a type of charge (security interest) used over the property of a company and it will usually include any land which the company has).

4.2.3.4 Certain trusts

Section 2(5) also expressly excludes 'the creation or operation of resulting, implied or constructive trusts.' This is in keeping with the terms of LPA 1925, s. 53(2), which excludes those trusts from the requirement in s. 53(1)(b) that declarations of trust must be in writing (see further 13.1.2.2).

This provision in s. 2(5) has proved to be far more important than might be expected at first sight. As we will see in 4.5, it is now playing a major part in the development of equitable relief for parties who mistakenly rely on invalid contracts.

4.2.4 How far does s. 2 extend?

Since s. 2 came into force, there have been a large number of cases in which the extent of the provision has been queried. After something of a 'free for all' in the early days, some principles have been established but, in some instances, things remain less certain. In the succeeding material, we consider the cases in which the application of s. 2 has been tested.

4.2.4.1 Options

In 2.6.3.2 it was explained that a property owner may give another person an option to acquire an estate in the property at a later date. Although it is clear that the option is enforceable by the contractual remedy of specific performance, there has always been some debate about the point at which the contract arises.

Some authorities describe the option to purchase as a conditional contract, because the vendor is bound to sell the property if the purchaser performs certain conditions (such as giving notice). Others reject this view, relying on the fact that only one party, the vendor, is bound, and prefer to describe the option as an irrevocable offer, with the contract only coming into existence when the option is exercised.

This debate about the nature of an option formed the background to the case of *Spiro v Glencrown Properties Ltd* [1994] Ch 537. The purchaser here had given notice that he wished to exercise his option and buy the property, but he did not complete the transaction and wished to avoid being compelled to do so. He therefore argued that it is the *exercise* of the option which is to be regarded as the making of the contract, and which therefore has to satisfy the requirements of s. 2. Since the vendor had not signed the document giving notice of the purchaser's intention to exercise the option, he argued that it was void for non-compliance with the requirement of signature by both parties.

The trial judge, Hoffmann J (at p. 544), took the view that:

> An option is not strictly speaking either an offer or a conditional contract. It does not have all the incidents of the standard form of either of these concepts. To that extent it is a relationship *sui generis* ['of its own type']. But there are ways in which it resembles each of them. Each analogy is in the proper context a valid way of characterising the situation created by an option. The question in this case is not whether one analogy is true and the other false, but which is appropriate to be used in the construction of s. 2.

In the view of the judge:

> Section 2 . . . was intended to prevent disputes over whether the parties had entered into a binding agreement or over what terms they had agreed. It prescribes the formalities for recording their mutual consent. But only the grant of the option depends upon consent. The exercise of the option is a unilateral act. It would destroy the very purpose of the option if the purchaser had to obtain the vendor's counter-signature to the notice by which it was exercised (at p. 541).

The court therefore held that the grant of the option, which satisfied the requirements of s. 2, was a valid contract, which became enforceable against the purchaser when he gave notice to exercise the option; he did not have to give notice in writing that, complying with s. 2, bore the signature of both parties. (You will see later at 5.4.2.2(4) that a similar question about the stage at which an option gives rise to a contract was considered in *Armstrong and Holmes Ltd v Holmes* [1993] 1 WLR 1482 in connection with registering the option as a land charge.)

While you are considering options, you may like to note that an option to surrender a lease is within the terms of s. 2 (*Commission for the New Towns v Cooper (Great Britain) Ltd* [1995] Ch 259), whereas a lockout agreement—by which a vendor agrees with a prospective purchaser not to negotiate with anyone else for a specified time—falls outside them (*Pitt v PHH Asset Management Ltd* [1994] 1 WLR 327).

4.2.4.2 Contracts to sell to a third party

In two first-instance cases (*Jelson Ltd v Derby County Council* [1999] 3 EGLR 91 and *RG Kensington Co Ltd v Hutchinson IDH Ltd* [2003] 2 P&CR 195) the High Court appears to have accepted that a contract between A and B which provides that A shall sell land to C falls within s. 2 and must satisfy its requirements. Discussion in both cases turned on whether s. 2 requires C to sign the contract (see further 4.2.2.6), thus by implication accepting that the section does apply to such a contract, but there was no express consideration of this wider question.

In *Nweze v Nwoko* [2004] EWCA Civ 379, the Court of Appeal referred briefly to contracts to transfer land to a named third party, saying merely that 'it may be' that s. 2 would apply (para. 24). By contrast, the court had no doubt on the facts before it that an agreement between A and B that A would market his property with a view to selling it to a buyer (who was as yet unknown) did not fall within the terms of the Act. The dispute arose from an oral compromise agreement between the parties (i.e., an agreement made in settlement of an earlier dispute) that Nwoko would sell his house and, after paying off the mortgage on it, would pay the balance of the proceeds of sale to the Nwezes. He did not, in fact, sell the property and withdrew the property from the market. When the Nwezes sought to enforce the compromise agreement, Nwoko claimed that it fell within s. 2 and was void for non-compliance.

The court had little difficulty in rejecting this suggestion. Although the words of the section ('contract for the sale or disposition of an interest in land') could 'as a matter of language' (para. 29) bear the meaning claimed by Nwoko, the court could find no case in which the provisions of s. 2 (or of its predecessors, dating back to the Statute of Frauds in 1677) had been given this wider meaning. The court explained that s. 2 relates to a contract which *effects* (or brings about) the obligation to sell or dispose of an interest in land, rather than to a contract which merely *results* in such a sale or disposition (per Sedley LJ at paras. 29–31). Here the contract did not place the 'vendor' under any obligation to complete a sale or disposition of any interest in the land; it was merely an agreement that the property would be marketed and that, if a buyer was found, the vendor would agree to sell the property to that buyer. Such an agreement did not place the 'vendor' under an obligation to convey any specific interest in the land and so did not give the other contracting party any kind of interest in the land, legal or equitable (see 2.6.3.1). As a result, s. 2 did not apply and the contract was enforceable as a **'parol'** (oral) agreement. Sedley LJ added that, as a matter of principle:

> A requirement for writing in a legal system which ordinarily recognises parol contracts as valid and enforceable is an exception to a rule and as such should be construed no more widely than is necessary.

4.2.5 Missing terms treated as separate contract

To comply with s. 2, *all the terms* of the contract must be recorded in the s. 2 compliant document (s. 2(1)). In some cases where an agreement has been partly recorded in writing but some part of the agreement has not been so recorded, the courts have taken the view that the written terms are complete and that the allegedly missing term of the contract is, in fact, a separate contract.

This approach was first adopted by the High Court in *Record v Bell* [1991] 1 WLR 853, where a purchaser failed to complete his purchase and then argued that the contract for sale was invalid because it did not include a condition, agreed between the parties' solicitors, about proof of title. It was held that there had been two contracts: one for the sale of the estate in land and the other a collateral contract that the title to the property would be revealed as described when the necessary paperwork was produced. The collateral contract was not in itself a contract for the sale of an estate or interest in land and thus was not subject to s. 2 and could be concluded orally. The collateral contract had been fulfilled and there was no defect in the contract for sale, which accordingly could be enforced.

This approach was also adopted by the Court of Appeal in *Tootal Clothing Ltd v Guinea Properties Management Ltd* [1992] 2 EGLR 80. The parties had entered into two formal written agreements, made on the same day and each signed by both parties. One of these was an agreement for the grant of a lease ('the lease agreement') and contained a term that the tenant would carry out shop-fitting works on the premises at his own expense. The other agreement was described as 'supplemental' to the lease agreement. It recited the terms of that agreement and provided that the landlord would pay £30,000 towards the costs of the shop-fitting. The lease was granted in accordance with the terms of the lease agreement and the tenant carried out the agreed works. However, the landlord refused to make his contribution towards the costs, claiming that his agreement to do so was a term of the agreement to grant the lease, and that its omission from that document made it void under s. 2.

The Court of Appeal held that the supplemental agreement was enforceable, but there is some doubt about why. The court noted that, if the contribution term was in fact a term of the parties' agreement for the lease, the recital of the lease agreement terms in the supplemental agreement meant that that agreement now recorded all the terms agreed between the parties and itself now satisfied the requirements of s. 2. The landlord's obligation to make the payment would therefore be enforceable under a s. 2 contract. If, on the other hand, the contribution term was not part of the parties' agreement for the lease, it was enforceable as a separate contract which did not involve the disposition of an interest in land and therefore was not subject to s. 2 requirements. The court also suggested that it was relevant that the contract had been partly performed, by the eventual grant of the lease itself, but this aspect of the reasoning is *obiter* and very controversial (see 4.4.1).

The Court of Appeal adopted a stricter approach in *Wright v Robert Leonard (Developments) Ltd* [1994] NPC 49. In this case the purchaser agreed to buy both a show flat and its furnishings, but the furnishings were not mentioned in the written contract. After completion, the purchaser found that the furnishings had been removed and, when he sought damages for breach of contract, was met with the argument that there was not sufficient writing to satisfy s. 2. It would have been relatively easy for the court to adopt the approach taken in *Record v Bell*, construing the agreement as creating two separate contracts. The Court of Appeal, however, declined to do this, taking the view that 'if the contract is all one arrangement, there is no collateral contract, and all the terms in it must be in writing, even those which do not refer to the land'. Here there was only one contract with two elements, and both should have been included in the written document (and note the similar approach adopted by the Court of Appeal in *Godden v Merthyr Tydfil Housing Association* [1997] NPC 1).

In later decisions the Court of Appeal appears to have switched attention from the idea of 'collateral contracts' and focused instead on how to decide whether the omitted term was truly a term of a 'land' agreement. *Grossman v Hooper* [2001] 2 EGLR 82 concerned an agreement for the transfer of a property from a man to a woman on the breakdown of their relationship. He subsequently claimed that she had undertaken to pay off a debt owed to a third party and that the omission of this from the written agreement invalidated the contract for transfer. The Court of Appeal held that the agreement about the debt was not part of the contract for transfer. Chadwick LJ commented (at para. 19), in relation to s. 2(1) of the 1989 Act that:

> the terms which the parties have expressly agreed means the terms . . . upon which the parties to the sale or other disposition have agreed that the relevant interest in land shall be sold or otherwise disposed of. The words do not refer to terms upon which the parties have agreed (albeit contemporaneously) that some other transaction should be entered.

The judge illustrated this statement by reference to a hypothetical agreement that a purchaser should take over a vendor's carpets and curtains. Whether or not a provision to this effect is a term of the contract of sale is a matter of fact in each case. It is for the court to decide whether the parties agreed that the sale of the house was conditional on the sale of the furnishings, in which case the term *is* part of the contract, or whether the agreement was for the sale of the house independently of the furnishings, in which case the agreement about carpets and curtains is *not* a term. In the court's view, its task of interpreting agreements of this type was not assisted by the notion of 'collateral contracts', which Sir Christopher Staughton described as 'elusive'.

Keay v Morris Homes (West Midlands) Ltd [2012] 1 WLR 2855 provides an important consideration of the 'missing terms' problem. The parties had made two written agreements. The first agreement was for the sale by the Keays ('the Ks') of their land to Morris Homes ('MH') for development, and the subsequent lease of part of the developed property to the Ks. The agreement was later varied by the second written agreement (the 'supplemental agreement') which provided for a reduction in the purchase price. The Ks alleged that at the time of making this later agreement, the parties also made a further oral agreement in which MH undertook to 'progress promptly' the development of the property to be leased to the Ks (the 'works obligation').

The sale and transfer were completed at the reduced price, but there was delay in the development work, and the Ks sought compensation for MH's breach of the alleged works obligation. MH denied that such an agreement had been made, but in the alternative claimed that, if it had been made, it was a term of the sale agreement, and that the supplemental agreement was invalidated by its omission. In response the Ks relied on *Grossman v Hooper*, claiming that the alleged oral agreement was a collateral contract and not part of the land agreement. Alternatively, if the works obligation was a term of the land agreement, the supposed principle in *Tootal Clothing Ltd v Guinea Properties Management Ltd* [1992] 2 EGLR 80 had converted it into a valid contract when the sale of the land was completed (see 4.4.1 on this aspect of the case).

The High Court refused the Ks' application for summary judgment, holding that the existence of the alleged oral contract and its relationship to the land agreement required consideration at a full trial. The Court of Appeal dismissed the Ks' appeal against refusal of summary judgment, agreeing with the judge that a trial was required to establish the facts in issue. The court's observations on the Ks' claim that the works obligation was a collateral contract and was not a term of the land agreement are therefore only *obiter dicta*, but it is worth noting that Rimer LJ described the judgment of Briggs J in the Court of Appeal decision of *North Eastern Properties Ltd v Coleman* [2010] 1 WLR 2715 as including 'some valuable statements of principle'. A quotation from that judgment encapsulates the present judicial approach. At paras. 46 and 54 of his judgment, Briggs J stated that, in seeking to avoid a land contract under s. 2:

> It is not sufficient merely to show that the land contract formed part of a larger transaction which was subject to expressly agreed terms which are absent from the land contract. . . . Nothing in s. 2 is designed to prevent parties to a composite transaction . . . from structuring their bargain so that the land contract is genuinely separated from the rest of the transaction in the sense that its performance is not made conditional upon the performance of some other expressly agreed part of the bargain. . . . By contrast, parties to a composite transaction are not free to separate into a separate document expressly agreed terms, for example as to the sale of chattels or the provision of services, *if upon the true construction of the whole agreement, performance of the land sale is conditional upon the chattel sale or service provision*. [emphasis added]

4.2.6 Rectification of the contract

One way of addressing the issue of a term that does form part of an agreement, but which is omitted from the written agreement may, in some instances, be to seek rectification of the written agreement. Section 2 might suggest that this is not possible because it says that no contract exists until all the terms are included in a s. 2 compliant document. However, s. 2(4) makes express reference to the possibility of rectification, and it appears from *Joscelyne v Nissen* [1970] 2 QB 86 that, as long as there is a pre-existing *agreement*, it is not necessary to establish that there was a pre-existing *contract* in order to obtain rectification. (If this were not so, it would of course be impossible to obtain rectification of a document which failed to satisfy s. 2 and so in consequence was not a valid contract.) In *Robert Leonard (Developments) Ltd v Wright* [1994] NPC 49 the Court of Appeal found itself able to assist the purchaser, holding that the case was one in which it was appropriate to grant the equitable remedy of rectification of the contract, saying that it was the intention of the Act that the 'all terms requirement should not be so inflexible as to cause hardship or unfairness where there has been a mistake resulting in a venial non-compliance with the Act'.

4.2.7 Section 2 does not apply to actual dispositions

It is important to note that s. 2 applies only to contracts to make a future disposition; it does not apply to an actual disposition of an interest in land. Actual dispositions are subject to different formality rules, which vary depending upon the type of disposition in question and which are contained in LPA 1925, ss. 52–4.

This point is illustrated by the decision of the Court of Appeal in *Rollerteam Ltd v Riley* [2017] Ch 109. That case arose from a family dispute about the ownership of properties and the payment of money in relation to a Sherlock Holmes museum that the family had been operating in Baker Street, London (not at 221B). The dispute had given rise to a complete breakdown of trust between members of the family, who ceased to speak to one another. However, on 8 April 2013, key members of the family did manage to have a meeting at which a settlement agreement was reached. The agreement included transfers of two properties and the payment of various sums of money. After the meeting, there were a number of emails recording the terms of the agreement; these did not satisfy the terms of s. 2 because they did not include all the terms of the agreement and they were unsigned. However, on 11 April, those concerned attended a meeting at a firm of solicitors and documents were executed declaring the two properties were held on certain trusts and some but not all the agreed money was paid. It was then argued that the total agreement was only recorded if one read all the emails and the documents together and that none of the documents satisfied s. 2. However, the Court was firmly of the view that, whatever the position on 8 April, on 11 April the parties were making actual dispositions of property (declaring trusts of the land) and were not entering into a contract to do so in future. As such, s. 2 did not apply and the declarations of trust were effective in creating trusts of the properties (see 13.1.2.1).

Similarly, in two recent High Court cases, *Mars Capital Finance Ltd v Hussain* [2021] EWHC 2416 and *Campbell v Chief Land Registrar* [2022] EWHC 200, the courts have rejected attempts to get the register altered on the basis that the contracts preceding entries on the register were void for non-compliance with s. 2. In both cases, the claimants had agreed to grant legal mortgages under contracts which, they argued, failed to comply with the requirements of s. 2 in full (e.g., because the lenders had not properly signed the documents). In both cases, the mortgages had ultimately been granted by deed and entered on the land register. The claimants then sought to get the mortgages removed from the register on the basis that the underlying dispositions had been void, and so their entry on the register was a mistake (see 6.7). As the judge explained in *Hussain*:

> Section 2 applies only to contracts for the sale or other disposition of interests in land, not to documents which create or transfer legal estates or interests in land ... Accordingly,

any non-compliance of the [contract] with section 2 would have had no impact on the validity of the disposition pursuant to which [the mortgagee] was registered as proprietor . . . and would therefore provide no basis for rectification of the title register.

Accordingly, when considering a set of facts to which s. 2 might apply, take care that you are in fact looking at an agreement to do something in the future and not an attempt to make an actual disposition. In the latter case, you need to apply the requirements of LPA 1925, ss. 52–4 and not those of s. 2 of the 1989 Act. If these are satisfied, nothing in s. 2 will prevent the actual disposition from taking effect, even if a previous *contract* to make the disposition was void for non-compliance with the section. For example, if Amina orally contracts to sell her freehold to Bertram, the effect of s. 2 is that Amina is under no obligation to perform her promise, Bertram is under no obligation to pay the purchase price, and he has no equitable interest in the property. But if Bertram in fact pays Amina and Amina then goes ahead and conveys the freehold to Bertram, using a deed that complies with s. 52 LPA 1925, Bertram will become entitled to the freehold under the deed and will become the owner of the legal freehold upon registration. Amina cannot seek to undo the conveyance, or get the register changed, by pointing to the unenforceability of the contract that has now been performed.

4.2.8 Consequences of the 1989 Act

It is obvious that the changes introduced by the 1989 Act affect the way in which contracts for the sale of a fee simple or an existing lease are made. The Act also has a considerable effect on the creation of equitable interests which arise from a contract to grant a legal estate or interest from a failure to use the correct form of grant (see 2.6.3). In order to treat an agreement or a failed grant as giving rise to an equitable interest, there now has to be a document which amounts to a written contract under the 1989 Act. This means that the help equity can give to informal transactions may well be more limited than in the past (see, e.g., the effect which the Act has had on informally created mortgages—22.5.2.1).

4.3 Contracts made before 27 September 1989

4.3.1 LPA 1925, s. 40

Before 27 September 1989 any contract relating to land could be made orally or in writing, but if made orally was not enforceable unless there was some written evidence of it or some act of part performance of the contract.

These requirements were imposed by LPA 1925, s. 40, which provided:

> (1) No action may be brought upon any contract for the sale or other disposition of land or any interest in land, unless the agreement upon which such action is brought, or some memorandum or note thereof, is in writing, and signed by the party to be charged or by some other person thereunto by him lawfully authorised.
>
> (2) This section . . . does not affect the law relating to part performance . . .

You will note that these provisions refer to 'any contract for the sale or other disposition of land or any interest in land'. This is substantially the same wording as that used in s. 2 of the 1989 Act, and thus the same range of transactions is covered by both statutory provisions.

We will now look in a little more detail at the s. 40 requirements, and consider the similarities and differences between them and the new rules considered in the previous section.

4.3.2 Requirements of s. 40

4.3.2.1 Contracts could be made in writing or orally

(1) *Written contracts* Section 40 provided for the possibility of a written contract, which was usually made in the same way as it would be today (i.e., by both parties signing the same document, or by each signing a copy and exchanging it with the other).

However, it was also possible for a written contract to arise through correspondence between the parties, in a way which *Commission for the New Towns v Cooper (Great Britain) Ltd* [1995] Ch 259 might suggest is no longer possible under the new rules (see 4.2.2.5).

(2) *Oral contracts* A valid contract could also be created by oral agreement between the parties. Unlike s. 2 of the 1989 Act, s. 40 did not require writing for the *formation* of the contract and this is the most significant difference between the old and new rules. An oral contract, however, was not *enforceable* unless there was some written evidence of it, or some act of part performance.

4.3.2.2 Oral contracts valid but unenforceable without writing or part performance

The wording of s. 40 did not render an oral contract either void or voidable: it was merely unenforceable by action in the courts. This may seem like splitting hairs but the distinction could be important, as is illustrated by the case of *Low v Fry* (1935) 51 TLR 322. In that case the parties made an oral agreement for the sale of an estate in land and the purchaser gave the vendor a cheque for a portion of the purchase price. Later the purchaser decided not to proceed with the transaction and told his bank to stop payment of the cheque. The vendor was unable to enforce the contract to sell because of s. 40, but was able to recover on the cheque: this was not a case in which a cheque had been issued for a consideration which had totally failed, because the contract, though unenforceable, was valid.

4.3.2.3 Written evidence of oral contract

(1) *Form* Section 40 required a written 'memorandum or note' of the agreement. There was no prescribed form for this, and all that was needed was a written document which showed that an oral agreement had been made and set out its terms.

(2) *Content* In order to satisfy s. 40, the note or memorandum had to contain certain essential details: the names of the parties (or a description which identified them); a clear description of the property; and the consideration. If any of these was missing from the document, the courts would not enforce the contract. In addition, any other material terms of the contract had to be included; however, if any term was omitted, the party affected might choose either to waive it or to perform it (as appropriate). Having done so, he could then enforce the balance of the agreement (*Scott v Bradley* [1971] 1 Ch 850). There is no scope for this approach under the 1989 Act (see 4.2.2.4 for the various ways in which the courts have dealt with omitted terms under the new rules).

(3) *Signature* The document had to be signed by the person against whom the contract was to be enforced. Thus if a purchaser alone had signed the document, he or she could not rely on it in suing the vendor—for fairly obvious reasons! However, there was no requirement that the document should be signed by the person seeking to enforce the contract, and this is another significant difference from the new rules, which require the written contract to be signed by both parties.

4.3.2.4 An alternative to writing: part performance

Even if there was no written evidence of an oral contract, it might still be enforceable if the plaintiff could show an act of part performance, that is that the plaintiff had already performed some of the obligations under the contract.

Part performance was an equitable doctrine which arose fairly soon after the Statute of Frauds 1677 first introduced the requirement for written evidence of contracts relating to land that eventually became LPA 1925, s. 40.

The Statute of Frauds was intended to combat the numbers of cases of perjured evidence in cases relating to land by requiring written, rather than oral, evidence of contracts. However, the statute soon caused its own problems since it became possible for a vendor to agree orally to sell land, allow the purchaser to move in and improve the land, and then claim the land back (plus improvements) on the ground that there was no contract enforceable at law. Not surprisingly at this point, equity intervened. To prevent the statute being used as an instrument of fraud, the equitable doctrine of part performance was developed. This doctrine provided that if a party to a contract had acted on the contract in reliance on the promise of the other party, then the contract would be enforced in equity, despite the lack of a written memorandum.

Requirements for the operation of part performance

In order to use the doctrine of part performance, a plaintiff had to show that acts had been done which pointed clearly to the existence of a contract. In essence, the plaintiff was claiming that he or she would not have acted in that way, had there not been a valid contract. In other words, the plaintiff's conduct was *evidence* of an agreement. At the same time, however, the courts emphasised their concern with general equitable principles: it would be *unfair* for anyone to escape from their obligations when the other side had already acted in reliance on the contract. Both of these explanations of the doctrine run throughout the cases and, in *Steadman v Steadman* [1976] AC 536, Lord Simon commented on 'the uneasy oscillation between regarding the doctrine as a principle vindicating conscientious dealing and as a rule of evidence' (at p. 560).

It is probably easiest to explain part performance by giving an example of the operation of the doctrine. In *Rawlinson v Ames* [1925] Ch 96, the defendant had agreed to take a lease from the plaintiff but had asked the plaintiff to do some work on the land before the defendant moved in. The plaintiff did the necessary work under the defendant's supervision but the defendant then refused to take the lease, relying on s. 40 as there was no written contract. In this case the plaintiff was granted an order for specific performance of the oral contract. The court concluded that the plaintiff would not have carried out the improvements to the land at the defendant's direction had there not been a pre-existing contract.

More generally, in cases of a contract to grant a lease, the tenant's act of taking possession and the landlord's permission for this were regarded as acts of part performance by each party, so that either of them could enforce the contract.

Since part performance was a creation of equity, it was discretionary in its application (as are all equitable remedies), and a court would decline to assist a party who relied on the doctrine if this would produce injustice, or if the party relying on the doctrine had 'dirty hands'.

The doctrine of part performance was specifically retained in 1925 by s. 40(2) which provided that the section 'does not affect the law relating to part performance'.

4.4 Part performance after the 1989 Act

4.4.1 Did the doctrine of part performance survive the 1989 Act?

The changes introduced by the 1989 Act to the rules governing contracts relating to land were based on the recommendations of the Law Commission Report on Formalities for Contracts of Sale etc. of Land 1987 (Law Com No. 164). The view of the Law Commission on part performance was that it should be abolished. It was suggested that the doctrine of estoppel might, in appropriate cases, be relied upon as an alternative (see 4.5), and the Law Commission concluded:

> We see no cause to fear that the recommended repeal and replacement of the present section as to the formalities for contracts for sale or other disposition of land will inhibit the courts in the exercise of the equitable discretion to do justice between parties in individual otherwise hard cases.

The 1989 Act makes no specific reference to the doctrine of part performance, neither continuing it nor abolishing it, and at first there was some judicial uncertainty about whether a party could still rely on part performance. In *Tootal Clothing Ltd v Guinea Properties Management Ltd* [1992] 2 EGLR 80 (see 4.2.5), Scott LJ said that:

> ... s. 2 is of relevance only to executory contracts. It has no relevance to contracts which have been completed. If parties chose to complete an oral land contract or a land contract that does not in some respect or other comply with s. 2, they are at liberty to do so. Once they have done so, it becomes irrelevant that the contract may not have been in accordance with s. 2. . . . Once the lease agreement had been executed by completion, s. 2 had no relevance to the contractual enforceability of the supplemental agreement, whether or not that supplemental agreement was negotiated as part of the one bargain that included the terms of the lease agreement.

This statement led commentators and a High Court judge (see the observations of Lewison J in *Kilcarne Holdings Ltd v Targetfollow (Birmingham) Ltd* [2005] 2 P&CR 8 at para. 198) to interpret *Tootal* as deciding that 'non-land terms' of an agreement invalidated by s. 2 would somehow become enforceable as valid contractual obligations, once the 'land' aspect of the agreement had been performed. This interpretation was, however, rejected by the Court of Appeal in *Keay v Morris Homes (West Midlands) Ltd* [2012] 1 WLR 2855. In that case, the court held that Scott LJ's dicta in *Tootal* did not provide authority for 'the proposition that a void contract can, by acts in the nature of part performance, mature into a valid one'—a proposition which Rimer LJ described as 'contrary to principle and wrong'. Since *Keay*, the courts have accepted that part performance has not survived the 1989 Act (see, for example, the recent High Court decision in *Ali v Dinc* [2020] EWHC 3055, at para. 216). Attention has switched to the question of whether there was any other equitable concept which might be able to take its place.

4.5 Estoppel and s. 2

The Law Commission assumed that hard cases could be handled by the rules of estoppel, and there are certainly considerable similarities between these rules and the doctrine of part performance. A proprietary estoppel may arise where some representation concerning property has been made by one party and relied upon by another to his detriment (see 2.6.7 and Chapter 19). In such cases, the courts may consider the outcome to be unconscionable; if so, they have a broad remedial discretion to remedy this unconscionability, which may range from ordering an outright conveyance of the promised property right to ordering the grant of some lesser right or ordering the payment of a money amount. Where A allows B to act to B's detriment in reliance on a belief that B will acquire an interest in A's property under an agreement which A knows is not a valid contract, it certainly could be argued that A's conduct is unconscionable in this sense, and that B should be entitled to a claim in proprietary estoppel.

However, while s. 2(5), among the other exclusions, says:

> . . . nothing in this section affects the creation or operation of resulting, implied or constructive trusts

it makes no mention of interests arising due to the operation of an estoppel. The usual rule of interpretation is that where a piece of legislation provides a list, unless it is clear that the legislative intended otherwise, the list is complete and anything omitted does not fall within the provision. This principle was traditionally expressed in Latin as *expressio unius exclusion alterius*. That means that the inclusion of one item excludes the others.

There has therefore been considerable doubt about whether estoppel can be used to assist parties who had failed to comply with the requirements of s. 2. Courts have generally been able to hold that a 'constructive trust' (which is expressly exempted from the rule by s 2(5)) exists in many of the cases where claims based on proprietary estoppel could also have succeeded. However, it remains unclear how far proprietary estoppel can be used to circumvent the operation of s. 2 in cases where no constructive trust can be found. The fullest treatment of this issue can be found in the Court of Appeal decision in *Yaxley v Gotts* [2000] Ch 162, which remains the leading case on this point.

4.5.1 *Yaxley v Gotts*

In this case the claimant and the first defendant ('Gotts Senior') had agreed that Gotts Senior would acquire the freehold of a large house, already divided into flats, and that the claimant, a builder, would carry out the necessary work and act as managing agent for the defendant. In return, the claimant was to be given the ground floor of the house, which he would divide into two flats and then let. No written contract was made, the claimant being content to rely on what he described as 'a gentleman's agreement'. Matters went ahead as agreed, save that the property was bought by the second defendant ('Gotts Junior'—son of the first defendant) and the property was registered in his name. No interest in the property was granted to the claimant. Some four years later, the parties fell out, and the claimant was excluded from the property. He then sought a declaration that he was entitled to ownership of part of the house.

At first instance, the judge held that, on these facts, a proprietary estoppel arose, and that it was to be satisfied by a grant to the claimant of a rent-free lease of the ground floor for 99 years. The defendants appealed against the first instance decision, raising for the first time the argument that the agreement in question was, in effect, a contract for the sale or disposition of an interest in land, and should have been made in writing. The defendant also relied upon what we will call the 'public policy' argument, namely the well-established principle (set out in *Halsbury's Laws of England*, 4th edn. Reissue, Vol. 16, pp. 849–50) that:

> the doctrine of estoppel may not be invoked to render valid a transaction which the legislature has, on grounds of general public policy, enacted is to be invalid.

The three members of the Court of Appeal agreed in dismissing the appeal and upheld the award to the claimant of the 99-year lease. However, they reached this conclusion by different routes, with the result that the decision as a whole is of some complexity.

Robert Walker LJ gave great weight to the argument based on public policy. He identified Parliament's requirement for written contracts as being based on the conclusion that the need for certainty in contracts relating to interests in land outweighed the disappointment of those who made informal bargains in ignorance of the statutory requirements, and concluded that:

> If an estoppel would have the effect of enforcing a void contract and subverting Parliament's purpose it may have to yield to the statutory law which confronts it [at p. 175].

In other words, Yaxley could not rely on estoppel to overcome the lack of a written contract.

Nevertheless, an alternative way of assisting those who act in reliance on an informal agreement was to be found in another equitable concept, the constructive trust. These trusts are considered in detail in 18.1.3, but, for the present, all you need to know is that a constructive trust arises by operation of law, when equity regards a property owner's behaviour as unconscionable and as a result requires the owner to hold all or part of the property in trust for some other person. One of the many situations in which a constructive trust may be imposed is that of 'common intention': that is, where the parties have agreed that one will have an interest in property belonging to the other, and the non-owning party has acted to his or her detriment in reliance on that common intention. Another scenario where a constructive trust may arise is in a 'joint venture' case (as in *Pallant v Morgan* [1953] Ch 43). These are cases where parties have agreed that they will acquire property in order to carry out a common purpose, one of them does acquire the property with the consent of the others, and then the person who has acquired the property seeks to keep it for his own advantage and without regard for the original common purpose.

There are clear similarities between the concepts of proprietary estoppel and the constructive trust, and the course of dealing between Yaxley and the Gotts family could equally well give rise to an estoppel or justify the imposition of a constructive trust. As we have already noted, s. 2(5) of the 1989 Act expressly excludes 'the creation of resulting, implied or constructive trusts' from the requirement of a written contract imposed by s. 2(1). In the judge's view, this section allowed:

> A limited exception . . . for those cases in which a supposed bargain has been so fully performed by one side . . . that it would be inequitable to disregard the claimant's expectations . . . [at p. 180].

Accordingly, Robert Walker LJ upheld the first instance decision, but on the basis of a constructive trust, rather than on the principles of proprietary estoppel.

The other two judges, Clarke and Beldam LJJ, agreed that the claimant could rely on a constructive trust, and that the appeal should be dismissed on that basis. However, in addition, they each expressed views on proprietary estoppel and its possible use in the context of the 1989 Act and both considered that in interpreting the Act greater weight could be given to the views of the Law Commission than was considered appropriate by Robert Walker LJ (see pp. 176, 182, and 190).

Beldam LJ considered that the Law Commission's report made it clear that its proposals were not intended to affect the court's power to give equitable relief through the principles of estoppel and constructive trusts. Moreover the general principle that a party could not rely on an estoppel in the face of a statute depended upon the nature and purpose of the enactment, and the social policy behind it. The 1989 Act was not:

> aimed at prohibiting or outlawing agreements of a specific kind, though it had the effect of making agreements which did not comply with the required formalities void. This by itself is insufficient to raise such a significant public interest that an estoppel would be excluded [at p. 191].

Thus, while agreeing that the facts justified the finding that the first defendant held the property subject to a constructive trust in favour of the claimant, Beldam LJ also considered that the trial judge was entitled to reach the same conclusion by finding a proprietary estoppel.

4.5.2 Developments after *Yaxley v Gotts*

4.5.2.1 Dicta in the House of Lords

There have been two important House of Lords decisions on proprietary estoppel since *Yaxley v Gotts*: *Cobbe v Yeoman's Row* [2008] 1 WLR 1752 and *Thorner v Major* [2009] 1 WLR 776. These cases are discussed in detail in Chapter 19, but for now it is simply important to note some important *obiter* comments, in both cases, on the relationship between s. 2 and claims in proprietary estoppel.

Cobbe concerned a written agreement between the claimant, Cobbe, an experienced property developer, and the defendant company, which owned a property suitable for development. The parties agreed that Cobbe would undertake the work and expense of obtaining planning permission for this property and, if successful, would buy the property at an agreed price. Both parties knew that this agreement was informal and not legally enforceable, and they intended to finalise the details and enter into a contract for sale at a later stage if planning permission was obtained. The process of obtaining planning permission was lengthy and expensive, and Cobbe spent time and money on the process. He was led to believe that the company regarded itself as bound in honour by the agreement and would not withdraw from it, but the company later decided that it would not honour the agreement and would require a considerably higher price for the property from Cobbe. However, it allowed Cobbe to continue his efforts on its behalf and did not tell him of its change of mind until planning permission had been obtained. Cobbe refused to pay the higher price asked by the company, and claimed to have acquired rights in the property by estoppel and/or a constructive trust.

The trial court's decision in Cobbe's favour was upheld by the Court of Appeal ([2006] 1 WLR 2964), which considered that the circumstances of the case gave rise to an estoppel, despite the fact that both parties knew that the agreement was not binding and that they intended to enter into a contract at a later stage. However, the Court of Appeal decision was reversed on appeal by the House of Lords in *Cobbe v Yeoman's Row Management Ltd* [2008] 1 WLR 1752, which held that Mr Cobbe did not have a claim in proprietary estoppel (see 19.4) *or* a claim based on a constructive trust (see 4.5.2.3). Lord Scott then went on to consider, *obiter*, the relationship between proprietary estoppel and s. 2 and said (at para. 29) that:

> Proprietary estoppel cannot be prayed in aid in order to render enforceable an agreement that statute has declared to be void. The proposition that an owner of land can be estopped from asserting that an agreement is void for want of compliance with the requirements of s. 2 is, in my opinion, unacceptable. The assertion is no more than the statute provides. Equity can surely not contradict the statute.

Note, however, that *Cobbe* was a case involving negotiations between commercial parties. In a family case, the courts are more likely to accept that an unwritten arrangement upon which one party has placed reliance has given rise to an estoppel and that this claim is *not* barred by s. 2. In *Thorner v Major* [2009] 1 WLR 776, which is also discussed in detail in Chapter 19, the owner of a farm led a relative to believe that he would leave him the farm if he worked on it. The relative duly worked on the farm, putting in long hours and abandoning any hope of other work, but on the farmer's death found that he had not been left the farm as promised. The case went to the House of Lords but any argument based on s. 2 was abandoned by the farmer's estate before the case came to the Lords. Commenting on this concession, Lord Neuberger said (at para. 99):

> The notion that much of the reasoning in Cobbe . . . was directed to the unusual facts of that case is supported by the discussion at para 29 relating to section 2 . . . Section 2 may have presented Mr Cobbe with a problem, as he was seeking to invoke an estoppel to protect a right which was, in a sense, contractual in nature . . . However, at least as present advised, I do not consider that section 2 has any claim such as the present, which is a straightforward estoppel claim without any contractual connection. It was no doubt for that reason that the respondents, rightly in my view, eschewed any argument based on section 2.

Thus, following *Thorner*, it seems that s. 2 will not pose a barrier to proprietary estoppel claims in cases involving informal family arrangements that are unlikely to rise to the level of certainty necessary for a binding contract anyway. In other cases, as Lord Scott acknowledged in *Cobbe*, it will often be possible to identify a 'constructive trust' instead. It is not clear how far s. 2 bars claims in proprietary estoppel where a constructive trust analysis is not available. In the recent case of *Howe v Gossop* [2021] EWHC 637, Snowden J held that Lord Scott's dicta in *Cobbe* only applied where the claimant was seeking to *enforce* the void contract, for example by compelling a conveyance of the very land that was supposed to be sold. Where a claim for proprietary estoppel could be relieved in other ways—for example, by preventing the owner of the legal estate from taking possession, or by ordering the grant of some lesser right—the court said that there could be no objection based on the policy of s. 2.

4.5.2.2 Cases involving constructive trusts

Since *Yaxley v Gotts*, the courts have considered a number of agreements which, under the old law, would have taken effect as oral contracts enforceable on the basis of part performance but which, under the new law, fail to create contracts because they do not satisfy the requirements of s. 2. In dealing with these cases, the courts have in general followed Robert Walker LJ in relying on constructive trusts, rather than on estoppel, to mitigate the effects of s. 2. In doing this, the courts have often emphasised the similarities between the two concepts. This process tends to conflate constructive trusts and proprietary estoppel, which may be a source of difficulty in itself. However, this approach can be illustrated by the decision of the Court of Appeal in *Kinane v Mackie-Conteh* [2005] EWCA Civ 45, [2005] WTLR 345.

The case concerned a loan by Kinane to a company of which Mackie-Conteh was managing director. The two men agreed that the loan, and interest on it, would be secured by a charge over the director's house, and Mackie-Conteh and his wife signed a letter ('the security agreement'), agreeing to create such a mortgage. Before the 1989 Act, this oral agreement, evidenced by the letter, would have created a contract which, if specifically enforceable, would have given rise to an equitable mortgage (see 2.6.4.2). However, under s. 2, of course, there was no contract and no equitable mortgage. Despite the agreement, no mortgage was executed.

In due course, Kinane sought to enforce the security agreement, claiming that he had acted to his detriment in reliance on the common intention of the parties that he would be granted a mortgage and was therefore entitled to relief under a constructive trust (para. 10). The court considered that the claimant had to show that there had been some representation by the defendant that the unenforceable security agreement was valid and binding, and that this representation consisted of more than merely providing him with that agreement.

The court was satisfied that there had been such a representation in this case. The claimant made it clear that he would not lend the money without security; the defendant responded by providing the security agreement, and thus persuaded the claimant to make the loan. By this conduct, the defendant represented to Kinane that the agreement was valid and binding (para. 28). Further, the claimant had relied upon this representation and acted upon it to his detriment by making an unsecured loan (para. 31), thus, in the court's view, meeting the requirements for establishing an estoppel.

A finding of estoppel was, however, not enough by itself: in order to bring the case within s. 2(5), the court must also be satisfied that the estoppel 'overlapped' with a constructive trust (para. 25), or, per Neuberger LJ at para. 45, that it was:

> an estoppel which can also properly be said to amount to a constructive trust.

Lord Justice Neuberger noted that there could be circumstances which gave rise to an estoppel but not to a constructive trust (para. 47). In his view, the essential characteristic of a proprietary estoppel which *did* give rise to a constructive trust was:

> the element of agreement, or at least expression of common understanding, exchanged between the parties, as to the existence, or intended existence, of a proprietary interest.

He concluded that there had been a common understanding that Kinane would acquire an interest in land by means of the mortgage. This gave rise to a 'common intention' constructive trust and accordingly this was a case in which the claimant could rely on s. 2(5). It is not altogether clear from the various judgments what relief was to follow from this conclusion, but Arden LJ's statement that 'an interest in land . . . is the appropriate relief in this case' (para. 33) suggests that she intended Kinane to receive a mortgage as security for the loan as originally intended.

4.5.2.3 Can an estoppel or constructive trust arise during pre-contractual negotiations?

Under the old law, in which a contract could arise by oral agreement between the parties, it was customary to label all preliminary negotiations as being 'subject to contract', in order to avoid the parties inadvertently becoming bound. Following the 1989 Act, it appeared for a time that this precaution was no longer necessary, but the decision in *Yaxley v Gotts* raised concerns that parties to unsuccessful negotiations might claim to have acquired rights to property under an estoppel or a trust. However, the House of Lords decision in *Cobbe v Yeoman's Row* suggests that it will be difficult to succeed in such a claim, at least in cases where the parties are commercial parties dealing at arms' length (see 4.5.2.1).

In *Herbert v Doyle* [2010] EWCA Civ 1095, Arden LJ expressed the view that no constructive trust was found in *Cobbe* because the terms of the agreement were not yet certain. She went on to say (at para. 57) that:

> If the parties intend to make a formal agreement setting out the terms on which one or more of the parties is to acquire an interest in property, or, if further terms for that acquisition remain to be agreed between them so that the interest in property is not clearly identified, or if the parties did not expect their agreement to be immediately binding, neither party can rely on constructive trust as a means of enforcing their original agreement.

It seems to follow that a common intention constructive trust can still, in principle, arise in a case where the parties have made a bargain that is unenforceable because of s. 2 but where all the terms are agreed and they believe their agreement to be immediately binding; detrimental reliance on such a bargain may then give rise to a common intention constructive trust. The idea that parties have to believe their agreement to be immediately binding does not necessarily mean that they must think everything has been done that needs to be done for a binding legal contract to arise. In *Matchmove Ltd v Dowding* [2016] EWCA Civ 1233, for example, the buyers had made an oral agreement to buy land from a company controlled by a friend. They had paid considerable sums of money, and improved the land, in reliance on the agreement, even though they were aware that there were some 'technicalities' that still had to be completed for the sale to take place. When they fell out with their friend, the company refused to convey part of the land that had been promised. The Court of Appeal held that this land was held on constructive trust for them, emphasising that all the essential terms had been agreed and that all the parties had behaved as if the agreement was immediately binding even though they were aware of some further steps that would eventually need to be taken to formalise the agreement.

Undoubtedly, therefore, the House of Lords' decision in *Cobbe* has made it difficult but not impossible for parties negotiating to buy land to claim that an estoppel or constructive trust has arisen during negotiations, where some terms of the agreement are not yet settled or where both parties are fully aware that an oral agreement is not binding. It is however possible to imagine a scenario in which a first-time buyer, who has no legal or business experience, acts to her detriment in reliance on a representation (which she believes to be binding in some sense) that the vendor will sell only to her. To guard against this danger, it would still be wise to ensure that negotiations continue to be labelled 'subject to contract' (for a decision which held that use of this phrase defeated an estoppel claim, see *James v Evans* [2003] 3 EGLR 1).

4.5.3 Promissory estoppel and s. 2

We saw at the start of 4.5 that the Law Commission were very much of the view that the doctrine of estoppel would be available in difficult cases; this included not only proprietary estoppel but also the related doctrine of *promissory* estoppel (see 19.2 for the distinction between proprietary and promissory estoppel). However, it is not clear how far the doctrine of promissory estoppel can assist a claimant in situations where claims based on proprietary estoppel or constructive trust are unavailable or unhelpful to the claimant. This will be the case, for example, where the claimant has detrimentally relied on some term of the void agreement other than the representation by the vendor that a property right in land will be conveyed; claims brought by the vendor herself, for example, will fall into this category.

This issue arose in *Dudley Muslim Association v Dudley Metropolitan Borough Council* [2015] EWCA Civ 1123. In that case, the Borough Council had granted a lease to the DMA for the purpose of building a mosque, subject to an option to reacquire the land if the mosque was not built within five years. For reasons beyond the DMA's control, there were delays obtaining planning permission to build the mosque and it was ultimately not completed within the promised time. The Borough Council sought to exercise its option to recover the land and the DMA argued that it was prevented from doing so by its representations that an extension of time would be given (which it argued gave rise to legitimate expectations that barred the council from exercising its powers under the option as a matter of public law).

While the Court of Appeal found that in fact there had been no such representations, and rejected the public law argument based on legitimate expectations, Lewison LJ added that any agreement to extend the time within which an option would be exercised represented a variation in the terms of a contract to dispose of an interest in land and would therefore have to comply with s. 2 to be enforceable as a contract. He then dealt with the estoppel argument and said that, while it was possible that claims in proprietary estoppel could be exempt from s. 2, because they were covered by the s. 2(5) saving of 'constructive trusts', claims in promissory estoppel could not:

> I will assume, for the purposes of argument, that a claim in proprietary estoppel is capable of outflanking section 2. But that is because it falls within an express exception which is itself part of section 2. When a defence is raised based on promissory estoppel there is no question of a constructive trust of land arising. And in the circumstances of this case, where the DMA [Dudley Muslim Association] already own the land, there is no relevant property which is capable of being held on trust for the DMA. Unless a case falls within section 2(5), to admit a defence based on promissory estoppel would be effectively to repeal the section by judicial legislation. . . .

We have spent quite a lot of time here on the estoppel and s. 2 issue but, as you can see from the discussion, the matter is very far from being as simple as the Law Commission suggested before s. 2 was passed. Indeed, the whole issue of estoppel is an area in which there is a considerable amount of case law and the cases are discussed in more detail in Chapter 19.

4.6 Effect of the contract: passing of the equitable interest

4.6.1 Purchaser gains rights in equity

The equitable maxim that 'Equity regards as done that which ought to be done' (2.6.3.1) has important results in land law. In the case of a contract to sell or grant an estate in land, 'that which ought to be done' is the completion of the sale by the execution of a deed which conveys the legal estate to the purchaser. Therefore, the application of the maxim means that, as soon as there is an enforceable contract, the purchaser is treated in equity as already having received the benefits of a conveyance, and as holding an equitable interest that mirrors the promised legal estate.

The effect of this rule depends on whether there has been a contract to *transfer* ('convey') an existing legal estate, already held by the vendor, or a contract to *create* ('grant') a new legal estate or interest in the land. A contract to convey a legal estate is said to give rise to a trust of that estate. The vendor remains the legal owner until the legal estate has been transferred to the purchaser, but the purchaser becomes a beneficiary under a trust of land—the so-called 'vendor–purchaser constructive trust'—as soon as the contract is concluded (*Lysaght v Edwards* (1876) 2 ChD 499, 506–10). Meanwhile, a contract to grant an easement gives the grantee an *equitable easement*, a contract to grant a lease gives the prospective tenant an *equitable lease* (*Walsh v Lonsdale* (1882) 21 ChD 9) and so on (see 9.3.2.3).

The 'vendor–purchaser constructive trust' is similar to a trust because, like a beneficiary under a trust, the purchaser has potential claims against third parties to whom the land is conveyed in breach of duty (subject to defences, see 5.5 and 6.5). If the vendor sells the land in breach of contract, the purchaser can also claim the proceeds of that sale in the hands of the vendor (*Luxe Holding Ltd v Midland Resources Holding Ltd* [2010] EWHC 1399). This is also a remedy that is typically available to a beneficiary under a trust. At the same time, the trust is unusual because the vendor does not owe the normal duties of a trustee and the purchaser does not have all the normal rights of a beneficiary (see 13.1.1). For example, unlike a normal trustee, the vendor is entitled to personally benefit from the use of the land until the sale is completed, and also has the right to demand the purchase price. Unlike a normal beneficiary, the purchaser is not entitled to go into occupation of the land before the sale is completed or to demand that the vendor account to him for his use of the land.

In *Scott v Southern Pacific Mortgages* [2014] UKSC 52, the issue was whether a purchaser under a contract for sale could grant rights to a third party that would then bind a subsequent mortgagee. The case resulted from a series of what appeared to be frauds, all of which followed a similar pattern and which came before the Supreme Court as a group. In this particular case, a third party had bought Mrs Scott's property and agreed to let it back to her, giving her to understand that she would be entitled to stay in the property for life and that, as well as the purchase price (which was reduced), she would be entitled to an additional lump sum payment in a further 10 years. The purchase was financed by a loan from Southern Pacific, who were led to believe that the property would be acquired with vacant possession. Southern Pacific was granted a charge over the property and when the transfer was registered, so was the charge. A few days later, Mrs Scott was granted a shorthold tenancy of the property by the new owner. Later the new owner vanished, having failed to make repayments on the mortgage, leaving Mrs Scott and Southern Pacific, who were both innocent parties, to sort out the resulting mess.

The question in *Scott* was whether Mrs Scott could have obtained rights from the purchaser that arose immediately after the exchange of contracts and which, therefore, arose earlier in time that Southern Pacific's mortgage. A beneficiary under a trust of land can usually grant rights to third parties—for example, by selling or transferring his beneficial interest, charging it to repay his debts, or creating a 'sub-trust' over it—and these rights will normally be capable of binding those who later take rights in the land. If the purchaser of the land from Mrs Scott had been a beneficiary under a normal trust, therefore, she could have granted such sub-rights to Mrs Scott and these rights would have bound a later purchaser like Southern Pacific (subject to defences, see 6.5.6.1). However, the Supreme Court concluded that a purchaser's equitable interest under a contract for sale does *not* enable the purchaser to grant property rights to others. Lord Collins said that, while it was true that a contract for sale gave the purchaser an equitable interest in the purchased land in some sense, this did not mean 'the purchaser has proprietary rights for all purposes.' (*Scott*, at [65]).

4.6.2 Risk passes to the purchaser

As the purchaser ('P') gains an equitable interest in the property from the date of the contract, the basic rule is that the risk passes to P at that point and P should obtain protection by insuring P's interest in the property. It is the equitable interest which is the valuable interest in the land and its owner should insure. Indeed, should a house on the property burn down after contract but before conveyance, the purchaser is still bound to complete the purchase and pay over the purchase price (*Paine v Meller* (1801) 6 Ves Jr 349). Again, if the land should become the subject of a compulsory purchase order after contract, the purchaser must still proceed (*Hillingdon Estates Co. v Stonefield Estates Ltd* [1952] Ch 627).

The contract could provide specifically that the risk is to remain with the seller until the estate is conveyed or transferred, but if such a term is not included the purchaser is at risk and should insure.

4.6.3 Notional conversion of property

If you refer back to the brief section on classification of property (2.10), you will realise that the process of buying and selling land brings about a significant change in the nature of the property owned by each party. The purchaser, who before completion owned personalty in the form of money, exchanges it for realty, the estate in land, and the vendor makes a corresponding change from realty to personalty. This change of classification is not so significant today, but under the old law it could have far-reaching consequences because, for example, the rules about inheriting realty and personalty were very different. If one of the parties died after the contract had been made but before the estate was conveyed, the question would arise of how the property should be classified and who should inherit it. Was it fair to treat it as being in its original form when it was really subject to a specifically enforceable obligation to convert it into the other kind of property?

Equity's answer to this conundrum was to treat the property as notionally converted from the date of the specifically enforceable contract, so that the purchaser's interest was regarded as realty and that of the vendor as personalty. This notional conversion still occurs today when the contract for sale is concluded, although as we shall see it no longer operates in the case of trusts for sale, which is the other situation to which it used to apply (see 14.1.1.2).

4.7 Remedies for breach of contract

Once a contract has been concluded both the parties are legally bound to carry out their parts of the contract. Should either party fail to do this, a number of possible remedies are available to the other. All we will do here is to draw your attention to the range of remedies which are available, emphasising those which are of most significance in the land law context.

4.7.1 Damages

The common law remedy for breach of contract is damages. The usual measure of damages is the loss which the claimant has sustained as a result of non-performance. Accordingly, it is usually possible for the wronged party to claim damages for the loss of the bargain. Liability in damages may arise in a number of ways, for example, through refusal by either party to perform the contract or due to misrepresentation by the vendor. The Law of Property (Miscellaneous Provisions) Act 1989, s. 3, has removed old rules which limited the measure of damages in certain cases and now ordinary contractual principles apply.

4.7.2 Specific performance

For many centuries equity has accepted that in cases concerning land the common law remedy of damages is likely to be inadequate. This is because each piece of land is unique in character, and a disappointed purchaser cannot take any damages and buy another identical property (as the purchaser might were the subject of the contract a car or a book). Accordingly, equity provided the remedy of specific performance, which can be used to compel the defaulting party to carry out his or her promise. The remedy is available to either party, so a vendor may also use it to force a purchaser to complete (*Hope v Walter* [1900] 1 Ch 257). This remedy is discretionary in nature and will be refused if the applicant has 'dirty hands', that is, if the applicant is in some way at fault in relation to the obligations under the contract.

As we have already seen, the availability of this remedy underlies a number of equitable interests (see 2.6.3.1 and 2.6.4.2), and accordingly this remedy is of particular importance to your study of land law.

4.7.3 Rescission

Rescission is a remedy which either party may elect to use should the other party break a term of the contract which is a condition precedent. Its effect is that the contract will be undone and any rights that passed under it will be restored. For example, if the vendor were unable to prove a good title to the land, the purchaser might choose to rescind the contract; this would mean the vendor was no longer obliged to convey his title to the land and the purchaser was no longer obliged to pay the agreed price. Rescission is an optional remedy and the wronged party might choose to affirm the contract instead and to seek damages for breach. It is only available in cases in which *restitutio in integrum* is possible: that is, it must be possible to return the parties to their original position.

Rescission of a transaction on the grounds of fraud, misrepresentation, or undue influence will be considered further in relation to mortgages in Chapter 23 (see 23.7.2).

4.7.4 Rectification

This remedy is available to correct an inaccurate written record of an oral agreement. The remedy is difficult to obtain as the court will require very strong evidence that the document does not record the oral agreement (*Joscelyne v Nissen* [1970] 2 QB 86 at p. 98), but you have seen an example of its use in *Robert Leonard Developments Ltd v Wright* [1994] NPC 49 to rectify a written agreement from which certain terms had been omitted (see 4.2.6).

4.7.5 Injunction

This equitable remedy is available to restrain a threatened breach of contract.

4.7.6 Declaration

In certain cases a declaration of the court on an issue may be a useful remedy, and LPA 1925, s. 49(1) provides for an application to be made to the court by vendor or purchaser. This process might, for example, be used if there were a dispute over the exact meaning of a term in the contract, or over a matter of proof of title.

4.8 Application to 2 Trant Way

We saw in Chapter 3 that Barbara Bell is thinking of buying 2 Trant Way from Victoria Ventnor. We can illustrate the changes in the law produced by the Law of Property (Miscellaneous Provisions) Act 1989, s. 2, by imagining that the two women have discussed the matter, have agreed that Miss Bell should have the property, and have settled the price. Miss Bell, thinking she should have the matter set out clearly before she goes to see her solicitor, has written to Miss Ventnor setting out the terms that have been decided upon.

If these events had occurred before 27 September 1989 the parties would have concluded a contract at the time at which they made their oral agreement. However, that agreement would not have been enforceable. When Miss Ventnor received Miss Bell's letter she would have come into possession of a document which satisfied LPA 1925, s. 40, provided that Miss Bell had signed her letter and that it was sufficiently detailed. Thereafter Miss Ventnor could enforce the contract against Miss Bell. Miss Bell could not enforce against Miss Ventnor because Miss Ventnor had not signed a s. 40 memorandum.

If these events occur on or after 27 September 1989 they do not create a valid contract. The document that exists does not comply with s. 2 of the 1989 Act because it is not signed by both parties. In addition it may only purport to record an existing agreement, whereas s. 2 requires that the contract be *made* in writing, and accordingly neither party would be bound until this had been done.

However, the best practice remains to sign nothing until your conveyancer has made checks, advised you, and a formal contract has been prepared. If none of the formalities have been met, but one of the parties has suffered loss by relying on the oral agreement, it is theoretically possible that claims in proprietary estoppel may be available or that a constructive trust would arise. To avoid any such result, parties are often well advised to label any correspondence between them as 'subject to contract'. This will often prevent a court from finding that it was reasonable to detrimentally rely on the agreement for the purposes of any of these doctrines.

FURTHER READING

Chitty on Contracts, 34th edn., Sweet & Maxwell, 2022, Chapter 5.

Formalities for the Contract of Sale, etc. of Land 1987 (Law Com No. 164) Parts IV and V (pp. 12–22).

Howell, 'Informal Conveyances and Section 2 of the Law of Property (Miscellaneous Provisions) Act 1989' [1990] Conv 441.

Lees, '*Keay v Morris Homes* and Section 2 Law of Property Act (Miscellaneous Provisions) Act 1989' [2013] 77 Conv 68.

Turner, 'Understanding the Constructive Trust between Vendor and Purchaser' (2012) 128 LQR 584.

Estoppel

Dixon, 'The Reach of a Proprietary Estoppel: A Matter of Debate' [2009] 73 Conv 85.

Feltham, Leech, Crampin, and Winfield, *Spencer Bower: Reliance-Based Estoppel*, 5th edn., Bloomsbury Professional, 2017, paras. 7.15–7.22.

Fetherstonhaugh, 'Proprietary Estoppel and s. 2—Where Are We Now?' [2009] EG 25 April (No 0916) 98.

Griffiths, 'Part Performance—Still Trying to Replace the Irreplaceable?' [2002] 66 Conv 216.

Griffiths, 'Proprietary Estoppel—The Pendulum Swings Again?' [2009] 73 Conv 141.

McFarlane, 'Proprietary Estoppel and Failed Contractual Negotiations' [2005] 69 Conv 501.

Moore, 'Proprietary Estoppel, Constructive Trusts and s. 2 of the Law of Property (Miscellaneous Provisions) Act 1989' [2000] MLR 912.

Smith, 'Oral Contracts for the Sale of Land: Estoppels and Constructive Trusts' (2000) 116 LQR 11.

Tee, 'A Merry-Go-Round for the Millennium' [2000] CLJ 23.

Thompson, 'Oral Agreements for the Sale of Land' [2000] 64 Conv 245.

You can visit the online resources to test your knowledge of this chapter with self-test questions at **www.oup.com/he/nair19e/**.

5
Unregistered land

5.1 Introduction: 2 Trant Way 69
5.2 Ownership of the estate 69
5.3 Checking for encumbrances 70
5.4 Land charges 71
5.5 Legal and equitable interests which are not land charges 79
5.6 Summary of searches to be made in relation to unregistered land 84
5.7 The conveyance 84
5.8 Application for first registration 86

5.1 Introduction: 2 Trant Way

You will remember that Barbara Bell wants to buy 2 Trant Way, the title to which is unregistered (see 3.1.2 and 3.2.3.2). In Chapter 4, we looked at what Barbara needed to do in order to create a binding contract for the sale of the land. She will only want to complete the contract, and acquire the land from Victoria Ventnor (the vendor), however, if it is safe to do so. As was explained in Chapter 3 (3.2.1), Barbara will need to check two things about the property she is planning to buy before completing the purchase. She needs to make sure that:

- Victoria Ventnor, the vendor, has a good title to the property she is offering to sell; and
- the property is free from any encumbrances (third-party rights) other than those which have already been revealed.

This chapter covers what Barbara (or, more likely, her professional adviser) will have to do, either before or after exchanging contracts, to answer these questions. We will now look at how she can do this where the land she is buying is unregistered.

5.2 Ownership of the estate

An owner of an estate in unregistered land proves (or 'deduces') his or her title to the estate by producing the title deeds to the property. These deeds are the documents by which the current owner and his or her predecessors have acquired the estate. Typically, they will include documents such as: conveyances on sale; transfers by the personal representatives of a deceased owner to the person entitled under the will or on intestacy (technically known as '**assents**'); mortgages affecting the property; and trust deeds. From this collection of deeds, it should be possible to show that the estate has been correctly conveyed from one owner to another over the years and that it was last conveyed to ('vested in') the current vendor.

Obviously, one cannot hope to produce an unbroken chain of deeds stretching right back to the Norman Conquest, and so the habit began of accepting a title which had been proved for a certain long period of years. English law recognises that the passage of time may extinguish old titles to land (by the process known as '**adverse possession**', discussed in Chapter 7) and so it will usually be safe for a purchaser to buy land where there is an unbroken chain of documents that covers at least the period of years necessary to extinguish old titles by the passage of time ('the **limitation period**'), plus a bit more. The parties to a contract for the sale of an estate may agree specifically on the length of the period which is to apply, but if no special agreement is made a standard provision is implied into the contract. Originally at common law the term implied was that one had to prove the devolution of the title for a period of at least 60 years, but this was reduced progressively by statute and the relevant period is now 15 years by virtue of LPA 1969, s. 23 (reflecting the current limitation period of 12 years, see 7.2.1.1).

In order to deduce title one has to start with a '*good root of title*'. This is a document which records a dealing with the whole legal estate in the land, unburdened by any trusts, and which contains nothing to cast any doubts on the validity of the title. Usually a conveyancer will insist on a document which evidences a dealing for value, such as a conveyance on sale or a mortgage. The reason for accepting such a document is that one presumes that the purchaser in that transaction had investigated the title for the necessary period and that taking the conveyance or lending money on mortgage indicates that he or she found no defect; any unknown equitable interests affecting the title at that date are also likely to have been extinguished by the conveyance for value to a bona fide purchaser (see 2.4.3). The document taken as a good root of title will be the first document which is as old as, or older than, the title period: that is, now, the first such document which is at least 15 years old. Accordingly, the good root of title might in fact be a document which is 16, 30, or even 100 years old, depending upon the history of the estate.

Once a good root of title has been shown, the vendor must produce every deed after the root of title which has affected the property. Under the current procedure, the vendor usually proves title by providing copies or summaries of the documents (an 'epitome of title' or an 'abstract of title') to the purchaser or the purchaser's conveyancer. At a later stage in the process the purchaser or conveyancer will check the copies or summaries provided against the originals.

5.3 Checking for encumbrances

Certain encumbrances may be revealed while the purchaser is checking the vendor's title, but a range of other enquiries and inspections are also needed. As we shall see, many third-party rights will bind the purchaser whether he or she knows of them or not, but there are still some other rights which will not bind a purchaser who can show that they have not been discovered, despite the making of all the right enquiries (see 5.5.2.2–3). The purpose of making these inquiries is therefore twofold:

- to inform the purchaser about encumbrances she will be bound by whether she knows about them or not; and
- to enable the purchaser to take 'priority' over ('take free of') certain encumbrances of which he or she is unaware.

Making such enquiries can be a complicated and time-consuming business, and to help the purchaser the 1925 legislation introduced a system of registering certain encumbrances as 'land charges'. This register—the Land Charges Register—is quite different from the Land Register that we will go on to look at in Chapter 6. Unlike the Land Register, it does not record the title to estates in land and then show encumbrances related to those estates. Instead, it is a freestanding list of particular encumbrances that are indexed by reference to the name of the owner of the affected estate. A number of third-party rights did not become registrable land charges and the purchaser has to rely on the old methods to find out about them.

In the next two sections we look first at land charges and their registration, and then at the legal and equitable interests which are not registrable as land charges and how a purchaser might discover these or avoid being bound by those she has not discovered.

5.4 Land charges

5.4.1 Nature of land charges

Land charges consist of those interests in land which are set out in LCA 1972 (which replaced LCA 1925). Only interests which are included on the list in the Act are land charges. Interests which appear on the list should be protected by registration on the Land Charges Register, which is one of the registers now kept by the Chief Land Registrar (LCA 1972, s. 1). This register used to be kept separately for each local authority and by the local authority in whose area the property stood. However, in recent years the register has, very sensibly, been centralised.

5.4.2 Classes of land charge

Land charges are divided by the 1972 Act into six classes (A to F) and certain classes are further subdivided.

5.4.2.1 Classes A and B

These are not particularly common. They consist of charges on land arising under statutory provisions.

5.4.2.2 Class C

This class is subdivided into four subclasses. Before considering these in detail it is important to note that rights of a type which fall within this class are registrable as land charges only if they were created on or after 1 January 1926 (the date upon which the 1925 legislation came into force) or, more unusually, if the right was created before that date but was itself transferred to some other holder at a later time (LCA 1972, s. 2(8)).

(1) *Class C(i), the puisne mortgage* The puisne mortgage is defined in LCA 1972, s. 2(4), as a legal mortgage which 'is not secured by a deposit of documents relating to the legal estate affected'.

When lending money on the security of a mortgage in unregistered land, a mortgagee will normally take the deeds to the property away from the estate owner in order to prevent further dealing with the property. If a legal mortgagee does take the deeds in this way, the mortgage is *not* a registrable land charge. It is supposed not to require registration, because the absence of the deeds is sufficient to alert any prospective purchaser from the mortgagor to the possible existence of the mortgage. (As noted at 3.2.3.2, the creation of new mortgages of a legal estate will now normally lead to the compulsory registration of the title to the legal estate which is subject to that mortgage.)

If the mortgagee does not take the deeds, the mortgage is a puisne mortgage and should be registered as a land charge. The puisne mortgage is a slightly unusual land charge because it is a legal interest in land, while most land charges are equitable or statutory interests.

(2) *Class C(ii), limited owner's charge* This is a land charge which arises when a tenant for life or statutory owner under the SLA 1925 (someone who has only a limited interest in the property—see Chapter 15), or another person with a similar interest, has paid tax under the Capital Transfer Tax Act 1984. Such persons may have a right to charge the repayment of the tax against the land (i.e., to recover from the rents and profits of the land money which they have paid out of their own pockets) and that right is a land charge.

(3) *Class C(iii), general equitable charge* This class of land charge forms a kind of 'dustbin' category. Into this class fall all equitable charges on property which are not specifically excluded from Class C(iii) by the Act itself. Charges excluded in this way, and therefore *not registrable* as land charges, include:
- any charge which is secured by a deposit of documents relating to the legal estate affected (this means that an equitable mortgagee who does not have the title deeds to the property can register a C(iii) land charge, but an equitable mortgagee who has the deeds cannot do so);
- interests arising under trusts of land (i.e., a beneficiary under a trust of land cannot register that interest as a land charge);
- any charge which falls into another class of land charge.

(4) *Class C(iv), estate contract* An estate contract is any contract to convey or create a legal estate in land, or any option to purchase a legal estate or any **right of pre-emption** in respect of a legal estate (a right of first refusal) (see 2.6.3). In addition to contracts for the conveyance of a fee simple, and contracts for the grant or **assignment** of a lease, this class of land charges also includes options to purchase the fee simple, and options contained in leases. These may include options for renewal (*Phillips v Mobil Oil Co. Ltd* [1989] 1 WLR 888) and options for the tenant to purchase the landlord's estate (known as the **reversion**, see 9.1.5).

Various statutes have added to this category of land charges: for example, the Landlord and Tenant (Covenants) Act 1995, s. 20(6), provides that a request for an **'overriding lease'** may be registered under the LCA 1972 as if it were an estate contract. (For overriding leases, see 11.2.1.3.)

Even where an option has been registered as a Class C(iv) land charge, it used to be suggested that there was a need for further registration of an estate contract after notice has been given to exercise the option. However, it was held in *Armstrong and Holmes Ltd v Holmes* [1993] 1 WLR 1482 that there is no need for further registration: the registration of the option gives sufficient warning to any other prospective purchaser of the estate, and any conveyance to such a purchaser will be subject to the estate contract which arises from the option once it has been exercised.

5.4.2.3 Class D

Class D is divided into three subclasses.

(1) *Class D(i), Inland Revenue charge* This is a land charge which arises in favour of the Inland Revenue when a liability to pay capital transfer tax in respect of land has not been discharged.

(2) *Class D(ii), restrictive covenants* This class comprises any covenants or agreements which are restrictive of the user of land, other than those between landlord and tenant, and which were created on or after 1 January 1926 (at which date the 1925 property legislation came into force). These covenants are discussed in more detail in Chapter 25. An example would be a covenant by a freeholder, entered into in 1940, not to keep pigs on a particular property. The same covenant would not have been a registrable land charge had it been created in 1920.

(3) *Class D(iii), equitable easements* This class consists of any easements, rights, or privileges affecting land which were created on or after 1 January 1926, and which are equitable only. Easements and profits à prendre are discussed in more detail in Chapter 24. It should be noted that only *equitable* easements and profits are registrable as land charges. Legal easements and profits are not.

5.4.2.4 Class E

These are very rare and consist of annuities created before 1926 and which are not registered on the register of annuities (which is one of the other registers maintained under the LCA).

5.4.2.5 Class F

This class consists of 'home rights' which were first created by the Matrimonial Homes Act 1967 and are now contained in the Family Law Act 1996 (as amended by the Civil Partnership Act 2004). These rights exist only in relation to couples who are legally married and to civil partners, and give a spouse or civil partner, who is not a co-owner of the matrimonial home, the right to occupy the home owned by the other spouse or civil partner. This right is considered in more detail at 21.3.3.1.

While all these classes of charge are important to a purchaser, who may find that the property which he or she is purchasing is less attractive or perhaps totally valueless because it is subject to a land charge, the ones that you will meet most commonly in your study of land law are classes C(i), (iii) and (iv), D(ii) and (iii), and F, and you should pay particular attention to these.

5.4.3 Registration of land charges

The application to register a land charge is made by the person who claims that right. Registration is not made against the address of the property, but against the *name* of the person who was the estate owner at the date that the charge was created. This choice of method for registration has caused a number of problems with the system.

5.4.3.1 Incorrect names

It is not uncommon for an estate owner to be known by a nickname or abbreviated name. If a registration is made against an incorrect version of a person's name, a search made against the true name may not reveal the entry. Or it may be that the registration has been made correctly but that the searcher searches an incorrect name. Once again such a search may well not reveal the relevant entry. These problems have produced a certain amount of litigation, and examples are to be found in such cases as *Diligent Finance Ltd v Alleyne* (1972) 23 P&CR 346 and *Oak Co-operative Building Society v Blackburn* [1968] Ch 730. Essentially, in order to be safe, the person making a search has to be certain of using full correct names.

5.4.3.2 Searching against the names of all past estate owners

When an estate changes hands, the existing registrations of land charges are not altered but remain against the name of the original estate owner. Accordingly it is not sufficient to make a search simply against the name of the current estate owner. To be certain of finding all registered charges one must search against the names of all the estate owners since 1925. This is, however, impractical in most cases, because in proving title a vendor is only obliged to go back to a good root of title, which may be only 15 years old.

The difficulties which this might cause may be illustrated by referring back to the title to 2 Trant Way. The history of No. 2 since 1925 has been as follows:

1926 The estate owner at the date at which the 1925 legislation came into force was Bill Brie.

1928 Land charge class D(ii) registered against the name Bill Brie.

1956 Bill Brie sold legal estate to Cathy Camembert.

1963 Land charge class D(iii) registered against the name Cathy Camembert.

1989 Cathy Camembert sold legal estate to Victoria Ventnor.

1989 Land charge class C(i) registered against the name Victoria Ventnor.

You will remember that Barbara Bell is considering buying 2 Trant Way from Victoria Ventnor. If Miss Bell agrees to purchase the estate, Miss Ventnor will produce the conveyance made to her by Cathy Camembert in April 1989 as the good root of title, but will not be required to produce any of the earlier deeds. Miss Bell will already know the name of her vendor, Victoria Ventnor, and will learn of Cathy Camembert from the 1989 conveyance. If she makes land charges searches against these names, she will discover the charges registered in 1963 and 1989. However, she will have no means of knowing that the property was once owned by Bill Brie and so will not discover the class D(ii) land charge registered in 1928. This land charge is a restrictive covenant and it is quite likely that it will still be capable of enforcement by a neighbouring landowner (see Chapter 25). Unfortunately for Barbara Bell, she will be deemed to have notice of this charge and will therefore still be bound by it (LPA 1925, s. 198). This is so even though Barbara had no means of discovering the registration.

This difficulty in the system was not originally envisaged as being of importance, because in 1926 vendors were required to provide a root of title going back 30 years and it was expected that the registered title system, which does not use the Land Charges Register, would be generally in force quite quickly. Delays in the introduction of the registered land system and the reduction of the title period to 15 years exacerbated the problem. As a result the law was amended by s. 25 of the LPA 1969, which provides that, should a purchaser of an estate or interest in the land suffer loss due to the existence of a registered land charge prior to the root of title, the purchaser may obtain compensation from a central fund administered by the Chief Land Registrar.

Now that we are many years on from this development, it is interesting to note that there has been very little call for compensation (one claim in the first 21 years following the introduction of the scheme: Land Registry Annual Report 1989–90, p. 11). It seems that the supposed difficulties were more apparent than real. Many land charges (such as mortgages) have a relatively short life, and are unlikely to be effective outside the search period. In the case of interests which may last for longer (such as rights under restrictive covenants or equitable easements), there are several ways in which a prospective purchaser may learn of them from the title deeds or associated papers. Thus conveyances within the period the purchaser is searching may well 'recite' previous dealings with the land and give details of the earlier conveyances which created the encumbrance. There is also the possibility of the purchaser having access to earlier land charge search certificates, which may be kept with the title deeds. It seems that in practice, therefore, the purchaser is not often bound by an active land charge of which he or she was not aware.

5.4.4 Effect of registration

Registering an equitable interest as a land charge ensures that anyone taking a later estate or interest in the land (most importantly, any purchaser of the legal estate) will take it subject to that right. This result is brought about by s. 198(1) of the LPA 1925 (as amended) which provides that:

> The registration of any instrument or matter in any register kept under the Land Charges Act 1972, . . . shall be deemed to constitute actual notice of such instrument or matter.

This refers back to the equitable doctrine of notice (see 2.6.3), and in effect introduces a form of 'statutory notice'. You may remember that a purchaser for value of a legal estate can avoid being bound by past equitable interests by showing that she is a bona fide purchaser for value without notice or 'equity's darling'. However, where an equitable interest appears on the Land Charges Register, s. 198 ensures that this defence is unavailable: every purchaser of the affected legal estate is treated as if they had actual notice (knowledge) of the registered charge and so the defence is not open to them even if they did not actually know about the charge because they failed to discover it in their searches of the register (see 5.4.3.2 for how this might happen).

It should be noticed that the fact that a charge appears on the register does not in any way guarantee that it is an effective charge. Under the Land Charges Rules 1974, r. 22, the Registrar is not concerned to check the accuracy of an application to register a charge. It is also possible that a charge may have been effective originally but is no longer so—for example, an equitable charge securing a debt could have been registered and never removed from the register, even though the debt has since been paid off and the charge, therefore, has ceased to be enforceable. Thus it may be that a purchaser may be contractually obliged to continue with a purchase even though the searches reveal registered charges. All that is necessary is that the vendor should show that the apparent encumbrance does not in fact affect his or her title (compare *Bull v Hutchens* (1863) 32 Beav 615).

5.4.4.1 Searches

The practical consequence of LPA 1925, s. 198, is to ensure that a careful purchaser makes a search of the Land Charges Register. Such searches may be made at any time and they do not require the prior consent of the current estate owner. The register is a public record, which is open to anyone who is prepared to pay the search fee (LCA 1972, s. 9). On receipt of a search requisition a search is made and the result is communicated to the searcher in the form of a search certificate.

5.4.5 Effect of non-registration of a land charge

In general terms, failure to register a land charge means that the person entitled to it is unable to enforce it against some later purchasers for value. The statutory rules on non-registration are very detailed, but the general policy is that, in order to bind a purchaser, the land charge must be registered before completion (i.e., the point at which the purchaser pays the money and receives the estate or interest), and that it cannot be enforced against the purchaser if it is not so registered. For the purposes of the Act, the term 'purchaser' is widely defined (s. 17(1)), so that it includes not only a person who buys a freehold estate, but also mortgagees, lessees, and the acquirers of other interests, both legal and equitable. Very importantly, nothing in the definition makes any reference to a purchaser *in good faith* or *without notice*. The courts have interpreted this to mean that, unlike the traditional 'equity's darling' defence, the Land Charges Act 1972 defences can apply in favour of purchasers who were fully aware of the existence of the unregistered right when they agreed to buy the property (see 5.4.5.4).

We will now look at the provisions in more detail, and you will see that basically there are two rules: one for land charges of classes A, B, C(i), (ii), and (iii), and F; and another for land charges of classes C(iv) and D(i), (ii), and (iii).

5.4.5.1 Classes A, B, C(i)–(iii), and F

The general rule with these land charges (with slight variations for class A) is that unless they are registered before completion they cannot be enforced against a purchaser for valuable consideration of an estate in the land or of any interest in the land (LCA 1972, ss. 4(2)(5) and (8) and 17(1)).

Thus even the purchaser of an equitable interest in the property can take an interest free from an unregistered charge. For example, suppose Clara has a puisne mortgage (C(i)) over Blackacre, which has not been registered. Later, the fee simple owner grants an equitable mortgage to Yasmin. Even though Clara has a legal mortgage and Yasmin has an equitable mortgage, it is Yasmin who will take free of Clara's rights (or, as is sometimes said, Yasmin's rights will take priority over Clara's). The practical result is that, if the estate has to be sold to pay back the sums due under the mortgages, the debt owed to Yasmin will be paid first and in full and Clara may find that there is not enough money to pay her in full (see Chapter 23).

5.4.5.2 Classes C(iv) and D(i)–(iii)

The rule to be applied to these land charges is that unless they are registered before completion they cannot be enforced against the purchaser of a legal estate for money or money's worth (LCA 1972, s. 4(6)). This is the only person who can take the land free of the charge and thus the purchaser of any lesser interest in the property will still be bound by the charge, even though it is unregistered. Thus, if an estate contract (C(iv)) has not been registered and later an equitable mortgage is created by the fee simple owner, the estate contract *can* be enforced against the equitable mortgagee: the equitable mortgagee is not the purchaser of a legal estate.

This rule was applied in *Sainsbury's Supermarkets Ltd v Olympia Homes Ltd* [2006] 1 P&CR 17. In that case, one Mr Hughes had contracted to buy unregistered land from a third party and, at the same time, granted Sainsbury's an option to purchase the land (to be used in case it needed the land to construct a roundabout giving access to its new supermarket). Sainsbury's failed to register its option on the Land Charges Register. Later, Mr Hughes failed to register himself as the first registered proprietor of the unregistered land that he was buying, meaning that he ceased to have any legal estate and instead became a beneficiary under a bare trust (see 5.8). Olympia Homes Ltd then bought Mr Hughes' interest in the land, which the court held was merely an equitable interest under a bare trust. It followed that, despite the lack of registration of Sainsbury's option as a land charge, it bound Olympia Homes as the purchaser for value of an equitable interest. (You should also note that Olympia Homes then went on to become the first registered proprietor of the legal estate, despite only being entitled to an equitable interest, and this raised issues about whether the Land Registration Act 2002 prevented the court from granting relief to Sainsbury's in the circumstances. See 6.3.4.1 for this aspect of the case.)

5.4.5.3 What is the difference between a 'purchaser for value' and a 'purchaser for money or money's worth'?

This question arises because s. 4(5) refers simply to a 'purchaser', who is defined in s. 17(1) as a 'purchaser for value', while s. 4(6) speaks of a 'purchaser for money or money's worth'.

'Purchaser for value' is the wider term, and includes not only purchasers who give money or money's worth but also those who give consideration of a sort which cannot be computed in financial terms. An example of non-financial consideration would be found in an agreement to convey land in consideration of marriage or the formation of a civil partnership. The purchaser would be regarded as giving valuable consideration (see LPA 1925, s. 205(1)(xxi), as amended by the Civil Partnership Act 2004) but not money or money's worth, since it is not possible to put a financial valuation on these relationships. Such non-pecuniary consideration is relatively rare today, and most purchases of the legal estate are likely to be for money or money's worth.

5.4.5.4 Judicial interpretation of rules about unregistered land charges

In considering the rules about non-registration of land charges, you need to be aware that:

- the courts will not enquire into the adequacy of the consideration given by the purchaser;
- the fact that a purchaser knew about an unregistered land charge does not make it enforceable against that purchaser.

Both these points are illustrated in the House of Lords' decision in *Midland Bank Trust Co. Ltd v Green* [1981] AC 513. Here a father had granted his son an option to purchase a farm for £22,500. This agreement came within the definition of estate contract given in LCA 1972, s. 2(4)(iv), and so was registrable as a land charge. The son failed to register his option. Later his father wished to avoid carrying through his promise and, acting on advice, he conveyed the legal estate in the property to his wife for £500. At the date of this conveyance the farm was actually worth £40,000. In the Court of Appeal, it was held that the sale at such a considerable undervalue was not a sale for 'money or money's worth'. However, the House of Lords reversed this decision, holding that the unregistered land charge was unenforceable against the purchaser, and relying on the contractual rule that the court will not enquire into the adequacy of consideration, as long as the consideration is real. It would therefore appear that a sale for 1p would satisfy s. 4(6), as long as it was genuinely intended that the money would be paid in exchange for the land.

Midland Bank Trust Co. Ltd v Green also illustrates the second important point: that a purchaser can take an estate free of an unregistered land charge even if the purchaser knows that the land charge exists and regardless of questions about good faith. It was clear that the mother had known about her son's interest, and that the goal of the entire transaction was to defeat the son's interest, but she was still able to take the estate free of it because he had not registered it.

5.4.5.5 Comparison with registered land

When you read Chapter 6 on registered land you will see that the result in *Midland Bank Trust Co. Ltd v Green* would have been very different if the title to the farm had been registered. It appears that the son was in actual occupation of the property and that his interest was known to his mother at the time of her purchase. Consequently, in the registered system, he could have claimed that his option was an overriding interest under s. 70(1)(g) of LRA 1925 (the forerunner of LRA 2002, Sch. 3, para. 2) and therefore binding on the purchaser (see 6.5.6).

A similar illustration of the difference between the two systems is to be found in *Lloyds Bank plc v Carrick* [1996] 4 All ER 630. Here, the defendant had sold her house on her husband's death, paid the proceeds to her brother-in-law, and moved into a maisonette owned by him, on the understanding that it would become hers. In 1982, when those events occurred, this agreement, supported by part performance, was sufficient to satisfy the requirements of LPA 1925, s. 40 (see 4.3.2.4), and accordingly there was an enforceable contract between the two parties. The defendant lived in the property for a number of years; the legal estate was never conveyed to her, and, predictably, she did not protect her position by registering a land charge. During this time her brother-in-law mortgaged the property, without her knowledge, as security for his own debts, and when he defaulted on the repayments, the bank sought possession of the property. The defendant argued that her brother-in-law, having received full payment for the maisonette, held his legal estate in it as a bare trustee for her, and that her interest under this trust was not a registrable land charge and so its enforceability against the bank depended on whether the bank had notice (see 2.6.3 and 5.5.2). The Court of Appeal, however, rejected this argument, as well as others based on constructive trusts and proprietary estoppel (see 13.2.3.2 and Chapter 19), holding that her rights arose from the contract with her brother-in-law. Since she had the benefit of an estate contract, her failure to protect that right by registration as a class C(iv) land charge meant that it was void against the bank, which accordingly was entitled to enforce its security and take possession. It was irrelevant that she was in actual occupation of the land; this would only have mattered if she had an equitable interest which was not a land charge, which would then have put the bank on constructive notice of her interest (see 5.5.2.3). Since notice is irrelevant under the Land Charges Act 1972 (see 5.4.5.4), actual occupation is irrelevant too.

In his judgment Morritt LJ drew attention to the fact that actual occupation would have made all the difference if title to the maisonette had been registered. In the case of registered land, *any* proprietary interest held by a person in actual occupation (including an estate contract) will be overriding and can bind a purchaser for value of a legal interest (see 6.5.6.1). By contrast, in unregistered land, actual occupation will only be relevant in situations where the doctrine of notice still applies—that is, where the claimant has an interest that is *not* a registrable land charge. As *Lloyds Bank v Carrick* illustrates, this can be problematic since the difference between equitable interests that *are* registrable land charges and equitable interests that are not can be quite complicated and may not be easy to draw in particular cases. However, the judge took the view that it was for Parliament, not the courts, to decide whether this distinction should continue.

5.4.5.6 Right still enforceable against original owner

Although the effect of non-registration is that the charge cannot be enforced against the new owner of the estate, the right does still remain enforceable against the original owner who granted it. This may not be so satisfactory for the person entitled; for instance, if that person has failed to register an equitable right of way (D(iii)) he or she will no longer be able to use the right over the land, but may well have a remedy in contract against the original owner and may be able to recover compensation. This is so even though it is the person entitled to the land charge who is really at fault, through failing to register it.

5.4.6 Importance of obtaining a search certificate

The certificate which shows the result of a search of the Land Charges Register serves a dual purpose for the prospective purchaser. It specifies the registered land charges which will bind him or her if the purchase proceeds, but, almost more importantly, it can be used to prove non-registration, since s. 10(4) provides that the certificate shall be conclusive in favour of the purchaser. For this reason, it is common for a purchaser to make two searches of the register, first during the investigation of title, to discover what encumbrances bind the property, and again just before completion to ensure that nothing new has been registered since the earlier search and to show the state of the register at completion.

For practical purposes, a system of priority notices operates, so that a purchaser can search the register up to 15 days before completion of the transaction, and will then take free of any land charges registered between that search and completion. (You are unlikely to need much knowledge of this procedure, which is more a matter of conveyancing than of land law, but if you want details you will find them in LCA 1972, s. 11(5) and (6).)

5.4.7 Other registers maintained under the Land Charges Act 1972

The other registers maintained under LCA 1972, s. 1 contain registrations of: pending actions relating to land; certain annuities created before 1926; court orders relating to land, and writs issued for the purpose of enforcing them.

5.5 Legal and equitable interests which are not land charges

5.5.1 Enforcement of legal interests

A purchaser will automatically be bound by all legal interests in the land which are not land charges (and, as we have seen, most legal interests are not on the land charges list). This rule is usually expressed by saying that 'Legal rights are good against the world'. Thus the purchaser will be bound, for example, by rights such as legal easements and legal leases, whether or not she knows about them or could have known about them. Similarly, if an estate is subject to a legal mortgage which is protected by a deposit of the title deeds, then anyone who buys the estate will buy it subject to the mortgage. (In practice the purchaser would insist that the vendor repay the debt on completion of the sale so that the mortgage is discharged and the purchaser is not affected by it; but if the purchaser did not know about the mortgage, and so did not require that this be done, it would bind the purchaser.)

5.5.2 Enforcement of equitable interests against the purchaser of the legal estate

We saw in Chapter 2 that the Court of Chancery developed the rule that equitable interests in land bound everyone who took the land *except* the bona fide purchaser of the legal estate without notice (see 2.6.3). Notice, in this context, does not only mean actual knowledge of the equitable interest ('**actual notice**'). It could also mean that a reasonable person in the purchaser's shoes *would* have known about the equitable interest ('**constructive notice**') if they had made proper inquiries. If the purchaser herself does not know and could not have known about the equitable interest, she will still be considered to have notice of it if her agent (e.g., the solicitor advising her on the sale) such knowledge or means of knowledge ('**imputed notice**'). In practice, the doctrine of notice used to impose a heavy burden on the purchaser of land, who had to make exhaustive enquiries in order to avoid being said to have constructive notice of equitable interests which he or she had failed to discover.

In the nineteenth century, this situation was considered to be problematic for everyone involved, especially where land was being purchased—as it often was—from trustees. Under the terms of a trust, it is very often perfectly proper for trustees to sell or otherwise dispose of the trust land for the benefit of the beneficiaries. For example, the land might be leased and the rental income might be paid to the beneficiaries, or it might be sold to raise funds to pay for the education of an infant beneficiary. A purchaser who buys land under these conditions will automatically take the land free from the interests of the beneficiaries, since there is no breach of trust involved in the sale. This is a process known as '**overreaching**': its effect is that the purchaser takes the land free from the trust, while the trustees hold whatever they have obtained from the purchaser—the proceeds of sale—on trust for the beneficiary. Because of the demands of the doctrine of constructive notice, purchasers in such circumstances had to undertake expensive inquiries in order to be completely sure that the trustees were not in breach of their duties in selling the land. They might, for example, have to get a receipt from the trustees to confirm that they had actually applied the proceeds of sale in accordance with the terms of the trust (paying it to the beneficiaries or for a purpose benefiting the beneficiaries). The need for inquiries of this type made sales of land expensive for the purchaser and slow and complicated for both sides of the transaction.

A major aim of the 1925 legislation, and of the statutory reforms which preceded it, was to facilitate the sale of land and to make this whole process less onerous for the purchaser. For this purpose, two new statutory mechanisms were introduced, which had the effect of making considerable inroads into the doctrine of notice in land law. The first, which we have already looked at, was land charges registration. The other was a method for extending the scope of overreaching by statute.

5.5.2.1 Statutory overreaching

Land charges registration was considered to be suitable for equitable rights such as restrictive covenants and easements, which must continue to bind the land if they are to benefit those entitled to them. However, in the case of trusts, such registration would have been unsuitable since it was not the goal of anyone involved in a sale for the benefit of the beneficiaries—the trustees, beneficiaries, or the purchaser—to ensure that the land was still bound by the equitable interests of the beneficiaries in the hands of the purchaser. Instead, the goal was to make it easier for purchasers to take land free from the beneficial interests, under a proper disposition by trustees, while still protecting beneficiaries from the risk that the trustees would defraud them by selling or disposing of the land to their disadvantage.

To facilitate this, a 'statutory overreaching' mechanism was introduced by a series of Acts, culminating in the 1925 legislation (see LPA 1925, s. 2(1)). Under this mechanism, an interest under a trust of land will be overreached by a disposition of the estate held on trust if any capital money arising under the disposition is paid to two trustees, or to a trust corporation. Provided this requirement is satisfied, the purchaser takes the legal estate free of the beneficiaries' interests, even if he has actual notice of them. The beneficiaries will instead have an interest in the proceeds of sale.

The beneficiaries' interests are supposed to be safeguarded in this process (in theory although not always in practice) by the rule that the money should only be paid to two trustees or a trust corporation. If the requirements relating to the payment of capital money are not satisfied, the beneficiaries' interests are not overreached, and the purchaser will take subject to them, unless the purchaser can establish no notice of them. In an era where many trustees were professional trustees, holding and managing land in which they themselves had no stake, this safeguard might have been very effective. Under modern conditions, as we shall see in Chapter 17, trusts of land frequently arise in informal domestic settings where the trustees and beneficiaries both have a stake in the land. In these situations, the requirement to pay two trustees has proved less of a safeguard against fraud.

In *City of London Building Society v Flegg* [1988] AC 54, for example, a Mr and Mrs Maxwell-Brown had acquired title to a house with the help of the wife's parents, the Fleggs, who lived with them. Since the Fleggs had contributed to the purchase price of the property, they had a beneficial interest under a trust of land, with the Maxwell-Browns holding their legal title on trust for themselves and the Fleggs in certain shares (a '**tenancy in common**', see 17.3). When the Maxwell-Browns mortgaged the property without the knowledge or consent of the Fleggs, to service their own separate debts, the payment of the mortgage money to two trustees was enough to overreach the beneficial interests. The bank was, therefore, entitled to possession of the land and the Fleggs were left to their remedy against the Maxwell-Browns who had of course spent the money and were bankrupt by the date of the litigation. Since *Flegg* concerned registered land, you will find further discussion of the case in chapter 6 (6.5.6.1) but you should note for now that the outcome would have been the same even if the land had been unregistered. A purchaser who pays two legal owners of an unregistered estate in land can be confident that if the legal owners hold that estate on trust for unknown beneficiaries, payment of the purchase price to both owners will have the effect of overreaching any unknown beneficial interests. The purchaser in this scenario does *not* need to investigate the basis on which the owners are holding to avoid being fixed with constructive notice of any trusts; overreaching renders the doctrine of notice irrelevant.

There are more details concerning overreaching, and the statutory provisions relating to it, at 14.9.2.

5.5.2.2 Doctrine of notice today

For purchasers of unregistered land the significance of the notice rules was reduced considerably by the 1925 reforms. However, the doctrine still applies to the following equitable rights:

- rights excluded from registration as land charges, such as pre-1926 restrictive covenants and equitable easements, and restrictive covenants made between landlord and tenant (see 5.4.2.2–3);
- beneficiaries' rights under a trust which have not been overreached because the proper procedures were not followed (e.g., because there was only one trustee); and
- equitable rights which had not been identified by the courts at the time of the 1925 legislation and so are not included in the scheme of land charge registration. These rights include, for example, rights arising from estoppel (see *Ives (E.R.) Investment Ltd v High* [1967] 2 QB 379) and certain rights of entry (*Poster v Slough Estates Ltd* [1968] 1 WLR 1515 and *Shiloh Spinners Ltd v Harding* [1973] AC 691).

In consequence, it remains essential for a purchaser of unregistered land to make thorough searches and enquiries in order to avoid being held to have constructive notice of any of these equitable rights.

5.5.2.3 What searches must a purchaser make to avoid constructive notice?

The searches required of the purchaser are of two types: first, investigation of the vendor's title correctly by examining the title deeds, and secondly, inspection of the land itself.

- *Constructive notice of matters revealed by examination of deeds.* A purchaser is bound by any right which would have been discovered on inspection of the vendor's title deeds for the statutory period (e.g., *Worthington v Morgan* (1849) 16 Sim 547, in which no investigation was made). As a result of this rule, it is common for the owners of equitable interests to insist that a note of their rights is made on the deeds (e.g., written on the back of a deed) so that future purchasers will have actual notice of their rights if they read the deeds and constructive notice if they omit to do so.

- *Constructive notice of matters revealed by inspection of land.* The rule that the purchaser must also inspect the land is commonly called the 'rule in *Hunt v Luck*'. In the case of *Hunt v Luck* [1902] 1 Ch 428, a purchaser was held to have notice of all the rights of a tenant who was in occupation of the land, but not of the rights of the landlord from whom the tenant derived his title. As a result, a purchaser runs the risk of having constructive notice of any rights belonging to anyone in actual occupation, and should ensure that enquiries are made of any such person.

Occupation by the owner's spouse

There used to be some uncertainty about the application of the rule in *Hunt v Luck* to property occupied by married couples. It has become increasingly common over the last 60 years for both parties to contribute to the cost of acquiring the matrimonial home. In consequence, a spouse in occupation of the land may have an equitable interest in the property under a constructive or resulting trust, even though the legal estate is vested only in the other spouse. (These trusts are discussed in more detail in Chapter 18.) At first, however, purchasers did not always think it necessary to enquire whether spouses in occupation had such an interest. This attitude was accepted in *Caunce v Caunce* [1969] 1 WLR 286, in which it was held that a purchaser was entitled to presume that a wife lived in the property because of her relationship with the estate owner, and that her presence did not put the purchaser of the estate on notice. However, this approach was heavily criticised by the House of Lords in the registered land case of *Williams & Glyn's Bank Ltd v Boland* [1981] AC 487 at p. 508 (see 6.5.6.2), and in *Kingsnorth Finance Co. Ltd v Tizard* [1986] 1 WLR 783 a wife's occupation of unregistered land was regarded as being separate from that of her husband. Accordingly, the rule in *Caunce v Caunce* should today be regarded as of historical interest only, marking the enormous change in social attitudes which has taken place since 1969.

Kingsnorth Finance Co. Ltd v Tizard is a very interesting case and well worth noting in detail. Mrs Tizard had contributed to the purchase price of the original matrimonial home. She therefore had a beneficial interest, under a resulting trust, both in that property and in a later house which was bought with the proceeds of sale from the first home, and conveyed into the sole name of her husband. Accordingly Mr Tizard held the property in trust for himself and his wife. After some years the marriage failed, and the wife left the matrimonial home, but lived nearby and came in each day to care for the children, leaving some clothes and other possessions at the house. Subsequently, the husband mortgaged the property without his wife's knowledge, having arranged for the preliminary inspection by the mortgagee's agent to be carried out in her absence. When the mortgage repayments fell into arrears, the mortgagee sought to enforce its security and was opposed by Mrs Tizard, who claimed that the mortgagee had had constructive notice of her beneficial interest in the property and therefore took subject to her rights.

The court held that Mrs Tizard had been in occupation of the property at the date at which the agent made his inspection and later when the charge was granted. It was said that occupation need not be exclusive, continuous, or uninterrupted. The court did, however, agree that someone inspecting property under the rule in *Hunt v Luck* was not obliged to go as far as opening drawers or hunting in cupboards (which, if done, would have revealed the wife's possessions). However, since the agent had been told of the recent separation and the fact that Mrs Tizard still lived in the area, the court considered that the mortgagee was put on notice and should have made further enquiries. The inspection of the property at a pre-arranged date did not amount to making sufficient enquiry.

As a result, the mortgagee, having constructive notice, took its legal interest in the property subject to Mrs Tizard's equitable rights as a beneficiary under the trust. This meant that the mortgagee could enforce its rights only against the husband's share, rather than against the whole property. In these circumstances Mrs Tizard agreed that the house should be sold and the proceeds divided between herself and the mortgagee, in proportion to their respective interests in the property. (For similar cases in which the court has ordered sale against the wishes of the beneficiary, see 14.8.5.)

The *Tizard* case, though only a first-instance decision, is of considerable importance because it widened the concept of notice beyond its previously presumed limits. The judgment is helpful in giving a detailed indication of the type of investigation which will be needed if a buyer or mortgagee is to be safe from hidden equitable interests, and certainly suggests that, in cases in which it is known that a vendor or mortgagor is married or has a civil partner, it is advisable to insist on obtaining written consent to the transaction from his or her spouse or civil partner.

5.5.2.4 Effect of purchase without notice

As we have already seen, the bona fide purchaser for value of the legal estate will take free of any equitable interests of which the purchaser does not have notice. An important consequence of this is that anyone who later acquires the legal estate from that purchaser also takes free of the equitable interest, even if he or she actually knows about it (*Wilkes v Spooner* [1911] 2 KB 473).

Although the equitable interest cannot be enforced against the purchaser without notice or against his or her successor, it does remain enforceable against the person who originally was subject to it (such as a trustee or a person who created the equitable right), but, as we have noted in the case of unregistered land charges (see 5.4.5.6), the only remedy available is likely to be damages for breach of contract or, where appropriate, an action for breach of trust.

5.5.3 Enforcement of equitable interests against later acquirers of equitable interests

Thus far we have considered the position of those who intend to buy a legal estate and who, if they do so, will take the property free of those equitable interests (which are not land charges) of which they have no notice, or which are overreached on sale. However, it is possible for someone to acquire only an equitable interest in the property, for example, by entering into a contract to buy the legal estate but never taking a conveyance of the legal estate or never applying for first registration where that is a requirement to retain the legal estate (see 5.8). We have already looked at an example of such a case in *Sainsbury's Supermarkets Ltd v Olympia Homes Ltd* [2006] 1 P&CR 17 (discussed at 5.4.5.2). In such a case the intending purchaser has an equitable right to the land under the contract (see 4.6.1) and the question then arises of the extent to which the purchaser is bound by pre-existing equitable interests.

Under the Land Charges Act 1972, as we have seen, a purchaser of an equitable interest can have a defence against some, but not all, unregistered land charges (at 5.4.5.2). By contrast, the 'equity's darling' rule only protects the bona fide purchaser of a legal estate in unregistered land. It does not protect a purchaser who acquires only an equitable interest in the property. For such a purchaser, the general rule is:

> Where the equities are equal, the first in time prevails.

Thus a later acquirer of an equitable interest will take priority over an earlier equitable interest only where the 'equities' are not equal. This may happen if the owner of the earlier equitable interest has been involved in a fraud on the later acquirer or possibly if the earlier equitable owner has been grossly negligent about protecting his interests (see further on this, in relation to mortgages of unregistered land, Chapter 23).

5.6 Summary of searches to be made in relation to unregistered land

To summarise, Barbara Bell (or her adviser) must make the following enquiries in respect of 2 Trant Way, in order to protect herself:

- a local land charges search (see 3.3.2.1);
- a thorough examination of the title deeds from the root of title onwards;
- a land charges search against the names of all the estate owners during the title period;
- since she is buying from a sole owner, an investigation of the occupancy of the land, including questioning any occupiers as to their rights.

5.7 The conveyance

Once Barbara Bell is satisfied with her enquiries and both parties have made the necessary arrangements, the time will have arrived for the completion of the transaction. She will pay the balance of the purchase price, provided either from her own resources or with money borrowed from a lender, to whom she will mortgage her newly acquired property. Victoria Ventnor, the vendor, will execute the deed (required by s. 52(1) of the LPA 1925), which will convey the legal estate to Barbara. An example of a very simple conveyance of 2 Trant Way is given in Form 5.1. Usually these documents are far longer and decidedly more complex than this example.

At the time of the conveyance the vendor will hand to the purchaser (or the purchaser's solicitors) the title deeds to the property (unless only part of the land covered by the deeds is being sold, in which case the vendor will give the purchaser an undertaking to produce the deeds should the purchaser ever require them). The purchaser should, of course, check the deeds to ensure that the copies previously seen are true copies of the original documents.

THIS CONVEYANCE is made the   day of

BETWEEN VICTORIA VENTNOR of 2 Trant Way, Mousehole, Stilton ST1 2XL ("the vendor") of the one part and BARBARA BELL of Oak Tree Cottage, Elmdale, Stilton EL4 9AJ ("the purchaser") of the other part.

WHEREAS the vendor is seised of the property hereinafter described for an estate in fee simple in possession free from incumbrances and has agreed with the purchaser for the sale thereof to her at a price of four hundred and sixty thousand pounds (£460,000).

NOW THIS DEED WITNESSETH as follows:

In consideration of the sum of four hundred and sixty thousand pounds (£460,000) paid by the purchaser to the vendor (the receipt whereof the vendor hereby acknowledges) the vendor with full title guarantee hereby conveys unto the purchaser all that piece or parcel of land known as 2 Trant Way, Mousehole, Stilton ST1 2XL which for the purposes of identification only is shown and delineated in red on the plan attached hereto **TO HOLD** the same unto the purchaser in fee simple.

IN WITNESS of which the vendor has executed this deed in the presence of the attesting witness the day and year first before written.

Signed and delivered }
as a deed by the said }   *Victoria Ventnor*
VICTORIA VENTNOR }
in the presence of }

Julia Possum

JULIA POSSUM
198 THE HIGH STREET,
MOUSEHOLE,
STILTON

I.T. CONSULTANT

Form 5.1 Conveyance of 2 Trant Way

5.8 Application for first registration

Although Barbara is now the legal owner of No. 2, there is still one more thing she must do. You will remember that the system of registered title was finally extended to all parts of the country (including Stilton) in 1990, and so all property, wherever situated, will now be in an area of compulsory registration. In consequence, most new owners who have taken a legal estate under the unregistered system of conveyancing must apply to the Land Registry for first registration as registered proprietor. The only exception is for those taking certain short leases (see 6.3.2). Since Barbara has bought a freehold estate, this requirement applies to her.

In order to compel purchasers to apply for first registration, LRA 2002, ss. 6 and 7 provide that if a registration is not made within two months of the date of the conveyance that conveyance shall become void, with the result that the legal estate that has been conveyed to the purchaser will revert to the vendor, who will hold it on a bare trust for the purchaser (see 6.3.2.3).

Thus, it is essential that once Barbara Bell has taken the conveyance of the legal estate in 2 Trant Way, she applies for first registration of her title without delay. We will see what this involves in Chapter 6.

FURTHER READING

Hanbury and Martin, *Modern Equity*, 22nd edn., Sweet & Maxwell, 2021, paras. 1-039–1-048 (doctrine of notice).

Harpum, 'Purchasers with Notice of Unregistered Land Charges' [1981] CLJ 213.

Harpum, 'Overreaching, Trustees' Powers and the Reform of the 1925 Legislation' [1990] CLJ 277.

Howell, 'The Doctrine of Notice: An Historical Perspective' [1997] Conv 431.

Megarry and Wade, *The Law of Real Property*, 9th edn., Sweet & Maxwell, 2019, Chapter 5.

Thompson, 'The Purchaser as Private Detective' [1986] Conv 283.

Thompson, 'The Widow's Plight' [1996] Conv 295.

Yates, 'The Protection of Equitable Interests Under the 1925 Legislation' (1974) 37 MLR 87.

You can visit the online resources to test your knowledge of this chapter with self-test questions at www.oup.com/he/nair19e/.

6
Registered land

6.1 Introduction **87**
6.2 Overview of the land registration system **88**
6.3 First registration of an unregistered estate **98**
6.4 Dealings with a registered estate: formalities **106**
6.5 Dealings with a registered estate: protection of purchasers **108**
6.6 Summary: the process of buying registered land **125**
6.7 Flawed dealings with a registered estate: alteration and indemnity **132**

6.1 Introduction

As we have explained, there is a key distinction between 'unregistered' and 'registered' land in modern English law (see 3.2.2). In Chapter 3, we saw that No. 1 Trant Way is 'registered land' and No. 2 Trant Way is 'unregistered land'. We have so far followed Barbara Bell in her quest to buy the unregistered title to No. 2 Trant Way from Victoria Ventnor. In this chapter, we will look at what it means to say that she must now to apply for "first registration" of the unregistered title to No. 2 Trant Way. We will then turn to No 1 Trant Way, which is 'registered land', and consider the case of Mr and Mrs Armstrong who intend to buy the registered title to the house from Victor Venn.

Where land is registered, information regarding title to that land appears on a public register maintained by a non-departmental government body, HM Land Registry. The functioning of this register is not merely a bureaucratic exercise in managing information. To make it work, the LRA 2002 creates new formality rules for the creation and transfer of estates and interests in land and new defences that give purchasers of land priority over certain pre-existing rights in that land. It also creates a new mechanism for the acquisition of rights in situations where someone has attempted a forged, fraudulent, or otherwise flawed disposition of land and the register is changed as a result.

This chapter introduces these core elements of the land registration system. We begin with an overview of the land registration system in England and Wales, explaining the concept and historic origins of title registration in this jurisdiction, the modern appearance of the register, and various aspects of how it works (see 6.2). We then look at how unregistered land becomes registered land, returning to the situation of Barbara Bell and her obligation to complete her purchase of unregistered land by getting her title registered (see 6.3). Next, we turn our focus to the Armstrongs and explain how rights in registered land may be created and transferred (see 6.4), the defences available to purchasers of such rights (see 6.5 and 6.6) and the consequences of registration where the underlying transaction is flawed in some way (see 6.7).

6.2 Overview of the land registration system

As we have seen, the process of buying land involves a process of discovering information about the land. Most fundamentally, purchasers want to know the quality of title to the land they are buying—whether the person who is purporting to sell them some estate in the land actually has the best title to that estate and a power to sell it, or whether there is some other person whose rights are superior or will override the sale and bind the purchaser. The existence of limited third-party rights, such as easements (see Chapter 24) and covenants (see Chapter 25), will also be important as such rights may significantly limit what the purchaser is free to do with the land once acquired.

Historically, the only way for a purchaser to discover this type of information was by inspecting the past history of transactions involving the land: the deeds, which would be privately held by those who had an estate or interest in the relevant land (see 5.2). This process, however, was regarded as risky for purchasers, cumbersome, and slow. Deeds could be lost, or difficult to interpret; where the sellers of land were trustees, the burdens of understanding the terms of the trust, and avoiding being fixed with 'constructive notice' (see 5.5) of a sale in breach of trust, were considerable. These burdens on purchasers were believed to make the market in land slow and inefficient.

Since the nineteenth century, law reform efforts have been directed at solving this problem and managing these risks, including by the introduction of public registers that made it easier for purchasers to discover what they needed to know. One effort led to the introduction of the Land Charges Register, discussed in Chapter 5: a limited record of specific encumbrances affecting land, which would not affect a purchaser if unregistered (see 5.4). The other and more ambitious effort led to the introduction of a much more comprehensive parallel register in English law: the 'title register'. This is the system that now covers most of the land in England and Wales and is governed by LRA 2002.

6.2.1 A brief history of title registration in England and Wales

Initial law reform efforts in England and Wales, in the early nineteenth century, focused on the idea of a national register of *deeds*. This register, mirroring the local deeds registries that then existed in Yorkshire and Middlesex, would require owners to deposit deeds creating or transferring rights in their land with a government office. Purchasers would then be protected from the risk of being bound by rights found in a lost deed. There is nothing inherently wrong with the idea; deeds registration and similar systems now successfully operate in many jurisdictions of the United States, for example. However, in England and Wales, this idea was superseded by the more ambitious proposal, in 1857, to introduce a system of registration of *title*. Unlike a register of deeds—where the state keeps a record of transactions affecting land but makes no comment on the legal effect of those transactions—registration of title involves a much more active role for HM Land Registry. Under this system, Land Registry interprets the total effect of the past transactions affecting the land and makes a declaration as to the nature and quality of the rights that now exist over that land.

The first land registration legislation in England and Wales was the Land Transfer Act 1862. This created a mechanism for landowners to *voluntarily* submit evidence of their title and apply for its registration. The idea of *compulsory* registration was first introduced by the Land Transfer Act 1897 but only in areas which were to be made areas of compulsory registration. Next, the Land Registration Act 1925 (LRA 1925) reformed the system, repealed the earlier legislation, and gave the government the power to actually designate areas of the country as areas of compulsory first registration, a process which began in 1926. However, the extension of compulsory registration to the whole of England and Wales was slowed by the economic recessions before and after World War II and was only completed in 1990. Finally, the whole system was revised and updated by LRA 2002, supplemented by the Land Registration Rules 2003 (LRR 2003); this is the legislation that now governs registered land in England and Wales.

In addition to modernising and simplifying the existing system, one major aim of LRA 2002 was to facilitate electronic conveyancing, making it possible to both investigate title to land and to deal with land entirely online. As the Law Commission noted in its 2018 Report on the subject of land registration (see 6.2.6.2), the model of electronic conveyancing envisaged by the LRA 2002 has not yet been systematically implemented and it is not clear when it will be. However, this remains an important long-term goal and the powers to introduce and manage electronic conveyancing, contained in the legislation, may well be used in the future once various technological and logistical obstacles have been addressed.

6.2.2 Registered and unregistered land

As has been explained, English law does not recognise the existence of titles to *land* as such, only to *estates in land* (see 1.5). Thus, when we speak of 'registered land', we are not talking about physical land but instead about some *estate* in that land, title to which is registered (LRA 2002, s. 132). It is possible for the same plot of physical land to be both 'registered' and 'unregistered' in this sense. For example, a 999-year leasehold title to the land may have been registered at the time that the lease was granted, while the fee simple title may never have been dealt with by its owner and hence never registered. In this scenario, any dealings with the freehold will count as dealings with unregistered land, governed by the rules described in Chapter 5 and triggering a requirement for first registration under the LRA 2002 (see 6.3.2). Meanwhile, dealings with the leasehold will count as dealings with registered land and regulated according to the rules applicable to registered land (see 6.4 and 6.5).

6.2.3 Appearance of the register

The 'register of title' consists of a number of individual registers, one for each estate registered (LRR 2003, r. 2). Since there may be more than one estate in one piece of land—for example, a fee simple and a lease—there may be several individual registers for the same piece of land.

The individual register for an estate consists of three parts:

- the property register;
- the proprietorship register; and
- the charges register.

While reading this section you may find it helpful to look at Form 6.1, which is a fictional register entry for 1 Trant Way. Each title is allocated a title number by the registry and you will see that CS1234 is the title number for 1 Trant Way.

6.2.3.1 Property register

This part of the register describes the property, including the type of estate ('freehold' or 'leasehold') that has been registered. It invariably refers to a filed plan of the physical land, which is prepared from the largest size of ordnance survey map; on the register

HM Land Registry

Official copy of register of title

Title number CS1234 **Edition date 26.07.2019**

— This official copy shows the entries in the register of title on 10 December 2019 at 09:20:59.
— This date must be quoted as the "search from date" in any official search application based on this copy.
— The date at the beginning of an entry is the date on which the entry was made in the register.
— Issued on 10 December 2019.
— Under s.67 of the Land Registration Act 2002, this copy is admissible in evidence to the same extent as the original.
— For information about the register of title, see www.gov.uk/land-registry.
— This title is dealt with by HM Land Registry Maradon Office.

A: Property register
This register describes the land and estate comprised in the title.

STILTON : MOUSEHOLE

1   (26.02.2010) The Freehold land shown edged with red on the plan of the above title filed at the Registry and being 1 Trant Way, Mousehole, Stilton ST14 3JP.

B: Proprietorship register
This register specifies the class of title and identifies the owner. It contains any entries that affect the right of disposal.

Title absolute

1   (26.02.2010) PROPRIETOR: VICTOR VENN of 1 Trant Way, Mousehole, Stilton ST14 3JP.

C: Charges register
This register contains any charges and other matters that affect the land.

1   (26.02.2010) REGISTERED CHARGE dated 19 November 2009.

2   (26.02.2010) PROPRIETOR: CORNISH YARG BANK of Apple Chambers, The Broadway, Mousehole, Stilton ST1E 7PO.

End of register

Page 1

Form 6.1 Register entry for 1 Trant Way

This document is Crown copyright and has been reproduced with the kind permission of Land Registry.

entry, the land concerned is shown edged in red. Usually, the description of the property is simply its postal address but a different type of description may sometimes be necessary (for instance, if the registration is of title to a field with no address).

The property register may also contain details of any legal interests that *benefit* the registered estate. Examples include easements, like a right of way over neighbouring land (see 24.2), or profits, like rights to fish on neighbouring land (see 24.3).

6.2.3.2 Proprietorship register

This part of the register gives the name and address of the registered owner of the estate described in the property register—known as the '**registered proprietor**' of that estate—and sets out the 'class of the title' that he or she has been registered with. The 'class' (or 'grade') of title is awarded on first registration and shows how reliable the title is considered to be, after the investigations made by Land Registry at the time of first registration (see 6.3.3.2); you can see from Form 6.1 that Victor Venn has been registered with 'title absolute' to the freehold estate in 1 Trant Way (see 6.2.7.1).

The proprietorship register will also record any limits that may exist on the power of the proprietor to deal with the land: as for example, where the registered proprietor is a trustee or a bankrupt, forbidden to deal with the land without the consent of named beneficiaries or trustees in bankruptcy. Entries on the register that reflect such limitations on the registered proprietor's powers to deal with the registered estate are known as '**restrictions**' (see 6.2.7.3).

6.2.3.3 Charges register

We have seen that the 'property register' includes any interests that *benefit* the registered estate, such as easements and profits. The charges register shows any interests that *burden* the registered estate, binding anyone who acquires that estate from its current registered proprietor. These include interests like charges (mortgages) on the property (see Chapter 22), covenants restricting the use of the land (see Chapter 25), and easements in favour of someone else's land (see Chapter 24). Entries on the register that record the existence of such interests are known as '**notices**' on the register of title (see 6.2.7.2).

In Form 6.1 you will see that Victor Venn holds his registered freehold estate subject to a registered charge (mortgage) in favour of a bank.

6.2.4 Rights that do not appear on the register: overriding interests

As the system outlined so far suggests, the aim of the title registration system is to ensure that any rights affecting land that can bind a purchaser should be made visible to such a purchaser on inspection of the register. That said, the system also makes provision for certain rights that continue to exist and can bind future owners of the land, despite not being included in an entry on the register. These are collectively known as '**overriding interests**', since they 'override' the provisions of the statute that otherwise would vest title in a registered proprietor free from the burden of any unregistered interest.

There are two lists of such interests in LRA 2002, in Sch. 1 and Sch. 3. Schedule 1 lists interests which override 'first registration', binding an owner of unregistered land even after he or she has been registered as proprietor of her estate and regardless of whether those interests have been entered on the register at the time of registration (see 6.3.4).

Schedule 3 lists interests which override a registered disposition of a registered estate. This means that they bind a purchaser from a registered proprietor, who has dealt with land that is already registered, even though they did not appear on the register when the land was bought (see 6.5.5 and 6.5.6). While there is a good deal of overlap between the two lists, there are also some important differences.

To understand why the Act provides two separate lists, it is important to understand the different functions of the rules governing first registration and the rules governing registered dispositions. Purchasers in this position will have relied on the information already on the register in making their decision to purchase the land. More pressing questions, therefore, arise when we are deciding which unregistered encumbrances should bind the property in the hands of purchasers of registered land.

By contrast, registering a disposition of a registered estate (either its transfer or the creation of a registrable interest granted out of it) does actually give the new owner a legal title which he or she did not have before, because legal title passes only on registration. Such purchasers *will* have relied on the information already on the register in making their to purchase the land. More pressing questions, therefore, arise when we are deciding which unregistered encumbrances should bind the property in the hands of purchasers.

6.2.5 The 'principles of title registration'

As we have seen, the aim of the title registration system is to protect purchasers of land from the need to make cumbersome and expensive inquiries into title and third-party rights. As the Law Commission puts it in its Report preceding the 2002 Act, the register is meant to be 'a complete and accurate reflection of the state of the title of the land at any given time, so that it is possible to investigate title to land on line, with the absolute minimum of additional enquiries and inspections'. From the perspective of protecting purchasers and reducing the costs of conveyancing, an ideal system would be one where the purchaser never needs to look either *behind* the register, to the transaction that explains why some entry now on the register was made, or *beyond* the register, to some fact that does not appear on the register at all.

However, in reality, this is not how the system works. There are situations where the entry now on the register may have become inaccurate, necessitating some inquiry into the facts behind registration. For example, the term of a registered lease may have expired, the registered proprietor may have died, or a fraudster could have used forged documents to be entered on the register as proprietor of some estate, even though there have been no actual dealings with the previous registered proprietor. In handling these situations, the law must decide if the register can be changed and how far persons who have suffered loss as a result of the inaccuracy can be compensated. The detail of the law on these questions is considered at 6.7.

There are also situations where a third party may have acquired rights in the land by some informal mechanism that has not led to any entry at all on the register (for example, by proprietary estoppel or constructive or resulting trust). In these situations, the law has to decide whether to protect the rights of the unregistered interest-holder, requiring a purchaser to look beyond the register to discover such rights, or whether to prefer the purchaser at the expense of the right-holder. The detail of the law in this area is considered at 6.5 and 6.6.

In all these situations, a balance has to be struck between the goal of protecting purchasers and facilitating cheap and quick conveyancing and other goals, such as deterring fraud, protecting the rights of owners, and protecting third parties who have informally acquired rights in the land. A former Chief Land Registrar, Theodore Ruoff, set out three principles that he considered should be used to strike this balance; these are frequently invoked in the literature surrounding title registration, and you may want to consider, as you go through the chapter, how far the detail of the system meets the demands of each principle. The principles are as follows:

1. *The mirror principle.* The register relating to a title should reflect accurately and completely, and beyond all argument, the facts that are material to that title from the perspective of a purchaser.
2. *The curtain principle.* The register should be the sole and definitive source of information for proposing purchasers but should *not* reveal information that would prejudice the position of a purchaser. These might include the terms of a trust, for example, as knowledge of such terms would then place the purchaser in a position where he or she had to determine if the transaction by the registered proprietor was or was not a breach of the trust.
3. *The insurance principle.* If the information on the register is defective or inaccurate in some way, then the person or persons suffering loss as a consequence of the error must be able to claim compensation.

6.2.6 Reform

6.2.6.1 Privatisation

On 24 March 2016, the Department for Business, Innovation and Skills (as it then was) issued a consultation on moving the operations of the Land Registry to the private sector. This concentrated on how such a privatisation might be carried out and any safeguards that would be necessary and not on whether there should be privatisation at all. This is despite the fact that a consultation in 2014, about the possibility of privatisation, produced responses overwhelmingly objecting to privatisation. In 2016, once again there was widespread objection to the idea. A public petition against this move was signed by over 300,000 members of the public. Indeed, even the Competition and Markets Authority objected to privatisation, on the basis that it would produce a dangerous monopoly. Those objecting also pointed out that currently the Land Registry produces a small profit.

Issues that were raised included:

1. the impact of any privatisation on the guarantee of accuracy of the register, which is currently backed by a state guarantee without any cap on liability;
2. concerns about security of personal data if the register is in non-Government hands; and
3. possible increases in costs of using the service.

In its Autumn Statement 2016 the Government announced that the Land Registry would remain in the public sector. The Chancellor of the Exchequer said:

> Following consultation, the government has decided that HM Land Registry should focus on becoming a more digital data-driven registration business, and to do this will remain in the public sector. Modernisation will maximise the value of HM Land Registry to the economy, and should be completed without a need for significant Exchequer investment.

This does not, of course, prevent the subject of privatisation being raised again in the future.

6.2.6.2 Law Commission recommendations

In July 2018, the Law Commission issued *Updating the Land Registration Act 2002*, Law Com No. 380 (which may be found online at https://www.lawcom.gov.uk/project/updating-the-land-registration-act-2002/). This is a very thorough analysis of the benefits of, and difficulties arising from, the LRA 2002 and contains recommendations for further reform, many of which have been accepted in principle by the Government. The report is well worth reading in full, as it summarises the current operation of the system in great detail and captures the policy concerns driving land registration reform in depth. We will touch on some of the recommendations in the report in this chapter, where they are relevant.

6.2.7 Types of entry on the register

As we have seen, there are three types of entry that can be made on the register. A person can be registered as proprietor of an estate, and the estate described in the property register. In addition, two further types of entry can be used to protect third-party rights affecting that estate. These are notices, entered in the charges register, and restrictions, entered in the proprietorship register. In addition, Land Registry maintains a separate register of cautions against first registration, which records alleged interests in unregistered land that must be investigated when the land comes to be registered.

6.2.7.1 Entry as registered proprietor

A person may be newly entered as proprietor of a registered estate in a number of situations. The first occasion will obviously be on first registration of the estate (see 6.3). When an estate is already registered, various types of dealings with that estate will trigger a requirement to update the register (see 6.4), causing a new person to be entered as proprietor or causing the property register to be amended to add new interests.

The legal effect of registration with title absolute (see 6.3.3.2) is to vest the legal estate in the registered proprietor. This outcome seems obvious in situations where registration is simply a formality requirement, the final step in completing an otherwise valid gift, sale, or other disposition. However, the legal effect of this type of registration goes beyond permitting title to pass once the formality of registration has been completed. It also works to *validate* the title of the new registered proprietor, even in situations where the transaction underlying the registration is flawed. This is the effect of s. 58 of the LRA 2002, which provides:

> (1) If, on the entry of a person in the register as the proprietor of a legal estate, the legal estate would not otherwise be vested in him, it shall be deemed to be vested in him as a result of the registration.
>
> (2) Subsection (1) does not apply where the entry is made in pursuance of a registrable disposition in relation to which some other registration requirement remains to be met.

This is known as the 'dispositive effect' of title registration, sometimes referred to as 'statutory magic'. It applies in situations where, but for registration, the new registered proprietor would not be entitled to the legal estate. Examples may include clerical errors leading to mistaken registration of the wrong person, or situations where Land Registry is misled by fraud into believing that the registered estate has been transferred to a new owner, even though the actual registered proprietor is completely unaware of the supposed transfer.

The effect is not as radical as it may seem, because the statute makes provision for the register to be altered on the application of a person affected by such an entry (see 6.7). Thus, for example, if s. 58 transfers the legal estate from the lawful registered proprietor to a fraudster who has relied on a forgery, the former registered proprietor may apply to have the fraudster's name deleted from the register and his or her own name restored. However, it is only by making such an application that the registered proprietor can get the estate back. The effect of s. 58 is that until such an application is successfully made, the estate remains genuinely vested in the new registered proprietor and this can have important consequences for third parties who deal with the new registered proprietor in the intervening period.

It is worth noting that this effect will only occur, as s. 58(2) provides, once *all* the requirements of registration are met (see 6.4.3). For example, creating an easement for the benefit of registered land requires both an entry in the property register of the benefited land and an entry in the charges register of the burdened land. Once both entries have been made, s. 58(1) kicks in and the registered proprietor of the benefited estate will have the benefit of the easement that now appears on the property register, even if the supposed grant of an easement underlying the registration is forged or void for some other reason.

6.2.7.2 Notices

The LRA 2002 defines a notice as 'an entry in the register in respect of the burden of an interest affecting a registered estate or charge' (s. 32(1)). The fact that an interest is the subject of a notice does not necessarily mean that the interest is valid (unlike registration under s. 58). However, if the interest *is* valid, the notice ensures both that it binds any purchaser for valuable consideration (s. 32(3)), and that he knows about it before he takes the estate. If there is no notice on the register reflecting an interest in registered land, a purchaser will escape being bound by that interest unless it happens to be an 'overriding interest' (see 6.2.4).

It is also a formality requirement for the creation of certain interests affecting registered land, such as easements, that they be entered on the charges register of the burdened land as notices; if this is not done, they will not arise at law but only in equity (see 6.4.2). For these reasons, it is important for a person who has or is acquiring an interest in registered land to ensure that a notice reflecting that interest appears on the register.

Agreed and unilateral notices

An *agreed notice* will be entered only with the agreement of the registered proprietor. Such a notice will be appropriate where the proprietor has created the interest, as for example in the case of a new restrictive covenant which burdens the land, or an equitable mortgage created to secure a loan.

A *unilateral notice* may be entered without the consent of the registered proprietor, possibly in circumstances in which the proprietor denies the existence of the interest. The proprietor must be informed of the entry of a unilateral notice and has the right to apply for its cancellation. If the person lodging the notice maintains the claim, there are procedures for determining its validity. If no objection is made, the notice protects the interest as adequately as an agreed notice.

Interests which cannot be protected by notice
There are certain interests which cannot be protected by notice (s. 33). The aim of keeping these off the register is to avoid cluttering up the register with information that may confuse or prejudice the position of a purchaser (see the *curtain principle*, 6.2.5). They include:

- interests under a trust of land or SLA settlement (for which see Chapters 14 and 15), which should be protected by a restriction;
- a lease for not more than three years, the title to which is not required to be registered (see 6.3.1.2 and 6.4.1); and
- a restrictive covenant between lessor and lessee, so far as it relates to the demised premises.

6.2.7.3 Restrictions
LRA 2002, s. 41(1) defines a restriction as:

> an entry in the register regulating the circumstances in which a disposition of a registered estate . . . may be the subject of an entry in the register.

In other words, it is a restriction on dealings with the registered estate. The restriction does *not* tell the purchaser anything about the underlying right that justifies the restriction, but only the conditions that must be complied with for a given transaction to be registered. A restriction is not an alternative to a notice: ss. 42(2) and 46(2) provide that a restriction must not be used to protect an interest which is capable of protection by notice.

Some restrictions may impose a complete ban on any dealing, as for example in the case where the registered proprietor has become a bankrupt. Others may impose conditions that must be met before any dealing will be registered. For example, a restriction can be used to ensure that any necessary consent is obtained for a transaction, or to require that capital money from a dealing with trust property is paid to two trustees or a trust corporation (i.e., so that requirements for overreaching the beneficiaries' interests are met (see 5.5.2.1)). In the latter case, the entry of such a restriction will also have the effect of indicating to a prospective purchaser that the property is subject to a trust but will protect the purchaser from knowledge of the terms of the particular trust.

Circumstances in which a restriction must or may be entered
There are certain circumstances in which the registrar *must* enter a restriction. For example, where two or more persons are registered as proprietor (with the result that a statutory trust arises—see 14.1.2.3), the registrar must enter a restriction designed to secure that interests capable of being overreached on the disposition of the estate are overreached (s. 44(1)). The registrar must also comply with any court order requiring him to enter a restriction.

Restrictions may also be entered on the application of the registered proprietor or of any person with a sufficient interest in the making of the entry, with or without the proprietor's consent. Where the application is without consent, the proprietor must be notified of it, and there is a process for dealing with any objections to the application.

Effect of entering a restriction
Where a restriction is entered in the register, the default rule is that no entry in respect of a disposition to which the restriction applies may be made in the register otherwise

than in accordance with its terms (s. 41(1)). The registrar does have the power, under s. 41(2), to make an order disapplying or modifying a restriction so that an entry that is inconsistent with its terms can be made. However, this can only be done in response to an application by a person who has an interest in the restriction, in the view of the registrar.

Effect of not entering a restriction
LRA 2002, s. 26 provides that:

> (1) Subject to subsection (2), a person's right to exercise owner's powers in relation to a registered estate or charge is to be taken to be free from any limitation affecting the validity of a disposition.
> (2) Subsection (1) does not apply to a limitation—
> (a) reflected by an entry in the register . . .

It has been argued that the effect of s. 26 is that the presence or absence of a restriction on the register might make a significant difference to the overreaching of beneficial interests under trusts of the registered title. The argument is that, by virtue of s. 26(1), limits on the powers of trustees of land can have no effect on a disponee from trustees *unless* those limits are reflected by an entry on the register (as required by s. 26(2)(a)). It follows that, in the absence of a restriction on the register, any disposition by a registered proprietor of registered land will **'overreach'** any beneficial interests affecting the title (see 5.5.2), whether or not the requirements for 'statutory overreaching' are met (see 5.5.2.1). This interpretation of s. 26 was upheld, *obiter*, by Lewison LJ in *Mortgage Express v Lambert* [2017] Ch 93 and by the High Court in *Kensington Mortgage Co Ltd v Mallon* [2019] EWHC 2512, although it was doubted by the High Court in *Ali v Dinc* [2020] EWHC 3055. Although the law on this point remains unclear, it seems that the absence of a restriction on the register might potentially make beneficiaries under trusts more vulnerable to overreaching than they otherwise would be and strengthens the case for entering such restrictions wherever possible.

6.2.7.4 **Cautions against first registration**

Finally, where a person claims to have an interest against an estate in unregistered land, that person may register a 'caution against first registration' (LRA 2002, ss. 15–22). These cautions are recorded on a separate register from the main title register, known as the 'cautions register'; each entry on the caution register has a title number, a description of the legal estate to which the caution relates, and a statement of the cautioner's claims in relation to that estate. Entries on this register must be dealt with during first registration (see 6.3.3.1), as part of the process of investigating title.

6.2.8 **Disputes concerning entries on the register**

Individuals apply to HM Land Registry to deal with matters such as first registration of unregistered land (see 6.3); registration of dispositions of unregistered land (see 6.4); entry of protective notices and restrictions; and alteration of entries in the register (see 6.7). Before the LRA 2002, any disputed application which could not be resolved by agreement between the parties was determined by a senior member of registry staff. In its review of the system prior to the LRA 2002, the Law Commission noted concerns that it might appear that decisions were being taken about property rights without any opportunity for the aggrieved party to have his case heard by an 'independent and impartial' tribunal, as required by Art. 6 of the Human Rights Convention (see the Report, para. 16.1).

As a result, the LRA 2002 (ss. 107–13 and Sch. 9) created a new office, originally called the **Adjudicator to the Land Registry**. Despite its name, the office was completely independent of the registry and there was provision for appeal on specified grounds from the Adjudicator to the High Court. It is through reports of these appeals that you are likely to come across the work of the Adjudicator; see, for example, the account later in this chapter (see 6.7.3) of the Court of Appeal's decision in *Baxter v Mannion* [2011] 1 WLR 1594.

The jurisdiction of the Adjudicator to the Land Registry has now been transferred to the new Property Chamber, which started work within the First-Tier Tribunal on 1 July 2013. The Chamber is divided into three sections, one of which deals with Land Registry cases and is headed by the Principal Judge for Land Registration, an office previously held by the former Adjudicator to the Land Registry.

In its 2018 Report, the Law Commission recommended an expansion of the jurisdiction of the Tribunal, giving it the power to determine boundaries, to determine how equities by estoppel should be satisfied, and to declare the extent of beneficial interests in land. These are issues that often arise in the course of disputed applications for entries on the register, and that the Tribunal currently does not have the power to determine. As of March 2021, these recommendations have been accepted in principle by the Government.

6.3 First registration of an unregistered estate

First registration is the process by which estates currently outside the registered title system are brought within it. The LRA 2002 makes provision for both compulsory and voluntary first registration.

6.3.1 Voluntary first registration

Section 3 of the LRA 2002 sets out the circumstances in which a person entitled to a registrable estate can voluntarily apply to the Land Registry to be registered as proprietor of that estate. All freehold estates, and certain leasehold estates, are capable of being registered under this process. In addition, certain non-possessory interests in land may be independently registered even though the estate in land that they affect is not on the register.

6.3.1.1 Leases with more than seven years to run

Under s. 3(3) of the LRA 2002, leases with an unexpired term of less than seven years are generally not registrable. This is because the registration of title to very short leases is administratively burdensome, given the amount of work involved for the registry in first registering them and then removing them from the register when they expire.

6.3.1.2 Leases which are registrable irrespective of term ('short registrable leases')

Section 3(4) permits the registration of a lease in which the right to possession is discontinuous. An example might include a timeshare arrangement for holiday accommodation, by which tenants are given rights of possession for specified periods each year. In a lease of this type, the fact that the tenant is not necessarily in possession of the land means that there is a real risk that a purchaser might buy the landlord's estate without discovering that it is subject to a lease and thus there is a real benefit to registration.

6.3.1.3 Registrable interests in land

The LRA 2002 also provides (in s. 3(1)) for the voluntary registration of title to the following legal interests:

- a rentcharge;
- a franchise; and
- a profit à prendre in gross.

The nature of a rentcharge has already been explained (see 2.5.1). Briefly, the nature of the other two rights is as follows.

(1) *A franchise* is a privilege which the Crown has allowed a subject to exercise. It gives the holder some particular right, for example to collect tolls or to hold a fair or market. Although medieval in origin, these can still be valuable property rights, but until the LRA 2002 came into force there was no way of registering title to them.

(2) *A profit à prendre* (see 24.3) is the right to take something (wood, gravel, fish, etc.) from another's land. The right may be '**appurtenant**', that is, attached to another piece of land and used for its benefit, or it can be 'in gross', which means that it exists for the personal benefit of its owner and is not attached to any land. Appurtenant profits may be included in the property register of title to the land which they benefit (see 6.2.3.1), but until the new Act there was no provision for the registration of title to profits in gross, although they can be of considerable value.

6.3.2 Compulsory first registration

Under s. 4 of the LRA 2002, certain dealings with an unregistered legal estate operate as 'triggers' for compulsory first registration, creating an obligation to apply for first registration of that estate (the 'requirement of registration'). These are:

1. The *transfer* of:
   - an unregistered freehold estate; or
   - an unregistered leasehold estate with more than seven years to run at date of transfer.
2. The *grant* of a lease (out of an unregistered estate) which:
   - is for more than seven years; or
   - is to take effect more than three months from date of grant
3. The creation of a first legal mortgage protected by deposit of title deeds over:
   - an unregistered freehold estate; or
   - an unregistered leasehold estate with more than seven years to run at the date on which the mortgage is created.

It is important to note that the requirement of registration may be triggered by these dealings even when they are not for value. The obligation to apply for first registration now arises where the transfer is made:

1. for value;
2. as a gift;
3. on a court order;
4. by assent, i.e., a form of conveyance used by personal representatives to transfer an estate to those entitled under the deceased's will or intestacy; or to the person next entitled under an SLA settlement (see Chapter 15);
5. by trustees partitioning trust land between beneficiaries;
6. to a newly appointed trustee.

6.3.2.1 Who has to apply for first registration?

Where the obligation to register arises on *the transfer or grant of an estate*, it is the new owner (e.g., the transferee of a freehold estate or the tenant of a new lease) who must make the application.

Where the triggering event is *the grant of a mortgage*, the application must be made by the mortgagor (the owner of the mortgaged estate), although the mortgagee (the lender) is entitled to apply for registration if the mortgagor fails to do so (s. 6(6) and r. 21 of LRR 2003).

6.3.2.2 Reform

In its 2018 Report, the Law Commission recommended two new triggers for compulsory first registration. These are:

1. The grant or transfer of rights to *mines and minerals*, which can currently be voluntarily registered but do not trigger compulsory first registration. This recommendation has now been rejected by the Government, subject to further consultation.
2. The *grant* or *transfer* of a *discontinuous lease* which can currently be voluntarily registered but does not trigger compulsory first registration (see 6.3.2). This recommendation has been accepted in principle by the Government.

6.3.2.3 What happens if application for first registration is not made?

In order to compel estate owners to apply for registration, s. 7(1) provides that if the application for registration is not made within two months of the triggering event (s. 6(4)) the transfer or grant of an estate or a mortgage will become void. Where the event in question was a transfer, the estate will revert to the transferor, who will hold it on trust for the transferee. Where the triggering event was the grant of a lease or a mortgage, the disposition will take effect as an estate contract, i.e., as a contract to grant the lease or mortgage (for the legal effect of such a contract, see 4.6.1). In all these circumstances, the person who failed to apply for registration will have to bear the costs of repeating the transaction and might also run into other problems.

6.3.2.4 2 Trant Way

You may remember that we left Barbara Bell at the end of Chapter 5, having just completed her purchase of the unregistered freehold estate in 2 Trant Way. This, of course, was an event which under s. 4 triggered the requirement to apply for first registration of her title, and she must do this within two months of the conveyance to her. If she does not do so in time, the conveyance will become void, and the estate will revert to Victoria Ventnor. She will hold it on trust for Barbara, who in due course will have to meet all the expenses involved in re-conveying it to her. There is also a risk that Victoria Ventnor, having reacquired the legal estate, might grant new rights to third parties, such as easements and covenants. These could potentially bind Barbara when she does finally obtain first registration of her title and so pose a problem for her (6.3.4.1).

6.3.3 The process of first registration

In this section we see what happens when Barbara Bell applies for first registration of title to her freehold estate in 2 Trant Way.

6.3.3.1 Investigation of title by the registry

One of the purposes of registration is to provide any prospective purchaser with reliable information about the estate being purchased. The purchaser will want to be sure that the registered owner owns the property offered for sale and that it is free from any encumbrances (third-party rights) other than those which have already been disclosed. In dealing with Barbara's application for registration, therefore, the registry will need to satisfy itself that she does indeed own the estate she wants to register and that as many third-party rights as possible are recorded on the register. It will do this by repeating the process her conveyancer undertook on the purchase of the property, scrutinising the title deeds and the results of searches and enquiries, all of which must be submitted with the application for registration. Indeed, the registry may be even more careful than a purchaser or a professional adviser would be, for the title once registered is guaranteed and, if the registry makes a mistake, it may have to compensate anyone who suffers a loss as a result (see 6.7). If necessary, the registry will raise queries with Barbara, and may even require her to make additional searches and enquiries to clarify uncertain points. It is important that she respond to these queries in a timely fashion, as a failure to respond might mean that the registry cancels her application (for an example of a case where this happened, see *Sainsbury's Supermarkets Ltd v Olympia Homes Ltd* [2006] 1 P&CR 17, discussed at 5.4.5.2).

6.3.3.2 Classes of title

The quality of the titles investigated may vary considerably: one title may prove to be entirely sound; another might be based only on the rights a squatter has established by possession of the land for some years (see Chapter 7); and another may suffer from some technical defect. Accordingly, the registration system provides for seven classes of title, three for freehold estates and four for leasehold estates (LRA 2002, ss. 9 and 10 respectively) as follows:

- classes of *freehold* title:
  - absolute freehold;
  - qualified freehold;
  - possessory freehold;
- classes of *leasehold* title:
  - absolute leasehold;
  - good leasehold;
  - qualified leasehold;
  - possessory leasehold.

Where an inferior class of title is awarded on first registration, the registrar may later upgrade it to a better class (s. 62); we will cover the circumstances in which this may be done as we consider each class of title.

Absolute freehold title

Absolute freehold title is the best class of title known to the registered land system. Section 9(2) provides that absolute title to a freehold estate may be registered where the title to the estate is such:

> as a willing buyer could properly be advised by a competent professional adviser to accept.

However, this does not mean that the registrar has to demand a perfect title, for s. 9(3) provides that in deciding to register an applicant with absolute freehold title, the registrar may disregard a defect in title if the registrar considers that it will not cause the title to be disturbed. The fact that the registrar may award an absolute title in these circumstances means that registration can have a curative effect and prevent future purchasers concerning themselves with technical, but unimportant, defects. This is one reason why owners sometimes choose to register their estates voluntarily.

Absolute leasehold title

As compared with the purchaser of a freehold estate, the purchaser of a leasehold estate has an extra dimension to consider when checking that the vendor can transfer the estate promised. Like the purchaser of the freehold estate, it is necessary to check the devolution of the title to the leasehold estate and that it has been correctly passed from one owner to another until it reached the vendor. However, in addition, the purchaser may want to be reassured that the landlord who granted the lease was actually entitled to do so. Thus the purchaser really needs to investigate the landlord's title to the superior estate in order to check that he or she had a good title to that estate and therefore had the right to grant the lease which the purchaser intends to buy.

Under s. 10(2), absolute leasehold title is granted only if the registrar is satisfied with both the lease *and* the superior title from which it is derived. Thus, if X, a freehold owner, grants a lease to Y, Y can be registered with absolute leasehold title only if the registrar is satisfied that the lease is good and that X's freehold title is good. This should cause no difficulty where X's estate is already registered or where Y has a contractual right to investigate the freehold title. If Y does not have this right, however, and the lease has been granted out of an unregistered estate, Y may well be unable to satisfy the registrar as to the landlord's title, and in such a case the leasehold estate could be registered only with good leasehold title.

It is also important to note that registration with an absolute leasehold title does *not* guarantee that the title register provides all the information about the lease that could be relevant to the purchaser. As was held in the recent case of *R (HCP (Hendon) Ltd) v Chief Land Registrar* [2020] EWHC 1278, it is still essential for the purchaser to inspect the actual lease that underpins the leasehold title (of which Land Registry will have a copy) in order to discover what land exactly is included in the lease and the content of any leasehold covenants (see Chapter 11).

Good leasehold title

This class of title is granted when the registrar is satisfied that the lease itself is good but where there is no evidence of the quality of the superior title (s. 10(3)). In such cases the registry cannot be absolutely sure that the lease was validly granted by a person with power to grant such an estate. Apart from the fact that the superior title cannot be guaranteed, good leasehold title has the same effect as registration with absolute leasehold title (s. 12(6)).

Good leasehold title may be upgraded to absolute title if the registrar is satisfied as to the superior title (s. 62(2))—as, for example, would become the case if title to that superior estate were registered at a later date.

Qualified freehold and leasehold titles

Qualified titles are extremely rare. Such a title is granted:

> if the registrar is of the opinion that the person's title to the estate has been established only for a limited period or subject to certain reservations which cannot be disregarded . . . (s. 9(4)).

The details of the defect will be entered on the register. Such a situation might arise if a purchaser of an estate in unregistered land had decided to take the risk of not investigating the title to the property as thoroughly as is usual. As we have seen in Chapter 5, it is normal to search back to a deed which is at least 15 years old. If the purchaser had accepted a deed made only 10 years ago and later applied for first registration, it is likely that he or she would be registered only with qualified title.

Qualified title may be upgraded to absolute title at any time if the registrar 'is satisfied as to the title to the estate' (s. 62(1))—for example, where the defect which led to the original classification is no longer a matter of concern.

Possessory freehold and leasehold titles

Possessory titles are less good than absolute titles but fortunately are fairly rare, occurring in only about 1 per cent of cases. Such titles are registered in cases in which the ownership of the estate is evidenced purely by the fact that the estate owner is in possession of the land, or is in receipt of the rents and profits from the occupant (s. 9(5)). This situation might arise if the deeds to the property had been lost, or if the estate owner had acquired rights merely through long use of the land (title by adverse possession—see Chapter 7).

In time, any competing claims to the estate would be extinguished by the Limitation Act 1980 (see Chapter 7) and so the possessory title would become quite safe from disruption. To take account of this, the system provides that, provided the registered proprietor is in possession of the land, the possessory title may be upgraded to absolute title after it has been registered for 12 years. It is also possible for possessory title to be upgraded to absolute title at any time if the registrar is satisfied as to the title to the estate (s. 62(1))—for example, if missing title deeds are found.

6.3.3.3 Interests affecting the registered estate

The Act imposes a duty on those applying for first registration or registration of a later disposition to inform the registrar of any 'overriding interests' that they know of (s. 71 and LRR 2003, rr. 28 and 57), while s. 37 provides that rights which would otherwise take effect as overriding interests may instead be protected by notice (see 6.2.4 and 6.2.7.2). These provisions are in accordance with the general policy of reducing the number of interests which can bind a disponee for valuable consideration without appearing on the register. It also benefits the person entitled to such an interest to have it protected in this way. As we shall see, several overriding interests depend upon fact-sensitive matters such as actual occupation or recent use by the person entitled, or on the state of the disponee's knowledge and the enquiries he or she has made. It is therefore much safer to protect such interests by notice.

6.3.4 Effect of first registration

Under s. 11 of the LRA 2002, the legal effect of first registration differs based on the class of title that has been awarded. Most applicants for first registration will be granted absolute freehold title and absolute or good leasehold title, and so we will consider the effect of these forms of registration in some detail here.

6.3.4.1 Effect of registration with absolute freehold title

Under s. 11(2)–(3), the effect of registration of a freehold estate with absolute title is to vest that freehold estate in the registered proprietor, together with all interests which benefit the estate (e.g., an easement, such as a right of way or a right of drainage which the estate enjoys over neighbouring land). In addition, s. 11(4)–(5) provides that a proprietor registered with absolute title takes the estate free from all interests that burden the estate, except for:

- interests noted on the register;
- overriding interests;
- squatters' rights of which the proprietor has notice; and
- rights of beneficiaries (where the registered proprietor holds the land as a trustee).

(1) *Interests noted on the register* On first registration, the registrar will aim to record on the estate's register of title as many as possible of the encumbrances which burden it. Depending on the nature of the right, this will be done either by entering a notice in the charges register or by putting a restriction in the proprietorship register. For example, on first registration of property subject to a legal mortgage, the registrar will register the mortgagee's title to the mortgage by entering it in the charges register of the mortgaged estate. Once this is done, the mortgage is known as a 'registered charge' and continues to bind the estate by virtue of its entry on the register.

(2) *Overriding interests* Schedule 1 lists certain interests that 'override' first registration or, in other words, will bind the estate although not entered on the register. The list includes:

- most leases for not more than seven years;
- interests of persons in actual occupation;
- legal easements and profits; and
- a range of legal and statutory rights.

The first of these, short leases, will not be entered on the register because they are of limited duration and, for the time being at least, the registry does not want to clutter the register with them. However, the other interests listed in Sch. 1 will be entered on the register if the registry is aware of them, and s. 71(a) and LRR 2003, r. 28 impose a duty on the applicant to inform the registry of any such interests of which the applicant is aware. Thus Sch. 1 really acts as a safety-net, to preserve those interests which bind the unregistered estate but are not identified and recorded on first registration.

(3) *Squatters' rights of which the proprietor has notice* The rules about adverse possession and squatters' rights are covered in Chapter 7. All you need to know at this stage is that if the owner of unregistered land loses possession of it to another person, the right to recover the land from the dispossessor may be extinguished after 12 years by the Limitation Act 1980. Once this has happened, the dispossessor (usually called an 'adverse possessor' or 'squatter') is regarded as the legal owner. Once ownership is acquired in this way, the squatter can go out of possession and still retain ownership.

Under the old Act (LRA 1925, s. 70(1)(f)), the rights of the adverse possessor were turned into rights under a trust of the registered title of the dispossessed owner. These rights were overriding and bound the estate on first registration and on any subsequent disposition. This meant that if a purchaser had bought the land and secured first registration without being aware of the squatter's rights, the purchaser could lose title to the estate if the squatter subsequently sought registration. One of the changes made by LRA 2002, Sch. 1 is to reduce the overriding effect of the squatter's rights, so that if the squatter is not in actual occupation of the property the rights do not override first registration, unless, under s. 11(4)(c), the proprietor has notice of them.

(4) **Beneficiaries' rights** A trustee who is registered as first proprietor is bound by those rights of beneficiaries under the trust of which the trustee has notice, even if they are not protected by entry on the register. The trustee cannot be freed from obligations to the beneficiaries merely by securing a registration which does not mention their interests.

It is also worth noting that the new registered proprietor might also end up being affected by rights that ought to have been registered at the time of her registration but were not, because of a mistake by Land Registry. For example, in *Sainsbury's Supermarkets Ltd v Olympia Homes Ltd* [2006] 1 P&CR 17, Olympia Homes Ltd was registered as proprietor of a legal estate in circumstances where an option to purchase the land, belonging to Sainsbury's, ought to have been put on the register but was not. (For the complex facts of this case, see 5.4.5.3). Sainsbury's then brought an action seeking to have the register altered to correct a mistake and was successful in this application (see 6.7). Where an existing interest in land has lost priority under s. 11 purely because of some error or omission by Land Registry at the time of registration, there is always the possibility of such alteration and so the new registered proprietor cannot simply rely on s. 11 to get rid of interests that would have bound her in the absence of such an error.

6.3.4.2 Effect of registration with absolute leasehold title

Registration with absolute leasehold title vests the leasehold estate in the owner subject to the encumbrances described in the case of absolute freehold title and, in addition, to all express and implied covenants, obligations, and liabilities imposed by the lease or incidental to the land (s. 12(3)–(5)).

The result of the registration is that the registrar will guarantee that the lease was effectively granted and will also show on the leasehold title any covenants which bind the freehold estate and which therefore bind the lease as well as the superior title (see Chapter 25).

6.3.4.3 Effect of registration with other classes of title

Registration with other classes of freehold and leasehold title occurs relatively seldomly, and has the following effects:

1. *Qualified title*
   Section 11(6) provides that registration with qualified title has the same effect as registration with absolute title:

   > except that it does not affect the enforcement of any estate, right or interest which appears from the register to be excepted from the effect of registration.

   Thus, if an estate is registered with qualified title because the applicant did not investigate title for the full statutory period, any later purchaser will run the risk of finding that the estate is subject to some defect which was not discovered on the earlier investigation of title.

2. *Possessory title*
   Section 11(7) provides that registration with qualified title has the same effect as registration with absolute title, except that it is subject to *any* adverse pre-registration estates, rights, or interests (not just those that appear from the register to be excepted from the effect of registration). The danger of having a title which is possessory only is that someone may appear who has a better claim to the estate (for example, the original owner who has been dispossessed by the squatter).
3. *Good leasehold title*
   Good leasehold title has the same effect as registration with absolute leasehold title (s. 12(6)), except that the superior title is not guaranteed.

6.3.5 First registration of title to the freehold estate in 2 Trant Way

If all goes well with the registrar's investigation, Barbara Bell will be registered with absolute title which, as we have already seen, means that she will hold the freehold estate free of all encumbrances except for:

- registered charges (which will include any mortgage she has granted to secure money borrowed to pay the purchase price);
- interests which are protected by a notice or restriction on the register;
- any right which overrides first registration under Sch. 1; and
- any interest acquired under the Limitation Act 1980 of which she has notice.

On completion of the registration process, Barbara Bell will receive a 'title information document', which consists of a cover sheet around official copies of the individual register and title plan. The copy of her register will be similar in appearance to that shown in Form 6.1, although of course with different details about the property. Note, however, that it is the register entry and not the title information document that is the record that should be relied on as proof of title.

6.4 Dealings with a registered estate: formalities

Once title to 2 Trant Way has been registered, it will become subject to statutory rules about how future dealings with the estate must be conducted if they are to have legal effect. If Barbara ever wishes to sell the house, to let it, to mortgage it, or to grant easements or certain other rights over it, she must not only use a deed (to satisfy LPA 1925, s. 52(1)) but must also comply with other requirements which are set out in LRA 2002, s. 27.

6.4.1 Dispositions which must be completed by registration

Section 27(2) sets out a list of 'registrable dispositions': that is, the dealings with a registered estate which must be completed by registration. They include:

- a transfer of the registered estate;
- the grant of a lease for more than seven years;
- the grant of certain leases irrespective of length, including discontinuous leases (see 6.3.1.2) and leases that do not take immediate effect in possession (see 9.3.1.1 for such leases);

- the express creation of interests under LPA 1925, s. 1(2)(a), (b), and (e), that is:
  - a legal easement or profit,
  - a legal rentcharge,
  - a right of entry in respect of a legal lease or a legal rentcharge;
- the grant of a legal charge (i.e., a mortgage).

The Act refers to persons taking under any of these registrable dispositions as **'disponees'**. This means the recipient of a disposition and it is a useful alternative to more specific terms (such as 'transferee', 'grantee', 'lessee', and 'mortgagee').

6.4.2 What happens if a registrable disposition is not completed by registration?

Section 27(1) provides that the dispositions listed at 6.4.1 do not take effect at law until registration requirements are met. These dispositions will not, therefore, create or transfer legal estates or interests until they are registered. This is a very important addition to the basic requirement for the use of a deed noted earlier (see 2.6.4.1), and it is essential to remember that, *where title is registered, you need a deed* and *registration to create or transfer a legal estate or interest*. An unregistered disposition may instead take effect in equity—that is, it will give the transferee an equitable right to the estate or will create interests such as equitable easements or mortgages (see 4.6.1).

6.4.3 Completing a disposition by registration: registration requirements

Schedule 2 of the LRA 2002 sets out the specific requirements that must be met for the different kinds of registrable dispositions to be completed. For a transfer of a registered estate, the requirement is simple: the transferee must be entered as the registered proprietor of that estate, replacing the previous registered proprietor. For a grant of a new registrable estate or interest—such as a lease, mortgage, rentcharge, or easement—two requirements must be met.

(1) *The grantee must be registered as owner of the new estate or interest.* In some cases, this involves opening a new individual register, and this is what will be done in the case of a lease or a rentcharge.

By contrast, easements and legal charges (i.e., legal mortgages) do not require their own separate registers, but are registered by entry on the title of a relevant estate:

- an *easement* is registered by adding it to the register of the estate which it *benefits*, where it will appear in the property register (see 6.2.3.1); and
- a *legal charge* is registered by entering it in the charges register of the estate which it *binds* (see 6.2.3.3), and is then known as a 'registered charge' (an example is shown in Form 6.1).

(2) *The estate or interest must be entered on the register of the estate which it burdens.* In general, this is done by putting a notice in the charges register of the title to the burdened estate. Thus, a notice of a lease will be put on the register of the landlord's estate, and a notice of an easement will be put on the register of the estate over which it is to be exercised. However, no separate notice of a registered charge is needed, because the actual registration of the charge is made by entry on the register of the burdened property.

6.5 Dealings with a registered estate: protection of purchasers

Having followed Barbara Bell's progress in buying a house with unregistered title and applying for first registration, we now need to turn our attention to the other house-hunters, Mr and Mrs Armstrong, who are planning to buy 1 Trant Way (see 3.1.1). The title to this property is registered (see 3.2.3.2), and like any other home-buyer, the Armstrongs will want to check two things about the property. They need to make sure that the vendor, Victor Venn, owns the estate he is offering to sell, and that it is free from any encumbrances other than those which have already been disclosed to them.

6.5.1 Does the vendor have the best title to the estate?

As we can see from the specimen register shown in Form 6.1 Victor Venn is the registered proprietor of the freehold estate in 1 Trant Way and is registered with absolute title. This is the best title available (see 6.3.4.1), and the Armstrongs can have reasonable confidence in buying the property, although they need to be aware that the system does provide for subsequent alteration of the register for various purposes, including the correction of mistakes (see 6.7).

The Armstrongs, or more likely their professional adviser, will need to obtain a copy of the register of title for 1 Trant Way or view it online. At some stage they will also need to make an official search of the register, but this is all that needs to be done to satisfy themselves that Victor does truly own the estate. There is no need to investigate title in the old way, described in Chapter 5 in respect to the purchase of unregistered land, which involved checking through past dealings with the property as shown by old title deeds. The register is conclusive evidence of the fact that Victor owns the freehold estate in No. 1.

6.5.2 Are there any encumbrances which bind the property?

Inspection of the register of title will tell the Armstrongs about the charge on the property (see Form 6.1). If the title to an estate is less than absolute (i.e., qualified or possessory) the purchaser will also be subject in addition to any exceptions appearing on the register (see 6.3.4.3); and where the estate is a leasehold one the purchaser will also be bound by obligations imposed by the lease but not noted on the register (s. 92(2)(a)(iii) and (b)). However, as Victor Venn is registered with absolute title to a freehold estate, so these additional encumbrances would not apply to the Armstrongs.

However, there could be other third-party rights not noted on the register, possibly including some that have come into existence since Victor acquired the property. How might the Armstrongs find out about these, and would they be bound by them if they bought the house? The answer to these questions is to be found in the rules governing the priority of interests in registered land.

6.5.3 Priorities: the general rule

Section 28 of the Act sets out the *general rule* governing competing interests in registered land, in the following words:

> (1) Except as provided by sections 29 and 30, the priority of an interest affecting a registered estate or charge is not affected by a disposition of the estate or charge.

(2) It makes no difference for the purposes of this section whether the interest or disposition is registered.

This means that each interest retains the priority it had at its date of creation. This priority does not depend upon registration, and it is not affected by any later dealing with the property. Thus under s. 28 anyone who acquires an interest in registered land takes it subject to all previous interests, and in turn will have priority over any further interests which are subsequently created—unless the exceptions in ss. 29 and 30 apply. In other words, 'the first in time prevails'. In fact, however, the s. 29 and s. 30 exceptions to s. 28 are so broad (see 6.5.4) that the principal function of s. 28 is to regulate the priority of rights only against those who have not given value and as between those who have acquired merely equitable, rather than legal, interests in the land.

For example, s. 28 will govern the priority of a person who acquires a purely equitable interest in registered land, such as a creditor who lends money on the security of an equitable mortgage or a tenant who has no formal lease but holds under an equitable one (see 2.6.4.2). Questions about the relative priority of such equitable interests can arise where, for example, the value of property subject to two equitable mortgages is not sufficient to repay both debts in full, or where an equitable mortgagee seeks to take possession of the property already occupied by a tenant under an equitable lease. In such cases, each newly-created interest is subject to all prior interests and will have priority over all those created at a future date.

The new general rule was considered for the first time by the High Court in *Halifax plc and Bank of Scotland v Curry Popeck* [2008] EWHC 1692 (Ch). The court was asked to determine the relative priorities of two equitable interests, one arising from a charging order imposed to enforce a judgment debt, and the other an equity arising from proprietary estoppel (which, under LRA 2002, s. 116 is now recognised as capable of binding successors in title—see 19.6.1.1). Both interests arose as a result of fraudulent mortgage transactions by a third party. The facts of the case are complicated but you simply need to note that the court applied s. 28, adding (at paras. 24–5) that the new provision removed the traditional qualification that priorities might be changed if the holder of the prior interest was at fault. As a result, the court held that the first interest to be created, the equity arising from estoppel, had priority over the later one.

6.5.4 Exceptions to s. 28: the 'special priority rule'

Section 29(1) provides:

> If a registrable disposition of a registered estate is made for valuable consideration, completion of the disposition by registration has the effect of postponing to the interest under the disposition any interest affecting the estate immediately before the disposition whose priority is not protected at the time of registration.

The Armstrongs' proposed purchase appears to satisfy the requirements of s. 29(1):

- the transfer of the registered estate in No. 1 would be 'a registrable disposition' (see 6.4.1);
- it is being made for 'valuable consideration' (the purchase price); and
- it will be 'completed by registration' when the Armstrongs get themselves registered as the new owners (see 6.4.3).

As a result, they will escape being bound by *all* previous interests, as they would otherwise be under s. 28. Instead, they will only be bound by those interests 'whose priority is protected at the time of registration'.

Section 29(2) then lists the categories of interests whose priority is protected. In summary, they are:

- registered charges (i.e., legal mortgages, which appear in the charges section of the register of title);
- interests protected by notice on the register (which also appear in the charges section of the register of title); and
- overriding interests, listed in Sch. 3.

6.5.4.1 The need for a registrable disposition

The provisions of s. 29(1) apply not only to a person who buys the registered estate, but also to those who take under any other registrable disposition for valuable consideration and complete the disposition by registration. Registrable dispositions are defined in s. 27 (see 6.4.1) and include the creation and transfer of all legal estates and interests in land, with the exception of certain short leases of less than seven years.

However, this does not mean that tenants under short leases do not have the protection of s. 29. Section 29(4) provides that, 'where the grant of a leasehold estate does not involve a registrable disposition', the section has effect *as if* the grant involved a registrable disposition. Thus, for example, a tenant who takes a six-year lease of registered land, for value, will gain priority over earlier interests in that land under s. 29(1) even though his or her lease will not itself be registered.

6.5.4.2 The need for a valuable consideration

A disposition of a registered estate that is not made for valuable consideration will not fall within the terms of s. 29 and as a result the disponee will take the title subject to all prior interests in accordance with s. 28. Thus, for example, the protection of s. 29 will not apply where the estate is transferred as a gift or under the will or intestacy of the previous owner. Completion of the disposition by registering the new owner will vest the title to the legal estate in that person but subject to all earlier encumbrances.

6.5.4.3 The need for completion by registration

The protection of s. 29(1) only kicks in when the disponee of a registered estate satisfies the requirements of registration of estate or interest in the land (see 6.4.2). As explained in 6.4.2, registrable dispositions do not create or transfer legal estates or interests until they are registered. Until then, the disponee has only an equitable interest in the property which, under s. 28, is subject to all earlier interests.

6.5.5 Exceptions to the 'special priority rule': overriding interests other than actual occupation

There are two categories of interests that bind disponees for valuable consideration, like the Armstrongs, under the terms of s. 29:

- interests protected by entry of a notice in the register; and
- interests that override a registered disposition.

As has been explained (at 6.2.7.2), all encumbrances which are not excluded by s. 33 may be protected by entry of a notice on the register. If the holder of such an interest has not entered it on the register as a notice, the purchaser of the registered estate for valuable consideration will take free of it unless it is overriding.

The interests that will override a registered disposition, binding a purchaser of the registered estate even though they do not appear on the register, are now to be found in Sch. 3 to the LRA 2002. They include:

- certain short leases (Sch. 3, para. 1);
- rights of persons in actual occupation of the land (Sch. 3, para. 2);
- certain easements and profits (Sch. 3, para. 3);
- certain miscellaneous interests, some of which remain overriding (Sch. 3, paras. 4–9) and some of which ceased to be overriding from 13 October 2013 (Sch. 3, paras. 10–14).

Of these, the rights of persons in actual occupation of the land is the broadest and has attracted a considerable body of case law. In this section, we will first look at the other categories of overriding interest and then go on to consider the rights of those in actual occupation in 6.5.6.

6.5.5.1 Short leases (Sch. 3, para. 1)

Schedule 3, para. 1 shortened the length of a lease which can be overriding from 'not exceeding 21 years' to 'not exceeding seven years'. This change is a consequence of the reduction in the minimum length of a registrable lease. Under LRA 1925, the title to leases for more than 21 years was compulsorily registrable, while leases over seven years could be registered but did not have to be. Now registration requirements apply to leases for more than seven years. Thus, para. 1 provides that leases which are not independently registrable (and therefore noted on the landlord's title) may take effect as overriding interests binding the landlord's estate.

Short registrable leases (see 6.3.1.2) are specifically excluded by para. 1 from the category of short leases which override registered dispositions.

This category of overriding interests is not expressly limited to legal leases, but it was held in *City Permanent Building Society v Miller* [1952] Ch 840 that the use of the word 'granted' in the equivalent provision of LRA 1925, s. 70(1)(k) excluded equitable leases, because they are not the subject of a grant. It seems that this interpretation also applies to the terms of para. 1.

6.5.5.2 Certain easements and profits (Sch. 3, para. 3)

Under LRA 1925, s. 70(1)(a) all legal easements and profits were overriding. In addition, it was held in *Celsteel Ltd v Alton House Holdings Ltd* [1985] 1 WLR 204 (based on a provision of the Land Registration Rules 1925), that certain equitable easements could be overriding. This very wide category of overriding interests was considerably reduced by the LRA 2002, but in order to understand how this is done, it is necessary to consider the way in which legal easements and profits are created.

These interests may be created expressly by granting another person a right over one's land, or by reserving a right over land which one is transferring to another person. In certain cases, where there is no express creation, the law may *imply* a grant or **reservation**, so that easements and profits can be created without any express words appearing in the documents relating to the burdened land. In addition, these rights can be created by a long period of use (known as prescription), again without any documentary evidence of their existence. You will find a full account of how easements and profits are created in Chapter 24, but at this point we need to focus on the status of these rights as overriding interests.

Schedule 3, para. 3, read in conjunction with other provisions of the Act, sets out the following conditions which must be met if an easement or profit is to take effect as an overriding interest, and in doing so greatly reduced this category.

(i) *The interest must be legal*
Paragraph 3 states at the outset that it applies only to *legal* easements and profits, so equitable interests of this kind cannot be overriding.

(ii) *The interest must arise otherwise than by express creation*
The rule that expressly created easements and profits cannot be overriding is not expressly stated in the LRA 2002, but results from a combination of the following provisions (most of which we have already noted at 6.4):

- in order to create a *legal* interest, an express grant or reservation of an easement must be completed by registration (s. 27(2));
- when the grant or reservation is registered, a notice is automatically put on the register of the burdened land (Sch. 2);
- rights protected by notice cannot operate as overriding interests (s. 29(3));
- if not completed by registration, an express grant or reservation creates only an *equitable* interest.

The effect of these provisions in respect of expressly created easements and profits is that:

- *those completed by registration* cannot (and need not) be overriding, because they are protected by a notice; and
- *those not completed by registration* cannot be overriding because they are only *equitable* (and para. 3 is limited to *legal* easements).

This means that the only easements or profits which can be overriding under para. 3 are those which arise from implied grant or reservation, by prescription, or as a result of the operation of LPA 1925, s. 62—for which see LRA 2002, s. 27(7), and 24.8 in Chapter 24. Such interests represent a danger to the purchaser; as overriding interests, they will not be entered on the register and yet may be very difficult to discover from an inspection of the property (as for example in the case of underground drains). To guard against this, para. 3(1)–(2) provides that a legal easement or profit arising otherwise than by express grant or reservation will be overriding only if it satisfies one of the following conditions:

(a) it is registered under the Commons Act 2006 (or its forerunner, the Commons Registration Act 1965) as, for example, might be the case with a profit of grazing; or

(b) the purchaser actually knew of its existence; or

(c) the purchaser did not know of it but it would have been obvious on a reasonably careful inspection of the land over which it is exercised; or

(d) even if it does not fall within (a) to (c), it has been exercised within the period of one year ending with the date of the disposition in question.

Thus, an easement or profit will be overriding only if:

- it is legal; *and*
- it has arisen by:
    - implied grant or reservation; or
    - by prescription; or
    - under LPA 1925, s. 62; *and*

- it satisfies one of the following requirements:
    - registration under the Commons Act; or
    - existence known by purchaser; or
    - obvious on reasonably careful inspection; or
    - used in the previous year.

6.5.5.3 Certain miscellaneous interests (Sch. 3, paras. 4–9)

Paragraphs 4 to 9 of Sch. 3 list various rights which were overriding under LRA 1925, s. 70(1) and which continue to override registered dispositions under the LRA 2002. They include customary and public rights, local land charges, and rights in connection with mines and minerals. You may remember from Chapter 3 that local land charges are recorded in their own register (see 3.3.2.1), and since these charges will override a registered disposition, that register should be checked by anyone buying registered land.

6.5.5.4 Miscellaneous interests that are no longer overriding (Sch. 3, paras. 10–14)

Paragraphs 10 to 14 of Sch. 3 list a range of interests described as 'miscellaneous', which include a franchise, a manorial right, and rights in respect of embankments, sea walls, and the repair of a church chancel. These were all overriding under LRA 1925, but gave rise to concern because they might be difficult to discover and could be burdensome. Their overriding status could not be abolished at once, because there were fears that this might contravene Article 1 of the First Protocol to the European Convention on Human Rights (by depriving the owner of a property right without due warning and an opportunity to protect their rights by registration). However, under s. 117 they ceased to be overriding from 13 October 2013 (that is, 10 years after the LRA 2002 came into force).

It is important to realise that these rights did not cease to exist in 2013: they merely lost their overriding status but continue to bind the estate if protected in the appropriate way. If an interest was not protected by the deadline, it would continue to bind the current owner of the title, because the owner would have taken subject to it when it was overriding, and thus there may still be time to make a protective entry. If this is not done, the interest will be lost at the next disposition for value.

6.5.6 Exceptions to the 'special priority rule': interests of those in actual occupation

Under Sch. 3, para. 2 certain interests of persons in actual occupation at the time of a disposition override that disposition and will bind the purchaser, despite the fact that they are not recorded on the register of title. The statute provides overriding status for:

> An interest belonging at the time of the disposition to a person in actual occupation, so far as relating to land of which he is in actual occupation, except for—
>
> (a) an interest under a settlement under the Settled Land Act 1925;
>
> (b) an interest of a person of whom inquiry was made before the disposition and who failed to disclose the right when he could reasonably have been expected to do so;
>
> (c) an interest—
>
>   (i) which belongs to a person whose occupation would not have been obvious on a reasonably careful inspection of the land at the time of the disposition, and
>
>   (ii) of which the person to whom the disposition is made does not have actual knowledge at that time;
>
> (d) [a future lease which is compulsorily registrable [see 6.3.1.2]] which has not taken effect in possession at the time of the disposition.

This provision is the successor of s. 70(1)(g) of the LRA 1925, which also conferred overriding status on person in actual occupation. There is a significant body of case law interpreting s. 70(1)(g) of the LRA 1925 and the courts have accepted that these cases provide authoritative guidance to the judicial interpretation of Sch. 3, para. 3 to the 2002 Act.

Thompson v Foy [2010] 1 P&CR 16 was the first decision in which Sch. 3, para. 3 was considered. In that case, T, the claimant, had inherited the family home when her husband died. She transferred the title to the house to her daughter, Mrs Foy ('F'), so that F could raise a large loan, secured by a mortgage of the property. It was agreed that the money so borrowed would be shared between mother and daughter. The property was mortgaged to The Mortgage Business ('TMB'), but F did not pay any of the money she raised over to her mother. T then claimed that her daughter had exercised 'undue influence' over her in persuading her to transfer the title, and that therefore she had a right in equity to set the transfer aside (for more information about the equitable doctrine of undue influence, see Chapter 23).

Lewison J found on the facts that F had not exercised undue influence over her mother. In consequence, T had no right to set the transactions aside and the issue concerning overriding interests did not arise. However, in case he was wrong in finding that there was no undue influence, the judge examined the arguments put forward in support of the claim to an overriding interest and indicated what his decision would have been on that issue (paras. 118–31). This section of his judgment does not, of course, form part of the ratio of the case, but the judge's observations on the circumstances in which actual occupation will be protective and the meaning of actual occupation where the interest-holder is temporarily absent from the land have been influential in the subsequent case law. In *Link Lending Ltd v Bustard* [2010] EWCA Civ 424 at para. 31, Mummery LJ described Lewison J's summary of the law in *Thompson v Foy* as 'accurate and helpful', and at para. 27 emphasised that:

> the construction of the earlier equivalent provisions by the House of Lords is binding on this court.

6.5.6.1 Interests that can override under para. 2

It should be noted that para. 2 does not create any new right to occupy the property, but rather gives overriding effect to any interest already belonging to the occupier, which has not been protected by an entry on the register.

Thus if the occupier is a tenant under a lease which gives the tenant an option to purchase the reversion (i.e., the right to 'buy out' his landlord's interest) the option may well be held to be overriding and enforceable against a purchaser of the landlord's estate, although there is no mention of it on the register of that estate (*Webb v Pollmount* [1966] Ch 584). Similarly, where a beneficiary under a trust is in actual occupation of the land, her rights have been held to be overriding and binding on the purchaser (see, for example, *Hodgson v Marks* [1971] Ch 892, and *Williams & Glyn's Bank Ltd v Boland* [1981] AC 487, discussed at 6.5.6.2).

However, the occupier's rights will be overriding only if they amount to a recognised interest in land that exists at the time of the disposition. As a result, when dealing with a problem concerning this class of overriding interests, you should begin by identifying the recognised property interest which the person is seeking to enforce and whether the right still exists, before going on to consider whether that person's rights are protected by occupation.

The occupier must have a proprietary interest in the land
This issue of the need to have rights capable of being protected by occupation was the foundation of the decision of the Supreme Court in an important recent case: *Southern Pacific Mortgages Ltd v Scott* [2015] AC 385 (see 4.6.1 for the details). Mrs Scott had sold her registered title to a third party who had agreed to let it back to her and let her live there for life. The purchase was funded by Southern Pacific Ltd, who were granted a charge by legal mortgage that was executed on the same day as the conveyance of the estate to the purchaser. It was clear that Mrs Scott was in occupation of the property at all relevant times. The question was whether she had rights that were of such a nature that they could be binding on Southern. As discussed in Chapter 4, the court concluded that Mrs Scott could only get *proprietary* rights over the land after the conveyance to the purchaser had been completed, since before then the purchaser only had an estate contract and so could only grant rights personally binding on her. However, because Southern Pacific Ltd had funded the mortgage, its charge arose at exactly the same moment in time as the purchaser's legal estate (following the earlier House of Lords decision in *Abbey National Building Society v Cann* [1991] 1 AC 56, discussed at 6.5.6.3). Since she gained her proprietary rights only after registration of the charge, she could not take priority over it and her actual occupation was irrelevant. This decision effectively left Mrs Scott without any protection, other than the very limited rights provided by the short lease that had been granted to her, which had come to an end. This emphasises the importance of the need to establish that there are rights in land capable of protection before considering in any detail whether there is actual occupation of the land.

The occupier's interest in the land must not have been overreached
As explained in Chapter 5 (5.5.2) the process known as 'overreaching' enables land subject to certain trusts to be sold free of the beneficiaries' interests, provided that the purchase price is paid to at least two trustees, who hold the money upon trust for the beneficiaries in place of the land. In *Boland*, the mortgage was granted and the money received by a sole registered proprietor, so that overreaching could not operate. However, in *City of London Building Society v Flegg* [1988] AC 54 mortgage money was paid to two legal owners who held the estate upon trust for themselves and the Fleggs (see 5.5.2.1 for the facts of this case). In these circumstances, the House of Lords held that the interests of the beneficiaries under the trust were overreached by that payment, even though they had been in occupation of the premises at the date of the charge. Since overreaching terminated the beneficiaries' equitable interest in the land, transferring it to the proceeds of sale, there was no 'interest in the land' to be protected by their actual occupation; the mortgagee was therefore able to sell the property free of their interests. The beneficiaries were left only with the right to sue the legal owners, their trustees, for breach of trust, since the legal owners had used the mortgage money for their own purposes.

The occupier must not have expressly or impliedly authorised the grant to the purchaser
In order to avoid the risk to purchasers, particularly mortgagees, posed by Sch. 3, para. 2, conveyancers have developed a practice of requiring anyone in occupation of the property, in addition to the mortgagor, to sign documents agreeing that any rights they may have will be subordinated to those of the mortgagee (such consent may, however, sometimes be set aside on the grounds of 'undue influence' (23.7.2)).

Even where there is no express agreement, it is possible that the occupier's rights will not prevail against a mortgagee. In *Paddington Building Society v Mendelsohn* (1985) 50 P&CR 244 the competition was between a beneficiary under a resulting trust, who was in occupation of the property and who had known that a mortgage advance would be needed in order to purchase the property, and the building society which had granted that mortgage. In such a case the Court of Appeal held that the occupier had impliedly consented to the creation of the mortgage since the possibility of acquiring an interest in the property was dependent upon that mortgage. Thus, the occupier could not claim an interest having priority to the rights of the building society. As a result of this decision the *Boland* and *Flegg* issues will usually arise now only in cases of second mortgages or sales.

More recently this approach was adopted by Lewison J in *Thompson v Foy* [2010] 1 P&CR 16, as the last stage in the hypothetical decision which he was outlining—that is, *if* T had the right to set the transaction aside for undue influence and *if* that right was overriding by virtue of her actual occupation, could the mortgagee take free of the right if it could show that she had agreed to the mortgage? The judge considered the decision in *Paddington Building Society v Mendelsohn* and held that on the evidence T knew about the mortgage and wanted it to happen. If he had been required to decide the point, he would have held therefore that T had agreed to the mortgage and could not enforce her right against the mortgagee.

The interest must relate to land of which the person is in actual occupation

Schedule 3, para. 3, grants overriding status to an interest belonging to a person in actual occupation 'so far as relating to land of which he is in actual occupation'. This requirement is designed to deal with situations such as that in *Ferrishurst Ltd v Wallcite Ltd* [1999] Ch 355, in which an occupier's overriding interest under LRA 1925, s. 70(1)(g) was held to extend to a part of the land comprised in the registered title which the person did not in fact occupy.

The occupier's interest in the land must not be specifically excluded by statute

You should also note that, in some instances, persons have rights and are in occupation but nonetheless their rights will not override because of a specific statutory exclusion. Thus, the right of a spouse or civil partner to occupy the home (see 5.4.2.5 and 21.3.3.1) is not capable of overriding and must be protected by means of an entry on the register if it is to bind a purchaser (Family Law Act 1996, s. 31(10)). As a result, it is necessary to check that there is no specific exclusion for the right that you are considering.

Two further exclusions are added by LRA 2002, Sch. 3, para. 2.

1. *Interests under a SLA settlement (para. 2(a))*
   The rights of a beneficiary under such a settlement must be protected by the entry of a restriction on the register (see 6.2.7.3), even if the beneficiary is in actual occupation.

2. *Future leases which are compulsorily registrable (unless they have already taken effect in possession at the time of the disposition) (para. 2(d))*
   We have already seen that leases of this type cannot be overriding under Sch. 3, para. 1, and para. 2(d) ensures that they do not become overriding by virtue of actual occupation.

6.5.6.2 **What is meant by 'actual occupation'?**

Judges have regularly emphasised that the question of whether a party is in 'actual occupation' is essentially a question of fact.

In the words of Lord Wilberforce in *Williams & Glyn's Bank Ltd v Boland* [1981] AC 487 at pp. 504–5, 'it is the fact of occupation that matters' and what is required is 'physical presence on the land and not some entitlement in the law'. The courts have been reluctant to suggest any test for what is 'essentially a question of fact', Lord Oliver pointing out in *Abbey National Building Society v Cann* [1991] 1 AC 56 at p. 93 that:

> ... 'occupation' is a concept which may have different connotations according to the nature and purpose of the property which is claimed to be occupied. It does not necessarily, I think, involve the personal presence of the person claiming to occupy. A caretaker or the representative of a company can occupy, I should have thought, on behalf of his employer. On the other hand, it does, in my judgment, involve some degree of permanence and continuity, which would rule out mere fleeting presence.

This is well illustrated by the decision of the Court of Appeal in *Lloyds Bank Plc v Rosset* [1989] 1 Ch 350. The Rossets had been allowed by their vendor to start work on renovating the property they wished to buy before contracts were exchanged. This involved the daily presence of builders on the site and regular visits to the property by the wife, who carried out a good deal of the work herself. At completion, the property was mortgaged to the bank by the husband (the sole transferee). Later, he defaulted on repayments and the bank sought possession of the property. The wife claimed that she had a beneficial interest in the house, arising from a common intention trust (see 17.5.1.2) and that this bound the bank as an overriding interest by virtue of her 'actual occupation' at the date of the mortgage. She succeeded in this claim at first instance, and the bank appealed against this decision.

In the Court of Appeal, Nicholls LJ said (at p. 377F) that he could see no reason:

> why a semi-derelict house . . . should not be capable of actual occupation whilst the works proceeded and before anyone has started to live in the building.

The court considered (Mustill LJ dissenting) that the physical presence of the wife when working on the property amounted to the necessary 'actual occupation' and in addition expressed the view that the presence of the builders as employees or agents of the Rossets was sufficient to establish the couple's occupation. Accordingly, the court rejected the bank's appeal and confirmed the lower court's decision.

This decision of the Court of Appeal was reversed by the House of Lords in *Lloyds Bank Plc v Rosset* [1991] 1 AC 107, on the grounds that the wife had not established her claim to a beneficial interest. As a result, their Lordships expressed no view on the question of her actual occupation, and the Court of Appeal's decision on this point has recently been relied upon by the High Court in considering very similar facts in *Thomas v Clydesdale Bank PLC* [2010] EWHC 2755 (see 6.5.6.5 and, for more on *Rosset*, 18.2.5).

A more extreme example of occupation of an uninhabitable site is provided by the Court of Appeal decision in *Malory Enterprises Ltd v Cheshire Homes (UK) Ltd* [2002] Ch 216, in which the land in question was awaiting development by Malory Enterprises Ltd, which claimed an overriding interest in respect of it under s. 70(1)(g). In the words of Arden LJ (at para. 80):

> If a site is uninhabitable . . . residence is not required, but there must be some physical presence, with some degree of permanence and continuity.

Here the company had maintained fences around the land, taken other physical measures to exclude trespassers, and had stored goods on the property. The court considered that this amounted to 'actual occupation'.

Under the terms of Sch. 3, para. 2, if occupation is established but the interest claimed was not known to the purchaser, the question will then arise of whether the occupation was 'obvious on a reasonably careful inspection of the land'. It seems possible that in a situation similar to that in *Malory Enterprises Ltd v Cheshire Homes (UK) Ltd* the court might hold that there was occupation but that it was not obvious, but this must of course be very much a decision on the facts.

What happens if the occupier is temporarily absent from the property?

The effect of temporary, possibly involuntary, absence was considered by the Court of Appeal in *Link Lending Ltd v Bustard* [2010] EWCA Civ 424. Ms Bustard ('B'), who suffered from a serious psychiatric condition, had been tricked into transferring the registered title of her house to a Mrs Hussain ('H'). The transfer was stated to be by way of sale, but B received no payment for the property. She remained in the house but, unknown to her, H mortgaged the property to Link Lending ('Link'), and later defaulted on the repayments. On Link's application for a possession order, it was claimed on B's behalf that she had a right to set the transfer aside, due to her lack of legal capacity, and that her right to do so bound the bank, because she had been in actual occupation at the date of the mortgage.

At trial, Link conceded that B had a right against H to set aside the transfer, but denied that she had been in actual occupation at the relevant date. At the time the mortgage was granted, B had been absent from the property for over a year, having been taken into residential psychiatric care under the Mental Health Act 1983. Nevertheless, the judge, guiding himself by *Thompson v Foy*, held that in the particular circumstances of the case B had 'a continuing intention to occupy' and so had remained in actual occupation of the property.

On Link's appeal to the Court of Appeal, Mummery LJ emphasised the fundamental point that the existence of actual occupation is essentially a question of fact, to be decided on the basis of evidence before the court. The factors to be weighed by a judge in a case such as this included (at para. 27):

> The degree of permanence and continuity of presence of the person concerned, the intentions and wishes of that person, the length of absence from the property and the reason for it and the nature of the property and personal circumstances of the person . . .

In this case, the facts were not all one way. Some of them supported B's claim, while others were against her. On balance, however, the trial judge had found that she was in actual occupation. The matters on which he had relied included: the presence of B's furniture and belongings in the house; the fact that she continued to regard the house as her home and was determined to return to live there; her brief but regular accompanied visits to the property; the payment on her behalf of bills relating to the property; and the fact that there had been no final decision by the medical authorities that she would never be able to live there again.

The Court of Appeal considered that the judge's finding that B was in actual occupation was a conclusion which he could properly draw from these circumstances, and accordingly dismissed Link's appeal.

One question remains: at what point in a period of prolonged absence will actual occupation come to an end? In *Stockholm Finance Ltd v Garden Holdings Inc* [1995] LTL

(26 October 1995), the court rejected a claim based on actual occupation in which the claimant had been absent from the property for a full year, Robert Walker J stating that:

> ... there must come a point at which a person's absence from his house is so prolonged that the notion of his continuing to be in actual occupation of it becomes insupportable ...

This decision was considered by the Court of Appeal in *Bustard*, but distinguished on its facts (see paras. 21 and 30).

Is the presence of possessions in the property enough to establish actual occupation?

It seems that in cases of temporary absence the presence of the occupier's belongings on the premises may help to establish actual occupation. However, it was held in *Strand Securities v Caswell* [1965] Ch 958 that the presence of belongings alone, without any previous occupation and intention to return, was not enough to establish occupation for the purposes of LRA 1925, s. 70(1)(g).

In this case, Caswell had a lease of a London flat. The lease, being for just over 39 years, fell into the category of leases which at that time could be registered, but did not have to be (a rule which was changed by LRA 1986). In fact, the title to the lease was not registered, nor was it protected by an entry on the landlord's title. Caswell kept some furniture and clothing at the flat but did not live there. The property was occupied by his stepdaughter who had moved in with his permission, because her marriage had broken down. She occupied the flat as a licensee (that is, as someone with permission—a licence—to do so). As we shall see in Chapter 23, the protection given by the law to licensees can vary considerably according to the individual's circumstances, but the general principle, which applied in this case, is that this type of agreement can be terminated at any time and gives the licensee no rights in the land.

The landlord sold its interest in the property, and the new owner claimed that the lease was void against it because the lease was neither registered nor protected by an entry against the landlord's estate. The Court of Appeal rejected the tenant's claim that he had an overriding interest under LRA 1925, s. 70(1)(g), because, although he had rights in the property (the lease), he was not in occupation. The presence of his belongings at the property did not amount to occupation for the purposes of the Act.

The stepdaughter was of course in occupation of the property, but unfortunately, she did not have any recognised property interest in the flat and so had no rights which were capable of being overriding. The court did suggest that, had she occupied the flat at the request of her stepfather and in order to look after it for him, he might have been regarded as being in occupation through an agent. However, on the facts as they stood, she was clearly there because of her own needs and not as Mr Caswell's agent. The House of Lords has since confirmed, in *obiter dicta* in *Abbey National Building Society v Cann* [1991] 1 AC 56, that occupation through an agent is possible.

The question whether the presence of belongings in the property was sufficient to establish actual occupation under Sch. 3, para. 2 was also considered in *Thompson v Foy* [2010] 1 P&CR 16 as a further point which would have arisen *if* T had been able to establish undue influence. By the time the mortgage was registered, T was no longer living in the property. Although her possessions remained there, and she went back at intervals to collect them, she had formed the intention of never returning to live there. The judge accepted that the presence of possessions in a property could establish actual occupation during temporary absence if there was an intention to return, but he considered that the presence of possessions without the intention to return was not enough.

He found therefore that T was not in actual occupation at the date of registration (paras. 130–1), although, as has been noted, he left open the question of whether actual occupation would have assisted her at this stage.

Can several people be in actual occupation of the property at the same time?

In the past, particular difficulties arose when the vendor and the person claiming under s. 70(1)(g) were both living in the property. This issue arose in *Hodgson v Marks* [1971] Ch 892, in which it was held that Mrs Hodgson was to be regarded as being in actual occupation of premises even though she shared the property with the registered proprietor. Mrs Hodgson had been the original owner of the estate and had transferred it to her lodger to hold on trust for herself. When the former lodger sold the property (in breach of his duties as trustee), the purchaser was held to be bound by Mrs Hodgson's rights to the property. Since she was the true beneficial owner of the property, the purchaser was in the position of a trustee and was compelled to convey the legal estate to her. This case illustrates very well the dangers of the s. 70(1)(g) overriding interest, since the purchaser had bought an estate which in reality was worthless.

Similar difficulties concerning shared occupation used to arise in the case of married women living in houses owned by their husbands. They might well have a beneficial interest under a trust, but their presence in the property was attributed to their marital status, and they were not regarded as being in occupation for the purposes of s. 70(1)(g) (*Bird v Syme-Thomson* [1979] 1 WLR 440).

However, a more modern approach to the role of the married woman was adopted by the House of Lords in *Williams & Glyn's Bank Ltd v Boland* [1981] AC 487. This case involved a wife who had acquired an interest in her husband's property by contributing to the purchase price, and so had become a beneficiary under a resulting trust of the land (see 13.2.2). She lived in the property with her husband, who was the sole registered proprietor. Mr Boland mortgaged the property to his bank and used the money raised in his business. Later, when he failed to make his mortgage repayments, the bank sought vacant possession of the premises, so that it could sell the estate in order to repay the loan. Mrs Boland then claimed that she had rights in the property and that, as she had been in occupation of the premises when the mortgage was granted, the bank's rights as mortgagee were subject to her prior beneficial interest. The House of Lords considered that the wife's occupation of the premises could be distinguished from that of her husband, and accordingly upheld Mrs Boland's claim that she had an overriding interest which bound the bank.

As a result of *Hodgson v Marks* and *Williams & Glyn's Bank Ltd v Boland*, it appeared that a purchaser or mortgagee could be bound by the rights of all those occupying the property with the vendor, including any of his relatives. It seemed possible that even children would be included in the category of those in actual occupation: they are certainly capable of having a beneficial interest in the property. However, the Court of Appeal held in *Hypo-Mortgage Services Ltd v Robinson* (1997), *The Times*, 2 January 1997, that a child cannot be a person in actual occupation for the purposes of s. 70(1)(g). The court made it clear that its ruling applied to all minors, not merely to those of 'tender years' (as in the case before it), explaining that children 'had no right of occupation of their own: they were only there as shadows of occupation of their parent'. No thought appears to have been given to minors over the age of 16, who could be married or cohabiting, and who could have acquired an interest in their homes through contribution. For a critical comment on this decision, see [1997] Conv 84.

Can use of an easement amount to actual occupation of the servient land?

In *Chaudhary v Yavuz* [2011] EWCA Civ 1314 the Court of Appeal rejected an argument that use of a right of way across a neighbour's land could amount to actual occupation of that land.

The case concerned two neighbouring properties, No. 35 and No. 37. They were separated by a narrow alleyway, which belonged to No. 35 and originally contained a wooden staircase giving access to the upper floors of that property. In 2006 Chaudhary ('C'), the owner of No. 37, extended his property by building upwards to create two flats, which were to be let to tenants. At his own expense and with the agreement of the current owner of No. 35, Vijay ('V'), C replaced the wooden stairs in the alleyway with metal stairs and a platform which gave access to the upper floors of both buildings. A deed was prepared granting C a right of way over the new structure but was never executed by V. In these circumstances, it would have been sensible for C to protect his interests by entering a notice on V's register of title, but he did not do so. The following year, V sold No. 35 to Yavuz ('Y'). Y regarded C's use of the stairs on his property as trespass and eventually removed that part of the structure which gave access to the upper floor of No. 37. C applied to the court for a declaration of his right of way over the stairs.

The trial judge held that C was entitled to an easement by estoppel, and that use of the right, coupled with the presence of the staircase on Y's land, amounted to 'actual occupation'. The easement was therefore an overriding interest under Sch. 3, para. 3 and enforceable against Y. On Y's appeal, the Court of Appeal reversed the lower court decision, holding that C was not in actual occupation and that therefore his easement was not an overriding interest. Lloyd LJ noted that there was no indication that the staircase was used otherwise than for 'passing and repassing' between the street and the upper floors of the two properties; in his view 'such use does not amount to actual occupation' (para. 31). He also rejected C's argument that the physical presence of the staircase in the alleyway amounted to occupation of the land on which it stood (para. 32). Referring to the principle that things attached to land become part of the land themselves (see briefly 1.8 of this text and in more detail at 26.2.1), he noted that the staircase thus became land, and:

> thus became part of what could be used or occupied. It makes no sense to say that its presence on the land [of Y] was itself occupation of the land by the person who paid for it to be put up in the first place. Occupation must be, or be referable to, personal physical activity by some one or more individuals ... The only such activity in the present case was that of [C's] tenants and their visitors coming to and fro on the staircase and the level area at the top of the stairs. That is use, not occupation.

This suggests that use of an easement cannot, in itself, amount to actual occupation conferring overriding status on that easement (unless it is independently overriding under Sch. 3, para. 3). However, in Chapter 24 there is a discussion of easements of storage and parking, both of which may allow presence on the servient land for considerably longer than the 'passing and repassing' involved in a right of way. It has taken the courts some time to accept that such rights may exist as easements and their extent is still not entirely clear (for details, see 24.2.3.2), but you may like to note the House of Lords' decision in *Moncrieff v Jamieson* [2007] 1 WLR 2620 in which Lord Neuberger expressed the view (at para. 143) that:

> A right can be an easement notwithstanding that the dominant owner effectively enjoys exclusive occupation, on the basis that the servient owner retains possession and control.

If this view prevails in future cases it will certainly be arguable that enjoyment of an equitable easement of storage or parking could amount to 'actual occupation', with the result that the easement would have overriding effect.

6.5.6.3 When must the person be in actual occupation?

There is normally a gap in time between the transfer of the estate and the completion of that transfer by registration at the registry. In dealing with claims to overriding interests based on actual occupation, the courts have had to decide at which point in this process it is necessary for the claimant to be in occupation. Section 70(1)(g) did not specify when the claimant had to be in occupation, and so the matter had to be considered in some detail by the House of Lords in *Abbey National Building Society v Cann* [1991] 1 AC 56. Although the facts involve the purchase of a registered estate, it was the concurrent grant by the purchaser of a mortgage which was said to be subject to the overriding interest. The facts were as follows.

Cann bought a property with the aid of a mortgage from the Abbey National, representing that the house was for his sole occupation, although he intended it to be occupied by his mother and uncle. On the day of the transfer and the creation of the charge, the Canns' furniture arrived at the property some 35 minutes before the completion of the transaction by execution of the deeds and payment of the vendor. At that point there were also removal men on the premises moving in items on the mother's behalf. The charge was not completed by registration until a month later, by which time Cann's mother and uncle were both in occupation of the premises. The mother claimed she had an equitable interest in the property, and, when Cann defaulted on the mortgage payments, she asserted that her rights had priority to those of the Society under s. 70(1)(g).

The House of Lords concluded that Mrs Cann's equitable interest could not have been first in time because her son could only have granted property rights to her after the deed of transfer, by which time the Society's charge had already taken effect in equity (see 4.6.1 on this aspect of the case). However, they also considered the question whether, if she had been first in time, her actual occupation at the date of registration would have given her priority and, if not, whether she was in actual occupation at the date of conclusion. They took the view that the purchaser is bound by most overriding interests in existence at the date of registration. However, there were difficulties in holding that a person who went into occupation between transfer and registration could acquire an overriding interest under s. 70(1)(g), because that section clearly contemplated that the purchaser would make enquiries of any person in occupation, and the proper time for making such enquiries is before the transfer. As a result, the House of Lords took the view that in order to succeed under s. 70(1)(g), Mrs Cann would have needed to show that she was in actual occupation at the date of the transfer. Any rights she might have would then be capable of being overriding interests, and, if those rights were still in existence at the date of registration, they would bind the purchaser.

Applying this to the facts of the case, the House of Lords held that the preparatory work of moving in furniture did not constitute actual occupation, and that accordingly Mrs Cann was not in occupation at the time of transfer, when the charge to the society was created.

Schedule 3, para. 2 defines the overriding interest as '[a]n interest belonging *at the time of the disposition* to a person in actual occupation' (emphasis added) but gives no guide as to whether the disposition occurs at the time of the grant or of the subsequent completion by registration. This point was considered by Lewison J in *Thompson v Foy* [2010] 1 P&CR 16, when indicating how he would have decided the case *if* Mrs Thompson ('T'), the claimant, had established the existence of undue influence. The distinction would have been of significance because the judge found as a fact that T had been in actual occupation of the property on the date at which a mortgage was granted but had given up occupation by the date of its registration.

Lewison J's conclusion on the question of the relevant date for occupation (at para. 121) was that:

> If actual occupation must exist at one date only, then in my judgment the date of disposition [i.e., the grant] is the relevant date.

His reasons for this view were:

> First, s. 27(2)(f) identifies the disposition as the grant of a legal charge, not its completion by registration. Second, the language of s. 29(1) contemplates that the time of the disposition and the time of registration may be different . . . Third, Sch. 3 para. 2(c) contemplates an inspection at the time of disposition. This must mean an inspection at the date when the legal documents are executed and the money is released.

However, the judge left open the question of whether there must be actual occupation at the date of registration as well as at the date of disposition. His own opinion was that the wording of Sch. 3, para. 2 indicated that occupation at both dates was required, but he noted that the leading texts of Ruoff & Roper and Gray & Gray took the contrary view, and he left the matter for consideration in some later case (see paras. 122–6). However, in summarising the facts in *Link Lending Ltd v Bustard* [2010] EWCA Civ 424, at para. 3 (see 6.5.6.2), Mummery LJ described the date on which the relevant mortgage was *registered* as being 'the key date'.

6.5.6.4 If asked about the interest, the person to whom it belongs must not have failed to disclose it 'when he could reasonably have been expected to do so' (para. 2(b))

This requirement is similar to that in LRA 1925, s. 70(1)(g) ('save where inquiry is made of such person and the rights are not revealed'), although the new version suggests that there could be some circumstances in which failure to disclose might be 'reasonable'. It is thus slightly less draconian than the earlier wording, under which non-disclosure automatically deprived the right of its overriding effect. The new wording gives rise to the question as to when non-disclosure would be reasonable. Would it be reasonable, for example, where a beneficiary under a resulting trust is unaware that, due to contribution to the purchase price, he or she has a beneficial interest in the property?

6.5.6.5 The occupation must have been obvious on a reasonably careful inspection of the land *or* the disponee must have had actual knowledge of the interest (para. 2(c))

In fact, para. 2(c) states these two requirements in the negative (i.e., occupation must not be obvious and interest must not be known to the disponee). Both conditions must be fulfilled if the interest is *not* to take effect as an overriding interest. However, it is easier to follow if rephrased in positive terms, and to see that satisfying either of them allows the interest to override the disposition. Do note, however, that it is the *occupation* which must be obvious, and the *interest* which must be known.

Thus, to summarise: an interest which satisfies the other conditions of para. 2 will override a disposition if:

1. the disponee actually knew about the interest, even if the occupation was not obvious on a reasonably careful inspection of the land; or
2. the occupation was obvious on such an inspection, even if the disponee did not know about the interest.

This means that provided the occupation is discoverable, the disponee may still be bound by an interest that is not discovered. To avoid this, it is essential that any persons seen to be in occupation should be asked whether they have any interests in the property, and in fact doing so has been standard practice since the decision in *Williams & Glyn's Bank Ltd v Boland* [1981] AC 487.

The two requirements derived from para. 2(c) were considered by the High Court in *Thomas v Clydesdale Bank PLC* [2010] EWHC 2755 (QB).

Clydesdale Bank PLC ('the bank') had obtained a county court order for possession of the family home owned by B, the former partner of Ms Thomas ('T'). T had claimed that she had a beneficial interest in the property, arising from a common intention constructive trust (see 17.5.1.2), and that this interest bound the bank because she had been in actual occupation of the property at the date of the mortgage. T had not attended the trial, and judgment was given against her in her absence. Her application to set aside the order was refused, and she appealed to the High Court. In order to succeed, T had to satisfy the court that 'she had a reasonable prospect of success at the trial'.

The mortgage had been granted after B had completed the purchase of the property, but before the couple moved into the house. At this time, major reconstruction work was being carried out, and T's claim of actual occupation was based on the presence of workmen on the site and her regular visits to the property. The court considered that on these facts T had reasonable prospects of establishing actual occupation. However, the bank claimed that even if there was actual occupation, T could not satisfy the requirements of para. 2(c), which raised the question of what was required to establish:

- that occupation was obvious on a reasonable careful inspection of the land; or
- that the bank must have had actual knowledge of the interest.

On the first point (at paras. 38–40) Ramsey J did not consider that:

> the objective phrase 'reasonably careful inspection' imposed any requirement that the person inspecting had any particular knowledge or was required to make reasonable enquiries . . . it is the visible signs of occupation which have to be obvious on inspection.

He considered that T would have reasonable prospects of establishing that a person carrying out an inspection would have been aware of the work being done on the property and of T's visits to it (para. 38).

On the second point (at paras. 47–9), the judge rejected the bank's suggestion that it could be said to have 'actual knowledge of the interest' only if it had received formal evidence of it (for example, from the submission of a deed). He noted that interests belonging to a person who relies on 'actual occupation' will rarely be ascertainable from a legal document. It would be sufficient to show that the bank had actual knowledge of the facts which were said to give rise to the alleged interest. Here the bank had been aware that B had a new partner, that T was intending to contribute to the cost of buying the property, and that it was to become the family home. On this second point, you may like to note the comment in Megarry and Wade at para. 6-093 that the judge's opinion that:

> the disponee has actual knowledge of an interest if he has 'actual knowledge of the facts which give rise to the alleged interest' . . . is neither what the 2002 Act says, nor what Parliament intended. What is required is 'real knowledge' of the existence of the interest.

The judge however was satisfied that T had reasonable prospects of showing both that her occupation was obvious and that the bank had actual knowledge of her interest, and accordingly allowed her appeal and set aside the order for possession. As so often happens, we do not know the outcome of the subsequent trial.

6.6 Summary: the process of buying registered land

As has been explained, a complex set of legal rules determine which encumbrances affecting registered land will bind a purchaser. In this section, we will look at the practical workings of those rules, taken together, and examine what the Armstrongs, the prospective purchasers of 1 Trant Way, should do in order to identify and protect themselves against encumbrances affecting the land.

6.6.1 Searching the register

The Armstrongs will of course have to make a search of the register: to satisfy themselves that Victor Venn is the registered proprietor of the estate, and to see whether any encumbrances have been noted on the register.

If an official search is made, a purchaser who completes within a specified period after an official search (the 'priority period') is not affected by any amendments made to the register in the interval.

A search should also be made of the local land charges register, because these charges are listed in Sch. 3 as overriding a registered disposition.

6.6.2 Inspecting the land

A physical inspection of the land should be made, from which the purchasers may discover overriding interests such as easements, and the existence of occupiers other than the vendor. Most important, in view of Sch. 3, para. 2, enquiries should be made of any such occupiers as to the nature of their rights and, as we have seen (6.5.6.1), the usual practice would be to require them to agree to waive any rights which they might have against the purchaser.

6.6.3 The role of notice or knowledge

This need to inspect the land and make enquiries of the occupiers may remind you of the rule in *Hunt v Luck* [1902] 1 Ch 428, which applies to unregistered land (see 5.5.2.3). It is worth now considering whether any similar doctrine of notice has any role to play in the registered title system. If the Armstrongs discover facts that might indicate the existence of an equitable interest in the land, even though no such right is on the register, are they at risk of being bound by such a right?

In *Williams & Glyn's Bank Ltd v Boland* [1981] AC 487, Lord Wilberforce said at p. 504:

> In my opinion . . . the law as to notice as it may affect purchasers of unregistered land . . . has no application even by analogy to registered land. . . . In the case of registered land, it is the fact of occupation that matters. If there is actual occupation, and the occupier has rights, the purchaser takes subject to them. If not, he does not. No further element is material.

Surprisingly, however, there were two later decisions of the Court of Appeal (*Lloyds Bank plc v Rosset* [1989] Ch 350 and *Abbey National Building Society v Cann* [1989] 2 FLR 265) in which the court apparently considered that the question of whether a purchaser could discover the rights through reasonable enquiries was relevant to the application of s. 70(1)(g). Moreover, Purchas LJ in *Rosset* even went so far as to say that the words of the subsection:

> clearly were intended to import into the law relating to registered land the equitable doctrine of constructive notice (at p. 403).

On appeal in both these cases, the House of Lords made no reference to this aspect of the judgments in the Court of Appeal (*Abbey National Building Society v Cann* [1991] 1 AC 56; *Lloyds Bank plc v Rosset* [1991] 1 AC 107).

In the Consultative Document that preceded the LRA 2002, the working party concluded that 'there should in general be no place for concepts of knowledge or notice in registered land' (para. 3.46), and recommended that the new Act should state that the doctrine of notice has no application in dealings with registered land except where the Act expressly provides to the contrary (para. 3.44). In fact, there is no express statement to this effect in LRA 2002, but the terms of ss. 28 and 29 leave no room for the operation of the equitable doctrine of notice: priority is conferred on a *purchaser* for valuable consideration, not a purchaser in good faith or without notice. As the Report puts it (at paras. 5.16–5.17):

> As a general principle, the doctrine of notice . . . has no application whatever in determining the priority of interests in registered land. [Apart from a number of very limited situations] issues as to whether [a] disponee had knowledge or notice of a prior interest, or whether he or she acted in good faith, are irrelevant.

The specific situations in which questions of knowledge, notice, or good faith *are* relevant under the Act are listed below.

(1) On first registration, the registered proprietor takes subject to those rights of an adverse possessor of which he or she has notice (s. 11(4)(c)), although before first registration the proprietor would have been subject to those rights, irrespective of notice. As the Armstrongs are not applicants for first registration, but purchasers of registered land, this provision does not apply to them.

(2) There are two special cases, involving Inland Revenue charges under the Inheritance Tax Act 1984 and dispositions by a proprietor who has become bankrupt. In these cases, the LRA 2002 follows the pattern of the legislation governing these matters, which does involve the concepts of notice and good faith (ss. 31 and 86). Thus, if the Armstrongs or their advisers discover facts that put them on notice of one of these two scenarios—Victor Venn is a bankrupt, or there is an Inland Revenue charge over the property—they should tread warily, as they may be fixed with constructive notice of the rights of the creditors in bankruptcy or the Revenue.

(3) Finally, and most broadly, the provisions of Sch. 3, paras. 2 and 3 (interests of persons in actual occupation and easements and profits à prendre which override a registered disposition) do involve requirements of actual knowledge or a reasonably careful inspection of the property. These may remind you of the rules about actual and constructive notice. However, the Report emphasises that these provisions are not drawn from notice-based principles, but are derived by analogy from the requirement of conveyancing law that a seller must disclose to the buyer certain incumbrances which are not obvious on a reasonably careful inspection of the land and of which the buyer does not have actual knowledge. (Report, para. 5.21.) If the Armstrongs discover someone in actual occupation of No. 1

Trant Way, or find evidence of a much-used path over the garden of No. 1 Trant Way to the neighbouring land, they are likely to be bound by any property right held by the occupier or any legal easement belonging to the neighbour. Outside these specific contexts, they may safely ignore any facts they come across that could indicate the existence of a third-party interest in the land.

6.6.4 Transfer and completion by registration: the 'registration gap'

Once the Armstrongs are satisfied with their enquiries and have made any necessary arrangements, the time will have come for the completion of the transaction. They will pay the balance of the purchase price, provided from their own funds or with money borrowed from a lender, to whom they will mortgage the property. Victor Venn will execute a transfer made by deed, using the appropriate Land Registry form. An example of such a transfer is given in Form 6.2.

The transfer of a registered estate is one of the dispositions which must be completed by registration, and does not take effect at law until this is done. This means that a transfer of a registered estate, unlike a conveyance of unregistered land, does not have the effect of conveying the legal title to the purchaser. The vendor remains the legal owner until the transfer has been registered, and meanwhile the purchaser has a merely equitable interest in the land, paralleling the rights he had under the estate contract prior to completion (see 4.6.1).

This period of time between disposition and registration is known as the 'registration gap' and can be dangerous to disponees. The risks which they run in not completing their transactions by registration are well illustrated by the decision in *Barclays Bank plc v Zaroovabli* [1997] Ch 321. Here the bank had been granted a mortgage by the registered proprietor in 1988, but did not register its charge until 1994. During the intervening six years, the mortgage took effect in equity only, and was not protected by any entry on the mortgagor's title. Although the terms of the mortgage provided that the mortgagor should not grant any lease of the property without the bank's consent, the mortgagor did in fact grant such a lease some two months after the creation of the mortgage. In 1995, when the mortgagor was unable to repay the loan, the bank sought possession of the property as a preliminary to selling the house and realising its security. The court held that the restriction on the mortgagor's power to grant leases operated only in the case of a legal mortgage, so that the lease created while the bank had only an equitable mortgage was a valid one. Since that lease had been granted before the mortgage was completed by registration, the tenant's lease, and her rights under the Rent Acts derived from the lease (see 9.2.1), were binding on the bank when it eventually acquired a legal mortgage on registration. As a result, the tenant was entitled to remain in the property, and the value of the bank's security was considerably reduced by the fact that there was a sitting tenant and the house could not be sold with vacant possession.

Baker v Craggs [2018] EWCA Civ 1126 is a recent case illustrating the protection available to the purchaser during the registration gap, and the limits of that protection. In that case, there had been a delay in making an application to register a transfer and the application then proved defective and was rejected by the Land Registry, leading to a second application. The result was that the purchaser, Craggs, was registered as proprietor only some five and a half months after the transfer. During the gap, the vendors had sold land they had retained and the purchasers of the retained land, the Bakers, had registered the burden of an easement over the yard that had already been sold to Craggs by the vendors.

At first instance, it was held that Craggs was bound by this easement. Although he had been in actual occupation of the land, including the yard, during the registration gap,

Newey J held that his interest under the vendor-purchaser constructive trust was 'overreached' by the grant of the easement and thus ceased to exist; by the time he acquired his legal title to the land, upon registration, the easement had already been granted and bound him. On appeal, the Court of Appeal rejected this application of the concept of overreaching, holding that the grant of a legal easement was not a 'conveyance... of a legal estate in land' for the purposes of the Law of Property Act 1925, s. 2(1) and so could not have overreaching effect. The result was that Mr Craggs still had his equitable interest in the land at the time that the legal easement was granted and, since he was in actual occupation of the land at that time, s. 29 of the LRA 2002 did not operate to confer priority on the grantees of the easement. This conclusion made it unnecessary to determine whether Mr Craggs' equitable interest in the land was of a kind that *could* have been overreached by a conveyance of an estate of land and Henderson LJ, in the Court of Appeal, expressly stated that he took no view on the question either way.

Thus, Mr Craggs was safe from the easement granted during the registration gap for two reasons: first, because he was in actual occupation of the land during the registration gap and, secondly, because the grant of an easement was not an overreaching transaction. If he had not been in actual occupation, he would have lost priority to the grantees of the easement under s. 29. If the vendors had, instead of granting an easement to a third party, conveyed the estate or granted a mortgage, it is not clear whether or not his equitable interest would have been overreached. An 'estate contract' is listed in s. 2(3) of the Law of Property Act 1925 as being among the equitable interests in land that cannot be overreached. However, at first instance in *Baker v Craggs* [2017] Ch 295, Newey J held that, once a contract for sale of land has been executed by the completion of the conveyance, the purchaser's interest in that land is no longer an 'estate contract' for the purposes of the section and so can be overreached; as we have seen, the Court of Appeal reserved its view on this question.

In the recent case of *Knight v Fernley* [2021] EWHC 1343, the High Court took the view that the purchaser's equitable interest in the registration gap *could* be overreached by a subsequent disposition by the vendors. In that case, Mrs Knight had bought a plot of land in Wiltshire and the conveyance in her favour had been executed in 2015. However, because of delays by her solicitors, no application to register her as proprietor was made until 2016. During the gap, the vendors had conveyed all their land—including, accidentally, the plot already sold to Mrs Knight—to the Fernleys, who were duly registered. When Mrs Knight belatedly applied to be registered as proprietor of the land she had bought, the Fernleys refused their consent to her application and Land Registry took the view that she was not entitled to be registered in the circumstances. The county court judge, whose decision was upheld by the High Court, held that her estate contract had been 'spent' by the execution of the conveyance in her favour, and she was left with a beneficial interest under a bare trust that had been overreached by the conveyance of the legal estate to the Fernleys. In the High Court, however, it was suggested that she might be able to argue that the entry of the Fernleys as registered proprietors of the entire plot was a 'mistake' that could be rectified (see 6.7.1.2) and she was given leave to amend her particulars of claim to make this argument.

It follows from these decisions that, if the Armstrongs go ahead with their purchase, it is essential that they complete the transaction by registration without delay, and do not risk leaving the legal estate in the hands of Victor Venn. If there is an unavoidable registration gap, it will be important that they go into actual occupation of the land during that gap, so that their equitable interest takes priority over any registrable disposition completed by Victor Venn in the gap. As Victor Venn is a sole legal owner, there is no risk that his transactions will 'overreach' their equitable interest in the land under s. 2(1) of

HM Land Registry
Transfer of whole of registered title(s)

TR1

Any parts of the form that are not typed should be completed in black ink and in block capitals.

If you need more room than is provided for in a panel, and your software allows, you can expand any panel in the form. Alternatively use continuation sheet CS and attach it to this form.

For information on how HM Land Registry processes your personal information, see our Personal Information Charter.

Leave blank if not yet registered.	1	Title number(s) of the property: CS1234
Insert address including postcode (if any) or other description of the property, for example 'land adjoining 2 Acacia Avenue'.	2	Property: 1 TRANT WAY, MOUSEHOLE, STILTON, ST14 3JP
Remember to date this deed with the day of completion, but not before it has been signed and witnessed.	3	Date:
Give full name(s) of **all** the persons transferring the property. Complete as appropriate where the transferor is a company. Enter the overseas entity ID issued by Companies House for the transferor pursuant to the Economic Crime (Transparency and Enforcement) Act 2022. If the ID is not required, you may instead state 'not required'. Further details on overseas entities can be found in practice guide 78: overseas entities.	4	Transferor: VICTOR VENN For UK incorporated companies/LLPs Registered number of company or limited liability partnership including any prefix: For overseas entities (a) Territory of incorporation or formation: b) Overseas entity ID issued by Companies House, including any prefix: (c) Where the entity is a company with a place of business in the United Kingdom, the registered number, if any, issued by Companies House, including any prefix:
Give full name(s) of **all** the persons to be shown as registered proprietors. Complete as appropriate where the transferee is a company. Also, for an overseas company, unless an arrangement with HM Land Registry exists, lodge either a certificate in Form 7 in Schedule 3 to the Land Registration Rules 2003 or a certified copy of the constitution in English or Welsh, or other evidence permitted by rule 183 of the Land Registration Rules 2003. Enter the overseas entity ID issued by Companies House for the transferee pursuant to the Economic Crime (Transparency and Enforcement) Act 2022. If the ID is not required, you may instead state 'not required'. Further details on overseas entities can be found in practice guide 78: overseas entities.	5	Transferee for entry in the register: ARNOLD ARMSTRONG and ARRIETY ARMSTRONG For UK incorporated companies/LLPs Registered number of company or limited liability partnership including any prefix: For overseas entities (a) Territory of incorporation or formation: (b) Overseas entity ID issued by Companies House, including any prefix: (c) Where the entity is a company with a place of business in the United Kingdom, the registered number, if any, issued by Companies House, including any prefix:

Form 6.2 Transfer relating to 1 Trant Way

This document is Crown copyright and has been reproduced with the kind permission of Land Registry.

Each transferee may give up to three addresses for service, one of which must be a postal address whether or not in the UK (including the postcode, if any). The others can be any combination of a postal address, a UK DX box number or an electronic address.	6	Transferee's intended address(es) for service for entry in the register: 1 TRANT WAY, MOUSEHOLE, STILTON, ST14 3JP
	7	The transferor transfers the property to the transferee
Place 'X' in the appropriate box. State the currency unit if other than sterling. If none of the boxes apply, insert an appropriate memorandum in panel 11.	8	Consideration ☒ The transferor has received from the transferee for the property the following sum (in words and figures): FIVE HUNDRED AND FIFTY THOUSAND POUNDS (£550,00) ☐ The transfer is not for money or anything that has a monetary value ☐ Insert other receipt as appropriate:
Place 'X' in any box that applies. Add any modifications.	9	The transferor transfers with ☒ full title guarantee ☐ limited title guarantee

Where the transferee is more than one person, place 'X' in the appropriate box.
 	
Complete as necessary.
 	
The registrar will enter a Form A restriction in the register *unless*:
– an 'X' is placed:
  – in the first box, or
  – in the third box and the details of the trust or of the trust instrument show that the transferees are to hold the property on trust for themselves alone as joint tenants, *or*
– it is clear from completion of a form JO lodged with this application that the transferees are to hold the property on trust for themselves alone as joint tenants.
 	
Please refer to *Joint property ownership* and *practice guide 24: private trusts of land* for further guidance. These are both available on the GOV.UK website.
	10	Declaration of trust. The transferee is more than one person and
		☒ they are to hold the property on trust for themselves as joint tenants
		☐ they are to hold the property on trust for themselves as tenants in common in equal shares
		☐ they are to hold the property on trust:

Insert here any required or permitted statement, certificate or application and any agreed covenants, declarations and so on.	11	Additional provisions

Form 6.2 (*Continued*)

The transferor must execute this transfer as a deed using the space opposite. If there is more than one transferor, all must execute. Forms of execution are given in Schedule 9 to the Land Registration Rules 2003. If the transfer contains transferee's covenants or declarations or contains an application by the transferee (such as for a restriction), it must also be executed by the transferee. If there is more than one transferee and panel 10 has been completed, each transferee must also execute this transfer to comply with the requirements in section 53(1)(b) of the Law of Property Act 1925 relating to the declaration of a trust of land. Please refer to *Joint property ownership* and *practice guide 24: private trusts of land* for further guidance. Examples of the correct form of execution are set out in *practice guide 8: execution of deeds*. Execution as a deed usually means that a witness must also sign, and add their name and address. Remember to date this deed in panel 3.	**12 Execution** Signed as a deed By Victor Venn In the presence of: Signature of witness: Name MICHAEL MOGGIE Address 14 The Broadway, Mousehole, Stilton ST1 3AY Signed as a deed By Arnold Armstrong In the presence of: Signature of witness: Name RITA RATTY Address 48 Downhole Way, Mousehole, Stilton ST9 4CH Signed as a deed By Arrietty Armstrong In the presence of: Signature of witness: Name RITA RATTY Address 48 Downhole Way, Mousehole, Stilton ST9 4CH

WARNING
If you dishonestly enter information or make a statement that you know is, or might be, untrue or misleading, and intend by doing so to make a gain for yourself or another person, or to cause loss or the risk of loss to another person, you may commit the offence of fraud under section 1 of the Fraud Act 2006, the maximum penalty for which is 10 years' imprisonment or an unlimited fine, or both.

Failure to complete this form with proper care may result in a loss of protection under the Land Registration Act 2002 if, as a result, a mistake is made in the register.

Under section 66 of the Land Registration Act 2002 most documents (including this form) kept by the registrar relating to an application to the registrar or referred to in the register are open to public inspection and copying. If you believe a document contains prejudicial information, you may apply for that part of the document to be made exempt using Form EX1, under rule 136 of the Land Registration Rules 2003.

© Crown copyright (ref: LR/HO) 07/22

Form 6.2 (*Continued*)

the Law of Property Act 1925. However, if there were two vendors in the case, with Victor Venn holding his registered title jointly with someone else, the position is more uncertain in the light of the reasoning in *Baker v Craggs* and *Knight v Fernley*.

6.7 Flawed dealings with a registered estate: alteration and indemnity

We have seen how a prospective purchaser of registered land, like the Armstrongs, can ascertain who owns the estate and obtain information about the encumbrances binding upon it. We now need to consider how safe it is to rely upon the register. There are different grades of title, and if one buys an estate with less than title absolute there will obviously be a degree of risk involved. The Armstrong's vendor is registered with title absolute (see Form 6.1), but they will want to know exactly how safe an absolute title is. Can they assume that the title is indefeasible and that, once they have been duly registered as proprietors of the estate, they will not be disturbed at some date in the future by someone else claiming the estate? Unfortunately, one would have to tell them that even an absolute title is not completely safe, for there are circumstances in which the register can be altered, even against a registered proprietor with absolute title.

In some cases a person who suffers loss due to an alteration of the register may apply for financial compensation from a central fund, and it is sometimes said therefore that in the case of registered land the State guarantees the title, because it provides a system of compensation for those who suffer from any deficiencies in the system. The 'State guarantee' concept is not altogether true, however, because, as we shall see, compensation is not available to every individual who suffers a loss.

6.7.1 Overview of the alteration and indemnity provisions of the LRA 2002

Under LRA 1925 the whole process of changing entries on the register was known as 'rectification'. While the joint working party had no major criticism of the substance of the Act's provisions about rectification, it commented adversely on the way in which they were drafted, saying that they tended to obscure the real nature of rectification and the manner in which it operated (Report, para. 10.4). It was thought that some of the difficulty was caused by the fact that the term 'rectification' was used to describe all alterations of the register, ranging from removing obsolete entries and remedying minor clerical slips to the correction of major errors which substantially affected existing property rights. In consequence, the provisions in the new Act about changes to the register (to be found in s. 65 and Sch. 4) use a different terminology, which is also important to the scope of the right to claim an indemnity (to be found in Sch. 8).

6.7.1.1 'Alteration'

The overall process of making changes to the register is now described as 'alteration of the register'. Under Sch. 4, paras. 2 and 5, the register may be altered on a court order or by the registrar without such an order, for the purpose of:

- correcting a mistake;
- bringing the register up to date; or
- giving effect to any estate, right, or interest excepted from the effect of registration.

In addition, the registrar has the power to remove superfluous entries.

Paragraphs 3(3) and 6(3) provide that an application to the court or registrar for alteration of the register must be approved, provided that the relevant body has power to do so, 'unless there are exceptional circumstances which justify not making the alteration'. There is thus an element of discretion in the process, but the Act indicates that the usual practice—in a case of alteration—must be to alter the register. However, the obligation to alter the register is radically qualified in the case of one particular type of alteration: 'rectification' that prejudicially affects the title of a proprietor in possession.

6.7.1.2 'Rectification'

The term 'rectification' is now used to describe a special form of alteration, and is defined in para. 1 as an alteration of the register which:

- involves the correction of a mistake; and
- prejudicially affects the title of the registered proprietor.

Where the registered proprietor is in possession of the land (as defined in s. 131), the power to rectify the register against that proprietor is limited by a further provision in paras. 3(2) and 6(2) that rectification *cannot* be made without his consent unless:

- the proprietor has contributed to the mistake by fraud or lack of proper care; or
- it would for any other reason be unjust for the alteration not to be made.

6.7.1.3 Indemnity

A person who suffers loss due either to a rectification of the register, or to a refusal to rectify, may be able to claim compensation (an 'indemnity') under LRA 2002, Sch. 8, para. 1(a) and (b). Compensation may also be paid to the person in whose favour the register is rectified for any loss he has suffered in spite of the rectification.

No compensation is payable where the loss suffered by a claimant is caused wholly or partly by his or her own fraud, or wholly by his or her negligence. Where the loss is caused only partly by the claimant's negligence, compensation is reduced to take account of his or her share in the responsibility (Sch. 8, para. 5).

6.7.1.4 The importance of defining the grounds for alteration or rectification: what is a 'mistake'?

The limitations on rectification against a proprietor in possession may well reassure the Armstrongs, assuming they have now taken possession of No. 1 Trant Way. Schedule 4 and Sch. 8, taken together, appear to promise that:

(1) the court or registrar will not normally award rectification of the register against them, in situations where they are not responsible for any mistake on the register and where it would not be unjust to refuse rectification (Sch. 4); and

(2) in those situations where rectification *is* awarded against them, compensation for any loss they suffer by reason of the rectification will be available (Sch. 8).

However, it is important to realise that these protections only apply in cases where an application to change the register does count as a 'rectification' within the meaning of the statute: i.e., where it involves the 'correction of a mistake' that 'prejudicially affects' their title. If someone applies to change the register for one of the other reasons—to correct a mistake that doesn't prejudicially affect them, or to 'bring the register up to date'—the protections will not apply. In such a situation, the court will normally alter the register with or without their consent and regardless of their own responsibility for the problem—and they will not be entitled to compensation, because their loss will not be by reason of a *rectification*. Thus, how the court draws the boundary between the different grounds for alteration—and, above all, how it defines the concept of 'correction of a mistake'—is of crucial importance to the position of the registered proprietor, both in terms of the security of their title and in terms of the availability of compensation in their favour.

Conversely, from the point of view of a party who wants to apply for a change in the register, it will be important to bring their case within the definition of the grounds for alteration set out in Sch. 4, paras. 4 and 5. If they do not have an interest that is excepted from the effect of registration, if there is no 'mistake' on the register, and no basis for arguing that the register needs to be 'brought up to date', there is no right to apply for alteration of the register. Nor is there any right to be compensated if their application to alter the register is refused: compensation is only available where their loss flows from a refusal to *rectify* the register. Again, therefore, what it means to 'correct a mistake' on the register is of crucial importance to such a person, both in determining whether they can make a successful application to change the register and in determining if they will get compensation if their application fails.

6.7.2 Mistake: the general definition

There is no statutory definition of 'mistake' in the LRA 2002, and the question of how it is to be defined has been the subject of much controversy. In *NRAM Ltd v Evans* [2017] EWCA Civ 1013, however, the Court of Appeal endorsed the following definition of 'mistake', proposed by the authors of Megarry and Wade (at para. 6-133 of the current edition):

> there will be a mistake whenever the registrar would have done something different had he known the true facts at the time at which he made or deleted the relevant entry in the register, as by:
>
> (i) making an entry in the register that he would not have made or would not have made in the form in which it was made;
>
> (ii) deleting an entry which he would not have deleted; or
>
> (iii) failing to make an entry in the register which he would otherwise have made.

It is important to note that, as Asplin LJ explained in *Antoine v Barclays Bank* [2019] EWCA Civ 2846, references to what the registrar would have done at the time do not depend on the subjective state of mind of the registrar, or what the registrar did know or could have discovered at the date of the registry entry. The key question is what the *legal* position was at the time of the decision to make or remove an entry from the register—that is, given the actual legal rights of the parties at that time, whether the registrar actually had a legal obligation or a legal power to alter the register in that way.

Examples of mistakes, under this definition, include:

- registering a person as proprietor under Sch. 6 to the LRA 2002, in the mistaken belief that his occupation of the land qualifies as adverse possession whereas in fact it does not (as in *Baxter v Mannion* [2011] 1 WLR 594);
- deleting a lease from the register of title of the freehold, under the mistaken belief that the lease has been terminated whereas in fact it has not (as in *MacLeod v Gold Harp Properties Ltd* [2014] EWCA 1084);

- registering a person as proprietor of a registered estate under the mistaken belief that there has been a valid transfer in her favour, whereas in fact the purported transfer is a forgery or void for some other reason (as in *Odogwu v Vastguide Ltd* [2009] EWHC 3565).

6.7.2.1 Giving effect to an overriding interest: alteration, not rectification

Under the LRA 1925 (s. 82(3)), altering the register to give effect to an overriding interest was specifically excepted from the protection given to the proprietor in possession. The danger to a purchaser who bought land subject to an overriding interest is well illustrated by the case of *Chowood Ltd v Lyall* [1930] 2 Ch 156 in which the registered proprietor of an estate was held to be bound by the rights of an adverse possessor, which were overriding under LRA 1925, s. 70(1)(f). In consequence, the register was altered by removing the portion of the property occupied by the squatter from the registered title. The fact that the registered proprietor was now in possession did not protect him, because the alteration was made for the purpose of giving effect to the overriding interest.

Under the LRA 2002 (Sch. 4, paras. 3 and 6), the protection of a proprietor in possession applies only to a particular type of alteration—rectification—which as we have seen is limited to an alteration which 'involves the correction of a mistake' and that prejudices the position of the registered proprietor. Altering the register to give effect to an overriding interest is not regarded as falling within this definition because, as we have seen, all registration of title is made subject to any overriding interest which may bind the estate. Thus, amending the register to take account of an overriding interest does not prejudice the position of the registered proprietor in any way, since he or she is bound by the overriding interest whether or not it appears on the register. An application to change the register in these circumstances is an application for 'alteration', not 'rectification', and so does not entitle the proprietor in possession to the benefits of paras. 3 and 6.

Similarly, as was later held in Re Chowood's Registered Land [1933] Ch 574, no indemnity is payable where the register is altered to give effect to an overriding interest. In such cases, the loss was caused by the proprietor acquiring an estate which was subject to an overriding interest. When the register was altered, the alteration gave effect to an existing state of affairs and did not cause any fresh loss (i.e., the loss was not due to the alteration). Under the 2002 Act, indemnity is payable only in respect of loss caused by rectification or refusal to rectify. As alteration of the register to give effect to an overriding interest does not constitute 'rectification', it remains the case that compensation is not payable in these circumstances.

This difference between alteration and rectification has become crucially important in cases where the registered proprietor has obtained a registered title by fraud or forgery. Unsurprisingly, it is uncontroversial that registration in these circumstances is a 'mistake' for the purposes of Sch. 4. It is therefore possible for the person who has lost their title in this way to apply for rectification of the register; these claims may or may not succeed, depending on whether the new registered proprietor is in possession and has contributed to the mistake by her own fraud or lack of proper care (see 6.7.3). However, it has also been argued that the previous registered proprietor also has the benefit of an overriding interest in this scenario, giving rise to the possibility of claims to *alter* rather than *rectify* the register in these scenarios.

In *Malory v Cheshire Homes* [2002] Ch 216, the Court of Appeal held that a person who acquired the legal estate by the operation of s. 69 of the LRA 1925 (the predecessor of s. 58 of the LRA 2002) did not thereby acquire the beneficial interest in the property, which remained vested in the previous registered proprietor. While it has been held that *Malory* was decided 'per incuriam' on this point (*Swift 1st v Chief Land Registrar* [2015] EWCA Civ 330), the idea that the new registered proprietor might sometimes become a trustee for the previous registered proprietor has not vanished from the law. In *Nasrullah v Rashid* [2018] EWCA Civ 685, the Court of Appeal held that a registered proprietor who had acquired the title by his own fraud (forgery, in the case of *Nasrullah*) thereby became a constructive trustee for the former registered proprietor that he had defrauded. Because of the length of time that had passed since the original fraud, this decision did not help the claimant in *Nasrullah* itself (see 7.2.2 and 7.3.2.5). However, if it had not been for the lapse of time, the decision would have meant that the former registered proprietor was entitled to apply for alteration—rather than rectification—of the register, with the result that the discretion of the court is considerably narrowed, and that no compensation is likely to be available to the current registered proprietor. This may seem fair enough in cases where the current registered proprietor is himself a fraudster, but it raises difficult questions about the position of successors in title who are bound by the 'constructive trust' because (for example) of the former registered proprietor's continued actual occupation of the land in question.

6.7.2.2 Removing derivative interests: the distinction between void and voidable dispositions

We have seen that there are many situations where registering a person as proprietor of a registered estate may be a 'mistake' within the meaning of Sch. 4. For example, in relation to No. 1 Trant Way, suppose Victor Venn had applied for registration as proprietor of the freehold title in reliance on a void deed of transfer, having forged the signature of the previous registered proprietor, Wanda Waynflete, on the form. He was then registered with title absolute because Land Registry mistakenly believed in the validity of the deed. If Wanda Waynflete then discovered what had happened, she could certainly apply for rectification of the register under Sch. 4, and have Victor Venn's details deleted from the proprietorship register and replaced by her own.

However, more difficult questions arise in a situation where the person who has mistakenly been registered goes on to transfer the estate, or to grant derivative interests in the estate, to a third party. In our example, suppose Wanda Waynflete discovers what has happened *after* Victor Venn has sold the estate to the Armstrongs, so that they are now the registered proprietors. Is their registration also a 'mistake', like his, allowing Mrs Waynflete to apply for rectification against them? Or, given that s. 58 of the LRA 2002 vested the legal estate in Victor Venn when he was registered with title absolute (see 6.2.7.1), can they argue that their registration was not a mistake and thus she has no right to seek rectification or alteration of the register in the circumstances?

Under the 1925 Act, the courts responded to this scenario by distinguishing between *void* and *voidable* dispositions. The leading cases were two decisions of the Court of Appeal, *Argyle Building Society v Hammond* (1985) 49 P & CR 148 and *Norwich and Peterborough Building Society v Steed* [1993] Ch 116. Both concerned the same dispute.

Mr Steed had been the registered proprietor of a property in London, which was occupied by his mother and his sister, Mrs Hammond. He alleged that his sister had used a fraudulent misrepresentation to obtain his signature to a power of attorney authorising his mother to sell the property. Subsequently, his sister and her husband had the property transferred to themselves and become the registered proprietors, relying on a deed in supposed exercise of the power of attorney, apparently signed by his mother. Mr Steed initially alleged that his mother's signature to the deed had been forged. The Hammonds agreed to grant a legal mortgage to the Argyle Building Society—later renamed the Norwich and Peterborough Building Society—and this charge was duly registered. When the Hammonds defaulted on the mortgage and the building society sought possession, Mr Steed sought to stay the warrant of possession on the basis that he had a prospect of obtaining rectification of the charges register to remove the mortgage. At first instance, the stay was denied on the basis that he had no prospect of success even if all his allegations were true.

In *Argyle Building Society v Hammond* (1985) 49 P & CR 148, the case was argued on the basis of Mr Steed's allegation that his sister had forged his mother's signature on the deed supposedly exercising the power of attorney. The Court of Appeal held that, if the allegation of forgery were true, the court would have a discretion under the LRA 1925 as to whether to remove the charges on Mr Steed's application. On this basis, the rectification claim was tried and returned to the Court of Appeal in *Norwich and Peterborough Building Society v Steed* [1993] Ch 116.

At this stage, Mr Steed had withdrawn his allegation of forgery but succeeded in showing that his sister had obtained his consent to the power of attorney by a fraudulent misrepresentation. This meant that the transaction in favour of the Hammonds was voidable—capable of being set aside by Mr Steed on application, but otherwise valid—rather than void. The Court of Appeal held that, in this case, there was no discretion to rectify the charges register. Since the Hammonds had a good legal title when they granted the charge, which Mr Steed had not yet applied to have set aside, they had been entitled to grant the mortgage and Land Registry had not made an 'error' (in the language of the LRA 1925) in registering that charge. Scott LJ said:

> The legal charge was executed by the Hammonds, who were at the time transferees under a transfer executed by Mrs. Steed as attorney for the registered proprietor. The voidable transfer had not been set aside. The registration of the Hammonds as proprietors took place at the same time as the registration of the legal charge. Neither registration was an error. Neither entry was made under a mistake.

There has been some uncertainty as to whether this reasoning applies to the somewhat different language of Sch. 4, of LRA 2002. In *Barclays Bank v Guy (No. 1)* [2008] EWCA Civ 452, the court appeared to take the view that the power to rectify the register did not include a power to remove derivative interests granted by a mistakenly registered proprietor. Even if a person became registered proprietor in reliance on a forgery or other void transaction, s. 58 vested the legal title in him or her and thus the registration of rights that she granted to others was not a 'mistake'. However, in *MacLeod v Gold Harp Properties Ltd* [2014] EWCA Civ 1084, the Court of Appeal rejected this view and held that the power to rectify the register included a power to remove derivative interests granted by a mistakenly registered proprietor. In the recent case of *NRAM Ltd v Evans* [2017] EWCA Civ 1013, the Court of Appeal upheld this view and held that the void/voidable distinction in the earlier case law offered 'principled and correct' guidance on when registration under a flawed transaction is a mistake.

Thus, in the scenario where Victor Venn had forged Wanda Waynflete's signature in order to become registered proprietor, the Armstrongs would be vulnerable to her claim for rectification. His registration in reliance on a forged transaction would have been a mistake—and so would the registration of the Armstrongs, in reliance on a disposition in their favour by a mistakenly registered proprietor. The Armstrongs would then need to resist her claim for rectification on the basis that they are innocent registered proprietors in possession (see 6.7.3) or, failing this, to seek indemnity from the Land Registry on the basis that they have suffered loss by reason of rectification (see 6.7.1.3).

By contrast, suppose Victor Venn had not forged Wanda Waynflete's signature but had, instead, obtained her signature on a transfer to himself by exercising undue influence or via a fraudulent misrepresentation. In this situation, the conveyance from Wanda Waynflete to Victor Venn would have been voidable, not void, and his registration would *not* have been a mistake. She would be entitled to apply to the court to set aside the transaction and have the title re-vested in herself, but her power to do this would lapse once he had conveyed the estate to the Armstrongs. She would have no right to seek rectification against them, and no claim to an indemnity under Sch. 8 as her loss is not by reason of a refusal to rectify the register.

6.7.3 How will the discretion as to rectification be exercised?

As we have seen, the decision that the court or registrar has a power to order a rectification of the register does not mean that such rectification will be ordered. Where rectification would be against a registered proprietor in possession, Sch. 4 gives the court or registrar a structured discretion: they should *not* grant rectification, unless the registered proprietor has caused the mistake by their own fraud or lack of proper care *or* it would for some other reason be unjust to deny rectification. Assuming that the Armstrongs are not complicit in Victor Venn's forgery, or could not have discovered it by reasonable care, rectification will not be ordered against them unless it is for some other reason held to be unjust.

Baxter v Mannion [2011] 1 WLR 1594 is an example of a case where rectification of the register *was* ordered against a registered proprietor in possession, on the grounds that it would be unjust not to do so. The case arose from an application by B to the Land Registry to be registered as owner of a field, of which M was already the registered proprietor. B based this application on a claim that he had been in adverse possession of the field for the last 10 years, making use of the new procedure introduced by ss. 96–8 and Sch. 6 of the LRA 2002 by which a squatter can claim title to land after a 10-year period of adverse possession (see 7.7). The registry gave the required notice of this application to M who, because of difficult family circumstances, failed to object within the prescribed period. As a result, B was registered as owner of the land. M later applied to the registrar for rectification of the register, claiming that B had never been in adverse possession of the land. Accordingly, his registration under Sch. 6 was a mistake, which should be corrected under the provisions of Sch. 4, para. 5.

Although B had not been in adverse possession before his application, it was accepted by both parties that he was in possession after his registration as proprietor. As a result, the register could be rectified against him only in the circumstances set out in Sch. 4, para. 6. In the High Court, Henderson J noted (at para. 63) that there was no evidence before the court to support a finding of fraud, but he had no hesitation in holding that the second limb of para. 6(2) applied:

> it is clear that [B] was never entitled to be registered as proprietor of the field, and in my view simple justice requires that, in the absence of strong countervailing factors, [M] should now be able to regain title to his property. I can discern no countervailing factors which would make it unjust for [B] to be deprived of his adventitious title to the field, and on the contrary I see every reason why he should.

The Court of Appeal upheld the judge's decision on this point, agreeing that it was a matter of 'simple justice'. It had been argued that M's failure to respond to the registry's notice in time had made it unjust to rectify the register against B, but Jacob LJ considered (at para. 42) that:

> Mere failure to operate the bureaucratic machinery is as thistledown to [M] losing his land and [B] getting it when he had never been in adverse possession.

B's appeal was accordingly dismissed, and the registrar was ordered to reinstate M as registered proprietor of the field.

You should also note that it is open to the court to *refuse* rectification in a case where it would otherwise be available—for example, because the registered proprietor is not in possession. This depends on showing that there are 'exceptional circumstances' justifying the refusal to rectify (see, for a recent example, *Dhillon v Barclays Bank* [2020] EWCA Civ 619).

6.7.4 Reform

In its 2018 Report, the Law Commission made a number of recommendations for reform of this area of law, proposing a significant rebalancing of the law in a number of respects. While these recommendations have been rejected by the Government pending further evidence that they are needed, you may like to take note of them. They are as follows:

- Where the proprietor of a registered estate has been removed or omitted from the register by mistake, he or she should be restored to the register if he or she is in possession of the land, unless it would be unjust to do so.
- The same protection should be available to a person who, but for the mistake, would have been a successor in title to the former registered proprietor.
- Where the current registered proprietors are in possession, rectification should not be awarded against them unless they have caused the mistake by their own fraud or lack of proper care or unless less than ten years have passed since the original mistake *and* it would be unjust not to rectify the register.
- After ten years have passed since the original mistake, the register should not be rectified to correct the mistake so as to prejudice the new registered proprietor even where the new proprietor is not in possession of the land.
- Where a chargee has been registered by mistake, it should not be able to oppose rectification by a removal of its charge but should instead be confined to its claim for indemnity under Sch. 8.

FURTHER READING

Cooke, *The New Law of Land Registration*, Hart Publishing, 2003.

Dixon, 'The Reform of Property Law and the Land Registration Act 2002: A Risk Assessment' [2003] 67 Conv 136.

Department for Business, Innovation and Skills, *Consultation on Moving Land Registry Operations into the Private Sector* (March 2016).

Gardner, 'The Land Registration Act 2002—The Show on the Road' (2014) 77 MLR 763.

Goymour, Watterson, and Dixon (eds), *New Perspectives on Land Registration*, Hart Publishing, 2018.

Land Registration for the Twenty-First Century: A Consultative Document, 1998, Law Com No. 254; in particular: Part I (need for reform); Part IV (overriding interests); and paras. 11.2–11.20 (electronic conveyancing).

Land Registration for the Twenty-First Century: A Conveyancing Revolution, 2001, Law Com No. 271; in particular: Part I (objectives of Land Registration Bill); and Part II (summary of changes).

Ruoff and Roper, *Registered Conveyancing*, Sweet & Maxwell, looseleaf edn., Pt. 1 General Principles.

Televantos, 'Overreaching and Trusts of Land' [2019] CLJ 516.

Updating the Land Registration Act 2002, 2018, Law Com No. 380.

You can visit the online resources to test your knowledge of this chapter with self-test questions at **www.oup.com/he/nair19e/**.

7

Acquisition of an estate by adverse possession

7.1	Introduction 141	7.6	Basis for the LRA 2002 reforms 156
7.2	Three systems of adverse possession 142	7.7	Adverse possession of registered land under LRA 2002 157
7.3	What constitutes 'adverse possession'? 145	7.8	What if the adverse possession is a crime? 164
7.4	Adverse possession of unregistered land 153	7.9	Adverse possession and human rights 165
7.5	Adverse possession of registered land under the old system 155		

7.1 Introduction

Thus far we have only considered estates in land which have been acquired in a formal manner, by the consent of a previous owner. However, it is also possible to acquire an estate in land by possession. It is an old rule of English law that any person who takes possession of land will thereby gain a *freehold estate* in that land, simply by virtue of the act of taking possession (*Asher v Whitlock* (1865) LR 1 QB 1). What this means is that the possessor can sue a stranger who has dispossessed her, and that this right to sue strangers is not limited in time but can go on forever. These rights of the person in possession can also be sold or given away. At the same time, the freehold title of the person in possession is only a *relative* title, not absolute ownership. There is no right to resist the claims of the actual owner, who will be entitled to evict a person whose title rests merely on possession and all her successors in title. This means that the rights of squatters are inherently quite weak and fragile—anyone with a better title will be able to evict the squatter and recover possession of the land. However, being in **adverse possession** for a period of time can change this, 'upgrading' the squatter's title to the best title available for that piece of land (effectively, absolute ownership). The LRA 2002 makes major changes to the process of acquiring ownership of registered land by adverse possession and greatly reduces its significance; but the old rules continue to apply to unregistered land (and to registered land where the period of adverse possession was completed before the new Act came into force).

7.1.1 No. 3 Trant Way

The current inhabitants of No. 3 are Oscar Oregano and his nephew, Nicholas. Nicholas has lived in Australia since he was a child and his family had lost touch with Oscar, but on a visit to England last year he discovered where his uncle was living and went to visit him. He found that Oscar was very old and frail, and so he stayed on to look after him. Oscar has become very fond of his nephew and told him recently 'when I am gone, the house will be yours'. However, he also told Nicholas that he has no title deeds to the property. He says that this is because he found the house apparently abandoned some years ago and, being homeless at the time, moved into it as a 'squatter'. He has stayed there ever since but unfortunately his memory is now very poor and he cannot remember how long he has been there. He assures his nephew that there is nothing to worry about and that he has 'squatters' rights', but Nicholas thinks that these 'rights' may not be very secure. He feels that, for Oscar's sake, he should get some advice about his uncle's position.

Before Nicholas seeks this advice, he needs to discover the answers to two questions:

- is the title to the house registered or unregistered? and
- how long has his uncle lived there?

Nicholas needs this information because there are now three separate systems under which a squatter may acquire ownership of property through adverse possession. These systems apply to:

- unregistered land;
- registered land in respect of which a squatter completed the required period of adverse possession before 13 October 2003 (when LRA 2002 came into force); and
- registered land governed by the new scheme under LRA 2002.

7.2 Three systems of adverse possession

7.2.1 Unregistered land

The position of a person in adverse possession of unregistered land is governed by the Limitation Act 1980.

7.2.1.1 Effect of the Limitation Act 1980

Most legal systems provide that a claimant must commence court proceedings within a prescribed time (the '**limitation period**') or lose the right to sue. Provisions of this sort are necessary to ensure that claimants bring their cases promptly, while the necessary evidence is available, and that defendants are not harassed by stale claims, which they may have difficulty in meeting when witnesses have disappeared and recollections have become blurred.

The current limitation provisions are contained in the Limitation Act 1980. Section 15, which now applies only to unregistered land (and to registered land, where the period of adverse possession was completed before LRA 2002 came into force on 13 October 2003) provides that the limitation period in respect of claims to recover land is 12 years. Thus generally, if someone with a prior estate in land allows it to be occupied by a squatter for 12 years, that prior owner will lose the right to recover the property from the interloper. At one time the original owner's title continued even after the limitation period had elapsed, so that although he could not sue to recover the land he could rely on his title as a defence if he took possession again without a court action. However, today the rule is that at the end of the limitation period the original owner loses both the right to sue and the unregistered title to the property (Limitation

Act 1980, s. 17). The effect of this is that the squatter is left with the best available title to the land, since the title of the only person entitled to evict him has been extinguished. As you would expect, there are detailed provisions about calculating the limitation period (see further 7.3.3.1).

7.2.1.2 Justification for adverse possession of unregistered land

It may seem somewhat surprising that our legal system allows one person to take land belonging to another and to keep it, and indeed this is sometimes described as 'land theft'. Cases of this sort always arouse public concern and comment when they hit the headlines and, as you will see later (7.9), were thought to be vulnerable to attack under the Human Rights Act 1998.

You should be aware, however, that many claims to title by adverse possession do not arise from a deliberate taking of another's property, but rather through some kind of mistake. Boundaries between neighbouring properties are often far from clear, and one owner may occupy a small strip of his neighbour's land in the genuine belief that it belongs to him. Other cases can arise from mistakes on the part of a vendor, who purports to sell the same piece of land to two different purchasers (as, for example, happened in *Bridges v Mees* [1957] Ch 475). In cases such as these, the rules of adverse possession can be beneficial in helping to bring the legal title into line with the position on the ground.

In fact, there are several good reasons for retaining a system which allows title to be acquired in this way (in addition, of course, to the general reasons underlying any form of limitation of claims, which we have noted at 7.2.1.1). There are some references at the end of the chapter, if you want to know more about these reasons.

In outline, there seem to be three main ways in which the system of adverse possession is beneficial, although, of course, they do not all apply in every case.

(1) *Mistake* Adverse possession may assist an innocent party who has spent money and time on land believing it to be his or her own, but who cannot establish a claim in proprietary estoppel (see Chapter 19), because there has been no encouragement or acquiescence by the owner.

(2) *Keeping land in use* The possibility of acquiring title in this way helps to ensure that land abandoned by its owner is not left to become derelict, or taken out of the property market because its occupier cannot prove title to it.

(3) *Facilitating investigation of title* Perhaps most importantly, it is said that the system of adverse possession facilitates and cheapens the investigation of title to unregistered land. This is because, in general terms, a purchaser is probably willing to assume that any claim to the land arising before the statutory period of title (currently a minimum of 15 years—see 5.2) has been barred under the 12-year limitation period, so that it will be safe to take a title shown for the minimum period.

7.2.2 Registered land: the old system under the Limitation Act 1980 and LRA 1925

Where a squatter completed a 12-year period of adverse possession before 13 October 2003, the provisions of the Limitation Act 1980 apply in the same way as they do to unregistered land, and the registered proprietor will have lost the right of action to recover the land. He or she must retain the legal title to the estate because this can only be taken away by altering the register, but under LRA 1925, s. 75(1) the registered proprietor now holds the legal estate in trust for the squatter, who is entitled to apply for registration as proprietor.

Over the years, it became apparent that the loss of registered title to an adverse possessor was incompatible with the basic principle that registered titles should be secure. As part of a review of the whole system of registered title, a number of problems relating to 'squatters' rights' were identified (see 7.6) and as a result the changes introduced by LRA 2002 included a completely new scheme for dealing with adverse possession of registered land. However, it is important to note that these changes only apply to those who complete the period of adverse possession *after* the commencement date of LRA 2002 (13 October 2003). For those who completed 12 years of adverse possession before this date, the old law still applies: that is, the registered proprietor is treated as holding the registered title on trust for the squatter.

In *Nasrullah v Rashid* [2018] EWCA Civ 685, the registered proprietor himself was an adverse possessor (see 7.3.2.5) who had got on the register by fraud and who had then completed 12 years of adverse possession by October 2002. In this scenario, the Court of Appeal held that the fraudster had originally held his registered title on trust for the previous registered proprietor who had been defrauded (for this aspect of the case, see 6.7.2.1). The question then became whether the passage of time had any effect. Lewison LJ suggested that there were two possible analyses of the effect of s. 75 LRA 1925 in the situation where the dispossessed owner was not the registered proprietor (and so could not hold his registered title on trust for the dispossessor). One possibility was that the fraudster held his registered title on trust for the dispossessed owner, but the dispossessed owner then held *his* interest under that trust on a trust for the fraudster (under s. 75). The other and simpler possibility was that the beneficial interest under the constructive trust was simply extinguished by the passage of time, leaving the adverse possessor as the sole legal and beneficial owner of the land. In either case, the effect of the completion of 12 years of adverse possession before 13 October 2003 was to extinguish, or render unenforceable, claims affecting the registered title that could have been made before that date.

7.2.3 Registered land: the new system under LRA 2002

The new rules about adverse possession introduced by LRA 2002 apply to any squatter who had not completed the 12-year limitation period before the Act came into force on 13 October 2003. The rules are designed to protect the rights of the registered proprietor, and as a result the squatter's chances of acquiring title to the land are greatly reduced by the new scheme. Time no longer runs against the owner under the Limitation Act 1980. All the squatter does acquire, after a minimum period of 10 years, is a right to apply for registration of title. The registered proprietor, and others with interests in the property, are notified of this application and given an opportunity to object. If the application is opposed, it will in general be rejected: there are only very limited situations in which the squatter may obtain registration despite opposition (see 7.7.3), or rely on the adverse possession as a defence in possession proceedings (see 7.7.4). This means that, apart from these cases, an adverse possessor can now acquire the registered title only if those notified of the application do not respond or raise any objection—which, although unusual, could happen if the property has been abandoned or is otherwise not wanted by those entitled to it. Certainly, it is no longer possible for the registered proprietor to lose title to a squatter against his or her will, and possibly even without knowing of it.

7.3 What constitutes 'adverse possession'?

Despite the differences between the systems, the requirements for establishing that a person has been in adverse possession remain the same in all of them. In order to claim title by adverse possession, the squatter must show that:

- he or she has been in possession of the land (7.3.1);
- the possession has been 'adverse' (7.3.2); and
- the adverse possession has lasted for the prescribed time (7.3.3).

7.3.1 Possession

The squatter must take possession of the land, either by dispossessing the owner or by entering at some time after the owner has discontinued possession. There are two essential elements of possession, both of which must be shown to exist:

- the fact of possession; and
- the intention to possess.

7.3.1.1 The fact of possession

What is required here is described by Slade J in *Powell v McFarlane* (1970) 38 P&CR 452 at p. 471:

> [W]hat must be shown as constituting factual possession is that the alleged possessor has been dealing with the land in question as an occupying owner might have been expected to deal with it and that no-one else has done so.

What the squatter actually does with the land depends on its nature. If it is a house, the squatter may live in it; if it is a piece of land adjoining the squatter's garden, he or she may have fenced and cultivated it. In some circumstances more occasional use may be enough, as in *Red House Farms (Thornden) Ltd v Catchpole* [1977] 2 EGLR 125, where shooting wildfowl was held to be a sufficient act of possession, because that was the only purpose for which the land could be used. Whatever the nature of the land, the squatter must be able to show that he or she has **exclusive possession** of it; sharing possession with the owner is not enough.

7.3.1.2 The intention to possess ('*animus possidendi*')

As well as taking physical possession of the land, the squatter must have the intention to possess it, defined by Slade J in *Powell v McFarlane* (1979) 38 P&CR 452 at p. 471 as:

> the intention, in one's own name and on one's own behalf, to exclude the world at large, including the owner with the paper title . . . so far as is reasonably practicable and so far as the processes of the law will allow.

The squatter must not only have this intention; the squatter must make it clear to the world, including the owner (if present), that the squatter intends to possess the land.

As the Court of Appeal put it in *Prudential Assurance Co. Ltd v Waterloo Real Estate Inc* [1999] 2 EGLR 85 at p. 87:

> [T]he claimant must, of course, be shown to have the subjective intention to possess the land, but he must also show by his outward conduct that that was his intention.

Proving the necessary intention

In general, the courts are loath to rely on the claimant's own statement about his or her intentions, because it may so easily be self-serving, and accordingly, they will tend to look for *conduct* from which the necessary intention may be inferred.

An example of conduct sufficient to show such an intention is to be found in *Buckinghamshire County Council v Moran* [1990] Ch 623, in which the adverse possessor had cultivated a piece of the council's land which adjoined his garden, fencing it and installing a gate which he chained and padlocked. In the view of the Court of Appeal (at p. 642), the locking of the gate amounted to a 'final unequivocal demonstration of the defendant's intention to possess the land' and to exclude the owner. In this context, it is important to emphasise that the mere installation of gates or fencing will not always and necessarily be enough to evidence the requisite intention: the question is always *why* these things are being done. For example, in the recent case of *White v Amirtharaja* [2021] EWHC 330 (affirmed on appeal at [2022] EWCA Civ 11), gates were found to have been installed for the purpose of protecting the claimant's use of a right of way from being disrupted by third parties. This was held to be too equivocal an act to demonstrate an intention to possess.

At the same time, you should note that all that is required here is *an intention to possess*; the squatter does not have to show that he or she intended to *acquire title* to the property. Thus in *Buckinghamshire County Council v Moran*, the squatter knew that the council had plans for the future use of the land, and made it clear that he intended to keep the land only until the council required it. The Court of Appeal was, however, satisfied that he intended to take possession of the land until that time, and this was sufficient, after completion of the limitation period, to enable him to claim title by adverse possession.

Conversely, it is not fatal to the squatter's claim if the squatter took possession believing that he or she was entitled to the property, either as a tenant or as the freehold owner. Thus in *Lodge v Wakefield City Council* [1995] 38 EG 136 the appellant, a former tenant of the council, had not paid any rent under the tenancy since 1974, but did not become aware of this fact until the late 1980s, believing, in the meantime that he was in possession of the land as a tenant. The Court of Appeal rejected the council's contention that time did not run against it until the possessor became aware of his true position, holding that the former tenant had had the necessary intention to possess the property and that his possession was adverse from the time he ceased to pay rent, even if he himself was not aware of this.

Similarly, it appears from the decision in *Hughes v Cook* (1994), (*The Independent*, 21 March 1994) that title by adverse possession can be acquired where the possessor occupies the land under a mistaken belief that he is already the owner of the estate, and indeed, such mistakes often form the background to cases of adverse possession. At the same time, it must be remembered that other cases can involve the deliberate taking of property which the squatter knows is not his or hers. The rules of adverse possession impose no requirement of good faith, and under the Limitation Act 1980 bad faith is relevant only in the exceptional case of the owner claiming that the squatter has acted fraudulently (see 7.3.3.1).

The owner's state of mind

Having considered what is required of the squatter by way of intention and knowledge, it may be helpful to deal here briefly with the owner's state of mind. There is no requirement that the owner should know about the adverse possession; use must be open, so that the owner has the opportunity of finding out about it, but the fact that the owner does not do so is no bar to the squatter's claim (*Powell v McFarlane* (1979) 38 P&CR 452), and the squatter is under no obligation to draw the owner's attention to what is happening (*Topplan Estates Ltd v Townley* [2005] 1 EGLR 90 at para. 85). Nor does the owner even have to be aware that he or she owns the land: adverse possession can operate against an owner who believes that the land already belongs to the squatter (see *Pye v Graham* (next) and Gray and Gray, para. 9.1.50).

Pye v Graham

The requirements for establishing adverse possession were considered and affirmed by the House of Lords in *J. A. Pye (Oxford) Ltd v Graham* [2003] 1 AC 419. In this case Pye, who were property developers, were the registered owners of fields adjoining the Grahams' farm. Pye hoped to obtain planning permission to build on the fields, but meanwhile permitted the Grahams to make limited use of them, at first under a written grazing licence for a period in 1983 and then by permission to cut hay in 1984. Further licences were requested in 1984 and 1985; these requests were not answered but the Grahams continued to use the land from 1986 to 1999. In 1997 Michael Graham, the current owner of the farm, registered a caution against dealings with Pye's registered title; a caution against dealings, under the LRA 1925, ensured that the person registered would be notified of any attempt to deal with the registered title and could object to such dealings. Pye sought to 'warn off' this caution (i.e. have it removed from the register) and in 1999 commenced proceedings for possession.

Although Neuberger J at first instance ([2000] Ch 676) held that adverse possession had been established, the Court of Appeal ([2001] Ch 804) considered that Graham's evidence showed that he did not have the necessary intention to possess the property to the exclusion of the owner. His evidence made it clear that he intended to carry on using the land in the hope that Pye would subsequently renew the grazing licence, and that he would have been willing to pay for the use of the land if asked to do so. In these circumstances, the court held that the intention to possess had not been established; there was thus no dispossession of Pye and time had not started to run against them under the Limitation Act.

On appeal, the House of Lords reversed the Court of Appeal decision, holding that the Grahams had been in adverse possession of the property and that time had run in their favour ([2003] 1 AC 419). In explaining this decision, Lord Browne-Wilkinson (with whom the others concurred) considered and approved the principles stated by Slade J in *Powell v McFarlane* (1977) 38 P&CR 452. At para. 40, Lord Browne-Wilkinson emphasised the need for both:

- the fact of possession—defined as 'a sufficient degree of physical custody and control'; and
- the intent to possess—defined as 'an intention to exercise such custody and control on one's own behalf and for one's own benefit'.

This second element, the intention to possess, was an essential ingredient in establishing adverse possession. The fact that physical control by itself was not enough could be illustrated by the hypothetical situation in which a person in occupation of a house in the owner's absence might be, depending on his intention, a friend of the owner who was looking after it for him, a temporary trespasser seeking only a night's lodging, or a squatter who intended to remain in the property. In order to establish adverse possession the occupier must show an intention to use the property for his or her own benefit, but did not have to intend to acquire ownership of it (*Buckinghamshire County Council v Moran* [1990] Ch 623 was approved on this point), and most significantly in the present case, a willingness to pay for the use of the land did not indicate an absence of intention to possess. As Lord Browne-Wilkinson put it (at para. 46):

> Once it is accepted that the necessary intent is an intent to possess not to own and an intention to exclude the paper owner only so far as is reasonably possible, there is no inconsistency between a squatter being willing to pay the paper owner if asked and his being in the meantime in possession. An admission of title by the squatter is not inconsistent with the squatter being in possession in the meantime.

Support for this view was to be found in the observations of Lord Diplock in the Privy Council decision in *Ocean Estates Ltd v Pinder* [1969] 2 AC 19, which it appeared had not been given sufficient weight by the Court of Appeal in the present case (para. 46).

In their Lordships' view, both the elements necessary for adverse possession were present in the Grahams' use of the land belonging to Pye. They had physical control of the property (the fields being surrounded by hedges and accessible only through gates which they controlled), and they had the necessary intention to use the land for their own purposes, maintaining and using it as though it was part of their farm. The Grahams were thus entitled to be registered as owners, but it should be noted that several of their Lordships expressed concerns about the apparent injustice of this result (see further 7.9).

7.3.2 Possession must be adverse

There is no statutory definition of 'adverse', but it may be understood as meaning possession which is inconsistent with the rights of the owner, (although it is clear that it does not have to be in any way hostile or aggressive). The adverse possessor is, in fact, in possession as a trespasser. In consequence, anyone taking possession with the consent of the owner, for example under a lease or a licence, will not be in adverse possession, and so cannot acquire rights under the Limitation Act. When a licence comes to an end or is withdrawn, time will, of course, start to run against the owner if the licensee remains on the land without acknowledging his title.

7.3.2.1 Possession by tenants under a lease

It is not possible for a tenant to lay claim to the freehold title because clearly the tenant occupies the land with the permission of the estate owner and in accordance with the terms of the lease. In the case of a lease for a fixed term, or a periodic tenancy granted in writing (see 9.1.2.1), time only starts to run against the former landlord if the tenant remains on the land at the end of the term or period, not paying rent or acknowledging the owner's title in some way. A tenant who holds the land under a periodic tenancy where there is no lease in writing is, however, in a special position. In the case of such oral tenancies, the Limitation Act 1980 (Sch. 1, para. 5) provides that the limitation period will run against the landlord as soon as the first period of the tenancy ends. However, should the tenant pay rent after this date the period will restart from the date that the rent was paid.

7.3.2.2 Possession by a licensee (i.e., with permission or consent of the owner)

Permission or consent may be given expressly, but it is also possible for the court to infer it from the circumstances of the case (an 'implied licence'). An example of this is to be found in *Colin Dawson Windows Ltd v King's Lynn, West Norfolk BC* [2005] 2 P&CR 19. The claimant ('Dawsons') had used land belonging to the defendant as a car park for some 16 years and claimed to have acquired title to it by adverse possession. The Court of Appeal, however, was satisfied that during this period there had been sporadic negotiations between the parties for the sale of the land to Dawsons, and held that as a result the claimant's continuing possession had been with the implied permission of the owner and was not adverse. In the words of Rix LJ (at para. 39):

> It is natural to draw an inference of permission where a person is in possession pending negotiations for the grant of an interest in that land.

The Court of Appeal adopted a similar approach in *Batsford Estates (1983) Company Ltd v Taylor* [2006] 2 P&CR 5. Here the owner of a farm, having made unsuccessful attempts to persuade a former tenant and his son (the defendant) to leave the property, decided to take no further action for the time being. The Court of Appeal considered that the continued possession by the defendant was with the implied permission of the owner, so that the defendant could not claim title by adverse possession.

7.3.2.3 Distinction between acquiescence and permission

In *Zarb v Parry* [2012] 1 WLR 1240 at paras. 26–8, the Court of Appeal emphasised the importance of distinguishing between mere *acquiescence* in the use of one's land by another, which is compatible with adverse possession, and *consent or permission*, which effectively prevents possession being adverse. This distinction is also relevant to prescription in relation to easements and we discuss it further in Chapter 24.

7.3.2.4 Land reserved by owner for specific purpose

A question which has arisen in a number of cases is whether a squatter's possession can be said to be 'adverse' when the owner is deliberately not using the land because the owner is keeping it for some special use in the future.

In *Leigh v Jack* (1879) 5 Ex D 264 the owner of some land had intended to use it to build a highway but no action had been taken to start the construction of the road. From 1854 onwards a neighbouring landowner had used the property to store materials used in his factory and in 1865 and 1872 he had erected fences on the land. The court held that none of these actions amounted to adverse possession of the disputed property, because the prior owner of the property had no intention to build upon or cultivate the land and therefore the actions of the neighbouring owner were not inconsistent with the intentions of the prior owner. In the words of Bramwell LJ (at p. 273):

> in order to defeat a title by dispossessing the former owner, acts must be done which are inconsistent with his enjoyment of the soil for the purposes for which he intended to use it: that is not the case here, where the intention of the plaintiff . . . was not either to build upon or cultivate the land, but to devote it at some future time to public purposes.

In later cases, this statement was treated as giving rise to the rule that an owner who was keeping land dormant for some particular purpose in the future was not dispossessed by a squatter who made use of it in the meantime. In a further development, this approach came to be supported by the idea that a person who occupied land for which the owner had no immediate use did so under an implied licence from the owner (*Wallis's Caytown Bay Holiday Camp Ltd v Shell-Mex and BP Ltd* [1975] QB 94).

The theory of an implied licence was, however, regarded as doubtful, and Sch. 1, para. 8(4) of the Limitation Act 1980 now specifically provides that the existence of such a licence shall not be assumed merely because the squatter's occupation is not inconsistent with the owner's present or future enjoyment of the land. (This does not, of course, prevent a court from inferring an implied licence from the actual circumstances of the case—see 7.3.2.2.)

The effect of this statutory provision on the 'rule' in *Leigh v Jack* was considered by the Court of Appeal in *Buckinghamshire County Council v Moran* [1990] Ch 623. In this case the council had acquired a plot of land in 1955, for the purpose of constructing a road diversion. It was known that the roadworks would not be carried out for many years and so the council merely fenced the plot from the road (but not from the neighbouring properties) and initially sent council workmen to cut the grass and keep the plot in order. From the late 1960s the owners of one of the neighbouring properties, to the knowledge of the council, began to cut the grass on the council's plot and keep it tidy. From that time on the council ceased to send its workmen to the plot. The neighbouring property changed hands several times and was bought by Moran in 1971. Moran knew that the title to the empty plot was vested in the council, but the plot appeared to form part of the garden of the property which he had bought and was always maintained as such. As we saw in 7.3.1.2, he erected a fence and a gate, which was secured with a lock and chain. In 1976 the council wrote a letter disputing his rights to use the plot but thereafter took no action to recover it for at least nine years. Thus by the time that the action was brought Moran and his predecessors in title had been using the plot as a garden for well over 12 years. The council argued, however, that as it had not had any use for the plot, other than to let it lie fallow until the road scheme could go ahead, the possession of Moran and his predecessors had not been adverse to the council's rights. The Court of Appeal held, however, that Moran had established a good claim to title by adverse possession over the plot of land. The court doubted the existence of any special rule applicable to these circumstances, and distinguished *Leigh v Jack* on the ground that the squatter in that case had not satisfied the court of his intention to exclude the owner.

The Court of Appeal's decision in *Moran* was expressly approved by the House of Lords in *J. A. Pye (Oxford) Ltd v Graham* [2003] AC 419, in which Lord Browne-Wilkinson described the suggestion that the adverse nature of possession depended not on the intention of the squatter but on that of the owner as 'heretical and wrong' (para. 45).

7.3.2.5 Whose consent? Adverse possession by the registered proprietor

In *Parshall v Hackney* [2013] EWCA Civ 240, an action was brought for rectification of the register on the basis that a plot of land had been mistakenly double-registered, as part of two different titles (for the process of correcting mistakes on the register generally, see 6.7). The mistake had happened in 1980, and the land had been in the possession of one of the two registered proprietors since 1988. It was argued that rectification should not be granted in the circumstances because any claims of the other registered proprietor had been extinguished by adverse possession. However, the Court of Appeal rejected this argument on the basis that the registered proprietor of land could not be in *adverse* possession of that land. By definition, the possession of a registered proprietor—in whom the legal estate was vested by registration—was inherently lawful, and so could not qualify as *adverse* for the purpose of extinguishing the claims of third parties (even where those third parties had themselves been registered as proprietors of the very same land).

However, in *Nasrullah v Rashid* [2018] EWCA Civ 2685, the Court of Appeal declined to follow its own earlier decision in *Parshall v Hackney*. Lewison LJ held that the reasoning in *Parshall* was inconsistent with the House of Lords decision in *J. A. Pye (Oxford) Ltd v Graham* [2003] 1 AC 419 and so could not be followed. After *Pye*, adverse possession could be made out simply by showing that a person was in possession of land 'in the ordinary sense of the word' without the consent of the owner: it was *not* necessary that the possession of an adverse possessor should also be 'unlawful'. The implication of this argument is that a registered proprietor might be found to be in adverse possession of registered land *if* the possession is without the consent of someone else with a better claim to become the registered proprietor. As Dixon has noted ((2020) 79 CLJ 415), this suggests that the registered proprietor of land is not always its 'owner', in the sense relevant to adverse possession, since the possession of a registered proprietor will always and necessarily be with his own consent.

7.3.3 Adverse possession must last for the prescribed time

7.3.3.1 Unregistered land and registered land under old scheme

A squatter who satisfies the requirements for adverse possession must then remain in possession for the period prescribed by the Limitation Act, which is generally 12 years (s. 15). Possession must be continuous; if the squatter gives up possession and then retakes it at a later date, the owner will have a new claim. Time will start to run afresh, and the squatter will have to complete the full limitation period after the second entry.

Although the period generally required to bar the owner's claim is 12 years (Limitation Act 1980, s. 15), one needs also to consider the circumstances in which:

- time starts to run; and
- an owner is given extra time in which to reclaim possession.

When does time start to run?
Time will start to run against a prior owner only once the owner has been dispossessed or has discontinued possession (Limitation Act 1980, Sch. 1, para. 1) and when adverse possession has been taken by another person (para. 8).

Postponement of limitation period
In the case of claims based on fraud or for relief from the consequences of a mistake, and in any case where a fact relevant to the claimant's claim has been deliberately concealed from him by the defendant, time does not start to run under the Act until the claimant has discovered the relevant matter, or could have done so with reasonable diligence (Limitation Act 1980, s. 32).

Extension of time within which owner may bring claim
The Limitation Act 1980 makes detailed provisions for extending the limitation period where the dispossessed owner is subject to a disability (i.e., is a minor or lacks capacity to conduct legal proceedings under the Mental Health Act 1983) and therefore unable to bring an action to recover the land during the normal limitation period (ss. 28 and 38(2) as amended by the Mental Capacity Act 2005, s. 67 and Sch. 6, para. 25).

Similarly, there are special rules relating to beneficiaries with future interests under settlements of land, enabling them to bring actions to recover the land when they become entitled to possession of it, even if this is outside the normal limitation period (s. 15(2)).

7.3.3.2 Registered land under the new scheme

Under LRA 2002, a squatter must show a minimum period of 10 years' adverse possession immediately before the application for registration or the commencement of proceedings in which adverse possession is relied upon as a defence.

Schedule 6 of the Act includes certain provisions similar to those of the Limitation Act:

- periods of adverse possession by different people may be added together, provided they form a continuous whole (para. 11(2));
- an application for registration may not be made while the registered proprietor is under certain mental or physical disabilities (para. 8(2)); and
- a squatter is not to be regarded as in adverse possession of an estate while it is subject to a trust for beneficiaries with future interests.

7.3.3.3 Preventing completion of a required period of adverse possession

Provided the required period of adverse possession has not yet been completed, it can be ended prematurely in a number of circumstances.

1. *The owner starts proceedings to recover the land.*

This requires no explanation.

2. *The owner retakes possession of the land.*

A dispossessed owner may choose to adopt this self-help remedy, but in doing so should avoid any use or threat of violence (Criminal Law Act 1977, s. 6).

The actions needed for successfully retaking possession were considered by the Court of Appeal in *Zarb v Parry* [2012] 1 WLR 1240. The Zarbs claimed ownership of a strip of land which formed part of the garden of their neighbours, the Parrys. On one occasion the Zarbs entered the strip and began to fence it off, but were prevented from completing the job and left the property. In subsequent proceedings to recover possession the Zarbs claimed that they had retaken possession by their entry and that this prevented the Parrys from establishing their defence under LRA 2002 (see 7.7.4).

The Court of Appeal upheld the finding of the trial judge that the attempt to retake possession had been unsuccessful. In reaching this conclusion the court considered earlier decisions on the action required to regain possession and interrupt adverse possession. It concluded that symbolic acts, such as putting up a notice or planting a flag, are not sufficient. In order to *acquire* adverse possession, the squatter 'has to show he has exclusive possession in the sense of exclusive physical control' (para. 38) and in order to *regain* possession from him the owner has to deprive him of this exclusive control by bringing his exclusive possession to an end (para. 40). If the Zarbs had succeeded in fencing the disputed area, it would have been sufficient to interrupt the period of adverse possession, but they had failed to do so.

3. *The squatter provides written acknowledgement of the owner's title.*

The owner may require this if the owner is content for possession to continue but wants to avoid losing his or her right to the land. However, such an acknowledgement may also be given inadvertently by the squatter if, for example, the squatter offers to buy the land from the owner (see *Edginton v Clark* [1964] 1 QB 367; and more recently *Ofulue v Bossert* [2009] 1 AC 990).

4. *The squatter goes out of possession, leaving the property vacant.*

This is obvious; you cannot claim if you are not in possession. If, however, another person (S2) takes possession of the property after a first squatter (S1), time will continue to run in S2s favour, and S2 can complete the limitation period by adding S2's time to that of his predecessor, S1. This is the case irrespective of whether S2 acquires the property with the cooperation of S1 (for example, by sale, gift, or on succession), or by dispossessing S1. S2 may bar the original owner simply by completing the limitation period (S1's time plus S2's time). However, if S2 dispossessed S1, S2 will have to hold for the full 12-year period from the time at which S2 acquired possession, if S2 is to bar S1's right to recover the property.

1965	1970	1975	1982	1987
O goes out of possession	S1 takes possession	S2 dispossess S1	O is time barred against S2	S1 is time barred against S2

Figure 7.1 A succession of squatters

Thus far in this chapter we have been considering rules which, unless otherwise indicated, are relevant to all adverse possession claims. However, we have now reached the point at which the various systems diverge, and in the next few sections we will deal with the special rules relating to:

- adverse possession of unregistered land (7.4);
- adverse possession of registered land under the old system (7.5);
- basis for the LRA 2002 reform of rules relating to registered land (7.6); and
- adverse possession of registered land under LRA 2002 (7.7).

7.4 Adverse possession of unregistered land

In this section we will look at the position of a squatter in adverse possession of unregistered land who has completed the limitation period of 12 years (Limitation Act 1980, s. 15).

As has been explained, the adverse possessor is regarded as having an estate in fee simple from the moment possession is first taken (*Leach v Jay* (1878) 9 ChD 42 at p. 45), although this title is always liable to be defeated by the owner until the limitation period has been completed. Thus, even before the period is completed, the squatter has the rights and powers of an owner, against everyone except the person dispossessed. This means that the possessor can sue for torts against the land (such as trespass and nuisance), and can recover the land if dispossessed by a third party. She can also sell her title to the land or leave it to others in her will (*Asher v Whitlock* (1865) LR 1 QB 1).

7.4.1 Completing the limitation period

When a squatter has completed the limitation period the dispossessed owner's right to recover the land is barred and his or her title to the estate is extinguished (Limitation Act 1980, s. 17). In other words, there is no longer anyone with a better title to the land.

It used to be thought that at the end of the limitation period the Limitation Acts vested the previous owner's estate in the squatter. This is what is meant by references you may see, in older cases, to 'a parliamentary conveyance'. It was, however, held in *Tichbourne v Weir* (1892) 67 LT 735 that the Acts did not have this effect. Instead, the previous owner's title is extinguished (as is now expressly provided by the Limitation

Act 1980, s. 17), and the squatter holds an estate in the land under their title, which has now become the best available title to the land.

7.4.2 Third-party rights over the land

The squatter takes the land subject to rights which affect that land, such as easements or restrictive covenants benefiting neighbouring landowners. The title to the land is acquired by operation of law, not by any transfer or conveyance. Consequently, the squatter is not a 'purchaser' in the technical sense (see 2.4.3.2), and so cannot take advantage of the rules which invalidate certain third-party rights against purchasers. As a result, the squatter is bound by such rights despite the fact that he or she has no notice of them or that they have not been protected by registration on the Land Charges Register (see, for example, *Re Nisbet & Potts' Contract* [1906] 1 Ch 386). Where an estate in land is held on trust, it was held in *Bolling v Hobday* (1882) 31 WR 9 that the squatter would not be affected by the trusts because it was the legal estate of the trustees—not the land itself—that was subject to the trusts. Since the squatter had not taken the estate of the trustees by a Parliamentary conveyance but had instead acquired a fresh estate by the act of taking possession, he was not bound by the trusts. However, the Limitation Act 1980 (s. 18) now addresses this problem by providing that the legal estate of trustees cannot be extinguished by adverse possession until such time as the beneficiaries' own interests are also extinguished.

7.4.3 Completing the limitation period against a tenant

Completion of the limitation period against a tenant will bar that tenant's right to recover the land and extinguishes the tenant's title against the squatter. Despite the fact that the dispossessed owner held only a leasehold estate, the squatter is regarded as holding a freehold estate. The squatter does not take over the leasehold estate which was held by the tenant, and so does not enter into any relationship with the landlord or become liable as a tenant on the covenants in the lease.

Although completing the limitation period bars the tenant's rights against the squatter, it does not affect the position of the landlord. The landlord has no right to physical possession of the land (and therefore no claim against the squatter) until the lease comes to an end. The squatter may complete the limitation period against the tenant and be able to stay on the land for the duration of the lease. Thus, in *Spectrum Investment Co v Holmes* [1981] 1 WLR 221, when a squatter barred the rights of a tenant who held the land under a 99-year lease, the squatter could not be removed during the remainder of the 99-year period. However, once the lease comes to an end, the landlord *will* be able to recover possession from the squatter. It is only if the squatter remains on the land for a further limitation period after the lease has ended that the squatter will be able to bar the landlord's rights and extinguish the landlord's estate.

7.4.4 No. 3 Trant Way

You will have realised that there are a number of factors to be taken into account when deciding whether a claim to recover unregistered land is time-barred. These include the need for possession to be adverse; the possibility that the person who has been dispossessed is a tenant or is under a disability; and the chance that there are persons entitled to future interests in the land. It should not, therefore, be too readily assumed that occupation of another's land for a simple period of 12 years will necessarily allow one to obtain good title as against any prior owners.

All the same, if the title to No. 3 proves to be unregistered and Oscar can show that he has been living there for 12 years, it is at least possible that he has extinguished the former owner's title and could raise this as a defence in any proceedings for possession. However, he would be in a very different position if the former owner (who presumably would have the title deeds) were to sell the property to a third party, who applied for first registration of title. Provided Oscar was in actual occupation at the time of registration, his right to the property would be overriding (LRA 2002, Sch. 1, para. 2—see 6.3.4.1(2)), and the purchaser would be bound by it. If, however, Oscar was not in occupation at that time, the purchaser would be bound only if he had notice of the right (LRA 2002, s. 11(4)(c)—and see further 6.3.3.2).

To avoid finding himself in this situation, Oscar would be well advised to apply for first registration of his title to the property. If he can show that he has satisfied the requirements for acquisition of the estate by adverse possession, he will be registered with a possessory title, which in time could be improved into absolute title (see 6.3.3.2). As well as protecting him from the consequences of any sale by the former owner, registration will facilitate the conveyancing process if he should wish to sell the property, and will also reduce the chances of any future squatter being able to acquire title against him.

7.5 Adverse possession of registered land under the old system

In this section we will look very briefly at the position of a squatter in adverse possession of registered land who completed the limitation period of 12 years before LRA 2002 came into force on 13 October 2003.

Under the old law relating to registered land time ran against the registered proprietor in exactly the same way as it did against the owner of unregistered land, and the right of action against the dispossessor was barred under the Limitation Act 1980, s. 15 at the end of 12 years. However, some variation of the existing rules was needed at the end of the limitation period, to take account of the fact that the registered proprietor remained owner of the estate until someone else was registered in his place. Accordingly, LRA 1925, s. 75(1) provided that the proprietor's title was not extinguished at the end of the limitation period (as it would be in unregistered land), but would be held in trust for the squatter, who could then apply for registration in his place (s. 75(2)).

7.5.1 No. 3 Trant Way

If the title to No. 3 is registered and Oscar can show that he had lived in the property for a full 12 years before LRA 2002 took effect, he will be protected by the transitional arrangements of that Act. These provide that where the completion of the limitation period had given rise to a trust before the Act came into force, the squatter is entitled to be registered as proprietor of the estate (Sch. 12, para. 18(1)). Provided Oscar stays in actual occupation of the land, his rights under the trust will be overriding (under LRA 2002, Sch. 3, para. 2—see 6.3.4.1.(2) and (3)), and so will bind anyone who buys the land from the dispossessed owner. However, if he is not in actual occupation at the date of the transfer to the purchaser his rights will no longer be overriding, and the purchaser will take free of them. Therefore, if Oscar completed the limitation period before 13 October 2003, he should be advised to make an immediate application for registration of his title to the estate.

7.6 Basis for the LRA 2002 reforms

We have already seen in Chapter 6 that a Joint Working Party of the Law Commission and the Land Registry made major proposals for the reform of the registered title system, most of which have been enacted in LRA 2002. The Consultative Document (*Land Registration for the Twenty-First Century: A Consultative Document*, 1998, Law Com No. 254) identified a number of problems in relation to adverse possession of registered land, and we will note these briefly.

(1) *Rules based on unregistered system of title* The adverse possession rules were developed by reference to unregistered land, where title is relative, and were inappropriate in a system where title is absolute and depends on registration. Adjustments had been made to the basic rules in their application to registered land (most notably in the imposition of the statutory trust by LRA 1925, s. 75(1)), but these were not thoroughly thought through and appeared inadequate to deal with the sort of questions raised in recent litigation. (For further information on this point see Consultative Document, paras. 10.27 and 10.42.)

(2) *Adverse possession undermines registered title* The registered proprietor ought to be able to rely on registration as safeguarding his title, but could in fact lose it to a squatter in substantially the same way as if it were not registered. The fact of registration did nothing to preserve the proprietor's title.

The possibility of adverse possession also affected the purchaser (P) from the registered proprietor. P should be able to buy relying on the state of the register and P's own inspection of the land. However, the overriding interests of the squatter (S) under LRA 1925, s. 70(1)(f) could constitute a trap for P, since once S had completed the limitation period, S could leave the land while still retaining her equitable interest in it.

(3) *Difficulty in justifying adverse possession of registered land* We have seen that adverse possession can be of benefit in simplifying the investigation of title of unregistered land (7.2.1.2), but this does not apply to registered land, where title depends on the register. Ability to justify the process as being in the public interest (rather than simply benefiting the squatter) became even more important with the advent of the Human Rights Act 1998 (see 7.9).

Despite these problems with the existing law, the working party considered that there was still a role for adverse possession in respect of registered land, most notably to facilitate dealings with properties that had been abandoned by their owners, and should not be allowed to become derelict and unmarketable. However, it proposed a number of changes to the system then in operation. It recognised that these would increase the differences between the rules for registered and unregistered land, but considered that this was inevitable and that it was time to accept that the two systems involve differences in substantive law as well as in conveyancing procedures.

Accordingly, the Consultative Document recommended the introduction of a completely new system of adverse possession for registered land, and this new system was introduced by LRA 2002.

7.7 Adverse possession of registered land under LRA 2002

7.7.1 Introduction

The modern scheme for dealing with adverse possession of registered land is set out in ss. 96–8 and Sch. 6 of LRA 2002. It applies to all claims to title based on adverse possession of a registered estate in which the squatter had not completed the required period of such possession before LRA 2002 came into force on 13 October 2002. At that date the old rules ceased to apply and as a result time will not run against the registered proprietor under the Limitation Act 1980, however long the period of adverse possession may be.

Under LRA 2002, the only way in which a squatter can acquire title to a registered estate is to obtain registration as its proprietor from HM Land Registry, following a minimum period of 10 years' adverse possession. The Act prescribes the process by which a squatter may apply for registration (see 7.7.2), and also provides for two cases in which the court may order registration of a squatter as proprietor of the registered estate after unsuccessful possession proceedings against the squatter (see 7.7.4).

Where an application for registration is made by an adverse possessor, the registered proprietor is informed by the registry and given an opportunity to oppose the application. This means that in general the registered proprietor is no longer at risk of losing the property against his or her will, and possibly even without knowledge of the loss. Of course, this depends on the registered proprietor actually receiving the notification of the claim from the registry, which need not be the case (particularly if the registered proprietor has abandoned the property and so is not checking for post at that address).

It is important to remember that a squatter who makes such an application still has to establish that he or she has been in adverse possession, and to do this must satisfy the rules we considered earlier in 7.3. Schedule 6, para. 11(1) provides that:

> [a] person is in adverse possession of an estate in land for the purposes of this Schedule if, but for section 96, a period of limitation under s. 15 of the Limitation Act 1980 would run in his favour in relation to the estate.

Section 96 provides that time does not run under the Limitation Act in respect of any registered estate. So para. 11(1) is saying, in effect, that if we disregard s. 96, the conditions for establishing adverse possession under the old rules apply also to the new scheme. Schedule 6 also includes provisions similar to those contained in the Limitation Act 1980 in respect of adverse possession against persons with certain mental or other disabilities, and against beneficiaries with a future interest under a trust (see 7.3.3, and Sch. 6, paras. 8(2)–(4) and 12).

For a decision to rectify the register against an applicant who had achieved registration without satisfying the requirements for adverse possession, see *Baxter v Mannion* [2011] 1 WLR 1594 (noted at 6.7.3).

7.7.2 Application by adverse possessor for registration

The process by which an adverse possessor may apply for registration of title is set out in Sch. 6 of the Act.

7.7.2.1 The application

Schedule 6, para. 1 provides that the squatter may apply to the registrar to be registered as proprietor of a registered estate if the squatter has been in adverse possession of that estate:

> for the period of ten years ending on the date of application

Thus it is essential that the squatter is still in adverse possession when the application is made. This requirement emphasises the difference between the new system and the old rules, under which the squatter acquired rights of ownership on completion of the limitation period and retained these even if he or she subsequently went out of possession. By contrast, under LRA 2002 the only right acquired by the squatter is to apply for registration while he or she is still in adverse possession.

7.7.2.2 Notification of registered proprietor and others

On receiving the application, the registrar must give notice of it to the registered proprietor, and to a number of other people with interests in the property, including any legal mortgagees and, where the estate in question is leasehold, the freehold owner and any intervening landlords.

7.7.2.3 Deciding the application

Where such notice is given and the recipients either do not respond, or respond but do not oppose the application, the applicant may be registered as proprietor of the estate (para. 4). Thus in such cases, which will usually arise where the property has been abandoned, the minimum period for acquiring title by adverse possession is reduced from 12 to 10 years.

Where the proprietor or some other recipient of the notice does respond and opposes the application, it will in general be rejected. However, Sch. 6, para. 5 provides that in three special cases the application may be accepted despite opposition to it. These exceptional cases may be summarised as involving:

- estoppel;
- some other right to the land; and
- reasonable mistake as to boundaries.

There is more about these exceptional cases in 7.7.3.

7.7.2.4 Right to make a further application

If the application for registration has been opposed and consequently rejected, the registered proprietor (or other interested person) now has the opportunity to recover the property from the squatter. However, if this is not done and the applicant remains in possession for a further two years from the date of the rejection, he or she may then make a further application under para. 6 for registration and in such a case is entitled to be entered in the register as the new proprietor (paras. 6 and 7).

Thus a minimum period of 12 years' adverse possession continues to give title to the property, by entitling the possessor to be registered as proprietor, but in circumstances in which the proprietor has been informed of the squatter's presence at the 10-year mark and given an opportunity to safeguard his title.

Finally, it is essential to note that the periods of 10 and 12 years involved in this process are *minimum* periods. A squatter may well be in adverse possession for a much longer time before applying for registration, but the squatter cannot acquire title to it save through the process of registration.

7.7.3 Three special cases in which squatter may be registered despite opposition to application

We will now consider in a little more detail the exceptional cases in which an applicant may be registered after a minimum of 10 years' adverse possession despite opposition from the registered proprietor. Provision for this aspect of the new scheme is made by para. 5 of Sch. 6, and is based on the recommendations of the Joint Working Party, which considered that in these three cases 'the balance of fairness plainly lies with the squatter and he or she should prevail' (Consultative Document, para. 14.3.6).

7.7.3.1 Estoppel

Under para. 5(2) the applicant is entitled to be registered if:

(a) it would be unconscionable because of an equity by estoppel for the registered proprietor to seek to dispossess the applicant; and
(b) the circumstances are such that the applicant ought to be registered as proprietor.

As explained in 2.6.7, an estoppel may arise where one person has made a representation to another (by words or conduct) and the other has acted in reliance on that representation to his or her detriment (see further Chapter 19). In such circumstances, the representor is estopped from going back on the representation and the situation is said to give rise to an equity in the claimant (i.e., the right to some relief). It is for the court to decide how that equity is to be satisfied.

In the case of applications under Sch. 6, the relief may take the form of registering the applicant as owner of the land in question. If it is considered that the circumstances do not warrant registration, the case must be referred to the Property Chamber of the First-Tier Tribunal, which will decide how the equity is to be satisfied.

It may seem strange to talk of adverse possession in this context, but the working party explained that if a person with such rights is in possession of the land, it will be easier and cheaper to apply for registration under Sch. 6 than it would be to seek to enforce the rights through the courts (*Land Registration for the Twenty-First Century: A Conveyancing Revolution*, 2001, Law Com No. 271, para. 14.37—'the Report'). The same considerations apply to the next special case.

7.7.3.2 Some other right to the land

Paragraph 5(3) provides for registration if:

the applicant is for some other reason entitled to be registered as the proprietor of the estate.

This category is intended to cover situations in which the adverse possessor does in fact have some right to the land. The examples given by the working party include situations where the applicant is entitled to the land under the will or intestacy of the deceased proprietor or where a prospective purchaser of the estate is entitled to it under a bare trust, which has arisen because he or she has paid the full purchase price to the vendor but has not taken a transfer of the legal estate (the Report, para. 14.43).

7.7.3.3 Reasonable mistake as to boundaries

The third special case arises under para. 5(4), which provides for registration of the applicant if:

- the land in question is adjacent to land belonging to the applicant;
- the exact boundary between the two has not been determined by land registry procedures; and
- 'for at least ten years of the period of adverse possession ending on the date of the application the applicant (or any predecessor in title) reasonably believed that the land to which the application relates belonged to him'.

This right to registration may also be raised by a squatter as a defence in possession proceedings. There is more about this in the following section, and a note of two Court of Appeal decisions which interpret the requirement of 'reasonable belief'.

Thus, under the new scheme, a squatter who has been in possession for just 10 years will be able to acquire title to the estate by registration if a claim can be made under one of the three exceptions noted above. For critical comment on these provisions, see Dixon, 'Adverse Possession and the Land Registration Act 2002' [2009] 73 Conv 169 at 174.

7.7.4 Defence to proceedings for possession

So far we have been considering the situation in which the adverse possessor takes the initiative and applies for registration. However, the question of the squatter's entitlement to the estate may be raised in a very different way, by the registered proprietor bringing proceedings against him or her to recover possession. In general an adverse possessor has no defence in such proceedings because, under LRA 2002, that person has no right to the land enforceable against a person with superior title until registered as proprietor. Exceptionally, however, s. 98 gives a defence to an action for possession if the squatter can show that on the day immediately before the proceedings started:

- he or she satisfies the conditions for a successful application for registration on the grounds of reasonable mistake about boundaries (s. 98(1) and Sch. 6, para. 5(4)); or
- he or she is entitled to be registered, having remained in adverse possession for two years after the rejection of the previous application (s. 98(3) and Sch. 6, para. 6).

If the squatter succeeds in establishing either of these defences, the court must order the registrar to register him or her as proprietor of the estate in question (s. 98(5)).

You may wonder why the other two special cases in which a squatter may be registered despite opposition to the application (i.e., estoppel and some other right to the land—see 7.7.3), are not specified in s. 98 as defences to possession proceedings. The reason for this is that the defences given by LRA 2002 are additional to any other defences and thus the Act does not mention other existing defences.

Next we can consider the requirement that the defendant or applicant who relies on Sch. 6, para. 4 must have 'reasonably believed' that the land in question belonged to him.

7.7.4.1 Reasonable belief

A squatter who relies on Sch. 6, para. 5(4)(c) must (together with any predecessors in title) have had a reasonable, although mistaken, belief in his or her ownership of the land for at least 10 years *immediately before* the application for registration or, in the case of a defendant, before the commencement of proceedings against the defendant. This means that someone who may have been in possession of a strip of a neighbour's land for well over 10 years, reasonably believing that the apparent boundary line is the correct one, could lose the right to registration if, for example, he or she is persuaded by the neighbour's arguments that the possessor may be wrong. It is also important to note that the possessor must have a reasonable mistaken belief *as to the position of the boundary* between his land and adjacent land and that a reasonable mistaken belief about the ownership of the land generally will not suffice to engage this exception (*Dowse v Bradford MBC* [2020] UKUT 202). The question of whether a 'reasonable belief' could survive despite disputes ending in litigation was one of the points considered by the Court of Appeal in *Zarb v Parry* [2011] EWCA Civ 1306, [2012] 1 WLR 1240.

Zarb v Parry

The case concerned a boundary dispute between two neighbours: the claimants, Mr and Mrs Zarb, the registered owners of Daisymore, and the defendants, Mr and Mrs Parry, registered owners of Fleet House. The boundary between the two properties was marked by a hedge, and the dispute concerned a piece of land ('the Strip') that lay on the defendants' side of the hedge. For 10 years before the defendants bought Fleet House, their predecessors in title had believed that the Strip belonged to them. When the claimants bought Daisymore, they claimed that the hedge was located within their property and that they owned the Strip. However, they took no action about the matter. When the defendants bought Fleet House in 2002, they were aware that there had been some dispute about the boundary but understood that this had been resolved. In 2007, the claimants raised the question again. The parties tried to resolve the matter by jointly instructing a surveyor, who concluded that the correct boundary lay through the middle of the hedge. The claimants rejected this finding and in June 2009 began proceedings to recover possession of the Strip. The defendants claimed that they owned the Strip or, alternatively, that the periods of adverse possession by themselves and their predecessors in title, under the belief that they owned the land, entitled them to registration of title to it under Sch. 6, para. 5(4).

At first instance, the judge found that the Strip was part of the claimants' registered title, but held that the defendants and their predecessors in title had been in adverse possession of the property for well over the required 10 years and so were entitled to be registered as its owners. On appeal, the claimants argued that the defendants did not satisfy the Sch. 6, para. 5(4)(c) requirement of reasonable belief.

The trial judge had found on the evidence that the defendants' predecessors in title had believed that the Strip was theirs, and by implication was satisfied that their belief was reasonable. Although his decision also implied that the defendants had the necessary reasonable belief, he made no express reference to this point. Arden LJ therefore considered whether the evidence before the judge would support such a finding and at para. 51 outlined her reasons for holding that the defendants' belief was reasonable. When they bought Fleet House, the dispute was dormant, and remained so for the next five years, and when arguments arose, the surveyor's report confirmed their belief that the physical boundaries were the correct ones. Although Arden LJ does not say so specifically, one can infer that she considered this evidence sufficient to establish not merely that they had the necessary belief but also that they retained it until the claimants began their action. This part of the judgment is brief and there is no discussion of the standard to be used in assessing whether the belief is reasonable. For that, we need to refer to the second Court of Appeal decision on the s. 98 defence: *IAM Group PLC v Chowdrey* [2012] EWCA Civ 505, [2012] 2 P&CR 13.

IAM Group PLC v Chowdrey

The case concerned two attached properties, both with registered title: No. 26 owned by the claimant, IAM Group PLC ('the Company') and No. 26a owned by the defendant, Mr Chowdrey. The structure of the two properties was somewhat unusual, there being no access from the ground floor of No. 26 to the two floors above it, while there was access to those floors from No. 26a.

The defendant bought No. 26a in 1993, having already occupied it since 1990 as a tenant. During his time as tenant and later as owner he had possession of the two upper floors of No. 26 and the tenants of No. 26 made no attempt to use that part of the building. At the time of his purchase, he believed that he was buying exactly the same property he had previously rented. There was no material change in the layout of the two buildings between 1990 and the Company's commencement of possession proceedings some 20 years later (para. 16). As a result, he believed throughout this period that he owned the upper floors of the neighbouring property.

The title deeds of the properties, however, told a very different story. The two buildings had originally been in common ownership, and a lease of No. 26a granted for 27 years in 1918 had included the upper floors of No. 26. By 1928, the properties were separately owned, and a deed of that date confirmed that the title to No. 26 included the upper floors of the building. Moreover, the land registry plans of the two properties gave no indication that part of No. 26 was included in the title of No. 26a, and in fact showed a vertical division of the boundary between them (para. 18).

The Company bought No. 26 in 2000, at which time the ground floor was occupied by a tenant who regarded the upper floors as belonging to the defendant. Some eight years later, he notified the Company that he was the owner of part of No. 26. In response, the Company asserted its title to the property, supported by copies of the relevant land registry entries, and subsequently began proceedings to recover possession of the disputed property.

At first instance the judge concluded that the disputed property was within the Company's registered title and that there was a clear vertical boundary between the two properties. Nevertheless, he dismissed the Company's claim, holding that the defendant had established his s. 98 defence by satisfying the requirements of Sch. 6, para. 5(4)(c), and that he was entitled to be registered as owner of the disputed property.

On appeal, the Company asserted that the trial judge had erred in finding that the defendant had 'reasonably believed' that he owned the disputed property. The Company did not doubt that he 'did subjectively (that is honestly and actually) believe that he owned the property' (para. 21). However, the question of whether the belief was 'reasonable' must be judged objectively: that is, by the test of what a reasonable man would believe in the circumstances of the case. There was documentary evidence in both the 1928 deed and in the land registry documents that his title did not include the disputed property. When he bought No. 26 in 1993, his solicitors either knew or ought to have known this, and this knowledge should be imputed to him. Further, even if he had a reasonable belief at the outset, he could not claim to have retained this after receiving copies of the land registry entries from the Company.

The Court of Appeal rejected the Company's argument, Etherton LJ saying (at para. 27):

> We are not here concerned with knowledge in the context . . . of imputing an agent's knowledge to the principal . . . [but] with the requirement as to the reasonable belief of a particular person. . . . What is in issue therefore is not imputed knowledge but rather whether that particular person was reasonable in holding the belief that he or she did in all the circumstances.

Applying this test could involve considering whether the person should have asked his solicitors whether certain property was included in his title, but there was nothing in the circumstances of the defendant's purchase of No. 26a to suggest to him that he needed to ask whether his title included property 'of which he had enjoyed exclusive possession without challenge or question from the time he first acquired an interest in 1990 and the access to which [was] obtained solely from No. 26a' (at para. 28).

On the further point of whether the defendant retained a reasonable belief in his ownership after receiving copies of the land registry entries, Etherton LJ observed (at paras. 29–30) that:

> it is clear from *Zarb v Parry* that the mere fact that a paper title owner challenges the asserted ownership of land by the adverse possessor is not in every case sufficient to render unreasonable any continuing belief of ownership on the part of the adverse possessor . . . the question in every case is what, in all the circumstances, is the proper conclusion as to the reasonableness or otherwise of the continued belief as to ownership. . . .

In the circumstances of this case, the defendant had enjoyed unchallenged **exclusive occupation** for some 18 years before his title was challenged, and the judge was right to conclude that the challenge did not result in his continuing belief in his title ceasing to be reasonable. Accordingly, the court dismissed the Company's appeal.

For a critical consideration of this decision and that in *Zarb v Parry*, together with a suggestion of an alternative interpretation of Sch. 6, para. 4(c), see [2012] 76 Conv 342.

7.7.5 What does an adverse possessor obtain on registration?

Under Sch. 6, a successful applicant will be registered as proprietor of the estate held by the person who has been dispossessed and this may well mean that he or she becomes the new freehold owner. However, if the applicant has dispossessed a tenant holding under a registered lease, the applicant will be registered as the new proprietor of that leasehold estate and the freehold title will not be affected.

7.7.6 No. 3 Trant Way

If title to No. 3 is registered and Oscar did not complete the limitation period before LRA 2002 came into force, his position is not as secure as he believes it to be. The registered proprietor retains his title to the estate and will continue to do so however long Oscar remains in adverse possession. Adverse possession gives Oscar a purely relative title to the land, so, if the registered proprietor were to sell her superior title, he could not claim an overriding interest binding on the purchaser under LRA 2002, Sch. 3, para. 2 (interests of persons in actual occupation).

The only right which Oscar has under the Act is to apply for registration with supporting proof that he has been in adverse possession for a minimum of 10 years immediately before his application. It does appear that the property has been abandoned, so if Oscar is lucky there will be no response when the registry notifies the registered proprietor: in that case Oscar will be registered as the new owner. If his application is opposed, it will be rejected as it seems unlikely that any of the Sch. 6 para. 5 requirements are satisfied on the facts. The registered proprietor has not made any representations to Oscar that would generate an equity by estoppel as a result of detrimental reliance. There seems to be no other reason why Oscar has become entitled to be registered as proprietor. Finally, the land is not a strip of land adjacent to land already belonging to Oscar, so that he could say he had a reasonable mistaken belief as to the location of the boundary. Oscar's only hope then would be that the registered proprietor will continue to neglect his property and will fail to recover possession, with the result that after a further two years Oscar will be entitled to make a further application and will then obtain registration.

7.8 What if the adverse possession is a crime?

Over the centuries, the adverse possession of land belonging to another was purely a civil matter of trespass between the original owner and the person who had taken possession. The possession was not a crime, although the refusal to comply with an order for possession obtained by the owner would be. However, this situation changed in some cases with the passage of s. 144(1) of the Legal Aid Sentencing and Punishment of Offenders Act 2012 ('LASPOA 2012'):

> (1) A person commits an offence if—
> (a) the person is in a residential building as a trespasser having entered it as a trespasser,
> (b) the person knows or ought to know that he or she is a trespasser, and
> (c) the person is living in the building or intends to live there for any period.

After the introduction of this new crime of residential trespass, the question arose as to whether a squatter could rely on a period of possession that constituted an offence under the new provisions in order to claim title by adverse possession. In this respect it is important to note that s. 144(7) specifically covers the case of someone who entered into possession before the introduction of the new offence. It is a general principle of the law that one cannot use a statute as 'an engine of fraud', to use the old terminology used in the past to describe this principle ('the illegality principle'). The argument was that to rely on the adverse possession provisions in Sch. 6 to the LRA 2002, where the possession was a criminal offence under s. 144 of LASPOA 2012, was to use the LRA 2002 provisions to obtain a benefit from behaviour that was now a criminal offence.

In *R (Best) v Chief Land Registrar* [2015] EWCA Civ 17, [2016] QB 23 the Court of Appeal was called upon to resolve a dispute concerning a person (Best) who was seeking registration of title to registered land by adverse possession, in reliance on more than 10 years as a 'squatter' in the property. When the 2002 Act was passed, there would have been no problem with the Land Registrar dealing with Best's application to register, subject to suitable evidence of possession for the required period.

The Land Registrar declined to register Best's title because at least part of the 10 years of possession on which his application depended constituted a criminal offence under s. 144 of LASPOA 2012. The registrar relied on earlier court decisions on a long-standing principle that a wrongdoer cannot rely on his or her wrongdoing to found a claim (see, for example, *Les Laboratoires Servier v Apotex Inc* [2014] 3 WLR 1257). The registrar relied particularly on a decision of the Administrative Court in *R (Smith) v Land Registry* [2009] EWHC 328 (Admin). In that case the judge had concluded that the registrar was correct to refuse to register title where the possession relied upon involved a criminal obstruction of the highway.

After earlier decisions on the *Best* application, the dispute between Best and the Chief Land Registrar came before the Court of Appeal (composed of Arden LJ, McCombe LJ, and Sales LJ). In summary, the decision was that the fact that the possible offence under s. 144 of LASPOA 2012 did not prevent Best relying on that period for the purposes of Sch. 6 of LRA 2002.

At para. 50, Sales LJ said:

> I do not consider that the enactment of section 144 and the commission of an offence under it has any material effect on the operation of the law of adverse possession.

See also the further comments to the same effect in para. 75 of the judgment.

Sales LJ pointed to a recent immigration and employment case as the best guide to the correct approach to the *Best* case (*Houga v Allen* [2014] 1 WLR 2889). That case involved an employee who had illegally been brought from Nigeria to the UK by her employer. The employee was then dismissed by the employer and the employee claimed the dismissal was discriminatory and went to the Industrial Tribunal. The problem was that her contract of employment was unlawful because it involved her employment as an illegal immigrant. When the case reached the courts, the decision was that the employee could bring a claim for unlawful discrimination, even if the employment contract relied upon was in itself unlawful.

In the *Best* case the Court emphasised that the whole area of law about which wrongs can or cannot be relied upon is inherently based on public policy (see paras. 57–9). Very careful consideration of later legislative provisions will be needed in order to determine what the precise intention of the legislature was. The decision suggests very clear wording will normally be required in order to make creation of an offence necessarily override the earlier legislation.

Even in relation to the *Best* type of case, Sales LJ said (para. 67) that he reserved his opinion about a hypothetical case he posited, in which a squatter was not only in breach of s. 144 of LASPOA 2012 but stayed in occupation by bribing a police officer who came to remove him. This indicates that the public policy background to this area of law might produce different results in different instances due to the precise facts of each case.

7.9 Adverse possession and human rights

At one time it was said by some that acquisition of title by adverse possession might be incompatible with the provisions of the European Convention on Human Rights ('the Convention') (see further 2.9).

In the case of unregistered land, completion of the necessary period extinguishes the owner's title to the land, without any reference to a court (Limitation Act 1980, s. 17). The owner is deprived of his property without compensation, arguably in breach of both Art. 1 of the First Protocol (protection of property) and Art. 6 (right to a fair trial).

Similar considerations apply to adverse possession under the old rules relating to registered land where the registered proprietor loses first his or her beneficial interest in the land (under the statutory trust imposed by LRA 1925, s. 75(1)) and later his or her legal title, again without reference to any court and without compensation. Although there is scope under the Convention for justifying interference with certain rights as being in the public interest, it was thought that loss of title to registered land would be particularly difficult to justify. Adverse possession of unregistered land can be said to be of general benefit by simplifying and shortening the investigation of title (7.2.1.2). However, this consideration would not apply in the case of registered land, where investigation of title has already been simplified by registration, and the possibility of future challenges on human rights grounds were among the concerns which led to the new system of adverse possession introduced by LRA 2002.

7.9.1 *Pye v Graham*

Human rights issues were raised in *J. A. Pye (Oxford) Ltd v Graham* [2003] 1 AC 419 (see 7.3.1.2). They were dealt with fairly briefly in the House of Lords, because HRA 1998, which came into effect on 2 October 2000, does not have retrospective effect and so did not apply to the case. Nevertheless, concerns about the human rights implications of this case were expressed both by the trial judge and in the House of Lords. At first instance ([2000] Ch 676 at p. 710) Neuberger J described the supposed justification for adverse possession in no uncertain terms:

> A frequent justification for limitation periods generally is that people should not be able to sit on their rights indefinitely . . . However, if as in the present case the owner of land has no immediate use for it and is content to let another person trespass on the land for the time being, it is hard to see what principle of justice entitles the trespasser to acquire the land for nothing from the owner simply because he has been permitted to remain there for 12 years. To say that in such circumstances the owner who has sat on his rights should therefore be deprived of his land appears to me to be illogical and disproportionate. Illogical because the only reason that the owner can be said to have sat on his rights is because of the existence of the 12-year limitation period in the first place; if no limitation period existed he would be entitled to claim possession whenever he actually wanted the land . . . disproportionate because, particularly in a climate of increasing awareness of human rights including the right to enjoy one's own property, it does seem draconian to the owner and a windfall to the squatter that, just because the owner has taken no steps to evict a squatter for 12 years, the owner should lose . . . land to the squatter with no compensation whatsoever.

These views were shared by at least some members of the House of Lords ([2003] 1 AC 419), Lord Bingham saying (para. 1) that he would echo the misgivings expressed by Neuberger J, and Lord Hope speaking of the 'apparent injustice of the result' (para. 67).

7.9.2 *Pye v United Kingdom*

On losing the appeal to the House of Lords the former owners, Pye, began proceedings against the UK government in the European Court of Human Rights ('ECtHR').

In *J. A. Pye (Oxford) Ltd v United Kingdom* [2005] 3 EGLR 1, the ECtHR held that Pye's rights under the Convention had been violated and that they were entitled to compensation for the loss of their land. However, this decision was later reversed by the Grand Chamber of the ECtHR on appeal by the United Kingdom government. In *J. A. Pye (Oxford) Ltd v United Kingdom* [2007] ECHR 700, the Grand Chamber held by a majority (10 out of the 17 judges) that there had been no violation of Pye's rights.

The judgments on both the application and the appeal follow the same pattern, and in effect consider three questions.

7.9.2.1 Did the statutory provisions on adverse possession amount to an interference by the state with the applicant's rights under the Convention?

The Grand Chamber held that there had been an interference with Pye's rights under the Convention, and that the Chamber had been correct in dealing with the case under Art. 1 of the First Protocol ('the Article'). It thus rejected the government's claim that the case should have been determined only by reference to Art. 6 of the Convention, which deals with the right to a fair trial. However, the Article contains three distinct rules and the Grand Chamber did not agree with the original decision as to the part of the Article that was applicable in the case. The Article provides:

> Every . . . person is entitled to the peaceful enjoyment of his possessions. No one shall be deprived of his possessions except in the public interest and subject to the conditions provided for by law and by the general principles of international law.
> The preceding provisions shall not, however, in any way impair the right of a State to enforce such laws as it deems necessary to control the use of property in accordance with the general interest . . .

On hearing Pye's application, the Chamber had considered that their loss of property amounted to a 'deprivation of possessions', within the second sentence of the first paragraph. By contrast the Grand Chamber held that the case was one of 'control of use' by the state under the second paragraph. The Grand Chamber considered a number of its previous decisions on the circumstances which bring a case within one or other of these provisions, and concluded (at para. 66) that:

> The statutory provisions which resulted in [Pye's loss of ownership] were thus not intended to deprive paper owners of their ownership, but rather to regulate questions of title . . .

If you are not familiar with the case law on human rights you may find it difficult to understand the significance of the distinction that is being made here, but it is relevant to the question of liability to pay compensation.

Under the Article, interference with property rights may be justified on the grounds of 'public interest' (in the case of deprivation of possessions) or of 'general interest' (in the case of control of use under the second paragraph), and this led to the second question of whether adverse possession could be justified.

7.9.2.2 Could the law of adverse possession be justified on the grounds of general interest?

In judging what is in the general interest the ECtHR accepts that national authorities are better placed than an international judge to appreciate what is required in a particular state. It therefore respects the judgment of the state legislature unless that judgment is manifestly without foundation. The Grand Chamber concluded that many Member States had similar rules and that the UK legislature must have considered the rules to be in the public interest at the time of LRA 1925.

Thus, the control of the use of property through the rules of adverse possession could be justified as being in the general interest. However, the method used for exercising such control must be proportionate.

7.9.2.3 Did the rules of adverse possession produce a proportionate result?

In considering this question, the ECtHR has to weight the interests of the individual against the general interest: in this case, to decide whether the outcome for Pye represented a fair balance between general and individual interests (i.e., whether it was proportionate).

It is on this third question that the judgment of the Grand Chamber differed completely from that of the original Chamber, although the same arguments were put forward again by both parties and the same test was applied on both occasions (see para. 75), namely:

> whether a fair balance has been struck between the demands of the general interest and the interest of the individuals concerned.

It simply appears that the Grand Chamber found the arguments put forward by the UK Government more compelling than those relied upon by Pye. Thus the Grand Chamber gave greater weight to the fact that the rules of adverse possession had been in force for many years, that the limitation period was a relatively long one, and that it would have taken very little action on the part of Pye to have stopped time running against it (paras. 77 and 78).

By contrast, the Grand Chamber was dismissive of the main points on which Pye relied (points which, interestingly, had been considered so significant by those who were critical of the English system).

1. Lack of compensation

Interference with Pye's rights arose from control of use, rather than from the deprivation of possessions which meant that the case law on compensation was not directly applicable (para. 79). Moreover, the Grand Chamber accepted the Government's argument that permitting claims for compensation would undermine the whole purpose of a limitation system, which is designed to promote certainty by preventing the bringing of stale claims (para. 79).

2. Absence of procedural protection

The court accepted that Pye had not been without procedural protection, since they could have recovered possession by court action at any time during the limitation period and even afterwards they could argue in the courts (as they had done) that the squatter had not been in 'adverse possession'. The Grand Chamber also noted that the LRA 2002 had provided additional procedures to protect the paper owner.

3. Size of Pye's loss and the squatter's gain

The Grand Chamber commented, rather unsympathetically, that the acquisition of rights by an adverse possessor must go hand in hand with a corresponding loss of property rights for the former owner (para. 83), adding that limitation periods, if they are to fulfil their purpose, must apply regardless of the size of the claim. The value of the land could not therefore be of any consequence to the outcome of the case (para. 84).

Taking all these matters into account, the Grand Chamber concluded that the fair balance required by the Article between the general interest and the interest of the individual involved 'was not upset in the present case' (para. 85), and as a result held that there had been no violation of Art. 1 of the First Protocol.

7.9.3 What is the status of *Pye v UK* in English law?

This question was considered by the Court of Appeal in *Ofulue v Bossert* [2009] Ch 1. There is no need to consider the facts of the case, save to note that it concerned adverse possession of registered land and that, as in *Pye v Graham*, the limitation period had been completed before the Human Rights Act 1998 came into force.

On appeal, the dispossessed owners, the Ofulues, argued that the court should make its own assessment in each case of whether the English rules of adverse possession had a legitimate aim, and whether they maintained a fair balance between the general interest and the interests of the dispossessed owner. They said that their own case differed from that in *Pye v Graham*.

In dismissing the appeal, the court emphatically rejected this approach. English courts are currently required to take account of judgments of the ECtHR, and would have to have very good reasons for departing from the jurisprudence of that court (paras. 30–3). Accordingly, the court considered that it should follow the decision in *Pye v UK* (para. 4) and it would not be appropriate for the present court to re-examine these matters from the perspective of individual cases (paras. 52 and 53).

Accordingly, the current rules on adverse possession are compliant with the ECHR and thus with the Human Rights Act 1998.

FURTHER READING

Dockray, 'Why Do We Need Adverse Possession?' [1985] Conv 273.

Gray and Gray, *Elements of Land Law*, 5th edn., Oxford University Press, 2008, paras. 9.1.6–9.1.13 (the rationale of acquisition by adverse possession).

Megarry and Wade, *The Law of Real Property*, 9th edn., Sweet & Maxwell, 2019, Chapter 7.

Rostill, *Possession, Relative Title, and Ownership of Land*, Oxford University Press, 2021, chapter 7 (historical origins of adverse possession).

Proposals for reform

Land Registration for the Twenty-First Century: A Consultative Document, 1998, Law Com No. 254, Part X (in particular, 10.1–10.19, and 10.43–10.64).

Land Registration for the Twenty-First Century: A Conveyancing Revolution, 2001, Law Com No. 271, Part XIV (in particular, 14.1–14.8—summary of changes).

LRA 2002

Dixon, 'Adverse Possession and the Land Registration Act 2002' [2009] 73 Conv 169.

J.A. Pye (Oxford) Ltd v United Kingdom (Grand Chamber)

Dixon, 'Adverse Possession, Human Rights and Land Registration: And They All Lived Happily Ever After?' [2007] 71 Conv 552.

Dixon, 'Human Rights and Adverse Possession: The Final Nail?' [2008] 72 Conv 160 (note on *Ofulue v Bossert*).

Radley-Gardner and Small, 'Shut out of Europe' [2007] EG—15 September 2007 (No. 0737) 228.

IAM Group PLC v Chowdry and Zarb v Parry

Milne, 'Mistaken Belief and Adverse Possession—Mistaken Interpretation?' [2012] 76 Conv 342.

You can visit the online resources to test your knowledge of this chapter with self-test questions at **www.oup.com/he/nair19e/**.

PART III
Legal estates

Introduction

Having considered the general background to the modern law relating to land, this Part examines in detail the nature of the two legal estates.

You will recall that, under the provisions of LPA 1925, s. 1(1), there are two legal estates in land:

(a) the fee simple absolute in possession—the freehold estate;
(b) the term of years absolute—the leasehold estate.

The fee simple estate is the larger of the two legal estates, being capable of lasting indefinitely, and it underpins everything else in this book. Leasehold estates, for example, are created out of the freehold (or out of a superior lease which is itself derived directly or indirectly from the freehold) and thus derive their validity from the existence of the fee simple.

Chapter 8 deals with the freehold estate, including the fee simple absolute in possession. Further material on the nature of the estate will also be found in Chapter 26, which addresses the rights which a freehold owner has over land and the nature of land itself.

By contrast with the freehold estate, you will find the landlord and tenant relationship is quite complex. Chapter 9 considers the nature and characteristics of a lease, and the ways in which it is created and brought to an end. Chapter 10 deals with the rights and duties of the landlord and tenant who are the parties to the lease. Chapter 11 explains the enforcement of leasehold covenants. Chapter 12 discusses the remedies available to one party to a lease when the other is in breach of duty.

PART II

Legal estates

8

The freehold estate

8.1	Introduction 173	8.4	In possession 176
8.2	Fee simple 174	8.5	Intervention of public policy 178
8.3	Absolute 174	8.6	Commonhold 179

8.1 Introduction

8.1.1 4 Trant Way

The estate in fee simple in 4 Trant Way (i.e., the freehold) is owned by David Derby. He has decided to give the estate to one of either of his two nephews or his niece and is considering the following three possible dispositions:

- giving the estate to his niece Erica 'on condition that she does not marry';
- giving the estate to his nephew Frank 'until he finds full-time employment' (Frank is at present a student);
- giving the estate to his friend George for life and then to his nephew Hal for life, 'provided that Hal marries before George dies'.

You will remember that s. 1(1) of LPA 1925 provides that only a fee simple absolute in possession can be a legal freehold estate in land and all attempts to create a lesser freehold will take effect only in equity. In this chapter, we consider whether each of these three possible gifts would vest in the nephew/niece or friend concerned a legal fee simple absolute in possession, or whether the gift would create an equitable interest in land.

You may find it helpful when reading this chapter to refer to Table 8.1, which sets out the eventual position in relation to each of the options that Mr Derby is considering.

Table 8.1 Dispositions of freehold estate

Nature of disposition	Result
To E on condition that she does not marry.	E gets a conditional fee simple, a legal estate. Condition may be void for public policy reasons. See 8.3.1.
To F, until he finds full-time employment.	F gets a determinable fee, which is an equitable interest. D retains a 'possibility of reverter'. Gives rise to a trust. See 8.3.2 and 8.4.2.
To G for life, and then to H for life provided that H marries before G dies.	G gets an equitable interest for life.
	H gets a contingent equitable interest. If he marries before G dies, H gets at that point a future equitable interest.
	G has the reversion in equity.
	Gives rise to a trust. See 8.4.1 and 8.4.2.

As described in Chapter 1, the phrase 'fee simple absolute in possession' in s. 1(1) of LPA 1925 imposes a series of requirements, all of which must be satisfied if the estate is to qualify as a legal one. This chapter covers these requirements in more detail, and considers whether David's proposed gifts would satisfy them.

8.2 Fee simple

It has already been explained (at 1.5.1.2 and 1.7.1.1) that a fee simple used to be an estate in land which was inheritable by the general heirs of its owner. This distinguished the fee simple from the life estate (which was not inheritable) and the fee tail (which was inheritable only by a restricted class of heirs, typically 'heirs of the body male'). When the rules of intestate succession were changed in 1925, so that both real and personal property were treated alike, the concept of 'the heir' became in the main obsolete. Before 1926, unlike personal property, real property (see 1.7.1.1) passed automatically on death to the legally-defined class of 'heirs'. However, since the Administration of Estates Act 1925, real and personal property are treated alike: if a person dies intestate, both types of property will now pass to her administrators who are obliged to distribute it among her statutory next of kin. As a result, it is no longer correct to define the fee simple as being inherited by the general heirs. It is, however, still true that the fee simple is an estate which lasts indefinitely, so long as there is anyone entitled to take the property under the will or on the intestacy of the previous owner.

The other two freehold estates which used to exist (the life estate and the fee tail) do not come within the definition of legal estates in LPA 1925, s. 1(1), and, since they are not on the list of legal interests in s. 1(2), they therefore take effect after 1925 as equitable interests under s. 1(3). This meant that the legal fee simple had to be held on trust to give effect to such interests. As a result of TOLATA 1996, it is no longer possible to create a new entailed interest in land (1.7.1.4).

8.3 Absolute

The word 'absolute' in s. 1(1) indicates that there must be no provision in the grant of the fee simple which might cause it to end prematurely while there is still someone qualified to take it. Fees which are subject to such provisions are known as 'modified' fees, and can arise in two forms:

- conditional interests; and
- determinable interests.

The disposition of 4 Trant Way to Erica Derby 'on condition that she does not marry' would be a conditional interest, while a disposition of the property to Frank Derby 'until he finds full-time employment' would be a determinable interest.

8.3.1 Conditional interests

A conditional interest arises where a fee simple is granted subject to a limitation which provides that the grantor will be able to re-enter the property at some date in the future on the occurrence (or non-occurrence) of specified events. In such a case the grantor initially confers a fee simple absolute, but then reserves the right to recover the land (usually described as a right of re-entry). It is only when the right of re-entry is exercised by the grantor that the fee simple comes to an end. This type of arrangement is said to be an interest subject to a condition subsequent. Such interests did not comply with the requirements of LPA 1925, s. 1(1), and so, under the terms of that statute, could not amount to legal estates.

However, this rule gave rise to immediate problems when the 1925 legislation came into force, because many estates had been sold as subject to rentcharges, as part of a practice of vendors selling freehold land in exchange for a promise to make periodic payments of 'rent' rather than lump sums (sometimes called 'fee farm rents', see 2.5.2). These usually provided that the owner of the rentcharge would be entitled to re-enter the land if the payments secured by the rentcharge were not made. In certain parts of the country (e.g., Bristol and Manchester) most of the fee simple estates were then subject to rentcharges, and the effect of s. 1(1) was to turn all these estates into equitable interests, since they were all subject to a right of re-entry on occurrence of a specified condition.

As a result, the Law of Property (Amendment) Act 1926 was passed, and the Schedule to that Act amended LPA 1925, s. 7(1), to read:

> [A] fee simple subject to a legal or equitable right of entry or re-entry is for the purposes of this Act a fee simple absolute.

This wording was, however, wider than was necessary to deal solely with the problem caused by rentcharges and produced the result that all fees simple subject to a right of re-entry became legal estates. Thus a conditional fee simple will be a legal estate within the meaning of LPA 1925, s. 1(1). Therefore, in principle, if 4 Trant Way is given to Erica Derby in fee simple on condition that 'she does not marry', Erica will receive a legal estate: she will be treated as having a fee simple absolute in possession, although her fee simple could come to an end if David or his successor exercise their right of re-entry (which they will be entitled to do if she marries). This form of words might, however, be open to objections on the grounds of public policy (see 8.5).

8.3.2 Determinable interests

A determinable fee is one which according to its terms will last only until a specified event occurs, or does not occur. Thus, a grant of the fee simple in 4 Trant Way to Frank Derby 'until he finds full-time employment' is a determinable fee. The fee lasts only until Frank gets a job. The fee would still be determinable even if it is very unlikely that the specified event will ever occur, because, from the outset, the period of the interest has been cut down. Such interests are not within LPA 1925, s. 1(1), and are not saved by s. 7(1) as amended. Since they are not included in the list of legal interests in s. 1(2), they take effect as equitable interests under s. 1(3).

The grantor retains an interest in the land, known as the **'possibility of reverter'**, and when the determining event occurs the property reverts automatically to him.

8.3.3 Differences between conditional and determinable fees

Whether a grant creates a conditional fee or a determinable fee may well be an accident of wording, and the grantor may not intend to create one rather than the other. The same arrangement can often be expressed in either way. Thus a grant 'to A on condition that he does not become a lawyer' is a conditional fee and creates a legal estate, subject to a right of re-entry; while a grant 'to A until he becomes a lawyer' is a determinable fee, which can only be an equitable interest. Because of this many students (and even courts, see *Re Moore* (1888) 39 ChD 116) find it difficult to distinguish between the two classes of right. The following lists of expressions which have been categorised as creating either conditional or determinable fees may help in identifying the nature of a particular grant:

Conditional	Determinable
'on condition that . . .'	'until . . .'
'providing that . . .'	'as long as . . .'
'but if . . .'	'for the duration of . . .'
	'while . . .'

However, although the distinction between the two types of fee appears to be a matter of form, rather than of substance, the difference can be of considerable importance to the grantee. We have already seen that a conditional fee takes effect as a legal estate, while a determinable fee can exist only as an equitable interest. A further difference will be experienced if the specified event occurs. In the case of the determinable fee, the interest will immediately come to an end and the grantee has no further right to the land. By contrast, the fee subject to a condition subsequent will in fact continue until the grantor, or the grantor's successor in title, exercises the right of re-entry. Thus, the grantee could be able to remain on the land indefinitely, as the grantor might choose not to exercise the right of re-entry. In such a case, you should also note that the right of re-entry could be extinguished by the Limitation Act 1980. This will happen if 12 years pass after the condition has occurred and the holder of the right has still not exercised his right to recover the land (see 7.2.1.1).

Thus a distinction which might seem to the grantor to be little more than a matter of style can have far-reaching consequences for the grantee and, as Parker MR said in *Re King's Trusts* (1892) 29 LR Ir 401 at p. 410, the difference between the two produces a rule which is 'little short of disgraceful to our jurisprudence'.

8.3.4 Reverter to transferor on failure to apply for first registration

We saw in 6.3.2.3 that, where a transfer of unregistered land triggers a requirement of first registration, the legal estate will revert to the transferor if the transferee fails to apply for registration within the prescribed period. Where the estate in question is a fee simple, the possibility that this might happen could give rise to doubts as to whether it is a fee simple absolute. Accordingly, LRA 2002, s. 7(4) provides that the possibility of such reverter is to be disregarded for the purposes of determining whether a fee simple is a fee simple absolute.

8.4 In possession

8.4.1 Future interests

Landowners may wish to create future interests in their property, that is, interests which will come into existence on the happening of some future event such as the performance of a condition *precedent* (i.e., a condition which has to be fulfilled before the grantee can enjoy the property: contrast the condition *subsequent* discussed at 8.3.1). An illustration of such a condition is provided by the grant of 4 Trant Way to David Derby's friend George 'for life', and then to his nephew Hal for life, 'provided that Hal marries before George dies'.

If the gift was made in these terms, Hal would, at the outset, have no interest in the property, but merely a chance of acquiring one in the future. Rather confusingly, he is said to have a 'contingent', or 'conditional', interest, but in fact no interest in the land will arise until the condition is met. Should Hal marry before George's death, he will have satisfied the condition and will then have a vested future interest in the property: that is, an interest entitling him to possession of the house in the future. For two reasons, this interest would not be capable of being a legal estate: not only is it for life, but it also takes effect in the future, and so does not satisfy the requirement of LPA 1925, s. 1(1), that to be legal a fee simple must take effect in possession. Thus, under the Act, a future interest, even in fee simple, cannot be legal and takes effect only in equity.

8.4.2 Remainders and reversions

We must now mention two technical terms used to describe future interests: '**reversions**' and '**remainders**'.

A *'reversion'* arises where a grantor gives away an estate, or series of estates, which will last for a shorter time than his own estate. The gifts to George and Hal are an example of this, for David Derby has a fee simple, which is capable of lasting forever, and he would have given away, at the most, only two life interests. When they came to an end, the property would revert to Mr Derby, or, if he was dead, would form part of his estate and devolve according to the terms of his will, or by the rules of intestate succession. The grantor therefore has a future right to the property from the date of the gift, and that future right is called a 'reversion'.

If, however, the grantor were to give away his full estate to a series of people, he will have kept no reversion in the property and the future interests he has created will be called *'remainders'*. Thus, if Mr Derby were to provide that, after George and Hal have died, the property should belong in fee simple to Ian, the grantor will have no reversion, and Hal and Ian would both be said to have remainders (Hal would have a life estate in remainder, and Ian would have a fee simple in remainder). George would have a life interest in possession, which means he would be entitled to enjoy the property immediately the gift took effect.

We have seen that the full fee simple absolute in possession is the only freehold estate which can exist in law, and that, with the exception of the conditional interest for Erica Derby (see 8.3.1), all the other dispositions which David Derby wants to make can take effect only in equity. In order to give effect to his wishes, therefore, it would be necessary to make use of a trust, so that the legal fee simple would be held by trustees and Mr Derby's niece/nephews and his friend would be entitled to equitable interests for the period and on the conditions stated in the grant. Trusts of this type are discussed in Chapter 14 (trusts created after 1997) and Chapter 15 (trusts created before 1997). You should also note that this type of control over the future enjoyment of land is only allowed for a limited period of time, known as the 'perpetuity period'. The rule against perpetuities, which invalidates trusts that seek to extend a previous owner's control of the future enjoyment of land too far into the future, is discussed in Chapter 17.

8.5 Intervention of public policy

It should not be thought from what has gone before that an estate owner is entitled to grant estates or interests subject to any limitations that he or she wishes. The courts will intervene in cases in which a limitation is considered to be contrary to public policy. Thus, in general a grant of an estate 'on condition that A does not marry' will be regarded as being contrary to public policy and the grant will take effect absolutely and free of the objectionable condition (*Kelly v Monck* (1795) 3 Ridg Parl Rep 205). It is permissible, however, to make a provision the purpose of which is simply to provide for someone until he or she marries, rather than to prevent marriage (*Jones v Jones* (1876) 1 QBD 279). Thus, normally an estate which is determinable on marriage is not so objectionable. David Derby, therefore, would be well-advised to reconsider the proposed grant to his niece Erica, for the present wording could result in a fee simple absolute free from condition.

It should also be noted that there are other cases in which public policy will intervene, e.g., where a disposition might have the effect of discouraging parents from exercising their own judgment about the religious education of a child (*Re Borwick* [1933] Ch 657) or preventing an adult taking public office or being employed in the armed services (*Re Edgar* [1939] 1 All ER 635; *Re Beard* [1908] 1 Ch 383). Obviously, however, the views expressed by the courts on such clauses are likely to vary with the times and courts have generally been cautious in deciding that a gift should be void on the grounds of public policy, because of their respect for the countervailing principle of freedom of testation (the freedom to decide the terms of one's will).

In *Blathwayt v Baron Cawley* [1976] AC 397, for example, the House of Lords refused to void a gift of a life interest subject to a condition that its holder should not 'be or become a Roman Catholic', holding that the gift was not contrary to public policy merely because the testator had chosen to prefer members of one religion over another. It was suggested that a gift that required trustees to discriminate on the grounds of religion was contrary to public policy, given the anti-discrimination legislation that had been enacted in England and Wales in the 1960s (see now the Equality Act 2010), and the provisions of the European Convention of Human Rights (see 8.5.2). Rejecting this argument, Lord Wilberforce said:

> My Lords, I do not doubt that conceptions of public policy should move with the times and that widely accepted treaties and statutes may point the direction in which such conceptions, as applied by the courts, ought to move. It may well be that conditions such as this are, or at least are becoming, inconsistent with standards now widely accepted. But acceptance of this does not persuade me that we are justified, particularly in relation to a will which came into effect as long ago as 1936 . . . in introducing for the first time a rule of law which would go far beyond the mere avoidance of discrimination on religious grounds. To do so would bring about a substantial reduction of another freedom, firmly rooted in our law, namely that of testamentary disposition.

8.5.1 Restrictions on alienation

One class of conditions or determining events to which the courts have always taken strong exception consists of provisions by which the grantor tries to restrict the power of the recipient to dispose of the property freely. Ever since the statute *Quia Emptores* in

1290 (see 1.4) it has been a principle of the law that generally an estate owner should have a free and unfettered power to alienate his or her property. Across the centuries the courts have continued to enforce this principle. Thus, in *Hood v Oglander* (1865) 34 Beav 513 at p. 522 it was said that a condition preventing **alienation** at any time would be void. The courts will, however, tolerate some restrictions on disposal of an estate which fall short of an absolute bar and indeed in some cases have been remarkably tolerant in dealing with restrictions which prevent disposal outside a particular family. Thus, in *Re Macleay* (1875) LR 20 Eq 186 a disposition to someone 'on condition that he never sells it out of the family' was upheld. One cannot guarantee, however, that modern courts would be so generous and in any event this decision was rather more limited in its scope than may first appear: the recipient alone was bound by the condition, it did not bind anyone to whom he transferred the estate, and it only prevented a *sale* outside the family; the recipient could *give* the property to anyone. Despite this limited approval given to such a restriction upon disposal, it is best to avoid such arrangements for fear that they may be struck down, leaving the estate owner with a free power to alienate the property. However, as you will see (14.5.2) it may be possible under TOLATA 1996 to create a trust for the specific purpose of retaining land, and it is certainly possible to provide that trust property cannot be alienated without the consent of specified persons.

8.5.2 Implications of Human Rights Act 1998

It is suggested in Gray and Gray at para. 3.1.33 that the Human Rights Act may be effective in striking down objectionable limitations:

> Although, like the determinable fee simple, the conditional fee has spawned a rich case law, some of the common law elaboration of this form of estate ownership may have been rendered redundant by the advent of the Human Rights Act 1998. The capacity for invidious discrimination so freely offered to the eccentric testator may in certain instances fall foul of Convention-based guarantees of individual freedom (if such guarantees are given horizontal effect).

It is certainly possible to imagine limitations which might infringe the prohibition of any discrimination which might affect the enjoyment of Convention rights (Art. 14) or violate rights such as those to respect for private and family life (Art. 8) or to freedom of conscience and religion (Art. 9). However, the lack of 'horizontal effect' in relation to such rights seems likely to produce a position in which the relevant human right does not assist (see 2.9), unless by influencing a court's judgment on whether a particular disposition is contrary to public policy.

8.6 Commonhold

In your reading, you may come across mention of a twenty-first century invention, called 'Commonhold'. This was a new concept introduced by Part 1 of the Commonhold and Leasehold Reform Act 2002, which came into force in September 2004. 'Commonhold' sounds as though it ought to be a novel form of tenure and an estate in land. However, commonhold simply makes use of existing forms in order to create a new arrangement.

Commonhold is designed to facilitate *freehold* ownership of 'interdependent properties'; that is, individual units such as flats in an apartment building, homes in a retirement village, and workshops or offices on an industrial estate. Although these sound like very different types of property—some residential and some commercial—they have several similarities. For a start, there are likely to be 'common parts' in all these developments—such as stairs, lifts, and car parks—which do not belong to any individual unit but are used by all unit holders. Arrangements have to be made for ownership and upkeep of these areas.

The other similarity between all these developments is that, in the interests of all the owners, there need to be rules controlling the use of individual units, and requiring each to be kept in a proper state of repair. If a flat in a block is allowed to deteriorate it can have an adverse effect on those above and below it, and obviously excessive noise or other anti-social behaviour will be of immediate concern to the neighbours. What is needed is a web of mutually enforceable covenants under which each unit holder takes on certain duties with the understanding that each also has the right to enforce the same obligations against other owners in the development. This is often done by giving the unit holders long **leasehold** estates in their units (see Chapter 9) and creating leasehold covenants that govern the use of each unit (see Chapters 10 and 11). It is much harder to create a similar web of obligations for freehold land, because covenants by freeholders that govern the use of their land ('freehold covenants') will normally bind and benefit later purchasers of the land only in a limited range of situations (see Chapter 25). At the same time, there are significant disadvantages to leasehold as a way of managing long-term ownership of land. The most obvious of these, from the point of view of the unit-owner, is the possible liability to pay a **'ground rent'** to the freeholder for the entire duration of the long lease (see 9.2.6).

Commonhold provides a system which is meant to address this problem and facilitate freehold ownership of interdependent properties. It can apply to both new and existing developments. Each unit holder owns the freehold estate in his or her property, and enters into a range of covenants, which—unlike normal freehold covenants—are enforceable between all unit holders in the property, and run to bind and benefit the new owner when a property changes hands. All unit holders are members of the 'commonhold association', a company limited by guarantee, which owns the freehold of the common parts and is responsible for all aspects of managing the property. Unit holders take part in decisions affecting the commonhold through their membership of the association.

In practice, commonhold has not yet been widely used. Developers seem still to be wary of it and tend to continue to use leasehold to address the issues raised by such developments. However, following widespread concerns that developers are tending to grant leases in new properties, rather than to sell the freehold estate, and that rents and other burdens are making such properties difficult to sell, the Government asked the Law Commission to reconsider the position on commonhold. The Law Commission Report *Reinvigorating Commonhold: The alternative to leasehold ownership* (Law Com No. 394), was published in July 2020. It proposed a series of measures to make it easier to convert existing leasehold estates into a commonhold structure and a number of reforms to the commonhold model designed to make it more attractive to property developers, prospective buyers of interdependent properties, and mortgage lenders. The Government has not yet formally responded to these recommendations. However, a Commonhold Council has now been established to look into what needs to be done to increase the popularity of commonhold as a mode of freehold ownership of interdependent properties and it is not yet clear what the outcome of this will be.

FURTHER READING

Megarry and Wade, *The Law of Real Property*, 9th edn., Sweet & Maxwell, 2019, paras. 3-028–3-045 (types of fee simple).

Smith, *Property Law*, 8th edn., Pearson Longman, 2014, pp. 35–43 (freehold estates).

You can visit the online resources to test your knowledge of this chapter with self-test questions at www.oup.com/he/nair19e/.

9

The leasehold estate

9.1	Introduction 182		9.5	Determining a lease 217
9.2	Basic requirements for a lease 189		9.6	Leases as contracts 225
9.3	Creation of leases 206		9.7	Summary 234
9.4	Transfer of leases 216			

9.1 Introduction

This is the first of three chapters on the leasehold estate, and the relationship between landlords and tenants. It explains the nature of a **lease** and the basic requirements for creating a valid lease (9.2). It then goes on to explain how leases may be created and transferred (9.3 and 9.4), how they come to an end (9.5) and the dual nature of the lease as a legal estate in land and as a contractual relationship (9.6). The summary at the end (9.7) offers a glossary of the many technical terms introduced in this chapter, which you may find helpful in revising its content. In later chapters, we will look at the content of the obligations that landlords and tenants may owe to each other (Chapter 10), who can be bound by those obligations and who can enforce them (Chapter 11), and the remedies for their breach (Chapter 12).

9.1.1 5 Trant Way

A few weeks ago, the Stilton Recorder carried the following advertisement in its property section:

> 5 Trant Way, Mousehole, Stilton.
> Leasehold maisonette. 99-yr. lease
> Pleasant maisonette, being ground and first floor of this elegant Victorian property.
> 2 recep. 2 bedrm. Bathrm. Sep WC. Spacious kitchen/breakfast rm.
> £450,000.

The current freehold owner of No. 5 is Fingall Forest, who is a widower with no children. He has lived there for many years, and title to the property is still unregistered. Mr Forest has decided that the house is too large for his needs and he has had it divided into three sections:

- a flat, consisting of the second floor of the property, in which he lives;
- the ground and first-floor maisonette, which is now for sale 'leasehold' (a 99-year lease); and

- the basement, which Mr Forest has let on a weekly tenancy to an old friend, Gerald Gruyère, at a rent of £175 a week.

Mr Forest's estate agent has now found a prospective purchaser for the maisonette, James Harding.

These two transactions, the sale of the maisonette on a 99-year lease and the letting of the basement on a weekly tenancy, seem at first glance to have very little in common. However, we shall see that, although Mr Gruyère and Mr Harding seem to have very different rights to occupy land, these rights both fall into the legal category of leases (or tenancies).

9.1.2 Leases as legal estates in land

As we have seen, s. 1(1) of the Law of Property Act 1925 provides that a lease, or 'term of years absolute', is one of the two legal estates in land recognised in English law. This means that, like a fee simple absolute in possession, it is a legal right to possess land for a period of time. Unlike a fee simple absolute in possession, however, a leasehold estate cannot go on forever but is limited to a defined period or 'term': 99 years in the case of Mr Harding, and a week in the case of Mr Gruyère.

A right to possess land for a week is, of course, very different from a right to possess land for 99 years. However, the content of the right—for as long as it lasts—is the same. A leaseholder, whatever the term of his or her lease, has a right to exclude others from the land for the duration of the lease: this includes not only the landlord, but also any successors in title. Suppose, for example, that Mr Forest attempted to move into the maisonette or the basement flat, having already let them to Mr Harding and Mr Gruyère. Since they are both leaseholders, they would both be entitled to resist such a move on his part and to bring an action in trespass against him. If he left his freehold title to a third party in his will—say, a charity—the leaseholder's rights would bind this new freeholder as well; the charity would be obliged to wait a week before it could begin the process of evicting Mr Gruyère (see 9.5.1), and 99 years before it could evict Mr Harding.

Like freeholders, leaseholders also have the standing to sue trespassers and other third parties who encroach on their possession of the land. A squatter who took over the basement flat could be evicted by Mr Gruyère, just as a squatter who took over the maisonette could be evicted by Mr Harding and one who occupied the second floor could be evicted by Mr Forest. In other words, although all the parties have rights to possession that will last for very different periods of time—Mr Forest for as long as there is someone to inherit (see 1.7.1.1), Mr Harding for 99 years, and Mr Gruyère for a week—each has a right that has a similar basic content, so far as third parties are concerned. They are all legal estates in land.

9.1.2.1 'Term of years'

LPA 1925, s. 1 requires that a leasehold estate should be for 'a term': that is, for a defined period, rather than for an indefinite one. It is this requirement of a defined term that distinguishes the leasehold estate from the various lesser freehold estates (see 1.6) that were demoted from the status of legal estates to equitable interests by the LPA 1925.

Like a leasehold estate, many of the estates that used to be recognised as freehold estates before 1926 were also likely to come to an end at some point. For example, a fee tail (see 1.5.1.3) would end when the original grantee ceased to have qualifying heirs, e.g., if his grandson died a bachelor without leaving any direct descendants. A life estate (see 1.5.1.1) ends when the grantee dies. The leasehold estate can be distinguished from the old limited freehold estates of this kind because its duration is not only limited but is also *fixed*. When a fee tail was granted, it could be not known at the date of the grant when, if ever, the condition for expiry of the estate would be met and the final heir of the body of the grantee would die. When a life estate is granted, it cannot be known at the date of the grant when exactly the grantee will die and the estate will come to an end. When a 99-year lease is granted, by contrast, it can be known from the outset that the lease will last for a maximum period of 99 years, no more. It is for this reason that, in *Lace v Chantler* [1944] KB 368, it was held that a purported lease 'for the duration of the war' could not take effect as a legal estate. At the time that the lease was granted, the exact period for which it would continue to exist could not be known and so the grant was not for a 'term'.

It might be thought that the expression 'term *of years*' in s. 1 means that a lease must be granted for a fixed term of more than one year, so that a 99-year lease would qualify but a lease for a week or a month would not. However, this impression is misleading. LPA 1925, s. 205(1)(xxvii), provides that:

> the expression 'term of years' includes a term for less than a year, or for a year or years and a fraction of a year or from year to year.

Accordingly, it is possible to grant a valid legal lease for a very short period. For example, in *Smallwood v Sheppards* [1895] 2 QB 627 it was held that a legal lease could be created for a period of three successive bank holidays, that is, for three separate days. More recently, it has been accepted that a time-sharing arrangement, giving the right to use a holiday cottage for one week a year over an 80-year period can amount to a legal lease for 'a single discontinuous period' (*Cottage Holiday Associates Ltd v Customs and Excise Commissioners* [1983] 1 QB 735).

1. Fixed term and periodic tenancies

As we have seen, a leasehold estate differs from a freehold estate because its duration is limited to a defined period or 'term'. In the case of the lease of the maisonette to Mr Harding for 99 years, it is obvious that the grant complies with this requirement. Mr Harding, and his successors, will be entitled to possession for a known period of time—99 years—and their right to possession will terminate, at the latest, on the expiry of this period. This is an example of a lease for a *fixed term*.

By contrast, the letting of the basement to Mr Gruyère is an example of a *periodic tenancy*. It does not seem to be granted for a single week, or for a fixed number of weeks: instead, it will run on indefinitely, from week to week, until one of the parties does not want to continue the arrangement, and therefore gives notice to the other. Tenancies can run on in this way from week to week, month to month, quarter to quarter, or year to year, being known as weekly, monthly, quarterly, or yearly tenancies respectively; the term intended by the parties to such a lease can usually be deduced by the frequency at which it is agreed that the tenant shall pay rent. In each case, what is technically happening is that the tenant initially receives an estate for a single period—a week, month, quarter, or year—and then impliedly agrees with the landlord to extend the term for a further week, month, quarter, or year. The principle, as explained by the House of Lords in *Hammersmith LBC v Monk* [1992] 1 AC 478 at p. 490, is that:

> the tenancy continues no further than the parties have already impliedly agreed upon by their omission to serve notice to quit . . . it is by his omission to give notice of termination that each party signifies the necessary positive assent to the extension of the term for a further period.

Therefore, even the tenant with a periodic tenancy does have a lease for a certain term, which is thus capable of being a legal estate under LPA 1925.

2. Leases for life or until marriage

You might think that a grant 'for T's life' or 'until T marries' cannot be a lease because the duration of such a lease is not certain. Before 1926, such grants created freehold estates (see 8.3.2), which could last for an uncertain time; they were often created as part of family settlements but they could also be commercial agreements, involving rent or other payment by the life tenant. As we have seen, the effect of the 1925 legislation was to abolish life estates and determinable estates as legal estates in land. Those created as part of family settlements would, in future, take effect as equitable interests under a trust (see 1.7.1.4 and 8.2). On the other hand, commercial leases for life were specially legislated for, under the provisions of LPA 1925, s. 149(6).

Under s. 149(6) (as amended by the Civil Partnership Act 2004, s. 81 and Sch. 8, para. 1), where a lease for life—or until marriage or the formation of a civil partnership—is granted at a rent or in consideration of a **fine** (a payment of a fixed sum), it will take effect as a fixed term of 90 years, determinable on the specified event (the death or the marriage). The term, it should be noted, does not terminate automatically as soon as the event takes place. Instead, it terminates if, after the event, either party to the agreement (including the tenant's personal representatives in the case of death) serves one month's notice on the other.

A lease comes within s. 149(6) even if it is granted 'to T for the lifetime of X': the life specified need not be that of the tenant but might be that of a third party, or of the landlord himself. The section applies to all cases of leases determinable on marriage, civil partnership, or death, provided they are granted for value. Thus, even if L grants T a lease for '100 years determinable on T's earlier death' this will also be converted into a term of 90 years determinable on death.

3. Tenancies at will

Tenancies at will are rather anomalous. Such a tenancy is said to arise in any case where the tenant occupies the land with the permission of the landlord, on terms that the tenancy may be terminated by either party at any time. Such tenancies may be expressly granted in situations where parties do not wish to commit themselves to a fixed period (as in *Manfield & Sons Ltd v Botchin* [1970] 2 QB 612). They may also arise by implication from the acts of the parties. A common example occurs when a former tenant continues to occupy the property with his landlord's consent after his lease has expired (as in *Dean and Chapter of the Cathedral and Metropolitan Church of Christ Canterbury v Whitbread* (1995) 72 P&CR 9). Alternatively, an owner may allow friends or members of the family to occupy a property for an indefinite period, and this arrangement may give rise to a **tenancy at will**. It has also been held that such a tenancy will arise where an attempt has been made to grant a lease for a longer term, but the applicable formality rules (see 9.3.1) have not been complied with (as, for example, in *Proctor v Proctor* [2021] EWCA Civ 167).

Parke B once described the tenancy at will as being the lowest estate known to the law (*Doe d Gray v Stanion* (1836) 1 M & W 700), although at an earlier date Littleton had said that a tenant at will 'hath no certain nor sure estate'. A tenancy at will, being for an uncertain period, appears to fall outside the definition of 'term of years' provided by the 1925 legislation, and thus be incapable of amounting to a legal estate. As a result, it used to be suggested that the tenancy would take effect in equity, but this of course involves the notion of a trust, which seems remarkably cumbersome in the usual circumstances of a tenancy at will. Megarry and Wade (at para. 17-106) suggests that:

> Probably the best analysis of [the tenancy at will] is that it is a form of tenure but one that confers no estate. Although an estate cannot exist without tenure, there seems no reason why tenure should not exist without any estate. A may hold land of B, but for no fixed period and merely for so long as B may allow.

In other words, the parties may stand in a landlord and tenant relationship (see 9.1.3) but it is questionable whether the tenancy at will itself gives the tenant any right to possession of the land of a kind that can be enforced against third parties, like successors in title to the landlord (see 9.1.2). The tenant at will does have the right to exclude trespassers, but it has been suggested that this is because of the fact that she has gone into possession rather than because she has obtained such a right from her landlord (see 7.1).

9.1.2.2 'Absolute'

The inclusion of this word in the definition of the leasehold estate is difficult to explain. When used to describe the fee simple it means, as we have seen (8.3), that the estate is not conditional or determinable, liable to end early if some condition is met. However, leases often provide for determination before the term has run its full course; for example, it is common practice to provide that the landlord may forfeit the lease for any breach of covenant by the tenant (see 12.4.1). Indeed some long leases even contain provisions ('**break clauses**') allowing either the landlord or tenant, or both, to terminate the lease early on notice. It has never been suggested that such a clause prevents the lease taking effect as a legal estate, even though it cannot be described as absolute in the same sense as the fee simple. As Megarry and Wade have put it (at 6-019) the word in this context appears not to be 'used . . . in any intelligible sense . . . '.

9.1.2.3 No requirement for the leasehold estate to be in possession

One further difference between the statutory definitions of the two legal estates may be noted here. We have seen that, in order to be legal, a fee simple absolute must take effect 'in possession', and that a future interest—for example, a grant of a fee simple estate from 1 January 2030—cannot take effect as a legal estate. There is no similar provision in LPA 1925, s. 1(1) with regard to leases. Accordingly, leases may be granted to take effect in the future and still have the status of legal estates. Suppose, for example, that on 1 January 2020, Mr Forest had granted Mr Harding a 99-year lease of the maisonette to commence on 1 January 2025. The 2020 grant would be immediately effective in granting a legal estate to Mr Harding, even though he would be able to exercise his right to possession under that estate only on 1 January 2025.

A lease that does not start immediately but at some time in the future is called a '**reversionary lease**' (not to be confused with a '*leasehold* reversion', see 9.1.5). Such leases are incapable of being created orally even if they are **short leases** but must be created by deed (see 9.3.1.1). In order to prevent landowners from tying up land in this way for very long periods of time, LPA 1925, s. 149(3) provides that any lease expressed to commence more than 21 years from the date of the instrument that creates it is to be void. For example, suppose that on 1 January 2020, Mr Forest had granted Mr Harding a 99-year lease of the maisonette to commence on 1 January 2045. Such a grant would be void and would confer no rights on Mr Harding, who would not be entitled to take possession when the date came.

A *contract* to grant a lease, which, when granted, will take effect more than 21 years from the date of the grant, is also void. On this point, it is important to distinguish between the date of the contract to grant a lease and the date of the grant itself. (For the general distinction between a contract to make a grant and the grant itself, see 3.3.1). The time limit specified in s. 149(3) relates to the period between the grant of the lease and the commencement of the term. It does not impose any restriction on the length of time that may elapse between entering into the contract to grant a lease and actually making the grant. For example, suppose that on 1 January 2020, Mr Forest had *contracted to grant* Mr Harding a 99-year lease of the maisonette on 1 January 2045. Since lease granted on 1 January 2045 would take immediate effect on that date, nothing in s. 149(3) invalidates such a contract. Mr Harding would obtain a contractual right to require Mr Forest to make the grant when the time came, as well as an equitable interest in the land capable of binding third parties (see 4.6 and 9.3.2.2).

For this reason, the section does not prevent a landlord from validly covenanting to grant, if the tenant wishes, a further term when the present lease ends (an option for renewal). Any such option can be exercised at the end of the lease, however long the original term may be.

9.1.3 Leases as contracts: the landlord and tenant relationship

As we have seen, one aspect of the relationship between a leaseholder and a freeholder is that it simply mirrors the relationship between the leaseholder and anyone else who does not have a superior right to possession: the leaseholder is entitled to keep the freeholder, like anyone else, out of possession and to sue if he encroaches on the tenant's possession of the land. However, this is not all there is to the relationship.

First, a lease will normally be created by a contract that sets out the exact terms on which the leaseholder (the tenant) is to enjoy his possession of the land, and that places certain obligations on the person who has let him into possession (the landlord). Thus, for example, Mr Gruyère is contractually obliged to pay his weekly rent to Mr Forest. Other terms of the contract may provide that Mr Gruyère is not entitled to keep pets or hang paintings, and that Mr Forest is obliged to pay for or perform any repairs that may become necessary during the term of the lease. Ordinary contract law principles have a role to play in defining these obligations of landlords and their tenants in particular cases, and settling what happens if they are not performed or become impossible to perform (see 9.6).

Secondly, over and above the ordinary principles of contract law, there are special rules that govern the landlord and tenant relationship. Leases are a very distinctive form of contract, of considerable social and economic importance, and the courts and Parliament have adopted a number of special rules and principles that regulate the relationship of landlord and tenant. These are unique principles that define the content of the obligations owed by landlords and tenants (see Chapter 10), the people by and against whom those obligations can be enforced (see Chapter 11), and the remedies that are available when they are breached (see Chapter 12).

In general, the landlord and tenant relationship and the 'term of years absolute' go hand in hand. A contract that gives rise to a landlord and tenant relationship for the purposes of the special rules that apply to that relationship will normally also give the tenant a legal estate in land under the Law of Property Act 1925, and vice versa. It appears, however, from the House of Lords' decision in *Bruton v London & Quadrant Housing Association* [2001] 1 AC 406 that it is possible for a lease to create the relationship of landlord and tenant between the parties *without* giving an estate in land to the tenant. *Bruton* is a controversial case, and the decision and its implications are addressed in more detail later (see 9.6.2). Usually, however, a tenant in a landlord and tenant relationship will also hold a legal estate in the land. Meanwhile, the holder of a term of years absolute will always be a tenant in a landlord and tenant relationship. It is this feature of the leasehold estate that has attracted criticism in recent years, since a person who takes a very long lease (say a term of 999 years) will normally consider herself to be the absolute owner of the land for all practical purposes. At the same time, the landlord and tenant relationship will arise between her and the freeholder who originally granted that lease, with the result that she may owe obligations that are considered repugnant to the notion of ownership. Liability to pay rent in such cases has proved particularly controversial and has led to recent legislation, the Leasehold Reform (Ground Rent) Act 2022 (discussed at 9.2.6 and 10.3.1).

9.1.4 Leases, subleases, and underleases

As we have seen, a landlord and tenant relationship will always exist between a freeholder and the leaseholder to whom he has granted a lease. So, for example, if Mr Harding were to buy the 99-year lease of the maisonette, he would become a tenant and Mr Forest would be his landlord.

However, a landlord need not always be a freeholder. It is open to a tenant to grant a second lease of the premises (a '**sublease**') to another person (a '*subtenant*') for a shorter period than the original lease (the '*head lease*'). When this happens, the leaseholder under the head lease becomes a landlord so far as the subtenant is concerned, and their relationship is governed by the special rules that apply to landlord and tenant relationships. The same principle will apply if the subtenant goes on to grant a third lease of the same premises (an '**underlease**') to yet another person (an '*undertenant*'), for a shorter period than the sublease. Each grantor of a lease, in this chain, will stand in a landlord and tenant relationship to his grantee. (Although this terminology of 'sublease' and 'underlease' is commonly used, it is not used consistently by all lawyers and you may sometimes find cases of what here are called 'underleases' being called 'subleases'.)

For example, suppose that Mr Forest granted a 99-year lease of the maisonette to Mr Harding on 1 January 2020. As we have seen, the effect of such a grant is that Mr Harding gains a legal estate in the land and becomes a tenant (T) to Mr Forest's landlord (L). Suppose that Mr Harding then decides not to occupy the maisonette, and instead grants a sublease to Mrs Smith for 25 years. Mrs Smith will gain a legal estate in the land—entitling her to exclude both Mr Harding and Mr Forest for the 25 years of her term—and become a subtenant (S) to Mr Harding's landlord. Suppose Mrs Smith then decides she will only need to move into the premises in 2025, and lets the property to Mr Underhill on a monthly periodic tenancy until then. Mr Underhill will gain a legal estate in the land—entitling him to exclude Mrs Smith, Mr Harding, and Mr Forest for as long as his monthly tenancy is renewed—and will have become an undertenant (U) to Mrs Smith's landlord. These relationships can be expressed diagrammatically in Figure 9.1.

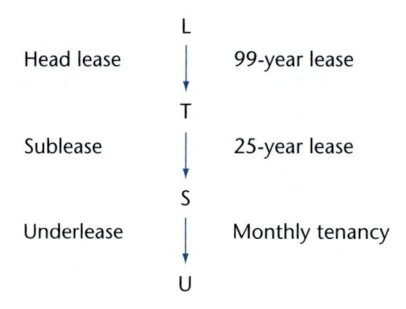

		L		
Head lease		↓		99-year lease
		T		
Sublease		↓		25-year lease
		S		
Underlease		↓		Monthly tenancy
		U		

Figure 9.1 Leasehold structures

Alternatively, you may like to picture these transactions as shown in Figure 9.2, in which each person is pictured as 'carving' a lesser estate out of their own estate—Mr Forest (L) hands 99 years of his indefinite right to possession to Mr Harding (T), Mr Harding hands 25 of his 99 years to Mrs Smith (S), and so on.

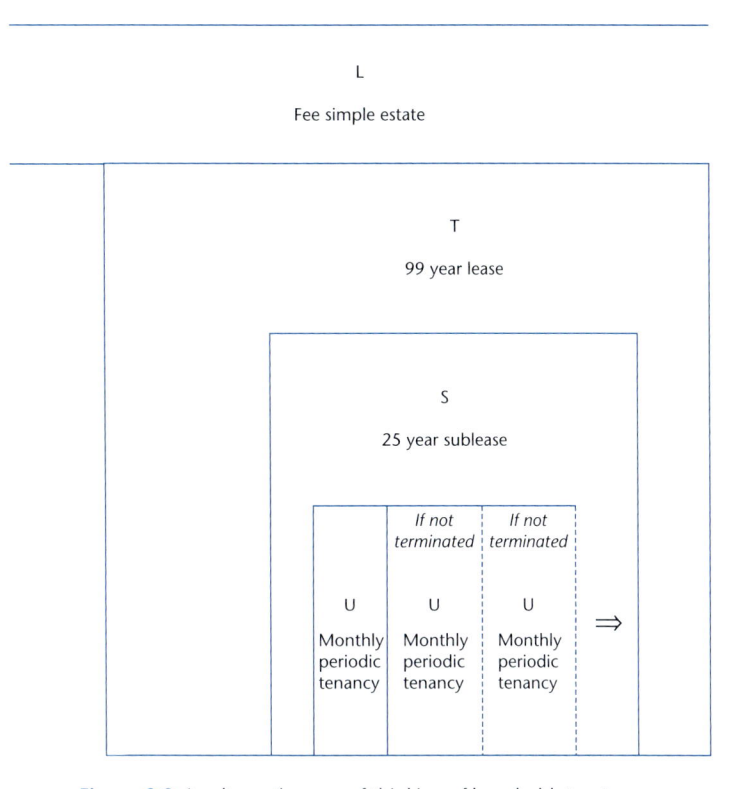

```
                    L
             Fee simple estate

                    T
              99 year lease

                    S
            25 year sublease

              If not       If not
          terminated    terminated

        U       U           U
      Monthly  Monthly    Monthly      ⇒
      periodic periodic   periodic
      tenancy  tenancy    tenancy
```

Figure 9.2 An alternative way of thinking of leasehold structures

In both figures, L (Mr Forest) is a landlord, T (Mr Harding) and S (Mrs Smith) are both tenants and landlords, and U (Mr Underhill) is a tenant only.

9.1.5 Freehold and leasehold reversions

In the example above, only Mr Underhill is entitled to immediate physical possession of the land. Everyone else in the chain is entitled to possession of the land—they all have legal estates in the land—but they can take physical possession only after someone else's right to possession has ended. Thus, Mrs Smith may recover possession of the maisonette by bringing Mr Underhill's monthly periodic tenancy to an end. Mr Harding will be entitled to immediate physical possession when Mrs Smith's 25-year term expires, and Mr Forest—or, more realistically, his successors in title—will become entitled when Mr Harding's 99-year term expires. All three have a right that possession of the land will revert to them on the termination of the estates that they have carved out of their own: a *'reversion'*. Since Mrs Smith and Mr Harding are owners of leasehold estates they are each said to have a *'leasehold reversion'*. Mr Forest has a **'freehold reversion'**.

9.2 Basic requirements for a lease

Agreements that allow one person to occupy land belonging to another can take a number of forms. For example, a student may be entitled to occupy a room on a university campus for the duration of a semester, a freeholder may allow a friend to stay in her house for a few weeks to keep an eye on her pets, or an employee may be entitled to live in a cottage belonging to his employer for the purposes of doing his job. Not all these contracts, or arrangements, will count as leases in either of the two senses we have looked at. If the basic requirements for a lease are not met, the contract will sometimes give rise to some lesser property right, such as an easement (see Chapter 24). More usually, it will give rise to a licence, which is a purely personal permission to be on the land (see Chapter 20).

9.2.1 Leases and licences: why the basic requirements matter

Showing that an agreement gives rise to a lease, rather than a licence, can make a significant practical difference to the situation of the would-be tenant. A lease, if made in the proper form, will normally give rise to a legal estate in the land. Thus it gives the leaseholder a right to use the land for the term of the lease, and this right will bind both the landlord and his successors in title. By contrast, a licence is just a permission and can readily be revoked. While a licensor may have an obligation not to revoke a licence—for example, if the licensor has contractually promised that he or she will not do so—this obligation is binding only against the licensor, and is usually unenforceable against a successor. (For the rare situations in which a licence of this kind can give rise to obligations affecting a person other than the original licensor, see 20.5).

For example, we have seen that Mr Gruyère occupies the basement of 5 Trant Way and pays a rent of £175 a week. Since Mr Forest has agreed to allow Mr Gruyère to occupy the property in consideration for his promise to pay a weekly sum, he cannot treat Mr Gruyère as a trespasser and seek to evict him. He is contractually obliged to leave him alone, or to terminate the arrangement only in accordance with its terms. Suppose Mr Forest then dies, leaving his freehold title to a charity. If his arrangement with Mr Gruyère meets the basic requirements for a weekly tenancy—a lease—the charity will be under the same obligations as Mr Forest was. It will not be able to evict Mr Gruyère, without first bringing the tenancy to an end according to its terms. If, on the other hand, Mr Gruyère's right to occupy the land does not meet the basic requirements for a lease and is merely a licence, the default rule is that the charity will not be bound by his rights. It will be entitled to require him to leave, whatever the terms of his agreement with Mr Forest.

In addition to this essential difference, arising from the nature of the lease as a property right, there are many other situations in which the distinction between leases and licences matters. One of the most important is security of tenure. From time to time, Parliament has legislated to protect tenants of residential property from eviction in certain circumstances (see 9.5.1) and this legislation does not apply to licensees. While some of these statutory protections have become less significant since the Housing Act 1988, the distinction remains very important for leases granted before that Act came into force, on 15 January 1989. The distinction also affects the process by which a landlord may recover possession (see, for example, *Gray v Taylor* [1998] 1 WLR 1093), the protection of business tenants under the Landlord and Tenant Act 1954, and the imposition of statutory duties upon landlords (see Chapter 11). During the pandemic, it was this legislation that was temporarily amended by the Coronavirus Act 2020 to give tenants a longer notice period before landlords could evict them during the lockdown. As such, this protection from eviction extended only to leaseholders and did not extend to licensees. Certain procedures for recovering possession of land are available against licensees but not against tenants (*Crancour Ltd v Da Silvaesa* [1986] 1 EGLR 80; and *Esso Petroleum Co. Ltd v Fumegrange Ltd* [1994] 2 EGLR 90).

Apart from proprietary protection and security of tenure, the lease/licence distinction also matters in a broad range of other contexts. For example, in determining whether a tenant has breached a covenant against subletting (see 11.2.2.2; *Brent LBC v Cronin* (1997) 30 HLR 43), the court will ask whether he has granted a sublease or a licence. There are formality requirements for the creation of leases, unlike licences. Compensation for compulsory acquisition of land is payable to an occupier with a legal or equitable interest in the land, but not to a licensee (*Rochester Poster Services v Dartford BC* (1991) 63 P&CR 88). In tort law, the traditional view is that claims in trespass and nuisance can be brought only by a person who has a property right in the affected land, not by a mere licensee. (See, however, *Manchester Airport plc v Dutton* [2000] 1 QB 133 with reference to trespass, and the speeches of some members of the House of Lords in *Hunter v Canary Wharf Ltd* [1997] AC 655, when considering a claim in nuisance). In *Appah v Parncliffe Investments Ltd* [1964] 1 WLR 1064, the availability of a claim in negligence depended on showing that the claimant was a licensee rather than a tenant. The claimant's property was stolen from a room that she occupied, because the lock on her door was defective. It was held that the defendant, who owned the property, owed her a duty to take reasonable care of her property because she was a licensee; had she been a tenant, no such duty would have been owed.

9.2.2 Overview of the basic requirements

The lease has been defined (see *Woodfall's Law of Landlord and Tenant*, Sweet & Maxwell, para. 1.003) as 'the grant of a right to the exclusive possession of land for a determinate term less than that which the grantor has himself in the land'. This definition identifies three essential elements of a lease, which are considered in detail in the following sections:

- exclusive possession (9.2.3),
- determinate (certain) term (9.2.4),
- term less than that of the grantor (9.2.5).

At one time, it was thought that an arrangement that met all these basic requirements for a lease might nevertheless be a licence, if the grantor meant it to have this effect. This gave rise to difficulties, especially where landlords wanted to avoid statutory protections for tenants by granting licences rather than leases. In *Street v Mountford* [1985] AC 809, the House of Lords rejected the view that the parties' intention to create a licence was of decisive importance. If the landowner had agreed to grant the occupier exclusive possession for a term, he would normally have granted a lease even if the contract expressly stipulated that the occupier was only a licensee.

In *Street v Mountford* [1985] AC 809, Mr Street and Mrs Mountford had entered into a written agreement allowing her to occupy some rooms belonging to Mr Street. It was accepted that this agreement gave Mrs Mountford exclusive possession of the rooms for a term. However, the contract stated that it only granted a 'licence', and referred to the payment of a 'licence fee' rather than rent. Mrs Mountford signed a declaration that she understood and accepted that 'a licence in the above form does not and is not intended to give me a tenancy protected under the Rent Acts'. Rejecting the argument that this made any difference to the effect of the contract, Lord Templeman said (at p. 819):

> If the agreement satisfied all the requirements of a tenancy, then the agreement produced a tenancy and the parties cannot alter the effect of the agreement by insisting that they only created a licence.

To put it another way:

> The manufacture of a five-pronged implement for manual digging results in a fork even if the manufacturer, unfamiliar with the English language, insists that he ... has made a spade (at p. 819).

In other words, if the agreement satisfies the criteria for the creation of a lease, the parties cannot avoid that result by labelling it as something else. Mrs Mountford was, therefore a tenant, and—despite the declaration she had signed—entitled to the protection of the Rent Acts.

A recent application of this principle, but in a reverse direction, is provided by *obiter dicta* in *Berrisford v Mexfield Housing Co-operative Ltd* [2011] UKSC 52. Having decided the case on other grounds (see 9.2.4), the Supreme Court considered whether an agreement that purported to grant a lease, but failed to do so for want of a determinate term, could instead take effect as a contractual licence. Lord Neuberger said that the fact that the parties had described their agreement as a lease would not prevent the court from regarding it as creating a contractual licence, if it was only capable of taking legal effect in this way.

9.2.3 Exclusive possession

Exclusive possession is the right to use premises to the exclusion of all others, including the landlord himself. It is a necessary, though not sufficient, ingredient of a lease; without exclusive possession, there can be no lease (although there may be a grant of exclusive possession without the creation of a lease: see 9.2.3.5). The first step in deciding whether some agreement to allow a non-owner to occupy land has created a valid lease, therefore, is to decide whether it grants exclusive possession to the occupier.

In *Street v Mountford* [1985] AC 809, Lord Templeman said:

> The tenant possessing exclusive possession is able to exercise the rights of an owner of land, which is in the real sense his land albeit temporarily and subject to certain restrictions. A tenant armed with exclusive possession can keep out strangers and keep out the landlord.

Clearly, someone who occupies a hotel room or lives in someone else's house as a paying guest cannot be said to have the power to keep out strangers *and* to keep out the landowner in this way; such a person cannot have a tenancy. In deciding whether or not an agreement has granted exclusive possession to an occupier, therefore, it is often helpful to look at the rights of continued access to the land that the landowner has retained. To quote Lord Templeman again (at p. 818):

> The occupier is a lodger [i.e., not a tenant] if the landlord provides attendance or services which require the landlord or his servants to exercise unrestricted access to and use of the premises. A lodger is entitled to live in the premises but cannot call the place his own.

9.2.3.1 Written terms inconsistent with exclusive possession

However, although terms that entitle the landowner to *unrestricted* access to and use of the premises are inconsistent with a grant of exclusive possession to an occupier, this does not mean that a lease cannot reserve any rights of access for a landlord. A lease may reserve the right for the landlord to enter the premises on certain occasions and for limited purposes (e.g., to inspect the state of repair of the property). Such a right must be exercised at reasonable hours and in a reasonable manner and does not prevent the tenant having exclusive possession. By contrast, a right for the landowner to come and go as he pleased, without the occupier's permission, would be inconsistent with a grant of exclusive possession.

For example, in *Appah v Parncliffe Investments Ltd* [1964] 1 WLR 1064, the claimant occupied a room in a house in which 17 such rooms were separately occupied. Each room had some cooking facilities but the bathroom was shared. The agreement provided that (a) no notice was required if an occupant wished to leave; (b) the fee simple owner retained the right to enter the room to empty gas and electricity meters and to clean; and (c) rules were made specifying that guests had to leave by 9.30 p.m. and otherwise regulating the use of the premises. The court held that this agreement could not amount to a lease, since the claimant did not have any right to exclude the landlord and the contract included detailed rules concerning her use of the premises that were inconsistent with the rights of an owner of an estate in the land. A more recent example of a case where the terms of an agreement were inconsistent with a grant of exclusive possession is *Camelot Guardian Management Ltd v Khoo* [2018] EWHC 2296. The agreement in that case included terms stating that there was no right to occupy any specific room within the (shared) premises, no right to use the property to hold 'meetings, parties or other similar gatherings', and no right to host overnight guests or more than two guests as visitors during the day. These terms were inconsistent with the grant of exclusive possession to the occupiers.

However, the mere existence of such terms in a *written* agreement will not conclusively prove that the occupier has not been granted exclusive possession. This is because the existence of statutory protections for tenants, but not for licensees, gave landlords an incentive to reserve rights in written agreements that they had no intention of enforcing, in order to avoid the appearance of granting exclusive possession to the occupier. The courts have refused to treat such 'sham' or 'pretence' terms as a genuine part of the agreement for the purposes of determining whether it grants exclusive possession to the tenant.

For example, in *Antoniades v Villiers* [1990] 1 AC 417, Mr Antoniades had granted a 'licence' of a small one-bedroom flat to a couple, on terms that provided that Antoniades could move into the property himself or introduce any other occupier if he wished. The House of Lords held that, given the relationship between the tenants and the nature of the flat, the landlord could have had no real intention of exercising his rights under this clause: that would have involved either sharing the couple's bedroom or introducing a stranger into it. Rather he had inserted the clause purely as a sham or a pretence in order to avoid conferring a right to exclusive possession—and thus statutory protection—on the couple. The term was therefore disregarded for the purpose of deciding whether the couple had a lease (see 9.2.3.2). Other terms that have been disregarded for the same reason include: the retention of keys by the landlady, coupled with the reservation of her right to enter the premises at any time (*Aslan v Murphy (Nos. 1 and 2)* and *Duke v Wynne*, both reported at [1990] 1 WLR 766); the limitation of the hours at which the occupier might use the property (*Crancour Ltd v Da Silvaesa* [1986] 1 EGLR 80 and *Aslan v Murphy (Nos. 1 and 2)* [1990] 1 WLR 766); and provisions that the landlord might share the premises with the occupier, or permit others to do so (*Hadjiloucas v Crean* [1988] 1 WLR 1006; *Antoniades v Villiers* [1990] 1 AC 417).

At the same time, the courts have emphasised that express terms of the agreement between the parties will *not* be disregarded unless they clearly meet the test that neither party genuinely intends the term to be enforceable. In *Camelot Guardian Management Ltd v Khoo*, for example, it was argued that many of the terms of the occupation agreement should be disregarded because they were never enforced and had been included purely to ensure that the occupier's rights did not qualify as a tenancy. However, the High Court rejected the view that lack of enforcement proved that the contractual terms were mere pretences or shams that should be disregarded. The context and purpose of the agreement had to be considered. In *Camelot*, the purpose of the agreement was to provide temporary occupiers for vacant property to protect it from incursion or damage (see 9.2.3.4 for a broader discussion of such 'property guardianship' arrangements). To achieve that purpose, it was essential that the occupiers should *not* have tenancies and both parties knew this. Butcher J went to say (at [34]):

> In entering into the Agreement, as both parties knew and must be taken to have intended, the basis of the arrangement was that CGML was providing some protection to temporarily-vacant premises against vandals and trespassers by arranging for accommodation by Guardians. . . . [I]t was essential to such an arrangement that the Guardians should not have tenancies. The inference I would draw is that CGML did indeed intend, when entering into the Agreement, that its terms would be enforceable by and capable of being enforced against it. It was in its interests that they should be.

This passage from Butcher J's judgment in *Khoo* was approved by the Court of Appeal in the recent case of *Global 100 Ltd v Laleva* [2021] EWCA Civ 1835 (at [54]).

9.2.3.2 Exclusive possession and land in shared occupation

A number of cases since *Street v Mountford* have involved the shared occupation of accommodation. As we have seen, a grant of exclusive possession means that the tenant is entitled to keep all others out of the premises, including the landlord. Exclusive possession cannot exist where a landlord genuinely reserves, and intends to exercise, a right to move into the premises himself or to introduce others into occupation of the premises.

However, this does not mean that there can never be a lease of premises shared by multiple people. As we have seen, in *Antoniades v Villiers* [1990] 1 AC 417, the House of Lords held that a lease had been granted to a young couple even though, of course, they had no right to exclude each other from the premises. This is because, as we will see in Chapter 17, it is possible for a single legal estate to be held by several people. It is, therefore, open to a couple, or a group of friends, to take a *joint* lease of premises that they plan to occupy together: in such a case, there is a single right of exclusive possession that is jointly held by all the tenants and enforceable against the rest of the world. Alternatively, each person might have an individual right to exclude the others from some defined part of the shared premises (e.g., a bedroom or self-contained suite). In such a case, there might be separate individual leases held by each occupier, in relation to their own room or part of the premises, subject to rights to share the common parts that belong to the landlord.

In *AG Securities v Vaughan* [1990] 1 AC 417, the House of Lords held that multiple people could jointly hold a single lease only if they were all co-owners of a particular kind: 'joint tenants'. As we will see, this form of co-ownership can exist only if certain requirements, known as the 'four unities', are satisfied (see 17.2.1). In general terms, this means that all the co-owners must be entitled to possession of the whole property (unity of possession), rather than having separate possession of the various parts, and their interests in the property must start at the same time (unity of time), be derived from the same transaction (unity of title), and be identical in their nature and duration (unity of interest). This last requirement, of unity of interest, 'imports the existence of joint rights and obligations' (*Mikeover Ltd v Brady* [1989] 3 All ER 618 at p. 627), meaning that each co-owner is both jointly and severally (i.e., individually) liable for any duties that attach to the enjoyment of the estate. Thus, where there is a joint tenancy of a lease, each tenant is liable for the full rent due on the lease, even though in practice each may pay only a share of it.

It was against this background that the House of Lords considered two flat-sharing agreements, which came before it in 1988. In *Antoniades v Villiers* [1990] 1 AC 417, as we have seen, a couple took a one-bedroom flat under written agreements that they each signed separately; these agreements were in identical terms and were signed by both parties on the same day. Having dismissed certain terms in this agreement as a mere pretence (see 9.2.3.1), the House of Lords held that the true agreement did not grant separate rights of occupation to the two tenants but instead represented a single contract, granting a single lease to them both to hold jointly.

By contrast in *AG Securities v Vaughan*, also reported at [1990] 1 AC 417, the House of Lords reached the opposite conclusion. In that case, the landowner owned a four-bedroom flat, which was occupied by four people who did not know one another but were selected by the landowner. Each had moved in at a different time and each paid a different amount for the use of the flat. Each had the use of one bedroom and the use of the other rooms in common with the other three. The owner did not dictate which room each occupier should have: that was agreed between the current occupiers. If an occupier left, the owner replaced him with a new occupier but then left it to the four occupiers to agree the new room allocation. The House held that this arrangement constituted a licence because the occupiers did not have a single joint right to exclusive possession of the whole flat. Nor did each occupier have an individual right to exclusive possession of a defined space within the flat, since the choice of bedroom turned on the agreement of the other occupiers rather than a grant of exclusive possession of that very room by the landlord.

In the recent case of *Proctor v Proctor* [2021] EWCA Civ 167, it was held that a lease had been granted by the joint owners of land (A and B) to themselves and one of their siblings (A, B, and C). One argument against this conclusion was that this was not possible at common law because the supposed tenants (A, B, and C) could not exclude the supposed landlords (A and B) and so exclusive possession had not been conferred. However, this argument was rejected, and the Court of Appeal held that there was no conceptual problem with landlords granting a lease under which they themselves were among the tenants (although it is not possible for landlords to grant a lease under which they are the *sole* tenants, since it is not possible for a person to enter into a contract with himself). Lewison LJ explained the position as follows:

> Following the grant of the tenancy, A and B are entitled to possession in two capacities; and to two different types of possession. As joint landlords they are entitled to possession in the sense of receipt of rents and profits (as contemplated by section 205 of the Law of Property Act 1925); and as joint tenants they are entitled, together with C, to physical possession of the land. Put another way, they have exchanged their right to physical possession of the land for symbolic possession in the shape of receipt of rents and profits.

Thus, it seems that an occupation agreement that requires the tenants to share with the landlord need not automatically fail to qualify as a lease. *Proctor v Proctor* suggests that such a lease might be valid if it can be interpreted as a grant of a joint right to exclusive possession by the landlord to all the tenants, *including himself*. However, as Lewison LJ's analysis suggests, this does depend on showing that the landlord is acting in two separate capacities—granting a right to physical possession to himself and the other tenants jointly, as well as reserving a right to receive rents and profits to himself individually—and that the intention of the parties is to create a joint tenancy. The four unities must therefore still be satisfied. It is likely that this analysis will apply, in other words, only in those relatively rare cases where the landlord has agreed to share the obligations of all the other tenants, including the obligation to pay any rent due under the lease.

9.2.3.3 Exclusive possession and accommodation for the homeless

A number of cases have considered the status of occupiers of hostels, or other accommodation provided for the homeless, and rejected the view that, for policy reasons, special rules should apply in these cases.

In *Family Housing Association v Jones* [1990] 1 WLR 779, the appellant, who was homeless, was given a flat in premises licensed to a housing association by a local authority. (For the relevance of the fact that the housing association itself was a licensee with no estate in land, see 9.6.2.) The housing association kept a set of keys in order to enter the premises to offer help to the occupier, to give her advice, and to inspect the condition of the premises. The Court of Appeal found that the occupier had the right of 'sole occupation' for a term on payment of an accommodation charge. Applying *Street v Mountford*, the Court held that this arrangement created a lease and not a licence. Following its earlier decision in *Aslan v Murphy* [1990] 1 WLR 766, the Court considered that the retention of a key by the housing association was not decisive; in this case it had been done to assist the occupier, and did not prevent a tenancy from arising. In holding that the occupier was a tenant, the Court of Appeal rejected the suggestion that the housing association's role in providing temporary accommodation for the homeless should be considered as an 'exceptional circumstance' which took the case outside the approach in *Street v Mountford*.

In *Westminster City Council v Clarke* [1992] 2 AC 288, the House of Lords adopted a similar approach, but reached a different conclusion on the facts. The council provided hostel accommodation for homeless single men under an agreement which included the provision that an occupier could be required to change rooms or to share his room with another occupant. The House of Lords accepted that these provisions were genuine, being necessary for the proper management of the hostel, and were not included for the purpose of avoiding the Rent Acts. Accordingly, the occupier did not have exclusive possession of his room, and was a licensee and not a tenant. If you read the report of *Westminster City Council v Clarke*, you will see that the headnote describes the decision as overruling *Family Housing Association v Jones*; however, this does not appear to be entirely accurate, since the House of Lords considered only one aspect of the decision in *Jones*. Moreover, the decision in *Jones* was later approved by the House of Lords in *Bruton v London & Quadrant Housing Trust* [2000] 1 AC 406, a case in which the court again refused to accept that the provision of housing for the homeless was a special circumstance which could negative the finding of a tenancy.

9.2.3.4 No lease despite an apparent grant of exclusive possession

As these cases suggest, the presence or absence of exclusive possession is critical to showing that a lease exists. However, the fact that an occupier appears to have been given exclusive possession is not conclusive proof that he or she is a leaseholder. A person may be in possession of land and yet not be a leaseholder, a point emphasised by Lord Templeman in *Street v Mountford* (at p. 818):

> There can be no tenancy unless the occupier enjoys exclusive possession; but an occupier who enjoys exclusive possession is not necessarily a tenant. He may be owner in fee

simple, a trespasser, a mortgagee in possession, an object of charity or a service occupier. To constitute a tenancy the occupier must be granted exclusive possession for a fixed or periodic term certain in consideration of a premium or periodical payments.

In *Watts v Stewart* [2016] EWCA Civ 1247, it was argued by counsel that this dictum in *Street v Mountford* must be wrong, on the basis that any person who has been granted a right to exclusive possession is necessarily a tenant of the grantor (if only as a tenant at will, assuming the other requirements for a valid lease are not met: see 9.3.3 for such implied leases). In response to this argument, the Court of Appeal drew a sharp distinction between *legal* exclusive possession on the one hand and a merely personal right of exclusive occupation on the other, and said that Lord Templeman's dictum applied in cases where a person lacked genuine legal exclusive possession but had a personal right of exclusive occupation instead. Sir Terence Etherton said:

> Legal exclusive possession entitles the occupier to exclude all others, including the legal owner, from the property. Exclusive occupation may, or may not, amount to legal possession. If it does, the occupier is a tenant. If it does not, the occupier is not a tenant and occupies in some different capacity. In the reported cases, including the passage in *Street v Mountford* which [counsel] has criticised, the expression 'exclusive possession' does not refer to legal possession but to exclusive occupation.

As this analysis suggests, an occupier in factual possession of land will not be a tenant where there was no intention on the part of the supposed landlord to grant her a right to exclude all others, including the landlord, from the property. This may be true where:

- the landowner has no intention to create legal relations, either because he has not given permission for the occupier to be in possession (as in the case of the trespasser) or he had no intention to create legal relations in doing so (as in the case of the object of charity);
- the occupier's possession is attributable to some other property right that he has (e.g., where he is a mortgagee in possession) or some other legal relationship that he has with the landowner (e.g., where he is an employee or a 'service occupier').

1. No intention to create legal relations

A number of decisions have held that, despite being granted apparent exclusive possession, an occupier is only a licensee. Early examples include *Foster v Robinson* [1951] 1 KB 149, in which a former farm worker was allowed to remain rent-free in his cottage after retirement, and *Errington v Errington* [1952] 1 KB 290, in which a young married couple occupied a house belonging to the husband's father (see further 20.5.3). An arrangement whereby a homeless family was given possession of a house rent-free has also been held to create only a licence (*Heslop v Burns* [1974] 1 WLR 1241), and the same result is to be found in respect of possession of a room in an old people's home (*Abbeyfield (Harpenden) Society Ltd v Woods* [1968] 1 WLR 374) and almshouses provided by charitable trustees (*Gray v Taylor* [1998] 1 WLR 1093; *Watts v Stewart* [2016] EWCA Civ 1247).

The common theme in most of these cases was summarised as follows by Denning LJ in the case of *Facchini v Bryson* [1952] 1 TLR 1386 at p. 1389:

> In all the cases where an occupier has been held to be a licensee there has been something in the circumstances, such as a family arrangement, an act of friendship or generosity, or such like, to negative any intention to create a tenancy.

This statement draws attention to two issues: first, a motive of the landowner that is inconsistent with an intention to create legal relations (family arrangements, friendship, generosity) and, second, the importance of the landowner's intention in such cases. We have seen, in *Street v Mountford*, that the law is prepared to disregard the intentions of a landowner who has conferred a legal right to exclusive possession for a term on an occupier but has labelled that agreement a 'licence': in such a case, the occupier is a tenant even if the landowner intends him to be a licensee. However, in addressing the prior question whether the occupier does in fact have a *legal* right to exclusive possession, intended to be enforceable against the landowner, intention is all-important.

2. Exclusive possession attributable to another property right or relationship

In *Street v Mountford*, Lord Templeman suggested a wide range of situations in which an occupier could be in possession of land that do not depend on the grant of a legal right of exclusive possession under a tenancy. The occupier might be:

- an owner in fee simple;
- a trespasser (see Chapter 7);
- a mortgagee in possession (see 22.7.2);
- a purchaser allowed into possession of the property before completion (e.g., *Cameron Ltd v Rolls-Royce plc* [2008] L&TR 22); or
- a service occupier, i.e., an employee, such as a housekeeper or gardener who occupies residential accommodation belonging to an employer for the better performance of the duties of the post.

The distinction between possession attributable to a tenancy and possession attributable to some other relationship has recently arisen in the context of the relatively new practice of 'property guardianship'. (see Bevan (2023) 139 LQR 79 for a fuller discussion of this practice and the cases dealing with it). These are arrangements under which people are allowed to occupy temporarily vacant land in order to protect it from squatters, vandalism, or becoming derelict through disuse. The landowner may contract with a company that provides 'property guardianship' services, and it is the company that then enters into arrangements with the people it identifies as suitable property guardians and sets the terms of their occupation. Property guardianship arrangements vary but it seems the occupier often pays some type of 'rent' and is subject to various obligations to ensure the property is not left vacant and is kept in good condition.

The question whether a 'property guardian' is a leaseholder or a licensee has been considered in two recent cases. In *Camelot Guardian Management Ltd v Khoo*, as we have seen, the terms of the property guardianship agreement were such that the court found that exclusive possession had not been granted. In *Global 100 Ltd v Laleva* [2021] EWCA Civ 1835, the Court of Appeal took the view that, even if a property guardian was in apparent exclusive possession of some part of the premises, her occupation was that of a service occupier. Although property guardians are not employees of the companies providing the property guardianship services, they will normally have been let into occupation for the purpose of providing those services and under contractual obligations to remain in occupation for that purpose. As such, on the approach taken in *Global 100 Ltd v Laleva*, such occupiers are unlikely to be treated as tenants.

9.2.3.5 Exclusive possession and exclusive occupation

Before leaving the topic of exclusive possession, it is worth mentioning the apparently similar phrase, 'exclusive occupation', which may cause you some confusion.

The two phrases are best used to describe two different situations. A hotel guest will expect to have exclusive occupation of a room, in the sense that he or she will not be required to share it with another person. Such a guest will not, however, have exclusive possession, in the sense of being entitled to exclude the proprietor and staff of the hotel, since they will have unrestricted access to the room for cleaning and the provision of other services.

The same distinction can be made in the case of longer-term residential accommodation. Clearly, in the absence of a joint tenancy (see 9.2.3.2), an occupier who does not have exclusive occupation of premises—because, for instance, she is sharing with other occupiers selected by the owner—cannot claim to have exclusive possession of those premises either. However, it does not follow that a person who *is* in sole or exclusive occupation automatically has a right to exclusive possession, in the sense of controlling access to the land and being entitled to exclude the owner (as noted by the Court of Appeal in *Watts v Stewart*, see 9.2.3.4).

This point is important because some confusion between the two phrases has arisen from their use by Lord Templeman in *Street v Mountford* and *AG Securities v Vaughan*. In his judgment in *Street v Mountford*, he referred throughout to 'exclusive possession', save for one occasion when he substituted the phrase 'exclusive occupation' (at p. 822). In *AG Securities v Vaughan* [1990] 1 AC 417 at p. 455, he explained that:

Exclusive possession means either exclusive occupation or receipt of rents and profits.

He then used the phrase 'exclusive occupation' throughout the rest of his speech in apparently the same sense in which he had spoken of 'exclusive possession' in *Street v Mountford*. Although other members of the House of Lords in *AG Securities v Vaughan* continued to speak of 'exclusive possession', Lord Templeman's usage has sometimes been adopted in later cases, for example in *Family Housing Association v Jones* [1990] 1 WLR 779, where Balcombe LJ (at p. 788) emphasised the fact of sole occupancy as bringing the agreement within the terms of *Street v Mountford*. Despite this, however, it is probably best to follow the language of *Street v Mountford* and in general use the phrase 'exclusive possession', since an exclusive occupier need not have exclusive possession in the relevant sense (see 9.2.3.4) and joint tenants might have exclusive possession without, individually, having exclusive occupation.

9.2.4 The requirement of a determinate term

The Law of Property Act 1925 requires that a leasehold estate should be for 'a term', that is, for a fixed period rather than for an indefinite one. In addition, the commencement of the period must also be certain. Normally, if the agreement says nothing about the date at which the lease takes effect, it will be deemed to start immediately (*Furness v Bond* (1888) 4 TLR 457). If, however, one has only an agreement for a reversionary lease (see 9.1.2.3), it will be void unless it is clear at what date the lease is to start, either from an express term in the contract or by inference (*Harvey v Pratt* [1965] 1 WLR 1025).

9.2.4.1 Attempts to avoid the certainty of term requirement

In some circumstances a landlord may want to permit the use of the property for an uncertain period. This was the position with wartime lettings during World War II, where leases were made 'for the duration of the war'. As we have seen (see 9.1.2.1), such attempts failed (*Lace v Chantler* [1944] KB 368). More recent cases have involved owners who intend to redevelop their land at some uncertain future date, and so want to avoid creating leases for fixed periods that might delay them when they are ready to start work.

For a time, it was thought that this could be achieved by creating a periodic tenancy with a provision that the landlord would not give notice to quit until he or she was ready to redevelop the land. This gave the tenant some measure of security, but enabled the landlord to regain possession when needed. An example can be found in *Re Midland Railway Co.'s Agreement* [1971] 1 Ch 725. Here the landlord claimed to have ended a periodic tenancy by giving notice, in breach of a term of the lease that it would only do so if the property was required for its own business. The Court of Appeal held that the restriction on the right to give notice was enforceable, and that the notice given by the landlord was therefore ineffective in terminating the lease. The court rejected the argument that the restriction made the term of the lease uncertain and therefore void under the rule in *Lace v Chantler*, holding that this rule did not apply to periodic tenancies.

Some 20 years later, however, a similar provision restricting the right of a landlord to give notice to determine a periodic tenancy was held to be void by the House of Lords in *Prudential Assurance Co. Ltd v London Residuary Body* [1972] 2 AC 386. As Lord Templeman explained in that case:

> A tenancy from year to year is saved from being uncertain because each party has power by notice to determine at the end of any year. The term continues until determined as if both parties made a new agreement at the end of each year for a new term for the ensuing year.

A term in a periodic tenancy that fetters the power of the landlord to determine it at the end of the relevant period, therefore, is inconsistent with the requirement of a determinate term.

In *Prudential Assurance* itself, the freehold owner of a shop with frontage to the street had sold the front strip of his property to the local authority in 1930, to enable it to widen the road. The authority then leased the strip back to its former owner, the lease providing that it was to continue until the landlord required the property for the road-widening work. It was obviously intended that this arrangement would be for a relatively short period, but the land was never needed for this purpose, and the lease was still in existence some 40 years later. The current landlord had no road-widening powers and, if the restriction on giving notice were valid, it would never be able to end the lease.

The House of Lords reviewed earlier cases which had led to the decision in *Lace v Chantler* and held that the certainty rule applied to periodic tenancies just as much as to leases (overruling the Court of Appeal's decision in *Re Midland Railway Co's Agreement*). Since the restriction on the landlord's right to give notice made the term of the lease uncertain, the lease had been void from the outset. However, the fact that the tenant had gone into possession and paid an annual rent meant that he had an implied yearly periodic tenancy (for which, see 9.3.2), and this could be ended by six months' notice.

Although the decision in this case was unanimous, several of their Lordships expressed regret and dissatisfaction with the result, which left the shop owner with no frontage to the street. Lord Browne-Wilkinson in particular commented (at p. 396) that it was difficult to think of a more unsatisfactory outcome or one further from what the parties to the 1930 agreement could ever have contemplated, and ended by expressing the hope that the Law Commission would consider:

> whether there is in fact any good reason for maintaining a rule which operates to defeat contractually agreed arrangements between the parties . . . and which is capable of producing such an extraordinary result.

Twenty years after *Prudential*, during which there had been no review of the certainty rule, the hope that the Law Commission would look into the matter was once again expressed, this time by the Supreme Court in *Berrisford v Mexfield Housing Co-operative Ltd* [2011] UKSC 52.

9.2.4.2 *Berrisford v Mexfield Housing Co-operative Ltd* [2011] UKSC 52

Facts

Ms Berrisford ('B') was the tenant of a property belonging to a housing association, Mexfield Housing Co-operative Ltd ('Mexfield'). Mexfield, and many other housing associations of the same type, used a standard occupancy agreement, which purported to grant each tenant a periodic tenancy and set out the terms of the tenancy, including provisions for bringing it to an end. The tenant could end the tenancy by giving one month's notice, but there was no equivalent power on the part on the housing association; instead, the contract provided that the association could end the tenancy only in specified circumstances, which included the tenant being in arrears of rent or in breach of other terms of the agreement.

These provisions, restricting the landlord's right to give notice, had been widely used by housing associations before *Prudential* and continued in use after it, apparently because the effect of that decision was not recognised. However, it seems that at some stage Mexfield became aware of the position and, wishing to end B's tenancy, purported to do so by giving a month's notice. B refused to vacate the property and Mexfield sought an order for possession.

Both the High Court and the Court of Appeal followed *Prudential* in holding that the restriction on the landlord's right to end the lease by notice resulted in uncertainty about the length of the term and therefore invalidated the purported grant of a periodic tenancy. Instead, B held under an implied periodic tenancy, arising from her entry into possession and her payment of rent. That monthly tenancy could be ended by the landlord giving one month's notice, and so Mexfield was entitled to possession of the property. Although Mexfield did not seek to enforce the order against B, and granted her a fresh lease on terms identical to the previous lease, it nevertheless resisted her appeal against the decision to grant the order for possession up to the Supreme Court. This was because it had granted about 500 other leases on identical terms to other tenants, and wanted the matter settled by *Berrisford* as a test case.

Supreme Court decision

It seemed that the Supreme Court appeal in *Berrisford* would provide an opportunity for a reconsideration of the certainty rule. However, B's counsel conceded that the lease *was* void for uncertainty, and successfully based the appeal on the submission that the agreement between the parties created a tenancy for life, which was converted into a 90-year term by LPA 1925, s. 149(6) (see 9.1.2.1).

This somewhat surprising argument was supported by authority, which was accepted by all members of the court and forms the basis for their individual judgments allowing B's appeal. The stages of the argument are set out clearly by Lord Neuberger and are as follows.

From the mid-thirteenth century onwards, an attempt to grant a lease for an indefinite period was treated by common law as creating a freehold life estate (paras. 39–41). Estates created in this way would end on the death of the tenant, but could also be ended on any earlier event which had been specified as determining the purported lease (para. 50). Thus, if the agreement between B and Mexfield had been made at any time before 1926, it would have created a life estate, determinable either on B's death or earlier in accordance with the provisions of the agreement.

- When the 1925 legislation came into force (on 1 January 1926) all such estates would have been converted into 90-year terms under LPA 1925, s. 149(6); although the statute refers to the term ending only on the death of the tenant, the Supreme Court was satisfied that the provisions for earlier determination on the occurrence of a specified event would also have been carried on into the new terms (para. 50).
- The effect of s. 149(6) was not limited to leases in existence when the legislation took effect. The purported grant made by Mexfield to B in 1993 thus had the effect of creating a 90-year lease determinable on B's death or as provided in the agreement.
- Accordingly, the court allowed B's appeal, holding that Mexfield was not entitled to possession.

Limits of the Berrisford approach

Berrisford appears, therefore, to have rescued many leases that would otherwise have been invalid because they have an uncertain term. Where a lease is void for uncertainty of term, the Supreme Court's analysis in *Berrisford* suggests that it can nevertheless be effectively enforced according to its terms. If the agreement would have been treated as granting a life estate before 1926, the courts will conclude that it has given rise to a 90-year lease, determinable earlier on the death of the tenant or the occurrence of the uncertain event stipulated in the agreement. On this analysis, the *Lace v Chantler* [1944] KB 368 agreement could have given rise to a valid 90-year lease, which would have ended earlier when the tenant died or—in accordance with the intentions of the parties—when the war ended.

However, this solution will not be available in all cases. The argument depends on showing that an uncertain lease would have been interpreted as giving rise to a life estate before 1926, and this interpretation is not available for every uncertain lease.

The most important exception is for leases granted to corporations. A corporation is not a natural person, with a natural lifespan, and so cannot be the grantee of a life estate. Thus, the *Berrisford* analysis will not help a company that has been granted a lease for an uncertain term; such leases will still be invalidated by *Prudential*. The *Berrisford* analysis will also only apply to an agreement that complies with the formality requirements (see 9.3.2.1) for creating a long lease (*Hardy v Haselden* [2011] EWCA Civ 1387), and so cannot rescue an uncertain short or periodic tenancy that has been created informally.

Finally, in *Southward Housing Co-operative v Walker* [2016] Ch 443, the High Court held that the *Berrisford* analysis will not apply where there is evidence that the parties did not actually intend to grant a lease for life. Hilyard J noted that, in *Berrisford* itself, the factual context was consistent with an intention that B should be allowed to occupy the property for the rest of her life; B had been a former freehold owner of the premises, who had sold it to Mexfield under a mortgage rescue scheme that was designed to allow her to retain the land as her home. On this basis, he distinguished *Southward*, where the parties envisaged that the tenants would stay at the property for a long time but had had no intention that they should be legally entitled to remain there for life. If this is right, and the *Berrisford* analysis will only apply where it can be shown that the parties had a genuine intention that the tenant should have a lease for life, then its scope is far more restricted than was initially thought and its application in commercial contexts is likely to be limited.

9.2.4.3 Other ways of avoiding the requirement of a determinate term

In *Berrisford*, members of the Supreme Court joined in deploring the effect of the certainty rule: there was no practical justification for the rule (para. 34), and its consequences were described as 'bizarre' and as 'having an Alice in Wonderland quality' (at paras. 95 and 88). In fact, the court's decision in the present appeal only added to the problem, Lord Clarke commenting (para. 105) that:

> It is a mystery to me why in 2011 the position of a tenant who is a human being and a tenant which is a company should in this respect be different.

The court echoed the words of Lord Browne-Wilkinson in *Prudential*: change was needed, and this would best be undertaken by Parliament, preferably following a full review by the Law Commission. We are, however, still waiting for any reaction from Parliament or the Law Commission; the Law Commission's current programme of law reform includes a project on residential leasehold but its terms of reference do not, for the moment, include any review of the certainty of term requirement.

Meanwhile, it is worth noting the following ways in which prospective landlords and tenants can avoid being bound for fixed periods, without falling foul of the certainty rule:

- granting a lease for a fixed term with a provision for earlier determination on the occurrence of a certain event. For example, a lease for a fixed term could have been granted during the war with a provision for determination if the war ended earlier, and this would have satisfied the certainty rule (see *Lace v Chantler* [1944] KB 368);
- granting a periodic tenancy that provides that, during a prescribed period, the landlord shall not give notice, unless for a specified purpose. Thus in *Breams Property Investment Co. v Stroulger* [1948] 2 KB 1 the landlords agreed not to give notice for three years, unless the property was needed for their own use, and this was held to create a valid lease;
- creating an express tenancy at will, as in *Manfield & Sons Ltd v Botchin* [1970] 2 QB 612;
- creating a contractual licence. In *Berrisford* itself, the Supreme Court gave obiter consideration to the circumstances in which a failed attempt to create an uncertain lease would be treated as an agreement to create a contractual licence. (See 9.2.1 on the legal difference between creating a lease and creating a licence.)

9.2.5 Term less than that of the grantor

An owner in fee simple is able to grant a lease of his property for any term because the fee simple is itself effectively perpetual (see 1.7.1.1). Thus there is nothing to prevent a fee simple owner granting a lease to a tenant for 9,000, or even 90,000 years. In fact 99-year leases are common and 999-year leases can also be found in practice.

A fee simple owner may also grant a lease to multiple tenants in respect of the same piece of land. Such leases are known as **'concurrent leases'**. Suppose, for example, that L grants a 21-year lease of a house to T, and then grants a 99-year lease of the same house to A. A cannot take physical possession of the house, because T has a better immediate right to possession, and so A's lease will take effect as a lease of L's freehold reversion. What this means is that A will be entitled to collect and keep rents paid by T, and to enforce the covenants owed by T under the lease (see Chapters 10 and 11).

In our example, the lease to A is longer than that to T and so A will eventually—once T's 21 years are up—be able to take physical possession of the property. If, instead, the second lease is for the same period as the first or a for a shorter one, A will never be able to enter, and will instead act simply as T's landlord for the term of A's lease, collecting any rent due and enforcing covenants in the lease.

Thus in Figure 9.3, L, the fee simple owner granted a lease for 25 years to T in 2000 and then in 2010 granted a 15-year lease of the same property to A. A became T's landlord and will be able to collect and keep rent from T and to enforce T's covenants until 2025. As the leases of both T and A end on the same date in 2025, A will never be able to take physical possession of the property; if, however, A's lease had been for longer than 15 years, A would be able to enter the property when T's lease ended.

L
Freehold estate–perpetual

T
25-year lease

2000

A
15-year lease

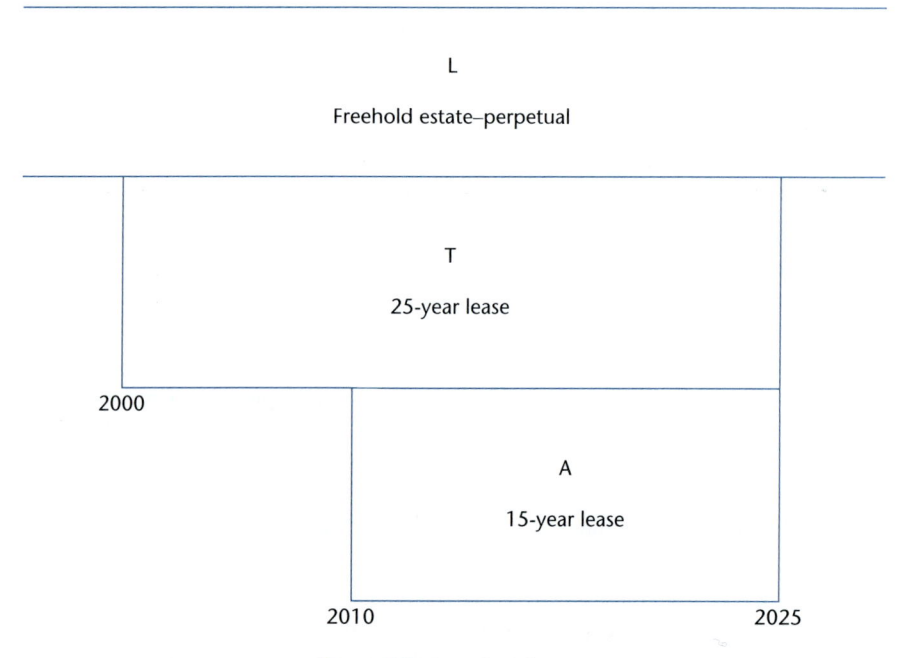

2010   2025

Figure 9.3 Concurrent leases

In the past, concurrent leases were not granted very often, except as a conveyancing device, which permitted the creation of successive mortgages of the same estate (see 22.4.1). However, under the Landlord and Tenant (Covenants) Act 1995, a landlord may, in certain circumstances, be required to grant a **lease of the reversion** (described by the Act as 'an overriding lease'), and as a result concurrent leases may become more common. Chapter 11 explains how the 'overriding lease' works (see 11.2.1.3).

We have also seen that a leaseholder may also carve shorter leases out of his own estate, by making grants to subtenants and undertenants (see 9.1.4). This process of creating further terms out of a leasehold estate may continue almost indefinitely, so long as each subsequent lease will end before the end of the term belonging to the person who grants it. If the grantor attempts to create a lease as long or longer than his own term, no new lease will be created and instead the grant will operate as an *assignment* (i.e., a transfer) of the grantor's own lease.

9.2.6 Rent?

The three essential elements identified in Woodfall's definition of a lease have now been considered. You may have noticed that that definition makes no mention of the payment of rent as an essential characteristic of a lease. This is because, although the payment of rents or a premium is usual, it is not an essential characteristic of a lease. LPA 1925, s. 205(1)(xxvii), defines a term of years absolute as:

a term of years . . . whether or not at a rent.

The limitation of other provisions in that Act to leases *at a rent or premium* (for example, s. 149(3) and (6)) implies that a valid lease can exist where there is no provision for payment in either form. Such leases are likely to be found as a part of family settlements, or as conveyancing devices, for instance, in connection with mortgages.

There was, therefore, some surprise when Lord Templeman in *Street v Mountford* [1985] AC 809 appeared to suggest that the payment of a premium or rent was necessary to constitute a tenancy. However, in *Ashburn Anstalt v Arnold* [1989] 1 Ch 1 the Court of Appeal confirmed that rent is not an essential characteristic of a lease and said that the remarks in *Street v Mountford* were not to be read as introducing such a requirement. In *Ashburn Anstalt v Arnold*, a purchaser of a leasehold estate had given the vendor the right to exclusive possession of the premises rent-free until a specified date, the agreement to continue thereafter until terminated by a quarter's notice. This arrangement was held to be a lease and Fox LJ said, at p. 10:

. . . the reservation of rent is not necessary for the creation of a tenancy.

Ashburn Anstalt v Arnold was overruled on other grounds by the House of Lords in *Prudential Assurance Co. Ltd v London Residuary Body* [1992] 2 AC 386. However, the long-established principle that it is possible to have a lease without payment of rent has been affirmed by the Court of Appeal in *Skipton Building Society v Clayton* (1993) 66 P&CR 223.

Despite the fact that rent is not an essential characteristic of a lease, it is true that leases are usually commercial arrangements in which the tenant pays for his use of the land. This may be done either by regular instalments throughout the lease ('rent') or by a lump sum at the start of the lease (called a *'premium'* or *'fine'*), or by a combination of both. These different types of payment are illustrated by the arrangements that Fingall Forest is making with his new tenants (see 9.1.1). The basement of 5 Trant Way is being let on a weekly tenancy at a rent of £175 a week; this is typical of periodic tenancies, in which rent is payable at regular intervals (e.g., weekly, monthly, quarterly, or annually). With a long lease for a fixed period (e.g., a 99-year lease), it is more usual for the tenant to pay a premium or fine at the start of the lease, and then to pay a smaller, sometimes almost nominal rent, usually called '**ground rent**', on a yearly or half-yearly basis. It is also possible, although less usual for shorter tenancies, to have a lease in consideration of one initial payment of a lump sum, rather than in consideration of the periodical payment of rent (*Hill v Booth* [1930] 1 KB 381).

We know from the newspaper advertisement for Fingall Forest's maisonette that the 99-year lease is to be granted at a premium of £450,000, but there is no mention of a ground rent, and this is something that Mr Harding will need to check before entering into a contract for the lease. Until last year, it was open to a landlord like Fingall Forest to attach substantial ground rents to long leases, an aspect of the long lease structure of homeownership that has been much criticised by consumer groups. Under the Leasehold Reform (Ground Rent) Act 2022, which came into force for most tenancies on 30 June 2022, this is likely to no longer be possible. The new legislation forbids landlords who have granted certain leases ('regulated leases') from requiring their tenants to pay a 'prohibited rent'. A prohibited rent is one that has a value greater than that of one peppercorn (i.e., any rent that has any financial value is forbidden). A regulated lease is a lease of a single dwelling, granted for a term of more than 21 years and for which a premium has been paid. Tenancies for business purposes are excluded, as are leases granted before the commencement date of the legislation (30 June 2022 in most cases). Leases granted in performance of contracts entered into before the commencement date are also excluded.

Thus, if Mr Harding has not yet bought or contracted to buy his 99-year lease of the maisonette, and if the maisonette is considered to be a 'single dwelling' within the meaning of the legislation, Mr Forest cannot include an enforceable term in the lease that requires him to pay a ground rent that exceeds a peppercorn in value. Even if such a term is included in the lease, Mr Forest will not be able to demand payment of the prohibited portion of the rent and, if he receives such payment without making a demand, he must refund it within 28 days. By contrast, if Mr Harding contracted to buy the 99-year lease of the maisonette on 29 June 2022, at a particular yearly rent, it will be open to Mr Forest to compel him to take the lease at that higher rent.

9.3 Creation of leases

We now turn to consider the different ways in which leases can be created. Leases arise by the express agreement of the parties, by implication from their conduct, and by operation of law. This section covers:

- express grant of a legal lease (9.3.1);
- leases that arise in equity when the requirements for creating a legal lease are not observed (9.3.2);
- implied grant of a legal lease (9.3.3);
- leases arising by estoppel (9.3.4);

9.3.1 Express grant of a legal lease

As has been explained, the general rule imposed by LPA 1925, s. 52(1) is that a deed must be used to create or transfer a legal estate (see 2.6.4.1) and LRA 2002 provides that certain legal estates and interests must be registered to take effect at law (see 6.4.1). The application of these formality rules to leases depends on the type of lease that is being created. Different rules apply to:

- leases for a term of three years or less, which satisfy the requirements of LPA 1925, s. 54(2);
- leases that do not satisfy these requirements and that have a term of seven years or less;
- leases for a term of more than seven years.

9.3.1.1 Short leases that satisfy LPA 1925, s. 54(2)

LPA 1925, s. 54(2) provides that a lease may be granted orally or in informal writing (the technical term is 'by parol'), provided that the lease:

- has a term of three years or less;
- takes effect in possession; and
- is at the best rent reasonably obtainable; and
- does not require the payment of a premium ('fine').

The provision that no premium is payable is self-explanatory (see 9.2.6 on the meaning of the term 'premium' in this context), but the other requirements are worth further consideration.

(1) *The lease must have a term of three years or less*. This includes periodic tenancies, as was decided in *Hammond v Farrow* [1904] 2 KB 332. However, as has been explained, the exception does not apply where a lease has an uncertain term and has been converted to a long lease as a result (see 9.2.4.2). In such a case, the exception does not apply even if the lease could potentially determine within three years of its grant, and the formality rules for creating a long lease must be met.

(2) *The lease must take effect in possession*. This means that the lease must begin at the date of the grant, not at some time in the future (see 9.1.2.3). As a result a reversionary lease, even one for less than three years, is excluded from the scope of the exception. For an application of this rule, see *Long v Tower Hamlets LBC* [1998] Ch 197.

(3) *The lease must be granted 'at the best rent'*. The Court of Appeal confirmed in *Fitzkriston LLP v Panayi* [2008] EWCA Civ 283 that 'best rent' means 'market rent'. In that case, it was argued for the tenant that the rent agreed between a landlord and tenant must be taken to be the best rent available at the time of grant (the unexpressed reason being, of course, that if anyone else was willing to pay a higher rent, the landlord would not have let the property to the current tenant). This argument was rejected by Rix LJ, who commented (at para. 27) that if it was correct:

> the statute calling for a best rent would be meaningless, because, in every case, the best rent in question would be the agreed rent.

In this particular case, a valuation of the property, prepared independently and before the grant of the lease, had regarded it as capable of fetching a much higher rent than was subsequently agreed. Thus there was clear evidence that the lease did not satisfy the requirements of LPA 1925, s. 54(2), and accordingly the tenant failed to establish his claim to a periodic tenancy.

In practice, most short leases do take effect in possession and satisfy the requirement for the best rent, and accordingly are granted without a deed, in a simple written form or by word of mouth. It is most unlikely that Mr Gruyère, the weekly tenant of the basement flat at 5 Trant Way, has a deed setting out his lease. Indeed, he may well have no written document at all. Nonetheless, Mr Gruyère is likely to have a legal lease, assuming his rent of £175 a week satisfies the 'best rent' test.

Short leases that do not satisfy these requirements are, however, subject to the general rule in s. 52(1) of LPA 1925, and must be created by deed. Thus, suppose Mr Gruyère's rent is not a market rent, but is significantly cheaper than what the basement flat would fetch on the open market. In this situation, he will not have a legal estate if his agreement with Mr Forest was merely oral or in a simple written form. Such leases must be created by deed. Grants of leases taking effect in possession more than three months after grant, and leases giving discontinuous possession (e.g., under timeshare schemes), must also be completed by registration whatever their term (see 9.3.1.3).

9.3.1.2 Seven-year leases

Leases which are longer than three years, but not more than seven years, are subject to the requirement of a deed in LPA 1925, s. 52(1) but not the registration requirements in the LRA 2002 (see 9.3.1.3). This means that such leases must be created by deed—signed, witnessed, and delivered in accordance with the requirements of the Law of Property (Miscellaneous Provisions) Act 1989, s. 1—but need not be put on the register of title to take effect as legal estates.

9.3.1.3 Leases for a term longer than seven years

Leases for more than seven years must be granted by deed in accordance with LPA 1925, s. 52(1), and must also be registered as required by LRA 2002. The registration requirements differ, depending on whether the grantor's estate in the land is already registered.

(a) *Registered land:* Where the owner of a registered estate grants out of it a lease for more than seven years, the grant is a registrable disposition, and does not operate at law until registration is complete (LRA 2002, s. 27(1) and (2)). When the lease is registered, a notice of it will be entered on the landlord's registered title (LRA 2002, Sch. 2, para. 3).

(b) *Unregistered land:* Where a lease for more than seven years is granted by the owner of an estate which is itself not yet registered, the grant of the lease is a trigger for compulsory first registration of the new lease (LRA 2002, s. 4) and the tenant must apply for registration of title to that estate. If the application is not made in the prescribed time, the legal estate ceases to exist (LRA 2002 ss. 4(1)(c) and 7(2)(b)) and the grant operates as a contract to grant the lease (see 9.3.2).

In accordance with these rules, the proposed grant of the 99-year lease of the maisonette at 5 Trant Way should be made by deed and followed by an application for registration of Mr Harding as proprietor of the lease. If Mr Forest's freehold estate had been registered already, it would also have been necessary to enter a notice of the lease on the register of his title to the freehold.

9.3.2 Non-compliance with requirements for legal grant

There are two situations in which the parties might fail to comply with these requirements for the grant of a legal lease:

- the parties make an agreement for a lease, but never proceed to the formal grant; or

- the parties attempt to make the formal grant but fail to do it properly, e.g., the grantor purports to grant a lease for more than three years, but does not use a deed, or does use a deed but fails to observe the registration requirements for a lease for more than seven years.

In both situations, the parties have not created the legal lease they intended. While it is possible that the tenant may obtain some other form of legal tenancy, if he goes into possession in reliance on the defective grant (see 9.3.3), this will differ significantly from the term which the parties originally intended to create. Equity, however, may come to the aid of the tenant if the defective grant has been made for value and, therefore, can be interpreted as a contract to grant a lease.

9.3.2.1 Formality requirements for contracts relating to land

In order to invoke equity's aid where a contract to grant a legal estate in land has not been performed, the parties must first show that a valid legal contract to grant such an estate in fact exists. As we have seen in Chapter 4, there are statutory formality requirements for contracts relating to land (see 4.2). The rules for the form of such contracts are dealt with in detail in that chapter, but it may be helpful to summarise them here.

1. Contracts made before 27 September 1989

Contracts to create or transfer legal estates in land could be made orally, but were not enforceable unless evidenced in writing, or, for the purposes of equity, by part performance (LPA 1925, s. 40).

- *Written evidence* There might be written evidence of the contract itself or, where the parties attempted to grant a lease but failed to do it properly, the defective grant might constitute sufficient written evidence for the transaction to be treated as such a contract.

- *Part performance* If the tenant had been allowed to enter into possession of the property and had paid rent, these actions amounted to sufficient acts of part performance by both parties and the contract would be enforceable in equity (see *Rawlinson v Ames* [1925] Ch 96).

2. Contracts made on or after 27 September 1989

Under the Law of Property (Miscellaneous Provisions) Act 1989 contracts to create or transfer legal estates in land must:

- be made in writing;
- contain all the terms agreed between the parties; and
- be signed by both parties.

Contracts to grant leases for not more than three years are exempted from these requirements.

As we have seen in Chapter 4, it is generally accepted that the doctrine of part performance can no longer apply to rescue contracts that do not comply with these requirements, although there may be cases in which equity will assist by means of proprietary estoppel or the constructive trust (see 4.5). There is also some doubt as to whether a defective deed of grant of a lease is likely to meet the current statutory requirements for a written contract (see Howell [1990] Conv 441), but this would of course have to depend on the exact nature of the documents in any particular case.

9.3.2.2 Equitable leases arising from specifically enforceable contracts

A valid contract to grant a legal estate in land, such as a lease, will normally entitle either party to seek an order for specific performance of the contract. Such an order would involve directing that the relevant formalities be complied with, and the grant of the legal lease be executed. The equitable maxim that 'equity sees as done that which ought to be done' will come into play in this situation (See 2.6.3.1 and 4.6.1). In the eyes of equity, the effect of a specifically enforceable contract to grant a lease is the same as if an order for specific performance had already been made and the lease executed. As a result, the tenant is treated as having obtained a lease in equity from the date of the contract. Exactly the same approach is adopted where there is no contract preceding the attempt to grant a lease for value, since a defective grant is treated by equity as a contract to make the grant (C (1858) 2 De G & J 559).

The existence of an equitable lease depends, however, on the availability of specific performance, and it is important to remember that this is a discretionary remedy and subject to the usual equitable rules. Thus the party seeking to enforce the contract must not delay unduly and must 'come to equity with clean hands'. Accordingly, he must not himself be in breach of any of the terms of the agreement. Although the court in *Parker v Taswell* (1858) 2 De G & J 559 said that equity would not usually refuse its help unless the applicant's breaches are 'gross and wilful' (at p. 573), there are several cases where relief has been refused because of the applicant's behaviour. In *Coatsworth v Johnson* (1886) 55 LJ QB 220, in which the tenant of a farm was in continuing breach of an obligation to cultivate the land in a proper manner, the tenant was refused an order for specific performance. A similar position arose in *Cornish v Brook Green Laundry Ltd* [1959] 1 QB 394, in which the performance of certain works by the plaintiff was a condition precedent to the grant of lease and those works had not been performed. However, you may like to note the view expressed in Gray and Gray at para. 4.2.85 that, 'the courts tend not to refuse equitable assistance in circumstances where relief against **forfeiture** would normally be granted under a legal lease' (for relief against forfeiture, see 12.4.5).

There may, of course, be reasons other than the applicant's behaviour which make the court unwilling to grant specific performance, as, for example, in *Warmington v Miller* [1973] QB 877, where the effect of granting the order would have been to procure the breach of a term in a superior lease.

In cases where, for one reason or another, specific performance is not available, the contract will not give rise to an equitable lease, and the only remaining possibility for redress would be to seek damages at law for breach of contract.

9.3.2.3 Effect of the equitable lease: *Walsh v Lonsdale*

The interaction of common law and equitable rules and of the provisions of the Supreme Court of Judicature Act 1873, s. 25(11), is clearly illustrated by the leading case of *Walsh v Lonsdale* (1882) 21 ChD 9. In that case, the claimant had purported to let a mill to the defendant for seven years by a written agreement that was not under seal and so, at that time, could not be a deed (see, now, the Law of Property (Miscellaneous Provisions) Act 1989, s. 1). The rent was to vary according to the productivity of the mill and it was agreed that the tenant would pay annually, in advance, if the landlord so demanded. The tenant thereupon took possession of the mill and paid rent at six-monthly intervals, in arrears, for a year and a half. At this point the landlord demanded the next year's rent in advance, in accordance with the written agreement. The tenant refused to pay and the landlord accordingly distrained for the rent, seizing the tenant's goods (a 'self-help' remedy—see 12.3). The tenant thereupon sued, claiming that the distraint was unlawful, and applied for an interim injunction to restrain the landlord.

It is clear that the relationship between the landlord and tenant in this case differs depending upon whether one looks at the position at law or in equity.

At law, the tenant had an implied legal lease arising from possession of the property and the payment of rent (see 9.3.3). Payment of rent at six-monthly intervals gives rise to an annual periodic tenancy and, since rent had been paid and accepted in arrears, the law would presume that it was a term of the implied legal lease that rent should be paid in this manner.

In equity, however, the act of entering the property and paying rent merely supports the written agreement, which was an agreement for a lease of seven years with rent payable annually in advance. Provided that the party seeking to enforce had done nothing wrong, this contract would have been enforced by equity with an order for specific performance, producing the lease originally intended. In the meantime, since 'Equity regards as done that which ought to be done', the tenant would be regarded by equity as already having a seven-year lease, under which rent was payable annually in advance.

Which lease then prevailed: the legal periodic tenancy or the seven-year equitable lease? Only if the equitable lease prevailed would the landlord's action in distraining be proper. The Supreme Court of Judicature Acts 1873 and 1875 required that, where the rules of law and equity conflict, the equitable rule should prevail (a provision now contained in the Supreme Court Act 1981, s. 49(1)). The court applied this provision, and accordingly held that the equitable lease prevailed and that therefore the landlord's actions were lawful.

For a modern application of these principles, see *R v Tower Hamlets LBC, ex parte Von Goetz* [1999] QB 1019. Here the Court of Appeal held that a written lease for 10 years created an equitable estate which was a sufficient 'term of years' to entitle the applicant to a renovation grant under the Local Government and Housing Act 1989. The council had refused the grant because it regarded the equitable interest as too precarious, but in Mummery LJ's view:

> There may be circumstances in which an equitable lease is overridden, but in most cases a person with an equitable lease is in the same position as a person who has had a legal estate vested in him by deed.

9.3.2.4 Is an equitable lease as good as a legal lease?

Since normally an equitable lease can be converted into a legal lease by obtaining an order for specific performance, and since in the meantime equity will uphold the rights of the parties as though the legal lease had already been granted, it has often been said that, 'A contract for a lease is as good as a lease' (see *Re Maughan* (1885) 14 QBD 956). However, this is not entirely true, for a variety of reasons.

1. Equitable remedies are discretionary

Recognition of an equitable lease depends upon the availability of an order for specific performance. Whereas a legal remedy (e.g., damages) will be available without reference to the behaviour of the claimant, an equitable remedy is not available where the claimant has 'dirty hands'. Thus a contract for a lease is only 'as good as a lease' if the circumstances are such that an order for specific performance can be obtained.

2. Enforcement against third parties

As has been explained (see 2.4.3), equitable interests differ from legal estates in their effect on third parties. Legal estates usually bind the world in general; equitable interests, by contrast, are subject to the defence of bona fide purchase and to various statutory defences that apply to land.

Let us assume that L, a freehold owner, agrees to give T a five-year lease of property and properly complies with all the formality requirements for granting the lease at law. If L then sells his fee simple title to P, P will automatically be bound by T's legal lease. If, on the other hand, no formal grant is executed but the contract is specifically enforceable, T will have an equitable lease of the property. When L sells his fee simple title to P, whether P is bound by T's lease will depend on the application of the various statutory defences that apply to equitable interests in land.

If the land is *unregistered land,* T's equitable lease will be an estate contract, a C(iv) land charge, under LCA 1972, s. 2(4) (see 5.4.5). It will, therefore, bind P only if it was registered as a land charge before the date of the conveyance to him (LCA 1972, s. 4(6)). If it is not registered, P will not be bound by it. By contrast, a legal lease of unregistered land will 'bind all the world', including a purchaser for value, regardless of registration or notice.

If title to the land is *registered*, P, as a person taking the registered estate for valuable consideration, will take free of T's equitable lease unless it has been protected by a notice on the register of title to that estate, or is capable of taking effect as an overriding interest (LRA 2002, s. 29 and Sch. 3). It is very unlikely that an equitable lease will be treated as an overriding interest under Sch. 3, para. 1, which is limited to *legal* leases (6.5.5.1). However, if at the time of the transfer to P, T was occupying the property and could satisfy the other requirements of Sch. 3, para. 2, T could claim that the equitable lease was overriding as the interest of a person in actual occupation. Nevertheless, as *Strand Securities Ltd v Caswell* [1965] Ch 958 shows, there are circumstances in which a tenant may not be in actual occupation at the relevant time, and a tenant with an equitable lease would therefore be well advised to protect his position by making an entry on the register. By contrast, a *legal* lease for seven years or less will always override under Sch. 3, para. 1, and a longer lease—which will have required completion by registration to take effect at law—will appear as a notice on the landlord's title and so bind a purchaser of that title.

Thus, while a legal lease will bind any purchaser, an equitable lease will only be binding in certain circumstances. Since such equitable leases usually only arise in cases in which the parties are unaware of the legal formalities for the creation of a lease, it is most unlikely that the tenant will know that he has to take further steps to protect his interest.

3. Enforcement of covenants in the lease

A further defect of the equitable leases arises in relation to the covenants in the lease. Each party to a lease will usually undertake certain duties, such as to pay rent or to keep the property in repair. As we will see in Chapter 11, such covenants are not only enforceable between the original parties to the lease, but, provided the lease is legal, will normally bind and benefit both a purchaser from the landlord and a purchaser from the tenant. However, this has traditionally depended on the purchaser acquiring an estate in the property; in the case of a purely equitable lease there is no legal estate in existence, and so the benefits and burdens of the covenants do not pass automatically if the tenant assigns his interest, although they probably do so on an assignment by the landlord.

However, the Landlord and Tenant (Covenants) Act 1995 substantially alters the applicable rules in respect of leases granted on or after 1 January 1996 (s. 1(3)). The old and new rules relating to equitable leases are covered in Chapter 11 (see 11.2.2.2 and 11.3.2.4).

4. A contract is not a conveyance

By LPA 1925, s. 62, a 'conveyance' automatically carries with it the grant of certain rights enjoyed in connection with the land (see 24.8). The grant of a legal lease comes within this section, and so brings these additional rights with it for the benefit of the tenant. The creation of an equitable lease by a specifically enforceable contract does not come within the definition of a 'conveyance' for the purposes of LPA 1925, s. 62, and so does not carry with it such benefits (*Borman v Griffith* [1930] 1 Ch. 493).

5. An equitable tenant is not a purchaser for value of a legal estate

A further difference is that the various defences that protect purchasers for value from being bound by earlier equitable interests in land are usually only available to purchasers for value of *legal* estates (see 2.4.3.3). Where title to the land is unregistered, a purchaser of an equitable lease cannot claim to be a 'bona fide purchaser of a legal estate for value'; such purchasers will be bound by rights to which the doctrine of notice applies whether or not they have notice. Nor can such purchasers claim the benefit of LCA 1972, s. 4(6); they will be bound by class C(iv) and D land charges even if they are unregistered. (The purchaser of an equitable lease will, however, be a purchaser within s. 4(5) and (8) of the Act and will take the property free of unregistered class C(i)–(iii) and F land charges (see 5.4.5).) Similarly, where title to the land is registered, the purchaser will not be a purchaser for value of a registered estate—only legal estates are registrable—and so will not be able to claim the protection of LRA 2002, s. 29 (see 6.5.4.1).

9.3.3 Implied grant of a legal lease

Because a lease for not more than three years may be created at law without any formalities, it is possible for certain leases to arise at law by implication from the actions of the parties.

9.3.3.1 Implied periodic tenancy

Where it could be shown that a person was in possession of land with the owner's consent and that rent calculated on a periodic basis was paid and accepted, the common law would presume the existence of a periodic tenancy (*Martin v Smith* (1874) LR 9 Ex 50). This is a presumption as to the intention of the parties and so could, of course, be rebutted by showing that they had a contrary intention. However, in the absence of any evidence about what the parties had intended, the common law would usually fill the gap by inferring the creation of a periodic tenancy.

In more recent times, however, the introduction of various forms of statutory protection for tenants meant that it was no longer safe to presume the intention to create a tenancy, and the courts now emphasise the importance of discovering the real intentions of the parties (see *Cardiothoracic Institute v Shrewdcrest Ltd* [1986] 1 WLR 368). Thus, as Nicholls LJ said in *Javad v Mohammed Aqil* [1991] 1 WLR 1007, at p. 1012:

> the inference sensibly and reasonably to be drawn will depend upon a fair consideration of all the circumstances, of which payment of rent on a periodical basis is only one, albeit a very important one.

In that case, the occupier had gone into possession in the course of negotiations for a fixed-term lease, and had paid a quarterly sum described as 'rent'. When the negotiations broke down, and the owner sought to recover possession, the occupier claimed that a quarterly tenancy had arisen from the payment and receipt of rent. The Court of Appeal, having regard to all the circumstances, including the continuing negotiations, refused to infer an intention to create a periodic tenancy, and held the occupier to be a tenant at will only (see 9.1.2.3). Other decisions in which the courts have refused to infer an implied grant include *Manfield & Sons Ltd v Botchin* [1970] 2 QB 612 (express grant of a tenancy at will), and *Tickner v Buzzacott* [1965] Ch 426 (landlord was unaware that the person paying rent was not the person he had in contemplation).

In many cases, however, it may well be found that the parties' intentions are consistent with the grant of a periodic tenancy. The occupier may have gone into possession under a contract to grant a fixed-term lease, which is never performed, or under a defective grant (e.g., a lease for more than three years not made by deed); on the other hand, he may 'hold on' in the property after a previous lease has come to an end. In these circumstances, if rent is paid and accepted on a periodic basis, a periodic tenancy may arise by implication.

The type of periodic tenancy arising by implication will in general depend upon the period for which the rent is said to be due rather than upon that for which it is paid. Thus a yearly tenancy will arise by implication if the tenant is in possession of the land and is paying a rent which is stated as an annual sum, even if payments are actually made in monthly instalments (*Ladies' Hosiery and Underwear Ltd v Parker* [1930] 1 Ch 304). However, this is only the general rule, and it is possible for the period of the tenancy to be determined by other terms of the agreement which indicate a particular period (e.g., reference to provisions for notice), or by local or business custom.

It is important to note that such leases arising by implication from conduct come within the terms of LPA 1925, s. 54(2) (relating to informal creation of leases for not more than three years), and so are legal leases.

9.3.3.2 Tenancy by sufferance

Implied periodic tenancies may be contrasted with tenancies by sufferance, which arise purely by operation of law and entirely without any form of agreement between the landlord and the tenant. They arise in cases in which the tenant originally had a valid tenancy but continues to occupy the property after the expiration of that term. This occupation must be without the landlord's consent and without the landlord's protest: if the tenant remains with the landlord's assent, he or she holds as a tenant at will rather than at sufferance, while if the landlord dissents the former tenant is in the position of a trespasser.

Thus, in *Remon v City of London Real Property Co. Ltd* [1921] 1 KB 49 where a tenant remained in possession of the premises after a valid notice to quit had expired, the tenant was held not to be a tenant at sufferance since his landlords had taken action to endeavour to remove him from the premises. Scrutton LJ said (at p. 58):

> [T]enants by sufferance seem to have been confined to persons who held over without the assent or dissent of their landlords, and not to have included persons who held over wrongfully in spite of the active objection of their landlords.

In such a case there is no real tenancy, despite the name **'tenancy at sufferance'** and no real relationship of landlord and tenant. The landlord cannot sue for rent (but may make a restitutionary claim for the use of the land—called **'mesne profits'**). Should the landlord accept rent, this will normally give rise to a fresh periodic tenancy (*Mann v Lovejoy* (1826) Ry & M 355 and *Doe d Clarke v Smaridge* (1845) 7 QB 957). At common law, the tenant at sufferance was in a very precarious position, because the landlord was able to recover possession of the premises, even by force. However, the landlord's rights are now subject to s. 6 of the Criminal Law Act 1977 and, in the case of residential accommodation, to s. 3 of the Protection from Eviction Act 1977.

9.3.4 Tenancies by estoppel

So far, it has been assumed that leases are created by landlords who have the power to grant an estate or interest in the premises, by virtue of having a fee simple or leasehold title to the land. It may be, however, that the person purporting to grant the lease has a defective title to the land. In earlier cases, leases were sometimes granted by mortgagors who, under pre-1926 law, had already conveyed their legal estates to mortgagees. In more recent times, the purported landlord may only have an equitable lease (as in *Industrial Properties (Barton Hill) Ltd v Associated Electrical Industries Ltd* [1977] 1 QB 580), or might be in the process of buying a legal title to the property, but not yet have completed the purchase (*Church of England Building Society v Piskor* [1954] Ch 553). Yet again, as in *Bruton v London & Quadrant Housing Trust* [2000] 1 AC 406, the grantor may be only a licensee.

9.3.4.1 Estoppel by representation and estoppel by grant

There are two ways in which a tenancy by estoppel may arise in these situations. The prospective landlord may make a specific representation about his or her title—for example, reciting in the document granting the lease that he or she is the fee simple owner of the property. The landlord is then estopped by this representation from denying the title. However, even if there is no such statement, the fact that a landlord purported to grant the lease is considered sufficient to create an estoppel, by virtue of the common law principle that a grantor is precluded from disputing the validity and effect of the grant (see *First National Bank v Thompson* [1996] Ch 231 at p. 237, a decision which, though dealing with a mortgage by estoppel, states the general principles which apply equally to tenancies). Although both forms of estoppel may prevent denial of the landlord's title, there are some differences in their operation.

Estoppel by grant arises only where the grantor has no legal estate at all in the land at the date at which the purported grant was made. If the supposed landlord had a legal estate that was less in extent than that which he or she purported to grant, the whole estate would pass to the grantee and no tenancy by estoppel would arise. Thus, if the landlord had, for example, a leasehold estate for five years and attempted to grant a sublease for a longer period than that lease (e.g., for 25 years) the purported grant of the sublease would not create a lease by estoppel but would operate as an assignment of the existing five-year term.

Estoppel by representation, by contrast, estops a grantor who has made a specific representation about his or her title from denying he or she has the particular estate represented. The fact that he or she has some lesser estate does not prevent the estoppel operating, so that a tenancy by estoppel for the full period that was purportedly granted will come into existence.

9.3.4.2 Rights and duties under a tenancy by estoppel

As between themselves, a tenancy by estoppel gives the parties all the rights and duties of a landlord and tenant. Moreover, such a tenancy can be assigned and in general binds the grantor's successors, although the rules on this vary depending on whether the estoppel arises by grant or by representation (see further Megarry and Wade, paras. 17-125–17-132). The tenancy is also regarded as a lease for the purpose of various statutory codes protecting the tenant (e.g., the Rent Acts).

Thus, unless an owner with superior title intervenes, a tenancy by estoppel is generally as effective and binding as any other lease (*Gouldsworth v Knights* (1843) 11 M & W 337). If, however, at any time the superior owner does assert his or her claim to the property, then the tenant may become liable to compensate this superior owner for the use of the land. In such a case, or if evicted by a superior owner, the tenant may then dispute the landlord's title and successfully resist a claim for rent. In the *Industrial Properties* case [1977] 1 QB 580 Lord Denning MR said (at p. 596):

> Short of eviction by title paramount, or its equivalent, . . . the tenant is estopped from denying the title of the landlord. It is no good his saying: 'The property does not belong to you but to a third person' unless that third person actually comes forward and successfully makes an adverse claim . . . If the third person . . . makes no adverse claim or is debarred from making it, the tenant remains estopped from denying the landlord's title.

9.3.4.3 Feeding the estoppel

If at any time during the continuance of the lease by estoppel the landlord obtains a full legal title to the land, this acquisition of title is said to 'feed' the lease by estoppel, which thereupon becomes a full legal lease (*Rawlin's Case* (1587) Jenk 254). Thus, if a purchaser, before taking a conveyance of the fee simple estate, should purport to grant a lease of the property, that lease will take effect only as a lease by estoppel, but will become a full legal lease as soon as the fee simple is conveyed to the purchaser.

This can cause problems when the purchaser obtains a mortgage in order to finance the purchase of the estate but later fails to keep up his mortgage repayments. Both the lease and mortgage must have been created after title to the estate vested in the purchaser, but which comes first? If the first thing that happened was the **feeding of the estoppel**, the property over which the mortgage was granted was the estate subject to the lease and thus the mortgagee (the lender) would be bound by the pre-existing legal lease. If, however, the mortgage took effect before the legal lease arose, the result would be different: the mortgage would take priority and the mortgagee could sell the mortgaged estate free of the lease.

It used to be thought that, even if all the documents were prepared and signed in advance, there must be a moment ('a scintilla of time') between the vesting of the legal estate in the purchaser and the creation of the mortgage, during which the estoppel could be fed (see *Church of England Building Society v Piskor* [1954] Ch 553). The defendant in *Abbey National Building Society v Cann* [1991] 1 AC 56 relied upon this argument (although not in relation to tenancy by estoppel), claiming that there had been a scintilla of time between the transfer to Cann and his grant of the mortgage to the building society, and that in this brief moment her beneficial interest took effect and became an overriding interest under LRA 1925, s. 70(1)(g) (see 6.5.6.3 for more on this case). The House of Lords rejected this argument, holding that the transfer to Mr Cann and the grant of the mortgage, both of which occurred on the same day, were to be regarded as happening together, and overruling *Church of England Building Society v Piskor*. The result was that the mortgagee took priority. Since this decision it seems, therefore, that although a tenancy by estoppel may be fed by the acquisition of the legal estate, it cannot thereby gain priority over a mortgage created at the same time (see *Scott v Southern Pacific Mortgages* [2014] UKSC 52, discussed at 4.6.1, on the same point).

9.4 Transfer of leases

We have so far looked at the rules that govern the creation of a new lease. A tenant may also acquire a lease by transfer or *'assignment'*, as where the original tenant sells or gives away the lease to a new tenant. Assignment of an existing lease is to be contrasted with the creation of a new sub-tenancy by the original tenant (see 9.1.2.3), to which the general rules that govern the creation of leases apply.

9.4.1 Express assignments

Since the assignment of a lease is the conveyance or transfer of a legal estate it should be made by deed (LPA 1925, s. 52(1)). This rule applies even to leases for not more than three years, because s. 54(2) provides an exception only for the original grant of such leases and does not apply to assignments (see *Crago v Julian* [1992] 1 WLR 372).

However, a defective assignment will be regarded in equity as a contract to assign, provided that it satisfies the formalities for a contract relating to land (see 9.3.2.1). Where such a contract arises, either party may then apply for an order for specific performance in order to effect a full legal assignment. Meanwhile, of course, equity 'regards as done that which ought to be done', and will regard the transaction as an equitable assignment.

9.4.2 Assignments by operation of law

An exception to the requirement for a deed arises in cases in which the assignment takes effect by operation of law. This can be important in cases in which a tenant purports to grant a sublease of the property but grants a term that is equivalent to, or greater than, the unexpired portion of his own lease. Such a disposition takes effect as an assignment of the lease rather than as the creation of a sublease. The reason for this is that a sublease can only be created if the tenant retains some interest in the property when granting the sublease: he or she must be in a position to recover the property at some point in the future in order to have a **leasehold reversion** (see 9.1.5). If the tenant parts with the property for the whole of the remainder of the head lease, there is no leasehold reversion and the transaction can only take effect as an assignment of the head lease and not as a sublease (*Beardman v Wilson* (1868) LR 4 CP 57).

If the purported sublease is for not more than three years it will probably have been made orally or in writing (in reliance on s. 54(2)). If the effect of the agreement is to transfer the whole remaining term of the head lease to the 'sublessee' (in fact, the assignee) the result appears to be a valid legal assignment without the use of a deed. Lord Greene MR seems to have accepted this reasoning in the case of *Milmo v Carreras* [1946] KB 306 at p. 312, on the ground that such an assignment arose by operation of a rule of law and so s. 52(1) LPA 1925 did not apply to it. This approach has more recently been followed in *Parc (Battersea) Ltd v Hutchinson* [1999] 2 EGLR 33.

9.5 Determining a lease

Leases can be brought to an end in a number of ways. Some of these methods of determining a lease have a reduced effect today, however, due to the provisions of various statutory codes, relating respectively to residential accommodation, business premises, and agricultural holdings. For the detail of these various statutory provisions, which are in general outside the scope of this book, reference may be made to a suitable specialist text on the law relating to landlord and tenant.

9.5.1 Some general points about statutory protection

There are three general points about the statutory protection of tenants, however, which it may be helpful to mention here.

- In general, the introduction of a new form of statutory protection does not supersede the earlier rules, which will continue to apply to tenancies already created under them. Thus, in respect of residential accommodation, the Rent Act 1977 continues to govern those tenancies within its terms which were granted before 15 January 1989, when the Housing Act 1988 came into operation.
- The statutory codes employ a wide variety of technical terms, including, for example: 'protected tenancy', 'statutory tenancy', 'restricted contract', 'protected shorthold tenancy', 'assured tenancy', and 'assured shorthold tenancy'. These terms are mentioned here simply because you may come across references to some of them, either elsewhere in this book or in reports of cases. For the purposes of this book, you do not need to know anything more about these terms beyond the fact that they are created and defined by the relevant statutes.
- The protection given to tenants by some of these codes is very extensive. For example, security of tenure under the Rent Act 1977 could pass on the tenant's death to any member of the family who was living with the tenant at that time, and there could be a further similar transmission on the death of that second tenant. The landlord's inability to recover possession, and the fact that the rent that could be charged was subject to statutory control, form the background to many of the decisions about residential licences which are considered in 9.2.3, and explains why landlords were so anxious to avoid the statutory provisions by granting licences rather than leases.

9.5.2 Common law rules for determining leases

Despite the statutory provisions noted, the older common law rules governing the determination of a lease are still of great importance, because in general the statutory rules which protect the tenant at the end of the lease do not come into effect until after the contractual tenancy has been terminated. Accordingly, a landlord who wishes to end a tenancy may first have to terminate the contractual tenancy and then take further action in order to bring to an end the tenant's statutory protection.

At common law a lease may be determined in any of the following ways:

1. expiry;
2. notice to quit;
3. surrender;
4. merger;
5. enlargement;
6. disclaimer;
7. forfeiture.

In addition, there are modern decisions that suggest that the contractual doctrines of frustration and repudiation by fundamental breach may apply to leases (see 9.6).

9.5.2.1 Expiry of term

A fixed-term lease gives rise to few problems, since it will expire automatically once the specified term comes to an end. In such cases it is not necessary for either party to the lease to take any action in order to terminate the lease.

In addition, if a lease is granted for a fixed term but is subject to earlier termination on the occurrence of a specified event, then the lease terminates automatically when the event occurs (see *Doe d Lockwood v Clarke* (1807) 8 East 185 and *Great Northern Railway Co. v Arnold* (1916) 33 TLR 114). Commercial leases determining on death, marriage, or the formation of a civil partnership are affected by the provisions of LPA 1925, s. 149(6), requiring notice, and do not terminate automatically (see 9.1.2.2).

Some fixed-term leases contain clauses ('*break clauses*') allowing one party, or both, to determine the lease on notice before the term expires. The break clause may be exercisable on the occurrence of certain events (for example, if the landlord wants to redevelop the property), or at specified intervals throughout the term (e.g., at the end of the 7th or 14th year in a 21-year lease). Such a lease will usually provide for notice to be given before the break clause is exercised.

9.5.2.2 Notice to quit

Parties may contractually agree the form and period of notice required to terminate a lease. In the absence of such agreement, there are standard common law rules that apply. The statutory codes designed to protect tenants have also created a number of requirements as to the form and timing of notices to quit, which cannot be varied by agreement.

(1) *Form of notice* In general, there appears to be no requirement at common law that notice must be given in writing, at least in the case of tenancies created orally (*Timmins v Rowlinson* (1765) 3 Burr 1603). However, under s. 5(1) of the Protection from Eviction Act 1977, notice to quit in respect of residential premises must be given in writing. Any such notice must be given in a form specified by the statute, drawing to the attention of the tenant the fact that there may be an entitlement to security of tenure under statutory provisions. The provisions of Part I of the Housing Act 1988 thereafter generally prevent the landlord from recovering possession of such premises without a court order. Most business tenancies must also be terminated by written notice, in the statutory form, under the provisions of the Landlord and Tenant Act 1954.

(2) *Period of notice* The correct period for notice will vary according to the type of lease or tenancy involved. However, there are certain statutory rules which apply to leases of dwellings, business premises, and agricultural holdings, and to long residential tenancies at low rent. These rules are more appropriately dealt with in a detailed text on landlord and tenant law, but you should note that any notice to quit residential premises must be given not less than four weeks before the date on which it is to take effect (Protection from Eviction Act 1977, s. 5(1)) unless the lease falls within one of the excluded categories set out in s. 3A.

In the absence of any express agreement between the parties (which must not, of course, exclude the statutory provisions), the common law will govern the length of notice required. Save in the case of a yearly tenancy, the correct period for notice is a full period under the lease. Thus, for a quarterly tenancy, one gives a quarter's notice, for a monthly tenancy a month's notice, and for a weekly tenancy a week's notice. The notice should expire at the end of one period of the lease. A yearly tenancy, however, can be terminated by half a year's notice, expiring at the end of a year (*Doe d Shore v Porter* (1789) 3 TR 13).

(3) *Excluding the right to give notice* It is clear from *Breams Property Investment Co. Ltd v Stroulger* [1948] 2 KB 1 that the landlord's right to give notice does not have to be identical with that of the tenant, and that one party's right to give notice may be restricted for a defined period. We have already seen that is difficult to exclude the

right to give notice for an indefinite period (9.2.4.1), because this has the effect of making the periodic tenancy uncertain, and therefore void under the rule in *Lace v Chantler* [1944] KB 368, as applied by the House of Lords in *Prudential Assurance Co. Ltd v London Residuary Body* [1992] 2 AC 386.

When a purported grant is invalidated in this way, the 'tenant' may be able to claim to have an implied periodic tenancy, arising from going into possession and paying rent on a periodic basis. Such a tenancy will then be determinable by the appropriate notice. Where the 'tenant' is an artificial person, such as a company or corporation, this outcome will be the best it can hope for (unless it chooses to claim to hold under a contractual licence). As we have seen, the Supreme Court decision in *Berrisford v Mexfield Housing Co-operative Ltd* [2011] UKSC 52 may allow a *human* tenant to claim that the purported grant created a lease for life, which has been converted into a 90-year term under LPA 1925, s. 149(6). Such a lease will be determinable by notice on the death of the tenant, or during his lifetime in accordance with the termination provisions in the purported grant (see 9.2.4.2).

9.5.2.3 Surrender

A surrender takes place when a tenant relinquishes the lease to the landlord, with the agreement of the landlord. Its effect is to release the tenant from any future liability under the lease, but not to release him from liability for past actions, such as past breaches of covenant (*Richmond v Savill* [1926] 2 KB 530). Accordingly, the landlord would still be able to seek compensation for any past losses arising from such breaches. It should be noted, however, that the circumstances of the surrender may be such that the landlord will be taken to have waived his right to compensation for past breaches (*Dalton v Pickard* [1926] 2 KB 545).

(1) *Express surrender* Since a surrender is a dealing with a legal estate in land, it should be done expressly and by deed. This is true even where one wishes to surrender a short lease, for the exemption in LPA 1925, s. 54(2), applies only to the grant of such leases and not to their surrender. A defective surrender (e.g., a surrender which, due to mistake, is unwitnessed) may operate in equity as a contract to surrender the lease, under the usual principles (see 9.3.2).

(2) *Surrender by operation of law* No deed is required, however, in cases in which the lease is surrendered by operation of law (LPA 1925, s. 52(2)(c)). In practice this is quite common, since often the surrender is evidenced by the actions of the parties who would thereafter be estopped from denying the fact of the surrender (*Foster v Robinson* (1951) 1 KB 149). Such surrenders commonly arise when a landlord accepts possession of the property and agrees that the tenant will be under no further liability. Thus in *Phené v Popplewell* (1862) 12 CB NS 334 a surrender was held to have been made without formalities when the landlord agreed to take back the premises, painted out the name of the former tenant on a signboard, and put up a board advertising the property as available to let. However, since a surrender requires the agreement of both parties, no surrender will arise from a purely unilateral act (e.g., the tenant returning the key without the landlord's assent, *Cannan v Grimley* (1850) 9 CB 634), and the other party to the lease may insist on the continued performance of the obligations under lease. A more recent example of this is to be found in the Court of Appeal decision in *Bellcourt Estates Ltd v Adesina* [2005] 18 EG 150, where the tenant had abandoned the premises and returned the key to the landlord and where the landlord had ceased to make

demands for payment of rent. The Court noted that a mere omission to do anything on the part of the landlord would not count as acceptance of a surrender, in the absence of unequivocal acts demonstrating such acceptance.

(3) Surrender by operation of law may also occur in situations where landlord and tenant have agreed variations to the terms of the current lease, which are so significant that they can take effect only through the creation of a new lease. Such a new lease could not be granted except on the basis that the old one had been surrendered, and the law will achieve the result sought by the parties by implying both a surrender of the old lease and a grant of a new one.

9.5.2.4 Merger

A merger arises when the tenant acquires the immediate reversion to his lease or a third party acquires both the lease and the immediate reversion (see 9.1.5). In such an event the tenant would, in theory, become his own landlord, or the third party would become both landlord and tenant. Unless there is some specific reason for wishing the lease and the reversion to remain separate, such as the new owner's wish or obligation to preserve lesser rights benefiting or burdening the leasehold estate alone, the lease will merge into the reversionary estate when they come into the hands of the same owner and disappear. However, this only occurs where it is the intention of the owner that the estates should merge, and LPA 1925, s. 185, preserves the equitable rule to this effect.

Since a merger involves the acquisition of the superior estate, the events which give rise to it can usually only be effected by deed (LPA 1925, s. 52(1)).

9.5.2.5 Enlargement

In practice, this is very rare, because under the provisions of LPA 1925, s. 153, it can only be done in the case of a lease originally granted for 300 years or more and upon which no rent of any money value is payable. Where the numerous conditions of s. 153 are satisfied, the tenant may execute a deed of **enlargement**, which has the effect of increasing his interest to that of an estate in fee simple, and thereby extinguishing the title of the previous fee simple owner.

9.5.2.6 Disclaimer

A right to disclaim a lease normally arises by statute. The most common examples are the rights of trustees in bankruptcy and liquidators of companies to disclaim certain 'onerous' property under the provisions of the Insolvency Act 1986. A **disclaimer** releases the tenant from future liabilities under the lease.

9.5.2.7 Forfeiture

In certain circumstances, it is possible for a landlord to forfeit a lease for breach, by the tenant, of one of the terms of the agreement. This method of determining a lease is considered in detail in Chapter 12, dealing with the landlord's remedies for breach of leasehold covenants (see 12.4).

9.5.3 Effect on subtenant of determination of head lease

As you have seen (9.1.4), a tenant may grant a second lease of the premises, giving a subtenant an estate for a shorter period, which has been carved out of the lease. The resulting position is portrayed in Figure 9.4.

```
                         L
        Head lease       │
                         ▼
                         T
        Sublease         │
                         ▼
                         S
```

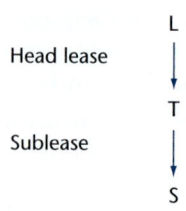

Figure 9.4 Freehold, lease and sublease

In this situation, S's term clearly depends upon the continuance of T's head lease, and the general rule is that it comes to an end automatically if the head lease expires, or is determined by L's giving T notice to quit or forfeiting the lease for breach of covenant.

9.5.3.1 Effect of surrender or merger

The general rule described above does not, however, apply where the head lease is determined by surrender or merger, which are recognised as exceptions to it.

Thus, in the situation illustrated in Figure 9.4, a surrender of the head lease by T will not end the sublease which T has granted to S. In the words of Cockburn CJ in *Mellor v Watkins* (1874) LR 9 QB 400 at p. 404:

> ... when a person voluntarily surrenders his lease, he cannot by so doing put an end to an undertenancy created by himself...

Instead, once T's head lease is gone, S will become L's tenant, on the terms and conditions of the sublease. The effect of the surrender on the subtenant is thus merely to alter the person to whom the rent is to be paid and to whom S owes a duty to observe the covenants in the sublease (LPA 1925, s. 150).

Similarly, if T's head lease and L's reversion merge, either in T or in some third party, the new owner of the single remaining estate will hold it subject to the sublease, and S's position will be in all respects the same as described in relation to surrender. In both cases, there is no hardship in the head landlord, or his successor, being bound by the sublease, because he has consented to the arrangement which has produced this situation.

9.5.3.2 Head lease ended on tenant's initiative

The general effect on the subtenant of the determination of the head lease is well established. Until recently, however, there has been some uncertainty about the subtenant's position in cases where the head lease was brought to an end on the initiative of the tenant under the head lease. A tenant may do this by operating a break clause or by giving notice to quit to his landlord (sometimes called an '**upwards notice**'): in such a case, does the sublease survive and bind the head landlord or will it be extinguished with the head lease?

Despite various *obiter dicta* on this matter, and one unreported first-instance decision (*Brown v Wilson* (1949)), it emerged in *Pennell v Payne* [1995] QB 192 that there was no authority on this point binding on the Court of Appeal. The court was therefore required to decide as a matter of policy between the competing interests of a hypothetical subtenant and head landlord (hypothetical because no sublease had actually been granted in the case itself). If the sublease were to survive the determination of the head lease, the tenant would have imposed the subtenant on the landlord against the landlord's will. If, on the other hand, the sublease were to end, the tenant, by ending his or own lease, would have destroyed the interest he had created, thus derogating from the grant to the subtenant. Faced with this choice, the Court of Appeal took the view (at p. 270) that:

> the considerations against allowing a tenant unilaterally to foist his subtenant upon the landlord are in total compelling

The court held that if a tenant terminated a lease by an upwards notice, the landlord would be entitled to regain the land from the subtenant. This decision was subsequently approved by the House of Lords in *Barrett v Morgan* [2000] 2 AC 264.

In such a case, it is likely that the tenant would be liable to his subtenant for breach of his covenant for quiet enjoyment (as to which, see 10.2.1). Lord Millett, in *Barrett v Morgan*, suggested that a subtenant could seek an injunction to restrain his landlord (the tenant under the head lease) from serving the upwards notice if forewarned.

9.5.3.3 Head lease ended on landlord's initiative

Finally, where a head lease comes to an end because of the landlord's notice to quit to the head tenant, the sublease will be destroyed when the head lease comes to an end. This is the case even where the landlord's notice to quit is served by pre-arrangement with the tenant who does not oppose it, because he wants to determine the sublease. In *Barrett v Morgan* ([1999] 1 WLR 1109), the Court of Appeal had held that, in such circumstances, the notice was consensual rather than unilateral and the termination of the lease by such notice was indistinguishable from surrender; accordingly, the sublease survived the determination of the head lease and bound the landlord.

This decision was, however, reversed on appeal by the House of Lords (*Barrett v Morgan* [2000] 2 AC 264), Lord Millett (at p. 274) describing the lower court's decision as having:

> the extraordinary result that the parties to a tenancy cannot achieve together by agreement what either can achieve alone without it.

To the House of Lords, the essential distinction was not between consensual and unilateral acts, but between agreements made by the parties to the head lease before and after the grant of the sublease. A subtenant takes the sublease already subject to the terms of the head lease, which were agreed *before* the tenancy was created. A subtenant's title cannot, therefore, survive the termination of the head lease in accordance with those terms (e.g., by the head landlord giving notice). By contrast, the subtenant's title cannot be prejudiced by any agreement (such as for surrender) between the parties to the head lease made *after* the creation of the sublease.

9.5.3.4 Effect of agreement between the parties

The impact on these rules of an agreement between the parties arose for decision in *PW & Co. v Milton Gate Investments Ltd* [2004] Ch 142. The case concerned a head lease which included a break clause exercisable by the tenant, and also a provision that a penalty was payable by the tenant on premature determination of the lease, unless at that time at least 75 per cent of the building was sublet. The lease also provided that any subleases would survive the ending of the head lease and would bind the head landlord. However, by the time the tenant ended the head lease, the original landlord had assigned its reversion and the new landlord (Milton Gate Investments Ltd) demanded payment of the penalty despite the fact that the property had been sublet. Accordingly, PW & Co. sought a declaration that it was not liable to pay the penalty because the subleases continued in existence and the property was therefore sublet.

The court refused the declaration, holding that the general rules applied and could not be varied by contrary provisions in the lease. As a result, the subleases came to an end with the ending of the head lease. In reaching this decision, the court emphasised that a lease is not merely a contract but also creates an estate in land, and that a sublease cannot last longer than the estate out of which it has been created.

9.5.4 Effect on joint tenant of determination of head lease

As you will see in Chapter 17, it is possible for a legal estate (either freehold or leasehold) to be owned by several people together, in the form of co-ownership known as 'joint tenancy' (see 9.2.3.2 and 17.2). In general, the rules about leases that we so far have considered apply to joint tenants of the estate in exactly the same way as to a sole tenant. However, there are special principles governing the termination of a lease that is jointly owned.

As Lord Bridge explained in *Hammersmith LBC v Monk* [1992] 1 AC 478 at p. 490:

> . . . all positive dealings with a joint tenancy require the concurrence of all joint tenants if they are to be effective. Thus a single joint tenant cannot exercise a break clause in a lease, surrender the term, make a disclaimer, exercise the option to renew the tenancy or apply for relief from forfeiture.

This requirement that all joint tenants should agree to all dealings with the estate has a somewhat unexpected result when applied to the ending of a periodic tenancy. As explained in 9.1.2.1, the theory underlying periodic tenancies is that their running on from one period to another depends on the will of the landlord and the tenant that they should continue in this way. The notice to quit is an indication by one side to the other that the person giving notice does not want the lease to be renewed for another period.

In the context of a jointly owned periodic tenancy, this means that all the joint tenants must want the tenancy to continue by being renewed for another period. If one of the tenants does not want to continue, the necessary agreement for renewal is not present and accordingly the periodic tenancy will come to an end. This means that, as the House of Lords held in *Hammersmith LBC v Monk* [1992] 1 AC 478, a notice to quit given by one joint tenant, even without the concurrence of the other(s), is effective to determine a periodic tenancy.

The facts of *Monk* were that a cohabiting couple held a joint periodic tenancy of a council flat, which was terminable on four weeks' notice. After some time, the woman left her partner and moved out of the flat. The local authority agreed to rehouse her if she ended the periodic tenancy she already held from it, and she therefore gave the appropriate notice to quit without her co-tenant's knowledge or consent. The House of Lords held that this was a valid notice to quit which brought the periodic tenancy to an end, and the council was entitled to recover possession of the flat and evict the other tenant. Members of the House of Lords agreed that, at first sight, it seems amazing that one co-owner, acting unilaterally, can terminate the other owner's rights in his home. However, their decision was based both on the nature of periodic tenancies and general contractual principles:

> If A and B contract with C on terms that are to continue in operation for one year in the first place and thereafter from year to year unless determined by notice at the end of the first or any subsequent year, neither A nor B has bound himself contractually for longer than one year . . . the agreement is intended to continue beyond the initial term only if and so long as all parties to the agreement are willing that it should do so (at p. 483).

The fact that the decision in *Monk* is consistent with the basic principle, however, does not alter the fact that its effect is to deprive the other co-owner of the property and home, and it is arguable that this way of ending a tenancy may well be challenged on human rights grounds (see 2.9). In *Sims v Dacorum Borough Council* [2014] UKSC 63, however, the Supreme Court rejected this argument. There was no breach of the right to peaceful enjoyment of possessions under Article 1 of the First Protocol because it was not a "deprivation" of a property right for that right to come to an end according to its own terms, which was what happened when a jointly held periodic tenancy was terminated by one co-owner giving notice. Nor was there a breach of the right to respect for the home, under Article 8 of the Convention, because the other joint tenant was a private party who had a right to serve such a notice. Where the landlord was a public authority, the Article 8 right to a home was adequately protected by the fact that the proportionality could be considered at the stage when the landlord sought an order for possession. But the termination of the lease by service of a *Monk* notice was not, in itself, a violation of the right to respect for the home.

9.6 Leases as contracts

As we have seen, the lease operates on two levels, being both a contract between the landlord and the tenant and a conveyance creating an estate in the land. The common law rules for the determination of the lease that we have so far concerned are peculiar to the estate in land, explaining how a tenant's right to possession may come to an end. In addition, as you may know if you have already studied the law of contract, there are a number of ways in which contracts may be discharged so that the parties no longer have any obligations under them.

9.6.1 Determination of leases by termination of contract

Two forms of discharge, frustration and repudiatory breach, have been held by the courts to be applicable to leases, and therefore constitute two further ways in which a lease may be brought to an end.

9.6.1.1 Frustration

In general, the doctrine of frustration applies where external factors prevent the parties to an agreement performing their obligations under the contract. As explained by Lord Simon in *National Carriers Ltd v Panalpina (Northern) Ltd* [1981] AC 675, at p. 700:

> Frustration of a contract takes place when there supervenes an event (without default of either party and for which the contract makes no significant provision) which so significantly changes the nature (not merely the expense or onerousness) of the outstanding contractual rights and/or obligations from what the parties could reasonably have contemplated at the time of its execution that it would be unjust to hold them to the literal sense of its stipulations in the new circumstances; in such case the law declares both parties to be discharged from further performance.

It may well happen that property let to a tenant becomes unusable, through no fault of either landlord or tenant, and the tenant may claim that as a result the lease is frustrated. It used to be thought that this would not succeed, for the tenant had an estate in the land and duties under the lease attach to that estate. Thus, if the house on the property was destroyed by fire, the tenant was still obliged to pay any rent due under the lease, for there was still an estate in the land (*Matthey v Curling* [1922] 2 AC 180). In the old case of *Paradine v Jane* (1647) Al 26, a tenant was evicted from the property by the King's army during the Civil War. The tenant was held to be liable to pay the rent on the property, for the risk of such interference was to be borne by the current legal occupier of the land. This rule generally favours others who have an interest in the land which is derived from the tenant's estate (e.g., a mortgagee who has taken a mortgage of the tenant's estate), who would otherwise be deprived of their interest or security.

At the date of *Paradine v Jane*, the doctrine of frustration of contract had not been developed. Even after it had emerged in the nineteenth century, there was for many years considerable uncertainty whether the doctrine could ever apply to a term of years. The issue appears to have been settled, at long last, by the House of Lords in *National Carriers Ltd v Panalpina (Northern) Ltd* [1981] AC 675. In that case, the lease was of a warehouse. For some 20 months, the local authority had closed the street that gave access to the premises because a neighbouring derelict property was in a dangerous condition. The tenants were thus prevented from using the warehouse for that period. They failed to pay rent and defended an action for its recovery by claiming that the lease had been frustrated. The House of Lords considered that in the circumstances the lease had not been frustrated because the interruption of 20 months (in a 10-year lease) did not destroy the entire contract. Their Lordships did, however, accept the principle that the doctrine of frustration could apply to a lease. Lord Wilberforce said (at p. 697):

> [T]hough such cases may be rare, the doctrine of frustration is capable of application to leases of land. It must be so applied with proper regard to the fact that a lease, that is, a grant of a legal estate, is involved. The court must consider whether any term is to be implied which would determine the lease in the event which has happened and/or ascertain the foundation of the agreement and decide whether this still exists in the light of the terms of the lease, the surrounding circumstances and any special rules which apply to leases or to the particular lease in question.

In reaching this conclusion, their Lordships considered in some detail the argument that a lease is more than a contract, because it creates an estate in land. They were not, however, persuaded that this was any reason for refusing to apply the doctrine of frustration, if justice required its use. Frustration would have the effect of ending the estate prematurely, but a leasehold estate is already capable of ending prematurely, for example on the occurrence of some prescribed event, or on forfeiture for breach of covenant. The argument that termination of the estate could prejudicially affect third parties (such as mortgagees) was noted, but was not regarded as a sufficient reason for excluding the doctrine. In dealing with the questions raised by this case, several members of the House of Lords found support from developments in the United States and in Canada, in which the doctrine of frustration has been applied to leases. It was accepted that in reality the question is one of where the risk of unforeseen events should fall: upon the tenant or upon the landlord.

The circumstances in which a lease may be frustrated remain to be seen, but would almost certainly include the destruction of the land itself (by cliff-fall, rising sea levels, or other natural occurrence), and possibly the total destruction of buildings (by analogy with *Taylor v Caldwell* (1863) 3 B & S 826, in which a contract granting a licence for use of buildings was held to be frustrated when the premises were destroyed by fire). Views expressed in the House of Lords suggest that frustration may also apply where property is let for a specific use which then becomes illegal (as, for example, during the Prohibition era in the United States when tenants were discharged from their obligations to pay rent for premises which they had taken for the specific purpose of using as liquor saloons). However, the House of Lords emphasised that frustration of a lease is likely to occur only very rarely.

9.6.1.2 Repudiatory breach

This method of discharging a contract involves a breach by one party of an obligation under the contract which is so fundamental that its breach is tantamount to his repudiating or rejecting the contract as a whole. In such a situation, the innocent party may accept the repudiation and treat it as terminating the contract, or may choose to ignore it and treat the agreement as continuing.

1. Breach by the landlord

In *Hussein v Mehlman* [1992] 2 EGLR 87 the question arose whether repudiatory breach could apply to a three-year residential lease (described throughout by the court as 'a contract of letting'). Under covenants implied by the Landlord and Tenant Act 1985, s. 11, the landlord was under a duty to keep in repair the structure and exterior of the house, and the installations for the supply of water, gas and electricity, and for space and water heating. He was in serious breach of these covenants, and the court found that he had no intention of performing them. In the view of the judge 'the tenants suffered real hardship as a result of the breach and were deprived of an essential part of what they had contracted for . . . the breach vitiated the central purpose of the contract of letting' (at p. 91). After 15 months, the tenants handed back the keys and vacated the property, claiming that the landlord's behaviour constituted repudiatory conduct which they accepted, thus ending the lease and their obligations under it.

In the county court, Assistant Recorder Sedley QC considered whether a repudiatory breach of a contract of letting was legally possible, and held that it was. An earlier opinion that repudiation was not applicable to leases (*Total Oil Great Britain Ltd v Thompson Garages (Biggin Hill) Ltd* [1972] 1 QB 318 at p. 324) was based on the view that a lease is essentially different from other contracts, and derived support from the then-accepted principle that the doctrine of frustration did not apply to leases. However, as we have already seen, the House of Lords in *National Carriers Ltd v Panalpina (Northern) Ltd* [1981] AC 675 had more recently emphasised the contractual dimension of the lease and specifically accepted that, in exceptional circumstances, a lease can be frustrated. This enabled the court in *Hussein v Mehlman* to conclude that *Total Oil* had ceased to be authority for the proposition that a lease cannot be terminated by acceptance of a repudiatory breach of its terms. Support for the view that a lease could be repudiated was to be found in a number of nineteenth-century cases in which it was treated as 'axiomatic that a contract of letting could be terminated by an innocent party without notice if the other party failed to fulfil a fundamental term of the contract' (at p. 89). Thus the judge held that a lease can be ended on repudiation by the other party and that, on the facts before him, the landlord's behaviour constituted repudiatory conduct, which had been accepted by the tenants. The lease had come to an end, and both parties were released from their obligations under it.

Although the decision in *Hussein v Mehlman* was only at first instance and in the county court, it has received considerable attention, and is recognised as a significant development. Its effect at present is to introduce into English land law another method of terminating a lease, which is already recognised in other jurisdictions.

Some five years after the decision in *Hussein v Mehlman*, repudiation of a lease was accepted by the Court of Appeal, apparently without question, in *Chartered Trust plc v Davies* (1997) 76 P&CR 396. In that case, the tenant of a unit in a shopping mall withheld rent because the business carried on in the premises was adversely affected by the landlord's failure to control the activities of other tenants in the mall. The tenant claimed that the landlord had broken his covenant not to derogate from his grant (see 10.2.2), and that this was so serious that it amounted to a repudiatory breach. This claim was accepted at first instance and the decision was upheld by the Court of Appeal. The judgment, given by Henry LJ, deals in some detail with derogation from grant, but does not discuss repudiation, merely saying at the end that the trial judge's finding of repudiation was one which he was entitled to make (at p. 409). Despite its brevity, and the fact that no mention is made of *Hussein v Mehlman*, this would seem to support the view that a lease can now be treated as repudiated. However, you may like to note the view expressed in Megarry and Wade at para. 18-106 that success in claiming repudiation may depend on the length of the lease:

> Clearly, both the length and the terms of the lease will be relevant to whether there has been a breach that will justify treating it as terminated. The longer the lease, the more artificial it is to regard it as other than an estate in land. It is therefore only in relation to shorter lettings that an allegation of discharge by breach is normally likely to be successful.

2. Breach by the tenant

In *Hussein v Mehlman* [1992] 2 EGLR 87 at p. 90 the judge considered that the concept of repudiatory breach could be used against the tenant as well as against the landlord:

> If the obligation to pay rent is as fundamental as the obligation to keep the house habitable, it will follow that a default in rent payments is a repudiatory act on the tenant's part.

Such breaches of covenant by the tenant are at present dealt with by the remedy of forfeiture which (see 12.4.2) is subject to statutory controls that protect the tenant, giving an opportunity to remedy the breach and avoid forfeiture. The Assistant Recorder suggested that the landlord's right to terminate on repudiatory breach by his tenant might in some way be modified by the provisions in the lease relating to forfeiture, so as to provide similar safeguards against repudiation. As yet, however, there has been no reported case in which a landlord has acted upon a repudiatory breach by a tenant.

In 2006, the Law Commission proposed major changes to the law of forfeiture, some of which would increase the protection available to tenants (see 12.4.8). The report, *Termination of Tenancies for Tenant Default* (2006, Law Com No. 303 Cm 6946) mentions at para. 2.3 that its proposals would not affect the ability of the tenant to bring a tenancy to an end by accepting repudiatory breach by the landlord. By contrast, the proposed new termination procedure (see 12.4.8.3) would abolish the landlord's right to terminate the lease by any other means, such as forfeiture or acceptance of a repudiatory breach by the tenant (see draft Bill in App.1 of the report, and explanatory note on cl. 1).

These recent developments emphasise the contractual nature of the lease and play down its proprietary aspects. In *Panalpina* the House of Lords applied the contractual doctrine of frustration to leases, while in *Monk* it was guided by general contractual principles in considering the effect of notice given by one of two joint tenants. Again, the Court of Appeal in *Chartered Trust* apparently accepted that leases can be determined by acceptance of repudiatory breach.

These examples all relate to the process of ending a lease. However, the trend is also apparent in other cases. For example, in *C. H. Bailey Ltd v Memorial Enterprises Ltd* [1974] 1 WLR 728 (on retrospective increases in rent following a rent review) Lord Denning rejected the suggestion that the matter was to be governed by considerations derived from feudal conceptions about the landlord-tenant relationship, saying:

> It is time to get away from the medieval concept of rent . . . in modern law, rent is not conceived of as a thing, but rather as a payment which a tenant is bound by his contract to make to his landlord for the use of the land.

The importance of the contractual relationship was also emphasised by Lord Browne-Wilkinson in *Prudential Assurance Co. Ltd v London Residuary Body* [1992] 2 AC 386 as he queried the justification for the ancient rule which requires leases to be certain, a rule which he described as operating to 'defeat contractually agreed arrangements between the parties'.

By contrast, Morritt LJ, in his dissenting judgment in *Ingram v IRC* [1997] 4 All ER 395 at p. 422, considered that:

> It is easy to make too much of the contractual nature of the relationship. The feature of a tenancy which distinguishes it from a licence or merely contractual right of occupation is the **lessee's** right to exclusive possession. But this right is a consequence of the ownership of the legal estate; it is not merely a contractual right, or it could not be the feature which distinguishes a lease from a licence.

It seems that this approach was favoured by the House of Lords, which reversed the decision of the Court of Appeal ([2001] 1 AC 293), Lord Hoffmann saying that, in the particular circumstances of the case, 'the contractual nature of the lease seems to me a matter of conveyancing theory rather than substance' (at p. 304). A similar emphasis on the lease as a property interest is to be found in *PW & Co. v Milton Gate Investments Ltd* [2004] Ch 142 (for which, see 9.5.3.4).

Nevertheless, despite *Ingram*, it remains true that recent developments reveal a tendency by the courts to view the lease, at least initially, primarily as a contract. The development is summed up by one writer (Bright [1993] Conv 71) as follows:

> when determining leasehold issues the courts will start from the premise that their foundation is in contract, instead of being reluctant to apply more general contractual principles to leases because of the fact that as property interests they are somehow special and sheltered from the rigours of contract.

9.6.2 *Bruton v London & Quadrant Housing Trust* [2000] 1 AC 406

The developments noted in this section have been, so far, one of emphasis. *Bruton v London & Quadrant Housing Trust* [2000] 1 AC 406, however, introduced what seems to some commentators to be a new explanation of the nature of leases. It appears now that it is possible to have a contractual or non-proprietary lease, which gives rise to a landlord and tenant relationship but does not create an estate in the land.

In the *Bruton* case, the housing trust held various properties (which were awaiting redevelopment) as a licensee of Lambeth Borough Council. The trust used the properties to provide short-term housing for the homeless, entering into 'licence agreements' with the individual occupiers. One of the occupiers, Mr Bruton, subsequently claimed that he had exclusive possession of his self-contained flat and that, despite the wording of the agreement, he was therefore a tenant under the principles of *Street v Mountford*. His purpose in doing this was to bring himself within s. 11 of the Landlord and Tenant Act 1985, which imposes a repairing obligation on landlords in respect of certain tenancies (see 10.2.4.1), but does not apply to licences. The housing trust itself had no estate in the land, and so could not grant a tenancy, but it was alleged that it was estopped from denying that it had done so. In other words, the occupier sought to combine the principles of *Street v Mountford* and the doctrine of tenancy by estoppel.

The occupier's claim was rejected by the Court of Appeal (see [1998] QB 834). At this stage, it seems to have been accepted by both parties that the trust could not have granted a tenancy because it had no estate in the land. In other words, it could not give what it had not got. It is in such circumstances that a tenancy by estoppel may arise, and it was a tenancy of this nature that the occupier claimed.

The Court of Appeal, however, considered that the situation in this case did not give rise to a tenancy by estoppel. In the words of Millett LJ (at pp. 842–3) such a tenancy is based on the principle that:

> A man who purports to grant a tenancy is not permitted to deny that he has done so by asserting his own want of title. If he has none, the grant creates a tenancy by estoppel.

In this case, the trust did not purport to grant a tenancy, because it was aware of its lack of title and specifically granted a licence. There was, therefore, no purported grant which the trust could be estopped from denying, and accordingly no tenancy by estoppel arose.

The decision of the Court of Appeal was reversed by the House of Lords ([2000] 1 AC 406), which held that a tenancy had been created between the parties. On the facts of the case, Mr Bruton had been granted exclusive possession for a term at a rent; this raised a prima facie conclusion that he was a tenant, and the House of Lords did not agree that the special nature of the trust (as a charitable body providing short-term accommodation) was sufficient to take it out of the rule in *Street v Mountford* (see 9.2.3.3).

In holding that Mr Bruton held a lease and was not just a tenant by estoppel, the House of Lords rejected the argument that the housing trust could not create a lease because it had no estate in the land. Lord Hoffmann explained that the creation of an estate is the usual consequence of a lease, but is not essential; an agreement which creates a landlord and tenant relationship is a lease, even though the landlord is unable to grant an estate to the tenant. In the words of Lord Hoffmann (at p. 415):

> ... the term 'lease' or 'tenancy' describes a relationship between two parties who are designated landlord and tenant. It is not concerned with the question of whether the agreement creates an estate or other proprietary interest which may be binding on third parties. A lease may, and usually does, create a proprietary interest called a leasehold estate or, technically, a 'term of years absolute'. This will depend upon whether the landlord had an interest out of which he could grant it. *Nemo dat quod non habet* [no one can give what he has not got]. But it is the fact that the agreement is a lease which creates the proprietary interest. It is putting the cart before the horse to say that whether the agreement is a lease depends upon whether it creates a proprietary interest.

A similar view was expressed by Lord Hobhouse (at p. 418):

> The present case does not depend upon the establishing of an estoppel nor does any problem arise from the fact that the housing trust did not have a legal estate. The [appellant's] case depends upon his establishing that his agreement with the housing trust has the legal effect of creating a relationship of tenant and landlord between them. That is all. It does not depend upon his establishing a proprietary title good against all the world.

Thus, although the trust could not create a proprietary interest, the agreement between the parties satisfied the requirements of *Street v Mountford* and created a lease within the meaning of s. 11 of the Landlord and Tenant Act 1985.

We should note at this point that the House of Lords also took the opportunity to explain the operation of tenancy by estoppel. In what follows, their Lordships were presumably referring to the form of tenancy by estoppel which arises from the purported grant of a lease, rather than from the landlord's representation as to title (see 9.3.4), since it is clear on the facts that the trust had made no such representation. To quote Lord Hoffmann once more (at p. 415):

> I think Millett LJ [in the court below] may have been misled by the ancient phrase 'tenancy by estoppel' into thinking that it described an agreement which would not otherwise be a lease or tenancy but which was treated as being one by virtue of an estoppel. In fact ... it is not the estoppel which created the tenancy, but the tenancy which created the estoppel. The estoppel arises when one or other of the parties want to deny one of the ordinary incidents or obligations of the tenancy on the ground that the landlord had no legal estate. The basis of the estoppel is that having entered into an agreement which constitutes a lease or tenancy, he cannot repudiate that incident or obligation.

And again (p. 416):

> ... it is the fact that the agreement between the parties constitutes a tenancy that gives rise to an estoppel and not the other way round. It therefore seems to me that the question of tenancy by estoppel does not arise in this case. The issue is simply whether the agreement is a tenancy.

9.6.3 Implications of the decision in *Bruton*

Although Lord Hoffmann speaks as though his analysis of the nature of a lease is well established and, indeed, obvious, it came as a considerable surprise to many lawyers. In relation to tenancies at will (9.1.2.1), we have seen that it is possible to have the relationship of landlord and tenant without the creation of an estate, but this appeared to be an unusual but useful way of explaining an anomalous situation. Historically, of course, the lease did begin as a purely contractual relationship between the parties that gave no estate in the land; once the notion of the leasehold estate had developed, however, it was generally thought that a lease inevitably created such an estate. As Millett LJ put it in the Court of Appeal in *Bruton* ([1998] QB 834 at p. 845): 'A tenancy is a legal estate'.

In the light of the House of Lords' decision, however, it seems that we now have to divide leases into two categories; the proprietary lease, which creates an estate in the land, and the contractual or personal lease—which does not. Lord Hoffmann makes it clear that leases will usually create a proprietary interest, but the possibility of a non-proprietary lease, even if rare, raises a number of questions. These include the following.

9.6.3.1 When may a non-proprietary lease be created?

Does it arise only where the grantor has no title, or may it be created in other circumstances?

9.6.3.2 How is a non-proprietary lease to be created?

The requirement of a deed in the case of leases for more than three years is imposed by the general rule in LPA 1925, s. 52(1) that a deed must be used for the conveyance or creation of a legal estate. Since no estate is created by a non-proprietary lease, it presumably can be created orally or in writing, whatever its length, and a contract for such a lease would not need to be made in writing.

9.6.3.3 In what circumstances will a court find a tenancy by estoppel?

If the agreement between the parties creates a non-proprietary lease, their rights and obligations must surely arise from that lease, and not from any estoppel. It is at first sight difficult to envisage the future use of tenancy by estoppel or, indeed, to understand why the concept has been used in the past if the non-proprietary lease has always been available to the courts.

9.6.3.4 What is the effect of a non-proprietary lease on third parties?

While the non-proprietary lease may be sufficient to determine the parties' rights and duties between themselves, its effect on third parties is far from clear. As we have seen, tenancies by estoppel bind and benefit not only the parties but their successors. Will the non-proprietary lease recognised in *Bruton* have the same effect, and will the benefit and burden of obligations under it run to the parties' successors? Presumably, rights under the tenancy could be assigned, like many other contractual rights, but the transfer of burdens would be ruled out by the privity of contract rules. As will be explained (11.2.2.2), courts have experienced considerable difficulties in dealing with the running of covenants in equitable leases. Non-proprietary leases seem likely to pose even greater problems. Such problems might be resolved, however, if the parties to the contractual lease were estopped from denying the existence of a proprietary lease and the estoppel bound and benefited their successors in the established way. This does not, however, explain why courts in the past have needed to rely on the concept of estoppel in dealing with the rights and duties of the original parties to the agreement.

As far as we know, there has as yet been no decision on this point, but you may like to note an observation of Lord Neuberger in *Berrisford v Mexfield Housing Corporation Ltd* [2011] UKSC 52. In *obiter dicta* the Supreme Court considered whether a purported grant of a lease which was void for uncertainty could instead be regarded as creating a contractual licence. It was suggested that such a notion might be inconsistent with the reasoning in *Bruton*. Lord Neuberger briefly explained (at para. 65) that there was no inconsistency, and, summarising the *Bruton* decision, stated that the tenancy which had been created between Bruton and the trust:

> ... would thus have been binding as such not only on Mr Bruton and the trust, but also on any assignee of Mr Bruton or the trust.

Tantalisingly, nothing more was said on this point—and as it stands, it simply adds to the uncertainty arising from *Bruton*.

These questions, and a number of others, were posed in various case notes and articles in the legal journals, and there are references to some of them in the section on further reading at the end of this chapter. Although writers speculated on the nature and characteristics of what one author describes as 'a beast long thought extinct' (Dixon [2000] CLJ 25 at p. 27), it had to be accepted that questions would remain unanswered until *Bruton* was interpreted in later decisions.

9.6.4 Decisions after *Bruton*

So far, the only later decision to note is that of the Court of Appeal in *Kay v Lambeth Borough Council* [2005] QB 352 (note that the appeal in this case to the House of Lords, reported at [2006] 2 AC 465, related to human rights issues and does not affect the aspect of the decision with which we are concerned here).

Following the House of Lords' decision in *Bruton*, Lambeth Borough Council terminated the housing trust's lease of the property (which had replaced the original licence) and sought to recover possession from the individual occupiers. Kay, and others, resisted the possession proceedings on a number of grounds, all of which were rejected by both the trial judge and the Court of Appeal. As far as most of the defendants' arguments are concerned, the fact that they held non-proprietary leases made no difference to the outcome, which would still have been the same if they had held proprietary leases giving them estates in the property.

Only one of the arguments put to the court is of interest in considering the effect of the non-proprietary lease. It arises from the replacement of the trust's original licence by a lease. You saw in that in general a sublease ends with the ending of the head lease, but that exceptionally, where the head lease is surrendered, the head landlord is bound by any subleases (9.5.3). In *Kay*, the occupiers argued that this rule about surrender of a lease applied equally to the trust's surrender of its original licence (in exchange for the grant of the lease): at that point, the Council became bound by the occupiers' non-proprietary leases, remained subject to them thereafter, and so was not entitled now to recover possession of the property.

The Court of Appeal rejected this argument, apparently on the ground that the rule about surrender was limited to the surrender of a head lease, and should not be extended to the surrender of a licence. However, it appears to have accepted the Council's argument that the occupiers could not take advantage of the surrender rule if they had no estate in the land (see generally paras. 74–86).

This case does not add a great deal to our understanding of the non-proprietary lease, and most of the questions still remain unanswered.

For an article which discusses the Court of Appeal decision in *Kay*, notes further questions raised by *Bruton*, and contains useful references for further reading, see Lower [2010] 74 Conv 38.

9.7 Summary

This chapter has introduced you to a wide range of new concepts and technical terms that are special to leases. These concepts are crucial both to understanding this chapter, and to understanding later chapters on other aspects of the landlord and tenant relationship. You may wish to review Table 9.1 to clarify the meaning of technical terms that recur throughout the chapter, or in order to revise the topic of leases generally.

Table 9.1 Terminology

Word or phrase	Definition	For more information
Types of lease		
Bruton tenancy	A tenancy that is not a legal estate in land, having been granted by a person who lacks an estate in land	9.6.2–9.6.3
Concurrent lease	A lease the term of which overlaps with another lease in respect of the same land	9.2.5
Equitable lease	A lease created by a specifically enforceable contract to grant a lease, which has not yet been performed by a formal grant of a legal lease (by deed and/or registration)	9.3.2
Freehold reversion	A freeholder's right to recover possession of land upon termination of a lease of that land	9.1.5
Head lease	The lease held by a tenant who has granted a shorter lease to a subtenant	9.1.4
Leasehold reversion	A leaseholder's right to recover possession of land upon termination of a sublease of that land	9.1.5
Periodic tenancy	A tenancy that automatically runs from one period to another (week to week, month to month, year to year, etc.) until terminated by one of the parties giving notice	9.1.2.1, 9.2.4.1, 9.3.1.1, 9.3.3.1, 9.5.4
Reversionary lease	A lease that does not start immediately but at some time in the future	9.1.2.3

Short lease	A lease that of three years or less that complies with the requirements of LPA 1925, s. 54(2) and so can be created by parol	9.3.1.1
Sublease	The lease held by a tenant who has been granted a lease by a leaseholder with a longer term	9.1.4, 9.5.3
Tenancy at will	A right to possession of land with the permission of the landlord, on terms that the tenancy may be terminated by either party at any time	9.1.2.1.3
Tenancy by sufferance	A right to be in possession of land arising at the end of a lease, when the tenant remains in possession without the consent of the landlord and without objection by the landlord	9.3.3.2
Tenancy by estoppel	A tenancy granted by a landlord with a defective title, who is estopped from denying the validity of the grant	9.3.4
Term of years absolute	A right to possession of land for a certain term; a legal lease	9.1.2
Underlease	The lease held by a tenant who has been granted a lease by a subtenant with a longer term	9.1.4

Requirements of a lease

Certainty of term	The requirement that a lease be for a defined term rather than an indefinite one	9.1.2.1, 9.2.3
Exclusive occupation	A right to occupy land without sharing that occupation with others	9.2.3.4
Exclusive possession	A tenant's right to exclude all others from the land, including the landlord	9.2.3
Fine	A lump sum paid by a tenant to a landlord at the start of the lease; a premium	9.1.2.1
Four unities	The requirements needed to prove that land in shared occupation is occupied by the tenants as joint owners of a lease, rather than as separate licensees	9.2.3.2
Ground rent	Periodic payments to a landlord by a tenant of a long lease	9.2.6
Lease for life	A right to possession of land for life, granted in consideration for the payment of rent or a premium; by LPA 1925, s. 149(6) takes effect as a lease of 90 years, determinable earlier if the tenant dies.	9.1.2.1, 9.2.4.2
Premium	A lump sum paid by a tenant to a landlord at the start of the lease; a fine	9.2.6
Rent	Periodic payments to a landlord by a tenant throughout the term of the lease	9.2.6
Sham or pretence	Terms in a written lease that the parties have no real intention of enforcing, inserted for the purpose of avoiding the appearance of granting exclusive possession to the tenant	9.2.3.1

Creation and transfer of leases

Assignment	The transfer of an existing lease by the tenant	9.4
Estoppel by grant	Tenancy by estoppel that arises when the purported grantor of the lease has no estate at all in the leased land	9.3.4.1

Estoppel by representation	Tenancy by estoppel that arises when the purported grantor of the lease represents to the tenant that he has a more extensive estate than he in fact has	9.3.4.1
Feeding the estoppel	When a tenancy by estoppel is turned into a legal lease, as a result of the landlord acquiring a full legal title to the land	9.3.4.3
Implied tenancy	Short lease or periodic tenancy arising without formality or express words, by implication from the conduct of the parties	9.3.3
parol lease	Lease arising orally or from informal writing	9.3.1.1
Walsh v Lonsdale doctrine	The rule that a specifically enforceable contract to grant a legal lease will give rise to an equitable lease	9.3.2.3
Termination of leases		
Break clause	A clause in a fixed-term leases that allows one party, or both, to determine the lease on notice before the term expires	9.1.2.2, 9.5.2.1
Disclaimer	Termination of a lease by the exercise of a statutory power to reject the lease, by persons such as a trustee in bankruptcy or liquidator	9.5.2.6
Enlargement	Termination of a lease by the tenant's decision to enlarge his long leasehold estate into the freehold estate, in compliance with LPA 1925, s. 153	9.5.2.5
Forfeiture	Termination of a lease by the exercise of the landlord's power to terminate the lease upon a breach of a covenant by the tenant	9.5.2.7, 9.6.1.2
Merger	Termination of a lease by the tenant's acquisition of his landlord's estate with the intention of terminating the lease	9.5.2.4
Notice to quit	The giving of notice by a landlord or a tenant with the intention of terminating a lease that can be terminated by such notice (e.g., a periodic tenancy, a fixed-term lease with a break clause)	9.1.2.1, 9.5.2.2, 9.5.4
Surrender	Termination of a lease by the tenant's decision, with the landlord's agreement, to relinquish the lease to the landlord	9.5.2.3
Upwards notice	The giving of notice to terminate a lease by a tenant to a landlord	9.5.3.2

FURTHER READING

Certainty of term

Bridge, 'Periodic Tenancies and the Problem of Certainty of Term' [2010] 74 Conv 492 at 496–7.

Bright, 'Uncertainty in Leases—Is It a Vice?' (1993) 13 LS 38.

Megarry and Wade, *The Law of Real Property*, 8th edn., Sweet and Maxwell, 2012, paras. 17-068–17-074 (*Mexfield Housing Co-operative Ltd v Berrisford*).

Smith, 'What Is Wrong with Certainty in Leases?' [1993] Conv 461.
Smith, 'An Uncertain Shift' [1998] Conv 326.

Javad v Aqil
Bridge, 'Tenancies at Will in the Court of Appeal' [1991] CLJ 232.

Repudiation
Bright, 'Repudiating a Lease—Contract Rules' [1993] Conv 71.
Harpum, 'Leases as Contracts' [1993] CLJ 212.
Pawlowski and Brown, 'Repudiatory Breach in the Leasehold Context' [1999] 63 Conv 150.

You can visit the online resources to test your knowledge of this chapter with self-test questions at www.oup.com/he/nair19e/.

10

Obligations of landlord and tenant

10.1 Introduction **238**
10.2 Landlord obligations **242**
10.3 Tenant's obligations **250**
10.4 Shared responsibilities **256**
10.5 Summary **257**

10.1 Introduction

Every lease, even the most informal, imposes some obligations on the landlord and tenant under the lease. Defining these obligations is, in part, a matter of contract law. Where parties have entered into a contractual relationship like a lease, the law will identify and enforce their intentions—the express and implied terms of their contract—in accordance with the normal principles of contractual interpretation. In *Liverpool CC v Irwin* [1977] AC 239, for example, the House of Lords drew on contract law principles to hold that a landlord was under an obligation to take reasonable care that lifts and stairs used by tenants remained in a state of reasonable repair and usability; such a term had to be implied into the lease, since the contract would be 'inefficacious, futile and absurd' (per Lord Salmon at p.262) without it. The principles of contractual interpretation, therefore, apply to leases as they do to all contracts, and a detailed discussion of these principles may be found in textbooks on contract law.

However, above and beyond these general rules, there are some special rules that apply to leases, which we examine in this chapter. First, certain terms are standard in leases and use terms of art that are peculiar to the leasehold context. In this chapter, we will look at the rules of construction that define the exact content of the obligations imposed by these standard terms.

Secondly, there are also some terms that will be implied by law into a lease, simply because it is a lease. Not every lease spells out the exact obligations intended by the parties. While a formally granted long lease might be detailed and complex, spelling out the obligations of landlord and tenant in a long document, a weekly periodic tenancy may not even be embodied in writing and the express terms actually agreed by the parties in such a case may be minimal. Certain fundamental obligations of landlord and tenant will be implied in to any such lease by operation of law.

Finally, statute has intervened to regulate certain key obligations of landlord and tenant, whether these are expressly covenanted for or require implication by law. There is often an inequality of bargaining power between a landlord and a tenant, to the disadvantage of the tenant, and Parliament has therefore intervened in their relationship to place certain burdens on landlords and to limit landlords' exercise of their rights under leases. Some of this regulation concerns the landlord's remedies for a breach of covenant, and will be examined in Chapter 11, but Parliament has also occasionally shaped the content of landlord and tenant obligations and these rules are considered in this chapter.

10.1.1 5 Trant Way: basement flat

You will recall from the last chapter (9.1.1) that the basement flat at 5 Trant Way has been let by Fingall Forest, the fee simple owner, to his friend Gerald Gruyère at a rent of £175 per week. This agreement was made orally and no further terms were specified. Mr Gruyère has been in possession of the flat for some time and pays his rent regularly. If a pipe begins to leak and Mr Gruyère wants Mr Forest to repair it, or the council tax goes unpaid and each party alleges that the other ought to pay it, the dispute between the parties cannot be solved by reference to the express terms of their agreement. It will have to be solved by reference to obligations that the law implies into their lease, because it is a lease.

10.1.2 5 Trant Way: maisonette

The ground and first-floor maisonette of 5 Trant Way is to be let by Fingall Forest to James Harding. The lease term is to be 99 years and Mr Harding is to pay a premium of £450,000 and a ground rent of £100 per annum, for the first 10 years, with a provision for regular increases thereafter. The draft lease, which has been prepared by Mr Forest's solicitor for approval by Mr Harding's legal adviser, is a very detailed document, over 40 pages long.

In this lease, which will be made by deed and must be completed by registration (see 9.3.1.3), the tenant may undertake a long list of obligations, such as a promise not to keep pets, not to assign, sublet, or part with possession without the landlord's consent, and to contribute to the cost of maintaining the structure of the premises. The landlord may also make a number of promises, including a promise to keep the building insured (though, in such a case, the tenant will pay a major share of the insurance premium). If a dispute arises—say, if Mr Harding wants to assign his lease and Mr Forest refuses his consent to the assignment on the grounds that he dislikes the new prospective tenant—the starting point for addressing the dispute will be found in the express terms of the agreement. However, the effect of these express terms will depend on rules of construction that are special to leases and on limits imposed on their content by Parliament.

10.1.3 6 Trant Way

The fee simple title to 6 Trant Way was owned by Irene Ivy. On 25 March 1989, Mrs Ivy granted a 40-year lease of the property to John Jarlsberg. The lease was made by deed and is in the form shown at Form 10.1 As you can see, this document uses a number of terms of art that are peculiar to the leasehold context. Its effect will depend, like the agreement between Fingall Forest and Mr Harding, on the application of special rules of construction peculiar to leases as well as statute.

> THIS LEASE made the 25th day of March 1989 between IRENE IVY of 15 Proudie Street, Grantchester in Stilton (hereinafter called 'the landlord') of the one part and JOHN JARLSBERG of 63 Upper Terrace, Mousehole in Stilton (hereinafter called 'the tenant') of the other part WITNESSETH as follows:
> 1. The landlord hereby demises unto the tenant ALL THAT messuage or dwelling-house, together with the garden, offices and outbuilding thereto belonging, known as 6 Trant Way, Mousehole in the County of Stilton, which premises for the purposes of identification only are outlined in red on the plan attached hereto, TO HOLD the same unto the tenant from the 25th day of March 1989 for the term of 40 years YIELDING AND PAYING therefore the

yearly rent agreed or determined in accordance with the provisions of clause 2 hereof by equal quarterly instalments in advance on the usual quarter-days (the first payment to be made on the date hereof).

2. (a) The rent shall be £3,000 per annum for the first five years of the said term.
   (b) [Rent review clause for later portion of term.]
3. The tenant hereby COVENANTS with the landlord as follows:
   (a) To pay the rent hereby reserved on the days and in the manner aforesaid without any deductions whatsoever.
   (b) To pay all rates, taxes and outgoings of an annual or recurring nature in respect of the demised premises.
   (c) Not to use or permit the use of the demised premises or any part thereof otherwise than as a private dwelling-house.
   (d) Not without the prior written consent of the landlord to assign, sublet or part with possession of the whole or part of the demised premises.

[Further covenants by the tenant.]

4. The landlord hereby COVENANTS with the tenant as follows:
   (a) That the tenant paying the rent hereby reserved and observing and performing the covenants on his part herein contained shall peaceably and quietly hold and enjoy the premises hereby demised during the said term without any interruption or disturbance by the landlord or any person claiming under or in trust for the landlord.
   (b) That if at any time during the continuance of the term hereby created the tenant shall desire to purchase the fee simple reversion in the demised premises the landlord on receipt of six months' notice in writing from the tenant shall assure the demised premises unto the tenant in fee simple in consideration of a sum equal to 95 per cent of the market value of the premises, such value to be assessed as at the date upon which such notice shall expire.

[Further covenants by the landlord, including one 'to keep in repair the structure and exterior of the premises'.]

5. PROVIDED ALWAYS and it is hereby expressly agreed and declared as follows:
   (a) That if at any time the rent hereby reserved or any part thereof is 21 days in arrears (whether formally demanded or not) or if the tenant has failed to observe or perform any of the tenant's covenants herein contained, the landlord may re-enter upon the demised premises or any part thereof in the name of the whole and thereupon the term hereby granted shall absolutely determine but without prejudice to any claim by the landlord against the tenant for any antecedent breach of the covenants herein contained.

IN WITNESS where of the hand and seal of the landlord and of the tenant have been hereunto set the day and year first above-written.

SIGNED SEALED AND DELIVERED
by the said landlord   [Signature of Irene Ivy] SEAL
in the presence of:

[Signed by witness]

SIGNED SEALED AND DELIVERED

by the said tenant   [Signature of John Jarlsberg] SEAL
in the presence of:

[Signed by witness]

[There follows a plan of the property.]

Form 10.1 Example lease

10.1.4 Covenants and conditions

Obligations in a lease may be imposed in one of two ways: by covenants or by conditions. The distinction matters because the consequences of a breach of condition differ from the consequences of a breach of covenant.

A *'covenant'* is a promise made by one party (the **'covenantor'**) for the benefit of another party (the **'covenantee'**) that is contained in a deed. Leasehold covenants—promises made by landlord and tenant to each other in a deed—traditionally attract special rules as to their interpretation and their enforceability against persons other than the original landlord and tenant (Chapter 11). For long leases, which must be made by deed to take effect at law (LPA 1925, s. 52) all promises made in the document creating the lease will count as covenants for the purposes of these rules. Short leases, however, can be created informally (s. 54(2))—without a deed—and so the promises made by landlord and tenant under these leases will not technically count as covenants but only as contracts. However, it has been held that the same rules that apply to leasehold covenants will also apply to the contractual promises in short leases (see *Boyer v Warbey* [1953] 1 QB 234 and *Weg Motors Ltd v Hales* [1962] Ch 49).

Covenants must be distinguished from *'conditions'*. A lease may contain a provision that the continuance of the term is conditional upon the fulfilment by the tenant of his or her obligations (see, for example, Form 10.1, cl 5). If the tenant breaks that condition, the landlord will have an automatic right to bring the lease to an end and evict the tenant (see Chapter 12 on the process by which this may be done). By contrast, a landlord does not automatically have a right to end the lease for breach of a covenant, and must make express provision for this in the lease.

Covenant or condition? The question of whether a particular term in a lease is a covenant or a condition depends on the intention of the parties. Generally, the courts presume that the terms of the lease are covenants, unless clear words are used to show that the obligation is intended to be a condition. Most obligations, even the most fundamental (e.g., to pay rent), will be covenants rather than conditions, unless the parties expressly spell out their intentions to the contrary. In *Doe d Henniker v Watt* (1828) 8 B & C 308, for example, a term in which the tenant 'stipulated and conditioned' that he would not assign or sublet the property was a condition rather than a covenant.

10.1.5 Express and implied covenants

As we have seen, some leases—typically long leases, like Mr Harding's lease of the maisonette at 5 Trant Way—will contain a very large number of detailed *express covenants*. Others—like Mr Gruyère's orally created weekly tenancy of the basement flat at 5 Trant Way—will not. However, Mr Gruyère's lease will include certain fundamental covenants, even though these are not spelt out in the agreement; the law includes these *implied covenants* in every lease.

Implied covenants can usually be excluded or limited by express terms of the lease. So, for example, where a lease expressly includes a covenant for quiet enjoyment (10.2.1) that is qualified or limited in some way, the law will not also imply a broader obligation for quiet enjoyment into the same lease (*Miller v Emcer Products Ltd* [1956] Ch 304). Statutory covenants for repair (10.2.4) are an exception to this rule.

Where there are ambiguities in the language of an express covenant, the courts will usually construe it in favour of the tenant rather than the landlord. This is because of a principle that a grant of rights is to be interpreted against the grantor, who has control of its terms, and in favour of the grantee who does not have such control. Where there is real doubt as to what was intended by an express covenant (*Spring House (Freehold)*

Ltd v Mount Cook Land Ltd [2001] EWCA Civ 1833), therefore, the court will adopt the interpretation that most favours the tenant.

10.1.6 Usual covenants

Certain leasehold covenants are conventionally described as the **usual covenants**. It is an implied term of every contract to grant a lease that the lease, when granted, will contain at least the 'usual covenants'. Where the creation of a lease is preceded by a contract, as is the usual conveyancing practice in the case of long leases, the parties can thus be obliged to expressly include the 'usual covenants' when the lease is finally granted.

The class of usual covenants is not entirely fixed and will vary depending on the location of the land or because of the nature of a trade run from the premises. In *Flexman v Corbett* [1930] 1 Ch 672, it was suggested that a covenant must be regarded as 'usual' if nine out of ten leases of the same kind would include the term. It was also pointed out that 'what is normal in Mayfair or Bayswater is not usual . . . in Whitechapel' (per Maugham J at p. 678). The following covenants are, however, always regarded as 'usual':

- the tenant will pay rent (10.3.1);
- the tenant will pay rates and taxes (other than those which statute provides must be borne by the landlord) (10.3.5);
- the tenant will keep the premises in repair (10.3.3);
- if the landlord has expressly covenanted to repair, that the landlord will be allowed reasonable access to view and repair the premises (10.3.4);
- the landlord will allow the tenant quiet enjoyment and will not derogate from his or her grant (10.2.1 and 10.2.2); and
- the landlord will have a right to re-enter should the tenant fail to pay his or her rent (but not in the case of the breach of other covenants). For rights of re-entry, see Chapter 12.

Chester v Buckingham Travel Ltd [1981] 1 WLR 96 provides an example of the court accepting a wider range of covenants as being 'usual' in a modern commercial lease, including both restrictions on the use or alteration of the buildings, and a right of re-entry for the landlord for breach of any covenant in the lease.

10.2 Landlord obligations

Covenants by the landlord for quiet enjoyment (10.2.1) and non-derogation from grant (10.2.2) are implied into every lease that does not expressly provide for them. Subject to the obligations imposed by these covenants, there is at common law no implied covenant that the premises will be fit for any particular purpose. This is the case even where the premises are domestic in character and yet prove to be unfit for human habitation. In *Lane v Cox* [1897] 1 QB 415, for example, a tenant's visitor had suffered injury because of a defect in the staircase of the house and sued the landlord. The Court of Appeal held that the landlord was under no duty, either to the tenant or to the visitor, to ensure that the premises were safe. Lopes LJ said (at p. 417):

> A landlord who lets a house in a dangerous or unsafe state incurs no liability to his tenant, or to the customers or guests of the tenant, for any accident which may happen to them during the term, unless he has contracted to keep the house in repair.

This general rule represents an application of the principle of **caveat emptor** ('let the buyer beware'); it is for the prospective tenant to examine the property and decide whether it is fit for the intended purpose. However, the general rule is modified by statute in relation to short leases, where there is now a requirement of fitness for human habitation (10.2.3) and a duty to perform certain repairs (10.2.4). A tenant who wishes to impose more extensive responsibilities on his or her landlord would be well advised to insist on express covenants spelling out the landlord's responsibility.

It is also common for leases to expressly include covenants by the landlord to renew the lease, and grant a further term, if the tenant wishes. These covenants can give rise to problems if they are badly drafted and there is some case law about their interpretation (10.2.5).

10.2.1 Quiet enjoyment

The effect of this covenant is that the landlord must let the tenant into possession of the premises and that the landlord will be liable if the tenant's enjoyment of the property is substantially disturbed by any action of the landlord or by the action of someone deriving an interest in the property from the landlord. As the holder of a legal estate in land, the tenant will in any case be entitled to sue the landlord—or anyone else—if they interfere with the possession or use of the land to such an extent that their conduct amounts to the tort of nuisance or of trespass. The covenant for quiet enjoyment can make the landlord liable for actions that disturb the tenant's use of the land even if these fall short of an actionable tort (*Southwark LBC v Tanner* [2001] 1 AC 1).

It should be noted that the covenant for 'quiet enjoyment' is not about noise made by the landlord. It is a wider concept involving any acts that prevent the tenant from using the demised premises. The creation of considerable amounts of noise might, of course, have this effect (as was accepted by the House of Lords in *Tanner*), but the word 'quiet' in this context means 'uninterrupted', rather than 'noiseless', enjoyment of the property, and most of the cases involve something other than noise.

There are some dicta suggesting that the covenant for quiet enjoyment can only be breached by *physical* interference with the premises (e.g. *Browne v Flowers* [1911] 1 Ch 219, per Parker J at p.228) and most common examples of breach do involve such physical interference by the landlord. However, in *Southwark LBC v Tanner* [2001] 1 AC 1, the House of Lords expressed the *obiter* view that the covenant could in principle be breached by factors such as the emission of excessive noise from neighbouring land retained by the landlord.

10.2.1.1 Examples of breach

An obvious example of the breach of this covenant is the case of *Perera v Vandiyar* [1953] 1 WLR 672, where the landlord tried to force the tenant out of the premises by continual harassment of a serious nature, including having the gas and electricity supplies cut off. Apart from involving a breach of the landlord's obligations, behaviour of this kind can also amount to a criminal offence under s. 1(3) or 1(3A) of the Protection from Eviction Act 1977 if the landlord's intention is to force the tenant to leave the premises (see 12.2.1).

It has also been held to be a breach of the covenant to erect scaffolding which prevents the tenant gaining access to the premises (*Owen v Gadd* [1956] 2 QB 99), to remove windows and doors (*Lavender v Betts* [1942] 2 All ER 72), and to cause the land to subside by carrying out mining activities beneath the surface (*Markham v Paget* [1908] 1 Ch 697).

10.2.1.2 No breach arising from condition of premises at the time of grant

The covenant for quiet enjoyment is prospective in effect: it entitles the tenant to object to actions of the landlord that take place after the tenancy has begun. It cannot, therefore, help a tenant in a case where his or her enjoyment of the premises is disturbed by factors resulting from the condition of the property from the beginning of the lease.

In *Southwark LBC v Tanner* [2001] 1 AC 1 the tenants of a block of flats complained that the noise from each other's flats was seriously affecting their quality of life—in the words of Lord Millett at p.18, it rendered life in the flats 'intolerable'. It was accepted that the neighbouring tenants were not themselves responsible for the disturbance, since they were using their flats in a normal manner; rather, the disturbance was attributable to the lack of soundproofing between the flats, which were old and not constructed to modern standards. The tenants claimed that, by failing to soundproof the flats, their landlord was in breach of its covenant for quiet enjoyment.

The House of Lords accepted that excessive noise may, in principle, constitute a substantial interference with the tenant's enjoyment of the premises, and could amount to a breach of the covenant for quiet enjoyment. However, this would only be the case if the cause of the noise were some act of the landlord, or of those claiming under the landlord, that took place after the tenancy had begun. Here, the cause of the problem was not the conduct of the tenants but the lack of soundproofing, which had existed before the premises were let and before the landlord had given its covenant for quiet enjoyment.

In *Southwark LBC v Tanner* [2001] 1 AC 1, the House also drew attention to the fact that at common law (subject to statutory intervention—see 10.2.3) there is no implied warranty by the landlord as to the condition or fitness of the premises; it is understood that the risk is on the tenant, who takes the property as it is ('caveat lessee'—'let the lessee beware'). In Lord Hoffmann's words (at p. 12):

> It would be entirely inconsistent with this common understanding if the covenant for quiet enjoyment were interpreted to create liability for disturbance or inconvenience or any other damage attributable to the condition of the premises.

Whether such a liability should be created, with its resulting financial burdens on private and public landlords, was a question for Parliament not for the judges.

10.2.1.3 Acts of persons claiming under landlord

A landlord may sometimes be liable under this covenant even where a third party commits the act amounting to a breach. However, this is only liability for the lawful actions of those deriving their title under the landlord, or for the actions of his or her agents acting within the scope of their authority. The landlord is not liable for actions committed by persons who are acting in excess of their own legal rights or authority.

In *Sanderson v Berwick-upon-Tweed Corporation* (1884) 13 QBD 547, for example, a tenant complained that he was unable to make normal use of the demised premises (a farm) because of flooding from drains on two neighbouring farms, which were also owned by the landlord. Both neighbouring farms were also let to tenants. On one farm, the drains were in good order but the flooding was caused by excessive use of them by the tenant: here, the tenant was acting in excess of his lawful rights, and the landlord was not liable for the damage caused by his actions. On the second farm, the tenant was using the drains perfectly properly, but flooding was being caused by a defect in the drain: here, the tenant was acting within his lawful rights and the landlord was liable for the damage caused. You should also note that the landlord may be liable where a neighbouring tenant has done something that would normally be a breach of the covenants in her own lease, but the landlord has licensed the action (compare *Duval v 11–13 Randolph Crescent Ltd* [2020] UKSC 18).

10.2.1.4 Acts of persons with superior title to the landlord

The landlord is not responsible for acts committed by a person with a title that is superior to—rather than derived from—the landlord's title. Thus, suppose Mr Harding sublets his maisonette to Mrs Smith for 25 years and she grants an underlease to Mr Underhill (see 9.1.4). Mr Underhill may complain of actions by Mrs Smith herself that interfere with his quiet enjoyment of the land, but he cannot make her liable if the person with a superior title, Mr Harding, does something that interferes with his enjoyment.

This rule creates a substantial danger for the tenant, as is demonstrated by the case of *Jones v Lavington* [1903] 1 KB 253. In that case, a tenant, who had only 8½ years left to run on his own lease, purported to grant a sublease of the property for 10½ years. As you have already seen (9.5.3.2), such a purported grant in fact operates as an assignment of the lease. In due course, the freehold owner recovered the property from the 'subtenant' two years before the 'sublease' should have ended. The 'subtenant' could not resist the claim of the freehold owner because the original tenant had no power to give more than he had got (*nemo dat quod non habet*) and could only give an 8½-year term. An action by the 'subtenant' against the tenant also failed because the tenant was not liable for actions by someone with a superior title (the freehold owner). However, the Court of Appeal has taken the view that a subtenant can have a claim for breach of this covenant if the landlord determines the head lease by giving notice to quit to the head landlord, thus acting in such a way as to destroy the lease (*Pennell v Payne* [1995] QB 192 and see 9.5.3.2).

10.2.2 Non-derogation from grant

It is a general principle of law that you must not take away with one hand what you have given with the other; to do so is to derogate from your grant (*Palmer v Fletcher* (1663) 1 Lev 122). Under this covenant, therefore, a landlord must not act in a way that makes it impossible for the tenant to use the land for its intended purpose. To a certain extent, this covenant overlaps with the covenant for quiet enjoyment, since acts that breach that covenant will also involve the landlord derogating from his or her grant. However, since the covenant not to derogate from the grant can certainly be breached without any interference with the physical premises, it is still worth considering it separately.

10.2.2.1 Examples of breach

A good illustration of the point is provided by *Aldin v Latimer Clark, Muirhead & Co.* [1894] 2 Ch 437. In that case, premises had been let to a tenant subject to a covenant that the tenant would use the property to run the business of a timber merchant. The demised premises included a shed used for the purposes of drying wood; its use for this purpose depended on a natural flow of air from neighbouring land, which also belonged to the landlord. Buildings were erected on the neighbouring land which prevented the free flow of air to the drying shed and thereby rendered it useless. This did not amount to a breach of the covenant for quiet enjoyment because there was no interference with the physical use of demised premises. These facts did, however, amount to a breach of the landlord's obligation not to derogate from his grant, because the action complained of prevented the very use for which the demised premises had been let.

Another example is provided by *Harmer v Jumbil (Nigeria) Tin Areas Ltd* [1921] 1 Ch 200, in which land was let to store explosives. In order to store such items, the tenant had to obtain a licence; it was a condition of the licence that there should be no other buildings within a specified distance. Accordingly, the tenant was entitled to prevent the landlord from building on neighbouring land, which he also owned, because this would lead to the loss of the tenant's licence and prevent him from using the premises for the purpose for which they were let.

10.2.2.2 No breach

A landlord will only be in breach of this covenant where his or her actions are inconsistent with the use of the land actually contemplated by both parties at the time of the grant. The tenant who relies on this principle must, therefore, have made it clear to the landlord at the time of the grant what use he or she has in mind for the land (*Robinson v Kilvert* (1889) 41 ChD 88). If the tenant is complaining of the landlord's use of neighbouring land, there will be no claim if he or she knew at the time of the grant that the landlord was going to use that land in that way (*Lyttelton Times Company Ltd v Warners Ltd* [1907] AC 476).

In addition, the act complained of must actually interfere with the contemplated use; it is not sufficient to say that the landlord's actions have made the use more expensive or less profitable. Thus, permitting a competing business to be run from a neighbouring property has been held not to be derogation from grant (*Port v Griffith* [1938] 1 All ER 295—a decision considered and applied in *Romulus Trading Co. Ltd v Comet Properties Ltd* [1996] 2 EGLR 70).

Finally, it has been held that the obligation imposed by the covenant is essentially restrictive or negative in character. The tenant can invoke the covenant to stop the landlord from doing something that interferes with the intended use of the land, but it cannot be used to make the landlord take positive steps to promote that use (*William Old International Ltd v Arya* [2009] EWHC 599 (Ch)).

10.2.2.3 Acts of persons claiming under landlord

As in the case of the covenant for quiet enjoyment, a landlord may be liable for the actions of other people, provided they have derived their title from that landlord (*Aldin v Latimer Clark, Muirhead & Co.* [1894] 2 Ch 437). *Chartered Trust plc v Davies* (1997) 76 P&CR 396 is a good example. The landlord had leased several units in a shopping mall to different tenants. One tenant complained that his trade was affected by the activities of neighbouring shopkeepers—such as blocking access to the shop—that were held at first instance to constitute nuisance. The common landlord had the power to stop the activities complained of, but did not do so. He was held by the Court of Appeal to have continued or adopted the nuisance committed by his other tenants, and thus to have derogated from his grant.

10.2.3 Covenant that premises be fit for purpose

As has been explained, apart from the obligations imposed by the covenant for quiet enjoyment and non-derogation of grant, there is in general no implied covenant that the premises will be fit for any particular purpose. However, the general rule is modified in the case of furnished houses at common law. In addition, statute has implied a landlord covenant that premises are fit for human habitation into certain leases. For leases granted before 20 March 2019, these are only leases at a very low rent. However, most short leases that are granted in England after 20 March 2019 are now subject to this implied covenant under the Homes (Fitness for Human Habitation) Act 2018.

10.2.3.1 Furnished houses

It is clear from a number of authorities that if a house is let furnished then it must be fit for human habitation at the start of the term (*Smith v Marrable* (1843) 11 M & W 5). It should be noted that this implied condition relates only to the state of the premises at the commencement of the term, and the landlord is not liable under this head if the premises become unfit during the lease term (*Harrison v Malet* (1886) 3 TLR 58; *Sarson v Roberts* [1895] 2 QB 395).

10.2.3.2 Low-rent housing

A covenant by the landlord that the premises are fit for human habitation was implied into certain leases at a low rent by the Landlord and Tenant Act 1985, s. 8. The levels of rent prescribed are, however, so low that today very few premises come within this section of the Act. By the Homes (Fitness for Human Habitation) Act 2018, s. 1, this legislation now applies only to Wales, where the law governing residential leases has in any case been completely overhauled by the Renting Homes (Wales) Act 2016. In England, it has been superseded for the future by the Homes (Fitness for Human Habitation) Act 2018.

10.2.3.3 Leases subject to the Homes (Fitness for Human Habitation) Act 2018

This legislation amends the Landlord and Tenant Act 1985, introducing new ss. 9A–9C that apply to residential short leases granted after the commencement date of the 2018 Act on 20 March 2019. Like the provisions which create the landlord's statutory covenant to repair (see 10.2.4), the new covenant to keep the premises fit for human habitation is implied only into leases for a term of less than seven years and excludes certain agricultural, business, and Crown tenancies, as defined in s. 14 of the 1985 Act. Like the statutory covenant to repair, the new covenant to keep the premises fit for human habitation cannot be excluded or limited by the express terms of a lease.

The covenant requires the landlord to ensure that the dwelling 'is fit for human habitation at the time the lease is granted' *and* that it 'will remain fit for human habitation during the term of the lease' (Landlord and Tenant Act 1985, s. 9A(1)). However, it does not include any obligation to carry out works and repairs for which the tenant is responsible under the covenant to use the land in a tenant-like manner (Landlord and Tenant Act 1985, s. 9A(2)), or any obligation to repair the premises where the reason why the premises are unfit for human habitation is because of a breach of covenant by the tenant (Landlord and Tenant Act 1985, s. 9A(2)).

Unfitness for human habitation is defined by s. 10 of the Landlord and Tenant Act 1985. This provides that, in deciding if a home is unfit for human habitation, the court shall consider various matters—such as state of repair, stability, lighting, sanitation, ventilation, freedom from damp and, after the 2018 Act, the presence of any 'hazards', which are from time to time defined by regulations under the Housing Act 2004. However, the mere presence of a defect with the lighting or ventilation, etc. will not render a home unfit for habitation: the court will need to decide if the defects are so significant that the home 'is not reasonably suitable for occupation in that condition'.

10.2.4 Landlord's covenant to repair

In general, there is no implied covenant that the landlord must maintain or repair the property (for a tenant's obligations to repair, see 10.3.3 and 10.4.1). However, statute has intervened to imply such obligations into certain leases, and to associate the landlord's duty of repair with broader duties of care to keep others safe from injury arising from defects in the premises.

10.2.4.1 Short leases

Under ss. 11–14 of the Landlord and Tenant Act 1985, certain covenants by the landlord are implied into all leases of dwellings for a term of 'less than seven years' (s. 13). The covenants implied by s. 11 are:

(a) to keep the structure and exterior in repair; and

(b) to keep in repair and working order the facilities for the supply of water, gas, electricity, sanitation, space heating, and water heating.

The effect of this provision is that, in the case of a weekly tenancy like that of Gerald Gruyère (10.1.1), the landlord will bear the responsibility to perform certain repairs, including repairs to a broken pipe or the heating system. Where the lease is for a longer term, like James Harding's 99-year term (10.1.2) or John Jarlsberg's 40-year lease (10.1.3), the landlord will owe no such obligation unless the lease includes an express covenant to this effect.

1. Excluding or limiting the statutory covenants

Unlike other implied covenants, the statutory covenants to repair cannot be simply excluded or limited by the express terms of a lease. Provisions in a lease that purport to exclude or limit the statutory covenants or to penalise the tenant for enforcing these covenants are void (s. 12(1)) unless the county court has given permission for them to be excluded or modified in a particular case. In deciding whether to permit the exclusion of the statutory covenants, the county court must consider what is reasonable in all the circumstances of the case, including the other terms of the lease (s. 12(2)).

2. Scope of the covenant to keep the 'structure and exterior' in repair

In the recent case of *Edwards v Kumaraswamy* [2016] UKSC 40, the Supreme Court examined the scope of the landlord's obligations under these statutory covenants to repair. The Court held that a duty to keep 'the exterior' of the leased premises in repair extended only to the actual physical building—'the floors, ceilings, walls and doors'—leased by the tenant. The duty did not extend to paths or steps that might be used by the tenant to access the building but that did not form part of the subject matter of the lease. In *Kumaraswamy* itself, for example, the tenant had tripped over an uneven paving stone on a path that led from the car park to the leased premises. The Court held that the statutory covenant did not place the landlord under any obligation to keep the path in good repair, since it did not form part of the 'exterior' of the leased premises. Lord Neuberger SJC said at [18]:

> . . . given that the section imposes obligations on a contracting party over and above those which have been contractually agreed, one should not be too ready to give an unnaturally wide meaning to any of its expressions.

10.2.4.2 Duty of care

Where a landlord is under a duty to repair (either by reason of express covenant or under the statutory provisions), s. 4 of the Defective Premises Act 1972 also imposes a duty of care in tort on him. This requires him to ensure that all persons who might reasonably be expected to be affected by defects in the state of the premises are reasonably safe from personal injury or property damage caused by such defect. Under the Act, the landlord will also be liable to any person who acquires an interest in a dwelling which was built by the landlord, or where the landlord has done any work in connection with its provision.

Originally there was some doubt as to whether this duty was owed to the tenant. However, the Court of Appeal held in *Sykes v Harry* [2001] QB 1014 that the tenant is included in the category of 'persons who might reasonably be expected to be affected'. The landlord in that case was, therefore, held liable for physical injury caused to his tenant by a defective gas fire. (Landlords are now required to have annual checks of gas appliances.)

In the later decision of *Alker v Collingwood Housing Association* [2007] 1 WLR 2230 the Court of Appeal emphasised that the landlord's liability under s. 4 of the Defective Premises Act 1972 arises only if the defect that has caused injury or damage can be attributed to a failure to repair or maintain the property. The claimant in this case had been seriously injured when she put her hand through a pane of glass in her front door. The glass was of a type which is today regarded as a safety hazard (although probably acceptable when the property was built), but it had not been damaged in any way before the accident and was not in need of repair.

At first instance, Mrs Alker succeeded in her claim against the landlord for compensation for breach of its statutory duty of care, but the Court of Appeal reversed this decision. The court reviewed its earlier decisions on such claims, and at para. 10 quoted the words of Gibson LJ in *McNerny v Lambeth Borough Council* [1989] 19 EG 77 at p. 83:

> . . . statutory protection for those in occupation of defective premises is geared to the landlord's obligation to repair the premises. It goes no wider than the repair covenant.

For this reason, the duty to repair or maintain could not be said to include an obligation to make the property safe by dealing with defects in it which did not arise from disrepair. To hold otherwise would be to transform the statutory obligation to protect against the effects of disrepair into a statutory warranty that the premises were reasonably safe (paras. 16 and 17). Such a warranty would impose a major liability on landlords:

> if it were to be desired to impose such a liability, it would be for Parliament to effect it.

10.2.5 Obligation to grant a further term

A lease may sometimes include an express covenant by the landlord to renew the lease for a further period, on the expiration of the first term. Such a covenant gives the tenant the benefit of an option. The tenant is free to choose whether or not to exercise the right to renew; if the tenant does so, the landlord is bound to grant the further term.

10.2.5.1 Enforcement against successors in title

Like other covenants (Chapter 11), this covenant is enforceable against the landlord's successor or assignee. However, it has been held that such an option in a lease of unregistered land is a class C(iv) land charge (*Beesly v Hallwood Estates Ltd* [1960] 1 WLR 549). As such, rather surprisingly given the landlord–tenant context, it must be registered on the Land Charges Register if it is to be enforced against a purchaser of the landlord's legal estate for money or money's worth.

10.2.5.2 Perpetually renewable leases

In *Northchurch Estates Ltd v Daniels* [1947] Ch 117, a lease for a year contained a clause which gave the tenant a right to renew the lease at the end of the year 'on identical terms and conditions'. Unfortunately this clause, if interpreted literally, meant that the second term included an identical provision allowing the tenant to call for a third term, the third term a clause providing for a fourth, and so on. As a result, the tenant was held to have a right to renew the lease perpetually. This caused considerable difficulties for the landlord, who would be able to terminate this perpetual lease only if the tenant broke a term of the agreement or forgot to give notice of his or her wish to renew.

Such **perpetually renewable leases** are subject to s. 145 and Sch. 15 of the Law of Property Act 1922 (which applies to all leases created after 1925). These provisions convert the affected lease into a fixed term of 2,000 years, subject to a right of the tenant to terminate the lease on 10 days' notice in writing on any occasion on which the original lease would have expired if it had not been renewed. The landlord has no similar right to terminate.

The effect of this interpretation is, therefore, that landlords are heavily penalised for the careless drafting of the original lease. Usually, it is quite clear that the original intention of the parties was that the tenant should have the right to renew the lease for a second term, with a further right to a third and final term at the tenant's choice. In *Northchurch Estates Ltd v Daniels* the real intention of the parties was that the tenant should have a lease for one year with a right to renew the lease twice if he so chose. The unfairness of transforming such an agreement into a 2,000-year term, when three years were intended, is obvious. Accordingly, in more recent decisions, the courts have reversed their earlier tendency to apply a literal interpretation of such clauses and have adopted a more liberal approach, in order to prevent tenants from obtaining an unjustified windfall through poor drafting (see, e.g., *Marjorie Burnett Ltd v Barclay* [1981] 1 EGLR 41).

10.3 Tenant's obligations

It is common for leases to include express covenants by the tenant regarding the payment of rent (10.3.1), and the tenant's exercise of powers to assign or sublet the premises or otherwise part with possession (10.3.2). Statute has intervened to regulate the landlord's control over the tenant's decisions to assign or sublease, and there is a good deal of case law surrounding the interpretation of such clauses and the statutory controls surrounding them.

In addition, the law implies certain tenant covenants into leases, flowing from the tenant's status as the person with day-to-day control of the land. These include obligations to avoid damaging alterations to the state of the land (10.3.3) and to pay rates and charges associated with the occupation of land (10.3.5). Where the landlord has a duty of repair (see 10.2.4), there is also an implied covenant by the tenant to allow the landlord to enter the land in order to perform these repairs (10.3.4).

10.3.1 Rent

Very few leases are concluded without there being an express agreement between the parties about the payment of rent. As we have already seen (9.2.6), it is perfectly possible to have a valid lease without an obligation to pay rent. Accordingly, a covenant to pay rent will not be implied automatically into every lease. However, the payment of rent is usual and it will normally be the intention of the parties that it should be paid. Where the grant of a lease is preceded by a contract, it is an implied term of the contract that the tenant shall pay the rent that the parties have agreed upon in the contract (10.1.6) and so the landlord can compel the tenant to insert an express covenant to do so in the final lease. Following the Leasehold Reform (Ground Rent) Act 2022, however, such covenants in certain long leases are no longer enforceable (see 9.2.6 for the details). A landlord who demands payment of a 'prohibited rent', or does not refund such a payment once made, will not only be liable to repay the tenant but may also be subject to a financial penalty (Leasehold Reform (Ground Rent) Act 2022, s. 9).

There are, of course, many situations in which a landlord continues to be entitled to impose an obligation to pay rent. This will be the case for all leases under a term of 21 years and for certain other 'exempt' leases as well (e.g., leases that are not of a single dwelling and leases where the tenancy is for a business purpose). In these cases, it is a general rule that the rent must be certain (a court cannot enforce an uncertain agreement) but this rule may be satisfied by providing a means whereby the rent is to be determined (e.g., rent to be set by a surveyor chosen by a named body). It is also common to include a clause whereby the rent is to be reviewed (usually with a view to increasing it) at intervals during the lease: see cl. 2(b) in the lease at 10.1.3. A great deal of technical case law on the interpretation of such rent-review clauses exists, but this is beyond the scope of this book. For more information about rent-review clauses, you should consult specialist works on landlord and tenant law.

10.3.2 Obligation not to alienate

As the owner of a legal estate in land, a tenant has inherent legal powers to alienate that estate, by selling it or granting lesser rights out of it (such as subleases, mortgages, easements, etc.). However, tenants may—and frequently do—bind themselves by express covenants not to exercise these powers. Most landlords take great care when selecting tenants, e.g., to ensure that they are of good character and can pay the rent. Quite reasonably, they will wish to ensure that the premises do not come into the hands of some less desirable person through assignment or subletting.

Accordingly, it is common to include in a lease a covenant that restricts the tenant's right to assign, sublet, or otherwise part with possession of the demised premises. The effect of such a covenant is to place the tenant under a personal obligation not to assign, sublet, or part with possession; it is not to abolish or invalidate the tenant's inherent legal power to enter into these transactions. If he or she assigns the lease or sublets in breach of the covenant, therefore, the transaction will still be legally effective in conferring a legal estate in land upon the assignee or subtenant (*Parker v Jones* [1910] 2 KB 32: subletting; *Old Grovebury Manor Farm v W. Seymour Plant Sales* [1979] 3 All ER 504: assignment). However, the tenant will be personally liable for her breach of covenant and the landlord's remedies for breach of covenant may have the effect of destroying the assignee or subtenant's estate in land (see 12.4).

It should be noted that covenants of this type are strictly interpreted against the landlord. Accordingly, a covenant forbidding 'assigning' does not prevent the creation of a subtenancy or a licence; similarly a covenant against 'subletting' does not prevent an assignment or the creation of a licence.

10.3.2.1 Qualified and absolute covenants against alienation

Covenants against assigning, subletting, or parting with possession come in two forms:

- an absolute covenant, i.e., not to assign, etc.;
- a qualified covenant, i.e., not to assign, etc., without the landlord's consent.

In the case of the absolute covenant, it is open to the tenant to ask the landlord to allow a particular disposition, but the landlord is under no obligation to agree to this, even if he or she is acting quite unreasonably in refusing. By contrast, if the covenant is in the qualified form that the tenant may not assign etc. *without consent*, the position is affected by s. 19(1)(a) of the Landlord and Tenant Act 1927, which implies into such a covenant the proviso that 'consent is not to be unreasonably withheld'.

10.3.2.2 Unreasonable withholding of consent

Although the Landlord and Tenant Act 1927 implies the proviso that 'consent shall not be unreasonably withheld', it gives no guidance on what would constitute reasonable grounds for refusal. We must, therefore, turn to case law to determine what this means.

The leading case is the decision of the House of Lords in *Ashworth Frazer Ltd v Gloucester CC* [2001] 1 WLR 2180. In that case, Lord Bingham identified three 'overriding principles' (see [2001] 1 WLR 2180, paras. 3–5), which should guide the courts in deciding whether a landlord's refusal of consent is unreasonable.

> (i) *A landlord is not entitled to refuse consent to an assignment on grounds which have nothing to do with the relationship of landlord and tenant in regard to the subject matter of the lease* In stating this first principle, his Lordship adopted the approach of the Court of Appeal in *Houlder Bros v Gibbs* [1925] Ch 575. It is important to realise that satisfying this test is only the first step in the process of deciding whether the landlord's refusal is reasonable. The reason for refusing may well relate to the nature of the assignee or the proposed use of the property, and may still be regarded by the court as unreasonable.
>
> (ii) *The question whether the landlord's conduct is reasonable or unreasonable is a question of fact* The House of Lords in *Ashworth Frazer* emphasised that the question whether the landlord's conduct is reasonable is always a question of fact, to be decided on the circumstances of each particular case. Previous decisions on similar reasons for refusal may be referred to for guidance, but they should not be regarded as laying down legal rules as to what is or is not reasonable.

The House of Lords was particularly concerned to emphasise this because, in the case before it, the Court of Appeal had held itself bound by an earlier decision that particular grounds for refusal were unreasonable. In *Ashworth Frazer*, the landlord had refused consent to an assignment because it considered that the assignees' proposed use of the property would be in breach of a covenant in the lease. At first instance, the landlord's refusal had been held not to be unreasonable. However, on appeal by the tenant, the Court of Appeal considered itself bound by its earlier decision in *Killick v Second Covent Garden Property Co. Ltd* [1973] 1 WLR 658, where the court had held that the landlord's belief that the assignee would use the premises in breach of a user covenant was not a reasonable ground for refusing consent to assign. If assignment took place, the landlord would still be able to enforce the covenant, and would be in no worse position than if the assignor himself had proposed to breach it. In *Ashworth Frazer*, the Court of Appeal treated the *Killick* decision as establishing a rule that consent could not reasonably be refused in such circumstances, and accordingly held that the landlord's refusal in the case before them was unreasonable.

In reversing the Court of Appeal's decision on this point, the House of Lords overruled *Killick*. In Lord Rodger's words (at para. 68):

> . . . it cannot be said as a matter of law, that the belief of a landlord, however reasonable, that the proposed assignee intends to use the demised premises for a purpose which would give rise to a breach of a user covenant, cannot, of itself, be a reasonable ground for witholding consent to the assignment.

The correct approach would be to ask what the reasonable landlord would do when asked to consent in these circumstances. While it was true, as had been said in *Killick*, that the landlord would have the same ability to enforce the covenant against the assignee as he or she would have had against the assignor, a reasonable landlord might well consider the assignment to make a significant practical difference. After the assignment, the landlord could be faced with the trouble and expense of enforcing the covenant, whereas the previous tenant might have been prepared to comply with it without legal action. The probability that the assignee might breach the covenant could be enough to justify the withholding of consent.

Whether refusal on such grounds was reasonable must, however, be decided as a question of fact in the circumstances of each case. Lord Rodger was at pains to emphasise that, in overruling *Killick*, the House of Lords were not substituting a contrary rule of law that it would always be reasonable to refuse consent on these grounds; there could be circumstances where refusal of consent for such a reason would be unreasonable. Accordingly, the case was remitted to the Chancery Division, for consideration whether, in the particular circumstances of the case, the landlord's refusal was reasonable.

(iii) **The landlord is required to show that a refusal was reasonable, not that it was right or justifiable** Not a lot is said in *Ashworth Frazer* about this third principle, but it has been considered and explained by the Court of Appeal in *NCR Ltd v Riverland Portfolio No. 1 Ltd* [2005] 22 EG 134. As Carnworth LJ put it (at para. 31):

> It is of course of the essence of a reasonable decision that there were reasons for it, which can be justified at some level, even if only by showing that they were genuine and not wholly fanciful . . . What is not required, however, is for those reasons to be justified by reference to some objective standard of correctness.

In other words, it is sufficient if the landlord's refusal was based on concerns about the proposed transaction which a reasonable person might have, even though others might take a different view (para. 33).

While bearing in mind the House of Lords' warning that previous decisions on refusal of consent must be regarded as illustrative only and not taken as laying down rules of law, it is still often helpful to consider previous decisions on specific grounds of refusal. Examples of acceptable reasons for refusal have included: the unsatisfactory nature of the assignee's references (*Shanly v Ward* (1913) 29 TLR 714); the fact that the proposed assignment would interfere with the future development of the property (*Pimms Ltd v Tallow Chandlers Co.* [1964] 2 QB 547); and the fact that assignment back to the original tenant would enable him to operate a break clause and bring the lease to an end (*Olympia & York Canary Wharf Ltd v Oil Property Investments Ltd* [1994] 2 EGLR 48).

By contrast, it has been held unreasonable to refuse consent on the ground that a proposed tenant has diplomatic immunity (*Parker v Boggon* [1947] KB 346) or because the landlord wants to recover possession for himself (*Bates v Donaldson* [1896] 2 QB 241). In *International Drilling Fluids Ltd v Louisville Investments (Uxbridge) Ltd* [1986] Ch 513, the Court of Appeal held that landlords could in some circumstances be said to be acting unreasonably in refusing consent if they did not take into account the effect that this would have on their tenants (at p. 521):

> there may be cases where there is such a disproportion between the benefit to the landlord and the detriment to the tenant if the landlord withholds his consent . . . that it is unreasonable for the landlord to refuse consent

The court considered that the case before it was of this type, and accordingly held that the landlord's refusal was unreasonable.

In *No.1 West India Quay (Residential) Ltd v East Tower Apartments Ltd* [2018] EWCA Civ 250, a residential landlord had refused consent to the assignment of two long residential leases for three reasons, one of which was considered to be unreasonable. In the High Court, it was held that the bad reason vitiated the good reasons so that the overall decision to refuse consent was unreasonable. The Court of Appeal, however, overruled this decision and held that the test was 'whether the decision would have been the same without reliance on the bad reason' (per Lewison LJ, at [41]); if so, 'the decision (looked at overall) is good' and the landlord's refusal was reasonable.

10.3.2.3 Landlord's duty to deal with request for permission

Before the Landlord and Tenant Act 1988, a landlord could cause a tenant serious inconvenience and even financial loss by delay in dealing with a request for permission to assign, or by unreasonably refusing such permission. The tenant had no redress for any damage caused in this way (see *Design Progression Ltd v Thurloe Properties Ltd* [2005] 1 WLR 1, paras. 1–3). To deal with this situation, the 1988 Act imposed several statutory duties on the landlord and provided remedies for breach of these duties.

Thus:

- The landlord must respond to the tenant's request for consent 'within a reasonable time' (s. 1(3)).

- The landlord must reply to the request in writing and, if refusing consent, must give the reasons for refusal in that reply (s. 1(3)).

- In the past, there was uncertainty as to whether a landlord who has to justify a decision in subsequent court proceedings may rely on reasons for refusal which were not given to the tenant at the time. In interpreting the provisions of the Act, it has now been held that the landlord cannot subsequently rely on reasons that were not given in the original written response (*Footwear Corp. Ltd v Amplight Properties Ltd* [1998] 3 All ER 52, approved by the Court of Appeal in *GoWest Ltd v Spigarola* [2003] QB 1140, at para. 18).

- The burden of proof is on a landlord who refuses consent, to prove that refusal was reasonable (s. 1(6)). This is a change from the pre-Act rule, under which the tenant was required to prove that the landlord's refusal was unreasonable.

- The tenant is given the right to sue the landlord for breach of these statutory duties (s. 4).

10.3.2.4 Agreement on grounds for refusal in advance of a request

While the provisions of the 1927 and 1988 Acts have the effect of improving the tenant's position, an amendment to s. 19(1) of the 1927 Act, introduced by the Landlord and Tenant (Covenants) Act 1995, s. 22, is designed to assist the landlord. It applies only to 'new tenancies' as defined by the Act (in outline, those created on or after 1 January 1996—see further at 11.1.3), and specifically excludes residential leases.

In the case of leases to which it applies, the effect of s. 22 is that the landlord and tenant may enter into an agreement specifying the circumstances in which the landlord may in the future withhold consent to any assignment, etc. and the conditions subject to which any consent may be given. If the landlord subsequently withholds consent on the ground that such circumstances exist or attaches such conditions to the granting of consent, the refusal of consent will not be considered unreasonable.

The agreement need not be contained in the lease, and can be made at any time before the tenant seeks consent.

10.3.2.5 Tenant's choices upon a refusal of permission

Where a lease contains a covenant not to assign, etc. without consent, the tenant who wishes to assign should, of course, first ask the landlord for permission. However, if the tenant asks for permission and it is refused there are three courses of action available:

- The tenant may seek a declaration from the court, under s. 19 of the 1927 Act, that the landlord's refusal is unreasonable and that he or she is therefore entitled to assign, sublet, or part with possession.
- The tenant may seek a remedy (damages or an injunction) for the landlord's breach of statutory duty under the 1988 Act (s. 4). (For an exceptional award of exemplary or punitive damages where the landlord had been 'deliberately obstructive', see *Design Progression Ltd v Thurloe Properties Ltd* [2005] 1 WLR 1.)
- The tenant may take the risk and make the disposition, which will be effective even if it is in breach of covenant. It should be remembered, however, that the proposed assignee or subtenant may well refuse to proceed unless the landlord's consent has been obtained, as to do otherwise could well cause problems in the future. If the tenant does take this course of action, the landlord may sue for breach of covenant and possibly seek to forfeit the lease (see 12.4).

10.3.3 Waste

If a lease makes no express provisions about duties of repair, a tenant comes under a duty in tort to avoid '**waste**'. Waste may be defined as an act or omission that alters the state of the land, and can even include changes which *improve* the land ('*ameliorating waste*'). The issue here, however, is the sort of behaviour that may damage the property and it is usual to divide such waste into two categories:

1. voluntary waste—which consists of doing something which should not be done, such as knocking down a wall; and
2. permissive waste—which consists of leaving undone something which ought to be done, such as failing to prevent a wall falling down.

The distinction is, therefore, between causing damage and failing to prevent damage. Liability for permissive waste thus has the effect of imposing a duty to repair on the tenant. The extent of liability for waste depends on the type of lease involved and so we will consider the various types separately.

10.3.3.1 Weekly, monthly, and quarterly tenancies

The general rule is that a weekly tenant is liable for voluntary waste but not for permissive waste: in other words, such a tenant may not knock a wall down but can let it fall down (*Mint v Good* [1951] 1 KB 517). The same rule applies to monthly and quarterly tenancies. The scope of the duty is increased beyond this point, however, by the further obligation to use the premises in a 'tenant-like manner' (per Denning LJ, *Warren v Keen* [1954] 1 QB 15 at p. 20). This means that the tenant must clean the premises, mend the electric light if it is fused, unstop blocked sinks, and generally 'do the little jobs about the place which a reasonable tenant would do'. The exact duties of the tenant under this head are not entirely clear, however, and each case must be judged on its facts.

10.3.3.2 Yearly tenancies

As in the case of other periodic tenancies, a yearly tenant is obliged to avoid voluntary waste. In addition, a yearly tenant is deemed to be obliged to keep the premises wind- and water-tight (*Wedd v Porter* [1916] 2 KB 91). This obligation is, however, rather watered down by the further rule that the tenant is not liable for 'fair wear and tear' (*Warren v Keen* [1954] 1 QB 15). This means that the tenant is not responsible for the gradual deterioration caused by normal use or by the normal action of the elements (*Haskell v Marlow* [1928] 2 KB 45), so does not have to replace stone steps which are worn down by use or tiles which are blown off the roof by the wind.

10.3.3.3 Fixed-term leases

A tenant with a fixed term of years is certainly liable for voluntary waste. In addition, as the High Court held in *Dayani v Bromley LBC* [1999] 3 EGLR 144, a tenant for years will also be liable for permissive waste. Thus, if a lease for a fixed term makes no express provision about repairs, there will be an implied term that such a tenant should maintain the premises in the condition in which they were at the start of the term. However, it is very likely that a longer lease will include some express covenants concerning duties of repair (10.4.1) and, in such cases, the landlord is more likely to sue on the covenant than to bring an action for waste.

10.3.4 Obligation to allow landlord entry

In general, as the tenant has exclusive possession, the landlord can be excluded from the premises (see, further, 9.2.3). However, where the landlord is under a duty to repair, a term allowing the landlord to enter the premises will be implied (*Saner v Bilton* (1876) 7 ChD 815). This will give the landlord a right, to be exercised reasonably, to enter and inspect and carry out necessary repairs. A similar implied term is also included where statutory provisions require a landlord to repair (10.2.4).

10.3.5 Tenant's covenant to pay rates and other taxes on the premises

The tenant is under an implied obligation to pay all the rates and taxes for which the landlord is not made expressly liable, either by the terms of the lease or under a rule of law. Because tenants are impliedly liable for the rates and similar obligations, such as council tax, they should take care to ascertain whether their rent is inclusive or exclusive of these charges before they enter into the agreement, as fairly large sums can be involved.

10.4 Shared responsibilities

As we have seen, there are certain obligations that inherently relate to the status of landlord or tenant: it is only landlords who are obliged to guarantee the tenants' quiet enjoyment of land, and it is only tenants who are likely to be obliged to pay rent. The burden of other duties regarding the use and maintenance of the land, however, may be distributed between landlord and tenant in very different ways for different leases. Duties of repair (10.4.1) that may be reasonable to place on a landlord in the case of a weekly tenancy (10.2.4) are more likely to be expressly shouldered by a tenant in the case of a 99-year lease. Duties to insure the premises (10.4.2) are similar in this respect.

10.4.1 Repair

Most leases for any period, other than the shortest, will contain detailed express covenants obliging the landlord or the tenant to effect certain repairs. These covenants vary considerably with the circumstances, but in the case of a long lease (e.g., 99 years) it is quite normal for the tenant to be obliged to undertake all necessary repairs, including structural repairs to buildings. In shorter leases, the burden may well be shared, with the tenant undertaking to decorate and to carry out internal repairs, while the landlord agrees to maintain the structure.

A covenant 'to repair' involves not only the maintenance of the existing property but will include replacement of parts which are irreparable (*Lurcott v Wakeley* [1911] 1 KB 905) and even complete rebuilding if the structure is destroyed, for example, by fire (*Bullock v Dommitt* (1796) 2 Chit 608). Obviously, it is wise to insure against such risks.

10.4.2 Insurance

In some cases the landlord will covenant to insure premises (though the tenant may have to agree to pay some, or all, of the premium), while in others the tenant will undertake this obligation. Such covenants will be breached if the property is uninsured for any period, however short, and even if no damage occurs during that time (*Penniall v Harborne* (1848) 11 QB 368).

10.5 Summary

Having examined the nature of a lease as an estate in land (Chapter 9), we have now looked at how a lease also gives rise to obligations between the landlord and the tenant. These obligations, as we have seen, are largely contractual in nature and arise—with the exception of a few cases of Parliamentary intervention—in response to the express or implied intentions of the parties to the original lease. In the next chapter (Chapter 11), we will see how these obligations, once created, can become attached to the estates in land of the landlord and the tenant. Chapter 11 examines how these leasehold covenants can bind new landlords and tenants, who acquire estates from the original parties to the lease, and how the original parties to the lease can escape their liability when they give up their estates.

FURTHER READING

Covenant not to assign

Fancourt, 'Licences to Assign: Another Turn of the Screw?' [2006] 70 Conv 37 (rather detailed, but worth reading selectively).

Covenant to repair

Burn and Cartwright, *Cheshire and Burn's Modern Law of Real Property*, 18th edn., Oxford University Press, 2011, pp. 227–37, and 246–50.

You can visit the online resources to test your knowledge of this chapter with self-test questions at **www.oup.com/he/nair19e/**.

11

Enforcement of leasehold covenants

11.1 Introduction **258**
11.2 Old leases **261**
11.3 New leases **271**
11.4 Position of a subtenant **277**

11.1 Introduction

We have now looked at some of the standard obligations that landlords and tenants may owe to each other (Chapter 10). Enforcement of these obligations between the original parties to the lease, while they remain in the landlord and tenant relationship, is a relatively straightforward application of contract law. A tenant who has promised to pay rent can be sued for a failure to keep that promise because such non-payment represents a breach of contract; similarly, a landlord who has promised to perform repairs can be sued for a failure to keep that promise as a matter of contract law.

However, the situation becomes more complicated where the tenant's lease or the landlord's reversion has been assigned (see 9.1.5), or where a sublease is carved out of the lease (see 9.1.4). When this happens, the original landlord or tenant may have given up possession of the land and a new person will have gained new rights to physical possession of that land. Three problems of enforcement can then arise, which are considered in this chapter:

1. enforcement by or against the original parties to the lease, who were parties to the original contract (*'privity of contract'*) but who are no longer in a landlord and tenant relationship with each other;
2. enforcement by or against the successors in title of the original landlord and/or tenant, who never had any contractual relationship with each other but are in a direct landlord and tenant relationship (*'privity of estate'*);
3. effect of covenants in a head lease or sublease on a head landlord and a subtenant, between whom there is neither privity of contract nor privity of estate (neither a contract, nor a direct landlord and tenant relationship).

11.1.1 Old and new leases

Following recommendations made by the Law Commission in 1988 (*Landlord and Tenant Law: Privity of Contract and Estate* (Law Com No. 174)), the Landlord and Tenant (Covenants) Act 1995 ('the 1995 Act') has made major changes to the law governing the enforceability of leases by or against the original parties to the lease, and by or against their successors in title. Most of these changes are not retrospective in their effect, despite the Law Commission's recommendation that they should be. As a result, there are now two very different sets of rules in operation for 'old leases' and 'new leases'.

Section 1(3) of the 1995 Act defines *'new tenancies'* as tenancies granted on or after the date on which the Act came into force: 1 January 1996. All the provisions of the 1995 Act apply to these leases. By contrast, only a few provisions of the 1995 Act apply to leases granted before this date (see 11.2.3). Apart from these few provisions, such *'old leases'* are still governed by the common law rules and the provisions of the LPA 1925 that dealt with leasehold covenants before the 1995 Act. Since leases may be created for very long periods of time, old leases are still very important in the modern law and the rules governing these leases remain of considerable practical importance.

11.1.2 6 Trant Way—an old lease

As we have seen (10.1.3), 6 Trant Way was held by John Jarlsberg on a 40-year lease granted in 1989, well before the operative date of the 1995 Act. Some time ago, Mr Jarlsberg moved away to a different part of the country to take up a new job. With the consent of his landlord, Irene Ivy, he sold his lease to Keith Kale. Later, Irene Ivy sold her fee simple estate in 6 Trant Way to Liam Lyle, who became the first registered proprietor of the estate. The legal relationship between the new landlord and the new tenant—Keith Kale and Liam Lyle—will be governed by the law as it was before the 1995 Act came into force (see 11.2.2). So will the relationship between the parties to the original contract, Irene Ivy and John Jarlsberg (see 11.2.1), with the exception of a few provisions protecting former tenants like John Jarlsberg from some forms of liability (see 11.2.3).

The situation is expressed diagrammatically in Figure 11.1.

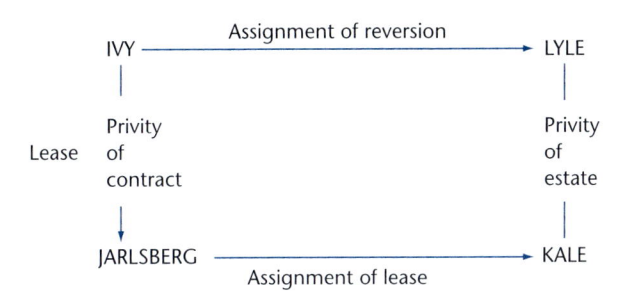

```
                    Assignment of reversion
         IVY ─────────────────────────────────→ LYLE
          │                                      │
          │                                      │
         Privity                                Privity
Lease    of                                    of
         contract                              estate
          │                                      │
          ↓                                      │
       JARLSBERG ──────────────────────────→ KALE
                    Assignment of lease
```

Figure 11.1 Position after dispositions of 6 Trant Way

11.1.3 5 Trant Way: maisonette—a new lease

By contrast, the lease of the ground and first-floor maisonette at 5 Trant Way (see 10.1.2), which James Harding has contracted to buy from Fingall Forest, will have been granted on 1 January 2018. All the provisions of the 1995 Act will apply to this new lease. Suppose that Fingall Forest were to decide to move to a retirement home a few months later, selling his freehold title to 5 Trant Way to Melanie McAdams. The 1995 Act will govern the relationship between James Harding and his ex-landlord, Fingall Forest (see 11.3.1), as well as the relationship between Mr Harding and the new landlord, Melanie McAdams (11.3.2).

11.1.4 Enforcement between the original parties to the lease: privity of contract

Where the parties to the original lease remain in the landlord and tenant relationship, enforcement of the leasehold covenants between them is a straightforward matter of contract law. Difficult problems can arise, however, when the parties to the original lease have transferred their estates in the land to others. In such a situation, having given up the rights to the land itself, the parties may also wish to escape the obligations that were originally associated with those rights.

For example, suppose that Keith Kale had moved into 6 Trant Way and then failed to pay the rent due under the lease and allowed the property to fall into a state of disrepair (see 11.1.2). John Jarlsberg has moved away and no longer has any connection with 6 Trant Way or control over the land; he will wish to avoid liability for Mr Kale's behaviour. However, Irene Ivy may argue that his original covenants—to ensure that rent is paid and the property is kept in repair—are still binding on him personally, as a matter of contract law. If Mr Kale cannot afford the repairs and is unable to pay the rent arrears, she might turn to Mr Jarlsberg to indemnify her for the loss.

This is a problem that arises from applying the doctrine of privity of contract—the rule that the original parties to a contract may sue and be sued upon that contract—to leases. The application of privity of contract to new leases has been heavily modified by the 1995 Act (see 11.3.1), but the Act only makes limited changes to its operation in the case of old leases, with the aim of protecting former tenants from its most onerous consequences (see 11.2.3).

11.1.5 Enforcement between successors in title: privity of estate

New landlords and/or tenants will normally wish to enforce the obligations created by the original lease, even though they were not party to the contract that gave rise to the lease. For example, suppose that James Harding refuses to pay his ground rent to Melanie McAdams or fails to keep up with his other obligations under the lease granted to him by Fingall Forest. She will wish to enforce those obligations against him directly.

However, unlike Fingall Forest, she will not normally be able to argue that James Harding owes her a *contractual* obligation to perform the covenants. She was not a party to the original contract, and so the default rule is that she cannot enforce the obligations under that contract. This is also an application of the doctrine of privity of contract—the rule that *only* the original parties to a contract may sue and be sued on the contract. A special exception to this rule, which applies in the landlord and tenant context, is known as *'privity of estate'*. Its effect is that a new landlord or tenant can enforce some of the covenants in the original lease, and is bound by those covenants, even though he or she was not party to the original lease.

The application of the doctrine of privity of estate to new leases has also been heavily modified by the 1995 Act, which redefines which covenants will be binding against successors in this way (see 11.3.2). Old leases remain subject to the common law rules, as modified by the LPA 1925 (see 11.2.2).

11.1.6 Subtenants

Finally, special problems arise when a sublease has been granted (see 9.1.4). In this scenario, the original tenant still has his or her rights to the land, and is still in a landlord and tenant relationship with the head landlord. The lease has not been transferred to the subtenant, who has simply received a fresh estate carved out of the original lease. However, the subtenant is now entitled to immediate physical possession of the land.

7 Trant Way is an example of such a situation. Martin Mount has the fee simple title to the property, which is divided into two parts: the ground floor (7A) has been adapted for use as a shop, while the upstairs (7B) provides office accommodation. The entire property was let to Nigel Norman in 1998 for 99 years. The lease was made by deed and included a number of covenants on the part of Mr Norman, including covenants to pay rent, at present £2,000 per month, to keep the property in good repair, and not to keep any animals on the property.

Immediately after completion of the lease, Mr Norman sublet 7A to Olav Orion, who uses it as a showroom for his antiques business, and 7B to Paula Primrose, who carries on a small employment agency from the premises. The two subtenants both have monthly tenancies, which were granted in writing and which contain covenants identical in form to those in the head lease.

This situation is expressed diagrammatically in Figure 11.2.

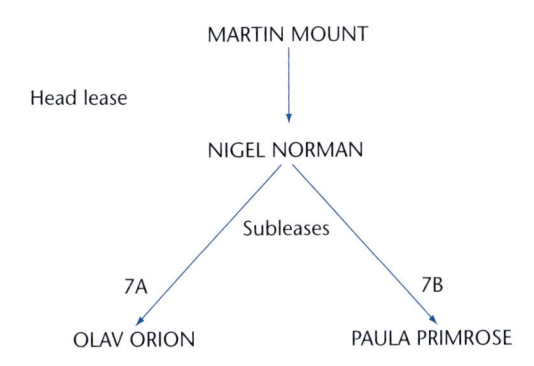

Figure 11.2 Position after dispositions of 7 Trant Way

In such a situation, Mr Mount may wish to complain of what Mr Orion or Miss Primrose are doing on the land or Miss Primrose may want to compel Mr Mount to perform the covenants in the head lease, even though there is no direct relationship—no contract, and no landlord and tenant relationship—between them. In this context, the law that applies to new and old leases is broadly similar, although the 1995 Act has made some limited changes in cases where the head lease is a new lease (11.4).

11.2 Old leases

As you would expect, old leases include all tenancies granted before 1 January 1996. However, the category also includes leases granted after that date if they are made under an agreement or a court order that existed before the Act came into force (s. 1). Options to renew an existing lease are agreements to grant leases within the meaning of this provision; as a result, it is likely that the effect of the old law will be further prolonged by the exercise of options to renew contained in long leases.

11.2.1 Privity of contract

Covenants in leases are usually phrased in terms that make the covenantor responsible for the acts and omissions of his or her successors in title, as well as his or her own actions. Apart from any wording in a particular lease, such an obligation will be implied by LPA 1925, s. 79 which provides that:

> A covenant relating to any land of a covenantor . . . shall, unless a contrary intention is expressed, be deemed to be made by the covenantor on behalf of himself his successors in title and the persons deriving title under him . . .

Accordingly, tenant covenants in old leases will be deemed to relate not only to the tenant's own conduct, but also to that of all future assignees ('successors in title') and subtenants ('persons deriving title under him'). A tenant who covenants not to do a specific act is taken to have promised, also, that his or her assignees and subtenants will not do that act. In this way, a tenant who has disposed of the estate remains potentially liable to her former landlord for any breaches committed by future tenants (*Thursby v Plant* (1690) 1 Saund 230). Such a tenant will be liable for the acts not only of the particular person to whom he or she has chosen to assign the lease but also of all future assignees for the rest of the term of the lease.

The same general principles apply to landlords under old leases, who are also presumed to have covenanted for themselves and their successors in title under LPA 1925, s. 79. An original landlord will thus remain liable on the leasehold covenants after assigning the reversion, and so could be sued by the tenant for breaches of covenant committed by the assignee of the reversion, the new landlord. As in the case of tenants, the landlord's potential liability covers the acts and omissions of all subsequent landlords for the rest of the term of the lease.

From a legal point of view, continuing liability under old leases could have been excluded by the parties at the time of grant, by covenanting in terms that excluded the operation of s. 79 and which specified that liability would cease on assignment. (For the impact of the 1995 Act on continuing liability under new leases, see 11.3.1). In reality, however, no landlord would accept a covenant in these terms from a prospective tenant, and a properly advised tenant would be unlikely to agree to such a limitation of the landlord's liability.

It is worth noting that this continuing liability applies only to an original covenantor—that is, the landlord or tenant who was party to the original grant of the lease. It does not apply to an assignee of the original lease or reversion, when they assign in their turn. This is because an assignee comes under obligations to perform the leasehold covenants only because of privity of estate, not privity of contract (see 11.2.2); when the relationship of privity of estate ceases to exist, because the assignee has in turn assigned the lease or reversion to a new landlord or tenant, the liability to perform the covenants also ceases (see *City of London Corporation v Fell* [1994] 1 AC 458 at p. 465).

11.2.1.1 Original covenantor's remedies

If an original covenantor (whether tenant or landlord) does have to compensate for a breach of covenant committed by an assignee, he or she will naturally want to recoup the losses and may do so in one of two ways. To illustrate this, we will assume a series of assignments of a lease, which is shown diagrammatically in Figure 11.3.

Figure 11.3 Successive assignments of lease

L has recovered damages from T in respect of a breach of covenant by A3, and two courses of action are now open to T.

Proceeding against A3
T may seek to recover directly from A3, relying on the rule in *Moule v Garrett* (1872) LR 7 Ex 101 that:

> where one person is compelled to pay damages by the legal default of another, he is entitled to recover from [that person] the sum so paid.

However, the fact that L did not sue A3 himself but instead preferred to sue T may suggest that it will not be worthwhile to proceed against A3, who may be difficult to find or insolvent, and so T may prefer the second course of action, recovering from A1.

Proceeding against A1
T is able to do this because any assignment of a lease includes an implied covenant by the assignee to indemnify the assignor for any breach of covenant in the lease. (See, for *registered land*, LRA 2002, s. 134 and Sch. 12, para. 20; for *unregistered land*, see LPA 1925, s. 77.)

Thus, T may sue A1, because A1 covenanted to indemnify T against such claims. Thereafter, A1 may sue A2 and A2 may sue A3, also on the basis of the indemnity covenant implied into every assignment.

It is, of course, important to realise that in the situations we have just been considering, where a claimant has a choice of whom to sue, the claimant can recover only one set of damages; there is no question of gaining double recovery by proceeding against two different defendants in respect of the loss caused by the same breach of covenant.

11.2.1.2 Hardship caused by privity of contract

The fact that the original tenant remained liable for any breach of covenant by successors throughout the whole term of the lease had always been capable of producing unfair results, largely because the original tenant was often unaware of the provisions of LPA 1925, s. 79, and did not appreciate fully the obligations being assumed. However, economic difficulties during the 1980s intensified the hardship experienced by original tenants. Many tenants found themselves being held liable for breaches of covenant committed by current tenants, who were in financial difficulties and could not afford to pay rent or perform other covenants. The lease had often passed through a series of assignments, and it might well be that the original tenant knew nothing of the current leaseholder, and certainly had no control over their actions. It was these difficulties that led to pressure for change, and to Parliament's enactment of the Law Commission's 1988 recommendations in the form of the 1995 Act.

As Clarke has pointed out ([2015] Conv 191), it is one of the ironies of the legislation that the individuals whose plight motivated Parliament to legislate—parties who had been tenants under leases granted before 1996, and who were being pursued by former landlords for later assignees' failures to pay rent—were not actually benefited by the major provisions of the 1995 Act, which applied only prospectively. However, ss. 17–20 of the 1995 Act, which apply to 'both new and other tenancies' (s. 1(2)), do offer some limited help to such tenants.

11.2.1.3 Protection of former tenants under the 1995 Act

These sections of the Act assist the former tenant in three ways:

1. by restricting the arrears that can be recovered;
2. by ensuring that the former tenant is not made subject to increased liability by variation of the terms of the lease; and
3. by giving the former tenant an opportunity to acquire a landlord's rights over the current tenant (the assignee), in the form of an **'overriding lease'**.

These provisions of the 1995 Act also apply to guarantors of the former tenant. It is common practice for a landlord to require a tenant or assignee of a lease to provide guarantors or sureties for the performance of the covenants in the lease. The practice is a common one, and guarantors can be seriously affected in times of recession by the inability of tenants to meet their commitments. The protection given to the tenant by these sections is accordingly extended to any guarantor, and references to the former tenant in the following account of ss. 17–21 should be read as including guarantors.

1. Restriction of liability for rent or service charge

Section 17 provides that a landlord cannot recover arrears of rent or other fixed payments—such as service charges—from a former tenant, unless the landlord has notified the former tenant of the amount due, and of the intention to recover the money, within six months of the money becoming due. This provision was intended to target landlords who had allowed arrears to accumulate over a period of years before having recourse to the former tenant, who meanwhile had no knowledge that the current tenant was in breach of covenant.

2. Restriction of liability where tenancy is subsequently varied

It is always possible to vary the terms of a lease by agreement between the landlord and the tenant and such a variation may result in an increased liability for the tenant. Accordingly, the Act provides that the former tenant shall not be liable to pay any charge which arises from a variation of the tenant's obligations agreed after the assignment of the lease (s. 18(2) and (3)).

It is a different matter, however, if the original lease itself provided for some future variation of the tenant's obligations (for example, by a rent review clause). In such a case, the original tenant might well be bound by the enhanced obligation.

3. Right to an overriding lease

A former tenant who remains liable on the leasehold covenants may be described as having responsibility without power, since there is liability for breach of covenants committed by assignees of the lease without any control over the conduct of these assignees. It is true that the original tenant selects the first assignee, but there is no control over any subsequent assignment unless special contractual arrangements are made for this. The original tenant may be unaware of breaches of covenant by an assignee, or have no way of compelling the landlord to take action.

A solution to these difficulties is offered by s. 19 which gives the former tenant the right to require the landlord to grant him an 'overriding lease'. This will take effect as a concurrent lease, or a lease of the reversion (see 9.2.5), and its effect is to make the former tenant the immediate landlord of the defaulting current tenant. This means that the former tenant has the landlord's power to enforce the covenants in the lease against the current tenant; if there are further breaches, he or she can take action to remedy them, if necessary by forfeiting the lease and seeking to re-let the property.

For a practical account of the ways in which this new device may assist the former tenant, see Williamson (2006) EG No. 0605 267.

11.2.1.4 Original tenant's liability to a new landlord

One final point is worth mentioning because it often causes confusion. As we will see (11.2.2), the benefit of certain covenants in a lease can be passed on to an assignee of the reversion and enforced by a new landlord who was not a party to the original lease. The courts have held that such an assignee of the reversion can also enforce the covenants against the original tenant, even though there has never been privity of contract or privity of estate between the new landlord and the original tenant (see, for example, *Parker v Webb* (1693) 3 Salk 5 (91 ER 656) and *Milverton Group Ltd v Warner World Ltd* [1995] 2 EGLR 28). It has been suggested that a new tenant might enforce against the original landlord in a similar way, again without any privity of estate or contract between them, but there is no decision on this point. (See further, Megarry and Wade, paras. 20-015–20-017.)

11.2.2 Privity of estate

Although the original covenantor remains liable for breach of covenant, as we have seen, most covenantees would in general find it more convenient to proceed against the person who has actually caused the breach and currently has rights to the land. Accordingly, it is often essential to know whether an assignee of a covenanting tenant, or a purchaser of a reversion from a covenanting landlord, can be made directly liable for breaches of covenant. Similarly, such an assignee or purchaser may well wish to know whether he or she can enforce the original covenants in the lease.

The problem, as has been explained, is that the assignee is not a party to the contract between the original landlord and tenant and it is a basic principle of contract law that duties under a contract cannot be passed to a person who was not a party to the original contract. However, as the leasehold estate developed, it became clear that it was essential to find ways of continuing to enforce the covenants despite successive changes in the ownership of the lease and the reversion. In the words of Lord Templeman in *City of London Corpn v Fell* [1994] 1 AC 458 at p. 464:

> ... common law, and statute following common law, were faced with the problem of rendering effective the obligations under a lease which might endure for a period of 999 years or more beyond the control of any covenantor.

Common law developed the doctrine of *'privity of estate'* to deal with this problem, and the operation of this doctrine was modified by statute. These rules, however, apply only to old leases created by deed. The rules that apply to old leases made without a deed are to be found in 11.2.2.2. The rules applicable to new leases are to be found in 11.3.1.

11.2.2.1 Leases made by deed

Two requirements must be satisfied before a leasehold covenant can be enforced by or against an assignee of the lease or the reversion:

1. there must be privity of estate between the relevant parties; and
2. the covenants in question must 'touch and concern the land' or 'have reference to the subject-matter of the lease'.

1. Privity of estate
Privity of estate arises when there is a direct relationship of landlord and tenant between the parties: in technical terms, a relationship of tenure. Where privity of estate exists, some leasehold covenants will be enforceable between the current landlord and tenant, even although there is no privity of contract between them.

If the situation in Figure 11.4 exists then there is both privity of contract and privity of estate between L and T. They are parties to a contract, and also stand in a landlord and tenant relationship.

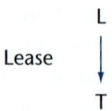

Figure 11.4 Privity of contract and of estate

If T later assigns the lease to A, A becomes L's tenant and L becomes A's landlord. There will be privity of contract between L and T but only privity of estate between L and A, as depicted in Figure 11.5. L and A have never entered into any contract with each other, but they are landlord and tenant by virtue of the estates in land that they now hold.

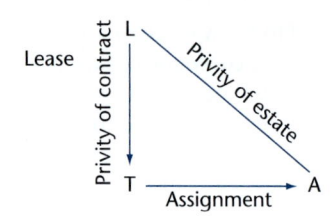

Figure 11.5 Position after assignment of the lease

Similarly, if the landlord, L, sells the reversion to P, a purchaser, there will continue to be privity of contract between L and T but there will be only privity of estate between T and P, as shown in Figure 11.6.

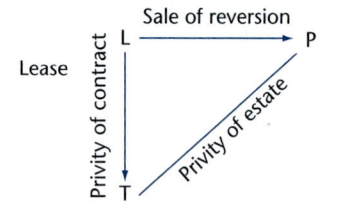

Figure 11.6 Position after sale of the reversion

If the landlord sells the reversion and the tenant assigns the lease the situation illustrated in Figure 11.7 will arise.

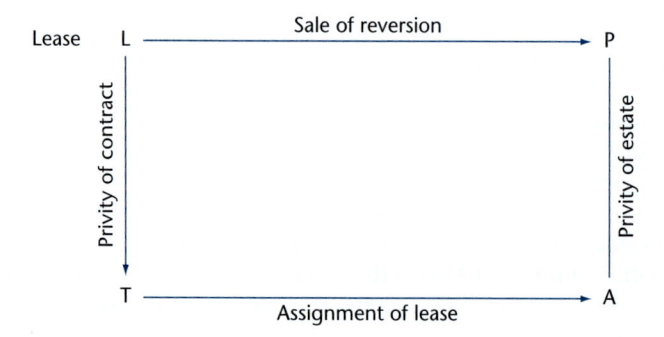

Figure 11.7 Position after sale of the reversion and assignment of the lease

Thus, there will be no privity of contract between the purchaser of the reversion, P, and the assignee of the lease, A, but there will be privity of estate; P and A are, respectively, the new landlord and the new tenant. Any covenants in the lease that touch and concern the land will be enforceable by or against A; any that have reference to the subject matter of the lease will be enforceable by and against P. Since neither of them were party to the original contract, none of the other covenants in the original lease will bind or benefit them.

2. Covenants must 'touch and concern' the land or 'have reference to the subject-matter of the lease'

The common law rule in *Spencer's Case* (1583) 5 Co Rep 16a applies whenever a tenant assigns a lease. Its effect is that all covenants that 'touch and concern' the demised premises will bind and benefit the assignee of the lease, the new tenant. Meanwhile, when a landlord assigns a reversion, the statutory provisions under LPA 1925, ss. 141 and 142 apply. The rule here is that all covenants that 'have reference to the subject-matter of the lease' will bind and benefit the assignee of the reversion, the new landlord.

It is generally accepted that these two phrases—'touching and concerning' and 'having reference to the subject-matter of the lease'—have the same meaning, and any covenant that meets one test will meet the other. Unfortunately, it has proved very difficult to define either phrase in such a way as to provide a clear test for identifying those covenants which will run on assignment, and all we can do here is to note certain suggestions that have found favour with the courts.

In *Breams Property Investment Co. Ltd v Stroulger* [1948] 2 KB 1 at p. 7, the Court of Appeal approved a passage in Cheshire's Modern Real Property (still to be found in the 18th edition of Cheshire and Burn—see p. 304) which suggested that the appropriate test for identifying a covenant which 'touched and concerned' the land was:

> whether the covenant affects the landlord qua [as] landlord or the tenant qua tenant. A covenant may very well have reference to the land, but, unless it is reasonably incidental to the relation of landlord and tenant, it cannot be said to touch and concern the land . . .

It may be thought that this test only substitutes one formula for another, and is not particularly helpful in practice. It does, however, explain the decision in *Woodall v Clifton* [1905] 2 Ch 257, in which it was held that an agreement by the landlord giving the tenant an option to purchase the reversion did not come within the rule in *Spencer's Case*, because the covenant did not affect the parties as landlord and tenant but as vendor and purchaser.

A further statement of the process to be followed in deciding whether a covenant 'touches and concerns' is to be found in *P & A Swift Investments v Combined English Stores Group plc* [1989] AC 632 in which Lord Oliver drew together criteria from earlier decisions and (at p. 642) set out what he described as 'a satisfactory working test' for whether a covenant touches and concerns the land. The case under consideration concerned the assignment of the reversion and Lord Oliver formulated his test accordingly, but it can be expressed more generally by saying that a covenant touches and concerns the land if three conditions are met:

(i) The covenant is of benefit to the covenantee only while holding an estate in the land: that is, while remaining a landlord or a tenant. Thus, for example, a tenant's covenant to repair the property benefits the original landlord only while that landlord retains an interest in the land: after assigning the reversion, the covenantee is not affected by the state of the property and so is not benefited by the tenant's performance of the covenant.

(ii) The covenant affects the nature, quality, mode of user, or value of the covenantee's land (for an earlier statement of this condition see Russel LJ in *Horsey Estate Ltd v Steiger* [1899] 2 QB 79 at p. 89).

(iii) The covenant is not stated to be personal; that is, it is not worded so as to bind only a specific covenantor or to benefit only a specific covenantee.

Despite this guidance from the courts, it remains difficult in borderline cases to predict whether or not a covenant will run on assignment. As long ago as 1931 Romer LJ, in *Grant v Edmondson* [1931] 1 Ch 1 at p. 28, described the rules as being:

> purely arbitrary, and the decisions for the most part quite illogical.

This criticism has continued to the present day (see, for example, Gray and Gray, paras. 4.5.42–4.5.54), and eventually resulted in major reform of the rules by the 1995 Act (see 11.3.2). The old rules, however, continue to apply to leases granted before the Act came into force, and so it is necessary to note a few examples of covenants which do and do not 'touch and concern'.

Covenants which 'touch and concern' It would be impossible to compile a complete list of all that covenants which satisfy the rule in *Spencer's Case*. All the standard covenants discussed in Chapter 10 will certainly do so, unless they are worded in such a way as to make it clear that they are intended to be merely personal.

Covenants which do not 'touch and concern' Covenants which do not 'touch and concern' land and so do not run on assignment may be described as 'collateral' covenants. They include: non-competition clauses (*Thomas v Hayward* (1869) LR 4 Ex 311); covenants to keep property other than the demised premises in repair (*Dewar v Goodman* [1909] AC 72); and covenants to repair chattels which are not fixed to the land (*Williams v Earle* (1868) LR 3 QB 739).

Personal covenants Any covenant that would normally be regarded as touching and concerning the land, and therefore capable of binding and benefiting an assignee, may be worded in terms that prevent it from having this effect: if the parties make it clear that a particular covenant is meant to be a personal covenant, benefiting or binding only the original tenant or landlord, the relevant burden or benefit will not run on assignment. It is also possible to create a covenant which is personal to one party but not to the other. Thus, for example, a covenant could give a personal right to a tenant, the benefit of which could not be passed on to an assignee but the burden of which would run with the reversion and bind the landlord's assignees (see *System Floors Ltd v Ruralpride Ltd* [1995] 1 EGLR 48).

Covenants that do not touch and concern the land are sometimes also described as 'personal' covenants in the case law, because they do not run on assignment and so are enforceable only between the original parties. However, you should note the difference between covenants that can never run ('collateral' covenants) and covenants that could run, but are prevented from doing so by the agreement of the parties ('personal' covenants).

11.2.2.2 Leases not by deed

The rules covered thus far apply only to leases made by deed. The rules applicable to legal leases granted orally or in writing (see 9.3.1.1), and to equitable leases (see 9.3.2) are different.

1. Legal parol leases

The old rule, expressed in *Elliott v Johnson* (1866) LR 2 QB 120, was that covenants did not run on the assignment of a parol lease: the principles in *Spencer's Case* applied only to legal leases made by deed. However, in *Boyer v Warbey* [1953] 1 QB 234, it was held that the rule in *Spencer's Case* applied to a written lease that met the requirements of LPA 1925, s. 54(2); accordingly, a tenant's covenant to pay £40 towards repairs at the end of the term bound an assignee of the written lease. It seems probable that the same approach would be adopted in the case of oral leases within the s. 54(2) exception, but no mention was made of this in *Boyer v Warbey*, so the position remains uncertain.

2. Equitable leases

The rule in *Spencer's Case* depends upon the assignee's acquiring an estate in the land. This means that the assignee of an equitable lease—which is not an estate, merely an equitable right to specific performance of an agreement for a lease—will not automatically get the benefits and burdens of the covenants in the agreement. While the benefit of a right to enforce a contract may be expressly assigned, the duties are not transferable in the same way. If, for example, the tenant under an equitable lease agrees to decorate the interior of the property, the burden of this agreement cannot be transferred to a person buying the lease from the tenant. The original tenant will remain contractually liable for any breach of the agreement, but the landlord will not be able to take action against the new tenant (*Purchase v Lichfield Brewery Co.* [1915] 1 KB 184).

It is doubtful whether the same principle applies to the statutory provisions dealing with the assignment of the reversion to a new landlord (ss. 141 and 142 of the LPA 1925). There are a number of decisions that equitable leases are covered by the statutory provision that the benefit of the lessee's covenants runs with the reversion (see, for example, *Rickett v Green* [1910] 1 KB 253, interpreting s. 10 of the Conveyancing Act 1881, the forerunner of LPA 1925, s. 141). There has as yet been no decision on whether the burden of the landlord's covenants runs to the assignee under LPA 1925, s. 142, but the reasoning of the decisions on the running of the benefit would seem equally applicable to the running of the burden (see Megarry and Wade, para. 20-062).

In *Boyer v Warbey* [1953] 1 QB 234, Denning LJ suggested, in *obiter dicta*, that the position on this issue had been altered by the Judicature Acts 1873–5:

> . . . since the fusion of law and equity, the position is different . . . There is no valid reason nowadays why the doctrine of covenants running with the land—or with the reversion—should not apply equally to agreements under hand as to covenants under seal; and I think we should so hold, not only in the case of agreements for more than three years which need the intervention of equity to perfect them, but also in the case of agreements for three years or less which do not.

As has been explained, *Boyer v Warbey* involved a written legal lease for three years and not an equitable lease. These remarks, therefore, are mere *obiter dicta* and have not been taken up in any later decision.

11.2.3 Breach committed before assignment

Where a tenant or a landlord has breached a covenant before assignment, they remain liable for that breach. If the burden of the covenant is capable of running on assignment, the assignee is bound by it for the future, but does not take on liability for pre-existing breaches. This seems almost self-evident, but if authority is needed it can be found in *Duncliffe v Caerfelin Properties Ltd* [1989] 2 EGLR 38.

The right to take action for any pre-existing breach of covenant by the tenant passes to the new landlord with the assignment of the reversion (LPA 1925, s. 141, as interpreted in *Re King* [1963] Ch 459), and the former landlord loses the right to sue the tenant. By contrast, where it is the lease that has been assigned, the former tenant may still sue the landlord in respect of breaches that occurred during the currency of the lease even after assignment. This right may be valuable if money has been spent to remedy a breach for which the landlord was responsible, and which had to be remedied before the assignee would agree to take the lease: see for example *City and Metropolitan Properties Ltd v Greycroft Ltd* [1987] 1 WLR 1085.

11.2.4 Applying the rules—6 Trant Way

It may now be helpful to consider how these rules might apply in an example. As we have seen (at 11.1.2), 6 Trant Way was originally held by John Jarlsberg on a 40-year lease, granted by Irene Ivy in 1989—that is, well before the operative date of the 1995 Act. He subsequently assigned his lease to Keith Kale, and Irene Ivy assigned her reversion to Liam Lyle.

Suppose that Keith Kale has now decided that he would like to take advantage of the option to purchase the freehold that the original lease gave to the original tenant (cl. 4(b), see 10.1.3). Mr Kale has served written notice on Mr Lyle of his intentions. He has also been having some problems lately with the tile cladding on part of the exterior wall of the house and wants Mr Lyle to sort this out, under the landlord's repairing covenant in the lease, before the purchase of the freehold goes ahead. Meanwhile, Mr Lyle is concerned that Mr Kale has fallen into arrears on his rent a few times in the last year and would like to know if he has the option of suing Mr Jarlsberg if Mr Kale proves unable to pay off these arrears.

In this situation we must consider:

- the scope of the continuing liability of Mr Jarlsberg, as the original tenant; and
- which of the terms in the original lease bind or benefit Mr Kale, the tenant's assignee; and
- which of these terms bind or benefit Mr Lyle, the purchaser of the freehold reversion.

11.2.4.1 Continuing liability of original landlord and tenant

Both Mrs Ivy and Mr Jarlsberg remain liable on their covenants, even though both of them have given up all connection with the property. This means that if, for any reason, Mr Lyle fails to carry out the necessary repairs, Mr Kale may be able to seek compensation from Mrs Ivy. Similarly, Mr Lyle does have the right to sue Mr Jarlsberg for the unpaid arrears of the rent owed by Mr Kale. However, he must comply with the requirements of ss. 17–20 of the 1995 Act in order to enforce this right (see 11.2.1.3). In particular, if he wants to sue Mr Jarlsberg for any particular sum of unpaid rent, he must give him proper notice of his intention and the amount due within six months of that payment becoming due; he cannot wait for a year or more for arrears to accumulate and then sue Mr Jarlsberg for the whole amount.

11.2.4.2 Enforcement of covenants between assignees of lease and reversion

Mr Lyle is now Mr Kale's landlord. There is privity of estate between them. Thus, Mr Lyle will be bound by those landlord covenants (LPA 1925, s. 142)—and will benefit from those tenant covenants (s. 141)—that have 'reference to the subject-matter' of the lease. Similarly, Mr Kale will automatically receive both the benefit and the burden of any covenants in the original lease which 'touch and concern' the land (*Spencer's Case* (1583) 5 Co Rep 16a).

This means that Mr Kale is bound by Mr Jarlsberg's covenants to pay rent, to obtain the landlord's consent before assigning or subletting, and not to use the premises otherwise than as a dwelling. Mr Lyle has the right to enforce these covenants against him. In his turn, Mr Lyle is bound by Mrs Ivy's covenants for quiet enjoyment and for the repair of the exterior, and Mr Kale has the right to enforce these against him. It follows from this that Mr Kale should be able to require Mr Lyle to remedy the problems he is experiencing with the exterior wall.

11.2.4.3 Option to purchase the reversion

The question whether Mr Kale has the right to enforce the option to purchase against his landlord is more complicated. It has been held that this covenant does not touch and concern the land: the option does not affect the parties qua landlord and tenant but qua vendor and purchaser (*Woodall v Clifton* [1905] 2 Ch 257). Accordingly, this right does not automatically benefit Mr Kale or burden Mr Lyle. The option did, however, give the original tenant, Mr Jarlsberg, an equitable interest in the fee simple estate. The benefit of that right could have been assigned to Mr Kale, as can the benefit of any chose in action, but a clear assignment of the right will be required if Mr Kale is to establish a claim to it.

Even if Mr Kale can prove that the benefit of the right has been assigned to him, he must still establish that the option is binding on Mr Lyle, who has bought the unregistered legal estate in fee simple and become the first registered proprietor of it. Mr Lyle will be bound by the equitable interest only if it had been protected as a C(iv) land charge before he purchased the fee simple title (see *Phillips v Mobil Oil Co. Ltd* [1989] 1 WLR 888 and 5.4.2.2). If the option had not been registered, it will not bind Mr Lyle and cannot be enforced against him.

11.3 New leases

As has been explained, the 1995 Act was enacted with the aims of relieving original covenantors from their continuing liability under leases and of simplifying the rules governing the running of leasehold covenants to assignees. For leases granted after 1 January 1996, the 1995 Act provides a complete code on both these issues. Importantly, it is not possible to contract out of this code; s. 25(1)(a) of the 1995 Act provides that any agreement that has 'effect to exclude, modify or otherwise frustrate the operation of any provision of this Act' is void to the extent that it has such an effect.

11.3.1 Privity of contract

The 1995 Act provides mechanisms whereby original covenantors—both former landlords and former tenants—can be released from their covenants on assigning the estate. However, it distinguishes between former landlords and former tenants in this context. The original tenant is automatically released on assignment, subject to certain exceptions. The original landlord, however, can obtain a release only with the consent of the tenant or under a court order.

11.3.1.1 Release of the original tenant

When a tenant assigns a new lease, s. 5 of the 1995 Act provides that, as from the date of the assignment, the tenant is released from the burden of the covenants and ceases to be entitled to the benefit of the landlord's covenants; s. 30(4)(a) of the Act provides that LPA 1925, s. 79 shall not apply to new tenancies. The Act also protects anyone who acted as a guarantor of the original tenant's performance of the covenants, releasing such a guarantor from liability under s. 24(2).

1. Circumstances in which the tenant remains liable

It is important to note that there are certain circumstances in which the tenant will not be freed from continuing liability. The tenant continues to be liable in the case of 'excluded assignments', which are defined in s. 11(1) of the 1995 Act as:

(a) assignments in breach of a covenant in the tenancy, i.e., assignments of the lease by a tenant in breach of an absolute or qualified covenant against assignment; and

(b) assignments by operation of law, for example, on death, where the estate vests in the deceased's personal representatives, or on bankruptcy, where the estate vests in the trustee in bankruptcy.

Where the tenant (or the tenant's estate) remains bound by covenants after assignment, the tenant will be freed by the next assignment of the lease that is not an excluded one (1995 Act, s. 11(2)(b)). In these situations, where continuing liability under a new lease remains possible, the provisions of ss. 17–20 of the 1995 Act (see 11.2.1.3) will apply to protect the tenant and his or her guarantor from the most onerous consequences of such liability.

2. Authorised guarantee agreement

Although the original tenant may be freed automatically from continuing liability on covenants, it should be noted that the landlord may require the tenant to enter into an 'authorised guarantee agreement', by which the original tenant guarantees the immediate assignee's performance of the covenants in the lease (s. 16). The landlord is permitted to do this only when:

(1) the landlord's consent to the assignment is required under the lease; and

(2) the landlord makes the giving of the guarantee a condition of his consenting to the assignment.

The guarantee is to last only while the immediate assignee is liable under the covenants of the lease and must end when this liability ceases—that is, the tenant giving the guarantee cannot be required to guarantee performance by successive assignees. Thus, although it may look at first sight as though the 1995 Act is taking away with one hand what it has just given with the other, the tenant's position is in reality still considerably better than it would be under the old rules. Unlike liability as original covenantor, liability under the guarantee agreement will not continue throughout the full period of the lease and cannot cover the actions of future assignees whom the original tenant has not selected. The provisions of ss. 17–20 of the 1995 Act (see 11.2.1.3) also apply to liability under an authorised guarantee agreement.

3. Assignment to original guarantor void

In *EMI Group Ltd v O & H Q1 Ltd* [2016] EWHC 529 (Ch), the High Court held that the operation of s. 24(2) of the Act would be frustrated if a tenant could assign the original lease to its own guarantor, since the effect would be to subject the guarantor—which would otherwise have been released from its obligations under s. 24(2) of the Act—to the same set of obligations in its new capacity as a tenant. Since such an assignment would have the effect of frustrating the effect of these provisions of the 1995 Act, therefore, s. 25 rendered it void.

The result is that a tenant may never assign a new lease to its own guarantor as a new tenant, since such an assignment will be void and ineffective for the purpose of passing the legal estate under s. 25. This may have significant practical implications in the context of commercial leases, as a lease may often be assigned from one company within a group to another related company within the same group, as part of corporate restructuring. The parent company will now need to be careful to ensure that the assignee company is not one that has previously been used as a guarantor of the obligations under the covenant.

11.3.1.2 Release of the original landlord

The 1995 Act provides for the release of the landlord from covenants on the assignment of the reversion (s. 6), but this release does not take place automatically on the assignment as it does for the tenant. Instead, s. 8 of the Act creates a procedure by which the landlord is required to give notice to the tenant of the proposed or actual assignment of the reversion, and to request release from the covenants. The landlord will be released if the tenant consents, or does not respond within the prescribed period. If the tenant refuses consent, the landlord may apply to the court, which may either uphold the tenant's objection or declare that it is reasonable for the covenant to be released.

The provisions of s. 11 relating to excluded assignments apply also to assignments by the landlord, with the result that assignment by operation of law does not end the continuing liability of the original landlord.

Where a landlord is not released from liability (for example, because the assignment is an excluded one, or because the tenant successfully opposes the landlord's application), the landlord may apply for release on any future assignment of the reversion (1995 Act, ss. 7 and 11(3)(b)).

The provisions of the 1995 Act in relation to the landlord may appear to be less favourable than those applying to the tenant, but it must be remembered that the tenant has no say in the landlord's choice of an assignee (despite the fact that the assignee will become the tenant's new landlord). By contrast, it is often the case that a landlord's consent is necessary for any assignment of the lease to take place and this gives the landlord an adequate opportunity to 'vet' any prospective new tenant. The creditworthiness of a new landlord can be very relevant to a tenant, for example where the landlord has repairing obligations under the lease; if there is any doubt about the financial standing of the assignee, therefore, the tenant may well want the current landlord's liability to continue, and so oppose the application for release.

11.3.1.3 No release of personal covenants

As we shall see, most covenants in a new lease will be enforceable between the new landlord and tenant (see 11.3.2). However, any covenant may be worded so as to make it clear that it is intended to be a *personal covenant*, benefiting or binding only the original tenant or landlord. In *BHP Petroleum Ltd v Chesterfield Ltd* [2002] Ch 194 the question arose of whether a covenantor who assigns the lease can be freed from liability on such personal covenants.

In that case, the original landlord had undertaken to carry out certain remedial work to the premises and it was clear from the agreement that this was to be a personal obligation which would not be enforceable against the landlord's successors (see para. 17). On assigning the reversion, the landlord served a notice on the tenant seeking release from its covenants and the tenant did not respond. Subsequently, the tenant sought to enforce the obligation to remedy certain defects against the original landlord, and the defendant claimed that it had been released from the obligation by its assignment of the reversion and the tenant's failure to serve a counter-notice. The Court of Appeal rejected this argument, holding that the provisions of the Act concerning release applied only to a 'landlord covenant' (see 11.3.2.1) which, relying on the definition of 'landlord' in s. 28(1) of the Act, the court defined (at para. 59) as:

> an obligation falling to be complied with by the person who may from time to time be entitled to the reversion on the tenancy.

By contrast, an obligation under a personal covenant by the landlord does not bind successors; it therefore falls outside the definition of a 'landlord covenant', and so does not come within the statutory provisions for release from 'landlord covenants'. The court considered that this interpretation accorded with the basic principle underlying the statutory provisions for release which, in the words of Lightman J at first instance (quoted with approval by the Court of Appeal at para. 29), was:

> that the release of a landlord or tenant from a covenant was intended to be sequential upon, and only sequential upon, a parting by the landlord or tenant with his interest in the property let and the successor taking his predecessor's place as the party responsible for complying with that covenant.

Accordingly, the original landlord remained liable on his personal covenant and was obliged to remedy the defects that the tenant had identified.

11.3.1.4 Express exclusion of continuing liability

In the case of old leases, it was theoretically possible for a covenantor to avoid continuing liability by express provisions in the covenant; this rarely happened in practice because such terms were not likely to be acceptable to the other party. However, in the important case of *London Diocesan Fund v Phithwa* [2005] 1 WLR 3956, such an exclusion in a *new* lease—and its compatibility with s. 25 of the 1995 Act—did arise for consideration by the House of Lords. (Some reports refer to this decision, and proceedings in the lower courts, as *Avonridge Property Co. Ltd v Mashru*—see for example [2006] 01 EG 100—but both references concern the same case.)

In 2002, Avonridge Property Co Ltd ('Avonridge') acquired an existing lease of various small shops, which it sublet to individual tenants in exchange for large initial payments and nominal rents. Each sublease contained a covenant by Avonridge that it would pay the rent due on the head lease to the head landlord, the London Diocesan Fund ('LDF'), but with the additional provision that it would not continue to be liable to its tenants on this covenant if it disposed of its interest in the property (i.e., if it assigned the head lease).

Very shortly after granting the subleases, Avonridge assigned the head lease to Phithwa, who failed to pay the rent due to the head landlord and subsequently disappeared. The head landlord began proceedings to forfeit the head lease (which would destroy the subleases). The subtenants applied for relief against forfeiture under the relevant statutory provisions (see 12.4.5.2) and succeeded; they were granted new leases to be held directly from LDF at a market rent. This meant that the subtenants were very much out of pocket: they had paid for the value of their leases by way of the premium and were now required to pay market rent as well.

Accordingly, the subtenants sued their former landlord, Avonridge, for breach of its covenant that it would pay the rent due under the head lease, claiming that it remained liable on this covenant despite the term in the covenant that liability should end on its assignment of the reversion. The effect of that term would be to free the landlord from its covenant without complying with the statutory procedure for release, and the claimants alleged that the term was designed to avoid that procedure and was therefore void under s. 25 of the 1995 Act.

The House of Lords rejected this argument (Lord Walker dissenting). Their Lordships held that the provisions of the Act were designed to address those situations in which the covenantor's liability continued after assignment, not to limit the means by which a covenantor could exclude that liability. It had always been possible, before the Act, for the covenantor to provide expressly that any liability would end on assignment, and there was nothing in the Act that changed this. Avonridge had not sought to avoid the statutory provisions, but had simply continued to exercise a right that had always existed and was not affected by the Act.

11.3.1.5 Loss of benefit with loss of burden

When, under the statutory provisions, an assignor is released from the burden of any covenants, the assignor also ceases to be entitled to the *benefit* of the other party's covenants under the lease (ss. 5(2)(b) and 6(2)(b)). However, s. 24(4) specifically provides that this loss of benefit does not affect any rights arising from an earlier breach of covenant (see 11.3.3).

11.3.2 Privity of estate

The 1995 Act makes very considerable changes to the rules relating to the running of covenants on the assignment of the lease or the reversion. In doing so, it introduces two new technical terms: 'landlord covenants' and 'tenant covenants'.

11.3.2.1 Landlord covenants and tenant covenants

These covenants are defined in s. 28(1) as the covenants to be performed by the landlord and tenant respectively; in other words, the classification of the covenant is determined by considering who is to bear its burden. For an interpretation of the statutory definition of these terms, see *BHP Petroleum Ltd v Chesterfield Ltd* [2002] Ch 194; as noted in 11.3.1.3, the Court of Appeal held that 'landlord covenants' are those which fall to be complied with by the person who may from time to time be entitled to the reversion (i.e., the current landlord), and do not include personal covenants by the original landlord. Although the court in this case was concerned only with landlord covenants, it seems most likely that a similar approach will be adopted in defining 'tenant covenants'.

11.3.2.2 Transmission of benefit and burden of covenants and rights of re-entry

Section 3 of the 1995 Act provides that the benefit and burden of *all* landlord and tenant covenants in the tenancy shall be annexed to the whole and each and every part of the demised premises and of the reversion in them, and shall pass on the assignment of the whole or any part of the premises or of the reversion. Section 4 makes a similar provision in respect of the landlord's right of re-entry (i.e., to repossess the property for breach of covenant).

Thus, in general, all the covenants in the lease—with the exception of personal covenants, which are specifically excluded by s. 3(6)(a)—will run on the assignment of the lease or the reversion. For new leases, there is no need to consider whether covenants 'touch and concern the land' or 'have reference to the subject matter of the lease' (see 11.2.2.1). The 1995 Act specifically states that its provisions apply to a landlord covenant or a tenant covenant 'whether or not the covenant has reference to the subject matter of the tenancy' (s. 2(1)(a)), and the 1995 Act further provides that nothing in LPA 1925, ss. 141 and 142 shall apply to new tenancies (s. 30(4)(b)).

11.3.2.3 Requirement of registration for options

Thus, the old distinction between leasehold covenants and collateral covenants is no longer relevant to new leases; the old 'collateral covenants' will, under the Act, benefit and burden assignees of new leases and their reversions unless the parties choose to express them to be personal. However, this does not affect the requirement of registration for covenants that depended on registration for their impact on assignees under the old law, such as options to purchase the reversion or to renew the lease (see 11.2.4.3).

The 1995 Act specifically provides that it shall not operate to make enforceable against any person any covenant which would otherwise be unenforceable against that person by reason of its not having been registered under the LRA 2002 or the LCA 1925 (s. 3(6)(b), as amended by LRA 2002). Thus options to renew the lease or to purchase the reversion will still continue to require protection by entry on the register of title or by registration as a class C(iv) land charge.

11.3.2.4 Equitable leases

A further welcome change is that, by virtue of s. 28(1), which defines 'tenancy' as including an 'agreement for a tenancy', the new rules about the running of covenants apply to equitable leases just as they do to legal ones, thus freeing the parties to new agreements from the problems noted at 11.2.2.2.

11.3.3 Breach committed before assignment

It has been noted that, when an assignor is freed from the burden of covenants, the assignor also loses the benefit of the other party's covenants. However, s. 24(4) specifically provides that this does not affect any rights the assignor may have arising from a pre-existing breach of covenant. As a result, the right to sue for earlier breaches of covenant by the tenant remains with the former landlord. Consistently with this, s. 23(1) provides that the new landlord cannot sue for breaches which have occurred before the reversion was assigned, since the tenant remains liable to the former landlord for these breaches; however the new landlord can, under s. 23(3), still re-enter and forfeit the lease for such a breach.

11.3.4 Applying the rules—5 Trant Way

By contrast with the lease of 6 Trant Way, the lease of the ground and first-floor maisonette at 5 Trant Way (see 11.1.3), which James Harding is to take from Fingall Forest, will fall within the main provisions of the 1995 Act.

11.3.4.1 Release of original covenantor

James is taking on a number of obligations under the lease. However, he can be assured that he will be released from any continuing liability under these tenant covenants if he assigns the lease in the future, provided he is not so foolish as to assign the lease without his landlord's consent, thus making an 'excluded assignment'.

By contrast, assigning the reversion would not relieve Fingall Forest automatically from his liability on the landlord covenants. However, he could seek release from his current tenant or, in case of refusal, from the court. If for any reason he was not released, he could make a further application on any occasion in the future when the reversion was assigned again.

11.3.4.2 Enforcement of covenants between assignees of lease and reversion

Assignees from the original landlord and tenant will take the reversion and the lease with the relevant benefits and burdens of the tenant and landlord covenants (i.e., all covenants by the original landlord and the original tenant, except those which are expressed to be personal to the original parties). There will be no need to ask whether the covenants touch and concern the land (*Spencer's Case*) or have reference to the subject matter of the lease (LPA 1925, ss. 141 and 142); all that will be needed is a reference to the terms of s. 2 of the 1995 Act, which provides that the benefit and burden of all landlord covenants and tenant covenants are annexed to the premises and to the reversion, and pass on assignment.

11.4 Position of a subtenant

As we have seen, when a tenant assigns the lease, certain covenants in the lease are enforceable between the landlord and the assignee, the new tenant. A different situation arises, however, if the tenant, T, instead creates a sublease. In such a case the subtenant, S, becomes the tenant of T and has no landlord and tenant relationship with L, the head landlord. Accordingly, there is neither privity of contract nor privity of estate between L and S, but there is both privity of contract and privity of estate between L and T and between T and S. This is expressed in diagrammatic form in Figure 11.8.

```
                L
Head lease      ↓      Privity of contract and estate between L and T
                T
Sublease        ↓      Privity of contract and estate between T and S
                S
```

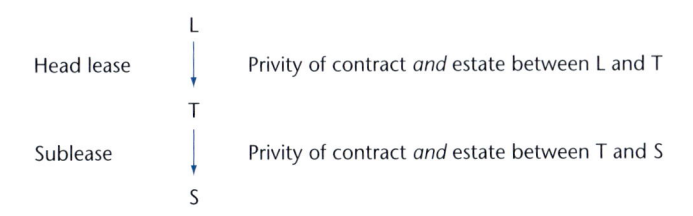

Figure 11.8 Position between head landlord and subtenant

As a result, covenants in the head lease are not usually enforceable against a subtenant. However, the head tenant will usually be liable for the actions of persons who derive their title from him and can be sued by the landlord if the subtenant acts in a manner inconsistent with the terms of the head lease. T would, therefore, want the power to take action against S for such actions so as to protect himself from any liability to L. He could do this by taking the precaution of including in the sublease all the tenant covenants in the head lease.

11.4.1 Exception in respect of restrictive covenants

As we will see in Chapter 25, promises by a landowner to restrict the use of his property in some way—restrictive covenants—can sometimes be enforced by the successors in title of the landowner to whom those promises were made. It has been held this rule applies between a head landlord and a subtenant as well. Thus, the only covenants in the head lease which could be enforced by L against S are those which restrict the use of the property and satisfy the rules relating to restrictive covenants derived from *Tulk v Moxhay* (1848) 2 Ph 774 (see Chapter 25 for the details). An example is provided by

Hemingway Securities Ltd v Dunraven Ltd [1995] 1 EGLR 61, in which it was held that a covenant not to assign or sublet without the landlord's consent was a restrictive covenant within the doctrine of *Tulk v Moxhay*, and could be enforced by the head landlord directly against the subtenant. This exception applies to both old and new leases.

11.4.2 New leases

In relation to new leases, s. 3(5) of the 1995 Act now provides that:

> Any landlord or tenant covenant of a tenancy which is restrictive of the user of land shall, as well as being capable of enforcement against an assignee, be capable of being enforced against any other person who is the owner or occupier of any demised premises to which the covenant relates, even though there is no express provision in the tenancy to that effect.

The full effect of this provision remains to be seen, as does its relationship to the rule in *Tulk v Moxhay*, but it is certainly clear that it will enable the head landlord to enforce restrictive covenants directly against the subtenant without reference to the equitable rules governing the running of the burden of restrictive covenants.

11.4.3 Effect of assignment of sublease or reversion

The same principles, shown in Figure 11.9, will apply if S assigns his sublease to SA and if L assigns his reversion on the head lease to P.

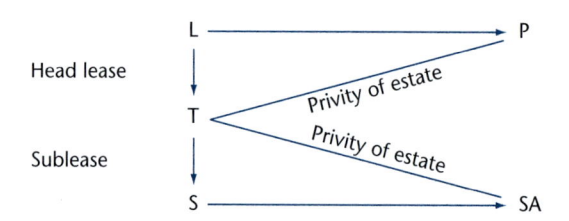

Figure 11.9 Position after sale of reversion and assignment of sublease

P becomes T's landlord, and, depending on the date when the head lease was granted, covenants in it may be enforced between them under either LPA 1925, ss. 141 and 142, or the 1995 Act.

SA becomes T's tenant, and, again depending on the date of the lease, covenants in the sublease will be enforceable between them under either the rule in *Spencer's Case* (1583) 5 Co Rep 16a or the 1995 Act.

There is, however, no relationship of any kind between P and SA, and no covenants (except those within either the *Tulk v Moxhay* rule or s. 3(5) of the 1995 Act) can be enforced between them.

11.4.4 Attempts by head landlord to enforce covenants in sublease

So far, we have been considering the extent to which the head landlord might be able to enforce covenants in the *head lease* against the subtenant. In these situations, the problem is with showing that subtenants can be bound by a contract—the head lease—to which they were not a party. However, different issues arise when the head landlord tries to enforce covenants in the *sublease* against the subtenant. Here, the subtenant is undoubtedly bound by the burden of these covenants, as a contracting party. The problem for the head landlord is to show that he or she can have the benefit of the covenants, despite not being party to the contract.

An example of an occasion on which a head landlord tried to do this is to be found in *Amsprop Trading Ltd v Harris Distribution Ltd* [1997] 1 WLR 1025. In that case, the subtenant had covenanted with *his* landlord that he would repair the property, and that, if he did not do so, the head landlord might enter and do the repairs, at the expense of the subtenant. The head landlord sought to enforce this covenant directly against the subtenant, relying on LPA 1925, s. 56, which provides that:

> a person may take . . . the benefit of any . . . covenant . . . respecting land, although he may not be named as a party to the conveyance [in which the covenant is made].

The landlord's claim was rejected because the covenant did not purport to be with him (i.e., did not name him as a covenantee), a requirement that has been developed by the courts in their interpretation of s. 56. Had this requirement been met, it seems that the head landlord could have relied on the section and enforced the covenant against the subtenant.

11.4.5 Attempts by subtenant to enforce covenants in headlease

There may well be similar situations in which a subtenant wishes to enforce a covenant in the head lease against the head landlord. The head landlord may, for example, be in breach of repairing obligations, and the subtenant, who suffers the effects of disrepair, might prefer to claim directly against the head landlord, instead of having to leave it to the head tenant to take action. It is possible that a subtenant under an 'old' lease (i.e., one granted before 1 January 1996) could do this by relying on LPA 1925, s. 78, as interpreted in *Smith and Snipes Hall Farm Ltd v River Douglas Catchment Board* [1949] 2 KB 500 (see 25.4.1.4), but even if this were so it would not help a subtenant under a new lease (granted after 1995), to which s. 78 no longer applies (s. 30(4) of the 1995 Act).

Where the lease in question is made on or after 11 May 2000, it seems possible that both head landlord and subtenant will be able to rely on the provisions of the Contracts (Rights of Third Parties) Act 1999, which came into force on that date. In outline, the Act provides that persons who are not party to a contract ('third parties') may enforce a term of the contract if either the contract expressly provides that they may do so, or if the term purports to confer a benefit on them, and the parties have not excluded the statutory provisions. As yet, there has not been any reported attempt to rely on the 1999 Act in this context, and many leases are so drafted as to expressly exclude the statutory provisions. However, it is theoretically possible that head landlords and subtenants could use the Act in these circumstances, provided that the lease or sublease in question does not include a term expressly excluding the operation of the 1999 Act. (See further Law Commission Report, 1996, No. 242, para. 2.11.)

11.4.6 Applying the rules—7 Trant Way

An example of the working of these rules is to be found at 7 Trant Way (see 11.1.6). In this situation, Mr Mount can enforce the tenant's covenants in the head lease against

Mr Norman, because there is privity of contract between them. There is, however, neither privity of contract nor privity of estate between Mr Mount and Mr Orion, or between Mr Mount and Miss Primrose, and so Mr Mount cannot take any action against either of the subtenants for breach of any of the positive covenants in the head lease.

Accordingly, should Mr Orion and Miss Primrose act in a manner inconsistent with these tenant covenants—for example, if they both allow the shops under their control to fall into a state of disrepair—Mr Mount will not be entitled to sue them directly for breach of those covenants. Instead, he is entitled to sue Mr Norman, on the basis of his obligation to control the actions of persons deriving title from him. Mr Norman should then take action against Mr Orion and Miss Primrose, enforcing the obligations to keep the property in a state of good repair that they owe to him under their subleases.

However, the position would be different if the covenant breached were a *restrictive* covenant—if, for example, Mr Orion and Miss Primrose were both keeping pets in breach of the covenant not to keep animals on the property. In such a case, Mr Mount would be able to directly sue them, either under the special rules in *Tulk v Moxhay* (1848) 2 Ph 774 or—since the head lease is a new lease—under s. 3(5) of the 1995 Act.

Since the subleases do not contain express terms excluding the operation of the 1999 Act, it is also theoretically possible that Mr Mount may try to enforce the covenants in the sublease against the subtenants, instead of enforcing the covenants in the head lease to which he is a party. He may argue that he is entitled to directly enforce the covenants in the sublease, on the grounds that the subleases purport to confer a benefit on a party in his position. A parallel argument may be available to Mr Orion and Miss Primrose, if they wish to directly enforce the covenants in the headlease against Mr Mount.

FURTHER READING

'Touching and concerning'
Smith, *Property Law*, 8th edn., Pearson Longman, 2014, pp. 441–4.

1995 Act
Davey, 'Privity of Contract and Leases—Reform at Last' (1996) 59 MLR 78.
Walter, 'The Landlord and Tenant (Covenants) Act 1995: A Legislative Folly' [1996] Conv 432.
Williamson, 'The best way to deal with a nasty surprise' [2006] EG–4 February 2006 (No. 0605) (overriding leases).
Clarke, '20 years on—the 1995 Act' [2015] Conv 191.

Contracts (Rights of Third Parties) Act 1999
Elias, 'Third party benefits' [1999] EG (No. 9913) 117.

You can visit the online resources to test your knowledge of this chapter with self-test questions at **www.oup.com/he/nair19e/**.

12

Remedies for breach of leasehold covenants

12.1 General contractual remedies 281
12.2 Tenant's remedies against a defaulting landlord 284
12.3 Landlord's remedy of distress 285
12.4 Landlord's remedy of forfeiture 287

The previous two chapters considered the typical covenants that may be contained in a lease, and how the rights and duties arising from them may pass to assignees of the lease and the reversion. This chapter covers what happens if some of these covenants are breached. It deals first with general contractual remedies, which are available for breaches of leasehold covenants as they are for any other breach of contract. It then considers in more detail some special remedies that are peculiar to leases. Tenants have certain statutory protections against defaulting landlords, in addition to their contractual remedies (12.2). Meanwhile, landlords have certain distinctive remedies for breach of covenant that have been heavily regulated by statute. The power to confiscate a defaulting tenant's goods ('**distress**') is discussed at 12.3, and the power to bring the lease to an end and to evict the tenant ('forfeiture') is discussed at 12.4.

12.1 General contractual remedies

Where a party to a lease is in breach of covenant, the usual contractual remedies are available to the other party. Thus, for example, either landlord or tenant may seek specific performance of a covenant by the other party to repair. Similarly, if a tenant uses the premises to run a business, contrary to a covenant to use the premises only as a dwelling, the landlord could seek an injunction to restrain the continuing breach. Further, either party might decide to claim damages for breach of contract as an alternative or additional remedy. Finally, since *Hussein v Mehlman* [1992] 2 EGLR 87 (see 9.6.1.2), the possibility of acceptance of repudiatory breach as a way of terminating the lease should also be borne in mind as a possible response to a breach of covenant by either landlord or tenant.

Further information on contractual remedies is available in any standard textbook on the law of contract. There are, however, some important decisions on the specific enforcement of certain covenants in leases, which are covered here.

12.1.1 'Keep-open' covenants and specific performance

If you think of your local shopping precinct, you may see that one store, perhaps a grocery supermarket, is clearly a major attraction, bringing customers to the area and thus providing passing trade for other smaller shops in the precinct. In recognition of this fact, the landlords of such shopping areas may require the tenants of the major store to enter into a 'keep-open' covenant, i.e., to covenant that they will continue to trade in the premises leased to them for the period of their lease, or, if they no longer wish to carry on business there, until they have assigned or sublet the property with their landlord's consent.

It had always been thought that such covenants were not enforceable by an order for specific performance. This was because such an order, compelling the tenant to carry on business, would involve the court in supervising the way in which this was done, a role which the court is not willing to undertake. However, to everyone's surprise, an order of specific performance of such a covenant was granted by the Court of Appeal in *Co-operative Insurance Society Ltd v Argyll Stores (Holdings) Ltd* [1996] Ch 286. Thus Argyll Stores, which had closed its Safeways store in Hillsborough shopping centre in breach of its keep-open covenant, was required to continue to trade there until the end of the lease in 2014, or until it could assign or sublet the premises with its landlord's consent.

The Court of Appeal's decision was, however, reversed by the House of Lords in *Co-operative Insurance Society Ltd v Argyll Stores (Holdings) Ltd* [1998] AC 1. Lord Hoffmann, in a speech adopted by the other Law Lords, gave a number of reasons for holding that it was inappropriate to compel a defendant to carry on a business; while none of the reasons would necessarily be sufficient on its own, he said (at p. 16), that the cumulative effect seemed to show that the settled practice of refusing to order specific performance of such an obligation is based upon sound sense. Those reasons included: the difficulty of defining precisely what the defendant was required to do; the hardship caused to him by requiring him to carry on a loss-making business; the perpetuation of conflict between the parties who were required to continue in a hostile relationship; and the need for continuing supervision by the court.

In terms of the principles governing the grant of specific performance, possibly the most significant of the reasons discussed by Lord Hoffmann relates to the need for continuing supervision. The suggestion that performance will require supervision by the court has often been given as a reason for refusing the order, because the court has no mechanisms by which it can ensure such supervision. Lord Hoffman's speech helpfully clarifies what is meant by 'continued supervision': not that the judge or some court official actually supervises ongoing performance, but that any failure to perform entitles the aggrieved party to return to court seeking the defendant's committal for contempt. An order to carry on an activity, such as a business, over an extended period of time, would give rise to the possibility of repeated applications to the court, alleging incidents of non-compliance. It would thus be expensive both to the parties and to the resources of the judicial system. A clean break, with the payment of damages for breach, would be a far better solution.

By contrast, an order to achieve a defined result, such as to repair property, does not involve the court in ongoing supervision. Provided the required outcome could be defined sufficiently precisely when the order was made, the court would, at most, have to decide on one further application whether the work had been done to a satisfactory standard, i.e., whether the desired result had been achieved. As you will see (12.1.2.2), this distinction between carrying on an activity and achieving a required result has

12.1.2 Repairing covenants and specific performance

Although this text does not deal in any detail with repairing covenants, you should be aware that either party to the lease may be subject to an obligation to repair, either by express agreement or under certain covenants implied by common law or statute (see 10.4.1). In considering remedies for breach of such covenants, we need to note first some special statutory provisions which protect the tenant, and then case law developments which have made the remedy of specific performance available against both landlord and tenant.

12.1.2.1 Leasehold Property (Repairs) Act 1938

The background to this Act is to be found in the activities of property speculators, who would buy tenanted property in a poor state of repair at a low price, with a view to enforcing the tenants' repairing covenants and evicting them (by forfeiture proceedings) if they were unable to carry out the repairs. The Act applies to leases of not less than seven years, with at least three years left to run, and provides that proceedings to recover damages or to forfeit the lease for failure to repair may be brought only with leave of the court. Such leave is to be given only on specified grounds, which in general involve satisfying the court that the landlord has a valid reason for requiring repairs to be done immediately rather than at the end of the lease (e.g., that lack of repair is injurious to other occupiers of the property, or that leaving the repairs until later will substantially increase their cost).

12.1.2.2 Specific performance of repairing covenants

It used to be thought, on the supposed authority of *Hill v Barclay* (1810) 16 Ves Jun 402, that specific performance of a covenant to repair was not available against either a landlord or a tenant. Several reasons were suggested for this rule, including the problem of continued supervision by the court, as discussed in connection with the *Argyll* case.

Where the landlord was in breach of a repairing obligation, therefore, the tenant's only remedy was to do the repairs, and then recover the cost from the landlord, either by withholding rent (*Lee Parker v Izzet* [1971] 1 WLR 1688) or by suing for damages for breach of covenant. More recently (see 9.6.1.2), if the breach is sufficiently serious, the tenant may regard it as repudiatory and treat the contract as discharged, freeing the tenant from further obligation but at the same time retaining the right to seek damages for breach.

Where it was the tenant who was in breach, the landlord could seek damages or forfeiture, subject of course to the provisions of the Leasehold Property (Repairs) Act 1938.

1. Specific performance against a landlord

The first change to the old approach is to be found in *Jeune v Queen's Cross Properties Ltd* [1974] Ch 97, where a landlord who had covenanted to maintain and repair the structure of a block of flats was ordered to reconstruct an exterior balcony which had collapsed. The balcony did not form part of the property leased to any of the plaintiff tenants; since they did not have possession of it, they would have had difficulty in following the usual route of doing the repairs and recovering the cost from the landlord.

The court reviewed the supposed authority of *Hill v Barclay* (1810) 16 Ves Jun 402, and considered that it did not preclude the grant of an order of specific performance against a landlord in breach of a repairing covenant. Statutory power to order specific performance of a landlord's repairing covenants is now to be found in the Landlord and Tenant Act 1985, s. 17, replacing the Housing Act 1974, s. 125.

2. Specific performance against a tenant

In *Jeune v Queen's Cross Properties Ltd*, *Hill v Barclay* was said in *obiter dicta* to be an authority for the proposition that specific performance of a repairing covenant could not be awarded against a tenant. However, some 25 years later such an award was made in a first-instance decision: *Rainbow Estates Ltd v Tokenhold Ltd* [1999] Ch 64. The facts of the case were unusual, in that the original landlord who granted the lease was a company controlled by the individuals to whom the lease was granted, and, possibly in consequence of this, there was no provision either for forfeiture for breach of covenant or for the landlord to enter and do repairs if the tenant failed to do so. The property was a listed building, in a serious state of disrepair; if the current landlords were not able to obtain specific performance of the tenants' repairing covenant, there was no way in which they could effect repairs until the lease ended in some six years' time. In these circumstances the judge considered it appropriate to grant an order against the tenants for specific performance of their repairing obligations.

In doing so, he reviewed the reasons which used to be given for refusing specific performance to either landlord or tenant, and concluded that today 'there is little or no life in these reasons' (at p. 69). In particular, the supposed need for continued supervision by the court was no longer seen as a problem. An order to repair was an order to achieve a specified result, rather than to carry on an activity, and so, on the distinction drawn in the *Argyll* case (see 12.1.1), need not involve repeated applications to the court.

A further point which the judge had to consider was that the remedy of specific performance does not fall within the provisions of the Leasehold Property (Repairs) Act 1938. In consequence, a landlord would not need to obtain leave from the court before seeking this remedy (as he would have to do if seeking damages or forfeiture), and applications for specific performance could therefore be used to harass or oppress a tenant. In the judge's view, it would not be right to extend the Act by judicial interpretation to cover applications for specific performance, but the court would take care to ensure that such applications were not used to bring about the mischief which the Act was designed to remedy. An order for specific performance against a tenant was likely to be appropriate only in rare cases, but:

> subject to the overriding need to avoid injustice or oppression, the remedy should be available when damages are not an adequate remedy (p. 73).

12.2 Tenant's remedies against a defaulting landlord

As we have seen, the tenant has all the usual contractual remedies against the landlord in case of breach. In addition, there are various statutory provisions which give the tenant additional protection against harassment or eviction, and offer alternative ways of ensuring that the landlord complies with his repairing obligations.

12.2.1 Harassment or eviction

A landlord who treats a tenant in a manner calculated to drive that tenant out of residential accommodation is in breach of the covenant of quiet enjoyment (see 10.2.1); in addition, such treatment may also amount to the criminal offence of harassment. This offence is committed where acts are done which are likely to interfere with the tenant's peace or comfort or where services, reasonably required for occupation of the premises as a residence, are withdrawn (Protection from Eviction Act 1977, s. 1(3) and (3A)). Only the local authority may institute proceedings for this offence, and the original provisions gave no real assistance to the tenant who wished to obtain a remedy in civil proceedings. However, the Housing Act 1988, s. 27, also provides a tenant who is a residential occupier with a statutory cause of action, should he be evicted by his landlord. The ingredients of this tort are the same as those of the criminal offence under the Protection from Eviction Act 1977 but it is not necessary for a criminal conviction to have been obtained before the tenant brings his action. In addition to this statutory claim, the tenant may also be able to found an action upon trespass, nuisance or even, if appropriate, assault, as well of course as on breach of contract.

12.2.2 Landlord's failure to repair

We have already considered the tenant's contractual remedies for the landlord's breach of a covenant to repair (10.2.4). However, it may be that a tenant wants to avoid a direct confrontation in the courts with the landlord (possibly because the tenant cannot afford the legal costs) and yet wants to ensure that repairs to the property are made. You should therefore be aware that failure to repair can, in some circumstances, be dealt with by the local authority, under statutory powers contained in the Housing Act 1985, Pt VI; in some cases, therefore, a tenant may be able to seek the assistance of the local authority. These statutory provisions are, however, only of assistance when the defects are serious in nature.

12.3 Landlord's remedy of distress

When the tenant fails to pay rent, the landlord may sue to recover it as a debt or may take the more extreme measure of bringing the lease to an end by forfeiture (12.4). One of the other traditional landlord remedies was the self-help remedy of distress, which allowed a landlord to enter the premises to seize goods belonging to the tenant (either personally or by using a bailiff) and then to sell them and keep the proceeds towards the unpaid rent.

12.3.1 The need for reform

Distress was a popular remedy with landlords, who regarded it as a quick and inexpensive way of recovering rent arrears without court proceedings and as a deterrent to future non-payment of rent. Although certain goods were protected against seizure (such as clothing, basic household equipment, and tools of the tenant's trade), the use of this remedy could cause considerable hardship to the tenant. The landlord's right to distrain arose the day after the rent became due and could be used without giving any notice to the tenant. The goods could be sold soon after their seizure by auction and rarely produced a good price, leaving the tenant deprived of the goods and still in debt to the landlord.

The operation of this remedy was reviewed and criticised, as being out of date and unfair to the tenant, on a number of occasions from the mid-1960s onwards. The enactment of the Human Rights Act 1998 provided additional reasons for seeking reform. The law of distress allowed the landlord to enter premises (very often the home of the tenant) without permission or warning, and to deprive the tenant of property without consideration of the matter by a court. There were concerns that distress, like other self-help remedies such as peaceful re-entry by a landlord without a court order or by a mortgagee (see 12.4.4.1 and 22.7.2) might prove to be a breach of rights guaranteed under the European Convention on Human Rights, such as those to a fair trial (Art. 6), to respect for private and family life and the home (Art. 8), and to the peaceful enjoyment of possessions (Art. 1 of the First Protocol) (see 2.9).

In *Fuller v Happy Shopper Markets Ltd* [2001] 2 EGLR 32 at p. 36 Lightman J warned landlords of the dangers involved in levying distress:

> The ancient (and perhaps anachronistic) self-help remedy of distress involves a serious interference with the right of the tenant, under Article 8 of the European Convention on Human Rights, to respect for his privacy and home, and, under Article 1 of the First Protocol, to the peaceful enjoyment of his possessions. The human rights implications of levying distress must be in the forefront of the mind of the landlord before he takes this step, and he must fully satisfy himself that taking this action is in accordance with the law.

12.3.2 Abolition of distress

Following a consultation by the Lord Chancellor's Department in May 2001 (*Enforcement Review Consultation Paper No. 5: Distress for Rent*), the Tribunals, Courts and Enforcement Act 2007, Part 3 and Sch. 12 made provision for the reform of the law of distress. After considerable delay, these provisions were brought into force on 6 April 2014. The new scheme:

- abolished the common law remedy of distress;
- prevents landlords of *residential* property from seizing tenants' goods for non-payment of rent;
- provides landlords of *commercial* property with a new statutory procedure known as 'commercial rent arrears recovery' (or 'CRAR').

Details of the new procedure are set out in the Taking Control of Goods Regulations 2012.

12.3.2.1 CRAR

Under CRAR, landlords of commercial property can still take and sell tenants' goods. However, there are new safeguards for tenants (including a requirement for seven days' notice) and the procedure is subject to supervision by the courts.

12.3.2.2 Resolution of human rights concerns

Does the new legislation address the human rights concerns mentioned in *Fuller v Happy Shopper Markets Ltd* [2001] 2 EGLR 32? It seems that the answer is almost certainly, 'yes'. First of all, the availability of the self-help remedy of distress is altogether removed in the case of residential property. Thus, the reform of the old law does away with any threat to 'home and family life', under Article 8.

In the case of commercial premises, the new CRAR remedy is available but protection is afforded to the tenant by the requirement to give seven days' notice of the landlord's intention to use this remedy. This would allow a commercial tenant to apply to the court, if the use of the remedy were opposed for any reason. This enables judicial control to be imposed, should the tenant consider that the proposed use of CRAR is an improper interference with his or her rights in relation to possessions at the premises (Protocol 1, Article 1, right to peaceful enjoyment of possessions).

While no doubt specific issues relating to the use of the CRAR regime will arise as time passes, the new rules thus appear to meet the past criticisms of the old law of distress. In practice, however, the requirement to give notice to the tenant may cause difficulties for the landlord because seven days may allow a wary tenant plenty of time to remove any valuable possessions from the premises or even to dispose of them. The change is, therefore, not one that has been welcomed by commercial landlords.

12.4 Landlord's remedy of forfeiture

A landlord may, in some circumstances, respond to a tenant's breach of a covenant by bringing the lease to a premature end, and recovering possession of the land from the tenant. This remedy is known as *'forfeiture'* of the lease. Its effects on the tenant and those who derive rights from the tenant can be draconian, and so its operation has been carefully monitored by the courts and heavily regulated by statute. This section addresses the following topics:

- Does the landlord have a right to forfeit the lease? (12.4.1)
- What must the landlord do before forfeiture for breaches other than non-payment of rent? (12.4.2)
- What must the landlord do before forfeiture for non-payment of rent? (12.4.3)
- How does the landlord forfeit the lease? (12.4.4)
- Can there be any relief against forfeiture? (12.4.5)
- What is the effect of forfeiture on holders of derivative interests? (12.4.6)
- Application of forfeiture and relief rules to tenancies in Trant Way (12.4.7)
- Reform of law of forfeiture (12.4.8)

12.4.1 Does the landlord have a right to forfeit the lease?

The right to forfeit a lease is not an automatic remedy, available to all landlords for all breaches by a tenant. It will only arise if:

- there is a provision in the lease permitting 're-entry' in the event of breach; and
- the landlord has not waived the breach of covenant.

12.4.1.1 Provision for re-entry

A right of re-entry is a right to recover possession of land if certain conditions are met. In the case of a lease, there are two ways in which a landlord may reserve such a right.

First, the lease may describe certain obligations of the tenant as *'conditions'*; where a tenant's obligation is labelled as a condition, the landlord has an automatic right to re-enter if that obligation is breached (see 10.1.4). Where the obligation is phrased as a *covenant*, however, the remedy of forfeiture for breach of that obligation will be available only if there is a specific provision in the lease authorising forfeiture for breach of that covenant. An example of a typical clause is given in cl. 5(a) at Form 10.1 in 10.1.3.

12.4.1.2 Waiver of breach

Where a lease gives the landlord a right of re-entry for breach of a particular obligation, and a breach of that obligation has taken place, the landlord will have an immediate right to forfeiture. However, this right can be lost if the landlord can be shown to have waived the breach: that is, if the landlord has said that the lease should continue despite the breach, or has acted in a way that suggests he or she means the lease to continue. Waiver may be express (e.g., as where the landlord tells the tenant that a particular breach will be ignored) or may be implied from conduct.

1. Implied waiver

Implied waiver may cause difficulties to landlords, since they may be taken to have waived breaches when they did not intend to do so. For a waiver to be implied the landlord must first know that a breach has occurred and thereafter have acted in a way that treats the lease as still continuing. The most common instance of waiver occurs where the landlord claims or accepts rent from the tenant, in the knowledge that a breach has occurred (*Segal Securities Ltd v Thoseby* [1963] 1 QB 887). However, in the recent case of *Faiz v Burnley BC* [2021] EWCA Civ 55, the Court of Appeal decided that a landlord will not be treated as having waived a breach merely because they have demanded, or accepted, a payment of rent after finding out about the breach. What matters is whether they have demanded or accepted a payment that only became due *after* the breach—that is, could only have become due if the lease continued to exist past the date of breach—and if they knew this at the time of the demand or acceptance. Lewison LJ said (at [28]):

> It does not matter whether the rent accrued due before or after the date of the landlord's knowledge; but whether it accrued due before or after the date of the breach of which the landlord (now) has knowledge.

Other acts that treat the lease as continuing will also qualify as instances of implied waiver (*Ward v Day* (1864) 5 B & S 359). However, as Slade LJ in *Expert Clothing Service and Sales Ltd v Hillgate House* [1986] 1 Ch 340 at p. 360 emphasised, where some act other than the acceptance of rent is in question:

> the court is . . . free to look at all the circumstances of the case to consider whether the act . . . relied on [as constituting waiver is] so unequivocal that, when considered objectively, it could only be regarded as having been done consistently with the continued operation of a tenancy . . .

Waiver by demand or acceptance of rent may cause problems for the landlord because landlords may be bound by the actions or knowledge of their agents. Thus, if the landlord's agent accepts rent that fell due after a breach at a date at which the landlord knows of a breach, this amounts to waiver. Of course, where the breach of covenant in question is a failure to pay rent, making the formal demand which may be a necessary step in forfeiture proceedings (see 12.4.2.1) will not constitute waiver.

You may wonder what happens these days when so many payments are made automatically by standing order or direct debit, and come into the creditor's account without any action on his part. This point was noted briefly by the Court of Appeal in *Thomas v Ken Thomas Ltd* [2007] 1 EGLR 31, in which Neuberger LJ quoted with approval the statement in *Woodfall on Landlord and Tenant,* 2006, vol. 1 at para. 17.098 that:

> It is considered that where the rent is paid directly into the landlord's bank account (e.g., by banker's order) it is not accepted if the landlord rejects the payment or repays it as quickly as possible.

2. Effect of waiver: 'once and for all' and continuing breaches

In considering the effect of a waiver, it is helpful to distinguish between these two types of breach. For example, a covenant to develop property by a fixed date is breached 'once and for all' if development is not completed by that date. Waiver will entirely deprive the landlord of his right to forfeit for breach of that covenant. By contrast, breach of a covenant to keep property in repair continues throughout the whole period of disrepair. If the property remains unrepaired after the waiver, and beyond the time during which the landlord knew the breach would continue, a fresh right to forfeit will arise, unaffected by the previous waiver (*Segal Securities Ltd v Thoseby* [1963] 1 QB 887).

12.4.2 Forfeiture for breach of non-rent covenants: s. 146 LPA 1925

Forfeiture for breach of covenants other than that to pay rent is governed by LPA 1925, s. 146. The section imposes a requirement upon the landlord to serve notice on the tenant in a prescribed form before the right to forfeit the lease can be exercised. The aim is to give a tenant a chance to remedy the problem before the ultimate sanction of forfeiture is imposed. If the notice is not served, or is not served in the proper form, the landlord has no right of forfeiture and cannot get an order for possession against the tenant.

12.4.2.1 Form of the s. 146 notice

The s. 146 notice must:

(a) specify the breach;

(b) require that the breach be remedied, if it is remediable; and

(c) require the tenant to pay financial compensation for the breach.

Item (a) must be contained in all notices; item (c) need not be included if the landlord does not require financial compensation (*Lock v Pearce* [1893] 2 Ch 271). It is item (b), requiring the breach to be remedied, which has given rise to considerable problems of interpretation.

The landlord is required to ask for the breach to be remedied only if it is 'capable of remedy'. If the breach is of a kind that cannot be remedied, it is enough for the notice to specify the breach; the landlord may then proceed to forfeit the lease. In order to adopt this approach, however, the landlord must know which breaches a court will consider to be incapable of being remedied; if the landlord serves a notice that does not include any demand to remedy the breach, and a court subsequently considers that the breach could have been remedied, the notice will be invalid and the landlord will not be able to proceed to forfeiture.

12.4.2.2 Breaches that are not capable of remedy

As Harman J commented in *Hoffmann v Fineberg* [1949] Ch 245 at p. 253:

> in one sense, no breach can ever be remedied because there must always . . . be a time in which there has not been compliance with the covenant.

However, s. 146 clearly contemplates that there are some breaches of covenant that are capable of being remedied, which the landlord must give the tenant a chance to remedy before exercising the right of forfeiture. The courts, therefore, have sought to identify when a breach is of a kind that cannot be remedied for these purposes.

In the early case law, the courts attempted to define certain types of breach as intrinsically incapable of being remedied. It was suggested that breaches of positive covenants could be remedied but that breaches of negative covenants could not, or that continuing breaches could be remedied but 'once and for all' breaches could not. However, in *Expert Clothing Service & Sales Ltd v Hillgate House Ltd* [1986] 1 Ch 340, the Court of Appeal held that the important question was whether the *harm* to the landlord could be remedied.

In that case, the tenants had breached two covenants: (a) to give notice to the landlord of any charge created over the property and (b) to reconstruct the premises for occupation by a stated date, or as soon as possible thereafter. The tenant charged the premises without giving notice, and allowed the specified date to pass without making the reconstruction. The landlord served a notice under LPA 1925, s. 146, which complained of the two breaches but did not require them to be remedied, and in subsequent court proceedings was granted an order for possession. On appeal, the Court of Appeal held that both of these breaches were remediable; accordingly the landlord's notice was invalid, and it was not entitled to possession.

In giving judgment, Slade LJ emphasised (at p. 358) that the principal object of s. 146 is to give the tenant the opportunity to remedy the breach:

> An important purpose of the s. 146 procedure is to give even tenants who have hitherto lacked the will or the means to comply with their obligations one last chance . . . before the landlord re-enters.

In considering whether a breach was remediable, the court should focus on the harm that had been done to the landlord and on whether that harm could be remedied. The test was said (at p. 358) to be whether compliance with the covenant (albeit late), together with financial compensation, would:

> have effectively remedied the harm which the lessors had suffered or were likely to suffer from the breach.

In other words, emphasis shifts from attempting to remedy the breach (by 'undoing' it or trying to put the clock back to the situation before breach) to remedying the harm that that breach has caused.

In certain cases, compliance plus compensation would not be enough to remedy the harm caused by the breach, and in these cases the breach would be irremediable.

12.4 Landlord's remedy of forfeiture

However, in *Expert Clothing Service & Sales Ltd* itself, any damage caused by breach of the covenants was capable of being remedied by the late performance coupled if necessary with compensation.

1. Positive and negative covenants

At first instance in *Rugby School (Governors) v Tannahill* [1934] 1 KB 695 at p. 701, MacKinnon J had also suggested that breach of a positive covenant could be remedied, but breach of a negative one could not:

> A promise to do a thing, if broken, can be remedied by the thing being done. But breach of a promise not to do a thing cannot in any true sense be remedied; that which was done cannot be undone.

However, *obiter dicta* in the Court of Appeal's judgment in the same case ([1935] 1 KB 87 at pp. 90–1) cast some doubt on this proposition, and suggested that in some cases—although not in the one before the court—breaches of a negative covenant might be remedied by immediately ceasing the activity prohibited by the covenant and giving an undertaking against further breach.

In *obiter dicta* in *Expert Clothing Service & Sales Ltd v Hillgate House Ltd* [1986] 1 Ch 340, the Court of Appeal suggested that even negative covenants are very often capable of remedy by compliance, by ceasing to do the act complained of. For instance, if a covenant has been broken by the erection of window boxes, the tenant can remedy the harm by removing the boxes and paying for the repair of any damage done.

Some 10 years later, this approach to the question of remediability was applied by the Court of Appeal in *Savva v Hussein* (1997) 73 P&CR 150. The landlord had treated the breach of negative covenants (not to put up signs or alter the premises without the landlord's consent) as being irremediable. The court referred with approval to the approach adopted in *Expert Clothing Service & Sales Ltd v Hillgate House Ltd*, stating that the question posed there in relation to positive covenants was equally relevant to negative covenants. There was nothing in the statute or in logic that required the courts to differentiate between these two forms of covenant. The court accepted that it was established law that breach of a covenant not to assign without the landlord's consent could not be remedied—citing *Scala House and District Property Co. Ltd v Forbes* [1974] QB 575—but was of the opinion that failure to seek consent for other actions did not, by itself, make the breach irremediable. There was a remedy if the mischief caused by the breach could be removed. In the present case, removing the signs or restoring the property to its original condition would have remedied the breaches, and the landlord's failure to require the tenant to remedy his breaches made the s. 146 notice invalid.

2. Continuing breaches and 'once and for all' breaches

In *Rugby School (Governors) v Tannahill*, the Court of Appeal suggested, in *obiter dicta*, that a 'once and for all' breach of covenant—a covenant that is breached on the occurrence of some event—is incapable of being remedied. For example, a positive covenant to make alterations to a building by a prescribed date was broken once and for all when the work was not done by that date; a negative covenant against making alterations to the property without the landlord's consent was broken once and for all when the alterations were made without that consent. In the court's view, such breaches could not be remedied; the breach had occurred on a given event in the past, and there was no way in which the tenant could rewrite history to make it appear that it had not. This approach, however, cannot survive the decisions in *Expert Clothing Service & Sales Ltd v*

Hillgate House Ltd and *Savva v Hussein* (1997) 73 P&CR 150. In both decisions, the Court of Appeal is explicit that certain once and for all breaches—such as failures to seek consent for certain actions or failures to complete some promised action by a particular date—are capable of remedy within the meaning of s. 146, provided that the harm inflicted on the landlord can be remedied.

3. Breaches causing irremediable harm

Following these two modern decisions of the Court of Appeal, it now appears that most breaches of covenant can be remedied. However, there are still certain breaches that continue to be regarded as irremediable. A number of earlier decisions regarded the use of premises for immoral purposes (*Rugby School (Governors) v Tannahill* [1935] 1 KB 87) or for gambling (*Hoffmann v Fineberg* [1949] Ch 245) as irremediable breaches of covenant, because the improper use would cast a stigma on the premises, which could not be removed by merely ceasing the use or paying compensation. (Note, however, that in *Glass v Kencakes Ltd* [1966] 1 QB 611 the tenant was held to have remedied his breach when he forfeited the sublease of his subtenant, who had used the premises for immoral purposes.) In more recent cases, breach has been held to be irremediable where the premises were used for the sale of pornographic material (*Dunraven Securities v Holloway* (1982) 264 EG 709), or for activities in breach of the Official Secrets Acts (*Van Haarlem v Kasner* (1992) 64 P&CR 214).

Although it is important to remember that social changes may make some activities less injurious to the property than they might have been formerly, it seems clear that breaches which in modern times would be seen as casting a stigma on the property would not satisfy the *Expert Clothing* test, and would therefore still be regarded as irremediable.

Other examples of breaches that cause irremediable harm to the landlord may be found in various hypothetical cases considered by the Court of Appeal in *Expert Clothing*. They include: breach of covenant to insure against fire, which would be irremediable after the property had burned down; and failure to alter or repair property where there is insufficient time to complete the work required before the end of the lease.

4. Breach of covenant against assignment

These examples of irremediable breach are all consistent with the modern principle that a breach is remediable if the harm caused to the landlord can be remedied. However there is one further example that is not consistent with that principle: the breach of a covenant against assigning, etc. cannot be remedied even if the harm caused to the landlord could be undone. On this point the Court of Appeal continues to regard itself as bound by its earlier decision in *Scala House & District Property Co Ltd v Forbes* [1974] QB 575 (see *Expert Clothing Service and Sales v Hillgate House* [1986] 1 Ch 340 at p. 363; and *Savva v Hussein* (1997) 73 P&CR 150 at p. 154).

The matter was considered yet again by the Court of Appeal in *Akici v LR Butlin Ltd* [2006] 1 WLR 201. In this case the tenant was in breach of a covenant against sharing possession of the premises and at first instance the judge considered himself bound by *Scala* to hold that the breach was not capable of remedy. In the Court of Appeal, Neuberger LJ referred disparagingly to the *Scala* decision, describing it as 'demonstrably fallacious and inconsistent with common sense' (para. 74). If the matter had been free from authority, he would be attracted to the view that breaches of covenants against assigning and subletting could be remedied by reassignment or surrender of the sublease. The judge accepted that the present court was bound by its earlier decision, but regarded it as applying only to transactions in breach of covenant which created or transferred a legal interest (i.e., to assignments and subleases; and, he suggested, also to mortgages granted in breach of covenants requiring the landlord's consent (para. 67)).

There was, however, no need to extend the rule, and he considered that a breach of a covenant against sharing or parting with possession fell outside the terms of *Scala* and was capable of being remedied (para. 73). Observations to the contrary by Slade LJ in *Expert Clothing* were dismissed as being *obiter dicta* (para. 75).

You may like to note that these observations on the scope of *Scala* are themselves *obiter dicta*, since the decision of the Court of Appeal in favour of the tenant was based not on whether the breach could be remedied but on the invalidity of the landlord's s. 146 notice on other grounds (because it had failed to specify the breach accurately).

12.4.2.3 Effect of serving the s. 146 notice

The effect of a valid s. 146 notice depends on whether it asks the tenant to remedy the breach. If the landlord is not asking for the breach to be remedied, the tenant must be given a reasonable (albeit short) time in which to consider the position before the landlord takes any further steps to forfeit the lease (*Horsey Estate Ltd v Steiger* [1899] 2 QB 79 at p. 91). If the notice does require the tenant to remedy the breach, the landlord must give the tenant a reasonable time in which to do so.

Obviously, some breaches may be swiftly remedied, while others may take some time. Where a reasonable time has elapsed without remedial action by the tenant, the landlord may proceed to forfeit the lease. If the tenant acts on the notice, remedying the breach and paying any compensation required, the matter is at an end and the landlord cannot take any further action. An unsatisfactory aspect of this, from the landlord's point of view, is that the landlord cannot be rid of an unsatisfactory tenant, who commits repeated breaches of covenant but always remedies them at the last moment.

12.4.3 Forfeiture for non-payment of rent

The notice procedure under LPA 1925, s. 146, does not apply where the forfeiture is for non-payment of rent, since it is easier for a tenant to get relief against forfeiture (see 12.4.5.1) when a lease is being forfeited for breach of this particular covenant.

Unless the lease provides otherwise, a lease cannot be forfeited for non-payment of rent unless the landlord has first made a *formal demand* for the rent: that is a demand at the demised premises between the hours of sunrise and sunset on the day on which payment is due (see *Duppa v Mayo* (1669) Saund 282 at p. 287 n. 16).

However, this is usually rendered unnecessary by a clause in the lease which specifies that the landlord may forfeit for non-payment of rent 'whether formally demanded or not' (see, for a typical example, cl. 5(a), at 10.1.3). In any event, s. 210 of the Common Law Procedure Act 1852 dispenses with the need for a formal demand in cases where the rent is at least half a year in arrears and the landlord cannot use CRAR to recover the arrears, either because the CRAR regime is not available or because there are insufficient goods on the premises to satisfy the debt in full (s. 210A of the Common Law Procedure Act 1852, as amended by the Tribunal, Courts and Enforcement Act 2007).

12.4.4 Methods of exercising the right to forfeiture

Traditionally there were two ways in which the landlord could end the lease and regain possession of the property:

- by self-help; or
- by seeking a court order for possession.

Both methods were available irrespective of the reason for forfeiture.

12.4.4.1 Self-help by physical re-entry

It used to be open to the landlord to forfeit the lease by taking possession of the premises; the lease automatically came to an end with the landlord's entry on the property. Today this right is considerably restricted. Under the Protection from Eviction Act 1977, s. 2, it cannot be used to forfeit leases of residential property. In cases where self-help is available, such as in leases of commercial property, the landlord must ensure that any such entry is peaceable and without force (Criminal Law Act 1977, s. 6).

In *Billson v Residential Apartments Ltd* [1992] 1 AC 494 the House of Lords accepted that this method of forfeiture still existed for commercial property, but was very critical of it, referring to the actions of the landlord as 'a dawn raid' (p. 540) and describing physical re-entry as a 'dubious and dangerous method of determining the lease' (p. 536). In addition, there are concerns that this process may infringe rights under the Human Rights Act 1998 by depriving the tenant of property (the estate in the land) without reference to a court.

12.4.4.2 Seeking an order for possession

The alternative and more acceptable method—the only method in respect of residential property today—is to obtain a court order for possession. It is important to note that even where the landlord chooses to regain possession by court order, the lease is regarded as being forfeited at the outset, by the commencement of court proceedings. Although the former tenant may in fact remain on the land for some considerable time, pending the court action and enforcement of any resulting order, he is no longer a tenant and the landlord cannot enforce any of the obligations in the lease against him during this period. A sum of money for use of the land during this period can be recovered, but technically this is not rent, but represents the 'mesne profits' payable by trespassers occupying land.

12.4.4.3 Statutory restrictions

Although the statutory protection of tenants is in general too detailed for this book (see 9.5.1), you should be aware that there are a number of provisions which regulate the operation of forfeiture procedures in relation to particular types of tenancies. An example, in respect of long leases of residential property, is to be found in ss. 168–9 of the Commonhold and Leasehold Reform Act 2002, which provides that a notice under s. 146 may not be served by the landlord, unless the tenant has admitted a breach of covenant or the fact that a breach has occurred has been determined by a leasehold valuation tribunal or in other court or arbitration proceedings.

12.4.5 Relief against forfeiture

Even when the landlord has taken steps to forfeit the lease, the tenant is entitled to seek relief from the court (i.e., to be allowed to keep his lease).

12.4.5.1 Relief where the tenant has failed to pay rent

In case of failure to pay rent, a tenant can have a statutory right, under the Common Law Procedure Act 1852 and the County Courts Act 1984, to stay proceedings by paying the rent due. This statutory framework is very complex, and its details are beyond the scope of this book. In addition, and at the discretion of the court, a tenant can obtain equitable relief against forfeiture for non-payment of rent. Usually, relief will be available on payment of the arrears of rent and any costs incurred by the landlord. However, the availability of relief is always discretionary, so that a court may refuse relief when it would be inequitable to do so: this may be the case where there have been unreasonable delays in applying for relief and a third party would be prejudiced (see, for example, the recent case of *Keshwala v Bhalsod* [2021] EWCA Civ 492, where there was an unexplained delay of several months and the landlord had re-let the property to a third party in the meantime).

12.4.5.2 Relief where the tenant has breached another covenant

In the case of breach of covenants other than that to pay rent, LPA 1925, s. 146(2) allows the tenant to apply to the court for relief. If the landlord has forfeited the lease by starting court proceedings, the tenant may seek relief at any time before the landlord actually re-enters the property. In *Billson v Residential Apartments Ltd* [1992] 1 AC 494, it was held that, where the landlord uses the self-help method of retaking possession without reference to the court, the tenant may still seek relief after that re-entry. However, as was explained in *Gibbs v Lakeside Developments Ltd* [2018] EWCA Civ 2874, such relief must be sought with 'reasonable promptitude'. In that case, the tenant sought relief 18 months after the re-entry, and this was held to be too late.

The tenant will usually obtain relief on remedying the breach. However, relief can also be available where the breach is technically irremediable (*Scala House & District Property Co. Ltd v Forbes* [1974] QB 575). In such cases, the court may need to weigh the harm caused to the landlord by the breach against the advantage gained by recovering the property. Thus, in *Van Haarlam v Kasner* (1992) 64 P&CR 214 the court considered that the value to the landlord of forfeiting a lease with some 80 years left to run was out of all proportion to the damage caused by the tenant's irremediable breach, and indicated that it would have been willing to grant relief had the question arisen.

12.4.6 Effect of forfeiture on holders of derivative interests

A number of people may hold interests derived from the lease, which will be lost if the lease itself is forfeited. Subtenants and mortgagees are both in this position and are entitled to seek relief against forfeiture. However, the landlord is not obliged to tell them that the tenant is in breach of covenant, and they may not find out about the impending forfeiture until a late stage of the proceedings. The law makes special provision to protect these parties. There may also be others with an interest in the lease—for example, a person with an option to purchase the leasehold estate—who currently have no protection from forfeiture.

12.4.6.1 Protection for subtenants

Under LPA 1925, s. 146(4), a subtenant may apply to the court for relief if the head lease from which the title is derived is forfeited. If relief is granted, the subtenant will become an immediate tenant of the head landlord, but for the period of the sublease, not for that of the head lease. The court may impose any conditions it sees fit upon the subtenant (e.g., compliance with covenants in the original head lease or payment of a higher rent—as in *London Diocesan Fund v Phithwa* [2005] 1 WLR 3956 (see 11.3.1.4)).

A similar provision in the County Courts Act 1984 (s. 138(9A)) enables the subtenant to seek relief within six months where the forfeiture is for non-payment of rent.

12.4.6.2 Protection for mortgagees

Relief against forfeiture may also be sought under s. 146(4) by a mortgagee who has lent money to a tenant on the security of a mortgage of the leasehold estate. If the landlord then forfeits the lease for breach of covenant, the mortgagee will lose its security and could suffer considerable financial loss. As you will see in Chapter 22, a mortgage of leasehold property is made by giving the mortgagee a sublease of the property, or a charge that gives the mortgagee the same rights as if the mortgage had been made by sublease. Accordingly, the mortgagee may seek relief from forfeiture in the same way as any other subtenant, and, if successful, will hold a lease directly from the landlord that it can use as security for its loan.

12.4.7 Application of the forfeiture and relief rules to tenancies at 7 Trant Way

You may recall from 11.1.6 that the current situation with regard to 7 Trant Way is as shown in Figure 12.1.

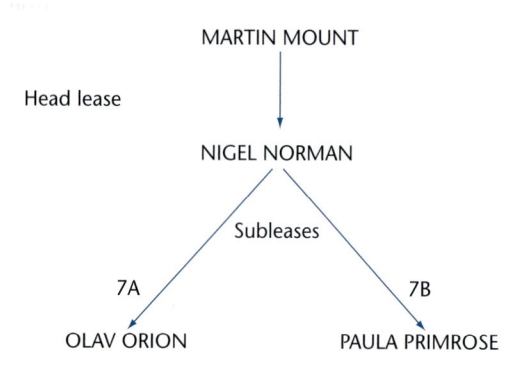

```
                    MARTIN MOUNT
                          |
        Head lease        |
                          ↓
                    NIGEL NORMAN
                      ╱        ╲
                 Subleases
               ╱                ╲
            7A                    7B
            ↓                     ↓
       OLAV ORION           PAULA PRIMROSE
```

Figure 12.1 Position at 7 Trant Way

The head lease and both subleases contain covenants, (a) against keeping animals on the property, and (b) to keep the premises in good repair. Both reserve a right of re-entry on the part of the landlords if these covenants are breached. Nigel Norman is also bound by a covenant to pay rent of £900 per month. For the last five months, Mr Norman has not paid his rent to Mr Mount, even though both the subtenants, Mr Orion and Miss Primrose, have been paying their rent regularly to Mr Norman. In addition, for the last three months Mr Orion has been stabling his daughter's pony in a shed at the back of the property. What can Mr Mount do to enforce the covenants?

12.4.7.1 Enforcement of covenant against keeping animals

As you have seen already (11.4), there is no privity of contract or estate between a head landlord and a subtenant, and generally they cannot take action directly against each other. However, the covenant against keeping animals is a negative one, restricting the use of the property, and therefore Mr Mount could proceed directly against Mr Orion, seeking an injunction to restrain the breach, under the *Tulk v Moxhay* doctrine described in Chapter 25.

Alternatively, or additionally, Mr Mount may wish to take action against his tenant, Mr Norman. Provided the operation of LPA 1925, s. 79, was not expressly excluded in the lease, Mr Norman will have covenanted on behalf of 'persons deriving title under him', and so will be liable for behaviour of his subtenant that is inconsistent with the terms of the covenant.

Since the lease gives Mr Mount a right of re-entry in the event of breach of this covenant, he has a right to forfeiture. Once he becomes aware of the breach, he should be careful to avoid any actions that might constitute a waiver of the breach (such as demanding rent from Mr Norman). He should serve a s. 146 notice on Mr Norman. It is likely that this breach will be regarded as remediable (see *Savva v Hussein* (1997) 73 P&CR 150) and so the notice should ask that the situation be remedied. After service of the notice, Mr Mount must allow Mr Norman a reasonable period within which to remedy the breach. On receipt of the s. 146 notice, Mr Norman would be well-advised to serve a similar notice on Mr Orion, who is himself in breach of a covenant in the sublease of 7A. The result will be either that Mr Orion ceases to keep the pony on the premises or that the sublease will be forfeited for the breach. Either result will have the effect of remedying the breach of the covenant in the head lease.

12.4.7.2 Forfeiture for non-payment of rent

The head lease contains the usual clause exempting the landlord from making a formal demand for the rent and also contains a clause allowing him to re-enter the premises if any covenant is broken. Accordingly, unless Mr Mount has in some manner waived the breach complained of, he may start proceedings against Mr Norman to forfeit the lease for the non-payment of the rent. (He cannot use the self-help remedy of physical re-entry, since the property is residential.) At or before the hearing, Mr Norman may ask for relief against forfeiture, and this will normally be granted as long as he pays the arrears of rent due and the costs of the action. In practice, the court will accept any offer of payment, as long as it is reasonable (e.g., by instalments over a prescribed period). If, however, Mr Norman cannot make a reasonable offer, the lease will be forfeited for breach of the covenant to pay rent.

12.4.7.3 Relief of subtenant

If, for any reason, the head lease is forfeited, Miss Primrose is placed in a difficult position. Although she has behaved perfectly properly, she is in danger of losing her own lease because it is dependent upon Mr Norman's head lease. Accordingly, Miss Primrose should apply for relief under LPA 1925, s. 146(4). As she is wholly innocent, it is very likely that, if Mr Norman's head lease is forfeited, Miss Primrose will be protected. If this happens, she will become a direct tenant of Mr Mount, for the period and upon the terms of her sublease but subject to any altered terms imposed by the court. If, however, Mr Norman manages to avoid forfeiture of the head lease, Miss Primrose has nothing to fear. As long as the head lease is valid the sublease will be safe, provided, of course, that Miss Primrose continues to observe the covenants in her own sublease.

12.4.8 Reform of the law of forfeiture of leases

It has long been accepted that the current rules about forfeiture of leases are in urgent need of reform. One defect in the present system is its complexity, arising from having different rules for covenants and conditions and for failure to pay rent and for other breaches of covenant. In addition, there are substantive defects that are unsatisfactory to both landlords and tenants.

12.4.8.1 Defects from the perspective of landlords

Aspects of the process that are unsatisfactory for landlords include:

- dangers of inadvertent waiver;
- inability to get rid of a tenant who persists in breaching covenants but always remedies the breach 'just in time';

- the fact that the lease ends when the landlord begins proceedings for forfeiture, so that the landlord is no longer entitled to rent or the performance of other obligations;
- the need to include clauses in leases providing for forfeiture and excluding the formal demand for rent.

12.4.8.2 Defects from the perspective of tenants

Aspects of the process that are unsatisfactory for the tenant include:

- the fact that the s. 146 notice is not required to give any details of the remedy required;
- the fact that forfeiture of a long lease may result in considerable loss of capital invested in its purchase;
- the lack of adequate protection for those with interests derived from the lease, other than subtenants and mortgagees.

12.4.8.3 Law Commission proposals for reform

For over 20 years now, the Law Commission has been putting forward proposals for reform of forfeiture, most recently in the report *Termination of Tenancies for Tenant Default*, 2006, Law Com No. 303 Cm 6946.

The 2006 Report recommends the complete abolition of the current law of forfeiture and its replacement with a statutory scheme for the 'termination of tenancies for tenant default' (a useful overview of which is given in Part 2 of the Report). The scheme would apply to all commercial leases and to residential leases for more than 21 years (shorter residential leases being in general protected by statutory provisions for security of tenure which are outside the scope of this book). Two methods of terminating a tenancy would be available to the landlord:

- making a 'termination claim' to the court; or
- using a 'summary termination process', which would not involve the court unless the tenant wished to do so.

The proposed scheme is designed to deal with all the defects in the current law. It thus covers the following issues:

- **Simplifying the law.** The new process would apply to all breaches of a tenant's obligations under the lease, whether imposed by covenant or condition; and there would no longer be any difference between procedures for non-payment of rent and for other breaches.
- **Improving the position of the landlord.** The concept of waiver of breach would have no place in the new scheme, and the lease would continue until the end of the termination proceedings, so that the landlord could continue to receive rent while taking steps to end the lease. Where a tenant repeatedly failed to observe obligations under the lease, the fact the current default had been remedied would not prevent the landlord from seeking termination.
- **Improving the position of the tenant.** Where the landlord required him or her to remedy a default, the tenant would be given details of what was required. Where the landlord sought to terminate the lease, the court would have power to make a range of alternative orders, including an order for sale of the property, as a result of which the tenant might be able to recover some of the capital invested in buying the lease.

- **Improving the position of derivative right-holders.** The scheme would recognise a wide category of interests derived from the lease, including not only subleases and mortgages, but also equitable charges, options, and rights to acquire an overriding lease under the Landlord and Tenant (Covenants) Act 1995 (see 11.2.1.3). The Report recommends that holders of these interests (to be known as 'qualifying interests') should have the same rights to information and protection as are given to the tenant himself under the proposed scheme.

There is, as yet, no indication of whether the recommendations of the Law Commission will be adopted. In 2015, the Government stated that it was still considering the proposals but no decision has yet been reached on their implementation. The Law Commission is now reviewing its original recommendations in this report, as part of a broader review of leasehold and commonhold that has been ongoing since 2019.

FURTHER READING

Specific performance

Luxton, 'Are You Being Served? Enforcing Keep-Open Covenants in Leases' [1998] 62 Conv 396.

Tettenborn, 'Absolving the Undeserving: Shopping Centres, Specific Performance and the Law of Contract' [1998] 62 Conv 23.

Protection from harassment

Cowan, 'Harassment, and Unlawful Eviction in the Private Rented Sector—A Study of Law in (-) action' [2001] 65 Conv 249 (research findings on effectiveness of Protection from Eviction Act).

Distress

Dale, Rivers, and Allen, 'Gently Does It' [2007] EG—6 October 2007 (No. 0740) 264 (an account of the new CRAR procedure).

Humphreys, 'Has CRAR Been Lost Forever?' [2009] EG—18 April 2009 (No. 0915) 96.

Karas and Maurici, 'The Human Rights Factor' [1999] EG—4 November 2006 (No. 9917) 126 (the human rights implications for distress and other self-help remedies).

Walton, 'Landlord's Distress—Past Its Sell By Date?' [2000] 64 Conv 508.

Forfeiture

Bridge, 'A Dinosaur Close to Extinction' [2006] EG—4 November 2006 (No. 0644) 187 (an account of the Law Commission's proposals by one of the commissioners).

Gravells, 'Forfeiture of Leases for Breach of Covenant: Pre-Action Notices and Remediability' [2006] JBL 830 (discusses *Akici v LR Butlin Ltd*, and some aspects of Law Commission Consultation Paper, 2004, No. 174).

Landlord and Tenant Law: Termination of Tenancies Bill, 1994, Law Com No. 221—Appendix C—defects in current law of forfeiture.

Termination of Tenancies for Tenant Default, 2006, Law Com No. 303 Cm 6946—see in particular paras. 1-7-1-12 (problems of the current law) and Part 2 (overview of proposed scheme).

You can visit the online resources to test your knowledge of this chapter with self-test questions at **www.oup.com/he/nair19e/**.

PART IV
Trusts

Introduction

This part of the book covers more complex forms of ownership, in which ownership at law is burdened by obligations arising in equity. This is the area of trusts, with which you may have some general familiarity from your other studies. If, however, you have never previously had occasion to consider the law of trusts, you may find it helpful to read an introductory book on trusts and equity before going on to consider the special rules relating to trusts which have an estate or interest in land as the trust property.

Chapter 13 contains introductory material, plus an account of how trusts arise. An explanation of the 'trust of land', which is the modern type of trust used for trusts of land, is in Chapter 14.

In Chapter 15 you will find a short note about the Settled Land Act settlement, the other form of trust which still exists in relation to land, and in Chapter 16 there is a very brief account of the 'rule against perpetuities'.

Chapter 17 deals with the rules relating to co-ownership of land, which are included in this part because all co-owned estates are subject to the statutory imposition of a trust (these days, the modern 'trust of land').

Finally, trusts of the family home are considered in Chapter 18 and Chapter 19 covers the doctrine of proprietary estoppel that sometimes gives rise to trusts or other equitable rights in property.

13

Express and implied trusts

13.1 Introduction   303
13.2 Implied trusts   305
13.3 Terms of trusts affecting land   309
13.4 Co-ownership and statutory trusts   312

13.1 Introduction

13.1.1 Separation of title and enjoyment

As explained briefly in Chapter 2 (2.6.2), the essential characteristic of the trust is the separation of the title to property from the right to enjoy it for one's own benefit. The trustees are the owners of the property (they have the legal 'title') but hold it not for themselves but for the beneficiaries, who have the right to have the property used for their benefit. The beneficiaries are protected by equity and accordingly have an equitable interest in that property. This equitable interest is sometimes described as 'the beneficial interest', and here both terms are used interchangeably.

In general, the trustee will have the *legal* title to the trust property (i.e., in a trust of land, the trustee will usually hold the legal estate). However, it must be realised that it is also possible to create a trust of an equitable interest: for example, a beneficiary under a trust may declare that she holds her own beneficial interest on trust for some third party. For example, Theresa may declare that she holds her legal freehold estate in land on trust for Bob absolutely. This will make her a trustee for Bob and place her under obligations to use her freehold only and exclusively for Bob's interests: for example, if the property is let out, any rental income must be paid by Theresa to Bob, and she must not use the property at all for her own benefit. *Bob* may then declare that he holds his beneficial interest on a second trust for Clara absolutely. This will turn Bob into a trustee of his rights against Theresa: for example, if she pays him the rental income from the property, he must account to Clara for what he has received. Thus, the interest of the beneficiary under a trust is always equitable, but that of the trustee may be legal *or* equitable, according to the nature of the property which is subject to the trust (see Figure 13.1). In such cases, there will always be someone who holds the legal estate as a trustee, but this trustee may be holding for the benefit of a beneficiary who is herself a trustee (e.g., because she has declared a trust of her beneficial interest in favour of another person).

TITLE	BENEFICIAL INTEREST
(usually legal, but could be equitable)	(always equitable)
Trustee/s	Beneficiary/ies

Figure 13.1 Title and beneficial interests

13.1.2 Classification of trusts

In Chapter 2 you saw that trusts may be created by express declaration or may arise without any express declaration for other reasons. It is convenient to describe this second category of trusts, those which are not expressly created, as 'implied trusts'; this terminology was adopted by the court in *Cowcher v Cowcher* [1972] 1 WLR 425 at p. 430. This usage is convenient, as long as you are not confused by the fact that the phrase 'implied trust' is also used in LPA 1925, s. 53(2), to describe one type of non-express trust—see 13.1.2.2.

If you have studied trusts in more detail, you will know that they may be classified in a number of different ways. For the purposes of this book, however, we need only to distinguish between:

- express trusts;
- non-express or implied trusts; and
- statutory trusts.

13.1.2.1 Express trusts

A trust may be created by the owner of the trust property (the 'settlor') declaring an intention to hold that property on trust or transferring the property to an intended trustee with instructions to hold on trust for the beneficiaries. However, in the case of land, such a trust will not be *enforceable* unless there is some written evidence of that declaration. LPA 1925, s. 53(1)(b) provides:

> a declaration of trust respecting any land or any interest therein must be manifested and proved by some writing signed by some person who is able to declare such a trust or by his will.

Thus, while a trust of land may be *created* orally, a beneficiary will not be able to *enforce* any interest under it unless the trust is evidenced in writing. The trust will be valid, but unenforceable unless written evidence becomes available. For example, suppose Theresa tells Bob on the telephone that she intends to hold her freehold title to land on trust for him absolutely. This is a valid declaration of trust, and a trust will arise from the moment that Theresa makes the declaration. However, Bob will not be able to sue Theresa, if she fails to perform her duties as a trustee, *unless* he can provide written evidence that such a declaration was made (or unless a trust is held to have arisen for some other reason: see 13.2). If Theresa writes Bob a signed letter that references her previous declaration of trust, this will satisfy the requirement and he will be able to treat her as his trustee as from the date of that declaration (see, on this point, *Gardner v Rowe* (1828) 5 Russ. 258).

It is always possible for a landowner to provide that property should be held by trustees on trust for one adult beneficiary who is solely entitled to it (a *'bare trust'*). Such a trust gives the trustees no power to do anything with the trust property, except at the direction of the beneficiary. Under the rule in *Saunders v Vautier* (1841) 4 Beav 115, an adult beneficiary solely entitled to trust property can also 'collapse' the trust by ordering the trustee to transfer the legal estate to her, and so uniting the legal estate and the beneficial interest. As such, these trusts are often relatively short-lived, intended to allow one person temporarily hold the legal estate for the benefit of another who is ultimately expected to take the estate. More often, however, trusts are expressly created with a view to longer-term management of the property by the trustee(s) in the interests of the beneficiaries, because:

- the intended beneficiary is still a minor, i.e., under the age of 18 years (see 14.1.2.3);
- the property is to be enjoyed by several people in succession as, for example, where land is given 'to A for life and then to B'. Where successive interests like these are created by a disposition, the arrangement is known as a '*settlement*'; or
- two or more people are to have the benefit of the property at the same time (see 13.4).

13.1.2.2 Implied (non-express) trusts

Implied trusts are not created expressly, but arise in circumstances in which equity considers it appropriate to recognise or impose a trust. As a result, writing is not required for the creation or enforcement of these trusts. LPA 1925, s. 53(2) provides that the earlier part of the section (which imposes the requirement for evidence in writing, under s. 53(1)(b)):

> does not affect the creation or operation of resulting, implied or constructive trusts.

These terms are explained in 13.2.

13.1.2.3 Statutory trusts

In certain circumstances statutes provide that property is to be held on trust. Thus, for example, statutory trusts operate in all cases of co-ownership of land—that is, where two or more people are entitled to enjoy the property at the same time (LPA 1925, ss. 34(2) and 36(1)). Similar trusts are applied to property where the owner has died without making a will (Administration of Estates Act 1925, s. 33(1)).

In the rest of the chapter you will look in more detail at three topics mentioned briefly in this introduction:

- implied trusts (13.2);
- terms of trusts affecting land (13.3); and
- co-ownership and statutory trusts (13.4).

13.2 Implied trusts

13.2.1 '... resulting, implied and constructive trusts'

As already noted, LPA 1925, s. 53(2) specifies three types of trust for which writing is not required: resulting, implied, and constructive. There is no shortage of material about resulting and constructive trusts, but it is not easy to say exactly what is meant by the term 'implied trust' in this context. Hanbury and Martin, *Modern Equity*, 22nd edn., at para. 2–028, briefly outlines some suggestions as to what this category may include, but concludes that the classification of implied trusts:

> serves little purpose, and the examples commonly given might preferably be regarded as express, resulting or constructive trusts, as the case may be.

None of the possible types of implied trust, in this narrower sense, has any immediate relevance to your study of land law, so is not covered further here. What follows deals in more detail with resulting and constructive trusts.

13.2.2 Resulting trusts

The term *'resulting'* trust describes a trust under which the beneficial interest in property 'jumps back' (or 'results to') to the person making a transfer of property. The idea is that these are trusts that arise where A transfers property to B and B then holds on trust for A (the legal title passes from A to B, but the beneficial interest is said to go back, or 'result,' to A). There are several recognised situations in which the court finds that a particular transaction has given rise to a trust in favour of a person who has transferred land or the money that was used to buy land, although there has been no express declaration that meets the requirements of s. 53(1)(b).

13.2.2.1 Incomplete or invalid express declarations

In some cases, the former owner of property has transferred it to another person on terms that mean the other person is not supposed to keep the property for himself. One example is to be found in the creation of an express trust, where the settlor directs the trustees to hold on trusts which do not dispose fully of the beneficial interest in the property—that is, where the terms of the trust do not explain what is supposed to happen in all circumstances (e.g., a direction to hold 'for A for life', without any explanation of what is supposed to happen after A dies). In these circumstances, the trustees will hold the property on a resulting trust for the settlor in respect of that undisposed of part of the beneficial interest (e.g., where the express instruction is simply to hold 'for A for life', the trustee will hold for A for life, with the remainder going to the settlor). The same rule applies where the former owner of property has transferred it to another person on the terms of a trust that cannot be performed (e.g., to hold for the benefit of a person who has already died). In these cases, the trustee will instead hold for the benefit of the settlor absolutely.

13.2.2.2 Presumed resulting trusts

In other situations, where an owner conveys property to a 'volunteer' (someone who does not give value for it), the law will presume that the new owner was intended to hold on a resulting trust for the transferor—provided that the volunteer is *not* able to show that the property was given for some reason, for example as a gift or a loan. The same principle applies where property is bought with money belonging wholly or in part to another. In these circumstances, the acquirer, who becomes the legal owner, holds the property on a resulting trust for the person who paid the purchase price, unless she can show that the payment was made with the intention that she take the property for her own benefit (i.e., the payment of the money was a gift or a loan). This is the rule that applies when property is bought with money *wholly* supplied by someone else (*Dyer v Dyer* (1788) 2 Cox 92). Where the acquirer has also made some contribution to the purchase price, the presumption is that the acquirer will hold the property in trust for herself *and* the other contributors in proportion to their contributions (*Dewar v Dewar* [1975] 1 WLR 1532). An overview of the situations in which the presumption of resulting trust arises, and the effect of the presumption if there is no contrary evidence to rebut it, is given in Table 13.1.

Table 13.1 Resulting trusts

A buys property using money provided by B	Trustee = A
	Beneficiary = B
A buys property using money provided by A and B	Trustee = A
	Beneficiaries = A & B

In these situations, the courts' recognition of the resulting trust appears to be based on the presumed intention of the person who has conveyed the property or provided the purchase money. This presumption is, however, rebuttable, and can be displaced by evidence of a contrary intention, for example to make a gift or a loan. You have already seen an example of such a trust arising in the case of the matrimonial home in *Kingsnorth Finance Co. Ltd v Tizard* [1986] 1 WLR 783 (see 5.5.2.3), although you should note that recent case law has limited the role of presumed resulting trusts where the land is meant to be the family home of those contributing to its acquisition (see Chapter 18).

13.2.3 Constructive trusts

Constructive trusts arise by operation of law rather than by the intention of the parties. The court recognises such a trust as being imposed by equity upon the owner of property, so that instead of enjoying the property as beneficial owner, the owner is required to hold it, in whole or in part, for the benefit of some other person.

We have already seen an example of such a trust arising under a specifically enforceable contract for the sale of land, with the result that the vendor is regarded as, in some sense, holding the legal title in the property in trust for the purchaser (see 4.6).

Unfortunately, it is almost impossible to give a simple explanation of what constitutes a constructive trust or to explain when it will arise. In *Carl-Zeiss Stiftung v Herbert Smith & Co. (No. 2)* [1969] 2 Ch 276, Edmund Davies LJ said, at p. 300:

> English law provides no clear and all-embracing definition of a constructive trust. Its boundaries have been left perhaps deliberately vague so as not to restrict the court by technicalities in deciding what the justice of a particular case may demand.

The best approach, therefore, to understanding the nature of constructive trusts is to note the circumstances in which they have arisen. Megarry and Wade states (para. 10-017), 'Despite uncertainties over its true nature there are a number of well-known situations in which it has been held that a constructive trust is imposed.' These situations may be categorised in a number of different ways (see, for example, Megarry and Wade, paras. 10-018–10-025). Here we simply cover a few cases which are particularly relevant to land law. You will find a more extensive discussion of these cases in Chapters 18 (informally declared trusts), 19 (proprietary estoppel), and 20 (contractual licences).

13.2.3.1 Constructive trusts and proprietary estoppel

You will already have seen in this book a number of statutory provisions requiring formalities for contracts to deal with land (LPA 1925, ss. 40 and Law of Property (Miscellaneous Provisions) Act 1989, s. 2) and for actual conveyances of estates and interests in land (LPA 1925, s. 52(1) and LRA 2002, s. 27). Where someone has detrimentally relied on an informal agreement—for example, spending money on improving land they believe has been given to them (*Dillwyn v Llewellyn* (1862) 4 De G. F. & J. 517)—the courts will sometimes hold that they have obtained certain rights in equity, by way of a constructive trust or a claim in proprietary estoppel (see 4.5). You will find a more detailed explanation of these cases in Chapter 19.

13.2.3.2 Constructive trusts and informally declared trusts

Many statutory formality provisions are derived from earlier statutory rules, in some cases dating back to the Statute of Frauds in 1677. At a fairly early stage, the courts of equity became concerned at the use which was being made of these statutory provisions, particularly the predecessor of s. 53(1)(b) LPA 1925 (s. 7 of the Statute of Frauds 1677). Estate owners who had acquired property subject to some oral understanding or agreement to hold it on trust and then sought to avoid that undertaking were considered to be acting in a fraudulent manner in the eyes of equity. In these circumstances, the courts evolved the maxim that equity would not allow a statute to be used 'as an instrument of fraud' and held that the transferee would be compelled by the court to hold the property on trust (*Rochefoucauld v Boustead* [1897] 1 Ch 196).

The approach in *Rochefoucauld v Boustead* [1897] 1 Ch 196 was applied by the Court of Appeal in *Bannister v Bannister* [1948] 2 All ER 133. In this case a purchaser had bought a cottage from his sister-in-law, on the understanding that she would be allowed to live in it rent-free for the rest of her life. The understanding between the parties was not recorded in any document. When the purchaser went back on his agreement and tried to obtain possession of the cottage, the defendant claimed that the oral agreement amounted to an informal declaration of trust—that is, that the purchaser would hold the property upon trust for her for her lifetime. As we have seen, such a declaration of trust would normally need to be evidenced in writing under LPA 1925, s. 53(1)(b), but the court held that the unconscionable conduct of the purchaser in seeking to avoid his undertaking gave rise to a constructive trust. He had promised his sister-in-law that she would have a life interest in the property and, consequently, held the property on trust to give effect to that interest. (You should note that the effect of this decision was that the sister-in-law had become a 'tenant for life' under an SLA settlement: see 13.3 and Chapter 15.)

13.2.3.3 Constructive trusts and contractual licences

In *Binions v Evans* [1972] Ch 359, a widow had been given the right to live in a cottage for her lifetime. According to the express terms of the agreement, she was to be a tenant at will, and she agreed to take care of the premises while she had the use of them. The property was then sold to purchasers, who agreed with the vendor that they would allow the widow to remain, and accordingly paid a reduced price for the cottage. Later, they sought to eject her, and the court had to consider the nature of her rights and whether they bound the purchasers for value. The Court of Appeal held unanimously that, although the agreement described the widow as a tenant at will, its terms were inconsistent with such a tenancy. The majority of the court (Megaw and Stephenson LJJ) held that the agreement had given the widow a life interest, and accordingly had made her a tenant for life under an SLA settlement. By contrast, Lord Denning MR considered that the agreement gave rise to a contractual licence. You will see in Chapter 20 that there are considerable difficulties in seeking to enforce such a licence against a purchaser from the original licensor, but Lord Denning considered that the circumstances justified the imposition of a constructive trust on the purchasers. The contract of sale had stipulated that the purchasers were to take subject to the widow's rights, and they paid a reduced price because of this. In Lord Denning's view (at p. 368):

> In these circumstances this court will impose on the [purchasers] a constructive trust for [the widow's] benefit; for the simple reason that it would be utterly inequitable for [them] to turn [her] out contrary to the stipulation subject to which they took the premises.

The argument that a 'constructive trust' arises in these cases, and can be used to enforce a contractual licence against a purchaser, has been very controversial and later cases have sought to limit the scope of the principle articulated by Lord Denning MR in *Binions v Evans*. You will find a more detailed explanation of these cases in Chapter 20.

13.2.3.4 Common intention constructive trusts

Some 'constructive trusts' arise in response to the common intention of the parties (see 4.5.1). Over the last 40 years, courts have relied increasingly on trusts of this type in dealing with claims of one partner in a family relationship to have a share in the family home that differs from the way in which the legal estate is held. In some cases, the legal estate might be held in the sole name of one partner, while the other argues that the estate is held on trust for them both. In others, the legal estate might be held jointly by both partners, but one partner argues that it is held on trust for them in unequal shares. The constructive trusts recognised in these decisions have come to be known as 'common intention constructive trusts' and their nature and development are covered in Chapter 18.

13.3 Terms of trusts affecting land

13.3.1 The old law

Before 1997 there were two ways of settling land on trust:

- by creating a *strict settlement* (giving rise to what is usually called 'settled land'), the ancient form of settlement, governed largely after 1925 by the Settled Land Act 1925 (SLA 1925); and
- by using a **trust for sale**, which was a form devised later in time than the strict settlement and which, after 1925, was largely governed by the LPA 1925.

Since 1997, following the enactment of TOLATA 1996, these old forms of trusts have limited relevance to the modern law. Trusts for sale that existed before 1997 have now all been converted into 'trusts of land', governed by TOLATA 1996. Meanwhile, it is no longer possible to create a *new* strict settlement (although settlements created before 1997 continue to exist). Although this book avoids excursions into historical matters, you will need a very short explanation of these two older forms of trust and how they developed, so that you can understand the modern trust of land discussed in later chapters.

13.3.1.1 Strict settlements (or 'Settled Land Act settlements')

It helps if you know that strict settlements arose under a system which began in the Middle Ages, and developed to meet the needs of families who owned considerable amounts of land. The landowner who made the sort of strict settlement described here probably owned at least several large country estates, and at a later period may also have had a London town house, a 'hunting-box' in the shires, and a grouse moor in Scotland. The settlement in its developed form was designed for large landowners, like the Victorian author Trollope's Duke of Omnium or, to use a TV example, the Earl of Grantham, rather than those of small modern owner-occupiers. The purpose of making a strict settlement was in the main to ensure that the family estates (to which there might well be some sentimental attachment) remained in the family, passing intact to the male heir, while at the same time making provision from the income of the estate for wives, daughters, and younger children.

In a typical marriage settlement, made by a male fee simple owner on his marriage, the settlor would deprive himself of his absolute title to the estate and create a mere life estate for himself, followed by a fee tail in favour of his eldest (unborn) son (see 1.5.1.3). He would also make provision for payments from the income of the estate: a personal allowance to his wife ('pin-money') during the marriage, with a larger sum to support her during her widowhood, if she survived him, and 'portions' for the daughters and younger sons to support them in later life. The settlor had thus split the legal fee simple into several smaller estates (a life estate, a fee tail, and a reversion in favour of his general heirs—see 1.6 and 8.4.2), which was possible at law before 1926.

An alternative way of making the same provision was to give the full fee simple to trustees, directing them to hold on trust for the family on similar terms, so that the settlor and his heir took equitable interests under the trust equivalent to the life estate and the fee tail, and money payments were provided for the rest of the family.

Whichever form was adopted, the result was similar: although the land could be sold or mortgaged if all those entitled under the settlement were of full age and agreed to act together, there was no one person who by himself could dispose of the whole legal and beneficial interest. Thus the chances of the property being lost to the family were greatly reduced.

Settling property in this way certainly had the desired effect of keeping land in the family, but preventing alienation had its own disadvantages. Some settlements did permit limited sale and mortgaging, so that money could be raised to improve the rest of the estate, but if such powers were not expressly provided, the current owner of the estate might well find himself unable to raise money for much-needed repairs and improvements, and as a result the property would deteriorate. Meanwhile, it was expensive for prospective buyers and lenders to acquire the fee simple or to lend money on a mortgage of the fee simple, since it was necessary to negotiate with all those entitled under the settlement in order to get their consent to the sale or mortgage.

A series of nineteenth-century Acts, culminating in the Settled Land Act 1882, gave the current beneficiary (the 'tenant for life') powers to deal with settled land and even to sell it, despite the settlor's intentions. Eventually, as explained in Chapter 1, the 1925 property legislation put an end to the practice of settling land by splitting the fee simple into a series of smaller legal estates, and from 1 January 1926 these lesser estates took effect as equitable interests under a trust of the legal fee simple absolute in possession. It is now no longer possible to create new strict settlements, but settlements created before 1997 continue to exist and are briefly discussed in Chapter 15.

13.3.1.2 Trusts for sale

As we have seen, the strict settlement was designed for landowners with a family attachment to land which had probably been owned by their relatives for hundreds of years. It was not, however, particularly appropriate in the case of land which had been bought relatively recently, and as an investment rather than for occupation. Land on which housing estates or factories were built might be of no sentimental value to its owners, and they usually intended to hold it as long as the yield was satisfactory, but to sell and reinvest the proceeds when better bargains were available. Yet, all the same, such landowners might want to make settlements, in order to keep their wealth intact for later generations and to provide for the present members of their families. Their needs were met by the development of the trust for sale.

Title would be vested in trustees, who would be under a duty to sell the property and reinvest the proceeds, but who could postpone sale until the time was right. The income generated by the property before sale, and the resulting capital realised after sale, could be held on trust for a series of beneficiaries, as defined in the trust instrument, and so the settlor could provide an income for family members without dividing the capital between them. The major defining factor in these trusts was that they imposed upon the trustees a *duty* to sell the trust property but usually also included a *power* to postpone the sale, so that the trustees could choose the best moment at which to realise the trust investment in the property.

However, the fact that the trustees were under a *duty* to sell brought into operation the equitable doctrine known as 'conversion'.

Doctrine of conversion

In any case where there is a specifically enforceable obligation to convert land into money, or money into land, the maxim that 'equity regards as done that which ought to be done' leads equity to treat the property as notionally converted from the moment the obligation arises. This notional conversion operates when any contract to buy or sell land is made (see 4.6.3), and because of the duty to sell, also applied to all trusts for sale. The trustees for sale could be compelled to perform their duty to sell the trust property and so such property was treated by equity as though it had been sold already, and the beneficiaries were regarded as having interests in money rather than in the land. This used to matter, for example, when the rules governing the devolution of personal property on death differed from the rules governing the devolution of real property (see 1.7.1.1 and 8.2). The whole concept may appear somewhat strange today, but seemed appropriate when the trust for sale was first developed as a commercial alternative to the strict settlement; what mattered was the value of the land, rather than the land itself.

13.3.2 Disadvantages of the old law

In origin, as we have seen, each type of settlement had its own specific purpose, the strict settlement being used where particular land was to remain in the family, and the trust for sale being employed where the land was an investment which changed from time to time. Both forms were retained in the 1925 property legislation, but in more recent years a number of problems became apparent.

The machinery for dealing with a settlement under the Settled Land Act 1925, although intended to facilitate the sale of the land, often appeared cumbersome and expensive. Moreover, the fact that the tenant for life now had a statutory power to sell the land meant that a settlement made in this form could no longer be relied upon to keep the land in the family.

Over the years, clever lawyers managed to construct trusts for sale which gave most of the benefits of the SLA settlement, while retaining the advantages provided by the greater flexibility of the trust for sale. Although the trust for sale imposed a duty on the trustees to sell the property, it was possible to provide that the land should not be sold without the consent of certain named individuals. Paradoxically, it therefore became easier to prevent the sale of family land by means of a trust for sale with provision for consents, rather than by relying on a SLA settlement. An example of this is to be found in the facts of *Re Inns* [1947] Ch 576 (for which see 14.5.2).

Gradually most property owners who wanted to create a settlement came to use a trust for sale and relatively few settlors would intentionally create a SLA settlement. Yet avoiding the creation of such a settlement required careful drafting and the fact that it could be created unintentionally constituted a trap for the unwary, particularly for those who made 'home-made' wills without legal advice. As a result, the availability of two methods of settling land came to be seen as a disadvantage to settlors rather than as a benefit.

13.3.3 The modern trust of land

In the main, the two old forms of settlements were replaced by a new type of trust introduced by the Trusts of Land and Appointment of Trustees Act 1996 (TOLATA 1996), which came into force on 1 January 1997. The changes made by the Act are described in detail in Chapter 14, but in outline the difficulties created by the existing methods of settling land were resolved as follows (see Table 13.2):

- a new 'trust of land' was introduced, which
  - applies to all trusts that include land,
  - becomes the only way of creating new settlements;
- trusts for sale were abolished, and
  - existing trusts for sale were converted into trusts of land,
  - attempts to create new trusts for sale now take effect as trusts of land;
- no new SLA settlements may be created,
  - but existing SLA settlements continued and are still governed by SLA 1925,
  - and attempts to create new SLA settlements take effect as trusts of land.

Table 13.2 Rules from 1 January 1997 onwards

NEW TRUSTS	PRE-EXISTING TRUSTS	
All become trusts of land. Governed by TOLATA 1996.	Trusts for sale	Become trusts of land. Governed by TOLATA 1996.
	Strict settlements	Continue as strict settlements. Governed by SLA 1925.

13.4 Co-ownership and statutory trusts

13.4.1 1925 legislation

The 1925 property legislation imposed statutory trusts for sale on most forms of co-ownership (LPA 1925, ss. 34(2) and 36(1)). This meant that from then onwards co-owners of land held the legal estate in their land on trust for themselves as beneficiaries, on terms that placed them under a duty (to each other) to sell but gave them a power to postpone sale. Up to this point in the book, the terms 'trustees' and 'beneficiaries' have been used as though they were different people, but it is possible for the same people to fulfil both roles, and this is what usually happens in cases of co-ownership.

The provision that co-owned property was subject to a trust for sale must be related to the overall policy of the 1925 legislation: to simplify conveyancing and to make it easier for a purchaser to buy land. The fact that co-owned property was subject to a trust enabled the purchaser to take advantage of the overreaching machinery (explained in 5.5.2). Provided the purchase money was paid to two trustees, the purchaser would take free of the beneficial interests and need not worry about questions of who was entitled in equity and whether they agreed to the sale. The overreaching process operated where co-owners received the purchase money as trustees, even though they were also the beneficiaries of the trust. Moreover, the fact that the statutory trust was a trust for sale meant that the doctrine of conversion applied. As a result, it was thought at one time that the beneficiaries had interests in money rather than in the land itself, and this provided further reassurance for the purchaser. However, this view was shaken by the decision of the House of Lords in *Williams & Glyn's Bank v Boland* [1981] AC 487 that a beneficiary under a trust for sale did have an interest in the land itself that could bind a third party like a bank that had been granted a mortgage by a sole trustee (see 6.5.6.2 for the facts of this case).

The imposition of the statutory trust for sale from 1926 does not seem to have caused any particular problems at the outset. This may well be because co-ownership was relatively uncommon at that time and was most likely to arise through inheritance. In such cases, where several people were entitled under a will or on intestacy, the usual course of action, even before the statutory trust, would be to sell the land and divide the proceeds between the beneficiaries.

During the twentieth century, however, a rise in home ownership, combined with the change in the status of women, meant that co-ownership of smaller residential property became increasingly common. Couples who bought a house or flat generally regarded it as their future family home. The idea that they were under a duty to sell the property that they had just acquired would have seemed astonishing (or, as Lord Wilberforce put it in *Williams & Glyn's Bank v Boland*, rejecting the view that a wife in this situation had no interest in the land itself, 'just a little unreal'—[1981] AC 487 at p. 507). Indeed, some solicitors have said that they never tried to explain this part of the law to their clients.

While relations between the co-owners remained happy, the nature of their rights and duties under the trust for sale would not be significant, but if disagreement arose between the owners the trust could cause real difficulties. In particular, difficulties were experienced on the breakdown of family relationships, where one partner might move out of the property and demand that it should be sold, leaving the remaining partner and any children without a home. The remaining partner might find it problematic to oppose sale in these circumstances because the co-owners, as trustees of a trust for sale, were under a *duty* to sell and had only a *power* to postpone sale. Following the decision in *Re Mayo* [1943] Ch 302, the power to postpone sale had to be exercised unanimously. If the trustees were not unanimous in agreeing to postpone sale, they must perform their duty and sell the property. Thus, one co-owner who wished to sell could compel the other to do so against his or her wishes.

As it became apparent that the statutory trust was having unintended consequences for modern home-owners, the courts tried to mitigate its effects by developing a concept known as 'the doctrine of continuing purpose'.

13.4.1.1 Doctrine of continuing purpose

This doctrine was developed by the courts in dealing with applications by one co-owner for an order for sale (under LPA 1925, s. 30) against the wishes of the other co-owner.

An early illustration of its use is to be found in *Re Buchanan-Wollaston's Conveyance* [1939] Ch 738. In this case a group of neighbours had jointly bought a piece of land adjoining their properties with the intention of keeping it as an open space and thereby preventing further building. Later one neighbour sold his house and wished also to realise the money he had tied up in the open land. His application for an order for sale of the co-owned property was rejected on the ground that the land had been bought for a particular purpose and that purpose was continuing to be satisfied by the retention of the property.

Other examples of the idea of the continuing purpose are to be found in cases about the matrimonial home. In *Jones v Challenger* [1961] 1 QB 176, a husband and wife jointly acquired property as a matrimonial home. After divorce proceedings the wife sought an order for sale. The court granted the order because the purpose for which the property was bought had ended on the divorce. However, it indicated that despite the statutory trust for sale an order might be refused in a case where there were children of the marriage and a home was still being provided for them and the other partner (in other words, where the purpose of providing a family home was still continuing, even though one partner had left it). In *Rawlings v Rawlings* [1964] P 398 Salmon LJ considered that in such a case an order for sale should be delayed until the children were grown up.

In these ways, the courts did their best to deal with the unforeseen consequences of imposing a trust for sale on co-owners, but by the end of the twentieth century it seemed desirable to make some statutory change to the rule.

13.4.2 TOLATA 1996

Under s. 5 of TOLATA 1996, the old trust for sale was replaced by the new trust of land (see 13.3.3) as the trust which is imposed by various statutes in specified circumstances, including those of co-ownership. This clarifies the right of beneficiaries under trusts of land to occupy the trust property in some situations, as well as modernising the law on the availability of orders for sale where co-owners disagree about whether land ought to be sold. We turn to the specific provisions of TOLATA 1996 in Chapter 14, and go on to discuss how it affects disputes between co-owners of land in Chapter 17.

FURTHER READING

Clements, 'The Changing Face of Trusts' [1998] MLR 56.

Transfer of Land: Trusts of Land, 1989, Law Com No. 181 (in particular, Part I on problems of existing law and Part II on proposals for reform, which paved the way for the changes introduced by TOLATA 1996).

You can visit the online resources to test your knowledge of this chapter with self-test questions at **www.oup.com/he/nair19e/**.

14

Trusts of land

14.1 Introduction 315
14.2 Creating a settlement of 9 Trant Way 319
14.3 How many trustees are needed and who appoints them? 320
14.4 What do trustees do? 322
14.5 Are there any controls over the exercise of trustees' powers? 324
14.6 Can beneficiaries be involved in the management of the trust property? 328
14.7 Do beneficiaries have a right to occupy the trust property? 330
14.8 How are disputes about the trust property resolved? 334
14.9 Is it safe for purchasers to buy trust property? 341

14.1 Introduction

Chapter 13 explained the ways in which trusts relating to land may arise, and outlined some of the reasons for which a property owner may create such a trust. In particular, it explained that, in the past, an owner might want to give several people *successive interests in land* (known as a 'settlement'), allowing the person creating the trust (the 'settlor') to control how the benefits of the property will be used in the future (e.g., with provision for a spouse during her lifetime, and with future provision for children and grandchildren). As was explained in Chapter 13, the 1925 legislation ensured that a settlor seeking to achieve this goal had to choose between two forms: a Settled Land Act (SLA) settlement and a trust for sale. Both these types of settlement involved the use of a trust, but were governed by very different rules and procedures, which could be confusing for settlors. Meanwhile, an owner might also want to give people *concurrent interests in land* (by way of co-ownership), with all the co-owners being entitled to some benefit from the use of the property at the same time. You have seen that most, but not all, forms of co-ownership were subject to a trust for sale imposed by the LPA 1925 and that the rules governing these statutory trusts were not always appropriate to the needs of the co-owners. Finally, an owner might wish to give the benefit of property to one person absolutely but prefer to leave the title to the estate, and its management, in the hands of trustees (known as a 'bare trust'). The 1925 property legislation made no specific provision for such an arrangement, and consequently there could be uncertainty about the application of statutory rules to such a trust.

These problems with the trust structures applicable to land became increasingly apparent over the course of the twentieth century and resulted in the enactment of The Trusts of Land and Appointment of Trustees Act 1996 (TOLATA 1996), which came into force on 1 January 1997. This Chapter provides an overview of TOLATA 1996, with a special focus on the impact of the Act on beneficiaries and trustees under settlements of land created after 1 January 1997. The impact of TOLATA 1996 on co-ownership of land is considered in Chapter 17.

14.1.1 The new 'trust of land'

The Act introduced a completely new trust, the 'trust of land', which is defined by s. 1(1)(a):

> 'trust of land' means any trust of property which consists of or includes land.

Section 1(2)(a) expressly provides that the reference in s. 1(1) includes all descriptions of trust, including express, implied, and resulting trusts; trusts for sale; and bare trusts.

14.1.1.1 A new way of making settlements

Since 1 January 1997 the *trust of land* is the only way in which a new trust may be created.

TOLATA 1996 provides that no new *SLA settlements* may be created (s. 2(1)). Any attempt to create such a settlement will take effect as a trust of land. Section 2(6) and Sch. 1 deal with certain specific circumstances which formerly would have given rise to SLA settlements (see 14.10). Also, an attempt to create a *trust for sale* will simply take effect as a trust of land under the statutory definition in s. 1(2)(a) (see further 14.1.2.2). This prevents the old problems associated with having had two different ways of creating trusts conferring successive interests (see 13.3.2).

14.1.1.2 A new way of regulating co-ownership

TOLATA 1996 provided that the statutory trust imposed on co-owners became a trust of land rather than a trust for sale. It did this by amending the relevant provisions of LPA 1925: see s. 25(1) and Sch. 3, paras. 3 and 4. This means that co-owners are no longer under a duty to sell their land and are not subject to the doctrine of conversion. (See further Chapter 17.)

14.1.2 Effect on settlements and trusts for sale

14.1.2.1 What happened to existing SLA settlements and trusts for sale?

SLA settlements which were in existence on 1 January 1997 continue to exist in their original form and were not converted into trusts of land. You will find a brief note about these settlements in Chapter 15.

Trusts for sale which were in existence on 1 January 1997 were converted overnight into trusts of land, as a consequence of s. 1(2)(b), which made it quite clear that the statute catches trusts created or arising before the commencement of the Act. This change affected both expressly created trusts for sale and also those imposed by statute, as, for example, in cases of co-ownership. As a result of the change in the nature of the trust, the trustees ceased to be under an automatic duty to sell the co-owned property and the trust property ceased to be subject to the doctrine of conversion.

In general, the existing trusts for sale which were converted into trusts of land are subject to the new statutory rules about the trust of land in this chapter. There are, however, a few exceptional cases of existing trusts for sale to which some of the new rules do not apply (if you need to know about these, see s. 3(2) and s. 11(2)(b)).

14.1.2.2 What happens if a settlor tries to create a new trust for sale?

Section 1(2)(a) specifically provides that trusts for sale are included within the statutory definition of the new trusts of land. Thus, although a settlor may still create a trust for sale (either by describing it as such or by imposing upon the trustees a duty to sell the trust property), the trust will nonetheless be categorised as 'a trust of land' and will operate within the framework of rules provided by TOLATA 1996.

The Act contains two important provisions which prevent trusts for sale operating as they once did:

(1) the trustees have an *implied power to postpone sale* (s. 4(1)), which cannot be excluded by the settlor (see 14.4.2.6); and

(2) the doctrine of conversion no longer operates on property held under a trust for sale.

No conversion under a trust for sale
Section 3(1) provides that:

> Where land is held by trustees subject to a trust for sale, the land is not to be regarded as personal property . . .

In other words, the land is not to be regarded as converted into money (a type of personal property—see 2.10), and this means that the doctrine of conversion is no longer brought into operation by the trustees' duty to sell the trust property. You should note, however, that despite the marginal note to s. 3 ('Abolition of doctrine of conversion') notional conversion continues to apply in other circumstances where there is a specifically enforceable obligation to convert land into money, or vice versa—as for example under a contract to buy or sell land.

14.1.2.3 What happens if a settlor tries to create a new strict settlement?

No new SLA settlements can be created after 1997, and any new arrangements which create successive interests in land will take effect as trusts of land. There are, however, three particular dispositions that under the old law would have taken effect as SLA settlements or as a trust for sale and for which TOLATA 1996 makes specific provision in s. 2(6) and Sch. 1.

Conveyance to a minor or minors
The 1925 legislation introduced the rule that a minor—that is a person or persons under 18 years of age—cannot hold a legal estate in land (LPA 1925, s. 1(6)). Before 1997, attempts to convey such an estate to a minor operated as a contract to create an SLA settlement, and until this was done the person making the conveyance held the estate on trust for the minor. Where a conveyance was made to an adult and a minor, the adult held the legal estate on a trust for sale for himself or herself and the minor.

Under TOLATA 1996, a purported conveyance (and this will include LRA transfers) to a minor or a group of minors operates instead as a declaration of trust (Sch. 1, para. 1(1)). Thus, in such a case, a minor can only become a beneficial (equitable) owner. The legal estate will have to be vested in an adult or adults as trustee(s).

Where a legal estate is conveyed to a minor or minors *and* an adult or adults, Sch. 1, para. 1(2) provides that that estate will vest in the adult(s) upon trust for the minor(s) and the adult(s) in question. You will see an example of this in the transfer of 8 Trant Way (17.2.5).

Charges 'by way of family arrangement'

As we have already seen in Chapter 13 (13.3.1.1), a typical settlement would ensure that the property would pass to a single heir (usually the settlor's eldest son), but would also provide for the maintenance of the settlor's widow and younger children. For this purpose, the settlement would create charges over the property, which gave these members of the family the right to receive payments from the income of the estate. Although less common today, this practice does still continue in some cases and this sort of arrangement is now governed by para. 3 of Sch. 1 to TOLATA 1996, which provides that, in such a case, the land becomes subject to a trust of land and is held on trust for the purpose of giving effect to the charge. Thus, were Sherlock to vest his legal estate in Moriarty (his eldest son) but subject to periodic payments by Moriarty to his sister Enola, this arrangement would create a trust of land, which would be subject to the provisions of TOLATA 1996.

Entails

As we saw in 1.5.1.3, an entailed interest (before 1926 known as a fee tail) was created by a disposition in favour of 'the heirs of the body' of a specified person. If the holder of such an interest had no lineal descendants, the interest came to an end at his or her death and the property reverted to the donor or the donor's successors, who were said to have a 'reversion' in it. Usually, such grants were to 'heirs of the body male', which could cause problems when there was no male heir: see Jane Austen's *Pride and Prejudice* and the TV programme *Downton Abbey* for examples of the problems caused. This succession of interests took effect as an SLA settlement (see further 13.3.1.1).

This form of settlement was regarded as inappropriate in modern law and under TOLATA 1996 it is no longer possible to create an entailed interest. Schedule 1, para. 5(1) provides that a purported grant of an entailed interest does not create that interest but instead takes effect as a declaration that the property is held in trust absolutely for the intended grantee. If a settlor purports to create an entailed interest in himself or herself, the whole disposition is ineffective (para. 5(2)). Thus, no new entailed interests can be created. They were already quite rare and in time most will come to an end.

14.1.2.4 Summary of changes under TOLATA 1996

The changes introduced by TOLATA discussed in this section may be summarised as follows.

- With the exception of SLA settlements created before 1 January 1997, all trusts relating to land now operate as trusts of land.
- The new trust of land includes:
    - all expressly created trusts, whether they be for one beneficiary (a bare trust) or for several beneficiaries in succession (creating a settlement) or concurrently (as in co-ownership), and whether or not they impose a duty to sell on the trustees;
    - all implied trusts, whether resulting or constructive; and
    - all trusts imposed by statute—as in cases of co-ownership.
- Even where an express trust imposes a duty to sell upon the trustees, they have a power to postpone sale, which cannot be excluded, and the doctrine of conversion no longer applies to such a trust.
- It is no longer possible to create a trust that limits the descent of the beneficial interests in land to 'heirs of the body' of the grantee (an entail). Attempts to make such trusts of land will now take as trusts in favour of the grantee absolutely.

14.1.3 Contents of this chapter

The operation of the new trust of land is regulated by Part 1 of TOLATA 1996, and the rest of this chapter deals with these provisions. In this chapter, these provisions are illustrated by reference to Mary Brown, the owner of 9 Trant Way, who needs advice about creating a settlement by will (see 14.2). In Chapter 17, we will consider the case of six students who hold 8 Trant Way as co-owners (see 17.1.2), and are therefore subject to a statutory trust of land.

14.2 Creating a settlement of 9 Trant Way

The fee simple estate of 9 Trant Way is owned by Mary Brown, who lives there with her wife, Janet. Mary has not yet made a will, although her wife keeps urging her to do so. Mary has no doubt about what she wants to happen to the house and her investments when she dies: she wants them all to go to her wife, if she survives her, and then at her death to pass on to their two married daughters concurrently. Mary Brown's plans are illustrated in Figure 14.1.

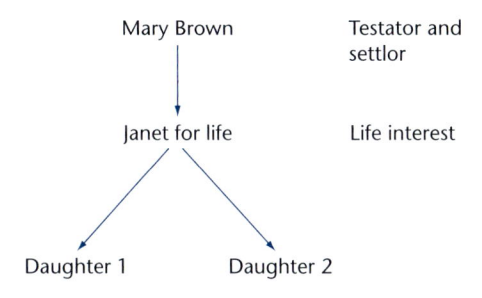

Figure 14.1 Mary Brown's will

In legal terms, what Mary wants to do is to create a settlement, giving successive interests to members of the family: a life estate to her widow and a remainder in fee simple to their daughters. She is, however, very uncertain about how to achieve this. She remembers reading a newspaper article years ago, which said that all this could be done with a trust, but warned that there were several different types of trust and that it was important to choose the right one. Apparently, it was possible to make the wrong one by mistake, and this worries Mary, and has deterred her from doing anything. However, as we have already explained, settlors no longer have to choose between two forms of settlement and any trust of No. 9 which Mary might make would take effect as a trust of land under TOLATA 1996.

If Mary's will is professionally drafted, it will almost certainly contain an express provision that at her death her property is to pass to trustees to hold on trust for her wife during her lifetime and then for their daughters. The trust will be a trust of land and will be governed by the provisions of TOLATA 1996.

If, however, Mary prefers to make her own will, she may simply provide that her property is to go to her wife and then to their daughters, without referring to any trust. Before 1997, this sort of provision in a home-made will would have created an SLA settlement, with resulting expense and inconvenience, but you know from s. 2(1) of TOLATA 1996 that it is no longer possible to create such a settlement. Rather confusingly, the Act does not make any express provision for treating such a disposition as giving rise to a trust of land, and the fact that it does so has to be worked out from general principles. You may remember from Chapter 1 that, after 1925, life estates and future interests can no longer exist as legal estates. Thus, dispositions creating such interests can take effect only in equity, with the result that the legal fee simple must be held on trust to give effect to such interests. Under s. 1(1), such a trust will now take effect as a trust of land and thus, if Mary makes such a disposition, she will in fact create a trust of land, even though she does not say so in so many words.

14.2.1 Mixed trusts

We must remember that Mary owns some investments, which she also wants to leave successively to her wife and daughters. In order to constitute a trust of land, it is sufficient that the trust property 'includes land' (s. 1(1)(a)). Thus, mixed trusts, containing both land and personalty, will also be subject to the rules in TOLATA 1996. This is a useful rule because it allows a house and its contents, or, indeed, all the settlor's property, to be held under a single trust. As a result, Mary Brown will be able to create one trust which will apply to both her house and her investments.

14.2.2 What a settlor will want to know

If Mary is advised to create a trust of land, she will probably have questions about it, such as:

- how many trustees are needed and who appoints them;
- what do trustees do;
- are there any controls over what the trustees do;
- will her wife be involved in looking after the property;
- can she be sure that her wife will be able to live in the house as long as she wishes, but also be free to sell it if she wants to move to something smaller;
- what will happen if her wife and the trustees disagree about what is to be done with the house;
- will the fact that the house is subject to a trust make it more difficult to sell if her wife wants to move?

The answers to all these questions are now affected by the provisions of TOLATA 1996, and are covered in the following sections.

14.3 How many trustees are needed and who appoints them?

The rules about the number and appointment of trustees are to be found partly in the Trustee Act 1925 and partly in TOLATA 1996.

14.3.1 Number of trustees

It is usual to have a minimum of two trustees because the 'overreaching' provisions, which are designed to protect purchasers, will lead anyone dealing with the trust to demand signatures from at least two trustees on any receipt for capital money (see 14.9.2).

A trust can, however, function with only one trustee, as for example where the owner of the legal estate holds it in trust for himself or herself and a friend who has contributed to the cost of buying the property (a 'resulting' trust, see 13.2.2.2). In such a case there is no need to appoint an additional trustee until the question of receiving capital money arises.

It is not possible to have more than four trustees of a legal estate. Where there is an attempt to appoint more than four, the Trustee Act (TA 1925), s. 34(2) will vest the legal estate in the first four of full age (that is the first four listed but omitting anyone who is named but who is under 18 when the disposition takes effect).

14.3.2 Who appoints trustees?

In the case of an express trust, it is normal for the disposition creating the trust to specify who are to be the trustees. Thus, if Mary Brown decides to create a trust by will, she will most probably name the trustees, who could be family members (including any of the intended beneficiaries who are adults), or friends, but could also be drawn from her professional advisers, such as her solicitors or bank.

The settlor may also nominate a person or persons to appoint trustees, including any additional or replacement trustees who may be needed in the future. If no appointor is named in the document creating the trust, any new appointments will be made by the existing trustees or, if they have all died, by the personal representatives of the last surviving trustee. If there is no one able or willing to appoint, the appointment may be made by the court, which can also make an order vesting the trust property in the new trustee(s). (For further details, see TA 1925, ss. 36, 41, and 44.)

Appointments of trustees must be made in writing and should be made by deed because a deed is needed in order to ensure that the legal estate in the land which is the trust property vests in the new trustee (TA 1925, s. 40).

14.3.3 Replacement and retirement of trustees

Section 36 of TA 1925 specifies the following circumstances which permit the replacement of a trustee: where a trustee dies; is out of the United Kingdom for more than 12 months; wishes to retire from the trust; refuses or is unfit to act (this would cover dishonesty or bankruptcy among other things); is incapable of acting (illness or mental incapacity); or is an infant (under 18).

A trustee may also retire, without a replacement being made, under TA 1925, s. 39, but only if there remain at least two trustees or the remaining trustee is a trust corporation. Trust corporations are defined in s. 68(18) and include the Public Trustee and certain other corporations.

14.3.4 Control by beneficiaries of appointment and retirement

The impact of TA 1925, s. 36, is now modified by TOLATA 1996, ss. 19–21, which give powers to the beneficiaries to direct the person with the right to appoint under TA 1925, s. 36, so that the choice of new trustee is in fact no longer always controlled by the person who actually appoints. In addition, s. 19 allows beneficiaries to require trustees to resign from the trust. The combination of these powers means that in many cases beneficiaries will be in a position to replace the trustees entirely should they disagree with them or replace particular trustees to whom they object. You should note, however, that the beneficiaries are not given the actual power to make the appointment but just the power to select the person(s) to be appointed.

You should also note that the beneficiaries' new powers do not apply to every trust. They do not apply if the settlor has, in the trust instrument, specified a person who is to appoint new trustees: in such a case the express wishes of the settlor take precedence and the beneficiaries have no power to direct the appointment of trustees of their choice (s. 19(1)(a)).

The new powers also only apply where the beneficiaries are all of full age and capacity and (taken together) are absolutely entitled to the trust property (TOLATA 1996, s. 19(1)(b)). Those are the conditions which would have to be satisfied in order to allow the beneficiaries to elect to end the trust under the rule in *Saunders v Vautier* (1841) 4 Beav 115 and to vest the trust property in themselves absolutely or to resettle on new trusts with fresh trustees (which was the only way that, in the past, the beneficiaries could control the choice of trustee). Thus, TOLATA 1996 simply allows the beneficiaries to control the appointment of new trustees without the expense, and usually adverse tax consequences, of ending the old trust and creating a new one.

In order to exercise their powers under s. 19, the beneficiaries must be unanimous; they must all agree on the new appointment (or retirement) and must give a direction in writing (s. 19(2)). If the beneficiaries cannot agree, they cannot exercise the new power to give directions and as far as appointments are concerned the choice of the new trustee(s) remains with the person who has power to appoint under TA 1925, s. 36.

Finally, note that powers in TOLATA 1996, ss. 19–21, apply to all trusts and not just to the new trusts of land. Thus, they apply also to existing SLA settlements and to trusts of pure personalty. It would be a mistake to think that TOLATA 1996 relates solely to trusts of land: the provisions of Part II of the Act are general in their application.

14.4 What do trustees do?

Whatever the nature of the trust property, trustees will own that property and be responsible for managing and maintaining it in the interests of the beneficiaries. The general topic of trustees' powers and duties is well beyond the scope of this book, so only the specific provisions relating to trusts of land which are to be found in TOLATA 1996 are covered here.

14.4.1 Trustees hold the legal estate

If Mary Brown's will does create a trust of land in respect of No. 9 Trant Way, the legal estate in the property will be transferred after her death to the trustees, who will hold it for the duration of the trust. You should note that this would have been different if Mary's settlement had been created before 1 January 1997 and was still governed by SLA 1925. In that case, the legal estate would have been vested in the life tenant—Mary's widow—and there would be separate 'trustees of the settlement' who perform certain trust functions (see 15.2).

14.4.2 Trustees' powers under TOLATA 1996

14.4.2.1 Powers of an absolute owner

Section 6(1) provides that:

> For the purpose of exercising their functions as trustees, the trustees of land have in relation to the land subject to the trust all the powers of an absolute owner.

This means that Mary's trustees will be able to manage the property as they think fit without automatically being in breach of trust, since the 'powers of an absolute owner' include the ability to sell the land, to mortgage it, to grant leases, and to create other rights over it, such as easements or options. (For the principles that govern how the trustees are supposed to exercise these powers to avoid being in breach of trust, see 14.5.)

In addition to these very general powers given by s. 6(1), the Act makes specific provision for five particular powers:

- to acquire land;
- to delegate functions to beneficiaries;
- to partition the trust land between the beneficiaries;
- to compel the beneficiaries to accept a conveyance of the trust land to themselves; and
- to postpone sale under a trust for sale.

14.4.2.2 Power to acquire land

Section 6(3) (as amended by the Trustee Act 2000, so as to include a reference to s. 8 of that Act) gives the trustees the power to acquire:

freehold or leasehold land in the United Kingdom.

The trustees' power under s. 6(3) may be used to acquire land as an investment, or for occupation by a beneficiary 'or for any other reason' (TA 2000, s. 8(1), replacing an identical provision in s. 6(4) of TOLATA 1996). The provision in TOLATA 1996 resolved an earlier uncertainty as to whether it was permissible to use trust funds to buy a home for a beneficiary. Mary can therefore be assured that if she leaves the house in Trant Way in trust for her widow, her trustees will be able to sell the property and buy another home for her widow, if she ever wants to move.

14.4.2.3 Power to delegate functions to beneficiaries

Section 9(1) gives the trustees the power to delegate any of their functions to one or more of the beneficiaries. This power is covered in more detail in 14.6.

14.4.2.4 Power to partition

Section 7 gives the trustees power to partition the land between the beneficiaries, where the beneficiaries are all of full age and absolutely entitled. While of little use in the majority of cases, this power may assist where it is intended to divide a large estate between beneficiaries or even where a large house can effectively be partitioned into smaller lots. Partition requires the consent of the beneficiaries (s. 7(3)) and, where title to the land is still unregistered, also requires each of them to apply for first registration of title to his or her plot (see 6.3.2.1).

14.4.2.5 Power to compel beneficiaries to take conveyance

A new power for the trustees is contained in s. 6(2), which only applies where all the beneficiaries are of full age and absolutely entitled. This is a power which is designed to permit the trustees to force the beneficiaries to take a conveyance of the trust land, effectively making the beneficiaries themselves the trustees. This will enable the trustees, if they wish, to discharge themselves from the obligations under a settlement where it is no longer necessary for them to be involved.

It appears from the wording of this section that this power applies only where there are two or more beneficiaries. Where there is one beneficiary solely entitled to the trust property, the trustees may bring the trust to an end by conveying the property to him or her, and do not need specific statutory authority to do so.

14.4.2.6 Power to postpone sale under a trust for sale

Section 4(1) gives trustees of a trust that expressly places trustees under a duty to sell an implied power to postpone sale. This power cannot be excluded by the settlor; it is implied by s. 4(1):

> in the case of every trust for sale created by a disposition . . . despite any provision to the contrary made by the disposition.

This marks a change from the old law, since the power to postpone which was formerly implied under LPA 1925, s. 25(1) could be excluded by the settlor's expressing 'a contrary intention'. Section 4(1) applies to all trusts where the trustees have a duty to sell, even those which were already in existence before the Act came into force, and which, therefore, might have contained an express exclusion of the power implied by LPA 1925, s. 25(1).

Situation where trustees disagree about postponing sale

Although TOLATA 1996 makes it impossible for the settlor to exclude the power to postpone, there is no provision in the Act which prevents a minority of trustees refusing to postpone and insisting on sale, in reliance on the rule in *Re Mayo* [1943] Ch 302. There must be unanimous agreement among the trustees to exercise their implied power to postpone sale; even if only one of them disagrees, they must perform their duty of selling the property.

Thus, if the trust contains an obligation to sell and one trustee does not wish to postpone sale, the property will have to be sold even against the wishes of the majority of the trustees. In such a case, if the beneficiaries disagree with the one trustee, they may be able to prevent the sale by exercising their power under s. 19, to require that trustee to retire (if that power applies on the facts of the case). This may require fast action on the part of the beneficiaries, however, and they will have to agree about requiring the trustee's retirement. If this is not possible, another way of seeking to stop the sale could be an application to the court under s. 14 (considered later in 14.8.3).

14.5 Are there any controls over the exercise of trustees' powers?

It may appear from the previous section that trustees have very wide powers under TOLATA 1996. Settlors like Mary Brown may be worried by the extent of those powers, fearing that they may be used to override the wishes of the beneficiaries or perhaps even be misused in the trustees' own interests. It may reassure Mary to know that there are provisions in the Act which can have the effect of considerably limiting the trustees' powers and that in addition trustees are subject to strict duties in equity.

In outline, the conduct of trustees of a trust of land may be controlled as follows:

- by the settlor excluding or restricting their powers under TOLATA 1996;
- by the settlor requiring trustees to obtain prescribed consents before exercising powers;

- by the statutory requirement that trustees consult the beneficiaries and give effect to their wishes;
- by trustees' duties, breach of which amounts to breach of trust.

Each of these methods of control is considered in this section.

14.5.1 Exclusion and restriction of powers by settlor

The Act recognises that the wide powers it confers on trustees may not always be appropriate. Accordingly, s. 8(1) allows the settlor to exclude the powers contained in ss. 6 and 7 by making express provision in the disposition which creates the trust. This will still give the settlor who is creating an elaborately drafted express trust the chance to select the precise powers which the trustees should have in order to carry out the settlor's intentions, but means that in badly prepared, accidentally created, or statutorily imposed trusts the trustees will have very wide powers, which will allow them the best chance to produce a good result for the trust.

The wide terms of s. 8(1) mean that there is nothing to stop the settlor excluding the trustees' power to sell the property, and thus ensuring that the land would remain unsold for the duration of the trust. This possibility could be seen as an undesirable return to control by the 'dead hand' of the settlor; for possible ways of escaping its grip, see Watt [1997] 61 Conv 263. However, it remains possible to apply to the court for an order for sale (see 14.8.3) even where there is no formal power of sale in the trustees (meaning the trustees would be in breach of their duties to the beneficiaries if they sold without a court order). For an example of the circumstances in which the court may authorise sale by the trustees, despite the settlor's exclusion of their power to do so, see *Alexander v Alexander* [2011] EWHC 2721 (Ch), in which the settlor had intended to provide a home for his granddaughter but: (1) the property was close to being derelict; (2) the trustees were receiving no income to use for repairs; and (3) the granddaughter had been living outside the UK for many years and was very unlikely ever to wish to live in the property.

14.5.1.1 Two powers which cannot be restricted or excluded

As already noted, the implied power to postpone sale, given to trustees under a duty to sell by s. 4(1) of TOLATA 1996, cannot be restricted or excluded by the settlor. There is also no provision for the settlor to exclude or limit the trustees' powers to delegate functions to beneficiaries under s. 9(1) (see further 14.6).

14.5.2 Requirements for consents imposed by settlor

If the settlor wishes, the trustees can be required to obtain the consent of named individuals before exercising some or all of their powers. Section 8(2) says that where the settlor has done this:

> . . . the power may not be exercised without the consent.

This means that if the trustees act without all the prescribed consents their act will constitute a breach of trust, and the beneficiaries could seek an injunction to restrain the breach, or could claim compensation from the trustees if it had already occurred.

The persons chosen by the settlor as persons whose consent should be obtained do not have to be beneficiaries or even persons who are in any way connected with the trust, but usually there will be some form of connection. Thus, Mary Brown, for example, could provide that her trustees must not exercise their power to sell 9 Trant Way without the consent of her widow and her daughters.

Should it prove impossible to obtain the consent of a person specified in the trust instrument, it will be necessary for the trustees to protect themselves by making an application to the court under s. 14, which expressly mentions the possibility of the court making an order relieving the trustees of an obligation to obtain any consent before exercising a power.

Section 10(3) also contains provisions to deal with cases in which the person whose consent is required is a minor (under 18) at the time at which the need for consent arises. In this case the trustees should obtain the consent of a person who has parental responsibility for the minor.

The consents rules permit settlors to tie the hands of their trustees by requiring that they obtain consent from someone who will be guaranteed to refuse. Although the trust of land no longer carries with it the obligation to sell which was a feature of the trust for sale, the power to sell is always available to the trustees under s. 6(1) which, as you have seen, provides that the trustees are to have 'all the powers of an absolute owner'. It is true that the power of sale could be excluded by the settlor under s. 8(1) of the Act, but an alternative is to use the requirement of consent to prevent the sale.

An old case that illustrates what can be done in this regard is *Re Inns* [1947] Ch 576, in which the settlor had left a large house by his will to his widow during her lifetime and thereafter to the district council, for use as a hospital. The trust instrument also provided that should the council use the property as a hospital, it would receive an additional gift of £10,000 to pay for equipment. It was also specified that the property could not be sold without the consent of both the widow and the council. The widow wished to sell the property because it was too large and expensive for her to maintain but the council was forced to refuse its consent because, if it gave consent, it would lose its interest in remainder in the trust property and the additional £10,000 (because there would be no house to use as a hospital). The court held that these provisions in the trust instrument were valid and both consents were required in order to sell, even though the effect of enforcing them was to ensure that the property would never be sold.

14.5.3 Statutory requirement for consultation

You will realise that provision for consents will only be capable of being used in an express (and properly drafted) trust, because it is necessary to insert consent provisions into the trust instrument if they are to work. Accordingly, there has long been provision in trusts legislation requiring some degree of consultation of beneficiaries by trustees before the trustees exercised their powers, even where there is no express provision for such consultation in the trust instrument. In the case of the trust for sale this requirement for consultation appeared in LPA 1925, s. 26(3). The advantage of these rules was that they applied automatically to a trust which arose by operation of law where the settlor might not really have been aware that a trust was being created and so would not, or could not, have provided for consents. The old requirements did not, however, work in an entirely satisfactory manner because they did not apply to expressly created trusts unless specifically included by the settlor.

Accordingly, the old requirements were adapted and extended in TOLATA 1996, s. 11(1), which provides:

> The trustees of land shall in the exercise of any function relating to land subject to the trust—
>
> (a) so far as practicable, consult the beneficiaries of full age and beneficially entitled to an interest in possession in the land, and
> (b) so far as consistent with the general interest of the trust, give effect to the wishes of those beneficiaries, or (in the case of dispute) of the majority (according to the value of their combined interests).

The mandatory requirement to consult and to 'give effect to the wishes' of the majority means that the wishes of the beneficiaries can take priority over even an obligation to sell (where the settlor has imposed this). However, you should bear in mind that the requirement to follow the wishes of the beneficiaries applies only 'so far as consistent with the general interest of the trust' and that s. 11 therefore gives beneficiaries less control over what the trustees do than an express term requiring their consent would do.

If the trustees do not consult as required by s. 11(1), or ignore the results of consultation, the beneficiaries may seek an injunction to restrain any intended breach of trust by the trustees, or may claim compensation should the transaction to which they object have been completed.

14.5.3.1 Cases where there is no duty to consult

The duty to consult can be expressly excluded by the settlor in the disposition by which the trust was created (s. 11(2)(a)). The wording of the statutory provision suggests that the exclusion could be either total or in part (for example, excluding the need to consult a particular beneficiary). This rule reverses the old position under which trustees of an express trust were under a duty to consult only if this was expressly provided; a requirement to consult is now implied unless expressly excluded.

Another case in which the duty to consult will not apply is where the trustees are using the power under s. 6(2), to force the beneficiaries to take a conveyance of the trust property. In that case consultation is obviously pointless because this power would not be used unless there were disagreement and the aim of s. 6(2) is to allow the trustees to free themselves of their trust obligations without the agreement of the beneficiaries.

14.5.4 Trustees' duties

Even if the settlor does not exclude or restrict the trustees' very wide powers or impose requirements for consent, the trustees are not free to do exactly what they want with the trust property. They are, of course, subject to all the general equitable rules about how trustees must conduct themselves. Thus, in all their dealings, the trustees must act in the interests of the trust as a whole and not, for example, for any personal advantage, for that would constitute a breach of trust.

The Act seeks to reinforce the general duties of trustees by a number of statutory provisions.

- *Section 6(1)* gives the trustees all the powers of an absolute owner 'for the purpose of exercising their functions as trustees', which could be interpreted as meaning that they could not exercise these powers for an improper purpose.
- *Section 6(6)* requires that the powers 'shall not be exercised in contravention of . . . any other enactment or any rule of law or equity'. Thus, for example, powers of investment must still be exercised in accordance with the requirements of the Trustee Act 2000.
- *Section 6(5)* provides that in exercising their powers the trustees shall have regard to the rights of the beneficiaries.

These provisions may at least help to reassure settlors worried by the extent of the trustees' powers.

14.6 Can beneficiaries be involved in the management of the trust property?

14.6.1 Power to delegate

Section 9 allows trustees in appropriate cases to delegate any of their functions as trustees which relate to the land. The functions which may be delegated are those 'which relate to the land' (s. 9(1)) and in consequence the trustees cannot for example delegate their power of choosing investments for any capital money which may arise from dealing with the land. Moreover, the Act specifically provides (s. 9(7)) that beneficiaries to whom trustee functions have been delegated shall not be regarded as trustees for other purposes—in particular, for the receipt of capital money.

The trustees' power of delegation cannot be excluded by the settlor. There is no provision in s. 9 for the expression of 'a contrary intent' and the power is not included in the general provisions for exclusion or restriction contained in s. 8(1).

14.6.2 To whom may trustees delegate?

Section 9(1) authorises delegation to:

> any beneficiary or beneficiaries of full age and beneficially entitled to an interest in possession in land subject to the trust.

It is important to emphasise that in order to be eligible under this provision, the beneficiary or beneficiaries must be 'entitled to an interest in possession'. Where a trust is designed to benefit several individuals in succession (as, for example, it would be if Mary Brown leaves her property to her wife for life and then after her death to their two daughters), the beneficiary entitled to actual enjoyment of the property (in this example, Mary's widow) is said to have an interest 'in possession', while the later beneficiaries merely have 'future interests'—although in due course they too will have 'interests in possession'. Thus under s. 9(1) the trustees may delegate only to the beneficiary or beneficiaries who are currently entitled to enjoy the property. This means that the trustees could delegate some or all of their functions to Mary's widow (which answers the question about whether she could be involved in looking after the property), but they could not delegate to her daughters during her lifetime.

Where more than one beneficiary is entitled 'in possession' the trustees may delegate to one or more of them. A delegation to several beneficiaries can be expressed to be 'joint', in which case all the delegates must agree to any exercise of power, or 'separate', in which case decisions could be taken by one delegate alone. It is also possible to delegate on terms that the power may be exercised 'jointly or separately'.

14.6.3 Form of delegation, and its duration and revocation

Section 9 regulates various matters relating to the delegation. It must be made by all the trustees jointly, by power of attorney, that is by an authority given by deed to act as agent. The delegation may be for any period or indefinitely, and may be expressly revoked by one or more of the trustees. Further, it is automatically revoked by the appointment of a new trustee (so that the new trustee can consider whether he or she wishes to delegate the functions), and also by the delegate ceasing to be a beneficiary under the trust.

14.6.4 Liability of delegates and trustees

As we have seen, the trustees have the powers of an absolute owner for the purpose of exercising their functions (s. 6(1)), and it is, therefore, possible for a delegate of those functions to enter into major transactions affecting the property. If the delegate acted unwisely and in some way caused loss to the other beneficiaries, who would be liable?

Section 9(7) of the Act provides that beneficiaries to whom functions have been delegated:

> are, in relation to the exercise of the functions, in the same position as trustees (with the same duties and liabilities). . . .

This means that they would be liable for any behaviour which would constitute a breach of trust, and this potential liability may help to ensure that they act responsibly. If they fail to do so, however, and do not have the means to compensate the other beneficiaries for resulting loss, questions may well arise about the liability of the trustees, who made the delegation and thus enabled the beneficiaries to engage in these transactions.

In such a situation, the liability of the trustees was, under the original terms of the Act, surprisingly limited. Under s. 9(8) the trustees were required to exercise 'reasonable care' when deciding to delegate, but were not required to monitor the performance of the delegate thereafter, and so were not responsible for any loss which might be caused.

Section 9(8) was repealed and replaced by the Trustee Act 2000, which inserted a new s. 9A, dealing with both the decision to delegate and supervision after delegation. Under s. 9A(1), trustees considering delegation are subject to a duty of care, defined by the Trustee Act 2000, s. 1, as the duty of each trustee 'to exercise such care and skill as is reasonable in the circumstances', having regard to any special knowledge or experience that the trustee has (or, if a professional trustee, might be expected to have). Section 9A(2) imposes a duty on trustees who make a revocable delegation to keep that delegation under review, and if necessary to intervene by, for example, giving directions to the delegate or revoking the delegation. A trustee is not liable for any act or default of the delegate, unless the trustee has failed to comply with the duty of care in making or reviewing the delegation (s. 9A(6)).

14.7 Do beneficiaries have a right to occupy the trust property?

This is obviously an important question for a settlor like Mary Brown, whose main purpose in making a trust is to enable her widow to continue to live in the family home.

14.7.1 Before 1997

The question whether a beneficiary had a right to occupy trust land caused real difficulty under the old law. It was clear that the current beneficiary of an SLA settlement (the 'tenant for life') was entitled to occupy the property (see Chapter 15). By contrast, in the case of trusts for sale the doctrine of conversion meant that the beneficiaries' interests were notionally in money and not in land and, in such circumstances, it was argued that a beneficiary had a no right to occupy the land itself. As a result, settlors who wanted their beneficiaries to have this right had to make express provision for it when creating the trust. Unless this was done, a beneficiary had no *right* to occupy but might be permitted to do so at the discretion of the trustees.

The statutory trust for sale imposed in cases of co-ownership caused particular difficulty, because equitable interests under such a trust were notionally in money and not in land and therefore could not give a beneficiary the right to occupy. This conclusion, however, was so inappropriate in the case of family homes that the courts did not apply the concept of conversion in this way. Thus, in *Bull v Bull* [1955] 1 QB 234 the Court of Appeal held that an equitable tenant in common had a right to occupy the property until sale and could not be evicted by the legal owner, and the House of Lords in *Williams & Glyn's Bank v Boland* [1981] AC 487 held that a beneficiary under a trust for sale had an interest in the land itself (see 6.5.6.2 and 13.4.1).

14.7.2 Under TOLATA 1996

However, the fact that a beneficiary has an interest in land is not the end of the story. The interest is not in itself sufficient to give the beneficiary the right to occupy the property, since usually trust property should be regarded as an investment for the trust as a whole, and not as something for the personal use of one or more beneficiaries. Accordingly, s. 12 makes specific provision for the right to occupy.

14.7.3 Statutory right to occupy

TOLATA 1996, s. 12(1) provides:

> A beneficiary who is beneficially entitled to an interest in possession in land subject to a trust of land is entitled by reason of his interest to occupy the land at any time if at the time—
>
> (a) the purposes of the trust include making the land available for his occupation (or for the occupation of beneficiaries of a class of which he is a member or of beneficiaries in general), or
>
> (b) the land is held by the trustees so as to be so available.

Section 12(2) adds that the beneficiary has no right to occupy the land if it is 'either unavailable or unsuitable' for occupation by the beneficiary.

You will note that by using the phrase 'entitled to an interest in possession' the Act limits this right to those beneficiaries who are entitled to actual enjoyment of the property and excludes those who currently have only a future interest (see 14.6.2). Thus, under the proposed trust of No. 9, only Mary's widow would have the right to occupy the property during her lifetime, although at her death her daughters would acquire 'interests in possession' and consequently thereafter have a right to occupation.

Under the terms of s. 12(1), it seems that in an express trust it will be best to state expressly whether occupation is, or is not, one of the purposes of the trust. However, even in the absence of such a provision s. 12(1)(b) will allow a claim to exercise the right where the property is in fact available and suitable for occupation. Thus, land held as an investment (for example, factories or office buildings) would not be suitable for residential occupation, while a house might be suitable for occupation but unavailable because it was let to a tenant or in the process of being sold by the trustees.

14.7.3.1 Exclusion or restriction of right to occupy

Where several beneficiaries are 'entitled in possession' and therefore have a right to occupy, s. 13 authorises the trustees to choose between them:

> Where two or more beneficiaries are . . . entitled under section 12 to occupy the land, the trustees of land may exclude or restrict the entitlement of any one or more (but not all) of them.

In addition, the trustees may impose reasonable restrictions on occupying beneficiaries (s. 13(3)). This will tend to mean that a set of terms for occupation will have to be drawn up and these may well draw on the sort of terms usually included in leases as a pattern. In a domestic case, in order to protect the trust as a whole, one might expect conditions as to keeping the premises clean and in reasonable order, requirements to decorate from time to time, obligations not to use the premises for certain purposes, obligations to pay outgoings (see s. 13(5)) and other such terms.

14.7.3.2 Occupation by co-owners

Although ss. 12 and 13 speak of separate trustees and beneficiaries, their provisions apply also to cases of co-ownership where both roles are likely to be held by the same people. If there are disputes about occupation between the co-owners, the trustees' power under s. 13 to choose who shall occupy is unlikely to resolve the conflict, and it will probably be necessary for the court to deal with the matter on an application under s. 14 (see 14.8.3).

14.7.4 Payments by co-owner in occupation

Section 13(6) permits the trustees to require any occupying beneficiary to make compensation payments to other beneficiaries who are not allowed to occupy, or to forgo other payments under the trust to which they would be entitled. The court has also always had the power, under a process known as 'equitable accounting', to require a beneficiary who remained in occupation to pay an 'occupation rent' to a beneficiary who was excluded from the property. There has been some doubt about whether the traditional equitable accounting approach has been superseded by the statutory compensatory regime, but recent cases have continued to treat the traditional remedy as available in cases where the TOLATA 1996 regime does not apply (e.g., where the conditions for a statutory right of occupation are not met).

14.7.4.1 Statutory compensation

A claim to a compensation payment under s. 13(6) may arise between co-owners, for example at the end of a relationship when one of the partners moves out of the family home and has to pay for alternative accommodation. This provision applies only where there is a statutory right of occupation under s. 12: as a result, it applies only where several beneficiaries are simultaneously 'entitled in possession' and, therefore, have a right to occupy the property. Mary Brown can be assured that it does not mean that her widow will have to pay rent to her daughters in order to be allowed to occupy the family home!

Where the parties cannot settle the matter by agreement, a claim for compensation will involve an application to the court under s. 14 of the Act. The court will consider the matters which it is required by s. 15 to take into account under any such application, including the intentions of the settlor, the purposes of the trust, the welfare of any minors in occupation of the trust property, and the interests of secured creditors of any beneficiary (see 14.8.3–4). In *Stack v Dowden* it was thought that the statutory process would not result in very different results from the principles of equitable accounting, Lord Neuberger expressing the opinion (at para. 150) that:

> it would be a rare case where the statutory principles would produce a different result from that which would have resulted from the equitable principles.

However, in *Murphy v Gooch* [2007] EWCA Civ 603, the Court of Appeal took a different view of the significance of the change, Lightman LJ commenting (at para. 14) that under the equitable doctrine the court was concerned simply with achieving a just result between the parties, whereas:

> The wider ambit of relevant considerations means that the task of the court must now be . . . to do justice between the parties with due regard to the relevant statutory considerations and in particular (where applicable) the welfare of the minor, the interests of secured creditors and the circumstances and wishes of the beneficiaries specified. It remains to be seen whether taking these further considerations into account results in any significantly different outcome between the parties.

14.7.4.2 Occupation rent: continuing role of equitable accounting

In two High Court decisions, *French v Barcham* [2009] 1 WLR 1124 and *Davis v Jackson* [2017] EWHC 698, it has been held that the principles of equitable accounting could still apply in circumstances where the s. 13 jurisdiction did not. In both cases, a married couple had jointly held their title to a house on trust for themselves in equal shares. One of the spouses had then become bankrupt, and the trustee in bankruptcy of the bankrupt spouse claimed occupation rent from the spouse who had remained in occupation. In both cases, it was argued that, since a trustee in bankruptcy had no statutory right of occupation under s. 12, no claim under s. 13(6) was available in his favour and the old doctrine of equitable accounting had been effectively abolished by TOLATA 1996. This argument was rejected. In *French v Barcham*, Blackburn J said (at [20]):

> Where the scheme [under s. 13(6)] applies, it must be applied. But where it plainly does not I do not see why the party who is not in occupation of the land ... should be denied any compensation at all if recourse to the court's equitable jurisdiction would justly compensate him.

French v Barcham was followed on this point by Snowden J in *Davis v Jackson* [2017] EWHC 698. He said (at [47]):

> ... if sections 12–15 of TOLATA were held to be an exhaustive regime, it would have the surprising result in practice that neither a bankrupt nor the trustee in bankruptcy would ever be able to claim a credit or payment under section 13 in respect of the occupation by a co-owner of jointly-owned domestic property for the period after the appointment of the trustee in bankruptcy, because neither would be able to establish a statutory right to occupy under section 12. The bankrupt would no longer have any beneficial interest in the house so as to fall within section 12(1) because his interest would have vested in the trustee. And a claim by the trustee would inevitably be defeated by section 12(2) which provides that a beneficiary does not have a right to occupy land if it is 'unsuitable for occupation by him'. . . . [T]his would undoubtedly have amounted to a major change in the law in a very obvious category of cases, which plainly neither Baroness Hale nor Lord Neuberger had in mind when they both commented [in *Stack v Dowden*] that they thought that it would be a rare case in which application of the TOLATA regime would have any different result than under the old equitable principles.

14.7.4.3 Occupation rent: principles of equitable accounting

The traditional rule in equity is that beneficiaries under trusts who have concurrent interests in the property are equally entitled to occupy the property and neither is, therefore, entitled to charge the other rent for her occupation. The default rule is that no occupation rent is payable by a co-owner in occupation to a co-owner who is not in occupation, except where the circumstances make it fair and equitable for such payments to be ordered.

In *French v Barcham*, Blackburne J took the view that the applicable test was whether the absent beneficiary had 'voluntarily chosen' not to occupy the property and had no good reason for this choice: if so, he was not being excluded from the property and no occupation rent would be payable. On the other hand, if there was a good reason for the beneficiary's refusal to occupy the property, he was entitled to occupation rent from the other beneficiaries. Applying this test, he held that a trustee in bankruptcy would normally be acting reasonably in refusing to occupy the family home of the bankrupt and so would usually be entitled to receive an occupation rent from a spouse who remained in occupation. This was the decision on the facts of *French v Barcham* itself.

However, in *Davis v Jackson* [2017] EWHC 698, Snowden J doubted this approach. He said that, for an occupation rent to be payable:

> there ought to be some conduct by the occupying party, or at least some other feature of the case relating to the occupying party, to justify a court of equity concluding that it is appropriate or fair to depart from the default position and to order the occupying party to start paying rent.

On the 'unusual facts' of *Davis v Jackson* itself, no occupation rent was held to be payable to the trustee in bankruptcy. This was partly because the bankrupt husband had never been intended by the parties to have any right of occupation, and his trustee in bankruptcy could not be in any better position. The couple had been estranged at the date of the purchase of the house, which had been acquired only for the purpose of providing a home for the wife and the children. The later deed of trust was executed only when the wife fell behind on her mortgage payments and they decided to jointly remortgage the property; the declaration of trust was a condition imposed on them by the mortgagee. In the circumstances, it was not equitable to require the wife to pay occupation rent to the husband's trustee in bankruptcy, even though it was true that the trustee in bankruptcy had acted reasonably in not attempting to occupy the property.

In the recent case of *Ali v Khatib* [2022] EWCA Civ 149, the Court of Appeal approved Snowden J's approach, in preference to that adopted by Blackburne J in *French v Barcham*, which was confined to its facts. Andrews LJ said:

> The starting point in every case is that a co-owner in occupation is not obliged to pay occupation rent merely because he is living in the property and the co-owner is not. Something more has to be shown which makes it just and equitable that he should pay that other owner for his use and occupation of the property—for example, that he is exploiting the property for his own financial gain, or that he has precluded the co-owner from exercising a right of occupation that he (or she) wished to exercise. The focus should therefore be on the behaviour of the person in occupation.

14.8 How are disputes about the trust property resolved?

14.8.1 Opportunities for dispute

Under TOLATA 1996 a number of people may be involved in decisions about managing or disposing of the trust property. These include:

- beneficiaries entitled in possession, who:
    - must be consulted by the trustees,
    - may be permitted to occupy the property,
    - may have trustees' functions delegated to them; and
- persons whose consent is expressly required by the settlor for the exercise of some or all of the trustees' functions.

Each of these people may have very different views about what ought to be done with the trust property. In particular, where a family home is involved, there may be real difficulty in securing agreement about whether or not to sell it. In addition, the trustees themselves may disagree, or be uncertain, about how to exercise their powers. In an express trust, of the sort that Mary Brown may make, consultation and decision-making may be relatively straightforward for the trustees, since during the widow's lifetime she would be the only beneficiary 'beneficially entitled in possession' and therefore the only person whose wishes would be considered.

The situation is more complicated where two or more beneficiaries are entitled in possession. This could happen under an express trust (for example, where a settlor gives a life interest to two people), and is always found in the case of the statutory trust imposed on co-owners.

14.8.2 Disputes between co-owners

The statutory trust imposed on co-owners is subject to all the provisions of TOLATA 1996, including the requirement for consultation. When you read s. 11(1) (see 14.5.3), it sounds as though deciding on a course of action, such as selling the property, is relatively simple, the decision being taken by a majority of the beneficiaries who will direct the trustees what to do. In real life, however, it is likely to be a much more complicated matter, especially in cases of co-ownership. The same people may be acting as both trustees and beneficiaries, they are very often connected by marriage or some other close relationship, and the property in question is their only home. The majority decision to sell may deprive the minority of a home and the proposal to sell may be only part of a larger dispute about the parties' future together. It therefore must not be assumed that having 'consulted the beneficiaries', the trustees can always readily give effect to the wishes of the majority, and a particular problem arises where the minority refuses to move out so that the property can be offered for sale with vacant possession. This issue is considered further in Chapter 17.

In practice, the solution in any situation involving disputes that cannot be resolved about the trust property, is to apply to the court for an order under s. 14. We can now look at the powers of the court under this section.

14.8.3 TOLATA 1996, s. 14

Section 14(1) provides:

> Any person who is a trustee of land or has an interest in property subject to a trust of land may make an application to the court for an order under this section.

14.8.3.1 Who may apply to the court?

Applications under this section may be made not only by trustees and beneficiaries, but also by anyone else with an interest in the property, such as a mortgagee or a trustee in bankruptcy.

A mortgagee is a creditor who has lent money and been granted an interest in the borrower's land as security for the loan. If the loan is not repaid, the mortgagee has a right to sell the land and take the proceeds of sale to satisfy the debt (for details, see Chapter 22). Thus, if the trustees have mortgaged the legal estate or a beneficiary has mortgaged his or her beneficial interest, the mortgagee may want the property to be sold, against the wishes of the beneficiaries.

Similarly, if one of the beneficiaries becomes bankrupt, that person's beneficial interest under the trust will vest in the trustee in bankruptcy, who may want the trust property to be sold so that the bankrupt's share of the proceeds can be used to pay his or her debts.

14.8.3.2 What orders may be made by the court?

Under s. 14(2) the court is authorised to make any such order as it thinks fit relating to:

- the exercise of the trustees' functions; or
- the nature and extent of a person's interest in the trust property.

In practice, however, the applicants will have to specify the remedy they seek.

1. Exercise of the trustees' functions

Under s. 14, the trustees may apply for directions about the exercise of their functions, and in particular may seek orders releasing them from requirements to obtain consent or to consult the beneficiaries (s. 14(2)(a)). Beneficiaries who are dissatisfied with the way in which trustees have exercised their powers may want to raise questions about such matters as lack of consultation, delegation of powers, or occupation of the property. The court can restrain any proposed exercise of the trustees' powers or conversely can order them to act where they are failing to do so.

As we have seen, one of the questions which is most likely to raise problems, particularly among co-owners, relates to the sale of the trust property, and the court can order sale on the application of the trustees or of any person with an interest in the property.

2. Nature and extent of a person's interest in the trust property

Questions about the nature and size of an interest under a trust are particularly likely to arise in cases of implied trusts, where there may be real doubt about the existence or value of a beneficiary's interest under such a trust. The court can resolve such questions on an application under s. 14.

14.8.4 TOLATA 1996, s. 15

Section 15 provides guidance for the court on matters it must consider when determining an application. Section 15(1) reads:

> The matters to which the court is to have regard in determining an application for an order under section 14 include—
>
> (a) the intention of the person or persons (if any) who created the trust,
> (b) the purposes for which the property subject to the trust is held,
> (c) the welfare of any minor who occupies or might reasonably be expected to occupy any land subject to the trust as his home, and
> (d) the interests of any secured creditor of any beneficiary.

The matters which the court is required to consider are said to 'include' those listed in s. 15(1). This means that the court may also take other relevant matters into account (for example, the health of one of the parties—*Bank of Ireland Home Mortgages Ltd v Bell* [2001] 2 FLR 809).

Another point to note is that s. 15(1) gives no guidance on the relative importance of each of the factors mentioned, although in practice the court will have to weigh one against the other. For example, there may well be a conflict between the interest of a mortgagee in recovering a loan through the sale of the property and the welfare of a child who needs the property as a home. It is for the court to decide how much weight should be attached to each consideration and we will see how this works in practice in 14.8.5.

As well as considering the matters mentioned in s. 15(1), the court is required to consider the circumstances and wishes of the beneficiaries (s. 15(2) and (3)).

14.8.4.1 Application by a trustee in bankruptcy

Where a trustee in bankruptcy applies for an order for sale under s. 14, s. 15 does not apply. Instead, the matters which the court should consider are to be found in s. 335A of the Insolvency Act 1986, a new section inserted by TOLATA 1996 (Sch. 3, para. 23).

This new section provides that, where the property in question includes the home of the bankrupt, or of his spouse or civil partner, the court considering the application for sale shall take into account:

- the interests of the bankrupt's creditors;
- the conduct of the spouse or civil partner in relation to the bankruptcy (essentially, whether he or she was a party to any fault);
- the needs and financial resources of the spouse or civil partner; and
- the needs of any children.

This accords with other provisions of the Insolvency Act 1986, which are designed to provide some short-term protection for the spouse or civil partner and children of a bankrupt, but at the same time to ensure that creditors can realise the bankrupt's assets within a reasonable period. Accordingly, the section goes on to provide that where the application for sale is made more than a year after bankruptcy, the court must assume that the interests of the creditors outweigh all other considerations 'unless the circumstances of the case are exceptional' (s. 335A(3)).

14.8.5 How are these provisions working in practice?

The brief explanation of the rules in ss. 14 and 15 given at 14.8.4.1 cannot really indicate the approach of the courts to applying their powers. It is therefore worth looking at the development of the courts' approach to their use of the powers under s. 14.

14.8.5.1 *Mortgage Corporation v Shaire* [2001] Ch 743

The first detailed consideration occurred in this case. The facts in this case were complicated, but the key issue for s. 14 purposes can be stated quite briefly. Mrs Shaire and her partner were the legal owners of their house, which they held on the statutory trusts imposed in cases of co-ownership (originally a trust for sale, converted into a trust of land by TOLATA 1996). Mrs Shaire was held to be entitled to 75 per cent of the value of the property, while her partner was entitled to 25 per cent. After his death, it was discovered that he had mortgaged the property to secure a loan, having forged Mrs Shaire's signature on the documents. The mortgage repayments were in arrears and in order to enforce its security the chargee (i.e., mortgagee) sought an order for sale under TOLATA 1996, s. 14. The court concluded that Mrs Shaire's share was not affected by the forged mortgage but that the mortgagee was entitled to the 25 per cent share in the property which had belonged to the deceased. The mortgagee could recover this only if the property was sold but Mrs Shaire wanted to remain in the property.

In dealing with whether to order sale, Neuberger J began by considering the position on the old law before the Act. There was clear authority (*Re Citro* [1991] Ch 142) that, save in exceptional cases, sale would be ordered on any application by a trustee in bankruptcy and that a similar approach was adopted in dealing with applications by mortgagees or chargees (*Lloyds Bank plc v Byrne & Byrne* [1993] 1 FLR 369). As we have seen, this approach in cases of *bankruptcy* is now given statutory force by the new s. 335A added to the Insolvency Act 1986 by TOLATA 1996. Should applications by *mortgagees and chargees* continue to be treated in the same way, or had the 1996 Act changed the law?

In the view of Neuberger J, the law on this point was changed by s. 15 and it was no longer necessary to apply the same approach to applications by chargees as one would to those by trustees in bankruptcy. Among the reasons given for this view was the fact that 'the interests of the secured creditor' is just one of four factors to be taken into account under s. 15(1) and there is no suggestion that it is to be given any more importance than the interests of the children living in the house (p. 758). Further (at p. 760) the judge thought it not unlikely that:

> the legislature intended to relax the fetters on the way in which the court exercised its discretion . . . so as to tip the balance somewhat more in favour of families and against banks and other chargees. Although the law under [LPA 1925,] s. 30 was clear following *Citro* and *Byrne*, there were indications of judicial dissatisfaction with the state of the law at that time.

In the judge's opinion, s. 15 had changed the law and the court now had greater flexibility in dealing with applications of this sort. In doing so it must take account of the factors set out in s. 15(1) and the circumstances and wishes of the beneficiaries under s. 15(3). In addition, there might be other factors in a particular case which the court could or should take into account. Once the relevant factors to be taken into account had been identified, it was a matter for the court as to what weight to give to each factor in a particular case.

There were, also in *Shaire*, a number of more general observations worth noting. In particular, the judge commented (at p. 758) on the change of emphasis resulting from the replacement of the statutory trust for sale by the trust of land:

> . . . the very name 'trust for sale' and the law as it has been developed by the courts suggests that under the old law, in the absence of a strong reason to the contrary, the court should order sale. Nothing in the language of the new code as found in the 1996 Act supports that approach.

The judge also considered the extent to which the case law which grew up around LPA 1925, s. 30 may be relevant in interpreting ss. 14 and 15 of the new Act. An earlier county court decision, *TSB Bank plc v Marshall* [1998] 3 EGLR 100 considered that the old case law remained relevant in interpreting the new provisions (thus confirming the view advanced by the Law Commission when the legislation was prepared). However, this led the judge, on facts very similar to those in *Shaire*, to apply the old rules in *Citro* and *Byrne*—which as we have just seen, were thought in the later case to be no longer applicable to chargees. Neuberger J accordingly disagreed with the conclusions reached in *TSB Bank v Marshall*, and (at p. 761) explained his own view on the extent to which old authorities would be of assistance in interpreting the Act:

> On the one hand, to throw over all the wealth of learning and thought given by so many eminent judges to the problem. . . . seems somewhat arrogant and possibly rash. On the other hand, where one has concluded that the law has changed in a significant respect so that the court's discretion is significantly less fettered than it was, there are obvious dangers in relying on authorities which proceeded on the basis that the court's discretion was more fettered than it now is. I think it would be wrong to throw over all the earlier cases without paying them any regard. However, they have to be treated with caution, in light of the change in the law, and in many cases they are unlikely to be of great, let alone decisive, assistance.

In case you are wondering what happened to Mrs Shaire, it was held that the interest of the chargee in realising his security outweighed Mrs Shaire's wish to remain in her home, particularly given her ability to buy another house with her share of the proceeds. The judge was, therefore, minded to order sale, unless Mrs Shaire found herself able to take on the amount owed to the chargee as an additional loan on which she would pay interest. He, therefore, postponed making an order so as to give the parties time to reach an agreement—and we know no more.

While the decision in *Shaire* gave adequate protection to the mortgagee's interest, Neuberger J's view of the radical changes introduced by ss. 14 and 15 were seen by some commentators as likely to cause anxiety and concern among professional lenders. As Pascoe put it ([2000] 64 Conv 315 at 327):

> Neuberger J's approach is not one of consolidation and rationalisation; rather he is wiping the slate clean and starting afresh with secured creditors the likely casualties of the new approach. It will be a welcome change in the law for spouses, partners and children living in the property, but an inexpedient, prejudicial and financially detrimental development if one is a secured creditor.

However, a somewhat more conservative approach was subsequently adopted by the Court of Appeal in *Bank of Ireland Home Mortgages Ltd v Bell* [2001] 2 FLR 809.

14.8.5.2 *Bank of Ireland Home Mortgages Ltd v Bell* [2001] 2 FLR 809

In outline, Mr and Mrs Bell were the legal owners of a house bought with a loan secured by a mortgage of the property, on which repayments were in arrears, the marriage having broken down. On an application by the mortgagees for an order for sale under s. 14, the trial judge accepted the wife's claim that her husband had forged her signature on the relevant mortgage documents, and in consequence held that the mortgage operated only as an equitable charge over his beneficial interest in the property. Although the wife's interest in the property was relatively small (10 per cent at most), the judge refused to order sale. In doing so, he took into account the fact that the property was purchased as a family home and was currently occupied by Mrs Bell and her son, who at that stage was still under age. He also took into account the fact that Mrs Bell was in poor health.

On appeal by the mortgagee, the Court of Appeal reversed the decision and ordered sale, holding that the trial judge had erred in exercising his discretion under s. 15. The matters to which he had given weight in reaching his decision should either not have been regarded or deserved only slight consideration. The acquisition of the property as a family home and its continued occupation by the wife, on which the trial judge had relied, had ceased to be relevant considerations under s. 15(1)(a) and (b) with the departure of the husband on the break-down of the marriage. The occupation by the son might be relevant under s. 15(1)(c), but at the time of the trial he was not far from the age of majority, and his welfare 'should only have been a very slight consideration' (per Peter Gibson LJ at para. 28). The court agreed that the judge could properly have regard to the wife's poor health, but considered that this would be a reason for postponing sale rather than for refusing to order it.

By contrast, the trial judge had not mentioned the matter that the Court of Appeal regarded as most significant: that, with the addition of interest, the debt had now grown to more than £300,000. This was more than the value of the house, and was increasing daily. Peter Gibson LJ commented (at para. 31) that before 1996 the creditors' interest would prevail over that of the spouse and family of the debtor save in exceptional circumstances, and went on to say:

> The 1996 Act, by requiring the court to have regard to the particular matters specified in s. 15, appears to me to have given scope for some change in the court's practice. Nevertheless, a powerful consideration is and ought to be whether the creditor is receiving proper recompense for being kept out of his money, repayment of which is overdue.

By refusing to order sale the judge required the bank to go on waiting for its money with no prospect of recovery from the Bells, and that seemed very unfair to the bank. The other two members of the Court of Appeal agreed with this approach, and sale of the property was ordered.

As far as the actual outcome for the parties is concerned, there is no significant difference between the decisions in *Shaire* and in *Bell*, the respective courts being willing in principle to order sale in both cases. However, there is a considerable difference in the views expressed about the overall effect of s. 15, Neuberger J treating it as producing a significant change in the law, and Peter Gibson LJ seeing it as giving 'some scope for change in the court's practice'.

Following these cases, the courts have in fact become quite adept at considering the various factors which they are required to consider. The tendency has been to emphasise that each case must turn on its own facts. However, there are signs that the courts can become quite creative in their use of the powers under s. 14.

14.8.5.3 *Bagum v Hafiz and Hai* [2016] Ch 241

In this case, there had been an express decision to create a trust of domestic property, in which Mrs Bagum lived with her two sons, Hafiz and Hai (and their wives). It was agreed that all three should have an equal beneficial interest in the property and all three should be trustees. Unfortunately, over time, the relationship between the two brothers broke down and Mr Hai left the property. Thereafter, the three could not agree what should be done about the property. Mr Hafiz offered to buy his brother's share and his brother refused to do this, saying he wanted the property sold. At first instance, Horney J clearly concluded that the best solution for the parties would be for Mr Hafiz to acquire his brother's share. This would avoid Mrs Bagum and Mr Hafiz having to move and would satisfy Mr Hai's claims to the property. Unfortunately, wide as it is, s. 14 does not give the court power to require a beneficiary to sell his interest because this is not something that the trustees themselves could require. However, the judge ordered that: (1) the property should be sold; but (2) the sale was to be delayed for up to six weeks, during which Mr Hafiz was to have the chance to purchase the property at a price to be set by the court.

On appeal, the Court of Appeal confirmed that the court has no power under s. 14 to require one beneficiary to sell a beneficial interest to another. The court confirmed that the decision made in the lower court was possible and that the judge had exercised her powers within the limits of her discretion and her decision had minimised the risks to each of the parties involved in the case. Furthermore, the court confirmed that ss. 14 and 15 confer on the court a wider discretion than trustees themselves might have. Briggs LJ said (at para. 23):

> ... I consider that the clear object and effect of sections 14 and 15 is to confer upon the court a substantially wider discretion, exercised on the basis of wider considerations, than might be enjoyed by the trustees themselves, acting without either the consent of

their beneficiaries or an order of the court. For example, section 15(1)(c) requires the court to consider the welfare of a minor in occupation of the trust property as his home, whether or not that minor is a beneficiary of the trust. Section 15(1)(d) requires the court to have regard to the interests of secured creditors (rather than merely to respect their strict legal rights) . . . Section 15(1)(a) may bring into play the intention of the person who created the trust that benefits be conferred upon particular beneficiaries. All this departs from the general rule of equity which requires the trustees single-mindedly to advance the interests of the beneficiaries as a class, without preferring some of them over others.

Accordingly, you should note that the powers of the court under s. 14 are very wide and that the court will not hesitate to use its powers, in order to achieve a sensible solution in the light of the facts as a whole and the s. 15 considerations.

14.9 Is it safe for purchasers to buy trust property?

When Mary Brown is thinking about creating a trust, she may wonder whether doing so might make it more difficult to sell the house if her widow needed to move. The trustees would have the power to sell, but would any purchaser want to buy?

It is certainly true that many years ago, there were considerable dangers in buying trust property. We explained earlier (2.6.2) the general principle that if trustees sold property which was subject to a trust the purchaser would take the property subject to the rights of the beneficiaries if the purchaser knew (or ought to have known) of them. The purchaser in such a case, on acquiring the property, became no more than a trustee and held the property for the beneficiaries. However, during the nineteenth century, it became necessary to change this approach in some way. Economic reasons made it desirable to facilitate the sale of land held within family settlements and accordingly a series of statutes, culminating in the 1925 property legislation, established the process of 'overreaching' the rights of beneficiaries, and in addition introduced other measures designed to protect the purchaser (see 5.5 and 6.5).

14.9.1 Protection of the purchaser

TOLATA 1996 imposes a number of duties upon trustees which are designed to protect the beneficiaries. These include duties:

- to obtain any consents required by the settlor (s. 8(2));
- to consult the beneficiaries (s. 11(1)), and to have regard to the beneficiaries' rights when exercising trustee powers (s. 6(5));
- to take care in making and reviewing the delegation of functions to beneficiaries (s. 9A); and
- to observe all statutory, legal, and equitable rules in exercising trustee powers (s. 6(6)).

If trustees do not observe the relevant statutory requirements on these matters, they will be in breach of trust. Would this have any adverse effect on a purchaser from the trustees, and must the purchaser check that the trustees are behaving correctly in their dealings? If this were necessary (for example, checking that four or five consents required by the settlor had been obtained), buying trust property could be very onerous and this would deter prospective purchasers.

There is also the possibility that the trustees' statutory powers have been limited in some way by the settlor under s. 8. What if the trustees ignored the limitation and entered into some transaction which was outside their powers? Does a purchaser have to check whether there are any such restrictions?

The LPA 1925 contained several measures designed to protect the purchaser and reduce the enquiries he or she might have to make. These are re-enacted, with a number of additional provisions, in TOLATA 1996.

(1) *Consents* Where trustees are required to obtain more than two consents, the purchaser need only check that at least two consents have been obtained (s. 10(1)).

(2) *Consultation* A purchaser is not required to check that the trustees have complied with the statutory requirements for consulting the beneficiaries or having regard to their rights (s. 16(1)).

(3) *Delegation* Where trustees have purported to delegate their functions, a purchaser is entitled to presume that the delegate is a person to whom the delegation can be made, unless the purchaser knows otherwise (s. 9(2)).

(4) *Duty to exercise powers in accordance with statutory, legal, and equitable rules* Where trustees act in breach of this duty, any conveyance to a purchaser who has no actual notice of the breach is valid (s. 16(2)).

(5) *Limitation of trustees' powers* The trustees should inform a purchaser of any such limitation, but it will not invalidate any conveyance to a purchaser who does not have actual notice of it (s. 16(3)).

When considering these provisions it is important to realise that they operate only in favour of the *purchaser*. If the *trustees* fail to observe the full statutory requirements they will be in breach of trust, but this will not invalidate the sale or make the purchaser liable to the beneficiaries in any way.

These provisions of TOLATA 1996 protect a purchaser of land held on trust by ensuring that such a purchaser is not fixed with 'constructive notice' of a breach of trust (see 5.5.5.2). As such, they are usually thought to matter only in cases where a purchaser needs to show that she has the benefit of the equity's darling defence, including that she lacks notice of the breach of trust. In the modern law, however, there are various ways in which a purchaser of trust land can avoid being bound by the trusts even where she does not have the benefit of the equity's darling defence. The most important of these is the defence under s. 29 of LRA 2002, which applies in favour of a purchaser for value of a registered estate and which does not depend on showing that she lacks notice of any adverse interests that are not overriding (see 6.5). This defence is not peculiar to trusts and its requirements have already been discussed in Chapter 6. The key point to note here is that a buyer of registered land will not need to rely on the purchaser-protective rules under TOLATA 1996 to avoid liability to a beneficiary under a trust of that land and so these rules are only relevant to unregistered land.

Meanwhile, for both registered and unregistered land, there is a special mechanism for purchasers to avoid being bound by interests under trusts in particular: overreaching (see 5.5). This section outlines the requirements of overreaching in more detail, and the question whether TOLATA 1996 has made any difference to those requirements.

14.9.2 Overreaching

You have seen how overreaching works (5.5) and you will remember that it is a process by which, provided the proper procedures are followed, the beneficiaries' interests are lifted from the existing trust property and attached instead to the money paid by the purchaser, and in due course to any property in which the trustees may invest that money. Where overreaching operates, the purchaser will acquire the property free of the interests of the beneficiaries, even if the purchaser knows of those interests.

The statutory provisions which govern overreaching in relation to a trust of land are contained in LPA 1925, s. 2(1)(ii) and s. 27, as amended by TOLATA 1996, Sch. 3, para. 4(1). These provisions apply to both registered and unregistered land. In order to be protected, the purchaser must ensure that the capital money (purchase price or other capital sum arising on the transaction, such as a mortgage advance or the premium paid on the grant of a lease) is paid to no fewer than two trustees or to a trust corporation (see 5.5.2.1). The money must not be paid to the beneficiaries (unless they also happen to be the trustees and even then it will be usual to require a receipt from them in their capacity as trustees). It is for this reason that TA 1925, s. 39 seeks to ensure that there are never fewer than two trustees unless the trustee is a trust corporation. If a trust has, for some reason, only one trustee for the time being, a purchaser should insist on the appointment of a second trustee before he pays over any purchase money.

The importance of the second trustee is well illustrated by the two cases of *Williams & Glyn's Bank Ltd v Boland* [1981] AC 487 and *City of London Building Society v Flegg* [1988] AC 54, discussed in Chapters 5 (see 5.5.2.1) and 6 (see 6.5.6.2 and 6.5.6.1). It will be recalled that, in the *Boland* case, capital money (in the form of a secured loan from the bank) was paid to the sole registered proprietor, with the result that Mrs Boland's equitable rights were not overreached, so that the mortgagee took subject to her interest in the property. By contrast, in *Flegg* the mortgage advance was made to the two registered proprietors, who held as trustees for themselves and the Fleggs, and in consequence the Fleggs' interest was overreached. As a result, they no longer had an interest in the land which could be asserted against the mortgagee, but only an interest in the money in the hands of the trustees. Theoretically, beneficiaries in this situation are protected by their rights against the capital money, but in practice, of course, this may be illusory. In *Flegg*, the money had been applied for the trustees' own purposes, and although they might be liable to the beneficiaries for breach of trust, any judgment against them would be worthless if they did not have the financial means to meet it.

14.9.2.1 Overreaching and TOLATA 1996

It is usually thought that the outcome in *Flegg* would have been different had the trustees actually exceeded their powers, since *ultra vires* transactions (i.e., transactions 'outside the powers' of the trustees) do not overreach the beneficiaries' interests (*State Bank of India v Sood* 1997 Ch 276 at p. 281). However, in *Flegg*, the House of Lords took the view that the transaction in question was within the powers of the trustees, even if it was in breach of trust. This was because the trust was a statutory 'trust for sale' and the trustees undoubtedly had the power, under such a trust, to mortgage the land.

It has been suggested that TOLATA, in replacing the old trust for sale by the new trust of land, might have altered this (See Ferris and Battersby [1998] 62 Conv 168). This is because, although s. 6 of TOLATA gives trustees broad powers (see 14.4.2), s. 6(6) provides that the powers 'shall not be exercised in contravention of, or of any order made in pursuance of, any other enactment or any rule of law or equity'. If this is interpreted to mean that an exercise of a power in contravention of any rule of law or equity is *ultra vires*, it might be thought that no transaction that involves a breach of trust could be an overreaching transaction (reversing *Flegg*). However, as has been noted, purchasers of unregistered land are protected by the provisions of s. 16(2), which provides in effect that contravention by the trustees of 'any rule of law or equity' shall not invalidate the conveyance to a purchaser who has no actual notice of the contravention. This provision does not, however, apply to registered land (s. 16(7)).

14.9.2.2 Overreaching and LRA 2002

It has been suggested that excluding registered land from the protection of s. 16 could put a purchaser at risk (Ferris and Battersby [1998] 62 Conv 168). While this view has been criticised (see for example Dixon [2000] 64 Conv 267, and a further article by Ferris and Battersby [2001] 65 Conv 221), the point was addressed by the enactment of LRA 2002, s. 26, which relates to the protection of disponees (i.e., those who take under a disposition of registered land). Section 26 provides that, subject to an exception for limitations protected by an entry on the register or imposed by the Act:

> a person's right to exercise owner's powers in relation to a registered estate or charge is to be taken to be free from any limitation affecting the validity of a disposition.

Section 26(3) adds that this provision has effect:

> only for the purpose of preventing the title of a disponee being questioned (and so does not affect the lawfulness of a disposition).

According to the Law Commission report preceding the Act, this provision protects a purchaser who takes registered land under an ultra vires transaction from trustees, while the beneficiaries will retain their rights against the trustees for any breach of trust. If this is correct, it follows that a purchaser from trustees of registered land need only ensure that she has paid two trustees, in compliance with the terms of any restriction that appears on the register. There is no requirement to investigate whether the transaction is within the powers of the trustees or to check if the trustees have complied with their duties under TOLATA 1996.

The point is well illustrated by the recent case of *N3 Living Ltd v Burgess Property Investments Ltd* [2020] EWHC 1711, where a purchaser who had contracted to buy land refused to complete the sale upon discovering the possible existence of a trust of land. The vendor proposed to appoint a second trustee, to ensure that the conveyance to the purchaser had overreaching effect, but the purchaser's solicitors argued that this would not be effective in overreaching the interests under the trust if any breach of duty was involved. Rejecting this argument, and requiring the purchaser to complete the sale in accordance with the contract for sale, Morgan J pointed out that the beneficiary was not in actual occupation of the land and so the purchaser would take free of her interests under s. 29 of LRA 2002 regardless of whether overreaching took place. However, he went on to consider the position if the purchaser did need to rely on overreaching to be sure that he could not be bound by any duty to the beneficiary, and concluded that s. 26 would protect the purchaser from any liability in the event of a breach of trust as between the trust beneficiary and the trustee-vendors. Although the point was *obiter*, since there was no evidence of an intended breach of trust on the facts of the case, it is a useful illustration of the normal practice of purchasers buying registered land that is held on trust and the strong protection for purchasers who comply with that normal practice.

14.9.2.3 What happens if the capital money is not paid to two trustees?

The Law of Property Act 1925 does not say what the position would be if a purchaser does not comply with s. 27. Accordingly, one must in such a case consider the ordinary rules which determine whether a purchaser is bound by an equitable interest in land.

Unregistered land

The purchaser who is a bona fide purchaser for value without notice will take free of such interests in unregistered land. Therefore, it is possible to obtain a legal estate free of the beneficial interests, even where capital money is not paid to two trustees (*Caunce v Caunce* [1969] 1 WLR 286) although only if the purchaser can avoid the rigours of actual, constructive, and imputed notice (see 2.4.3.4). The provisions of TOLATA 1996 may be invoked by a purchaser to avoid being fixed with constructive notice of certain breaches of which she has no actual notice.

Registered land

You will remember from Chapter 6 that a purchaser of registered land is always at risk from overriding interests (which are binding without any entry on the register). In the case of trust property, the interests of beneficiaries who are in actual occupation of the land could bind the purchaser under LRA 2002, Sch. 3 para. 2, just as Mrs Boland's interest bound the mortgagee under the earlier provisions of LRA 1925, s. 70(1)(g) in *Williams & Glyn's Bank v Boland* [1981] AC 487. Where the beneficiaries are *not* in actual occupation, a purchaser of registered land will automatically take free of their interests under s. 29. However, if there is a restriction on the register, the purchaser will normally need to comply with the terms of that restriction, or to apply for its discharge or modification, in order to get on the register in the first place and so get the benefit of the s. 29 defence.

14.9.2.4 Overreaching in the absence of a payment of capital money

A slightly different problem arose in *State Bank of India v Sood* [1997] Ch 276, in which the issue was whether overreaching can *only* take place under s. 27 or whether there are other occasions upon which beneficial interests can be overreached. The issue arose in this case because there had been no payment of capital monies at the time of the disposition in question.

The case involved a house that was registered in the names of the first and second defendants but which was held on trust by them for themselves and for the third to seventh defendants. All seven defendants occupied the premises and thus the beneficial interests under the trust were overriding interests under LRA 1925, s. 70(1)(g) in relation to later dispositions. The disposition in question was a mortgage of the premises to the bank. Normally, a mortgage will give rise to a mortgage advance and that advance would constitute capital money (that was the case in *Flegg*) but in this instance the trustees mortgaged the property as security for the discharge of their existing debts and for any future indebtedness. No actual moneys were advanced at the time the mortgage was granted.

Later, one of the trustees was made bankrupt and the bank tried to enforce its security, relying on the principle set out in *Flegg* that where overreaching occurred it was irrelevant that the beneficial interests were overriding interests under the LRA 1925, s. 70. The problem was that the bank could not rely on LPA 1925, s. 27 because no capital money had been paid. Nonetheless, the Court of Appeal held that in this case the interests of the beneficiaries had been overreached, saying that s. 27(2) was relevant only where capital money actually arose and that it did not mean that there could be no overreaching without capital money. In reaching this conclusion Peter Gibson LJ adopted the analysis of the position set out in Harpum's article 'Overreaching trustees' powers and the reform of the 1925 legislation' [1990] CLJ 277 that:

> the exercise intra vires of a power of disposition which does not give rise to any capital money, such as an exchange of land, overreaches just as much as a transaction which does.

The case clearly establishes that the courts will consider whether other overreaching events have arisen. You may like to note that Peter Gibson LJ's judgment also provides a useful analysis of the overreaching provisions in the LPA 1925. (Also see Oldham, 'Overreaching Where No Capital Monies Arise' [1997] CLJ 494.)

14.9.2.5 What happens to capital money paid to trustees?

You may be wondering what happens to the proceeds of sale when they have been paid to the trustees and the rights of the beneficiaries have been overreached. This depends on the terms of the trust. It may be that the capital money is to be paid over to a sole beneficiary or divided between several beneficiaries. On the other hand, if the trust is to continue, the trustees could invest in any authorised investments, and their power to do so would include the purchase of any estate in land for any purpose (TOLATA 1996, s. 6(3)). Of course, where this power is exercised the trustees will again hold land and this will give rise to a trust of land.

14.9.3 Protecting a purchaser who buys land that is no longer subject to a trust

A trust of land comes to an end:

- when the trustees transfer the legal estate to beneficiaries who are absolutely entitled; or
- when a joint tenant becomes solely entitled to both the legal estate and the equitable interest by right of survivorship.

A trust may come to an end when the beneficiaries are of full age and are absolutely entitled to the property (i.e., the interest of any earlier beneficiary has come to an end and there are no other conditions to be fulfilled before the beneficiaries may enjoy the property). This is the situation which might arise under a settlement created by Mary Brown, if she provides that the property is to go unconditionally to their daughters after the death of her wife. When the widow dies, the daughters will be absolutely entitled and the trustees may convey the legal estate in the house to them. The conveyance to the beneficiaries will bring the trust to an end, and the trustees should execute a '**deed of discharge**', declaring that they are discharged from the trust (s. 16(4) and (5)). Any restrictions on the register that reflect the existence of the trust should be removed at this stage.

Anyone who wishes to buy unregistered land after it has been transferred to the beneficiaries in this way should insist on seeing the deed of discharge, which will show that the property is no longer subject to a trust; if this is not done, there is a risk of being fixed with constructive notice of the trusts if it turns out that they have not come to an end. If such a deed cannot be produced, the purchaser should insist on paying the money to two trustees, to ensure that any remaining trusts are overreached. Meanwhile, a purchaser of registered land should take the usual steps of obtaining the consent to the sale of any persons in actual occupation of the property and ensuring that any restrictions on the register are either complied with or discharged.

These rules should cover all Mary might want to ask about trusts of land (14.2.2). However, there is still one matter that probably would not concern Mary, but which you need to know about. Accordingly, the next chapter covers the SLA settlements that may still exist if created before TOLATA 1996.

FURTHER READING

Megarry and Wade, *The Law of Real Property*, 9th edn., Sweet & Maxwell, 2019, Chapter 11.

Barnsley, 'Co-owners Rights to Occupy Trust Land' [1998] CLJ 123.

Clements, 'The Changing Face of Trusts' [1998] MLR 56.

Dixon, 'To Sell or Not to Sell: That Is the Question: The Irony of the Trusts of Land and Appointment of Trustees Act 1996' (2011) 70 CLJ 579.

Hopkins, 'The Trusts of Land and Appointment of Trustees Act 1996' [1996] Conv 411 (and see Sydenham [1997] Conv 242).

Martyn, 'Co-Owners and Their Entitlement to Occupy Their Land Before and After the Trusts of Land and Appointment of Trustees Act 1996: Theoretical Doubts Are Replaced by Practical Difficulties' [1997] Conv 254.

Oldham, 'Overreaching Where No Capital Monies Arise' [1997] CLJ 494.

Smith, 'Trusts of Land Reform' [1990] Conv 12.

Watt, 'Escaping s. 8(1) Provisions in 'New Style' Trusts of Land' [1997] 61 Conv 263.

TOLATA 1996, s. 12

Bright, 'Occupation Rents and [TOLATA] 1996: From Property to Welfare?' [2009] 73 Conv 378.

Pascoe, 'Right to Occupy under a Trust of Land: Muddled Legislative Logic' [2006] 70 Conv 54 (in general, too detailed; but see pp. 58–62 on questions arising from s. 12(1)).

TOLATA 1996, s. 15

Pascoe, 'Section 15 of the Trusts of Land and Appointment of Trustees Act 1996—A Change in the Law?' [2000] 64 Conv 315.

Probert, 'Creditors and Section 15 of the Trusts of Land and Appointment of Trustees Act 1996: First among Equals?' [2002] 66 Conv 61 (case note on *Bank of Ireland Homes Mortgages Ltd v Bell*).

You can visit the online resources to test your knowledge of this chapter with self-test questions at www.oup.com/he/nair19e/.

15

Settled Land Act settlements

15.1 Who holds the legal estate in settled land? **348**

15.2 Are there trustees? **349**

15.3 What sort of property may be subject to an SLA settlement? **349**

It is no longer possible to make new Settled Land Act settlements but it is important to remember that settlements created before TOLATA 1996 continue to exist and, unlike trusts for sale, were not converted into the new trusts of land (which is why you will still find references to them in LRA 2002). Just in case you come across one of these continuing settlements, this chapter deals briefly with the following three questions:

- who holds the legal estate in settled land?
- are there trustees?
- what sort of property may be subject to an SLA settlement?

15.1 Who holds the legal estate in settled land?

Although there are 'trustees of the settlement', the legal title to the settled land is held by the beneficiary currently entitled to the enjoyment of the property, who is known as the **'tenant for life'**. In addition to being the legal owner and having the right to occupy the property, the tenant for life has wide powers to deal with the property, being able to sell all or part of the settled land, to grant leases over it and to raise money by mortgage for specified purposes. You saw in Chapter 13 that land tied up in family settlements often deteriorated because the beneficiaries could not raise money for repair and development (see 13.3.1.1) and these statutory powers were designed to remedy this problem. Consequently, the SLA 1925 provides that the powers of the tenant for life under the Act may not be excluded by the settlor and attempts to restrict them in any way are void. This is very different from the position under TOLATA 1996, where the settlor can limit or exclude the wide powers given by the Act to the trustees, with the result that even the power to sell the property can be excluded (see 14.5.1).

It is important to realise that, although the tenant for life has these wide and unrestricted powers, he or she holds the estate on trust for all the beneficiaries, and when exercising powers must have regard to the interests of all parties entitled under the settlement (SLA 1925, s. 107).

If there is no tenant for life (because for example, the current beneficiary is a minor), the powers of the tenant for life will be exercised by the **'statutory owner'**.

15.2 Are there trustees?

Although the tenant for life holds the legal estate and has the power to deal with it, the Act requires the appointment of 'trustees of the settlement'. Their most important function is to receive any capital money arising from dealings with the property, in order to ensure that the beneficial interests under the settlement are overreached and the purchaser is not bound by them (see 14.9.2). Apart from this, the trustees' powers and duties are fairly limited. Their *consent* is required for certain major dealings by the tenant for life (such as the sale of the 'principal mansion house'), but in general the tenant for life is required only to give *notice* to the trustees of any intention to exercise certain powers, and normally the trustees have no right to prevent the proposed transaction. The rights and powers of 'trustees of the settlement', as compared to the tenant for life, are summarised in Table 15.1.

Table 15.1 Summary of rights and powers under SLA

Tenant for life	Trustees	Other beneficiaries
• Holds legal estate • Has power to sell • Other powers to manage the property	Receive capital money	Hold equitable interests in the property

15.3 What sort of property may be subject to an SLA settlement?

You may well think that SLA settlements are relevant only to the rather grand country estates described in 13.3.1.1. However, it must be remembered that these settlements could also be created 'by mistake' in home-made wills, with the result that a small semi-detached house could become subject to all the machinery of the SLA 1925. It was also possible for a settlement to arise in the most unexpected circumstances, as it did in *Binions v Evans* [1972] Ch 359 (see 13.2.3.2), in which a landowner allowed the widow of his former employee to remain in their cottage for the rest of her life, and thus inadvertently created an SLA settlement.

So these settlements are not just for the rich and powerful—you may still come across them in the most unlikely places!

You can visit the online resources to test your knowledge of this chapter with self-test questions at **www.oup.com/he/nair19e/**.

16

The rule against perpetuities

16.1 Future interests **350**

16.2 The old rules **351**

16.3 Legislative modifications before 2010 **352**

16.4 Breadth of application of old rules **352**

16.5 The Perpetuities and Accumulations Act 2009 **353**

16.1 **Future interests**

Before leaving the subject of trusts, you need to be aware of the rules which govern the kind of future interests which can be created under them, and so this chapter will be concerned with the 'rule against perpetuities'.

Common law has always disliked uncertainty in relation to future interests in land, and sought to limit the 'dead hand' control of a past owner of land on the freedom to deal with the land of the present owners. Uncertainty tends to make the property inalienable for some time, and common law has always opposed any arrangement which restricts free alienation. For example, should a settlor, who as yet has no children, wish to settle land upon 'the first of my great-grandchildren to obtain a law degree', it could easily be 70 or 80 years before the great-grandchild who is to take the gift can be ascertained. For that period of time there would be no one absolutely entitled to the property and, under the early trusts rules, there would have been no one with a power to dispose of it absolutely. As a result, the courts developed rules ('against perpetuities') which invalidated certain future interests if they did not vest within a defined period of time (the 'perpetuity period'). Unfortunately, the rigid application of these rules frequently led to ridiculous results, with the creation of very complicated rules and their extension beyond family settlements to capture commercial arrangements (such as options to purchase land in the future). Eventually, statutory amendments were made by the Law of Property Act 1925 (to a limited extent) and the Perpetuities and Accumulations Act 1964. Unfortunately, this legislation did not replace the older rules and, by simply modifying them, made the law more (rather than less) complicated. Now the older rules have been considerably simplified, and narrowed in their scope, by the Perpetuities and Accumulations Act 2009, which came into force on 6 April 2010. Here the old rules are covered in a very outline fashion, simply in order to indicate their complexity.

You should first note that the rule against perpetuities is about grants or gifts that are to *vest* at some point in the future, because at the time the grant takes effect the eventual beneficiary is not identified or it is not certain that the intended beneficiary will actually get the interest. It is not about grants or gifts that belong to some identified person now, but can only be enjoyed in the future. Such interests are vested ('vested in interest', as distinct from 'vested in possession') and outside the scope of the rule. Thus, a grant to

> A for life and then to B

is not caught if A and B are both living and named people at the date of the grant. In this case, both A and B have an existing *vested* interest. A's interest is an immediate benefit ('vested in possession'), whereas B's will confer a benefit in future ('vested in interest'). However, B already has rights that are vested—he or she already owns a future vested interest. It does not matter if A then lives for a very long time, so that B's interest vests in him only after the perpetuity period has passed. The perpetuities rules relate to cases in which the recipient of the future interest does not actually gain that interest under the grant, but will only do so at some future time. For example, they relate to cases in which the future recipient is not an identifiable person at the point of the grant, such as a grant to 'A's first child to reach the age of 21'. In such a case, unless A already has a child aged 21 at the date of the grant, the actual beneficiary will only be identified and the future interest vest in him or her when one of A's children reaches 21. The rule is therefore sometimes described as a rule against remoteness of vesting.

16.2 The old rules

The basic perpetuities rule was that a contingent (conditional) future interest had to take effect, if it were to be valid, within the period of a 'life in being plus 21 years (plus any period of gestation)'. A 'life in being' was the life of any person connected to the disposition who was alive at the date that it was made. Any purported creation of an interest that *could possibly vest* more than 21 years after the death of such a person was, until legislative changes were made in the twentieth century, invalid from the start.

A simple example will serve to illustrate some of the problems that resulted. If a settlor made a gift to

> the first child of X to become an accountant

the gift was invalid under the old rule. This is because, unless X already had a child who was a qualified accountant, it is possible that X would have a child born later and who qualified as an accountant more than 21 years after the death of X. Even if X already had an adult child who had nearly qualified, it was theoretically possible that that child might never qualify and that X might have another child born later, who qualified more than 21 years after X's death. Because of this, even if this possibility was highly unlikely, the whole gift was void. X is the only possible 'life in being' and the possibility that the gift would result in the contingent gift to the child vesting more than 21 years after his or her death would have made the whole gift invalid.

To make matters even more difficult, over time, rules were developed about presumptions as to who could or could not have children and as to which lives did or did not count as 'lives in being'. The resulting complexities in the law constituted a dreadful trap for the unwary.

16.3 Legislative modifications before 2010

In 1925 some limited reforms were made to the rules, to deal with cases in which the only problem with the grant was that a disposition vested in someone at an age greater than 21 (raising the possibility that the intended recipient would die before reaching that age, and the interest would vest in the next possible recipient at a date after the perpetuity period had passed). Thus, this addressed the following type of grant:

> to A for life and then to the first of A's children to reach the age of 25.

This was void under the basic rules (unless A already had a 25-year-old child) because, even if A already had a 24-year-old child, that child might die and a child born after the date of the gift might reach 25 more than 21 years after A's death. Section 163(2) of LPA 1925, allowed the age specified to be reduced to 21 in order to save the grant. This worked because it was thought that A's child must necessarily reach 21 no longer than 21 years after A's death (plus any period of gestation—which was already permitted under the older rules). (At the date of the legislation, questions raised by modern practices like the freezing of genetic material or of embryos were not in anyone's mind.)

Far more extensive reforms were made by the Perpetuities and Accumulations Act 1964. Of these, the most important were the introduction of:

- a 'wait and see' rule, that saved gifts until such time as it become clear that vesting could not take place within the perpetuity period;
- statutory provisions as to who is a 'life in being' in any case;
- further age reduction rules (and repeal of the 1925 provision);
- presumptions concerning fertility; and
- the possibility of choosing a fixed period of 80 years for the perpetuity period.

The most important in practice was 'wait and see', which, instead of making the grant void from the start because it might break the rules, allowed you to wait through the perpetuity period to see whether in fact the grant did vest before the end of the period. Therefore, in the case of the grant to

> the first child of X to become an accountant

you could now wait to see whether a child of X qualified in time, rather than having an entirely ineffective grant right from the start. The gift would only fail if X's first child in fact failed to qualify as an accountant and it later became clear that no subsequent child would be able to qualify within 21 years of X's death.

16.4 Breadth of application of old rules

The old perpetuities rules applied not only to settlements but also to options and rights of **pre-emption** (rights of first refusal). They also applied in relation to options to acquire interests and to future easements and restrictive covenants that are to take effect in the future and in relation to some areas of law outside the scope of this book (notably in relation to pensions).

16.5 The Perpetuities and Accumulations Act 2009

The perpetuities and accumulations rules had, over the years, attracted a great deal of criticism because of their complexity and the fact that they applied to a wider range of arrangements than just trusts (for which they were designed) and thus had implications (for example) for commercial arrangements like pensions, options to purchase, some rights of pre-emption, and future easements. In its report on *The Rules Against Perpetuities and Excessive Accumulations*, 1998, Law Com No. 251, the Law Commission recommended a radical overhaul of the rules and their confinement to trusts and settlements.

The Perpetuities and Accumulations Act 2009 (PAA 2009) was the outcome of these recommendations. The Act came into force in full on 6 April 2010. This Act replaced all the old rules as far as new trusts are concerned. The new system applies to trusts that take effect after the commencement of the Act and to will trusts where the will is made after the coming into force of the Act (PAA 2009, s. 15). Pre-existing will trusts, even where the testator was still alive, were preserved, so that it was not necessary for everyone to reconsider and rewrite any wills they had already made. However, this means that the old rules will be relevant to some trusts for many years to come, which may be a trap for the unwary.

16.5.1 Interests affected

Section 1 of the PAA 2009 specifies those arrangements to which the new rules apply and specifies that the rules will apply only to the arrangements specified. The effect is to remove from the ambit of the rules everything except successive interests under trusts.

16.5.2 Perpetuity period is 125 years

The main change made by the 2009 Act is that now the perpetuity period is 125 years in all cases (s. 5). This period applies even if the deed or will creating the trust purports to specify another perpetuity period (s. 5(2)). This imposition of a universal statutory period renders the old common law rules about lives in being irrelevant for trusts created on or after 6 April 2010.

16.5.3 Adoption of fixed period in old 'royal lives' trusts

In the past, in order to make the applicable period as long as possible, those drafting trusts sometimes elected to use all the living descendants of a particular monarch as their 'lives in being'. One did not have to choose individuals who are related to the trust in any way. The PAA 2009 does have some implications for such pre-existing trusts because it allows the trustees to elect to adopt a perpetuity period of 100 years instead, if the trust period was to be determined by a 'royal lives' clause (s. 12). The trustees will have to execute a deed in order to apply the 100-year period. They are not obliged to change but may wish to do so if it has become difficult or inconvenient to determine which royal descendants are still lives in being (the Royal College of Arms keeps a list to assist with the determination of such issues). For example, if the trust was subject to a period which depended on the lives of the descendants of Queen Elizabeth II, the trustees of this old trust could now elect to impose instead a fixed perpetuity period of 100 years from the commencement of the trust.

16.5.4 Rules on duration preserved

Do not forget that the perpetuity rule is not a rule about how long a trust can endure. It is simply a rule about remoteness of vesting. The rules about the duration of non-charitable purpose trusts (a matter of trusts law rather than land law and thus not covered here) are preserved by s. 18 of the PAA 2009.

16.5.5 Changes to accumulations rules

The PAA 2009 also makes important changes to the certain rules of trusts law that limited the ability of trustees to accumulate income arising under a trust. These rules, which are primarily a matter for general trusts law and raise no special issues in relation to trusts of land, are preserved only for charitable trusts (ss. 13 and 14).

16.5.6 Old rules are still important

The new perpetuity rules have made things much easier for all those called upon to advise on the drafting of new trusts but it should be noted that the old rules continue to apply to:

- trusts that existed before 6 April 2010; and
- will trusts where the testator died before 6 April 2010.

Thus the old rules could have a lifespan of at least the next 100 years.

The application of the 1964 Act is restricted to the older arrangements, which will continue to be subject to the old rules (PAA 2009, s. 16).

Therefore, it will be essential in each case to check exactly when the deed giving effect to the trust was created or the testator of a will trust died, in order to apply the correct set of rules.

FURTHER READING

Cheshire & Burn's Modern Law of Real Property, 18th edn., Oxford University Press, 2011, Chapter 15 (Future Interests).

Gallanis, 'The Rule Against Perpetuities and the Law Commission's Flawed Philosophy' (2000) 59 CLJ 284.

Law Commission 'The Rules Against Perpetuities and Excessive Accumulations', 1998, No. 251.

Lawson and Rudden, *The Law of Property*, 3rd edn., Oxford University Press, 2002, Chapter 13 (The Control of Endowment).

Maudsley, *The Modern Law of Perpetuities*, Butterworths, 1979.

Megarry and Wade, *The Law of Real Property*, 9th edn., Sweet & Maxwell, 2019, Chapter 8 (Perpetuities and Accumulations).

Wilson, 'Grave Consequences' [2007] EG 134.

You can visit the online resources to test your knowledge of this chapter with self-test questions at www.oup.com/he/nair19e/.

17

Co-ownership

17.1 Introduction 355
17.2 Necessary conditions for a joint tenancy 359
17.3 Joint tenancy or tenancy in common: effect of express declaration 360
17.4 Presumption of a tenancy in common 363
17.5 Presumption of a joint tenancy: the family home 364
17.6 Severance of a joint tenancy 370
17.7 Relationship between co-owners 378
17.8 Ending co-ownership 379
17.9 8 Trant Way 380

17.1 Introduction

17.1.1 Background

Before the twentieth century, the normal pattern of land ownership in Britain was that the estate in land, unless it was a large property subject to a complex settlement, was vested in one person as sole beneficial owner. The family home, whether leasehold or freehold, tended to be held by the man, who was regarded as head of the household. Changes in social conditions, and the alteration of attitudes to women, have meant that today sole ownership has become less common and it is normal for the family, domestic property to be the subject of co-ownership.

Co-ownership may be created by an express act of the parties because the property is conveyed to two or more persons as co-owners, or may arise in response to conduct, as for example where one person contributes to the purchase price of property bought by another and is thus presumed to acquire an equitable interest in the property under a resulting trust (13.2.2 and Chapter 18).

In studying co-ownership, you need a clear understanding of the distinction explained in Chapter 13 between the legal title to the property and equitable or beneficial interests (see 13.1.1). There can be co-ownership of the legal title, or of beneficial interests, or of both. For example, in Figure 17.1, a husband and wife may be co-owners both at law and in equity (i.e., both of them own the legal estate and both are entitled to the equitable interest).

LAW	EQUITY
Legal estate	Beneficial interest
H and W	H and W

Figure 17.1 Ownership at law and in equity

Alternatively, one of them (in Figure 17.2, the husband) owns the legal estate, but holds it on trust for himself and his wife, either because of a specific provision for this in the conveyance to him, or because there is some agreement between them, express or inferred, which gives her an equitable interest under an implied trust (see 13.2 and Chapter 18).

LAW	EQUITY
Legal estate	Beneficial interest
H	H and W

Figure 17.2 Differing ownership at law and in equity

This chapter concentrates on the rules which apply where there is co-ownership of the *legal* estate, with the legal co-owners also holding on trust for themselves in equity. Chapter 18 explains the second possibility, in which the legal estate is held by a single owner, in trust for himself and others as co-owners of the beneficial interest.

17.1.2 Co-ownership in Trant Way

Mr and Mrs Armstrong have completed the purchase of the fee simple estate in 1 Trant Way (see 6.5 and 6.6.4). The property was transferred 'to Arnold Armstrong and Arriety Armstrong' and they have now been registered as proprietors by the Land Registry.

8 Trant Way was bought last year by six friends who are all studying Outer Mongolian history on a four-year course at Mousehole University. The friends each contributed one-sixth of the purchase price and, because they were short of money, one of their number did the conveyancing. The property was transferred to all six: i.e., to Alice, Brian, Colin, David, Eric, and Fanny. At the date of the conveyance Alice was 17 and all the others were 18. The intention was that the house was to be kept until all six graduated and that it should then be sold. Unfortunately, this 'do-it-yourself' conveyancing was not entirely successful: there are a couple of errors in the transfer, and these are described in 17.2.2.1.

10 Trant Way belongs to a firm of chartered surveyors. The partners in the firm are Sidney Search and Frederick Find and the legal estate, a 99-year lease, has been registered in the names of the two partners.

17.1.3 Two forms of co-ownership

In modern law, there are two forms of co-ownership:

- **joint tenancy**; and
- **tenancy in common**.

17.1.3.1 Nature of a joint tenancy

The joint tenancy is, in a way, the more perfect of the two types of co-ownership. It is a method of ownership in which the co-owners are *not* regarded as having 'shares' in the land but as together owning the whole estate. It is as though the co-owners are not really treated as separate owners but as a single group owner. Thus, if Arnold and Arriety Armstrong are joint tenants in respect of 1 Trant Way, we cannot say that

Arnold owns half and that Arriety owns half. We must say that Arnold and Arriety together own the whole estate. In the notation used in this chapter joint tenants are placed inside brackets:

(Arnold and Arriety)

to indicate this relationship.

While a joint tenancy exists, neither joint tenant can make decisions about the right they jointly hold without the consent of the other and neither of them can separately deal with their interest in the property. Very importantly, joint tenants have a 'right of survivorship' or *jus accrescendi*. Since a joint tenant is not regarded as having a distinct share in the co-owned land, he or she is not able to dispose of his or her interest by will on death, nor will it pass on intestacy if no will is made. Instead, on the death of one joint tenant, the interest of the deceased person ceases to exist and the remaining joint tenants are left as the remaining owners of the property. This is the natural result of regarding joint tenants as a kind of unified and indivisible group. The last survivor of the group will of course become a sole owner and will be able to dispose of the property as he or she pleases on death. With the joint tenancy it pays to be long-lived!

A joint tenancy may exist either at law alone, or both at law and in equity. What this means is that the legal estate may be held by more than one person as joint tenants, but the joint tenants at law may hold the legal estate subject to a range of different trusts. Joint tenants at law might hold for themselves as joint tenants in equity as well. This means their beneficial interest in the property will also have to be dealt with by them together and they will not be treated as each having individual beneficial interests under the trust of the property. If one of them dies, survivorship will operate in equity as well as at law; the survivor will hold the legal estate alone, and will owe no duties to anyone else in equity.

However, it is equally possible that joint tenants at law might hold the legal estate subject to some other arrangement in equity. For example, they might hold the legal estate on trust for themselves *and others* as joint tenants, as where Mary and Norma hold as joint tenants at law on trust for Mary, Norma, and Oona as joint tenants in equity. Alternatively, they might hold the legal estate on trust for completely different people who are themselves joint tenants in equity, as where Mary and Norma hold as joint tenants at law on trust for Oona, Prithvi, and Rehan, who are joint tenants in equity. Finally, joint tenants might hold the legal estate as joint tenants on trust for beneficiaries who are *tenants in common* rather than as joint tenants in equity. This is the most typical alternative to joint tenancy in equity in cases of co-ownership: i.e., Mary and Norma hold as joint tenants at law on trust for themselves in certain shares, which may be equal (50/50) or may be unequal (e.g., 80% to Mary and 20% to Norma).

17.1.3.2 Nature of a tenancy in common

Unlike a joint tenancy, *tenants in common* have separate shares of the co-owned property, which they can deal with individually as they please. Survivorship does not operate as between tenants in common, so each person can leave their share to others in a will and the shares will pass to the statutory next of kin of each tenant who dies intestate.

Before 1926, co-owners were able to hold the legal estate as either joint tenants or tenants in common. However, the 1925 legislation provided that tenancies in common of the legal estate could no longer be created (LPA 1925, s. 34(1)). This change was designed to facilitate the transfer of land: it meant that a buyer of a legal estate could deal with all the joint tenants collectively to buy the single jointly-held legal estate, rather than needing to separately negotiate with each tenant in common to buy their share of the estate.

It follows that, while a joint tenancy may exist both at law and in equity, a tenancy in common can exist only in equity. In the unlikely event that a modern conveyance purports to convey the legal estate to new owners as 'tenants in common', they would still take that estate as joint tenants. However, in such a case, equity would give effect to their intentions by imposing a trust and treating the co-owners as joint tenants at law, holding the legal estate on trust for themselves as tenants in common in equity.

17.1.3.3 Statutory trusts imposed on co-owners

The 1925 legislation also provided that in most forms of co-ownership the joint owners of the legal estate would hold it on trust for themselves, at first on a trust for sale (LPA 1925, ss. 34(2) and 36(1)) and, since 1997, on a trust of land (see Chapter 14). This has various advantages. It means that anyone who buys the legal estate from joint tenants can take advantage of the overreaching machinery: provided the money was paid to two trustees, the purchaser will take free of the beneficial interests under the trust. It also means that tenancies in common can still be created *in equity*, with the legal joint tenants holding in trust for themselves as tenants in common of the beneficial interest.

It is important to note that the statutory trust of land, imposed in most cases of co-ownership, is an unusual trust because the trustees are also beneficiaries and so are normally entitled to act in their own best interests when making decisions about the property (unlike in a normal trust, where trustees owe beneficiaries duties to act in their exclusive best interests and not to act in ways that put them in a position of conflict of interests). For example, you may recall that, where a periodic tenancy is held by joint tenants, one joint tenant can bring the tenancy to an end by unilaterally giving notice to the landlord (see 9.5.4); this is one of the few decisions that a joint tenant can make, affecting the legal estate, without the consent of the other joint tenant. In the recent case of *Procter v Procter* [2022] EWHC 1202, it was held that a joint tenant of a lease who held the lease on trust for herself and the other joint tenants was in breach of trust in giving notice to terminate the lease in the circumstances. However, this was because the terms of the trust in the case were more elaborate than the terms of the bare trust imposed by statute on all co-owners and placed the joint tenant in question under special obligations to them. Where the trust in question is a simple bare trust, imposed on the parties by statute because they are co-owners, no such liability will arise (see *Pile v Pile* [2022] EWHC 2036).

17.1.3.4 Severance of a joint tenancy

A relationship which begins as a joint tenancy need not continue as one, for it is possible for one or more of the joint tenants to sever the tenancy and convert the relationship with the other co-owners into a tenancy in common. Since 1926, a joint tenancy of the *legal estate* can no longer be severed (because the resulting tenancies in common may no longer be created at law), but **severance** of a joint tenancy of the *beneficial interest* remains possible. You will see later the ways in which a joint tenancy may be severed (see 17.6), but should note here that the result of doing so is that each of the co-owners becomes entitled to an equal share under the resulting tenancy in common (*Goodman v Gallant* [1986] Fam 106, approved by the House of Lords in *Stack v Dowden* [2007] 2 AC 432, at para. 49). Thus, if two co-owners sever their joint tenancy, each will be entitled to a half share in the beneficial interest; if one of three co-owners severs, that one will be entitled to a one-third share, while the other two owners will continue as joint tenants of the remaining two-thirds of the beneficial interest.

17.1.4 Contents of this chapter

In this chapter, we look first (17.2) at the necessary conditions for the creation of a joint tenancy, both at law and in equity, including the 'four unities' that must be established for a joint tenancy to exist and rules about the age and number of joint tenants. Next, we look at how the court determines which form of co-ownership exists in equity, first considering the effect of express declarations (17.3) and then looking at the situations where the law presumes a tenancy in common (17.4) or, in relation to the family home, a joint tenancy (17.5). We go on to look at the severance of joint tenancies (17.6), the process by which parties who have once been joint tenants in equity become tenants in common in equity. Next, we consider how disputes that arise between co-owners are resolved (17.7), under the provisions of TOLATA 1996 that apply in cases of co-ownership because of the imposition of the statutory trust of land (17.1.3.3). Finally, we look at how co-ownership comes to an end (17.8) and conclude with an overview of how the law might affect the students who have bought 8 Trant Way (17.9).

17.2 Necessary conditions for a joint tenancy

A joint tenancy cannot exist at law unless four requirements, known as the four unities, are satisfied. In the absence of the four unities in relation to the legal estate, there will be no co-ownership at law; only one person will have the legal estate. In the absence of the four unities in relation to the beneficial interest, there can be no joint tenancy in equity. Instead, parties holding as joint tenants at law will necessarily hold on some other trusts in equity. You should note that only one of the four unities is necessary for the creation of a tenancy in common in equity, unity of *possession*. If there is no unity of possession, the parties are treated as having separate entitlements to separate parts of the land and there is no co-ownership between them.

17.2.1 The 'four unities'

The unities are:

(a) *Time* This unity requires that the interests of all the co-owners should vest (be acquired) at the same time. Thus in a disposition, 'to J for life and then to K and L', K and L have the unity of time because the interest of each vests on the death of J. In the case of Mr and Mrs Armstrong this unity exists because the interest of each vested when 1 Trant Way was transferred to them as co-owners at the same time.

(b) *Title* This requires that the co-owners should all have acquired their title by the same means, e.g., all from the same document. In the case of Mr and Mrs Armstrong they both derive their title from the transfer that, on registration, vested the legal estate in them.

(c) *Interest* For a joint tenancy to exist, the interests of all the co-owners must also be identical. Each interest must be of the same duration and of the same nature and extent. Thus, if one co-owner has a life interest and the other an interest in fee simple, they cannot be joint tenants because this unity is not present.

(d) *Possession* Finally, the co-owners must be equally entitled to the possession of the whole land. If one of them could point to a portion of the land and say, 'That portion is mine alone', then there would be no co-ownership. In such a case each would be a sole owner of a smaller part of the land. This would arise, for example, if two people were to divide one parcel of land between themselves and each take a different portion.

17.2.2 Number and age of joint tenants

To prevent a trust having an inordinate number of trustees, the Trustee Act 1925, s. 34(2), limits the number of trustees to a maximum of four, and provides that where more than four are named, the property vests in the first four listed. Thus, the imposition of the statutory trust in cases of co-ownership means that there cannot be more than four owners of the legal estate, who will hold it on trust for themselves and any additional co-owners.

17.2.2.1 8 Trant Way

We have seen that the transfer of 8 Trant Way purported to vest the legal estate in the six students, one of whom, Alice, was at that time only 17 years old. Section 1(6) of LPA 1925 provides that a legal estate in land cannot be held by an 'infant' (i.e., a person under the age of 18 and today known as a 'minor'. See further 14.1.2.3.)

As a result of these statutory rules, the title to the legal estate in No. 8 must be registered in the name of the first four named in the transfer who are over 18 (Brian, Colin, David and Eric), while Alice and Fanny will be owners in equity only (see Table 17.1).

Table 17.1 8 Trant Way; the start

Law	Equity
(Brian, Colin, David, Eric)	• Alice, Brian, Colin, David, Eric, Fanny
	• Beneficiaries under the trust
Must be a joint tenancy	• Can be joint tenants or tenants in common

17.3 Joint tenancy or tenancy in common: effect of express declaration

A joint tenancy *cannot* arise in equity unless the requirements above, including the four unities are satisfied. However, these requirements are necessary but not sufficient conditions for a joint tenancy to arise instead of a tenancy in common. It is perfectly possible for a conveyance that satisfies the four unities to give rise to a tenancy in common in equity, because this is thought to reflect the true intentions of the parties. Such an intention can most obviously be identified where the parties expressly declare the terms on which they intend to hold the legal title.

LAW	EQUITY
Legal estate	Beneficial interest
(M and N)	M and N
Joint tenancy	Tenancy in common

Figure 17.3 Tenancy in common in equity only

17.3.1 Making an express declaration

Like any other declaration of a trust of land, a declaration of how co-owners intend to hold their title in equity must satisfy the requirement of s. 53(1)(b) of LPA 1925 that a declaration must be evidenced by signed writing to be enforceable (see 13.1.2.1). This can most easily be done where the conveyance or transfer to the co-owners itself makes express provision as to the way in which they are to hold the beneficial interest. A conveyance or transfer will always be a deed, and therefore any declaration of trust in such a document will satisfy the requirement of signed writing.

17.3.1.1. Unregistered land

Where the title to the property is still unregistered, the conveyance could provide that the legal estate is conveyed to co-owners as joint tenants, either to hold for themselves as tenants in common in equity or as 'beneficial joint tenants' (joint tenancy in equity).

It is also possible to make an express declaration of an equitable tenancy in common by providing that the beneficial interest is to be held in 'undivided shares', the technical term sometimes used as a synonym for 'tenancy in common'. In fact, any words suggesting that the owners are to be regarded as owners of *shares* in the property, rather than as a kind of group sole owner, would prevent the creation of an equitable joint tenancy and would create a tenancy in common instead. Such phrases, known as **'words of severance'**, include:

- 'in equal shares'—*Payne v Webb* (1874) LR 19 Eq 26;
- 'equally'—*Lewen v Dodd* (1595) Cro Eliz 443;
- 'share and share alike'—*Heathe v Heathe* (1740) 2 Atk 121;
- 'to be divided between'—*Peat v Chapman* (1750) 1 Ves Sen 542;
- 'between'—*Lashbrook v Cock* (1816) 2 Mer 70.

17.3.1.2 Registered land

In the case of registered land, the transfer form now in use gives the transferees the opportunity to indicate whether they are to hold the property in trust for themselves as joint tenants or as tenants in common. If you look at Box 10 of the specimen transfer form in Form 6.2, you will see that the Armstrongs have chosen to hold their beneficial interest as joint tenants. The transfer form also gives transferees the opportunity to say that they wish to hold as tenants in common in equal shares, while those who wish to hold as tenants in common of *unequal* shares could provide for this by completing the third option in Box 10.

However, completing this part of the form is not compulsory. Failure to do so does not invalidate the transfer, but the absence of any declaration about the nature of the purchasers' beneficial interests can cause them considerable difficulty and possibly expensive litigation at a later stage. It has always been possible to make the necessary declaration in a separate document at the time of acquisition and the Land Registry has issued a form for such a declaration, in the hope that purchasers and their legal advisers will find this more convenient. The option of completing the box on the transfer form still remains as an alternative.

17.3.2 Conclusiveness of express declaration

An express declaration of the nature of the beneficial interest can always be set aside on equitable grounds such as fraud or undue influence. That apart, such a declaration is conclusive, unless it is varied by subsequent agreement or affected by proprietary estoppel arising from a later representation (*Goodman v Gallant* [1986] Fam 106, approved by the House of Lords in *Stack v Dowden* [2007] 2 AC 432 at para. 49; and on the estoppel point, see *Clarke v Meadus* [2010] EWHC 3117 (Ch) at para. 56).

The conclusive nature of such an express declaration was emphasised by the Court of Appeal in *Pankhania v Chandegra* [2012] EWCA Civ 1438. The parties bought a house as legal joint tenants and made an express declaration in the transfer that they would hold the beneficial interest as tenants in common. It appears that the trial judge did not appreciate the significance of this declaration, and thought that he was obliged to infer the parties' intentions from the circumstances surrounding the purchase. Following this approach, he concluded that the parties' real intentions at the time of the transfer were that the whole beneficial interest in the property would belong to C. Applying the principle in *Goodman v Gallant*, the Court of Appeal reversed this decision, holding that it must give legal effect to the express declaration. In the words of Patten LJ (at para. 22):

> The effect of executing the declaration of trust was . . . to make [P] an equitable tenant in common regardless of what the parties may have subjectively intended and to estop [C] from denying his title.

17.3.3 Position where there is no express declaration

It may be that a conveyance or transfer to co-owners says nothing about how they intend to hold the beneficial interest. Historically, equity preferred the tenancy in common, because it considered that the notional entitlement to a share in the property and the owner's ability to dispose of this share at his death was a fairer form of co-ownership. Despite this preference, however, equity would in general follow the law: in other words, if the legal estate was held on a joint tenancy, the equitable or beneficial interest would follow the legal estate and would also be held on a joint tenancy.

There were, however, certain situations in which equity regarded the right of survivorship as being so unfair or inappropriate that it considered it unlikely that the parties had really intended it to apply. In such circumstances equity would presume that the parties held as tenants in common despite the fact that all the requirements for a legal joint tenancy were satisfied. With one major exception (relating to the family home—see 17.5), this presumption still operates today. It is, of course, always open to a party to rebut the presumption by showing that the co-owners had in truth intended to hold the beneficial interest as joint tenants, despite the apparent disadvantages.

17.4 Presumption of a tenancy in common

In the following situations, equity will presume that joint tenants of the legal estate hold the beneficial interest as tenants in common, in the absence of an express declaration to the contrary.

17.4.1 Unequal contributions

If the co-owners have contributed unequal amounts to the purchase price, equity considers it unfair to impose upon them the equality of the joint tenancy and the effects of the right of survivorship, for it might be that the tenant who has contributed least will prove to be the longest lived, and thus become the sole owner of the whole property. Accordingly, in such cases equity has always presumed that unequal contributors hold the property as tenants in common, each co-owner having a share in the property proportional to his or her contribution to the purchase price (*Lake v Gibson* (1729) 1 Eq Rep 290; and, in modern law, *Bull v Bull* [1955] 1 QB 234). Another way of expressing this, using the language of trusts rather than of co-ownership, is to say that the property was held on a resulting trust (see 13.2.2), with shares in the beneficial interest quantified according to the amount contributed. The presumption could, of course, be rebutted by clear evidence of an intention to the contrary: either that the parties should, after all, hold as joint tenants, or that the size of their shares under a tenancy in common should not correspond to the amount of their respective contributions.

This presumption has always been applied irrespective of the nature of the property or its owners, but in *Stack v Dowden* [2007] 2 AC 432 the House of Lords held that it was no longer appropriate in certain cases involving 'domestic property' (i.e., the family home). There is more about this decision in 17.5.

It appears that unequal contributions to the cost of *commercial property* will continue to give rise to a presumption of a beneficial tenancy in common, and the burden of proving a contrary intention so as to rebut that presumption will lie on the party who alleges a joint tenancy (although note the hint of a future reconsideration in *Jones v Kernott* [2011] 3 WLR 1121 at para. 53).

17.4.2 Partnership property

Where the co-ownership is of a commercial character, the right of survivorship appears to equity to be inappropriate even in the case of equal contributions to the purchase price. Thus, in the case of property belonging to business partners, equity favours the tenancy in common, and so would presume that the beneficial interest in 10 Trant Way (owned by the chartered surveyors—see 17.1.2 and Figure 17.4) is held on a tenancy in common (*Re Fuller's Contract* [1933] Ch 652).

SEARCH & FIND
Chartered Surveyors

LAW
(S + F)
Joint tenants

EQUITY
S F
Tenants in common

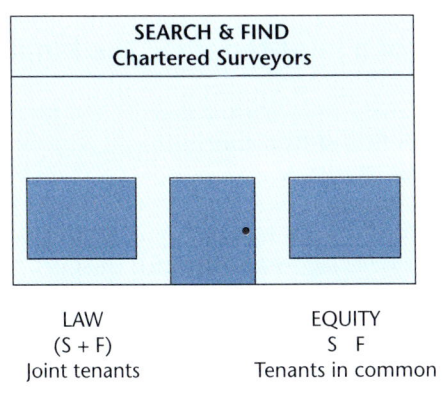

Figure 17.4 Search and Find

17.4.3 Estate or interest used to secure a loan

As is explained in Chapter 22, a mortgage is created by a borrower ('the mortgagor') who grants an interest in land to the lender ('the mortgagee') as security for the loan. Where two or more people lend money secured by the same mortgage, equity presumes that the beneficial interest in the land granted to them as security is held on a tenancy in common (*Morley v Bird* (1798) 3 Ves Jr 628). Thus, the money owed to each creditor is secured on an identifiable share in the beneficial interest and that share would pass with the lender's estate if he or she died before the loan was repaid.

17.4.4 Other circumstances

It had been suggested that the three situations described earlier were the only ones in which joint tenants of the legal estate would be regarded by equity as tenants in common of the beneficial interest in the property. However, this view was rejected by the Privy Council in *Malaysian Credit Ltd v Jack Chia-MPH Ltd* [1986] 1 AC 549.

This case concerned joint tenants of leasehold business premises. As joint tenants, each was entitled to possession of the whole of the property (see 17.2.1(d)), but in practice they occupied separate and unequal areas of it, and rent and other outgoings were divided between them in proportion to the area that each occupied. When a dispute arose between them, the plaintiff, who occupied the smallest area, claimed that they were joint tenants in both law and equity, and sought an order for sale and the equal division of the proceeds between them. The two owners were not in partnership with each other, so did not come within the equitable presumption relating to partnership property, and there were no words in the grant of the lease that indicated an intention to hold as tenants in common. Despite this, the Privy Council considered that the beneficial interest in the property was held on a tenancy in common. In reaching this conclusion their Lordships were clearly influenced by the unequal contributions to outgoings, which they regarded as analogous to those unequal contributions to the purchase price of a property that would support a presumption of tenancy in common. Nevertheless, they rejected the plaintiff's suggestion that the circumstances in which such a presumption could operate were strictly limited. In Lord Brightman's words (at p. 560):

> Such cases are not necessarily limited to purchasers who contribute unequally, to co-mortgagees and to partners. There are other circumstances in which equity may infer that the beneficial interest is intended to be held by the grantees as tenants in common . . . one such case is where the grantees hold the premises for their several [i.e., separate] individual business purposes.

17.5 Presumption of a joint tenancy: the family home

Until recently the rules about co-ownership described so far in this chapter applied to all types of land, regardless of its nature or the purpose for which it was bought. However, in *Stack v Dowden* [2007] 2 AC 432 the House of Lords adopted a new approach to 'domestic property' or, more specifically, to property bought jointly by partners in a relationship for use as a family home. In this chapter, we will look at this decision, and the later Supreme Court case of *Jones v Kernott* [2011] UKSC 53, from the perspective of co-ownership: that is, we will look at how the law decides whether *joint* legal owners of a family home are joint tenants or tenants in common in equity. In Chapter 18, we will look again at these cases and consider their implications for cases where the legal title to the family home is held in the *sole* name of one partner and the other partner is arguing that the title is held on trust for them.

17.5.1 Resulting and constructive trusts of the family home: before *Stack v Dowden*

In the family home context, the rights of the parties are often discussed in terms of resulting and constructive trusts (for more about these 'implied' trusts see 13.2). This is because it is frequently the case that couples buying homes together do not expressly declare the terms on which they intend to hold the property as against each other.

17.5.1.1 Resulting trusts

As has been explained, in many situations, equity presumes that joint tenants of the legal estate who have made unequal contributions to the purchase price would hold in trust for themselves as tenants in common of the beneficial interest, in shares proportionate to the amount which each had contributed. These *'resulting trusts'* were often found to arise in cases where couples had bought homes in their joint names, with one partner contributing more to the purchase price than the other.

17.5.1.2 Common intention constructive trusts

Another way in which an enforceable trust can arise, in the absence of a written express declaration, is where the parties have agreed that the title will be held on particular trusts, and one person has acted to his or her detriment in reliance on this shared understanding. The cases describe these trusts as *constructive trusts*, obliging the parties to give effect to their shared or common intentions about the nature of their beneficial interests (hence the name 'common intention constructive trust'). This type of constructive trust has been developed during the last 40 years in disputes about entitlement to a share in the family home. It differs from the resulting trust in a number of ways (for a more detailed discussion, see 18.1.3).

First, the common intention might be evidenced by unequal contributions to the purchase price of the property *or* other types of unequal financial contribution (e.g., mortgage payments, which do not trigger the presumption of resulting trust) as well as by types of behaviour that do not involve financial contribution (e.g., physical labour towards the improvement of the property).

Secondly, there is no necessary connection between the financial value of a person's contribution and the terms of the trust that is found to exist. If Peter and Mary buy a title in their joint names, and Peter contributes 20% to the purchase price and Mary contributes 80%, the presumption of resulting trust would have treated them as tenants in common in 80/20 shares. By contrast, the search for their common intention, under a constructive trust analysis, would not necessarily lead to such a strict one-to-one correspondence between the level of financial contribution and the terms of the ultimate trust. Looking at the parties' behaviour in the round, and taking into account their discussions with each other, a court might instead decide that Mary's 80% financial contribution had to be considered in the context of Peter's contribution to physically improving the property, and reach the conclusion that their true intention was to hold on 60/40 or 70/30 shares.

Thirdly, unlike the resulting trust, the conventional understanding of a common intention constructive trust is that it is enforceable only if there has been detrimental reliance on the common intention (see *Hudson v Hathway* [2022] EWCA Civ 1648, discussed at 17.5.5). However, where the evidence of common intention is financial contribution to the value of the property, making mortgage payments or undertaking physical work, it is likely that the evidence of intention will also serve as evidence of detrimental reliance on that intention.

17.5.1.3 Implied trusts in *Stack v Dowden*

In *Stack v Dowden* the House of Lords drew on principles established in sole-name cases and applied them in a joint-names dispute. As a result, the judges use the language of trusts, rather than that of co-ownership: for example, they focus on whether the parties intended their shares under the trust to be equal or unequal, but do not relate this specifically to an intention to create a tenancy in common. As a result, you may find at first that it is not always easy to relate what is said in this case to the rules described in the earlier part of the chapter.

Also, some statements in these decisions appear to suggest that joint tenants are entitled to individual shares in the property. These are really references to potential shares—that is, the shares that would be acquired if a joint tenancy was severed, but for the avoidance of doubt you need to understand now that *joint tenants, as a group, own the whole property and are not to be regarded as owning individual shares in it*. The question of 'shares' arises only if the parties intended at the outset to hold the beneficial interest as tenants in common, or if an existing beneficial joint tenancy has been converted into a tenancy in common by severance.

The rest of this section gives a relatively brief account of *Stack v Dowden* and *Jones v Kernott* as they relate to cases where legal title is jointly held by co-owners and the question is on what terms. You will find a fuller description of these two decisions in Chapter 18 which deals in detail with cases where the legal title is held by a sole owner and the question is whether any trust of land exists at all.

17.5.2 *Stack v Dowden*: the facts

In this case the parties were an unmarried couple who had bought a house as a home for themselves and their children, and were registered as joint tenants of the legal estate. The Land Registry transfer form in use at that time did not give transferees any opportunity to state that they were holding the property in trust for themselves or to describe the way in which they wished to hold the beneficial interest. When the parties' relationship came to an end, Ms Dowden served a notice of severance on her former partner which, if they were joint tenants in equity, would convert them into tenants in common.

Mr Stack then obtained a court order that the house should be sold and the proceeds divided equally between himself and his former partner. However, Ms Dowden had provided more than 50 per cent of the cost of acquiring the property and she appealed against this decision, claiming that she was entitled to a greater share. The Court of Appeal held that she was entitled to a 65 per cent share, and Mr Stack appealed from this decision to the House of Lords. He claimed that the parties had been joint tenants of both the legal estate and the beneficial interest, and relied on the rule in *Goodman v Gallant* [1986] Fam 106 that severance of a beneficial joint tenancy produces a tenancy in common in equal shares.

17.5.3 *Stack v Dowden*: the House of Lords' decision

Lady Hale, in a speech with which Lord Hoffmann, Lord Hope, and Lord Walker all agreed, started from the principle (already noted at 17.3.3) that where there is no express declaration about how the beneficial interest is to be held:

> it should be assumed that equity follows the law and that beneficial interests reflect the legal interests in the property (para. 54).

In other words, the fact that Stack and Dowden held the legal estate together as joint tenants raised the presumption that they were also joint tenants of the beneficial interest. However, they had made unequal contributions to the cost of acquiring the property, and it might be thought that this would give rise to the presumption of a tenancy in common or, to use the language of trusts, to a resulting trust. Nevertheless, the majority considered that determining the nature of interests in a family home solely by reference to the size of contributions to the purchase price was inappropriate in modern society (unless of course that was what the parties had intended—see Lord Walker at para. 31 and Lady Hale at paras. 60 and 69). Such an approach would not reflect the intentions which most couples in relationships today would have when deciding to buy a home together.

Accordingly, the House of Lords rejected the presumption of a resulting trust in cases involving the family home, and by implication also rejected the presumption of a tenancy in common arising from unequal contributions to the purchase price of such a property. Where property had been bought in joint names as a family home, the appropriate presumption was that *equity follows the law*. Purchase in joint names therefore indicates an intention to hold the beneficial interest on a joint tenancy, with all that that entails: that is, right of survivorship and equal shares on severance. This recognition of constructive trusts in joint-name cases enabled their Lordships to adopt a more flexible approach (already developed by the Court of Appeal—see 18.3.2) to discovering the intentions of the parties about their ownership of the home.

17.5.4 Rebutting the presumption of a beneficial joint tenancy

This presumption of a beneficial joint tenancy in the family home could be rebutted by proof that both parties intended their beneficial interests to be different from their legal interests, that is, they both intended to hold the legal estate in trust for themselves as tenants in common, in equal or unequal shares. However, Lady Hale and Lord Walker emphasised that rebutting the presumption would not be easy, and would occur only in very unusual cases (paras. 14 and 68).

Where a party attempted to rebut the presumption of beneficial joint tenancy, but could not show any express discussion or agreement on the matter, courts should apply the principles developed in sole-name cases and, in Lady Hale's words (at para. 60) seek to:

> ascertain the parties' shared intentions . . . with respect to the property in the light of their whole course of conduct in relation to it.

At para. 69, Lady Hale noted some of the factors which she considered could be relevant in establishing the parties' true intentions about their ownership of the family home, and you will find a list of these in Chapter 18 at 18.4.5.

Stack v Dowden itself proved to be one of the 'unusual cases' in which it was possible to rebut the presumption of a beneficial joint tenancy. At paras. 87–92, Lady Hale noted the factors from which she was able to infer that the parties did not intend to hold the beneficial interest as joint tenants. These factors included not only the greater financial contribution made to the cost of the house by Ms Dowden, but also the fact that her partner took responsibility only for certain clearly-defined areas of expenditure in relation to the house, and that both parties kept all their property, apart from the house, completely separate—there were no joint savings or investments. To Lady Hale, this conduct strongly indicated that the parties did not intend their shares in the house to be equal, and certainly did not intend the beneficial interest to be held on a joint tenancy with rights of survivorship. It follows from this that, from the outset, the beneficial interest must have been held on a tenancy in common in unequal shares although Lady Hale does not specifically say so. She simply states that there was no intention to hold as beneficial joint tenants and in the next sentence says that Ms Dowden has made good her claim to a 65 per cent share (para. 92).

17.5.5 Changing intentions: *Jones v Kernott*

The principles in *Stack v Dowden* were explained and developed by the Supreme Court in *Jones v Kernott* [2011] 3 WLR 1121. The facts of this case were in many ways similar to those of *Stack v Dowden*. Mr Kernott and Ms Jones were an unmarried couple who bought a house as a home for themselves and their children and were registered as joint tenants of the legal estate without making any statement about how they intended to hold the beneficial interest. When their relationship ended, Mr Kernott moved out of the property, and Ms Jones and the children continued to live there for the next 14 years, during which time she paid the mortgage instalments and all other outgoings on the property. At the end of this time, Mr Kernott asked for payment of his share in the property, and then purported to sever the beneficial joint tenancy. Meanwhile, Ms Jones had commenced proceedings, seeking a declaration that she was entitled to the whole beneficial interest in the property. She accepted that there had originally been a joint tenancy of the beneficial interest, and that if that tenancy had been severed when the parties separated, each would have been entitled to a 50 per cent share. However, she claimed that their intentions had changed during the period since their separation.

In *Stack v Dowden* it had been accepted, in *obiter dicta*, that intentions about the family home could change over a period of time (para. 62). In this case, there was no evidence of any express discussion or agreement, but the trial judge considered that the conduct of the parties since their separation enabled him to infer that they no longer intended to hold the beneficial interest as joint tenants. He was, however, apparently unable to infer any intention about the respective size of their shares but, relying on the Court of Appeal decision in *Oxley v Hiscock* [2005] Fam 211 (see also 18.3.2.3) he considered what would be fair and just between the parties, and accordingly held that J was entitled to 90 per cent of the value of the property and K to 10 per cent. This decision was reversed by the Court of Appeal (*Kernott v Jones* [2010] 1 WLR 2401), but upheld by the Supreme Court, although there was some difference of judicial opinion about the process by which the judge had quantified the shares.

In *Marr v Collie* [2017] 3 WLR 1507, the same approach was taken by the Privy Council in relation to a male couple who had lived together for 17 years, and it was accepted that intentions can change over time. However, there the lower court had refused to hear evidence as to the intentions of the parties and thus the case was remitted to the lower court for a further hearing on these matters.

The decision that a change in the intentions of the joint tenants can work such a change in the terms of the trust on which the property is held raises a puzzle about severance. The decision that Mr Kernott and Ms Jones were entitled to unequal shares must surely mean that at some stage in their relationship that joint tenancy turned into a tenancy in common. This could have been done by severing the joint tenancy, and severance may be effected by mutual agreement inferred from the conduct of the parties (see 17.6.4.2). However, severance of a joint tenancy entitles each party to an *equal* share under the resulting tenancy in common. There seems to be an unbridged gap between inferring severance (if that is what the court did) and holding that the parties were entitled to unequal shares. For a comment on this puzzle, see Dixon [2012] 76 Conv 83 at pp. 84–5.

In the recent case of *Hudson v Hathway* [2022] EWCA Civ 1648, the Court of Appeal addressed the question of how a change of common intention could alter beneficial interests under a trust. In that case, it was conceded that Mr Hudson and Ms Hathway had acquired a title to a house as joint tenants at law and in equity. When they later separated, they exchanged emails about the future division of their assets: in one of his emails, Mr Hudson said that he had no further interest in the house, and that Ms Hathway should 'take it'. She agreed that she would make no claims in relation to any of his assets, and subsequently took over making the mortgage payments on the property.

The Court of Appeal held that, in order for Ms Hathway to show that she had become solely entitled to the property, it was necessary to show *either* that Mr Hudson had formally released his interest in the property to her *or* that she had detrimentally relied on his informal agreement that he would do so. Lewison LJ explained that, while one joint tenant cannot *assign* his interest in the property to the other joint tenant—since each joint tenant is already considered to be jointly entitled to the whole value of the property—it *is* possible for one joint tenant to *release* his beneficial interest in the property to the other. Such a release does not bring about a transfer of the interest of one joint tenant to another, but simply extinguishes it, leaving the other joint tenant as the sole beneficial owner of the property. Such a decision to extinguish one's beneficial interest under a trust, however, was a disposition of an equitable interest, caught by s. 53(1)(c) of the LPA 1925, which requires a disposition of a beneficial interest under a subsisting trust to be made in signed writing. On the facts, the court held that the emails exchanged by the parties, all of which had been signed by the insertion of their names, met the formality requirement for the release of a beneficial interest. If they had not, Ms Hathway would have needed to prove detrimental reliance in order to justify a finding of a common intention constructive trust, to which the formality rule did not apply. Lewison LJ accepted the first instance judge's findings on the facts that Ms Hathway *had* detrimentally relied on Mr Hudson's emails, although he rejected the judge's alternative view that no evidence of detrimental reliance was necessary to make out a common intention constructive trust (see 18.4.4.6).

In *Hudson v Hathway* [2022], the parties had ceased to be beneficial joint tenants and one co-owner was left as the sole beneficial owner. It is less clear how this analysis might apply in a case like *Jones* where the parties cease to be joint tenants and are instead left as tenants in common holding in *unequal* shares. By analogy with Lewison LJ's analysis in *Hudson v Hathway*, it might be argued that the parties have first agreed a severance and then one party has agreed to assign a partial share of her own interest to the other. However, the outcome is not explained in this way in *Jones v Kernott*, in which the judges make no reference to the notion of severance as a necessary step in the process of turning a joint tenancy into a tenancy in common.

17.5.6 Scope of presumption of beneficial joint tenancy

The equitable presumption of a beneficial joint tenancy was described in *Stack v Dowden* as applying to 'the family home' or, to use another phrase, to 'domestic property'. It appears almost certain that it would apply to property of this type jointly owned not only by cohabitants, but also by married couples and civil partners, and it has been held to apply also to the parent and child relationship (see *Adekunle v Ritchie* [2007] BPIR 1177). Questions remain about homes jointly owned by other family members, such as siblings or cousins, or indeed by close friends who are not in a relationship together but may have pooled their resources to provide a home for themselves, perhaps in old age. In *Laskar v Laskar* [2008] 1 WLR 2695, a resulting trust was found to exist in relation to a property that was not the family home. The case concerned a house bought as an investment by a mother and daughter and registered in their joint names. The property was let to tenants and was never used by the owners as a family home. The daughter had contributed just over 4 per cent to the cost of the property, but subsequently claimed to be entitled to a 50 per cent share, relying on the *Stack v Dowden* presumption that the beneficial interest was held on a joint tenancy. The court considered that, although the relationship between the parties was among those contemplated by the House of Lords, the presumption did not arise in respect of property bought as an investment (which is akin to commercial cases) and not as a family home, and accordingly held that the parties' respective shares should reflect their contributions to the purchase price. However, in *Marr v Collie* [2017] UKPC 17, the Privy Council took the view that this did not mean there was a rigid distinction between 'domestic' and 'commercial' property held by people in a family relationship and that *Stack v Dowden* only applied to the domestic property. There was no 'strict line of demarcation' between the two and the question was one of discovering the actual common intentions of the parties in each case.

17.5.7 Significance of *Stack v Dowden* in context of co-ownership

The decision broke new ground in the distinction it makes between 'domestic' and 'commercial' cases and in the majority opinion that the equitable presumption arising from unequal contributions should not be applied in family cases. In the absence of any express declaration of a tenancy in common, it will now be presumed that where the legal estate is held by both cohabitants the beneficial interest will be held on a joint tenancy (despite unequal contributions to acquisition costs), unless the party who alleges that it is held on a tenancy in common can rebut the presumption by satisfying the court that this is what both partners intended. Since the trust in question is a common intention constructive trust, not a resulting trust, it is necessary to show that the party seeking a larger share of the value has relied to her detriment on that common intention.

17.6 Severance of a joint tenancy

17.6.1 Turning a joint tenancy into a tenancy in common

A relationship which begins as a joint tenancy need not remain so, for in certain circumstances it is possible for a joint tenant to sever his or her interest and thereby convert it into a tenancy in common. A primary reason for severance may be to avoid the effects of the right of survivorship—that is, to create separate shares in the property, which can then be passed by will or intestacy on the death of a co-owner. It is never possible these days to sever a joint tenancy of the legal estate, for to do this would be to create a legal tenancy in common, which is prohibited by LPA 1925, s. 34(1). Accordingly, LPA 1925, s. 36(2) provides that:

> No severance of a joint tenancy of a legal estate, so as to create a tenancy in common in land, shall be permissible.

Severance of an equitable joint tenancy is, however, still possible and when this is done the former joint tenant becomes entitled to an equal portion of the beneficial interest as a tenant in common (see 17.2.6).

17.6.2 Methods of severance

Severance may be effected in a number of ways, which are set out in the proviso to s. 36(2) (as amended by TOLATA 1996, Sch. 2, para. 4(3)):

> Provided that, where a legal estate (not being settled land) is vested in joint tenants beneficially, and any tenant desires to sever the joint tenancy in equity, he shall give to the other joint tenants a notice in writing of such desire or do such other acts or things as would, in the case of personal estate, have been effectual to sever the tenancy in equity, and thereupon the land shall be held in trust on terms which would have been requisite for giving effect to the beneficial interest if there had been an actual severance.

In summary, this provision:

- creates a new method of severance by written notice; and
- authorises the continued use of existing methods of severance, namely 'such other acts or things as would, in the case of personal estate have [severed] the tenancy in equity'.

17.6.3 Notice in writing

This is probably the simplest way of severing a joint tenancy today. There is no prescribed form for the notice, but it is essential that it contains a clear expression of the intention to sever.

Statements made by one joint tenant in documents initiating court proceedings have been held to be effective notices of severance. In *Re Draper's Conveyance* [1969] 1 Ch 486, an application to the court by a wife for an order for the sale of the former matrimonial home and the division of the proceeds according to the parties' interests in the property was held to have severed their beneficial joint tenancy. Despite some criticism of this decision in later cases, it was described by the Court of Appeal in *Burgess v Rawnsley* [1975] Ch 429, 440A as not being 'wrongly decided', and in *obiter dicta* (at p. 447F–G) Sir John Pennycuick said that he could not see why:

> The commencement of legal proceedings by writ or originating summons or the swearing of an affidavit in those proceedings, should not in appropriate circumstances constitute notice in writing within the meaning of s. 36(2) [LPA 1925].

More recently, in *Quigley v Masterson* [2011] EWHC 2529 (Ch) the High Court held that the beneficial joint tenancy in a house owned by Mrs Masterson ('M') and her former partner, Mr Pilkington ('P'), had been severed by M's statement in earlier Court of Protection proceedings that she and P each owned a 50 per cent share in the property. As a result, on P's death his share passed to his daughter Mrs Quigley as his executor, to be distributed according to the terms of his will.

17.6.3.1 Service of the notice

The notice must be served on all the joint tenants, by leaving it at their last known address or by posting it to that address by registered or recorded delivery (LPA 1925, s. 196(3) and (4); Recorded Delivery Service Act 1962, s. 1 and Sch. 1, para. 1).

Once the notice has been served in one of these ways it will be effective and will sever the joint tenancy, even if the co-owner does not in fact receive it. In *Re 88 Berkeley Road NW9* [1971] Ch 648 the two joint tenants both occupied the premises. One co-owner served notice of severance on the other joint tenant by registered post to the property. It later became clear that, when the letter was delivered, it was received and signed for by the person who had sent it and that it was never handed to the addressee. This was held nonetheless to amount to good service and the joint tenancy had accordingly been severed.

Lest you should think that *Re 88 Berkeley Road* was an isolated case, something very similar happened in *Kinch v Bullard* [1999] 1 WLR 423. Here a husband and wife were beneficial joint tenants of the matrimonial home. In 1995 the wife began divorce proceedings and, being aware that she was terminally ill, also instructed her solicitors to serve notice of severance on her husband because she wished to ensure that the right of survivorship would not have effect. While the letter was in the post, the husband had a heart attack. When the letter was delivered, it came into the hands of the wife, who had changed her mind by that point about wanting to sever and destroyed the letter without showing it to her husband. The husband died a few days later and the wife died in the following year. If the letter of severance was effective, the husband's share passed on his death under his will but, if it were not effective, on his death the right of survivorship operated, and the wife's estate could claim the entire property.

Neuberger J held that the notice had been served effectively, severance had occurred, and the husband's estate was entitled to his share. The fact the husband had not received the letter personally was not relevant because service was effected when the letter was 'left' at the premises and not when the person being served actually read the letter. The wife's change of mind was irrelevant because she could not withdraw the letter once it had been served: the severance took effect at the moment of service, when the letter was left at the premises. It was accepted, however, that it may be possible to withdraw a notice if the sending co-owner said to the other *before* the letter was served, 'I have sent a notice but I have changed my mind'. However, this view is *obiter* and tentatively expressed (at p. 429C).

In this case, it was in the interests of the wife and her estate to argue that the notice was *ineffective*. What would the position be if, by contrast, she had wanted to claim that the notice was *effective* even though her husband had not seen it? Neuberger J considered that if the wife had wished to argue that her notice was effective, she would not have been entitled to do so because she had taken positive steps to ensure that the letter did not ever come to her husband's attention. The judge indicated that to permit her to rely on the notice would be to permit the statutory provisions about severance by notice 'to be used as an engine of fraud' and would therefore be contrary to longstanding equitable principles (p. 431E).

Another interesting case on severance is *Grindal v Hooper* [1999] EGCS 150 (and see the article on the case at [2000] Conv 461). Here, in the conveyance to themselves, joint tenants had agreed that any notice purporting to sever their joint tenancy would not be effective unless it had been annexed to the conveyance to them. (This term takes one step further a usual, unregistered land, conveyancing practice, under which notice of severance is noted on the title deeds as a warning to later acquirers.) One joint tenant served a notice that complied with s. 36(2) but was not annexed to the conveyance. On his death the survivor claimed that there had been no valid severance in this instance. The court held that the agreement between the joint tenants could not displace the effect of the statutory rule that a notice complying with s. 36(2) did effect severance. The parties had been tenants in common in equity from the point at which notice was validly given.

17.6.4 'Such other acts or things as would, in the case of personal estate, sever the tenancy in equity'

It may seem strange that methods of severing appropriate to personal property are prescribed here but it must be remembered that the old statutory trust for sale had the effect of notionally converting the beneficiaries' interest into an interest in money (i.e., personal property (see 2.10 and 13.3.1.2)). Although this conversion no longer occurs, due to TOLATA 1996, s. 3, the statutory provision has not been altered. In fact, however, the pre-1926 rules for severing a joint tenancy in real property were the same as those for personal property, so in reality the same methods were continued by s. 36(2) (see *Nielson-Jones v Fedden* [1975] Ch 222 at p. 229).

What 'acts or things' bring about severance in equity? The classic statement, to which later decisions usually refer with approval, is that of Sir William Page Wood V-C in *Williams v Hensman* (1861) 1 John & H 546 at p. 557:

> A joint tenancy may be severed in three ways: in the first place, an act of any one of the persons interested operating upon his own share may create a severance as to that share ... Each one is at liberty to dispose of his own interest in such manner as to sever it from the joint fund losing, of course, at the same time, his own right of survivorship. Secondly, a joint tenancy may be severed by mutual agreement. And, in the third place, there may be a severance by any course of dealing sufficient to intimate that the interests of all were mutually treated as constituting a tenancy in common.

These three methods are now considered in turn.

17.6.4.1 'An act . . . operating upon his own share'

Sale

The example of this method given in *Williams v Hensman* is that of disposing of one's own interest in such a way as to sever it from the joint property—for example, on sale. This creates severance because it has the effect of destroying one of the unities essential to the joint tenancy: that of title. The purchaser does not share the unity of title with the other co-owners, for that person takes under a different document and so cannot be a joint tenant with them. At law, severance used to occur when the estate was conveyed to the purchaser, but in equity, it takes place as soon as there is a specifically enforceable contract to sell. It will be remembered that equity recognises the purchaser as owner from the date of the contract (see 4.6) and the change of equitable ownership is enough to destroy the unities.

Where severance is effected by sale of the beneficial interest, the joint tenant cannot transfer an interest in the legal estate to the purchaser, for to do so would amount to severance of the legal joint tenancy, which is forbidden (LPA 1925, s. 36(2)). So, even after the joint tenant has disposed of the beneficial interest, the joint tenant at law continues to hold the legal estate as a trustee, and can only cease to be a trustee by releasing his interest to his fellow joint tenants or by retiring from the trust (Trustee Act 1925, s. 39).

Mortgage

Another example of alienation arises when one joint tenant mortgages an interest in the property. Acting alone, the joint tenant can only affect his or her own interest (the equitable interest) and can only mortgage it if it constitutes a share separate from that of the other co-owner. Thus, mortgaging one's own interest severs the joint tenancy (the legal owners would have to act together as trustees to charge the legal estate). In *First National Securities v Hegarty* [1984] 1 All ER 139, Bingham J held that the same effect occurred where a husband purported to mortgage the legal estate by resorting to the forgery of his wife's signature. The result was an equitable charge operating only on the husband's interest, which severed the joint tenancy in equity.

Bankruptcy

An example which falls within this category (although this may at first seem odd) arises if one of the joint tenants is declared bankrupt. This is an involuntary effect of the law relating to bankruptcy which transfers the bankrupt's interest to the trustee in bankruptcy when a bankruptcy order is made. Thus, while not really an act of the bankrupt co-owner, it nonetheless does create a separate share in the property by means of a transferring disposition of the beneficial interest in the property.

17.6.4.2 Mutual agreement

Severance can be effected by the agreement of all the joint tenants. The agreement may, of course, be express, but can also be inferred from the conduct of the parties. The leading modern case which illustrates this method of severance is *Burgess v Rawnsley* [1975] Ch 429. Here it was held that an oral agreement by one joint tenant to purchase the share of the other had effected a severance (because the parties were thinking in terms of 'shares'), even though such an agreement would not be legally enforceable because there was no written memorandum or part performance to satisfy LPA 1925, s. 40 (the predecessor to the Law of Property (Miscellaneous) Provisions Act 1989, s. 2). You saw in 17.6.4.1 that a contract must be specifically enforceable if it is to constitute severance under the first rule in *Williams v Hensman*; but in *Burgess v Rawnsley* [1975] Ch 429 at p. 444, Browne LJ emphasised that this requirement:

> only applies where the suggestion is that the joint tenancy has been severed by an alienation by one joint tenant to a third party and does not apply to severance by agreement between the joint tenants.

The principle that an unenforceable agreement can serve as evidence of a common intention to sever was confirmed in *Hunter v Babbage* [1994] EGCS 8, in which a divorcing couple's unenforceable agreement was held to sever the joint tenancy, although the husband had died before the agreement could be formalised.

Another example of severance by agreement is to be found in *Re Woolnough* [2002] WTLR 595. Here, the joint tenants were brother and sister. They went to their solicitor together and both made wills, each leaving his or her interest in the property to the other but with a remainder to their niece. After the sister's death the brother changed his will and it became essential to know whether the joint tenancy had been severed by the making of the earlier wills. The court held that it had. This is because for each to make a will leaving a share to the other there must have been an intention on the part of both to treat themselves as each having a share. If they agreed that each had a share they must both have regarded themselves as having interests in common (rather than joint) because joint interests do not give rise to shares that can be disposed of by a will.

No severance by will
In considering the decision in *Re Woolnough* it is important to realise that the will-making was treated as evidence of a mutual agreement to sever, and that it was the *agreement* which effected severance. A joint tenancy cannot be severed by one tenant making a will which purports to dispose of that person's interest in the property, when the other party is unaware of this decision and has not agreed to it. The will does not take effect until the death of the joint tenant. The right of survivorship operates at the moment of death, with the result that the deceased had no interest in the property to pass under the will.

17.6.4.3 'Any course of dealing [which shows] that the interests of all were mutually treated as constituting a tenancy in common'

In *Burgess v Rawnsley*, members of the Court of Appeal expressed views on this third category, although they emphasised that as the decision was based on the second ground (mutual agreement), these views were necessarily *obiter dicta*. Thus, Sir John Pennycuick explained that it includes 'negotiations which, although not otherwise resulting in any agreement, indicate a common intention that the joint tenancy should be regarded as severed' (at p. 447).

It should be noted that Lord Denning MR gave a slightly wider interpretation (at p. 439), which seems to cover a unilateral declaration by the party wishing to sever:

> It is sufficient if there is a course of dealing in which one party makes clear to the other that he desires that their shares should no longer be held jointly but be held in common.

This does not seem to fit too well with the requirement of mutual behaviour stated in *Williams v Hensman*, and it should be noted that Sir John Pennycuick expressly states that in his view 'a mere verbal notice' (i.e., an *oral* notice) by one party to the other cannot operate as severance (p. 448). *Written* notice, of course, is validated by the statutory rules in LPA 1925, s. 36(3) and (4). Certainly, in *Gore v Carpenter* (1990) 60 P&CR 456 (ChD) it was held that an agreement 'in principle' for one joint tenant to acquire the interest of the other, but without a final agreement, did not suffice to sever.

17.6.5 Forfeiture as a result of homicide

One final method of severance, not covered by LPA 1925, s. 36(2) or *Williams v Hensman* (1861) 1 John & H 546 must be noted briefly. Should one joint tenant kill the other, it seems that the right of survivorship cannot operate because this would allow the killer to benefit from his or her criminal act. The general principle that this is not permitted is to be found in *In the Estate of Hall* [1914] P 1.

The Forfeiture Act 1982, s. 2(1) and (2) gives the courts the power to modify the effect of forfeiture in cases of an unlawful killing which does not constitute murder. The power can only be exercised where 'the justice of the case so requires'. In *Dunbar v*

Plant [1998] Ch 412, these rules were applied in a case in which there had been a suicide pact between two people but one person had, despite the joint attempt, survived. Note, however, in *Chadwick v Collinson* [2014] EWHC 3055 (which was not a severance case) the forfeiture rule was applied in full in a case in which the person who had killed was suffering from diminished responsibility. Here the court felt that, despite his mental condition, the killer still had a degree of responsibility for his actions and thus relief from forfeiture should not be given.

You may wish to note that where there *is* a tenancy in common and the killer stands to inherit a share of the deceased's property as part of the residuary estate of the deceased, s. 46A of the Administration of Estates Act 1925 (inserted by s. 1 of the Estates of Deceased Persons (Forfeiture Rule and Law of Succession) Act 2011) states that the estate will be disposed of as though the killer had died immediately before the person killed. This allows those deriving an interest under the killer to inherit if they are themselves not convicted of the killing. In the past, the killer lost any interest due to forfeiture and his or her innocent spouse or children were therefore also deprived of any chance of benefiting from the estate (for example, the grandchildren of a grandparent murdered by a child would also lose any possibility of an inheritance). In such an instance, the new rule permits the grandchildren to inherit as though their convicted parent had died immediately before the death of their grandparent.

17.6.5.1 8 Trant Way: example of the operation of the severance rules

You saw in 17.2.2.1 that despite the fact that the transfer of this property purported to convey the legal estate to all six students, rules about the age and number of legal owners resulted in the estate vesting in the first four students named in the transfer who were over 18 (Brian, Colin, David, and Eric), who hold the estate in trust for themselves, Alice and Fanny.

You have also seen in the course of this chapter that the way in which the students hold the beneficial interest depends on the presence of the four unities and the absence of any words of severance (that is, any words in the transfer indicating an intention to hold as tenants in common in equity). The four unities appear to be satisfied by the transfer, and it appears that there were no words of severance. All six contributed equally to the purchase price, so it is possible that equity will presume a tenancy in common in equal shares, unless the rule in *Stack v Dowden* applies. Since the parties do not seem to intend a shared family life together, and it is unlikely that they intend (for example) survivorship to operate between them, it is likely that the presumption of resulting trust rather than the presumption of a beneficial joint tenancy will apply. Suppose, however, the parties had taken under a conveyance that expressly conveyed the title to them as 'beneficial joint tenants'. This language would constitute an express declaration of a joint tenancy in equity, which would be conclusive. In this scenario, there would be joint tenancies of both the legal estate and the beneficial interest, as shown in Figure 17.5.

LAW	EQUITY
Legal estate	Beneficial interest
(B, C, D, and E)	(A, B, C, D, E, and F)

Figure 17.5 Co-ownership of 8 Trant Way at the start

The effect of the severance rules can be illustrated by assuming that the following events occur:

(a) Alice serves notice of severance on Brian, Colin, David, Eric, and Fanny;
(b) Brian sells his interest to Wilfred;
(c) Colin dies.

This produces the devolution of title to the legal estate and the equitable interest shown in Table 17.2.

Table 17.2 Effect of severance rules on co-ownership at 8 Trant Way

Event	Law	Equity	Explanation
	(B, C, D, and E)	(A, B, C, D, E, and F)	At start all are joint tenants in law and equity.
(a)	(B, C, D, and E)	A (B, C, D, E, and F)	Position at law not affected. A becomes tenant in common in equity with a one-sixth share, but others remain joint tenants inter se ('between themselves') as to five-sixths.
(b)	(B, C, D, and E)	A, W (C, D, E, and F)	Position at law not affected. In equity, severance by destruction of unities. W becomes tenant in common with a one-sixth share. C, D, E, and F remain joint tenants inter se of four-sixths.
(c)	(B, D, and E)	A, W (D, E, and F)	Right of survivorship operates in law and equity. B, D, and E hold the legal estate as joint tenants. A and W each own a one-sixth share of the equitable interest. D, E, and F jointly own four-sixths of the equitable interest.

17.6.6 How should the former joint tenant protect an interest in the property after severance?

Before severance, the last surviving joint tenant would have become solely entitled to the property by the right of survivorship. To avoid any risk that such a survivor might conceal the fact of severance and pretend to be solely entitled to the property, it is important that the severance should be noted on the title.

In the case of *unregistered land*, this is done by endorsing a memorandum of severance on the original conveyance to the joint tenants. This serves two purposes. It protects the interest of those who inherit the share in the property created by the severance. It also warns any prospective purchaser that the property remains subject to a trust and that the purchaser will be bound by it unless the beneficiaries' interests are overreached by payment of the purchase money to two trustees (see 5.5.2.1, 14.9.2).

Where title to the land is *registered*, the tenant who has severed an interest should ensure that a restriction is placed on the register of title (see 6.2.7.3). This will indicate that the survivor of the legal joint tenancy cannot give a valid receipt for capital money. It thus protects those who have a share in the beneficial interest and also alerts any prospective purchaser to the existence of the trust.

17.7 Relationship between co-owners

It is not uncommon for co-owners to have differences of opinion about the management of their property. In the case of family homes, in particular, disputes often arise when relationships break down and one owner may want to exclude the other from the property or even to sell it against the other's wishes. In considering how to deal with such problems, it is important to remember that co-owned land is always subject to a trust of land and accordingly is governed by the provisions of TOLATA 1996, which were discussed in Chapter 14. You may find it helpful at this point to review this discussion in Chapter 14 (14.7 and 14.8), which will be briefly recapitulated below.

17.7.1 Is one co-owner able to sell the property against the wishes of the other(s)?

Where one co-owner wishes to sell the property (i.e., the legal estate) and cannot secure the agreement of the other(s), that co-owner will have to seek an order for sale from the court under TOLATA 1996, s. 14. There is no other way of proceeding. If the other co-owners hold the legal estate with that person, a conveyance or transfer cannot be made without their cooperation. For details of the statutory jurisdiction to order a sale, and the considerations that a court must take into account in deciding on whether to do so, see 14.8.

17.7.2 Does one co-owner have the right to exclude the other from the property?

As was explained in Chapter 13, the imposition of the statutory trust for sale, coupled with the doctrine of conversion, made it difficult for some co-owners to claim that they had a right to occupy the land. Where the legal estate was vested in all the co-owners, each one had a legal right to possession of the property and one could not lawfully be evicted by another. It was different, however, when the legal estate was held by one person in trust for himself and another, who consequently had only an equitable interest under the trust. Under the doctrine of conversion, the equitable interest was regarded as being in money and not in the land itself, and it was difficult to see how such an interest could give a right to occupy the land.

This problem was considered by the Court of Appeal in *Bull v Bull* [1955] 1 QB 234. Here a financial contribution by the mother to the purchase price of a house conveyed to her son created a resulting trust, in which the son held the legal estate in trust for himself and his mother as tenants in common. The house was bought to provide a home for both, but after his marriage the son wanted his mother to move out, and finally sought a possession order against her. The court held that, while the trust for sale imposed a duty to sell, each beneficiary was entitled to occupy the property until it was sold. The son could not evict his mother by obtaining an order for possession. If he wished to bring the co-ownership to an end and could not do so by agreement, he should seek an order for sale from the court (under LPA 1925, s. 30), and on sale should divide the proceeds between himself and his mother. In effect, the court in this case 'glossed over' the effect of the notional conversion of the property, and after this decision the courts appeared willing to protect the occupation of equitable co-owners and did not press the statutory trust for sale to its logical conclusion.

With TOLATA 1996, however, the old difficulties disappeared. The trust imposed on co-owners is now a trust of land, not a trust for sale, and the doctrine of conversion no longer applies. Under the trust, co-owners have interests in the land itself, and in certain cases have a statutory right to occupy the property under s. 12 of TOLATA 1996. Where several beneficiaries have this right and all wish to occupy the property, the trustees have the power to balance their interests under the provisions of s. 13, and may permit some to occupy while excluding others. Of course, in the case of the statutory trust imposed on co-owners, where the same people may be both trustees and beneficiaries, this may simply lead to further conflict, which will have to be resolved by the court under TOLATA 1996, s. 14. For details of the statutory right of occupation and the court's power to deal with disputes between co-owners, as well as the possibility that a co-owner who is *not* in occupation may seek a payment of 'occupation rent' from another who is, see 14.7.

17.8 Ending co-ownership

There are three ways in which co-ownership may come to an end.

17.8.1 Partition

Where the land is sufficiently extensive it may prove convenient for the co-owners to decide to partition the premises between themselves. In this way each becomes a sole beneficial owner of a portion of the land. Such partition can always be effected by agreement between all the co-owners. Under TOLATA 1996, s. 7(1), trustees may partition the land and convey the portions thus created to the co-owners. Before exercising this power the trustees are required to obtain the consent of each beneficiary to whom a conveyance of a portion of the land is to be made (s. 7(3)).

Where title to land is still unregistered, partitioning it in this way is one of the new triggers inducing first registration (see 6.3.2), so each beneficiary who acquires land in this way will need to apply for first registration of the title to each plot.

17.8.2 Sale of the property and division of the proceeds

Again, this may be done by agreement or, where necessary, on the order of the court following an application under TOLATA 1996, s. 14.

17.8.3 Union of interests in one of the co-owners

17.8.3.1 On death

Where the beneficial interests are held by several co-owners as joint tenants, the survivor will become solely entitled to the property by right of survivorship.

This could create difficulties if the survivor wanted to sell the property, because it was almost impossible to prove to a prospective purchaser that the beneficial joint tenancy had not been severed at some time in the past. If there had been severance, the tenants would have been holding shares in the beneficial interest under a tenancy in common, and these shares would have passed on death to those entitled to take them. If this had happened, the sole survivor, who appeared to be absolutely entitled, would in fact be holding the legal estate as trustee for himself and others.

Unregistered land
In the case of unregistered land it is usual to make a note of any severance on the original conveyance to the joint tenants. However, it is not compulsory to do this, and so the absence of such a note is no guarantee that severance has not occurred. To guard against this, a purchaser might well insist on paying the purchase money to two trustees to take advantage of the overreaching procedure (see 5.5.2), and this would involve the seller in the delay and expense of appointing another trustee. This problem has been resolved by the Law of Property (Joint Tenants) Act 1964. This statute ensures that where a sole surviving joint tenant sells, the purchaser will obtain good title free of any equitable interests and need not worry about the possibility of an earlier severance unless a memorandum of severance has been endorsed on or annexed to the conveyance which vested the property in the joint tenants. Accordingly, if a joint tenant does sever and wishes to avoid the possibility of the 1964 Act being used by a sole survivor of the original co-owners the serving person should ensure that a memorandum of severance is so endorsed.

The 1964 Act does not apply to registered land (s. 3).

Registered land
Where title to the land is registered, the severing tenant or those who inherit his share should enter a restriction on the register of title to protect their interests (17.6.6). If this is not done, a disponee for valuable consideration would in general take free of their interests (see 6.5), but there is a risk that if beneficiaries are in 'actual occupation' of the land their interests might override the disposition and bind the purchaser (see 6.5.5).

17.8.3.2 By agreement
It is also possible in any co-ownership situation for one owner to acquire the interests of the others by agreement, and thus become solely entitled. An agreement of this kind will involve the *release* of beneficial interests in the case of a joint tenancy and an *assignment* of beneficial interests in the case of a tenancy in common. These are both 'dispositions' of equitable interests under subsisting trusts for the purposes of s. 53(1)(c) of the LPA 1925 (as decided by the Court of Appeal in *Hudson v Hathway* [2022] EWCA Civ 1648, discussed at 17.5.5, in the case of a release). It is therefore necessary for the parties to use signed writing to bring a co-ownership arrangement to an end in this way. If one of the co-owners has detrimentally relied on the other's informal promise to assign or release the other person's rights, the court may give effect to the agreement by way of a constructive trust (see 17.5.5).

17.9 8 Trant Way

Co-ownership and trusts of land are very closely linked and one cannot really understand one without also knowing the other. In particular, you could have difficulty in dealing with a problem about co-owners unless you know something of the TOLATA 1996 provisions about:

- consultation of beneficiaries (14.5.3);
- beneficiaries' right of occupation (14.7); and
- the powers of the court under s. 14 of TOLATA 1996 (14.8).

To apply the law to the facts of 8 Trant Way, we must look at the latest position. See Table 17.2 for the current ownership in law and in equity.

Recently, Eric and Fanny got engaged to each other and want to move out of No. 8 and find a separate flat, while David has lost interest in the history of Outer Mongolia and plans to withdraw from his course and go travelling. All three of them want to sell the house and take a share of the proceeds. However, Alice, who is in the second year of her course, wants to continue to live in the house until she graduates, and Wilfred also wants the house to remain unsold.

If trustees Brian, David, and Eric apply for an order for sale, those who want to sell will be in the majority, since between them they hold four-sixths of the beneficial interest. However, the trustees cannot simply go ahead and sell the property. In order to sell, they will need vacant possession, and *Bull v Bull* [1955] 1 QB 234 makes it clear that the minority cannot simply be evicted. The problem could be solved by Alice and Wilfred buying out the interest of the other three, but if they cannot afford to do this those who want to sell will probably seek a court order under s. 14.

The relevant matters for consideration by the court on such an application would include the purpose for which the property is held (s. 15(1)(b)) and the wishes of the majority of the beneficiaries (s. 15(3)). In opposing the application, Alice will undoubtedly argue that the house was bought to provide accommodation for the students while at the university, and that she still wants to use the property for that purpose. In interpreting the reference to 'purpose' in s. 15(1)(b) the court may consider the 'continuing purpose' decisions on earlier applications under LPA 1925, s. 30 (see 13.4.1.1) but the indications are that in a case like this the court is more likely to be influenced by the need to balance the interests of the parties, as far as is possible. Since Alice is now the only one of the original owners who wants to live in the house, unless Wilfred is able to produce some compelling argument for retaining the house, it seems more likely here that the court will give effect to the wishes of the majority and will order sale.

FURTHER READING

Megarry and Wade, *The Law of Real Property*, 9th edn., Sweet & Maxwell, 2019, Chapter 12.

Severing a joint tenancy

Crown, 'Severance of Joint Tenancy of Land by Partial Alienation' (2001) 117 LQR 477.

Gravells, 'Co-ownership, Severance and Purchasers—The Law of Property (Joint Tenants) Act 1964 on Trial?', [2000] 64 Conv 461 (case note on *Grindal v Hooper*).

Hayton, 'Joint Tenancies—Severance' (note on *Burgess v Rawnsley* and *Nielson-Jones v Fedden*) [1976] CLJ 20.

Percival, 'Severance by Written Notice—A Matter of Delivery?' (note on *Kinch v Bullard*) [1999] Conv 61.

Tee, 'Severance Revisited' [1995] Conv 105.

You can visit the online resources to test your knowledge of this chapter with self-test questions at www.oup.com/he/nair19e/.

18

Trusts of the family home

18.1 Introduction **382**
18.2 Sole-name cases: establishing a beneficial interest **386**
18.3 Sole-name cases: quantifying the beneficial interest **392**
18.4 Joint-names cases **396**
18.5 Joint-names cases after *Stack v Dowden* **403**
18.6 Sole-name cases after *Stack v Dowden* **406**
18.7 Detrimental reliance **407**

Chapter 13 explains the nature of resulting and constructive trusts and the circumstances in which they arise. In recent years these trusts have played a major role in resolving disputes about ownership of the family home, and this has now become a fairly specialised area of law with some special principles that apply particularly in the domestic context. It is now time to look at this topic in more detail.

18.1 Introduction

18.1.1 Who owns the family home?

It is always open to partners in a family relationship (whether they be spouses, civil partners, or cohabitants) to make express arrangements about their respective property interests in the family home. In so-called '*joint-names*' cases, in which the property is conveyed to family partners as *co-owners*, there is an opportunity for them not only to state that they are holding the legal estate on trust for themselves but also to indicate the nature of their beneficial interests (i.e., whether they hold the beneficial interest as joint tenants or tenants in common (see 17.1), and, if the latter, what is to be the size of their respective shares). In '*sole-name*' cases, in which the conveyance or transfer is to one of the parties only, it could still include a declaration that the property is held in trust for both partners, and if the property had in fact been acquired by one partner before the relationship began, that person could always make a separate declaration of trust.

For a variety of reasons, however, many couples do not regulate their interests in the family home in this way. In recent years difficulties have arisen in joint-names cases where the parties hold the legal estate as co-owners in trust for themselves but fail to specify the nature of their beneficial interests. Moreover, although co-ownership of the family home has become more common during the past 50 years, there are still many cases in which the more traditional approach is adopted, thus vesting the title in only one of the partners without any declaration of trust. Where one partner holds the legal title in this way, and there is no express declaration of trust, he or she is presumed to be entitled to sole beneficial ownership, and this presumption is rebutted only if the other partner can prove entitlement to a share in the property under a resulting or constructive trust. Further, even where such a trust is established (either expressly or by implication), the size of the partners' interests under it may be uncertain and require determination by the court.

In general, questions about entitlement to a share in the family home come before the courts in two situations. They may arise from disputes between former partners who are separating at the end of their relationship, or may arise between a third party with an interest in the property and one of the partners who claims to have rights which take priority over that interest.

18.1.2 11 Trant Way

The fee simple in 11 Trant Way is vested in Mark Mould, who bought the property in 1999 as the sole holder of the legal estate. The house is also occupied by Sally Mould, Mark's wife, and their two children. Mrs Mould has not worked outside the home during the marriage, and has been fully occupied in bringing up the children and looking after the house and garden.

The Moulds' marriage appears to be a happy and successful one and they have no money worries. However, if things did go wrong, either with their relationship or their finances, the considerations explained in this chapter could be very relevant, as they would also be in any joint-names case, in which the co-owners had not declared the nature of their beneficial interests.

18.1.2.1 Property adjustment orders on divorce or dissolution of civil partnership

If the Moulds' marriage were to end in divorce, they would find that the court has wide powers, under Part II of the Matrimonial Causes Act 1973, to make property adjustment orders, which require the transfer of property from one party to the other. Similar provisions apply on the dissolution of a civil partnership under the Civil Partnership Act 2004, s. 72 and Sch. 5, Part 2 and para. 21.

In exercising its statutory powers, the court is authorised to take into account a range of matters, which include: the financial resources and commitments of each party; their age; the duration of the marriage; and the contribution which each has made or is likely to make to the welfare of the family by looking after the home or caring for the family (Matrimonial Causes Act 1973, s. 25(2)). These provisions were not introduced, however, until 1970 (under the Matrimonial Proceedings and Property Act 1970) and before then the only way of obtaining a share in the former matrimonial home owned by the other spouse was by establishing entitlement under a trust.

18.1.2.2 Claims between cohabitants

The provisions relating to property adjustment orders do not apply when a relationship between cohabitants who are neither married nor civil partners comes to an end. It is essential to be aware that cohabitation, however long the period, does not give rise to the family law rights mentioned in 18.1.2.1. Nor will a form of marriage that is not legally recognised in England and Wales, as is the case with some religious marriages.

In these cases, any claim to a share in the family home has to be decided according to the rules of property law, rather than by any consideration of what each party needs or deserves. As Millet J put it in *Windeler v Whitehall* [1990] 1 FLR 505 at p. 506, when considering a claim by a woman to a share in her former partner's property:

> It is not enough for her to persuade me that she deserves to have such a share. She must satisfy me that she already has it.

18.1.2.3 Claims involving a third party

Many cases arise when couples, whether married or not, find themselves in financial difficulties and their mortgagees seek possession of the property. When this happens, one partner may claim to have a share in the house, which takes priority over the mortgage, so that the mortgagee cannot enforce its rights against that share. We have already seen examples of this in earlier chapters in *Kingsnorth Finance Co. Ltd v Tizard* [1986] 1 WLR 783 (5.5.2.3) and *Williams & Glyn's Bank Ltd v Boland* [1981] AC 487 (6.5.6.2). Thus, if the Moulds were to find themselves in financial difficulties, Sally Mould might want to claim that she was entitled to a share in the family home, although the legal title is in her husband's name, because this may delay sale of the property.

In such a case, where the dispute is not between the family partners themselves but between one of the partners and the mortgagee, the existence and size of any share in the beneficial interest will have to be decided in accordance with basic trust principles.

Similarly, if one partner becomes bankrupt or is subject to a confiscation order following a criminal conviction (see, for example, *Gibson v Revenue & Customs Prosecution Office* [2008] EWCA Civ 645 or the recent case of *R v Lam* [2022] EWCA Crim 448), the other partner will have to establish that any right claimed in the property can be shown to arise under a trust.

In dealing with these family home cases, the courts have developed existing doctrines concerned with 'resulting' and 'constructive trusts' to determine the legal consequences of the parties' actions in the absence of an express declaration (see 13.2). However, note that the courts have sometimes failed to distinguish between resulting and constructive trusts when describing the trusts that arise in the context of the family home. This can be misleading and, in fact, it is important to be able to distinguish between the two.

18.1.3 Distinguishing between resulting and constructive trusts

18.1.3.1 Failure to distinguish

Lord Diplock in *Gissing v Gissing* [1971] AC 886 at p. 905, in referring to resulting, implied, and constructive trusts, said:

> It is unnecessary for present purposes to distinguish between these three classes of trust.

This statement may be acceptable when taken in context, but it led other judges to use the phrases almost interchangeably. Thus, Lord Denning MR in *Hussey v Palmer* [1972] 1 WLR 1286 at p. 1289 said that although the plaintiff alleged that there was a resulting trust:

> I should have thought that the trust in this case . . . was more in the nature of a constructive trust: but this is more a matter of words than anything else. The two run together.

As a result of this approach being adopted over a number of years, it is often unclear which type of trust is involved in a particular decision, and as a result it is difficult to give a clear account of the circumstances in which each of these trusts operates.

This somewhat cavalier approach by the courts might suggest to you that the distinction is unimportant, and that you too could say: 'It doesn't matter which it is!'. However, a very different approach was taken in later cases, beginning with the Court of Appeal decision in *Drake v Whipp* (1995) 28 HLR 531.

18.1.3.2 Importance of distinction

In *Drake v Whipp* Peter Gibson LJ described the earlier judicial statements as 'a potent source of confusion' (at p. 533). It is now clear that the distinction between resulting and constructive trusts is of crucial importance in determining:

- the nature of the evidence that can give rise to a finding that a trust was intended; and
- the approach to be adopted by the court in determining the size of each party's share in the property.

1. Evidence justifying a finding of a trust

The only evidence which can be relied upon to establish a resulting trust are financial contributions made at the time the property was acquired (i.e., contributions to the purchase price paid to the vendor before transfer). These contributions can include liabilities undertaken at the time of acquisition, such as taking on a liability to make payments under a mortgage that is taken out to fund the acquisition of the property (*Laskar v Laskar* [2008] 1 WLR 2695). Later contributions, such as paying instalments due under the mortgage, do not create a resulting trust in favour of the party making the payments (*Curley v Parks* [2005] 1 P & CR DG 15).

By contrast, the payment of mortgage instalments, and a range of other contributions, as well as other types of conduct or discussions between the parties, can be relevant in establishing a constructive trust (see 18.2). A constructive trust of the family home can arise without any financial contribution by one of the partners, provided that there is other evidence of their common intention that the property be held on trust for both and provided that there has been detrimental reliance on that common intention.

2. Size of share in property

Under a *resulting trust*, the beneficiary's share is strictly proportionate to the amount he or she has contributed at the time of acquisition and later payments cannot be taken into account.

Under a *constructive trust*, the court has a much greater freedom to decide on the respective shares of the parties, which are not necessarily proportionate to their financial contributions (see 18.3). The question in a constructive trust case is what the parties' likely common intention as to their shares might be, and it is open to the court to take a range of evidence into account in deciding what they intended; there is no presumption, unlike in the resulting trusts context, that they intend each person to get only a share proportionate to her contribution.

3. Relevance to family homes

Following *Stack v Dowden* [2007] 2 AC 432 and *Jones v Kernott* [2011] 3 WLR 1121, it is clear that the presumption of resulting trust is no longer available in the context of the family home, at least in cases where the property is held in joint names (see 17.5). A court will not, therefore, presume an agreement to hold in unequal shares purely because parties have contributed unequally to the acquisition of a family home in their joint names. It is less clear whether such a presumption is still treated as arising in sole-name cases, but it is at the least a doubtful question: where parties have contributed unequally to the acquisition of a family home in the name of one of them, this will often be evidence of a *common intention* that the property be held on trust and, in the family home setting, courts have tended to look beyond the proportionate contributions of the parties to decide what shares were in fact intended (see 18.3).

18.1.4 Sole-name and joint-names cases

Until *Stack v Dowden* [2007] 2 AC 432 (in which the parties were co-owners of the legal estate), many of the decisions which establish the principle of the common-intention constructive trust had arisen from claims by one partner (spouse or cohabitant) to a share in the family home, which was owned by the other partner.

In these cases of *single legal ownership*, the court is required to consider two questions:

- is the claimant entitled to a share in the beneficial interest, i.e., does the legal owner hold the property on trust for himself and the claimant?
- and, if so, what is the size of the claimant's share in the beneficial interest?

By contrast, in cases of *joint legal ownership* the partners hold the legal estate on a statutory trust for themselves (LPA 1925, ss. 34(2) and 36(1)). As a result, there is usually no difficulty in establishing that each is entitled to some beneficial interest in the property, but problems can arise about the nature and size of their interests. We have already seen that the courts now respond to these situations by presuming a joint tenancy in equity unless there is evidence to suggest a contrary intention (see 17.5). In this chapter, we will consider what type of evidence can be used to show a contrary intention.

Sections 18.2 and 18.3 describe the development of the common-intention constructive trust in sole-name cases, and 18.4 covers how the principles developed in these cases have been applied where the family home is jointly owned.

18.2 Sole-name cases: establishing a beneficial interest

18.2.1 The starting point

In the words of Lady Hale in *Stack v Dowden* [2007] 2 AC 432 at para. 56:

> The starting point where there is sole legal ownership is sole beneficial ownership.

Equity is presumed to follow the law, with the result that the owner of the legal estate is presumed to be solely entitled to enjoy all the benefits of his property. The burden of displacing this presumption rests on the person who claims to be entitled to any part of the beneficial interest in property belonging to another. The circumstances in which the presumption may be displaced in disputes involving the family home were considered by the House of Lords in *Gissing v Gissing* [1971] AC 886.

18.2.2 Gissing v Gissing

You have seen that a contribution to the purchase price is presumed to give rise to a resulting trust, and it has always been possible for a spouse or cohabitant to claim an interest in the property because of such a contribution. However, in the early 1970s, just before property adjustment orders were introduced, the House of Lords had to consider two cases in which the claim of a divorced spouse to a share in the family home was based not on direct financial contribution but on, in the one case, work done on the house and in the other, on relatively minor contributions to household expenses. In *Pettit v Pettit* [1970] AC 777, the house was owned by the wife. Her divorced husband's claim to a share in the proceeds of sale was based on redecorations and improvements to the property which he had carried out, and which he claimed had increased its value. In *Gissing v Gissing* [1971] AC 886 a wife, whose marriage had ended in divorce after some 30 years, sought to establish a claim to a share in the family home which was owned by her husband, relying on financial contributions she had made over the years in buying items of furniture and equipment, and paying for some improvements to the garden.

In each of these cases, the Court of Appeal had considered that the applicant was entitled to a share in the property, but the House of Lords did not share this view, and in both cases held that the claimants had no share in the beneficial interest. While the speeches in both decisions are of interest, it is Lord Diplock's speech in *Gissing v Gissing* which has received the most attention, as setting out the requirements for the modern common-intention constructive trust. The relevant passages (at pp. 905 and 906) run as follows:

> A resulting, implied or constructive trust—and it is unnecessary for present purposes to distinguish between these three classes of trust—is created by a transaction between the trustee and the [beneficiary] in connection with the acquisition by the trustee of a legal estate in land, whenever the trustee has so conducted himself that it would be inequitable to allow him to deny to the [beneficiary] a beneficial interest in the land acquired. And he will be held so to have conducted himself if by his words or conduct he has induced the [beneficiary] to act to his own detriment in the reasonable belief that by so acting he was acquiring a beneficial interest in the land.
>
> This is why it has been repeatedly said in the context of disputes between spouses as to their respective beneficial interests in the matrimonial home that if at the time of its acquisition . . . an express agreement has been made between them as to the way in which the beneficial interest shall be held, the court will give effect to it—notwithstanding the absence of any written declaration of trust. Strictly speaking this states the principle too widely for if the agreement did not provide for anything to be done by the spouse in whom the legal estate was not to be vested, it would be a merely voluntary declaration of trust and unenforceable for want of writing. But in the express oral agreements contemplated by these dicta it has been assumed . . . that they provide for the spouse in whom the legal estate . . . is not vested to do something to facilitate its acquisition. . . . What the court gives effect to is the trust resulting or implied from the common intention expressed in the oral agreement between the spouses that if each acts in the manner provided for in the agreement the beneficial interest in the matrimonial home shall be held as they have agreed . . .
>
> But parties to a transaction in connection with the acquisition of land may well have formed a common intention that the beneficial interest in the land shall be vested in them jointly without having used express words to communicate this intention to one another. . . . In such a case . . . it may be possible to infer their common intention from their conduct.

Thus, it appears that there are two stages in establishing a common intention trust of this sort:

- an agreement; and
- some detrimental act in reliance on it.

18.2.2.1 The agreement

There must be an agreement between the parties at the time the property is acquired or, exceptionally, at a later stage, that the partner without the legal estate is to have a beneficial interest in the land. This agreement may be:

- express; or
- inferred from conduct.

1. Express agreement

Lord Diplock's requirement of an express agreement suggests that the parties must have agreed in so many words that one should have a share in the other's property. However, as applied in later cases and subsequently reworded by Lord Bridge in *Lloyds Bank v Rosset* ([1991] 1 AC 107 at pp. 132–3), the requirement appears to be slightly less precise and becomes:

> any agreement, arrangement or understanding reached between [the parties] that the property is to be shared beneficially.

Before finding such an agreement or arrangement, the court requires 'evidence of express discussions between the parties'. However, provided there is evidence of such discussion, the courts have been willing to accept that there was an agreement and an intention, common to both parties, although in at least two cases the discussions might equally well suggest that there was no such intention on the part of the owner. Thus, in both *Eves v Eves* [1975] 1 WLR 1338 and *Grant v Edwards* [1986] Ch 638, there was evidence that one partner had made excuses to the other for having the property conveyed to him alone, rather than to both of them. A bystander hearing the conversation might suspect that the owner did not want his partner to have a share in the property, but on both occasions the court accepted that discussions of this nature about title to the property were sufficient to establish a common intention to share. Lord Bridge in *Lloyds Bank v Rosset* treats these decisions as examples of express agreement under Lord Diplock's first category (see [1991] 1 AC 107 at pp. 132–3), although you might be forgiven for thinking that the agreements were really inferred by the court.

2. Agreement inferred from conduct

In the absence of an express agreement, the court may be able to infer (i.e., deduce) the existence of a common intention from the conduct of the parties. After the passage we have quoted, Lord Diplock went on to outline the type of conduct from which such an intention could be inferred. All the examples he gave involved reasonably direct contributions to the cost of acquiring the property, such as contributions to the outright payment of the price, or to the deposit and legal charges, or to the mortgage instalments. Indirect contributions to the mortgage repayments would also be acceptable if, for example, the claimant paid other outgoings, so as to enable the estate owner to use his funds to pay off the mortgage debt. Such contributions, however, must be clearly referable to the acquisition of the property; it must appear that the contributor was meeting those expenses *in order to* facilitate mortgage repayments. In the absence of such evidence, mere contributions to household expenses by itself would not be enough.

18.2.2.2 Action by claimant to his detriment in reliance on agreement

Under LPA 1925, s. 53(1)(b) a declaration of a trust of land must be evidenced in writing. Thus, simply establishing the agreement between the parties would not be enough to give the non-owner an enforceable share in the beneficial interest, unless the court could find an implied, resulting, or constructive trust (for which writing is not required—s. 53(2)).

This explains Lord Diplock's second requirement: that the claimant has been induced to act to his or her detriment in the belief that an interest is being acquired. For the owner to go back on the agreement after this has happened would be inequitable, and it is this that justifies the recognition of some sort of implied trust.

Lord Diplock's speech in *Gissing v Gissing* suggests that the sort of acts required to establish detriment are very much the same as those noted previously from which an agreement may be inferred: contributions direct or indirect to the cost of acquisition. He did not exclude the possibility that other acts might be sufficient and for a time (under the influence of Lord Denning) the courts accepted a wider range of activities which do not involve financial contribution (see 18.2.3). However, more recently there has been a notable retreat from that approach.

18.2.2.3 How were these principles applied to the facts of *Gissing v Gissing*?

The House of Lords considered that there was no evidence of any express agreement between the parties at the time the house was bought. Nor were the contributions by the wife sufficient to support the inference of a common intention. The contributions she made were not sufficiently referable to the acquisition of the property and, in consequence, the wife's claim to a share in the house belonging to her husband was rejected.

18.2.3 Lord Denning's interpretation of *Gissing v Gissing*

The immediate result of the decision in *Gissing v Gissing*, at least at Court of Appeal level, was an increased use of implied trusts to achieve a fair result between the parties when a strict application of legal rules would appear inequitable. This development was very much associated with Lord Denning MR who read Lord Diplock's words as authorising the use of what Lord Denning described as 'a constructive trust of a new model' wherever it was equitable to do so.

It was Lord Denning's view (expressed in *Hussey v Palmer* [1972] 1 WLR 1286 at p. 1290) that a non-express trust was imposed by law 'whenever justice and good conscience require it' and that it was to be applied:

> in cases where the legal owner cannot conscientiously keep the property for himself alone, but ought to allow another to have the property or the benefit of it or a share in it . . .

The Court of Appeal's approach during this period can be illustrated by two decisions, both of which involved cohabitants.

In *Eves v Eves* [1975] 1 WLR 1338 the woman had made no financial contribution (direct or indirect), but had done a good deal of manual work in restoring the house and garden, and had looked after her partner and cared for their children. In Lord Denning's view, it would in these circumstances have been inequitable for her partner to deny her a share in the house; equity would impose a constructive trust under which she would receive a quarter share.

In *Hall v Hall* [1982] 3 FLR 379 the parties had lived together for seven years. The woman had made no direct payments towards the cost of acquisition, but had paid for furnishings, bought a car, and contributed to housekeeping expenses. The Court of Appeal considered that these contributions gave rise to a trust in her favour, Lord Denning saying (at p. 381):

> It depends on the circumstances and how much she had contributed—not merely in money—but also in keeping up the house; and if there are children, in looking after them.

18.2.4 A change of approach: *Burns v Burns*

The mid-1980s saw a change in the Court of Appeal's approach, and a more careful application of the principles in *Gissing v Gissing*. This can be seen most clearly in *Burns v Burns* [1984] 1 Ch 317, which concerned an *unmarried* couple who had been living together for 19 years. The man was the legal owner of the house and had provided the initial deposit and paid the mortgage instalments. For some time the woman stayed at home and cared for their children. Later she undertook paid work and used her salary to pay some domestic bills and to buy furniture and equipment for the house and clothes for the children. She also redecorated the interior of the house.

On the approach adopted by Lord Denning, one would have expected these facts to support the recognition of some form of implied trust. On this occasion, however, the Court of Appeal followed very closely the principles laid down by Lord Diplock in *Gissing*, emphasising the need for some agreement, express or inferred from conduct. The conduct from which an agreement could be inferred was summarised in *Gissing* terms, as essentially involving some money payment referable to the acquisition of the property. A substantial contribution to housekeeping expenses would be sufficient if its intended effect was to enable the other partner to pay the mortgage instalments but such contributions by themselves *without such an intention* were not enough.

Mrs Burns' financial contributions were small and could not be said to be referable to the acquisition of the house and were no evidence of a common intention that she was to have a share. The decorating work she had carried out did not help her, the court following the view expressed on this by the House of Lords in *Pettit v Pettit* [1970] AC 777. Finally, the court had to consider the claim that the performance of domestic duties (running the household and looking after her partner and the children) was a sufficient contribution to entitle Mrs Burns to a share. In *Hall v Hall* Lord Denning considered that such a contribution could be taken into account. The court in *Burns v Burns* considered that his view was not supported by precedent, nor was it consistent with principle; or, as May LJ put it more bluntly (at p. 342), Lord Denning's *dictum* 'was wrong'.

A useful summary of the court's position is to be found towards the end of the judgment of May LJ:

> When the house is taken in the man's name alone, if the woman makes no 'real' or 'substantial' financial contribution towards either the purchase price, deposit or mortgage instalments by the means of which the family home was acquired, then she is not entitled to any share in the beneficial interest in that home even though over a very substantial number of years she may have worked just as hard as the man in maintaining the family in the sense of keeping the house, giving birth to and looking after and helping to bring up the children of the union.

18.2.5 Lloyds Bank v Rosset

Twenty years after its decision in *Gissing v Gissing*, the House of Lords attempted to restate the law on common intention constructive trusts in *Lloyds Bank v Rosset* [1991] 1 AC 107. Here property was purchased with money provided by the husband's family trust. On the insistence of the trustees, the property was registered in the sole name of the husband. The house required a great deal of alteration and the necessary building work was paid for by the husband, with money obtained on an overdraft from his bank, secured by a charge on the property. Mrs Rosset made no financial contribution to the cost of the property, but was heavily involved in its renovation, giving instructions to the builders and later doing much of the decoration of the premises herself. The marriage broke down, with the husband moving out and failing to repay the loan, and the bank sought possession of the house. The wife claimed that she had a beneficial interest in the property under a constructive trust and that this took effect as an overriding interest binding on the bank under LRA 1925, s. 70(1)(g) (see 6.5.6.2). Thus, this was a dispute between the claimant and her spouse's mortgagees and her claim, therefore, had to be decided on basic trust principles, rather than on the statutory provisions which would have applied if she had been asserting it against her husband in divorce proceedings.

Mrs Rosset's interest was said to derive from an express agreement reached in conversations with her husband, in reliance on which she had made a significant contribution to the acquisition of the property by the work she had done on its renovation. The judge at first instance rejected the claim of an express agreement but was prepared to infer a common intention from the wife's conduct in undertaking the work of renovation. This finding was, however, rejected by the House of Lords. The monetary value of the work done was trifling when compared with the cost of the property as a whole, and their Lordships doubted whether it would even have been enough to constitute detrimental reliance in the case of an express intention, let alone sufficient to support an inferred agreement. In Lord Bridge's view, the work done by Mrs Rosset was the sort of work which any wife might do to prepare a new home for occupation; it could not be said to be the sort of work which she would not have undertaken if she had not been expecting to acquire an interest in the house.

Lord Bridge, in a speech adopted by his brethren, decided against Mrs Rosset's claim on the simple basis that she had not established any agreement with her husband, express or inferred, that she was to have a share in his property. This was, in essence, a decision on the facts, and Lord Bridge doubted whether any further analysis of the relevant law would be helpful. Unfortunately, he went on to draw attention to what he described as 'one critical distinction', and in doing so created further confusion in this already complicated and difficult area. The passage in question (at p. 132) reads:

> The first and fundamental question which must always be resolved is whether, independently of any inference to be drawn from the conduct of the parties in the course of sharing the house as their home and managing their joint affairs, there has at any time prior to acquisition, or exceptionally at some later date, been any agreement, arrangement or understanding reached between them that the property is to be shared beneficially. The finding of an agreement or arrangement to share in this sense can only, I think, be based on evidence of express discussions between the partners, however imperfectly remembered and however imprecise their terms may have been. Once a finding to this effect is made it will only be necessary for the partner asserting a claim

> ... to show that he or she has acted to his or her detriment or significantly altered his or her position in reliance on the agreement in order to give rise to a constructive trust or a proprietary estoppel.
>
> In sharp contrast with this situation is the very different one where there is no evidence to support a finding of an agreement or arrangement to share, however reasonable it might have been for the parties to reach such an arrangement if they had applied their minds to the question, and where the court must rely entirely on the conduct of the parties both as the basis from which to infer a common intention to share the property beneficially and as the conduct relied on to give rise to a constructive trust. In this situation direct contributions to the purchase price by the partner who is not the legal owner, whether initially or by payment of mortgage instalments, will readily justify the inference necessary to the creation of a constructive trust. But, as I read the authorities, it is at least extremely doubtful whether anything less will do.

This passage may well have been intended as a restatement or summary of the rules in *Gissing v Gissing*, but the reference in the second paragraph to the need for direct contribution to establish an inferred agreement seems to limit the scope of the principles as understood at the time, and to rule out the indirect contribution to mortgage repayments by meeting household expenses which was accepted as sufficient in both *Gissing v Gissing* and *Burns v Burns*.

In addition, some writers take the view that what is described in the second paragraph is really a resulting trust (see Thompson [1990] Conv 314), although the Court of Appeal in *Oxley v Hiscock* [2005] Fam 211 at para. 40 continued to regard Lord Bridge's second category as consisting of inferred common intention constructive trusts.

18.2.6 Stack v Dowden

Lord Bridge's statement in *Lloyds Bank v Rosset* was criticised by the House of Lords in *Stack v Dowden* [2007] 2 AC 432, Lord Walker (at para. 26) doubting if it took full account of the views expressed in *Gissing v Gissing*, and adding:

> Whether or not Lord Bridge's observation was justified in 1990, in my opinion the law has moved on, and your Lordships should move it a little more in the same direction ...

Lady Hale also commented that the law had moved on 'in response to changing social and economic conditions' (para. 60), and suggested that Lord Bridge may have 'set the hurdle' rather too high in describing the contributions needed to establish a common-intention constructive trust (para. 63). Similar criticism is to be found in the Privy Council decision in *Abbott v Abbott* [2007] UKPC 53, in which Lady Hale quoted with approval from her own and other speeches in *Stack v Dowden*.

18.3 Sole-name cases: quantifying the beneficial interest

If the claimant can establish entitlement to a beneficial interest—whether under a resulting or constructive trust—the court will then have to quantify the share—that is, decide the proportion of the beneficial interest to which the claimant is entitled.

18.3.1 Resulting and constructive trusts

We have already noted (at 18.1.3.2) that the share taken by a beneficiary under a *resulting trust* is strictly proportionate to the amount of the original contribution at the time the property was acquired, and that later contributions to mortgage instalments or improvements to the property cannot be taken into account.

By contrast, under a *constructive trust*, the size of each share depends upon the intention of the parties, and in *Gissing v Gissing* [1971] AC 886 (at pp. 908–9) Lord Diplock gave the following guidance on quantifying shares under a common intention constructive trust:

- an express agreement between the parties as to the size of their shares would be conclusive;
- if there was no express agreement, the court might infer an intention from the conduct of the parties. In doing so, it might take into account any contribution made by the claimant, not only at the outset but during the course of the relationship as well;
- if no intention as to size of share could be inferred, the court might infer that the parties had intended the non-owner to have a share but had left the size of the share to be determined later:

when the mortgage was repaid or the property disposed of, on the basis of what would be fair having regard to the total contributions, direct or indirect which each spouse had made by that date. Where this was the most likely inference from their conduct it would be fair for the court to give effect to that common intention of the parties by determining what in all the circumstances was a fair share;

- in the last resort, if no intention could be inferred the court would apply the maxim 'equality is equity' and regard each party as being entitled to a half-share.

The rest of Lord Diplock's speech makes it clear that the contributions on which he would rely in inferring the parties' intentions were all of a financial nature. However, over the last 20 years three decisions of the Court of Appeal have shown a more flexible approach to discovering the intentions of the parties about the size of their shares.

18.3.2 A new approach to quantifying shares

18.3.2.1 *Drake v Whipp* [1995] 28 HLR 531

This is the decision in which Peter Gibson LJ emphasised the importance of distinguishing between resulting and constructive trusts. The parties in this case were an unmarried couple who bought a barn for conversion into a house, the property being conveyed to the man alone. The woman made a substantial contribution to the purchase price, but the costs of conversion, which were considerably greater than the purchase price, were largely borne by her partner. When the couple separated, the woman claimed a share in the beneficial interest proportionate to her contribution to the purchase price (40 per cent), while her former partner claimed that her share should be determined by reference to her contribution to the overall cost of purchase and conversion (which amounted to just under 20 per cent).

If the property were held on a resulting trust, the size of the share would depend simply on the contribution to the cost of acquisition, and the cost of subsequent enhancement would be irrelevant. However, if the property were subject to a constructive trust the court could adopt 'a broad brush' approach to determining the parties' respective shares (p. 536), and thus could take into account their individual contributions to the overall cost of the property.

On the facts before it, the Court of Appeal considered that the requirements for a constructive trust were satisfied (i.e., common intention plus detriment—p. 536), and the court was therefore able:

> [to] approach the matter more broadly, looking at the parties' entire course of conduct together (at p. 537).

Accordingly, the court took into account a wide range of matters which included: direct financial contributions; the work each party did to improve the property; that the joint bank account was fed mainly by the man's earnings; and the fact that the woman paid for food and some other household expenses and took care of the housekeeping for them both. In the light of these circumstances, the court considered that the woman was entitled to a one-third share of the current value of the property.

A similar approach, based on the recognition of a constructive trust, is to be found in *Midland Bank v Cooke* [1995] 4 All ER 562 and *Oxley v Hiscock* [2005] Fam 211.

18.3.2.2 *Midland Bank v Cooke* [1995] 4 All ER 562

This case arose out of possession proceedings by a mortgagee, in which a wife claimed that she had a share in the family home which was binding on the mortgagee. The Court of Appeal was satisfied that the wife had made a direct contribution, albeit a small one, to the purchase price of the matrimonial home owned by her husband, and apparently accepted that there had been sufficient agreement between husband and wife to give rise to a *constructive* trust. At first instance, the size of the wife's interest had been quantified by reference to the size of her contribution to the purchase price, and in consequence she was held to have a 6.47 per cent share in the house. On the wife's appeal, it was argued against her that this mathematical approach must be adopted in the absence of any express agreement between the parties as to their relative shares. Moreover, the parties had actually stated that they had not considered the matter at all when acquiring the property.

Surprisingly, Waite LJ considered (at p. 575) that:

> positive evidence that the parties neither discussed nor intended any agreement as to the proportions of their beneficial interest does not preclude the court, on general equitable principles, from inferring one.

In such a case the court should:

> undertake a survey of *the whole course of dealing between the parties relevant to their ownership and occupation of the property* and their sharing of its burdens and advantages [and should] take into consideration all conduct which throws light on the question of what shares were intended (our emphasis).

Accordingly, the Court of Appeal held that it was not bound to deal with the matter on the strict basis of the trust resulting from the cash contribution to the purchase price, and was free to attribute to the parties an intention to share the beneficial interest in some different proportion—in this case, in equal shares.

18.3.2.3 *Oxley v Hiscock* [2005] Fam 211

The methods used by the courts in quantifying shares by reference to the original intentions of the parties were reviewed at length by the Court of Appeal in this case, which was another constructive trust case involving an unmarried couple and their family home. The woman had made financial contributions to the purchase price, but had been persuaded by her partner that the conveyance should be to him alone, to avoid any problems with her former husband. After the relationship ended, the woman applied under TOLATA 1996, s. 14 for a declaration that her former partner held the property on trust for both of them in equal shares.

The trial judge, following *Midland Bank v Cooke*, looked at 'the whole course of dealing' between the parties and from this inferred an intention that they would share the property equally. The defendant appealed from this decision, claiming that the property was held on a resulting trust with the shares proportionate to each party's contribution to the purchase price. This argument was rejected by the Court of Appeal, which confirmed the trial judge's finding of a constructive trust but varied her award to a 60:40 split in favour of the appellant.

The real interest of the case, however, lies in the observations of Chadwick LJ about the methods used in previous decisions to infer intention from the conduct of the parties. This process has always seemed rather artificial and the judge clearly regarded this approach as being unsatisfactory, describing it (at para. 71) as 'an unnecessary fiction' to attribute a common intention to the parties when the evidence showed that they had given no thought to the matter. By contrast the judge favoured an entirely different approach, saying that in his opinion what really happened in these cases was that the court itself decided on a fair division of the property between the parties. When dealing with questions about the size of shares:

> It must now be accepted that (at least in this Court and below) the answer is that each is entitled to that share which the court considers fair having regard to the whole course of dealing between [the parties] in relation to the property.

In *Stack v Dowden* [2007] 2 AC 432, however, Lady Hale appeared to reject this approach, saying:

> The search is still for the result which reflects what the parties must, in the light of their conduct, be taken to have intended . . . it does not enable the court to abandon that search in favour of the result which the court itself considers fair.

However, in the case of *Jones v Kernott* [2011] 3 WLR 1121, at para. 53, Lady Hale described *Stack v Dowden* as giving 'qualified approval' to the statement in *Oxley v Hiscock*, and it has been adopted by the Supreme Court as a guide to courts required to 'impute', rather than to 'infer', the parties' intentions. There is more about this later (18.4.5).

18.3.2.4 Significance of the Court of Appeal decisions

The three decisions mentioned in 18.3.2.1–3 mark two changes in the court's approach to quantifying shares in a sole-name case.

(i) The court shows *a clear preference for the recognition of a constructive trust*. Once the necessary common intention to share the beneficial interest is established, the presumption of a resulting trust arising from contribution to the purchase price appears to be rebutted, and the parties move into the greater freedom of the constructive trust, in which size of share does not depend solely on contributions to the purchase price.

(ii) The court adopts *a wider interpretation of the conduct from which the parties' intentions can be inferred*, taking into account 'the whole course of dealing between the parties relevant to the ownership and occupation of the property' (*Midland Bank v Cooke* [1995] 4 All ER 562 at p. 575).

These developments by the Court of Appeal were approved in *Stack v Dowden* [2007] 2 AC 432, you will see in the next section that they were carried forward by the House of Lords in that case and by the Supreme Court in *Jones v Kernott* [2011] 3 WLR 1121. Both these decisions were joint-names cases, and so it is now important to consider how principles developed in sole-name cases are relevant to situations in which the legal estate in the family home is owned jointly by both partners.

18.4 Joint-names cases

18.4.1 Co-ownership

Chapter 17 explains co-ownership, but the next paragraphs summarise the basic points that you need to understand before reading the rest of this chapter.

Since the 1925 legislation, co-owners of a legal estate hold it as 'joint tenants' under a statutory trust for themselves (LPA 1925, ss. 34(2) and 36(1)). They may choose to own the beneficial interest under the trust in one of two ways.

(1) *As joint tenants* i.e., in the same way in which they hold the legal estate. Joint tenants are together regarded as owning the whole interest (as a sort of 'group' owner); the individual tenant is not entitled to a specific share, and when he dies, ownership remains with the survivors, under the right of survivorship (or '*ius accrescendi*').

(2) *As tenants in common*, entitled to notional individual shares in the property, which they can transfer during their life and which pass with their estates on death.

A tenancy in common of the beneficial interest may come into existence in the following ways.

- *Under an equitable presumption* that purchasers who make unequal contributions to the purchase price intend to hold as tenants in common (see 17.4.1). This presumption, which can be rebutted by evidence that the purchasers intended to hold as joint tenants, has always applied to all forms of co-owned property, but it now appears from *Stack v Dowden* [2007] 2 AC 432 that it is no longer applicable to the purchase of the family home (see 17.5).

- *By an express declaration* of the intention to hold as tenants in common, which should be made by the purchasers at the time of acquisition. If they do not do this, the presumption that 'equity follows the law' will come into play and they will hold the beneficial interest in the same way as the legal estate (that is, on a joint tenancy).
- *By severance*, which can turn joint tenancy of the beneficial interest into a tenancy in common (for details of how this is done, see 17.6). When this occurs, each of the former joint tenants obtains an equal share of the property under the rule in *Goodman v Gallant* [1986] Fam 106.

18.4.2 *Stack v Dowden* and *Jones v Kernott*

Both of these cases concerned disputes between former cohabitants about the nature of their beneficial interests in family homes held in their joint names (see 17.5.2 and 17.5.5 for the facts). In the few years between these two decisions, the Appellate Committee of the House of Lords was replaced by the new Supreme Court. However, two of the Lords of Appeal in Ordinary (Lady Hale and Lord Walker) who had considered *Stack v Dowden*, sat as members of the Supreme Court in *Jones v Kernott*, and this gave them the opportunity to explain and amplify what they had said some four years earlier. As a result, comments from *Jones v Kernott* are included in the following account of *Stack v Dowden*.

18.4.3 The presumption of a beneficial joint tenancy

You will recall, from the discussion in Chapter 17, that *Stack v Dowden* makes a novel distinction between domestic cases (usually involving family home) and commercial cases. The significance of the distinction was emphasised at the outset by Lady Hale who (at para. 40) described the issue in the case as being:

> the effect of a conveyance into the joint names of a cohabiting couple, but without an explicit declaration of their respective beneficial interests, of a dwelling house which was to become their home.

Their Lordships agreed in starting from the basic principle expressed by Lady Hale (at para. 54) that, in a family home case, where there is no express provision about how the beneficial interest should be held:

> it should be assumed that equity follows the law, and that the beneficial interests reflect the legal interests in the property.

So, the fact that Mr Stack and Ms Dowden held the legal estate together as joint tenants raised a presumption that they were also joint tenants of the beneficial interest.

18.4.4 Rebutting the presumption of a beneficial joint tenancy: the irrelevance of resulting trusts

In *Stack v Dowden*, the parties had made unequal contributions to the cost of acquiring the property, and you might expect this to give rise to the equitable presumption of a tenancy in common or, to use the language of trusts, to a resulting trust. This was the approach favoured by Lord Neuberger (see paras. 110–22), but it was rejected by his colleagues. The majority of the judges considered that questions about entitlement to shares in the family home should not depend solely on the size of financial contribution (unless, of course that was what the parties had intended—see Lord Walker at para. 31). In Lady Hale's words (at paras. 60 and 69):

> These days the importance to be attached to who paid for what in a domestic context may be very different from its importance in other contexts or long ago . . . In law, context is everything, and the domestic context is very different from the commercial world. Each case will turn on its own facts. Many more factors than financial contributions may be relevant in divining the parties' true intentions.

Accordingly, the House of Lords rejected the presumption of a resulting trust in cases involving the family home, and by implication also rejected the presumption of a tenancy in common arising from unequal contributions to the purchase price of such property. The view that the presumption of a resulting trust is not appropriate in a domestic setting was emphasised again by Lord Walker and Lady Hale in *Jones v Kernott* [2011] 3 WLR 1121 (at para. 25):

> The time has come to make it clear, in line with *Stack v Dowden*, that in the case of a purchase of a house or flat in joint names for joint occupation by a married or unmarried couple, where both are responsible for any mortgage, there is no presumption of a resulting trust from their having contributed to the deposit (or indeed the rest of the purchase) in unequal shares.

Thus, their Lordships shared the Court of Appeal's preference for recognising a constructive trust in family home cases, Lady Hale explaining in *Jones v Kernott* (at para. 15) that:

> . . . the principle in *Stack v Dowden* is that a 'common intention' trust, for the cohabitants' home to belong to them jointly in equity as well as on the proprietorship register, is the default option in joint names cases.

However, *Stack v Dowden* makes it clear that the presumption of a beneficial joint tenancy may be rebutted by evidence of a contrary common intention (which takes us to the third stage of the process).

18.4.5 Rebutting the presumption of a beneficial joint tenancy: evidence of contrary intention

Stack v Dowden made it clear (see Lady Hale at para. 68) that it is possible to displace the presumption of a beneficial joint tenancy by proving that at the time of acquisition (or, in some cases, at a later stage):

> the parties did intend their beneficial interests to be different from their legal interests and in what way.

Although Lady Hale does not say so, this statement must refer to an intention to hold as tenants in common, in equal, or unequal shares. The existence of such an intention has to be proved by the party who seeks to displace the presumption of a beneficial joint tenancy. However, their Lordships warned that this would be very difficult, Lord Walker describing it as 'a heavy burden' (para. 14) and Lady Hale saying that 'it is not a task to be lightly embarked upon' (para. 68).

Where a claimant (in this case, Ms Dowden) seeks to displace the presumption of beneficial joint tenancy, the court is being asked to infer the parties' intentions about two questions.

- Did they intend to have unequal shares in the beneficial interest (i.e., to create a tenancy in common)?; and, if they did so intend,
- What size did they intend those shares to be?

In seeking to discover the parties' intentions on these matters, the House of Lords approved and adopted the approach developed by the Court of Appeal in earlier sole-name cases (see 18.3.2).

Lady Hale noted that, since *Gissing v Gissing*, 'the law has indeed moved on in response to changing social and economic considerations', and went on to summarise the new approach to quantifying shares under a common intention trust in the following words (at para. 60):

> The search is to ascertain the parties' shared intentions, actual, inferred or imputed, with respect to the property in the light of their whole course of conduct in relation to it.

Later (at para. 69) her Ladyship indicated a range of matters which could throw light on the parties' true intentions in respect to their family home. She emphasised that in the domestic context there are many factors other than financial contributions which may be relevant, and a lengthy list of examples includes:

- advice or discussions at the time of the transfer;
- the purpose for which the house was acquired;
- the nature of the parties' relationship;
- whether they had children for whom they both had responsibility to provide a home;
- how the purchase was financed, both initially and subsequently;
- how the parties arranged their finances, whether separately or together or a bit of both;
- how they discharged the outgoings on the property and their other household expenses.

Finally, even the parties' individual characters and personalities 'may also be a factor in deciding where their true intentions lay'.

Reading through such a list makes one uneasily aware of the time and expense that could be involved in such an approach. Lady Hale herself appeared to be conscious of the dangers of opening the floodgates, for she noted that '[a] full examination of the facts is likely to involve disproportionate costs' (para. 68) and tried to discourage applications in similar cases by emphasising that it would be very unusual for a claimant holding under a legal joint tenancy to be able to convince the court that the parties had not intended the beneficial interest to be held in the same way. Unfortunately, this discouraging statement would have no effect in cases in which the legal title is held by only one of the partners, and one can imagine weighty files of evidence building up as legal advisers work their way through Lady Hale's 'checklist'.

One limitation of the matters which the court has to consider is the fact that the purpose of considering them is to discover the parties' intentions about the *property*. It does not have the wider purpose of drawing any conclusions about the nature of their *relationship*. (For Lady Hale's criticism of the trial judge for concerning himself with the relationship rather than with matters relevant to intentions about property, see para. 86.)

Despite several warnings (at paras. 14 and 69) of the difficulty that a claimant would face in attempting to show that legal joint tenants did not intend to hold the beneficial interest on a joint tenancy, Lady Hale was in fact able to find several factors in the case under consideration that showed just such an intention (see paras. 87–92). These factors included not only the greater financial contribution made to the cost of the property by Ms Dowden, but also the fact that her partner took responsibility only for certain clearly defined areas of expenditure in relation to the house, and that, apart from the house, both parties kept all their property completely separate—there were no joint savings or investments.

To her Ladyship, this conduct was a strong indication that the parties did not intend their shares in the house to be equal, and certainly did not intend the beneficial interest to be held on a joint tenancy with rights of survivorship. It follows from this that, from the outset, the beneficial interest must have been held on a tenancy in common in unequal shares although, rather confusingly, her Ladyship does not say so specifically. She simply states that there was no intention to hold as beneficial joint tenants and in the next sentence says that D has made good her claim to a share of 65 per cent of the property.

18.4.6 Changing intentions: *Jones v Kernott*

In *Stack v Dowden*, their Lordships accepted that the parties' intentions about ownership of the family home might change during the course of their relationship, Lady Hale noting (at para. 70) that in some cases there might be reason to conclude that:

> whatever the parties' intentions at the outset, these have now changed. An example might be where one party has financed (or constructed himself) an extension or substantial improvement to the property, so that what they have now is significantly different from what they had then.

The question of changed intentions, arising not from improvements to the property but from events occurring after the parties had separated, was considered in more detail by the Supreme Court in *Jones v Kernott* [2011] 3 WLR 1121. (See 17.5.5 for the facts).

At first instance, in *Jones v Kernott*, the county court judge applied the approach to discovering intention set out in *Stack v Dowden*, so that a broad range of factors could be taken into account not only in identifying the original intentions of the parties when they acquired the property but also any change in intention that occurred later. In *Jones v Kernott*, there had been no discussion or agreement about the house when the parties separated, but from the evidence before the court he was able to infer that their intentions about their beneficial interests in the property had changed. Matters relied on in drawing this inference included:

- the length of time since the separation, during which Mr Kernott had shown no interest in the house;
- the very substantial financial contributions made by Ms Jones, particularly in the 14 years since the separation; and
- the division of the proceeds of the insurance policy between the parties which, combined with Ms Jones's assumption of financial responsibility for the house, had enabled Mr Kernott to buy a new home for himself.

In the absence of any indication of the parties' new intentions about the size of their shares, the judge held himself bound by the Court of Appeal decision in *Oxley v Hiscock* [2005] Fam 211 (see 18.3.2.3) to consider what was fair and just between the parties, bearing in mind what he had found with regard to the whole course of dealing between them. Having done so, he held that Ms Jones was entitled to 90 per cent of the value of the house and Mr Kernott to 10 per cent. This decision was reversed on Mr Kernott's appeal to the Court of Appeal (*Kernott v Jones* [2010] 1 WLR 2401), but was affirmed by the Supreme Court. The court was satisfied that a change of intention about the parties' beneficial interests could be inferred from the factors identified by the trial judge and that his decision as to the size of each share was correct. The decision confirms the view expressed in *Stack v Dowden* that the intentions of parties to a common-intention trust can change during the life of the trust, and establishes that such a change of intention:

- can rebut the *Stack v Dowden* presumption that a conveyance of a family home into joint names indicates both a legal and beneficial joint tenancy; and
- can result in a change in the size of the share in the property to which each party is entitled.

Although all five members of the court agreed on these points and on the outcome of the appeal, there was some variation between them on the reasons for that decision, most notably on the question of whether the parties' new intentions about the size of their respective shares were to be *inferred* (that is, deduced by the court from the parties' conduct) or *imputed* (that is, attributed to the parties by the court).

18.4.7 Inferring or imputing intention: *Jones v Kernott*

In her speech, in *Stack v Dowden* (at para. 60), Lady Hale had referred to the search:

> to ascertain the parties' shared intentions, actual inferred or imputed. . . .

The suggestion that intentions could be 'imputed' as well as 'inferred' concerned Lord Neuberger (see paras. 125–7), who explained the difference between the two processes as follows:

> An inferred intention is one which is objectively deduced to be the subjective actual intention of the parties in the light of their actions and statements. An imputed intention is one which is attributed to the parties, even though no such actual intention can be deduced from their actions and statements, and even though they had no such intention. Imputation involves concluding what the parties would have intended, whereas inference involves concluding what they did intend.

Lord Neuberger considered that 'imputing an intention' was wrong in principle and conflicted with the earlier House of Lords' decisions in *Pettit v Pettit* [1970] AC 777 and *Gissing v Gissing* [1971] AC 886. In *Jones v Kernott*, however, the Supreme Court said that in cases where a court was required to quantify shares under a common intention trust, it would be permissible for the court to *impute* intentions about size of shares if there was no evidence from which such intentions could be *inferred*. In a joint judgment, Lord Walker and Lady Hale stated (at para. 31):

> ... we accept that the search is primarily to ascertain the parties' actual shared intentions whether expressed or to be inferred from their conduct. However ... where it is clear that the beneficial interests are to be shared, but it is impossible to divine a common intention as to the proportions in which they are to be shared ... the court is driven to impute an intention to the parties which they may never have had.

It is clear from this passage that the two judges regard the process of imputing intention as very much a 'last resort'. By contrast, Lord Kerr suggested (at para. 72) that courts should be willing to adopt the process of imputation at an earlier stage. He appreciated that:

> [t]here is a natural inclination to prefer inferring an intention to imputing one. If the parties' intention can be inferred, the court is not imposing a solution. It is, instead, deciding what the parties must be taken to have intended and where that is possible it is obviously preferable to the court's enforcing a resolution. But the conscientious quest to discover the parties' actual intention should cease when it becomes clear that this is simply not deducible from the evidence or that no common intention exists ... [t]he court ... should not be reluctant to recognise, when it is appropriate to do so, that inference of an intention is not possible and that imputation of an intention is the only course to follow.

Lord Kerr and Lord Wilson were in no doubt that intentions could be imputed, and although Lord Collins did not refer specifically to the point, he was in general agreement with the joint judgment. Thus, following *Jones v Kernott*, it now appears to be established that in certain circumstances the court may impute an intention to the parties about the size of their shares. The question then arises of how the court is to set about the task of doing this.

In the words of the joint judgment (para. 47):

> If [the court] cannot deduce exactly what share was intended, it may have no alternative but to ask what their intentions as reasonable and just people would have been had they thought about it at the time.

At a later stage in the joint judgment (para. 69), a further answer, approved by other members of the court (paras. 74 and 87), is provided by quoting the words of Chadwick LJ in *Oxley v Hiscock* [2005] Fam 211, at para. 69:

> The answer is that each is entitled to that share which the court considers fair having regard to the whole course of dealing between them in relation to the property.

The link between these two formulations is provided by Lord Wilson (para. 83) who observes that reasonable people would intend only what is fair.

At this point, there is some divergence in the reasons given by individual judges for their decisions. Three members of the court (Lord Walker, Lady Hale, and Lord Collins) accepted that the evidence before the trial judge was sufficient to enable him to infer both the change of intention and the size of the adjusted shares. By contrast, Lord Kerr and Lord Wilson held that, while the change in the parties' intentions could be inferred, it was not possible to infer any intention about the size of the shares. As a result, both judges imputed an intention to the parties to share the property between them in the proportions fixed by the trial judge, a division which Lord Kerr described as 'eminently fair'.

It is important to note that the Supreme Court's discussion of the possibility of imputing intentions to the parties relates only to the question about the size of shares, and that the first question (about the change of the original intention) was answered by drawing an inference from the evidence. It seems reasonably clear that at least three members of the court (Lord Walker, Lady Hale, and Lord Collins) considered that any change in the original common intentions of the parties must be deduced from their conduct and cannot be imputed to them on the basis of what the court considers fair (paras. 51(3) and 52). However, you may like to note a passage in Lord Wilson's judgment (para. 84), in which his Lordship observes:

> [This] case does not require us to consider whether modern equity allows the intention required by the first question also to be imputed if it is not otherwise identifiable. That question will merit careful thought.

The joint judgment, supported by Lord Collins, expresses the view (para. 32) that although the conceptual difference between 'inferring' and 'imputing' is clear, the difference in practice is not so great. By contrast, Lord Kerr (para. 67) considers that although the distinction may not in practice make a great difference to the outcome between the parties, it must result in the court reaching that decision by a very different process. He notes (at para. 74) that the exercise would be:

> wholly unrelated to ascertainment of the parties' views. It involves the court in deciding what is fair in light of the whole course of dealing with the property. As soon as it is clear that inferring an intention is not possible, the focus of the court's attention should be squarely on what is fair . . .

18.5 Joint-names cases after *Stack v Dowden*

In *Stack v Dowden*, both Lord Walker and Lady Hale warned that it would be difficult to displace the presumption of a beneficial joint tenancy (paras. 14 and 68), and predicted that attempts to do so would succeed only in 'very unusual cases'. In fact, the claimants in both *Stack* and *Jones* succeeded in their attempts, and further examples of rebuttal are provided by later case law. Since the inquiry is so fact-sensitive, it is difficult to deduce general principles that govern when the presumption will be rebutted and when it will not. Here, we present some examples of cases decided after *Stack v Dowden* as illustrative of the courts' approach in the aftermath of that decision.

18.5.1 *Adekunle v Ritchie* [2007] BPIR 1177

When Ritchie's mother had the opportunity to buy the house in which she and her son lived, she was not able to obtain the necessary loan by herself and Ritchie agreed to be a party to the mortgage and transfer. They were accordingly registered as joint tenants of the legal estate but the transfer contained no declaration about how they would hold the beneficial interest. Mrs Ritchie later died without making a will, and her administrators (Adekunle and another) applied for an order for sale of the house, so that the proceeds could be divided between the 10 children entitled under their mother's intestacy. Ritchie opposed the application. Relying on the *Stack v Dowden* presumption, he claimed that he and his mother had held the beneficial interest as joint tenants and that he was therefore solely entitled to the house by right of survivorship.

The trial judge accepted that the domestic relationship between mother and son gave rise to the *Stack* presumption of a beneficial joint tenancy, although he added (at para. 65) that:

> It may well be . . . that where one is not dealing with the situation of a couple living together, it will be easier to find that the facts are unusual in the sense that they are not to be taken to have intended a beneficial joint tenancy.

The judge then identified the factors which led him to regard the case as unusual. These included:

- the purchase and registration in joint names was undertaken to enable the mother to borrow money secured by a mortgage;
- the principal purpose of buying the house was to provide a home for the mother;
- the financial affairs of mother and son were kept separate; and
- the mother had nine other children and would not have intended the whole of her property to pass to Ritchie.

The judge accepted that there was a common intention that Ritchie should have some share in the beneficial interest, but these factors were a strong indication that the parties did not intend their shares to be equal (still less that the right of survivorship should operate on death). Ritchie had made some contribution to the mortgage repayments, but his overall contribution was considerably less than that of his mother, and the judge held that the parties 'are to be taken to have intended' that Ritchie should have a one-third share in the beneficial interest.

18.5.2 *Laskar v Laskar* [2008] 1 WLR 2695

For the facts of this case, and the decision of the Court of Appeal that the presumption of beneficial joint tenancy did not apply to property bought as an investment, see 17.5.6. In *obiter dicta* (at paras. 18–19) Lord Neuberger identified the following aspects of the parties' conduct which, if the presumption had applied, might have operated to rebut it:

- the parties' financial affairs were kept separate;
- the mother had several other children and there was no reason to think that she intended her daughter to receive a significant gift not shared with the other children;

- the parties' contributions to the purchase price were significantly different; and
- the daughter became a co-purchaser primarily because the mother could not afford the purchase on her own.

18.5.3 *Fowler v Barron* [2008] 2 FLR 831

This case is of considerable interest, not only because attempts to rebut the presumption of a beneficial joint tenancy failed, but because it illustrates the detail involved in the 'whole course of conduct' approach, and also provides an interesting contrast with the earlier Court of Appeal decision in *Burns v Burns* [1984] 1 Ch 317.

18.5.3.1 Facts

The parties were former cohabitants who had lived together, *unmarried*, for some 23 years. Early in the relationship, they had bought a house as a home for themselves and their baby son. Both the mortgage and the transfer were in joint names, but there was no declaration in the transfer about the nature of their beneficial interests. Throughout their relationship all payments relating to the acquisition of the property were made by Mr Barron, who also paid council tax and utility bills and other housekeeping expenses. When the parties separated, Miss Fowler claimed a half-share in the value of the family home. In opposing this claim, Mr Barron asserted that his intention in buying the property in both names was to enable Miss Fowler to inherit the house if she was still living with him at his death. He had not understood that doing this would give Miss Fowler an immediate beneficial interest in the property.

18.5.3.2 First instance decision

The trial judge held that there was no evidence of a common intention that each party should have an equal share in the property. In the absence of such an intention, the presumption of a resulting trust applied (this judgment was given before the House of Lords' decision in *Stack v Dowden*). Fowler had made no direct or indirect contribution to the cost of acquisition, and the judge held that she had no beneficial interest in the property.

18.5.3.3 Court of Appeal decision

Arden LJ referred to Lady Hale's statement in *Stack v Dowden* that the parties' whole course of conduct in relation to the property must be taken into account in ascertaining the parties' shared intentions about it, and held that the trial judge's concentration on financial contributions was an error of principle (paras. 29–31). Both parties had been registered as joint tenants of the legal estate and this gave rise to the presumption of joint beneficial ownership. A party seeking to rebut that presumption must satisfy the court that there was a common intention that the beneficial interest would be held in some other way. Both parties must have this intention, and the presumption could not be displaced by the intention of one party which had not been communicated to the other (para. 37).

In considering the parties' course of conduct in relation to the property, Arden LJ identified several matters which could assist the court to infer their common intentions. Although Fowler made no direct contribution to the cost of acquisition, she spent most of her income on family expenses, such as clothes for the children, outings, and family holidays. From this Arden LJ inferred (see paras. 41 and 46) that:

> The parties intended that it should make no difference to their interests in the property which party paid for what expense . . . There was no prior agreement as to who would

> pay for what... the parties simply did not care about the respective size of each other's contributions... the parties largely treated their incomes and assets as one pool from which household expenses [would] be paid.

A further significant point was that the parties had made mutual wills in favour of each other (para. 42). To Arden LJ this was evidence that they thought that they each had a beneficial interest in the property. Further relevant matters were added by Toulson LJ (paras. 53 and 56), who noted that Miss Fowler was a party to the mortgage and therefore jointly liable on it, and that during the 17 years of home ownership she had 'contributed to the life and wellbeing of the family in financial and other ways'.

The Court of Appeal concluded that there was no evidence of a common intention to hold the beneficial interest in any way other than as joint tenants. The presumption of joint tenancy had not been rebutted and Fowler was held to be entitled to a half share in the property after severance.

18.5.4 Barnes v Phillips [2015] EWCA Civ 1056

The new approach to such cases was followed in *Barnes v Phillips*, in which the creation of a mortgage under which 25 per cent of the value of the property had been paid to one co-owner, shortly before the collapse of their relationship, was taken by the Court of Appeal to be sufficient evidence of an intention to vary the interests of an unmarried couple who were previously joint tenants. The court also indicated that it was prepared to look at the whole history of financial contributions to child maintenance (or the lack of them) in order to ascertain the shares of each party, provided that doing so did not give rise to double counting.

18.6 Sole-name cases after *Stack v Dowden*

We must now return to the two-stage process involved in sole-name cases:

- establishing a claim to a share in the beneficial interest; and
- quantifying the size of that share.

18.6.1 Quantifying the beneficial interest

As you saw in 18.3.2, the practice of quantifying the claimant's share by reference to the parties' 'whole course of conduct in relation to the property' had been developed by the Court of Appeal in sole-name cases before *Stack v Dowden*. The effect of the House of Lords decision, coupled with that of the Supreme Court in *Jones v Kernott*, was to adopt and confirm this approach, with the additional possibility of imputing intention about the size of shares when there is no evidence from which it can be inferred.

18.6.2 Establishing a claim to a beneficial interest

By contrast, there has been considerable uncertainty about the effect that *Stack v Dowden* and *Jones v Kernott* would have on the first stage of the sole-name process. Would lower courts still follow the Court of Appeal's decision in *Burns v Burns* [1984] 1 Ch 317, and hold that the necessary agreement to share the beneficial interest could not be inferred from anything less than substantial financial contributions to the cost of acquisition (see 18.2.4); or would they adopt the less restrictive approach of considering the parties' 'whole course of conduct in relation to the property'? And what weight should now be given to Lord Bridge's much criticised dictum in *Lloyd's Bank v Rosset*?

It would certainly be possible, at least theoretically, for a court to distinguish *Stack v Dowden* from any sole-name case which might come before it, and continue to apply the more restrictive approach. In the joint-names case of *Stack v Dowden*, the House of Lords was not required to infer the common intention necessary to establish an implied trust, since both parties already had a beneficial interest in the property under the statutory trust imposed on legal co-owners. Thus, their Lordships were concerned only with the parties' intentions about the nature of that beneficial interest and, if relevant, the size of their respective shares in it. The critical comments about the *Rosset* dictum were themselves only *obiter dicta* and, although Lady Hale repeated them in the sole-name cases of *Abbot v Abbot* [2007] UKPC 53, they had no greater weight in that context: the legal owner of the family home had accepted that his wife had a beneficial interest in the property and the dispute between them related only to the size of their respective shares.

Thus technically at least it would be possible for the lower courts to continue along the old lines. However, there was no indication that judges would take that route, and indeed it is difficult to imagine that the Court of Appeal that was so ready to recognise the contribution made by Miss Fowler in the joint-names case of *Fowler v Barron* [2008] 2 FLR 831 (see 18.5.3) would maintain the hard-line approach of the earlier Court of Appeal in *Burns v Burns*. Indeed, from the start it seemed that the courts were beginning to consider a wider range of conduct from which to infer intention, and examples of this may be found in *Aspden v Elvy* [2012] EWHC 1387 (Ch), [2012] 2 FLR 435, *Geary v Rankine* [2012] EWCA Civ 555, [2012] 2 FCR 461, *Capehorn v Harris* [2015] EWCA Civ 955, and *R v Lam* [2022] EWCA Crim 448. At the same time, it remains necessary to provide some positive evidence of a common intention. The mere fact that land was purchased as a family home will not be sufficient (see, for example, *O'Neill v Holland* [2022] EWCA Civ 1583).

18.7 Detrimental reliance

Finally, it is important to note the continuing need to prove detrimental reliance in cases where the parties need to show that a common intention constructive trust has arisen (either because the presumption of a beneficial joint tenancy is being departed from, in a joint-names case, or because a trust is being asserted at all in a sole-name case). While some doubt has been expressed on whether there is such a need, recent Court of Appeal authority has made it clear that this is still a freestanding requirement: this was the decision in *Hudson v Hathway* [2022] EWCA Civ 1648 (joint names) and *O'Neill v Holland* [2022] EWCA Civ 1583 (sole names). In *Hudson v Hathway*, Lewison LJ surveyed the authorities on this point and said:

> The overwhelming weight of authority both before and after *Stack v Dowden* and *Jones v Kernott* is to the contrary. Moreover, to hold that an oral agreement, disposition or declaration of trust was binding without more would directly contradict two statutory provisions. Equity cannot repeal the statute.

At the same time, the range of factors that can be used to show detrimental reliance overlaps to some degree with the type of conduct that can be used to prove the common intention in the first place. Agreement to allow title to be conveyed into the sole name of one person, while there is a common intention that both parties take beneficially, may in itself be sufficient evidence of detrimental reliance. There can, therefore, be some overlap in the facts that justify a finding of a common intention and the facts that justify the finding of detrimental reliance on that intention. However, the courts have emphasised that both findings are important and parties seeking to show that a common intention constructive trust of the family home has arisen need to plead and prove both the existence of a common intention and detrimental reliance on that intention.

FURTHER READING

Clarke, 'The Family Home: Intention and Agreement' (1992) 22 Fam Law 72.

Dunn, 'Whipping Up Resulting and Constructive Trusts' [1997] Conv 467.

Eekelaar, 'A Woman's Place—A Conflict between Law and Social Values' [1987] Conv 93.

Gardner, 'Fin de siècle chez *Gissing v Gissing*' (1996) 112 LQR 378.

Georgiou, '*Marr v Collie*: The Ballooning of the Common Interest, Constructive Trust', (2019) 82 MLR 145.

Hanbury and Martin, *Modern Equity*, 21st edn., Sweet & Maxwell, 2018, Chapter 12.

Megarry and Wade, *The Law of Real Property*, 9th edn., Sweet & Maxwell, 2019, paras. 10-017–10-033.

Pawlowski, 'Imputing Intention and the Family Home' (2016) 46 Fam Law 189.

Pawlowski, 'Mixed Messages' (2018) 178 Fam Law 18.

Pawlowski, 'Fair Shares' (2019) 375 PLJ 18.

Oxley v Hiscock

Gardner, 'Quantum in *Gissing v Gissing* Constructive Trusts' [2004] LQR 541.

Thompson, 'Constructive Trusts: Estoppel and the Family Home' [2004] Conv 496.

Stack v Dowden

Cloherty and Fox, 'Proving a Trust of a Shared Home' [2007] CLJ 317.

Dixon, 'Case Note on *Stack v Dowden*' [2007] 71 Conv 352.

Dixon, 'The Never-Ending Story' [2007] 71 Conv 456—case note on *Abbott v Abbott*.

Etherton, 'Constructive Trusts and Proprietary Estoppel: The Search for Clarity and Principle' [2009] 73 Conv 104 (104–15).

Neuberger, Chancery Bar Association Annual Lecture, 2008, paras. 8–22—available at www.chba.org.uk.

Pawlowski, 'Beneficial Entitlement—No Longer Doing Justice?' [2007] 71 Conv 354.

Piska, 'Distinctions without a Difference? Explaining *Stack v Dowden*' [2008] 72 Conv 451 (451–60)—case note on *Fowler v Barron*.

Swadling, 'The Common Intention Trust in the House of Lords: An Opportunity Missed' [2007] 123 LQR 511.

Jones v Kernott

Briggs, Co-ownership—An Equitable Non-Sequitur' [2012] 128 LQR 183.

Dixon, 'The Still Not Ended, Never-Ending Story' [2012] 76 Conv 83.

Gardner and Davidson, 'The Supreme Court on Family Homes' (2012) 128 LQR 178.

Mee, '*Jones v Kernott*: Inferring and Imputing in Essex' [2012] 76 Conv 167.

Pawlowski, 'Imputed Intention and Joint Ownership—A Return to Common Sense' [2012] 76 Conv 149.

Yip, 'The Rules Applying to Unmarried Cohabitants' Family Home' [2012] 76 Conv 159.

Geary v Rankine, Aspden v Elvey

Lee, '"And the Waters Began to Subside": Imputing Intention under Jones v Kernott' [2012] 76 Conv 421.

Lees, '*Geary v Rankine*: Money Isn't Everything' [2012] 76 Conv 412.

You can visit the online resources to test your knowledge of this chapter with self-test questions at **www.oup.com/he/nair19e/**.

19

Proprietary estoppel

19.1 Introduction 410
19.2 Nature of proprietary estoppel 410
19.3 Expectations of future rights 412
19.4 Essential elements 414
19.5 Satisfying the equity 421
19.6 Nature of the equity arising from estoppel 424
19.7 Relationship between proprietary estoppel and constructive trusts 426

19.1 Introduction

This chapter provides more detail on proprietary estoppel, which was mentioned in Chapter 4 as a possible substitute for the doctrine of part performance in situations where a contract to dispose of land is rendered unenforceable by a lack of formality. However, estoppel is an area of law which is still very much in the developmental stage. Judges and academic writers are by no means sure how the various bits of the jigsaw fit together, and there is a good deal of debate on issues which in the main relate to classification. Do not, therefore, be too confused by variations in the labels attached to apparently similar forms of estoppel. The only classification point of importance is that proprietary estoppel differs from other forms of estoppel in that it can be used to ground a claim, rather than simply being relied on as a defence against another's claim. It is usual to say, and you may have come across this in your studies of contract law, that estoppel can be used as a shield but not as a sword. However, proprietary estoppel can very definitely be used as a sword (see, e.g. *Crabb v Arun DC* [1976] 1 Ch 179, and the observations of Cumming-Bruce LJ in *Pascoe v Turner* [1979] 1 WLR 431 at p. 436).

19.2 Nature of proprietary estoppel

Proprietary estoppel is usually said to be one of the two forms of equitable estoppel, the other being promissory estoppel.

The basis of equitable estoppel was explained by Lord Denning MR in *Crabb v Arun DC* [1976] 1 Ch 179 at p. 187 as follows:

> Equity comes in . . . to mitigate the rigours of strict law . . . it will prevent a person insisting on his strict legal rights . . . when it would be inequitable for him to do so having regard to the dealings which have taken place between the parties.

Thus, if one party promised not to enforce his legal rights and the other party acted upon this, equity would not allow the promisor to go back on his promise ('estopping' or stopping him from doing so), even though it might not be enforceable against him on a contractual basis. This aspect of equitable estoppel, promissory estoppel, may be familiar to you from the law of contract (see *Central London Property Trust Ltd v High Trees House Ltd* [1947] KB 130).

By contrast, proprietary estoppel arises from a representation by a property owner ('the representor') that another person ('the representee') has or will have some right in the representor's property. If the representee relies on this and acts to his detriment in some way (for example by spending money on the property), it would be inequitable or unconscionable for the owner to insist on his strict legal rights. In such a case, equity would regard him as being estopped from asserting his own rights to ownership of the land. A simple example is to be found in the hypothetical case discussed by Lord Cranworth in *Ramsden v Dyson* [1866] LR 1 HL 129 at pp. 140–1:

> If a stranger begins to build on my land, supposing it to be his own and I, perceiving his mistake, abstain from setting him right and leave him to persevere in his error, a court of equity will not allow me afterwards to assert my title to the land on which he had expended money on the supposition that the land was his own.

This sort of situation, in which the estoppel arises from the true owner's acquiescing in another's mistaken belief as to his own legal rights, has led to the suggestion that the estoppel arises only where the person seeking to rely on it believes that he or she has an existing right in the property. However, in modern decisions, the doctrine has been extended to cover situations in which the claimant is led to believe, possibly by a promise, that the claimant will have some right to the property in the future (see 19.3). In these cases, the remedy is not merely a refusal to allow the promisor to deny the promise in litigation but can take the form of an order to the promisor to convey rights to the promise or to take other steps to remedy the unconscionability involved in going back on the promise (for this explanation of the remedy in proprietary estoppel, see *Guest v Guest* [2022] UKSC 27, per Lord Briggs at [13], discussed at 19.3.1.4). An important feature of the doctrine is that these remedies may be available not only against the original promisor but also against those who have subsequently received the relevant property from him.

19.2.1 What is proprietary estoppel?

Promissory and proprietary estoppel are generally treated as two distinct forms of equitable estoppel. However in *Cobbe v Yeoman's Row Management Ltd* [2008] 1 WLR 1752 Lord Scott referred to proprietary estoppel as a 'subspecies of a promissory estoppel' and described Cobbe's claim as being to a 'promissory estoppel' (see paras. 14 and 23). In *Thorner v Major* [2009] 1 WLR 776, Lord Walker commented that he had some difficulty with Lord Scott's observation in the earlier case, but acknowledged that 'the terminology and taxonomy of this part of the law are . . . far from uniform' (para. 67). However, in that case (at para. 29), Lord Walker confirmed that the essential elements of proprietary estoppel were, as summarised in Megarry and Wade, 7th edn., (2008), para. 16-001, that an equity arises where:

> (a) the owner of land induces, encourages or allows the claimant to believe that he has or will enjoy some right or benefit over the owner's property,

> (b) in reliance on this belief, the claimant acted to his detriment to the knowledge of the owner; and
>
> (c) the owner then seeks to take unconscionable advantage of the claimant by denying him the right or benefit which he expected to receive.

(See now Megarry and Wade, 9th edn., (2019), para. 15-001.)

Lord Walker also confirmed that whether an assurance is clear enough to found a claim for a proprietary estoppel is '... hugely dependent on context' (para. 56). This approach was followed by the Court of Appeal in a later case, *Liden v Burton* [2016] Fam Law 687.

19.3 Expectations of future rights

A good example of an estoppel arising from expectations about future rights is to be found in *Crabb v Arun District Council* [1976] Ch 179. In this case, the claimant had a right of access to his land through a gate leading from a road owned by the Council over which he had a right of way. He wanted to sell the part of his land which adjoined the gate, but intended to retain the rest of it, which lay further along the road. The Council agreed informally to grant him a right of way along the further stretch of road and to permit him to gain access to his property by a new gate. Relying on this understanding, the claimant completed the sale without reserving any right of way to the existing gate, but the Council did not grant the extended right of way, and indeed fenced the road so that the plot retained by the claimant became landlocked.

The Court of Appeal held that the Council had led the claimant to believe that he would be granted the right of way, and thus had encouraged him to act to his detriment in selling part of his land without reserving an easement over it. This gave rise to an equity in the claimant's favour which the court would satisfy by requiring the Council to grant the necessary right of way and right of access.

Since *Crabb v Arun DC* the courts have often recognised that the encouragement of expectations relating to future rights (including an expectation of inheriting property) may give rise to an estoppel, with the result that the representor (or, after his death, his personal representatives) may be required to give effect to this expectation. This aspect of proprietary estoppel can be important in cases involving family arrangements. It provides an alternative route for spouses or partners who believed that they were to receive a share in the family home but cannot show the common intention necessary for a constructive trust. It may also be helpful when a person has been led to believe that he or she can continue to live in the house, but later has this permission withdrawn. This second situation is addressed in Chapter 20, in connection with licences.

19.3.1 Expectations as to future inheritance

Many influential decisions on proprietary estoppel arise from representations or assurances by a property owner about what will happen to the property at his or her death. Four of these cases are described briefly in this section, and are commented upon at relevant points throughout the rest of the chapter.

19.3.1.1 *Re Basham* [1986] 1 WLR 1498

Re Basham was the first modern decision to recognise a proprietary estoppel arising from expectations of inheritance. The plaintiff had spent time and money caring for her stepfather after her mother's death and, instead of moving away from the area, had continued to live near him, in order to help him. He led her to believe that she would inherit his house, but at his death she discovered that he had not made a will. As a result, the house would pass to members of his own family. The court was satisfied that the assurances had been given and that the plaintiff had acted to her detriment in reliance on them. This gave rise to an equity in the plaintiff's favour, which would be satisfied by declaring that the deceased's personal representatives held his house on trust for her.

19.3.1.2 *Gillett v Holt* [2001] Ch 210

In this case the claimant, Gillett, had been persuaded by Holt, a wealthy local landowner, to give up his plans for further education and leave school at an early age, to work for Holt on his farm. Over the years Gillett was treated almost as a member of his employer's family, took on increasing responsibilities for the management of the property and was led to believe that, in due course, he and his family would inherit the whole property and the farming business carried on upon it. There was evidence that, on several occasions when Gillett expressed concerns about his position, he received assurances that his future was secure and that the whole property would be left to him in Holt's will. Unfortunately, after some 40 years of a close working relationship, the two men fell out, Gillett was dismissed and Holt made a new will, leaving his property elsewhere. Gillett claimed that Holt was under an obligation founded on proprietary estoppel to bequeath to him substantially the whole of his estate.

At first instance, this claim was rejected, Carnwath J holding that the claimant had failed to establish that there was an irrevocable promise that Gillett would inherit. The judge also found against Gillett on the further ground that he failed to establish that he had suffered detriment due to relying on Holt's assurance.

The Court of Appeal reversed this decision, holding that there was no need for an express assurance that the promise would not be revoked ('it is the other party's reliance on the promise which makes it irrevocable' (p. 229)). The court was also of the opinion that there was clear evidence that Gillett had suffered detriment through relying on the assurances about Holt's testamentary intentions which he had received over a prolonged period of time (see further, 19.4.2). As a result, Gillett had a right to relief arising from proprietary estoppel. The position was different from that in other inheritance expectation cases, because Holt was still alive and could continue to use his property. Nevertheless, the court ordered that the farm and farmhouse currently occupied by Gillett and his family should be transferred to Gillett, together with a sum of £100,000.

19.3.1.3 *Thorner v Major* [2009] 1 WLR 776

The claimant, David Thorner ('David'), had worked without payment for nearly 30 years on the farm of his older cousin, Peter Thorner ('Peter'), who had no children of his own. Peter was a man of few words and there was never any direct conversation between him and David about what would happen to the farm after his death. Nevertheless, over the years David gained the impression from Peter's 'oblique remarks' (para. 24) that Peter intended him to inherit the farm. On one occasion some 15 years before his death, Peter gave David a document relating to his life assurance policies with the comment, 'That's for my death duties.' (para. 40). Peter did indeed make a will in which he left the farm to David (para. 44), but later revoked it because he intended to amend another disposition contained in it (not concerning David) but subsequently failed to make the new will. At his death, therefore, the farm with the rest of his property vested in his personal representatives who intended to deal with the property in accordance with the rules of intestate succession. David, however, claimed that he had a right to ownership of the farm and related property, arising from proprietary estoppel. He had relied on the representations or assurances of Peter that he would inherit the farm, with the result that he had not pursued other available opportunities to acquire employment or property and so had suffered detriment. This claim succeeded at first instance, the trial judge finding that the three ingredients of assurance, reliance, and detriment were all established. He therefore ordered that David should receive the farm and other assets of the farming business (para. 48).

This decision was reversed by the Court of Appeal, on the grounds that the assurances relied upon by David were not sufficiently 'clear and unequivocal' and that there was no finding by the judge that Peter had intended David to rely on his statements.

On David's appeal, the House of Lords held that the assurances received by David were sufficiently clear, that they were intended to be taken seriously and to be relied on, and that the property David expected to receive was sufficiently certain. The House of Lords therefore allowed David's appeal and restored the order made by the trial judge. The reasons for this decision are covered later in this chapter (see 19.4.1–2 and 19.7.3).

19.3.1.4 *Guest v Guest* [2022] UKSC 27

The claimant Andrew Guest ('Andrew') had spent his working life on the family farm, which belonged to his parents, David and Josephine Guest. The parents had represented to him that, as their eldest son, he would one day inherit the farm or at least a significant share of it. As a result, he had worked at lower than market wages on the farm and had given up on alternative opportunities (such as pursuing another career or buying a home elsewhere). Unfortunately, he subsequently fell out with his father and siblings, and his parents changed their will in consequence. Following the approach in *Thorner v Major*, it was held in the High Court that all the elements of a claim in proprietary estoppel were made out and the parents did not appeal this decision. However, they did appeal the judge's decision on the remedy. The High Court judge had ordered them to sell the farm—where they were still living—and pay Andrew a cash sum equivalent to his promised inheritance. The Court of Appeal upheld this decision, holding that the judge had the discretion to award such a remedy, and the parents appealed to the Supreme Court. There was a disagreement in the Supreme Court, with the majority and minority disagreeing about the principles that should be used to arrive at a remedy in proprietary estoppel cases. The majority concluded that, while Andrew was entitled to receive what he had been promised, the order to sell the farm and pay him a share gave him *more* than he had been promised, since it would mean receiving the promised inheritance much earlier than he otherwise would have. The appropriate remedy would either be to reduce the amount payable to take account of this benefit, or to allow the parents to remain in the property for their lifetime and give Andrew a share in the property after their death (by way of a trust). *Guest v Guest* is now the leading case on the remedy available to a claimant who has successfully brought a claim in proprietary estoppel, and the principles articulated in that case are considered later in this chapter (see 19.5).

19.4 Essential elements

Originally the scope of proprietary estoppel was much narrower than it is today. For an example of the early approach to the criteria for such an estoppel see *Willmott v Barber* (1880) 15 ChD 96. However, for many years now the courts have taken a wider approach to the issue and have warned against approaching the issue in too formulaic a manner. In *Taylors Fashions Ltd v Liverpool Victoria Trustees Co. Ltd* [1982] 1 QB 133, 151–2, Oliver

J suggested that, rather than trying to fit claims of proprietary estoppel into 'some preconceived formula', it would be better to adopt:

> a very much broader approach which is directed at ascertaining whether, in particular individual circumstances, it would be unconscionable for a party to be permitted to deny that which, knowingly or unknowingly, he has allowed or encouraged another to assume to his detriment . . .

This more flexible approach has been adopted with enthusiasm in a number of later cases. Lord Walker, in *Cobbe v Yeoman's Row Management Ltd* [2008] 1 WLR 1752 (paras. 56–8) referred with approval to *Taylors Fashions* as 'having put this part of the law back on the right track'. However, he also emphasised that, while unconscionable behaviour is an essential element, it is not enough in itself to give rise to an estoppel, Lord Walker saying (para. 46):

> Equitable estoppel is a flexible doctrine which the Court can use, in appropriate circumstances, to prevent injustice caused by the vagaries and inconstancy of human nature. But it is not a sort of joker or wild card to be used whenever the Court disapproves of the conduct of a litigant who seems to have the law on his side. Flexible though it is, the doctrine must be formulated and applied in a disciplined and principled way.

Similarly, Lord Scott (para. 16) emphasised that:

> Unconscionability of conduct may well lead to a remedy but . . . proprietary estoppel cannot be the route to it unless the ingredients for a proprietary estoppel are present.

These 'ingredients' for proprietary estoppel are:

- the representation as to the facts or law that is claimed to give rise to the estoppel;
- reliance;
- detriment; and
- unconscionability.

19.4.1 The representation

This may well, of course, be made in express terms, as it was in *Re Basham* [1986] 1 WLR 1498, and in some of the other cases considered in Chapter 23. It may however be made more indirectly, as for example by encouraging a course of action which it would not be sensible for the claimant to undertake unless he was to be granted some interest in the property—thus raising the expectation that such a grant is to be made.

An old example of this approach, though not expressed to be decided on this basis, is *Dillwyn v Llewellyn* (1862) 4 De G F & J 517 in which a son was 'given' land by his father and thereafter built a house upon the land. No formal conveyance of the estate was ever made. Despite the usual rule that equity will not assist a volunteer (one who acquires property without giving value) and accordingly will not perfect an imperfect gift, the court held that the son was entitled to a conveyance of the fee simple because he had expended his own money on building, in reliance on his father's representation.

A modern example of the same principle, and one which was expressly decided on the basis of estoppel, is *Inwards v Baker* [1965] 2 QB 29. Here a son, acting on a suggestion of his father, built a bungalow on his father's land (partly at the son's expense). Thereafter, the son occupied the bungalow in the belief that he would be able to remain there for his lifetime. However, when his father later died, the son discovered that the estate in the land had been left to other people. The Court of Appeal held that the son had a licence (i.e., permission) entitling him to remain in the property as long as he wished, because he had altered his position to his detriment in reliance on a belief induced by his father's conduct. In this case, Lord Denning MR suggested that the operation of the rules of estoppel gave rise to 'an equity' in favour of the son, and that this equity should be satisfied by the grant of a suitable remedy, in this case a licence for life. (For a contemporary comment on this decision, see Maudsley [1965] 81 LQR 183.)

Finally, *Ramsden v Dyson* [1866] LR 1 HL 129, established that representations can be made by conduct, including complete silence, as where an owner stands by and watches another mistakenly building on his land and does nothing to correct the mistake (sometimes described as 'estoppel by acquiescence').

19.4.1.1 *Cobbe v Yeoman's Row Management Ltd* [2008] 1 WLR 1752

You may recall (see 4.5.2.1) that *Cobbe* concerned a property developer who had been assured by a company that property would be sold to him at an agreed price if he succeeded in obtaining planning permission to develop the property. He knew, however, that this was not a legally enforceable contract and the House of Lords took the view that, in the commercial context in which the negotiations took place, it was not reasonable for him to have relied on the company's assurance that it was 'bound in honour' to enter into a binding contract with him later.

Lord Walker emphasised the commercial context in which these negotiations took place and the effect this had on Cobbe's expectations and his reliance on the company's representations:

> Mr Cobbe's case seems to me to fail on the simple but fundamental point that, as persons experienced in the property world, both parties knew that there was no legally binding contract, and that either was therefore free to discontinue the negotiations without legal liability—that is liability in equity as well as at law . . . [para. 91].

In his Lordship's view, Cobbe was running a risk (i.e., by spending time and money on obtaining planning permission without any certainty that the later negotiations would be successful), but he ran that risk 'with his eyes open'. He knew that he had no legally enforceable right arising from the agreement, and was not misled by the company. Although its behaviour, in allowing him to continue his efforts to obtain planning permission when it had already decided not to honour the agreement was 'unattractive' it was 'in the eyes of equity . . . not unconscionable' (para. 92). Lord Scott reviewed a number of earlier decisions which established that an essential element of proprietary estoppel is the claimant's belief that he has or will acquire a 'certain interest' in the property in question. Here Cobbe could not be said to have an expectation that he would acquire a certain interest. Such expectation as he had was of further negotiations which, if successful, would result in a formal written agreement for such an interest (paras. 18 and 20).

19.4.1.2 *Thorner v Major* [2009] 1 WLR 776

These points about the nature of the representation (or assurance) were considered by the House of Lords in *Thorner*. You saw in 19.3.1.3 that the House of Lords reversed the Court of Appeal decision, holding that Peter's assurances to his cousin David were sufficiently clear and that there was evidence that he intended David to rely upon them.

1. How clear must the representation be?

The House of Lords' answer to this question is delightfully simple but not very helpful. In Lord Walker's words (at para. 56):

> I would . . . say (while conscious that it is a thoroughly question-begging formulation) that to establish a proprietary estoppel the relevant assurance must be clear enough. What amounts to sufficient clarity, in a case of this sort, is hugely dependent on context.

In this case the context was quite unusual: that of two hardworking country men ('taciturn and undemonstrative men committed to a life of hard and unrelenting physical work'—see para. 59). The judge had heard detailed evidence about the nature and circumstances of the two men, was sensitive to the unusual circumstances and was satisfied that Peter's oblique remarks were sufficient assurance.

Lord Walker's test of 'clear enough' was adopted and amplified by Lord Rodger (para. 26):

> . . . it is sufficient if what Peter said was 'clear enough'. To whom? Perhaps not to an outsider. What matters, however, is that what Peter said should have been clear enough for David, whom he was addressing and who had years of experience in interpreting what he said and did, to form a reasonable view that Peter was giving him an assurance that he was to inherit the farm and that he could rely on it.

2. Must the representor intend the representee to rely on his assurances?

The Court of Appeal had concluded that there was no evidence that Peter had intended David to rely on his representations. The House of Lords noted that, in reaching this conclusion, the Court of Appeal had been concerned with what Peter himself had actually known and intended. As a result, it had been influenced by the fact that there was no evidence to show that Peter was either aware of other opportunities open to David or had intended him to rely on the assurances so as to encourage him to continue his unpaid work on the farm. In other words, it had adopted a subjective test of intention ('what did this particular man actually intend') rather than applying the objective test adopted by Denning MR (in *Sidney Bolsom Investment Trust Ltd v E Karmios & Co (London) Ltd* [1956] 1 QB 529 at pp. 540–1): a man must be taken to intend what a reasonable person would understand him to intend.

Thus, in Lord Hoffmann's words (para. 5):

> . . . the Court of Appeal departed from their previously objective examination of the meaning which Peter's words and acts would reasonably have conveyed and required proof of his subjective understanding of the effect which those words would have upon David. In my opinion it did not matter whether Peter knew of any specific alternatives which David might be contemplating. It was enough that the meaning he conveyed would reasonably have been understood as intended to be taken seriously as an assurance which could be relied upon.

A similar view was expressed by Lord Scott (paras. 15–17), and Lord Walker noted (at para. 60) that the trial judge had found on the evidence that Peter's assurances, objectively assessed, were intended to be taken seriously and relied on. In his Lordship's opinion, there was no sufficient reason for the Court of Appeal to reverse the trial judge's findings and conclusion.

3. Must there be an expectation of a well-defined property right?

The essence of proprietary estoppel is that the representee is led to believe that he or she has, or will acquire, rights in the representor's property. In *Cobbe*, one of the reasons for the failure of Cobbe's claim was that he did not have any expectation of receiving an interest in the company's property: merely an expectation of further negotiations which might result in a contract for such an interest. In *Thorner*, the extent of the farm had fluctuated over the years (parts being sold off and new areas being acquired). On David's appeal to the House of Lords (which was heard after the decision in *Cobbe*) the respondents claimed that, as a result of these changes to the area of the farm, the property which David expected to receive was not sufficiently certain. Their Lordships dealt with this issue fairly briefly, holding that there was no real uncertainty here. There was no reason to doubt that the common understanding was that Peter's assurances related to what the farm would consist of at his death (para. 62).

In considering the respondent's reliance on *Cobbe*, Lord Neuberger emphasised that that case was very different from the present one (paras. 94–5). In *Cobbe* there was no doubt about the physical identity of the property. However, there was total uncertainty as to the nature of the interest in the property, or other lesser benefit, which Cobbe expected to receive. By contrast, in the present case, the extent of the farm might change, but there was no doubt about the nature of the interest in it which David believed he would be given. In both *Cobbe* and *Thorner* their Lordships also stressed the importance of considering whether the relationship between the parties was 'entirely at arms' length and commercial' (as in *Cobbe*), or 'familial and personal', with neither party having much commercial experience (as in *Thorner*). Such differences in context might be particularly relevant to the question of whether the interest which the claimant expected to receive was sufficiently defined. In 'domestic' cases, the claimant's expectations might well not be defined in legal terms, because both parties thought in terms of the tangible property rather than of intangible legal rights. By contrast, where the relationship was a commercial one, the parties could be expected to understand the legal position and to know, for example, that 'a gentlemen's agreement' or 'being bound in honour' had no legal weight and so could not raise expectations of receiving a certain legal interest.

19.4.2 Reliance

It is an essential element in establishing estoppel that the claimant has relied on the representation, in the sense of being influenced or induced by it to act in a particular way. There are statements in earlier decisions which suggest that it is for the claimant to prove reliance, and this approach appears to have been adopted by Oliver J in *Taylors Fashions Ltd v Liverpool Trustees Co.* [1982] 1 QB 133 at p. 156. However, the contrary view finds strong expression in *Greasely v Cooke* [1980] 1 WLR 1306 at p. 1311, in which Lord Denning MR repeated a statement he had made in an earlier judgment (*Brikom Investments Ltd v Carr* [1979] QB 467 at pp. 482–3):

> Once it is shown that a representation was calculated to influence the judgement of a reasonable man, the presumption is that he was so influenced.

In *Gillett v Holt* [2001] Ch 210 the Court of Appeal accepted without question that reliance would be presumed, citing *Greaseley v Cooke* as authority for this.

Therefore, the burden is on the person who made the representation and is now contesting the estoppel, to show that the claimant *did not* rely upon it.

19.4.2.1 Mixed motives

In seeking to show non-reliance, it may well be suggested that the claimant acted as he or she did for a variety of reasons, and was not influenced solely by the representation. This problem of mixed motives was considered by the Court of Appeal in *Campbell v Griffin* [2001] EWCA Civ 990, the facts of which were as follows.

The claimant, Mr Campbell, had lived for many years as a lodger in a house jointly owned by an elderly couple, Mr and Mrs Ascough. As the Ascoughs became increasingly frail, they depended upon Campbell for practical help, and as time went by he gradually took on the role of an unpaid carer, preparing meals for them and helping them to wash and get to bed. At various times over the years he received assurances from them that he had a home for life. An attempt was in fact made by Mr Ascough to give effect to this assurance in his will, but by the time he did this his wife was suffering from senile dementia and was no longer capable of altering her own will to the same effect. Mr Ascough died before his wife, who took the whole property by right of survivorship (see 17.1.3.1), with the result that at her death the whole house passed to those entitled under her will. In these circumstances, the executors of the couple's wills were obliged to oppose Mr Campbell's subsequent claim of estoppel.

During the trial, the claimant admitted that he had been influenced by feelings of affection and responsibility towards the elderly couple, who had treated him as one of the family, and that he would have acted as he did even without an expectation of receiving an interest in the property. In the light of this, the trial judge held that Mr Campbell had not acted in reliance on the assurances, and that in consequence no estoppel was established.

On appeal, the court considered the position of a claimant who realises that he had several reasons for incurring the detriment on which he relies. In the words of Robert Walker LJ (at para. 29):

> It would do no credit to the law if an honest witness who admitted that he had mixed motives were to fail in a claim which might have succeeded if supported by less candid evidence.

His Lordship quoted with approval the words of Balcombe LJ in *Wayling v Jones* (1993) 69 P&CR 170 at p. 173:

> The promises relied upon do not have to be the sole inducement for the conduct: it is sufficient if they are an inducement.

The Court of Appeal accepted that the assurances given by the Ascoughs were among the inducements which led Mr Campbell to act as he did, and in consequence found that he was entitled to equitable relief.

19.4.3 Detriment

While reliance on the representation may be presumed, the detriment resulting from that reliance must be proved by the claimant (*Gillett v Holt* [2001] Ch 210 at p. 232, rejecting the suggestion that the detriment could be presumed).

The detriment relied upon may often involve the expenditure of money (for example on property in which one believes one has, or will have, an interest—see, for example, *Pascoe v Turner* [1979] 1 WLR 431), but it does not necessarily have to do so. In *Crabb v Arun DC* [1976] 1 Ch 179, the detriment consisted of the plaintiff's selling off part of his land without reserving a right of way over it. In *Greasely v Cooke* [1980] 1 WLR 1306, a former maid had continued to live in the house and look after the family 'when otherwise she might have left and got a job elsewhere' (at p. 1312). In *Re Basham* [1986] 1 WLR 1498, the plaintiff and her husband had looked after her stepfather, providing meals for him and working in his house and garden, and had continued to live in the neighbourhood so that they could continue to care for him, rather than moving away.

In *Gillett v Holt* [2001] Ch 210, the Court of Appeal identified a wide range of matters which in its view constituted detriment: the claimant had left school without academic qualifications at the request of the defendant; he and his wife had subordinated their wishes to those of his employer in a number of ways, most notably in connection with their sons' education; they had sold their own house (and so had 'stepped off the property ladder') and had lived as rent-paying tenants in a farmhouse owned by Holt, on which they had spent a good deal of their own money. In addition, by remaining in Holt's employment, Gillett had deprived himself of the chance to try to better himself in some way—although the court also accepted that he might have done less well with a different employer.

A difficulty sometimes experienced in seeking to establish detriment is that the claimant may appear to have derived considerable benefit from the arrangements to which he or she was a party. Thus, in situations such as those in *Dillwyn v Llewellyn* and *Inwards v Baker*, the claimants had had the advantage of occupying land without paying rent, while Gillett had found Holt to be a generous employer, and had benefited from gifts to the family and substantial help with school fees. While things were going well between the two men, it would not have appeared that Gillett was acting to his detriment, and it was this that apparently led the trial judge to consider that the necessary element of detriment had not been established. However, the Court of Appeal (p. 232) was at pains to point out that:

> The issue of detriment must be judged at the moment when the person who has given the assurance seeks to go back on it.

In elaborating this point, the court quoted with approval (at pp. 232–3) a passage from the judgment of Dixon J in the Australian case of *Grundt v Great Boulder Pty Gold Mines Ltd* (1937) 59 CLR 641 (at pp. 674–5):

> The real detriment or harm from which the law seeks to give protection is that which would flow from the change of position if the assumption were deserted that led to it. So long as the assumption is adhered to the party who altered his situation upon the faith of it cannot complain. His complaint is that when afterwards the other party makes a different state of affairs the basis of an assertion of right against him then, if it is allowed, his own original change of position will operate as a detriment.

19.4.4 Unconscionability

Although unconscionability is not sufficient by itself to give rise to an estoppel (*Cobbe*, paras. 16 and 46), it is essential that the behaviour of the representor, in 'going back' on his representation, is serious enough to appear unconscionable or inequitable. In *Cobbe*, Lord Walker described unconscionability as 'unifying and confirming' the other elements of proprietary estoppel and suggested (para. 92) that:

> If the other elements appear to be present but the result does not shock the conscience of the court, the analysis needs to be looked at again.

19.5 Satisfying the equity

You may have noted from the decisions mentioned so far, that the estoppel, when established, is said to give rise to an 'equity', by which the courts mean that the claimant has a right to some form of remedy in equity. Once the equity is established, the court has to consider how to 'satisfy' it—that is, to decide what relief should be given.

Over the years the courts have drawn on a range of remedies, including restraining the owner from exercising rights, requiring payment of compensation, and the grant to the claimant of some interest in the land.

In some cases the court has decided that the equity can be satisfied only by giving effect to the expectations which the representation has encouraged. Thus, in *Re Basham* [1986] 1 WLR 1498 the claimant received the estate she had expected to inherit, and in *Crabb v Arun DC* [1976] 1 Ch 179 the landowner was granted the rights of access and way on which he had relied. In *Greasely v Cooke* [1980] 1 WLR 1306 the former maid was allowed to remain in the house as long as she wished, and similarly in *Inwards v Baker* [1965] 2 QB 29 the son was in effect given a licence for life. In other cases, however, it has been either impossible or, in the view of the court, inappropriate to satisfy the expectations of the claimant in full.

For example, in *Sledmore v Dalby* (1996) 72 P&CR 196, the plaintiff sought possession of a house which she owned, and which the defendant, her son-in-law, had occupied for over 30 years, initially in exchange for rent but subsequently on a rent-free basis. The defendant relied on proprietary estoppel, claiming that during his wife's lifetime he had been led to believe that the house would be left to her on her parents' death, and that during that period he had made various improvements to the house at his own expense. He had remained in the house for some 12 years after his wife's death, and assumed that he would be allowed to live there rent-free for the rest of his life. At first instance, the court gave effect to this expectation, refusing the plaintiff's application for possession and declaring that the defendant had a personal licence to occupy the house during his life for so long as he wished.

The Court of Appeal, however, took into account the relative circumstances of the two parties. The defendant's children were grown up, and had either left home, or were capable of doing so; he was in employment; and he had the use of alternative accommodation, spending much of his time away from the house and using it on only one or two nights each week. By contrast, the claimant was an elderly woman who could no longer afford to remain in her present home, and accordingly needed the house to live in. The court emphasised (at p. 207) that in applying the equitable doctrine of proprietary estoppel:

> ... it is necessary to consider the extent of the equity created and what is, in the circumstances, the equitable way in which to give effect to it.

The court referred to a discussion of the law of estoppel to be found in a decision of the High Court of Australia (*Commonwealth of Australia v Verwayen* (1990) 170 CLR 394), and (at p. 208) quoted with approval the statement of Mason CJ that:

> A central element of [the doctrine of estoppel] is that there must be a proportionality between the remedy and the detriment which [it] is its purpose to avoid.

Having regard to these principles, and to all the circumstances of the case, the Court of Appeal considered that it was no longer inequitable to allow the expectation raised some 18 years earlier to be defeated, and accordingly made an order for possession against the defendant.

In *Jennings v Rice* [2003] 1 P&CR 8, Mr Jennings had spent many years working, originally as a gardener, for an elderly and wealthy widow, who gradually came to depend upon him as her carer. After a while she no longer paid him for his work, but assured him that he had no need to worry and that 'this will all be yours one day'. Despite this, she died without making a will, leaving an estate which was valued at over £1 million. At first instance the trial judge accepted that Mr Jennings had acted to his detriment in reliance on the assurances and that it was unconscionable for the deceased to go back on her word. In deciding how to satisfy the equity that had arisen, he rejected Mr Jennings's claim that he was entitled to the whole estate, holding that the claimant was unaware of the true extent of the deceased's wealth and therefore could not have expected to receive her whole estate. He also rejected the alternative claim to the house and furniture (valued at £435,000), considering that the house was not suitable for Mr Jennings to live in on his own and also that a reward of such value would be excessive. He took into account the fact that the cost of full-time nursing care would have been in the region of £200,000 and that Mr Jennings could probably buy a suitable house for £150,000, and accordingly awarded the claimant the sum of £200,000. On appeal by Mr Jennings, who sought a greater award, the Court of Appeal upheld the lower court's decision, holding that satisfying Mr Jenning's expectations in this case would be out of all proportion to the detriment suffered and that the court had a broad discretion as to remedy that allowed them to take into account a variety of factors, including:

> ... factors [such as the] misconduct of the claimant ... or particularly oppressive conduct on the part of the defendant. To these can safely be added the court's recognition that it cannot compel people who have fallen out to live peaceably together, so that there may be a need for a clean break; alterations in the benefactor's assets and circumstances . . .; and (to a limited degree) the other claims (legal or moral) on the benefactor or his or her estate. No doubt there are many other factors which it may be right for the court to take into account in particular factual situations.

19.5.1 How does the court decide on appropriate relief? *Guest v Guest* [2022] UKSC 27

The decisions considered earlier illustrate the range of approaches which the court may be asked to adopt in giving relief. While the claimant hopes that the court will give full effect to his expectations, those opposing the claim may suggest that it would be enough to compensate him for the detriment he has suffered through his reliance on the representation. In *Guest v Guest* [2022] UKSC 27, the facts of which are given at

19.3.1.4, Lord Briggs (with whom Lady Arden and Lady Rose agreed) surveyed some of the earlier Court of Appeal decisions and summarised the principles that the courts ought to apply in future cases (at paras. 74–80). This passage from the majority judgment of Lord Briggs in *Guest* is likely to now provide the guidance necessary for the lower courts in deciding how to award relief in future proprietary estoppel cases and so merits careful scrutiny.

Lord Briggs began by pointing out that the first stage of any inquiry was to determine whether the repudiation of the promise by the promisor was unconscionable in the first place, given the circumstances at the date of the repudiation. He said there might be circumstances—'such as the promisor falling on hard times and needing to sell the property to pay his creditors, or to pay for expensive medical treatment or social care for himself or his wife'—where it would not be. If this proved to be the case, there would be no claim in proprietary estoppel at all. *Sledmore v Dalby* was cited (at paras. 35–7 of the judgment) as an example of such a case.

In situations where a claim in proprietary estoppel was made out, Lord Briggs said the remedies stage ought normally to begin (at para. [75])

> . . . with the assumption (not presumption) that the simplest way to remedy the unconscionability constituted by the repudiation is to hold the promisor to the promise.

Thus, contrary to the views expressed by some academics and by the minority in *Guest v Guest*, the majority took the view that the starting point to remedy a claim in proprietary estoppel was to give effect to the expectations of the promisee—that is, to compel performance of the promised conveyance of land or other grant of rights. However, this was only a starting point. It would be open to the promisor to show 'why something less than full performance will negate the unconscionability and therefore satisfy the equity'. In this context, Lord Briggs affirmed the approach of the Court of Appeal in *Jennings v Rice* and framed the question in terms of deciding whether enforcing the promise would be 'out of all proportion to the cost of the detriment to the promisee'. Like Walker LJ (as he then was), he considered that the degree of certainty with which the promise and the detriment had been defined by the parties was an important consideration (at para. 77):

> There is in my view real merit in Lord Walker's spectrum (as he would now prefer to call it) between on the one hand a case where both the promise and the detriment are reasonably precisely defined by the time when the promise is repudiated, where the one is in a sense the quid pro quo of the other although falling short of contract, and on the other hand where either or both are left much less certain. The 'almost contractual' end of the spectrum is likely to generate the strongest equitable reason for the full specific enforcement of the promise if the reliant detriment has been undertaken in full, regardless of a disparity in value between the two. At the other end there may be much greater scope for a departure from full enforcement, even if there are no other problems making it just to do so.

Other reasons why the court might depart from a full enforcement of the promise included, as was suggested by the Court of Appeal in *Jennings v Rice* (see 19.5), the need for a clean break where relations between parties had broken down. It was also necessary to take account of the benefits to the promisee of receiving early performance of a promise of a future benefit (such as a promised inheritance). Lord Briggs emphasised that, in such cases, the fact that it was fair to depart from full enforcement would *not* mean that the promisee would have to be satisfied with compensation for his detriment (contrary to the view tentatively expressed by Lewison LJ in the earlier case of *Davies v Davies* [2016] EWCA Civ 463). Instead, the court would simply have to exercise its discretion, to the best of its ability (at para. 79):

> I can see no principled justification for treating a perceived need to abandon full enforcement as a reason for moving straight (or at all) to compensation on the basis of an attempt to value the detriment. That would suggest something approaching a binary choice which would be alien to the flexible and pragmatic nature of the discretion. I recognise that, in a case where there is perceived to be a large gap between the respective values of the promise and of the detriment this may leave the judge with a wide range of options with little in the way of rules as a guide . . . In an early receipt case the solution . . . may be a discount for acceleration of the expectation. In a case where there is a need to avoid enforced cohabitation the solution may be a financial proxy for the promise rather than enforcement in specie. But where the only objection to full enforcement is that it will be out of all proportion to the detriment then the court will . . . just have to do the best it can.

In *Guest v Guest* itself, there was the need for a clean break, since the relationship between Andrew and his parents and siblings who were still living and working on the farm had broken down. There was also the need to take account of the benefit of an early receipt of the promised benefit, since the parents were still living and there was no way to know when, in the ordinary course of events, the expectation of the inheritance would have crystallised. Rather unusually, Lord Briggs held that the solution to these problems lay in giving the parents a choice as to remedy. They could either sell the farm and pay a share to Andrew, with a discount for the early receipt, or remain in occupation under a trust of the farm, with the parents having a life interest and Andrew becoming entitled to a share of the reversion on their death.

19.6 Nature of the equity arising from estoppel

As you have seen, the equity which arises from proprietary estoppel entitles the claimant to some form of equitable relief. What happens if the landowner who made the representation and so is subject to the equity transfers the property to another person after the equity arose, but before the claimant seeks relief in the courts? Is the equity a purely personal right, enforceable only against the original representor or does it have the character of a proprietary right, binding those who take the land from that person?

A similar but less frequently considered question is whether an equity which would benefit the representee's land (for example, an equity which might be satisfied by the grant of an easement) could be enforced by the representee's successors in title.

19.6.1 Does the equity bind the representor's successors in title?

19.6.1.1 Registered land

At one time, there was little authority on the status of the equity in relation to registered land, although it appeared that it was the practice of the registrar to allow the protection of such an equity by means of a notice or caution on the register. There were also suggestions that the equity was capable of taking effect as an overriding interest under LRA 1925, s. 70(1)(g) (rights of persons in actual occupation), and this was supported by two decisions: *Habermann v Koehler (No. 2)* [2000] TLR 825 (see 20.5.5) and *Lloyd v Dugdale* [2002] 2 P&CR 13 167.

Shortly before the two decisions just noted, the position of the equity in relation to registered land was considered by the Joint Working Party of the Law Commission and the Land Registry, which developed the proposals for reform of registered title discussed in Chapter 6. The Working Party emphasised the increasing importance of the doctrine of proprietary estoppel, which in its view had become 'one of the principal vehicles for accommodating the informal creation of proprietary rights' (Consultative Document, 1998, Law Com No. 254, para. 3.33).

The status of the equity arising from estoppel was uncertain, but such authority as there was indicated that the equity was of a proprietary nature capable of binding successors, rather than a personal right against the original owner. It was desirable to clarify the status of the equity in relation to registered land, and during the consultation process it emerged that similar clarification was needed in respect of 'mere equities' (for which, see 2.6.6 and Report, Law Com No. 271, paras. 5.32–6).

Accordingly LRA 2002, s. 116 provides:

> It is hereby declared for the avoidance of doubt that, in relation to registered land, each of the following—
>
> (a) an equity by estoppel, and
>
> (b) a mere equity,
>
> has effect from the time the equity arises as an interest capable of binding successors in title (subject to the rules about the effect of dispositions on priority).

Thus, the equity arising from estoppel is now capable of binding a purchaser for valuable consideration of registered land if it is protected by an entry on the register or, alternatively, can take effect as an overriding interest if the person entitled is in actual occupation of the land (LRA 2002, Sch. 3, para. 2).

Section 116 of LRA 2002 was applied by the High Court in *Halifax PLC and Bank of Scotland v Curry Popeck* [2008] EWHC 1692, in which an equity arising from estoppel was recognised as an interest in land capable of binding the holder of a later equitable interest (see 6.5.3, but note the warning there that the facts of this case are complicated).

19.6.1.2 Unregistered land

There are a number of decisions relating to licences of unregistered land in which the equity arising from estoppel has been held to bind third parties, and these are covered in Chapter 20 (see 20.5.4).

19.6.2 Does the equity benefit the representee's successors in title?

There is relatively little authority on this point (for details see Megarry and Wade at para. 15-034), but recognition that the equity is capable of binding the representor's successors, and to that extent has a proprietary character, makes it seem more likely that the equity itself could pass to the new owners of the land it benefits.

There is in fact a recent decision of the Court of Appeal, *Joyce v Epsom and Ewell Borough Council* [2012] EWCA Civ 1398, in which a claimant succeeded in enforcing his predecessor's right to relief against the representor. Unfortunately, however, the parties and the trial judge all accepted without question that the right to do so had passed to the claimant. As a result, the matter was not open for discussion in the subsequent appeal (see para. 28) and therefore cannot be regarded as authoritative on this point. Despite this, the case is still worth noting, in particular because of the way in which the Court of Appeal limited the relief given to the claimant, Joyce ('J') so as not to exceed the expectations of his predecessor ('H').

H had expected the Epsom & Ewell Borough Council ('the Council') to grant him a right of way over a service road which the Council had constructed to provide vehicular access to the rear of H's property. In reliance on this, H moved his garage to the end of his garden and constructed a driveway to it from the service road. H and his immediate successors in title used the road for a number of years, but the right of way was never granted. Later J acquired the property intending to demolish the house and use the site for a residential development, which would considerably increase the use of the service road. The Council claimed that J's predecessors had used the road only as licensees (i.e., with the permission of the Council). It would grant J a right of way on payment of a premium, but this would be limited to access to the existing house and could not be used for the planned development. In his subsequent action, J claimed a right to unrestricted access along the service road, derived from the estoppel created by the Council's representations to H and the detriment H had incurred by moving his garage and constructing the drive.

At first instance, J was unsuccessful in this claim, but the Court of Appeal held that the requirements of estoppel were satisfied. The trial judge had indicated that if he had been satisfied of the estoppel, he would have ordered the Council to grant J an easement of way over the road, limited to use of the present single dwelling on the site (para. 49). The court agreed with this approach, saying that it was necessary to have regard to the expectations which H would have had. There was nothing to show that he had any expectation of future development of his property or any wish for more extensive vehicular access than was needed to serve the existing house. Moreover, the Council was responsible for the upkeep of the service road, and it did not seem right to the court that the Council should have to incur the increased maintenance obligations which would follow from an increased use of the way not contemplated at the time when the estoppel arose (paras. 51–2). Accordingly, the court allowed the appeal, and ordered the Council to grant J the limited right of way.

19.7 Relationship between proprietary estoppel and constructive trusts

While reading this account of proprietary estoppel you have probably been reminded of the rules about common intention constructive trusts, derived from *Gissing v Gissing* [1971] AC 886, which were considered in Chapter 18. The need for detrimental reliance in establishing an estoppel is reminiscent of the requirement that the party claiming a share under a common intention constructive trust must show that he acted to his detriment in reliance upon the agreement between the parties. Over the years, judges have expressed a wide range of views about the relationship between the two concepts, and some are noted in this section.

19.7.1 Assimilation?

As case law on the common intention constructive trust developed, several judges commented on the apparent similarities between that type of trust and proprietary estoppel. Thus, in *Grant v Edwards* [1986] 1 Ch 638 at pp. 656–7, Browne-Wilkinson VC based his decision on the existence of a constructive trust (at p. 657), but at p. 656 he suggested that:

> in other cases of this kind, useful guidance may in the future be obtained from the principles underlying the law of proprietary estoppel which . . . are closely akin to those laid down in *Gissing v Gissing* [1971] AC 886. In both, the claimant must to the knowledge of the legal owner have acted in the belief that the claimant has or will obtain an interest in the property. In both, the claimant must have acted to his or her detriment in reliance on such belief. In both, equity acts on the conscience of the legal owner to prevent him from acting in an unconscionable manner by defeating the common intention. The two principles have been developed separately without cross-fertilisation between them: but they rest on the same foundation and have on all other matters reached the same conclusions.

Similarly, Nourse LJ in *Stokes v Anderson* [1991] 1 FLR 391 at pp. 398–9, suggested that:

> It is possible that the House of Lords will one day decide to solve the problem [presented by earlier decisions] either by assimilating the principles of *Gissing v Gissing* and those of proprietary estoppel, or even by following the recent trend in other commonwealth jurisdictions towards more generalised principles of unconscionability and unjust enrichment.

A similar approach has been adopted in the Court of Appeal when dealing with cases arising from informal agreements for the sale or other disposition of an interest in land which do not satisfy the requirements of the Law of Property (Miscellaneous Provisions) Act 1989, s. 2 (see 4.5). In such cases concerns about public policy may prevent the court from basing its decision on proprietary estoppel which it was originally thought would take the place of part performance in helping deserving parties. Following *Yaxley v Gotts* [2000] Ch 162, the courts have been ready to find that the circumstances which give rise to proprietary estoppel will also support a finding of constructive trust, thus bringing the case within the s. 2(5) exception to the formal requirements.

The relationship between the two concepts when used in this context has been described in a variety of ways. In *Yaxley v Gotts* [2000] Ch 162 at pp. 176 and 180 it was said that they 'coincide' and 'are clearly akin to each other', while in *Kinane v Mackie-Conteh* [2005] EWCA Civ 45 (at paras. 31 and 48) estoppel was said to 'overlap' or 'amount to' a constructive trust. In *Kinane*, however, Neuberger LJ (at para. 47) provided some clarity by noting that not all estoppels give rise to a constructive trust:

> The essential difference between a proprietary estoppel which does not also give rise to a constructive trust, and one that does, is the element of agreement, or at least expression of common understanding, exchanged between the parties, as to the existence or intended existence, of a proprietary interest in the latter type of case.

An illustration of an estoppel situation which does not give rise to a constructive trust can be found in the hypothetical case discussed in *Ramsden v Dyson* [1866] LR 1 HL 129 (see 19.2) in which a claimant builds on another's land, having formed the mistaken belief, without any discussion with the owner, that he himself owns the land. This makes it reasonably clear that although the two concepts may overlap, like intersecting circles, they are not identical, and more recent judicial utterances have begun to focus on the differences between the two concepts, rather than on their similarities.

19.7.2 Emphasising the differences

Obiter dicta in several cases show that the tide has now turned against the idea of assimilation. Sir Andrew Park, sitting as a judge in the Chancery Division of the High Court, is reported as having said in *Lalani v Crump Holdings Ltd* [2007] EWHC 47 (Ch), [2007] 08 EG 136 (CS) that:

> While there was an affinity between the two types of claim for a beneficial interest, a common intention trust tended to focus upon the current state of affairs, whereas proprietary estoppel was concerned with promises to do something in the future that would change the pre-existing situation. Moreover, the remedies available to the court were different.

Even more significant, perhaps, is the comment of Lord Walker in *Stack v Dowden* [2007] AC 432 at para. 37 that in *Yaxley v Gotts* he had given some encouragement to the approach which emphasises the similarities between the two concepts, but:

> I have to say that I am now rather less enthusiastic about the notion that proprietary estoppel and 'common intention' constructive trusts can or should be completely assimilated. Proprietary estoppel typically consists of asserting an equitable claim against the conscience of the 'true' owner. The claim is a 'mere equity'. It is to be satisfied by the minimum award necessary to do justice . . . which may sometimes lead to no more than a monetary award. A 'common intention' constructive trust, by contrast, is identifying the true beneficial owner or owners, and the size of their beneficial interests.

19.7.3 *Thorner v Major* [2009] 1 WLR 776

A further contribution to the debate about the relationship between proprietary estoppel and constructive trusts is to be found in *Thorner*, in which Lord Scott suggested that each concept had a distinct role to play in cases arising from expectations of future rights. In his view (at para. 19):

> . . . a problem inherent in every case in which a representation about inheritance prospects is the basis of a proprietary estoppel claim is that the expected fruits of the representation lie in the future, on the death of the representor, and, in the meantime, the circumstances of the representor or of his or her relationship with the representee, or both, may change and bring about a change of intentions on the part of the representor.

The possibility of change of intention or circumstances had been recognised by other members of the Court, who briefly considered various hypothetical situations (breakdown of relationship between Peter and David; need for farm to be sold to provide support for Peter in old age, etc.), but the general view was that it was unprofitable to speculate on what might have been. To Lord Neuberger, for example (paras. 87–9), the short answer here was that Peter's intentions and circumstances had not changed; if they had, David might still have been entitled to some relief and the court would have assessed this by reference to all the facts as it did in *Gillett v Holt* [2001] Ch 210 (see 19.3.1.2).

Lord Scott, however, taking a more theoretical approach (paras. 19–21), noted that proprietary estoppel was the obvious remedy where the representations relied on related to the acquisition of a more or less immediate interest in the property. However, representations about interests to be acquired in the future were, in a sense, conditional and did not fit comfortably into the concept of estoppel. He suggested that they were better explained as giving rise to a constructive trust, created by the common intention or understanding of the parties on the basis of which the claimant has acted to his detriment.

Consequently, he would prefer (para. 20):

> to keep proprietary estoppel and constructive trust as distinct and separate remedies, to confine proprietary estoppel to cases where the representation . . . on which the claimant has acted is unconditional and to address the cases where the representations are of future benefits, and subject to qualification on account of unforeseen future events, via the principle of remedial constructive trust.

19.7.4 Still a matter of debate

The whole position of common intention constructive trusts and proprietary estoppel continues to develop and new cases on the issue seem to arrive by the day. The Further Reading list below indicates places to start, should you need more information, but does not attempt to be a complete survey of all the literature. The more important items in the list are marked with an asterisk.

FURTHER READING

Land Registration for the Twenty-First Century: A Consultative Document, 1998, Law Com No. 254, paras. 3.33–3.36.

*Land Registration for the Twenty-First Century: A Conveyancing Revolution, 2001, Law Com No. 271, paras. 5.29–5.36.

Battersby, 'Contractual and Estoppel Licences as Proprietary Interests in Land' [1991] Conv 36.

*Cooke, *The Modern Law of Estoppel* (Oxford University Press 2000).

*Dixon, 'Proprietary Estoppel: A Return to Principle?' [2009] 73 Conv 260.

*Dixon, 'Proprietary Estoppel: The Law of Farms and Families' [2019] Conv 89.

Fetherstonhaugh, 'Proprietary Estoppel and s. 2—Where Are We Now?' [2009] EG 25 April (No. 0916) 98.

Gardner, 'The Remedial Discretion in Proprietary Estoppel' (1999) 115 LQR 438.

*Gardner, 'The Remedial Discretion in Proprietary Estoppel—Again' (2006) 122 LQR 492.

Getzler, 'Quantum Meruit, Estoppel and the Primacy of Contract' (2009) 125 LQR 196 (at 196–203).

Griffiths, 'Proprietary Estoppel—The Pendulum Swings Again?' [2009] 73 Conv 141.

Haywood, 'Losing the Farm in a Family Feud', New LJ, 28 June 2019, 13.

*McFarlane, *The Law of Proprietary Estoppel* (Oxford University Press 2020).

Mee, 'Proprietary Estoppel and Inheritance: Enough is Enough?' [2013] 77 Conv 280.

*Megarry and Wade, *The Law of Real Property*, 9th edn., Sweet & Maxwell, 2019, paras. 10–024, 10–034, and Chapter 15.

Thompson, 'Estoppel: A Return to Principle' [2001] 65 Conv 78.

Thompson, 'Estoppel, Reliance, Remedy and Priority' [2003] 67 Conv 157.

Thompson, 'The Flexibility of Estoppel' [2003] 67 Conv 225.

Wells, 'The Element of Detriment in Proprietary Estoppel' [2001] 65 Conv 13.

Relationship between constructive trusts and proprietary estoppel

Etherton, 'Constructive Trusts and Proprietary Estoppel: The Search for Clarity and Principle' [2009] 73 Conv 104.

Ferguson, 'Constructive Trusts—A Note of Caution' [1993] Conv 114.

Hayton, 'Equitable Rights of Cohabitees' [1990] Conv 370.

Hayton, 'Constructive Trusts of Homes—A Bold Approach' (1993) 109 LQR 485.

Smith, 'Oral Contracts for the Sale of Land: Estoppels and Constructive Trusts' [2000] 116 LQR 11.

Thompson, 'Constructive Trusts, Estoppel and the Family Home' [2004] Conv 496 (at 505).

You can visit the online resources to test your knowledge of this chapter with self-test questions at www.oup.com/he/nair19e/.

PART V
Licences and rights to the family home

Thus far this book has explained the two legal estates in land and the way in which they may be held on trust. Before we turn to consider the legal and equitable interests in land we need to cover two further matters.

First, you need to understand the law relating to licences. Licences to use land are unusual in the sense that, although they are rights which concern the use of land, they create neither an estate nor an interest in land. Indeed, the term 'licence' covers a diversity of rights to use land. Chapter 20 explains the nature of licences and looks at the ways in which some of them can be enforced, including, in limited cases, against third parties.

Chapter 21 then goes on to pull together elements from various parts of the book to provide a summary of issues that can arise in relation to a family home.

PART V
Licences and rights to the family home

20

Licences and their enforcement

20.1 Introduction 433
20.2 Distinguishing a licence from other rights 435
20.3 Types of licence 436
20.4 Enforcement against the licensor 438
20.5 Enforcement against successors of the licensor 441
20.6 Are licences becoming interests in land? 448
20.7 Trant Way 449

20.1 Introduction

The starting point for any consideration of the nature of a licence is the classic statement made by Vaughan CJ in *Thomas v Sorrell* (1673) Vaugh 330 at p. 351, that:

> A dispensation or licence properly passeth no interest, nor alters or transfers property in any thing, but only makes an action lawful, which without it had been unlawful.

(Oddly enough this case concerned the granting of alcohol licences and had nothing to do with land law, yet ever since it has been regarded as crucial to any discussion of licences to use land.) Put more simply, this means that a licence does not give the licensee an estate or interest in the land but does make presence on the property authorised, so that the licensee is not a trespasser. Any permission to do something on land that, without the permission, would be a legal wrong is a 'licence' in this sense. The category is, therefore, very diverse. It extends from simple situations like a freeholder inviting a friend around for dinner (the friend's presence is not a trespass to the land because the invitation by the friend constitutes a 'licence') to more complex situations in which a landowner provides someone with permission to access to land that she is under a legal obligation not to revoke (e.g., under a contract to permit the licensee use the land for a designated purpose).

20.1.1 Trant Way

Number 1 Trant Way has a small front garden with a short path leading to the front door, on which there is a door-knocker. Every day the postman walks up to the front door in order to make deliveries and the owner has also employed a gardener who makes twice-weekly visits to the property to tend to the garden.

Barbara Bell has completed the purchase of 2 Trant Way (see Chapter 5) and has moved into the property. Her father, Bob Bell, has come to live in the 'granny flat' on the top floor. Mr Bell has his own separate front door and Barbara has given her father the only set of keys to the flat. She never enters her father's flat unless he invites her in. When Mr Bell moved in Barbara told him, 'You need never worry again, you will have a home here with me for as long as you live'. Since moving in, Mr Bell has used some of his savings to make improvements to the flat.

The fee simple estate of 12 Trant Way belongs to Mildred Mumps, who bought it in 1984. The basement is a self-contained flat (12A Trant Way) which has been occupied by Laura Lymeswold since 1985. Miss Lymeswold pays Mrs Mumps £120 a week for the use of the flat. However, Mrs Mumps was keen to ensure that Laura did not obtain any statutory protection, and has always refused to give her a written lease. She has always told Laura, 'You only have a licence, dear. You must go if I say so.' Mildred has kept a key to the front door of the flat and lets herself in once a month to empty the gas and electricity meters and to check that the flat is clean and in good order.

Mrs Mumps occupies the rest of 12 Trant Way herself, together with Henry Newton. Mildred and Henry are not married, but have lived together as a couple ever since Mildred first bought the property. They have two children, now grown up. Mildred has a very highly paid job and so, while she has always worked (apart from brief maternity leave when the children were born), Henry stayed at home to look after the children and still does all the cooking and cleaning. Henry is very clever at 'do-it-yourself' and, while he has never contributed financially to the purchase of the property or to the family living expenses, he has made considerable improvements to the property. Recently Mildred and Henry's personal relationship has been under some strain and now Mildred appears to be having an affair with another man. Henry is very worried that soon Mildred may tell him that she wants to end their relationship.

These four situations, summarised in Figure 20.1, are very different in nature, but each might give rise to a licence. One, the 'licence' of Laura Lymeswold, may cause considerable problems if considered by the courts, since it is likely that Laura will allege that the arrangement is not a licence at all but a lease which gives her extensive rights under the Rent Acts (see 9.2). Two of the situations, those concerning the positions of Bob Bell and Henry Newton, look like family arrangements which would only come before a court should the family relationships break down, but this seems likely to be the case for Henry (see Chapter 21). The other situation, the front path at No. 1, is one with which we are all familiar. Yet normally, when we walk on to someone else's land, we do not consider the nature of our right to do so.

It is clear that Bob Bell, Laura Lymeswold, and Henry Newton and the children could not possibly be regarded as trespassers; obviously they have permission to be on the

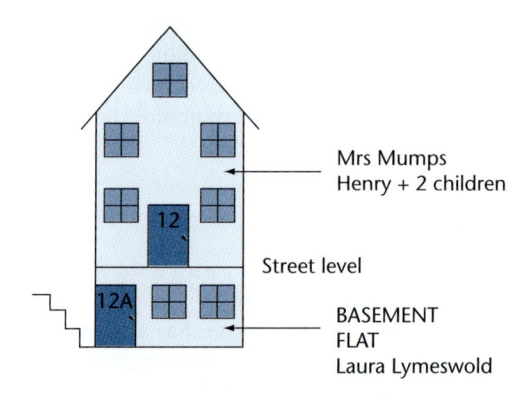

Figure 20.1 12 and 12A Trant Way

properties concerned. What about the postman, and others, who use the footpath leading to the front door of 1 Trant Way? In this case the owners of 1 Trant Way have not expressly given permission to each caller to walk up to the front door, but they have impliedly done so by providing the path and by putting a knocker on the door. Thus, someone who walks up to the front door and knocks would not be a trespasser, though a visitor who went further and prowled about the rest of the garden would have gone beyond the limits of the implied licence and would be trespassing. It is also open to the estate owner to limit the implied licence, e.g., by putting up a sign saying 'No sellers' at the garden gate, and then any person who is a seller and who fails to observe the restriction would also be a trespasser.

In addition to these examples, there are many other types of rights which can amount to a licence to use land, for example, a licence to walk across another's property (which may look very like an easement) or a licence to run the sweet counter in a cinema foyer. These assorted rights give rise to three main problems.

- What is the nature of a licence, and how can it be distinguished from other rights?
- Are these licences enforceable against the original grantors, or may they be revoked at will?
- Are these licences enforceable against successors in title of the original grantors?

20.2 Distinguishing a licence from other rights

Once one has established that a person who is on the land is not a trespasser, one then has to establish whether that person has an estate or interest in the land. If the person has no property ('proprietary') interest giving *the right* to be on the land, enforceable against third parties, then it is usually true to say that the person is there by *permission* and is a licensee of some kind. (Since the decision of the House of Lords in *Bruton v London & Quadrant HT* [2000] 1 AC 406 there is the further possibility of being a tenant under a non-proprietary lease, but this is a new and unfamiliar concept and its third-party effects seem to be limited: see 9.6.2.) The rights which are most commonly confused with licences are leases and easements.

20.2.1 Leases and licences

We have already looked at how the courts have attempted to distinguish leases from licences in the context of understanding the nature of a lease (see 9.2). In this context, the courts have held that any right that has the substantive characteristics of a lease—a legal grant of exclusive possession, for a term—cannot be a licence, however the parties choose to label it. You should therefore refer back to Chapter 9, on the nature of a lease, in deciding whether a particular agreement to occupy land is a lease or a licence: if it *could* be a lease, it *cannot* be a licence.

20.2.2 Easements and licences

If Carlos walks across David's land and it is clear from the circumstances that Carlos is not a trespasser, then one must establish whether Carlos has an easement (a *right* to walk across the land—a right of way) or a licence (he has *permission* to walk across the land). A similar question arises when Eva fishes in Farhana's lake: does Eva have a profit or a licence? Once again one has to distinguish between the ownership of a proprietary right and the existence of a permission that merely prevents the person using the land from being a trespasser. The distinction may well be very important, because the grant of an easement or profit creates a right which cannot be revoked, whereas often the permission given in a licence can be withdrawn (see 20.3). Moreover, if a third party interferes with the enjoyment of an easement or profit, the person entitled has a right of action for this infringement, whereas a licence would at best be enforceable against the licensor.

Unfortunately, there is no simple method of distinguishing between: (a) an easement or profit, and (b) a licence. It is clear that only some rights are *capable* of being easements or profits (see Chapter 24) but (unlike in the case of leases) it is not true that any right that *can* be an easement therefore is one: it might meet all the conditions for a valid easement or profit (see Chapter 24) but, because of the intention of the parties, be a mere licence. In some cases, therefore, the boundary can be drawn by showing that right claimed is incapable of being an easement or profit: if not, it can be only a licence. An illustration of this is to be found in *Hill v Tupper* (1863) 2 Hurl & C 121, in which it was held that the right to exclusively control the sailing of pleasure boats on a canal could only be a licence and not an easement, because it did not benefit the claimant's land and thus failed to meet one of the criteria for establishing an easement (see further 24.2.1.3). However, and unlike leases, even if the arrangement is capable of giving rise to an easement or profit, it will amount to no more than a licence if the intention to create an interest in land is missing (see *Fitzgerald v Firbank* [1897] 2 Ch 96). An example of the operation of this second principle is to be found in *IDC Group Ltd v Clark* [1992] EGLR 187, in which an agreement for a fire escape route through a neighbouring flat was held to create only a personal licence and not an easement binding on successors in title. The question here is one of determining the intention of the parties in making their agreement, and depends on the general contract law principles for identifying the objectively intended terms of an agreement.

20.3 Types of licence

Since a licence in itself gives no right in law and is a *mere permission*, it could be revoked at any time at the will of the licensor (with one exception, see 20.4.1). However, not all licences are so easily withdrawn by the licensor. There are some types of licence that have been held to be irrevocable by the licensor, because the surrounding circumstances place her under an obligation not to revoke the licence. There are also some decisions which suggest that licences may sometimes be enforceable against the licensor's successors, and this raises the question of whether it is really still true to say that a licence creates no interest in land.

Before considering these issues, however, you must first understand the various types of licence.

20.3.1 Licences coupled with an interest

Sometimes licences do not stand alone but are coupled with some other right. An example would be the grant of a profit allowing A to cut wood on B's land. Obviously, a licence must be implied into this agreement because A cannot exercise his or her right to cut wood unless A is permitted to go on B's land to do so. Another example of the operation of the rule is given in *Doe d Hanley v Wood* (1819) 2 B & Ald 724 at p. 738, in which it was said that if a man sells hay standing on his land he cannot later prevent the purchaser from entering the land to collect it (see also *Wood v Manley* (1839) 11 Ad & El 34 and *James Jones & Sons Ltd v Earl of Tankerville* [1909] 2 Ch 440).

20.3.2 Contractual licences

As the name suggests, a licence is a contractual one if it is conferred by contract, and this is so even if the right to enter land is only a secondary part of the contract (*Hounslow LBC v Twickenham Garden Developments Ltd* [1971] Ch 233). In most cases, however, the primary purpose of the contract is to grant the licence in return for consideration; everyday examples are to be found in the purchase of tickets for rail travel or for cinema and theatre visits and when booking into a hotel. Longer-term contractual licences are to be found in the licences to occupy premises, which were considered in the previous chapter. These are most usually commercial arrangements, granted in exchange for what is described as 'rent' or a licence charge, and are an important type of contractual licence.

Contracts giving rise to contractual licences will usually be expressly created, but you should notice that there have been occasions on which the courts were prepared to infer a contractual agreement giving rise to the licence. Thus, in *Tanner v Tanner* [1975] 1 WLR 1346 a contractual licence was inferred in favour of a woman who had given up a protected tenancy and moved into a home provided by her partner and there cared for the children of the relationship. Lord Denning MR said that the court should infer a contract that the woman should remain in the property for so long as the children were of school age and accommodation was reasonably required.

A contractual licence was similarly found in *Chandler v Kerley* [1978] 1 WLR 693 in which a man had bought a house from his mistress and her husband at less than the market price on the understanding that he and the woman would live there together and that eventually they would marry. When the relationship ended soon after the purchase, the Court of Appeal held that the woman had a contractual licence to remain, which could be terminated only on reasonable notice (a year in this instance). A contractual licence was also inferred between a mother and daughter-in-law in *Hardwick v Johnson* [1978] 1 WLR 683.

Other cases, however, show that the courts will not always be willing to accept the existence of a contract in such cases. Indeed, it seems unusual to construe arrangements of this nature as demonstrating the intention to create legal relations which is necessary in the law of contract. Thus, in *Horrocks v Forray* [1976] 1 WLR 230 a woman failed to establish that a contractual licence existed on the basis of a claim that she had subordinated her choice of residence and mode of life to the will of her former partner in return for a promise that she should have a permanent home. The Court of Appeal rejected her case on two grounds: first, the parties had no intention to enter into a legally binding agreement and, secondly, she had provided no consideration. (It should be recalled that the courts will not recognise consideration which they regard as being 'immoral' in character.) The situation in *Tanner v Tanner* was distinguished on the ground that in that case, '[T]he man and the woman were making arrangements for the future at arm's length' (at p. 745).

20.3.3 Bare licences

Bare licences may be seen as a sort of residuary category: permission to enter another's land may be described as a bare licence if it does not fall into any other category. These licences are essentially gratuitous, since if any charge was made for them, they would be regarded as contractual. A good example of a bare licence is the implied licence to walk up the garden path to the front door of 1 Trant Way (see 20.1). Most of us spend a large part of our lives as bare licensees, for every time we visit a friend's house, for example, or enter a shop we are acting as licensees (see *Davis v Lisle* [1936] 2 KB 434 at p. 440).

20.3.4 Estoppel licences

In certain situations, which we consider later, an owner may be estopped (precluded), by representations made, from denying that another person has a licence to be on his land or from revoking a licence already given (for the concept of estoppel, see Chapter 19). These situations are sometimes described as creating a distinct type of licence (licences by estoppel or estoppel licences), but they may equally well be seen as operating on the existing categories of bare and, possibly, contractual licences. To some extent this is no more than a question of presentation: what is important is that you are familiar with the relevant decisions and can recognise the occasions on which an estoppel is likely to arise. Some of the relevant decisions were covered in Chapter 19, and the application of estoppel to licence situations is covered in 20.4.4 and 20.5.4.

20.4 Enforcement against the licensor

The question to consider here is whether the licensee can continue to enjoy the licence over another's land, even if the owner changes his or her mind and purports to revoke or withdraw that licence. The answer to this question depends very much on the type of licence which has been granted.

20.4.1 Licences coupled with an interest

This type of licence is not revocable as long as the proprietary interest (for example, the profit) continues.

20.4.2 Bare licences

A bare licence may be revoked at any time. Once the licence is revoked the former licensee must be given a reasonable period in which to leave and once that period has elapsed will become a trespasser if still on the property. In *Robson v Hallet* [1967] 2 QB 939 some police officers went up to the door of a house and knocked. In doing this they were licensees and within their rights. However, in the absence of a search warrant or other authority permitting the officers to insist on remaining, their licence could be revoked, although the householder had to give them reasonable time to leave the property.

20.4.3 Contractual licences

Originally, when considering revocation by the licensor the courts do not appear to have distinguished between bare licences and those which were granted for consideration. Thus, in *R v Inhabitants of Horndon-on-the-Hill* (1816) 4 M & S 562 a licence to build a cottage on a piece of land, where the licensee made an annual payment for the right, was held nonetheless to be revocable at the will of the licensor.

The same view was taken in the famous case of *Wood v Leadbitter* (1845) 13 M & W 838, in which a race-goer was ejected by force from a racecourse even though he had paid one guinea (£1.05) for the right to enter the premises and view the racing. The race-goer was unsuccessful when he sued the race steward for damages for battery and false imprisonment. The court said that his licence was revocable at the will of the licensor, despite the fact that this was in breach of contract. Since he had refused to leave when told to go, the race-goer had become a trespasser and reasonable force could be used to remove him. The licensor might be acting in breach of contract, and the common law would award damages against him for breach. However, it would not compel him to perform his contract. This rigid view of the inherent revocability of any type of licence continued at least until the passing of the Supreme Court of Judicature Acts 1873 and 1875, after which time the availability of equitable remedies in all courts appears to have produced a considerable change in attitudes to the licence.

In *Hurst v Picture Theatres Ltd* [1915] 1 KB 1 a situation arose which was similar to that in *Wood v Leadbitter*. A cinema-goer was asked by the management to leave because it was believed, incorrectly, that he had not paid for his ticket. When he refused to leave, the cinema-goer was ejected with the use of force and later sued for assault and false imprisonment. Here the court found for the licensee cinema-goer. It was said that since the licensee had a contract with the cinema to watch the film, the equitable remedy of an injunction to restrain breach or an order for specific performance of the contract would have been available to prevent the breach of contract, had it been possible to obtain the remedy in the short time before the breach actually occurred. Accordingly, in equity the licensee did have a right to remain for the whole contractual period. In consequence he was not a trespasser and his removal was unjustified; and he was entitled to damages for assault and false imprisonment. Buckley LJ distinguished *Wood v Leadbitter* because that case had been heard in a court of law before the Supreme Court of Judicature Acts 1873 and 1875 had unified the courts of law and equity.

A rather surprising aspect of the majority judgment in *Hurst v Picture Theatres Ltd* (Phillimore LJ dissented) is that it treated the licensee's contractual right to view a spectacle (such as a film show or a race) as amounting to an 'interest'. The licence to enter the premises for this purpose was regarded as coupled with this interest, thus producing an irrevocable licence under the rules relating to licences coupled with a grant. Understandably, this approach has been much criticised; see for example the observations of Latham LJ in *Cowell v Rosehill Racecourse Co. Ltd* (1937) 56 CLR 605. However, although this approach forms the major part of the judgment in *Hurst v Picture Theatres*, Buckley LJ did offer another reason for the decision: the licence to view the spectacle contained an implied term that the permission would not be withdrawn before the end of the show, and equity would restrain revocation in breach of this term. It is this second approach which has been developed in later cases, so that a contractual licence is now regarded as enforceable against the original grantor according to its terms. Thus, a contractual licence for a specified period cannot be revoked by the grantor until the contractual period has expired (*Hounslow London Borough Council v Twickenham Garden Developments Ltd* [1971] Ch 233). Should the licence be for an unspecified period, a term will be implied that the licence can be terminated upon reasonable notice (*Winter Garden Theatre (London) Ltd v Millennium Productions Ltd* [1948] AC 173). The next time that you attend a cinema, theatre, or sporting event, look at the terms of the contract. Almost certainly they will make it clear that you can be removed at any time in order to ensure that you do not have a contractual right to remain until the end of the event.

If the licensor should purport to revoke the licence in breach of contract, the licensee may seek an injunction to restrain the breach or, in appropriate cases, an order for specific performance of the contract (as in *Verrall v Great Yarmouth BC* [1981] 1 QB 202).

20.4.4 Limited statutory protection

Where a licence constitutes a 'periodic licence' of a dwelling, s. 5(1A) of the Protection from Eviction Act 1977 (inserted by the Housing Act 1988) requires that the licence may not be terminated otherwise than after four weeks' notice in writing, such notice to be in the prescribed form. In addition, s. 3(2A) and (2B) now provide that in the case of such licences the licensor may only recover possession of the property by court order. By these amendments the Housing Act 1988 has conferred a limited protection upon certain licensees and given them some of the rights enjoyed by tenants. The term 'periodic licence' is not defined but is likely to be construed as covering those licences which resemble periodic leases. It is not certain whether the term extends to cover bare licences or only relates to contractual licences. However, the provisions are likely to be used largely in relation to those contractual licences that closely resemble tenancies, save perhaps that the licensee does not have exclusive possession (see Chapter 9 for the lease/licence distinction more generally). Sections 3 and 5 do not apply to 'excluded licences', the largest category of these being licences under which the licensee shares facilities with the licensor. At worst, Laura Lymeswold at 12A Trant Way, will have the benefit of this protection, should Mildred Mumps want to remove her and if her position is only that of a contractual licensee.

20.4.5 Licences protected by estoppel

In Chapter 19 you saw how the principles of proprietary estoppel may prevent an owner relying on his or her strict legal rights when the owner has encouraged another in the mistaken belief that that person has or will have rights in the property. This principle has been used in a number of cases to prevent a licensor revoking a licence (usually a gratuitous or bare one) and recovering possession from a licensee who has been led to believe that it will be possible to remain in the property.

An early example of estoppel preventing the revocation of a licence is provided by *Plimmer v Wellington Corporation* (1884) 9 App Cas 699. Plimmer occupied part of the foreshore of Wellington Harbour as a 'licensee at will' of the Crown. With the encouragement of the government, and indeed at its request, he incurred expenditure in first erecting and later extending a jetty. At a later stage, when questions as to the nature of his interest arose, he was held by the Privy Council to have acquired an irrevocable licence, because his dealings with the government:

> were sufficient to create in his mind a reasonable expectation that his occupation would not be disturbed (at p. 714).

Nearly a hundred years later, *Pascoe v Turner* [1979] 1 WLR 431 shows the Court of Appeal applying a very similar approach. The unmarried plaintiff and defendant had lived together as man and wife, in houses owned by the plaintiff, for almost ten years. When the relationship ended, the plaintiff moved out of their current house, telling the defendant that she had nothing to worry about: the house and its contents were hers. In reliance on this, she stayed in the house thinking that it belonged to her, and expended a considerable proportion of her small savings on repairs and improvements. In fact, the plaintiff did nothing to convey the property to her, so that she remained in occupation as a licensee; a couple of years later he gave her notice to terminate the licence and sought possession of the property.

At first instance, the judge considered that these events gave rise to a constructive trust, but the Court of Appeal did not agree. Instead, it identified the case as one of proprietary estoppel, holding (at p. 436) that the estoppel arose:

> from the encouragement and acquiescence of the plaintiff, when, in reliance upon his declaration that he was giving and, later, that he had given the house to her, she spent a substantial part of her small capital upon repairs and improvements to the house.

The court then had to decide how the equity, arising from the estoppel, was to be satisfied (see 19.5). The choice lay between granting the plaintiff a licence for life, and requiring the transfer to her of the fee simple. Having regard to the plaintiff's apparent determination to evict the defendant, and to the precarious nature of the licence ('she may find herself ousted by a purchaser for value without notice'—at p. 439), the court considered that it must compel the plaintiff to give effect to the defendant's expectations, and convey the fee simple to her.

A later example of the licensee being restrained from revoking a bare licence is to be found in *Matharu v Matharu* (1994) 68 P&CR 93, in which a licensor was estopped from recovering possession of a house from his daughter-in-law. The plaintiff owned a house which had been occupied by his son and daughter-in-law as their matrimonial home. He sought to recover possession from the daughter-in-law after the breakdown of the marriage and the death of his son. The Court of Appeal held that the defendant could establish an estoppel, arising from her mistaken belief, known to her father-in-law, that the house belonged to her husband, on which she had acted to her detriment in a number of ways. However, the court rejected the woman's claim that this entitled her to a beneficial interest in the property and held that she had no more than a licence to remain in the house 'for her life or such shorter period as she may decide' (at p. 103). Moreover, this limited right was subject to a requirement that she take on responsibility for some repairs to the property and for financial outgoings on it (including the mortgage repayments). Although there have been other decisions in which the equity recognised by the court has been satisfied by giving the licensee a mere right to remain in the property, this has not usually been coupled with such requirements, and it seems somewhat strange that the licensee here was required to pay off the mortgage debt without having any chance to acquire some share in the beneficial interest in the property.

There are a number of other decisions which make use of estoppel in the context of licences, but they involve enforcement against the licensor's successors, and these are considered in 20.5.4.

Note, however, that in these cases there is not really an example of a licence being protected by estoppel. Rather, they should be regarded as cases in which the relationship began as a licence but later was converted into another interest, arising from proprietary estoppel. However, the right arising from the estoppel may be satisfied by the award of a permanent or long-term licence (see, e.g., *Plimmer v Mayor of Wellington* (1884) 9 App Cas 699).

20.5 Enforcement against successors of the licensor

It may well happen that a licensor will sell the property to a third party, leaving the licensee with the problem of whether the licence can be enforced against the new owner, or whether eviction will follow. Similar questions arise when the licensor becomes bankrupt or dies, and the trustee in bankruptcy or those entitled under the will or on intestacy seek possession of the property. In the case of some of the various types of licence, these questions can be answered quite briefly. In the case of others, the law does provide a limited route for a licensee to get a remedy from some third parties. However, in recent years, the applicable rules have become increasingly demanding and it is now doubtful that a licensee will be able to bring an action against a third party, purely on the basis of her licence, except in cases where an equity by estoppel has arisen.

20.5.1 Bare licences

With the bare licence there is no problem: since these licences can be revoked at will by the grantor they can certainly be revoked at any time by a successor in title of the licensor. Such a licence also ends automatically if the licensor dies or assigns the property in relation to which the permission was given (see *Terunnanse v Terunnanse* [1968] AC 1086. This was a Privy Council case involving rights in relation to a temple in the then Ceylon).

20.5.2 Licences coupled with an interest

These licences will bind a successor in title of the licensor if the successor is bound by the interest to which the licence is coupled. As long as the licensee can enforce that interest, the licensee can insist on the continuance of his licence. Accordingly, the enforceability of these licences depends on issues outside the scope of this chapter, and the rules applicable will vary with the nature of the coupled interest.

20.5.3 Contractual licences

Hurst v Picture Theatres Ltd [1915] 1 KB 1 established that a contractual licence was enforceable just as any other contract is enforceable. This suggests that a contractual licence would not bind a successor to the original licensor, because such a person would not be a party to the original contract. It is part of standard contractual principles that while the benefit of a contract can be assigned to a third party the burden, or obligation, under the contract cannot be transferred. Indeed, in two cases, this rule has been applied to contractual licences. In *King v David Allen & Sons (Billposting) Ltd* [1916] 2 AC 54 the licensee had a contractual agreement under which it could display posters on the wall of a cinema. The House of Lords held that this contract could not bind a tenant who took a lease of the cinema from the licensor. In reaching this conclusion the court applied the normal rule that a contract creates a personal obligation enforceable only against the original parties. The Court of Appeal accepted the same principle in *Clore v Theatrical Properties Ltd* [1936] 3 All ER 483 and thus, while agreeing that the benefit of a licence could be *assigned* to a third party, said that the burden of the contract would not otherwise pass. Unfortunately for the licensee, this means that any contractual obligation to allow the licence to continue cannot bind a successor in title to the licensor.

This position was doubted in the case of *Errington v Errington* [1952] 1 KB 290. A father bought a house in order to provide a home for his son and daughter-in-law. The property was conveyed to the father, but it was agreed that if the son and his wife paid all the mortgage instalments he would then convey the property to them. In due course the father died, and the property vested in his widow as executrix (she was also a beneficiary under the will). Thereafter the son went to live with his mother while the daughter-in-law remained in the property and continued to pay the mortgage instalments. At this point the mother attempted to revoke her daughter-in-law's licence. The Court of Appeal held that this licence was not revocable by the new owner, even though she was a third party to the original agreement. Denning LJ said that the original contractual arrangement gave rise to an 'equity' in favour of the daughter-in-law which was enforceable against a third party according to the notice rules. Since the mother was a volunteer, having acquired the property as a gift, she was bound by the contract.

This decision can be criticised on the grounds that it flies in the face of normal contractual rules and is contrary to the decisions in two earlier, and binding, authorities. Furthermore, since at the date of the action the mother was still acting as executrix of her husband's estate and held the land in that capacity, she was not a third party at all but was bound as executrix by obligations which bound her husband's estate. The case, however, came to be regarded as authority for the proposition that in certain circumstances a contractual licence would bind a third party who acquired as a volunteer, or even one who bought the property with notice. In the view of Denning LJ (at p. 299):

> neither the licensor nor anyone who claims through him can disregard the contract except a purchaser for value without notice.

Errington v Errington was followed by a number of decisions in which a contractual licence was held to bind the licensor's successors. In *Binions v Evans* [1972] Ch 359 (see 13.2.3.2), the majority of the Court of Appeal based its decision on the existence of a Settled Land Act settlement, but Lord Denning MR regarded the arrangement as giving rise to a contractual licence, which would bind the purchaser with notice in accordance with the principle he had articulated in *Errington v Errington* (at p. 367). In addition, the fact that the plaintiff had expressly taken subject to the defendant's licence and accordingly paid a reduced price would justify the imposition of a constructive trust.

The consequences of imposing a constructive trust were considered in some detail by Browne-Wilkinson J in *In re Sharpe* [1980] 1 WLR 219. Here a nephew bought a house, the bulk of the purchase money being lent to him by his elderly aunt, who was to live with him and his wife and be cared for by them. The nephew was subsequently declared bankrupt, and the property vested in his trustee in bankruptcy, who sought possession of the house. The aunt claimed a right to remain in the house, at least until the loan was repaid.

In giving judgment, Browne-Wilkinson J confessed to feeling some uncertainty about the Court of Appeal decisions which spelt out irrevocable licences from informal family arrangements. He referred to decisions on both proprietary estoppel and contractual licences and decided that the aunt had the right, as against her nephew, to remain in the property:

> whether it be called a contractual licence or an equitable licence or an interest under a constructive trust (p. 224).

The more difficult question, however, was whether that right was enforceable against the nephew's trustee in bankruptcy. In general, the trustee steps into the debtor's shoes, and takes the property subject to all rights and equities affecting it; the trustee is, however, free to break any merely contractual obligations of the debtor. On which side of this line did the rights of the aunt fall: were they merely contractual obligations or did she have some interest over the property? In considering this question, the judge found guidance in *DHN Food Distributors Ltd v Tower Hamlets LBC* [1976] 1 WLR 852. If the licence was to be regarded as creating an interest in land, the use of a constructive trust was essential, since by virtue of LPA 1925, s. 40 (see 4.3.1), an enforceable interest in relation to land could not arise simply under an oral contract. Here, the court concluded that the aunt's contractual or equitable licence did confer an interest under a constructive trust, which accordingly bound the trustee in bankruptcy.

In reaching this conclusion, Browne-Wilkinson J made it clear that he had considerable reservations about the state of the law, describing it (at p. 226) as:

> very confused and difficult to fit in with established equitable principles.

Similar doubts about the decision in *Errington v Errington* and subsequent developments were expressed by a number of judges and academics, as for example by Russell LJ in *National Provincial Bank Ltd v Hastings Car Mart Ltd* [1964] Ch 665 at pp. 696–7. However, the House of Lords when considering the appeal in that case (under the name of *National Provincial Bank v Ainsworth* [1965] AC 1175) declined to express any final view on the matter, which accordingly remained unresolved for some considerable time.

The matter was, however, considered at some length by the Court of Appeal in *Ashburn Anstalt v Arnold* [1989] 1 Ch 1. Unfortunately, all the remarks of the court upon this subject constitute *obiter dicta* because in the case the agreement under consideration was held to be a lease and not a licence. Nonetheless, having heard lengthy argument upon the *Errington* problem, the court felt it proper to express its views upon this subject. After a detailed consideration of the authorities, Fox LJ concluded (at p. 22):

> Before *Errington* the law appears to have been clear and well understood. It rested on an important and intelligible distinction between contractual obligations which gave rise to no estate or interest in the land and proprietary rights which, by definition, did. The far-reaching statement of principle in *Errington* was not supported by authority, not necessary for the decision of the case and *per incuriam* in the sense that it was made without reference to authorities which, if they would not have compelled, would surely have persuaded the court to adopt a different *ratio*. Of course, the law must be free to develop. But as a response to problems which had arisen, the *Errington* rule (without more) was neither practically necessary nor theoretically convincing.

As a result, it seems most unlikely that it will be possible to argue that a contractual licence is binding on a third party to the contract and the contractual licence has been returned to its true place, which appears simply to be as part of the law of contract. The Court of Appeal did, however, accept that there might be cases in which the facts justified the imposition by the court of a constructive trust. It was emphasised that the courts will not take this step where the evidence is 'slender' and that the issue for the court in such cases is (at p. 27):

> whether the [third party] has acted in such a way that, as a matter of justice, a trust must be imposed . . .

The court agreed that the imposition of a constructive trust was justified by the facts of *Binions v Evans* [1972] Ch 359, where the purchaser had acted in breach of the term in his contract that he would take the property subject to the occupier's rights. Although the remarks of the Court of Appeal in *Ashburn Anstalt v Arnold* are theoretically only of persuasive authority, as a lease was found to exist in the case and so the comments on the enforceability of licences were *obiter dicta*, recent case law has followed this approach. In *Habermann v Koehler* (1996) 73 P&CR 515 at p. 523, the Court of Appeal referred to the case as being the decision which governs contractual licences, and in *Lloyd v Dugdale* [2002] 2 P&CR 13 167 at p. 183 Sir Christopher Slade cited *Ashburn Anstalt v Arnold* as authority for the principle that:

> Notwithstanding some previous authority suggesting the contrary, a contractual licence is not to be treated as creating a proprietary interest in land so as to bind third parties who acquire the land with notice of it, on this account alone.

He said that, in future cases, the test for the application of the principle in *Binions v Evans* was whether the conscience of the purchaser was affected and that:

> In deciding whether or not the conscience of the new estate owner is affected in such circumstances, the crucially important question is whether he has undertaken a new obligation, not otherwise existing, to give effect to the relevant incumbrance or prior interest. If, but only if, he has undertaken such a new obligation will a constructive trust be imposed.

This passage from *Lloyd v Dugdale* has been treated in later cases as providing the decisive test for whether a purchaser's knowledge of a pre-existing right available against the landowner (including a licence) can turn him into a constructive trustee for the holder of that pre-existing right (see, for example, the Court of Appeal decision in *Chaudhary v Yavuz* [2013] Ch 249).

20.5.4 Estoppel licences and successors in title

In a number of cases in which the licensor would be estopped from revoking the licence, the courts have had to deal with the additional question of whether his successors in title are subject to that estoppel.

Two cases, *Dillwyn v Llewellyn* (1862) 4 De G F & J 517 and *Inwards v Baker* [1965] 2 QB 29 (see 19.4.1), arose after the death of the licensor and involved questions about the extent to which those inheriting the deceased's property took subject to the licence. In both cases they were held to be bound by the rights which the licensee could have asserted against the licensor.

Similarly, in *Greasely v Cooke* [1980] 1 WLR 1306 the action to recover the property from the licensee was brought by family members who had inherited the property from the original licensor. The licensee, Miss Cooke, had lived in the house for nearly 40 years, having started work as a maid with the family when she was just 16. Over the years she came to be regarded as one of the family, living as the wife of one of the brothers, and caring for other members, including an invalid daughter. After the first 10 years she was no longer paid for her services, but was assured that she could regard the property as her home for the rest of her life. When her partner died, the younger generation, who inherited the house, sought to recover possession from her.

The Court of Appeal held that the various elements of proprietary estoppel were established in this case, and that the claimant had an equity arising from that estoppel, which, as in *Inwards v Baker*, should be satisfied by allowing her to remain in the house for as long as she wished. This was enforced against the new owners, taking by inheritance, who were not able to evict her.

Also, in *In re Sharpe* [1980] 1 WLR 219 elements of the judgment suggest that the circumstances could give rise to an estoppel, and so the case could be seen as illustrating the possibility of the enforcement of such an equity against the owner's trustee in bankruptcy.

All in all, these are cases in which, once again, the rights are best regarded as having started as licences but which later became a greater interest because of the effect of circumstances that gave rise to a proprietary estoppel.

20.5.4.1 Enforcement against purchaser for value

The decisions mentioned above involve enforcing the estoppel rights against successors who are volunteers or who for some other reason are regarded as stepping into the shoes of the licensor. The really interesting question about the enforcement of these licences arises when the licensor's successor is a purchaser for value: can the rights be enforced against a purchaser?

The first cases in which this question arose involved unregistered land, these cases are dealt with first and thereafter the position with regard to registered title is addressed.

Unregistered land

In *Inwards v Baker* [1965] 2 QB 29 at p. 37 Lord Denning MR stated that:

> any purchaser who took with notice would clearly be bound by the equity

but this must be considered as merely *obiter dicta*, since no purchaser was involved in the case.

In *Hopgood v Brown* [1955] 1 WLR 213, the Court of Appeal held that a purchaser for value was bound by an estoppel which had been binding on his vendor. However, there was little discussion of this point, and in part at least the court seemed to argue by analogy from the legal doctrine of tenancy by estoppel rather than relying on the equitable concept of proprietary estoppel.

However, in *E. R. Ives Investment Ltd v High* [1967] 2 QB 379, an equity arising from estoppel was enforced against a purchaser for value. A building company, while erecting a block of flats, mistakenly allowed the foundations of the new building to encroach on to land belonging to a neighbour. When the neighbour objected, he was persuaded to accept a right of way across the courtyard of the new block (allowing access to his back garden from the road) in compensation for the continuing trespass. Thereafter, the neighbour built a garage, access to which was only possible via the courtyard. Later the owner of the block of flats sold the property and it was eventually resold to the plaintiffs. They bought it subject to the neighbour's right of way but subsequently claimed that since this right amounted to an unregistered D(iii) land charge (an equitable easement) it was not binding on them. The Court of Appeal held that the neighbour's right to cross the courtyard did bind the plaintiffs.

This decision appears to be reached on two separate grounds. The first ground is that it is a basic rule of law that one cannot take the benefit of an agreement without accepting a related burden. (This principle is discussed further in Chapter 25 in relation to covenants relating to freehold land and the decisions in *Halsall v Brizell* [1957]

Ch 169—see 25.5.1.) Thus, as long as the plaintiffs wished to maintain their foundations on the neighbouring land they could not revoke the neighbour's right of way. This analysis causes few problems. It is the second reason given for the decision in this case which causes concern: that the actions of the original owner in allowing the neighbour to build his garage gave rise to an estoppel or, as Lord Denning MR put it, 'an equity arising out of acquiescence'. It was held that this 'equity', which is not a land charge and therefore was not void for non-registration, would bind a purchaser who bought with notice, as had the plaintiffs in this case. The decision is thus, to the extent that the second ground operates, an example of the enforcement of an estoppel licence against a purchaser for value, and seems to elevate the licence by estoppel into some kind of quasi-interest in land.

This departure from traditional ideas about licences led to criticism (see Crane (1967) 31 Conv NS 332), and it must be said that since the dispute in *E. R. Ives Investment Ltd v High* could have been resolved on the point of the related benefit and burden alone, the discussion of the 'equity' arising from estoppel was quite unnecessary. The case, however, stands as authority for the proposition that, in estoppel cases, rights that started as licences in respect of unregistered land can bind third parties, including a purchaser for value. The decision as a whole was referred to with approval by the Court of Appeal in *Thatcher v Douglas* (1995) 146 NLJ 282. It is also worth noting *obiter dicta* in *Lloyds Bank plc v Carrick* [1996] 4 All ER 630, in which Morritt LJ, referring to counsel's argument that proprietary estoppel cannot give rise to an interest in land capable of binding successors in title, observed that it was hard to see how that argument 'can surmount the hurdle created by the decision of this court in *E. R. Ives Investments Ltd v High*' (at p. 642).

Registered land

As you saw in 19.6.1.1, there was, until recently, little authority on whether an equity arising from estoppel would bind a purchaser of registered land, and none at all in the context of licences.

However, in 1996, the question of the overriding effect of this equity was raised before the Court of Appeal in the case of *Habermann v Koehler* (1996) 73 P&CR 515. The defendants' employer was the registered proprietor of a house which he made available to the defendants, giving them an oral promise that they could live there rent-free for the rest of his life, and could buy the property from him at a reduced price. The defendants moved into the house on the strength of the arrangement, and for some time worked without payment for their employer. The property was then mortgaged, and some 10 years later was sold to the mortgagee to meet the mortgage debt. The purchaser sought possession of the property from the defendants, who in their defence relied on proprietary estoppel. It seemed that at last all the unanswered questions about estoppel licences, on which, as the Court of Appeal observed, 'there is much controversy', would arise in an appellate court for decision. Tantalisingly, however, the Court of Appeal considered that too many relevant factual questions had not been dealt with at first instance and, accordingly, remitted the case for a new trial.

At that further trial, the judge held that the option to buy the property could not be enforced against the purchaser under LRA 1925, s. 70(1)(g) because the occupier had not disclosed it on enquiry. However, it appears that the licensee's right to remain in the property was held to bind the purchaser. The court ordered the execution of a declaration of trust giving effect to the occupiers' right to remain in occupation of the property for the lifetime of the previous owner (that is, the occupiers' previous employer, who had created the licence). This first instance decision is recorded in the report of *Habermann v Koehler (No. 2)* [2000] TLR 825, in which the occupiers appealed, unsuccessfully, against the decision that their option was unenforceable. The purchaser did not appeal against the decision on the right to occupy, and accordingly there is no reference to that part of the first instance decision in the Court of Appeal's judgment. Nevertheless, it does appear that an equity arising from proprietary estoppel in a licence situation was held binding on a purchaser for value of registered land, albeit at first instance only.

Fortunately, the issue has now been solved by LRA 2002, s. 116, which confirms 'for the avoidance of doubt' that an equity arising by estoppel and a mere equity are interests that are capable of binding successors in title. Thus they can be protected on the register and may form overriding interests if the holder of the rights is in occupation of the land.

20.5.5 Could a contractual licensee rely on estoppel?

This is a question to which there is no clear answer and it has generated a certain amount of academic debate. As Pawlowski puts it in *The Doctrine of Proprietary Estoppel*, 1996, at p. 8:

> There are conflicting views as to whether a contractual licence and proprietary estoppel can overlap.

The question of whether there could be such an overlap seems to be of particular importance in the context of enforcing a licence against the licensor's successor. Following *Ashburn Anstalt v Arnold* [1989] 1 Ch 1, it is generally accepted that a contractual licence will not bind a third party (unless, of course, there are special circumstances which lead the court to impose a constructive trust). By contrast, as we have seen, the equity arising from proprietary estoppel now appears to be enforceable against successors in title and, as in *Habermann v Koehler (No. 2)* [2000] TLR 825, can result in a licence being enforced against a purchaser for value. If a contractual licensee could establish that he has acted to his detriment in reliance on a representation by the licensor—for example that the licence would not be revoked—any resulting equity should be enforceable against a third party, in the circumstances in which other equitable rights would be enforceable against a third party.

20.6 Are licences becoming interests in land?

The start of this chapter referred to the traditional idea that licences are mere permissions and do not constitute interests in land. Having looked at the modern case law, it is worth considering whether this is still true, or whether modern decisions mean that the licence has become, or is becoming, an interest in land.

20.6.1 What is an interest in land?

The authorities seem to suggest that the crucial factor, in deciding whether a right amounts to an interest in land, is whether the right is enforceable against third parties. A right which cannot be enforced against a successor in title is clearly *not* an interest in land. However, since the answer to the question, 'What rights bind successors in title?' appears to be, 'Those which are interests in land', this definition seems to be distinctly circular in nature. It is nevertheless the best that can be offered, and so, in considering whether a right creates an interest in land, attention centres on whether it binds third parties, and in particular the purchaser for value. The answer depends, therefore, on how you interpret the cases we have already considered on whether a successor in title to the licensor can ever be affected by the licence, whether in proprietary estoppel cases or in cases like *Binions v Evans*.

The other essential characteristic of an interest in land is that it is capable of being transferred to another person, passing either by itself, or on the transfer of the land to which it is attached. Thus, in considering whether licences can be regarded as interests in land, you need to ask not only whether they bind the licensors' successors but also whether they are transferable.

20.6.2 Is a licence transferable?

Rights arising under a contract are usually assignable, subject, of course, to the specific terms of the contract (see *Clapman v Edwards* [1938] 2 All ER 507). An assignment would have to be made in writing and notice must be given to the licensor: LPA 1925, s. 136. The question of whether the benefit of an estoppel could be assigned was considered and answered affirmatively in the Australian case of *Hamilton v Geraghty* (1901) 1 SRNSW Eq 81. In *E. R. Ives Investment Ltd v High* [1967] 2 QB 379, Lord Denning described such an equity as being available also to the claimant's successors in title (at p. 395).

A bare licence cannot be assigned because it is a mere permission. However, a lack of objection from the licensor to the licensees' successor might well be taken to amount to the implied creation of a new licence for the successor: *Ives v High* at p. 404.

20.7 Trant Way

The matters discussed in this chapter could be relevant to two of the licensees described in para. 20.1. Henry Newton and Bob Bell are each living as licensees in property owned by another member of their family.

20.7.1 12 Trant Way

Henry is already worried about his position, fearing that Mildred wants to end their relationship, and possibly to turn him out of the house. If he could establish that he is entitled to a share of the beneficial interest under a common intention constructive trust, he would have the right to remain in occupation, as well as a right to a share in the capital value of the house (see Chapter 18).

If he cannot establish such a trust, he will be left trying to show that he has an irrevocable licence to remain in the house. Decisions on implied contractual licences (such as *Tanner v Tanner* [1975] 1 WLR 1346) might be thought to give him some comfort, but, as we have seen, the courts have not always been willing to adopt this approach (see 20.5.3). Even if Henry could establish such a contract, since *Ashburn Anstalt v Arnold* [1989] 1 Ch 1 he would be at risk from anyone to whom Mildred might sell or mortgage the house.

The other possibility for Henry would be to seek to establish an estoppel, but for this he would need to show that Mildred led him to believe that he would be allowed to remain in the house, and that he had acted in reliance on this to his detriment (see Chapter 19).

Failing all else, Henry does have a very limited statutory right to occupation under s. 36 of the Family Law Act 1996, and this and Henry's position more generally are considered in Chapter 21.

20.7.2 2 Trant Way

Although relations between Bob Bell and his daughter Barbara seem happy at the moment, it is worth noting that he might have a licence by estoppel which could be enforced against his daughter. Bob has spent money on his flat in reliance on her statement that he has a home for life. It is possible that if a dispute arose a court could hold that Bob had an irrevocable licence for life although the court would be free to satisfy the equity arising from estoppel in whatever way it thought best, and might choose to make only a money award, to compensate Bob for his expenditure.

FURTHER READING

Hill, 'Shared Accommodation and Exclusive Possession' (1989) 52 MLR 408.
Landlord and Tenant: Reform of the Law, 1987, Law Com No. 162, paras. 4.4–11.
Megarry and Wade, *The Law of Real Property*, 9th edn., Sweet & Maxwell, 2019, Chapter 33.
Sharples, *Land Licences*, Jordan (2011).
Street, 'Coach and Horses Trip Cancelled? Rent Act Avoidance after *Street v Mountford*' [1985] Conv 328.

Bruton v London & Quadrant HT
Bright, 'Leases, Exclusive Possession, and Estates' (2000) 116 LQR 7.
Dixon, 'The Non-Proprietary Lease: The Rise of the Feudal Phoenix' [2000] CLJ 25.
Hinojosa, 'On Property, Leases, Licences, Horses and Carts: Revisiting *Bruton v London & Quadrant HT*' [2005] Conv 114.
Lower, 'The Bruton Tenancy' [2010] 74 Conv 38.
Pawlowski, 'Occupational Rights in Leasehold Law: Time for Rationalisation?' [2002] Conv 550.
Routley, 'Tenancies and Estoppel—After *Bruton v London & Quadrant HT*' [2000] MLR 424.

Tenancies at will and licences
Bridge, 'Tenancies at Will in the Court of Appeal' [1991] CLJ 232.

Enforcement of licences
Battersby, 'Contractual and Estoppel Licences as Proprietary Interests in Land' [1991] Conv 36.
Crane, 'Estoppel Interests in Land' (1967) 31 Conv 332.
Everton, '"Equitable Interests" and "Equities"—In Search of a Pattern' (1976) 40 Conv 209.
Moriarty, 'Licences and Land Law: Legal Principles and Public Policies' (1984) 100 LQR 376.

You can visit the online resources to test your knowledge of this chapter with self-test questions at www.oup.com/he/nair19e/.

21

Special rights in relation to the family home

21.1 Introduction 451
21.2 Right to a share in the value of the property 453
21.3 Right to remain in occupation 456
21.4 Reform 458

21.1 Introduction

The purpose of this chapter is to pull together some matters about the family home which are mentioned at various points in the book, and to give you a little more information about certain statutory rights which members of a family may have in respect of their homes.

21.1.1 Family relationships

Throughout this chapter we will be concerned with three different family relationships, each of which gives rise to different rights in respect of the family home.

21.1.1.1 Marriage or civil partnership

These are both formal relationships, recognised by the state, which create legal rights and duties for each party. Note that here marriage only includes marriages that are legally recognised by the state. Some informal ceremonies (such as some 'handfasting' ceremonies) and some religious ceremonies are not recognised by the state and the couple must have also gone through a civil marriage or a civil partnership for them to have the rights described here as the rights of married persons.

21.1.1.2 Cohabitation

Many couples live together as though they were spouses or civil partners. A cohabitant has some statutory rights in respect of property belonging to the other partner, but is not as well protected as a party to a marriage or civil partnership. As you will see, this can cause major difficulties for couples if their relationships break down. The Law Commission has undertaken two major projects about the legal position of cohabitants, and in July 2007 published recommendations for a statutory scheme of financial relief on the breakdown of a relationship (*Cohabitation: The Financial Consequences of Relationship Breakdown*, 2007, Law Com No. 307 Cm 7182). There is more about these proposals in 21.4, but it should be noted here that in March 2008 the Ministry of Justice announced that, for the time being, it would not be taking action to implement the recommendations.

21.1.1.3 Other homesharing

Family members (and sometimes friends) may share a home together for a variety of reasons, including the provision of care for the old or infirm. This may well involve one person living in property belonging to the other and can lead to hardship when the arrangement comes to an end. Although these relationships may be of considerable social importance, there is very little legal recognition of them.

21.1.2 Trant Way

There are three inhabitants of Trant Way who are particularly relevant to this chapter:

- Sally Mould, who lives with her husband Mark at No. 11 (18.1.2);
- Henry Newton, who cohabits with his partner Mildred at No. 12 (20.1.1); and
- Bob Bell, who has moved in with his daughter, Barbara, at No. 2 so that she can look after him in his old age (20.1.1).

Although the circumstances of each person may be very different, they all have one thing in common. Each of them is living in a house owned by another member of the family; none of them has the legal title to the property he or she regards as home. This can give rise to problems if things go wrong, and this is what we want to focus on in this chapter. We will not concern ourselves with Mr and Mrs Armstrong, although they too occupy a family home, because they are both registered as legal owners of 1 Trant Way, and they have declared they hold the legal estate as beneficial joint tenants; the position of beneficial joint tenants has been explored sufficiently in Chapter 17.

21.1.3 What might go wrong?

It is always possible that relationships may break down, ending in divorce or dissolution if the parties are married or in a civil partnership, or in separation if they are cohabiting. Similarly, home-sharing arrangements between different generations within a family sometimes become unhappy and are no longer workable. We need to consider the position which Henry, Sally, and Bob would find themselves in if this happened to them. Could they go on living in their homes if they wanted to, and, even more important, could they claim a share in the capital value of the property which they could use to acquire alternative accommodation?

Even if all these characters are lucky enough to enjoy successful relationships (and Henry is already worried about his—see 20.1.1), a further possibility we have to consider is that their families may encounter financial problems. We do not know how the Moulds and Barbara Bell financed the purchase of their houses (although they may very possibly have had to borrow money to do so), but we do know that Henry's home is already mortgaged to the Red Leicester Building Society, and that his partner, Mildred, is planning to create a second mortgage to raise money for her business (see 20.1 and 22.2). If Mildred was unable to meet repayment obligations under a mortgage, the mortgagee would have the right to seek possession of the house and to sell it. We need to consider therefore what rights Henry might have in such a situation, and whether his position would differ in any way from that which Sally and Bob would face if their homes were subject to repossession by a mortgagee.

21.2 Right to a share in the value of the property

21.2.1 Rights against the other partner at the end of the relationship

21.2.1.1 Spouses and civil partners

When a relationship comes to an end, a spouse or civil partner is in a much better position than a cohabitant. On divorce or dissolution, the courts are empowered to make property adjustment orders, and can take into account a wide range of matters, including the needs of the respective parties and the contribution which each has made to the marriage (see 18.1.2.1). If Sally Mould's marriage were to end in divorce, she could rely on these provisions, so as to receive a fair share of what she probably regards as the 'family assets'. If there are children of the marriage, she might well be allowed to remain with them in the family home until they are grown up. Also, a spouse or civil partner will have 'home rights' under the Family Law Act 1996, or the Civil Partnership Act 2004, which will protect Sally Mould's right to occupy the matrimonial home (see further 21.3.3).

21.2.1.2 Cohabitants

By contrast with spouses and civil partners, there are no legal provisions governing arrangements when a relationship between cohabitants comes to an end.

Cohabitation contracts

These days, couples planning to live together are advised to discuss in advance what would happen if their relationship ended, and to draw up formal cohabitation contracts which would provide for matters such as the division of property. It used to be thought that such contracts were illegal, as encouraging immorality, but it seems that the judges have kept pace with social change, and it is unlikely that any court today would adopt such an approach. This view received support from *obiter dicta* in *Sutton v Mishcon de Reya*, *The Times*, 28 January 2004, in which Hart J stated that there was nothing to prevent cohabitors from entering into perfectly valid legal relations concerning their mutual property rights:

> Such a contract would not be a contract of cohabitation [that is, a contract for sexual relations outside marriage, which would be void] but a contract between cohabitors.

However, there is as yet no precedent for the enforcement of such a contract. In 2007, in its report on the financial consequences of relationship breakdown (Law Com No. 307 Cm 7182 at paras. 5.5–5.10) the Law Commission recommended that:

> legislation should provide, for the avoidance of doubt, that, in so far as a contract ('a cohabitation contract') governs the financial arrangements of a cohabiting couple during their cohabitation or following their separation, it should not be regarded as contrary to public policy.

The Commission suggested that this free-standing recommendation could usefully be implemented by itself, even if the rest of the recommendations in the report were not accepted, but so far this has not happened.

In any case, couples at the start of a relationship are understandably unwilling to contemplate that it may not succeed. As Waite LJ commented in *Midland Bank plc v Cooke* [1995] 4 All ER 562 at p. 575:

> for a couple embarking on a serious relationship, discussion of the terms to apply at parting is almost a contradiction of the shared hopes that have brought them together

and it is likely that in practice most couples will give no thought to such matters until it is too late.

Express trust

It is always open to Mildred to declare that she holds her title to No. 12 Trant Way on trust for herself and Henry. This will not be a cohabitation contract, since it will not address what is to happen to all the assets in the event of relationship breakdown, but it will give Henry an automatic entitlement to a share in the value of the property in the event that the relationship breaks down. It will also give him rights that could bind a third party, such as Mildred's mortgagee. As explained in Chapter 17, such a declaration of trust must comply with certain formalities but, if these formalities are satisfied, it will be treated as conclusive evidence of Henry's rights (see 17.3).

If Henry and Mildred have not made any specific arrangements, however, any claim which Henry might want to make to a share of the property would succeed only if he could establish the existence of a constructive trust or, possibly, proprietary estoppel.

Constructive trust

As explained in Chapter 18, Henry would have to show that he and Mildred had a common intention, arising either from an express agreement or to be inferred from their conduct, that he should have a share in her property, and that he had acted to his detriment in reliance on this in such a way as to give rise to a constructive trust. In the absence of any express agreement, it would have seemed very unlikely before *Stack v Dowden* [2007] 2 AC 432 that Henry would be able to establish such an intention, because he has not made the direct financial contribution to the cost of buying the house that the courts required. In fact, his position seems very similar to that of Mrs Burns (see *Burns v Burns* [1984] 1 Ch 317). As the decision in that case showed, where an unmarried couple was involved in a separation, only financial contributions were relevant and long-term commitment to the family and its welfare could not be taken into account. By contrast, where a marriage ends in divorce, or a civil partnership in dissolution, the court considering applications for property adjustment orders is specifically authorised to take into account the contributions which each party has made to family life (see 18.1.2.1).

However, in addition to running the household, Henry has made considerable DIY improvements to the property, and these may well have increased the value of the house. Could they entitle him to a share? Again, he would find himself at a disadvantage compared with a spouse or civil partner.

Under s. 37 of the Matrimonial Proceedings and Property Act 1970 a husband or wife who contributes in money or money's worth to the improvement of real or personal property belonging to the other spouse may claim a share (or an increased share) in that property. The contributions must be 'of a substantial nature'. A similar provision in respect of civil partners is to be found in the Civil Partnership Act 2004, s. 65. You should note that these provisions apply only to contributions to improvements and not to purchase. Where such a contribution is made it will be presumed that the parties intended the contributor to obtain a share, or an enlarged share, in the premises. This presumed intention may be displaced by express agreement to the contrary. The court is given a general discretion to assess the amount of the share thus obtained.

The improvements which Henry Newton has made to 12 Trant Way might have allowed him to claim under s. 37, were it not for the fact that he is not married to Mildred. This emphasises once again that cohabitants are at a disadvantage in this type of situation.

Despite the rather gloomy picture painted in the last few paragraphs, there may be some hope for Henry. It is clear from *Stack v Dowden* and the Supreme Court decision in *Jones v Kernott* [2011] 3 WLR 1121 that activities such as caring for the family and working on the property are part of the 'whole course of conduct' from which intentions may be inferred in joint-names cases. It must be remembered that in such cases, courts are concerned to discover the parties' intentions about the nature and size of their shares under an existing trust, and are not dealing with the preliminary intention required to establish a beneficial interest in property owned solely by the other partner. Nevertheless, as noted in 18.6.2, there were signs in decisions such as *Aspden v Elvy* [2012] EWHC 1387 and *Geary v Rankine* [2012] EWCA Civ 555 that the more liberal approach was making its way into sole-name cases. This seems to be confirmed by *Capehorn v Harris* [2016] 2 FLR 1026, in which it was said that, in relation to unmarried cohabitees or partners, the court should apply a two-stage process: One should first consider whether there was (a) an actual agreement that the non-owner should have a benefit; or (b) the sort of conduct from which an agreement can be inferred; and thereafter, the court may be able to impute that the intention was that the cohabitee or partner should have a *fair share*.

Thus, it may well be that Henry's non-financial contributions to the family will help him to establish a claim to a share in the former family home, if they are sufficiently extensive for an agreement to be implied and if he can show he has detrimentally relied on that agreement. If so, Henry's share will reflect the court's view of the terms of the agreement on which he has relied and, in the absence of any evidence of the terms, the court may be willing to impute an intention to do whatever is fair in all the circumstances.

Estoppel

The only other way in which Henry might succeed in claiming a share would be through the doctrine of proprietary estoppel (see Chapter 19). If he could show that Mildred, by words or conduct, had led him to believe that he would have a share, and that in reliance on this he had acted to his detriment, this would, by analogy with *Pascoe v Turner* [1979] 1 WLR 431, give rise to an equity by estoppel. Unlike a common intention constructive trust, a successful claim in proprietary estoppel will not always give Henry an interest under a trust of the property, since the court has a wide discretion in fashioning the remedy, but it is likely that Henry will get some such interest unless his expectations are out of all proportion to the detriment he has suffered or the circumstances have changed in such a way that it is less unconscionable than before for Mildred to go back on her word (see 19.5).

21.2.2 Against a mortgagee on a claim for possession

When a claim to a share in the beneficial interest is being asserted against a mortgagee, it makes no difference whether the parties to the relationship are married or in a civil partnership, or are cohabiting. Both Sally and Henry would have to establish their claims by virtue of a common intention trust or proprietary estoppel: the rights of a spouse or civil partner on divorce or dissolution have no application against a third party during the course of the relationship.

If the claimant's interest arose under a trust, its enforceability against the mortgagee would depend on the usual rules: notice in the case of unregistered land (*Kingsnorth Finance Co. Ltd v Tizard* [1986] 1 WLR 783), and enforcement as an overriding interest by virtue of actual occupation in the case of registered land. You should remember, however, that in practice the beneficiary may have waived these rights expressly, in order to enable the owner to obtain a mortgage. Where there is no express waiver, the court may also imply one where the beneficiary knew that a mortgage advance was needed in order to purchase the property (see 6.5.6.1).

If Henry or Sally based a claim on proprietary estoppel, rather than on a common intention trust, the position would most probably be the same, since it now appears that an equity arising from estoppel will be enforced against purchasers of both registered and unregistered land (19.7.1 and 20.4.4).

From what we know about Bob's story, it seems unlikely that he would be in a position to claim a share in his daughter's house, but he might very well need to assert a right to remain in occupation if Barbara tries to bring their arrangement to an end, and this is considered in the following section.

21.3 Right to remain in occupation

21.3.1 As a beneficiary under a trust

If Henry or Sally could establish a claim to a share in the beneficial interest, he or she would, as a beneficiary under a trust of land, have a right to occupy the property (TOLATA 1996, s. 12—see 14.7). This right would be enforceable against both the legal owner (Mildred or Mark), and against third parties such as mortgagees, on the principles you have already seen. However, as we have seen in *Mortgage Corporation v Shaire* [2001] Ch 743 and *Bank of Ireland Home Mortgages Ltd v Bell* [2001] 2 FLR 809 (see 14.8.5), the secured creditor (and, indeed, the owner) has the right under s. 14 of the Act to apply to the court for an order for sale, and the beneficiary may be ordered to give up occupation so that the property can be sold and the proceeds divided between those entitled. Further, even if the court refuses to order sale, the creditor may adopt the alternative route of suing for the money owed and bankrupting the debtor if he cannot pay, so that eventually the property will be sold under the provisions of the Insolvency Act 1986.

21.3.2 Under a contractual licence or by proprietary estoppel

In Chapter 20 you saw a variety of ways in which the courts have intervened to prevent licensors from revoking licences which arise from family arrangements. In Lord Denning's day, Henry Newton might have been advised to try to establish an implied contractual licence (by analogy with *Tanner v Tanner* [1975] 1 WLR 1346), but today both he and Bob Bell would be better advised to rely, if necessary, on the doctrine of proprietary estoppel.

Spouses are not usually regarded as occupying the matrimonial home as licensees (see *National Provincial Bank v Ainsworth* [1965] AC 1175 at pp. 1223–4), and Sally has in fact a statutory right to occupation, which would serve her better, provided she takes the necessary steps to protect it (as to which, see the next section).

21.3.3 Under a statutory right of occupation

This is another area of the law in which a married person or a civil partner is in a very much better position than a cohabitant or anyone else seeking to remain in occupation of the family home.

21.3.3.1 Home rights

In 1965 the House of Lords held in *National Provincial Bank Ltd v Ainsworth* [1965] AC 1175 that a wife who had no proprietary interest in the matrimonial home had no occupation rights which she could enforce against a purchaser. She did have a common law right to be supported and provided with a home, but this was a personal right enforceable against her husband only. Thus, a husband could desert his wife and family, and sell or mortgage the house in which they lived, leaving them homeless.

The decision in *Ainsworth* brought to an end an interesting development associated with Lord Denning MR, who had pioneered the concept of the 'deserted wife's equity'—that is, a right to remain in the matrimonial home which bound purchasers from her husband.

Although the House of Lords was unable to accept the existence of such a right, the earlier decisions by the Court of Appeal which had developed the concept had drawn attention to the wife's need for protection. Following the House of Lords' decision, new statutory rights of occupation were created in 1967. These rights were renamed 'matrimonial home rights' by the Family Law Act 1996, and have recently been renamed yet again as 'home rights' and made available to civil partners as well as to spouses by the Civil Partnership Act 2004. As their name suggests, home rights apply only to premises which have been a matrimonial home or a civil partnership home of the couple or were intended to be such a home.

The effect of s. 30 of the Family Law Act 1996 (as amended by the Civil Partnership Act 2004, s. 82 and Sch. 9, Part 1) is that where one spouse or civil partner ('A') owns the family home, the other spouse or civil partner ('B') has:

- a right not to be evicted or excluded if already in occupation; and
- a right, with the leave of the court, to enter and occupy if not already in occupation.

B's rights last as long as the marriage or civil partnership continues: that is, until one of the parties dies or the legal relationship is ended by divorce (in the case of marriage) or dissolution (in the case of a civil partnership).

Enforcement against a purchaser

Under s. 31, B's home rights constitute a charge on the estate or interest of A and will bind a later purchaser of the legal estate in the property for valuable consideration provided they are protected:

- *in the case of registered land*, by a notice on the register of title (they cannot take effect as overriding interests, even if B is in actual occupation—see s. 31(10)(b), as amended by LRA 2002, Sch. 11, para. 33(4)); or
- *in the case of unregistered land*, by registration of a class F land charge (see 5.4.2.5).

Occupation orders

Where B has home rights, s. 33 gives the court the power to make an 'occupation order', which can be used for various purposes including requiring A to let B into the premises, regulating the occupation of the premises, or even excluding A from the property. The order can last for a fixed period or indefinitely.

Accordingly, Sally does have a statutory right to remain in occupation of 11 Trant Way, but she should be advised to protect it by entering a notice on Mark's registered title, and should be warned as to the consequences of not doing so.

21.3.3.2 Cohabitants' occupation rights

The Family Law Act 1996, s. 62(1)(a) defines cohabitants as:

> two persons who are neither married to each other nor civil partners of each other but are living together as husband and wife or as if they were civil partners.

As a cohabitant, Henry has certain rights of occupation under the Act, but they give him much less protection than those enjoyed by Sally as Mark's wife.

Section 36 of the Act permits the court to make an order against a cohabitant who owns the family home, giving the other cohabitant:

- a right not to be evicted or excluded if already in occupation; or
- a right to enter and occupy if not already in occupation.

An order may also be made excluding the owning cohabitant from the property.

This sounds very similar to the protection given to a spouse or civil partner, but it is in fact very much more limited. An order under s. 36 can be made for a period of six months only, subject to one extension for another six months. Accordingly, the maximum period of security provided by s. 36 is one year. However, from Henry Newton's point of view, even this limited protection would be of value if Mildred told him to go.

21.3.3.3 Associated persons

Bob, as a father living in his daughter's house, has no right to an occupation order under the Family Law Act 1996. However, a few provisions of the Act do apply to what it terms 'associated persons', who are defined (in s. 62(3)) as including not only spouses, civil partners, and cohabitants, but also relatives and those who live or have lived in the same household.

The Act confers a limited range of rights on associated persons (in the case of spouses, civil partners, and cohabitants these are, of course, in addition to those we have already noted). Under s. 42 the court may make a non-molestation order, which prevents a person from molesting another associated person or a child living with either of them. These provisions replace and extend the earlier provisions of the Domestic Violence and Matrimonial Proceedings Act 1976, which applied only to couples who were married or were living together as man and wife.

Accordingly, if family relationships deteriorate seriously, both Henry and Bob could seek protection from domestic violence under s. 42 of the Act, but this by itself will not help them to deal with the very real problem of losing their homes.

21.4 Reform

The provisions of the Family Law Act 1996 and the Civil Partnership Act 2004 that are mentioned in this chapter take a step in the right direction by giving limited rights of occupation to cohabitants and by extending protection against domestic violence to a wider range of people who are likely to be sharing a home. However, there is still a great difference between the position of spouses and civil partners, with their long-term statutory rights of occupation and the opportunity to seek an adjustment of property on divorce or dissolution, and of a cohabitant like Henry, who has only a limited right of occupation under the Family Law Act, and who has to satisfy strict property law rules if he is to obtain a share in the family home. If his relationship with Mildred does break down and she tells him to move out, he will find himself in a very difficult position. As Waite J noted in *Hammond v Mitchell* [1991] 1 WLR 1127, the lack of any legal process to deal with the ending of a relationship can, due to property disputes, create even greater stress than that which arises on the breakdown of a marriage.

21.4.1 Law Commission reviews

In 1994, the Law Commission embarked on a review of the property rights of home-sharers, a move which was welcomed by members of the judiciary who have to deal with the very difficult problems created by the present law (see Waite LJ in *Midland Bank plc v Cooke* [1995] 4 All ER 562 at pp. 564–5, and Peter Gibson LJ in *Drake v Whipp* (1995) 28 HLR 531 at p. 533). The project was an ambitious one, the aim being to develop a scheme applicable to all home-sharers, irrespective of whether they were sexual partners, members of a family, or simply friends. However, the Law Commission was eventually compelled to admit that it was unable to devise any scheme that would be regarded as fair in its application to all home-sharers. For an account of the difficulties which made it impossible to formulate any recommendations, see *Sharing Home: A Discussion Paper*, Law Com, July 2002.

In 2006, the Law Commission embarked on a more limited project, publishing a consultation paper: *Cohabitation: The Financial Consequences of Relationship Breakdown* (Consultation Paper No. 179), which was followed in the next year by a report with the same title (Law Com No. 307 Cm 7182, July 2007).

21.4.2 Law Commission recommendations

The 2007 Report outlined the case for reform (Part 2), and recommended the introduction of a new statutory scheme for financial relief when a relationship ended on separation. The scheme would be of general application, and would enable couples who satisfied certain eligibility criteria to apply for financial relief from each other when their relationship came to an end, unless they had made a valid opt-out agreement. It is important to realise that the proposals related only to financial relief for partners; they did not deal with financial support for any children of the relationship, because there is already statutory provision for child support.

21.4.2.1 Eligibility criteria

The scheme would apply to couples who had cohabited for a prescribed minimum period and to those who had a child of the relationship, irrespective of how long they had been together. The report did not recommend a specific minimum period, since the Commission considered this to be a topic that required political decision.

21.4.2.2 What relief would be available?

The Commission emphasised that it was not proposing a system of relief similar to that which operates on divorce or dissolution of a civil partnership. Thus there was no question of dividing the former partners' property equally between them, nor of one partner being obliged to maintain the other. The Report commented there is no obligation on one cohabitant to maintain the other during the relationship, and that accordingly such an obligation should not be imposed on separation (para. 4.20). Instead the scheme, summarised at paras. 4.32–4.42, would seek to identify the 'economic impact' that the relationship had had on the former partners and to redress any resulting imbalance. Thus a former cohabitant applying for relief would have to show that, as a result of a contribution to the relationship made by the applicant:

- he or she was now under *an economic disadvantage*; or
- the former partner had acquired *a retained benefit*.

A typical contribution leading to the *economic disadvantage* of the applicant would be the giving-up of paid employment to look after home and family, with the resulting economic disadvantage of lack of savings, inadequate pension provision, and poor prospects for future employment.

The most obvious example of a contribution to a *retained benefit* would be the making of direct or indirect contributions to the acquisition of an asset, such as the family home, but it could include many other contributions, such as, for example, supporting a partner during training for a qualification, which created the retained benefit of improved earning power.

Where such a contribution, and the resulting benefit or disadvantage, were established by the applicant, the court would have a discretion to adjust the retained benefit, and/or to share the economic disadvantage equally between the former parties. A number of remedies would be available for this purpose, including the making of lump sum payments, property transfers, orders for sale, and pension sharing.

Some responses to the consultation on these proposals expressed concern about 'the potential complexity' of the proposed scheme (see para. 4.29). The Commission recognised that any scheme it devised would need to be capable of use without litigation (para. 4.3), but its proposals gave the court such wide discretion that it seemed unlikely that parties would be able to resist the temptation of 'trying their luck' in court, at least in the early years of such a scheme.

21.4.2.3 The Scottish experience

Shortly before the publication of the Law Commission Report in 2007, a scheme similar in many respects to that proposed by the Report had been introduced in Scotland (by the Family Law (Scotland) Act 2006) and research was to be undertaken to assess its cost and efficacy. In March 2008 the Ministry of Justice announced that it proposed to wait for the result of this Scottish research before taking any action on the Law Commission's recommendations for England and Wales. In a further announcement in 2011, the government stated that it did not intend to take any action on the recommendations during the last parliamentary term. In the words of Lord McNally (see Hansard, HL. Deb, 6 September 2011, c 119), the government had:

> taken the Scottish research on board, but it is . . . rather narrow, very early and not enough to persuade us that we should implement the recommendations now.

Thus hopes of any statutory reform in the immediate future were dashed again and, as yet, no further action has been taken.

If you want to know more about the Scottish scheme, you may like to look at *Gow v Grant* [2012] UKSC 29, a Supreme Court decision on a Scottish appeal. Lord Hope's judgment provides an interesting introduction to it, as well as illustrating its application in the particular case. Lady Hale, in a concurring judgment, noted various lessons which can be learnt from the Scottish experience, and reminds us yet again of the need for similar reform in England and Wales. She also noted (paras. 48–9) that as far as she was aware no research had been commissioned by the Scottish Executive into the costs and benefits of the Scottish scheme, and references to such research in the 2011 announcement appear to refer to a report published by the Centre for Research on Families and Relationships at the University of Edinburgh. Details of this report are given in the Further Reading section at the end of this chapter, and you may like to look in particular at Chapter 9 of the Report, which considers the implications of the Scottish experience for England and Wales.

21.4.3 What next?

In the past the courts have emphasised that any change in the law affecting the rights of cohabitants on separation must be introduced by Parliament, saying that it was not for the judges to bring about reform in such a politically sensitive matter. However, comments in *Stack v Dowden* [2007] 2 AC 432 suggest that the courts may be ready to take a more proactive approach. Referring to the fact that the Law Commission had been unable to devise a scheme suitable for all home sharers, Lady Hale commented (at para. 46) that:

> [w]hile this conclusion is not surprising, its importance for us is that the evolution of the law of property to take account of changing social and economic circumstances will have to come from the courts rather than Parliament.

At the time this comment was made, it was thought that there was a real chance that the Law Commission's recommendations about financial relief for cohabitants would be implemented (para. 47), but now that this appears unlikely, the ball seems to be back in the judges' court and, as we have seen, there are some indications that the courts are becoming more flexible in relation to constructive trusts. Perhaps there is hope yet for Henry Newton!

FURTHER READING

Deech, 'The Case against Legal Recognition of Cohabitation' [1980] Int. Comp. Law Quart 480.

Jackson, 'People Who Live Together Should Put Their Affairs in Order' (1990) 20 Fam Law 439.

Megarry and Wade, *The Law of Real Property*, 9th edn., Sweet & Maxwell, 2019, paras. 33-021–33-027.

Thompson, 'Home Sharing—Reforming the Law' [1996] Conv 155.

Law Commission

Sharing Homes: A Discussion Paper, July 2002.

Cohabitation: The Financial Consequences of Relationship Breakdown, 2006, Law Com, Consultation Paper No. 179.

Cohabitation: The Financial Consequences of Relationship Breakdown, 2007, Law Com No. 307 Cm 7182 (available at: www.lawcom.gov.uk).

Research on Scottish cohabitation provisions

CRFR Briefing 51: No longer living together: how does Scots cohabitation law work in practice? (available at: http://www.crfr.ac.uk/publications/research-briefings).

You can visit the online resources to test your knowledge of this chapter with self-test questions at www.oup.com/he/nair19e/.

PART VI
Rights in land

Introduction

In this part we move on to look at the major third-party rights in land. This group of rights includes mortgages and charges (Chapters 22 and 23), easements and profits à prendre (Chapter 24), and covenants affecting freehold land (Chapter 25). These are rights that are capable of existing as interests in land and you should already be familiar with the rules relating to the question of whether such rights will bind any later acquirer of an estate or interest in the land. However, in each chapter, as well as explaining the nature of the rights, we will also examine how the rules as to later acquirers operate in relation to each interest. As you will see, in some cases this can produce quite complex problems, which can be difficult for practitioners and are much beloved of examiners!

22

Mortgages and charges

22.1 Why are mortgages and charges needed? 465
22.2 Introduction 466
22.3 What is a mortgage or charge? 466
22.4 Legal mortgages 468
22.5 Equitable mortgages 472
22.6 Rights of the mortgagor 474
22.7 Rights of the mortgagee 479
22.8 Mortgagee's remedies 481
22.9 Right of certain third parties to redeem 490
22.10 Liability of mortgagees, receivers, and valuers for fraud or negligence 491
22.11 The end of a mortgage 496

22.1 Why are mortgages and charges needed?

Very few individuals or companies have sufficient liquid assets to pay for the purchase of property outright. The normal method of financing such a purchase is to obtain a loan from a bank, building society, or finance house. Since large sums of money are involved, the lender will seek security for the money advanced and this will normally take the form of a mortgage of the property to be purchased. Accordingly, a large proportion of real property in this country is mortgaged. In addition to such mortgages for purchase, it is also common to offer a mortgage of land as security for any sizeable loan. Such a loan might be taken in order to improve the land (e.g., to install central heating) or for purposes unconnected with the land (e.g., to finance the owner's business ventures or refinance other debts).

Thus far, we have mentioned only mortgages. 'Mortgage' is the traditional name for the arrangement by which property becomes security for a debt but, as you will see, the correct modern term is normally 'charge'. In practice, however, the two terms are often used interchangeably. You should also note that land is not the only form of property that can be used as security. It is not at all uncommon for valuable chattels also to be used as security for a debt and thus chattel mortgages are perfectly possible. Ships, aeroplanes, fleets of cars, and large pieces of factory equipment are often mortgaged as a way of financing their acquisition. The rules for chattel mortgages are not identical to those for mortgages of land or interests in land, though there are similarities. However, we deal here only with mortgages that relate to land.

This chapter examines the types of mortgages or charges of land or of interests in land which may be created. It also covers the rules regarding their administration. Chapter 23 covers their protection against other holders of interests in the land ('priority'), including some special rules that apply only to holders of security when they are competing against each other.

22.2 Introduction

When they purchased 1 Trant Way, the Armstrongs were able to pay their own removal expenses and legal fees, and provided 10 per cent of the purchase price of the property from their own resources. They obtained the remaining 90 per cent of the house price by way of a loan from the Double Gloucester Building Society (DGBS). As security for the loan, the society took a charge by deed over 1 Trant Way. This charge was registered at the same time as the transfer to the Armstrongs.

James Harding, who is buying a 99-year lease of the maisonette at 5 Trant Way, also needs to raise money by way of a mortgage. He plans to borrow 95 per cent of the price from his bank, the Wensleydale Bank plc.

Mildred Mumps wishes to borrow a large sum of money from her bank (the Royal Windsor Bank), in order to start her own business. The bank has insisted on security for the loan. 12 Trant Way is already mortgaged to the Red Leicester Building Society but Mildred has offered her bank a second mortgage on the property, as security for her business loan. Mildred has not told her partner, Henry Newton, of her plans.

Nigel Neep, the owner of an unregistered fee simple title to 14 Trant Way, has asked his bank manager for overdraft facilities for one month. The bank manager has said that this is possible, but has suggested that the bank take Mr Neep's title deeds and hold them as security for the loan. Mr Neep bought the property in 1989, raising the bulk of the purchase price by a loan secured by a mortgage. He finished repaying that debt in 2010. He is happy to deposit the title deeds (which are normally stored for safe-keeping by his solicitor) with the bank as suggested.

22.3 What is a mortgage or charge?

In *Santley v Wilde* [1899] 2 Ch 474 a mortgage was described as:

> a conveyance of land . . . as security for the payment of a debt or the discharge of some other obligation.

The purpose of a mortgage or charge is to provide a lender of money with security for the debt. If the borrower fails to repay the debt, the lender can use the property to recover the sum lent and any interest payable. This is usually achieved by the lender taking the property that has been used as security and selling it. The lender is then able to deduct the sums owed from the proceeds of sale.

22.3.1 Terminology

It is worth stopping here for a moment and considering the terminology that is used in relation to mortgages and charges, since it often causes confusion. In a mortgage the mortgage is granted by the property owner (the borrower), who is thus called the *mortgagor*. The lender, who receives the benefit of the security provided by the mortgage is called the *mortgagee*. It is therefore not the building society or bank that *grants* the mortgage, although in common parlance we often speak as though this is the case.

In the case of a charge, the correct terms are *chargor* (the owner who borrows) and *chargee* (the lender) but the terms 'mortgagor' and 'mortgagee' are often used even where the arrangement is technically a charge rather than a mortgage. Figure 22.1 may help you to remember these rules.

PROPERTY OWNER	BANK, BUILDING SOCIETY etc
BORROWER	LENDER
Mortgagor	Mortgagee
or	or
Chargor	Chargee

Figure 22.1 Who's who in mortgages and charges

22.3.2 Types of mortgage or charge

There are a number of different types of mortgage or charge that can be created, although in modern times, with the registration of title, one form has come to be by far the most common. That form is usually called the 'registered charge' and this is covered in some detail later. Some of the older methods of creating mortgages are no longer commonly used, particularly those that relate only to unregistered land, but they are explained because an understanding of how the forms of mortgage or charge developed can make some of the modern rules easier to follow.

22.3.3 Can be legal or equitable

As is the case with many interests in land, mortgages and charges can be either legal or equitable, although modern changes to the law have made equitable mortgages or equitable charges of legal estates much less common. It is also possible to use nearly any interest in land as security and not just a legal estate. The holder of an equitable lease could mortgage or charge his or her equitable interest as security for a loan. However, as this is a mortgage of an equitable interest, the mortgage or charge can only take effect in equity. Thus, while a legal estate or interest can be the subject of a legal or an equitable mortgage or charge, an equitable interest can only be the subject of an equitable mortgage or charge (see Table 22.1). In the past, it was not at all uncommon for an heir to a large settled estate to mortgage his equitable future interest in the property. However, in modern times, equitable mortgages of equitable interests are much less common.

Table 22.1 Legal and equitable mortgages

Estate or Interest Mortgaged or Charged	Type(s) of Mortgage or Charge Possible
Legal estate	Legal or equitable
Legal interest in land	Legal or equitable
Equitable interest in land	Equitable

22.3.4 The traditional method of creating a mortgage

The traditional form of mortgage is no longer possible in relation to a legal estate but it is nonetheless important to understand how it operated, both in order to see why some of the modern rules developed and also to understand some of the older cases. This method was abolished in 1926 (as a consequence of ss. 85–7 of the LPA 1925).

Originally, a mortgage was created by the mortgagor (the borrower) transferring his (in those days the owner was usually male) legal estate in the land to the mortgagee (lender) as security for the loan. If the mortgagor defaulted on his debt (failed to pay) the mortgagee could sell or let the property in order to reimburse himself. He could do this because he owned the estate in the property. The agreement made between the parties did, however, provide for the estate to be re-conveyed to the mortgagor if he repaid the loan in full (usually on a specified date). This was known as *'redemption'* of the mortgage.

There were a number of problems with this arrangement. One that arose early in the history of the mortgage was that lenders often tried to prevent the mortgagor being able to repay on the contractual date. This abuse was dealt with by equity developing the principle that the mortgagor has an equitable right to repay ('redeem the mortgage') *after* the contractual date. Another issue was that it was the borrower/mortgagor, rather than the lender/mortgagee, who would normally expect to occupy the mortgaged land, receive rents and profits from it, and so on; while the borrower was paying off the loan, there was no reason why the lender—despite technically having the legal estate—should take possession or exclude the mortgagor from the land. Equity dealt with this problem by treating the mortgagor as having an equitable interest in the land ('the *equity of redemption*') that entitled him to not only pay off the mortgage after the contractual date but also hold the mortgagee to account if it took possession of the land or otherwise improperly exercising its rights for purposes other than enforcing its security (see 22.6.2). The equity of redemption is a proprietary interest in the land, capable of binding a buyer from the mortgagee. Finally, because of the structure of the traditional mortgage, it was impossible for the mortgagor to create two mortgages over the same piece of property because the first mortgage conveyed the whole legal estate to the mortgagee. This problem was circumvented by the mortgagor granting the second mortgage over his equity of redemption. However, because that mortgage was of an equitable interest, the second mortgage itself had to be equitable and this led to many inconveniences in practice. These are just a few illustrations of how the pre-1926 rules caused unnecessary complications, which became unacceptable in a modern commercial world.

22.3.5 The LPA 1925 reforms

The LPA 1925 replaced the older form of legal mortgage with new forms that do not involve the conveyance by the mortgagor of his or her estate to the mortgagee. Instead, security is provided by either granting the mortgagee a long lease of the premises (LPA 1925, ss. 85 and 86) or by the mortgagor creating a charge over the property that gives the mortgagee the same rights as if the mortgagee had been granted a long lease (LPA 1925, s. 87). Over time the s. 87 charge became the form used by most banks and building societies. It is also the only form of mortgage or charge of a registered legal estate that is possible. The ss. 85 and 86 mortgages are technically possible in other instances but are relatively rare.

We will now look at the legal mortgages in more detail and then consider the equitable forms of mortgage.

22.4 Legal mortgages

22.4.1 Legal mortgage of a fee simple under LPA 1925, s. 85

Under the provisions of LPA 1925, s. 85, the mortgagor, instead of transferring the fee simple, grants a long lease of the property to the mortgagee. This lease will be expressed to be terminable when the loan is repaid: it is said to be subject to **'cesser on**

redemption'. This method has the advantage that the mortgagor retains his or her estate in the land, but the mortgagee also has an estate (the lease) which gives certain rights in relation to the land. To ensure that the lease will not end before the debt is repaid, it is normal to grant an extremely long term of years. Indeed, the statute provides that, should one try to create a mortgage by the old method of transferring the fee simple as security for a loan, this will automatically be converted into a grant of a lease for a term of 3,000 years from the date of the mortgage (s. 85(2)), and those drafting mortgages in accordance with s. 85 usually adopted a similar period of lease.

The s. 85 method of creating a legal mortgage has an advantage over the older form of mortgage. It allows the creation of a second legal mortgage over the same land, by giving the second mortgagee a lease which is longer than the lease of the first mortgagee. This creates a **leasehold reversion** in the second mortgagee, giving the second mortgagee the landlord's rights in relation to the first tenant (mortgagee). (As already explained, it is possible to grant several leases which take effect at the same time in the same piece of land—see Chapter 9.) It would not, in fact, matter if the leases given to the various mortgagees were all the same length, but it was usual to give a slightly longer term to each successive mortgagee.

22.4.2 Legal mortgage of a term of years under LPA 1925, s. 86

Before 1926, mortgages of leases were created by assigning the whole term of years to the mortgagee. However, LPA 1925, s. 86, provided for such a mortgage to be created by granting a sublease to the mortgagee. Again, the mortgagee was thereby given an estate in the land (a sublease), while the mortgagor retained the lease. Should an attempt be made to use the old method of mortgaging, the disposition would be converted into a sublease. The period of the sublease would be the unexpired period of the mortgaged lease, less 10 days (s. 86(2)). The 10-day gap allowed the creation of a second mortgage of the same lease, made by granting a sublease that is a day longer than the first sublease. Once again this allowed for the creation of two or more legal mortgages of the same term of years.

22.4.3 Charge by deed by way of legal mortgage under LPA 1925, s. 87

The third method of creating a legal mortgage is the method in normal use today. Instead of granting a lease or sublease to the mortgagee, the mortgagor merely executes a deed which declares that the estate is charged by way of legal mortgage with the repayment of the loan (plus interest). This form of **'charge'** may be used for both freehold and leasehold estates. LPA 1925, s. 87, provides that the effect of such a mortgage is to give the mortgagee 'the same protection, powers and remedies' as if the mortgage had been made by lease or sublease (whichever is relevant). Thus, the mortgagee is treated as though holding a lease or sublease, although in fact no such estate is created.

The effect of this provision is illustrated by *Grand Junction Co. Ltd v Bates* [1954] 2 QB 160, in which leasehold property had been charged by way of legal mortgage under s. 87. Later, the landlord began forfeiture proceedings under s. 146 for breach of covenant by the tenant. Had he succeeded, the mortgagee's security for the loan would have been totally destroyed, for the lease ceases to exist on forfeiture. If the mortgage had been made by sublease, the mortgagee would have been able to apply for relief as a subtenant under s. 146(4) (see Chapter 12), but the question arose whether a mortgagee could do this, since he had no legal estate in the property. However, the court held that the provisions of s. 87 gave him a right to apply for relief, just as though he held a mortgage by sublease.

The charge by way of legal mortgage does have several advantages over the other methods of creating a legal mortgage. It enables an owner to mortgage a freehold and a leasehold property in one document and, in the case of leasehold property, has the further advantage that, since no actual sublease is created, the grant of such a charge will not amount to breach of a covenant against subletting (see *Grand Junction Co. Ltd v Bates* per Upjohn J at p. 168).

As a result of its simple form (a brief example is given in LPA 1925, Sch. 5, form No. 1), and the fact that it can be used to mortgage both of the legal estates, the legal charge has become in modern times the most usual method of mortgage. The mortgages of both 1 and 5 Trant Way are likely to take this form. The sample format of such a charge given in the LPA 1925 does not, however, give a true picture of the type of document which one would expect to see today. Most modern charges add a long list of covenants between the mortgagor and mortgagee (e.g., preventing the mortgagor from granting leases or taking lodgers). There will also be detailed provisions concerning repayment of the sum advanced, together with interest, usually by instalments (and normally spread over a period of 20–25 years in the case of domestic mortgages). The modern mortgage is accordingly a very much longer document than the Act might suggest.

22.4.3.1 Registered land

The s. 87 charge is used when one is dealing with registered land. Section 23(1)(a) of the LRA 2002 expressly says that the powers of an owner in relation to a registered estate include the power to make any disposition permitted by the general law *except* a mortgage by demise or subdemise (see 22.4.1 and 22.4.2). Thus, the legal charge, since 12 October 2003, is the only form of mortgage to use for registered land. In line with the general policy applying to registered land, the completion of the deed does not, by itself, create a legal mortgage. It is the registration of the charge which perfects it (LRA 2002, ss. 4 and 27). In the absence of registration, the charge can only have effect in equity.

Recently, the Land Registry has been developing the use of 'digital charges', which are dealt with online and reduce the need for any paperwork. The first such charge was registered in April 2018.

Note that in relation to registered land a legal charge may be created (subject to the necessary formalities, such as the need for a deed) by the simple use of words that make it clear that the land is to be regarded as charged with the repayment of a loan. Thus, in registered land, it is not necessary to include the words 'by way of legal charge' in the deed, if the intention to charge is clear. This position in relation to the wording used in the LRA 1925, s. 25(2) was confirmed in *Cityland and Property (Holdings) Ltd v Dabrah* [1968] Ch 166, 171 and now is governed by s. 25 of the LRA 2002 and r. 103 of the Land Registration Rules 2003. Since r. 103 says that 'A legal charge of a registered estate may be made in [the form provided]', rather than that it must ('shall') be made in that form, it would appear that any wording that is clearly intended to create a legal charge will do.

22.4.3.2 Islamic mortgages

The methods of creation of mortgages discussed so far do not satisfy the need for the increasingly popular 'Islamic mortgage' because they are really designed for repayment mortgages that bear interest and so are a problem for religious prohibitions on usury (lending at an interest). The simplest method of providing finance without using the form of an interest-bearing loan is for the financial institution to purchase the property and grant a long lease (at a rent) to the intended acquirer, who also pays an additional monthly sum to acquire the estate in the property at a later date. In such cases there is no charge or mortgage under ss. 85–7 of LPA 1925. Instead of interest, rent is paid for the lease and a further sum is paid to acquire the estate at the end of the lease. This approach is something like a hire-purchase agreement, which is more normally used for chattels. There are other ways of creating non-interest-bearing arrangements but this provides an illustration of how such arrangements may be constructed.

22.4.4 Grant of legal mortgage as a trigger for first registration

The creation of a legal mortgage or charge of an unregistered estate may itself trigger a requirement to register both the estate charged and the mortgage or charge. Under LRA 2002, s. 4(1)(g), the creation of a 'protected first legal mortgage' of a qualifying estate gives rise to the requirement of registration. The 'protected first legal mortgage' is defined by s. 4(8) as follows:

> (8) For the purposes of subsection (1)(g)—
>
> (a) a legal mortgage is protected if it takes effect on its creation as a mortgage to be protected by the deposit of documents relating to the mortgaged estate, and
>
> (b) a first legal mortgage is one which on its creation, ranks in priority ahead of any other mortgages then affecting the mortgaged estate.

You will recall from the earlier discussion of land charges (see 5.4.2.2) that, in unregistered land, only mortgages that are not protected by deposit of title deeds can be protected as land charges. The effect of LRA 2002, s. 4 is that the creation of a legal mortgage in which the title deeds *are* deposited will lead to a requirement to register the estate charged, unless the mortgage is not a first mortgage (which is very unlikely because the first mortgagee normally takes the deeds). Section 6(2) makes it quite clear that it is the charged estate that must be registered and not just the mortgage or charge. Thus, the land will become registered land and then all charges must be protected in accordance with the land registration provisions.

Thus, if Mr Neep, the owner of 14 Trant Way, has to create a legal mortgage of his property as security for his bank loan, rather than using the informal method suggested by the bank manager, he will have to register his fee simple estate and the charge.

22.4.4.1 Registration of charges

Once the estate is registered, any legal mortgage or charge over that estate must itself be registered (s. 27(2)(f)). Once registered, the mortgage or charge will take effect as a charge by deed by way of legal mortgage, even if originally created as a different type of legal mortgage (LRA 2002, s. 51). Thus, if Mr Neep did create a new legal mortgage of his premises but incorrectly used the LRA 1925, s. 85 method (the grant of a lease), the effect would be that the s. 85 mortgage will be transformed into a charge by deed by way of legal mortgage (the s. 87 form) once it is registered.

22.4.4.2 Registration not triggered

All of this produces a constant movement towards all estates being registered and all legal mortgages of those estates becoming legal charges. However, even in future, there will still be cases in which registration is not triggered. Notably, these include the creation of a second legal mortgage of unregistered land and the creation of an equitable mortgage of unregistered land. Equitable charges of registered land are, of course, also possible but unlike legal charges are not protected by registration of the charge itself. We will look at this in more detail once we have considered how equitable mortgages and charges can arise.

22.5 Equitable mortgages

22.5.1 Contract to create a mortgage

Under the principle that 'Equity regards as done that which ought to be done', a contract to create a legal mortgage will be regarded as giving rise to an equitable mortgage from the date of the contract (see 4.6). Of course, due to s. 2 of the Law of Property (Miscellaneous Provisions) Act 1989, the contract itself must be made in writing. Reliance on the equitable rule is also dependent upon the contract being one which the courts would enforce by an order for specific performance (*Tebb v Hodge* (1869) LR 5 CP 73). A defective legal mortgage (e.g., one which has been signed but not witnessed) will be similarly treated, as long as specific performance is available. This is similar to the rule for defective leases (see *Walsh v Lonsdale* (1882) 21 ChD 9 and Chapter 9). However, specific performance will not be available in any of these cases unless the mortgage money has actually been advanced, for traditionally equity has declined to force someone to make a loan. In such cases, the mortgagor could fall back on his common law remedy of damages.

22.5.2 Informal mortgage by deposit of deeds

In the past, the willingness of equity to recognise and protect any transaction in which it was clear that an estate owner had intended to charge the property with the repayment of a loan, meant that many informal arrangements were regarded as equitable mortgages; equity regarded what had taken place as evidence of a contract to grant a mortgage. The classic example of the protection afforded by equity arose where an estate owner deposited the land certificate (in the days in which these were issued) or title deeds with the lender in return for the loan. This was recognised as creating an equitable mortgage of the property in *Russel v Russel* (1783) 1 Bro CC 269, and continued in modern law under the saving provisions of LPA 1925, s. 13. For this type of mortgage, until 1989, no written record of any kind was necessary, for the deposit of documents was regarded not only as constituting the contract to make the mortgage, but also as amounting to part performance for the purposes of LPA 1925, s. 40(2). Moreover, the deposit and receipt of the documents were regarded as part performance by each party respectively, so whichever side wished to rely on the doctrine might do so. Despite this, however, a written record was desirable, in order to provide clear evidence of the nature of the transaction. These mortgages were convenient and cheap where a short-term loan was envisaged.

22.5.2.1 Need for writing

The law relating to these informal mortgages was, however, changed by the Law of Property (Miscellaneous Provisions) Act 1989, s. 2, because that provision relates to:

> A contract for the sale or other disposition of an interest in land . . .

Accordingly, for an equitable mortgage to be enforceable it is now necessary to show that the agreement was made in writing. It will not do merely to have a later deed which states that the agreement exists (as was previously common practice) because that deed would merely purport to record an existing contract, which would not satisfy s. 2, and accordingly would not amount to a contract at all. This effect of s. 2 (which was unforeseen) was confirmed by the Court of Appeal in *United Bank of Kuwait plc v Sahib* [1997] Ch 107. This prevents the creation of the most informal old type of mortgage, in which deposit of deeds was used without anything more being done. Therefore, Nigel Neep's bank will be wise to insist that his mortgage is, at least, made by a written agreement which satisfies s. 2. If a mortgage is ineffective due to s. 2, the loan will become immediately repayable because the security has failed. However, old informal mortgages created before the 1989 Act are not affected by s. 2 and thus a few may still exist.

The one exception to this rule will be cases in which one of the parties (probably the intended mortgagee) can rely on the doctrine of constructive trust, as happened in *Kinane v Mackie-Conteh* [2005] EWCA Civ 45. However, it would appear that commercial lenders, like banks and building societies, will not normally be able to rely on this doctrine because of the need for belief in the existence of a mortgage relationship, whereas such organisations will be clear as to the need for a written contract compliant with s. 2.

22.5.3 Equitable charge

An equitable charge arises when a chargee 'appropriates' specific property to the repayment of a sum of money in such circumstances that a legal charge does not arise. This type of arrangement is relatively rare in relation to land and would normally require a written document. For an old example see *Matthews v Goodday* (1861) 31 LJ Ch 282.

22.5.4 Equitable mortgage of an equitable interest

One obviously cannot grant a legal mortgage of an interest that is recognised only in equity. This rule dates from the days of separate courts with separate jurisdictions. Common law did not recognise the equitable interests developed in the Chancellor's courts, and accordingly would not enforce any dealings with them. Therefore, any mortgage of an equitable interest in land had to be equitable in character. The method of creating such mortgages was not changed in 1925 and thus they continue to be made in the old-fashioned way by a transfer of the entire interest to the mortgagee, subject to an agreement that it will be returned to the mortgagor on repayment of the loan. The transfer must be made, at the least, by writing, in order to pass the equitable interest to the mortgagee under LPA 1925, s. 53(1)(c). (Note that this is a transfer and not an agreement to transfer.) Normally thereafter, the mortgagee should give notice of the transfer to the trustees of the trust under which the interest exists—usually the legal owners (see 23.2). Figure 22.2 sets out the required formalities.

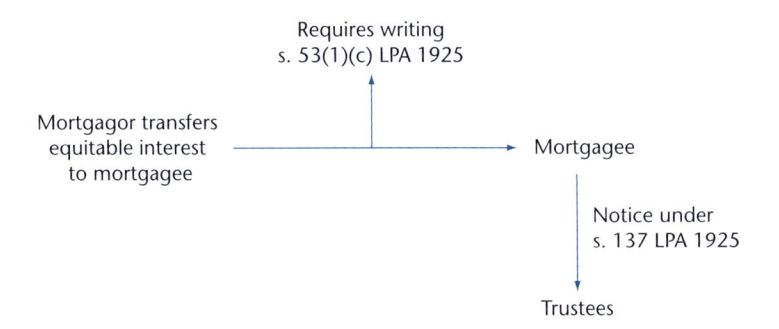

Figure 22.2 Equitable mortgage of equitable interest

22.6 Rights of the mortgagor

Having examined the methods of creating a mortgage we must turn our attention to the position of the parties after a mortgage has been made. This paragraph covers the rights of the mortgagor (the borrower).

22.6.1 Right to redeem

The primary right enjoyed by the mortgagor is the right to redeem the mortgage on repayment of the loan and payment of any interest provided for by the charge. This brings the mortgage to an end.

22.6.1.1 Right to redeem at law

At law the right to redeem is a matter of contract: the mortgagor can redeem on the date or dates and in the manner provided for in the mortgage. Thus, should the agreement provide that the mortgage should be redeemed on a particular date, the mortgagor has, at law, a right to redeem on that date only. The legal rules do not allow the mortgagor to insist on redeeming the mortgage either before or after the contractual date: see the discussion in *Kreglinger v New Patagonia Meat & Cold Storage Co. Ltd* [1914] AC 25 at p. 35. At common law, if the mortgagor did not pay on the contractual date, the land was forfeited to the mortgagee and the mortgagor could still be sued in contract for the repayment of the debt. Accordingly, the legal right to redeem was, and is, very limited.

22.6.1.2 Right to redeem in equity

Fortunately, equity took a very different view of the situation, particularly as there were examples of mortgagees hiding, so that it became impossible for the mortgagor to repay on the contractual date. Equity took the view that, as long as the advance and any interest were paid, the mortgagee should not be able to object to redemption because the purpose of the agreement was merely to provide the mortgagee with security for the loan. Originally equity intervened only in cases of fraud by the mortgagee but soon came to recognise a general right to redeem in all cases (*Salt v Marquess of Northampton* [1892] AC 1). Thus, equity allows the mortgagor to redeem even after the date fixed by the mortgage agreement for repayment has passed. Of course, since this right is enforceable in equity only, it is subject to the general principle that equitable remedies are discretionary in nature and all the equitable maxims (particularly the 'clean hands' doctrine) will apply. Furthermore, in deciding whether redemption is possible, equity will look at the substance of the agreement, not its form. Accordingly, a mortgage which is drafted to look like an outright transfer of the property, rather than the creation of an interest by way of security, will still be subject to the equitable right to redeem, if the facts are such as to indicate that only a grant by way of security was intended (*Darby v Read* (1675) Rep t Finch 226).

22.6.1.3 Instalment mortgages

So far, it has been assumed that the full sum owed becomes payable on one date. The modern mortgage is more likely to provide for repayment by instalments, spread over a number of years. However, usually it will contain a provision that if the mortgagor defaults on the payment of one instalment the whole sum will become due. At law, the mortgagor will then have to redeem the mortgage or lose the property for ever, but equity will moderate the rigour of this in the way already described.

22.6.2 The equity of redemption

Obviously, a legal mortgagor retains his or her legal estate or interest in the land but subject to the rights of the mortgagee (see 22.7). In equity, meanwhile, the mortgagor is described as owning the '**equity of redemption**'. This must be distinguished from the equitable right to redeem. The equity of redemption is the mortgagor's equitable interest in the property and it consists of the sum total of the mortgagor's rights in relation to the land (including the right to redeem). The equity of redemption is therefore an interest in land (*Pawlett v Attorney-General* (1667) Hardres 465 at p. 469) and can be dealt with like any other equitable interest. Table 22.2 summarises the rights of the mortgagor (the borrower).

Table 22.2 What does a mortgagor own?

At Law	Legal estate or interest
In Equity	Equity of redemption

22.6.3 No clogs on the equity of redemption

Equity is so protective of the mortgagor's equity of redemption that it will not tolerate any arrangement which either prevents or deters the mortgagor from exercising the right to redeem. Similarly, any burdens imposed by the mortgage on the mortgaged property that may continue after the date of redemption are generally regarded with disfavour. They derogate from the principle that the mortgage should provide security only, and that on redemption the mortgagor should recover the property without further fetter. In restricting the contents of mortgage agreements in this way, equity recognised the fact that the mortgagor is often unable to dictate the terms of the mortgage because of the need to obtain the mortgage advance. It was therefore appropriate that the mortgagor should be afforded some protection by the courts. However, in some cases this approach has been taken to undesirable lengths.

Equity's approach is summed up in the rule that there must be no **clogs** (restrictions) **on the equity of redemption**. This is applied to a number of situations, some of which are considered now.

22.6.3.1 Prevention of redemption

Any provision in a mortgage which would operate to prevent the mortgagor from redeeming will be disregarded by equity and will be void. Thus a mortgagee cannot include in a mortgage a term that, should a specified event occur, the land would become the mortgagee's absolutely (*Toomes v Conset* (1745) 3 Atk 261).

This rule has, however, been taken to extremes, so that it is not possible to give a mortgagee a valid option to purchase the estate as part of the mortgage transaction. The option, if exercised, would extinguish the mortgagor's right to redeem and is accordingly void. The original rationale for this rule was sound. As Lord Henley put it in *Vernon v Bethall* (1762) 2 Eden 110 at p. 113:

> there is great reason and justice in this rule, for necessitous men are not, truly speaking, free men, but to answer a present exigency will submit to any terms that the crafty may impose upon them.

However, in *Samuel v Jarrah Timber & Wood Paving Co. Ltd* [1904] AC 323 the House of Lords applied (albeit reluctantly) the same rule to an 'arm's-length' commercial transaction. Lord Linley referred to the old axiom, 'Once a mortgage always a mortgage' (meaning that the agreement could not covertly become something greater), and said (at p. 329):

> The doctrine . . . means that no contract between a mortgagor and a mortgagee made at the time of the mortgage and as part of the mortgage transaction, or, in other words, as one of the terms of the loan, can be valid if it prevents the mortgagor from getting back his property on paying off what is due on his security. Any bargain which has that effect is invalid, and is inconsistent with the transaction being a mortgage.

It was suggested that granting the option in a separate document might avoid the rule, but it seems that even this may not avail the mortgagee, unless the option is granted some time after the mortgage (this gives the mortgagor a chance to refuse an unfair agreement once the loan is paid): *Lewis v Frank Love Ltd* [1961] 1 WLR 261; but see also *Reeve v Lisle* [1902] AC 461, in which an option was upheld. The issue of whether a transaction made later could be acceptable was further considered by the Court of Appeal in *Jones v Morgan* [2002] 1 EGLR 125 and, in the particular circumstances of that case, a later transaction was nonetheless held to be a clog on the equity of redemption and thus invalid, probably because a transaction carried out three years after the initial creation of the mortgage amounted to a complete reconstruction of the debt arrangements, rather than being a separate transaction. The judgment of Chadwick LJ usefully provides a short history of the doctrine (see paras. 50–73). However, the case is perhaps chiefly notable for the acerbic comment of Lord Phillips MR that '. . . the doctrine of a clog on the equity of redemption is, so it seems to me, an appendix to our law which no longer serves a useful purpose and would be better excised' (para. 86).

22.6.3.2 Postponement of redemption

Any provision in a mortgage that attempts to postpone redemption to such an extent that the right to redeem becomes illusory may also be rendered void. The equitable right to redeem arises only once the contractual, legal date for redemption has passed. There is no general right in equity to redeem earlier (but see the Consumer Credit Act 1974, ss. 94 and 173, for cases of small mortgages which may be redeemed at any time and, if the mortgagor is a consumer, the Unfair Terms in Consumer Contracts Regulations may also assist). Accordingly, one way by which a mortgagee may try to obtain an irredeemable mortgage is to postpone the contractual date for redemption.

1. Freehold estates

In *Knightsbridge Estates Trust Ltd v Byrne* [1939] Ch 441 a company had mortgaged its freehold property to an insurance company on terms that the mortgage would be repaid over 40 years. Later the mortgagor wished to redeem the mortgage before that period had expired, but the mortgagee objected. The court held that the term postponing redemption for 40 years was valid. The agreement was a commercial one made by businessmen and the mortgaged property was a fee simple. Due to the great duration of the freehold estate (effectively it is perpetual), the company would recover an estate of equivalent worth when it did redeem the mortgage. The effect of this case is not, however, to make any postponement for a similar period valid. Were a domestic mortgage to be made irredeemable for such a long period, the court might still regard the bargain as oppressive and unconscionable. In fact most modern domestic mortgages expressly allow for early redemption, usually on payment of an extra sum.

2. Leasehold estates

Postponement of the date of redemption is rather more serious when one is concerned with a mortgage of leasehold property, because a lease is inherently of finite duration and therefore a wasting asset. In *Fairclough v Swan Brewery Co. Ltd* [1912] AC 565 the residue of a leasehold term of 20 years was mortgaged; the agreement being that the mortgage was not to be redeemed until a date six weeks before the lease was to end. Three years later the mortgagor sought to redeem early and the court upheld his right to do so. In this case, had the postponement been valid, the mortgagor would, on redemption, have recovered an estate which was nearly valueless and very different in character from the property mortgaged. Accordingly, in the case of leases, postponement of the contractual date for redemption is likely to be rather more objectionable, even where the mortgage is a commercial bargain made between businessmen.

22.6.3.3 Collateral advantages for the mortgagee

The final type of clog on the equity of redemption that is commonly encountered is the creation of further advantages for the mortgagee, which are collateral to the mortgage. These are common in certain types of commercial mortgage. Thus, breweries will often advance money on mortgage to the licensees of public houses, provided that the mortgagors agree that they will buy their beer from the mortgagee-brewery. Similar arrangements are made between petrol companies and garage owners.

Such collateral advantages (now, subject to the rules that they are not unconscionable or contrary to competition law), are valid while the mortgage continues (*Biggs v Hoddinott* [1898] 2 Ch 307). They will not, however, normally endure once the mortgage is redeemed (even if the mortgagor has accepted a term that they shall continue beyond redemption), for otherwise the mortgagor would recover an estate encumbered in a way the estate mortgaged was not (see also *Bradley v Carritt* [1903] AC 253). An advantage will not, however, invariably end once the mortgage is redeemed. In *Kreglinger v New Patagonia Meat & Cold Storage Co. Ltd* [1914] AC 25 a meat company mortgaged its property to a wool-broker (the mortgage was in the form of a floating charge, a special type of mortgage granted by companies). It was a term of the mortgage that the mortgagor would, for five years, offer its sheepskins (a by-product of its meat business) to the mortgagees for purchase. The mortgage was redeemed after two years but the House of Lords held that the mortgagor was obliged to continue to offer the mortgagees first refusal on the skins for the full five-year period. The option was regarded as being reasonable in its terms (it was for a short period and at the best price) and was to be regarded as a separate agreement not really forming part of the mortgage. It was also, of course, a commercial transaction which had been agreed to by business people with 'open eyes'. It seems unlikely that such a collateral advantage could validly continue after redemption of a domestic mortgage.

Collateral advantages may also be held to be invalid, even during the continuance of the mortgage, if they are unconscionable or oppressive. Thus, in *Cityland & Property (Holdings) Ltd v Dabrah* [1968] Ch 166 an agreement which imposed an extremely high premium, rather than requiring payment of interest, was rewritten by the court. In this case the mortgagor was allowed to redeem on repayment of the loan together with interest at a rate approved by the court. It is not, however, sufficient to show that the terms are unreasonable (certainly in a commercial bargain), even if they are extremely advantageous to the mortgagee. The agreement must be 'unfair and unconscionable' and imposed by the mortgagee 'in a morally reprehensible manner, that is to say, in a way which affects his conscience' (see *Multiservice Bookbinding Ltd v Marden* [1979] Ch 84 at p. 110 per Browne-Wilkinson J).

The issue is not, however, confined to commercial mortgages and charges. The extension of the range of services provided by lenders has led to concerns that mortgagors may be forced into agreements which require them to use a prospective mortgagee to provide, for example, removal vans or estate agency services. The mortgagor might be told that unless other such items were taken from the mortgagee the rate of interest on the mortgage would be higher. This problem was addressed by the Courts and Legal Services Act 1990, ss. 104–7 ('tying-in provisions'). These provisions have never been brought into force, but could be were 'tying-in' to become common.

Another approach some mortgagees have adopted is to apply unduly heavy rates of interest, if the mortgagor is ever late in making payment. The Office of Fair Trading has issued guidance to banks and building societies as to the rates of interest that properly can be charged to those who are 'locked into' mortgages (usually by means of high charges made on early repayment of the mortgage). Institutions that lend on mortgage security are also regulated under the Financial Services and Markets Act 2000 and the Financial Services Act 2012.

22.6.4 Right to grant leases

Having already granted a lease or sublease (or being in a similar position in the case of a charge by way of legal mortgage), the mortgagor would be unable, on general principles, to grant further leases of the same property which could bind the mortgagor and mortgagee. Any further lease created would operate as a lease of the reversion, and would not give the tenant any right to possession of the land as against the mortgagee. However, this caused difficulty, particularly in the case of large estates, where the mortgagor remained in possession of the land and continued to manage it, needing to grant new leases to, for example, tenant farmers and estate workers. The mortgagor is therefore given a statutory power by LPA 1925, s. 99: where he or she is still in possession of the land the mortgagor may create both leases and contracts for leases which will be binding on the mortgagee. Section 99 sets out a number of detailed requirements for the form and content of such leases, but in practice most mortgages will exclude the mortgagor's statutory power of leasing altogether, unless the mortgage is security for a business loan designed to allow the acquisition of a property for the purpose of letting it ('buy to let'). This is because, in general, the mortgagee does not want the land to be burdened with a sitting tenant, for this will reduce its value if the mortgagee needs to realise the security (obviously different arrangements are made for the management of large estates and in commercial cases where the plan is to let the property).

The statutory power of leasing will almost certainly be excluded in any domestic mortgage, such as that of the Armstrongs at 1 Trant Way, though mortgagees do sometimes agree to waive this exclusion in the case of approved tenants. Interestingly, in *Citibank International plc v Kessler* (1999) EGCS 40 a mortgagor tried to argue that such an exclusion was contrary to Article 48 of the Treaty of Rome as inhibiting the free movement of workers. However, unsurprisingly this claim failed even in that instance, in which a German worker had returned to Germany and could not sell the house in question because it had structural defects that would prevent anyone else obtaining a mortgage on the property.

Should the right to grant leases be excluded, any lease granted will nonetheless bind the mortgagor and tenant (a lease by estoppel) but will be void as regards the mortgagee and successors (*Iron Trades Employers Insurance Association Ltd v Union Land & House Investors Ltd* [1937] Ch 313). In *Starling v Lloyds TSB Bank plc* [2000] Lloyd's Rep 8, a mortgagor tried to argue that, where permission to lease had been sought, the mortgagee should be under a duty to consider that request properly. However, this claim was dealt with robustly by the Court of Appeal, who struck out the cause of action because there was no suggestion in the papers that the mortgagee had acted dishonestly or due to any improper motive. The court regarded as impractical the argument that the bank should, on receiving such a request, indulge in a balancing exercise between the interests of the mortgagor and the bank's interests.

22.6.4.1 Surrenders

The mortgagor has power under LPA 1925, s. 100, to accept surrenders of leases as well. This may be done, however, only in order to replace the surrendered lease with a fresh lease and the new lease must be made within one month of the termination of the old.

22.6.5 Right to sue

In some cases the rights of the mortgagor to sue in relation to the land might be hampered by the fact that the mortgaged estate is subject to the rights of the mortgagee. Any such problems are remedied by LPA 1925, s. 98, which allows a mortgagor in possession, who has not been notified that the mortgagee intends to take possession, to sue in a number of situations in which there might otherwise be difficulties. Generally, therefore, the mortgagor is free to bring any necessary action in relation to the land.

22.7 Rights of the mortgagee

22.7.1 Rights to title deeds or charge certificate

22.7.1.1 Unregistered land

Under the pre-1926 type of mortgage the mortgagee (the lender) necessarily had a right to hold the title deeds to the property, since the grant of the mortgage conveyed the legal estate to the mortgagee. Under the modern system, however, the mortgagee at most has only a lease or sublease and it is not normal for a tenant to hold the landlord's deeds. It is nonetheless desirable for the mortgagee to take any deeds, since this will usually prevent the creation by the mortgagor of later interests in the same property without the knowledge of the mortgagee (see 23.1). Accordingly, ss. 85(1) and 86(1) specifically provide that a first mortgagee has the right to take the title deeds from the mortgagor. A mortgagee under a charge by way of legal mortgage is expressly given similar rights (s. 87(1)).

LPA 1925, s. 96(1), gives the mortgagor the right to inspect the deeds and make copies, as long as this is done at a reasonable time and any costs incurred by the mortgagee are paid.

The equitable mortgagee has a similar equitable right to the deeds but, since the most common form of equitable mortgage was that which involved deposit of the deeds, this was rarely a problem.

22.7.1.2 Registered land

In the case of registered land, a legal charge is created only when the charge is substantively registered. Section 27(2)(f) of the LRA 2002, provides that the grant of a legal charge is a disposition that is required to be completed by registration. On the application being made, the Registrar will enter the chargee in the register as the proprietor of the charge. Before the 2002 Act, such a registration would then have led the Registrar to issue a new certificate in relation to the charged estate: a Charge Certificate. This was held by the chargee (rather like holding the title deeds of unregistered land). Now, however, such certificates are no longer issued, though you may still encounter old ones. All that matters is the content of the register itself.

22.7.2 Right to possession of the land

Since a legal mortgagee has a lease or sublease (or is treated as having one), the mortgagee has a right to possession of the land from the moment that the mortgage is created (see *Four-Maids Ltd v Dudley Marshall (Properties) Ltd* [1957] Ch 317 at p. 320 and *National Westminster Bank plc v Skelton* [1993] 1 WLR 72). This right may well be restricted by a term in the mortgage deed that possession will not be taken while the mortgagor makes regular payments (see, e.g., *Birmingham Citizens Permanent Building Society v Caunt* [1962] Ch 883).

Usually, the taking of possession is only normal as a preliminary to the remedy of sale and is not otherwise generally exercised. However, in some situations, lenders have sought possession of a property in order to let it. This may cause problems for a mortgagor because the interest payable under the mortgage will continue to mount. In *Palk v Mortgage Services Funding plc* [1993] Ch 330, the Court of Appeal said that where sale was preferable in the mortgagor's interests a sale would be ordered instead (see further 22.8.1.1 for the court's power to order sale).

The taking of possession must, in any event, be exercised peaceably (e.g., one may not break into premises—see Criminal Law Act 1977, s. 6) and this may necessitate an application to the court. However, if peaceable re-entry is possible without resort to the court this is perfectly acceptable (see *Ropaigealach v Barclays Bank plc* [1999] 1 QB 263 but note that the case proceeded on the assumption that the bank had taken possession peacefully but without those facts ever being established). In practice it may be difficult or impossible to regain possession peacefully in the absence of an application to the court. However, where the power of sale has become exercisable, and the mortgagee can find a buyer who is willing to buy without vacant possession, that buyer may get a right to evict the mortgagor as a trespasser (see *Horsham Properties Group Ltd v Clark* [2009] 1 WLR 1255, discussed below at 22.8.1.5).

22.7.3 Insuring at the mortgagor's expense

Normally, the mortgagee will wish to ensure that the property is properly insured, since, should it be damaged, the value of the mortgagee's security will be diminished. Accordingly, most mortgages include express terms concerning the maintenance of insurance. If there is no express agreement, LPA 1925, s. 101(1)(ii), implies into every mortgage made by deed a term allowing the mortgagee to insure the property against loss or damage by fire. The premiums paid become a charge on the property in addition to the mortgage advance. The amount of the insurance and the mode of application of any sums arising from the policy are further regulated by LPA 1925, s. 108.

22.7.4 Right to lease

A mortgagee who has taken possession has always had a right to grant leases. These, however, would be subject to the rule that there must be no clog on the equity of redemption and so would not survive redemption by the mortgagor, were it not for the statutory power to lease under LPA 1925, s. 99(1), which gives rights similar to those of the mortgagor described earlier. Any lease created under the statutory power will also bind the mortgagor. Since possession by the mortgagee was normally only a preliminary to sale, such leases used to be rare but have occurred on occasion in recent years as often the rent that can be achieved gives a better return on the security of the property, when sale prices are low in an area.

22.7.5 Right to tack further advances

This right is relevant only when there is a dispute about priorities, and is considered in the section on priorities (23.6).

22.7.6 Right to consolidate mortgages

This right applies when one mortgagee holds two or more mortgages which were both made by the same mortgagor. This might occur if James Harding (5 Trant Way) had already granted a mortgage of, say, his business premises at 15 High Street, Mousehole to the Wensleydale Bank plc. The Bank would have the right to **consolidate** the two mortgages if, as is normal, this is expressly provided for in the mortgage (LPA 1925, s. 93).

The effect of the right is to allow the mortgagee to refuse to allow the mortgagor to redeem one of the mortgages without also redeeming the other. In the case of Mr Harding's mortgages, this right might prove important to the bank should the value of 15 High Street fall below the sums outstanding on the mortgage of that property. If Mr Harding chose to redeem the mortgage on 5 Trant Way, rather than the mortgage of his business premises, the mortgagee bank would be left with a mortgage for which the security is defective. By consolidating, the bank can insist that Mr Harding redeems *both* mortgages.

The right to consolidate is an equitable one, and is an unusual example of equity permitting a clog or fetter on the equity of redemption. It may be seen as the 'price' which equity exacts for allowing the mortgagor to redeem the mortgage when this is no longer possible at law. Accordingly, the mortgagee has this right only after the contractual date for redemption has passed, when the mortgagor is relying on the equitable right to redeem. If the mortgagor should in fact repay the debt on the contractual date, the mortgagee would not be able to require payment of the other debt as well.

The doctrine can affect subsequent purchasers if they buy land subject to the mortgage. Thus, if someone bought 5 Trant Way from Mr Harding subject to the mortgage and then sought to redeem it, he or she would find that the bank's right to consolidate still applied, and that the mortgage on 15 High Street would also have to be redeemed. Fortunately, it is extremely rare for estates to change hands without any mortgages first being discharged.

This is a relatively simple account of the doctrine of consolidation, illustrated with a situation in which both mortgages are granted to the same mortgagee. This is not in fact an essential requirement: provided the mortgages are granted by the same person it does not matter that they are granted to different people. The rules governing the various different situations which may arise as a result of this are complicated, and beyond the scope of this book, but if you are interested you will find them fully discussed in Megarry and Wade, paras. 24-054–24-068, which also provides some useful diagrams.

22.8 Mortgagee's remedies

The whole purpose of a mortgage is to provide security that the mortgagee can realise if the mortgagor fails to repay the loan. Obviously, the mortgagee, like any lender, can always sue in contract for the repayment of the loan, but this may be a long process, in which enforcing payment, even once judgment is obtained, can be difficult.

The advantage of the mortgage is that it allows the mortgagee to use the charged land to repay the loan, sometimes without the need for any court proceedings at all. At one time the special remedies available to a mortgagee were of such importance that it was rare in the extreme for mortgagees to bother to sue for repayment as a simple matter of contract. However, fluctuations in property prices have sometimes made it more common, in appropriate cases, for mortgagees to seek a money judgment (since in cases of 'negative equity' the price realised by enforcement against the property will not repay the loan in full) or to use this remedy in addition to the special remedies available to a mortgagee. Despite this change, the additional protection provided by the security of a charge on property still makes mortgagees' remedies of crucial importance.

22.8.1 Remedies available to a legal mortgagee

22.8.1.1 Foreclosure

Foreclosure was the traditional remedy by which a mortgage was enforced. However, today it is rarely used.

Although equity would allow a mortgagor to redeem after the contractual date, there would come a time in many cases when it was obvious that the mortgagor would never have the means to repay the debt. Foreclosure proceedings in equity were therefore the means whereby 'the court simply removed the stop it had itself put on' (*Carter v Wake* (1877) 4 ChD 605 at p. 606) and enabled the mortgagee to realise the security. For this reason, foreclosure cannot be sought before the contractual obligation to repay has been broken (*Williams v Morgan* [1906] 1 Ch 804). A court order is required for foreclosure (*Re Farnol Eades Irvine & Co. Ltd* [1915] 1 Ch 22) and its effect is to vest the mortgagor's estate in the mortgagee in full settlement of the debt (LPA 1925, ss. 88(2) and 89(2)).

Should the property be worth more than the debt, the mortgagee is not liable to pay the balance in value to the mortgagor. Since this is normally the case, foreclosure is a remedy which is often unfair to the mortgagor (and to any subsequent mortgagees, who lose their security). Accordingly, on hearing an application for foreclosure, the court will give the mortgagor a period in which to redeem the mortgage (and will allow later mortgagees the chance to protect their security by redeeming the prior mortgage).

Generally, the mortgagor is in financial difficulties and is unable to repay the loan and redeem. Accordingly, the mortgagor has the right to ask for an order for sale instead of foreclosure (LPA 1925, s. 91(2)). This is an advantage because on sale the mortgagee may keep only the portion of the proceeds that represents the debt, plus interest and costs. The balance must be returned to the mortgagor, or paid to anyone else entitled, such as later mortgagees. Sale may also be appropriate in any case in which it produces a better financial result for the mortgagor (see *Palk v Mortgage Services Funding plc* [1993] Ch 330).

Another reason foreclosure is an unpopular remedy (but this time from the mortgagee's point of view) is that, even once a foreclosure order has been made, the court may reopen the whole situation and allow the mortgagor to redeem the property after all. *Campbell v Holyland* (1877) 7 ChD 166 (in which an order for foreclosure was reopened three months after it had been made absolute) sets out the various matters which the court will take into account in considering such an application. These include: the speed of the mortgagor's application; the reasons for failing to redeem before foreclosure; and the nature of the property.

As might be expected, the court would be less willing to reopen foreclosure if the mortgagee had already sold the property to someone else, although even in that case this is, in theory, still possible.

22.8.1.2 Possession and sale

The basic rules relating to possession have been given already. Generally, this right of the mortgagee is only used as a remedy and normally is a prelude to sale. The mortgagee might, however, take possession in order to repay the debt from the income produced by the premises (e.g., if the premises are let to a tenant). However, in such cases it is more common to appoint a receiver instead so that the mortgagee is not personally liable for any mismanagement of the land. The chief purpose of taking possession is therefore usually to ensure that on a subsequent sale the mortgagee will be in a position to give vacant possession to the purchaser. The power for the mortgagee to sell the land is implied into every mortgage made by deed by LPA 1925, s. 101(1)(i). This power arises when the mortgage money has become due (for instance, on the contractual date of redemption) but does not become exercisable until one of the conditions prescribed by LPA 1925, s. 103, has been met. These are that:

(a) a notice requiring payment has been served on the mortgagor and the default has continued for three months thereafter; or

(b) some of the interest payable is at least two months in arrears; or

(c) there has been breach of a covenant in the mortgage deed (other than that relating to the payment of money) or of some provision of the LPA 1925.

A purchaser must ensure that there is power to sell under the mortgage (that is, that it was made by deed and that the power has arisen), but does not have to check that one of the conditions for exercise of the power ((a) to (c) above) has been met (see *Bailey v Barnes* [1894] 1 Ch 25 at p. 35).

Sale has the advantage over foreclosure that it is generally not necessary to apply for a court order. The sale may be negotiated in any suitable manner (e.g., by auction or by private contract) and may be made subject to such conditions as the mortgagee sees fit (s. 101(1)(i)). Note that the mortgagee may be liable to the mortgagor, and others, for any loss caused through negligence in conducting the sale.

However, an order for possession (as a prelude to sale) may be delayed for a time if the court believes that the mortgagor may obtain a higher price if the mortgagor makes the sale. (See *Target Home Loans Ltd v Clothier* [1994] 1 All ER 439.) This possibility was also explored in *Palk v Mortgage Services Funding plc* [1993] Ch 330 and in *Barrett v Halifax Building Society* (1995) 28 HLR 634, and in these cases the courts seemed to take a generous approach to the use of the power under LPA 1925, s. 91(2) to direct sale of the property 'on such terms as it thinks fit', in order (for example) in the *Barrett* case to enable the mortgagor to carry out the sale himself. The reasoning was that the mortgagor is likely to get a better price for the property than the mortgagee (in practice this is almost inevitably the case). However, this approach was criticised in *Cheltenham & Gloucester plc v Krausz* [1997] 1 All ER 21, in which the Court of Appeal said that these powers and those under the Administration of Justice Act 1970, s. 36 (see 22.8.1.5) should not be used unless it is clear that the result will be that the mortgage debt will be repaid in full. Where the mortgagor is still faced with a debt greater than the value of the property (a 'negative equity' in common parlance) the mortgagee will still be entitled to immediate possession and sale. (See also Kenny, 'No Postponement of the Evil Day' [1998] Conv 223.)

When considering the possibility of sale, you should also bear in mind that where the land in question is held under a trust of land (which will be the case in all co-owned property which is not the subject of a SLA 1925 settlement) the mortgagee can also apply for sale under TOLATA 1996, s. 14, because the mortgagee has an interest in the property subject to the trust. For an example of this (in which sale was ordered despite the existence of a pre-existing overriding interest) see *Bank of Baroda v Dhillon* [1998] 1 FLR 524. However, in the cases since TOLATA 1996 the courts have expressed differing views as to the weight to be given to the interests of the mortgagee when carrying out the balancing exercise under ss. 14 and 15. See the cases discussed at 14.8.5.1.

It is worth noting when reading these cases that the mortgagee's remedies are cumulative and that, as a last resort, the mortgagee can also sue for repayment of the debt and (if necessary) make the mortgagor bankrupt. Due to the interaction of the various different legal principles and rules, such as s. 36 of the Administration of Justice Act 1970, the effects of TOLATA 1996, the possibility of undue influence (on which see 23.7.2) and the law of insolvency (which allows the trustee in bankruptcy to obtain a charge over the bankrupt's home—see Insolvency Act 1986, s. 313 and Enterprise Act 2002, s. 261), the law in this area is complex. A wise mortgagee takes great care before deciding on the exact approach to the issue in any case that is not entirely straightforward and, most certainly, in any case in which the sale of the property is unlikely to repay all the sums due under the mortgage.

22.8.1.3 Effect of sale

On sale, the mortgagee will convey to the purchaser a good estate or interest (for example, the fee simple) free of the interests of the mortgagor and of any estates, interests, or rights to which the mortgage has priority, but subject to any estates or interests having priority to the mortgage (LPA 1925, s. 104(1)). Thus, if 1 Trant Way were subject to two mortgages:

(a) to the Double Gloucester Building Society; and

(b) to the Mousehole Bank plc,

then on a sale by the DGBS the purchaser would take a title free of the second mortgage to the MB plc, but on a sale by the MB plc the purchaser would take an estate subject to the first mortgage to the DGBS.

It is perhaps worth emphasising that on sale the purchaser obtains the full estate belonging to the mortgagor, not just the long lease or sublease which was granted to the mortgagee (LPA 1925, ss. 88(1) and 89(1)).

As the purchaser takes the estate free of the mortgage, he or she can obtain an order for possession against the mortgagor, if the mortgagor is still in occupation. This became important in *Horsham Properties Group Ltd v Clark* [2009] 1 WLR 1255. Here the mortgagees appointed a receiver, who sold the property relying on a clause in the mortgage document but without obtaining possession. The purchaser then sought possession against the mortgagor, claiming that the mortgagor's rights had been overridden by the sale. The mortgagor claimed that the sale, whether under s. 101 or the terms of the agreement, conflicted with its rights under Art. 1 of Protocol I of the European Convention on Human Rights and the Human Rights Act because there had been no court order and thus no due process of law. The High Court rejected this view, saying that, contractually, possession by the mortgagor is always at the mercy of the mortgagee, who has a right to possession due to the leasehold estate or equivalent rights granted to the mortgagee by the mortgage. The judge also took the view that the deprivation of possession after default was in the public interest and proportionate, resting as it did on 200 years of history. Accordingly, the mortgage and s. 101 were ECHR compliant. This case confirms the approach in *Ropaigealach v Barclays Bank plc* [2000] QB 271–2, in which (before the HRA) it was accepted that no order for sale is needed (in that case re-entry had, it seems, been effected peaceably without a court order).

Despite this authority (which would always allow sale without a court order), the Council of Mortgage Lenders has agreed that their members will always seek a court order for possession or sale in the case of a domestic mortgage. The Ministry of Justice has proposed that the law should be changed in order to require a court order before sale (whether an order for possession or for sale) in the case of all residential owner-occupier mortgages. This is perhaps desirable because the *Horsham* case illustrates how little protection a mortgagee currently has. However, legislating may prove difficult, as it will be necessary to define what constitutes a residential owner-occupier mortgage. For example, what if another member of the family is living in the property? On the proposed reforms see the Ministry of Justice Consultation paper: *Mortgages. Power of Sale and Residential Property*, CP 55/09. To date, there has been no legislation on this specific topic. However, in 2013 a pre-action protocol for possession claims was issued by the Ministry of Justice and this was updated in June 2015 (see www.justice.gov.uk/courts/procedure-rules/civil/protocol/prot_mha). This protocol requires that the borrower who is in default be given the opportunity to make a voluntary arrangement with the mortgagee before the case goes to court.

22.8.1.4 Disposition of proceeds of sale

The selling mortgagee becomes a trustee of the proceeds of sale of the property (LPA 1925, s. 105), and should apply the proceeds in the following order:

(a) in payment of any sums needed to discharge any encumbrance prior to the mortgage and to which the sale was not made subject;

(b) in payment of the costs, charges, and expenses properly incurred in arranging the sale;

(c) in discharge of the mortgage debt, including interest and other sums due; and

(d) any balance should be paid to the mortgagor or the other person 'entitled to the mortgage property'.

Thus, in the example given in 22.8.1.3, were the DGBS to sell 1 Trant Way, it would first pay the costs of sale (e.g., legal expenses), and then would pay its own mortgage debt, interest, and costs. Thereafter, the balance of the proceeds of sale should be paid to the MB plc, which at the time of sale was next entitled to the property (*British General Insurance Co. Ltd v Attorney-General* (1945) 12 LJNCCR 113). The MB plc will in turn become trustee, and after repaying itself, should (if anything remains) pass the balance of the proceeds of sale to the mortgagors.

Should the sale not realise sufficient funds to repay the mortgagee, it may still sue in contract for the balance of the debt (*Rudge v Richens* (1873) LR 8 CP 358). Since the property itself may well have been the mortgagor's only valuable asset, it may prove difficult to obtain satisfaction of any judgment but there have been cases in which mortgagors voluntarily 'handed back' their property to permit sale by the mortgagee but were then sued some years later for sums not recovered on sale. Examples of this are to be found in *Bristol and West v Bartlett* [2003] 1 WLR 284, *Scottish Equitable plc v Thompson* [2003] HLR 48, and *West Bromwich Building Society v Wilkinson* [2005] 1 WLR 2303, which establish that any such action is subject to a 12-year limitation period. See also the article by Griffiths at [2005] Conv 469 on the complications in such actions.

22.8.1.5 Protection for the mortgagor

There are circumstances in which it would be unfair for the mortgagee to be allowed to sell the property. Thus, if the mortgage interest is only a few months in arrears and the mortgagor can show that it will be possible to repay the debts very shortly it would be undesirable to allow the mortgagee to insist on sale. Accordingly, the following means of protection is provided for the mortgagor.

As you have seen, the first step towards sale is usually for the mortgagee to obtain possession. The mortgagee may not do this by means of any force (e.g., by breaking a window) since this would constitute a criminal offence (Criminal Law Act 1977, ss. 5 and 6). Normally, therefore, an application to the court for possession will have to be made. This in itself will give the mortgagor extra time to pay and the court has inherent jurisdiction to postpone possession, although this power will be exercised sparingly (see *Cheltenham & Gloucester plc v Krausz* [1997] 1 All ER 21).

If the land is or includes a dwelling-house, further protection is given to the mortgagor by the Administration of Justice Act 1970, s. 36. Under this provision the court may, on hearing an application for possession of a dwelling, adjourn the proceedings, stay or suspend judgment, or postpone the date for delivery of possession, if it appears that 'the mortgagor is likely to be able within a reasonable period to pay any sums due under the mortgage'. This permits the court to give the mortgagor a 'second chance' to pay but will not be exercised where the mortgagor cannot make payments which will clear the debt within a reasonable time (while continuing to pay current instalments: see *First National Bank plc v Syed* [1991] 2 All ER 250).

As originally drafted, these provisions proved unsatisfactory when dealing with instalment mortgages, in which it is normal to provide that should one instalment be unpaid the whole sum becomes due. If the mortgagor has to pay 'any sums due' in such a case this would include the whole advance and few mortgagors could comply with this requirement (see *Birmingham Citizens Permanent Building Society v Caunt* [1962] Ch 883). Accordingly, an amendment was introduced by the Administration of Justice Act 1973, s. 8, and now in the case of instalment mortgages the 'sums due' are only those payments which are in arrears and a clause requiring repayment of the whole loan can be disregarded by the court when exercising its discretion under s. 36 of the 1970 Act. The 1973 Act also extends the powers of the court to foreclosure actions even where possession is not also sought (s. 8(3)). However, if peaceable re-entry can be effected without the need for an order for possession (if, for example, a dwelling is standing empty), s. 36 does not come into play: *Ropaigealach v Barclays Bank plc* [1999] 1 QB 263. Nor will s. 36 help if sale takes place while the mortgagor remains in occupation. In such a case the mortgagor's rights are overridden and the purchaser can obtain an order for possession: *Horsham Properties Group Ltd v Clark* [2009] 1 WLR (this was a commercial mortgage but the principle remains the same).

The court's powers under s. 36 of the Administration of Justice Act 1970, are also not available if the mortgagor has voluntarily given up possession but later realises that it would be in his or her best interests to delay sale. This is illustrated by *Barclays Bank plc v Alcorn* [2002] All ER (D) 146, in which the court said that in such a case it had no jurisdiction to exercise its discretion under s. 36(2). The case was also one in which, even had the court had powers under s. 36(2), it would not, on the facts, have exercised those powers in favour of the mortgagor because the mortgagor had failed to establish that she would be likely to pay the debts within a reasonable time.

The question of what is a 'reasonable period' to allow the mortgagor is a matter which is determined in the light of the circumstances of each case (see *National and Provincial Building Society v Lloyd* [1996] 1 All ER 630). In the case of a domestic instalment mortgage, the Court of Appeal indicated in *Cheltenham and Gloucester Building Society v Norgan* [1996] 1 WLR 343 that it would, in assessing what was a reasonable period, be appropriate for a court to take as its starting point the whole of the outstanding term of the mortgage. Indeed, that is an arrangement which had often been proposed voluntarily by mortgagees, where arrears were not too great.

Further regulation of consumer mortgages is now also provided by the 'Mortgage Conditions of Business' system, which was created under the Financial Services and Markets Act 2000.

At one time it was thought that the mortgagee owed no duty to the mortgagor when exercising the power of sale (other than the duty not to act fraudulently). However, it is now clear that the courts do consider in such cases that the mortgagee is under a duty to 'obtain a proper price'. This is a duty that arises in equity rather than in contract but is analogous to a duty of care in negligence (see *Raja v Lloyds TSB Bank plc* (2001) Lloyd's Rep Bank 113). For this reason, a mortgagee may elect to appoint a receiver rather than sell itself because then the duty of care will fall on the receiver, provided that the appointment itself is not unreasonable. (See 22.10 for more on the duties of receivers and mortgagees.)

22.8.1.6 Protection for tenants of the mortgagor

In the past, an order for possession granted against a mortgagor could produce a real problem for a tenant of the mortgagor, if the lease had been granted in breach of the terms of the mortgage. In such a case, the mortgagor's tenant could be obliged to leave the property immediately and without prior notice of the risks. Losing any rights to the property without any warning was obviously of grave concern to the tenant, who could be rendered homeless 'at a minute's notice'. Limited reforms were made by the Mortgage Repossessions (Protection of Tenants, etc) Act 2010. The new rights apply only to leases of a property which is or includes a dwelling-house. The Act requires service of a notice, in every case, before the mortgagee or chargee seeks to enforce an order for possession of such premises, whether or not there is a tenancy. This prevents the lender arguing that no notice was served because it did not know of the tenancy. The tenant may then apply to the court, which may postpone execution of the possession order for a period not exceeding two months. This is hardly generous but will allow a tenant unauthorised by the mortgagee a little time to find alternative accommodation.

22.8.1.7 Power to appoint a receiver

A receiver is a person who is appointed to take charge of the mortgaged land and either manage it (in order to produce an income to repay the debt) or sell it. Receivers are not commonly appointed in respect of mortgages of domestic property but are very frequently used in commercial mortgages.

The power to appoint a receiver may be granted expressly by the mortgage but in addition, provided the mortgage is created by deed, the right to appoint will be implied by LPA 1925, s. 101(1)(iii). The power arises and becomes exercisable in exactly the same way as the statutory power of sale.

The receiver is appointed by a written document executed by the mortgagee (LPA 1925, s. 109). The receiver appointed under the power in LPA 1925, s. 101, becomes an agent of the mortgagor (and not of the mortgagee who appointed him) and thus the mortgagee will not be liable for any negligence of the receiver (but see 22.10). Where a receiver obtains income from the land it should be applied in the following order:

(a) in payment of any outgoings in respect of the land (e.g., rates, and instalments on mortgages which have priority to that under which he was appointed);

(b) in payment of insurance premiums in respect of the land and the receiver's own commission (fees);

(c) in payment of interest on the loan;

(d) in payment of capital, if the mortgagee agrees; and

(e) payment of any balance should be made to the mortgagor (or other person entitled to income).

22.8.2 Problems regarding remedies when the mortgage is equitable

In describing the remedies available to the mortgagee, thus far you have seen the position of the legal mortgagee. It is, however, important to note that in a number of ways an equitable mortgagee may not be in such a strong position. In several instances an equitable mortgagee may, in the end, obtain the same remedy as a legal mortgagee, but will often do this only after the trouble and expense of obtaining a court order, whereas the legal mortgagee may often make use of such remedies without applying to the court. It must also be remembered that, in any event, remedies given by the court in protection of an equitable mortgagee will always be discretionary in character because of the basic nature of the equitable jurisdiction. The position is as follows.

22.8.2.1 Foreclosure

This causes little difficulty since it requires a court order in any event and being an equitable remedy applies to equitable mortgages just as it does to legal ones.

22.8.2.2 Possession

There appears to be no reason why an equitable mortgagee should not be regarded as having a right to possession in equity. It has, however, been said that the equitable mortgagee has no such right (see *Barclays Bank Ltd v Bird* [1954] Ch 274 at p. 280). By contrast, other authorities suggest that an equitable mortgagee may be so entitled (see *Ex parte Bignold* (1834) 4 Deac & Ch 259 and the article by Wade (1955) 71 LQR 204 and the decisions discussed in it). The weight of academic opinion certainly seems to be that an equitable mortgagee does have the right to possession (see Megarry and Wade, paras. 24-046–24-047).

It should be noted that the issue under discussion here is whether an equitable mortgagee has the right to take possession without a court order, for it is certainly possible for this to be done on an order from the court (*Barclays Bank Ltd v Bird*). These days, few mortgagees would risk taking possession without a court order, even when they are entitled to do so and so the whole question, although interesting, does seem largely a theoretical one.

Finally, it seems to be the case that a chargee under an equitable charge will have no right to possession, since the chargee cannot be regarded as having a contract for a lease or sublease, as can other equitable mortgagees (*Garfitt v Allen* (1887) 37 ChD 48). However, even this might be questioned if the equitable charge is regarded as a contract to create a charge by deed by way of legal mortgage, under which the chargee certainly does have a claim to possession.

22.8.2.3 Sale

The statutory power of sale under LPA 1925, s. 101(1)(i), applies only to mortgages made by deed, and therefore an equitable mortgagee will have no automatic power of sale unless such a deed exists. In consequence, an equitable mortgagee normally required execution by the mortgagor of a memorandum under seal evidencing the transaction, which would be sufficient to satisfy the statutory requirements. Today it is more likely that such a mortgage will be made by deed (at which point one might as well opt for a legal charge).

Even if the mortgagee has obtained such a deed there may be problems, since it has been held that an equitable mortgagee is not able to convey the legal estate because he or she has only an equitable interest in the property (*Re Hodson and Howes's Contract* (1887) 35 ChD 668). Although this view may be supported by the principle that one cannot give more than one has, the same argument might appear to apply to the legal mortgagee, who has only a lease but is enabled by statute to convey the full estate (LPA 1925, ss. 88(1) and 89(1)). It is difficult to see why the equitable mortgagee, selling in exercise of the statutory power, cannot rely on these provisions in the same way, and in *Re White Rose Cottage* [1965] Ch 940 Lord Denning MR expressed the view that there was no reason why an equitable mortgagee should not be able to convey the legal estate (at p. 951).

In order to avoid any difficulties, it has become usual to include in the deed a declaration of trust or grant of a power of attorney. Either will confer a separate power of sale.

However, these issues were considered further in *Swift 1st Ltd v Colin* [2012] Ch 206. In this case a charge of a registered estate was made by deed by way of legal mortgage in favour of the claimant but the charge was not registered. It was, however, entered in the register as an equitable charge. There were two subsequent charges. Later, the claimant exercised the power of sale under s. 101 but the Land Registry declined to register the purchasers as proprietors because the claimant's charge was not registered. The court held that the claimant did have the power of sale under ss. 101 and 104, and sale extinguished the subsequent charges by virtue of s. 88. The court held that the lack of registration made no difference in the case of a charge by deed by way of legal mortgage. Furthermore, the court was of the view that, even had the charge only been equitable due to lack of registration, the power to sell and convey the legal estate would still be available.

In the case of an equitable mortgage created without the formality of a deed the mortgagee may still apply to the court for an order for sale under LPA 1925, s. 91(2).

22.8.2.4 Appointing a receiver

The statutory power to appoint a receiver under LPA 1925, s. 101(1)(iii), applies only to equitable mortgages which are made by deed. However, any equitable mortgagee may apply to the court for the appointment of a receiver (Senior Courts Act 1981, s. 37).

22.8.3 Disadvantages of equitable mortgages

It can be seen that a mortgagee who accepts an equitable mortgage not made by deed may find the remedies available less satisfactory than those of a legal mortgagee. To some extent, although not entirely, these disadvantages may be overcome by the use of a deed.

Given the need for a deed to enable the equitable mortgagee to take advantage of the statutory remedies, a lender may regard it as being altogether easier to create a charge by way of legal mortgage (using a deed), and thereby avoid all the problems. In the case of the planned mortgage by deposit of deeds by Mr Neep of 14 Trant Way, his bank manager may well feel, on consideration, that, following the decision in *United Bank of Kuwait plc v Sahib* [1997] Ch 107, the best course as far as the bank is concerned will be to insist on taking a legal charge, rather than adopting a more informal method of creating a mortgage: writing will be necessary to create an equitable mortgage and very little more effort is required to produce a deed. The bank is most unlikely to be able to rely on the doctrine of constructive trust (see *Kinane v Mackie-Conteh* [2005] EWCA Civ 45) because it will be aware of the requirements of s. 2 of the Law of Property

(Miscellaneous Provisions) Act 1989, and thus will know that it is essential to make the mortgage in the prescribed manner. However, the grant of a legal charge would trigger a requirement to register the fee simple (LRA 2002, s. 4(1)(g)). Accordingly, Mr Neep may be able to persuade the bank to accept an equitable mortgage made by means of a written contract.

22.9 Right of certain third parties to redeem

The mortgagor and the mortgagee are not the only people who may have rights in respect of a mortgage, for others may be entitled to exercise the right to redeem. This arises because any person who has a right in the equity of redemption is also allowed to redeem (of course by repaying the sums secured by the mortgage) (*Peace v Morris* (1869) LR 5 Ch App 227). Thus, if Henry Newton manages to establish that he has an interest in 12 Trant Way, he will be entitled to redeem any mortgage of the property should he choose to do so. A spouse who has a right to occupy the matrimonial home has also been held to have a sufficient interest in the equity to allow him to redeem under this rule (*Hastings & Thanet Building Society v Goddard* [1970] 1 WLR 1544). This rule is expressly recognised in the case of married couples and civil partners by the Family Law Act 1996, s. 30(3), in favour of a spouse or civil partner with a right to occupy a dwelling.

22.9.1 Subsequent mortgagees

A second or later mortgagee is also a person who has an interest in the equity of redemption and may also claim to redeem a superior mortgage. This reference to 'later' and 'superior' mortgages brings us to the notion of priorities. Where there are several mortgages of the same property, those mortgages are ranked in order, with the mortgagees being entitled to receive the money owed to them according to their place in that ranking. Thus, if the property is not worth the full amount of the debts secured on it, those ranking first take their money in full and those coming later may receive nothing. The rules which determine the order of priorities are explained in Chapter 23 but for the moment it is enough to know that mortgages are ranked in this way.

Where a later mortgagee wishes to redeem an earlier mortgage and this can be arranged by agreement, there is no difficulty. It may be, however, that the earlier mortgagee refuses to accept payment, either because there is a dispute about what is owed or because this mortgagee is relying on the right to consolidate. In this case, the person wishing to redeem will have to seek a court order, and in doing this will discover the rule 'redeem up and foreclose down'. This is best explained by reference to the following illustration.

22.9.2 Redeem up, foreclose down

Assume that land is subject to mortgages in favour of different lenders, A, B, C, D, and E, the mortgages ranking for priority in that order. If D wishes to redeem the mortgage to B by court action, D is obliged to also redeem the intervening mortgage to C (redeem up). D does not have to redeem A's mortgage which simply keeps its priority. D is also required to bring foreclosure proceedings, which will extinguish the rights of E and the mortgagor (see Figure 22.3).

22.10 Liability of mortgagees, receivers, and valuers for fraud or negligence

Mortgagee D wishes to redeem mortgage B		
A		Unaffected. No action required
B	↑	Wants to redeem
C	↑	Must redeem
D		
E	↓	Must foreclose

Figure 22.3 Redeem up, foreclose down

This apparently harsh provision comes about because B will be required to account for any payments already received and show what is still owed. The later mortgagees and the mortgagor are all interested in this, because if D redeems B's mortgage D will take over B's position, and be entitled to recover that amount of money from the value of the property in priority to all those who rank after B. They must be made parties to the action between D and B, so that they can protect their own interests and be bound by the court's decision about the amount owed to B. However, it was felt to be unreasonable to put all these people to the expense of coming to court simply to watch the proceedings, and therefore the rule developed that, while they were there, their claims on the property must be dealt with as well. Therefore, as well as redeeming B's mortgage, D must take the opportunity to quantify and pay off the debts due to any intervening mortgagees (here, C), and must also take foreclosure proceedings to vest the property in D, free from the rights of later mortgagees (here E) and the mortgagor. Of course, if E or the mortgagor can pay off the debt owed to D, one or other of them can prevent D foreclosing. If neither of them has the resources to do that, it may be worth their while asking the court to order sale instead of foreclosure, in the hope that sale will produce enough money to pay off all the earlier mortgages and still leave enough for E and the mortgagor.

22.10 Liability of mortgagees, receivers, and valuers for fraud or negligence

As you have seen, a mortgagee has extensive powers to enter the property and to dispose of it. Alternatively, a mortgagee will often choose to appoint a receiver to take charge of the property and conduct any disposition. Inevitably, over the years the issue has arisen as to what liability the mortgagee or receiver has to the mortgagor, should the property be mismanaged or should the sale price be lower than expected. In some instances, the question of the liability of a valuer employed by the mortgagee or receiver has also arisen and whether a mortgagee or receiver who has innocently relied on a negligent valuation is liable to the mortgagor for any loss. The slump in the property market in the 1990s led to many cases in which sale of a property either did not repay the entire debt or realised far less than the mortgagee had expected. Unsurprisingly therefore, there were a number of important developments in the law in this area.

The leading case is the Court of Appeal decision in *Silven Properties v Royal Bank of Scotland plc* [2004] 1 WLR 997, in which in giving judgment Lightman J summarised nearly all the case law on this issue. The case involved 34 properties owned by two family property companies, all of which had been charged to the bank to secure extensive borrowing by the companies. In 1996 the total debt was nearly £5 million and the bank in that year appointed receivers in relation to all the properties, which were then sold over an 18-month period. The mortgagors complained that many of the properties were sold at an undervalue, though by the time of the appeal the issue was restricted to complaints in relation to only six of the sales, in relation to which the complaints were that:

(1) in some cases, a far better price would have been obtained had the receivers or mortgagees first obtained planning permission for development (initially permission had been sought but the receivers later decided to sell without waiting for it to be granted); and
(2) in other cases, a better price would have been obtained had possible leases of vacant property been completed before sale.

In some instances, the properties were sold by the receivers and in some cases by the mortgagees. Thus, helpfully, in giving judgment the court considered the duties of both. Each is considered in turn in the following paragraphs.

22.10.1 The duties of mortgagees

22.10.1.1 Mortgagee can elect not to exercise powers

In *Silven* Lightman J first restated the basic principle that a mortgagee is under no obligation to exercise any powers: 'He is entitled to remain totally passive.' Thus, the mortgagee cannot be forced to take possession or sell, even if the mortgagor would benefit were this to happen.

22.10.1.2 Mortgagee in possession must take reasonable care of premises

If, however, the mortgagee chooses to take possession of the property, the mortgagee becomes its manager and thereby assumes a duty to take reasonable care of the premises: on this see *Downsview Nominees Ltd v First City Corporation Ltd (No. 1)* [1993] AC 295 at p. 315A. See also the older cases, *White v City of London Brewery Co* (1889) 42 ChD 237 and *Hughes v Williams* (1806) 12 Ves Jr 493, which show that this concept is far from new.

22.10.1.3 Mortgagee is not a trustee of his powers

Secondly, Lightman J reiterated the time-honoured expression: 'A mortgagee is not a trustee of the power of sale for the mortgagor' (which also applies to the mortgagee's other powers). This means that the mortgagee may sell when the mortgagee chooses and may select the time of sale without regard to whether a different time may be more beneficial to the mortgagor: see *Raja v Austin Gray (a firm)* [2002] EWCA Civ 1965 (which also contains a useful summary of the basic rules), *China & South Sea Bank Ltd v Tan Soon Gin* [1990] 1 AC 536, and *Tse Kwong Lam v Wong Chit Sen* [1983] 1 WLR 1349 at p. 1355B. This principle can be traced back at least as far as *Nash v Eads* (1880) 25 Sol J 95 and *Warner v Jacob* (1882) 20 ChD 220, but note that these older cases proceeded on the basis that a mortgagee could only be liable for fraud (see also, for example, on the older approach, *Davey v Durrant* (1857) 1 De G&J 535). In *Silven*, Lightman J expressly rejected the suggestions made (*obiter dicta*) by Lord Denning MR in *Standard Chartered Bank Ltd v Walker* [1982] 1 WLR 1410 at pp. 1415G–H and 1416A that there might nonetheless be some restriction on the mortgagee, such as not being able to elect to sell at the worst possible time.

In *Meretz Investments NV v ACP Ltd* [2007] Ch 197, in a case in which it was alleged that a mortgagee had a range of motives for selling, including some that might be improper, Lewison J was called upon to consider what the implications were (if any) in a case in which the mortgagee might have had both valid and invalid reasons to wish to sell. After considering a number of earlier decisions (including *Nash v Eads*) he concluded that even where there are several motives for sale, as long as one reason is to enforce the security given by the mortgage, the sale is lawful, even if the mortgagee also had other motives. This, once again, underlines the strength of the right of a mortgagee to rely upon and enforce the security. The case, while a heavy read, is worth looking at, if only because it demonstrates how complex some modern property cases can be. It also provides a useful analysis of the case law in this area. Lewison J's reasoning is not affected by the subsequent appeal case (see [2008] Ch 244).

22.10.1.4 The mortgagee may sell the property as it is

Thirdly, in relation to the claims that the mortgagees should have taken steps to improve the position before selling, Lightman J said, 'The mortgagee is entitled to sell the mortgaged property as it is. He is under no obligation to improve it or to increase its value.' While accepting that there was a duty to preserve the property (see the first point in 22.10.1.2) the Court of Appeal in *Silven* declined to extend this to a duty to *improve*, whether by obtaining planning permission, granting leases, or in any other way. The mortgagee is free to take such steps but is not even obliged to continue with any steps taken.

You may wonder what protection the mortgagor has. Lightman J indicated that should the mortgagor wish to impose any such obligations on the mortgagee this should be done when entering into the mortgage or charge as part of its terms. This is, save in commercial transactions and perhaps not even there, likely to be impossible because the lender is likely to be in the position of dictating the terms of the agreement to the borrower. Thus, except in rare cases, this possibility is theoretical rather than practical. Lightman J also says that it is open to the mortgagor to redeem the mortgage, should there be risk if the mortgagee exercises the rights. Since the issue is only likely to arise in a case in which the mortgagor is already unable to make repayments on the mortgage, once again this is an option that is not likely to be a real one.

22.10.1.5 Duty to obtain market value

However, the mortgagee is not without any duties because, fourthly, the decision in *Silven* confirms that when selling, the mortgagee is under a duty in equity to take reasonable precautions to obtain the 'fair' or 'true market value' or 'proper price' for the property at the date of sale. In the conduct of the sale, the mortgagee must not unduly rush the transaction or sell at a low price that will simply cover the mortgage debt (*Palk* v *Mortgage Services Funding plc* [1993] Ch 330 at pp. 337–8). Lightman J says in *Silven*: 'He must take proper care, whether by fairly and properly exposing the property to the market or otherwise, to obtain the best price reasonably obtainable at the date of sale.'

In the circumstances in *Silven* this would include taking reasonable care to obtain any extra value that would arise as a consequence of drawing the attention of prospective purchasers to the possibility of obtaining planning permission or granting the leases that were under negotiation, but that is the full extent of the duty.

In *Standard Chartered Bank Ltd v Walker* Lord Denning MR seemed to suggest that this was a duty in negligence. The same approach was taken in the modern case that really started the concept of the possibility of liability in negligence for certain matters other than choice of time of sale (*Cuckmere Brick Co v Mutual Finance Ltd* [1971] Ch 949 at p. 969G). In that case the property had the benefit of one planning permission for houses and a second (an alternative scheme) for flats. Subsequently, there was a problem with meeting mortgage payments and the mortgagee moved to sell. The property was widely advertised but the advertisements failed to mention that there was planning permission for flats. The mortgagor asked for the sale to be delayed and better details advertised but the mortgagees went ahead with the sale. The property realised £44,000, although the mortgagor had a valuation saying that, with permission for flats, it was worth £75,000. When the matter came before the Court of Appeal it was held that, while a mortgagee was not a trustee of the power of sale for the mortgagor and, where there was a conflict of interests, was entitled to give preference to his or her own over those of the mortgagor (notably in deciding on the timing of the sale), when exercising the power of sale the mortgagee was not merely under a duty to act in good faith but also to take reasonable care to obtain whatever was the true market value of the mortgaged property at the moment chosen for sale. This was a clarification of the law at the time and the decision appears to be based on the concept of liability in negligence, although a curtailed liability due to the nature of the mortgagee's rights. However, the most recent cases have clearly said that this approach is incorrect, and the liability is not in tort for negligence but arises from a duty in equity. Thus, the correct remedy is not damages for negligence but that the mortgagee account to the mortgagor for the sums that would have been raised had the mortgagee complied with the duty. Also, it is a duty owed not just to the mortgagor but also to anyone who has an interest in the equity of redemption. This includes a later mortgagee or indeed a later acquirer of the estate, who takes subject to the mortgage (see *Freeguard v Royal Bank of Scotland plc* [2002] EWHC 2509).

22.10.2 The duties of receivers

It is normal for a mortgagee to ensure that any receiver who is appointed is appointed as an agent of the mortgagor. This enables the receiver to manage or sell in the capacity of agent but avoids the mortgagee becoming liable for any fault on the part of the receiver (unless the mortgagee 'inter-meddles' with the receiver's actions in some way). However, the supposed agency relationship has over the years given rise to a suggestion that the duties of the receiver to the mortgagor may differ from those owed by a mortgagee who elects to act in person. This issue was also discussed in *Silven*, in which it was argued that as agent of the mortgagors the receiver should have acted in their interests when selling.

22.10.2.1 Duty of receiver same as that of mortgagee when selling

In *Silven* the Court of Appeal confirmed the long line of cases which establish that a receiver when selling property owes the same equitable duty to obtain the market value as does a mortgagee. On this point see also the Court of Appeal decision in *Medforth v Blake* [2000] Ch 86 and also the decision in *McDonagh v Bank of Scotland plc* [2019] 4 WLR 12.

22.10.2.2 Receiver may not be passive

Since the receiver is appointed to manage or sell, he or she is under a duty not to remain passive, if to do so would be damaging to the mortgagor or anyone else interested in the equity of redemption. The receiver must be active in the protection and preservation of the property.

22.10.2.3 Otherwise duties are the same as those of a mortgagee

In *Silven* the Court of Appeal recognised that, while the receiver may, due to the terms of appointment, be an agent, the agency in question is very unusual in form. The main differences, as explained by Lightman J giving the judgment of the court (at para. 27), are:

(1) the mortgagor does not appoint the receiver and cannot give instructions to or remove the receiver;

(2) there is no contractual relationship and no duty in tort between mortgagor and receiver but only a relationship in equity;

(3) the receiver also owes a duty to the mortgagee and thus the relationship is tripartite;

(4) the duty owed to the mortgagor is in fact a duty to the whole class of persons who have an interest in the equity of redemption;

(5) the receiver's primary responsibility is to produce a situation in which the mortgage debt is repaid, rather than just to manage the property; and

(6) really the receiver is managing the security that is the property of the mortgagee for the mortgagee's benefit (in *Silven* this is regarded as a separate point but really seems to be an element of point (5)).

After reviewing all the case law, and considering a very influential article by the then Peter Millet QC in which he pointed out that the so-called agency was not really a true agency (see *The Conveyancing Powers of Receivers After Liquidation* (1977) 41 Conv (NS) 83 at p. 88), Lightman J concluded that the duties of receivers in respect of the exercise of the power of sale were the same as those of mortgagees. Accordingly, in *Silven* the receivers were not liable for not having obtained planning permission or granted leases prior to sale.

22.10.3 Setting aside sale in cases of fraud

While the remedies of a mortgagor are restricted in cases of negligence, the position is very much better where a sale of property is conducted fraudulently. In such a case the sale can normally be set aside, allowing a further sale to take place in a proper manner: see *Farrar v Farrars Ltd* (1888) 40 ChD 395. However, it is frequently difficult to establish fraud and a mere sale at an undervalue will not suffice, since it may arise simply due to negligence or the choice of the time of sale. Furthermore, not even the existence of some deception coupled with a sale at an undervalue will necessarily suffice. In *Corbett v Halifax Building Society* [2003] 1 WLR 964, a sale to the uncle of an employee of the Society at an undervalue and subsequent sub-sale to the employee, in breach of the terms of his employment, did not suffice to allow the transactions to be set aside. In this case the mortgagor was left to his remedy in damages.

22.10.4 Valuers

One of the ways in which both mortgagees and receivers endeavour to ensure that they comply with the duty to sell for the market value is to ensure that they take an independent valuation of the property before selling. It had been assumed that provided that reliance had been placed in a competent, qualified valuer the receiver or mortgagee would have done all that was necessary. However, the Court of Appeal decision in *Raja v Austin Gray (a firm)* [2002] EWCA Civ 1965 demonstrates that this is not necessarily the case, essentially because the liability of either receiver or mortgagee is not in the tort of negligence but is an equitable duty.

22.11 The end of a mortgage

22.11.1 Formalities

Obviously, apart from a termination by use of one of the remedies set out earlier, a mortgage normally ends when the mortgagor repays the debt. At that point any estate granted to the mortgagee will terminate automatically (cesser on redemption). However, the mortgagor will require evidence that the mortgage sums have been repaid, so that future purchasers can be assured that the land is free of any encumbrance.

In the case of registered land, the aim will be to remove the registered charge from the register, so that it is clear that the title has been freed of the charge. The procedure is governed by rr. 114 and 115 of the Land Registration Rules 2003 and the accompanying forms (which include an acknowledgement by the lender that the property is no longer charged as security for the repayment of sums due under the registered charge). Rule 115 also permits an electronic discharge. The registrar will, on receipt of the appropriate documents, then exercise his wide power under Sch. 4, para. 5 to LRA 2002 to bring the register up to date by removing the entry relating to the registered charge.

In unregistered land the necessary evidence of discharge is provided by asking the mortgagee to execute a memorandum of discharge, which is usually endorsed on the back of the mortgage deed itself.

22.11.2 Passage of time

Ashe v National Westminster Bank plc [2008] 1 WLR 710 is a reminder that a mortgage can also be brought to an end by prolonged inaction on the part of the mortgagee (see 7.2.1.1). In this case, the mortgagee bank had made a formal demand for the money in June 1992, but took no further steps to enforce its security and matters dragged on for some 14 years, during which time the mortgagor continued to live in the mortgaged house. The bank regarded the mortgage as continuing throughout this period and wrote to the mortgagor on several occasions reminding him that it would require full repayment when the property was eventually sold.

In 1993, the mortgagor had been declared bankrupt and all his property, including the right to redeem the mortgage, vested in his trustee in bankruptcy. The mortgaged property was the debtor's only asset; if it had not been subject to the mortgage it could have been sold by the trustee in bankruptcy and the proceeds applied towards paying debts owed to other creditors. The trustee therefore sought a declaration that the mortgage over the property had been extinguished by the provisions of the Limitation Act 1980.

As explained in Chapter 7, the Limitation Act 1980 provides that rights of action are extinguished after prescribed periods, and a 12-year period is specified for actions to recover possession of land (s. 15) and to recover money secured by a mortgage (s. 20). In the case before the court, the mortgagor had made no mortgage payments for over 12 years and also had done nothing to acknowledge the mortgagee's rights under the mortgage. The bank claimed that the limitation provision did not apply here, because the mortgagor had been allowed to remain in possession of the property with the bank's permission; he was therefore not in 'adverse possession' (see 7.3.2) and time did not run against the bank.

The Court of Appeal held that the mortgagors' rights to possession accrued, in the case of this mortgage, as soon as the mortgage was granted. Failure to require repayment meant that the contractual right to the sums due under the mortgage was time barred. Further, the court held that despite the fact that occupation of the premises by the mortgagors was within the intention of the mortgagees and arose from the mortgagors' legal title to the property, it was nonetheless 'adverse possession' due to the particular wording of para. 3 of Part I of Sch. 1 to the Limitation Act 1980. Therefore, more than 12 years having passed, the mortgagee could not enforce its right to possession of the premises. Time would stop running and the limitation period would begin again if the mortgagor made any payment after the money became due or acknowledged the mortgage in some way (i.e., acknowledged his indebtedness and legal liability to pay—per Kerr J in *Surrendra Overseas Ltd v Government of Sri Lanka* [1997] 1 WLR 565 at p. 575 (see ss. 29 and 30 of the 1980 Act)).

However, in *Ashe* there had been no payment and no acknowledgement. Accordingly, the Court of Appeal held that the bank's right to take possession of the property was statute-barred and that the mortgage itself was extinguished by s. 17 of the Limitation Act, which provides that:

> . . . at the expiration of the period prescribed by this Act for any person to bring an action to recover land . . . the title of that person to the land shall be extinguished.

Accordingly, in such a case the mortgagor could apply to the Land Registry to have any registered charge removed from the register.

FURTHER READING

Bently, 'Mortgagee's Duties on Sale—No Place for Tort' [1990] Conv 431.
Griffiths, 'Mortgages, Repossession and Limitation Periods' [2005] Conv 469.
Kenny, 'No Postponement of the Evil Day' [1998] Conv 223.
Megarry and Wade, *The Law of Real Property*, 9th edn., Sweet & Maxwell, 2019, Chapters 23 and 24.
Millet, 'The Conveyancing Powers of Receivers After Liquidation' (1977) 41 Conv (NS) 83, 88.
Ministry of Justice, 'Mortgages. Power of Sale and Residential Property' CP55/09.
Wade, 'An Equitable Mortgagee's Right to Possession' (1955) 71 LQR 204.

You can visit the online resources to test your knowledge of this chapter with self-test questions at **www.oup.com/he/nair19e/**.

23

Priorities in relation to mortgages and charges

23.1 Why are priorities important? 498
23.2 How to approach the issue 499
23.3 Priorities of mortgages or charges of an equitable interest 499
23.4 Priorities of mortgages or charges of a legal estate 501
23.5 Priorities where there are three or more mortgages or charges 507
23.6 The mortgagee's or chargee's right to tack further advances 508
23.7 Interests prior to the mortgagee: a cause for concern for a mortgagee or chargee 510

23.1 Why are priorities important?

Often, when a person (or, more usually, a bank) is asked to lend money on the security of a **mortgage**, or later comes to enforce that mortgage, it will be found that there are a number of people who have interests in the property. When Mildred's bank is considering her request for a loan secured by a mortgage of 12 Trant Way, it will have to take into account the claims of: (a) the first **mortgagee**, the Red Leicester Building Society (RLBS) (see 22.2); (b) Laura Lymeswold's lease/licence (see Chapter 20); and (c) Henry Newton's possible rights in equity (see Chapters 18 and 20). The bank will be concerned with these other rights, because it wants to be sure that if Mildred fails to repay the loan it will be able to sell the property (or exercise its other remedies) without any difficulty, and that the proceeds of sale will be sufficient to repay the debt. The bank therefore will need to consider the following issues.

- The amount of the loan secured by the first mortgage. If the property was sold, and the debt to RLBS discharged first, would there be enough left to repay the bank?
- The nature of Laura's interest. If she has a lease and this lease binds the bank, this would decrease the value of the property, because a purchaser is unlikely to pay as much for a house with a sitting tenant as for one with vacant possession. If Laura has a different claim enforceable against third parties (such as an estoppel licence), this would, of course, decrease the value of the property in the same way.
- Whether Henry Newton has any rights in equity, given his contribution to the value of the property, such as a claim in estoppel or an interest under a resulting or constructive trust. Either of these might give him a right to remain in the property and, if the right bound the bank, it would effectively prevent sale; and if he had an interest under a trust, the bank might find that the mortgage attached only to Mildred's share of the beneficial interest.

The existence of other interests in the property is therefore of considerable importance to mortgagees. The mortgagee needs to know which interests can largely be ignored because they are postponed to the mortgagee's rights, and which interests the mortgagee must take into account because they have priority to the mortgage.

The rules on priorities are, in the main, merely a practical application of the rules on the enforceability of legal and equitable interests against third parties, which were discussed in Chapters 5 and 6. However, these rules might appear rather confusing when applied to mortgages, because there are so many rules and there seem to be so many different situations to consider. In fact, if you can work out which situation is presented by the facts before you, you should find that applying the relevant rule is not too difficult.

23.2 How to approach the issue

23.2.1 Start with chronological order

When dealing with a question of priorities, it is best to begin by arranging the competing mortgages in chronological order, that is, according to their date of creation. The final order of priorities may be very different from this, but it at least provides a starting-point and a basis from which to apply the rules. Having done that, you will find it helpful to ask yourself a series of questions, in a prescribed order, which are worked through in the following pages, and which are set out in Figures 23.1–23.4. Figure 23.4 provides a diagrammatic representation of the rules as a whole but you will find greater detail in the separate Figures 23.1–23.3, which contain elements of Figure 23.4.

23.2.2 Application to other interests

In what follows, references are usually to competing *mortgages*, but in general the same principles will apply where questions of priority arise between a mortgage or charge and any other interest (such as that of a purchaser of the fee simple).

23.2.3 What has been mortgaged?

Begin by asking yourself:

> What is the nature of the property which is subject to the mortgage: is this a mortgage of the legal estate or of an equitable interest (such as a beneficiary's interest under a trust)?

Mortgages of the equitable interest will be dealt with straight away, because the rules can be stated relatively shortly, and you can then concentrate for the rest of the chapter on mortgages of the legal estate.

23.3 Priorities of mortgages or charges of an equitable interest

23.3.1 Where the equities are equal

You have already seen that any dealing with an equitable interest must itself be equitable, so you are concerned here only with successive equitable mortgages. Where there is a competition between equitable interests, the general rule is expressed in the maxim: 'Where the equities are equal, the first in time prevails'.

Therefore, the interests will rank chronologically, according to the date of creation, provided each mortgagee has, in equity's view, acted fairly in regard to those who come later.

23.3.2 The rule in *Dearle v Hall*

Where the property which is mortgaged consists of a beneficial interest under a trust, questions of priorities are regulated by special rules.

Competing assignments of the beneficial interest are regulated by the rule in *Dearle v Hall* (1823) 3 Russ 1, as applied to trusts of land by LPA 1925, s. 137. This rule applies to all successive assignments of the beneficial interest, and provides that priority of competing assignments (which include mortgages) depends on the order in which notice of the assignments is received by the trustees.

23.3.2.1 An example

In the following situation:

(a) mortgage to A,

(b) mortgage to B,

(c) B gives notice,

(d) A gives notice.

B would normally gain priority over A. However, since one is dealing with the equitable jurisdiction, B is not allowed to gain priority by giving notice first if he knew of the existence of A's mortgage when the second mortgage was created, for to allow this would be patently unfair. Thus, only a second mortgagee without notice can improve his priority under the rule (*Re Holmes* (1885) 29 ChD 786). If B had no notice at the date when his mortgage was created, but learned of A's mortgage before giving notice, B may still obtain priority by giving notice first (*Mutual Life Assurance Society v Langley* (1886) 32 ChD 460). It is important to note that the crucial time for the operation of the rule is the date at which the trustee receives the notice, rather than the time at which notice is given. Accordingly, a mortgagee who posted a notice through the trustee's letter-box one evening, was held not to have given notice until the following day when the notice was opened and read (*Calisher v Forbes* (1871) LR 7 Ch App 109).

23.3.2.2 Giving notice

When giving notice under *Dearle v Hall* the assignee of the equitable interest should take care to give notice to the correct persons. Usually, the trustees to be served will be the persons, or person, in whom the legal estate is vested. However, in the case of land which is settled under the SLA 1925, notice should be given to the trustees of the settlement and not to the tenant for life, in whom the estate is vested.

Great care should be taken to give notice to *all* the trustees, whatever the type of trust. If this is done, the notice is effective for priority purposes even if later those trustees who received the notice retire, or die in office, and leave their successors without any knowledge of the notice which was given (*Re Wasdale* [1899] 1 Ch 163). However, if, where there are several trustees, notice is given to one only, that notice becomes invalid when that trustee retires or dies, unless that trustee has told the others that he had received notice (*Timson v Ramsbottom* (1836) 2 Keen 35, but see also *Ward v Duncombe* [1893] AC 369). If giving notice proves unduly difficult or expensive, a 'purchaser' (this includes a mortgagee) can require that a memorandum be endorsed on the document which created the trust and under LPA 1925, s. 137(4); this is effective in place of giving notice to the trustees.

LPA 1925, s. 137(3) provides that '[a] notice, otherwise than in writing, . . . shall not affect the priority of competing claims of purchasers in that equitable interest'. The meaning of this provision is not entirely clear: it may mean that all notices for the purpose of *Dearle v Hall* must since 1925 be in writing, or it may be that an oral notice is sufficient to maintain an assignee's existing chronological priority, although inadequate to give him priority over an earlier assignee.

23.3.2.3 Registered land

Where the subject matter of the trust was registered land, the priority of assignments of the beneficial interest used to depend upon the order in which the assignments were entered in a special index called the Index of Minor Interests (LRA 1925, s. 102(2)). Relatively little use was made of the Index and therefore it was abolished by LRA 1986, s. 5. You should note that the LRA 2002 makes no special provision for the priority of competing equitable interests. This is because s. 28 simply provides that the registration of an interest makes *no* difference to its priority (see 23.4.1.1) and the ss. 29–30 exceptions apply only to buyers of *legal* estates and interest in land. As a result, the same rules apply to mortgagees of equitable interests in both registered and unregistered land: that is, the first in time prevails unless the equities are unequal (e.g. the earlier mortgagee has misled the later mortgagee about the existence of its interest) or unless the mortgaged interest is an interest under a trust, to which the rule in *Dearle v Hall* applies.

23.3.2.4 Summary

The principles for mortgages of an equitable interest are summarised in Figure 23.1.

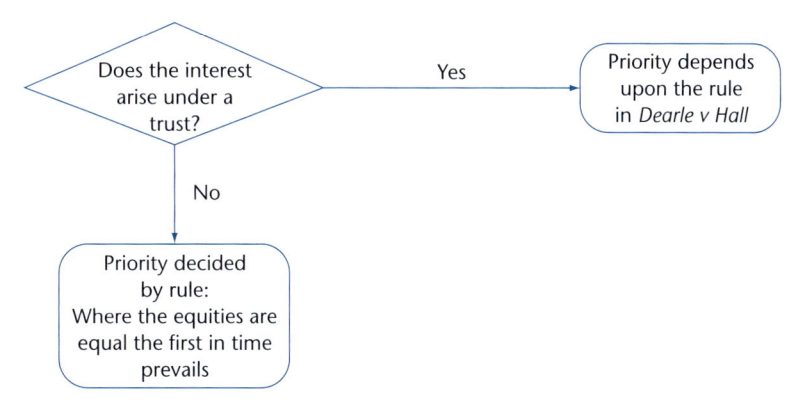

Figure 23.1 Priorities of mortgages of an equitable interest

23.4 Priorities of mortgages or charges of a legal estate

Where it is the legal estate which is subject to the mortgage, one begins by asking:

Is title to the estate registered or unregistered?

23.4.1 Registered title

The rules on priorities in relation to unregistered land are simply a practical application of the material already covered in Chapter 6. Accordingly, only a few key rules are covered here, since our focus is on the practical application of the rules to cases involving mortgages.

First, you should note the requirement in s. 27(1) and (2)(f) of the LRA 2002 to complete *legal charges* by registration. The creation of the charge takes effect only in equity until this is done. On registration, the chargee will be entered on the register as proprietor of the charge (Sch. 2, para. 8). This entry is made in the charges section of the register entry for the estate that has been charged. It is this completion by registration of the disposition that gives the mortgagee a legal charge and makes it possible to postpone the priority of earlier interests (see 23.4.1.2). Any *equitable charges* have to be protected by the entry of a notice in the register (s. 32(1)). Such notices will give the equitable chargee protection from *loss* of priority to a later legal mortgagee but will not postpone the priority of any earlier interests. Where no notice is entered on the register, the equitable chargee might lose priority to a later disponee of the land who takes a registered estate for value.

23.4.1.1 The basic principle

The effect of LRA 2002, s. 28 is that the priority of competing interests in registered land is determined by the order in which they were created. Thus, the section says that a disposition of the registered estate will not affect the priority of an existing interest in that estate. It further says that it makes no difference for the purpose of the section whether or not the earlier interest or disposition has been registered. To apply this rule to two competing charges one therefore simply asks which was created first, and that charge has priority even if it was not registered when the second charge was created.

23.4.1.2 The exceptions to the basic principle

However, ss. 29 and 30 provide cases in which the basic s. 28 rule is not to apply and in practice will mean that the simple 'first created gets priority' rule will not apply in a large number of situations. Section 29 is relevant where there is a registrable disposition of a registered estate. Section 30 applies where there is a registrable disposition of a registered charge. Note that you will normally be considering cases under s. 29 because usually you will be concerned with a later disposition made by the owner of the freehold or leasehold estate that is registered. Section 30 only applies in relation to dealings with the charge itself (e.g., a transfer for value of the charge from one lender to another lender).

Section 29

Section 29 applies where there is a registrable disposition of a registered estate for value, and that disposition is then registered. A registrable disposition is defined by s. 27 of LRA 2002 as a disposition that needs to be registered in order to take effect at law—the creation of most legal estates and interests in registered land fall within this category. However, you should also note that grant of a short legal lease of less than seven years is not a registrable disposition for the purposes of the formality rule in s. 27 but it is treated *as if* it is a registered disposition for the purposes of the rule in s. 29 (see s. 29(4)). The grant of a six-year lease for value, if it is made by deed and therefore takes effect as a legal lease, will give the tenant the benefit of the rule in s. 29 even though the short lease never appears on the register.

Where a right of this type is created or transferred in exchange for value, the rights of any person who has an interest affecting the estate before the registrable disposition is created (the first interest) are postponed to those of the owner of the interest conferred by the registered disposition (the second interest) unless the priority of the first interest had been protected by the time that the second interest is registered. 'Protection' in this context is defined in s. 29(2):

> ... the priority of an interest is protected—
> (a) in any case, if the interest—
>   (i) is a registered charge or the subject of a notice in the register,
>   (ii) falls within any of the paragraphs of Schedule 3, or
>   (iii) appears from the register to be excepted from the effect of registration; and
> (b) in the case of a disposition of a leasehold estate, if the burden of the interest is incident to the estate.

Thus, if an estate owner creates two registrable charges of the land in the order Charge 1 and then Charge 2, the basic rule in s. 28 is that they will rank for priority in the order: (1) Charge 1; and (2) Charge 2. If, however, Charge 2 is registered first, the rule in s. 29 will apply (a charge is always granted for value, since it secures a loan). Charge 1 will lose its priority, since it is not 'a registered charge or the subject of a notice in the register'. The result is that the rights will rank in the order: (1) Charge 2; and (2) Charge 1. This is a simple example involving two registrable charges and in such a case the charges each have to be protected by registration in order to maintain priority. However, this is not the only possibility. If Charge 1 is in the Sch. 3 class of unregistered interests, and has not previously been the subject of a notice (see s. 29(3)), it will override Charge 2. The different overriding interests are set out in detail in Chapter 6 (see 6.5); the key point to note here is that an equitable interest will only be overriding if it is combined with actual occupation (LRA 2002, Sch. 3, para. 2). As it is unlikely that the holder of Charge 2 will be in actual occupation of the land that is the subject matter of the charge, it is unlikely that the charge will be overriding in this example.

How to approach a problem

Thus, in the case of registered title, the first question to ask is:

> Is the later disposition a registrable disposition of a registered estate?

What this means is that the later disposition must involve the grant or creation of a legal estate or interest. If the disposition instead involves the grant of an equitable interest, s. 28 applies instead: the first in time prevails.

The next question to ask is:

> Is the later disposition for value?

If not, the usual rule is that the disposition will not gain priority over any earlier interest. If the disposition is for value, and any registration requirements have been complied with, assume that s. 29 applies. Then go on to ask:

> Is any earlier interest (1) a registered charge, (2) protected by a notice or (3) listed in Schedule 3 (overriding)?

If the answer is 'Yes', the earlier interest retains its priority. If the answer is 'No', the earlier interest loses its priority to the later interest (LRA 2002, s. 29) (see Figure 23.2).

```
                    ┌─────────────────┐
                    │ Is the later    │         No        ┌──────────────────────────────┐
                    │ disposition     ├──────────────────▶│ Earlier interest retains     │
                    │ for value?      │                   │ priority                     │
                    └────────┬────────┘                   └──────────────────────────────┘
                             │ Yes
                             ▼
              ┌──────────────────────────────┐
              │ Is the earlier               │
              │ disposition—                 │
              │ (1) a registered charge      │            ┌──────────────────────────────┐
              │ (2) protected by notice      │   Yes      │ Earlier interest retains     │
              │   or                         ├───────────▶│ priority                     │
              │ (3) listed in Sch. 3, LRA    │            └──────────────────────────────┘
              │ 2002 (overriding)?           │
              └──────────────┬───────────────┘
                             │ No
                             ▼
              ┌──────────────────────────────┐
              │ Earlier interest loses its   │
              │ priority to the later        │
              │ interest—s. 29 LRA 2002      │
              └──────────────────────────────┘
```

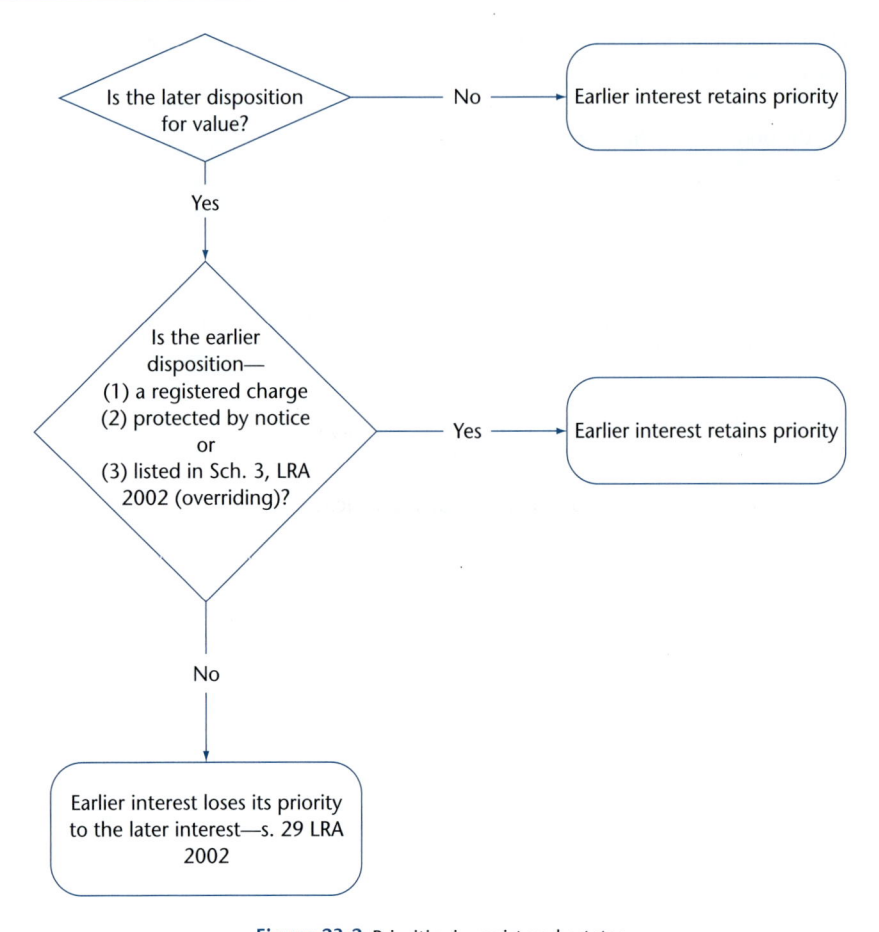

Figure 23.2 Priorities in registered estates

Section 28

Under s. 28, time of creation is all that matters and ss. 29 or 30 cannot change the priority. In addition, the complexities in unregistered land in relation to any equitable right arising from estoppel or any 'mere equity' are removed by LRA 2002, s. 116, which treats both as interests capable of binding successors in title.

In summary

This approach is designed to produce an admirable simplicity in the rules on priorities in registered land. The most obvious impact of these rules is that, where the mortgagee fears it may be bound by an earlier interest (e.g., because its holder is in actual occupation), it will need to get the consent of the interest-holder to the grant of the mortgage and to the mortgagee's priority. However, such consents are not always straightforwardly effective because one also needs to consider the impact of other rules of law. One of the most important of these, in the mortgage context, is the doctrine of undue influence (23.7.2).

23.4.2 Unregistered title

The rules on priorities in relation to unregistered land are simply a practical application of the material already covered in Chapter 5. Accordingly, here only a few key concepts are covered by way of reminder.

The basic points to remember are as follows.

(1) If there is a legal mortgage and the mortgagee does not have the title deeds, that mortgage must be registered on the Land Charges Register as a **puisne mortgage**, which is a Class C(i) land charge (see 5.4.2.2).

(2) If there is an equitable mortgage and the mortgagee does not have the title deeds, that mortgage must be registered on the Land Charges Register as a *general equitable charge*, which is a Class C(iii) Land Charge.

(3) If there is a legal mortgage and the mortgagee does have the title deeds, that legal mortgage will be good against the world (save in rare cases in which priority is lost due to carelessness with the deeds).

(4) If there is an equitable mortgage and the mortgagee does have the title deeds:

   (a) that mortgage will normally bind any acquirer of a later *legal* estate or interest because the absence of the deeds gives notice of the existence of the earlier mortgage;

   (b) that mortgage will normally bind any later acquirer of an *equitable* interest because of the rule that, 'Where the equities are equal, the first in time prevails'.

The way to work through the rules for unregistered land is summarised in Figure 23.3. Figure 23.4 gives a flowchart showing how all the priorities for both registered and unregistered land interact.

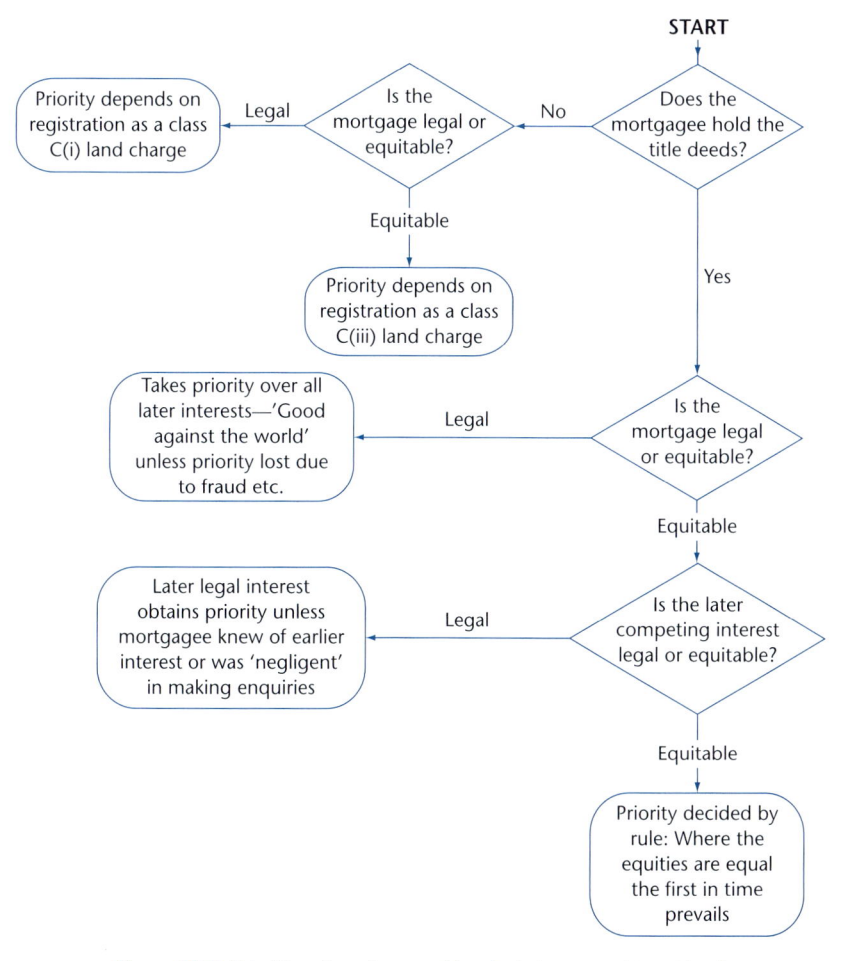

Figure 23.3 Priorities of mortgages of legal estate—unregistered land

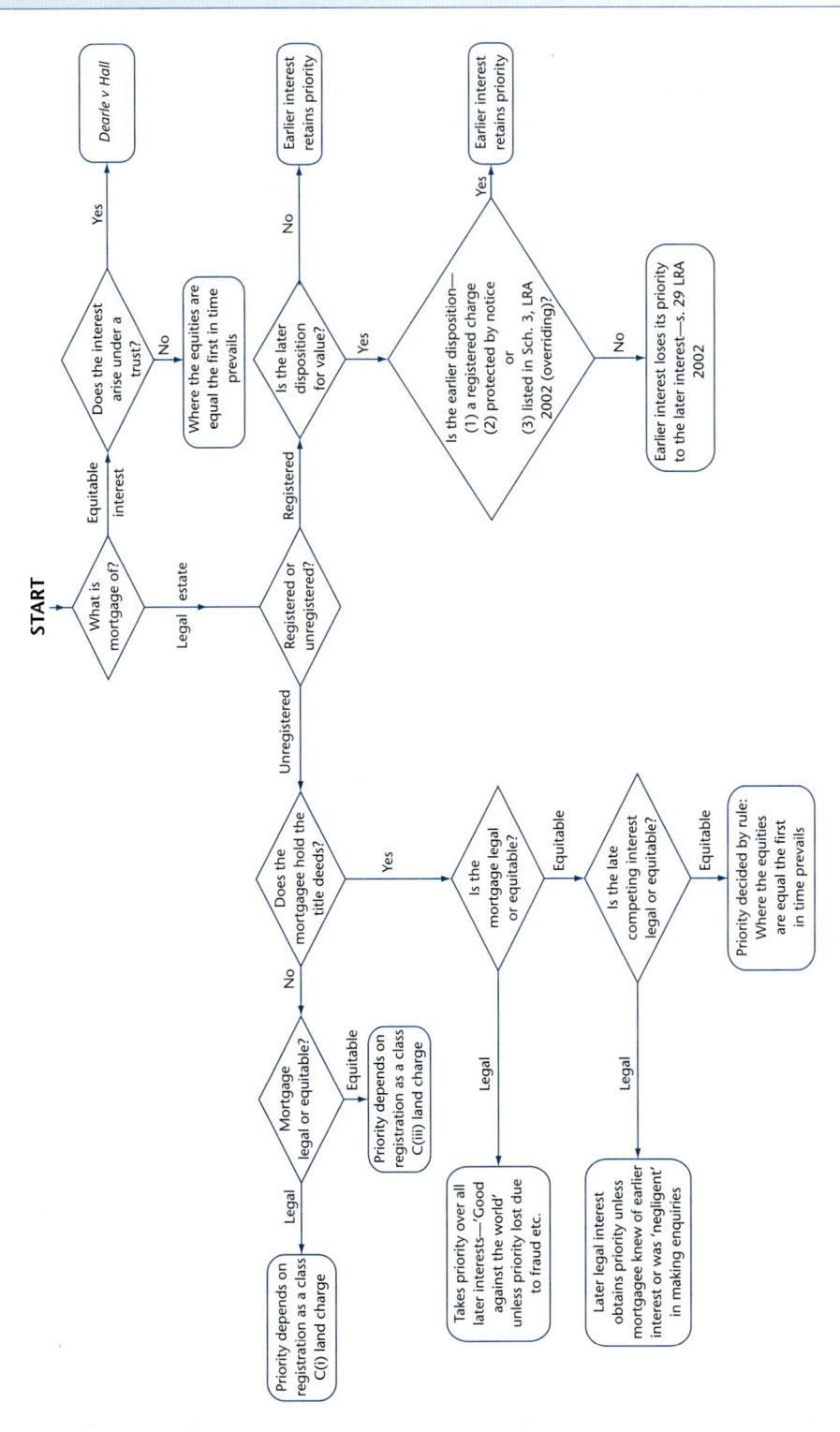

Figure 23.4 Priorities of mortgages in registered and unregistered land

23.5 Priorities where there are three or more mortgages or charges

So far, the rules about priorities have been addressed as though one is dealing only with a competition between two mortgages. It is, however, possible to have three or more mortgages of the same estate, and you may therefore have to deal with questions of priorities in such a situation. You should continue to apply the approach adopted so far: begin by listing the mortgages according to their date of creation, and then consider the earliest one in relation to each successive mortgage. When you have done this, take the next one to be created, and consider it in relation to each one that follows it. If you proceed in this way, considering each pair separately, you will often find that at the end you can list all the mortgages in order of priority.

23.5.1 A simple example

Take, for example, three old mortgages of a legal estate, title to which is not registered, which have been created in the following order:

(a) 1981, legal mortgage to A, who takes the title deeds;
(b) 1982, legal charge to B, who registers a class C(i) land charge; and
(c) 1983, equitable mortgage to C.

Now compare the mortgages in pairs:

(a) *A and B.* A has a mortgage protected by deposit of title deeds, which is therefore not a registrable land charge. He has a legal mortgage, so his right is good against the world, and there is no suggestion of any conduct on his part which would deprive him of his priority.
Result: A before B.

(b) *A and C.* The position is exactly the same as in the case of A and B.
Result: A before C.

(c) *B and C.* B has a legal mortgage not protected by deposit of title deeds. It is therefore a registrable class C(i) land charge and, having been registered as such, will bind all those who take a later interest in the property including C.
Result: B before C

On this occasion, then, this method of approaching the problem produces a clear and simple set of answers:

A before B
A before C
B before C

and the mortgages can be sorted into a neat straight line of priority:

A first
B second
C third

Although this is an old, unregistered land, example you will find that the LRA 2002 rules mean that in registered land it should normally be possible to 'sort' charges in a fairly straightforward manner. However, there has historically been a more complex possibility in relation to unregistered land.

23.5.2 A more complex unregistered possibility

It is possible to think of cases in which the order of priorities does not resolve itself so readily. For example, after applying the priorities rules to a set of mortgages in pairs you might theoretically come up with the following order of priorities, which produces a circle, as shown in Figure 23.5.

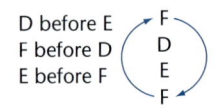

D before E
F before D
E before F

F
D
E
F

Figure 23.5 Circular priorities

How you break into this circle is unclear, because the point has never come before the courts. Two possible solutions are: (a) that all the mortgagees should bear an equal loss (for there is only a problem if the value of the property is less than the sums outstanding on all three mortgages), or (b) that the mortgages should rank in the order in which they were created. Some authorities have suggested applying the rules of subrogation, but this produces a manifestly unfair result. (See Megarry and Wade, para. 25-034, and Gilmore (1961) 71 Yale LJ 53.) Happily, the circular priority problem is now rarely likely to arise in practice, because a mortgage supported by deposit of title deeds will trigger a need for first registration of title. Thus, this possibility, though interesting, is very unlikely to occur in future.

23.5.3 Is that the end of the matter?

Once one has sorted out priorities according to the rules given above, it is not the end of the matter because there remain rules which cause the standard pattern of priorities to be disrupted (such as the rules relating to undue influence). A number of these issues are dealt with at the end of this chapter, when we look at the position of Henry Newton in more detail (see 23.7).

23.6 The mortgagee's or chargee's right to tack further advances

12 Trant Way is already subject to a first mortgage to the Red Leicester Building Society (RLBS), and a second mortgage may soon be created in favour of the Royal Windsor Bank (RWB). At some later date, after the creation of the second mortgage, Mildred, the owner of No. 12, might return to the RLBS and ask whether it would extend her mortgage to cover an additional advance. If the building society considers doing this, it will wish to know whether the fresh advance is effectively a third mortgage, ranking for

priority after the RWB's mortgage, or whether it can '**tack**' (add on) this further advance to the first mortgage, so as to gain priority for the later advance.

Again, the need to tack further advances will often arise where a mortgage has been given to a bank to secure the **mortgagor**'s overdraft. As each withdrawal is made from the account, the bank makes a further loan to the mortgagor, but it is obviously desirable, from the bank's point of view, that all these loans should rank for priority with the original mortgage.

The circumstances in which further advances may be tacked are governed by different statutory provisions in the case of registered and unregistered title.

23.6.1 Registered title

Under the LRA 2002, the rules on tacking in relation to registered land changed. LRA 2002, s. 49 provides that the proprietor of a registered charge may make a further advance that ranks in priority to any later charge, if the chargee has not received notice of the subsequent charge from the subsequent chargee. This places the onus on a new chargee to give notice to any earlier chargee of the creation of the new charge. A further advance may also be made with priority over any later charges if the advance is made in pursuance of an obligation and that obligation has been entered on the register (s. 49(3)), or if the parties to the earlier charge have agreed a maximum for which the charge is security and that agreement is entered on the register (s. 49(4)). Section 49(4) was an entirely new provision in 2002. Rules may be made to make certain variations to the position under s. 49(4) (see s. 49(5)). However, this power has not yet been used. In any other case, it is only possible to take and gain priority if the chargee of the later charge agrees (s. 49(6)).

23.6.2 Unregistered title

The rule is that under LPA 1925, s. 94, a mortgagee has the right to tack further advances in three situations.

(1) *Where all the subsequent mortgagees agree.*

   This is unlikely to happen.

(2) *Where the mortgagee seeking to tack did not have notice of the existence of the subsequent mortgage at the date at which the further advance was made.*

   It may be thought that this second category would be of little use to the earlier mortgagee if the later mortgage was registered as a land charge, since registration constitutes notice. However, under s. 94(2), the first mortgagee is not deemed to have notice of the second mortgage merely because it has been registered as a land charge, provided that:

   (a) the first mortgage was expressly made for the purpose of securing further advances; and

   (b) the second mortgage was not registered at the date when the first mortgage was created or when the first mortgagee last searched the register, whichever is the later.

   Therefore, if a later mortgagee wants to prevent tacking in these circumstances, the later mortgagee must give express notice of the position to the earlier mortgagee.

(3) *Where the first mortgage obliges the mortgagee to make further advances . . .*

Here the first mortgagee may tack even if he or she has notice of the later mortgage. Thus, should a mortgagee agree to finance the building of a new estate, it might be agreed that the advance should be paid in stages as each house is finished. In such a case the mortgagee can tack the separate loans together, even where there is knowledge of a later mortgage.

23.7 Interests prior to the mortgagee: a cause for concern for a mortgagee or chargee

23.7.1 12 Trant Way

Finally, before we leave mortgages, we need to look again at the position at 12 Trant Way. Mildred is seeking a loan from the Royal Windsor Bank (RWB) on the security of a second mortgage of No. 12, and the bank will need to consider the extent to which it will be bound by the existing interests in the property. The title is unregistered.

23.7.1.1 The mortgage

The RWB must first consider the earlier legal mortgage to the Red Leicester Building Society (RLBS). If the RLBS has the deeds (as is normal) and has not done anything to forfeit its natural priority, it will take priority over any second mortgage to the RWB. Should the RLBS not have the deeds, its mortgage still takes priority if it is registered as a class C(i) land charge. If it does not have the deeds, and its mortgage is not registered when the second mortgage is created, the second mortgagee will gain priority, even if the RWB knew of the earlier mortgage (*Midland Bank Trust Co. Ltd v Green* [1981] AC 513) (see Figure 23.6).

SITUATION IF UNREGISTERED LAND

RLBS Legal mortgage or charge	Has deposit of deeds	Does not have deeds Has registered C(i) land charge	Does not have deeds Has not registered land charge
RWB If it takes a mortgage or charge	RLBS gets priority RLBS gets paid first	RLBS gets priority RLBS gets paid first	RWB gets priority RWB gets paid first

Figure 23.6 Mortgages at 12 Trant Way, if title is unregistered

Accordingly, before making any advance, the RWB should check the situation with regard to the RLBS mortgage. Thereafter, it will need to have 12 Trant Way valued, and should ensure that it does not lend more than the balance of the value after deduction of the sums due to the RLBS.

23.7.1.2 Laura's rights

The RWB needs also to consider the situation of Laura Lymeswold, who has a licence or lease of 12A Trant Way (see Chapter 20). If she has a lease (see 9.2 for the requirements of a lease), the RWB will take a mortgage *subject to* the pre-existing legal estate vested in her. It should ensure that its valuation takes account of the existence of a sitting tenant. Should Laura have only a licence, it appears that it will not bind the bank (and a later purchaser on sale by the mortgagee) for the licence would be contractual: see *Ashburn Anstalt v Arnold* [1989] Ch 1 (the decision in this case was overruled in *Prudential Assurance Co. Ltd v London Residuary Body* [1992] 2 AC 386, but no criticism was made of the analysis of the position relating to licences).

23.7.1.3 Henry's rights

The greatest problem for the RWB would be the uncertain position of Henry Newton. If Henry were to have an equitable interest in the property under a trust, for example, this will bind the RWB, unless the bank could claim to be a bona fide purchaser for value of a legal estate without notice. Since Henry is in occupation of the premises the bank would be likely to have notice under the rule in *Hunt v Luck* (see 5.5.2.3).

The existence of such a binding interest would mean that the bank's mortgage would attach only to Mildred's interest in the property and not to Henry's share. Thereafter, since as an equitable co-owner Henry would have a right to reside in the property until sale (TOLATA 1996, s. 12) and as the mortgage would not affect his interest, Henry might be able to prevent the second mortgagee getting vacant possession of the property (compare the registered land case of *Williams & Glyn's Bank Ltd v Boland*). This would prevent realisation even of the partial security with which the bank would be left.

However, note the decisions in *Bank of Baroda v Dhillon* [1998] 1 FLR 524 and *Bank of Ireland Home Mortgages Ltd v Bell* [2001] 2 FLR 809 (discussed in more detail in Chapter 14) which demonstrate that, even where the bank is bound by a beneficial interest, it may be possible to obtain an order for sale of property held on trust (in the earlier case under LPA 1925, s. 30 but in the latter under TOLATA 1996, s. 14). Unlike the case where the bank is not bound by Henry's interest, however, there is no ability to sell without an order from a court. The mortgagee will also have to account to Henry for his share of the proceeds of sale, even if this means its own loan is not paid off in full.

The possibility of such interests arising has accordingly created considerable difficulties for the building societies and banks. One solution to the problem would be for Mildred to appoint another trustee to join with her in receiving the mortgage money, so that Henry's interest would be overreached and attach only to the mortgage advance (*City of London Building Society v Flegg* [1988] AC 54) and, where no capital moneys (mortgage advance) arise, see also *State Bank of India v Sood* [1997] Ch 276. However, anyone taking on the role of trustee would then have to address any claim to an interest Henry may make and may, therefore, be in a difficult position. Note that any mortgage granted will not trigger registration of the title because it will not be a first legal charge (LRA 2002, s. 4).

23.7.2 Undue influence

Of recent years, the professional mortgagees (e.g., building societies and banks) have been increasingly concerned about the position of people such as the mortgagor's family and friends, who occupy the property with him or her at the date of the mortgage and may have rights to the property which can be enforced against the mortgagee. Accordingly, the practice has grown up of asking a spouse or anyone else the mortgagee identifies as being resident in the premises to sign a document postponing his or her rights to those of the mortgagee. Also, where there are co-owners the mortgagee will have to seek the signatures of all involved (typically spouses or civil partners or a couple who are living together). However, in recent years, those who have signed such a document have often sought later to argue that they are not bound by the mortgage *despite* having signed the mortgage or some document acknowledging the mortgagee's priority.

The basis on which such claims are made is the equitable concept known as 'undue influence'. This is not a rule which is specific to land law but is a general principle that arose as part of the equitable jurisdiction to see that there was fair play between the parties when it comes to their consensual or contractual dealings. Accordingly, it might more properly be regarded as being better dealt with in textbooks on contract law, unjust enrichment, and equity, rather than land law. However, in recent years its importance in the law of mortgages particularly (and in relation to some other interests in land) has become so considerable that the position is summarised here.

23.7.2.1 The doctrine

The equitable doctrine of undue influence was developed to protect those who had entered into a transaction because of the inappropriate use of influence by a person in whom they reposed a particular level of trust because of the particular nature of the relationship between them. The most common example has therefore been that of a wife who agrees to something (such as signing a mortgage deed) due to the influence of her husband. However, the concept goes beyond the limits of marriage and civil partnership and can cover a far wider range of relationships. Thus, it can include cases in which elderly relations act under the influence of young family members on whom they depend, unmarried couples (like Mildred Mumps and Henry Newton) and even other relationships of close trust. For example, in *Allcard v Skinner* (1887) 36 ChD 145, in which a nun made a gift of all her property to her Mother Superior (for the religious order), the relationship was considered to be within the ambit of the doctrine of 'undue influence'. In such cases the transaction will be voidable as between the person influenced and the person exercising the improper level of influence, allowing the person influenced to apply to court for the transaction to be set aside.

23.7.2.2 Impact on third parties

The same doctrine can also affect a party who has not itself exerted influence but is party to the transaction procured by undue influence. The typical modern example is a case in which someone with rights to the property (e.g., a wife) is persuaded by another person (e.g., her husband) to sign an arrangement giving rights to a third party (such as a mortgagee). If this is a case in which there is no clear benefit to the wife (such as where the money raised is applied for something of benefit only to the husband), then as between the husband and wife the transaction might in many cases be set aside. However, really the wife will need the transaction not to bind her as regards the *mortgagee* as well, if she is to protect her rights effectively. Thus, increasingly in recent history people have claimed that the transaction should also not be enforceable by the third party. This is because, in certain circumstances, it can be argued that the third party knew or should have known that the transaction had been effected with use of undue influence. If such a claim succeeds, the transaction is also unenforceable by the third party (e.g., the mortgagee).

In *Mortgage Express v Lambert* [2017] Ch 93, the Court of Appeal confirmed that the right to set aside an unconscionable bargain was an 'equity' or 'mere equity', and that equity was capable of being an overriding interest in registered land under s. 116 of the LRA 2002.

23.7.2.3 Etridge

The leading case in modern law is *Royal Bank of Scotland v Etridge* [2002] 2 AC 773. In this case, following an absolute flood of claims of undue influence in the last few years of the twentieth century, the House of Lords considered eight conjoined cases in which undue influence had been raised and laid down general principles to be applied in future in such cases. The House of Lords also gave a clear statement of the steps that a third party, such as a mortgagee, should take in order to protect itself from being affected by any undue influence that might have occurred. In doing so, the court moved away from the somewhat convoluted approach to undue influence cases that had developed over the years.

As far as the original parties are concerned (such as Mildred Mumps and Henry Newton), Lord Clyde indicated (para. 93) that, where a relationship of trust exists, undue influence can arise in a range of ways. These include coercion, domination, victimisation, and also more insidious forms of persuasion (which may be harder to identify). In some relationships (such as marriage and civil partnership) it may be easier to infer that some influence has led to the transaction, rather than it being a matter of real free choice by the person adversely affected. However, each case will turn on its own facts and there are no rigid rules as to when undue influence will arise. In each case, one is looking for an element of breach of trust. This is not, however, in the strict legal sense of breach of trust but rather covers the case of someone abusing their position to persuade someone who would not otherwise have been persuaded to act as they did.

Third parties, such as mortgagees, should take steps to protect themselves, if there is anything in the facts to suggest a risk. This will normally be the case where, for example, a spouse or civil partner signs away rights with no advantage to themselves. In such cases, the third party should ensure that the person who may have been influenced is given the chance of having independent advice about the transaction and that she or he has had the full implications explained before deciding to proceed. In essence, normally the third party (usually a lender) will need to be sure that the person in question has had legal advice that is separate from that given to the person who will benefit from the transaction. This usually means a separate firm of solicitors must be instructed to act. Clearly, in some cases, even after such advice is received, a spouse, civil partner, or other person in a close relationship may decide to act in a manner that is not in their own best interests due to love, kindness, or a multiplicity of other possible reasons. However, the separate legal advice should ensure that they make this decision freely and in full possession of the facts. Without such advice, the improper 'influencer' and any mortgagee will both be at risk that the transaction will be set aside as against them.

23.7.2.4 12 Trant Way

If the RWB want to be sure that any rights Henry may have will not interfere with the RWB's rights to enforce their mortgage they would therefore be well advised to require Henry to sign a document that will postpone his rights to those of the bank, to tell Henry to take independent advice, and to insist that they have a certificate from his lawyer confirming that the nature and effect of the mortgage have been explained to him before he signed the release document. It should also be noted that, in the case of registered land, a signed release from a person in actual occupation may be of limited assistance in any event for reasons which have nothing to do with undue influence: see further on this *Woolwich Building Society v Dickman* (1996) 72 P&CR 470.

FURTHER READING

Capper, 'Undue Influence and Unconscionability: A Rationalisation' (1998) 114 LQR 479.

On the *Etridge* conjoined cases, see the case note by Thompson, in [2002] 66 Conv 174.

Gilmore, 'Circular Priority Systems' (1961) 71 Yale LJ 53.

You can visit the online resources to test your knowledge of this chapter with self-test questions at **www.oup.com/he/nair19e/**.

24

Easements and profits à prendre

24.1 Introduction 515
24.2 What is an easement? 517
24.3 What is a profit à prendre? 530
24.4 Easements and profits may be legal or equitable 531
24.5 Enforcement against purchaser of servient tenement 532
24.6 Acquisition by express grant or reservation 534
24.7 Acquisition by implied grant or reservation 535
24.8 Acquisition by express grant by virtue of LPA 1925, s. 62 540
24.9 Acquisition by prescription 546
24.10 Remedies 561
24.11 Extinguishment of easements and profits 564
24.12 Law reform 567

24.1 Introduction

The title '**easements** and **profits à prendre**' may make you imagine that this chapter is concerned with strange rights known only to land lawyers and having archaic names. In fact, both easements and profits are commonly encountered and most of us use such rights every day of our lives: for example, when we walk across the courtyard in the block of flats in which we live, or enjoy the continuing support of our houses that is provided by walls belonging to our neighbours. Once you have read this chapter you can, on your next train journey, play a variant on a children's game, and spot from the train windows the situations in which easements and profits are likely to arise. Is the woman driving up a shared driveway exercising an easement (a right of way)? Is the little girl leading her pony into that field exercising a profit (grazing)? Does the path across the back gardens of those terraced houses indicate an easement (right of way on foot)? From this you can see that the interests discussed in this chapter are often quite straightforward and some are essential to our daily life. The common strand to all these arrangements is that they are all rights exercised over land which belongs to another person, and so come into the category of third-party interests in land.

24.1.1 Trant Way

24.1.1.1 14–16A Trant Way

The plan of 14, 15, 16, and 16A Trant Way in Figure 24.1 may assist you when reading this chapter.

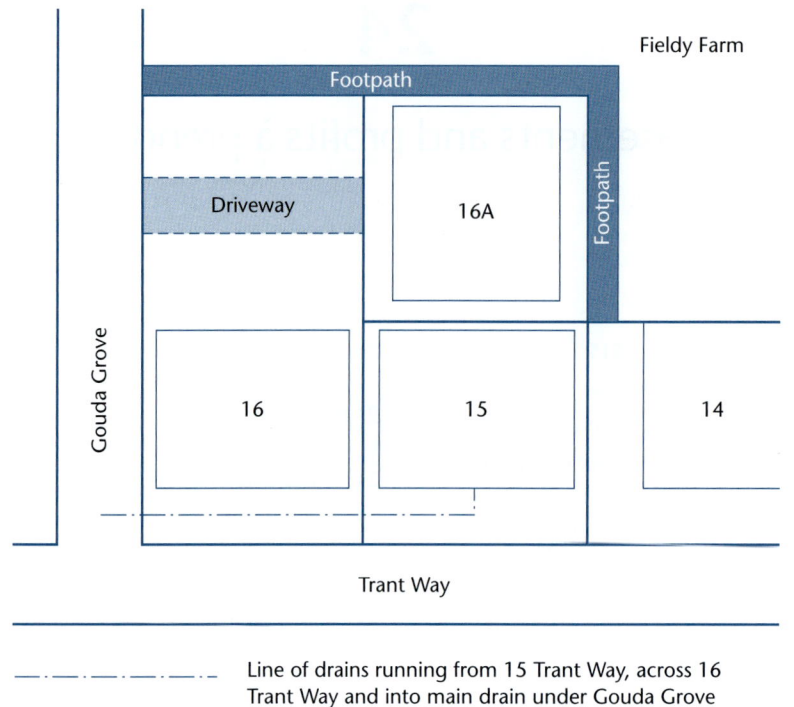

Figure 24.1 Nos. 14, 15, 16, and 16A Trant Way

In 1947, the then owner of 15 Trant Way decided to install modern drains in the property. The nearest main drain was in Gouda Grove. After discussion, the then owner of 16 Trant Way agreed that the drains could be laid across his front garden into Gouda Grove. A deed was drawn up which contained the following words:

> The grantor [the owner of 16] as beneficial owner hereby grants unto the grantee [the owner of 15] full right and liberty to use the sewer or drain marked with a dotted line on the plan attached hereto for the passage or conveyance of sewage water and soil from the said 15 Trant Way to the public sewer.

The current owner of 15 Trant Way is Charles Chive.

The current owner of 14 Trant Way (Nigel Neep) keeps a goat which he grazes on Fieldy Farm (to the rear of 14). Fieldy Farm is owned in fee simple by Farmer George.

There is a footpath leading from the back of 14 Trant Way to Gouda Grove. This path runs across Farmer George's land. The path has been in regular use by the owners of 14 Trant Way for many years.

For the last 50 years the fence separating 14 Trant Way from Fieldy Farm has been maintained by Farmer George or his father (who was his predecessor in title).

At one time 16 and 16A formed one plot of land. In 1980 the then owner of 16 Trant Way (Marjorie Marjoram) sold the freehold of the property now known as 16A Trant Way to Basil Borage. The only access to 16A is across the driveway on 16 Trant Way (see Figure 24.1) but this fact was not mentioned in the conveyance to Basil Borage. In 1996 Miss Marjoram sold 16 to Dan Dill (who made a first registration of title). Mr Dill dislikes Mr Borage and wants to prevent his use of the driveway.

At present 16 Trant Way enjoys an uninterrupted view of fields to the rear of the property over Fieldy Farm. Farmer George has just obtained planning permission to erect a corn silo on the farm and Dan Dill believes that this will spoil his view.

24.1.1.2 Basement flat: 5 Trant Way

You will recall from Chapter 9 that Fingall Forest, the fee simple owner of 5 Trant Way, has granted a tenancy of the basement flat at No. 5 to his friend Gerald Gruyère. When Mr Gruyère first moved in he had only an oral lease. At that time, he asked Mr Forest if he could keep his dustbin in the back garden of 5 Trant Way (which Mr Forest retained for his own use) and Mr Forest agreed. About two months ago the two friends decided to formalise their arrangement, and Mr Gruyère was given a written lease of the flat for a period of two years. The agreement was recorded in a written document which did not mention the right to keep the dustbin in the garden.

24.2 What is an easement?

Easements are rather like elephants: easy to recognise but very difficult to define. We are easily able to identify rights which are commonly accepted as being easements, for example, rights of way and rights of light. However, the label 'easement' covers such a wide range of interests that it may be difficult to discern any similarity between them. One might, as a result, be inclined to ignore the difficulties of definition and merely construct a list of rights which have been recognised as easements. However, although this may be helpful, it is not sufficient, for the courts have recognised that the list of easements is not closed and that the need for new easements will be met as the circumstances of life change (*Dyce v Lady James Hay* (1852) 1 Macq 305). For example, an easement allowing the erection of a satellite dish is obviously a modern addition to the list. We must accordingly address the question of a standard against which a claim to a new right can be tested. This standard is provided in the judgment of the Court of Appeal in *Re Ellenborough Park* [1956] Ch 131 which, although it does not define an easement, provides rules for its recognition.

24.2.1 The rules in *Re Ellenborough Park*

The original owners of Ellenborough Park also owned the surrounding land, which they sold off in plots for building purposes. Each conveyance granted to the purchasers the right to use the park, subject to an obligation to make a contribution towards the cost of maintaining it. The plaintiffs in the case acquired the park itself from the original owners, and intended to build upon it. The owners of the surrounding plots claimed the right to use the park and to be able to prevent the proposed building. The Court of Appeal upheld these claims, saying that the rights to use the park were legal easements. Since these rights were legal interests in unregistered land, they bound the purchasers of the park, and thus prevented them from building upon it. The court approved four rules of recognition for an easement:

(a) there must be a **dominant tenement** and a **servient tenement**;
(b) dominant and servient owners must be different persons;
(c) the easement must accommodate the dominant tenement; and
(d) the right claimed must be capable of forming the subject matter of a grant.

We will now look at these rules and their application in greater detail.

24.2.1.1 Need for a dominant and servient tenement

An easement is a right enjoyed over one piece of land (the 'servient tenement') for the benefit of another piece of land (the 'dominant tenement'). In the case of the easement of drainage given in the practical examples, 16 Trant Way is burdened and is the servient tenement, while 15 Trant Way is benefited and is the dominant tenement (see Figure 24.2).

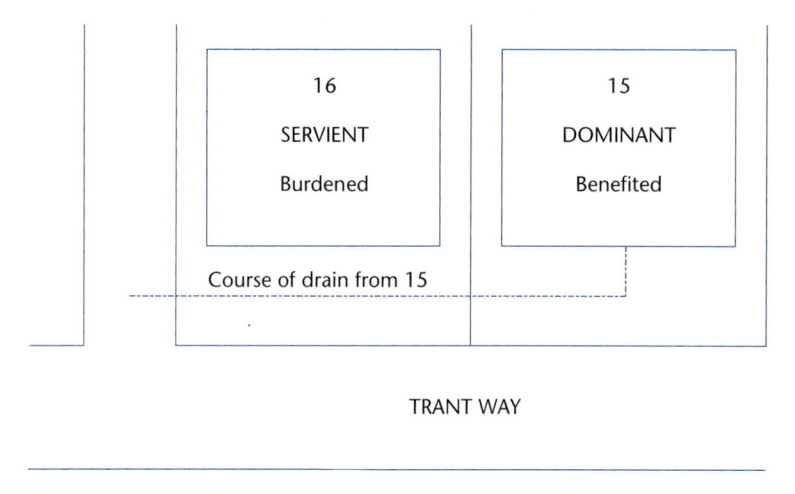

Figure 24.2 Dominant and servient tenements

It is essential that there is a dominant tenement, for an easement cannot exist 'in gross', that is, without being attached to a particular piece of land which derives benefit from it. It is this which distinguishes, for example, an easement of way from a public right of way: in the latter, anyone may use the way, whereas the easement is available only to those connected in some way with the dominant tenement.

Accordingly, when a claim is made to an easement, the two pieces of land must be readily identifiable and, therefore, when an easement is being created, care must be taken to ensure that the two properties are clearly identified. This is particularly important in the case of the servient tenement and, in the example of the right to drainage, the burdened land is clearly identified by the dotted line showing the line of the drain as it passes under 16 Trant Way. In a properly drafted document, the dominant tenement should also be clearly defined, thus the use of words such as 'for the benefit of the land known as 15 Trant Way' is desirable. However, it is not fatal if such an express mention is omitted as long as it is clear from the deed which land is to be benefited (see *Thorpe v Brumfitt* (1873) LR 8 Ch App 650).

Appurtenant to what?
In recent years there has been an interesting debate as to whether easements have to be appurtenant to land or to estates in land. In *Wall v Collins* [2007] EWCA Civ 444 the Court of Appeal took the view that easements were appurtenant to land. In this case, the benefit of an easement was granted to the owner of a 999-year lease. Later the current leaseholder acquired the freehold of the land and the leasehold estate merged into the freehold estate (see 9.5.2.4). If the benefit of the easement were only attached to the

leasehold estate, it would be extinguished on merger. The court, however, was of the view that it was appurtenant to land but lasted for the period of the lease.

However, in its 2008 Consultation Paper No. 186 (see 24.12.1), the Law Commission took the opposite view and proposed that an easement appurtenant to a lease should end when the lease ended. In its 2011 Report No. 327 (see 24.12.1) the Law Commission confirmed its general view, subject to limited exceptions and recommended that *Wall v Collins* be overturned by legislation. No further steps have been taken yet.

24.2.1.2 Dominant and servient owners must be different persons

This is how the rule is stated in *Re Ellenborough Park*, but it is perhaps easier to understand if one says that the two tenements must not be both owned and occupied by the same person. An easement is essentially a right over another's land for the benefit of one's own, and one cannot exercise a right against oneself. Thus, if a person owns two pieces of land and walks across one piece in order to reach another, this is not the exercise of an easement (*Roe v Siddons* (1888) 22 QBD 224 at p. 236). Sometimes, however, such a situation is said to give rise to a '**quasi-easement**': this is, as you will see (24.7.1.3), a potential easement which could develop into an easement if the plots came into separate hands.

We emphasise the requirement that the same person must not own *and* occupy the two tenements, because it is possible for a tenant to have an easement over other land belonging to his landlord, and equally for the landlord, during the period of the lease, to have an easement over land occupied by the tenant. Thus, in the case of Fingall Forest and Gerald Gruyère at 5 Trant Way it is perfectly possible for Mr Gruyère to have an easement in respect of the land owned and occupied by Mr Forest, although Mr Forest owns the fee simple of both dominant and servient tenements.

Should one person acquire both the servient and the dominant tenement this will extinguish a pre-existing easement, if at the same time the two properties come into common occupation. If, at some future date, the same person were to buy and occupy both 15 and 16 Trant Way, this would bring the easement over 16 Trant Way to an end. This is because one cannot have rights as against oneself, unless one is acting in different capacities (for example, where the owner of both tenements holds one of them on trust for another person).

24.2.1.3 The easement must accommodate the dominant tenement

This rule requires that the right must confer an advantage on the dominant land. It is not sufficient for the right to confer a merely personal advantage on the current owner. In *Re Ellenborough Park* the right to use the park was held to benefit the surrounding plots of land because a domestic property is always improved in character by the availability of a garden. Unfortunately, it is sometimes difficult to distinguish between personal benefits and benefits conferred on land. It may help to consider whether any possible owner of the property would regard the right as advantageous. In the case of 15 Trant Way, any owner would regard the availability of drainage into the main drains as an advantage.

A problem may arise where the right claimed tends to confer an advantage, not on the land itself, but rather on some trade or business which is being carried on upon the land. In *Hill v Tupper* (1863) 2 Hurl & C 121 the right claimed as an easement was the exclusive right to put pleasure-boats on the canal which bordered the 'dominant' land and to prevent anyone else sailing boats on that canal. It was held that this right did not amount to an easement, because it did not benefit *the land*. Rather it benefited the business which Mr Hill happened to be running upon his land. The fact that the right benefits a business is not necessarily fatal, however, to a claim that the right is an easement. In *Moody v Steggles* (1879) 12 ChD 261, a right to hang on neighbouring land, a sign pointing towards a public house, was held to be capable of being an easement. This may well be because it is common for land used as a public house to remain in such use for prolonged periods, sometimes for centuries, so that the business run on the land and the land itself become inextricably linked.

The requirement that benefit be conferred on the land does, however, mean that the servient tenement and the dominant tenement must be reasonably close together. Normally the two properties will adjoin one another (as is the case in all the practical examples given above) but this is not essential (*Pugh v Savage* [1970] 2 QB 373). The two pieces of land must, however, be close enough to support a claim that the dominant land receives an actual benefit from the right, and thus one could not have an easement exercisable over land at the other end of the country (*Bailey v Stephens* (1862) 12 CB NS 91 at p. 115).

The requirement for benefit to land has given rise to other issues, notably:

(1) what happens if the benefited land changes its character over time, so that the impact of the easement on the burdened land changes; and

(2) what is the position if the owner of the dominant land tries to use the easement to benefit other land he owns?

1. Change of character
This issue was considered in *Attwood v Bovis Homes Ltd* [2001] Ch 379, in relation to an easement of drainage. Here the land having the benefit of the drainage had ceased to be agricultural land and was being developed. It is important to note that here the easement had been obtained by long use (**prescription**—see 24.9) and not by an express grant. Thus, the owner of the dominant land argued that the easement should be restricted to the benefit conferred on land as it had been while the right was being acquired. This argument was rejected. However, as you will see from the decision and the older cases cited in it, a different result might be reached if the changed use of the dominant tenement led to a substantial increase in the burden or changed the nature of the burden (see also *British Railways Board v Glass* [1965] Ch 538). In *Attwood* it was accepted that the drainage had not been increased by the change in use. It appears that the court did consider that it was more likely to be accepted that there was a substantial increase or change in nature where the easement was a right of way. For an example of this, see *Wimbledon and Putney Commons Conservators v Dixon* (1875) 1 ChD 362. In *McAdams Homes Ltd v Robinson* [2004] EWCA Civ 214 the Court of Appeal held that an easement of drainage granted to benefit a bakery could not endure to benefit two large domestic properties that were later constructed on the same site. The Court of Appeal was of the view that the judge at first instance was entitled on the facts to conclude that at the time of the original creation of the easement the parties could not have contemplated that such a change in the character of the dominant land would come about.

2. Use to benefit additional land
In *Peacock v Custins* [2002] 1 WLR 1815 a farmer wanted to use a right of way in order to gain access to a field that was not part of the land expressed to be the benefited land in the conveyance creating the easement but which he farmed with the benefited land. The Court of Appeal held that the right of way could not be used to gain access to the extra field and confirmed that the right was determined by reference to the land mentioned in the conveyance. In *Das v Linden Mews Ltd* [2003] 2 P&CR 4, the same rule was

applied to prevent a right to drive across a private mews being used to gain access to a car-parking area that the owners of the dominant properties (houses on either side of the mews) had added by acquiring new land at the end of the mews. You will appreciate that this rule, while generally sensible in order to prevent increase in the burden of an easement, may cause a problem in some cases, if the user of a right of way has a primary purpose of reaching the dominant land but once there may decide to move on to the extra land. This issue was considered in *Macepark (Whittlebury) Ltd v Sargeant* [2003] 1 WLR 2284, in which it was indicated that access to such extra land was acceptable but that the right of way could not be used substantially for that purpose and that the access to the extra land had to be merely ancillary to the proper main use of the easement in relation to the benefited land. The same approach was adopted by the Court of Appeal in *Massey v Boulden* [2003] 1 WLR 1792.

24.2.1.4 The easement must be capable of forming the subject matter of a grant

Easements are interests in land which can be legal interests, and as such they must 'lie in grant'. This means that a right must be capable of being granted by deed if it is to be recognised as an easement. A number of rules result from this condition, which in *Re Ellenborough Park* (at pp. 175–6) was said to require consideration of whether an alleged easement was:

- too wide and vague;
- inconsistent with the proprietorship or possession of the servient tenement owner (i.e., must not deprive the servient tenement owner of possession); or
- a mere right of recreation and amusement.

The court must consider all these matters when it is asked to recognise a new easement, and they are covered in more detail, along with some other conditions, in 24.2.3.

The second important consequence of the rule that easements lie in grant is that, at the date at which the right arose, there must have been two persons who were capable respectively of granting and receiving the easement. This is of importance where easements are acquired otherwise than by express grant and will accordingly be discussed later when we consider methods of acquisition.

24.2.2 Some examples of easements

It is not possible to list all the rights which have been recognised as amounting to easements, but some of the most common are mentioned in the following paragraphs.

24.2.2.1 Rights of way

The right of way is an easement that you are likely to have encountered frequently in your daily life: it involves a right to pass over the servient land. It can be general (passage by any means) or limited (for example, on foot only, or exercisable only at certain times of the day).

Where one tenement has a right of way over another, questions may arise about which owner should construct or repair any path or road over the route. Should you need material on this, you will find a useful summary of the rules in *Carter v Cole* [2006] EWCA Civ 398, at para. 8. In outline, neither owner is obliged to do the work, but either of them may undertake it if he or she wishes to do so. Where the dominant tenement owner decides to do the work, he or she must pay for the work and is entitled to enter the servient tenement for the purpose.

24.2.2.2 Right to light

This must be a specific right, so that light is claimed for particular windows or skylights, and there cannot be a general claim for light over the whole piece of land (*Colls v Home & Colonial Stores Ltd* [1904] AC 179).

How much light?

The amount of light which one can claim is that which is necessary according to the ordinary notions of mankind. This rule relates to and, in essence, is derived from the rule in nuisance that the damage must be such as, 'materially to interfere with the ordinary comfort of human existence': *St Helen's Smelting Co. Ltd v Tipping* (1862) 11 ER 1483 and see *City of London Brewery Co. Ltd v Tenant* (1873) LR 9 Ch App 212.

The amount of light to be expected will also vary depending upon the nature of the property. Thus, this right would be infringed were the light so obstructed that in a dwelling the electric light had to be lit all day, but this might not be objectionable were the premises in question to be a warehouse (see *Colls*). In *Allen v Greenwood* [1980] Ch 119 a claim was made in relation to light to a greenhouse, used to grow tomatoes, which it was alleged was being obstructed by a fence and a parked caravan. The servient owner argued that there was no right to heat or the direct rays of the sun. However, Lord Justice Buckley said that in such a case there was a claim of light to a particular building (the greenhouse) and that:

> ... the amount of light to which a dominant owner is entitled ... is sufficient light, according to ordinary notions, for the comfortable or beneficial use of the building in question, again according to ordinary notions, for such purposes as would constitute normal uses of a building of its particular character. If the building be a dwelling house, the measure must be related to reasonable standards of comfort as a building house. If it be a warehouse, a shop or a factory, the measure must be related to reasonable standards of comfort or beneficial use . . . If the building be a greenhouse, the measure must . . . be related to its reasonably satisfactory use as a greenhouse.

Subsequently, however, in *Midtown Ltd v City of London Real Property Co. Ltd* (2005) 4 EG 166 (CS) it was held that owners of an office building could object to a *substantial* diminution of the light passing to it, even if all the rooms in the office were habitually lit by artificial light whenever they were in use. A mere diminution in the light is not sufficient, nor can one claim extra light because of the activities carried out on the land, unless the special use contemplated was known to the owner of the servient land at the time at which the easement was acquired.

24.2.2.3 Rights to water

One has no general right to water which percolates through the soil, but an easement may exist in respect of water in a defined channel, e.g., a pipe or stream. On this see *Race v Ward* (1855) 4 El & Bl 702 and *Dickinson v Grand Junction Canal Co. Ltd* (1852) 7 Exch 282 at p. 301.

24.2.2.4 Right to drainage

This is a common and important easement (see the example in 24.1.1.1). For a further discussion see *Attwood v Bovis Homes Ltd* [2001] Ch 379 and 24.2.1.3(1).

24.2.2.5 Rights to air

Once again there is no general right to the passage of air (*Webb v Bird* (1861) 10 CB (NS) 268) but a claim to air flowing in a defined channel can amount to an easement. This might include, for example, rights in respect of ventilation ducts (*Wong v Beaumont Property Trust Ltd* [1965] 1 QB 173).

24.2.2.6 Right to support

This right is very important where one is dealing with a semi-detached or terraced house. In such a case the boundary frequently runs down the centre of the connecting wall. Were one owner to remove his or her half, the remaining portion would probably soon collapse. Accordingly, an easement of support is recognised in this, and other similar, cases (*Dalton v Angus & Co.* (1881) 6 App Cas 740); this right is limited, however, so that while the servient owner may not pull the wall down it can be allowed to fall down for lack of repair (*Jones v Pritchard* [1908] 1 Ch 630 at p. 637).

The right to support is not, however, confined to walls (see *Jordeson v Sutton, Smithcoates & Drypool Gas Co. Ltd* [1898] 2 Ch 614, which related to quarrying at the bottom of a hill that resulted in part of the land in a neighbouring fruit farm being dislodged). This area of law interacts with the tort of nuisance (see 24.10.2.1 and *Holbeck Hall Hotel v Scarborough BC* [2000] QB 836).

24.2.2.7 Rights to use of facilities

Common examples include the use of a lavatory (*Miller v Emcer Products Ltd* [1956] Ch 304), of a letter-box (*Goldberg v Edwards* [1950] Ch 247), or a kitchen (*Haywood v Mallalieu* (1883) 25 ChD 357).

24.2.2.8 Rights of storage

Claims to rights of storage have given rise to a good deal of case law and academic debate, because they are sometimes said to amount to an unacceptable interference with the rights of the servient tenement owner. You will find more about the decisions on this point when we consider the rules for recognition of new easements—see 24.2.3.2(1). Mr Gruyère's claim to put his dustbin in Mr Forest's garden is an example of a claim to a right of storage.

24.2.2.9 Rights of parking

A popular modern claim is to an easement of parking. In a sense this is really only an extension of the easement of storage, giving rise to the same questions about interference with the rights of the servient owner, so we will postpone consideration of the relevant decisions until 24.2.3.2(2).

24.2.2.10 Easement of fencing?

In certain circumstances, a landowner may be under a duty to maintain a fence on the boundary with neighbouring land, and the courts have recognised the neighbour's right to enforce this obligation as being 'in the nature of an easement'. This is unusual, because easements do not usually impose expense on the servient tenement. For example, you have already seen that there is no requirement to make up or maintain a road or track across one's land and that similarly there is no duty to repair a wall which is supporting a neighbour's house. For this reason, the easement of fencing is sometimes described as a spurious easement, but its existence has nevertheless been recognised in at least three decisions of the Court of Appeal: *Jones v Price* [1965] 2 QB 618; *Crow v Wood* [1971] 1 QB 77; and *Egerton v Harding* [1975] QB 62.

It should be noted, however, that all these decisions arose in the context of disputes about cattle trespass in which A, the owner of cattle grazing on adjoining land, claimed that his neighbour, B, should have fenced his (B's) land in order to keep out A's cattle. Where this right to require one's neighbour to fence against cattle is found to exist, it has in general arisen through long use (i.e., by prescription) and in *Jones v Price* the Court of Appeal doubted whether it could be acquired in any other way. You will see later, however, that most forms of prescription are based on a fiction that the right in question was granted at some time in the past, with the consequence that the finding of prescription in *Jones v Price* ([1965] 2 QB 618) compelled Diplock LJ to admit that the right was in theory capable of being granted, although he added:

> There is no precedent in the books for such a grant. I find it difficult to envisage its form.

In the later case of *Crow v Wood* [1971] 1 QB 77, the requirements for establishing prescription were not satisfied, and the Court of Appeal, relying on *Jones v Price*, found that an easement of fencing had been created by implied grant, Edmund Davies LJ saying that 'a duty to fence against trespassers' could arise by express or implied grant and could also pass under LPA 1925, s. 62 (for which, see 24.8).

It is important to remember that these decisions were dealing only with the obligation to fence against cattle. There seems to be no decision on the duty to fence in other circumstances, and interestingly there is still no precedent for the grant of such an easement in any of the precedent books. The point is important because vendors selling off part of their land often wish to impose obligations to fence on purchasers and their successors in title. In Chapter 25, it is explained why this cannot be done by means of positive covenants, and it would be a mistake to assume too readily when considering a problem, that the solution is for the vendor to reserve an easement of fencing.

In *Churston Golf Club Ltd v Haddock* [2019] EWCA Civ 544, the Court of Appeal held that an obligation to fence that was drafted, expressly, as a covenant in a professionally prepared document, should be construed as a positive covenant and not as an easement. They declined to decide whether such an easement could be expressly granted and said that such an issue was best left to a case in which the issue was directly in point.

The types of easements described above merely provide some examples, and reference should be made to *Gale on Easements*, 20th edn., paras. 1-76 and 1-77, should you require a more detailed list.

24.2.3 Establishing a new easement

If one wishes to establish a claim to a hitherto unknown easement, one must first show that the right claimed satisfies the four rules of recognition adopted in *Re Ellenborough Park*. Thereafter it is necessary to satisfy the court that the claim to a new type of easement is justified. This is considerably easier if one can show that the nature of the right claimed is analogous to that of some existing easement. Thus, Mr Gruyère might wish to show that his claim to store a dustbin is similar in character to the right to store coal in a shed, which was accepted in *Wright v Macadam* [1949] 2 KB 744 (see 24.2.3.2(1)).

The first three rules of recognition described in *Re Ellenborough Park* are covered in 24.2.1, but at that point any consideration of certain conditions that arise from the fourth rule (that an easement must be capable of being granted) were postponed. It is now time to tell you about those conditions and to note a number of other requirements which the courts will take into account in considering whether to recognise a new easement.

24.2.3.1 Must not be too wide and vague

The right claimed must be specific and definable, for it would have to be carefully defined if included in a deed. This can be a problem if the right claimed involves issues of taste, since such matters cannot be defined. Thus one cannot claim a right to a prospect (a fair view) as an easement, for one cannot define such a right (*William Aldred's Case* (1610) 9 Co Rep 57b—'the law does not give an action for such things of delight'). Accordingly, Dan Dill at 16 Trant Way cannot complain about Farmer George's silo on the basis of an easement for a view. He should have made his complaints at the stage at which the farmer applied for planning permission (though he might not have been able to prevent the grant of permission).

The vague nature of the right claimed may also result in its failing this test. Thus, in *Dyce v Hay* (1865) 1 Macq 305, a claim to use land for general recreational purposes was held to be too vague to amount to an easement, although a right to use a garden for similar purposes was upheld in *Re Ellenborough Park* itself and, in *Regency Villas Title Ltd v Diamond Resorts (Europe) Ltd* [2019] AC 553, the Supreme Court held that sporting and recreational rights could, if sufficiently specifically defined, constitute easements. Lord Briggs said (at para. 48):

> I consider that *In re Ellenborough Park* should be taken to be dispositive of this issue for the purposes of English common law, to this extent, namely that it is not fatal to the recognition of a right as an easement that it is granted for recreational (including sporting) use, to be enjoyed for its own sake on the servient tenement. The question in every such case is whether the particular recreational or sporting rights granted accommodate the dominant tenement.

However, note that in *Chaffe v Kingsley* [2000] 79 P&CR 404, a claim to a right of way failed because the conveyance by which it was alleged the right was granted was insufficiently specific as to the area of land affected. Accordingly, care must be taken when claiming an easement, or when drafting one, to be as specific as possible about the details of the right claimed.

24.2.3.2 Must not deprive servient owner of possession

The courts will never accept as an easement a right which has the effect of excluding the servient owner from possession of his or her land. An easement is by nature a limited right, and if the dominant owner seeks to oust the servient owner that would be to claim a right that is considerably greater than that conferred by an easement.

Over the years this requirement has received a good deal of attention from the courts, particularly in the context of claims to:

(1) easements of storage; and

(2) easements of parking.

1. Easements of storage

It is generally accepted that a right to store goods on another's land can constitute an easement. However, the courts have had some difficulty in rationalising their recognition of this right, because use of a piece of land for storage does appear to involve excluding the owner from it (in practical terms, a landowner cannot use the garden shed if it is full of the neighbour's furniture). However, this problem was not discussed in *Wright v Macadam* [1949] 2 KB 744, and the Court of Appeal accepted without question that a tenant could have a right to store coal in her landlord's shed. The attention of the court focused on the question of how the right had been created, rather than on whether it satisfied the requirements for recognition as an easement.

By contrast, in *Copeland v Greenhalf* [1952] 1 Ch 488, the High Court rejected a claim by the owner of a workshop that he had a right to store vehicles awaiting repair or collection on a strip of land belonging to his neighbour. In the words of Upjohn J (at p. 498), the right claimed was:

> wholly outside any normal idea of an easement ... it is virtually a claim to possession of the servient tenement, if necessary to the exclusion of the owner; or, at any rate, to a joint use.

The court in *Copeland v Greenhalf* did not consider the earlier decision of the Court of Appeal in *Wright v Macadam*, and as a result it has been suggested that the judge's decision was *per incuriam* (although it is worth noting that it was referred to with approval by the Court of Appeal in *Re Ellenborough Park* [1956] 1 Ch 131 at pp. 176–7).

The apparent inconsistency between the two decisions was considered by Brightman J in *Grigsby v Melville* [1972] 1 WLR 355. The parties were the owners of two adjoining properties and the defendant claimed a right of storage in the cellar beneath his neighbour's house. The judge did not consider whether the right of storage claimed could amount to an easement, because he decided the case on other grounds. However, he indicated that, if he had been required to deal with that point, he would have followed *Copeland v Greenhalf*, since in his view the right claimed by the defendant amounted to exclusive use of the cellar.

For our purposes, the significance of *Grigsby v Melville* lies in the judge's comments on the supposed inconsistency between *Wright v Macadam* and *Copeland v Greenhalf*. In his view, it might well be that there was no inconsistency: we do not know how much coal was stored nor whether the landlord was prevented from using his shed. As Brightman J put it:

> To some extent a problem of this sort may be one of degree.

A similar approach was adopted by Judge Paul Baker QC in *London & Blenheim Ltd v Ladbrooke Parks Ltd* [1992] 1 WLR 1278 at p. 1286:

> The matter must be one of degree. A small coal shed in a large property is one thing. The exclusive use of a large part of the alleged servient tenement is another.

Thus, the courts seem to have arrived at a compromise conclusion: it is possible to have a right to store goods on one's neighbour's land—provided one does not try to store too much!

2. Easements of parking

In a sense, the right to park is really only an extension of the easement of storage, as can be seen from the words of Megarry VC in *Newman v Jones* (unreported, but quoted by Aldous J in *Handel v St Stephen's Close* [1994] 1 EGLR 70 at p. 72):

> In view of *Wright v Macadam* ... I feel no hesitation in holding that a right for a landowner to park a car anywhere in a defined area nearby is capable of existing as an easement.

As with the storage cases, however, an alleged right of parking raises questions about exclusion of the servient owner. In *London & Blenheim Ltd v Ladbrooke Parks Ltd* [1992] 1 WLR 1278 at p. 1288 Judge Paul Baker QC expressed the view that:

> The essential question is one of degree. If the right granted in relation to the area over which it is to be exercisable is such that it would leave the servient owner without any reasonable use of his land, whether for parking or anything else it could not be an easement though it might be some larger or different grant.

The 'compatibility' test As we have just seen, courts considering a claim of parking or storage have come to apply the test of whether the right claimed is so extensive that it would prevent the servient owner from making any reasonable use of his land or, as Gray and Gray put it (see para. 5.1.65) whether the right claimed is compatible with the beneficial ownership of the servient proprietor. It may occur to you at this point that this development seems to involve a slight shift in language: the earlier decisions speak of depriving the servient owner of *'possession'*, but from *London & Blenheim Ltd* onwards we find the courts talking about deprivation of *'use'*. (We will return to this point later when considering the House of Lords' decision in *Moncrieff v Jamieson* [2007] 1 WLR 2620.)

The London & Blenheim Ltd approach was followed by the Court of Appeal in *Batchelor v Marlow* [2003] 1 WLR 764, in which the court rejected a claim by the defendant that he had a right to park up to six cars on the plaintiff's land on weekdays between 8.30 a.m. and 6 p.m. The court considered that such an extensive right would leave the plaintiff without any reasonable use of his land, whether for parking or otherwise (paras. 15 and 18).

This decision by the Court of Appeal seemed to establish the 'substantial interference' test, which until then had been developed in lower-court decisions, and to confirm the limited nature of storage and parking easements. However, the whole question was reopened by the House of Lords' decision in *Moncrieff v Jamieson* [2007] 1 WLR 2620.

Moncrieff v Jamieson This case came to the House of Lords as an appeal from the Court of Session in Scotland. The Scots law on servitudes is in many respects similar to that of the English law of easements (paras. 45 and 111), so this case is of relevance to English land law, but if you read the case you should be aware of Lord Neuberger's warning against assuming that the two systems are the same in every respect (para. 136).

There is no need to note the facts of the case in any detail. All you need to know is that the respondent, Moncrieff ('M'), had succeeded at first instance and on appeal in establishing that he had an implied right to park on the land of the appellant, Jamieson ('J'). The appeal to the House of Lords raised a number of issues, but the only ones that concern us are: (a) J's claim that a right to park did not amount to an easement in law; and (b) that the claim was for an implied right to park.

The speeches of Lord Scott and Lord Neuberger contain interesting discussions of the principle against excluding the servient tenement owner, and its application to easements of storage and parking. Their Lordships emphasised that although the courts often speak of depriving the servient tenement owner of use, the real rule is that the owner must not be deprived of possession. At para. 55, Lord Scott distinguished between giving the dominant tenement owner 'sole use' of part of the servient tenement (which in his view would not prevent the right being an easement) and giving 'exclusive possession' of that part, which would not be consistent with the general principle:

> sole use for a limited purpose is not, in my opinion, inconsistent with the servient owner's retention of possession and control or inconsistent with the nature of an easement.

Lord Neuberger agreed with him, saying (at paras. 140 and 143) that he was not satisfied that:

> a right is prevented from being an easement simply because [it] would involve the servient owner being effectively excluded from the property . . . a right can be an easement notwithstanding that the dominant owner effectively enjoys exclusive occupation, on the basis that the essential requirement is that the servient owner retains possession and control.

Applying this approach to parking claims, Lord Scott (at para. 59) said that he would:

> reject the test that asks whether the servient tenement owner is left without any reasonable use of his land and substitute for it a test which asks whether the servient owner retains possession and, subject to the reasonable exercise of the right in question, control of the servient land.

As a result, both Lord Scott and Lord Neuberger expressed doubts as to whether *Batchelor v Marlow* had been correctly decided by the Court of Appeal (paras. 60 and 143). In the event, however, there was no need for either of them to reach any conclusion on this point, nor to express any final view on the degree of exclusion which is required to prevent a right being recognised as an easement (para. 143). The easement claimed by M was simply that of parking one or two cars somewhere on J's land at the end of a track which led to M's house. The case did not raise any difficult 'borderline' questions: it did not involve parking an excessive number of cars, nor was there any question of excluding the servient owner from any particular parking space. The claim in fact fell clearly within the situation originally envisaged by Megarry V-C in *Newman v Jones*, and their Lordships concluded that M was entitled to an easement of parking.

You will recall that the second issue in *Moncrieff* was that the claimant was seeking an implied right to park. This issue arose before the Court of Appeal in *Waterman v Boyle* [2009] EWCA Civ 115. This case concerned a property in relation to which there was an express right of way over a drive and an express right to park in two designated parking places. The owner of the dominant tenement was claiming in addition an implied right for visitors to park on the drive arguing that this was implied as necessary for enjoyment of the property as a dwelling. The Court of Appeal refused to recognise an implied right to park in such a case, saying the fact that a right to park was implied in *Moncrieff* was quite exceptional. Thus it seems now to be the case that while there can be express easements of parking, they will only be implied in very exceptional cases. See 24.7 for the general position on implied easements. However, of course, this does not preclude such easements from arising by prescription (see, for example, the recent case of *Poste Hotels Ltd v Cousins* [2020] EWHC 582).

24.2.3.3 Must not be a mere right of recreation and amusement

This is the third condition that the court in *Re Ellenborough Park* noted as arising from the requirement that an easement must be capable of forming the subject matter of a grant. It is derived from statements in *Mounsey v Ismay* (1865) 3 Hurl & C 486, a case concerned with an alleged right to enter land and hold horse races there. The requirement had some relevance to the right claimed in *Re Ellenborough Park* (i.e., that of using a garden), but it is unlikely to affect many claims to new easements, unless of course they involve the use of facilities for sport or other leisure time amusements (See *Regency*

Villas v Diamond Resorts (Europe) Ltd [2019] AC 553 and the discussion of that case at 24.2.3.1 and 24.2.3.6).

24.2.3.4 Must be a right

Any interest claimed must be in the nature of a *right*, rather than a permission (in which case it will amount to a licence). Thus, in *Burrows v Lang* [1901] 2 Ch 502 a claim to an easement to take water from an artificially filled pond was rejected, because exercise of such a right depended on the owner filling the pond and could not be enjoyed without his cooperation. The 'right' was, therefore, too precarious and could not qualify as an easement. In *Green v Ashco Horticultural Ltd* [1966] 1 WLR 889 a claim to a right to park a van failed because the claimant had always moved his van when asked to do so by the servient owner and accordingly exercised his right only as far as the servient owner permitted.

24.2.3.5 No new negative easements

Easements may broadly be divided into two categories: positive and negative. In the case of a positive easement the dominant owner must *do* something in order to exercise the right. A right of way is thus positive because the dominant owner must walk, drive, or ride on to the servient land in order to exercise the right. A negative easement protects a benefit which is enjoyed without any action by the dominant owner (e.g., a right to light, air, water, or support). Such easements impose a burden on the servient owner not to interrupt the dominant owner's enjoyment of the relevant benefit. In *Phipps v Pears* [1965] 1 QB 76 it was said that the courts would not readily accept the creation of new *negative* easements, because they tend to restrict the servient tenement owner and hamper development of the property. Thus, the court rejected a claim to an easement of protection from the weather, which was argued for by analogy with the easement of support and which, like that easement, would have the effect of preventing one from demolishing one's own property (on this see further *Rees v Skerrett* [2001] 1 WLR 1541).

In this context, it is worth noting that developments in the law of nuisance might allow a landowner to object to a neighbour's actions on his land, as an interference with her enjoyment of some aspect of her own property, without necessarily involving the recognition of an easement. The recent case of *Fearn v Board of Trustees of the Tate Gallery* [2023] UKSC 4 is a striking example of such a situation. The landowners in that case successfully sued the Tate Gallery in London for allowing strangers onto their land for the purpose of looking into the landowners' (glass-walled) flats. There was no suggestion that such a claim depended on showing an easement that restricted the servient owner from interfering with the landowners' freedom not to be looked at.

24.2.3.6 Not involving expenditure

Normally, the courts will not accept an easement which requires expenditure by the servient owner. Thus, in *Regis Property Co. Ltd v Redman* [1956] 2 QB 612 it was held that a claim to the supply of hot water was not an easement. The easement of fencing is an exception to this rule. In *Regency Villas v Diamond Resorts (Europe) Ltd* [2019] AC 553, it was argued that a right to make use of gym facilities, including a swimming pool, could not be a valid easement because it required the servient owner to expend money in maintaining the facilities in usuable form. However, the majority of the Supreme Court rejected that argument and held that the easement permitted the dominant owners to make use of the facilities even if the servient owner stopped maintaining them, by stepping in to perform the necessary maintenance themselves.

Subject to these general principles the list of easements will continue to expand as circumstances change and the courts seem happy to see new rights arise as and when they prove to be useful or necessary.

24.3 What is a profit à prendre?

A 'profit à prendre' is a right to take something from land which belongs to another person. The 'something' which is removed may either be part of the land itself (e.g., sand), or something growing on the land (e.g., grass), or wild creatures found naturally on the land (e.g., fish, deer, or pheasants). There are a number of traditional forms of profit, although others can still arise.

24.3.1 Examples of profits

(a) The *profit of pasture* is an ancient right but still commonly claimed today. It is a profit because the grazing animals take grass and other plants from the land. This cannot exist as a right to graze an unlimited number of animals as this would exhaust the land, and the traditional limit is the maximum number of animals which can be supported through the winter (*Mellor v Spateman* (1669) 1 Saund 339). Mr Neep's right to graze his goat would probably be a profit of pasture.

(b) The *profit of piscary* is the right to take fish.

(c) The *profit of turbary* is the right to cut turf or peat, usually in order to burn it.

(d) The *profit of estovers* is the right to take wood for use as fuel or for domestic or agricultural purposes (e.g., to build fences).

24.3.2 May be appurtenant or in gross

Unlike an easement, it is not necessary for a profit to be appurtenant to land. It may exist in gross, in which case it may be exercised for the personal benefit of its owner. Thus, a profit of piscary in gross would allow the person fishing to take fish in order to sell them, while a profit of piscary appurtenant allows fishing only to the extent of the needs of the land to which the right is attached (e.g., to feed those who reside there). Furthermore, profits may exist to the exclusion of the servient owner, as well as in common with the servient owners or other persons. Thus, Mr Neep's right to graze his goat may be for the benefit of 14 Trant Way (appurtenant), or for his own benefit (in gross), and may be to the exclusion of Farmer George (sole) or a right shared with Farmer George (in common).

24.3.3 Profit appurtenant can change character

One might expect that the character of a profit, particularly whether it is appurtenant or in gross, would be set at the point at which that profit is created and could not alter during the currency of the profit. However, despite the hundreds of years over which profits have been important land rights, this point had never been settled until the House of Lords' decision in *Bettison v Langton* [2002] 1 AC 27. When reading this case it is important to be aware that the Commons Registration Act 1965 required the registration of all commons and of all rights over commons. In the case of grazing rights, the Act required that the registration should be for a specified number of animals, thus bringing to an end the old common law limitation to the maximum number that could be supported during the winter (see 24.3.1).

In *Bettison v Langton*, the land in question enjoyed appurtenant rights of grazing, which had been registered in accordance with the 1965 Act. In 1987 Mrs Langton, the then owner of the land, sold the grazing rights to Mr and Mrs Bettison, while retaining the land. Some seven years later the land itself was sold by Mrs Langton's mortgagee (in exercise of his power of sale—see 22.8.1.2). The purchasers claimed that it was not possible for Mrs Langton to have severed the grazing rights from the land, or, in other words, they claimed that the rights were still attached to the land and had passed to them.

The House of Lords held that, if the scope of a profit appurtenant could be quantified otherwise than by the needs of the property to which it was annexed, that profit could be disposed of separately from the estate to which it had been annexed. Here, the rights had already been quantified on registration, and accordingly the disposal to the Bettisons was valid and the profit had become a profit in gross. As a result of the Commons Act 2006, s. 9, rights of grazing over common land can no longer be severed from the land they benefit, but *Bettison v Langton* will continue to be relevant where the right is enjoyed over land in private ownership.

A slightly different issue arose in *Lynn Shellfish Ltd v Loose* [2017] AC 599 in which there was a claim to rights of fishing on a sea shore, in which the seaward boundary of the right claimed varied with the lowest tidemark from time to time. Even though the area over which the right was claimed thus varied from day to day, the Supreme Court was content that the right could constitute a profit.

24.4 Easements and profits may be legal or equitable

Easements or profits, like other interests in land, may be legal or equitable. In order to constitute legal interests, they must satisfy certain rules concerning the period for which they last and the method by which they are created.

24.4.1 Prescribed period

The first requirement is derived from LPA 1925, s. 1(2), which defines legal easements and profits as being granted for a period 'equivalent to a fee simple absolute in possession or a term of years absolute'. This means that the easement or profit must last either, in effect, forever, or for a fixed period. Thus, an easement granted 'for 10 years' would be legal, while an easement 'for life' cannot be legal because it is not for a period equivalent to a legal estate. Note that, in an interesting article on equitable easements (see (1999) LQR 89), Professor Barnsley argues that it is in fact not likely that an equitable easement for life could exist. He concludes that the problem lies with the fact that an easement must be appurtenant to land, whereas an easement for life seems to have personal character. However, the answer here seems uncertain since rights can clearly relate to land while existing only for a lifetime.

Easements which do not satisfy the requirements of s. 1(2) necessarily take effect as equitable interests under s. 1(3), LPA 1925.

24.4.2 Creation by deed

The second requirement, concerning the method of creation, is found in the general rule that all legal estates and interests must be created by deed (LPA 1925, s. 52(1)). If no deed is used, the purported grant is ineffective in law but, provided the requirements of the Law of Property (Miscellaneous Provisions) Act 1989, s. 2 (see 4.2) are satisfied, equity may treat the arrangement as a specifically enforceable contract to grant an easement or profit and treat that right as being in existence from the date of the contract.

There is, at present, one apparent exception to the requirement for a deed for the creation of legal easements and profits. These rights can be acquired, without any formal grant, by 'prescription'; that is, by use over a long period of time. No deed is in fact used in such a case but, with only one exception, the various methods of prescription are all based on the fiction that a grant has been made in proper form, so that in this method, too, legal interests are created by deed—even if only by a fictitious one!

The Commonhold and Leasehold Reform Act 2002, s. 31(7), creates a further exception in relation to easements arising under a commonhold community statement, because that provision says that the duties imposed by the agreement will not require any other formality.

For completeness you should note that Professor Barnsley also identifies two other occasions on which an equitable easement will arise: (1) where the easement is created by an equitable owner; and (2) where the easement arises from an estoppel.

24.5 Enforcement against purchaser of servient tenement

Whether an easement or profit is legal or equitable is of great importance when one comes to enforce it against someone who has bought the servient tenement. The enforcement of third-party rights against purchasers has already been covered in detail (see 5.5 and 6.5) and so what follows is just a reminder of the relevant rules.

24.5.1 Registered land

Under LRA 1925, s. 70(1)(a), a legal easement or profit was an overriding interest and accordingly was automatically binding upon a purchaser. Generally, an equitable easement or profit was a **minor interest** and had to be protected by entry on the register for the servient tenement (but for an exception to this general rule, see *Celsteel Ltd v Alton House Holdings Ltd* [1985] 1 WLR 204). The position was changed very considerably by LRA 2002. The Act greatly reduced the number of legal easements and profits which can take effect as overriding interests, and ensures that the express creation of these rights results in their automatic protection by notice.

24.5.1.1 Easements and profits which can take effect as overriding interests

1. On first registration

All legal easements and profits take effect as overriding interests on first registration (LRA 2002, ss. 11 and 12, and Sch. 1, para. 3). This reflects the position in the unregistered system of title, and means that the rights which bound the estate owner in the unregistered system are carried forward and will continue to bind him when his title is registered for the first time. Where the registrar is aware of these encumbrances, they will be noted on the register of title and will continue to bind the estate on any future disposition.

2. On dispositions of the registered estate

All legal easements and profits created expressly after LRA 2002 came into force are automatically protected by notice on the register of the servient land, and cannot (and need not) take effect as overriding interests (for an explanation of how this works, see 24.5.1.2).

As a result, an easement or profit will be overriding (under LRA 2002, ss. 29 and 30, and Sch. 3, para. 3) only if:

1. it is a legal interest; and
2. it arises by implied grant or reservation, or by prescription, or under LPA 1925, s. 62; and
3. it satisfies one of the following conditions:
   (a) it is registered under the Commons Act 2006 (or its forerunner the Commons Registration Act 1965); or
   (b) the acquirer actually knew of its existence; or
   (c) the acquirer did not know of it but it would have been obvious on a reasonably careful inspection of the land over which it is exercised; or
   (d) even if it does not fall within (a) to (c) above, it has been exercised within the period of one year ending with the date of the disposition in question.

These provisions, depending as they do on factors such as the knowledge of the purchaser or the recent exercise of the right, pose considerable risks to the dominant tenement owner. Accordingly, the dominant owner would be well advised to take advantage of the fact that any easement or profit may be protected by entry of notice on the title of the servient tenement. Once such a notice is entered, the interest ceases permanently to be an overriding interest (s. 29(3)), but its enforcement against subsequent purchasers is ensured.

24.5.1.2 Easements and profits which are protected by entry of notice on title of servient tenement

1. Legal easements and profits which are expressly created

As you have seen, legal easements and profits which are expressly created (other than under LPA 1925, s. 62—for which see 24.8) are now automatically protected by entry of notice on the servient tenement's register of title. This is because the express creation of an easement or profit is one of the dealings with registered land that must be completed by registration (LRA 2002, s. 27(1) and (2)(d)). When the dominant tenement owner applies for this registration of a newly created easement, details of the easement will be entered in the property section of the register of title, and the registrar will automatically put a notice in the charges section of the register for the servient tenement.

If the new easement or profit is not registered in this way, the requirements for its legal creation will not be satisfied, and it will take effect only in equity (see Table 24.1).

2. Legal easements and profits arising other than by express creation

These may take effect as overriding interests, subject to satisfying the requirements of Sch. 3, para. 3, LRA 2002 but, as mentioned earlier, the dominant owner would still be well advised to protect them by notice.

3. Equitable easements and profits

There are no circumstances in which equitable easements and profits can take effect as overriding interests, unless enjoyment of the easement can be combined with actual occupation of the servient land (for a discussion of this doubtful possibility see the discussion of *Chaudhary v Yavuz* [2011] EWCA Civ 1314 in 6.5.6). They must be protected by notice on the register of the servient land and will not bind a purchaser unless this has been done.

24.5.2 Unregistered land

In the unregistered land system, a legal easement or profit is enforceable against any purchaser, under the principle that legal rights bind the whole world.

Table 24.1 Protection of easements

	PROTECTION OF EASEMENTS	
	REGISTERED LAND	
	Overriding interests	**Must protect by entry on register**
Legal easements and profits	On first registration of estate, all legal easements and profits. On later disposition ONLY IF arising by (1) prescription, or (2) implied grant or reservation, (3) or under s. 62, LPA 1925 AND (a) is registered under Commons Act, or (b) acquirer knew of it, or (c) would have been discoverable on reasonable inspection of land, or (d) exercised in the year before the disposition.	Expressly created easements and profits arising after first registration of estate. Expressly created easements which are not protected by entry of a notice on the register take effect in equity only.
Equitable easements and profits	Cannot be overriding	All must be protected by notice.
	UNREGISTERED LAND	
Legal easements and profits	Binding on all acquirers because legal rights are good against the world	
Equitable easements and profits	Created on or after 1 January 1926	Must be registered as a land charge to bind acquirer
	Created before 1 January 1926	Apply notice rules to determine whether binding on later acquirer

Equitable easements in unregistered land are registrable as land charges if created on or after 1 January 1926 (LCA 1972, s. 2), while equitable profits, and equitable easements that were created before 1926, are subject to the old equitable rules of notice.

24.6 Acquisition by express grant or reservation

The story of the installation of the drains of 15 Trant Way, given at the beginning of this chapter (24.1.1.1), shows that an easement or profit can arise by agreement between two owners who already hold separate properties. In such a case, the owner of the land which is to become the servient tenement executes a deed granting the easement to his neighbour and, where the servient land is registered, applies to enter a notice on the charges register of the servient land.

Very often, however, easements or profits are created when land is divided on sale. The vendor may sell only part of the land, keeping the rest (as happened with 16 and 16A Trant Way), and the vendor and the purchaser may each want to enjoy rights over the other's property. Where the purchaser is to be given easements or profits, they are granted by deed, usually by the same deed which conveys the legal estate. Where the vendor wishes to retain certain rights over the land, they must be 'reserved' in the conveyance or transfer. So a purchaser takes rights by express grant, while the vendor obtains rights by express reservation.

The reservation of an easement requires care because the document will be construed strictly against the vendor/grantor (*Cordell v Second Clanfield Properties Ltd* [1969] 2 Ch 9).

In addition to express grant and reservation, there are three other ways in which easements and profits may be acquired, and these are addressed in the following sections:

- implied grant and reservation (24.7);
- express grant by virtue of LPA 1925, s. 62 (24.8); and
- prescription (24.9).

24.7 Acquisition by implied grant or reservation

In certain cases in which a conveyance of land makes no mention of the grant or reservation of an easement or profit, it may be possible to say that one arises by implication. As you will see, it is easier to establish an implied grant, in favour of the purchaser, than it is to set up an implied reservation on behalf of the vendor.

24.7.1 Implied grant

Traditionally, it was said that easements, and in some cases profits, can arise by implied grant in the following cases:

(a) easements of necessity;
(b) intended easements and profits;
(c) easements under the rule in *Wheeldon v Burrows* (1879) 12 ChD 31.

However, *Nickerson v Barraclough* [1981] Ch 426 suggests that the first two of these are not really separate categories, and that easements of necessity are really a form of intended easement.

24.7.1.1 Easements of necessity

An easement of necessity is an easement which is so essential to the enjoyment of the land that the land cannot be used without the easement. The classic example of such an easement arises in the case of 'the land-locked close'. This is land which, like 16A Trant Way, is totally inaccessible, unless an easement to permit access is implied into the conveyance or transfer. On this basis an easement of way would have been implied in the conveyance of 16A Trant Way by Marjorie Marjoram to Basil Borage, as otherwise Mr Borage would have acquired a useless estate.

In many of the cases in which a grant of a way of necessity has been implied, the landlocked close has been completely surrounded by the land of the grantor. In *Adealon International Proprietary Ltd v Merton LBC* [2007] 1 WLR 1604, the Court of Appeal was required to consider whether it would make any difference to the outcome if some of the land surrounding the landlocked plot belonged to a third party. The claimant in this case was in fact claiming an implied reservation, rather than an implied grant, but the case is noted here because the court also expressed views on implying a grant in these circumstances, although these views are, of course, *obiter dicta*.

The court, differing from the trial judge on this point, considered that it was possible for an easement of necessity to be implied in such a situation. Where a grantee had acquired a landlocked close, there would normally be an expectation that access would be provided over land controlled by the grantor, and so the grant of an easement of necessity might well be implied, despite the fact that alternative access over land belonging to a third party might be a theoretical possibility (para. 16). For the court's views about an implied reservation in these circumstances, see 24.7.2.

Basis of the rule

It used to be suggested that the recognition of certain easements of necessity was based on considerations of public policy, because, for example, it was not in the public interest to allow land to become unusable through lack of access. However, the public policy argument was rejected in *Nickerson v Barraclough* [1981] Ch 426, in which the Court of Appeal stated that easements of necessity were to be seen simply as a type of intended easement. In the words of Buckley LJ (at p. 447):

> The law relating to ways of necessity rests not upon a basis of public policy but upon the implication to be drawn from the fact that unless some way is implied, a parcel of land will be inaccessible. From that fact the implication arises that the parties must have intended that some way giving access to the land should have been granted.

Thus an easement of necessity could not be implied where, as in the case before the court, the original vendor had expressly stated that no right of access was being granted.

Although this explanation of the basis of the doctrine appears to have been doubted in *Sweet v Summer* [2004] 4 All ER 288, it was quoted with approval and applied by the Court of Appeal in *Adealon International Proprietary Ltd v Merton LBC* [2007] 1 WLR 1604 at para. 11.

Overlap between necessity and intention

The overlap between necessity and intention can be illustrated by the older case of *Wong v Beaumont Property Trust Ltd* [1965] 1 QB 173, in which basement premises had been let upon the express understanding that the property was to be used as a restaurant. Later, after assignment by the original tenant, the assignee was required to improve ventilation if the restaurant business were to continue. The assignee claimed an implied easement for passage of air through a duct to be constructed on the landlord's property, and was successful on the ground that this was necessary if the contemplated use of the premises were to continue. On the facts, one can see that the case might have been similarly decided by implying that the parties intended all those rights that permitted the use of the premises as a restaurant.

Another important case in this area of the law is *Liverpool City Council v Irwin* [1977] AC 239 (see 24.2.3.6) in which easements were implied giving the right to use rubbish chutes, stairs, and lifts in a multi-storey block of flats. In addition, the grant of a flat was held to include an implied right to have the facilities maintained in a reasonable state of repair. Again, is this a matter of intention or is it that a lessee cannot make any real use of a flat at the top of a tall block unless there is a lift, which is kept in working order?

24.7.1.2 Intended easement and profits

As you have seen, it may be that rights which are necessary for the use of the land are to be presumed to be within the intention of the parties unless expressly excluded. This second category, however, includes more than easements of necessity, for under this heading a grantee may claim a profit or any easement, even though not necessary to the enjoyment of the property, provided it can be shown that both parties intended that it should be granted. An example of this is found in *Cory v Davies* [1923] 2 Ch 95, where a row of terraced houses had been built with a drive at the front and an exit to the road at each end. One of the owners barred the exit at his end of the terrace, requiring all traffic to go the other way. There was no express grant of an easement in favour of all the house owners over all parts of the drive, but the court found that the original parties had a common intention that the drive should be used in this way, and thus an intended easement was implied.

The decision in *Stafford v Lee* (1992) 65 P&CR 172 shows how the question of the intention of the parties was addressed in a case of 'land-locked' land and which therefore might properly appear to fall into the area of easements of necessity. Here the defendant's predecessor in title had conveyed an area of woodland and a pond to the plaintiffs' predecessors. The land fronted a drive but no right of way over the drive to the nearby highway was conferred. The plaintiffs wished to build a house on part of the land but the defendants said that there could be no right of way over the drive for residential purposes (including construction work). The court accepted that it was appropriate to infer an easement to give effect to the intentions of the original parties, but indicated that this could only be done in cases in which the parties intended that the dominant land should be used in some definite and particular manner. In this case because the plan on the relevant conveyance showed other neighbouring buildings the court was ready to infer that the woodland would be used for similar purposes. Accordingly, the claim to an easement for domestic purposes succeeded.

Another example of the recognition of intended easements is to be found in the Court of Appeal decision in *Kent v Kavanagh* [2007] Ch 1. A pair of semi-detached houses had been built by a developer early in the twentieth century on 99-year building leases. The boundary between the two plots ran down the middle of a shared pathway, which gave access to the back gardens of both properties. In 2003 a dispute arose between the current owners as to their relative rights over the path. The leases made no reference to its use and as a result the Court of Appeal was required to consider whether they could be said to contain implied grants and reservations of rights of way.

The court noted that the path was only three feet wide, with the result that it would have been obvious when the leases were granted that it could not be used by either tenant without passing over the half that lay on the neighbour's property. It therefore concluded that the original parties to the leases must have intended that the path would be used in this way. As a result, Chadwick LJ, citing *Cory v Davies* [1923] 2 Ch 95 as an authority, had no difficulty in inferring that each lease contained the implied grants and reservations of reciprocal rights that would enable the path to be used as intended (para. 63).

24.7.1.3 The rule in *Wheeldon v Burrows*

In order to understand this rule, it is necessary to remind ourselves about quasi-easements (see 24.2.1.2). Although a landowner may derive benefit from one piece of the owner's own land in favour of another, he or she cannot be said to have an easement, because there are no separate tenements. For example, if the owner enjoys the uninterrupted passage of light over the garden to the windows, he or she cannot say there is an easement of light, although, if the garden were in separate ownership there might be such a right. This situation is sometimes described as giving rise to a quasi-easement.

1. The rule

The rule in *Wheeldon v Burrows* (1879) 12 ChD 31 provides that if, in such a situation, the owner sells that part of the land which is benefited (e.g., the house) and retains the land which is burdened (e.g., the garden), the purchaser may acquire an easement over the land retained by the vendor. Thus, in the example given above, the quasi-easement would become a true easement of light.

In *Wheeldon v Burrows*, Thesiger LJ stated the principle as follows (at p. 49):

> [O]n the grant by the owner of a tenement of part of that tenement as it is then used and enjoyed, there will pass to the grantee all those continuous and apparent easements (by which, of course, I mean quasi easements), or, in other words, all those easements which are necessary to the reasonable enjoyment of the property granted, and which have been and are at the time of the grant used by the owners of the entirety for the benefit of the part granted.

2. Elements of the rule

There seem to be three elements of this rule, for the quasi-easement must be:

(a) 'continuous and apparent';
(b) 'necessary to the reasonable enjoyment' of the land sold; and
(c) in use by the owner at the time of the sale.

If all three requirements are satisfied then a grant of a legal easement is implied into the conveyance or transfer of the portion of the land which is sold. There has however always been some doubt as to whether it is necessary to show that the quasi-easement is both 'continuous and apparent' and 'necessary to the reasonable enjoyment of the property'. It has been suggested that these requirements should be viewed as alternatives, so that it is only necessary to show that the quasi-easement in question satisfies one or other of them. In *Ward v Kirkland* [1967] Ch 194 at p. 224, Ungoed-Thomas J put forward the alternative suggestion that each requirement applied to a different type of easement, positive easements (e.g., rights of way) being required to be 'continuous and apparent', while negative easements (e.g., rights to light) must be shown to be 'necessary to the reasonable enjoyment of the property'. However, in *Millman v Ellis* (1996) 71 P&CR 158 (a case involving a claim to a right of way), the Court of Appeal treated the two requirements as separate conditions, each of which had to be satisfied in order to bring the claim within the rule in *Wheeldon v Burrows*.

We can now look briefly at each of these three requirements.

(a) *'continuous and apparent'* Strictly speaking, 'continuous' easements are those which are enjoyed passively, such as rights to drainage, support, and light, and are therefore in use all the time. Although a right of way cannot be said to be in continuous use, the courts accept that it satisfies this test if there is a made-up road or some other clearly defined track (which of course is in place at all times) along which the right can be exercised (see *Borman v Griffiths* [1930] 1 Ch 493 at p. 499).

The requirement that the quasi-easement should be 'apparent' stems from the principle that underlies all types of implied grant, namely that a grantor must not derogate from his or her grant. Under the rule in *Wheeldon v Burrows*, a purchaser is to receive the easements expected: on inspecting the land visible signs of a quasi-easement were seen and the purchaser assumed that the benefit of such a right would be obtained on purchase of the property.

In the case of 16A Trant Way, if there was a house on the property when Mr Borage bought it and a driveway across No. 16 leading to it, the driveway would render apparent the quasi-easement being used by the vendor.

(b) *'necessary for the reasonable enjoyment of the property'* This requirement does not produce a test as strict as that for easements of necessity. All that is needed for *Wheeldon v Burrows* is that the right claimed should facilitate the reasonable enjoyment of the property. However, in *Wheeler v J. J. Saunders Ltd* [1996] Ch 19, a second access route to premises was held by the Court of Appeal not to be necessary for the reasonable enjoyment of the land, even though it was convenient, because the alternative route would 'do just as well'.

(c) *'in use by the owner at the time of the sale'* In considering this requirement, attention has always focused on the fact that the quasi-easement must be 'in use' at the time of the sale. The reason for requiring such use is that it leads the purchaser to believe that the right will pass with the property.

More recently, however, the Court of Appeal has emphasised the other aspect of the condition: it must be in use by the owner. In *Kent v Kavanagh* [2007] Ch 1, the court rejected a claim under *Wheeldon v Burrows* to an implied grant of a right of way, because at the relevant date the land benefited by the quasi-easement was occupied by a tenant and not by the owner himself. Chadwick LJ considered that it would be 'unnecessary and artificial' to hold that the vendor had been using quasi-easements over part of his land to benefit another part, when the part that received the benefit was in fact no longer occupied by him, but by a tenant (see paras. 44 and 45). Although the judge does not say so, the same argument would probably apply if the benefited land was occupied before the conveyance by a licensee.

It thus appears from this decision that one may need to add a further requirement to the rule in *Wheeldon v Burrows*, namely that an implied grant under this rule operates only where the land conveyed and the land retained were in both common ownership and common occupation immediately before the conveyance.

Simultaneous sales

So far in this explanation of the rule in *Wheeldon v Burrows*, it has been assumed that the vendor sells the quasi-dominant piece of land (which has been enjoying the quasi-easement) and retains the quasi-servient land. What happens if, instead, the vendor sells both pieces of land and both sales take effect on the same day (for example, on a sale at auction)? In such a situation, each purchaser acquires any quasi-easements which have been enjoyed with the piece of land acquired and will be entitled to enforce them against the land of the other purchaser (see *Hansford v Jago* [1921] 1 Ch 322 at p. 335).

24.7.2 Implied reservation

Easements and profits may arise by implied reservation in the following cases:

(a) easements of necessity;
(b) intended easements and profits.

There is, however, no possibility of an implied reservation under the rule in *Wheeldon v Burrows*, for the court in that case rejected the vendor's claim to an easement over the land he had sold. (It is interesting to note that the rule that takes its name from this case is in fact derived from *obiter dicta*, for the court was not dealing with any question about implied grant.)

In general, the courts will not readily accept a claim to the acquisition of an easement or profit by implied reservation because of the rule that documents are to be construed strictly against the grantor. This is because it is presumed that the grantor is in a position of strength, and is able to reserve any rights which he or she chooses to retain. Any failure to reserve these rights is the fault of the vendor. Moreover, it can be said that an implied reservation derogates from the grant, for the grantor has apparently given the grantee an unencumbered estate and is then trying to burden it with an easement or profit.

However, there are a few cases in which claims to have acquired an easement by implied reservation have succeeded. Thus, in *Peckham v Ellison* [2000] 79 P&CR 276, a successor to a council that had sold some properties under the 'right to buy' scheme, while retaining other neighbouring property, claimed that the council must have reserved a right of way by implication. Perhaps surprisingly, the Court of Appeal held that on the particular facts of the case, the judge at first instance had been entitled to conclude that there was no other possible explanation of the circumstances other than that the council and purchasers had intended that the council should reserve the easement. The case emphasises that the matter is one to be decided on the facts of each case.

For other successful claims, see *Richards v Rose* (1853) 9 Exch 218 (easement of support), and *Pinnington v Galland* (1853) 9 Exch 1 (right of access to landlocked close). More recently, the Court of Appeal in *Adealon International Proprietary Ltd v Merton LBC* [2007] 1 WLR 1604 (see 24.7.1.1) accepted that a right of way to landlocked property could be acquired by implied reservation, even in cases where there was theoretically a possibility of access across adjoining land owned by a third party. The court emphasised, however, the difficulty that faces a grantor who claims an implied reservation. In the words of Carnwath LJ (at para. 16):

> ... the presumption is that any rights [the grantor] requires over the land transferred will have been expressly reserved in the grant, and the burden lies on [him] to establish an exception.

In *Adealon*, there was no evidence of an intention at the time of sale that the vendor would access the retained land by means of a way over the sold land, and thus the presumption that the grantor would expressly reserve any right required had not been rebutted.

For other cases in which claims to implied reservations have been rejected by the courts, see *Re Webb's Lease* [1951] Ch 808, and *Chaffe v Kingsley* [2000] 79 P&CR 404.

24.8 Acquisition by express grant by virtue of LPA 1925, s. 62

24.8.1 Section 62

LPA 1925, s. 62(1), provides that:

> A conveyance of land shall be deemed to include and shall ... operate to convey, with the land, all buildings, erections, fixtures, commons, hedges, ditches, ... liberties, privileges, easements, rights, and advantages whatsoever, appertaining ... to the land, ... or, at the time of conveyance, ... enjoyed with ... the land.

At first reading the subsection appears to be nothing more than a word-saving provision, designed to make it clear that on the conveyance of an estate in land the grantee obtains the benefit of houses, fences and other things upon the land and any rights, interests, and privileges existing for the benefit of the estate, without any express mention of them being made in the conveyance. Express words to this effect used to be included in full in conveyances, but since the end of the nineteenth century statute has provided that such words are deemed to be included in the conveyance. Section 62 thus operates to pass any existing easements or profits that benefit the land conveyed, without any need to mention them in the conveyance.

24.8.2 Interpretation of s. 62

Rather surprisingly, s. 62 has been interpreted by the courts in such a way that it is capable of creating new easements and profits in favour of a purchaser, as well as transferring those that already exist. As a result, any conveyance that does not exclude the provisions of s. 62 will convert into legal easements or profits:

- certain quasi-easements and quasi-profits;
- licences.

It also appears from the decision of the Court of Appeal in *Wall v Collins* [2007] Ch 390 that s. 62 is capable of converting an existing easement for a fixed period into one that is equivalent to the freehold estate (see 24.8.2.3).

24.8.2.1 Conversion of quasi-easements and quasi-profits

The nature of quasi-easements was explained earlier in discussing *Wheeldon v Burrows* (24.7.1.3). In order to be converted by a conveyance under s. 62 into full easements binding the land retained by the vendor, the quasi-easement (or quasi-profit) must be 'continuous and apparent' and must have been in use at the time of the conveyance. There is no requirement that the right should be 'necessary for the reasonable enjoyment of the property', as there is in *Wheeldon v Burrows*.

24.8.2.2 Conversion of licences

The cases in which the courts have found that a licence has been converted into an easement by virtue of s. 62 all arose in situations in which, before the conveyance, the land to be benefited was already occupied by someone other than the grantor. The occupier was permitted to undertake some activity on other land owned by the grantor, such as using an alternative route of access across it (as in *International Tea Stores v Hobbs* [1903] 2 Ch 165, and *Goldberg v Edwards* [1950] Ch 247) or, for example, storing goods upon it (*Wright v Macadam* [1949] 2 KB 744). The grantor then conveyed the property, either on sale or on the grant of a lease, and the permissive use was converted into a legal easement, binding on the land retained by the grantor.

An examination of the case of *Wright v Macadam* [1949] 2 KB 744 illustrates how this may occur. While in possession as a protected tenant under the Rent Acts, Mrs Wright was given permission by her landlord, Mr Macadam, to store coal in a garden shed, which was retained by the landlord. Later a fresh lease of one year was made (in writing but not by deed, in accordance with LPA 1925, s. 54(2)), which did not refer to the shed. After some time, Mr Macadam tried to charge for the use of the shed and Mrs Wright refused to pay, claiming that she had an easement of storage. It was held, by the Court of Appeal, that the creation of the fresh lease was a 'conveyance' within the meaning of

LPA 1925 and that it operated to grant Mrs Wright a legal easement of storage. Thus, by virtue of s. 62, a conveyance had converted a pre-existing licence into a legal easement.

It is not easy to see why s. 62 should have this effect, for the words of the section would suggest that the licence should pass as a licence, rather than changing into a legal right (see Tee [1998] Conv 115). However, this approach to interpretation was first adopted in nineteenth-century decisions on similar provisions in earlier statutes and it is now well accepted and has been expressly recognised in LRA 2002, s. 27(7). To ensure that new rights are not created in this way, a landowner making a conveyance should either revoke any licences previously granted, or include a term in the conveyance that will exclude the operation of s. 62.

24.8.2.3 Conversion of existing easements

In *Wall v Collins* [2007] Ch 390, the Court of Appeal had to consider the question of what happens to easements enjoyed by a tenant over adjoining land belonging to the landlord when the tenant 'buys out' the landlord (i.e., acquires the reversion on the lease and becomes the freehold owner). This case is covered later (see 24.11.4), but you need to note here that the Court of Appeal considered that the conveyance of the freehold to the former tenant had the effect of converting his former easement, granted for a term of years, into one equivalent to the fee simple absolute in possession. Although most of the decisions on the effect of s. 62 have been concerned with activities permitted by licence, the court emphasised that the fact that the right in question here was already a legal easement made no difference:

> ... if at the time of the conveyance the occupier of No. 231 had enjoyed a permissive use of [the passageway] s. 62 would have converted it into a right attached to the freehold. It is hard to see why the occupier of No.231 should be in a worse position because his enjoyment is not simply permissive, but is protected for 999 years (per Carnwath LJ at para. 27).

24.8.3 Conditions for successful claims under s. 62

Any claim to be entitled to an easement or profit by virtue of s. 62 must satisfy certain conditions.

24.8.3.1 The right claimed must be capable of being an easement or profit (*Phipps v Pears* [1965] 1 QB 76)

This is, of course, a requirement that applies to all methods of acquisition, and you have already seen the various conditions for recognition as an easement (24.2.1 and 24.2.3).

24.8.3.2 There must be a conveyance upon which s. 62 can operate

The definition of 'conveyance' in LPA 1925, s. 205(1)(ii), in effect requires a written document, other than a will, which creates or transfers a legal estate or interest in land. In general most conveyances and transfers are made by deed, because as you will remember, dealings with a legal estate are ineffective unless made by deed. A short lease granted informally under LPA 1925, s. 54(2), will amount to a conveyance for the purposes of s. 62 if the grant is made by a written document (as it was in *Wright v Macadam*), but an oral lease has been held not to constitute a conveyance (see *Rye v Rye* [1962] AC 496, in which it was held that the definition of conveyance in LPA 1925, s. 205, requires there to be an 'instrument', i.e., a written document).

The requirement for a conveyance means that s. 62 does not operate upon contracts to grant or transfer an estate in land, despite the fact that such contracts may create equitable interests in the property (*Re Peck's Contract* [1893] 2 Ch 315). An illustration of this is to be found in *Borman v Griffith* [1930] 1 Ch 493, in which it was held that existing easements that benefited a property did not pass to the prospective tenant under a contract to grant a lease. It follows from this that there is no question of quasi-easements or licences being converted into easements by a contract for a lease and, as mentioned when considering equitable leases (9.3.2.2), this is yet another way in which a contract for a lease is not 'as good as' a legal lease.

24.8.3.3 The conveyance must not express a 'contrary intention'

Section 62 applies only in so far as a contrary intention is not expressed in the conveyance (s. 62(4)), and it is open to the grantor to exclude the section altogether (although this might create some practical drafting difficulties) or to make it clear that there is no intention to grant certain rights.

24.8.3.4 Must there be diversity of occupation?

In a number of cases, judges have said that new easements and profits arise under s. 62 only where the two properties were separately occupied before the date of the conveyance. This requirement is usually attributed to the decision in *Long v Gowlett* [1923] 2 Ch 177. In this case, the owner of a mill claimed the right to go on his neighbour's land to cut weeds on the river bank which impeded the flow of water to his mill. The two pieces of land had previously been in common ownership, and the owner had cleared and maintained the river banks in this way. The miller claimed that, when the mill was conveyed to him, s. 6(2) of the Conveyancing Act 1881 (the forerunner of s. 62) created an easement benefiting his mill and binding the other part of the land. The court rejected this claim, saying that in such a case there was no 'privilege, easement or advantage' being exercised at the date of such a conveyance, for the owner-occupier of both plots could not be exercising rights against himself. In such a case there were no rights which could mature into easements on the conveyance.

This view was endorsed by *obiter dicta* of Lord Wilberforce in *Sovmots Investments Ltd v Secretary of State for the Environment* [1979] AC 144, in which his Lordship said (at p. 169):

> The reason is that when land is under one ownership one cannot speak in any intelligible sense of rights, or privileges, or easements being exercised over one part for the benefit of another. Whatever the owner does, he does as owner and, until a separation occurs, of ownership or at least of occupation, the condition for the existence of rights, etc., does not exist.

This issue was considered further by the Court of Appeal in *Payne v Inwood* (1996) 74 P&CR 42. This case involved two houses in a terrace of three: No. 1 was the corner house and access to the rear of the house could be obtained by passing up the side of the house; No. 1A was the next house in the terrace and originally access to the rear of No. 1A could only be obtained by passing through the house itself. Both No. 1 and No. 1A had yards at the rear of the house which adjoined one another and in about 1964 the then owner of No. 1 had allowed the construction of a gate between the two rear yards (largely because the owners of the two properties were close friends and this permitted easy access between the houses). Thereafter it was possible to gain access to the rear of

No. 1A by walking up the side of No. 1, across the back yard of No. 1 and through the gate into the yard of No. 1A.

In 1971, No. 1 was bought by the then owner of No. 1A. She moved into her new property, but retained occupation of No. 1A until she sold it a week later. Some 20 years after this, a dispute arose between the then owners of the two houses, and the owners of No. 1A sought a declaration that they were entitled to a right of way over No. 1. At first instance, the judge rejected claims that an easement had arisen by prescription (i.e., by long use) or under the rule in *Wheeldon v Burrows*, but held that an easement had been created by the conveyance of 1971, which as a result of s. 62 had converted a licence to use the way into an easement.

On appeal by the owners of No. 1, this decision was reversed, the Court of Appeal holding that s. 62 cannot operate to convert a licence into an easement unless there was some diversity of ownership or occupation prior to the conveyance. At the time immediately before the 1971 conveyance, both houses had been owned and occupied by their common owner, albeit only for one week, and this prevented the creation of a new easement under s. 62.

In his judgment, with which other members of the Court of Appeal concurred, Roch LJ considered the case of *Broomfield v Williams* [1987] 1 Ch 602, which appears to conflict with the requirement for diversity of occupation. In this case the plaintiff claimed to have a right of light over adjoining land retained by his vendor. The two pieces of land had been both owned and occupied by the vendor before the conveyance, but the Court of Appeal held that the purchaser had acquired a right to light by virtue of the Conveyancing Act 1881, s. 6(2). In *Payne v Inwood* the court accepted that this earlier decision constituted a genuine exception to the requirement of separate occupation, but considered (at p. 51) that the exception was:

> to be confined to cases dealing with such advantages as light to buildings.

The right to light is often said to be an unusual easement with its own characteristics and so it did not seem unreasonable to distinguish *Broomfield v Williams* in this way.

However, in two recent Court of Appeal decisions a different approach has been taken, following a view advanced by Harpum (at [1979] 41 Conv 415 and [1979] 43 Conv 113). In *P & S Platt Ltd v Crouch* [2004] 1 P&CR 18 and *Wood v Waddington* [2015] EWCA Civ 538, a distinction was made between the effect of s. 62 on:

- licences, which are converted under s. 62 only if there is diversity of occupation; and
- continuous and apparent quasi-easements, which can become full easements on conveyance without separate occupation.

On this approach, the claim in *Long v Gowlett* did not succeed because there was no diversity of occupation *and* because the common owner's practice of walking along the river bank to cut the weeds was not 'continuous and apparent', there being no track or path which indicated this practice (see [1923] 2 Ch 177 at p. 199). By contrast, a right to light can be regarded as 'continuous and apparent' (the windows that receive light being a permanent feature of property) and *Broomfield v Williams* can therefore be explained as a case of a continuous and apparent quasi-easement being converted by the operation of s. 62 upon the conveyance.

P & S Platt Ltd v Crouch [2004] 1 P&CR 18 concerned a hotel, situated close to a river, and an adjacent piece of land which provided mooring facilities for guests arriving at the hotel by boat. The claimant bought the hotel from the common owner of both properties but, through failure to exercise an option in time, did not acquire the additional land. As a result, the hotel's customers were no longer able to use the moorings or to access the hotel from the river bank. The purchaser therefore sought a declaration that, on the conveyance of the hotel to him, he had acquired rights of access and mooring over the retained land by virtue of s. 62.

Although both properties had been in common ownership and occupation immediately before the conveyance, the purchaser succeeded in his claim, Peter Gibson LJ stating (at para. 42):

> The rights were continuous and apparent, and so it matters not that prior to the sale of the hotel there was no prior diversity of occupation of the dominant and servient tenements . . . Accordingly, I reach the conclusion that s. 62 operated to convert the rights into full easements.

Similarly, in *Wood v Waddington* [2015] EWCA Civ 538, Lewison LJ held (at para. 35):

> [I]n cases where there has been no diversity of occupation, all that is necessary to establish is that the exercise of the relevant rights has been continuous and apparent in the sense developed for the purposes of the rule in *Wheeldon v Burrows*.

He applied this principle to hold that rights of way had been implied into a conveyance by a vendor of land in his own sole occupation, despite the fact that there had never been diversity of occupation before the date of the conveyance. It seems settled, therefore, that s. 62 can be used to imply easements into a conveyance of part of his land by a sole owner-occupier who has retained land over which he has been exercising 'continuous and apparent' rights for his own benefit.

24.8.4 Trant Way

If we now consider the situation of Mr Forest and Mr Gruyère at 5 Trant Way (see 24.1.1.2), it seems very probable that Mr Gruyère has acquired the legal easement of keeping his dustbin in the garden. The dustbin is unlikely to take up too much space, and so would probably be acceptable as an easement of storage. The recent grant in writing of a two-year lease provides the necessary conveyance for the operation of s. 62 (*Wright v Macadam*) and the magic of s. 62 will therefore have converted what was a mere licence into a legal easement.

24.8.5 Nature of grant under s. 62

Since s. 62 operates by importing certain words into the conveyance, it has the effect of making an express, not implied, grant of the easement or profit (*Gregg v Richards* [1926] Ch 521). It is for this reason that LRA 2002 provides that the requirement to complete an express grant of an easement by registration does not apply to easements arising under s. 62 (LRA 2002, s. 27(7)). Despite this, some textbooks describe easements acquired by virtue of s. 62 as being 'impliedly granted', and there are several recent decisions in which judges have referred to s. 62 as giving rise to 'an implied grant' (although without any discussion of the matter). At present, the question of classification does not appear to be of any great significance, but it is mentioned here in case you are confused by it.

24.8.6 Comparison of the rule in *Wheeldon v Burrows* and LPA 1925, s. 62

Space does not permit a detailed comparison, and indeed it will be more useful to you to make this for yourself, but the main differences are as follows.

(a) *Wheeldon v Burrows* relates only to easements, while s. 62 applies to both easements and profits (see *White v Williams* [1922] 1 KB 727).

(b) *Wheeldon v Burrows* operates where, before the conveyance, the two pieces of land have been occupied by the same person, whereas, save in the case of continuous and quasi-apparent easements, diversity of occupation is required for s. 62.

(c) The types of easements which can pass under *Wheeldon v Burrows* are restricted by the three requirements of the rule, whereas there are no such restrictions in the case of s. 62 (save for the requirement that quasi-easements should be 'continuous and apparent').

(d) *Wheeldon v Burrows*, unlike s. 62, is apparently not limited to conveyances. Thus it seems that a contract to grant a lease may be sufficient to create an easement in favour of the tenant under *Wheeldon v Burrows* (*Borman v Griffith* [1930] 1 Ch 493) although it is not enough to pass even existing easements under s. 62.

This comparison may lead to you wonder what the remaining role of *Wheeldon v Burrows* might be: it would seem that s. 62 is a much easier test to satisfy in any case where there has been the continuous and apparent use of land by a sole owner. Following the decisions that diversity of occupation is not needed for s. 62 to apply in cases involving continuous and apparent quasi-easements, this is a well-founded question. It appears, now, that the only circumstance in which *Wheeldon* is useful would be in the case of a mere contract to convey that falls short of a conveyance. In these cases, *Wheeldon* may be used to imply the grant of equitable easements into the contract since s. 62 cannot play a role. It is also true that conveyances are sometimes drafted so as to expressly exclude the operation of s. 62. In such cases, and in the absence of an equivalent exclusion of the rule in *Wheeldon v Burrows*, a claimant may still need to rely on *Wheeldon* to show an implied easement has arisen in her favour.

24.9 Acquisition by prescription

Both easements and profits may be acquired as the result of long use, as well as by the means of grant and reservation. This method of acquisition is called 'prescription', of which there are three forms:

- common law prescription;
- the fiction of lost modern grant; and
- under the Prescription Act 1832.

All these types of prescription have three characteristics in common which are set out in the following paragraphs.

24.9.1 Common characteristics of prescription

24.9.1.1 Creation of legal interests

All three forms will give the acquirer a legal easement or legal profit, even though there has in fact been no grant by deed.

24.9.1.2 Acquisition based on a fiction

With the exception of one of the forms of prescription under the Prescription Act, all these methods are based on the fiction that a grant of the easement or profit has been made at some time in the past, and long use is regarded merely as evidence of that grant. Some of the rules about prescription that may seem strange will be more easily understood if you remember that they are designed to maintain this pretence.

24.9.1.3 Acquiescence of servient tenement owner

In claiming that an easement has been created by any form of prescription, it is essential to show that the owner of the servient land acquiesced in the use during the prescription period. In *Dalton v Angus* (1881) 6 App Cas 740 at pp. 773–4, Fry J stated that in his opinion the whole law of prescription rested upon acquiescence, and summarised the circumstances in which the servient owner can be said to acquiesce as being that:

- the servient owner knows of the use;
- the servient owner has the power to stop it; and
- the servient owner does not do so.

In establishing acquiescence, knowledge may be actual or imputed—that is, the owner will be taken to know facts of which he or she should have become aware 'as an ordinary owner of the servient land, diligent in the protection of his interests' (per Chadwick LJ in *Williams v Sandy Lane (Chester) Ltd* [2007] 1 EGLR 10). The claimant is not required to prove knowledge on the part of the owner: the owner is presumed to know of the use and has to rebut this presumption by showing that there was no knowledge (*Pugh v Savage* [1974] 1 WLR 1427 at p. 1434).

The need to show acquiescence can cause problems when the servient land has been occupied by a tenant for some or all of the prescription period, and you will see how the requirement operates in these circumstances later (see 24.9.2.2).

24.9.2 Basic rules for prescription

There are three basic rules which apply to all the methods of prescription; these are discussed first and then each of the three forms of prescription is considered in turn.

24.9.2.1 Use must be as of right

It is essential for the claimant to establish that, throughout the period of use, he or she has enjoyed the right claimed 'as of right'. The use (and that of any predecessors in title, if relevant) must be consistent with the fiction that the right was granted at some time in the past, and that the owner of the dominant land has been acting in reliance on this. Any inconsistent behaviour will be taken to show that the claimant does not have such a right. It appears that it is irrelevant that the claimant of the easement has been exercising the right in the mistaken belief that it has in fact been granted (*Bridle v Ruby* [1989] QB 169).

The traditional formulation of the test of whether the use is as of right is that the use must be **nec vi, nec clam, nec precario**.

1. Nec vi
This means that the right claimed must not have been exercised by force. Thus, if Farmer George were to have erected a gate blocking access to the footpath on his land, Mr Neep would be using the path by force if he broke down the gate, or even if he simply climbed over it. Even a protest by the servient owner can prevent user as of right, for ignoring

a protest is regarded as use by force (*Eaton v Swansea Waterworks Co.* (1851) 17 QB 267). The rule prevents people obtaining interests in land by use of 'strong-arm' tactics.

It was said at one time that acting illegally also prevented acquisition of an easement: *Hanning v Top Deck Travel Group Ltd* [1993] 68 P&CR 14. However, the House of Lords took the opposite view in *Bakewell Management Ltd v Brandwood* [2004] 2 AC 519, in which their Lordships distinguished between a use that could be or become lawful and a use that could never be lawful. They were of the view that public policy did not require that it be unlawful to acquire an easement by prescription, where the use relied upon would not have been a tort or a crime had an easement been granted expressly. Since in *Bakewell Management* the owners of the servient land could have given consent, the right could be acquired by prescription. On this point, see also *George Legge & Son Ltd v Wenlock Corporation* [1938] AC 204 and *Cargill v Gotts* [1981] 1 WLR 441.

2. Nec clam

The right must not be exercised secretly, for such use prevents the servient owner from objecting to the acquisition of the right and appears inconsistent with a claim of right. In *Liverpool Corporation v Coghill & Sons Ltd* [1918] 1 Ch 307 a claim to an easement of drainage was unsuccessful because the claimant's drain had entered the general sewer below ground and it was impossible for the corporation to ascertain that one more load of effluent had been added to its general burden. A similar result was caused by secret use in *Union Lighterage Co v London Graving Dock* [1902] 2 Ch 557, in which the claimed easement of support was being exercised secretly, below water level.

Thus, if Mr Neep had used the farmer's path only at dead of night and in a manner designed to conceal his use, he would be regarded as not having exercised an easement of way as of right.

3. Nec precario

This means that the right must not be enjoyed precariously, i.e., by permission. If the servient owner has given the claimant permission, the use is by licence, not as of right, and such permissive use is inconsistent with the fiction that an easement was granted at some time in the past. Thus, if Farmer George has given Mr Neep permission to use the path, his use is not 'as of right', and he will not be able to acquire a legal right of way by prescription. In some cases, of course, permission may have been given so long ago that it may be deemed to have lapsed, so that the more recent use may be regarded as not being by permission (*Arkwright v Gell* (1839) 5 M & W 203).

At this point, it must be emphasised that some claims under the Prescription Act are subject to special rules about permission, and these are covered later (see 24.9.6.2(1)).

Implied licence In *R (Beresford) v Sunderland City Council* [2004] 1 AC 889, the House of Lords indicated that, even in the absence of express permission, a claim to acquire by prescription can theoretically be displaced by evidence of implied permission. When you look at the case you will see that it did not concern an easement but was about public rights to use a recreational area. However, this is an area of law in which the same concept of user as of right applies and thus the case is also useful in relation to easements and profits. Lord Bingham said (at para. 5):

> I can see no objection in principle to the implication of a licence where the facts warrant such an implication. To deny this possibility would, I think, be unduly old-fashioned, formalistic and restrictive.

Here it was argued that because the Council had mown the grass and provided seating it had impliedly consented to the use being made (and thus given permission). The House of Lords did not, however, accept this view of the facts and held that the public use during the statutory period had not been by permission and thus was user as of right.

Distinguishing between acquiescence and permission It was said earlier that acquiescence by the servient owner is an essential element of prescription, and it seems now that permission from that owner will prevent time running against him or her. You may find this confusing, but the courts emphasise that the two concepts are completely different. An owner who acquiesces does nothing: the owner merely tolerates or 'puts up with' the use of his or her land. By contrast, permission requires some positive act: the giving of oral or written consent, or the doing of some act from which permission may be inferred. Such permission cannot be inferred from the mere inaction of a landowner with knowledge of the use to which his or her land is being put (per Lord Bingham in *R (Beresford) v Sunderland City Council* [2004] 1 AC 889 at para. 6). However, permission bars acquisition by prescription even if the dominant owner did not ask for permission: *Odey v Barber* [2008] 2 WLR 618.

24.9.2.2 The right must be acquired by a fee simple owner against a fee simple owner

Again, this rule originates in the pretence that the right has been properly granted at some time in the past, for the only way to explain its continuance is that it was granted in fee simple, rather than for a limited period of years. This implies a grant by a fee simple owner to a fee simple owner.

Prescription by a tenant

Even if the use in question is by a tenant, any easement or profit acquired as a result will attach to the fee simple in the dominant land, rather than to the tenant's lease (though of course the tenant will still have an interest in claiming).

As a result, it is never possible for a tenant of dominant land to acquire rights by prescription against his or her own landlord (*Gayford v Moffat* (1868) LR 4 Ch App 133), for such a tenant can only claim to acquire an easement on behalf of the landlord, and the landlord cannot have rights against himself or herself (*Ivimey v Stocker* (1866) LR 1 Ch App 396). This only means that a tenant cannot acquire easements against his or her landlord *by prescription*, for a tenant may acquire such rights by express or implied grant. Similarly, it was held in *Simmons v Dobson* [1991] 1 WLR 720 that a tenant could not obtain by prescription against another tenant of the same landlord (see also on this point *Wheaton v Maple* [1893] 3 Ch 48 and *Kilgour v Gaddes* [1904] 1 KB 457).

Prescription against a tenant (i.e., where the servient land is occupied by a tenant during the prescription period)

Where an easement is acquired by prescription it binds the fee simple estate in the servient land. If that land is let to a tenant during the prescription period it seems unfair to allow the dominant owner to claim the acquisition of an easement or profit by prescription. The tenant on the servient land may well not be concerned about the exercise of the right, while the fee simple owner may not be aware of the user since he or she has given exclusive possession of the land to the tenant. In these circumstances it would not really be true to say that the owner has acquiesced in the prescriptive use and, as we have noted, such acquiescence is an essential requirement. As a result, some claims under the Prescription Act are subject to special rules, which provide for periods of occupation under leases for more than three years to be deducted from the prescription period (see 24.9.6.2(3)). In all other forms of prescription, the matter is regulated by case law, and the relevant rules were reviewed and restated by the Court of Appeal in *Williams v Sandy Lane (Chester) Ltd* [2007] 1 EGLR 10.

This case involved claims to rights of way said to have been acquired by prescription over the defendant's land. Two different routes were involved. One, the 'secondary route', was held by the trial judge to have been abandoned and this aspect of the case is covered later (see 24.11.3). The claim to use the 'primary route' raised several issues about acquiescence, one of them being the claim that acquiescence by the freehold owner could not be established because part of the primary route lay on land occupied by a tenant during the prescription period. This argument was rejected by the Court of Appeal, because the rest of the route lay over land still occupied by the owner, who could have prevented the use. As a result, the court's observations on the rules relating to acquiescence in respect of tenanted land are *obiter dicta*, but are still important.

As summarised by Chadwick LJ (at paras. 22–4) the position is as follows:

(i) *If the use began before the grant of the lease* and the owner knew of it before making the grant, the owner can be said to have acquiesced in the use, and the prescription period will run against that person, despite the fact that the land is occupied by a tenant for part of the period. Thus, in *Pugh v Savage* [1970] 2 QB 373 an easement was acquired by prescription even though the servient land had been let for 10 years in the middle of the prescription period.

(ii) *If the use begins when the land is already let* the general rule is that the prescription period will only start when the fee simple owner re-enters at the end of the lease (*Daniel v North* (1809) 11 East 372; although note that there is some uncertainty in the case of certain claims under the Prescription Act see 24.9.6.2(2)). However, Chadwick LJ suggested (at para. 24) that despite the lease, the owner could be said to acquiesce if he or she:

> does have knowledge [actual or imputed] of the user and could (notwithstanding the tenancy) take steps to prevent that user, but does not do so.

In these circumstances, the prescription period would run despite occupation by the tenant.

It is therefore the rule that there should be no tenancy of the servient land at the start of the prescription period. If, however, the fee simple owner is in possession when the use begins, the owner has the opportunity to discover what has happened and, if the land is subsequently let, can make enquiries of the tenant in order to ascertain whether the use is continuing. Thus, in *Pugh v Savage* [1970] 2 QB 373 an easement was acquired by prescription even though the servient land had been let for 10 years in the middle of the prescription period. If, however, the land is let when the use began, the prescription period will only start when the fee simple owner re-enters (*Daniel v North* (1809) 11 East 372).

24.9.2.3 The use must be continuous

The infrequent use of a right is not sufficient if one is claiming an easement or profit by prescription. Thus, if Mr Neep had used Farmer George's path on only three occasions in the last 12 years this would not support a claim to an easement by prescription (see *Hollins v Verney* (1884) 13 QBD 304). As we have mentioned previously, the exercise of a right of way can never be continuous in a literal sense, but for the purposes of prescription regular usage will suffice. Also the right exercised should not generally be varied during the period for prescription, although in the case of *Davis v Whitby* [1974] Ch 186 it was regarded as acceptable if a minor variation was made for the sake of convenience (here the alteration was to the exact path used in the case of a right of way).

24.9.3 Prescription at common law

In order to establish a claim to an easement or profit by prescription at common law, it is necessary to establish that the interest has been enjoyed, as of right, since *time immemorial* or, to use the traditional phrase, 'from time whereof the memory of man runneth not to the contrary'. You may, however, be amused to discover that lawyers have a very definite view on when the 'memory of man' started. Under the Statute of Westminster the First (1275), c. 39, the date of legal memory is 1189 and this date has never been amended. Therefore this method of prescription requires that the right in question was in existence before that date.

You will appreciate that it is practically impossible to establish positively such a long period of use. Accordingly, the rule has developed that proof of use during living memory will raise a presumption that the right has been enjoyed since 1189. Originally user during living memory was established by asking the oldest inhabitants of the area whether the right had been exercised as long as they recalled. Today all that is needed is evidence that the right has been used for at least 20 years (*Darling v Clue* (1864) 4 F & F 329).

However, the presumption raised by the 20-year use is a rebuttable presumption, and the claim to prescription at common law can be destroyed by evidence which shows that the right claimed must have begun later than 1189. Thus if the claim were to an easement of light to the windows of a building, proof that the building on the dominant tenement had been built after 1189 would destroy the claim at common law (*Bury v Pope* (1588) Cro Eliz 118). Similarly, if the dominant and servient tenements have been in common ownership at any time since 1189 this claim at common law will fail because even if the right had been granted before 1189, it would have come to an end when the two pieces of land came into the same hands (see 24.2.1.2), and any grant when they separated again would be after the date of legal memory (*Keymer v Summers* (1769) Bull NP 74).

Thus, were Nigel Neep to claim his right to use the footpath on Farmer George's land by common law prescription, he would be able to raise the presumption of use since 1189 if he and his predecessors in title had used the path for 20 years, but his claim would easily be defeated if Farmer George could prove that 14 Trant Way and Fieldy Farm were once owned by one person (which might well be the case). As a result, claims by prescription under the pure common law rule are rarely successful today, although, as we shall see, some assistance is provided by the Prescription Act 1832.

24.9.4 Lost modern grant

Because it was so difficult to obtain an easement or profit under the general common law rules, the courts eventually developed a second method of prescription at common law, known as the fiction of the lost modern grant. This requires that the claimant should first establish user during living memory (for at least 20 years). Once this has been established the court is prepared to presume that the right is being exercised as the result of a modern grant by deed, but that the grant has been lost (see *Dalton v Angus & Co.* (1881) 6 App Cas 740). You should note, however, that the courts do admit that this is a clear fiction. In *Lynn Shellfish v Loose* [2017] AC 599, at para. 45, Neuberger LJ said:

> It is true that a prescriptive right can be said to be based on a notional grant but that grant is not merely notional: it is fictional. The essential point is that such a right is based not on an imagined document, but on actual use 'as of right', namely which is such as to 'bring home to the landowner that a right is being asserted against him' . . .

24.9.4.1 Rebutting the presumption that a grant was made

It appears that the presumption cannot be rebutted by proving that no grant has been made but it will destroy the claim if the servient owner can show that, at the date at which it is alleged the grant occurred, there was no person capable of making the grant (for example, because the land was subject to a SLA settlement, under which no grant could be made). Similarly, the claim may be opposed by showing that at the relevant time the dominant and servient tenements were in common ownership (see *Neaverson v Peterborough Rural District Council* [1902] 1 Ch 557).

24.9.4.2 Continued existence of this form of prescription

This method of prescription, based on a blatant fiction, was disliked in the nineteenth century, and it was hoped that the changes introduced by the Prescription Act 1832 would make it unnecessary to use it. However, as we shall see, this Act has proved to be most unsatisfactory, and although it had been thought that present-day courts would be unwilling to accept a claim based on such a fiction, the doctrine was revived by the Court of Appeal in *Tehidy Minerals Ltd v Norman* [1971] 2 QB 528 (see 24.9.8 for an account of this decision). Since *Tehidy*, this method of prescription has been relied upon in a number of modern cases.

The extent of the fiction is well illustrated by *Bridle v Ruby* [1989] QB 169. There a developer built and sold a number of houses. Originally it was intended that the purchaser of plot 12 was to be granted an express right of way over a drive. In fact the relevant clause was deleted from the conveyance so that the grant of the right was never made. The purchaser and his successors, in the mistaken belief that they had the right to do so, used the driveway for 22 years. Here the Court of Appeal held that the right could be claimed on the basis of lost modern grant. The fact that the relevant clause had been deleted from the original conveyance did not prevent the operation of the theory that, at a later date, a grant had been made. It was even irrelevant that the owners of plot 12 had used the right believing that the right to do so arose from the original conveyance. This case clearly demonstrates that the legal fiction is alive and well in the modern age. For further illustrations see *Mills v Silver* [1991] Ch 271, in which the Court of Appeal considered at length the issue of permission in relation to the doctrine of lost modern grant, and *England Environmental*

(Northern) Ltd v Arthur Jones & Sons (Contractors) Ltd [2017] EWHC 1903 (Ch), in which a landlord and his periodic tenant both gained a right of way over a neighbouring lane, due to 20 years of use.

24.9.5 Prescription Act 1832

The Prescription Act 1832 may very well have the dubious honour of being the worst drafted Act of Parliament on the statute book. Indeed, it is even generally presumed that there is a serious misprint in s. 8 of the Act and lawyers have accordingly adopted the habit of reading the section as though the misprint did not exist (thereby substituting the word 'easement' for the word 'convenient' where it appears in s. 8). The Act was intended to remove the difficulties which arose with the common law forms of prescription; however, it did not abolish the common law forms, so that the three forms now exist alongside one another. Furthermore, the Act introduced fresh complexities of its own.

The Act divides the easement of light from all other easements and profits and deals with it separately. Furthermore, it creates two different prescription periods (a 'short period' and a 'long period'), with different effects, for profits and easements other than light. The provisions relating to the short period merely assist a person claiming under the common law rules, but those relating to the long period introduce a form of statutory prescription, which does not depend on any fiction.

24.9.6 Profits and easements other than light under the Prescription Act 1832

24.9.6.1 Short period

The short period for easements is 20 years (Prescription Act 1832, s. 2), and for profits is 30 years (s. 1). The Act provides that, where use can be shown for the appropriate period, no claim to prescription at common law shall be defeated by showing that the right 'was first enjoyed at any time prior to such period'. The effect of this provision is quite simple but understanding why the statutory words have this effect is not so easy. The explanation is as follows. Legal memory does not go back before 1189, so, if the right was first enjoyed before that date, it would not be possible to show when it started. Thus the fact that one can show when it started means that that beginning must be after 1189, which would be fatal to a claim at common law. Therefore the Act is saying, in a roundabout way, that once the period had been completed, common law prescription cannot be defeated merely by showing that the use began after 1189.

The claim can still be defeated in any other way that would defeat common law prescription, such as showing that the use is not as of right, or that the right claimed lacks the characteristics of an easement or profit.

Deductions

In order to provide some protection for a servient owner who is subject to a legal disability, s. 7 of the Act provides that certain periods should be deducted when one computes the 20- or 30-year short period. The effect of these provisions, as modified by later reforms of the law, is that one should deduct any period during which the servient owner was:

(a) an infant;

(b) a patient under the Mental Health Act 1983 (or the Acts which preceded it); or

(c) a tenant for life.

Thus, if Nigel Neep had exercised his right of way for 35 years but for 20 of those years the owner of Fieldy Farm had been incapable (e.g., Farmer George's father had suffered from dementia for 20 years before his death) Mr Neep can only claim 15 years of user for the purposes of the short period. He can, however, add together the use before the old man's illness overcame his mental capacity and the use after Farmer George inherited on his father's death. He does *not* have to restart the period once the disability is removed (*Pugh v Savage* [1970] 2 QB 373).

24.9.6.2 Long period

The long period is 40 years for easements (s. 2) and 60 years for profits (s. 1). The benefit of proving use for the longer period is that the right claimed:

> shall be deemed absolute and indefeasible, unless it shall appear that the same was enjoyed by some consent or agreement expressly given or made for the purpose by deed or writing.

This is the statutory form of prescription, and does not depend on the common law rules, although use does still have to be as of right. It may also be the case that the long period does not rely upon any fiction that there must have been a grant at some time. This is the view this text has always taken and the view is shared by a number of others. However, in *Housden v The Conservators of Wimbledon and Putney Commons* [2008] 1 WLR 1172 the Court of Appeal considered this point (without deciding it) and drew attention to the difference of opinion on the point. See also *Staffordshire and Worcestershire Canal Navigation v Birmingham Canal Navigation* [1866] LR 1 HL 254.

1. Consents

It is clear from the statutory provisions mentioned earlier in this chapter that written consent can destroy a claim under the long period, whether it was given before the period started or during the period. At first reading this may seem to imply that purely oral permission cannot destroy the claim. However, this is not the case for it is still necessary for the dominant owner to show that the use of the easement or profit during the 40- or 60-year period has amounted to use as of right. As you have seen already, if the servient owner has given oral permission the use is precarious and not as of right. Accordingly, oral permission given during the long period will destroy the claim but oral permission given before the period can be ignored.

2. Does the use have to start against a fee simple owner?

At common law the prescription period could not start at a time when the servient land was let to a tenant. In *Davies v Du Paver* [1953] 1 QB 184 the Court of Appeal appeared to apply the same rule to a case brought under the Prescription Act 1832. However, in the earlier case of *Wright v Williams* (1836) 1 M & W 77 (which was not cited in *Davies v Du Paver*) it was held that the common law rule did not apply because of the positive wording of the Act. It would appear that the better view is that the rule does not apply, particularly as in s. 8 special provision is made for deduction of periods during which the servient land is subject to a lease (see Megarry (1956) 72 LQR 32).

3. Deductions

Deductions from the long period are governed by s. 8. It should be noted that these rules bear no real relation to the deductions from the short period prescribed by

s. 7. Assuming that the word 'convenient' in s. 8 is a misprint for 'easement', s. 8 provides for the deductions from the long period of any term during which the servient land was:

(a) held by a tenant for life;

(b) held by a tenant under a lease for more than three years.

However, the s. 8 deductions may only be made if the servient owner resists the claim to acquisition by prescription within the three years following the end of the life interest or lease.

4. Application of rules
The following example may make this clearer:

1 January 1979	The then owner of 14 Trant Way started to use the footpath on Fieldy Farm.
1 January 2007	Lease of Fieldy Farm for 10 years granted.
31 December 2016	Lease ends.
31 December 2018	40 years' use of right of way.

In this example, if Mr Neep had claimed under the longer period on 1 January 2019, Farmer George would have been able to claim a deduction from the period of use, under s. 8. For in these circumstances the servient tenement, Fieldy Farm, would have been subject to a lease for more than three years (10 years) and that lease would have ended less than three years before the date of the action. (Action started on 1 January 2019 and lease ended two years earlier on 31 December 2016.) If, however, the use continues, but no action were brought until 2020, more than three years would have elapsed since the end of the lease, and Farmer George would accordingly not be entitled to make any deduction. Thus, if the matter came to court in 2019 Nigel Neep would only have a claim based on 30 years' use (40 years' actual use, less 10 years during which the servient land was let), while if the case started in or after 2020 Nigel Neep can claim 41 years' use (no deduction is permitted). This result may seem odd at first sight but one should remember that the purpose of s. 8 is to provide limited protection for the reversioner who takes action swiftly on recovering the land. This may be particularly important to the freehold reversioner or a remainderman, following on after a tenant for life under an SLA settlement, who should accordingly make immediate enquiries about such matters as soon as his interest vests in possession.

24.9.6.3 Rules common to both short and long periods
Certain rules are common to both the long and the short periods.

1. User as of right
We have already seen that the Prescription Act 1832 does not exclude the common law requirement that the user relied upon must be as of right during the period claimed, and this has been held to mean not only that the use should be *nec vi*, *nec clam*, and *nec precario*, but also that use must be by and against fee simple owners (*Kilgour v Gaddes* [1904] 1 KB 457). It seems that any clear action taken to object to a claimed right will prevent user being as of right. Thus, in *Winterburn v Bennett* [2017] 1 WLR 646, the Court of Appeal held that user as of right of a car-park had been prevented by the

erection and replacement over time of a sign saying that the parking was private and for use of the patrons of a club only. The court was of the view that it was not necessary to go further and erect a barrier, or to start court proceedings, in order to establish that use was as a trespasser and not as of right.

2. Period must be 'next before some suit or action'
Under s. 4, the period relied upon must be:

> next before some suit or action wherein the claim or matter to which such period may relate shall have been or shall be brought into question . . .

Thus, a period of use which ceased some time before the commencement of an action cannot be relied upon for the purpose of statutory prescription, although it may be effective to support a claim to prescription at common law. Thus, in *Tehidy Minerals Ltd v Norman* [1971] 2 QB 528 claims based upon user which had ceased in 1941 (when the land was requisitioned by the army) were ineffective under the Act, although some claimants succeeded in establishing their rights under the principle of lost modern grant (see further 24.9.4).

Another effect of s. 4 is that no right to the easement or profit can exist under the statutory rules until some action is started, regardless of the length of use involved (*Hyman v Van den Bergh* [1908] 1 Ch 167). Of course, in order to secure the interest in the land, the dominant owner has only to apply to the court for a declaration that an easement or profit has been secured under the Act.

3. There must have been no interruption
A claim based on either period may be destroyed by proof that there has been some 'interruption' to the claimed interest and that the dominant owner has acquiesced in that interruption for the period of one year.

An 'interruption' is any action which interferes with the right claimed. In the case of the footpath on Fieldy Farm, Farmer George could create an interruption by erecting a gate, or other barrier, preventing access to the path. Thus, in *Davies v Du Paver* [1953] 1 QB 184, the servient owner erected a fence in order to exclude the dominant owner's sheep and thereby to prevent the acquisition of a profit. This case illustrates, however, that there must not only be an obstruction but that the obstruction must be acquiesced in for one year by the claimant. In *Davies v Du Paver* the dominant owner immediately protested at the erection of the fence, but did not issue proceedings to establish his claim to a profit until 13 months later. The Court of Appeal found that he had not acquiesced in the interruption for one year because his initial protest must have been effective for some period (at least a month) in which case at the start of the action there had been less than one year's acquiescence. Mere discontent which is not sufficiently communicated cannot amount to sufficient action to indicate a lack of acquiescence (*Dance v Triplow* [1992] 1 EGLR 190).

As a result of this provision about acquiescence, an interruption that begins during the last year of any of the statutory periods will not prevent the claimant succeeding under the Act. If an interruption were made, for example, to an easement after it had been used for 39 years and one day, the dominant owner could still issue proceedings 364 days later, as soon as the 40-year term is up, and claim that he had not acquiesced in the interruption for a year. By protesting at the interruption, he can extend the time still further. Thus, once usage has entered the last year of one of the periods, a servient tenement owner who objects to the use should commence proceedings immediately for trespass, for until the period is completed his opponent will *not* be able to rely on the existence of an easement or profit by prescription by way of defence.

24.9.7 Right to light under the Prescription Act 1832

24.9.7.1 One period only

The right to light is dealt with by the Prescription Act 1832 in a different way from its treatment of all other easements. There is only one period (not a 'short' and a 'long' period) and that requires use for a period of 20 years. Section 3 of the Act provides that if the 'use of light' to 'any building' has been:

> actually enjoyed . . . for the full period of 20 years without interruption, the right thereto shall be deemed absolute and indefeasible.

There are a number of differences between this provision and those relating to other easements and profits. In particular s. 3 does not require the satisfaction of the common law requirements for prescription. Accordingly, the use need not be as of right, nor is it necessary for the use to be by a fee simple owner against a fee simple owner. Thus, a tenant can acquire an easement of light by prescription against the landlord, or against a fellow tenant holding from the same landlord.

24.9.7.2 Interruption

The rules on interruption, however, do apply to easements of light in the same way as they apply to other rights claimed under the Act, and it has also been held that the 20-year period relied on must be next before suit or action, even though s. 3 does not specifically mention this (*Hyman v Van den Bergh* [1908] 1 Ch 167).

24.9.7.3 Preventing acquisition of right

It can be seen that it is far easier to acquire an easement of light than any other easement or profit. Accordingly, a 'servient' owner may well wish to take action to prevent a neighbour acquiring such a right. Unfortunately, in order to do this, he or she would need to interrupt the use of the right, and the erection of some structure (e.g., a hoarding) in order to do this will probably be contrary to the planning regulations applicable to the property. As a result, the Rights of Light Act 1959 was passed in order to provide a simple means by which a claim to light can be interrupted. Under this Act, instead of building a hoarding, a servient owner may, after taking certain preliminary steps, register a notice in the Local Land Charges Register specifying the size and position of the obstruction which would otherwise have been erected. The entry upon the register operates as though a real obstruction had been built and therefore if the dominant owner takes no action for a year he will be deemed to have acquiesced in the interruption.

24.9.8 How to apply the three forms of prescription

We have now looked at a bewildering variety of rules, and you must wonder how they fit together and which method to use.

There are three main methods to consider, and it appears that they should be applied in the following order. Begin with the long period under the Prescription Act 1832.

If there is not a sufficient period of use, or it is not 'next before the action', or for some other reasons that method does not succeed, apply the common law rules, assisted if possible by the short-period provisions of the Act. If that is not successful, as a last resort you should apply the doctrine of the lost modern grant. See Table 24.2 for a summary of this approach.

Table 24.2 Approaching a prescription problem

Step 1	Try applying the long period rules under the Prescription Act, s. 1 for profits (60 years), s. 2 for easements (40 years), and s. 3 for claims to light (20 years).
Step 2	Try applying the common law rules and, if they assist, the short period rules under the Prescription Act (30 years for profits, 20 years for easements).
Step 3	Try the lost modern grant rules.

This is in effect the order in which the various forms of prescription were considered in *Tehidy Minerals Ltd v Norman* [1971] 2 QB 528. This judgment of the Court of Appeal does provide a very good example for anyone who has to deal with a problem of this kind and so we will end this section with an account of that case.

The plaintiffs owned an area of downland on which local farmers had grazed their animals since the nineteenth century. For some time during and after the Second World War the down was requisitioned, and when grazing was resumed it appeared to be by permission. The plaintiffs fenced the down and tried to exclude the farmers, but they broke the fences. The plaintiffs alleged trespass and the defendants claimed that they had a profit of grazing.

It was not possible to make the claim under the long period of the Act, because user had ceased in 1941, when the land was requisitioned, and therefore the period of use was not 'next before the action', as required by s. 4. The long use, dating back to the nineteenth century did, however, enable some farmers to raise a presumption that the right had existed from time immemorial, and they succeeded at common law. The other defendants, however, could not rely on the common law, because their farms and the down had been in common ownership at some time after 1189. They were not assisted by the shorter period under the Act because, again, it was not 'next before the action'. They were, however, able to show over 20 years' use before the war, and the Court of Appeal held that this was sufficient to raise a presumption of a lost modern grant and found that they had acquired a profit by this means.

For another case in which a claim under the short period in the Act failed but the claimant won by relying on lost modern grant, see *Smith v Brudenell-Bruce* [2002] 2 P&CR 4.

By now you will have realised that the rules for identifying and acquiring easements and profits are quite complex in structure (though probably not in themselves difficult to understand). Figure 24.3 provides a basic summary of the structure of these rules and Table 24.3 provides a summary of the methods of acquiring easements by grant (or reservation), implied grant (or reservation), prescription, or contract.

Note that Table 24.3 does not set out exceptions or details (see the text for these) and that the right must also satisfy the other requirements for acquisition set out in Figure 24.3.

24.9 Acquisition by prescription 559

Is the right capable of being an easement?
Does it satisfy the requirements in
Re Ellenborough Park:
1. dominant and servient tenement;
2. dominant and servient owners must be different persons;
3. right claimed must accommodate the dominant tenement;
4. right claimed must be capable of forming the subject-matter of a grant.

↓ YES (NO → No easement)

Has it been created?
Has there been:
1. grant;
2. reservation; or
3. prescription.

(See Table 24.3)

↓ YES (NO → Is there a specifically enforceable contract to grant an easement? YES → EQUITABLE EASEMENT; NO → No easement)

Is the length equivalent to a fee simple absolute in possession or a term of years?

↓ YES (NO → Does the right take effect under s. 1(3) LPA 1925? YES → EQUITABLE EASEMENT; NO → No easement)

LEGAL EASEMENT
But note that if registered land, easement becomes a legal easement only when completed by registration—s. 27(1) LRA 2002

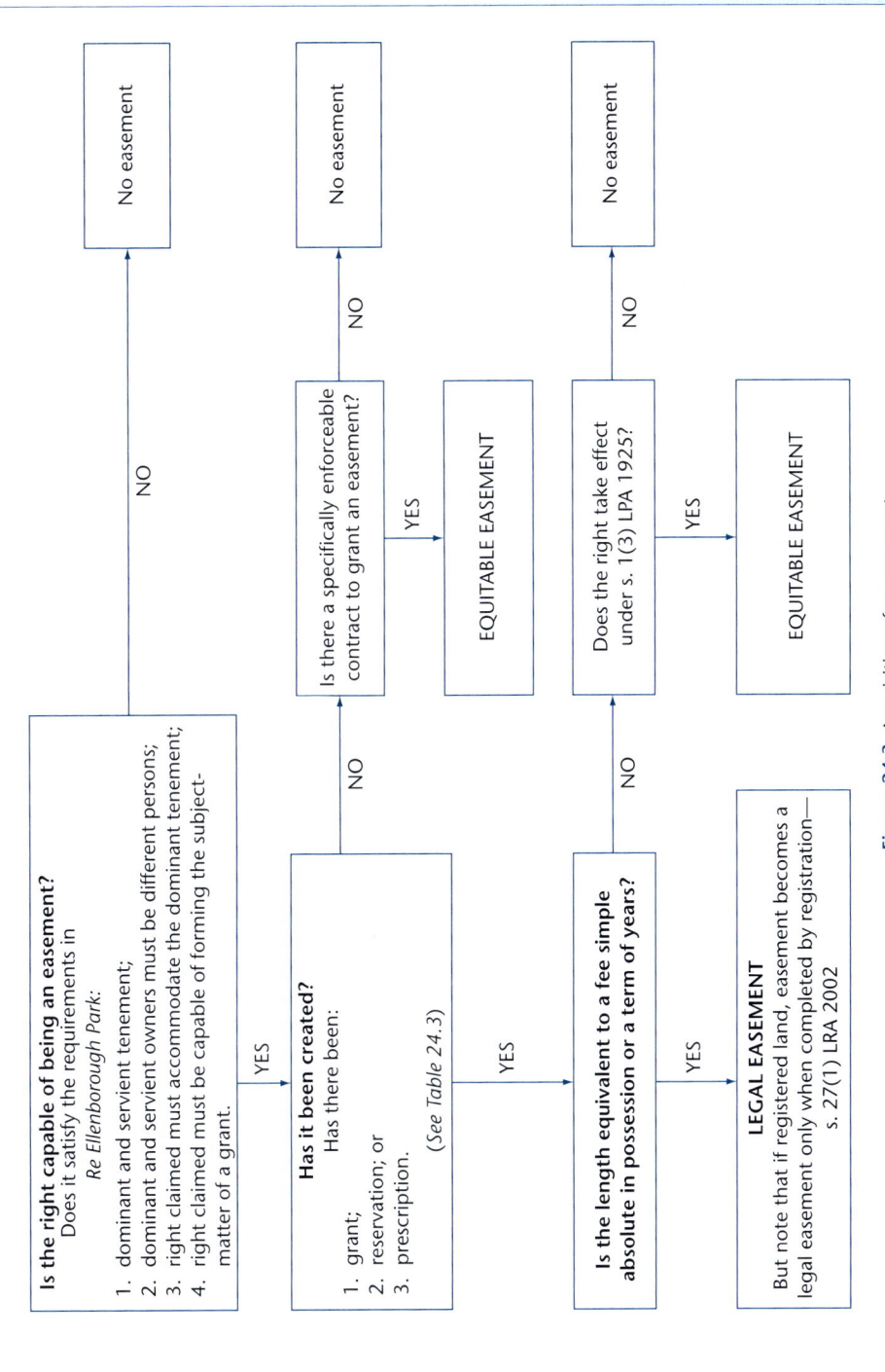

Figure 24.3 Acquisition of an easement

Table 24.3 Methods of creating an easement

Method	Requirements	Result
Express Grant or Reservation		
Agreement by the dominant owner	A deed complying with LPA 1925, s. 52(1) (plus, in the case of registered land, completed by registration—LRA 2002, s. 27(1)).	Legal easement
Section 62 LPA 1925	Legal grant or conveyance may carry with it existing rights (licences) and convert them into easements—see *Wright v Macadam* Note: applies only to legal grant—not relevant in equity, or to reservation	Legal easement
Implied Grant or Reservation		
Easements of necessity and intended easements, implied into a legal conveyance of land or a contract to convey	Court will look at the intention of the parties—see *Nikerson v Barraclough*	Legal easement if implied into a legal conveyance Equitable easement if implied into a contract to convey
Rule in *Wheeldon v Burrows*, implied into a legal conveyance of part of the land or into a contract to convey part of the land	Must be: (1) continuous and apparent; (2) necessary to the reasonable enjoyment of the land; (3) in use at the time the land was sold. Note: This applies to grant only—not relevant to reservation	Legal easement if implied into a legal conveyance Equitable easement if implied into a contract to convey
Prescription		
Common law prescription	Must be: 1. use as of right; 2. acquired by a fee owner against a fee simple owner; 3. continuous use; 4. possible to presume right has existed since time immemorial (1189)—a rebuttable presumption arises after 20 years' use. Note: The presumption after 20 years is rebutted by evidence which establishes that an easement cannot have existed since 1189 or that tenements have been in common ownership after 1189.	Legal easement
Common law prescription plus the benefit of the Prescription Act short period (rights other than light)	Must be: 1. use as of right; 2. by a fee simple owner against a fee simple owner; 3. without an interruption that has been acquiesced in for one year; 4. for 20 years next before a suit or action; 5. no evidence of express or implied consent either during or before the 20 year period. Note: The short period under the Act 'assists' acquisition at common law by removing the possibility that the presumption after 20 years can be rebutted by evidence which establishes that an easement cannot have existed since before 1189.	Legal easement

Table 24.3 Continued

Method	Requirements	Result
Prescription Act—long period *(rights other than light)*	Must be: 1. use as of right; 2. by a fee simple owner against a fee simple owner; 3. without an interruption that has been acquiesced in for one year; 4. for 40 years next before a suit or action; 5. no evidence of written consent either during or before the 40-year period or oral consent during the 40-year period	Legal easement
Prescription Act—rights to light	Must be: 1. used for 20 years; 2. before some suit or action; 3. without an interruption that has been acquiesced in for one year Note: There is no need for use as of right and the acquisition need not be by a fee simple owner against a fee simple owner.	Legal easement
Lost modern grant	Must be: 1. use as of right; 2. by a fee simple owner against a fee simple owner; 3. continuous use; 4. during living memory (20 years' use); 5. no evidence that a grant was impossible at the time any 'lost' grant must have been made.	Legal easement
	Contract to grant an easement	
Contract made on or after 27 September 1989	Must be made in writing—Law of Property (Miscellaneous Provisions) Act 1989, s. 2.	Equitable easement
Contract made before 27 September 1989	Must be: 1. recorded in writing and signed by servient owner—LPA 1925, s. 40; or 2. evidenced by part performance.	Equitable easement

24.10 Remedies

We can now consider briefly the remedies which may be used to protect an easement or profit.

24.10.1 Abatement

Theoretically, if any obstruction to the lawful exercise of a profit or easement is erected, the dominant owner may exercise a 'self-help' remedy and may simply 'abate' (remove) the obstruction. This may be done without informing the servient owner (*Perry v Fitzhowe* (1846) 8 QB 757) but the right should be used with care. The dominant owner must not use unreasonable force, nor may he or she injure any person in attempting to enforce the owner's rights. It would, however, be permissible to break down a fence or gate. A self-help remedy may also be appropriate in the case of an easement of support. As we noted in 24.2.2.6, such an easement does not require the servient owner to maintain the servient property in order to provide adequate support, and he or she can in fact allow it to collapse (see *Jones v Pritchard* [1908] 1 Ch 630 at p. 637). However, the dominant owner is not obliged to leave the servient property to collapse, thus depriving his or her own premises of support. Instead, the owner can enter the neighbour's land and carry out such repairs as are necessary to ensure that the support of the dominant property is maintained (see *Bond v Nottingham Corpn* [1940] Ch 429, per Greene MR at pp. 438–9).

In general, however, it is inadvisable for the dominant owner to rely upon self-help, and indeed in *Lagan Navigation Co. v Lambeg Bleaching, Dyeing & Finishing Co. Ltd* [1927] AC 226 at p. 245 Lord Atkinson indicated that the law preferred that a remedy be sought through the courts, and that abatement should only be used in cases of extreme urgency.

24.10.2 Action

Normally, a person claiming that his or her easement or profit has been infringed will apply to the courts for a suitable remedy. Obviously, it is possible to seek a *declaration* to clarify the rights of the parties (useful where a right is claimed by prescription). The claimant may, however, go further and seek *damages* to compensate for any loss caused by the infringement but, if this is done, must establish some serious interference with the rights, rather than some trivial incident (*Weston v Lawrence Weaver Ltd* [1961] 1 QB 402).

Generally, the remedy which will be sought is that of an *injunction* restraining the interference of which the dominant owner complains. Once again, the courts will not intervene where the act complained of is only a trivial interference with the dominant owner's rights (*Cowper v Laidler* [1903] 2 Ch 337). However, there is no right to alter the terms of an easement even where the dominant owner could not reasonably object to the change. Thus, it would not be a defence to a complaint of interference with a private right of way that a reasonable substitute had been provided (*Greenwich Healthcare National Health Service Trust v London and Quadrant Housing Trust* [1998] 1 WLR 1749). The relevant question is not whether the use left to the person with the benefit of the right is reasonable, but whether it was reasonable for that person to insist on all he or she had bargained for: see *Celsteel Ltd v Alton House Ltd* [1985] 1 WLR 204 at p. 217.

Even if the court considers that the applicant deserves a remedy, it has power under the Senior Courts Act 1981, s. 50, to award damages in place of an injunction if it considers that this would be a more appropriate remedy. When this power was first introduced in the nineteenth century, there was considerable discussion as to the principles which should guide the court in its choice of remedy. In *Shelfer v City of London Electric Lighting Co. Ltd* [1895] 1 Ch 287, at pp. 322–3, Smith LJ said that in his opinion damages in lieu of an injunction may be given if:

- the injury to the plaintiff's legal rights is small; and
- is capable of being estimated in money; and
- can be adequately compensated by a small money payment; and
- the case is one in which it would be oppressive to the defendant to grant an injunction.

These conditions had been considered and applied by the courts in two cases involving interference with easements of light: *Tamares (Vincent Square) Ltd v Fairpoint Properties (Vincent Square) Ltd* [2007] 1 WLR 2148 ('*Tamares*') and *Regan v Paul Properties Ltd* [2007] Ch 135 ('*Regan*'). In both cases the interference complained of resulted from development work on the servient land, which was already well advanced by the time the cases came to court. In *Tamares*, the judge considered that it would be oppressive to require the demolition of a major part of a new building, and awarded damages in lieu of an injunction, while in *Regan* the Court of Appeal held that damages would not be an adequate remedy and required the developer to reduce the height of the building. These cases turn very much on their own facts and you probably do not need to study them in any detail. All you need to note is that the court has the power to award damages in place of an injunction and that the decision as to whether to exercise that power is a matter for the court's discretion.

Then in 2010 the decision of the High Court in *HKRUK II (CHC) Ltd v Heaney* [2010] EWHC 2245 (Ch), as the Law Commission says, sent 'shock waves through the development industry'. In *HKRUK* the developer obtained planning permission in 2007 to erect two additional floors on the top of an existing five-storey building. The developer wrote to the adjoining landowner in 2008, conceding that the proposed development interfered with the neighbour's right to light and making an offer of compensation. This offer was rejected and the neighbour threatened action but then 'stood by' while the developer proceeded to construct the two new storeys. These were completed in 2009 and the two new floors were let to a tenant. At this point the neighbour finally went to court to protect his rights. The court awarded a mandatory injunction, requiring the demolition of the two new storeys. The injunction was granted on the basis that the impact on the dominant land was not small and was not capable of being remedied in damages, even though the actual loss of light did not seem particularly problematic and the cost of demolition of the offending two floors was in the region of £1–2 million. The court took notice of the fact that the breach of the right to light was acknowledged and that the developer had proceeded without first resolving the matter with the neighbouring owner. The effect of the case was to make developers very wary of proceeding in any case in which there was a risk of a claim of a right to light. Finally, in *Lawrence v Fen Tigers Ltd* [2014] AC 822 the Supreme Court made it clear that there should not be any slavish adherence to the 'good working rule' in *Shelfer v City of London Electric Lighting Co Ltd*. The court indicated that where there is a breach of property rights the prima facie position is that an injunction should be granted and that it is for the defendant to show why this should not be done (see para. 121). It was emphasised, however, that the eventual decision would depend very much on the facts of the particular case. You may wish to note, however, that Lord Sumption JSC (at para. 161) expressed the view that the whole jurisprudence of this issue needed to be reviewed and was of the view that, in the modern world, the time might have come to move towards a presumption in favour of damages being the appropriate remedy, at least in cases in which planning permission had been granted for the development in question. For the moment, however, it seems that a dominant owner is very likely to get an injunction, rather than merely an award of damages. Following this case, s. 237 of the Town and Country Planning Act 1990 has been used by developers to remove rights to light and also see s. 208 of the Localism Act 2011.

24.10.2.1 Claim in nuisance

One must also note that the inability to enforce an easement may not mean that a complainant has no remedy at all, because in some cases a claim in nuisance may be available. This may be particularly important in cases which, at first, seem to involve the easement of support. Where support is not being maintained, the dominant tenement owner may enter and repair the servient property. However, *Bradburn v Lindsay* [1983] 2 All ER 408 suggests that another right may be available even where abatement has not been practicable. The case concerned two semi-detached houses, separated by a party wall, which were owned respectively by Mrs Lindsay (No. 53) and the Bradburns (No. 55). In 1972 Mr Bradburn complained that dry rot had taken hold in the party wall between the properties. Over the next few years, No. 53 became derelict and eventually the council ordered it to be demolished, because of its dangerous condition. The house was accordingly pulled down, save for its half of the party wall.

The Bradburns, whose half of the house was thus left unsupported, brought a claim in nuisance and negligence. A claim based on the easement of support should not in this case (at least theoretically) have succeeded since Mrs Lindsay had merely allowed the dereliction to occur and the pulling down of the house had been carried out by the council under statutory powers. However, the court held that the Bradburns' claim could succeed. The decision appears to be based in part in nuisance and in part in negligence. Judge Blackett-Ord V-C said that the considerable dry rot at No. 53 constituted a nuisance, that Mrs Lindsay should have appreciated the risks to No. 55 and accordingly should have taken steps to prevent the damage. Accordingly, the Bradburns were able to recover the costs of works to strengthen and support No. 55.

It may be that this case does not conflict with the traditional view of the easement of support because, on a careful reading of the case, it seems that the decision is based on the principle that allowing spread of dry rot falls within the ambit of nuisance and goes further than simply allowing a structure to fall down. However, in practice the two may typically run together and thus nuisance might provide a useful alternative when the law relating to easements fails to provide a remedy.

There are two other cases that adopt this approach. In *Holbeck Hall Hotel v Scarborough BC* [2000] QB 836, it was said that a duty may arise in tort but this extends only to damage that is reasonably foreseeable. In *Holbeck* it could only have been foreseen had there been geological investigation and the defendant was not obliged to carry out such an investigation.

Rees v Skerrett [2001] 1 WLR 1541 concerned two terraced houses, one of which was demolished. As a consequence the party wall between the properties became unstable and it also was exposed to the weather. The instability was clearly a breach of the easement of support and the court held so. However, the owner of the affected (dominant) property had suffered additional loss due to the penetration of rain through the wall, which had caused damp in his house. This loss was not attributable to the loss of support. It was accepted that no easement could be claimed in relation to protection from the weather (*Phipps v Pears* [1965] 1 QB 76). However, the court held that the servient owner did owe an additional duty to take care when demolishing his house, to the extent necessary to prevent consequential damage to the dominant property. Thus a claim in relation to the damp could succeed.

24.11 Extinguishment of easements and profits

Once easements and profits have arisen they will, as interests in land, endure through successive ownerships of the land. Indeed, they may well endure for very long periods. It is therefore necessary to consider the means by which such rights are brought to an end.

24.11.1 Dominant and servient tenements coming into the same hands

Because a person cannot have rights against him- or herself, an easement, or a profit appurtenant to land, will be extinguished if the dominant and the servient tenements come into common ownership and possession. It is essential that both ownership and possession become common, and that both tenements are acquired for an estate in fee simple (*R v Inhabitants of Hermitage* (1692) Carth 239). Thus, if the fee simple owner of one tenement takes a lease of the other this does not extinguish the easement or profit. All that happens is that the exercise of the easement or profit as a right is suspended for a period of the lease and will revive when it ends (*Simper v Foley* (1862) 2 John & H 555). If, however, the two tenements do come into common ownership the easement or profit will be completely extinguished and will not revive if the plots are separated again at a later date.

24.11.2 Release

An easement or profit may be 'released' (given up) by the dominant owner at any time. Obviously, at law such a release should be effected by deed, but equity will recognise an informal release if it would be inequitable to allow the releasing owner to go back on his word (e.g., *Waterlow v Bacon* (1866) LR 2 Eq 514). The effect of a release is to return the easement or profit to the servient owner, at which point it merges with his or her estate and is thereby extinguished.

24.11.3 Implied release: abandonment

In general, the mere lack of use of an easement or profit, once it has been acquired, will not lead to the extinguishment of the right (*Seaman v Vawdrey* (1810) 16 Ves Jr 390), for one is never obliged to exercise the rights which one may have. However, a prolonged non-use may be adduced as evidence that the dominant owner has impliedly abandoned a right.

It should, however, be noted that if the dominant owner explains the non-use he or she may still be regarded as not having abandoned the right. Thus, in *James v Stevenson* [1893] AC 162 a right was not lost due to a long period of non-use because the dominant owner explained that he had simply had no occasion to exercise the right (but presumably might wish to in the future). In *Benn v Hardinge* (1992) 66 P&CR 246 the Court of Appeal said that non-use, even for 175 years, was not enough on its own to indicate an intention to abandon. The court also commented that the abandonment of such a right would not be lightly inferred. In *CDC 2020 plc v George Ferreira* (2005) 35 EG 112 this approach was again confirmed by the Court of Appeal, as was the fact that the dominant owner must make it clear that he or she was abandoning the right for himself or herself and successors and not just for the current owner.

If, however, the dominant tenement has been altered in such a way that the right claimed becomes unnecessary or impossible to exercise, then the alteration may be regarded as evidence of an intention to abandon the right. This presumption may be rebutted by evidence that the original character of the land may be restored in the future and that the need for the easement or profit would revive. Thus, in the case of a right to light, the easement will not be extinguished merely because the house on the dominant land is destroyed, as long as it is intended to erect another building in its place (*Ecclesiastical Commissioners for England v Kino* (1880) 14 ChD 213).

A more recent consideration of the rules about implied abandonment is to be found in the Court of Appeal decision in *Williams v Sandy Lane (Chester) Ltd* [2007] 1 EGLR 10. In this case, the servient tenement owner accepted that an easement over his land had been acquired by prescription, but he claimed that the right, over a path described in the case as 'the secondary route', had been abandoned when the claimant began to use a different route to access the dominant property.

At first instance, the trial judge had inferred an intention to abandon the right, relying among other matters on 30 years' non-use and various developments on the dominant tenement (fencing, creation of a bank of earth, and growth of vegetation) that made it difficult to use the path to gain access to the property. The Court of Appeal considered that none of the developments made the use of the route impossible (para. 57) and reversed the trial judge's decision, holding that he had taken into account matters which did not support an inference of the intention to abandon (para. 58).

24.11.4 Do easements benefiting a leasehold property end on the merger of lease and reversion?

When a lease and its reversion come into the same hands, the two estates merge and the lease comes to an end (see 9.5.2.4). In *Wall v Collins* [2007] Ch 390, the Court of Appeal considered the effect of such a merger on an easement granted by the lease over the landlord's adjoining land. Did it come to an end along with the lease, or did it survive for the period for which it was already granted and thus benefit the owner of the freehold estate?

The properties in *Wall v Collins* were two houses that had been built by a developer on a 999-year building lease. In 1911, he sold No. 231 (i.e., assigned the lease to the purchaser), while continuing to own No. 233. The assignment of No. 231 included the grant of a right of way along a passageway situated on the retained land. The freeholds of both properties were subsequently acquired by their respective lessees, that of No. 231 being bought in 1986 and that of No. 233 some years later in 1995. For some time the Land Registry maintained separate registers for the leasehold and freehold estates in the two properties, but by the time the litigation began the leasehold registers had been closed and the leasehold estates were regarded as having merged with their respective freeholds.

The case before the Court of Appeal arose from a dispute between the current owners of the two properties about the use of the passageway, and Wall (owner of No. 231) sought a declaration that he was entitled to a right of way over No. 233. At first instance, this claim was rejected, the trial judge holding that the easement granted in the assignment of the lease was attached to that lease and ceased to exist when the lease merged with the freehold.

This decision was reversed by the Court of Appeal, which rejected the view that the easement was attached to the lease and ended when the lease came to an end. An easement must be attached to a dominant tenement (i.e., attached to the piece of land that it benefits), but it is not necessarily attached to any particular interest in that land. The fact that a legal easement can be created for a 'term of years' (LPA 1925, s. 1(2)(a)) does not mean that it has to be attached to a leasehold estate of the same length. Consequently, the ending of the leasehold estate through merger with the freehold does not destroy the easement, which will continue to exist for the rest of the period for which it was granted. As a result, the easement granted in the 1911 assignment had survived the merger and Wall was entitled to a right of way along the passageway for the rest of the 999-year period (paras. 13–19).

You may remember that *Wall v Collins* was mentioned in connection with s. 62 (see 24.8.2.3). In case you are confused by what appear to be two different decisions, you should note that the court had heard argument on s. 62 as an alternative ground of appeal, and so gave judgment on this point as well. Thus, although the 999-year easement was accepted by Wall as 'amply sufficient for his purposes' (para. 19), the court also held that, by virtue of s. 62, the conveyance of the freehold to Wall's predecessor in title had converted the existing easement for a term of years into one equivalent to the freehold estate.

24.12 Law reform

24.12.1 The need for reform

By this point you may well have concluded that the law relating to easements and profits is sadly in need of reform. It may be of some comfort to know that we agree with this conclusion. The existence of three methods of prescription is in itself an unnecessary complication and the nightmarish quality of the Prescription Act 1832 has been a cause of complaint for generations. Indeed in 1966 the Law Reform Committee recommended that all the existing rules on prescription should be abolished and replaced by one simpler method of prescription providing for a single period of 12 years (14th Report, Cmnd 3100). In addition, in 1971 it was recommended that a more far-reaching reform be contemplated in order to bring the law relating to easements and freehold covenants in line with one another (Law Commission Working Party, Working Paper 1971, No. 36). In March 2008 the Law Commission published a further consultation paper: *Easements, Covenants and Profits à Prendre* CP No. 186. In June 2011 the Law Commission published a final Report on the need for reform in the areas of freehold covenants, easements, and profits à prendre, following extensive consultation on its earlier consultation paper: *Making Land Work: Easements, Covenants and Profits à Prendre* (2011) Law Com No. 327. The Report is long (257 pages) but well worth reading because it considers in a very clear fashion all the difficulties of the law relating to easements and profits and those relating to freehold covenants (on which see Chapter 25). It also provides, in Part 2 of the Report, a useful summary of the law relating to estates and interests in land, which you may find helpful.

The Law Commission identified the following problems with the law on easements and profits. First, those arising from the practicalities of the extent of use rules and the requirement that the servient owner should not be excluded from using his or her own land (see the cases on parking). Secondly, the fact that easements can be acquired relatively easily and they can be acquired by multiple means (including implied easements and those obtained by prescription). Thirdly, that the law on prescription is unduly complex and that it seems unnecessary to have three separate forms of prescription operating alongside one another. Fourthly, that, although long use can allow the acquisition of an easement, long-term failure to use an existing easement will not lead to it being lost. Fifthly, even if the factual background circumstances change considerably, the court has no power to modify or discharge a profit or easement (which is possible in the case of freehold covenants).

The Law Commission said that its aim was to have a law of easements and profits which is as coherent and clear as possible and that as far as possible the law relating to these rights and freehold covenants should be brought into line and that overlapping and alternative doctrines (such as the three forms of prescription) should be rationalised or eradicated.

24.12.2 The 2011 recommendations

The 2011 Report makes a wide range of recommendations in relation to easements and covenants and it really is best to read them in full. The Report includes a draft bill, which is also well worth study. However, we will summarise the main proposals in the Report. Here the paragraph numbers refer to paragraphs in the Report.

24.12.2.1 Creation of profits

The Report recommends that it should in future only be possible to create profits à prendre by express grant or reservation or statute. On this see para. 3.9 and clauses 18 and 19 of the draft Bill. Thus, implied profits and those arising by prescription would cease to be possible. The Law Commission was of the view that profits are usually commercial agreements and therefore little would be lost by requiring that they be formally created, and that this would also provide certainty as to the extent of the profit.

24.12.2.2 Implied easements

In para. 3.30, it is recommended that, in determining whether an easement is implied, it should not be material whether it takes effect due to implied grant or implied reservation. At present the courts are more likely to imply an easement where there is a grant rather than a reservation but the Law Commission felt that implied easements usually dealt with cases of inadvertence or mistake, which were just as likely in either case.

The Law Commission takes the view that there should be a single statutory test for implication, to replace all existing methods. The proposal is that an easement should be implied as a term of a disposition if at the time of the disposition it is *necessary for the reasonable use of the land* bearing in mind:

(1) the use of the land at the time of the grant;
(2) the presence on the land of any relevant physical features;
(3) any intention for the future use of the land which is known to both parties at the time of the grant;
(4) so far as relevant, the available routes for the easement sought; and
(5) the potential interference with the servient land or inconvenience to the servient owner.

(See clause 20 of the draft Bill.)

The Law Commission recommends that it should remain possible to prevent implied easements by express exclusion (para. 3.49). Thus express drafting will be possible in order to prevent their creation.

The proposals are not intended to have an impact on ancillary easements (e.g., a right of access to a pipe to repair it, which is ancillary to an easement to use the pipe). These arise from construction of the grant and really relate to the scope of the grant (para. 3.51).

24.12.2.3 Section 62 LPA 1925

The Commission views the effects of LPA 1925, s. 62, as better regarded as an aspect of the express creation of easements rather than as a form of implication (para. 3.11). This is unsurprising. This text has always taken the view that s. 62 gave rise to wording being implied into a grant and thus produces the creation of an express easement, arising from the wording implied into the document.

Para. 3.64 recommends that s. 62 should no longer operate to transform precarious benefits into legal easements or profits on conveyance (clause 21(1) of the draft Bill).

This would prevent licences becoming easements on conveyance and would overrule, for example, *Wright v Macadam* [1949] 2 KB 744.

The Report proposes that it should remain possible for s. 62 to upgrade leasehold easements to freehold easements (para. 3.66). However, this should not in future apply to leasehold profits (para. 3.68).

24.12.2.4 Prescription

Most consultees were against abolition of prescription, even though it can sometimes prove burdensome to the generous, who simply allow adverse conduct to continue over time without objection (para. 3.76). The Law Commission advises the abolition of the *present* law of prescription and its replacement by a new statutory scheme for prescription. See clauses 16, 17, and 18 of the draft Bill for the detailed provisions.

In formulating new rules, the Law Commission had the following objectives (see para. 3.116):

(1) simplicity;

(2) avoidance of litigation;

(3) compatibility with land registration principles; and

(4) ensuring the scope for prescription is not extended.

The proposed scheme is that an easement will arise:

(1) on completion of 20 years' continuous qualifying use;

(2) if the qualifying use is without force, without stealth, and without permission; and

(3) if that use is not a use that is contrary to the criminal law, unless the use can be rendered lawful by the dispensation of the servient owner.

See para. 3.123 and clauses 16 and 17 of the draft Bill. This provides one period for prescription and retains the traditional requirement that exercise of the right should have been *nec vi, nec clam*, and *nec precario*.

The intention is that qualifying use must be by and against a freehold owner (para. 3.150). Use is not to be qualifying use at any time when the freehold is vested in a person who, or body which, is not competent to grant an easement over it (para. 3.168).

Where land is let, it is recommended that use is not qualifying use as against the freeholder at any time at which the servient freeholder:

- does not have power to prevent the use during the currency of the lease; or
- does not know of the use or could not reasonably have discovered it.

Two exceptions to this approach are proposed:

(1) if the use began before the lease was granted; and

(2) if, when the lease was granted:

   (a) the landlord knew about the use; or

   (b) could reasonably have discovered it.

24.12.2.5 Prescription and rights to light

No special rules were proposed as to the right to light, in order to maintain consistency (para. 3.130). The proposed new rules should apply in the same way to all easements. Thus, the old distinctions between the right to light and other rights would be abolished and one common system introduced. However, in 2013 a further Consultation Paper was published on reform of rights to light: Law Com CP 210 (see 24.12.3).

24.12.2.6 Transitional provisions for prescription

The main recommendation is that the new rules should apply to cases in which the use started before any new Act comes into force: you would not apply the old rules to the earlier period of use. However, to cover the oddity that under the 1832 Act, interruption must be for at least a year and thus no interruption is effective once 19 years and one day have passed, it is proposed that the 1832 Act should remain in force for a year after implementation of the new rules, in order to allow potential claimants under these provisions to obtain an easement if they bring their claim promptly.

24.12.2.7 Interaction with proposals on land obligations

One of the important proposals in the 2011 Report is the creation of a new system of interests in land called '**land obligations**'. This issue is covered in more detail in Chapter 25 because, in the main, land obligations would replace rules relating to covenants in relation to freehold land. However, the proposals do have a read-across to the law on easements and profits, so those issues are discussed here.

As you have seen, the easement of fencing is an anomaly and para. 5.94 therefore recommends that in future an obligation to fence should only have effect in the form of a land obligation and not as an easement. This would prevent for the future any confusion as to whether the easement or land obligation rules should apply. This would be the case however the obligation was worded.

There are four easements that may be regarded as 'negative' because they prevent the servient owner from doing something. Those easements are the easements of:

(1) support;

(2) air;

(3) water; and

(4) light.

An easement of support prevents, for example, removal of a wall, whereas the other three negative easements prevent obstruction of the flow of air, water, or light. For the future any attempt to create any negative easement would have effect as a new 'land obligation' because no formal wording is to be required in order to create such an obligation. However, the Law Commission recognises that negative easements would continue to be capable of arising by means of prescription or as implied easements (para. 5.99) and makes no recommendation to change this situation.

24.12.2.8 Extensive use

In recent years there have been many cases in which a key element of a case was whether the use being made of land was too extensive to be an easement. (See *Dyce v Hay* (1852) 1 Macq 305.) This has been particularly an issue in cases involving a claim to a parking space. Currently, to be an easement the use must:

- not amount to exclusive possession;
- not prevent the servient owner making reasonable use of the land.

The Law Commission proposes the abolition of the second possibility, leaving only the requirement that an easement does not give exclusive possession. This would reverse the decision in *Batchelor v Marlow* [2003] 1 WLR 764. Thus, for example, an easement granting an exclusive right to park would become possible.

24.12.2.9 Extinguishment by abandonment

At present this is often difficult to establish. In *Benn v Hardinge* (1993) 66 P&CR 246 an easement not used for 175 years was nonetheless not regarded as abandoned because it might be of use in future. The Law Commission proposal is that where title is registered and an easement or profit has been entered on the register then abandonment should not be able to cancel the right. Where title is unregistered or the easement or profit has not been entered on the register of the servient title, it should be possible to claim abandonment. In such cases, where there has been no use for 20 years there should be a rebuttable presumption of abandonment.

24.12.2.10 Termination of the estate to which the interest is appurtenant

The recommendation is that the decision that an easement that benefits a lease should survive merger with the freehold should be reversed (*Wall v Collins* [2007] Ch 390). However, it is proposed that a statutory right be created that allows the person who would have obtained the benefit to elect to do so.

24.12.2.11 Reform of registered land rules

Four reforms are proposed in relation to easements and profits where title is registered.

1. Statutory magic and registered interests

Section 58 of the LRA 2002 provides a guarantee of validity of registered estates and interests. The Report recommends that it should be made clear that this does not apply where an entry is made on the register due to an instrument that purports to create an easement, if the right it purports to create does not in fact accommodate and serve the dominant land. This is because in principle an easement cannot exist in such a case (paras. 4.11–4.18).

2. Unity of seisin

One of the basic rules for an easement or profit is that the dominant and servient tenements must not be both owned and occupied by the same person. This causes problems in some cases in which properties are temporarily in common ownership and some other cases (paras. 4.25–4.40). The Report recommends that this rule should be abolished if title to both the dominant and the servient land is registered.

3. Express release of registered interests

Oddly, there is currently no requirement to enter on the register an express release (discharge) of a registered easement or covenant. A deed of release is effective, even if the register still shows the right as existing. It is therefore recommended that an express release should become a registrable disposition (para. 4.57).

4. Use of short forms for creation of easements

The Report proposes that the Land Registry should make Rules determining the wording of some easements (which easements being for the registry to decide). The Rules should then allow these forms of easement to be adopted by registrable instruments. The aim is to produce standard forms of popular easements that *may*, but not must, be adopted by those drafting registrable dispositions.

24.12.2.12 Jurisdiction of the Lands Chamber of the Upper Tribunal

The 2011 Report also recommends changes to the powers of the Lands Chamber, in order to facilitate the removal of barriers to the use of land that have become redundant over time. It is proposed that the jurisdiction of the Lands Chamber should in future extend to any new easements and profits created after the introduction of the new rules and to all of the proposed new land obligations (para. 7.35). Jurisdiction should also be extended to include powers in relation to leasehold land of any term (para. 7.38).

The grounds for modification or discharge should be those currently in s. 84 of the LPA 1925: para. 7.55 of the Report and see also Chapter 25 (25.7.2). However, it is recommended that it be made clear that, where several people can enforce the benefit, an order may be made even if differing grounds under s. 84 apply to each of them (para. 7.87). Thus an applicant would not have to show the same ground or grounds against all the benefited persons.

The Lands Chamber should only modify an easement or profit if it is satisfied that the modified interest will not be materially less convenient to the benefited owner and will be no more burdensome to the land affected (para. 7.60).

It is proposed (para. 7.83) that the power to modify easements and profits should include power to change the *nature* of the interest, if:

(1) the change appears reasonable; and

(2) the applicant seeking the modification does not object to the change.

This might, for example, allow the Lands Chamber to substitute a land obligation for an easement, if this appeared to be appropriate.

24.12.3 Rights to light

In 2013 the Law Commission issued a further Consultation Paper which addressed possible reforms of the law relating to rights to light: *Rights to Light, A Consultation Paper*, Law Com CP 210. As is the case with all Law Commission papers, this contains a useful analysis of the current law and the problems to which it gives rise and is well worth reading for this alone. The main proposals in the paper are:

(1) that the possibility of obtaining a right to light by long use (prescription) should be abolished;

(2) that a simpler, statutory, test should be provided for cases in which a court is called upon to consider whether damages should be awarded instead of an injunction in a right to light case;

(3) the possibility of a new statutory procedure that would allow those who wish to develop land to discover whether neighbours who have rights to light would seek to enforce their rights to prevent the development; and

(4) that the Lands Tribunal should have extended jurisdiction to discharge or amend rights to light, whenever those rights have arisen.

It should be noted that the proposals in this Paper were very tentative. On 4 December 2014 the Law Commission published a final Report on rights to light, including a draft Bill: *Rights to Light*, Law Com No. 356. It had been a major part of the earlier paper that the obtaining of rights to light by prescription should be abolished. However, it appears that there were a large number of objections to this proposal during the consultation and the Law Commission has abandoned this proposal in its final Report. A particular objection seems to have been that the result would have simply been to shift arguments about rights to light into the planning system, which would be unable to cope with the resulting burden of disputes. Instead, the Report proposes that rights to light should be added to the proposals made in its 2011 Report in relation to other easements obtained by prescription.

The other proposals made are as follows.

(1) After considering whether it would be possible to develop a new objective test for the extent of the right to light, the Report concludes that the law as stated in *Colls v Home and Colonial Stores Ltd* [1904] AC 179 and *Allen v Greenwood* [1980] Ch 119 (see 24.2.2.2) should remain unamended.

(2) Following *Coventry v Lawrence* [2014] UKSC 13, which introduced the need to consider matters of public interest when deciding to grant an injunction requiring demolition or simply to award damages, the Report and draft Bill propose that an injunction should not be granted where it would amount to a disproportionate means of protecting the dominant owner's easement of light. The Report lists a series of factors which should be taken to account when determining what is disproportionate. Clause 2(3) of the draft Bill lists them as:

   (a) the claimant's interest in the dominant land;
   (b) the loss of amenity attributable to the infringement;
   (c) whether or not damages would be adequate compensation for the injury to the claimant;
   (d) the claimant's conduct;
   (e) any unreasonable delay in claiming an injunction;
   (f) the defendant's conduct;
   (g) the impact of an injunction on the defendant; and
   (h) the public interest, so far as relevant.

Clause 2(4) of the draft Bill also makes it clear that the extent to which artificial light is relied on instead of or in addition to natural light is always to be relevant in assessing the loss of amenity caused by the infringement of the right to light.

(3) The Report refines the proposals for a Notice of Proposed Obstruction procedure and makes them more flexible. The draft Bill gives powers for the Secretary of State to make Regulations to govern the procedure. However, the process remains, in essence, the same and the owner of the dominant tenement will have to respond swiftly to a notice by applying for an injunction promptly, or will lose the right to an injunction and would be restricted to a possible claim in damages: see the Schedule to the draft Bill. The effect will be to allow a developer to identify ahead of a development whether a right to light will be claimed, which could imperil the construction once built. The new system would replace the system of registering a local land charge under the Rights of Light Act 1959.

(4) While recognising that the current position on the quantum of damages for breach of the right to light is far from ideal, the Law Commission has concluded that there is no consensus on any reform and has concluded that it has no better ideas of its own. Accordingly, the problem of the amount of damages in such cases has been handed back to the Government for further consideration at some point in the future.

(5) As far as abandonment of an easement is concerned, you have seen how difficult this is to prove. The Law Commission in the 2011 Report proposed that non-use of an easement (other than light) for 20 years should be evidence of abandonment. In the 2014 Report they propose the same approach to rights to light but that the period of non-use should only be five years. They point out that if a building has been demolished and not replaced within five years, or a window has been blocked up for five years, it is hard to see how it can be said that the dominant owner intended to continue to use the right to light.

(6) In relation to the possibility of discharging rights to light and all other easements, the Law Commission has concluded that its 2011 Report was too cautious and that the Lands Chamber should have jurisdiction to discharge or modify *all* easements, including the right to light. The Commission has also reached the view that this power should exist in the case of any easement and whether or not the easement was created before or after any amending Act is brought into force. The earlier Report had proposed that this power should arise only in relation to easements created after the Act.

24.12.4 The future for reform

Following the Law Commission's 2011 Report on profits and easements, the Lord Chancellor announced to Parliament that the Government would respond by 2014. In 2017, the Government announced that it would bring forward proposals in a draft Bill to implement the recommendations of the Law Commission so far as they concern freehold covenants (see Chapter 25). However, this has not yet happened and it is not clear whether there is any intention of also implementing the recommendations for reform of the law of easements and profits.

FURTHER READING

Megarry and Wade, *The Law of Real Property*, 9th edn., Sweet & Maxwell, 2019, Chapters 26–9.

Equitable easements
Barnsley, 'Equitable Easements—Sixty years On' (1999) 115 LQR 89.

Easements of storage and parking
Gray and Gray, *Elements of Land Law*, 5th edn., Oxford University Press, 2009, paras. 5.1.62–5.1.67.
Hill-Smith, 'Rights of Parking and the Ouster Principle After *Batchelor v Marlow*' [2007] Conv 223.
Zif and Litman, 'Easements and Possession: An Elusive Limitation' [1989] Conv 296.

LPA 1925, s. 62
Harpum, 'Easements and Centre Point: Old Problems Resolved in a Novel Setting' [1977] 41 Conv 415.
Harpum, '*Long v Gowlett*: A Strong Fortress' [1979] 43 Conv 113.
Jackson, 'Easements and General Words' [1966] 30 Conv NS 342.

Smith, 'Centre Point: Faulty Towers with Shaky Foundations' [1978] 42 Conv 449.

Tee, 'Metamorphoses and Section 62 of the Law of Property Act' [1998] Conv 115.

Thompson, 'The Acquisition of Easements' [1997] Conv 453 (case note on *Payne v Inwood*).

Prescription

Burns, 'Prescriptive Easements in England and Legal Climate Change' [2007] Conv 133.

Dixon, 'Prescriptive Easements: Acquisition, Abandonment and Leasehold Land' [2007] Conv 160 (case note on *Williams v Sandy Lane (Chester) Ltd*).

Land Registration for the Twenty-First Century: A Consultative Document, 1998, Law Com No. 254, Part X: Adverse Possession and Prescription, paras. 10.79–10.94.

Reform

Francis, 'Tinkering Really Won't Do the Trick' [2007] EG 28 July 2007 (No. 0730) 125.

Law Commission, 'Easements, Covenants and Profits à Prendre: A Consultation Paper', 2008 (Consultation Paper No. 186) (available on: www.lawcom.gov.uk).

Law Commission, 'Making Land Work: Easements, Covenants and Profits à Prendre', 2011, Law Com No. 327 (available on: www.lawcom.gov.uk).

Law Commission, 'Rights to Light', A Consultation Paper, 2013 (Consultation Paper No. 210) (available on: www.lawcom.gov.uk).

Law Commission, 'Rights to Light', 2014, Law Com No. 356 (available on: www.lawcom.gov.uk).

Lyall, 'What are Easements Attached or Appurtenent to?' [2010] Conv 300.

Reference

Bickford Smith and Francis, *Rights of Light: The Modern Law*, 3rd edn., Jordans, 2015.

Gale, *Easements*, 20th edn., Sweet & Maxwell, 2017.

Murphy, *The Law of Nuisance*, Oxford University Press, 2010.

Sara, *Boundaries and Easements*, 7th edn., Sweet & Maxwell, 2019.

You can visit the online resources to test your knowledge of this chapter with self-test questions at **www.oup.com/he/nair19e/**.

25

Freehold covenants

25.1 Introduction 576
25.2 Trant Way 576
25.3 Enforceability of covenants: original parties 578
25.4 Enforceability of covenants: successors of the original parties 580
25.5 The problem of positive covenants 597
25.6 Remedies 601
25.7 Discharge of covenants 603
25.8 Reform of the law 605

25.1 Introduction

We saw in Chapter 10 that it is usual for covenants to be included in leases. Similarly, covenants are quite commonly made in respect of freehold property, particularly if land is divided and the person selling part of the land wishes to ensure that his or her new neighbour does not behave in an inconvenient or disturbing manner. In the case of a new estate, the developer may well wish to impose covenants upon all the purchasers, in order to ensure that the estate is maintained in good order. Thus, covenants are frequently imposed upon freehold estates. However, while the covenants made will be binding between the original parties as a matter of the law of contract, once the land burdened with the covenant is sold, the question will arise whether the covenant is binding upon the purchaser of the property. Over the years, special rules have developed in order to settle the question of which covenants can run with freehold land. These rules have some links with the rules governing covenants in leases, but the two systems are not the same and should not be confused with one another. In many cases a covenant by a freehold owner will not bind a purchaser, although a similar covenant, if contained in a lease, would bind the tenant's assignee.

25.2 Trant Way

25.2.1 17 and 18 Trant Way

In 1988, Nos. 17 and 18 Trant Way were both owned in fee simple by Olive Orange. Miss Orange occupied 17 Trant Way, while No. 18 was let to a tenant. When the tenant left the property at the end of the lease, Miss Orange decided to sell 18 Trant Way. She sold the fee simple estate in the property to Robert Raspberry and, because she was concerned that her new neighbour should not inconvenience her, or alter the character of the neighbourhood, she insisted that Mr Raspberry should enter into a number of covenants in the conveyance. The covenants were:

(a) not to use No. 18 'for business purposes';
(b) to keep the exterior of No. 18 in good repair;
(c) to contribute one-half of the cost of maintaining the driveway shared with No. 17; and
(d) not to sell No. 18 to a family with children (Miss Orange was elderly and found the noise of children at play disturbing).

When she made these arrangements Miss Orange wanted to ensure that her neighbour at 19 Trant Way (Daniel Date) was also protected, in so far as was possible. Accordingly, she made Mr Raspberry covenant 'for the benefit of the owners for the time being of land abutting 18 Trant Way' and told Daniel Date about the arrangements she had made. Figure 25.1 shows 17–19 Trant Way at that point.

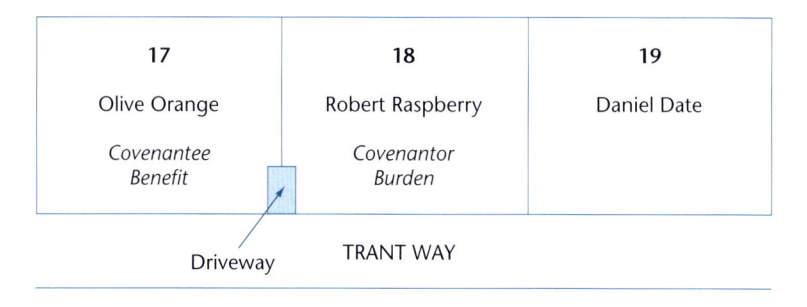

Figure 25.1 17–19 Trant Way

In 1995, Miss Orange died, and her executors sold 17 Trant Way to Paul Peach.

In 1998, Mr Raspberry sold 18 Trant Way to Silvia Strawberry. In the last year Mrs Strawberry has proved to be rather a difficult neighbour to Mr Peach and causes him considerable trouble. She has started to give piano lessons at home and the noise of children playing their scales throughout the day and early evening disturbs Mr Peach greatly. Furthermore, Mrs Strawberry has failed to repair the outside of No. 18, which has become something of an eyesore, and when Mr Peach had repairs made to the joint driveway she refused to contribute to the cost.

25.2.2 20 Trant Way

20 Trant Way was the old rectory, which had a very large garden and an orchard. In 1999, a development company, Big Builders plc, bought the old rectory, demolished it, and built a new crescent of six bungalows. The gardens of the properties were landscaped and are 'open plan' in style. The six bungalows have now been sold, and the new owners of the fee simple estates have been registered as proprietors at HM Land Registry. The crescent is called Rectory Crescent, and the bungalows have been numbered 1 to 6, and were sold in that order. 1 Rectory Crescent was bought by Alfred Alpha, and 6 Rectory Crescent was bought by Oscar Omega. On each sale, the purchaser covenanted with Big Builders plc not to fence the garden of the plot being purchased. See Figure 25.5 at 25.4.3.5 for a plan of Rectory Crescent.

We now need to consider the extent to which the covenants just described are enforceable, not only between the original parties but also between their successors in title.

25.3 Enforceability of covenants: original parties

25.3.1 Covenantor and covenantee: burden and benefit

When Olive Orange sold 18 Trant Way to Robert Raspberry in 1988, the covenants contained in the conveyance to Mr Raspberry constituted a contract between the parties. You have already seen that a covenant is a promise by deed (2.5.5). Here, Mr Raspberry is the 'covenantor', and assumes the 'burden' under the covenant, and Miss Orange is the 'covenantee', and takes the 'benefit'. If Mr Raspberry had broken a covenant, Miss Orange could have sued for damages for breach of contract or sought an injunction restraining the breach. In this situation, the basic rules of the law of contract apply.

As with any contract, it is important when drafting a covenant to make its exact limits entirely clear. However, *Dano Ltd v Earl Cadogan* [2003] 2 P&CR 10, provides an interesting example of a case in which the court seemed to accept that the exact meaning of a covenant might change over time. The covenant in question restricted use of premises to 'the housing of the working classes', and it was accepted that the interpretation of this covenant might change to mean (in modern times) those whose income was sufficiently low that they required inexpensive accommodation. However, an alternative approach to construction mentioned in the case was that, if one could find some persons who still clearly fell within the restriction, it was not necessary to be able to identify every person who did so. (However, in a later Court of Appeal decision on another issue in the same case (see *The Times*, 2 June 2003) it was held that since the document creating the covenant, when read as a whole, envisaged that the covenant lasted only as long as the benefited land remained settled and that had ceased to be the case, the covenant was not in fact enforceable.)

25.3.2 LPA 1925, s. 56

It is easy enough to see that Miss Orange and Mr Raspberry had a contractual relationship with one another, for both executed a deed which contained their agreement. However, it is possible for someone to take the benefit of such a covenant, even though he or she was not a party to the deed or perhaps did not even know that the contract had been concluded. In the case of 19 Trant Way, Daniel Date was not an express party to the deed which included the covenants made by Mr Raspberry. However, you will recall that Miss Orange included in that deed words which indicated that any owner of land abutting No. 18 (which is the case with No. 19) should also benefit from the covenant. This wording may have an important legal effect and may indeed allow Mr Date to sue on the covenant as if he had been a party to the deed. However, as we will see, this result depends upon the case law interpreting the effect of LPA 1925, s. 56(1), which provides that:

> A person may take . . . the benefit of any condition, . . . covenant or agreement over or respecting land, . . . although he may not be named as a party to the conveyance or other instrument.

In *Re Ecclesiastical Commissioners for England's Conveyance* [1936] Ch 430, it was held that the effect of s. 56 was that a person, expressed in the conveyance to be one for whose benefit the covenant was made, was to be regarded as an original covenantee, even though he was not a party to the deed. As a result, the covenant may confer enforceable benefits on other persons, even though they may have been unaware that such a covenant had been made! Accordingly, *Re Ecclesiastical Commissioners for England's Conveyance* seems to suggest that if Mr Raspberry broke the covenants Mr Date could sue him for breach of contract, provided that Mr Date could satisfy the court that the covenant did purport to be with him as covenantee, although he was not a party to the agreement (*Re Foster* [1938] 3 All ER 357 at p. 365).

However, in *Amsprop Trading Ltd v Harris Distribution Ltd* [1997] 1 WLR 1025, Neuberger J said that s. 56 was only effective in a case in which the covenant purported to be made *with* the person seeking to enforce and not where the covenant merely purported to be made *for the benefit of* that person. This appears to produce results that vary depending upon the exact wording used in the covenant in the case, but this may be unsurprising in a situation in which a statutory provision appears to be being stretched beyond what would appear to be its intended ambit. It may also be of importance that the case involved an attempt to circumvent the standard rules relating to covenants in leases. It concerned a covenant in a sublease which the head landlord, rather than the tenant/landlord of the sublease itself, was seeking to enforce. The head landlord could not use the leasehold rules (see Chapter 11) to enforce the covenant because there is no privity of estate or contract between the head landlord and the subtenant. However, the covenant in the sublease was expressed to give the head landlord power to enforce the covenant and thus he claimed to be able to enforce the covenant under the general covenant rules because the covenant was clearly intended to benefit the head landlord. Neuberger J held that, on the construction of the sublease in question, the covenant was not expressed to be made with the head landlord, although it was clearly intended to benefit him. In such a case, it was held that s. 56 did not operate to permit the head landlord to enforce the covenant.

One reason for the decision may have been that, were this interpretation not to be adopted, it would be easy to circumvent the standard leasehold rules and to allow enforcement of covenants by persons who have no privity of estate or of contract with the tenant in question. Unfortunately, however, the effect may be merely to make the result in such cases depend entirely upon the particular words used. If *Amsprop* is confined to its facts and Mr Date can rely on s. 56, the position would now be as shown in Figure 25.2.

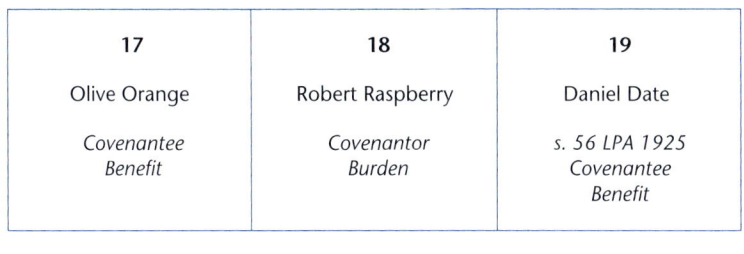

17	18	19
Olive Orange	Robert Raspberry	Daniel Date
Covenantee Benefit	Covenantor Burden	s. 56 LPA 1925 Covenantee Benefit

TRANT WAY

Figure 25.2 Operation of s. 56

25.3.3 The 'mischief' addressed by statute

In trying to decide what s. 56 will or will not do, it may be helpful to consider the mischief that the statutory provisions appear to have been addressing, even if to do so does require a short historical digression. The 'mischief' was the effect of the common law rule that a person could not sue on a deed unless he or she were actually named in that deed: a description which identified the person in question but without naming them would not do. Accordingly, if in an old deed one described one of the parties as 'the owner for the time being of 21 Trant Way', that would not have sufficed to enable the owner of that property at the time the deed was made to enforce the covenants in that deed. This was true even though the actual person involved was readily identifiable and there was no doubt as to who was intended by the description given. This rule was first modified by s. 5 of the Real Property Act 1845 and then by s. 56. Accordingly, courts might have been expected to view s. 56 as only removing the problem created by the common law rule, so that a person who was described in a document as a party but not named and who clearly was a contracting party could benefit. However, the courts have in fact gone further than this in their use of s. 56. The main limitation on s. 56 seems to be simply that the persons covered by the description in question can only benefit if they are existing and identifiable at the date that the covenant was made. The statutory provision does not (as some originally suggested) have the effect of setting aside altogether the principles of privity of contract (see the discussion in *Smith and Snipes Hall Farm Ltd v River Douglas Catchment Board* [1949] 2 KB 500 at p. 514 and *Beswick v Beswick* [1966] Ch 538 at p. 556).

25.3.4 An alternative

In addition to s. 56, it may be possible to rely on the general contractual provisions in the Contracts (Rights of Third Parties) Act 1999, which were designed to relieve some of the problems connected with the rules on privity of contract. The benefits and obligations conferred by that Act are in addition to those provided by s. 56 (see s. 7(1) of the 1999 Act), but are similar in many ways and normally use of s. 56 will suffice for land cases. However, you should remember this as a possible alternative approach.

25.4 Enforceability of covenants: successors of the original parties

In time, the benefited and burdened pieces of land will change hands, and pass to new owners. We must now consider whether the new owner of the benefited land obtains the right to enforce the covenants, and whether the duties under these covenants bind the new owner of the burdened land. In other words, do the benefits and burdens of the covenants run with the respective pieces of land?

25.4.1 Position after sale by the covenantee: does the benefit pass to the new owner?

In 1995 Olive Orange, the original covenantee in relation to the covenants burdening 18 Trant Way, died and her executors sold her fee simple estate in No. 17 to Paul Peach. At this time, the original covenantor, Robert Raspberry, was still the owner of 18 Trant

Way. If Mr Raspberry had broken one of the covenants contained in the 1988 conveyance to himself, could Mr Peach have enforced the covenant against him? At that point the arrangements at 17–19 Trant Way were as shown in Figure 25.3.

17	18	19
Olive Orange Covenantee ↓ Paul Peach Benefit	Robert Raspberry Covenantor Burden	Daniel Date s. 56 LPA 1925 Covenantee Benefit

TRANT WAY

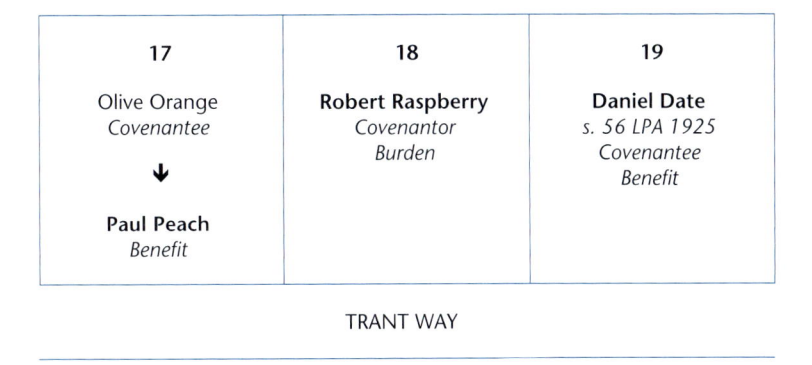

Figure 25.3 Position after sale of 17 Trant Way

Obviously, there is no privity of contract between Mr Peach and Mr Raspberry, but common law does allow the benefit of such a covenant to pass to a successor in title of the original covenantee, if four conditions are met:

(1) the covenant must 'touch and concern' the land of the covenantee;

(2) at the time when the covenant was made, it must have been the intention of the parties that the benefit of the covenant should run with the land to the covenantee's successors in title;

(3) at the time when the covenant was made, the covenantee must have held the legal estate in the land to be benefited; and

(4) the claimant must derive his title from or under the original covenantee (this is the common law rule as amended by LPA 1925, s. 78).

Each of these requirements is now considered in greater detail.

25.4.1.1 'Touching and concerning' the land of the covenantee

Common law rules do not allow the successor of the original covenantee to claim the benefit of a covenant unless, at the date when the covenant was made, the covenantee had land which was benefited by the covenant. This emphasises that only the benefit of covenants which are appurtenant to land can be claimed under these rules, although no such connection is required where the original contracting parties are concerned.

In addition, the covenant must 'touch and concern' the covenantee's land. The purpose of the rule is to distinguish between covenants which confer a benefit upon land and those which confer a purely personal benefit upon the covenantee. In *P. & A. Swift Investments v Combined English Stores Group* [1989] AC 632 at p. 642, Lord Oliver of Aylmerton provides a useful working test designed to ascertain whether a covenant 'touches and concerns' land. This is mentioned earlier in connection with leasehold covenants (see 11.2.2.1) but it is useful to note it here as well. The first element of the test is that the covenant must benefit the estate owner for the time being and that it would cease to be of benefit to the covenantee were it to be separated from the ownership of the benefited estate. Secondly, the covenant must affect the nature, quality, mode, of use or value of the benefited land. Thirdly, even if it satisfies the first two elements of the test, a covenant will not be regarded as 'touching and concerning' benefited land if the benefit is in some way expressed to be personal to the covenantee (this last element accordingly raises the issue of the intention of the parties). In the case of 17 Trant Way you may well feel that the covenant not to sell No. 18 to anyone with children was purely for the personal benefit of Miss Orange. Such a covenant does not seem to confer any benefit upon 17 Trant Way itself: the test here is the same as that used in relation to leases made before 1 January 1996 (the test in *Spencer's Case* (1583) 5 Co Rep 16a). The other covenants made by Mr Raspberry do, however, appear to confer a benefit upon No. 17.

25.4.1.2 The parties must have intended the benefit to run

This condition requires proof that, when the covenant was made, the parties intended that it should run to benefit successors of the covenantee. Evidence of such an intention can be provided by the covenantor expressly covenanting with 'the covenantee, his successors in title, and those deriving title under him'. These words are, however, now deemed to be contained in the covenant, by virtue of LPA 1925, s. 78(1):

> A covenant relating to any land of the covenantee shall be deemed to be made with the covenantee and his successors in title and the persons deriving title under him or them, and shall have effect as if such successors and other persons were expressed.

25.4.1.3 At the time when the covenant was made, the covenantee must have held the legal estate in the land

At common law, covenants attach to the legal estate and pass with it, and so it is essential that, at the time the covenant was made, the covenantee was the owner of the legal estate in the land on which the benefit is to be conferred (*Webb v Russell* (1789) 3 TR 393).

25.4.1.4 The successor claiming to enforce the covenant must derive title from or under the original covenantee

At one time, a successor claiming the benefit of a covenant at common law had to show that he or she had acquired the same estate as had been held by the original covenantee, for common law regarded the covenants as attaching to the estate, so that only a person who took the estate could obtain the benefit of the covenants. Thus, a purchaser of the fee simple from the covenantee could enforce a covenant, while a tenant acquiring a term of years (even if it were for 999 years) could not do so. Today, however, a tenant may claim the benefit of a covenant which is attached to the freehold estate in the land of which he or she is a tenant, because in *Smith and Snipes Hall Farm Ltd v River Douglas Catchment Board* [1949] 2 KB 500 it was held that LPA 1925, s. 78, has the effect of extending the right to enforce a covenant to such a person. In this case the original owner of the benefited land had sold it to a purchaser and that purchaser had granted a lease of the premises to a tenant. The Court of Appeal took the view that the effect of s. 78(1) was that the benefit of the covenant was enforceable not only by the successor in title to the freehold estate but also by the tenant, who derived title under that freeholder. Section 78 appears to have been intended to be merely a word-saving provision, but here and elsewhere has been held to create important substantive changes in the law. In this instance it was said that, because the section refers to persons 'deriving title under' the covenantee, it extends the benefit of such covenants to tenants, who derive their title under the covenantee (or his successors). Were the intention that such persons remain incapable of obtaining a benefit under the legal rules, the inclusion of the reference to them in s. 78 would be meaningless. Therefore, the section has been interpreted as creating an amendment to the law.

The benefit of a covenant amounts to a chose in action and thus it is possible for the holder of the benefit to assign it to any third party in accordance with the ordinary rules of law. Under LPA 1925, s. 136, any such express assignment should be made in writing and notice of it should be given to the covenantor.

25.4.1.5 Application of the rules

One can see from these rules that, when Miss Orange's executors sold 17 Trant Way to Paul Peach, he would have obtained the benefit of all Mr Raspberry's covenants; except probably that of the covenant not to sell No. 18 to a family with children, which appears to be purely personal in nature. Apart from this, the benefit of all the covenants, both positive and negative, would pass with the estate to the new owner, for at common law the benefit of both types of covenant can run to a successor of the covenantee.

25.4.2 Position after sale by covenantor: does the burden pass to the new owner?

In 1998, Mr Raspberry sold the fee simple in 18 Trant Way (the burdened land) to Silvia Strawberry, and it appears that Mrs Strawberry is in breach of a number of the covenants originally made between Mr Raspberry and Miss Orange. The current owner of the benefited land, Mr Peach, needs to know whether Mrs Strawberry is in fact bound by these covenants. Mr Peach wishes to establish, if possible, that the position at 17–19 Trant Way is now as is shown in Figure 25.4. Can he do this?

17	18	19
Olive Orange Covenantee ↓ Paul Peach Benefit	Robert Raspberry Covenantor ↓ Silvia Strawberry Burden	Daniel Date s. 56 LPA 1925 Covenantee Benefit

TRANT WAY

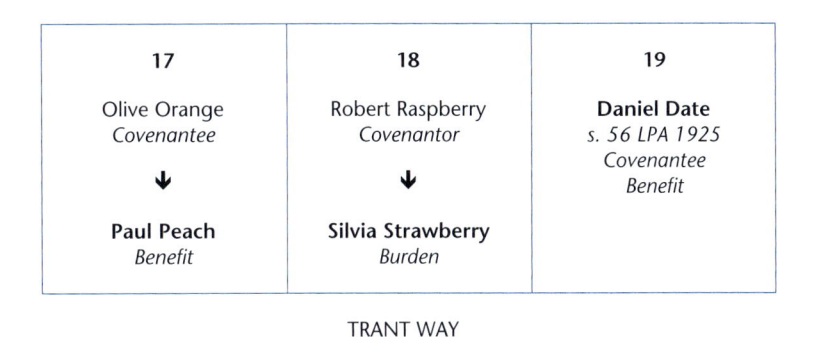

Figure 25.4 Position after sale of 17 and 18 Trant Way

25.4.2.1 Burdens do not run at common law

Unfortunately for Mr Peach, the basic rule is that the burden of covenants does not run at common law. Common law dislikes restraints being placed on your use of your own estate, and accordingly applies the strict rule of privity of contract in such cases. The leading decision on this issue is *Austerberry v Corporation of Oldham* (1885) 29 ChD 750, in which it was held that, at common law, the obligation to make up a road and keep it in good repair could not pass to the successor in title of the original covenantor. This position was reaffirmed by the House of Lords in *Rhone v Stephens* [1994] 2 AC 310, in the case of a covenant to maintain a roof. Thus, Mrs Strawberry will not be liable at law for breach of any of the covenants made in respect of 18 Trant Way. This is in line with the general principles of the law of contract, which allow the benefit of a contract to be transferred to a third party but not the burden. The rule arose principally because of the concerns at law to keep land freely alienable and to prevent it becoming burdened with incumbrances which might hinder sale. However, in the increasingly complex modern world, such a rule can be inconvenient since in many cases it may be quite reasonable to wish to impose restrictions when one sells, for example, part of one's property and to wish to ensure that those restrictions apply to anyone subsequently acquiring the part sold.

25.4.2.2 The burden of certain covenants can run in equity: *Tulk v Moxhay*

The common law rule caused considerable inconvenience, because the owner of benefited land could find that covenants became unenforceable merely because the burdened land changed hands. Equity took note of this difficulty and, through applying general equitable principles, arrived at the conclusion that where a purchaser acquired the burdened land with knowledge of the covenants it was quite fair that he or she should be bound to observe them. The enforceability of the burden of certain covenants against a successor in title to the covenantor was settled finally in the famous case of *Tulk v Moxhay* (1848) 2 Ph 774. In this case, the burdened land formed the centre of Leicester Square in London, and the original covenantor had covenanted with the owner of adjacent property that he would maintain the square as an ornamental open space. Later the square was sold, and the purchaser, relying on the common law rule that burdens do not pass on sale, intended to build on the property. It was held that the owners of the neighbouring benefited land had a right in equity to enforce the covenant against the purchaser of the burdened land, because he had known of the restriction when he acquired his estate.

In taking this view, the court attached great importance to the inequity of a purchaser who acquired with notice simply disregarding the restriction in question. Lord Cottenham in *Tulk v Moxhay* seems to be taking a fairly liberal view (for the period) of the power of the court to intervene in an inequitable case. However, the reasoning adopted may not be that strong because, if before *Tulk v Moxhay* the burden of covenants had not run (see *Keppell v Bailey* (1834) 2 My & K 517), a purchaser would surely be entitled to assume that although he or she knew of the covenant it would have no impact upon a purchaser. The decision to alter the law may have been a surprising result. Lord Cottenham seems also to have thought that if one bought at a reduced price due to the covenant, one should in conscience be bound by it. However, surely if the law (or rather equity) were clear that burdens did not run, then normally the vendor could sell at a higher price because he or she would know that the purchaser would not be bound by the covenant. If the vendor failed to claim a higher price in this way, the loss is the vendor's and that of the owners of the benefited land: the vendor loses solely due to ignorance of the law. It is difficult to see in such a case how the purchaser's conscience is affected. Accordingly, while the decision in *Tulk v Moxhay* proved to be an essential step towards the introduction of a more modern approach to the planning of land use, one wonders to what extent the reasoning in the case stands up to close scrutiny. In essence, the decision is an early example of an attempt to introduce land-use planning by non-statutory means. (The Leicester Square covenants were again the subject of litigation in *R v Westminster City Council, ex parte Leicester Square Coventry Street Association* (1989) 87 LGR 675.)

Since 1848 the courts have, in later cases, identified the rules which must be satisfied before equity will regard the burden of a covenant as passing under the *Tulk v Moxhay* doctrine. These rules are derived from *Tulk v Moxhay* but are not (apart from the last of them) expressly mentioned in the case. To a certain extent the rules step back from the very liberal and reforming approach taken in *Tulk v Moxhay*. In their modern form, they may be stated as follows:

(1) the covenant must be negative;

(2) at the date of the covenant, the covenantee must have owned land which was benefited by the covenant;

(3) the original parties must have intended that the burden should run to bind successors; and

(4) as the rule is equitable, general equitable principles (and the need for notice or its modern equivalent) apply.

1. The covenant must be negative

This rule may seem odd when one remembers that the covenant in *Tulk v Moxhay* was to maintain Leicester Square as an ornamental open space, which sounds like a positive obligation. However, it is the substance of the covenant which matters, and not the form in which it is expressed. Thus, the effect of the covenant in *Tulk v Moxhay* was that the owner should keep the square in an open state and not erect buildings.

In the case of the covenants relating to 18 Trant Way, the covenants to keep the exterior in good repair and to contribute to the cost of maintaining the driveway are both positive, and thus cannot run to bind Mrs Strawberry under the rule in *Tulk v Moxhay*.

This can produce rather inconvenient results, and reform of the law has been recommended (see 25.8.3). Indeed, some writers have argued that *Tulk v Moxhay* makes no mention of such a requirement, and that in the past positive covenants had been enforced against the covenantor's successors (see Bell [1981] Conv 55). However, this limitation on the rule has been accepted since the case of *Haywood v Brunswick Permanent Benefit Building Society* (1881) 8 QBD 403, in which Lindley LJ said that 'only such a covenant as can be complied with without expenditure of money will be enforced' against a successor in title. Thus, a covenant 'not to allow the premises to fall into disrepair' would be regarded as a positive covenant, even though it is worded in a negative form, because compliance with the covenant will require action, and expenditure, on the part of the owner of the burdened land.

The difference between positive and negative covenants was summarised by Cotton LJ in *Austerberry v Corporation of Oldham* (1885) 29 ChD 750 at pp. 773–4 in a passage in which it was explained that a covenant requiring someone to 'lay out money':

> . . . is not a covenant which a court of equity will enforce: it will not enforce a covenant not running at law when it is sought to enforce that covenant in such a way as to require the successors in title of the covenantor to spend money, and in that way to undertake a burden upon themselves. The covenantor must not use the property for a purpose inconsistent with the use for which it was originally granted: but in my opinion a court of equity does not and ought not to enforce a covenant binding only in equity in such a way as to require the successors of the covenantor himself, they having entered into no covenant, to expend sums of money in accordance with what the original covenantor bound himself to do.

This principle was reaffirmed by the House of Lords in 1994 in *Rhone v Stephens* [1994] 2 AC 310. In that case a large single property had been divided into two parts ('the house' and 'the cottage') and the cottage had been sold. The vendor retained the house. Due to the design of the properties the roof remained part of the house but protected both the house and the cottage. Accordingly, on sale, the vendor covenanted that he would maintain the roof for the benefit of the cottage. Over the years both the house and the cottage had been sold on and the current owner of the cottage sought to enforce the covenant to repair the roof, which had fallen into disrepair. The House of Lords was urged to overturn the rule which prevented such positive covenants binding successors and the many criticisms of the rule were argued against it. However, the traditional rule was reaffirmed, and it appears now that it can only be overturned by legislation. Lord Templeman said (at p. 321):

> For over 100 years it has been clear and accepted law that equity will enforce negative covenants against freehold land but has no power to enforce positive covenants against successors in title of the land. To enforce a positive covenant would be to enforce a personal obligation against a person who has not covenanted. To enforce negative covenants is only to treat the land as subject to a restriction.

Thus, in a situation like that in *Tulk v Moxhay*, in equity a successor to the covenantor can be prevented from putting the open space to an alternative use but cannot be forced to maintain it in good order, since the latter requires expenditure whereas the former merely prevents the successor taking certain types of action. (This was one of the reasons for the introduction of commonhold, discussed at 8.6.)

2. At the date of the covenant the covenantee must have owned benefited land

Equity will not enforce a covenant unless it confers a benefit upon land. This involves two requirements:

(a) that the covenant touches and concerns land; and

(b) that, at the date of the covenant, the covenantee must have retained land which was benefited by the covenant.

In *London County Council v Allen* [1914] 3 KB 642 a builder covenanted that he would not build on a particular piece of land. The covenantee was the council, which did not own land in the neighbourhood. Mrs Allen bought the plot with knowledge of the covenant, but was held not to be bound by it, because it was not made for the benefit of land owned by the council. This decision emphasises the fact that equity will protect only covenants which are appurtenant to land: see also *Morrells of Oxford Ltd v Oxford United Football Club Ltd* [2001] Ch 459, in which a covenant was construed as being personal only.

There are, however, some exceptions to the rule that the covenantee must retain land which is benefited by the covenant, which are as follows.

(a) If you think of the situation in Rectory Crescent, you will realise that Big Builders plc, after selling plot 6 to Mr Omega, did not retain any land in the Crescent, and so, on the basic rule, the burden of the covenant would not run with that plot to any new owner. However, if it can be established that the development of Rectory Crescent constituted what is known as a 'building scheme', the burden will run with the last plot, despite the fact that the developer did not retain any land in the area. Building schemes are explained later in this chapter (at 25.4.3.7).

(b) There are also statutory exceptions to the rule, for example in favour of local authorities or the National Trust. These exceptions allow such bodies to enforce covenants on behalf of the whole community (for example, to ensure that an area of natural beauty is not disturbed: National Trust Act 1937, s. 8).

(c) The rules relating to restrictive covenants in leases require a special mention in this context. Such covenants are capable of amounting to restrictive covenants binding under the rules of *Tulk v Moxhay*. This is of little importance where assignees of the tenant are concerned, for most of the covenants in the lease may be enforced against them under the rule in *Spencer's Case* (see 11.2.2.2) or pass under the Landlord and Tenant (Covenants) Act 1995. However, covenants which fall within the *Tulk v Moxhay* principle are binding on anyone who derives title from or under the covenantor, or one of his or her successors, and thus such covenants can be enforced against a subtenant, with whom the enforcing landlord has no privity of estate. You may remember this from the chapter on leases, which also says that in general the head landlord cannot enforce covenants in the lease against the subtenant. Where the restrictive covenant is contained in a lease, it is not necessary to show that the landlord has retained other neighbouring land which is benefited. It is enough to show that a benefit is conferred on the landlord's reversion (which is normally the case) (*Hall v Ewin* (1887) 37 ChD 74; *Regent Oil Co. Ltd v J. A. Gregory (Hatch End) Ltd* [1966] Ch 402).

3. The parties must have intended the burden to run

It is essential that the parties should have intended the burden to pass to later owners of the affected property. Normally this intention will be expressly evidenced by the covenantor covenanting on behalf of the covenantor and his or her successors in title, and those deriving title under the covenantor and successors. In the absence of an express provision, the covenantor is deemed to have covenanted in these terms by virtue of LPA 1925, s. 79. However, this provision may be excluded from the agreement by an express term to the contrary: for a case in which the court construed the document as a whole when deciding whether such an exclusion existed, see *Morrells of Oxford Ltd v Oxford United Football Club Ltd* [2001] Ch 459. If the document creating the covenant is silent on the matter, the parties will be presumed to intend that it will bind later owners. Section 79 only deals with the need for intention. Suggestions that its positive wording ('shall have effect') rendered the other traditional rules on running of burdens redundant have been disapproved by the House of Lords in *Sefton v Tophams Ltd* [1967] 1 AC 50 at pp. 73 and 81 and in *Rhone v Stephens* [1994] 2 AC 310 at p. 322. Thus, s. 79 on its own will not make the burden run to bind a successor.

4. The application of equitable principles, and the need for notice or its modern equivalent

If Mr Peach is to enforce the covenants relating to 18 Trant Way against Mrs Strawberry, he will be obliged to rely on the assistance of the equitable jurisdiction of the court. As we have seen, in *Tulk v Moxhay* Lord Cottenham regarded the decision of the court as being primarily based upon conscience operating as an equitable principle. As a result, the general equitable principles and maxims will apply to any action which he brings. The most important of these is that 'He who comes to equity must come with clean hands'. This may be of particular importance where there are reciprocal covenants between neighbouring owners (as we shall see, this is the case in Rectory Crescent), if the owner seeking to enforce is also breaking any of the covenants. In such a case, the court would almost certainly decline to assist the person who is also in breach of the agreement.

More importantly, the fact that the burden of the covenants runs only in equity means that one must bear in mind the need to protect the right to the covenant by entry on the register in the case of registered land or registration of a land charge in unregistered land. As we have seen, *Tulk v Moxhay* was decided primarily on the basis that the purchaser of Leicester Square bought with notice of the covenant restricting the use of the land.

25.4.2.3 Unregistered land

Where one is dealing with unregistered land and with restrictive covenants created *before* 1 January 1926 the old equitable doctrine of notice will still apply. You should not assume that such old covenants can be ignored, for they are still frequently encountered and can still be enforced where the rules in *Tulk v Moxhay* are satisfied.

Where the title to the land is unregistered, and the covenant was created on or after 1 January 1926, it requires registration as a class D(ii) land charge (LCA 1972, s. 2(5)). If such a covenant is not registered, it will be void against a purchaser of a legal estate for money or money's worth, regardless of notice (LCA 1972, s. 4(6)). The date by which the covenant must have been registered is the date on which the burdened land was conveyed to the purchaser. In the case of 18 Trant Way, Mrs Strawberry will not be bound by such restrictive covenants relating to the property unless they were registered as land charges before she bought the fee simple in 1998 (the land has not been sold since Mousehole became an area of compulsory registration in 1990).

25.4.2.4 Registered land

When she acquired the property, Mrs Strawberry was obliged to register her title to the land with HM Land Registry (see Chapter 6), because Mousehole became a compulsory registration area on 1 December 1990 (see 3.2.3.1). On any such registration, the purchaser must tell the registrar of any pre-1926 covenants of which he or she has notice and present to the registrar a land charges search, which will reveal any registered covenants made after 1925. When the estate is registered, the registrar will also enter on the register notice of any such encumbrances. At the time Mrs Strawberry purchased, this requirement arose from the Land Registration Rules 1925, r. 40; LRA 1925, s. 50(1). Today the requirement on the registrar arises from the Land Registration Rules 2003, r. 35. These burdens on the land will affect a purchaser only if entered on the register relating to the burdened land. Usually the registrar will insert a full copy of the terms of the covenant in the charges section of the register.

Any covenants created after the title becomes registered must also be entered against the burdened estate. Most new covenants are created on transfer of the estate, and in the transfer deed. These covenants will be entered automatically on the register by way of notice. In the case of a covenant created at another time, the person with the benefit of the covenant should apply to have his or her interest noted on the register of the burdened land (under LRA 2002, s. 32) by way of notice.

25.4.3 Where the burden runs in equity, the benefit must be made to run in equity

Having established that Mrs Strawberry may be bound by certain covenants burdening 18 Trant Way, it must still be established that Mr Peach has a right to enforce the covenants. When alleging that Mrs Strawberry is bound in equity by the covenants, he must also establish that he has obtained the benefit of the covenants according to equitable rules: it is not enough to show that the benefit passes at common law. However, in general the equitable rules are more generous to the person claiming the benefit and thus one would not wish to use the legal rules.

In equity, there are three ways in which a purchaser of the benefited land can acquire the right to enforce the covenant:

(1) by **annexation** (which may be express, implied, or statutory);
(2) by express assignment of the benefit of the covenant; and
(3) under the special rules relating to building schemes.

25.4.3.1 Express annexation

Where 'words of annexation' are used, the benefit of the covenant is annexed or attached to the land, so that forever afterwards it passes automatically with the land to the new owner. In order to achieve express annexation, it is necessary that the words of the covenant should show that the original parties intended the benefit to run, and one way of doing this is to state expressly that the covenant is made 'for the benefit of' named land (*Rogers v Hosegood* [1900] 2 Ch 388). Another method which will have the same effect is for the covenant to be made with the covenantee as 'estate owner', that is, describing him as the owner of the land to be benefited. For example, Mr Raspberry covenanted with Miss Orange as 'for the benefit of the owners for the time being of land abutting' No. 18 and that included Miss Orange. These words would have the effect of attaching the benefit of the covenants to No. 17. It is not enough, however, for the covenant to be made with the covenantee and his 'heirs, executors administrators and assigns' (or any similar set of words), for such a phrase does not link these people with the benefited land (*Renals v Cowlishaw* (1878) 9 ChD 125).

Where a claimant seeks to establish express annexation, a problem will arise if the wording of the deed creating the covenant purports to annex it to an area of land which is so large that it cannot reasonably be said that the covenant confers actual benefit on the whole property. In *Re Ballard's Conveyance* [1937] Ch 473, a covenant was said to be for the benefit of the whole of a large estate (approximately 690 hectares). In fact, the covenant could confer a benefit on only a small portion of that estate. Here the court said that, since the covenant did not confer a benefit on the whole estate, it could not run on a sale of the estate. Nor would it run when a part of the estate which was benefited was sold, because the court would not sever the covenant and attach it to parts of the land where the express wording of the deed did not allow for this (but see also *Earl of Leicester v Wells-next-the-Sea Urban District Council* [1973] Ch 110 and *Small v Oliver & Saunders (Developments) Ltd* [2006] 3 EGLR 141). As a result, when one drafts a covenant and wishes to attach it to a large area of land, it is wise (in order to avoid any disputes) to say that the covenant is for the benefit of 'the whole or any part of' the named land. This will allow the covenant to run with any part of the large estate which is actually benefited, and will also allow the benefit to be divided between several plots if the estate is ever sold off in that way (*Marquess of Zetland v Driver* [1939] Ch 1; and see *Morrells of Oxford Ltd v Oxford United Football Club Ltd* [2001] Ch 459 and at 25.4.3.3).

25.4.3.2 Implied annexation

Where words of express annexation are lacking, some cases suggest that it may still be possible for the court to identify the benefited land by looking at the circumstances. Where the facts are held to indicate with reasonable certainty the land which is to be benefited, the benefit will thereafter run with that land. This way of proceeding has been called 'implied annexation'.

The notion of implied annexation is usually said to be derived from two decisions: *Newton Abbot Cooperative Society Ltd v Williamson & Treadgold Ltd* [1952] Ch 286 (the 'Devonia' case) and *Marten v Flight Refuelling Ltd* [1962] Ch 115. The first of these cases was in fact concerned with assignment of the benefit, rather than with annexation, but it was welcomed as 'a useful guide' in *Marten v Flight Refuelling Ltd* (at p. 133). Here there had been no assignment of the benefit, and the court looked at the burdened land and the surrounding area, and came to the conclusion that the covenant had been taken for the benefit of land retained by the vendor. Wilberforce J mentioned with approval (at p. 132) that there seemed to be support for the view 'that an intention to benefit may be found from surrounding or attending circumstances'.

It has to be said that this decision stands very much on its own, and, further, that it has been suggested that the issue of annexation was not relevant (Ryder (1972) 36 Conv NS 26). The covenant was made with the executors of the previous owner, who were holding in trust for an infant beneficiary, and it was these executors and the former beneficiary, now absolutely entitled to the property, who sought to enforce the covenant. Thus, there was no transfer and the benefit did not need to run. The decision was also criticised as tending to increase the general uncertainty about the enforceability of covenants, for while questions of express annexation can in general be decided from a study of the documents, a claim of implied annexation cannot be decided without an application to the court (*Report of the Committee on Positive Covenants Affecting Land* (Chairman: Lord Wilberforce) (Cmnd 2719, 1968), para. 15).

However, in Shropshire County Council v Edwards (1982) 46 P&CR 270, at first instance, it was said explicitly that express words of annexation are not necessary if, on the construction of the relevant document, both the land to be benefited and an intention to benefit that land, 'can be clearly established' (see pp. 277–8). This may have resolved the matter but, in the majority of cases, no sufficiently clear intention can be discerned: see, for example, the Privy Council decision in *Jamaica Life Assurance Society v Hillsborough Ltd* [1989] 1 WLR 1101.

25.4.3.3 Statutory annexation

These rather complicated rules about express annexation, and the uncertainty about implied annexation, may be of less importance since the decision of the Court of Appeal in *Federated Homes Ltd v Mill Lodge Properties Ltd* [1980] 1 WLR 594, which introduced the idea that in certain cases statutory annexation may be effective.

The case before the court concerned a covenant by the defendant not to build more than a certain number of dwellings on the burdened land. It was clear from the wording of the document that the land to be benefited was neighbouring land retained by the covenantee, but there were no express words annexing the benefit of the covenant to that land. Later the covenantee sold this land and eventually it became the property of Mill Lodge Properties Ltd. In the case of part of the benefited land no problem about annexation arose, because the benefit of the covenant had been expressly assigned.

In respect of the other portion of the land, however, there had been no assignment, but the court held that this did not matter because it was clear which land was intended to benefit, and accordingly the covenant was annexed to that land by LPA 1925, s. 78. In the words of Brightman LJ (at p. 605):

> If, as the language of section 78 implies, a covenant relating to land which is restrictive of the user thereof is enforceable at the suit of (1) a successor in title to the covenantee, (2) a person deriving title under the covenantee or under his successors in title, and (3) the owner or occupier of the land intended to be benefited by the covenant, it must, in my view, follow that the covenant runs with the land, because *ex hypothesi* . . . every other owner and occupier has a right by statute to the covenant. In other words, if the

condition precedent of section 78 is satisfied—that is to say, there exists a covenant which touches and concerns the land of the covenantee—that covenant runs with the land for the benefit of his successors in title, persons deriving title under him or them and other owners and occupiers.

One strange feature of this case, is that the defendant was the original covenantor. There was no need, therefore, to show that the burden had run with the land in equity, and accordingly one would have thought that the court would have been concerned only with whether the benefit ran at common law. Consideration of the equitable requirement of annexation was, strictly, unnecessary for the decision of the case, and it would therefore be open to a later court to treat the statements about statutory annexation as *obiter dicta* (but see the discussion in *Roake v Chadha* [1984] 1 WLR 40). However, since that time it seems to have been accepted that s. 78 does have this effect in any case in which it is clear which land was intended to benefit. Also, it appears that the statutory annexation is to every part of the benefited land since the court assumed that every successor or derivative proprietor could claim under s. 78. If this is the effect of s. 78, it renders obsolete many of the traditional difficulties associated with express annexation, including the need to annex to the 'whole or any part' of the benefited land (if such a need exists—see 25.4.3.3).

You should note, however, not everyone accepted that the decision in *Federated Homes* was correct. See particularly two articles by G. H. Newsom on this subject in (1981) 97 LQR and (1982) 98 LQR 202, in which it is argued that the decision is wrong. What is clear is that there are arguments that suggest that the decision is problematic. These include the following points.

(1) The fact that a consequence is that covenants created before 1926 have to be treated in a different way. However, that is normally true with reforming legislation because it does not normally have retrospective effect.

(2) This interpretation took until 1980 (54 years) to be applied and it is easily possible to interpret the provision in a more limited way, to cover the points mentioned earlier in this chapter. A similar provision actually originated in 1881 and this extends the period of judicial blindness to almost 100 years. It is also notable that s. 79 has not been applied in the same way, despite the similarity of wording. It should, however, be noted that the provision in the Conveyancing Act 1881 has been said by some to give clearer evidence of an intention to annex.

(3) One might have expected the legislature to use clearer language to make such a marked change. The wording of ss. 76(6) and 77(5) show that where the legislature intended annexation to arise or be recognised, it uses clear language to produce that effect. Similarly, in s. 80(3) clear language is used to dispense with an old requirement for technical language in documents.

(4) In *Federated Homes* two members of the Court of Appeal said that they agreed entirely with the comments made on annexation by Hall V-C in *Renals v Cowlishaw* (1878) 9 ChD 125 at p. 130. Yet that reasoning does not seem to tally with a subsequent owner of the benefited land being able to take the benefit of the covenant even though he or she may not have known of it and perhaps could not even be sure that it benefited the land, because this would not be clear from the documents creating the covenant.

In *Crest Nicholson Residential (South) Ltd v McAllister* [2004] 1 WLR 2409, the Court of Appeal returned to the issue of statutory annexation and affirmed it as a possibility but also considered some further issues about when s. 78 can be relied upon. The case also provides an interesting discussion of the differences between ss. 78 and 79 of the LPA 1925 and whether s. 78 produces 'statutory annexation' where the benefited land is not identified in the documents creating the covenant.

The case involved an estate which had been sold off in plots in the early 1930s by two brothers and their company (the company had a beneficial interest in the property arising from a contract with the brothers). The conveyance of each plot said that the covenants in the conveyance were given by the purchaser 'to the intent that [the covenants would] be binding in so far as maybe on the owner for the time being' of the plot sold. The covenants were substantially in the same terms in the case of each plot and were as follows:

> The premises shall not be used for any purpose other than those of or in connection with a private dwellinghouse or for professional purpose.
>
> No dwellinghouse or other building shall be erected on the land hereby conveyed unless the plans drawings and elevation thereof shall have been previously submitted to and approved of in writing by [the brothers' company] but such approval shall not be unreasonably or vexatiously withheld.

Some time after the plots had all been sold, the brothers' company had been dissolved and therefore no longer existed as a legal person.

The claimant and the defendant were successors in title to the original purchasers of two of the plots of land. The owner of one (a property called 'Redruth') was Crest Nicholson, which wished to demolish the house on Redruth to build a new house and an access road to new houses on other plots also now owned by the same party. Mrs McAllister was the owner of another plot ('Newlyn'), at least part of which had been one of the original plots and which was sold after Redruth, and she contended that the development proposed by Crest Nicholson was in breach of the covenants and that she had the benefit of those covenants. Crest Nicholson brought the initial action in order to determine the effects of the covenants. On appeal the issue of whether the covenants had been annexed to the benefited land was raised. There had been no express annexation in the documents relating to some of the potentially benefited plots, including Newlyn.

At first instance there was no issue taken as to annexation but in the Court of Appeal the issue was raised. The Court of Appeal followed the 'statutory annexation' approach it had adopted in *Federated Homes v Mill Lodge Properties*. However, it concluded (see Chadwick LJ at para. 33) that the land intended to be benefited still had to be so mentioned or defined in the documents creating the covenant that it was easily ascertainable (the requirement in *Marquess of Zetland v Driver* [1939] Ch 1). It was insufficient, in the view of the Court of Appeal, for the benefited land to be identifiable from the surrounding circumstances. As the documents relating to the property that had come into Mrs McAllister's hands contained no references that could be relied upon to identify benefited land, the covenants were not annexed to Newlyn by operation of statute and could not be enforced by Mrs McAllister.

Indeed, such references as existed in any of the documents relating to the string of transactions (when one included documents relating to all the plots sold) only suggested annexation to such land as the company retained from time to time (suggesting that on a sale by the company it was intended that the annexation ended). The Court of Appeal was content that s. 78 gave way to anything in the documents that indicated that enduring annexation was not intended.

Thus, *Crest Nicholson* is authority for at least two propositions:

(1) the land benefited must be identifiable from the documents creating the covenant and not just from extraneous facts; and

(2) the effect of s. 78 gives way to anything in the documents that suggests that it was not intended that the benefit should be annexed so as to run with the land after sale.

In the recent case of *Bath Rugby Ltd v Greenwood* [2021] EWCA Civ 1927, the Court of Appeal revisited the general principles governing the statutory annexation of the benefit of restrictive covenants in equity. In that case, a 1922 conveyance had included a covenant not to build on the land or start a business there that could amount to 'a nuisance, annoyance or disturbance or otherwise prejudicially affect the adjoining premises or the neighbourhood'. Although the covenant was entered into before 1926, and the rules of statutory annexation did not apply, the general approach to identification of benefited land in *Crest Nicholson* was applied. The Court of Appeal held that a covenant for the benefit of 'the neighbourhood' did not sufficiently identify the benefited land and so annexation was not possible on the facts. Nugee LJ said:

> . . . it is not enough to see that the vendor owns adjoining property and that the covenant is plainly inserted with a view to benefiting the vendor accordingly; what is needed is an intention that the covenant is taken for the protection of defined lands of the vendor so that it goes with the land to successive owners, rather than being kept in the hands of the vendor for him to exploit.

Finally, there is authority that—even for covenants created before 1926—the benefit of a covenant may be annexed to each and every part of the benefited land. In *Small v Oliver & Saunders (Developments) Ltd* [2006] 3 EGLR 141, the covenant in question was a covenant made in March 1925 and thus before the 1925 legislation came into force at the start of 1926. The claimant owned only a portion of the land that had been retained by the covenantee at the point that the covenant was made. The covenant was expressed to be for the benefit of the retained land and was worded to be made 'to the intent that such covenant shall enure for the benefit of and be annexed to the remainder of the Beech Hill Park Estate'. However, the 'magic' wording 'for the whole or any part of' was missing. One issue was therefore whether these words or, perhaps more accurately, this intention, could be implied prior to s. 78 coming into force.

Mark Herbert QC, sitting as a Deputy Chancery Division Judge, relied on statements of Brightman LJ and Megaw LJ in *Federated Homes v Mill Lodge Properties* [1980] 1 WLR 594, at p. 606 and p. 608 respectively to the effect that a covenant annexed to the whole of land must necessarily be annexed also to every part of that land. He concluded that those statements were:

> . . . statements of principle that, in the absence of any contrary intention, annexation to identified land of the vendor, whether statutory or express, enures for the benefit of every part of the land (para. 31).

If this is correct, then the impact of s. 78 was less extensive than once had been suggested. It seems annexation to parts as well as the whole may apply even in relation to pre-1926 covenants, provided that there is nothing in the documents to suggest that the annexation was only intended to be to the whole of the retained property.

25.4.3.4 Assignment

Even where the benefit of a covenant has not been expressly annexed to land, it has always been the case that the covenantee could transfer that benefit by express assignment. The benefit of a covenant, like the benefit of any other contract, is a chose in action and can be assigned at will. If one relies on this method it is, however, necessary to show that there is an unbroken chain of assignments, so that on each sale of the benefited land the benefit has been passed to the new owner and has finally come to the person who now seeks to enforce the covenant (*Re Pinewood Estate* [1958] Ch 280). It is also essential that the right should be assigned to the purchaser of the estate at the time of the conveyance to him: an assignment made after the estate has been transferred is not acceptable (*Re Union of London & Smith's Bank Ltd's Conveyance* [1933] Ch 611 at p. 632).

25.4.3.5 Building schemes

Some of the rules discussed would cause difficulty when applied to the development of a new estate, such as Rectory Crescent. As we have seen, each purchaser entered into covenants with the developer, but now the estate is completed Big Builders plc has sold all of its plots in the area and will move on to work elsewhere and will not be concerned with enforcing these covenants. What the purchasers want is to be able to rely on a sort of 'local law' for the area (*Re Dolphin's Conveyance* [1970] Ch 654 at p. 662), which each householder can enforce directly against all the others. To a large extent, this could be achieved by the ordinary rules for freehold covenants, but this would be complicated and would depend on knowing the exact order in which the plots had been sold.

Once the new properties built on the old Rectory land had been built and sold the position in Rectory Crescent was as shown in Figure 25.5.

3 Gail Gamma		4 Dolly Delta
2 Bertie Beta	RECTORY CRESCENT	5 Ewan Epsilon
1 Alfred Alpha		6 Oscar Omega

TRANT WAY

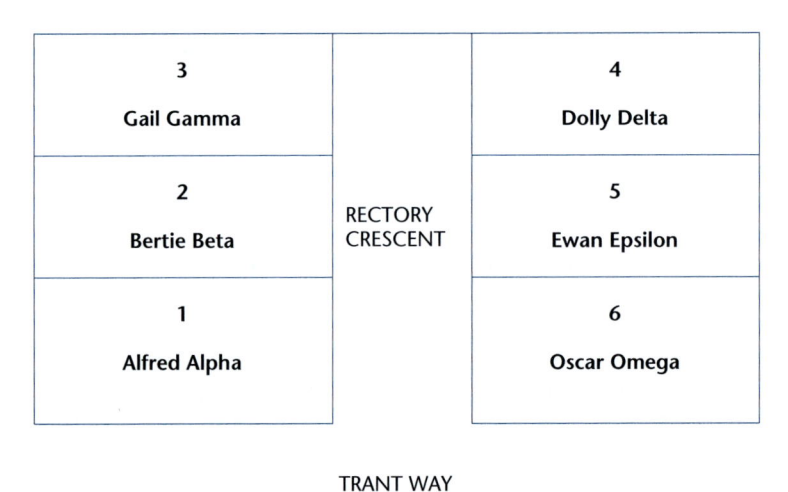

Figure 25.5 Position after construction and sale of 1–6 Rectory Crescent

1. Rectory Crescent: the position without a building scheme

In this example, plots 1 to 6 Rectory Crescent were sold in that order. If some time in the future, the successor of the original purchaser of No. 3 should fence the garden in breach of the covenant, those holding plots sold after No. 3 (i.e., 4 to 6) could claim that they held land retained by the developer at the time of the sale of No. 3. The benefit of that purchaser's covenant would be annexed to the retained land, assuming of course that the covenant had been drafted correctly. Therefore, it would have passed to them, or their predecessors in title, when the later plots were sold. Those who bought before the sale of No. 3 (i.e., 1 and 2) might be able to rely on LPA 1925, s. 56, if the covenant purported to be with the owners of those plots and provided that, if they are not the original purchasers, they can show that the benefit has passed to them under the usual rules.

Proceeding in this way may not seem too difficult, but that is because we have simplified matters by saying that plots 1 to 6 were sold in that order. In real life, the houses on a new estate may be sold in no particular order, as purchasers make their choices. Fifty years or so later it could be quite difficult to know, in respect of a particular breach, who could proceed under s. 56 and who could rely on annexation.

There is, further, the problem mentioned earlier that, because Big Builders plc retained no land when the last plot was sold, an essential rule for the running of the burden is not satisfied on the sale of that plot. Therefore, the successor to the original purchaser of No. 6 would take free of the covenant.

However, all these difficulties are avoided if it can be established that the development satisfies the legal requirements of a 'building scheme'.

2. Requirements for a building scheme

The traditional requirements for a building scheme were established in the Edwardian case of *Elliston v Reacher* [1908] 2 Ch 374, in which a building society had laid out an area for development in separate plots and had sold these using identical conveyances and imposing identical covenants upon each purchaser. The court held that the covenants were enforceable against all the successors to the original covenantor and set out four rules to be satisfied in order to establish a building scheme (sometimes called a 'scheme of development'):

(a) the purchasers must derive their titles from a common vendor;

(b) before selling, the vendor must have laid out the land in lots (or plots);

(c) on sale, the same restrictions must be imposed on all the plots, and it must be clear that those restrictions are intended to be for the benefit of all the plots sold; and

(d) each purchaser must have acquired a plot on the understanding that the covenants were intended to benefit all the other plots in the scheme.

3. Developments after *Elliston v Reacher*

In later cases, however, it has been established that these four rules provide only guidance, and that what is crucial is the intention of the parties to create a building scheme. Accordingly, a scheme was found in *Baxter v Four Oaks Properties Ltd* [1965] Ch 816, even though the whole area had not been divided into lots in advance of the first sale. In this case the developer had wished to allow purchasers to choose lots of varying sizes. Again, in *Re Dolphin's Conveyance* [1970] Ch 654, a single scheme was established, even though the purchasers had not acquired from a common vendor. The first sales were made by two co-owners, but later the land came into the hands of their nephew, who continued the sale of plots and imposed covenants identical to those imposed by his aunts. The court considered that this satisfied the essential requirement, since it was quite clear that the various vendors did intend to create a local law for the area. If, however, a common intention cannot be established—for example, because the covenants vary between the plots of land—a building scheme will not exist (see *Emile Elias & Co. Ltd v Pine Groves Ltd* [1993] 1 WLR 305 and *Small v Oliver & Saunders (Developments) Ltd* [2006] 3 EGLR 141).

4. Advantages of establishing a building scheme

Rectory Crescent would appear to be a clear example of such a scheme. Once a scheme has been established, it is necessary to consider what benefits will accrue. Although it is still necessary to establish that the rules in *Tulk v Moxhay* have been satisfied, the first benefit of a building scheme is that these rules are modified slightly in one respect, so that the burden will run with the last plot sold (here, No. 6). This happens despite the fact that the developer does not retain any land capable of being benefited. With this exception, all the other basic rules have to be observed: so there is no question of the burden of positive covenants being enabled to run under a building scheme, and the usual registration or protection by entry on the register is needed if successors of the covenantors are to be bound.

The second benefit of a building scheme is that all purchasers of plots in the scheme are enabled to enforce the covenants between themselves, irrespective of the date on which they, or their predecessors in title, bought their plots. There is thus no need to distinguish between the earlier purchasers, proceeding under s. 56, and the later purchasers, who rely on express annexation. Earlier purchasers will be able to obtain the benefit of later covenants, and that benefit will run with their plots automatically, provided that they can establish that a building scheme has been created.

The third advantage of a building scheme is that, in equity, it will ensure that the benefit of the covenants imposed on other plots will automatically run to all successors of the original purchasers, without the need for express annexation or for assignment (although this may be less important since *Federated Homes Ltd v Mill Lodge Properties Ltd* [1980] 1 WLR 594).

Besides the three advantages of the building scheme, such a scheme appears not to be subject to some of the other general principles relating to covenants. In *Brunner v Greenslade* [1971] Ch 993, it was established that both the benefit and the burden of covenants in a building scheme will run to affect someone who acquires only part of the original plot. Thus, where a plot is subdivided, the purchaser of one part may enforce the covenants against the purchaser of the other part and against all the other owners of plots forming part of the scheme. This rule was accepted because the aim of the scheme is to create a type of local legal system, and this aim would not be fulfilled if 'islands of immunity' developed in which covenants could not be enforced (as would happen if the owners of subplots could not enforce the covenants between themselves).

Similarly, it appears that, should two plots come into common ownership and then later be divided again, the original covenants will revive automatically between the subsequent owners (*Texaco Antilles Ltd v Kernochan* [1973] AC 609). In general law this would not occur, for the common ownership would extinguish the covenants as between the two plots and the rights and duties created by the covenants would not revive when the plots were once more separated. The only way in which the covenants could be revived would be for the common vendor to require fresh covenants from each purchaser. However, when a building scheme can be established, the rights and duties under the original covenants will spring up again automatically when the plots are separated. Thus, the building scheme provides a useful exception to the ordinary rules on this point.

Another interesting issue is what happens if the covenants cannot be shown to benefit the whole of the area described as falling within the scheme. In *Whitgift Homes v Stocks* [2001] 48 EG 130 (CS) the claimants were owners of 55 properties on an estate built in the 1920s. The defendants were owners of two properties, which they proposed to develop in a manner that was in breach of some of the covenants imposed by the original developer. The Court of Appeal accepted that LPA 1925, s. 78 would be effective to annex the benefit of the covenants to all the plots on the estate. However, it was also held that in this case the building scheme tests could not be passed for the estate as a whole. At first instance it was held that this did not prevent it being possible to establish a scheme in relation to part of the whole estate. However, the Court of Appeal pointed out that it was necessary for the scheme to apply to a defined area (*Reid v Bickerstaff* [1909] 2 Ch 305), and said that here this was not possible because one could not clearly identify which of the properties on the estate formed part of the scheme.

25.4.3.6 Letting schemes

At this point it is worth noting that the building scheme rules are also capable of application to leasehold properties that are let as a scheme and, in such cases, allow the tenants to enforce some of the covenants in their leases against one another. An example is *Williams v Kiley (trading as CK Supermarkets Ltd)* [2003] 1 EGLR 47, in which five shops in a shopping parade had been leased and one tenant claimed that it was able to enforce a covenant against another tenant on the basis of a letting scheme. Here each lease dovetailed with the others to ensure each business did not compete with the others and this was held to demonstrate a sufficient reciprocity of obligation for a scheme to exist and thus for one tenant to enforce against the others. In *Hannon v 169 Queen's Gate Ltd* (*The Times*, 23 November 1999), it was held that where a block of flats that was covered by a letting scheme was extended upwards, the scheme could stretch to cover that development. The court said that there was only a limitation in the horizontal plane. Thus, it should be borne in mind that the letting scheme can change in area over time but only upwards or, presumably, downwards.

25.5 The problem of positive covenants

The fact that the burden of a covenant will not normally run at law, and that equity declines to enforce a positive obligation against the successor of the original covenantor, can prove decidedly inconvenient. You will recall that when 18 Trant Way was sold originally to Mr Raspberry he undertook to contribute towards the cost of the maintenance of the driveway which is shared with No. 17. Undoubtedly, the same conveyance gave him an easement of way over the same drive. When Mrs Strawberry bought No. 18, she will have acquired the benefit of the legal easement, but may claim that she is not obliged to contribute to the maintenance of the drive, as the burden of positive covenants does not run to the covenantor's successors. This would produce an unfair result, and over the years conveyancers have developed a number of ways in which positive obligations can be made to bind successors. In addition, the common law has recognised one exception to the basic rule that it will not enforce burdens on later owners of the covenantor's land. These methods of avoiding the disadvantages of the basic rules can accordingly be of considerable importance, and they are now considered individually.

25.5.1 The exception to the rule: *Halsall v Brizell*

In the case of *Halsall v Brizell* [1957] Ch 169, the purchaser of a plot of land on an estate had been given various easements including an easement of way over the estate roads, and in return had covenanted to contribute to the cost of maintaining the roads, walls, and other facilities from which he derived a benefit. A successor of the original purchaser claimed the benefit of the easements affecting the property but denied that he was obliged to make any payment, on the basis that the burden of a positive covenant would not run at law or equity. The court refused to accept this argument, holding that the successor in title could not take the benefit of an agreement unless he was also prepared to accept the related burdens (see also *E. R. Ives Investment Ltd v High* [1967] 2 QB 379, and *Tito v Waddell (No. 2)* [1977] Ch 106 at p. 290). For the rule to apply, the burden and benefit do have to be related to one another in some way. Comments by Megarry V-C in *Tito v Waddell (No. 2)*, which suggested that the benefits and burdens did not have to be interrelated provided that they were part of the same transaction, were expressly disapproved by the House of Lords in *Rhone v Stephens* [1994] 2 AC 310, in which Lord Templeman said (at p. 322):

> It does not follow that any condition can be rendered enforceable by attaching it to a right nor does it follow that every burden imposed by a conveyance may be enforced by depriving the covenantor's successor in title of every benefit which he enjoyed thereunder. The condition must be relevant to the exercise of the right. In *Halsall v Brizell* there were reciprocal benefits and burdens enjoyed by the users of the roads and sewers.

Accordingly, under this rule only related burdens can be enforced and, where there is no necessary relationship between the benefit exercised and the burden for which enforcement is sought, the courts will not act.

The problems that this approach can produce when dealing with modern estate housing are illustrated very clearly by *Thamesmead Town Ltd v Allotey* (1998) 37 EG 161. Here the original covenantor had covenanted to pay a service charge to maintain roads, sewers, and landscaped and communal areas on an estate. Mr Allotey acquired a property from the original covenantor and was held not to be liable to make payments in relation to the landscaped and communal areas because he had obtained no entitlement to benefit from these areas. He did, however, have to pay the service charge in relation to the roads and sewers, which he had a right to use and did use. The possible arguments that may arise where someone argues that they never use a facility and thus are not going to pay for it can be imagined. However, if they have a right but simply do not choose to use it, this argument should fail.

A recent example of the difficulties that can arise in relation to positive covenants can be found in *Elwood v Goodman* [2014] Ch 442, which, inter alia, concerned the effect of the burden in equity of a positive covenant to contribute to the cost of maintaining a road in the case of registered land. You will recall that the aim of the land registration legislation is to produce a register that can be relied upon as accurate to the interests applicable on purchase of a property, subject to those interests that are made to override. However, the burden in equity of a positive covenant is not capable of creating an estate or interest in registered land and therefore it is not registrable under what was s. 20(1) of the LRA 1925. Accordingly, it does not have to be registered to be binding on a successor of the original covenantor. As the obligation could prove to be an expensive one, this constitutes an unhelpful gap: the register is a mirror of title but does not necessarily reveal all the positive obligations that may arise in connection with ownership of the property. You will see in this case that the court was of the view that the covenant to pay for an estate road was accordingly binding on a purchaser of the burdened estate in land.

The principle in *Halsall v Brizell* may assist the current owner of 17 Trant Way, in compelling Mrs Strawberry to contribute to the cost of the repairs recently made to the shared driveway. The rule is also frequently of considerable importance when one is dealing with a building scheme in which positive covenants for the maintenance of shared facilities may be necessary.

25.5.2 Evasion of the rules by techniques of drafting

There are numerous ways in which the burden of a positive covenant can be imposed on a later acquirer of burdened land.

25.5.2.1 Granting leases

Where a lease is granted, covenants in the lease which fall within the rule in *Spencer's Case* or pass under the Landlord and Tenant (Covenants) Act 1995 will bind the tenant's assignees (see Chapter 11). In such cases, the law makes no distinction between positive and negative obligations, and covenants to contribute to the cost of maintenance or to an insurance premium are common. As a result, a vendor may well choose to grant a long lease of property, rather than selling the fee simple estate. In the case of blocks of flats, where the enforcement of positive obligations may be crucial, it is exceptionally rare for the flat owners to hold estates in fee simple, and leases are the norm. In such cases, the purchaser may well pay as much as would have been paid to acquire a freehold estate, but will obtain only a wasting asset. In addition, the tenant's ownership will be subject to the landlord's rights of re-entry and to a continuing obligation to pay ground rent. The tenant may also encounter the difficulty that mortgagees may be less willing to lend money on the security of a leasehold property. All this is quite a high price to pay to enable the vendor to ensure that the burden of positive covenants passes to the successors in title of the covenantee. The new commonhold system was designed to meet these problems but it has not proved popular in practice (see 8.6). In practice, the issue is sometimes addressed by the leaseholders acquiring the freehold and vesting it in a management company in which they each hold a share.

25.5.2.2 Indemnity covenants

Another method of circumvention is to impose upon the covenantor an obligation to require an indemnity covenant from his successor. Should the covenant be broken, the covenantee can then sue the original covenantor, who remains liable on the covenant; he or she will sue their successor, and so on down the line. This method is not, however, very effective, because it is dependent on the maintenance of an unbroken chain of indemnity covenants. In the case of *Thamesmead Town Ltd v Allotey* (25.5.1) this approach broke down on the first transfer. In addition, after some years it may prove impossible to find the original covenantor in order to enforce against him or her.

25.5.2.3 Creating estate rentcharges

Another possible method is for a vendor to require the purchaser to grant the vendor an **estate rentcharge** over the land. You will remember that a rentcharge imposes a duty on the current estate owner to make regular payments of money to the person entitled to the charge (see 2.5.1), and so a rentcharge can be useful where it is wished to impose an obligation to contribute to the cost of maintenance; it might, for example, have been used in relation to the shared driveway at 17 and 18 Trant Way. However, in addition to this, the rentcharge can be used to enforce other positive obligations beyond the mere payment of money, for the owner of the charge has a legitimate interest in maintaining the value of the land, and so can require the estate owner, when the rentcharge is granted, to enter into covenants for repair and maintenance. The rentcharge, and its associated obligations, run with the land to bind successive owners. The right of re-entry which supports the rentcharge enables the owner of the charge to enter on the land and do the work, if the estate owner fails to repair.

The estate rentcharge was exempted from the general bar on the creation of rentcharges imposed by the Rentcharges Act 1977 (see s. 2), and so may still be created. It takes effect as a legal interest in land. In the case of registered land, the rentcharge must be substantively registered in order to be legal. Where a rentcharge is granted in relation to a registered estate, its creation does not operate at law until the registration requirements are met (LRA 2002, s. 27). If the rentcharge is granted for a term of years of up to and including seven years' duration, the requirement is to enter a notice on the register of the burdened land (LRA 2002, s. 27(4) and Sch. 2 para. 7). In the case of any other rentcharge the person granted the charge must be registered as proprietor of the rentcharge and a notice must be entered against the register relating to the estate that has been charged (LRA 2002, s. 27(4) and Sch. 2 para. 6). In the case of unregistered land, it is good against the world (LPA 1925, s. 1(2)).

The decision in *Orchard Trading Estate Management Ltd v Johnson Security Ltd* [2002] 18 EG 155 illustrates the use that may be made of the estate rentcharge. The court considered the application of the tests in the Rentcharges Act 1977 for a valid estate rentcharge and the decision indicates how they will be applied in practice. It concerned a rentcharge enabling the recovery of 'all . . . expenditure incurred by [the respondent] in or about the maintenance and proper or convenient management of the estate'. The appellant argued that the rentcharge failed to comply with the requirements of the Rentcharges Act 1977 because payment of rates in respect of the common parts of the estate were not for the benefit of the land charged and there was no limitation to reasonable sums. The court was, however, content that the payment of rates was necessary to enable holding of the common parts for the benefit of all the properties on the estate and the reasonableness requirement did not have to be expressly stated, particularly as here the sums covered were only actual expenditure. The latter point does not, however, seem to deal with the possibility of the person who is spending the money on the maintenance of common parts not doing so in a reasonably cost-effective manner.

25.5.2.4 Creating long leases which are then converted to freehold estates

A long lease with more than 200 years to run, which satisfies the other requirements of LPA 1925, s. 153, may be converted by the tenant into a freehold estate. On such conversion, any obligations on the tenant, including positive covenants, will become burdens enforceable against the freehold estate. This method is rarely used as it is very cumbersome, and, in the main, untested, but it is usual to include it in the list of devices enabling positive covenants to run with the land.

25.5.2.5 Covenants restraining sale of registered land without consent of the original vendor

Under LRA 2002, s. 40, a vendor of registered land may place on the register a restriction preventing the transfer of the registered estate to any person without the vendor's consent. The use of this provision would enable the vendor to require an intending purchaser from the 'covenantee', to enter into fresh positive covenants with the original vendor before he will consent to the sale.

25.5.2.6 Fencing

It should be remembered that, in some circumstances, an obligation to maintain a fence may constitute an easement of fencing, rather than a positive covenant, and the obligation will then run with the servient tenement (*Crow v Wood* [1971] 1 QB 77). However, see 24.2.2.10 on the 'spurious' nature of such an easement and, in *Churston Golf Club Ltd v Haddock* [2019] EWCA Civ 544, the Court of Appeal held that an obligation of this type that had been drafted expressly as a covenant would *not* create an easement but was simply a positive covenant.

25.5.2.7 Commonhold

In cases involving a number of units, such as blocks of flats, the use of a commonhold scheme will enable positive covenants to be enforced against successors of the original owners (see 8.6 for the details of a commonhold scheme). However, these schemes may prove unduly complex where only two or three units are involved and thus far commonhold has not been a popular option.

25.5.3 Statutory powers of local authorities

Local authorities are able to impose positive obligations and to enforce them against successive owners, under the provisions of a number of statutes. For example, under s. 72 of the Town and Country Planning Act 1990, a local planning authority, on granting planning permission, may impose conditions and these will be enforceable against future owners of the land. For this reason, it is advisable to check when purchasing a property that all planning conditions have been observed because planning authorities have quite Draconian enforcement powers available to them.

25.6 Remedies

25.6.1 Contractual remedies

Should a covenant be broken, the normal contractual remedies of damages for breach, or an injunction restraining breach may be sought. However, where one is dealing with a successor in title to the original covenantor a claim to damages cannot be brought in contract because of the lack of privity (see *Rhone v Stephens* [1994] 2 AC 310). However, it is possible to seek an injunction and/or damages under the Senior Courts Act 1981. (See also *Surrey County Council v Bredero Homes Ltd* [1993] 1 WLR 1361, which emphasises that the covenantee's claim is for the actual loss and not for the profit that the covenantor will make as a consequence of the breach.) In many cases the resulting damages may be surprisingly low (see *Small v Oliver & Saunders (Developments) Ltd* [2006] 3 EGLR 141 and the discussion at 24.10.2).

In cases in which a positive covenant has been broken, an order for specific performance or a mandatory injunction may be the most suitable remedy. In the case of a negative covenant, the court is unlikely to order demolition of property built in breach of covenant: *Wrotham Park Estate Co. v Parkside Homes Ltd* [1974] 1 WLR 798 and see also *Small v Oliver & Saunders (Developments) Ltd* on this point. *Surrey County Council v Bredero* was discussed by the House of Lords in *A-G v Blake* [2001] AC 268 (a case unrelated to land law, being about the breach of a duty of confidentiality owed by a former member of the security services) and Lord Nicholls indicated that he preferred the approach in *Wrotham* to the assessment of damages. In *Wrotham*, while refusing an injunction to remove buildings, the court awarded damages at a rate of 5 per cent of the developer's expected profit. In *Bredero*, only nominal damages were given, because the value of the benefited land had not been reduced.

25.6.2 Need to avoid delay

Where an equitable remedy is to be sought, it is essential not to delay in seeking the appropriate remedy. This is particularly true where the owner of the dominant estate is aware that the servient owner is expending money (for example, by carrying out building work in breach of covenant). Indeed, in an appropriate case, the dominant owner who has remained silent about breaches for a prolonged period may be regarded as having acquiesced in the breach and thus as having lost his right to relief for breach of covenant.

These possibilities are well illustrated by *Gafford v Graham* (1998) 77 P&CR 73, in which the servient owner, in breach of covenant, between 1986 and 1989 constructed and ran, on the servient land, a riding school. The covenants binding the land permitted only certain buildings and prohibited other building without the consent of the dominant owner (which had not been obtained). The covenants were broken. The first complaint of the breaches had been a solicitor's letter, written three years after the first of the breaches commenced. Nourse LJ held that, in relation to most of the construction, the delay (three years) in making a complaint was such that the dominant owner's rights to any relief for breach were entirely barred. The complaint in relation to the construction and operation of a riding school was much closer to the events of which complaint was made and in relation to these the dominant owner was not taken to have acquiesced. However, the dominant owner had not sought an immediate (interlocutory) injunction to prevent the building work continuing but had waited until the full hearing of the action and sought there a final injunction (which would have required the removal of the riding school). Nourse LJ concluded that in these circumstances it was not appropriate to grant the injunction sought in relation to the riding school. However, he did award £25,000 damages for the breach of covenant involved in its construction and operation. The sum awarded as damages was to be calculated by reference to the amount that might reasonably have been expected in payment for an agreement to relax the covenant permanently in relation to the riding school.

The message for the aggrieved dominant owner is accordingly not to be tolerant of breaches and to seek a remedy swiftly, obtaining interim relief as appropriate. In such a case, where the servient owner acts flagrantly in breach of covenant and ignores warnings, the court may require any building constructed to be demolished (*Wakeham v Wood* [1981] 43 P&CR 40) but will not do so as an invariable principle. However, in *Mortimer v Bailey* [2005] 2 P&CR 9, the Court of Appeal even granted a mandatory injunction requiring demolition a year after a building had been completed and even though no interim injunction had been obtained to prevent building works continuing. For an older example of acquiescence defeating a claim see *Sayers v Collyer* (1885) 28 Ch D 103, where a complainant lost his case in respect of a beershop that had been constructed in breach of covenant because of evidence that he had made regular use of the premises!

25.6.3 Declaration under LPA 1925, s. 84(2)

In many cases, the real problem with a covenant is not in enforcing it, but in establishing whether it is binding on a particular person, or whether the person seeking to enforce it is entitled to do so. Suitable relief in the case of such a dispute is provided by LPA 1925, s. 84(2), as amended by LPA 1969, s. 28(4), which allows an applicant to ask the court to declare whether or not land is affected by 'a restriction imposed by an instrument' and 'the nature and extent' of the restriction. In addition, a declaration may be sought 'whether the same is or would in any given event be enforceable and if so by whom'.

For an excellent summary of the remedies available and some of the difficulties encountered in enforcement, see the article by Professor Martin on this subject in [1996] Conv 329.

25.7 Discharge of covenants

25.7.1 Common ownership

A covenant will be extinguished automatically should the burdened and benefited land come into common ownership and occupation (*Re Tiltwood, Sussex* [1978] Ch 269) but remember the special rule relating to plots within a building scheme (*Texaco Antilles Ltd v Kernochan* [1973] AC 609). Otherwise, it is open to the parties affected to agree to discharge the obligation (the discharge itself being made by deed). Apart from these methods, a covenant would continue to affect land in perpetuity, under the rules of common law and equity. This causes considerable inconvenience, where after the passage of many years the covenant has become redundant or unreasonable. As a result, a statutory method has been provided whereby certain covenants may be discharged or varied.

25.7.2 Application to Lands Chamber

Under LPA 1925, s. 84, as amended by the LPA 1969, an application to discharge or modify, 'any restriction arising under covenant or otherwise as to the user [of land] or the building thereon' may be made to the Lands Chamber of the Upper Tribunal (formerly the 'Lands Tribunal'), which may modify or discharge the restrictive covenant in whole or in part. The party who is applying must establish one of four grounds on which he seeks discharge or modification of the covenant.

First, the applicant may show that the restriction has become obsolete due to 'changes in the character of the property or the neighbourhood' or to other relevant circumstances. This would apply, for example, to a covenant to use premises only as a dwelling, if the surrounding area had come into business or mixed use. Secondly, it may be established that the covenant impedes a reasonable user and either does not provide any practical benefit of substantial value to any person or is contrary to the public interest and, in either case, money would be adequate compensation for the loss or disadvantage (if any) that would be suffered due to the discharge or modification. Thirdly, it may be established that those entitled to the benefit have agreed, expressly or impliedly 'by their acts or omissions' to the discharge or modification. Fourthly, the claimant may be able to establish 'that the proposed discharge or modification will not injure the persons entitled to the benefit of the restriction'.

In considering applications for discharge, the Lands Chamber must take into account the development plan for the area and any declared or ascertainable pattern for the grant or refusal of planning permission (s. 84(1B)). *In re University of Westminster* [1998] 3 All ER 1014 sets out the approach that should be adopted by the Lands Chamber on any application made under s. 84 and in *Dobbin v Redpath* [2007] 4 All ER 465 it was indicated that the existence of a building scheme would be a material factor if an amendment were sought in such a case. If the Lands Chamber agrees to discharge or modify a covenant on any ground, it may require the payment of compensation to the owners of the benefited land. It should be noted that the wording of s. 84 is such that the powers of the Lands Chamber do not apply to positive covenants.

The s. 84 jurisdiction to discharge or modify a restrictive covenant has recently come before the UK Supreme Court for the first time, in *Millgate Developments Ltd v Alexander Devine Children's Cancer Trust* [2020] UKSC 45. The facts of that case provide an interesting illustration of the role of restrictive covenants and of the discretion to discharge or modify them. In *Millgate*, a children's hospice had the benefit of a restrictive covenant that prohibited building on the neighbouring land. The development company had then built several affordable housing units on this land, in breach of the terms of the covenant. At the time of carrying out the building works, it was aware of the covenant and was also aware of the possibility that it could have obtained planning permission to build in a way that was consistent with the terms of the covenant. Having completed the work, the company later sought to discharge or modify the covenant on the basis that the covenant impeded a reasonable user and was contrary to the public interest.

The Lands Tribunal modified the covenants to permit the limited building work undertaken by the company, on the basis that it was contrary to the public interest for the affordable housing project to be impeded. On appeal, it was argued that the developer's knowledge that it was in breach of the covenant at the time of building meant that it was not in the public interest to encourage this type of 'cynical' breach of a known covenant; on this basis, it was argued that the Lands Tribunal had no jurisdiction to discharge or modify the covenant, since the 'public interest' element of the relevant ground for discharge was not made out. This argument succeeded in the Court of Appeal but was rejected by the Supreme Court, which held that the Tribunal *did* have the jurisdiction to discharge or modify the covenant. Lord Burrows, giving the judgment of the majority, said:

> It is of central importance that the question that has to be asked is not the wider one of whether in all the circumstances of the case it would be contrary to the public interest to maintain the restrictive covenant. Rather the wording requires one to focus more narrowly on the impeding of the reasonable user of the land and to ask whether that impediment, by continuation of the restrictive covenant, is contrary to the public interest.

However, the Supreme Court held that, when exercising its discretion under the jurisdiction, the Lands Chamber ought to have considered the cynical breach of the covenant; in particular, they should have given special weight to the fact that the developer *could* have obtained planning permission to build in a way that respected the rights of the hospice and chose not to. Since the Lands Chamber had erred in law in failing to take this into account in excercising its discretion, the Supreme Court therefore overturned the decision of the Lands Chamber and refused the application to modify or discharge the covenant.

25.7.3 Housing Act 1985, s. 610

A further statutory power to discharge a covenant requiring property to be kept as a *single* dwelling exists under Housing Act 1985, s. 610. This permits a county court to authorise an alteration of the property in breach of a covenant (for example, into several flats) if the property cannot be disposed of readily as one unit due to a change in character of the neighbourhood. The aim of this provision is to prevent land falling into disuse because of a limitation imposed by a covenant, and thereby to prevent a diminution in the number of dwellings available for occupation.

25.8 Reform of the law

After reading this chapter, you may well be left with the impression that the rules relating to covenants and freehold are in considerable need of reform. This is a generally accepted opinion.

25.8.1 Some proposals for reform

The rules relating to the running of covenants have been particularly heavily criticised and have been the subject of three major reports over the years: (a) the Law Commission, *Report on Restrictive Covenants* (Law Com No. 11, 1967); (b) the Wilberforce Committee, *Report on Positive Covenants Affecting Land* (Cmnd 2719, 1968); and (c) the Law Commission, *Report on the Law of Positive and Restrictive Covenants* (Law Com No. 127, 1984). The last of these reports was a detailed attempt to make some sense of the confusion of the rules relating to easements and covenants. The position regarding positive covenants was particularly criticised, since such covenants do not run to bind a subsequent owner, and accordingly the original covenantor, who remains liable on the contract, can be held responsible for the acts of some later owner long after the covenantor's own interest in the land has ceased (para. 4.3 of the Report). This problem has now been addressed in relation to covenants in leases (see 11.3) but no reform has yet been made of the law in relation to freehold covenants. In 1998 the Lord Chancellor announced that the Law Commission Report of 1984 (No. 127) would not be implemented but said that the issues it raised would be considered further by the Law Commission in the light of other proposals for reform. With the intention of producing a coherent scheme that is compatible with the LRA 2002, the rules on commonhold and the position in relation to easements, the Law Commission published a Consultation Paper in 2008 (Law Com No. 186: *Easements, Covenants and Profits à Prendre*) and a new 'final' Report in 2011 (Law Com No. 327: *Making Land Work: Easements, Covenants and Profits à Prendre*). For more on these recent developments see 25.8.4.

25.8.2 Problems of the current rules

The horrors of the rules regarding restrictive covenants were cogently summarised in para. 4.9 of the 1984 Law Commission Report:

> The burden of a restrictive covenant does not run at all at law, but it does run in equity if certain complicated criteria are met. The benefit, by contrast, runs both at law and in equity, but according to rules which are different. These rules are, if anything, more complicated than the rules about the burden, and some of them are particularly technical and hard to grasp: as examples one may cite the rules about 'annexation' and those about 'building schemes'.

For some years now there has been further pressure to reform the rules about covenants, as part of a wider campaign for changes in the law to facilitate the sale of flats as freehold rather than as leasehold properties.

25.8.3 Past proposals for reform

25.8.3.1 Land obligations

The 1984 Law Commission Report took the view that the existing rules on covenants should be abolished and a new class of rights, 'land obligations', should be created to replace them. Such rights would be subject to rules similar to those applying to easements (which the Commission regarded as more satisfactory), and should subsist as legal interests in land, binding on successive owners under normal rules. After sale, the original parties would lose their contractual rights and obligations, thus destroying the present continuing contractual liability of the original covenantor (see para. 4.22 of the 1984 Report). Under such a scheme, no distinction would be made between positive and negative covenants.

25.8.3.2 Commonhold

The various suggested reforms were, to some extent, drawn together in the consultation paper on 'Commonhold' presented to Parliament in November 1990 (Cmnd 1345 (1990)). Thus far, the introduction of commonhold itself is the only change that has been made but further reform of the commonhold regime remains under consideration.

25.8.4 Law Commission Report 2011

As explained in Chapter 24, in March 2008 the Law Commission published yet another paper (Consultation Paper No. 186) dealing with the law relating to covenants. This followed a very serious review of the law relating to easements, profits, and covenants and the Report is well worth reading. The Report concluded that the law on covenants relating to freehold land is seriously in need of urgent reform and their recommendations build on the earlier consideration of the possibility of creating new 'land obligations'. Following consultation, a final Report was published in June 2011: *Making Land Work: Easements, Covenants and Profits à Prendre*, Law Com No. 327. This Report, while long, is well worth study for the detailed analysis of the problems in this area of law and proposals for a solution. The Report includes a draft Bill, which is also worth attention. The text that follows, identifies the areas of difficulty and gives a short summary of the proposals.

The Law Commission identified the following important flaws in the current law on freehold covenants:

(1) the burden of positive covenants will not run with land unless complex drafting devices are employed, which do not always work satisfactorily;

(2) burdens can run but only in equity and only if complex and technical conditions are met;

(3) while the benefit of covenants can run with land in both law and equity, different rules apply to law and equity and the rules are even more complicated than those applying to burdens;

(4) there is no need for the document creating an easement to describe the benefited land without doubt, as extrinsic evidence can be introduced in the case of conflict in order to establish what vague wording means, which reduces certainty;

(5) there is no need for benefits to be registered in any way, which makes it difficult to establish at a later date what benefits do attach to land;

(6) the original parties to a covenant remain contractually bound and benefited even after they have disposed of the affected land because they are bound to one another in a contractual agreement. This can leave a covenantor who has disposed of the burdened land at risk of being sued if there is a breach of covenant by the new owner.

The availability of commonhold is noted in paras. 5.16 and 5.17 of the Report but it is said that commonhold is designed for truly interdependent developments with shared facilities and structures. No mention was made of the fact that commonhold has not been widely adopted, even in cases in which it might be appropriate. The Report does, however, point out that commonhold does not cover all possible cases.

The Law Commission's conclusion is that there should be a fairly extensive reform of the law relating to freehold covenants, both positive and negative.

25.8.4.1 Land obligations

The main proposals are to be found in paras. 5.69 and 5.70 of the 2011 Report. The key intention is to create a new type of interest in land. In the earlier Reports from the Law Commission this new interest was called a 'land obligation', but the Bill attached to the latest Report merely calls them 'obligations'. However, the Report acknowledges that it is easiest to call the new rights 'land obligations' and that approach is adopted here. If the new rights are ever introduced, this will probably become their usual name, in order to distinguish these new rights in land from other types of obligation that can be enforced.

25.8.4.2 Land obligations may be negative or positive

The first detailed proposal is that an estate owner should be able to create both negative and positive land obligations, to take effect as legal interests appurtenant to another estate in land and which are registrable interests under the LRA 2002, provided that:

(1) the benefit of the land obligation touches and concerns the benefited land;
(2) the land obligation is:
   (a) an obligation not to do something on the burdened land; or
   (b) an obligation to do something on the burdened land or on the boundary between the burdened and benefited land; or
   (c) an obligation to make a payment in return for the performance of an obligation of the type mentioned in (b); and
(3) the land obligation is not a covenant between lessor and lessee relating to the demised premises (this excludes leasehold covenants).

It is proposed that land obligations should not operate as covenants but as legal interests in the burdened land, which are appurtenant to the benefited estate in land. This would make them more like easements. Land obligations would replace entirely the existing law on the enforceability of covenants in relation to any new obligations over freehold land (whether worded as covenants or land obligations): see paras. 5.70–5.73 of the Report.

25.8.4.3 Abolition of old rules on freehold covenants

Paragraph 5.89 of the Report proposes that following the introduction of the new land obligations it should no longer be possible to create freehold covenants enforceable under *Tulk v Moxhay*.

25.8.4.4 Creation of land obligations

Paragraphs 6.1–6.53 rehearse in more detail the manner in which land obligations will operate. Key points are that, as legal rights, they must be granted by deed and, if the estate is registered, the grant must be completed by registration. Paragraph 6.57 proposes that where title to the burdened land is unregistered the burden of the land obligation should be registrable as a land charge under the LCA 1972 (as a new class G land charge).

The Commission advises that the new land obligations should arise only expressly. They should not be capable of arising by implication or prescription and LPA 1925,

s. 62 should not operate to create a land obligation or to convert one from a leasehold to a freehold interest (para. 6.62).

25.8.4.5 Land obligations and registered titles

It is proposed that land obligations will be registrable interests in registered land. They are not to be overriding interests (para. 6.68). Normally, they will have been registered as land charges if created in relation to unregistered land and will be automatically entered on the register on first registration of the title.

25.8.4.6 Enforceability of benefit of land obligations

As the land obligation is to be a legal *interest* in land, it will pass to an acquirer of any *estate* in the benefited land to which it is appurtenant. However, the Commission proposes that it should not be transmitted with derived interests (para. 6.98). Therefore, a land obligation cannot be transmitted as appurtenant to another land obligation. This would prevent the decision in *Re Salvin's Indenture* [1938] 2 All ER 498 applying to the new land obligation. In that case a water company had rights over the dominant land but no estate in it. Nonetheless an easement claimed by the water company to lay a pipe over the servient land was regarded as possible and transmissible because it was appurtenant to the other rights that the water company had, even though the water company had no estate in the dominant land.

It is possible that a number of dominant owners may have the right to enforce an obligation. Therefore, the Report proposes that where the land obligation is to contribute to the cost of something, only the owner who has incurred expenditure is to be able to enforce the obligation. Thus, if landlord A and his tenant B have an obligation to repair a fence and the neighbour C has an obligation to pay half the cost, if tenant B carries out the repairs only B can obtain compensation from C. A cannot claim (para. 6.99).

25.8.4.7 Enforceability of burden of land obligations

It is indicated that the proposed registration provisions will deal with any issues of whether the burden of a land obligation runs with the land when the burdened estate is disposed of as a whole. Thus, where a burdened estate is sold to a purchaser of the whole estate, the purchaser takes the land subject to the burden provided the disposition creating the burden has been registered on the register of the burdened land (registered land) or as a class G land charge (unregistered land) (para. 6.101).

The situation is not so straightforward where an estate is *derived from* a burdened estate (e.g., if a lease is created out of the burdened estate). In such a case should the lessee be bound by the land obligation—or more correctly, is the leasehold estate to be bound? Similarly, if only part of the burdened land is disposed of, should the burden run to bind the part of the land?

1. *Restrictive obligations*

In both these cases the Law Commission proposes replicating the current law where the land obligation in question is *restrictive* (para. 6.103). This will perpetuate the need to distinguish between negative and positive interests. Therefore, para. 6.104 proposes that the burden of a restrictive land obligation should pass onto all estates and interests derived from the burdened estate and to all occupiers of the burdened estate. The exceptions would be:

(1) where the derived estate or interest has priority to the land obligation;

(2) where the occupier is authorised by the owner of an estate or interest that has priority to the land obligation (e.g., a licensee of such an owner); and

(3) where the derived estate or interest is a mortgage and the mortgagee is not in possession of the land.

2. Positive obligations

Different rules are proposed in relation to the passing of the burden of *positive* land obligations. This is because of the particularly onerous nature of such obligations, which require expenditure to be made. Thus, for example, the Law Commission would not regard it as right for a weekly tenant of the burdened land to be obliged to pay a large sum for the maintenance of a driveway.

Thus, it is proposed that, while generally a land obligation should pass down with any estate derived from a burdened estate, there should be an exception where the derived estate is a lease granted for a term of seven years or less. The burden should also pass to mortgagees when they come into possession of the burdened estate. On all this see paras. 6.106–6.116.

Some protection is to be provided to lessees who do have to take the burden of a land obligation. Where a lessee suffers loss due to the lessor's breach of covenant, the lessee is to be able to recover from the lessor, unless the lease expressly provides otherwise: see para. 6.116 and clauses 5 and 6(3) of the draft Bill. It is, of course, likely that leases would, in future, be drafted to cover this point.

3. Transmission of part of the burdened land

The Commission started from the point of view that there should be no difference between dealings with the whole or with a part of the land (para. 6.118). However, they recognised that this approach might cause problems where the acquirer of part could not comply with the obligation. This might arise with an obligation to repair a fence in a case in which the part of the burdened land disposed of provides no access to the fence. With positive covenants, it may also be necessary to apportion the obligation to pay money.

Accordingly, in para. 6.126, it is recommended that where burdened land is divided, the resulting estates should be jointly and severally liable in relation to the obligation. However, liability as between the burdened estates should be apportioned relative to the area of land covered by each burdened estate, unless an express apportionment has been made. Where an express apportionment is agreed, the obligations between the various burdened estates are themselves to be land obligations (para. 6.131).

4. Burdens and adverse possession

Taking account of the changes made to the law relating to adverse possession by the LRA 2002, the proposal is that any adverse possessor of land should be bound by any land obligations that bound the estate of the dispossessed estate owner (para. 6.144).

25.8.4.8 Remedies

Breach of a land obligation is to be enforceable by action (para. 6.148 and clause 7 of the draft Bill).

A person bound by a *negative* land obligation is to be in breach if he or she does something it prohibits or if he or she permits or suffers someone else to do so. *Positive* obligations are breached when the obligation is not performed. See para. 6.154.

The normal remedy will be an injunction or an order to perform a positive obligation. In some cases damages may be an appropriate substitute (paras. 6.160 and 6.165).

Normal contractual principles should apply to calculation of any damages (para. 6.166).

The limitation period for bringing any action is to be the 12 years that is normal in relation to land (para. 6.171).

It is to be possible to draft 'self-help' remedies into land obligations (such as a right to enter the servient land and do repairs). Where this is done, the Commission advises that failure to exercise the rights should not reduce any damages payable for breach. Where such rights are used, the costs are to be recoverable from the dominant owner, in so far as the costs are reasonable and the work is done to a reasonable standard (paras. 6.176 and 6.177).

25.8.4.9 Powers of the Lands Chamber of the Upper Tribunal

The Lands Chamber of the Upper Tribunal (formerly the 'Lands Tribunal') already has an important jurisdiction in relation to the release of old rights that provide a bar to proper use of land. However, these powers are subject to restrictions. The Law Commission recommends that the powers of the Lands Chamber should be extended and enhanced and that the jurisdiction of the Lands Chamber should extend to all land obligations (para. 7.35).

Jurisdiction should be extended to include powers in relation to leasehold land of any term (para. 7.38).

The grounds for modification or discharge should be those currently in LPA 1925, s. 84 (para. 7.55). However, it is recommended that it be made clear that, where several people can enforce the benefit, an order may be made even if differing grounds under s. 84 apply to each of them (para. 7.87). Thus, an applicant would not have to show the same ground or grounds against all the benefited persons.

The Lands Chamber should have power to modify or discharge a *positive* land obligation if, as a result of changes in circumstances, performance of the obligation (para. 7.69):

(1) has ceased to be reasonably practicable; or

(2) has become unreasonably expensive by comparison with the benefit it confers.

Where a positive land obligation is modified or discharged the Lands Chamber should be able to modify or discharge any reciprocal financial obligation (e.g., to pay towards the expense of performance) and to rearrange apportionments between those subject to obligations (paras. 7.70, 7.71, and 7.75).

As you can see, the proposed changes would be quite extensive. In 2017, the Government announced in a White Paper that it intended to 'simplify the current restrictive covenant regime by implementing the Law Commissions recommendations for reform', promising that a draft Bill to this effect would be published for consultation. However, as yet no Bill has been published.

25.8.4.10 Conservation covenants

In 2013 the Law Commission issued a further consultation paper, *Conservation Covenants: A Consultation Paper* Law Com CP 211. A conservation covenant is an agreement between a covenantor and a public body or charity that the covenantor will do or not do something on his or her land for a conservation purpose. The Law Commission proposed the replacement of existing statutory and other powers ('workrounds') by a statutory scheme for conservation covenants.

A final Report was published on 24 June 2014: *Conservation Covenants*, Law Com No. 349. This recommended a new statutory scheme of conservation covenants. A conservation covenant would:

- be formed by the agreement of two parties, comprising (1) a freeholder or a leaseholder who has a term of years with more than seven years to run and (2) a responsible body drawn from a limited class of organisations;

- be able to contain both restrictive and positive obligations;
- be capable of binding the freeholder's or leaseholder's successors in title.

There would be no need for the responsible body to own neighbouring land that could be benefited by the covenant. Such a covenant would have to be made for the public good and for the purpose of conserving, protecting, restoring, or enhancing:

(1) the natural environment, including flora, fauna, or geological features of the land;
(2) the natural resources of the land;
(3) cultural, historic, archaeological, architectural, or artistic features of the land; or
(4) the surroundings, setting, or landscape of any land which has any of those features.

Enforcement of any such covenant would be by the responsible body and the provisions of the Bill attached to the Report are said to enable swift and effective action, when required. Any such covenant is to be capable of being discharged or modified by agreement between the parties or on application to the Lands Chamber of the Upper Tribunal.

The Commission comments that the result would be to create a simple method of:

(1) unlocking currently missed conservation opportunities by overcoming the legal difficulties faced when seeking to create long-term binding obligations;
(2) facilitating better ways to deliver conservation objectives; and
(3) providing assurance of long-term conservation benefits.

The *Conservation Covenants* Report was welcomed, in January 2016, by the Secretary of State for Environment, Food and Rural Affairs and, in 2018, the Government stated that it would review and take forward the conservation covenants proposal as part of its wider environment plan. However, at the time of writing, no indication has yet been given as to whether, and if so when, any legislation may be introduced.

25.8.5 In summary

The Law Commission has advised extensive reforms of the interlinked issues of profits, easements, and freehold covenants. The proposals seem to be a considerable improvement on the currently unsatisfactory state of the law, even if one does not necessarily agree with all of the details. However, as yet no reforming Bill has been introduced and the matter may now be somewhat bound up in more recent proposals in relation to the reform of commonhold.

FURTHER READING

Bell, '*Tulk v Moxhay* Revisited' [1981] Conv 55.

Dixon, 'Is There Any Value in Restrictive Covenants? Enforceability and Remedies' [2007] 71 Conv 70 (casenote on *Small v Oliver & Saunders (Developments) Ltd*).

Gravells, 'Enforcement of Positive Covenants Affecting Freehold Land' (note on *Rhone v Stephens*) (1994) 110 LQR 346.

Hayton, 'Revolution in Restrictive Covenant Law?' (1980) 43 MLR 445.

Law Commission Consultation Paper No. 186 on *Easements, Covenants* and Profits à Prendre, 2008 (available at www.lawcom.gov.uk).

Law Commission Report, *Making Land Work: Easements, Covenants and Profits à Prendre*, Law Com No. 327, 2011 (available at www.lawcom.gov.uk).

Law Commission Consultation Paper No. 211 on *Conservation Covenants: A Consultation Paper* 2013 (available at www.lawcom.gov.uk).

Law Commission Report, *Conservation Covenants*, Law Com No. 349, 2014 (available at www.lawcom.gov.uk).

Martin, 'Remedies for Breach of Restrictive Covenants' [1996] Conv 329.

Megarry and Wade, *The Law of Real Property*, 9th edn., Sweet & Maxwell, 2019, Chapter 31.

Newsom, 'Universal Annexation' (1981) 97 LQR 32 (see also Newsom (1982) 98 LQR 202).

Report of the Committee on Positive Covenants Affecting Land (Cmnd 2719, 1968) 583.

Ryder, 'Restrictive Covenants: Problem of Implied Annexation' (1972) 36 Conv NS 26.

Todd, 'Casenote on *Roake v Chadha*' [1984] Conv 68.

Todd, 'Annexation after *Federated Homes*' [1985] Conv 177.

Wade, 'Casenote on *Halsall v Brizell*' [1957] CLJ 35.

Wade, 'Covenants—A Broad and Reasonable View' [1972B] CLJ 157 (see pp. 171–5: 'What is wrong with section 78?').

For reference only

Gastowicz, *Scamell and Gastowicz on Land Covenants*, 2nd edn., Bloomsbury, 2018.

Jessel, *Positive Covenants and Freehold Land*, Wildy, Simmonds & Hill, 2019.

You can visit the online resources to test your knowledge of this chapter with self-test questions at **www.oup.com/he/nair19e/**.

PART VII

In conclusion

This final part contains a more detailed consideration of what, in the law of England and Wales, constitutes land (Chapter 26).

26

What is land?

26.1 The statutory definition **615**
26.2 Earth, minerals, buildings, and fixtures **616**
26.3 Hereditaments **618**
26.4 Real and personal property (or, realty and personalty) **619**
26.5 How far up and down? **621**
26.6 A practical approach to land law **626**

26.1 The statutory definition

Thus far very little has been said in this book about the definition of land. At first it may seem odd that there should be any question about the matter at all: surely everybody knows what land is? However, as you will see, the word 'land' to a lawyer means far more than it does when the word is used in normal speech. As well as defining 'land', this chapter explains some of the other terminology which is applied to estates and interests in land, as this is relevant to the rather complex statutory definition of land.

26.1.1 LPA 1925, s. 205

'Land' is defined in LPA 1925, s. 205(1)(ix), as follows:

> 'Land' includes land of any tenure, and mines and minerals, whether or not held apart from the surface, buildings or parts of buildings (whether the division is horizontal, vertical or made in any other way) and other corporeal hereditaments; also . . . a rent and other incorporeal hereditaments, and an easement, right, privilege, or benefit in, over or derived from land . . .

This definition is, of course the one that is used in the LPA 1925. The SLA 1925 has the same definition in s. 117(1)(ix) and the same words appear in s. 68(6) of the TA 1925 and s. 3(viii) of the LRA 1925. Accordingly, this provides the general rule when you are dealing with the 1925 legislation.

Section 25(2) of TOLATA 1996 adopts the LPA 1925 definitions but you should note that Sch. 4 to TOLATA 1996 repealed some words that used to appear at the end of s. 205(1)(ix) ('but not an undivided share in land'). Those words are no longer relevant after the introduction of the new trust of land rules and the changes made to the doctrine of conversion by s. 3 of the 1996 Act, because a beneficial interest under a trust of land is an interest in land, unlike an interest under a trust for sale, which was in money.

As a consequence of all these provisions, when you are dealing with any of the main property statutes mentioned in this book you will be using the same definition of land.

26.1.2 Interpretation Act 1978

If, however, you are construing other legislation you may need to refer to the definition in Sch. 1 to the Interpretation Act 1978 (but note that this only applies to statutes passed on or after 1 January 1979, with any earlier legislation you should refer to earlier versions of the Interpretation Act):

> 'Land' includes buildings and other structures, land covered with water, and any estate, interest, easement, servitude in or over land.

Note that both the LPA 1925 and the Interpretation Act definitions are merely inclusive and not exclusive and thus it would remain theoretically possible for other things also to constitute land (if one could think of an example of such a thing). Also, any other Act may contain its own definition.

You can see that there is a relationship between the two definitions given and both contain similar terms. Here, because we are primarily concerned with the property legislation, we will concentrate on the LPA 1925 definition. That definition requires some thought and so we will now consider its individual parts.

26.1.3 Other definitions

Were you to be construing a document other than an Act of Parliament you would, of course, have to look to see whether a special definition had been provided for that document and in drafting any such document yourself you might need to provide a definition (perhaps by expressly adopting the LPA 1925 definition).

26.2 Earth, minerals, buildings, and fixtures

26.2.1 The basic rule

It is easy to accept that 'land' includes the earth beneath our feet and any minerals contained therein. However, the legal definition of land goes further and includes in the definition plants growing on the land *and* any other thing which is actually fixed to the land. 'Buildings' and 'parts of buildings' are actually mentioned in s. 205(1)(ix), and, after a moment's thought, it is not altogether surprising that they are included in the term 'land'.

It is perhaps more surprising, at first thought, when one discovers that any item affixed to the land becomes land itself. Thus in *Buckland v Butterfield* (1820) 2 Brod & Bing 54, it was held that a conservatory which was attached to a house by eight cantilevers, each 9 inches long, formed part of the land. This is important, because should one wish to retain and remove such a fixture when selling the freehold estate in the land, one must specifically contract to exclude the fixture from the sale. Thus, should a vendor intend to remove the rose bushes from the garden of a house when selling, this should be provided for when the contract for sale is made and may have to be specified in the final conveyance or transfer, if the items have not been removed before that document is executed.

Buckland v Butterfield also illustrates the point that since the house is land, because it is fixed to the earth, anything fixed to the house also becomes land. However, something which is merely placed upon the land, and not fixed to it, will not be regarded as forming part of the land, however heavy it is and even if it would be very difficult to move it. In *Berkley v Poulett* (1976) 242 EG 39, a large statue, made of marble and weighing nearly half a ton, was not regarded as part of the land, because it was not fixed down in any way.

The basic rule is therefore that anything annexed to land is land. However, the courts have long accepted that something which is affixed merely to facilitate its display, or in order to steady it, is not to be regarded as becoming part of the land. Thus in *Leigh v Taylor* [1902] AC 157, a tapestry tacked to strips of wood, which were then affixed to the wall, was not regarded as being part of the land. The degree of **annexation** in this case was merely that which was necessary for the display of the tapestry. In *Hulme v Brigham* [1943] KB 152, printing machines weighing between 9 and 12 tons were not regarded as fixtures, even though they were attached to motors which were fixed to the floor. In this case the degree of annexation was slight and was necessary merely to render the motors stable. The *purpose* of annexation is important in deciding whether something attached to the land (or a building) has thereby become part and parcel of that land (or that building). For example, in *Marlborough Knightsbridge Management Ltd v Fivaz* [2021] EWCA Civ 989, it was argued that the external doors of a flat leased to a tenant were not part and parcel of the land leased to the tenant because they were only attached with hinges. The Court of Appeal rejected this argument on the basis that they 'were an essential part of the structure, since they afforded privacy and security to the tenant(s)'. It was the function served by the annexed doors, not just the physical extent of connection between the doors and the building, that explained why they were to be treated as part of the building and, therefore, as part of the land.

26.2.2 Items not fixed to the land

In rare circumstances something which is not actually fixed to the land but which appears to form an integral part of it may be regarded as forming part of the land for legal purposes.

The best example of this is *D'Eyncourt v Gregory* (1866) LR 3 Eq 382, in which stone statues, seats, and garden vases were held to be part of the land, even though they were free-standing, as were certain tapestries and pictures hanging upon the walls. The basis of the decision is that the ornaments formed an integral part of the architectural design of the house on the property. Thus it appears that the existence of a 'master plan' concerning the property may render items part of the land, even though there is no real annexation.

Another illustration was supplied by Blackburn J in *Holland v Hodgson* (1872) LR 7 CP 328 at p. 335, when he explained that a pile of stones lying in a builder's yard would obviously not form part of the land upon which it lay. However, were the same stones to be constructed into a drystone wall (which uses no mortar and no method of fixing the wall to the ground) on a farm, the wall obviously would form part of the land of the farm.

A modern example is provided by *Elitestone Ltd v Morris* [1997] 1 WLR 687, which concerned a chalet bungalow, which had been placed on concrete blocks but which was not attached to them in any way. The blocks were attached to the land. The land was occupied by the defendants under an agreement which purported to be a licence but which the court of first instance held to be a lease. However, for the defendants to have Rent Act protection the bungalow itself had to be land and the landlord argued that this was not the case because the building was not fixed to land in anyway but merely rested on the blocks. The case was finally decided in the House of Lords, who concluded that in this instance the bungalow was land despite the absence of physical annexation. Lord Lloyd of Berwick said (at pp. 692–3):

> Many different tests have been suggested, such as whether the object which has been fixed to the property has been so fixed for the better enjoyment of the object as a chattel, or whether it has been fixed with a view to effecting a permanent improvement of the freehold. This and similar tests are useful when one is considering an object such as a tapestry, which may or may not be fixed to a house so as to become part of the freehold. . . . These tests are less useful when one is considering the house itself. In the case of the house the answer is as much a matter of common sense as precise analysis. A house which is constructed in such a way so as to be removable, whether as a unit, or in sections, may well remain a chattel, even though it is connected temporarily to mains services such as water and electricity. But a house which is constructed in such a way that it cannot be removed at all, save by destruction, cannot have been intended to remain as a chattel. It must have been intended to form part of the realty.

This decision emphasises that what is of primary importance is the 'intention' involved. However, Lord Clyde (at p. 698) indicated that the use of this word may be misleading because it is the purpose which the object in question is serving which matters and not the intention or purpose of the person who put it there. Thus, Lord Clyde said that the test was objective and not subjective. The relevant issue is whether the object is 'designed for the use or enjoyment of the land or for the more complete or convenient use or enjoyment of the thing itself'.

Although this may sound complicated, the case in fact indicates that the courts are really applying a common-sense test, rather than relying on technical arguments about the degree of annexation. These principles were applied in *Chelsea Yacht and Boat Club Ltd v Pope* [2000] 1 WLR 1941 in which the attachment of a houseboat to pontoons, and to the river bed and banks by means of an anchor and rings, were held to be insufficient to make the boat real property, rather than a chattel. However, by way of contrast see also *Cinderella Rockerfellas Ltd v Rudd* [2003] 1 WLR 2423, in which a permanently moored vessel was regarded as forming part of a hereditament for the purposes of rateable valuation. You should, however, note that in giving the judgment of the court Potter LJ appears not to be saying that the vessel in question was land but that it was a chattel which was, for rating purposes, sufficiently connected to the land to be capable of being regarded as part of the rateable property. Accordingly, the apparent conflict with the *Chelsea* case is not a real conflict: the vessel is a chattel but can be taken into account in assessing the rates payable in respect of the land (which includes the water above the land on which the vessel floats as well as the bank to which it is moored).

26.3 Hereditaments

26.3.1 LPA 1925 definition

Before 1926, '**hereditaments**' were those rights which were capable of passing to heirs by way of inheritance. The term is defined in LPA 1925, s. 205(1)(ix), as 'any real property which on an intestacy occurring before the commencement of this Act might have devolved upon an heir'. This includes the estates and interests in land discussed in this book, and which are not purely personal rights. Thus a licence is not a hereditament because it is a personal permission and not an interest which would have passed to an heir.

26.3.2 Corporeal and incorporeal hereditaments

Having defined 'hereditaments' as 'inheritable interests', the common law went on to distinguish between 'corporeal' and 'incorporeal' hereditaments. Corporeal hereditaments are physical objects: the physical land and its attachments. Incorporeal hereditaments are rights, not things, and there is a fixed list of such hereditaments, which includes rentcharges, easements, and profits.

This traditional classification may cause you some surprise, for the two groups, corporeal and incorporeal, seem strangely unrelated, though they are supposed to be subdivisions of one category. To paraphrase Austin (*Jurisprudence*, 5th edn., vol. 1, p. 362): one class consists of intangible rights over objects (incorporeal), and the other of physical objects over which rights may be exercised (corporeal). Further, the notion of corporeal hereditaments seems to conflict with the basic principle of English land law, which was emphasised in Chapter 1, that one cannot own the land itself, but only an estate in it. No provision for estates in land seems to be made in this classification: they are certainly not within the accepted list of incorporeal hereditaments, but one cannot describe them as corporeal because they are intangible rights rather than tangible objects.

This is a classification which has always caused difficulty and debate and the reason for explaining it is the fact that you will see references to 'hereditaments' in the statutory definition of land. It is also important that you should realise that easements, profits, and rentcharges are not merely interests in land but are themselves 'land' within the statutory definition. However, it is probably enough to note the meaning of the terms and you should not spend too much time on this rather difficult point until your studies of land law are very advanced.

The statutory definition of 'hereditaments' includes the term 'real property' and this leads to the next set of technical terms.

26.4 Real and personal property (or, realty and personalty)

26.4.1 The meaning of 'real'

Often you may see references to 'real property' which suggest that this term is synonymous with 'land' (e.g., in the book title, Megarry and Wade's *The Law of Real Property*). This is not, however, entirely true, for some interests in land do not amount to real property.

The distinction between real and personal property is an ancient one and is still of importance today. The term 'real' property refers to that property which the early courts would protect by a 'real' action (an action *in rem*). In this context the adjective 'real' does not have its usual modern meaning of 'genuine' but is used in a technical sense. The word 'real' derives from the Latin word *res* (thing). A 'real action' was one in which the court would order that the property itself (the *res*) be restored to an owner who had been dispossessed, rather than giving the defendant the choice of returning the property or paying damages to compensate for the loss. If someone takes your table, a remedy in damages will usually suffice, for you may take the money and buy another table. However, land is unique in its character and, at a time when status in society depended upon one's relation to land, it was felt that where land was lost it was essential that it should be recovered. Thus, there was a distinction between 'real' property (where the property could be recovered by an action *in rem*) and 'personal' property, so called because it could be protected only by an action *in personam* (an action against the person of the wrongdoer). Where an action *in personam* was concerned the wrongdoer would in general pay damages rather than return the property. Thus the history of English forms of action has led to a labelling of property which is still used today.

26.4.2 Exceptions

Most of the rights considered in this book amount to real property because they are rights in land which would have been subject to an action *in rem*. There have been, however, two main exceptions.

26.4.2.1 Rights of beneficiaries under trusts

The first of these was the right of a beneficiary under a trust for sale. Since the doctrine of conversion notionally transformed the trust property into money (a form of personal property) the beneficiaries' interests under the trust were seen to be interests in personalty. The doctrine of conversion was abolished in relation to trusts for sale by TOLATA 1996 and now the interests of beneficiaries under *trusts of land*, which replaced trusts for sale, *are* interests in land.

26.4.2.2 Leases

The other exception is not so obvious and results once again from the manner in which the law has developed. When leases first came into common use, they were regarded as commercial contracts creating rights *in personam* between the parties. Unlike freehold estates they did not affect the tenant's position on the feudal ladder, and were not subject to one of the real actions. If the tenant were dispossessed by his or her landlord, the tenant could not recover the land but would only be awarded damages for breach of contract. Since it was protected only by an action *in personam* the lease came to be regarded as personal property. After a time, the tenant was enabled to recover the land by action, whether he or she was dispossessed of the land by the landlord or by some third party, but by this time it was too late to alter the classification of the lease. A lease was therefore a 'chattel' (another name for personal property, derived from a French word from which 'cattle' is also derived, livestock being an important form of personal property). However, recognition of the rather special nature of the lease led to the rather paradoxical nomenclature of 'chattel real', which emphasises its hybrid nature.

Leases remain personal property to this day and the distinction can sometimes prove to be of importance. Thus if a testator were to make the following disposition in his will: 'All my real property to my son Alfred and all my personal property to my son Bernard', Alfred would receive any freehold property owned by his father, but Bernard would be able to claim any leasehold property, together with all his father's chattels. In this case the freehold property is obviously an estate in land. It should be recalled, however, that the lease, while being personal property, is also an estate in land (LPA 1925, s. 1(1)).

26.5 How far up and down?

26.5.1 The extent of ownership

It is often said that a freehold owner owns the land up to the skies and down to the centre of the earth. This theory is usually expressed in the Latin maxim *Cuius est solum eius est usque ad coelum et ad inferos* ('whoever's is the soil, it is theirs all the way to heaven and all the way to hell'). However, in practice this theory is far from true and in any event lawyers throughout the centuries, while espousing this theory, appear to have had problems with some of the logical consequences.

However, while the title to the land may be vested in the freehold owner, this does not mean that all the elements of the physical land are his or hers to use. To give an example to illustrate this point, while there are limited cases in which it is possible for a land owner also to own the title to the coal in a piece of land, normally the freehold title to coal is vested in the Coal Authority, regardless of who owns the freehold to the surrounding land (see the Coal Industry Act 1994, s. 7(3)).

The law recognises that the general theory can be disrupted in some cases and also that land can be owned in layers. Thus, it appears perfectly possible for the freehold title to land to be vested in A down to a certain depth and for the title to the land below that depth to be vested in B. This is confirmed in s. 205(1)(ix) of the LPA 1925 (see 26.1.1) which expressly says that both horizontal and vertical division of land is possible.

You will realise that there must be restrictions on a freehold owner's rights to use his or her estate in land because otherwise every plane overflying the land would commit a trespass. However, in *Mitchell v Mosley* [1914] 1 Ch 438, 450, Cozens-Hardy MR confirmed that the grant of land includes the surface and everything above it (such as trees and houses) and everything that is within it (such as earth, clay, and mines). Swinfen Eady LJ and Phillimore LJ concurred and said that this was a recognised rule of law.

26.5.1.1 Above the land—flying

This view, if taken literally, would suggest that overflying land without permission would constitute a trespass. However, in *Baron Bernstein of Leigh v Skyviews & General Ltd* [1978] QB 479, Baron Bernstein failed in a claim that a company that had overflown his land to take pictures of it had committed a trespass. Griffiths J accepted that overflying at a height which interfered with the normal use and enjoyment of the land could constitute a trespass but that overflying at a height that could not interfere with such use and enjoyment could not constitute a trespass. He said that above that level the landowner has no more rights to the sky than any other member of the public. This conflicts with the 'up to the heavens' element of the classical expression of the extent of the rights of the owner, which would suggest that overflying was a trespass (but might attract only nominal damages due to the lack of a real loss when the overflying was at a great height).

26.5.1.2 Below the land—fracking

Is land use similarly restricted below the ground? This issue came before the Supreme Court for consideration in *Bocardo SA v Star Energy UK Onshore Ltd* [2010] 1 AC 380. Section 1 of the Petroleum (Production) Act 1934 vests property in petroleum in strata below ground in the Crown. Star Energy had a licence granted by the Crown under s. 2 of the 1934 Act to bore, search for, and get oil from a petroleum reservoir lying under land in Surrey. To reach the reservoir, Star bored at an angle beneath land belonging to

Bocardo, who sued for trespass. The Supreme Court held that the classical statement of the rights of an owner did apply in this case and that because Star had obtained no right to drill through Bocardo's land, the company had committed a trespass for which damages would be awarded. In this case, Lord Hope of Craighead DPSC reviewed the entire history of *cuius est solum, eius est usque ad coelum et ad inferos*, and concluded that this was a proposition of law that commanded general acceptance and should be applied in the current case. He accepted, however, that it did not apply in the *Baron Bernstein* type of aviation case. In relation to how far down towards the centre of the earth the maxim held good, Lord Hope said:

> There must obviously be some stopping point, as one reaches the point at which physical features such as pressure and temperature render the concept of the strata belonging to anybody so absurd as to be not worth arguing about. But the wells that are at issue in this case, extending from about 800 feet to 2,800 feet below the surface, are far from being so deep as to reach the point of absurdity. Indeed the fact that the strata can be worked upon at those depths points to the opposite conclusion.

The effect of *Bocardo* was that energy companies would have to acquire rights to get access to minerals by obtaining (for example) access easements from neighbouring owners or buying their estates. Neighbouring owners were not obliged to grant rights or sell. So *Bocardo* rendered the licensing regime unusable in many cases. This was a considerable blockage on government plans to promote the exploitation of mineral reserves by the process called 'hydraulic fracturing' or, more commonly, '**fracking**'. It is rare for fracking to be possible by buying land and going straight down to mineral reserves by drilling straight down through that land. In practice, access under neighbouring land at an angle is often essential.

With its plans for use of subsoil energy reserves crippled, it was no surprise that the government decided that it should take measures to change the effects of *Bocardo*. However, fracking is a very unpopular topic with the UK public and consultation was needed. In 2014, the Infrastructure Bill was introduced in the House of Commons. However, despite including a wide range of property issues, the Bill did not address fracking when it was introduced. Instead, fracking provisions (which use the term 'hydraulic fracturing') were inserted by the Government by amendment at a later stage in the House of Commons. When the Bill reached the House of Lords, there was something of a revolt about the content of the fracking provisions and the government was forced to agree to a late amendment to them.

The law on fracking is now to be found in ss. 43–8 of the Infrastructure Act 2015. This gives a new statutory right to use certain land for certain purposes. You will need to look at the provisions in detail but the key provision is s. 43(1):

> A person has the right to use deep-level land in any way for the purposes of exploiting petroleum or deep geothermal energy.

The right only applies to deep-level land that is within a landward area (s. 43(2)). Deep-level is defined in s. 43(3) as 'any land at a depth of at least 300 metres below land'. So the new right does not apply to land where it is necessary to mine or drill closer to the surface. In those instances, the energy company will still have to obtain rights to mine from the estate owners and the estate owners can refuse. That was one of the protections built into the new provisions. Figure 26.1 illustrates the new rules.

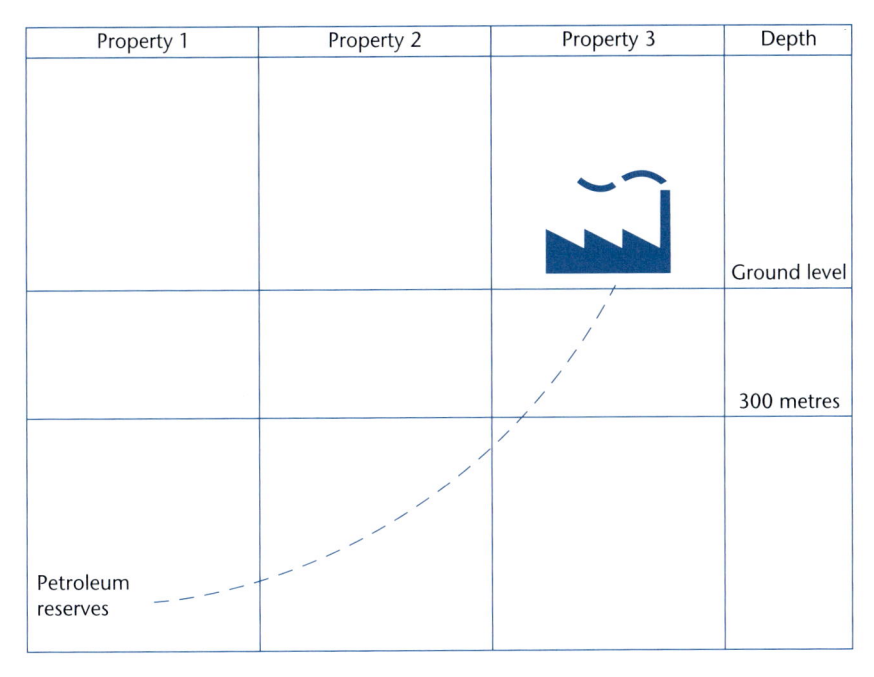

Figure 26.1 Rights of access to petroleum reserves—Fracking

Assume that there are petroleum reserves under Property 1. To get access to those reserves, assume that the energy company will need to create mining access under the adjoining Property 2 and the next piece of land, Property 3. The access and facilities under Properties 1 and 2 will be below 300 metres. In those cases, the energy company will be able to rely on the new statutory right and the owners of the estates in those properties will not be able to prevent the fracking proceeding. However, access at Property 3 is to the surface and goes above 300 metres. In the case of Property 3, the company must obtain rights of access from the estate owner in accordance with *Bocardo*, in relation to the land that is above 300 metres.

Section 44(1) and (2) gives a wide, 'inclusive' definition of the ways and purposes for which the new right may be used. The new right of use is also given an equivalence to a legal interest in land by way of s. 44(4). This is done by saying the power to use the land does not give a power, 'greater than, or different from, the power that [the energy company] would have had if the right had been granted by a person legally entitled to grant it'. Note that this does not make the right to use into one of the rights in land about which you have learnt. It just makes the right of use operate like one.

The problem for the estate owner comes in s. 44(3), which allows the energy company to leave the deep-level land in a different state from the state it was in at the start. So permanent changes to the subsoil can be made. However, the Secretary of State has powers under s. 45 to make a payment scheme by Regulations (secondary legislation), requiring energy undertakings to make compensation payments. Also, s. 46 permits the Secretary of State to make Regulations imposing a notice procedure before the new right is exercised. The secondary legislation may impose enforcement provisions on the energy suppliers, including financial penalties for breach (s. 47(1)).

The Infrastructure Act 2015 received Royal Assent on 12 February 2015. The fracking provisions came into force in April 2015. It appears that the Government does *not* currently intend to make notice or compensation Regulations. If the energy industry complies with the public undertakings it has given to do such things on a voluntary basis, no Regulations will be made. If there are future problems, Regulations may be made to compel the industry to give proper notice and pay appropriate compensation.

Section 50 of the Infrastructure Act 2015 makes some changes for the process under which the Secretary of State licenses (consents to) use of subsoil reserves for fracking. This amends the safeguards in relation to such licences. Regulations must be made in order to cover some of the detail. The Regulations required by s. 50 of the Infrastructure Act (see subsections (4)–(6) of the new Petroleum Act 1998, s. 4B), which specify protected areas, were laid before Parliament in draft in July 2015 and were approved in December 2015, after considerable complaint that they allowed fracking to take place below national parks. See now the Onshore Hydraulic Fracturing (Protected Areas) Regulations 2016.

Section 25 of the Wales Act 2017 amends the fracking provisions of the Infrastructure Act in order to confer powers on the Welsh Ministers in relation to land in Wales.

In 2019, the Government 'suspended' fracking. In summer 2022, the suspension of fracking was lifted in some places, but the suspension was reimposed by the new Prime Minister in October 2022. At the time of writing, this remains the case.

26.5.2 The problems of a 'flying freehold'

If it is generally accepted that it is possible for different owners to own different strata in the subsoil and rights in the air, it should follow that it would be possible for layers of a building to be similarly divided and thus for a freehold to be conveyed, for example in a flat above ground level, without the owner also having to own the fee simple in the land at ground level. Surprisingly, however, this seems to be a concept that lawyers have over the centuries found hard to accept, although it should follow logically from the cases mentioned.

One could spend a long time arguing about why the concept of what is usually called a 'flying freehold' should have given problems in England and Wales. However, one explanation is that, despite the theory of estates, early land law was very much centred upon physical land, the control of physical land, and the relationships within society that were built upon the foundation of tenure of land. Interestingly, the idea of a leasehold estate in a stratum above the ground does not appear to have ever given the same problems. The reason for this may be rooted in the fact that early leases were viewed solely as commercial agreements that did not give rise to the same tenurial incidents as the freehold estate or have the same impact upon the owner's place in society. Accordingly, while many seem to have struggled with the possibility of a freehold estate in 'thin air', the law of leases accepted that if a tenant had a lease of an upper floor and the building burned down, the lease continued and rent had to be paid: *Cricklewood Property and Investment Trust Ltd v Leighton's Investment Trust Ltd* [1945] AC 221 (but see 9.6.1.1 for the modern rule as to frustration and leases). It is this reasoning, as well as the benefits of a lease in relation to the running of positive covenants (see Chapter 11), that has made it standard practice for the estate granted in flats to be a leasehold estate rather than a freehold estate, with the freehold of the whole property being vested either in the owner of the ground floor flat or in some other person (sometimes to be held upon trust for all the leaseholders but often as a commercial investment in its own right).

This approach to the freehold estate seems, however, to be an unnecessary complication and it has been pointed out for centuries that there is no real justification for the view that there is some difficulty involved in creating a flying freehold. The same approach does not apply elsewhere; for example, Scottish law appears to have no difficulty with the concept of the Scottish equivalent to freehold in an upper floor flat and this can prove beneficial to the owner, since a major defect of a lease is that it is a time-limited estate. Although the disadvantage of the time limitation can be overcome by giving the leaseholder the right to renew the lease when it expires, the wish to avoid the use of the flying freehold has, in recent history when tenurial relationships are unimportant, probably arisen solely from the practical problems that can arise because of the freehold rules on running of covenants (see Chapter 25). If the difficulty of ensuring compliance with suitable covenants, including positive covenants where necessary, could be overcome, there seems to be no genuine reason for English law not to accept that a flying freehold can be a useful concept in practice.

One of the very real problems in the past has been that there has been no means of requiring a freehold owner to maintain the building in a proper state of repair. While it is a nuisance if your neighbour allows the neighbouring house to become derelict (and may even affect the value of your neighbouring property), the problem is not severe if your property does not depend upon the other for support. Where support was crucial, the law developed a limited right to support by means of an easement (see 24.2.2.6) but still did not oblige the neighbour to keep the neighbouring property in good repair. This difficulty becomes acute if the safety of your own property depends upon that neighbour keeping neighbouring premises in good repair (which would be true if the neighbour's property were a lower flat and yours an upper flat) and thus there was a tendency to adopt the known path of granting leaseholds, with the benefit that, in a lease, positive covenants could be imposed that would bind later acquirers of the estate.

However, even in the past, in particular circumstances, this issue was found not to be impossible of solution and it is perhaps amusing to note that one example of the use of flying freeholds in England has been in relation to some of the properties forming part of Lincoln's Inn in London. It appears that Chancery barristers were less troubled by the concept than other lawyers, or perhaps that they were happier to rely on the careful drafting of agreements, in order to ensure that the flying freeholds did not cause insuperable problems. Away from legal London, they are also occasionally found in other places, including in at least one small terrace of country cottages where, as a previous co-author of this text discovered from personal experience, a bedroom 'flying' over the next-door property was not regarded as unusual.

Having said that flying freeholds should not cause insuperable difficulties to the careful, it is perhaps worth looking at a case that illustrates how things can go wrong if insufficient thought is given when a flying freehold is created. In *Abbahall Ltd v Smee* [2003] 1 All ER 465, a house had been separated so that the upper two floors constituted a flying freehold owned by Miss Smee, while the ground floor was owned by Abbahall Ltd. Miss Smee had allowed some parts of the property to fall into disrepair and water thus leaked onto the ground floor and there was a danger of falling masonry. Abbahall therefore obtained a court order allowing it to enter Miss Smee's premises in order to repair the roof. It then brought further proceedings to recover the costs of the repairs from Miss Smee, on the basis that the roof must form part of her premises. The Court of Appeal agreed that both parties were responsible for the roof but that their liability to pay depended on the extent of the benefit to each. On the facts of the particular case, they determined that the parties should each be responsible for half of the costs of the repairs. The case therefore leaves much room for dispute in any future case in which it is not clear to what extent each party benefits from the element of the property in question.

Therefore, it is the case that flying freeholds are perfectly possible in the law of England and Wales, even if they are very rare. However, the provisions to be included when creating such an estate require careful thought and meticulous drafting.

26.5.3 Commonhold

Interestingly, the concept of commonhold advanced by the Law Commission in its Report *Commonhold: Freehold Flats and Freehold Ownership of Other Independent Buildings* (Cm 179, July 1987) decided not to build solely upon the idea of flying freeholds but on an adaptation of the existing model used for flats, where each flat owner has a lease of the flat and is a member of a management company, which owns the freehold. The commonhold scheme provided by the Commonhold and Leasehold Reform Act 2002 involves each flat owner owning the freehold estate in his or her flat and being a member of a company, the commonhold association, which owns the freehold of the common parts of the building (see 8.6 for the details). Bear in mind that there can be no 'flying commonhold', thus the issues mentioned in 26.5.2 cannot arise.

26.6 A practical approach to land law

This whole area of law provides an excellent example of how lawyers are affected by both society and custom (the early influence of tenurial incidents and relationships) and practicalities (making covenants work or allowing aviation to continue) rather than by absolute theories. The practising lawyer, while being a person who has to understand and apply concepts and theories that are often extremely complex, is mainly driven by the need to find a practical solution to a problem. Where there is doubt, the lawyer will usually prefer a proven solution to the risks of experimenting with uncertainties. The push for growth or reform comes when existing approaches no longer meet all the practical needs of those affected.

It was said at the start of this book that it was intended to avoid a discussion of purely historical matters. However, you will have found that historical issues have intruded rather often into this last chapter. The reason for this is that modern land law is still, to a certain extent, tied to its past. The 1925 property legislation was not a complete break with the past but rather reformed and built upon the existing law, which had developed over the centuries. This trend has continued in more modern legislation. The relationship between land law ancient and modern is particularly noticeable when dealing with the technical definition of 'land' because in this area the 1925 statutes attempted no radical reforms. Accordingly, although a knowledge of the historical development of land law is not essential to the modern student, it may be of interest and assistance to those who wish to deepen their understanding of the subject. We hope that this book has shown you that land law is a fascinating and lively subject and that you have been encouraged to extend your reading into such areas.

FURTHER READING

Cheshire and Burn's Modern Law of Real Property, 18th edn., 2011, pp. 3–12.

Gray, 'Property in Thin Air' [1991] CLJ 252 (on flying freeholds).

Gray and Gray, *Elements of Land Law*, 5th edn., 2009, 1.1 and 1.2.

Lawson and Rudden, *The Law of Property*, 3rd edn., Clarendon Press, 2002, Chapter 2 (The Classification of Things).

Smith, *Property Law*, 9th edn., Pearson, 2017, pp. 3–11 (Basic Property Principles).

On fracking

House of Commons briefing paper Number SN06073, 'Shale Gas and Fracking', 15 January 2016 (which may be found at researchbriefings.parliament.uk).

You can visit the online resources to test your knowledge of this chapter with self-test questions at **www.oup.com/he/nair19e/**.

BIBLIOGRAPHY

Austin, *Jurisprudence*, 5th edn., Murray, 1885.

Cheshire and Burn, *Cheshire and Burn's Modern Law of Real Property*, 18th edn., Oxford University Press, 2011.

Beale, *Chitty on Contracts*, 34th edn., Sweet & Maxwell, 2022.

Cooke, *Land Law*, 2nd edn., Oxford University Press, 2012.

Fry, *A Treatise on the Specific Performance of Contracts*, 6th edn., Stevens, 1921.

Gale, *Gale on Easements*, 21st edn., Sweet & Maxwell, 2020.

Gray and Gray, *Elements of Land Law*, 5th edn., Oxford University Press, 2009.

Hanbury and Martin, *Modern Equity*, 22nd edn., Sweet & Maxwell, 2021.

Lawson and Rudden, *The Law of Property*, 3rd edn., Oxford University Press, 2002.

Maitland, *Equity*, Cambridge University Press, 1936.

McFarlane, *The Law of Proprietary Estoppel*, 2nd edn., Oxford University Press, 2020.

Megarry and Wade, *The Law of Real Property*, 9th edn., Sweet & Maxwell, 2019.

Morris and Leach, *The Rule against Perpetuities*, 2nd edn., Stevens, 1962.

Oakley, *Constructive Trusts*, 3rd edn., Sweet & Maxwell, 1996.

Pawlowski, *The Doctrine of Proprietary Estoppel*, Sweet & Maxwell, 1996.

Preston and Newsom, *Restrictive Covenants Affecting Freehold Land*, 11th edn., Sweet & Maxwell, 2020.

Ruoff and Roper, *Registered Conveyancing*, Sweet & Maxwell, looseleaf edn.

Smith, *Property Law*, 10th edn., Pearson Longman, 2020.

Woodfall, *Law of Landlord and Tenant*, Sweet & Maxwell, looseleaf edn.

GLOSSARY

abatement A 'self-help' remedy by which the owner of the dominant tenement may remove an obstruction to the exercise of an easement.

absolute interest An interest which is not determinable or conditional (see 1.7.1.2), i.e., it is not granted on such terms that it is liable to end prematurely on the occurrence of some specified event.

Adjudicator to the Land Registry See 6.2.8.

administrators See '**personal representatives**'.

adverse possession (acquisition of title by) The process of acquiring title to land by dispossessing the previous holder and occupying the land until: (1) the owner's right to recover it is time-barred under the Limitation Act (unreg. land); (2) the adverse possessor is registered as proprietor (reg. land).

alienation The act of disposing of one's property, i.e., passing it from one owner to another.

annexation The procedure of attaching the benefit of a restrictive covenant to the land of the covenantee, so that it will run automatically with that land, without any need for the benefit to be assigned (transferred) to the new owner when the land changes hands.

appurtenant See '**profit à prendre**'.

assent A disposition by personal representatives, by which property is vested in the person entitled under the deceased's will or on his intestacy.

assignment A transfer of property (used particularly in respect of the transfer of a lease or a reversion).

break clause A clause in a fixed-term lease that allows one party, or both, to determine the lease on notice before the term expires.

Bruton tenancy A tenancy that is not a legal estate in land, having been granted by a person who lacks an estate in land (see 9.6.2).

caution, inhibition, notice, restriction Methods of protecting interests in registered land by entry on the register under LRA 1925; under LRA 2002 only notices and restrictions are used.

caveat emptor Let the buyer beware.

cesser on redemption The process by which a mortgage automatically comes to an end when the obligation which it secures is performed.

charge An encumbrance securing the payment of money.

charge by way of legal mortgage See 2.5.2 and 22.4.3.

chattels real Leases—see 2.10.2.3 and 26.4.2.2.

choses in action See 2.10.2.2.

choses in possession See 2.10.2.1.

clog (on the equity of redemption) Any restriction imposed by the mortgage on the mortgagor's right to redeem the mortgaged property.

concurrent lease A lease the term of which overlaps with another lease in respect of the same land (see 9.2.5).

conditional fee See 1.7.1.2.

consolidate (right to) The right of the mortgagee to refuse to allow the mortgagor to redeem one mortgage unless some other mortgage is redeemed at the same time.

conversion A change in the nature of property, from realty to personalty, or vice versa. Actual conversion of this kind occurs when land is sold, so that the purchaser's property changes from money into land, and that of the vendor changes from land into money. Under the equitable doctrine of conversion, this change notionally takes place at an earlier stage, as soon as the contract to sell is concluded (see 4.6.3). This doctrine was abolished by TOLATA 1996 in relation to trusts of land.

conveyance An instrument (other than a will) which transfers property from one owner to another.

co-ownership A form of ownership in which two or more people are entitled to possession of the property at the same time. See '**joint tenancy**' and '**tenancy in common**'.

corporeal hereditament See 26.3.2.

covenant A promise made by deed.

covenantee The person with whom a covenant is made, who takes the benefit of the covenant and has a right to enforce the promise.

covenantor The person who makes a covenant, and has the burden or duty of performing the promise.

deed A document which is signed in the presence of a witness as a deed and is then delivered (see 2.6.4.1).

deed of discharge See 14.9.3.

determinable fee See 1.7.1.2.

disclaimer Termination of a lease by the exercise of a statutory power to reject the lease, by persons such as a trustee in bankruptcy or liquidator.

disponee A person to whom a disposition is made.

distress (to levy distress, to distrain) The legal seizure of chattels in order to satisfy some debt or claim; in particular, may be used by the landlord against the tenant in respect of unpaid rent.

dominant tenement A piece of land which is benefited by some right (see '**easement**').

easement A right enjoyed over one piece of land (the 'servient tenement') for the benefit of another piece of land (the 'dominant tenement'), e.g., rights of way, rights of drainage, rights of light. See also '**quasi-easement**'.

encumbrance A liability burdening property.

enlargement Termination of a lease by the tenant's decision to enlarge his long leasehold estate into the freehold estate, in compliance with LPA 1925, s. 153.

entail See '**entailed interest**'.

entailed interest An interest in land inheritable only by the issue (child, grandchild, etc.) of the original grantee; existed only as an equitable interest after 1925 and can no longer be created after TOLATA 1996.

equity of redemption The mortgagor's interest in the property during the continuance of the mortgage.

estate An interest in land which entitles its owner to exercise proprietary rights over that land for a prescribed period.

estate contracts A contract to sell or grant an estate in land. Both parties are bound by the contract, so that either can enforce against the other. The statutory definition of estate contracts which are registrable as class C(iv) land charges (LCA 1972, s. 2(4)(iv)) includes two further rights, the option to purchase and the right of pre-emption, but these do not create the reciprocal rights and duties of the full estate contract.

An option (to purchase an estate or to renew a lease) gives the person entitled the right to compel the owner to sell or grant the estate, but does not impose on him any duty to buy. He is free to exercise the option or not, as he chooses.

A right of pre-emption (or right of first refusal) gives the person entitled a right to be offered the property if the owner decides to sell, but does not impose any duty to sell on the owner, nor any duty to buy on the person entitled.

estate rentcharge A rentcharge (q.v.) created to ensure that the owner of the land, subject to the charge, contributes to maintenance costs or performs some other positive obligation (see 25.5.2.3).

exclusive possession A tenant's right to exclude all others from the land, including the landlord.

estoppel by grant Tenancy by estoppel that arises when the purported grantor of the lease has no estate at all in the leased land.

estoppel by representation Tenancy by estoppel that arises when the purported grantor of the lease represents to the tenant that he has a more extensive estate than he in fact has.

executors See '**personal representatives**'.

fee simple absolute in possession The larger of the two legal estates in land (the other being the term of years absolute: LPA 1925, s. 1) which will last indefinitely, as long as there are persons entitled to take the property under the will of the previous owner or on his intestacy.

fee tail See '**entailed interest**'.

feeding of the estoppel When a tenancy by estoppel is turned into a legal lease, as a result of the landlord acquiring a full legal title to the land.

fine A lump sum paid by a tenant to a landlord at the start of the lease; a premium.

fixed-term tenancy See 9.1.2.1.

foreclosure The procedure by which a mortgagee asks the court to extinguish the mortgagor's equitable right to redeem, and his other rights to the property, and to permit the mortgagee to take the property in satisfaction of the debt or other obligation for which it is security.

forfeiture Termination of a lease by the exercise of the landlord's power to terminate the lease upon a breach of a covenant by the tenant.

fracking The commonly used name for hydraulic fracturing of land.

freehold estate An estate in land for an indefinite term. The only legal freehold estate is the fee simple absolute in possession.

freehold reversion A freeholder's right to recover possession of land upon termination of a lease of that land.

ground rent Periodic payments to a landlord by a tenant of a long lease.

head lease The lease held by a tenant who has granted a shorter lease to a subtenant.

hereditament See 26.3.

incorporeal hereditament See 26.3.2.

infant A minor; a person who has not attained the age of majority, being under the age of 18.

in gross See '**profit à prendre**'.

inhibition See '**caution**'.

in possession Denotes that an interest so described gives a right to present enjoyment of the property, rather than to enjoyment that will not commence until some time in the future.

instrument A legal document whereby a right is created or confirmed or a fact recorded.

intestacy The condition of dying without having made a will.

implied lease Short lease or periodic tenancy arising without formality or express words, by implication from the conduct of the parties.

joint tenancy The form of co-ownership in which each owner is entitled to the whole property, rather than to an undivided share in it. The right of survivorship (*jus accrescendi*) applies here, so that the last surviving tenant becomes solely entitled to the whole property, while those joint tenants who predecease him have no share in the property to pass with their estates. (Compare '**tenancy in common**'.)

land obligation A right in land proposed by the Law Commission as a replacement for covenants in freehold land and some easements (see Chapters 24 and 25).

lease The second legal estate in land ('term of years absolute', LPA 1925, s. 1(1)); an interest which gives the person entitled exclusive possession of the land for a fixed period of time, usually but not essentially, in consideration of the payment of rent. The term 'lease' is used to describe both the estate and the contract creating it. (See also '**tenancy**'.)

lease of the reversion See '**concurrent lease**'.

leasehold estate The term of years absolute.

leasehold reversion A leaseholder's right to recover possession of land upon termination of a sublease of that land.

lessee Tenant under a lease.

lessor Landlord under a lease.

licence Permission (in this context, usually permission to use land).

limitation period The procedure whereby the right to bring an action is barred after the lapse of a prescribed period of time.

merger Termination of a lease by the tenant's acquisition of his landlord's estate with the intention of terminating the lease.

mesne profits The profits lost to the owner of land by reason of his having been wrongfully dispossessed of his land.

minor interest An interest in registered land which required protection by an entry on the register (LRA 1925). The term is not used in LRA 2002.

mortgage The grant of an interest in property as security for the payment of a debt or the discharge of an obligation.

mortgagee The person to whom a mortgage is granted and the interest in the mortgaged property conveyed (see '**mortgage**').

mortgagor The person who creates the mortgage and conveys an interest in his property as security for the payment of a debt, etc. (see '**mortgage**').

nec vi, nec clam, nec precario Literally, 'not by force, nor by stealth, nor by permission'. The phrase describes the way in which one who claims an easement or profit by prescription must have acted during the prescription period.

notice 1. An entry on the register of title to registered land reflecting the existence of an interest binding on the purchaser. 2. Knowledge. (a) actual notice—real knowledge; (b) constructive notice—knowledge which a person is deemed to have, usually because he failed to make the necessary enquiries and is taken to know what they would have revealed; (c) imputed notice—notice belonging to an agent which is ascribed to his principal. Relevant to the "equity's darling defence" available to a purchaser of unregistered land against some equitable interests.

notice to quit The giving of notice by a landlord or a tenant with the intention of terminating a lease that can be terminated by such notice (e.g. a periodic tenancy, a fixed-term lease with a break clause).

option See '**estate contract**'.

overreaching The statutory procedure which enables a purchaser to take the legal estate free from certain equitable interests (arising, for example, under a trust of land or a Settled Land Act settlement), provided the purchase money is paid to two trustees or a trust corporation.

overriding interest An interest in registered land, which does not require protection by entry on the register and binds the registered proprietor and all who acquire later interests in the land (LRA 2002).

overriding lease A concurrent lease, which a landlord may be required to grant under the Landlord and Tenant (Covenants) Act 1995. See 11.2.1.3.

parol lease Lease arising orally or from informal writing.

partition The physical division of land between several co-owners, so that each becomes the sole owner of a separate plot.

periodic tenancy A tenancy that automatically runs from one period to another (week to week, month to month, year to year etc.) until terminated by one of the parties giving notice.

perpetually renewable lease See 10.2.5.2.

personal property (personalty) See 2.10.2 and 26.4.

personal representatives Persons authorised to administer the estate of a dead person. There are two types: executors, who are appointed by will; and administrators, who are appointed by the court in cases of intestacy (i.e., where the deceased leaves no will), or where there is no executor willing or able to act.

personalty See '**personal property**'.

possibility of reverter The right of a grantor to recover the land if a determinable interest comes to an end.

pre-emption (right of) See '**estate contract**'.

prescription A method of acquiring easements or profits by long use.

profit à prendre The right to take something (such as sand, wood, pasture) from land belonging to another. A profit may be appurtenant to a piece of land, that is, it may benefit that land and run with it; or it may be in gross, that is, it may belong to an individual without being attached to a specific piece of land which is benefited by it.

puisne mortgage A legal mortgage of unregistered land which is not protected by the deposit of the title deeds with the mortgagee, and so is registrable as a class C(i) land charge (LCA 1972, s. 2(4)).

purchaser A person who takes an estate or interest by act of parties rather than by operation of law (see 2.6.3.2). When used as a technical term, the word does not have its colloquial meaning of 'buyer', and so one who buys has to be described as 'a purchaser for value'.

quasi-easement A potential easement. The term is used to describe the situation in which land, which is owned and occupied by one person, is used in a way which would constitute an easement if the land was divided into two tenements which were separately owned or occupied (see 24.2.1.2).

real property (realty) See 2.10.1 and 26.4.

registered proprietor The person registered as the owner of a legal estate in registered land.

remainder An interest in land granted under a settlement to take effect after some previous interest (e.g., to A for life, remainder to B in fee simple). A remainder gives a right to possession of the land in the future and so, since 1925, exists only in equity.

rentcharge A right entitling the holder to receive a periodic sum of money from the owner of land charged with that payment. Provision may be made, for example, for the payment of annuities in this way. See also '**estate rentcharge**'. A rentcharge should be distinguished from rent service—the rent due from a tenant to a landlord under a lease.

rent service Payments (generally in money, although sometimes in goods or services) made to a landlord by a tenant holding under a lease.

reservation A method of creating an easement or profit, whereby a grantor retains these rights over the land which he conveys to the grantee.

restriction An entry on the register of title to registered land, setting conditions that must be complied with for the register to be changed.

reversion The right remaining in a grantor after he has granted some interest shorter in duration than his own. The term is used in respect of both settlements and leases. 1. Settlements: the owner of a fee simple, for example, who grants a life interest or (before they were abolished by TOLATA 1996) an entailed interest, has not disposed of his full estate, and therefore retains a right to the land when the interests he has granted come to an end (the property will 'revert' to the grantor). Such a reversion gives a right to possession of the land in the future and so, since 1925, exists only in equity. 2. Leases: an estate owner who grants a lease retains his own legal estate in the land (fee simple or superior lease) throughout the duration of the lease. This interest in the land, which includes the right to receive rents and profits, if any, during the lease, and to recover the physical possession of the land at the end of the term, is called the 'landlord's reversion'.

reversionary lease A lease that does not start immediately but at some time in the future. Contrast the 'lease of the reversion', which arises when a landlord grants concurrent leases over the same land.

rights in personam Rights enforceable against only certain categories of persons.

rights in rem Rights in respect of a piece of land which are enforceable against any person who acquires an estate or interest in that land, e.g., in the case of unregistered land, a legal easement or a legal lease.

seisin Possession (historically, the type of possession enjoyed by the holder of a freehold estate).

servient tenement A piece of land which is burdened by some right (see **'easement'**).

settlement A disposition of property, made inter vivos or by will, whereby the settlor (the estate owner making the settlement) creates a series of successive interests in the property, e.g., a grant to A for life, remainder to B in fee simple.

severance The procedure by which a joint tenant converts his relationship with the other co-owners into that of a tenant in common, so that he has a notional undivided share in the property and is no longer affected by the right of survivorship. Distinguish 'words of severance'.

short lease A lease that of three years or less that complies with the requirements of LPA 1925, s. 54(2) and so can be created by parol (see 9.3.1.1).

socage The surviving form of tenure, by which land in England and Wales is held of the Crown.

statutory owner A person who acts where there is no tenant for life of a Settled Land Act Settlement (see 15.1); if there is no express appointment by settlor, the role is assumed by trustees of settlement.

sublease A lease held by a tenant who has been granted that lease by another leaseholder with a longer term.

surrender Termination of a lease by the tenant's decision, with the landlord's agreement, to relinquish the lease to the landlord.

tack (right to) The right to add a further advance (i.e., a later loan) to an earlier debt secured by a mortgage, so that the additional loan shares the priority of the earlier debt and thus takes priority over any intervening mortgages.

tenancy A lease; the two terms, 'tenancy' and 'lease', are used interchangeably throughout the book.

tenancy at sufferance A right to be in possession of land arising at the end of a lease, when the tenant remains in possession without the consent of the landlord and without objection by the landlord.

tenancy at will A right to possession of land with the permission of the landlord, on terms that the tenancy may be terminated by either party at any time.

tenancy by estoppel A tenancy granted by a landlord with a defective title, who is estopped from denying the validity of the grant.

tenancy in common The form of co-ownership in which each owner has a notional, although undivided, share in the property, which passes with his estate at his death; the right of survivorship does not apply to this form of co-ownership. Compare 'joint tenancy'.

tenant for life The beneficiary under a Settled Land Act settlement who has the right to present (current) enjoyment of the property. Under the Act, the tenant for life holds the legal estate and has statutory powers of management over the settled land.

tenure The set of conditions on which a tenant held land from his feudal lord.

term of years absolute A lease.

title A person's right to property, or the evidence of that right.

transfer The deed used to pass the legal estate in registered land from one owner to another.

trust corporation The Public Trustee or a corporation either appointed by the court in any particular case to be a trustee or entitled by rules made under the Public Trustee Act 1906, s. 4(3), to act as a custodian trustee (LPA 1925, s. 205(1)(xxviii)).

trust for sale A trust which imposes a duty to sell the property. Under TOLATA 1996 this form of trust now takes effect as a trust of land.

trust of land The new form of trust relating to land introduced by TOLATA 1996. Any trust in which some or all of the trust property is land constitutes a 'trust of land'.

undivided shares The interests of tenants in common; sometimes used as another name for tenancy in common.

upwards notice The giving of notice to terminate a lease by a tenant to a landlord.

usual covenants A term of art, denoting a fixed list of covenants to be included in a lease (see 10.1.6).

underlease A lease held by a tenant who has been granted that lease by a subtenant with a longer term.

volunteer A person who takes property without giving value for it.

waste (liability for) The liability of a limited owner, such as a tenant under a lease or a tenant for life of settled land, for any act or omission which alters the state of the land whether for better or worse.

words of severance Words in a grant of property to co-owners, which indicate an intention that the grantees should hold as tenants in common and not as joint tenants.

INDEX

Note: Tables and figures are indicated by an italic "t" and "f ", respectively, following the page number.

abandonment 565–6
abatement 561–2
absence, involuntary 118
absolute (definition) 10
absolute freehold title 102, 174–6
  conditional and determinable fees, differences between 175–6
  conditional interests 174–5, 177
  determinable interests 174–5
  first registration of unregistered estate 104–5
  reverter to transferor on failure to apply for first registration 176
absolute leasehold title 102, 186
  beneficiaries' rights 105
  first registration of unregistered estate 105
  interests noted on register 104
  overriding interests 104
  squatter's rights of which proprietor has notice 104–5
absolute ownership 141, 322–3
absolute right 30
absolute title 103, 108, 155
abstract of title 70
accumulations *see* perpetuities and accumulations
acquiescence 547, 550, 556
  and permission distinction 149, 549
acquisition 323
  adverse *see* adverse possession
  by express grant or reservation 534–5
  by implied grant *see under* easements and profits à prendre
  see also acquisition by prescription
acquisition by prescription 546–61
  acquiescence of servient tenement owner 547
  acquisition based on a fiction 547
  applying three forms of prescription 557–8
  basic rules 547–51
  common characteristics 546–7
  common law 551
  legal interests, creation of 546
  lost modern grant 552–3
  Prescription Act 1832 533
  profits and easements other than light 533–7
    application of rules 555
    consents 554
    deductions 533–5
    long period 554–5
    no interruption 556–7
    period must be 'next before some suit or action' 556
    rules common to both short and long periods 555–7
    short period 533–4
    use to start against fee simple owner 554
    user as of right 555–6
  right must be acquired by fee simple owner against fee simple owner 549–50
  prescription against tenant 549–50
  prescription by tenant 549
  use began before grant of lease 550
  use begins when land is already let 550
  right to light under Prescription Act 1832 557
    interruption 557
    one period only 557
    prevention acquisition of right 557
  use must be continuous 551
  use must be as of right 547–9, 555–6
    acquiescence and permission distinction 549
    implied licence 548–9
    nec clam 548
    nec precario 548
    nec vi 547–8
action by claimant to his detriment in reliance on agreement 388–9
action *in personam* 622
action *in rem* 621–2
actual occupation 50, 78, 126, 127–8
  see also under purchaser protection on registered land
adverse possession 141–69
  acquiescence and permission distinction 149
  burdens and 611
  crime, as 164–5
  human rights 165–9
    general interest grounds 167–8
    proportionate result 168–9
    statutory provisions amounting to interference by state with applicant's rights 167
  land reserved by owner for specific purpose 149–50
  licensees (with permission or consent of owner) 149
  limitation period 142–4, 146, 148, 151, 153–8, 166, 168–9
  LRA 2002 reforms 156–7
  mortgages and charges 497
  must last for prescribed time 151–3
  necessary intention, proving 146
  owner's state of mind 147
  possession 145–8
    fact of 145, 147
    intention to possess 145–8
    must be adverse 148–51
  preventing completion of required period of 152–3
  registered land 103, 104–5, 126, 134, 135, 138, 141, 142, 156, 166, 169

adverse possession (*Cont.*)
  new system 144, 152
  old system 143–4, 151, 155–6
  registered land under LRA 2002 157–64
    application by adverse possessor for registration 158–9
    defence to proceedings 160–3
    squatter registered despite opposition to application 159–60
    what adverse possessor obtains on registration 163
  registered proprietor 150–1
  squatter goes out of possession leaving property vacant 152–3
  squatter provides written acknowledgement of owner's title 152
  tenants under lease 148
  time starts to run 151
  time within which owner may bring claim, extension of 151
  unregistered land 70, 142–3, 151, 153–5
    justification for 143
    limitation period 142–3, 153–4
    third-party rights 154
  unregistered system of title 156
agricultural holdings 219
air, rights to passage of 523, 570
alienation
  restrictions 178–9
  see also non-alienation obligation
allodial land 5, 23t
alteration *see under* registered land
amenity, loss of 573
animals, keeping of, enforcement of covenant against 296–7
annexation 596, 620
  degree of 619
  express 590, 591–2, 597
  implied 590–1
  purpose of 619
  statutory 591–4
appurtenant easements 519
appurtenant profits 91
appurtenant rights 99
appurtenant to land 531
arm's length commercial transaction 476
assault 285, 439
assents 69
assignment 72
  breach committed before 269–70, 276
  breach of covenant against 292–3
  by operation of law 217
  co-ownership 380
  defective 217
  excluded 272, 276
  express 217
  freehold covenants 595, 597
  landlord and tenant obligations 245, 250, 251, 255
  leasehold covenants 271, 282
  leasehold estate 205, 216–17

  of sublease or reversion, effect of 278
  to original guarantor void 272–3
associated persons, right to remain in occupation 458
assurance 414, 417
auctions 47
authorised guarantee agreement 272

bankruptcy 20–1
  application by trustee in 336–7
  family home 384
  leasehold covenants 272
  leasehold estate 221
  licences and their enforcement 442–4, 446
  mortgages and charges 484, 496
  registered land 91, 96, 126
  severance 374
  trusts of land 332–3, 334, 335, 337, 345
bare licences 437–8, 440, 441, 442
bare trust 78, 304, 316, 318
  adverse possession 160
  co-ownership 358
  registered land 128
  trusts of land 315
  unregistered land 76, 86
beneficial interest 24, 144, 340, 349
  co-ownership 357–9, 361–4, 366–7, 368, 370, 374, 376, 379–81
  establishing claim to in sole-name cases 406–7
  family home 382, 384, 456
  joint-names cases (family home) 396, 397, 404
  registered land 97, 98, 117, 120, 128
  sole-name cases (family home) 306, 392–6
  trusts 305, 306
  unregistered land 81, 82–3
  see also equitable interest
beneficial joint tenancy 361, 370, 397, 403
  rebutting presumption of 367–8, 397–400
beneficial owner 24, 317
beneficiaries 24, 81, 105
  under a trust 16, 17, 24, 114, 456, 622
  see also under trusts of land
best rent (market rent) 207–8
bona vacantia (unowned property) 9
breaches
  continuing 290, 291–2
  gross and wilful 210
  not capable of remedy 290–3
  'once and for all' breaches 289, 290, 291–2
  waiver of 288–9
break clauses 186, 219, 222, 223
bribery 165
building schemes 595–8, 604
burdens 599, 611
business or trade, right to prevent use of in a dwelling 15
'buy to let' mortgages 478
buying a house *see* house purchase

car parking *see* parking, rights of
cautions register 97
caveat emptor 243
caveat lessee 244
certainty rule 201, 203
certainty of terms requirement, attempt to avoid determinate term of 199–201, 203
cesser on redemption 468–9, 496
character, change of 520
chargees 337, 466
charges
  'by way of family arrangement' 318
  equitable 502
  limited owner 72
  register 91
  see also land charges; mortgages and charges
charging order 109
chattel mortgage 465
chattels 31, 622
Chief Land Registrar 71, 74
children and minors 120, 151, 305, 317, 326, 338, 360
choses in action 31
choses in possession 31
civil partners *see* spouses or civil partners
classes of title 91, 101–3
  absolute freehold 102
  absolute leasehold 102
  freehold 101
  good leasehold 102–3
  leasehold 101
  possessory freehold and leasehold 103
  qualified freehold and leasehold 103
co-ownership 16, 355–81, 396
  disputes, resolving 335
  ending 379–80
    agreement, by 380
    death 379–80
    partition 379
    sale of property and division of proceeds 379
    union of interests in one of co-owners 379–80
  equitable presumption, under 396
  exclude other(s) from property, right to 378–9
  express declaration 397
  family home 382, 383, 386
  first registration 379
  leasehold estate 194–5
  new way of regulating 316
  payments by co-owner in occupation 331–4
  relationship between co-owners 378–9
  sale of property against wishes of other(s) 378
  severance 397
  statutory trusts 312–14, 358
  tenants in common 396
  trusts 305

trusts of land 315, 318, 319, 330, 334–5, 336, 337
see also joint tenancy; tenancy in common
coercion 20
cohabitants 451–5
  cohabitation contracts 453–4
  constructive trust 454–5
  estoppel 455
  express trust 454
  occupation rights 458
  see also spouses or civil partners
collateral contract 49, 51
collateral covenants 268, 276
commercial leases/property 219, 418
  co-ownership 370
  joint-names cases (family home) 397
  landlord and tenant obligations 242
  leasehold covenants 273, 286–7, 294, 298
  for life 185
  perpetuities, rule against 350
commercial rent arrears recovery (CRAR) 286, 287
common intention 62, 309, 429, 537
  contract 58, 61
  detrimental reliance 408
  family home 385–6, 454, 456
  joint-names cases (family home) 404, 405
  plus detriment 394
  sole-name cases (family home) 388, 392, 407
  to share beneficial interest 396
  see also common intention constructive trusts
common intention constructive trusts 117, 398–9, 402, 428
  co-ownership 369, 370
  detrimental reliance 407
  family home 365–6
  licences and their enforcement 449
  proprietary estoppel 427
  registered land 124
  sole-name cases (family home) 387, 393
commonhold 179–80, 602, 607, 608, 628
  association 180
  community statement 532
compensation
  adverse possession 167, 168
  compulsory acquisition of land 191
  financial 290–1
  house purchase 39
  leasehold estate 220
  registered land 133, 134
  statutory 332
  trusts of land 325, 327
completion
  by registration 109–10
  conveyancing 38, 40
compulsory registration 36–7, 86, 88–9, 208
concurrent interests in land 315
concurrent leases 204
condition precedent 176–7
condition subsequent 177

conditional contract 47
conditional fees 10, 179
   and determinable fees, differences between 175–6
conditional interest 174–5, 177
conduct of the parties 388, 390, 393, 396, 403, 408, 416
confiscation order following criminal conviction 384
conquest, by right 23t
consent 342, 349, 554
   imposed by settlor, requirements for 325–6
   unreasonable withholding of 252–4
conservation covenants 612
constructive notice 21, 80, 82, 83, 88, 126, 346
constructive trusts 19, 24, 305–6, 307–9, 318
   adverse possession 144
   co-ownership 367, 380
   cohabitants 454–5
   common intention 309
   contracts 43, 57, 58–63
   contractual licences 308–9
   detrimental reliance 408
   inferred common intention 392
   informally declared trusts 308
   joint-names cases (family home) 398
   leasehold estate 209
   licences and their enforcement 441, 443–5, 448
   mortgages and charges 473, 498
   proprietary estoppel 308, 412, 427–9
   registered land 91, 92, 136
   sole-name cases (family home) 387, 389, 392, 393, 394, 395–6
   unregistered land 78, 82
   vendor-purchaser 64
   see also common intention constructive trusts; *and under* family home/property
consultation, statutory requirement for 326–7
content, differences of 18–19
continuing breaches 289
continuing purpose, doctrine of 313–14, 381
contracts 41–68
   are not a conveyance 212–13
   collateral 49, 51
   conditional 47
   conveyancing 40
   equitable interest 64–5
      notional conversion of property 65
      purchaser gains rights in equity 64–5
      risk passes to purchaser 65
   estate 19, 25, 72
   estoppel 57–63
      constructive trusts 60–3
      promissory 63
   formality requirements 209
   house purchase 38
   interpretation 238
   made on or after 27 September 1989 42–53, 67–8
      auction 47
      by correspondence 43–5
      land, contracts for sale or other disposition of interest in 42
      missing terms treated as separate contract 49–51
      options 47–8
      rectification 51–2
      short leases 46–7
      signed by both parties 45–6
      third parties 48–9
      trusts 47
      under Financial Services Act 1986 47
      variation 43
      written 42–6
   made before 27 September 1989 53–6, 67
      oral contracts 54–5
      part performance 54, 55–6
      written contracts 54–5
   remedies for breach 66–7
   to create mortgage 472
   variation 43
   see also determination of leases by contract termination; leases as contracts *under* leases; privity of contract
contractual lease 230, 232
contractual licences 192, 203, 308–9, 437, 438–40, 442–5, 456
   implied 449
contractual promises 241
contractual remedies 602
contrary intention 324, 386, 398–400
conversion, doctrine of 311, 313, 330, 378, 617, 622
conveyancing 15, 38–40
   compelling beneficiaries to take 323–4
   completing transaction 40
   contract 40
   electronic 45, 89
   investigating title 40
   two-stage process 38–9
      local land charges 39–40
   unregistered land 84–5
   see also under registered land
corporation leases 202
court, applying to 335
court order 335–6, 482, 485
covenants 15
   collateral 268, 276
   and conditions 241
   conservation 612
   covenantee 241
   covenantor 27, 241, 262–3
   express 241–2, 243, 250, 251, 257
   fit for purpose 246–7
   freehold *see* freehold covenants
   implied 241–2
   indemnity 263, 600
   insurance 292
   'keep-open' 282–3
   landlord 274–5

leasehold *see* leasehold covenants
must 'touch and concern' the land or 'have reference to subject-matter of the lease' 267–8
negative 290, 291, 296, 584, 586–7, 602, 607, 608
personal 268, 273–4
positive *see* positive covenants
registered land 88, 101, 105
restraining sale of registered land without consent of original vendor 601
restrictive *see* restrictive covenants
criminal offences 164–5, 243
see also forgery; fraud; trespass
Crown 5, 6, 9, 10, 12, 23*t*
curtain principle 93, 96
custom 214
customary rights 113

damages 25
contracts 66–7, 602
easements and profits à prendre 562–3, 572, 573
exemplary or punitive 255
freehold covenants 602, 611
landlord and tenant obligations 255
leasehold covenants 262–3, 281, 283
licences and their enforcement 439
'dead hand' control 325, 350
death 37, 272, 311, 412, 442
co-ownership 357, 359, 370, 373, 379–80
leasehold estate 185, 202, 218, 219, 220
trusts of land 318, 319, 322, 331, 337
see also intestacy; wills
debenture 47
declarations 562
contracts 67
trust 304, 317, 382, 489
under LPA 1925 s.84(2) 603–4
see also express declaration
deductions 533–5
deed(s) 19, 25, 26, 40, 88, 106
of discharge 346
executed on or after 31 July 1990 26
executed before 31 July 1990 26
defective assignment 217
defective grant 209, 210, 214
defective lease 472
defective legal mortgage 472
defective title 215
delay, need to avoid 603
delegation and trusts of land 342
demise or subdemise 470
deprivation of possessions 167
depriving tenant of property without reference to a court 294
derivative interest holders, effect of forfeiture on 295–6, 299
derivative interests, removal of 136–8
derogation *see* non-derogation from grant
deserted wife's equity 457

determinable fee 10
determinable interest 174–5
determinate term 199–203
certainty of terms requirement, attempt to avoid 199–201, 203
determination of leases by contract termination 226–30
frustration 226–7
repudiatory breach 227–30
detriment 28, 414, 415, 420–1, 423, 455
detrimental reliance 62, 164, 366, 369, 385, 391, 407–8, 427, 454
devolution of property 311
digital charges 470
'dirty hands' 56, 66
disability, mental or physical 151, 152, 154, 157, 554
discharge 604–5
electronic 496
memorandum of 496
disclaimer 221
discontinuous lease 100
discontinuous possession 208
discrimination, prohibition of 30, 178, 179
disponees 107
dispositions
proceeds of sale 485
testamentary 178
which must be completed by registration 106–7
see also registrable dispositions
dispositive effect (statutory magic) 94–5
disputes
concerning entry on register 97–8
see also under trusts of land
dissolution of marriage *see* divorce or dissolution
distress 285–7
see also distress, landlord's remedy of *under* remedies for breach of leasehold covenants
diversity of occupation 546
divorce or dissolution 314, 339, 372, 383, 387, 391, 452–4, 456–7, 459
domestic violence, protection against 458
dominant tenements *see under* easements and profits à prendre
donees or volunteers 20
double-registration 150
drainage, right to 15, 104, 112, 518, 519, 520, 522, 534
driveways, right to use 15
duty of care 329
in negligence 487

earth, minerals, buildings and fixtures 618–20
easements and profits à prendre 15, 18, 24, 515–75
abandonment 574
acquisition 534–61, 559*f*

easements and profits à prendre (Cont.)
  acquisition by express grant by virtue of LPA
    1925 s.62 540–6
  comparison of rule in *Wheeldon v Burrows*
    and LPA 1925 s.62 546
  conditions for successful claims
    under 542–5
  conveyance must not express a contrary
    intention 543
  diversity of occuption 543–5
  interpretation of s.62 541–2
  must be conveyance upon which s.62 can
    operate 542–3
  nature of grant under 545
  right claimed must be capable of being an
    easement or profit 542
  s.62 540–1
  acquisition by express grant or
    reservation 534–5
  acquisition by implied grant 535–9
  basis of the rule 536
  intended easement and profits 537
  necessity, easements of 535–6
  necessity and intention, overlap
    between 536
  rule in *Wheeldon v Burrows*
    537–9
  acquisition by prescription *see* acquisition by
    prescription
  action 562–4
  adverse possession 149, 154
  air, rights to passage of 523, 570
  ancillary 568
  arising other than by express creation 533
  by estoppel 121
  contract 562*t*
  conveyance must not express a contrary
    intention 543
  creation of 560–1*t*
  diversity of occupation 543–5
  dominant and servient tenements 15,
    517–22, 525, 529, 533
    appurtenant 518–19
    change of character 520
    coming into same hands 565
    easement of forming subject matter of
      grant 521
    easement must accommodate dominant
      tenement 519–21
    owners must be different persons 519
    use to benefit additional land 520–1
  drainage, rights to 15, 104, 112, 518, 519,
    520, 522, 534
  easement (definition) 517–30
  easement examples 521–30
  easement use amounting to actual
    occupation of servient land
    120–1
  enforcement against purchaser of servient
    tenement 532–4
    registered land 532–3, 534*t*
    unregistered land 533–4

  equitable 27, 532, 533, 534, 546
    contract 64
    land charges 73
    licences and their enforcement 446
    for life 531
    unregistered land 74, 81
  estovers, profit of 530
  existing easements, conversion of 542
  express easement 568
  express grant or reservation 560*t*
  express release of registered interests 571
  expressly created 533
  extensive use 570–1
  extinguishment 564–7
    by abandonment 565–6, 571
    dominant and servient tenements coming
      into same hands 565
    easements benefiting leasehold property
      ending on merger of lease and
      reversion 566–7
    implied release 565–6
    release 565
  facilities, rights to use of 523
  fencing, easement of 523–4, 529,
    601–2
  flying freehold 626–8
  freehold covenants 569, 607, 609, 612
  future easements 353
  hereditaments 621
  implied easements 546, 567, 568, 570
  implied grant *see* implied grant
  implied rights 528
  landlord and tenant obligations 251
  Lands Chamber jurisdiction
    571–2
  law reform 567–75
    future of 574
    interaction with proposals on land
      obligations 570
    Law Commission recommendations
      2011 568–72
    light, rights to 572–4
    LPA 1925 s.62 568–9
    necessity for 567
    registered land rules 571
  leasehold estate 190, 569
  legal or equitable 29, 79, 531–2
    creation by deed 531–2
    prescribed period 531
  licences, conversion of 541–2
  light *see* light, right to
  long period 554–5, 557–8, 567
  must be conveyance upon which s.62 can
    operate 542–3
  necessity, easements of 535–6
  negative easements 538, 570
  new easement, establishment of 524–30
    compatibility test 527
    must be a right 529
    must not be mere right of recreation and
      amusement 528
    must not be too wide and too vague 525

must not deprive servient owner of possession 525–8
no new negative easements 529
not involving expenditure 529–30
non-use 565
overriding interests 532–3
  dispositions of registered estate 532–3
  first registration 532
  protection by entry of notice on title of servient tenement 533
parking, rights of 121, 523, 526–7, 528, 570–1
pasture, profit of 530
piscary, profit of 530
positive easements 529, 538
prescription 520, 524, 532, 533, 544, 560–1t, 567, 569–70, 572
profits à prendre
  appurtenant can change character 530–1
  appurtenant or in gross 530
  creation of 568
  definition 530–1
  examples 530
proprietary estoppel 425
qualifying use 569
quasi-easements see quasi-easements
registered land 88, 91, 95, 99, 101, 104, 106–7, 111–13, 125–8
release 565
remedies 561–7
  abatement 561–2
  action 562–4
  nuisance, claim in 563–4
right claimed must be capable of being an easement or profit 542
rights of way see rights of way
rules in Re Ellenborough Park 517–21
servient tenement 517–18, 520, 523, 527–8, 529, 533, 534
short forms for creation of easements 571
short period 533–4, 558
spurious easements 523
statutory magic and registered interests 571
storage, rights of see storage, rights of
support, right to 523, 529, 540, 562, 564, 570, 607
termination of estate to which interest in appurtenant 571
trusts of land 323
turbary, profit of 530
unity of seisin 571
unregistered land 80
water, rights to 15, 522, 529, 570
electronic discharge 496
embankments 113
encumbrances 17, 108, 132
enforcement
  against purchaser 457
    for value 446–8
  against successors in title 249
  against third parties 211–12

of covenants between assignees of lease and reversion 270–1, 277
of covenants in the lease 212
leasehold covenants see under leasehold covenants
enlargement, deed of 221
entailed interest 7, 10, 318
entry on register, types of see under registered land
entry, rights of 18, 23, 81
epitome of title 70
'equality is equity' 393
equitable accounting 331–4
equitable charges 502
equitable estoppel 410–11, 415
  see also promissory estoppel; proprietary estoppel
equitable interests 8, 9, 10, 19, 20, 21, 23–8, 473
  beneficiary under trust of legal estate 24
  co-ownership 355–6, 374, 378
  contracts 64–5
  estate contracts 25
  former legal estates becoming 10
  freehold estate 174, 175, 176
  in land 18
  leasehold covenants 271
  leasehold estate 183, 185, 187, 191
  mortgages and charges 467, 505
  not created formally 26–7
  options 25
  other rights to equitable relief 28
  priorities see under mortgages
  proprietary estoppel 28
  registered land 109, 110, 112, 127–8
  restrictive covenants 27
  trusts 303, 310, 313
  trusts of land 330, 344
  unregistered land see under unregistered land
equitable leases 27, 215
  arising from specifically enforceable contracts 210
  compared with legal leases 211–13
  contract 64
  effect of 210–11
  leasehold covenants: enforcement 268, 276
  leasehold estate 212–13
  mortgages and charges 467
  privity of estate 269, 276
equitable mortgage see under mortgages and charges
equitable ownership 532
equitable presumption 396
equitable principles, application of and need for notice or modern equivalent 588–9
equitable remedies 28
  discretionary 211
equitable right to redeem 475
equities are equal 499–500
equity arising from estoppel, nature of 424–6
  benefiting representor's successors in title 426

equity arising from estoppel, nature of (*Cont.*)
    binding representor's successors in
        title 425–6
equity follows the law 367, 397
equity of redemption 468, 475, 481, 494–5
'equity regards as done that which ought to
        be done' 25, 27, 64, 210, 211, 217,
        311, 472
equity, satisfying in proprietary
        estoppel 421–4
equity will not assist a volunteer 416
'equity's darling' 20, 75, 76, 84
escheating 6, 7, 9
estate contracts 19, 25, 72
estate in fee simple absolute in possession
        see freehold estate
estate, privity of *see* privity of estate
estates in land 3–13, 89
    meaning 5–6, 11–12
    tenure 6
    see also commonhold; freehold estates;
        leasehold estates; legal estates; privity
        of estate
estoppel 16, 28
    adverse possession 159, 160, 164
    by acquiescence 416
    cohabitants 455
    contracts 43, 56, 57–63
    easements and profits à prendre 532
    equitable 410–11, 415
    licences 440–1, 449–50, 498
    mortgages and charges 504
    promissory 63, 410–11
    registered land 98
    unregistered land 81
    used as shield not a sword 410
    see also proprietary estoppel; tenancies by
        estoppel
estovers, profit of 530
eviction 190, 225, 285, 480
exceptional circumstances 139, 159, 228
exclusion of others from property, right to
        enforce 378–9
exclusion or restriction of right to occupy 331
exclusive occupation 163, 197, 198–9
exclusive possession 145, 192–9
    attributable to another property right or
        relationship 198
    exclusive occupation, and 198–9
    homeless, accommodation for 196
    land in shared occupation 194–6
    leasehold estate 205
    no intention to create legal relations 197–8
    no lease despite apparent grant of 196–8
    written terms inconsistent with 192–4
executors 372
exempt leases 251
existing settlements and trusts for sale, effect
        on 316–18
express agreement 206, 283, 388
express covenants 241–2, 243, 250, 251, 257

express declaration
    co-ownership 397
    joint tenancy and tenancy in
        common 360–2
    conclusiveness 362
    making express declaration 361–2
    no express declaration 362
    registered land 361–2
    unregistered land 361
express exclusion 568
    of continuing liability 274–5
express grant 214, 524, 545, 549, 568
    legal lease 206–8
    lease for term longer than seven years 208
    seven-year leases 208
    short leases satisfying LPA 1925 207–8
express terms 199, 238, 239, 247
express trusts 304–5, 306, 316, 318, 321, 331,
        334, 454
extensive use 570–1
extinguishment 564–7, 571

facilities, rights to use of 523
fair trial, right to 30, 166, 167, 286
false imprisonment 439
family arrangements, friendship or
        generosity 197–8, 412
family home/property 314, 382–408
    co-ownership 355, 362, 363, 378
    cohabitants, claims between 383–4
    constructive trusts *see* resulting and
        constructive trusts *below*
    detrimental reliance 407–8
    family relationships 451–2
    homesharing 452
    ownership 382–3
    potential problems 452
    property adjustment orders on divorce or
        dissolution 383
    reform 458–61
        available relief 459–60
        eligibility criteria 459
        future prospects 461
        Law Commission recommendations/
            reviews 459–61
        Scotland 460–1
    resulting and constructive trusts 365, 383,
        384–6
        distinction importance of 385
        evidence justifying finding of 385
        failure to distinguish between
            384–5
        relevance to family homes 385–6
        size of share in property 385
        sole-name and joint-names cases 386
    right to remain in occupation 456–8
        beneficiary under trust, as 456
        contractual licence or by proprietary
            estoppel, under 456
        statutory right of occupation, under
            457–8

right to share in value of 453–6
  cohabitants 453–5
  mortgagee in claim for possession, against 455–6
  spouses and civil partners 453
special rights 451–61
  reform 458–61
  right to remain in occupation 456–8
  right to share in value of property 453–6
third parties, claims involving 384
trusts 307, 309, 310, 312, 314
trusts of land 330, 334, 339
see also joint-names cases; sole-name cases; and under joint tenancy
family relationships 451–2
  breakdown of 313
  cohabitation 451–2
  homesharing 452
  marriage or civil partnership 451
family settlements 185, 205, 348
fee farm rents 175
fee simple 7, 8, 9–10, 11, 22, 29, 174, 549–50
  landlord and tenant obligations 239
  leasehold estate 203–4, 215
  registered land 89
  in remainder 177
  trusts 310
  trusts of land 319, 320
  unregistered land 76
fee simple absolute 11
  free from condition 178
  in possession 12, 18, 19
fee tail 7, 8, 174, 183, 310
  see also entailed interest
fees, modified 174
fencing easements 523–4, 529, 601–2
financial compensation from central fund 132
fines 185
first created gets priority rule 502
first refusal, right of 72
first registration of unregistered estate 86, 98–106
  compulsory first registration 99–101
    reform 100
    what happens if application not made 100
    who has to apply 100
  effect of 104–6
    absolute freehold title 104–5
    absolute leasehold title 105
    good leasehold title 106
    possessory title 106
  freehold estate 106
  process 101–3
    classes of title 101–3
    interests affecting registered estate 103
    investigation of title by registry 101
  voluntary first registration 98–9
    leases with more than seven years to run 98
    registrable interests in land 99
    short registrable leases 98–9
'first in time prevails' 109

fishing rights 531
  see also piscary, profit of
fit for purpose covenant 246–7
  furnished houses 247
  leases subject to Homes (Fitness for Human Habitation) Act 2018 247
  low-rent housing 247
fitness for human habitation requirement 243
fixed term lease 17, 19, 22, 148, 184, 203, 214, 218–19, 256
fixed-term in old 'royal lives' trusts 353
flying freeholds 626–8
flying (overflying land) 623
foreclosure 482, 486, 488
forfeiture 210, 221, 222, 229, 283, 375–6
  see also under remedies for breach of leasehold covenants
forgery 135–7, 138, 337, 339, 374
formality rules 19, 502
former tenants, protection of 263–4
four unities 194, 196, 360, 376
  unity of interest 194–5, 360
  unity of possession 194, 359, 360
  unity of time 194, 359
  unity of title 194, 359
fracking 623–6
franchise 99, 113
fraud 20, 28, 66, 308
  adverse possession 144, 146, 151
  co-ownership 362, 372
  registered land 93, 95, 109, 133, 135–6, 138, 139
  setting aside sale in cases of 495
  see also liability for fraud/negligence under mortgages and charges
fraudulent misrepresentation 136–8
freedom of conscience and religion 179
freedom of testation 178
freehold covenants 180, 577–613
  annexation
    express 590
    implied 590–1
    statutory 591–4
  application of rules 584
  assignment 595
  benefits 599
  building schemes 595–8
  burden can run in equity 585–9
  burdens and adverse possession 611
  burdens do not run at common law 584–5
  commonhold 602, 604, 607
  conservation covenants 612
  covenantee must have owned benefited land 587–8
  discharge 604–5
    common ownership 604
    Housing Act 1985 s.610 605
    Lands Chamber, application to 604–5
  easements 607
  enforceability: original parties 579–81
    alternative 581

freehold covenants (*Cont.*)
   burden and benefit 579
   LPA 1925 s.56 579–80
   mischief addressed by statute 581
   enforceability: successors of original parties 581–98
     after sale by covenantee: benefit passes to new owner 581–4
     after sale by covenantor: burden passes to new owner 584–9
     burden and benefit to run in equity 589–98
     equitable principles, application of and need for notice or modern equivalent 588–9
   estate rentcharges, creation of 601
   fencing 601–2
   granting leases 600
   indemnity covenants 600
   intention for burden to run 583, 588
   land obligations *see* land obligations
   Lands Chamber, powers of 611–12
   legal estate in land held by covenantee 583
   letting schemes 598
   local authorities: statutory powers 602
   long leases which are then converted to freehold estates 601
   negative covenant 586–7
   old rules, abolition of 609
   positive covenants, problems of 598–602
     evasion of rules by drafting techniques 600–2
     exception to the rule: *Halsall v Brizell* 598–600
     local authorities, statutory powers of 602
   positive obligations 610
   reform 606–13
     current rules, problems of 606
     Law Commission Report 2011 607–12
     past proposals 606–7
     proposals 606
   registered land 589
   remedies 602–4, 611
     contractual 602
     declaration under LPA 1925 s.84(2) 603–4
     delay, need to avoid 603
   restraining sale of registered land without consent of original vendor 601
   restrictive obligations 610
   successor claiming to enforce covenant must derive title from or under original covenantee 583–4
   'touching and concerning' 582–3
   transmission of part of burdened land 610–11
   unregistered land 589
freehold estate 6–7, 8, 9–10, 12, 22, 101, 173–80
   absolute (definition) 10
   absolute freehold title 174–6
   adverse possession 141, 154
   commonhold 179–80
   estates in land 6–7, 9–10
   fee simple 7, 9–10, 174
   fee tail 7
   first registration of unregistered estate 106
   former legal estates becoming equitable interests 10
   leases for life or until marriage 185
   life estate 7
   old rules relating to 6–7
   in possession (definition) 10
   possessory freehold title 176–7
   public policy, intervention of 178–9
     alienation, restrictions on 178–9
     human rights aspects 179
     redemption postponement 476
   registered land 89, 91, 98
   term of years 183
freehold reversion 189, 204
freehold tenure 6
freehold title 103
   see also possessory freehold title
frustration 218, 229
furnished houses 246, 247
further term, obligation to grant 249–50
   enforcement against successors in title 249
   perpetually renewable leases 249–50
future easements 353
future enjoyment of land 177
future inheritance 412–14
future interests 10, 176–7, 320, 328
   adverse possession 151, 152, 154, 157
future leases, compulsorily registrable 116
future rights, expectations of 412–14

gambling on premises 292
gazumping 38
gazundering 39
general equitable charge 72, 505
general heirs 7, 9
general interest 169
general trusts 354
gentlemen's agreement 418
gift(s) 350, 351–2, 416, 443, 512
   adverse possession 153
   estates in land 7, 10
   express and implied trusts 306, 307
   family home 404
   house purchase 33, 37
   interest in land 20
   leasehold estate 173, 177, 178
   registered land 94, 100, 110
   trusts of land 326
'good against the world' 19
good faith 20, 21, 77, 126, 494
good root of title 70, 74
grant 99, 100, 111, 112, 350, 600
   defective 209, 210, 214
   see also express grant; implied grant; non-compliance with requirements for legal grant; non-derogation from grant
gratuitous licence 440
grazing rights 15, 112, 147, 530–1, 558

see also pasture, profit of
gross, right in 99
ground rent 180, 206, 239
guarantors 264, 272

harassment 285
hardship caused by privity of contract 263
'have reference to the subject matter of the lease' 270, 275
'he who comes to equity must come with clean hands' 210, 474, 588
head lease/head landlord 188, 233–4, 580
  attempts to enforce covenants in sublease 278–9
  landlord and tenant obligations 245
  lease ended on landlord's initiative 223
  lease ended on tenant's initiative 222–3
  leasehold covenants 258, 260, 274, 277, 278–9, 295–6
hereditaments 620–1
  corporeal and incorporeal 621
  LPA 1925 definition 620–1
home rights 16, 73, 453, 457–8
home-sharing agreements 452
homeless persons
  accommodation for and exclusive possession 196
  and licence agreements 230
homicide, forfeiture as result of 375–6
hostel accommodation 196
house purchase 35–40
  properties and parties 35
  two systems of title 36–8
    compulsory registration 36–7
    investigating title 38, 40
    registered system 36, 37–8
    unregistered system 36, 38
    what buyer wants to know 36
    which system applies 36–8
  see also conveyancing
housing associations 196, 201
housing, low-rent 247
housing trusts 230–1, 233
human rights 29–30, 165–9, 179, 225, 233, 286–7
hydraulic fracturing *see* fracking

illegality principle 164
immorality 292, 437
implied grant 112, 213–14, 524, 533, 539–40, 545, 549, 560t
  'continuous and apparent' 538–9
  elements of the rule 538–9
  'necessary for reasonable enjoyment of the property' 539
  rule 538
  simultaneous sales 539
  'in use by owner at time of sale 539
implied power to postpone sale 317, 325
implied release: abandonment 565–6
implied terms 238
implied trusts 24, 304, 305–9, 316, 318

co-ownership 356
constructive trusts 305–9
family home 366, 384
resulting trusts 305–7
sole-name cases (family home) 387, 389, 407
trusts of land 336
imputing intention 401–3
in personam rights 19–20
in rem rights 19
incapacity *see* disability, mental or physical
incorrect names 73
indemnity
  covenants 263, 600
  see also under registered land
index map search 38
Index of Minor Interests 501
inferred common intention constructive trust 392
inferred intention 396, 401–3
informal mortgage by deposit of deeds 472–3
informally declared trusts 308
inheritance
  trusts 313
  see also entailed interest
injunctions
  contracts 67
  easements and profits à prendre 562–3, 573
  freehold covenants 602, 611
  interim 603
  landlord and tenant obligations 255
  leasehold covenants: remedies for breach 281
  licences and their enforcement 439, 440
  mandatory 602, 603
  trusts of land 325, 327
Inland Revenue charges 72, 126
inspecting the land 125
instalment mortgages 474, 486
insurance 93, 257, 480
  covenants 292
intangible rights 31, 621
intention 198, 213, 241, 395, 417–18, 436, 583, 620
  change of 368–9, 400–1, 429
  contrary 324, 386, 398–400
  express 257
  implied 257
  imputing 406
  inferred 396, 401–3
  proving necessary intention 146
  subjective test of 417
  to occupy, continuing 118
  to possess 145–8
interdependent properties 179–80
interest
  contingent or conditional 177
  determinable 174–5
  entailed 7, 10, 318
  equitable *see* equitable interests
  first 502
  'in gross' 519
  individual 168

interest (*Cont.*)
　noted on register for absolute leasehold
　　　title 104
　in possession 331
　prior to mortgagee 510–13
　　undue influence 511–13
　proprietary 231, 438
　second 502
　subject to condition subsequent 175
　unregistered 503
　see also future interests; interests in land;
　　　overriding interests
interest rates 478
interests in land 12, 14–31
　allodial land 23*t*
　any other similar charge on land not created
　　　by an instrument 23
　charge by way of legal mortgage 22
　conquest, by right of 23*t*
　Crown 23*t*
　entry, rights of 23
　equitable interests 23–8
　human rights 29–30
　law and equity distinction 18–21
　legal 18, 19, 22, 79
　life interest 10
　modern approach to protection of rights 29
　multiplicity of rights 28–9
　property, classification of 30–1
　rentcharges 22
intestacy 7, 9, 413, 442, 620
　adverse possession 160
　co-ownership 357, 370
　registered land 100, 110
　succession on freehold estate 174, 177
　trusts 305, 313
　trusts of family home 404
　unregistered land 69
investigating title *see* house purchase
irremediable harm, breaches causing 292
irrevocable licence 440
irrevocable offer 47
Islamic mortgages 470–1

joint tenancies 194
　beneficial 361, 370, 397, 403
　co-ownership 356–7, 396
　effect on, of determination of head
　　　lease 224–5
　express declaration 360–2
　family home 364–70, 382
　　beneficial joint tenancy, scope of
　　　　presumption of 370
　　changing intentions 368–9
　　co-ownership 370
　　common intention constructive
　　　　trusts 365–6
　　implied trusts 366
　　　rebutting presumption of beneficial joint
　　　　tenancy 367–8
　　resulting trusts 365
　four unities requirements 359–60
　joint-names cases *see* joint-names cases
　leasehold estate 196, 199, 229
　necessary conditions 359–60
　number and age of joint tenants 360
　severance 358–9, 370–7
　　bankruptcy 374
　　forfeiture as result of homicide 375–7
　　joint tenancy into tenancy in
　　　　common 370–1
　　methods of 371
　　mortgage 374
　　mutual agreement 374–5
　　no severance by will 375
　　notice in writing 371–3
　　protection of former joint tenant's interest
　　　　after 377
　　sale 373–4
　　service of notice 372–3
　　'sever tenancy in equity' 373–5
　　tenancy in common 375
joint venture 58
joint-names cases 382, 383, 396–406
　after *Stack v Dowden* 403–6
　beneficial joint tenancy, presumption of 397
　changing intentions: *Jones v Kernott* 400–1
　co-ownership 396–7
　contrary intention, evidence of 398–400
　inferring or imputing intention: *Jones v
　　　Kernott* 401–3
　rebutting presumption of beneficial joint
　　　tenancy 397–400
　resulting and constructive trusts 386
　resulting trusts, irrelevance of 397–8
　Stack v Dowden and *Jones v Kernott* 397

'keep-open' covenants 282–3
keeping land in use 143
knowledge
　actual or imputed 547
　role of 125–7

land 617–28
　commonhold 628
　definition 617–18
　earth, minerals, buildings and
　　　fixtures 618–20
　　basic rule 618–19
　　items not fixed to land 619–20
　flying freeholds 626–8
　hereditaments 620–1
　land-locked 535, 537, 540
　ownership, extent of 623–6
　practical approach to land law 628
　real and personal property 621–2
　reserved by owner for specific
　　　purpose 149–50
　settled 309–10
　in shared occupation 194–6
　tax 18, 23
　theft 143

unavailable or unsuitable for occupation 331
land charges 71–9
  Class A 71, 76
  Class B 71, 76
  Class C 71–2, 74, 76–7, 78, 213, 249, 276, 505, 506f, 507, 510, 633, 637
  Class D 72–3, 74, 76–7, 589
  Class E 73
  Class F 73, 76, 457
  nature of 71
  non-registration 75–9
    judicial interpretation 77
    purchaser for value and purchaser for money or money's worth distinction 77
    registered land, comparison with 78
    right still enforceable against original owner 78–9
  registered land 108
  registration 73–5
    incorrect names 73
    searching against names of all past estate owners 74–5
  search certificates, importance of obtaining 79
  unregistered land 70
Land Charges Register 29, 70–1, 75–6, 79, 88, 249, 505
land obligations 606–7
  creation of 609
  enforceability of benefit of 609
  enforceability of burden of 609–11
  freehold covenants 606–7
  negative or positive 608–9, 611
  registered titles 609
Land Registry 19, 29, 37, 38, 40
  adverse possession 157
  co-ownership 362
  easements and profits à prendre 566
  error or omission 105
  mortgages and charges 489
  registered land 87, 88, 91, 93, 97, 98, 127, 128, 136–7
  unregistered land 86
Land Registry Annual Report 74
land-locked land 535, 537, 540
landlord and tenant obligations 238–57
  covenants and conditions 241
  express and implied covenants 241–2
  fit for purpose covenant 246–7
  further term, grant of 249–50
  landlord entry to premises 256
  landlord's intention to force tenant to leave premises 243
  non-alienation obligation 251–5
  non-derogation from grant 245–6
  physical interference by landlord 243
  quiet enjoyment 243–5
  rent 250–1
  repair (landlord's) covenant 247–9
  shared responsibilities 256–7
  insurance 257
  repair 257
  tenant's covenant to pay rates and other taxes on premises 256
  usual covenants 242
  waste 255–6
landlords
  covenants 274–5
  failure to repair 285
  peaceful re-entry by 286, 480, 486
  repairing obligations see repair and maintenance obligations of landlord
  rights of entry obligation 256
  and tenants relationship 187–8
  see also forfeiture, landlord's remedy of under remedies for breach of leasehold covenants; landlord and tenant obligations
Lands Chamber of the Upper Tribunal 571–2, 574, 604–5, 611–12
law and equity distinction 18–21
  content, differences in 18–19
  formality rules, differences in 19
  third parties, different effect on 19–21
leasehold covenants 204, 227, 276
  enforcement 258–80
    assignees 262
    old leases 258–9
    see also leasehold covenants under subtenants
  enforcement - new leases 271–7
    between assignees of lease and reversion 277
    breach committed before assignment 276
    privity of contract 271–5
    privity of estate 275–6
    release of original covenantor 276
  enforcement - old leases 261–71
    between assignees of lease and reversion 270–1
    breach committed before assignment 269–70
    continuing liability of original landlord and tenant 270
    option to purchase reversion 271
    privity of contract 260, 261–5
    privity of estate 260, 265–9
  new leases 258–9
  remedies for breach see remedies for breach of leasehold covenants
  subtenants 260–1
leasehold estate 6, 8, 9, 11, 17, 182–236
  adverse possession 154, 158
  commonhold 180
  creation 235–6t
  estates in land 8, 11
  freehold and leasehold reversions 189
  inference 199
  leasehold covenants 295
  no requirement to be in possession 186–7
  redemption postponement 477

leasehold estate (*Cont.*)
  registered land 89, 98
  requirements 235t
  reversion 186, 189, 217, 469
  termination 236t
  title 101, 102–3, 106
  transfer 235–6t
  types of 234–5t
  see also leases
leasehold title, possessory and qualified 103
leases 11, 16, 96
  basic requirements 189–206
    determinate term 199–203
    exclusive possession 192–9
    importance of basic requirements 190–1
    overview of 191–2
    rent 205–6
    term less than that of grantor 203–5
  by estoppel 478
  concurrent 204
  as contracts 225–34
    Bruton tenancy 230–4
    determination of leases by contract termination 226–30
    landlord and tenant relationship 187–8
    non-proprietary lease creation 232
    non-proprietary lease and third parties 232–3
    tenancy by estoppel, court finding 232
  corporation 202
  creation 206–16
    express grant of legal lease 206–8
    implied grant of legal lease 213–14
    implied periodic tenancy 213–14
    non-compliance with requirements for legal grant 208–13
    tenancies by estoppel 215–16
    tenancy by sufferance 214
  defective 472
  determination 217–25
    common law rules 218–21
    disclaimer 221
    effect of agreement between parties 223–4
    effect on joint tenant of determination of head lease 224–5
    effect on subtenant of determination of head lease 221–4
    effect of surrender on merger 222
    enlargement, deed of 221
    forfeiture 221
    head lease ended on landlord's initiative 223
    head lease ended on tenant's initiative 222–3
    merger 221
    notice to quit 219–20
    statutory protection 218
    surrender 220–1
    term, expiry of 218–19
  discontinuous 100
  effect of agreement between parties 223–4
  equitable *see* equitable leases
  exempt 251
  fixed term 17, 19, 22, 148, 184, 203, 214, 218–19, 256
  future leases, compulsorily registrable 116
  implied 197
  leasehold covenants: remedies for breach 298
  legal 79, 211–12
  as legal estates in land 183–7
    absolute 186
    fixed term and periodic tenancies 184
    leases for life or until marriage 185
    no requirement for leasehold estate to be in possession 186–7
    tenancies at will 185–6
    term of years 183–6
  legal parol 268–9
  for life or until marriage 185
  long *see* long leases
  made by deed 265–8
  new 278
  non-proprietary 230, 232, 233–4
  overriding 72, 263, 264
  perpetually renewable 19, 249–50
  personal 232
  proprietary 232
  real and personal property 622
  regulated 206
  reversionary 186, 199, 204, 207, 221
  right to grant 478–9
  right to (mortgagee) 480–1
  seven-year 208
  short *see* short leases
  subject to Homes (Fitness for Human Habitation) Act 2018 247
  subleases *see* subleases
  superior 171
  for term longer than seven years 208
  transfer 216–17
    assignments by operation of law 217
    express assignments 217
  underleases 188–9, 204, 245
    see also head lease/head landlord
legal charges 107, 502
legal easements 29, 79, 532
legal estates 10, 11, 12
  in land 8–9, 190
  see also legal estates in land *under* leases
legal interests 191, 546
  in land 18, 19, 22, 79
legal leases 79, 212
  implied 211
legal memory 553
legal mortgage *see under* mortgages and charges
legal owner 24
legal parol leases 268–9
'legal rights are good against the world' 79
legal title 303, 355
letting schemes 598

liability 262
  for fraud/negligence *see under* mortgages and charges
  of original landlord and tenant, continuing 270
  restriction of
    for rent or service charge 264
    where tenancy is subsequently varied 264
licences 16, 433–50
  bare 437–8, 440, 441, 442
  charge 437
  contractual 192, 203, 308–9, 437, 438–40, 442–5, 456
  distinguished from easements 435–6
  distinguished from leases 435
  enforcement 436
  estoppel 438
    licences protected by 440–1
    licences and successors in title 445–8
    reliance on 448
    and successors in title 445–8
  gratuitous 440
  implied 149–50, 548–9
  interest, coupled with 436–7, 438, 442
  interests in land, whether becoming 448–9
  irrevocable 440, 443, 450
  landlord and tenant obligations 251
  leasehold estate 193, 195, 197–8
  licensor, enforcement against 438–41
  mortgages and charges 511
  periodic 440
  permanent or long-term 441
  proprietary estoppel 426
  residential 218
  statutory protection, limited 440
  successors of licensor, enforcement against 441–8
    against purchaser for value 446–8
  transferability 449
  types of 436–8
licensee 16, 119, 149, 196
  at will 440
lie in grant 521
life estates 7, 8, 174, 183–4, 319–20
  in remainder 177
life interest in possession 177
life tenancy 185, 201, 322
light, right to 15, 517, 522, 529, 537–8, 544, 557
  acquisition by prescription 551, 553
  amount of light 522
  extinguishment 565
  interruption 557
  one period only 557
  prevention of acquisition of 557
  reform 569–70, 572–4
  remedies 563
limitation period 70, 176, 186, 485, 607, 611, 627
  adverse possession 142–4, 146, 148, 151, 153–8, 166, 168–9
living memory (at least 20 years) 552

loans 5, 39, 296, 364, 443
  contract 61, 64
  express and implied trusts 306, 307
  family home 391, 404
  interests in land 17, 22, 30
  mortgages and charges 465–74, 476–8, 481–2, 486, 488, 498, 503, 509–11
  registered land 95, 114, 120, 127
  trusts of land 335, 336, 337, 339, 343
local authorities: statutory powers 602
local land charges 39–40, 113
Local Land Charges Register 557
lockout agreement 48
long leases 207, 241, 242, 251, 257, 294, 298
  converted to freehold estates 601
long period 554–5
loss of benefit with loss of burden 275
lost modern grant 552–3, 556, 558
  continued existence of the form of prescription 552–3
  rebutting presumption that grant was made 552
low-rent housing 247
lump sum payment (premium or fine) 205–6

maintenance *see* repair and maintenance obligations of landlord
manorial right 113
marriage settlement 310
mental incapacity *see* disability, mental or physical
mere equity 28, 425, 428, 448, 504, 512
mere life estate 310
mere permission 436
mere pretence 195
merger 221
mesne profits 214, 294
mines and minerals 100, 113
  see also fracking
minor interest 532
minors *see* children and minors
mirror principle 93
mischief addressed by statute 581
misrepresentation 66
mistake 28, 133–8, 139, 349
  adverse possession 143, 150, 151, 160
  correction of 108, 133, 135
  reasonable mistake as to boundaries 160
mistaken belief 161, 164
mixed motives 419–20
mixed trusts 320
money judgment 482
Monk-notice 225
mortgagee *see under* mortgages and charges
mortgages and charges 17, 30, 465–97
  creation of mortgage 467–8
  end of mortgage 17, 496–7
    formalities 496
    passage of time 496–7
  equitable mortgage 27, 29, 76, 95, 109, 467, 472–3

mortgages and charges (*Cont.*)
  contract to create mortgage 472
  disadvantages of 489–90
  equitable charge 473
  of equitable interest 473
  informal mortgage by deposit of deeds 472–3
  remedies, problems with 488–9
instalment mortgage 474, 486
Islamic mortgages 470–1
landlord and tenant obligations 251
leasehold estate 205
legal mortgage 18, 29, 76, 79, 99, 107, 467, 468–71, 489, 502
  charge by way of 22, 469–71
  defective 472
  fee simple, of 468–9
  grant of as trigger for first registration 471
  registration of charges 471
  registration not triggered 471
  second mortgage 116, 468, 469
  term of years, of 469
liability for fraud/negligence 491–6
  mortgagees, duties of 492–4
  receivers, duties of 494–5
  setting aside sale in cases of fraud 495
  valuers 496
LPA 1925 reforms 468
mortgagees 22, 337, 364, 454, 466, 498
  can elect not to exercise powers 492
  on claim for possession, against 455–6
  collateral advantages for 477–8
  duties 492–4
  duty to obtain market value 493–4
  is not a trustee of his powers 492–3
  legal 482–8
  may sell property as it is 493
  in possession 197
  in possession must take reasonable care of premises 492
  protection for 295–6
  receiver 30
  subsequent 490
mortgagees, remedies of 481–90
  disposition of proceeds of sale 485
  foreclosure 482, 488
  legal mortgagee 182–8
  possession and sale 483–4, 488
  protection for mortgagor 485–7
  protection for tenants of mortgagor 487
  receiver, appointing 487–8, 489
  sale, effect of 484–5, 488–9
mortgagees, rights of 479–81
  insuring at mortgagor's expense 480
  right to consolidate mortgages 481
  right to lease 480–1
  right to possession of land 480
  right to tack further advances 481
  rights to title deeds or charge certificate 479–80

mortgagors 22, 466
  co-ownership 364
  equity of redemption 475
  instalment mortgages 474
  insuring at mortgagor's expense 480
  no clogs in equity of redemption 475–8
  overdraft 509
  protection for 485–7
  right to grant leases 478–9
  right to redeem at law and in equity 474
  right to sue 479
  rights 474–9
  surrenders 479
  necessity for 464
  priorities 498–513
    application to other interests 499
    chronological order 499
    importance of 498–9
    interests prior to mortgagee 510–13
    right to tack further advances 508–10
    three or more mortgages or charges 507–8
    what has been mortgaged 499
  priorities of equitable interest 499–501
    equities are equal 499–500
    giving notice 500–1
    registered land 501
    rule in *Dearle v Hall* 500–1
  priorities of legal estate 501–6
    registered title 502–4
    unregistered title 504–5
  puisne mortgage 71–2, 76, 505
  redemption
    redeem up, foreclose down 490–1
    subsequent mortgagees 490
    third parties 490–1
  registered land 91
  right to consolidate mortgages 481
  second mortgage 116, 468, 469
  severance 374
  tenants of mortgagor, protection for 487
  terminology 466
  types 467
mortgagors *see under* mortgages and charges
mutual agreement 374–5

national conversion 317
nec clam 548, 555, 569
nec precario 548, 555, 569
nec vi 547–8, 555, 569
necessity, easements of 535–6
necessity and intention, overlap between 536
negative covenants 290, 291, 296, 584, 586–7, 602, 607, 608
negative easements 538, 570
negative equity 482, 483
negligence 133, 191, 494, 564
  see also liability for fraud/negligence
  see under mortgages and charges
nemo dat quod non habet 231, 245
new trust of land 343
no clogs in equity of redemption 475–8, 480

no conversion under trust for sale 317
no intention to create legal relations 197–8
no lease despite apparent grant of exclusive possession 196–8
noise, excessive from neighbouring land 243, 244
non-alienation obligation
  agreement on grounds for refusal in advance of a request 254–5
  landlord's duty to deal with request for permission 254
  qualified and absolute covenants against 251–2
  tenant's choice upon refusal of permission 255
  unreasonable withholding of consent 252–4
non-charitable purpose trusts 354
non-competition clauses 268
non-compliance with requirements for legal grant 208–13
  equitable lease, effect of 210–11
  equitable lease and legal lease comparison 211–13
    contract is not a conveyance 212–13
    enforcement against third parties 211–12
    enforcement of covenants in the lease 212
    equitable remedies are discretionary 211
    equitable tenant is not a purchaser for value of legal estate 213
  equitable leases arising from specifically enforceable contracts 210
  formality requirements for contracts relating to land 209
    on or after 27 September 1989 209
    before 27 September 1989 209
non-derogation from grant 242, 245–6
  acts of persons claiming under landlord 246
  breaches 245–6
  no breach 246
non-express trusts 304, 389
non-molestation order 458
non-payment of rent, forfeiture for 293, 297
non-performance 66
non-possessory interests in land 98
non-proprietary leases 230, 232–4
notice 78, 81–2, 349, 358, 589
  actual 21, 79, 82, 126
  agreed 95–6
  constructive 21, 80, 82, 83, 88, 126, 346
  effect of serving s. 146 notice 289–90, 293, 297
  imputed 21, 80
  leasehold estate 184, 185, 186, 200, 201, 203, 213, 214, 219, 229
  oral 375
  priorities of equitable interest 500–1
  registered land 91, 95–6, 103, 112, 125–7
  rule 20
  service of 487
  seven days 286–7
  statutory 75
  unilateral 95–6
  in writing 371–3, 375
    service of notice 372–3
  see also notice to quit
Notice of Proposed Obstruction 573
notice to quit 219–20, 222, 223, 224, 245
  excluding right to give notice 219–20
  form of notice 219
  period of notice 219
nuisance 153, 191, 243, 246, 285, 594
  easements and profits à prendre 522, 523, 529, 563–4

objectionable limitations 179
obligations
  positive 610
  restrictive 610
  see also landlord and tenant obligations; land obligations; non-alienation obligations
occupation
  by co-owners 331
  by owner's spouse 82–3
  orders 457–8
  rent 379
    continuing role of equitable accounting 332–3
    principles of equitable accounting 333–4
  see also actual occupation; statutory right of occupation
'once and for all' breaches 289, 290, 291–2
onerous property 221
options 25, 47–8, 271, 323
oral tenancies 148
out of possession (squatter) leaving property vacant 152–3
overreaching 342–6, 349, 358, 380
  in absence of payment of capital money 345–6
  capital money not paid to two trustees 344–5
  capital money paid to trustees 346
  and LRA 2002 344
  registered land 128, 345, 9607
  statutory 80–1, 97
  TOLATA 1996 343–4
  trusts of land 320, 341
overriding interests 104, 252, 345, 425
  adverse possession 156, 163
  easements and profits à prendre 532–3
  leasehold estate 212, 216
  mortgages and charges: priorities 503, 511
  other than actual occupation 110–13
  registered land 91–2, 95, 103, 111, 116, 120, 121, 122, 123, 135–6
overriding lease 72, 263, 264
ownership
  equitable 532
  extent 623–6
  statutory 348
  see also co-ownership

parking, rights of 121, 523, 526–7, 528, 570–1
parliamentary conveyance 153
parol 207
part performance 78, 209, 410, 427, 472
   contract 28, 54, 55–6, 57
partition 323, 379
'party walls' 564, 574, 607
passage of time 496–7
pasture, profit of 530
peaceful enjoyment of possessions 30, 167, 286–7, 538–9
   see also quiet enjoyment, covenant to allow
peaceful re-entry by landlord 286, 480, 486
pensions 352, 353
periodic licence 440
periodic sum 22
periodic tenancies 17, 148, 175, 203, 358
   implied 213–14
   leasehold estate 184, 189, 200, 201, 205, 207, 211, 214, 220, 224–5
perpetually renewable leases 19, 249–50
perpetuities and accumulations 22, 177, 350–4
   future interests 350–1
   legislative modifications before 2010 352
   old rules 351–2
   Perpetuities and Accumulations Act 2009 353–4
     accumulation rules, changes to 354
     duration rules preserved 354
     fixed period in old 'royal lives' trusts 353
     interests affected 353
     old rules, importance of 354
   perpetuity period 350, 353
personal covenants 268
   no release of 273–4
personal leases 232
personal property 30–1, 174, 373
   chattels real 31
   choses in action 31
   choses in possession 31
personal representatives 21, 37
personalty *see* real and personal property
physical possession 10, 145, 189, 195–6, 204
physical presence 116–17
piscary, profit of 530
pornographic material, sale of on premises 292
positive covenants 22, 524
   breach 290
   flying freehold 626, 627
   forfeiture, landlord's remedy of 291
   freehold covenants 584, 586–7, 602, 606–7, 608, 610
positive easements 529, 538
possession
   definition 10
   discontinuous 208
   entitlement to 331–2, 334
   of land, right to 480
   order 30, 118, 294, 486–7
   physical 10, 145, 189, 195–6, 204
   retaking, without reference to court 295

   and sale 483–4, 488
   vacant 381
   see also exclusive possession
possessory title 103, 108, 155
   first registration of unregistered estate 106
   freehold 103, 176–7
     future interests 176–7
     remainders and reversions 177
postponement of sale under trust for sale 324
power of attorney 136–7, 489
practical approach to land law 628
pre-emption rights 72, 352, 353
premium 239
prescription 111, 112
   see also under acquisition by prescription; easements and profits à prendre
priority
   general rule 108–9
   notices 79
   period 125
   see also special priority rule *under* purchaser protection on registered land
private and family life, right to respect for 30, 179, 286–7
privatisation of registered land 93–4
privity of contract 27
   freehold covenants 581, 584
   leasehold covenants 258, 260, 265–6, 277, 280
   leasehold estate 233
   new leases 271–5
     assignment to original guarantor void 272–3
     authorised guarantee agreement 272
     circumstances in which tenant remains liable 272
     express exclusion of continuing liability 274–5
     loss of benefit with loss of burden 275
     no release of personal covenants 273–4
     release of original landlord 273
     release of original tenant 271–3
   old leases 261–5
     hardship caused by 263
     original covenantor's remedies 262–3
     original tenant's liability to new landlord 264–5
     protection of former tenants 263–4
     restriction of liability for rent or service charge 264
     restriction of liability where tenancy is subsequently varied 264
     right to an overriding lease 264
privity of estate
   leasehold covenants 258, 260, 262, 277
   new leases 275–6
     equitable leases 276
     landlord covenants and tenant covenants 275
     requirement of registration for options 276

transmission of benefit and burden
of covenants and rights of
re-entry 275–6
old leases 265–9
covenants must 'touch and concern' the
land or 'have reference to subject-
matter of the lease' 267–8
equitable leases 269
leases made by deed 265–8
leases not by deed 268–9
legal parol leases 268–9
procedural protection, absence of 168
profits à prendre *see* easements and profits à
prendre
prohibited rent 206, 251
promises, contractual 241
promisor 27
promissory estoppel 63, 410–11
proper care, lack of 135, 138, 139
property adjustment orders 383, 453, 454
property, classification of 30–1
property guardianship arrangements 194, 198
property, protection of 166
property register 89, 91
proportionality 30
proprietary estoppel 19, 78, 92, 109, 143, 209,
362, 392, 410–29
assimilation 427–8
constructive trusts, and 308, 427–9
assimilation 427–8
debate on 429
differences 428
contract 57–61, 63
definition 411–12
detriment 420–1
domestic cases 418
equitable interests 28
equity arising from estoppel, nature
of 424–6
equity benefiting representor's successors
in title 426
equity binding representor's successors in
title 425–6
equity, satisfying 421–4
essential elements 414–21
family home and special rights 454, 455, 456
future rights, expectations of 412–14
future inheritance 412–14
leasehold estate 209
licences and their enforcement 440, 441,
443, 446, 447–8
mixed motives 419–20
nature of 410–12
reliance 418–20
relief, court deciding 423–4
representation 415–18
clarity of 417
expectation of well-defined property
right 418
intention 417–18
unconscionability 421

proprietary interest 231, 438
proprietary lease 232
proprietary protection 191
proprietorship register 91
protection, statutory 218
public policy/public interest 58–9, 175, 178–9,
427, 484, 604–5
adverse possession 156, 165, 166, 167–8
easements and profits à prendre 529, 548,
573
public rights 113
Public Trustee 321
puisne mortgage 71–2, 76, 505
purchase without notice, effect on 83
purchaser 17
bona fide 20
must acquire legal estate 21
must give value 20–1
must not have notice of equitable interest 21
for value 20
and purchaser for money or money's
worth distinction 77
see also purchaser protection on registered
land
purchaser protection on registered
land 108–24
best title to estate (vendor) 108
easement use amounting to actual
occupation of servient land 120–1
encumbrances binding property 108
priorities: general rule 108–9
special priority rule 109–10
completion by registration, necessity
for 110
registrable disposition, necessity for 110
valuable consideration, necessity for 110
special priority rule exceptions: interests of
those in actual occupation 113–24
actual occupation (definition) 116–21
future leases which are compulsorily
registrable 116
interest must relate to land of which
person is in actual occupation 116
interests that can override 114–16
interests under SLA settlement 116
non-disclosure and 'when he could
reasonably have been expected to
do so' 123
obvious occupation or actual knowledge of
interest 123–4
occupier must have proprietary interest in
land 115
occupier must not have expressly or
impliedly authorised grant to
purchaser 115–16
occupier temporarily absent from
property 118–19
occupier's interest in land must not be
specifically excluded by statute 116
occupier's interest in land must not have
been overreached 115

purchaser protection on registered land (*Cont.*)
   presence of possessions in property enough to establish actual occupation 119–20
   shared occupation at same time 120
   when persons must be in actual occupation 122–3
  special priority rule exceptions: overriding interests other than actual occupation 110–13
   easements and profits 111–13
   miscellaneous interests 113
   short leases 111
pure personalty trusts 322

qualified title 103, 105, 108
qualifying interests 299
quasi-easements 519, 537–8, 539, 541, 543, 544, 546
  'continuous and apparent' 541, 544, 546
quiet enjoyment, covenant to allow 223, 243–5, 256
  acts of persons claiming under landlord 244–5
  acts of persons with superior title to landlord 245
  breaches 243
  landlord and tenant obligations 241, 242
  leasehold covenants 271, 285
  no breach arising from condition of premises at time of grant 244

re-entry
  peaceable 286, 297, 480, 486
  physical 294, 297
  right of 175–6, 242, 275, 287–8, 295, 296, 484, 600
real and personal property 30–1, 65, 174, 621–2
  exceptions 622
  real (definition) 621–2
  rights of beneficiaries under trusts 622
realty *see* real and personal property
reasonable belief 160–3
reasonable mistake as to boundaries 160
reasonable period 486–7
receivers 487–8, 489, 494–5
recognition, rules of 524
rectification 51–2, 67, 132, 135–9, 150
  definition 133
redemption 468
  equity of 468, 475, 481, 494–5
  postponement of 476–7
  prevention of 475–6
  right 474
reform
  easements and profits à prendre 567–75
  family home/property 458–61
  freehold covenants 606–13
  registered land 93–4
  remedies for breach of leasehold covenants 298–9

registered charge 104, 467
registered interests, express release of 571
registered land 87–139
  adverse possession *see* adverse possession
  alteration and indemnity 132–9
   alteration (definition) 132–3
   derivative interests, removal of: void and voidable dispositions distinction 136–8
   indemnity (definition) 133
   mistake 133–8
   overriding interest 135–6
   rectification (definition) 133
   rectification, discretion as to 138–9
   reform 139
  best title to estate 108
  co-ownership 377, 380
  conveyancing process 125–32
   inspecting the land 125
   notice or knowledge, role of 125–7
   registration gap 127–8
   searching the register 125
   transfer 129–31
  death 380
  disputes concerning entry on register 97–8
  easements and profits à prendre 533, 571
  enforcement against purchaser of servient tenement 532–3, 534*t*
  entry on register, types of 94–7
   cautions against first registration 97
   notices 95–6
   registered proprietor 94–5
   restrictions 96–7
  family home and special rights 456, 457
  first registration *see* first registration of unregistered estate
  formalities 106–7
   dispositions which must be completed by registration 106–7
   registrable disposition not completed by registration 107
   registration requirements 107
  freehold covenants 589, 599, 601, 609, 610
  historical background 88–9
  house purchase 40
  indemnity 135, 137
  joint tenancy and tenancy in common 361–2
  leasehold estate 208, 212
  legal mortgage 470
  licences 447–8
  mortgages and charges 470, 496, 508, 513
  new system and adverse possession 144
  old system and adverse possession 143–4
  overreaching 345
  overriding interests 91–2
  priorities of equitable interest 501
  proprietary estoppel 425–6
  purchasers, protection of *see* purchaser protection on registered land
  reform 93–4
   Law Commission recommendations 94

privatisation 93–4
register, appearance of 89–91
 charges register 91
 property register 89, 91
 proprietorship register 91
 rights to title deeds or charge certificate 479–80
 title registration, principles of 92–3
 trusts of land 246, 342–3, 344
 and unregistered land 89
registered proprietor 91, 94–5, 150–1
registered title 89, 502–4, 509, 609
registers 89–91
 charges 91
 property 89, 91
 proprietorship 91
 see also Land Charges Register; Land Registry; Local Land Charges Register
registrable dispositions 106, 109
 necessity for 110
 not completed by registration 107
registration
 of charges 471
 compulsory 36–7, 86, 88–9, 208
 gap 127–8
 house purchase 36
 for options, requirement of 276
 triggering 37
 voluntary 37
regulated leases 206
relative title 141
release
 of original covenantor 276
 of original landlord 273
 of original tenant 271–3
reliance 414, 415, 418–20
relief, court deciding 423–4
remain in occupation, right to see under family home/property
remainders 177
remedies 611
 contracts 66–7, 602
  damages 66
  declaration 67
  injunction 67
  rectification 67
  rescission 66
  specific performance 66
 discretionary equitable 211
 easements and profits à prendre 561–7
 equitable 28
 self-help 294, 295, 297, 561–2, 611
 see also remedies for breach of leasehold covenants
remedies for breach of leasehold covenants 238, 281–99
 distress, landlord's remedy of 285–7
  abolition of distress 286–7
  commercial rent arrears recovery (CRAR) 286, 287
  human rights concerns 286–7
  reform, necessity for 285–6

forfeiture, landlord's remedy of 287–99
 assignment, breach of covenant against 292–3
 breaches not capable of remedy 290–3
 continuing breaches 291–2
 defects in present system 297–8
 derivative interest holders, effect of forfeiture on 295–6, 299
 form of s. 146 notice 289–90, 293
 irremediable harm, breaches causing 292
 keeping animals, enforcement of covenant against 296–7
 methods of exercising right to forfeiture 293–4
 mortgagees, protection for 295–6
 non-rent covenants 289–93, 297
 'once and for all' breaches 291–2
 order for possession, seeking 294
 positive and negative covenants 291
 re-entry, provision of 287–8
 reform of law 297–9
 relief against forfeiture 294–5
 right to forfeit lease 287–9
 self-help by physical re-entry 294
 statutory restrictions 294
 subtenant, relief of 297
 subtenants, protection for 295
 tenant has breached another covenant 295
 tenant's failure to pay rent, relief for 294–5
 waiver of breach 288–9
general contractual remedies 281–4
 'keep-open' covenants and specific performance 282–3
 repairing covenants and specific performance 283–4
reform proposals 298–9
tenant's remedies against defaulting landlord 284–5
 harassment or eviction 285
 landlord's failure to repair 285
rent 205–6
 formal demand for 293
 ground rent 180, 206, 239
 owner 22
 prohibited 206, 251
 review clauses 251, 264
rent-free possession 197
rentcharges 18, 22, 23, 29, 175, 601, 621
 tithe 23
repair and maintenance obligations of landlord 241, 243, 247–9, 250, 256, 257, 268, 271, 611
 duty of care 248–9
 leasehold covenants: remedies for breach 292, 296
 short leases 248
 specific performance 283–4
  against landlord 283–4
  against tenant 284
  Leasehold Property (Repairs) Act 1938 283
repossession by mortgagee 452

representation 415–18, 423
repudiatory breach 218, 227–30, 281, 423
  by landlord 227–8
  by tenant 228–30
rescission, remedy for breach of contracts 66
reservation 111, 112
  agreements 39
  implied 112, 533, 539–40
residential licences 218
residential property 199, 218, 219, 286–7, 294
  see also family home/property
restitutio in integrum 66
restrictions 91, 96–7
restrictive covenants 15, 19, 29
  adverse possession 154
  equitable interests 27
  exception in respect of 277–8
  freehold covenants 588, 589, 594, 605, 606
  land charges 73
  leasehold covenants: enforcement 280
  perpetuities, rule against 352
  registered land 95, 96
  unregistered land 74, 80, 81
restrictive obligations 610
resulting trusts 19, 24, 305–7, 316, 318, 321
  co-ownership 363, 378
  incomplete or invalid express
      declarations 306
  irrelevance of 397–8
  joint-names cases (family home) 398, 405
  mortgages and charges: priorities 498
  presumed 306–7
  registered land 92, 115, 120, 123
  sole-name cases (family home) 386, 387, 389,
      392, 393, 395
  unregistered land 82
  see also under family home/property
reversion 7, 72, 114, 310, 318
  freehold estate 189, 204
  leasehold covenants 258, 262, 264, 266–9,
      273, 274, 275, 276
  leasehold estate 189, 222, 224
  possessory freehold title 177
reversionary lease 186, 199, 207, 221
reverter 175–6
rights of way 517–18, 520–2, 525, 528, 538–9,
      545, 550, 552–3
  adverse possession 146
  interests in land 15, 19, 29
  licences and their enforcement 446–7
  proprietary estoppel 426
  registered land 91, 104, 120–1
  remedies 562
  unregistered land 78
root of title 70, 74
'royal lives' trusts 353

sale 7
  adverse possession 153
  against wishes of other(s) 378
  and division of proceeds 379

  effect of 484–5, 488–9
  houses see house purchase
  power to postpone 313
  severance 373–4
  simultaneous 539
  trusts see trusts for sale
Scottish law 460–1, 527, 627
sea walls 113
searches 75, 82–3, 84, 125
section 106 agreements 46
security of tenure 190–1, 218, 219, 298
self-help remedies 294, 295, 297, 561–2, 611
servient tenements 15, 251–2
  see also under easements and profits à prendre
Settled Land Act settlements 309, 310, 311,
      316, 348–9
  easements and profits à prendre 552, 555
  property concerned 349
  registered land 96, 116
  tenant for life 349t
  trustees 349
  trusts 312
  trusts of land 315, 317, 318, 319, 322, 330,
      346
  trusts for sale 316–17
  who holds legal estate 348
settlements 8
  by will 319
  creating 319–20
  family 185, 205, 348
  new way of making 316
  trusts 305
  trusts of land 315
  and trusts for sale, effect on 316–18
settlor tries to create new strict
      settlement 317–18
settlor tries to create new trust for sale 317
severance 369, 376–7, 397
  equal shares on 367
  memorandum of 377, 380
  words of 361
  see also under joint tenancies
sham or pretence 193–4
share in property, size of 385
short leases 186, 248
  contracts 46–7
  excluding or limiting statutory
      covenants 248
  landlord and tenant obligations 241, 243,
      246, 257
  registered land 110, 111, 115
  satisfying LPA 1925 207–8
  scope of covenant to keep 'structure and
      exterior' in repair 248
short period 533–4
signature 19, 26, 44, 45–6, 48, 55
  forgery of 136–8, 337, 339, 374
single discontinuous period 184
sitting tenant 127
socage 6
sole beneficial ownership 383

sole occupancy 196, 199
sole-name cases 382, 386–92
  action by claimant to his detriment in reliance on agreement 388–9
  after *Stack v Dowden* 406–7
    beneficial interest, establishing claim to 406–7
    beneficial interest, quantifying 306
  agreement 388
  agreement inferred from conduct 388
  beneficial interest, quantifying 392–6
  change of approach in *Burns v Burns* 390
  express agreement 388
  Gissing v Gissing 386–90
  Lloyds Bank v Rosset 391–2
  new approach to quantifying shares 393–6
  resulting and constructive trusts 393
  Stack v Dowden 392
special priority rule *see under* purchaser protection on registered land
specific performance 25, 27
  contracts 47, 66
  freehold covenants 602
  and 'keep-open' covenants 282–3
  leasehold covenants 269, 281
  leasehold estate 210, 211, 217
  licences and their enforcement 439–40
  mortgages and charges 472
  and repairing covenants 283–4
specific use which then becomes illegal 227
sporting and recreational rights 525, 548
spouses or civil partners 16, 73, 83, 116, 337, 412, 451, 453–4, 456–8, 490, 512–13
squatters 37, 101, 104–5, 106, 135, 138, 183
  see also adverse possession
standard occupancy agreement 201
standard terms 238
state guarantee concept 132
state of mind (owner) 147
statutory magic and registered interests 571
statutory right of occupation
  family home/property 330–1, 457–8
    associated persons 458
    cohabitants' occupation rights 458
    enforcement against purchaser 457
    home rights 457–8
    occupation orders 457–8
statutory trusts 305, 316
  adverse possession 156, 166
  co-ownership 312–14, 360
  joint-names cases (family home) 396
  registered land 96
  for sale 373, 378–9
  sole-name cases (family home) 407
  trusts of land 315, 319, 334–5, 337–8
stigma on property, causing 292
storage, rights of 15, 121, 523, 525–6, 541–2, 545
strict settlements *see* Settled Land Act settlements
sub-trust 65

subleases 188–9, 233
  freehold covenants 580
  landlord and tenant obligations 245, 250, 251, 255
  leasehold covenants 258, 274, 282, 292, 296, 297
  leasehold estate 191, 217, 224
  mortgages and charges 469, 478
  see also subtenants
subrogation rules 508
substantial interference test 527
subtenants 188
  determination of headlease 221–4
  freehold covenants 588
  landlord and tenant obligations 245
  leasehold covenants 260–1, 262, 277–80
    assignment of sublease or reversion 278
    attempts by head landlord to enforce covenants in sublease 278–9
    attempts by subtenant to enforce covenants in headlease 279
    new leases 278
    restrictive covenants exceptions 277–8
  leasehold estate 205, 223
  protection for 295
  relief of 297
succession 153
successive interests in land *see* settlement
successors in title 28, 262
sue, right to 479
superior lease 171
supervision, continuing 282, 283
supplemental agreement 49–51, 56
support, right to 523, 529, 540, 562, 564, 570, 607
  see also 'party walls'
surrender 220–1, 233–4
  by operation of law 28, 220–1
  defective 220
  express 220
  on merger, effect of 222
  mortgagors 479
survivorship, right of 346, 419
  co-ownership 357, 363, 367–8, 370, 372–3, 375–7, 379–80
  joint-names cases (family home) 396, 400, 404

tack further advances, right to 481, 508–10
  registered title 509
  unregistered title 509–10
tangible objects 31
temporary absence from property 118–19
tenancy 184, 256
  by sufferance 214
  circumstances court will find 232
  express 203
  life 185, 201, 308–11, 322, 330, 348, 349*t*
    see also Settled Land Act settlements
  new 259
  oral 148

tenancy (*Cont.*)
  periodic *see* periodic tenancies
  trusts 308
tenancy at will 29, 185–6
tenancy by estoppel 28, 215–16, 230–2
  feeding estoppel 216
  representation and estoppel by grant 215
  rights and duties under 215–16
tenancy in common 81, 382, 397
  co-ownership 357–8, 361, 366, 367, 369, 376, 378, 379, 380, 396
  equitable 330
  express declaration 360–2
  from joint tenancy 370–1
  severance 375
tenant 6, 16
  covenant to pay rates and other taxes on premises 256
  failure to pay rent, relief for 294–5
  has breached another covenant 295
  liability 272
  liability to new landlord 264–5
  obligations *see* landlord and tenant obligations
  privity of estate 275
  sitting 127
  under lease and adverse possession 148
tenure 5, 6, 185
  security of 190–1, 218, 219, 298
term, expiry of 218–19
term less than that of grantor 203–5
term of years absolute 19, 183–6, 187, 205, 231
  see also leasehold estate
termination 298, 571
testamentary disposition 178
third parties 10, 19–21
  adverse possession 146, 151, 153, 154, 155
  co-ownership 374
  contracts 41, 46, 48–9, 50, 64–5
  easements and profits à prendre 532, 536, 540
  family home and special rights 383, 454, 456
  freehold covenants 585
  house purchase 36, 38
  interests prior to mortgagee 512
  landlord and tenant obligations 244
  leasehold covenants 279, 295
  leasehold estate 183, 185, 186, 187, 216, 221, 222, 227, 231
  licences and their enforcement 436, 441–2, 443–5, 447, 448–9
  mortgages and charges 498–9, 513
  proprietary estoppel 426
  purchaser must acquire legal estate 21
  purchaser must be bona fide 20
  purchaser must give value 20–1
  purchaser must not have notice of equitable interest 21
  registered land 88, 92–3, 94, 95, 101, 108, 109, 127–8, 136

trusts 303
unregistered land 70–1, 76
  see also encumbrances
time immemorial 551
time starts to run 151
time within which owner may bring claim, extension of 151
timeshare arrangements 98–9, 208
title
  absolute 91, 132, 136
  defective 215
  and enjoyment, separation of 303
  epitome of 70
  information documents 106
  legal 303, 355
  register 88
  registered 89, 502–4, 509, 609
  registration, principles of 92–3
  relative 141
  unregistered 504–5, 509–10
  written acknowledgement of 152
title deeds 74, 84, 479–80
'touching and concerning' the land 270, 275, 582–3
transfer 7, 15, 40, 99, 100, 129–31
transmission
  of benefit and burden of covenants and rights of re-entry 275–6
  of part of burdened land 610–11
trespass
  adverse possession 153, 166
  easements and profits à prendre 557–8
  landlord and tenant obligations 243
  leasehold covenants 285
  leasehold estate 183, 186, 191, 197, 214, 225
  licences and their enforcement 435, 438–9
  mesne profits 294
  mortgages and charges 480
  possession as a 148
  residential 164
trust corporations 321, 343
trustees 10, 24, 80–1, 88, 348, 349
  see also trusts of land: trustees
trusts 10, 16, 22, 24, 303–14
  adverse possession 154
  bare *see* bare trust
  by will 321
  charitable 354
  classification 304–5
  co-ownership and statutory trusts 312–14
    continuing purpose, doctrine of 314
    LPA 1925 312–13
    TOLATA 1996 314
  collapse the trust 305
  common intention *see* common intention trusts
  constructive *see* constructive trusts
  contracts 47
  express *see* express trusts
  freehold estate 174, 177, 179

general 354
housing 230-1, 233
implied *see* implied trusts
informally declared 308
land *see* trusts of land
leasehold estate 185
mortgages and charges: priorities 500
non-charitable purpose 354
non-express 304, 389
pure personalty 322
registered land 88, 96, 97
resulting *see* resulting trusts
'royal lives' 353
separation of title and enjoyment 303
statutory *see* statutory trusts
terms of trusts affecting land 309-12
   conversion, doctrine of 311
   modern trust of land 312
   old law 309-12
   Settled Land Act settlements 310
   trusts for sale 311, 312
unit 47
unregistered land 80
will 353
trusts of land 309, 315-46
   beneficiaries and right to occupy trust property 330-4
   before 1997 330
   exclusion or restriction of right to occupy 331
   occupation by co-owners 331
   occupation rent: principles of equitable accounting 332-4
   payments by co-owner in occupation 331-4
   statutory compensation 332
   statutory right to occupy 330-1
   TOLATA 1996 330
beneficiary involvement in management 328-9
   form of delegation, duration and revocation 329
   liability of delegates and trustees 329
   power to delegate 328
   to whom trustees may delegate 328-9
charges 'by way of family arrangement' 318
co-ownership, new way of regulating 316
creating a settlement 319-20
disputes, resolving 334-41
   applying to court 335
   bankruptcy, application by trustee in 336-7
   between co-owners 335
   new provisions in practice 337-41
   opportunities for disputes 334
   orders of court 335-6
   person's interest in trust property, nature and extent of 336
   TOLATA 1996 335-7
   trustees' functions, exercise of 336
entails 318

existing settlements and trusts for sale, effect on 316-18
mixed trusts 320
new trust of land 316
no conversion under trust for sale 317
perpetuities, rule against 354
'in possession' 328-9
purchaser protection 341-6
   consents 342
   consultation 342
   delegation 342
   duty to exercise powers in accordance with statutory, legal and equitable rules 342
   limitation of trustees' powers 342
   overreaching 342-6
   purchase of land no longer subject to trust 346
realty and personalty 622
Settled Land Act settlements and trusts for sale 316-17
settlements, new way of making 316
settlements and trusts for sale, effect on 316-18
settlor tries to create new strict settlement 317-18
   minor(s), conveyance to 317
settlor tries to create new trust for sale 317
TOLATA 1996, summary of changes under 318
trustees *see* trusts of land - trustees
what settlor will want to know 320
trusts of land - trustees 320-8
   appointment and retirement 321-2
   beneficiaries compelled to take trust property 327
   duties 322-4, 327-8
   functions of trustees of 336
   holding legal estate 322
   number of 320-1
   postponing sale, trustees disagreeing about 324
   powers 322-4
      absolute owner 322-3
      acquisition of land 323
      compel beneficiaries to take conveyance 323-4
      consents imposed by settlor, requirements for 325-6
      consultation, statutory requirement for 326-7
      controls over 324-8
      duty to consult excluded 327
      exclusion and restriction of powers by settlor 325
      no duty to consult 327
      partition, power to 323
      postpone sale under trust for sale 324
      which cannot be restricted or excluded 325
   replacement and retirement 321

trusts for sale 309, 311, 312, 315, 316, 317, 330, 337–8, 343
turbary, profit of 530
turning a blind eye 21
twenty-year use 551
tying-in provisions 478

uncertain term 207
unconscionable behaviour 28, 57–8, 411, 415, 421, 423, 427, 477
underleases/undertenants 188–9, 205, 245
undue influence 28
  co-ownership 362
  contract 66
  interests prior to mortgagee 511–13
  mortgages and charges 484, 504, 508
  registered land 114, 115–16, 119, 122, 138
unenforceable agreement 374
unforeseen events 227
unilateral notice 95–6
uninhabitable site/house 117
unit trust 47
United States 88, 227
unities see four unities
unity of seisin 571
unjust enrichment 427
unmarried couples see cohabitants; spouses or civil partners
unregistered interests 503
unregistered land 69–86, 89
  adverse possession 141, 142–3, 156, 166
  cautions against first registration 97
  co-ownership 373, 377, 379, 380
  conveyance 84–5
  death 380
  easements and profits à prendre 517, 532
  encumbrances, checking for 70–1
  enforcement against purchaser of servient tenement 533–4
  equitable interests enforcement against purchaser of legal estate 76–8, 79–83
    effect of purchase without notice 83
    notice doctrine 81–2
    searches required to avoid constructive notice 82–3
    statutory overreaching 80–1
  family home and special rights 456, 457
  first registration application 86
  freehold covenants 589, 601, 609, 610
  freehold estate 176
  house purchase 36, 38, 40
  interests prior to mortgagee 510f
  joint tenancy and tenancy in common 361
  landlord and tenant obligations 249

leasehold estate 208, 212, 213
legal interests, enforcement of 79
licences 446–7
mortgages and charges 467, 471, 496, 501, 504, 508
notice or knowledge 125
overreaching 345
overriding interests 92
ownership 69–70
proprietary estoppel 426
rights to title deeds or charge certificate 479
searches 84
trusts of land 342–3, 346
see also adverse possession; land charges
unregistered title 504–5, 509–10
upwards notice 222–3
use, control of 167, 168
use must be as of right 547–9, 555–6
usual covenants 242

vacant possession 381
valuable consideration 109–10
valuers 496
vendor-purchaser constructive trust 64
void
  leasehold estate 186, 199–200, 201, 202, 220
  registered land 100, 135
  for uncertainty 233
  and voidable dispositions distinction 136–8
volunteer 20, 306

'wait and see' rule 352
waste 255–6
  ameliorating 255
  permissive 255, 256
  voluntary 255, 256
water, rights to 15, 522, 529, 570
way, rights of see rights of way
'where the equities are equal, the first in time prevails' 500, 505
whole course of conduct approach 405, 407, 455
will trusts 353
wills 69, 110, 313, 442
  adverse possession 153, 160
  co-ownership 357, 370, 374–5
  freehold estate 174, 177
  home-made 312, 319, 349
  mutual 406
  see also intestacy; survivorship, rights of
written evidence 209
written terms inconsistent with exclusive possession 192–4